THE ANGLO-AFRICAN WHO'S WHO

AND

BIOGRAPHICAL SKETCHBOOK

1907

Edited by

Walter H. Wills

JEPPESTOWN

Published by Jeppestown Press, 10A Scawfell St, London, E2 8NG, United Kingdom.
First published 1907 by L. Upcott Gill, Drury Lane, London, United Kingdom.

Arrangement and introduction copyright © David Saffery 2006

ISBN   0-9553936-3-9
ISBN-13   978-0-9553936-3-1

The

Anglo-African Who's Who

AND

Biographical Sketch-Book

EDITED BY

WALTER H. WILLS

1907

LONDON

L. UPCOTT GILL, Bazaar Buildings, Drury Lane, W.C.
South Africa: Juta and Co.
New York: Chas. Scribner's Sons, Fifth Avenue
City Agents: Walter Judd, Ltd., 5, Queen Victoria St., E.C.

Contents

Introduction

The Anglo-African Who's Who was published in three editions biennially between 1905 and 1909. The first edition was edited by Robert Barratt (q.v.) and Walter H. Wills, and the 1907 (of which this work is a reprint) and 1909 editions compiled by Walter Wills alone.

Walter Wills' enthusiasm for African journalism and politics inform the content of this book. Many of the subjects are journalists, men, and occasionally women, who wrote for the plethora of impecunious newspapers and magazines concerned with mining and Africa that tottered precariously from issue to issue (occasionally folding while only halfway there) in the years between the start of the southern African mineral revolution and the First World War.

Wills was at the centre of this world: his brother, William, was a business partner of Sir Henry Rider Haggard, who had been one of the British colonial administrators responsible for annexing the Transvaal in 1880, before returning to Britain and taking up the profitable theme of southern Africa in popular fiction (*King Solomon's Mines, She, Allan Quartermain…*). Haggard was also one of the proprietors of the influential *African Review of Mining* periodical, for which William wrote a history of the Matabele Rebellion in 1894.

It is evident from the content of Walter Wills' entries that many of the people listed in this book were personally known to him, and his comments—sometimes expressed in a quirky, throwaway style—in some cases quite unexpectedly illuminate our knowledge of them. We also learn about Wills in the course of leafing through this book: an enthusiastic and unapologetic British imperialist, deeply suspicious of Afrikaner nationalism and dismissive of the aspirations of black Africans towards equality and independence. Wills fades from public view after 1919, and I have not been able to trace his death record in England, South Africa or even Zimbabwe. Every effort has been made to trace the owner of the copyright in this work, if it still exists; he or she is invited to contact the publisher.

In the course of preparing this work for reprinting, I have corrected a few obvious spelling mistakes and typographical errors that appear in the original text, and have provided an index. I have also taken a number of biographical entries which originally appeared in an addendum of some thirty pages and incorporated them into the main body of the book, as there seems to be no compelling reason why they should be kept separate.

My sincere thanks to Stephen Stopes for the kindness with which he took time out from his Ph.D. studies to respond courteously to my questions and generously share information about the Wills family.

Abbreviations

A.A.G. Assistant Adjutant-General.

A.B.C. African Banking Corporation;

Acct. Account(ant).

Acct.-Gen. Accountant-GeneraL

A.D.C. Aide-dc-Camp.

Ad. eund. grad. Admitted to the same degree.

Adjt. Adjutant.

Adjt.-Gen. Adjutant-General.

A.M.I.C.E. Associate Member of the Institute of Civil Engineers.

A.M.S. Army Medical Staff.

Apr. April.

A.R.A. Associate of the Royal Academy.

A.R.1.B.A. Associate of the Royal Institute of British Architects.

A.R.M. Assistant Resident Magistrate.

A.S.C. Army Service Corps.

Assist., Asst. Assistant.

Assoc. Associate, Association.

Aug. August.

B.A. Bachelor of Arts.

Bart. Baronet.

Batt. Battalion.

B.B.P. Bechuanaland Border Police.

B.C.L. Bachelor of Civil Law.

B.D. Bachelor of Divinity.

Beds. Bedfordshire.

B.P.P. Belingwe Field Force.

Br., Brev. Brevet.

Brig. Brigade; Brigadier.

Brig.-Genl. Brigadier-General.

Bro. Brother.

Bros. Brothers.

B.S. Bachelor of Surgery.

B.S.A. British South Africa(n).

B.S.A. Co. British South Africa (Chartered) Co.

Camb. Cambridge.

Capt. Captain.

C.B. Companion of the Bath.

C.C. Cape Colony; Cape Colonial; Civil Commissioner.

C.C.F. Cape Colonial Forces.

C.D.F. Colonial Defence Force.

C.E. Civil Engineer; Church of England.

C.G.R. Cape Government Railways.

Chm. Chairman.

C.I.C. Commander-in-Chief.

C.1.E. Companion of the Indian Empire.

C.I.V. City of London Imperial Volunteers.

C.M. Church Missionary.

C.M.G. Companion of St. Michael and St. George.

C.M.R. Cape Mounted Rifles.

C.M.S. Church Missionary Society.

Co. County; Company.

C. of E. Church of England.

Col. Colonel; Colony; Colonial.

Coll. College.

Comdt. Commandant.

Comm. Commission(er.)

Cos. Companies.

Coy. Company.

Cr. Created.

C.S.I. Companion of the Star of India.

C.S.O. Chief Staff Officer

C.T. Cape Town.

C.V.O. Commander of the Royal Victorian Order.

d. Died.

D.A.A.G. Deputy-Assistant Adjutant-General.

D.A.G. Deputy Adjutant-General.

D.A.Q.M.G. Deputy-Assistant Quartermaster-General.

Dau. Daughter.

D.C.L. Doctor of Civil Law.

D.C.O. Duke of Cambridge's Own.

D.D. Doctor of Divinity.

D.D.G.M. Deputy District Grand Master.
Dec. December.
D.E.O.V.R. Duke of Edinburgh's Own Volunteer Rifles.
Dept. Department(al).
D.F.H. Diamond Fields Horse.
D.G. Dragoon Guards.
Dist. District.
D.L. Deputy-Lieutenant.
D.M. Diamond Mine(s).
D.M.T. District Mounted Troops.
D.P.H. Diploma of Public Health.
Dr. Debit.
D.R. Dutch Reformed.
D.Sc. Doctor of Science.
D.S.O. Distinguished Service Order.
E. East(ern).
E.C. East Central.
Ed. Editor; edited.
Edin. Edinburgh.
Eng. England.
F.A.S. Fellow of the Society of Arts
F.C. Football Club.
Feb. February.
Fel. Fellow.
F.G.S. Fellow of the Geological Society.
F.I.Inst. Fellow of the Imperial Institute.
F.L.H. Frontier Light Horse.
F.L.S. Fellow of the Linnaean Society.
F.R.A.S. Fellow of the Royal Astronomical Society.
F.R.C.I. Fellow of the Royal Colonial Institute.
F.R.C.P. Fellow of the Royal College of Physicians.
F.R.C.P.E. Fellow of the Royal College of Physicians, Edin.
F.R.C.S. Fellow of the Royal College of Surgeons.
F.R.C.S.E. Fellow of the Royal College of Surgeons, Edinburgh.
F.R.G.S. Fellow of the Royal Geographical Society.
F.R.Hist.S. Fellow of the Royal Historical Society.

F.R.Hort.S. Fellow of the Royal Horticultural Society.
F.R.Met.S. Fellow of the Royal Meteorological Society.
F.R.M.S. Fellow of the Royal Microscopical Society.
F.R.S. Fellow of the Royal Society.
F.R.S.E. Fellow of the Royal Society of Edinburgh.
F.S.A. Fellow of the Society of Antiquaries.
F.R.S.S. Fellow of the Royal Statistical Society.
F.Z.S. Fellow of the Zoological Society.
G.C.B. Knight Grand Cross of the Bath.
G.C.M.G. Knight Grand Cross of St. Michael and St. George.
G.C.I.E. Knight Grand Commander of Indian Empire.
G.G. Grenadier Guards.
G.C.S.I. Knight Grand Commander of the Star of India.
Gen. General.
Gen. Man. General Manager.
Glos. Gloucester(shire).
G.M. Gold Mine; Gold Mining; Grand Master (Masonic).
Govt. Government.
G.P.O. General Post Office.
Gram. Grammar(ian).
Gren. Grenadier.
H.B.M. His (Her) Britannic Majesty(s).
N.E. His Excellency.
H.E.I.C.S. Honourable East India Company's Service.
Herts. Hertfordshire.
Hon. Honourable, Honorary.
H.M. His (Her) Majesty.
H.M.S. His (Her) Majesty's Ship.
H.R.H. His (Her) Royal Highness.
H.S.H. His (Her) Serene Highness.
I.Br. Im. Breisgau.
I.C.S. Indian Civil Service.
I.D.B. Illicit Diamond Buying.
I.G.R. Illicit Gold Buying.
I.L.H. Imperial Light Horse.

Ill. Illinois.
Imp. Imperial.
Imp. Yeo. Imperial Yeomanry.
I.M.R. Imperial Military Railways.
Ind. Med. Indian Medical.
Inf. Infantry.
Invest. Investment.
Intell. Intelligence.
I.S.C. Indian Staff Corps.
I.S.O. Imperial Service Order.
I.W. Isle of Wight.
I.Y. Imperial Yeomanry.
Jan. January.
J.M.R. Johannesburg Mounted Rifles.
J.P. .Justice of the Peace.
K.A.R. King's African Rifles.
K.C. King's Counsel.
K.C.B. Knight Commander of the Bath.
K.C.M.G. Knight Commander of St. Michael
and St. George.
K.C.S.I. Knight Commander of the Star of
India.
K.F.S. Kitchener's Fighting Scouts.
K.G. Knight of the Garter.
K.L.H. Kimberley Light Horse.
Knt. Knight.
K.R. Kaffrarian Rifles.
K.R.R. King's Royal Rifles.
K.W.T. King William's Town.
L.C.C. London County Council.
Ld. Lord; Limited.
L.I. Light Infantry.
Lieut. Lieutenant.
Lieut.-Col. Lieutenant-Colonel.
Lieut.-Gen. Lieutenant-General.
Lit. Literary.
LL.B. Bachelor of Laws.
LL.D. Doctor of Laws.
LL.M. Master of Laws.
L.M.S. London Missionary Society.
Lond. London.
L.R.C.P. Licentiate of the Royal College of
Physicians.
Ltd. Limited.

M.A. Master of Arts.
Maritzburg. Pietermaritzburg.
Maj. Major.
Maj.-Gen. Major-General.
M.B. Bachelor of Medicine.
M.C.C. Marylebone Cricket Club.
Mch. March.
M.D. Doctor of Medicine.
M.E. Mining Engineer.
Med. Medical; Medicine.
Mem. Member.
M.I. Mounted Infantry.
M.I.E.E. Member of the Institution of
Electrical Engineers.
M.I.M.E. Member of Institution of Mechanical
Engineers.
M.Inst.C.E. Memb. of Institution of Civil
Engineers.
M.L.A: Member of Legislative Assembly.
M.L.C. Member of Legislative Council.
M.M.P. Mashonaland Mounted Police.
M.O.O. Money Order Office.
M.P. Member of Parliament.
M.R. Main Reef.
M.R.A.S. Member of Royal Asiatic Society.
M.R.C.I. Member of the Royal Colonial
Institute.
M.R.C.P. Member of the Royal College of
Physicians.
M.R.C.P.E. Member of the Royal College of
Physicians, Edinburgh.
M.R.C.S. Member of the Royal College of
Surgeons.
M.R.C.S.E. Member of the Royal College of
Surgeons, Edinburgh.
Mus. Bac. Bachelor of Music.
M.V.O. Member of the Royal Victorian
Order.
N. North.
Nat. National; Native.
N.B. North Britain; *Nota bene* (note well)
N.C. Natal Carabineers.
N.C.O. Non-Commissioned officer.
N.E. North-east.
N.M.P. Natal Mounted Police.

No. Number.
Northants, Northamptonshire.
Nov. November.
N.S.W. New South Wales.
N.W.P. North-West Province.
N.Z. New Zealand.
Oct. October.
O.F.S. Orange Free State.
O.H.M.S. On His (Her) Majesty's Service.
O.M On Maine; Order of Merit.
O.R.C. Orange River Colony.
Oxon. Oxford, Oxfordshire.
P.A.G. Prince Alfred's Guards.
P. and O. Peninsular and Oriental Steam
Navigation Co.
P.C. Privy Councillor.
P.E. Port Elizabeth.
P.H.Paget's Horse.
Ph.D. Doctor of Philosophy.
P.G.D. Past Grand Director (Masonic).
P.G.M. Past Grand Master (Masonic).
P.M.B. Pietermaritzburg.
P.M.G. PostmasterGeneral
P.M.O. Principal Medical Officer.
P.O. Post Office.
Priv. Private.
Prof. Professor.
P.R.I. President of the Royal Institute of
Painters in Water Colours.
P.B.S. President of the Royal Society.
P.S.C. Passed Staff College.
Pub. Public.
P.W. Public Works.
Q.C. Queen's Counsel,
Q.M. Quartermaster
Q.M.G. Quartermaster General
Q.M.I. Queenstown Mounted Infantry.
q.v. *Quod vide*, which see.
R. Royal.
R.A. Royal Academician; Royal Artillery.
Raad. Volksraad.
R.A.M.C. Royal Army Medical Corps.
R.E. Royal Engineers.
Regt. Regiment(al.
Rev. Reverend.

R.F.A. Royal Field Artillery.
R.G.A. Royal Garrison Artillery.
R.H. Roberts' Horse.
R.H.A. Royal Horse Artillery.
R.H.V. Rhodesia Horse Volunteers.
R.M. Royal Marine(s); Resident Magistrate.
R.M.A. Royal Marine Artillery.
R.M.L.I. Royal Marine Light Infantry.
R.M.S. Royal Mail Steamer.
R.N. Royal Navy; Royal Naval.
R.N.R. Royal Naval Reserve.
R.R. Rand Rifles.
R.S.O. Railway Sub-Office.
Rt. Right.
R.V. Rifle Volunteers,
S. South.
s. Son.
S.A. South Africa(n).
S.A.C. South African Constabulary.
S.A. Coll. South African College.
S.A.L.H. South African Light Horse.
S.A.M.I.F. South African Mounted Infantry
Forces.
S.A.R. South African Republic; South African
Railways.
S.D. Senior Deacon (Masonic).
Sc.D. Camb. Doctor of Science, Cambridge.
Sch. School; Scholar.
S.E. South-east; Stock Exchange.
Sec. Second; Secretary; seconded.
Sept. September.
Secy. Secretary.
S.F.F. Somaliland Field Force.
S.H. Scottish Horse:
S.L.F.F. Sierra Leone Field Force.
S.M.O. Senior Medical Officer.
Soc. Society.
Squad. Squadron.
St. Street; Saint.
S.V.O. Senior Veterinary Officer.
Supt. Superintendent.
Surg. Surgeon.
Surg.-Capt. Surgeon-Captain.
Trans. Transvaal; translate.

Univ. University.
U.K. United Kingdom.
U.S. United States.
U.S.A. United States of America.
v. Against.
V. Van, von.
V.C. Victoria Cross.
V.D. Veterinary Department; Volunteer
Officers' Decoration.
v.d. van der.
Ven. Venerable.
Vice.Pres. Vice-President.
Vol(s). Volume(s), Volunteer(s).
W. West.
W.A. West Africa(n).
W.A.F.F. West African Field Force.
W.C. West Central.
Wilts. Wiltshire.
W.M.R. Winterberg Mounted Rifles.
Yorks. Yorkshire.

The Anglo-African Who's Who

ABBAS HILMY, II., Khedive of Egypt, was born July 14, 1874, is great-great-grandson of Mehemet Ali, the founder of the present Egyptian dynasty, great-nephew of the reactionary Annas I., and son of the late Tewfik Pasha, who succumbed to an attack of influenza in 1892. The present Khedive was educated at Lausanne and at the Theresianum Academy at Vienna, and had supplemented his college training with a course of European travel when, at the age of eighteen, he succeeded his father, with no knowledge of the art of government, but with a strong disinclination to submit to the chafing restrictions which the occupying Power so frequently has had to impose. Thus it was that from the outset the young ruler, not fully appreciating the position and responsibilities of the British in Egypt, adopted an antagonistic attitude towards the introduction of reforms. The differences between Lord Cromer (q.v.) and the Khedive culminated in strong and uncomplimentary expression of opinion by the latter on the value of the Egyptian Army. Lord Cromer took full advantage of the unpleasant occasion to explain to the Khedive the exact relations in which was necessary for the two countries to stand towards one another, and so clearly was the explanation made that there has bever since been visible any recurrence of friction or opposition from the Abdin Palace, a happy consummation, as much attributable to the good sense and intelligence of his Highness as to the character and firmness of the Consul-General. In fact, the former's earlier attitude has since given place to one of cordial co-operation with those who are mainly responsible for progree in Egypt and the welfare of its people. From implacable enmity to everything British he has come to the wise conclusion that "British rule was the best; the people were happier, less taxed, better supplied with water, and that there was no difference made in the administration of justice between the rich and the poor."

Abbas Hilmy Pasha has visited England on five occasions: first as a boy, and again in 1899. In 1900 he stayed as the guest of Queen Victoria, when her late Majesty conferred upon him the Grand Cross of the Royal Victorian Order. He paid a private visit as the guest of Sir Ernest Cassel in June, 1903, and in June, 1905, he was again a guest at Windsor Castle. During these visits he had many intimate conversations with the late and present Sovereigns, and he is said to entertain a warm regard for the British Royal Family and for English institutions; while in Cairo he dispenses hospitality with a charm of manner which never deserts him. He is a great linguist, speaking, besides Arabic, Turkish, English, French and German perfectly, and some Italian.

Abbas II is said to have a very full technical knowledge of machinery, but he principally devotes his leisure to agricultural pursuits on a scientific scale and to horse-breeding. At his model farm and village at Koubeh, near Cairo, he has elaborate poultry establishments, a fine stud of Arab and English-bred horses, and well-stocked kennels. He is much interested in housing reform, and the model dwellings on his estate are far in advance of the objectionable abodes of the ordinary fellah. No rent is charged for these two-roomed houses, the only conditions being that they shall be kept clean and that the children under ten years shall be sent to the Khedive's free school. He is a good musician, and maintains a private band of over fifty performers. He eschews wine, spirits and tobacco, and is, like his father, a monogamist, although as a Mohammedan his religion allows him four wives. His heir is Prince Mohammed Abdul Monem, who was born in the Palace of Montazah, near Alexandria, Feb. 20, 1899. Besides the Order before mentioned, the Khedive was decorated with the G.C.B. in 1892, and was previously made a K.C.M.G.

ABBOTT, Lieutenant Augustus Wathen John Frederick, was born Nov. 16, 1873, and joined the Army Service Corps in 1901. He served in the South African War in 1899-1900 (Queen's medal with three clasps).

ABBOTT, Lieut. Col. Frederick William D.S.O., of Abbotts Road, Auckland, N.Z., and of the Auckland Club, was born in 1865. He entered the New Zealand Volunteers in 1898, and served in the late S. African War with the 7th, 8th, and 9th New Zealand Contingents (despatches, Queen's medal with four clasps, King's medal with two clasps, and the N.Z. Veterans' medal). He married, in 1903,

Annie, dau. of the late P. G. Ritchie, of Wellington, N.Z.

ABERCORN (James Hamilton), Duke of, P.C., K.G., C.B., of 60 and 61, Green Street, W.; Baronscourt, Newtown Stewart, Ireland; Duddingston House, Edinburgh; and of the Carlton, Travellers', Turf, and Marlborough Clubs; was born in 1838. He succeeded the first Duke in 1885, and is looked upon nowadays as an Irish magnate, but, of course, his family is of purely Scottish origin, his oldest title being that of Baron Paisley, created by James the Sixth in 1587, and now borne as a courtesy designation by the Duke's grandchild, Lord Hamilton's little son. The Duke of Abercorn is one of the three nobles who enjoy peerages in all three divisions of the United Kingdom. He owns property in more than one Scottish county, besides his large estate in Ireland; but his only possession in England is his house in Mayfair, the lease of which he holds of the Duke of Westminster. He is also Knt. of the Danneburg Order, of St. Anne of Russia, and of the Iron Crown of Austria. The Duke of Abercorn is the son of one of the most remarkable and interesting personages in the British peerage. His mother, the late Dowager, who only died in 1905, at the age of ninety-two, was the second daughter of the sixth Duke of Bedford. She lived in five reigns, and had over two hundred descendants, almost half the peerage being thrown into mourning by her death. The family is a long-lived one, the grandfather of the late Duchess having been born 195 years before her death. She had seven sons and seven daughters, of whom there were still living at the time of her death the present Duke of Abercorn, Lord Claud Hamilton, Lord George Hamilton, Lord Frederick Hamilton, Lord Ernest Hamilton, Harriet Countess of Lichfield, the Duchess of Buccleuch, the Countess Winterton, the Marchioness of Blandford, and the Marchioness of Lansdowne. Her sons were all famous in one field or another, with the exception of the fourth and fifth, both of whom died young. The second son, Lord Claud, held many posts under the Government, and is chairman of the Great Eastern Railway Company. Her third son, Lord George, has been First Lord of the Admiralty, Secretary of State for India, and chairman of the London School Board. The sixth son, Lord Frederick, was a diplomatist, and is also a well-known literary man; while the seventh, Lord Ernest, is also a politician and novelist. The late Duchess was hostess at Dublin Castle when the King was installed as Knight of St. Patrick in 1868. She was again at Dublin Castle from 1874 to 1876, when her husband resigned the Lord-Lieutenancy of Ireland because of the state of health of the Duchess. She saw five sons in Parliament at the same time-one in the Lords and four in the Commons. Three of her grandsons—the Duke of Marlborough, the Earl of Durham, and the Earl of Lichfield—sit in the Lords, with three of her sons-in-law, the Duke of Buccleuch, the Marquis of Lansdowne, and Lord Mount-Edgcumbe, while no fewer than twenty-two of her descendants fought in the last South African war. She was the grand-daughter, the daughter, the wife, the mother, and the grandmother of dukes, and their titles represented all the three countries which comprise the United Kingdom. These are the Duke of Gordon, the Duke of Bedford, the first Duke of Abercorn, the present Duke, the Duke of Marlborough, and the Duke of Leeds. She was also half-sister to Lord John Russell. The present Duke of Abercorn was educated at Harrow and Christ Church, Oxford, where he graduated M.A. He was Hon. Col. of Donegal Militia from 1860-91; represented Donegal as Conservative M.P. from 1860-80; was Lord of the Bedchamber to the Prince of Wales from 1866-86; and is President of the Ulster Assoc.

For many years, which date from the inception of the Company, the Duke of Abercorn has taken a strong personal and political interest in the Chartered Company, of which he is president, lending the full weight of his influence and a great deal of his time to the development of Rhodesia. He has travelled through the country and is in no sense merely a figurehead, his counsel and advice always carrying great weight with the directors and shareholders. The Duke has also lately become a trustee for the debenture-holders of the Victoria Falls Power Company, which is destined to be the largest electrical power transmission company in the world. The story of the occupation and settlement of Rhodesia is one which suggests much romance, not a little tragedy, and a great deal of live comedy, and much of this may be gleaned from various biographical references in this book. But a

SIR WILLIAM ARBUCKLE

THE DUKE OF ABERCORN

few further remarks concerning Rhodesia—a country larger in area than France, Germany, Austria, and Italy combined—may not inaptly be given in connection with the Duke of Abercorn's name. At a time when more than one European Power was anxious to establish itself in Africa, the British Imperial Parliament could not undertake the vast responsibilities involved in the acquisition of such an extensive territory as that which has for years borne the name of Rhodesia; and had it not been for the foresight and patriotic enterprise of Mr. Cecil Rhodes and his associates in the formation of the Chartered Company, Matabeleland and Mashonaland would probably have fallen to either one of these Powers, or would have become part of the South African Republic. Early in 1888 Lobengula entered into a treaty with Great Britain, and the Royal Charter was granted just a year later. The company having decided to open up Mashonaland first, organised a pioneer expedition under Major Frank Johnson (June, 1890), consisting of about 200 Europeans and 150 native labourers. The aim of the expedition was to cut a road 400 miles long from Macloutsie, passing through the south of Matabeleland and terminating at Mount Hampden, in Mashonaland. This was duly accomplished, and having founded Fort Salisbury at a spot twelve miles south-east of Mount Hampden (September 12, 1890), the column was disbanded, and immediately set to work prospecting and occupying the country. Much was done by the company in the next four years to develop the country, there being then about 1,000 white men in the country. Mining commissioners were appointed, townships laid out, roads constructed to different parts, a postal system inaugurated, and measures taken generally for the settlement of the country. For the protection of the community forts were built, at Tuli, Victoria, Charter, and Salisbury, and a military police force was enrolled. The strength of the force in 1891 reached 650, but was reduced as soon as possible to 140 whites and 15 native police, and a volunteer force ('Mashonaland Horse') 500 strong, raised locally by Major Forbes, took its place; the remainder of the settlers forming a burgher force in case of need. The Chartered Company arranged for the extension northwards of the Cape telegraph and railway from Mafeking, and the surveys for the Beira Railway, connecting Mashonaland with the East Coast, were begun in 1891. A commission of prominent South African farmers came up in 1891 to look into the agricultural prospects of the country, and gave a most satisfactory report, resulting in the organisation of the 'Moodie trek' of farmers with their families, which left the Orange Free State in May, 1892, and founded the settlement of Melsetter, in Gazaland, early in 1893. The first sign of native trouble was in 1893, when Lobengula's young bloods crossed the Mashonaland border in defiance of the white man. Dr. Jameson's pioneers were but a handful, but the sturdy and disciplined adventurers who had made light of the hardships of the early occupation made less of the Matabele hordes who faced their fire, and in three months these descendants of Tshaka surrendered Matabeleland to the representatives, by proxy, of Britain, one regrettable incident only having occurred-the massacre of Major Alan Wilson and his gallant fellows at the Shangani River. But the peace was short-lived, and in 1896 a series of massacres by the natives led to the war which was prolonged well into 1897. These, however, were not the only troubles that retarded the progress of Rhodesia. Rinderpest had practically denuded the country of cattle, unprecedented swarms of locusts laid bare the fields, and no sooner were these difficulties overcome, than the South African war practically closed the country for three years. In spite of these serious drawbacks, however, Rhodesia is now making marked headway. A regular output of gold—steadily increasing, if not magnificent—is being recorded, and considerable attention is now being devoted to agriculture. Much invaluable experience has been accumulated, which is now available for a settler's guidance. Experts have studied the conditions under which he can cultivate semitropical products of high commercial value, such as tobacco, oil, cotton, fibre, and (in special districts) rubber. Fruit-growing has been established as a remunerative branch of farming. The conditions under which the farmer can raise grain of all kinds, both European and indigenous, are far better understood than they were ten years ago, and an important point lies in the fact that by the completion of the Trunk Railway System of Southern Rhodesia, and the establishment of through communication between the port of Beira on the Indian Ocean, the Cape ports and the Victoria Falls, South African as well as external markets have now been opened to local produce.

In this short sketch it is impossible to refer even briefly to all that has been achieved in Rhodesia, or to all the sources of wealth that await its further development. Those, who have but a superficial idea of these interesting possibilities may have their imagination stirred by the vivid pictures photographed by the Cape to Cairo Bioscope Expedition, the Rhodesian section of which was privately shown at the Palace Theatre in Feb. 1907, at the invitation of the Duke of Abercorn and the Directors of the Chartered Company, the subjects representing a most varied and instructive collection of incidents which the general public will have many opportunities of enjoying during the current year. The financial position of the Chartered Company is now more sound than ever before, and it is, of course, very largely interested in the huge electrical power scheme at the Victoria Falls, the possibilities of which are immense.

His Grace married in 1889 Lady Mary Anna Curzon, dau. of the first Earl Howe.

ABERDARE; Lord, D. L., of Duffryn, Mountain Ash, Glam., and of 83, Eaton Square, London, S.W., was born in 1851, and is son of the 1st Baron, whom he succeeded in 1895. He was educated at Rugby, and spent his earlier years in travelling in out-of-the-way places, notably in the then little-known regions of North Africa.

Subsequently he had a long and distinguished career in the House of Commons. Lord Aberdare's powers of organisation have proved valuable for the Princess Mary Village Homes for Poor Children, another of his philanthropic hobbies is the Children's Hospital in Great Ormond Street. He is also an art connoisseur, and has priceless treasures both at his town house and country seat. Lord Aberdare is Hon. Col. of the 3rd Vol. Battn. Welsh Regt. He married, in 1880, Constance, dau. of the late Hamilton Becket and Hon. Mrs. Becket. Lord Aberdare's eldest son and heir, Hon. Henry Lyndhurst Bruce, married Miss Camille Clifford, the well-known American actress.

ACLAND-HOOD, Sir Alexander Fuller, Bart., M.P., of St. Audries, Bridgwater, was educated at Eton, Oxford Univ., and Sandhurst, and entered the Grenadier Guards in 1875. He served in the Egyptian campaign of 1882, and after having acted as A.D.C. to Lord Linlithgow, when the latter was Governor of Victoria from 1889 to 1891, he began the real work of his life in politics. Ten years after he had left the Army he became (1902) Chief Whip to the Conservative Party in the House of Commons.

ABRAHAMSON, Louis, M.L.A., is of German extraction, and belongs to the Jewish community He went to S. Africa from Melbourne as a youth, and was engaged in business in Cape Colony for several years. Going up to the Rand in the early days, he was amongst the first to take an interest in floating the deep levels, including the May Deep, S. Primrose, Wemmer, Worcester, and Robinson Deep. Returning to the Cape he settled down to farming in the Somerset East Dist., and in 1894 was nominated by the Bond to contest Somerset East, for which constituency he was returned at the top of the poll. In July, 1904, he was elected as M.L.A. for one of the new seats for Cape Town. Although he was originally a supporter of the Bond, he subsequently threw in his lot with the Progressives, not approving of the later trend of the Bond policy. He married in 1892 the eldest dau. of Hougham Hudson, late C.C. of Graaff Reinet.

ABRUZZI, Duke of, was born in 1873, and is son of the late Duke of Aosta. He is a keen mountaineer, and in the spring and summer of 1906 he succeeded in gaining the summit of the highest peak of Mount Ruwenzori, never before. touched by human foot. The three highest points he named after King Edward, King Leopold, and King Victor Emmanuel. The Duke has also explored farther into the Arctic regions than has been known before.

A'COURT, Lieut. Col. Charles, C.M.G., of 29, Victoria Road, Kensington, W., was born in 1858, and entered the Rifle Brigade in 1878; in the same year he served in Afghanistan (medal with clasps); the Sudan Expedition in 1898 (despatches, Khedive's and British medals with clasp and brevet Lieut.-Col.); and the South African War in 1899-

1900 with the S. African Light Horse and on the Staff, being present at the relief of Ladysmith and the action at Spion Kop (despatches, Queen's medal with three clasps and C.M.G.).

ACUTT, Ernest Leslie, C.M.G., J.P., of Waverton, Essenwood Road, Berea, Durban, and of the Durban Club, was born at Durban, Nov. 26, 1855, is son of Robert Acutt, of Natal, and formerly of Torquay, Eng. He was educated at Hilton Coll., Natal, is a Government valuator by appointment, was formerly Mayor of Durban, and married, in 1890, Madeline Churchill Gillespie.

ADAMS, Major Sir Hamilton Goold- (See Goold-Adams.)

ADAMS, Dr. Percy Targett, D.P.H., M.R.C.S., of the Public Health Dept., Government Buildings, Bloemfontein, O.R.C., and of the Bloemfontein and Royal Yacht (India) Clubs, was born in England in 1863. He was educated at Durham Univ. and Guy's Hospital. For several years he was Resident Surgeon and afterwards Hon. Asst. Surgeon to the Kent County Ophthalmic Hosp., and has held several other appointments, including Deputy and Assistant Med. Officer of Health for the Borough of Maidstone, Assistant Port Health Officer for Bombay, Assistant Medical Officer to the G.P.O., London, and now holds the post of Government Analyst and Deputy Med. Officer of Health for the O.R.C.

ADAMS, Rev. W. S., formerly curate-in-charge at Harrowbarrow in the St. Dominic parish of Cornwall, volunteered and was accepted for service in the Government leper settlement in Kaffraria, S. Africa, in May, 1906.

ADAMS, Major William Augustus, 5th (Royal Irish) Lancers; of the Junior United Service and Authors' Clubs; was born in Dublin, May 27, 1865, and is eldest son of the Rev. B. W. Adams, D.D. He was educated at Harrow, Dublin University, and Sandhurst, taking first honours in Classics and Modern History; Senior Moderator and Gold Medallist in Modern Languages and Literature. Major Adams was gazetted in 1887, obtained his majority in 1905, and has passed Staff

College. He is an interpreter in Russian, French, Hindustani, etc., and has served in India, Canada, West Indies, and S. Africa, going through the Boer War, 1899-1902, and taking part in the defence of Ladysmith (Queen's medal with four clasps and King's medal with two clasps). He was on special service in Japan in 1903-5, and he published *Rus Divinum*, *Norae Fugaces*, *The Lonely Way*, and *Japanese Conversation in Six Months*. Recreations, rowing, polo, travelling, tennis, literature, etc. Unmarried.

ADAMSON, George, of Johannesburg, is Editor of the *Rand Daily Mail*, and was in 1904 decorated by the Portuguese Government with the important Order of Santiago. The Order was conferred in special recognition of the manner in which the policy of the Transvaal, regarding Delagoa Bay as its natural outlet, had been dealt with by Mr. Adamson.

ADENDORFF, A. R., M.L.A., was elected as Bond representative of Fort Beaufort in the Cape House of Assembly at the general election in 1904.

AGBEBI, Pastor Mojola, M.A., D.D., was born April 10, 1860, in the up-countries of the Colony of Lagos, West Africa. His father was of the Ekiti tribe and his mother of the Kossoh tribe. Removing to Lagos for school advantages, he qualified as a schoolmaster, and subsequently occupied himself as author, poet, leader-writer, preacher, and church organiser. His honorary degrees were conferred on him for literary ability by colleges in Liberia, West Africa, and the United States. He has travelled twice in England and once in America, lecturing on the customs of Africa, and the idiosyncrasies of the native African. He belongs to the school of Africans who, among other things, believe in independent church government for their peoples. He is a Fellow of the Royal Colonial Institute, Organising Secretary of the African Institute, Colwyn Bay, and member of the Toussaint L'Ouverture Republican Club, New York.

AINSWORTH, John, C.M.G., (1900), F.R.G.S., of The Residency, Nairobi, East Africa Protectorate, was born at Manchester, June 16, 1864. He was appointed to charge of the Imperial British East Africa Co.'s transport at Mombasa in

1890, and was given administrative charge of the district of Machakos (Wakamba) in 1892. On the transfer of the company's territory to the Imperial Government in July, 1895, he was appointed H.M. Sub-Commissioner in charge of interior districts; concluded treaties with the Masai, and brought them within effective control of H.M. Govt., and later (1904) he was instrumental in the peaceful introduction of Masai reserves in the Protectorate. During the years 1900-4 he laid out the town of Nairobi, introducing the municipal system; founded the East Africa Agricultural and Horticultural Soc. in 1901, and started an East African quarterly publication in 1904. From 1896 he was Vice-Consul for the interior districts of the East Africa Protectorate until 1904, when such appointments ceased to be in force, and he is now H.M. Sub-Commissioner for the Ukamba Province, E.A.P., Commissioner of Mines, Pres. of the Nairobi Municipal Council, and a 1st class magistrate. He married in 1897 Miss Ina Cameron Scott.

AIRD, Sir John, Grand Cordon of the Medjidieh, of 14, Hyde Park Terrace, London, W., was born Dec. 3, 1833, and was educated privately. He was Unionist M.P. for North Paddington until his retirement at the end of 1905, and is head of the great engineering firm of John Aird and Co., the contractors for the Nile barrage and Assuan reservoir. He is Lieut.-Col. in the Engineer and Railway Staff Corps, and married in 1855, a dau. of Mr. Benjamin Smith.

AITKENS, Ferdinand, J.P., was born at Bournemouth, Jan. 14, 1861; was educated at Bedford Grammar Sch. and Camb. University (non-collegiate). He was a Lieut. in the 3rd Battn. Royal Irish Rifles 1878-80, served in the Louis Riel Rebellion in Canada in 1885, Capt. in the Salisbury Field Force in the Matabele Rebellion in 1896, joined Mr. Coryndon's expedition to Barotseland in 1897, was Assistant to the B.S.A. Co.'s representative in Barotseland in 1898, and received his present appointment as District Commissioner Barotse District in 1900. He is J.P. for N.W. Rhodesia. Unmarried.

ALBEMARLE, Earl of, of Quidenham, Norfolk, and of the Carlton Club, is titular head of the 'Fighting Keppels', a grandson of the earl who fought at Waterloo, and grand-nephew of the late 'Father of the Fleet', and a brother of Mr. Derek Keppel, Equerry to the Prince of Wales. The title dates back to the seventeenth century, when it was conferred on Arnold Joost van Keppel, who came to England with the Prince of Orange in 1688. It was the Earl of Albemarle who as Lord Bury stood for Birkenhead in 1892, after issuing an election placard which has since become historic. The Liberal candidate had decked every hoarding in the constituency with bills bearing the heading: "The Flowing Tide is With Us". Lord Bury immediately outflanked them with another—"Vote for Bury and Dam the Flowing Tide". And he was elected by a big majority.

Lord Albemarle is Brig.-Gen. of the Norfolk Volunteers, and commanded an infantry battn. in the South African War. He is an enthusiastic yachtsman, sportsman, and cyclist, and married, in 1881, the only dau. of the 1st Earl Egerton of Tatton.

ALBU, George, of the firm of G. and L. Albu, of Winchester House, London, E.C., and of Johannesburg, is the chief of one of the most progressive combinations operating on the Rand. The Albu group, as a whole, is managed on up-to-date lines, and a feature in the working of the mines is the introduction of labour-saving and other appliances, with a view to economising expenditure. That the controlling company, the General Mining and Finance Corporation, is well managed is evident from the success which has hitherto attended its operations. In addition to the General Mining and Finance Corporation, the group consists of the Meyer and Charlton, Roodepoort United Main Reef, New Goch, Cinderella Deep, Van Ryn, Aurora West, New Steyn Estate, West Rand Mines, Sacke Estates, Violet Consolidated, and the Midas East Estate G.M. Co., Limited.

Mr. Albu is universally popular, is fond of music, horses, and outdoor sports, but is not in the least attracted by cards or games of chance. He is married and has several children.

ALBU, Leopold, of Winchester House, London, E.C.; Bentley Priory, Stanmore, Middlesex; 4, Hamilton Place, London, W. and of Johannesburg, Transvaal, is a partner in the firm of Messrs. G. and L. Albu, South African merchants, of Winchester House, London, and of Johannesburg. He is brother to George Albu (q.v.), and is a Director of the Aurora West United Gold Mining Co., Ltd., Cinderella Deep, Ltd., Frontier Exploration Syndicate, Ltd., General Mining and Finance Corp., Ltd., of which he is Chairman of the London Board, Meyer and Charlton Gold Mining Co., Ltd., New Goch Gold Mines, Ltd., Rand Collieries, Ltd., New Steyn Estate Gold Mines, Ltd., Roodepoort United Main Reef Gold Mining Co., Ltd., Van Ryn Gold Mines Estate, Ltd., West Rand Consolidated Mines, Ltd., West Rand Mines, Ltd., and the West Rand Trust, Ltd. Married.

ALDERSON, Brig.-Gen. Edwin Alfred Hervey, C.B. (cr. 1900), of the Marlborough and Naval and Military Clubs, son of Col. Edward Mott Alderson, of Poyle House, Ipswich; was born in 1859; was educated at Ipswich Grammar Sch.; entered 97th Regt. 1878, became Capt. Roy. W. Kent Regt. 1886, Major 1896, Brevet Lieut.-Col. 1897, and Brevet Col. 1900. He served in the Transvaal Campaign with Mounted Inf. in 1881; during Egyptian Campaign of 1882, with Mounted Inf., being present at actions of Mahuta and Masameh, battles of Kasassin and Tel-el-Kebir, and the occupation of Cairo (medal with clasp, bronze star); in the Sudan Campaign 1884-5 with Mounted Inf. Camel Regt., when he was present at the battles of Abu Klea, El Gubat, and Metemmeh (two clasps). He did good work in Mashonaland, 1896, with Mounted Inf. and in command of troops (despatches, medal, Brevet Lieut.-Col.), and in S. Africa 1899-1902 in command of four different Mounted Inf. Brigs., being present at relief of Kimberley, battles of Paardeberg and Driefontein, and the occupation of Bloemfontein and Pretoria (several times mentioned in despatches, C.B., A.D.C. to the King, Brevet Col.); was D.A.A.G. and Comdg. Mounted Inf., Aldershot, 1897-9; appointed to command Mounted Inf. in S. Africa

1900, Inspector-Gen. thereof, with rank of Brig.-Gen.; appointed Brig.-Gen.-on-Staff Comdg. 2nd Brig. (lst Div.) lst Army Corps, 1903; has been an extra A.D.C. to H.M. Queen Victoria and H.M. King Edward VII. Since 1900; received Royal Humane Society's medal 1885; author of *With the Mounted Infantry and the Mashonaland Field Force, 1896*; also of *Pink and Scarlet, or Hunting as a School for Soldiering*. He married in 1886 Alice Mary, 2nd dau. of Rev. O. P. Sergeant.

ALEXANDER, Lieut. Boyd, F.Z.S., was born Jan. 16, 1873; joined the Rifle Brigade in 1900, and served in the Gold Coast Constabulary and with the West African Frontier Force in the relief of Kumasi; made an ornithological survey on the Gold Coast, and in Sept., 1902, proceeded to the Benin Islands to investigate their avifauna. Early in 1904 Lieut. Boyd Alexander left England in charge of an expedition to conduct a survey of part of the eastern portions of the Northern Nigerian Protectorate, and also to make zoological collections. He has for several years made a special study of West African birds, and on a previous journey in the interior of the Gold Coast Colony Lieut. Alexander collected a series of a thousand birds, representing 283 species, six of which were new to science. On the last expedition this indefatigable ornithologist and his collectors proceeded from Lokoja, Nigeria, and before reaching Lake Tchad came into conflict with the Marghi tribe, who attacked with poisoned arrows. Having taken the Marghis' entrenched stockade the expedition proceeded, and, arriving at Lake Tchad, cut a passage through the lake-jungle to the little island kingdom of the Buduma tribe. A base camp was established, and much time was occupied in exploring the lake and the region between the S.E. of Tchad and the Congo. Then, striking the caravan route from the South Sahara, the explorers eventually reached the Nile by means of the Yei tributary, arriving in England in Feb., 1907.

ALEXANDER, James Dalison, of 2, St. Helen's Place, London, E.C., is a partner in the firm of Alexander, Fletcher and Co., and is chairman of the Eastern Gold Farms Syndicate, Ltd., and director of the African Banking Corp., Ltd. (See W. J. Thompson.)

ALING, Gerrit, entered the Cape Civil Service in 1894 as Clerk in the High Commissioner's Office. He was employed in the Agricultural Dept. in 1896; acted as Private Secy. to the Minister in 1895, and as Second-Class Clerk in 1899.

ALLDRIDGE, T. J., J.P., F.R.G.S., F.Z.S., F.R.C.I., of Godalming, Surrey; Government House, Bonthe, Sherbro, W.C. Africa, and the Royal Societies Club, was born in 1847; is 2nd son of the late R. W. Alldridge, of Old Charlton, Kent, and was educated at the Blackheath Proprietary School. He was travelling Commissioner for Sierra Leone 1889-93, doing pioneer work to the remote hinterland, especially in the Upper Mendi country, placing many of the paramount chiefs in treaty with the British Govt. He made peace between the Yonnis and Timinis at Robari in 1890, and was on other peace missions. He served through the native rebellion in 1898 (medal and clasp), and was awarded the Cuthbert Peek grant in 1900 in recognition of his geographical work in the interior of Sierra Leone. He is J.P. for the Colony; Commissioner of the Court of Requests; Coroner for Sherbro District; Hon. Corresponding Secy. of the Royal Colonial Institute, and the author of *The Sherbro and its Hinterland*.

ALLEN, Francis, of Egypt, is a director of the Alexandria Bonded Warehouse Co., Ltd., Alexandria Central Buildings Co., Allen, Alderson and Co., Ltd., and the Khedivial Mail Steamship Graving Dock Co., Ltd.

ALLEN, John Alfred, of 6, Westmoreland Buildings, London, EC., is a director of the Akrokerri (Ashanti) Mines, Ltd., and the Gold Coast United, Ltd.

ALLEN, Lewis A., of 1, Pinner's Court, London, E.C., is a partner in the firm of L. Allen and Co., Ltd., and is a director of the Abassi (Wassau) Gold Mines, Ltd. and the Gold Coast Development Syndicate, Ltd.

ALLEN, Rev. Henry William Charles, of Utrecht, Natal; was ordained in the Zululand diocese; was Priest-in-charge of St. Andrew's Mission, Lower Tugela; Priest-in-charge of Annesdale (Zululand) for three years, and was then preferred to the living of Utrecht.

ALTHAM, Col. Edward Altham, C.B., (1904), C.M.G. (1901), 3rd Class Order of the Sacred Treasure (Japan), of 114, Earl's Court Road, London, S.W., and of the Junior Naval and Military Club, Lond.; was born Apr. 13, 1856, at Wilton, Somersetshire, and is the second son of Major W. S. Altham, of Bridgwater. The Althams are a very old family. A younger son was Lord Chief Baron of the Exchequer in Queen Elizabeth's reign, and a daughter of one of the Altham line was wife of Sir John Bankes, who pluckily held Corfe Castle—under historic circumstances—against a siege by Roundheads during the Civil Wars. Col. Altham was educated at Winchester, and Christ Church, Oxford. He joined the Royal Scots in 1876, and was employed with the M.I. Co. of that regt. through Sir Chas. Warren's Bechuanaland expedition in 1884-5; was District Adjt., Cape Town, 1885-7; P.S.C., 1889; D.A.A.G., I N.W. Dist. 1893-6, and was employed in the Intelligence division of the War Office from 1896 to 1899, except from July, 1896, to Mch., 1897, when he was Mil. Secy. to the G.O.C. in S. Africa, Sir W. Goodenough. During the S. African War Col. Altham served as A.A.G. for Intelligence on Sir Geo. White's staff up to the relief of Ladysmith, and subsequently on Lord Methuen's staff in the O.F.S. (medal with four clasps, and promoted Lt.-Col.); was appointed A.Q.M.G. of the strategical branch of the War Office on the re-organisation of the H.G. Staff in 1901, and retired on half-pay in 1904. Col. Altham married in 1880 Emily Georgina, dau. of W. Macpherson Nicol, of Inverness.

AMERY, Leopold Charles Maurice Stennett, M.A., of 2, Temple Gardens, E.C.; All Souls' Coll., Oxford, and of the Royal Societies and Alpine Clubs, was born in India, Nov. 22, 1873, and is son of the late C. F. Amery, of the Indian Forest Service. He was educated at Harrow, and Balliol Coll., Oxford (Exhibitioner, B.A., took a first-class in Moderations, 1896; Fellowship at All Souls' Coll., 1897). He gained the Ouseley Scholarship for knowledge of Turkish at the Imperial Institute in 1895. He acted as private sec. to the Rt. Hon. L.

H. Courtney, M.P., in 1896-7, and travelled in Europe and the Near East in 1897-8, contributing articles on travel and politics to the *Times*, *Manchester Guardian*, and *Edinburgh Review*. He joined the regular staff of the *Times* in 1899 as asst. foreign editor, and acted as correspondent in Berlin for part of that year, subsequently going out to S. Africa. He was in the Boer laager at Sandspruit when the war broke out, and was sent back by Gen. Joubert to Cape Town, where he was appointed by the *Times* to organise and direct their staff of correspondents during the war. He edited the *Times* history of the war, in six vols., leaving S. Africa in 1900 for that purpose. After completing Vol. II he revisited S. Africa at the close of war, in order to examine battlefields. He is on the council of the Imperial S. African Association, and contested E. Wolverhampton as Unionist candidate. He was champion of the gymnasium at Harrow; ran for Oxford against Cambridge in the cross-country race in 1896; is also a keen mountaineer; and is fond of boat sailing and travelling.

AMPHLETT, Captain Charles Edward, was born Nov. 30, 1879, and joined the 6th Dragoons in Aug., 1898, as 2nd Lieutenant, becoming Captain in 1902. He served in the South African Campaign in 1899-1901, taking part in the operations in the Orange Free State in 1900, including the actions at Vet River and Zand River; the operations in the Transvaal in May and June, 1900, and being present at the actions near Johannesburg, Pretoria, and Diamond Hill; the operations in the Transvaal east of Pretoria, including the actions at Riet Vlei and Belfast; the operations in Cape Colony south of the Orange River, including the actions at Colesberg in Jan. and Feb., 1901; and the subsequent operations in the Transvaal (Queen's medal with five clasps).

AMPHLETT, George Thomas, F.R.C.I., of Uhlenhorst, Rondebosch, Cape Colony, and the Imperial Colonies Club, was born in London Jan. 1, 1852; was educated at the Philological School, Marylebone, and King's Coll., London. He was one of the only two who passed the first exam. of the English Bankers' Inst., and is Secy. in Cape Town of the Standard Bank of S.A. He won the sculling championship of Hamburg in 1874, and is

Vice-Pres. of the Mountain Club of S.A. In February, 1902, he rescued three N.C.O.s from a perilous position on Devil's Peak, Cape Town, after 55 hours' detention on a narrow ledge, receiving the thanks of the Chief Army Paymaster and Staff with a presentation. During the late S.A. War he was Capt. in the Town Guard, Cape Town. He is an Assoc. of the Inst. of Bankers; mem. of the Philosophical Society (C.T.); mem. of the S.A. Assoc. for the Advancement of Science, and is Past Grand Warden of the Provincial Grand Lodge of South Africa.

AMYAND, Arthur. (See Major E. A. Haggard.)

ANCKETILL, Henry, M.L.A., is 4th son of the late M. J. Ancketill, J.P., D.L., of Ancketill's Grove, Co. Monaghan, Ireland, where he was born May 4, 1855. He entered the Royal Navy in 1869, but left the service in 1875, and read for Holy Orders, going through a course at Chichester Theological College. Finally he devoted himself to social and economic questions, writing extensively in various publications. He became an enthusiastic follower of Henry George, and in 1886 went to the U.S.A., where he was associated with him in *The Standard*. He returned to England in 1889, and became organising secretary of the English Land Restoration League. Early in 1896 Mr. Ancketill settled in Durban, and in Sept., 1901, won one of the seats for the Natal capital in the Legislative Assembly. He is one of the vice-presidents of the English League for the Taxation of Land Values, and never loses an opportunity of advocating reform in this connection both in and out of Parliament. He is also a strenuous advocate of woman suffrage, and was the first member to present a petition from the women of the Colony to the Natal Parliament in 1904. He married in 1900 Miss Oona Recson, of Durban, an artist who has gained some distinction as a portrait painter.

ANDERSON, D. M., of Bloemfontein, O.R.C., entered the Orange River Colony Postal Service in 1903 as Assistant at Philippolis, and was transferred to the Post Office Savings Bank at Bloemfontein in 1904.

ANDERSON, Ebenezer Thomas, of The Residency, Beaufort West, Cape, Colony, was born in the Oudtshoorn dist. of the Cape Colony, Dec. 11, 1855; is grandson of the Rev. Wm. Anderson, L.M.S., the founder of Griquatown, and son of Rev. B. E. Anderson, of Oudtshoorn. He was educated at the Diocesan Coll., Rondebosch, and entered the Cape Civil Service in 1873 as clerk to the C.C. and R.M. at Port Elizabeth. He was subsequently chief clerk to the High Sheriff and Master of the Supreme Court at Cape Town; and has since served as C.C. and R.M. at Barkly West (1889); Prince Albert (1895), Humansdorp (1901), and Beaufort West (1904). He married in 1881 Fanny, dau. of the Rev. Hy. Kayser, of Port Elizabeth.

ANDERSON, Edgar, of 20, Copthall Avenue, London, E.C., is chairman of the Sudan Exploration, Ltd. , and a director of the North Nile Valley Co., Ltd.

ANDERSON, Rev. Frederick Ingall, M.A., of Savoy House, Cairo, was born at Chester in 1874, and is son of the Rev. F. Anderson, of Chester. He was educated at Bradfield Coll., and Jesus College, Cambs.. (Mathematical Scholarship, Senior Optime, Mathematical Tripos, 'Lady Kaye' Scholar, 3rd class Theological Tripos); was one of the Cambridge Univ. Football XI. in 1895, and also played in the Corinthian team in that year. He was ordained by the Bishop of Ely in 1898, and has since been curate at Holy Sepulchre Church, Cambs., curate-in-charge at Westward Ho!, N. Devon, Chaplain to the Forces at Aldershot, and is at the present time Chaplain to the Forces at Cairo. He married, Jan. 20, 1903, Dora, eldest dau. of the late Gen. Channer, C.B., V.C., Indian Army.

ANDERSON, Ralf William, has been employed in the Audit Department of the Orange River Colony since 1901, being appointed Assistant Auditor there in 1902.

ANDERSON, Thomas Johnson, M.L.A., represents Cape Town in the Progressive interest in the House of Assembly; he was last elected at the general election in 1904.

ANDERSON, Lieut.-Col. William Campbell, D.S.O., of Earlywood, Windlesham, Surrey, was born in 1868. He joined the 15th (King's) Hussars

in 1890, and was promoted in 1892 and 1896. In the latter year he was selected for duty in the Niger Coast Protectorate, and subsequently became assistant inspector of the Gold Coast Constabulary at Accra. In February, 1900, he was appointed adjutant of the 5th Imperial Yeomanry, and rose to the command in South Africa (despatches, two medals and clasps, and D.S.O.). He is now in command of the 4th Batt. Border Regiment, and married in 1894 Elizabeth, dau. of the late Ed. Barnes.

ANDREWS, Martindale Stewart, Director of Telegraphs, Gold Coast Colony; of the Blenheim Club, was born Nov. 20, 1865, and was educated at Merchant Taylors' Sch. Joining the Eastern Tel. Co. in 1881, he was at Alexandria at the time of Arabi's rebellion in 1882, and remained there until in 1886 he was transferred to the African Direct Tel. Co. at Bathurst, Gambia, and in 1887 to Accra, as superintendent, becoming Director of Govt. Telegraphs in 1891. Mr. Andrews served with the Ashanti Field Force under Sir Jas. Willcocks in 1900, being mentioned in despatches (medal). He is an official member of the Accra Town Council, and married in 1892 Catherine Elizabeth, widow of Rev. Bell Grant, and only dau. of the late W. Large, of Ogbourne St. Andrew, Marlborough.

ANGEHRN, Adolf, of Cape Town, South Africa, is managing director of the Federal Supply and Cold Storage Co., of South Africa, Ltd.

ANNAN, John, of 21, Ironmonger Lane, London, E.C., is chairman of the Durban Navigation Collieries, Ltd., Gold Coast Amalgamated Mines, Ltd., New York City Free hold Estates Corp., Ltd., United Gold Coast Mining Properties, Ltd., and the Wassau (Gold Coast) Mining Co., Ltd., and is director of the Abbontiakoon Block 1, Ltd., Abbontiakoon (Wassau) Mines, Ltd., Chida (Wassau) Mines, Ltd., Effuenta (Wassau) Mines, Ltd., Gold Coast Investment Co., Ltd., Gold Coast Pioneer Syndicate, Ltd., New Gold Coast Agency, Ltd., the West African Gold Trust, Ltd., and a few other companies.

ANSON, Hon. F. C. M., of Lagos, W. Africa, was formerly for twenty years in the Civil Service of

British Guiana; then served for a short while as Treas. of St. Lucia, prior to his present appointment as Colonial Treas. of Lagos.

ANTILL, Lieut.-Col. John Macquaire, C.B.; of Sydney, and of the Australian Club, was born in N.S.W. Jan. 26, 1866. He raised and commanded a squadron of Mounted Rifles at Picton, N.S.W. in 1889; was selected by the general officer commanding for training with the Imperial troops in India, 1893-4, where he gained certificates as an instructor. He joined the General Staff as Permanent Adjt. of the Mounted Rifle Regt. in S. Africa, 1894, and commanded the lst contingent of Mounted Rifles there; served in the S. African War in 1899-1901, chiefly in De Lisle's corps under Generals Ian Hamilton, Alderson, and Hutton. Until Feb., 1900, he was in command of a detachment N.W. of Cape Colony, when he joined Lord Roberts' advance and was present at the relief of Kimberley, Paardeberg, Poplar Grove, Driefontein, the occupation of Bloemfontein, actions at the Vet and Zand Rivers, Johannesburg, and Pretoria (June 4), Diamond Hill, and the operations in connection with the pursuit of De Wet in the Wittebergen (mentioned in despatches, and created C.B.). On his return to N.S. Wales he was appointed Chief Instructor of the Australian Light Horse, A.D.C. to the Governor-General, and promoted Lieut.-Col. for his services. He married Oct. 24, 1901, Agnes, eldest dau. of Thomas Polk Willsallen, of Gunnedale, N. S. W.

ANTROBUS, Reginald Lawrence, C.B., B.A. Oxon., of 19, Cranley Gardens, London, S.W., was born Sept. 5, 1853; is son of the late Rev. Geo. Antrobus, M.A., Vicar of Beighton, Derbyshire, and was educated at Winchester and New Coll., Oxon. He entered the Colonial Office in 1877; was private secretary to the Earl of Derby 1882-5, and to Col. the Rt.. Hon. F. A. Stanley, M.P. (now Earl of Derby) 1885-6, and to Earl Granville, 1886; acted as Governor of St. Helena, 1889-90, and was appointed Under-Secretary of State for the Colonies in 1898. He married lst, in 1880, Selina Jane (dau. of the Rev. A. Leighton Irwin), who died in 1900; and 2nd, Edith Marion, dau. of John Robinson, of Liverpool.

APTHARP, Major K.P., was educated at Charterhouse, and entered the Royal Irish Regt. in 1881. He took part in the Nile Expedition in 1885 (medal with clasp and Khedive's star); the Black Mountain Expedition in 1888 (medal with clasp); acted as A.D.C. to the Lieut.-Governor of the Punjab from 1889-91, Special. Service Officer at Lucknow from 1892-94, and Adjutant in the Oudh Light Horse from 1894-99; served in the South African War in 1900-1, including the operations in the Orange Free State and Cape Colony (despatches, medal with two clasps and Kings medal). In 1900 he was appointed a District Commissioner in the Orange River Colony; joined the S. African Constabulary in 1901; appointed Secy. of the O.R.C. Land Settlement Board in 1901, and Director of Land Settlement in 1905, which position he still holds.

AQUA, King; one of the chiefs of the Cameroons, in German West Africa, who was condemned to nine years' imprisonment by Herr von Puttkamer (q.v.). King Aqua has a son, Aqua, educated in Germany, who is well versed with the language and the law.

ARBUCKLE, Hon. Sir William, Knt., M.L.C., J.P., of 26, Victoria St., London, S.W., and of the Victoria (P.M.B.) and Durban Clubs, was born of Scottish parents in 1839 and served a long apprenticeship in a mercantile business, of which he ultimately became manager, subsequently carrying on a merchant business of his own formation in Durban, from which he has since retired. Sir William was many times Mayor of that borough, and first became a member of the old Natal Legislative Council in 1884, when he was elected for Durban County. On the establishment of Responsible Government in 1893 he was nominated M.L.C. for Maritzburg, and was appointed Chairman of Committees. In 1897 he joined Sir Henry Binns' Cabinet as Treasurer, and in January, 1902, became Pres. of the Natal Legislative Council, being knighted in the same year. He succeeded Sir Walter Peace as Agent-General for Natal in London in 1905, and in the following year was appointed a Commissioner of Oaths for Natal in London. Sir William married in 1865 the eldest dau. of Henry Shire, one of the pioneers of sugar cultivation in the garden colony.

ARCHER, Hon. Francis Bisset, M.Exec.C., M.L.C., J.P., of Bathurst, the Gambia; of 72, Bishop's Mansions, Bishop's Park Road., S.W.; and of the Grosvenor Club; eldest son of Capt. F. G. Archer, late of the Commissariat Dept., by a niece of Sir Henry Fox Bristowe, late Vice-Chancellor of the Duchy of Lancaster, and grandson of Commissary-Gen. Archer, was born in British Honduras Aug. 1, 1868. In Feb., 1894, he joined the Colonial Service as Principal Clerk, Col. Secy.'s. Office, Gold Coast; promoted Chief Clerk 1896, and acted as Asst. Col. Secy., Clerk of Executive and Legislative Councils. He held a commission in the Gold Coast Volunteers, acting as adjt. for some time, and holds a Field Officer's certificate. In 1897 he was transferred to Lagos as Asst. Col. Secy.; 1st Asst, in 1899, and had charge of the Dept, during the various periods when Sir Geo. Denton (q.v.) administered the Govt. between 1899 and 1902; he acted as Col. Treasurer, as Member of the Legislative and Executive Councils, and was appointed Receiver-Gen. of the Gambia Jan., 1903. He acted as Col. Secy. Feb.-Aug., 1903, and June, 1904-May, 1905; also as Dep.. Governor April-May, 1905, and is J.P. for the Colony. Mr. Archer is author of the *History and Development of the Gambia*, and compiled the *Lagos Official Handbook*. He married, Mch. 15, 1894, Daisy, youngest dau. of the late Dr. J. G. Thompson, D.D., M.A.

ARCHIBALD, Robert Montgomery, M.L.A., J.P., of Umzinto, Natal, has been for years one of the representatives of Alexandra County in the Natal House of Assembly, and succeeded Sir James Hulett (q.v.) as Speaker in Nov., 1902. He is a prosperous sugar planter, trader, and farmer.

ARROL, Sir William, Knt., M.P., LL.D., of Seafield, Ayr, was born in 1839. He is chairman of and senior partner in the engineering firm of William Arrol and Co., and constructed the Forth and Tay bridges; is also a member of the Union-Castle Mail Steamship Co., Ltd. (see Sir Donald Currie), and a director of J. & P. Coats, Ltd., Stewarts and Lloyds, Ltd., and the Union Bank of Scotland, Ltd. He married, first in 1864, and secondly, in 1905, Miss Hodgart, of Lockerbank, Ayr.

ASCHAM, Roger, Organist to the Municipality of Port Elizabeth, of Harrowden, Havelock St., Port Elizabeth, and of the Deutsche Liedertafel Club, was born at Bonner Rd., Victoria Park, Aug. 28, 1864, and was educated at the Royal Normal College of Music for the Blind, Upper Norwood. Mr. Ascham comes of musical parents, and received his first tuition in music when six years old at the hands of his mother. A few years later he joined the choir of St. Clements, Bournemouth, studying under the church organist, Dr. Linter. On the departure of Dr. Linter he succeeded him as organist, at the age of thirteen years, and held the post for two years. As the services of St. Clement's were 'high' and the music somewhat elaborate, the youthful organist might have justly been regarded as an infant prodigy. After leaving Bournemouth the young musician went to the Royal Normal College in Upper Norwood as music reader, where he remained 32 years, teaching the piano during his last year. At this time he was studying under Fritz Hartvigson (piano) and Dr. Hopkins (organ), choral singing under W. H. Cummings, and harmony under the late H. C. Banister. After leaving the College Mr. Ascham became Organist and Choirmaster of All Saints' Church, Wellingboro', Northamptonshire, and during this period frequently gave recitals at Northampton, Kettering, Oundle, Stamford, etc. In 1890 he went to S. Africa, having accepted the post of Music Master to the Girls' Collegiate School at Port Elizabeth, which position he holds at the present day, together with the Organship of Trinity, the principal church at the Bay. Mr. Ascham has held the appointment of Town Organist at Port Elizabeth since 1893, but it is as a pianist he is most widely known. He has written a large number of compositions, of which over fifty are published. They include principally works for the piano; also violin, organ, and violoncello, and German and English songs. One of his most popular compositions for the organ is entitled *Slumber and Rest*; of his songs two favourites are *Annabel Lee* and *Ich Liebe Dich*. He married first, July 20, 1885, Miss Margaret Jane Reece, a former student of the Royal Normal College, who was blind (died 1837), and secondly, in 1903, Miss Alice Thompson, formerly of Wellingboro'. He has 3 children living by his first wife.

Mr. Ascham is an enthusiastic Freemason, and has twice been the W.M. of the. Good Hope Lodge, No. 863 (1902-1903 and 1904-1905), and has published a complete Masonic Musical Service (Vincent Co.).

ASHBURNHAM, John Anchitel, of Bloemfontein, O.R.C., was born Feb. 6, 1865. He is son of John Woodgate Ashburnham, belonging to an old Sussex family, whose ancestor, Bertram Ashburnham, was Constable of Dover Castle at the time of the Conquest, and was beheaded by the Conqueror immediately after his accession. Mr. J. A. Ashburnham was educated at Lancing Coll., and Exeter Coll., Oxford. In 1888 he was appointed Secy, to the British Bechuanaland Administration. He was Asst. Commissioner, Bechuanaland Protectorate, 1895-1901, Actg. Resident Commissioner 1901, and became Resident Magistrate at Bloemfontein in the same year. This position he still holds. He accompanied the High Commissioner to the conferences between H. E. and the Pres. of the late S.A.R. at Brignant's Pont in March, 1890, and at Colesburg in April, 1893, and was Chairman of the Land Laws Enquiry Commission, O.R.C., Oct., 1901. He acted as Colonial Secretary of the Orange River Colony from lst April, 1904, for six months. He, married, June 20, 1894, Jean, dau. of the late Rev. R. Price.

ASHMORE, Sir Alexander Murray, K.C.M.G., after serving in Ceylon, the Gold Coast, and Cyprus, was appointed Government Secretary of British Guiana in 1900, and administered the Government of that Colony in 1901. Sir Alexander also acted as Commissioner to inquire and report on the Transvaal Concesssions in 1900. He was created K.C.M.G. on the occasion of the King's birthday, 1905.

ATHERSTONE, Guybon Damant, M.Inst. C.E., M.R.C.I., of Grahamstown (Cape Colony), and of the Port Elizabeth, Bloemfontein, and Albany (Grahamstown) Clubs, was born at Grahamstown June 20, 1843; is son of the late Hon. W. G. Atherstone, M.D., M.L.C., and was educated at St. Andrew's Coll., Grahamstown, and King's Coll., London, of which he is an Associate. Mr. Atherstone was employed as engineer to the Cape Govt. Railways from July, 1873, to Dec. 31, 1896,

when his services were transferred to the Railway Dept. of the O.F.S., of which he was Chief Engineer until March, 1900, when this office was abolished and he was pensioned. However, he is now re-employed by the Cape Govt. as engineer in charge of the Alexandria Surveys.

ATHERSTONE, Dr. Walter Herschel, of Port Alfred, Cape Colony, was acting District Surgeon at Bathhurst, and Medical Officer at Kowie Convict Station in 1888; was appointed Surgeon Superintendent at Port Alfred Asylum in 1889; Medical Superintendent there in 1898; and acted as Senior Medical Officer at Robben Island from 1896-1901, when he was appointed Medical Superintendent at Port Alfred, which appointment he still holds.

ATHERSTONE, W. J., of Rhodesia, was selected at the latter end of 1903 for the office of Surveyor-Gen. of S. Rhodesia in succession to Mr. J. M. Orpen (q.v.).

ATKINSON, Lewis, of 73, Basinghall St., London, E.C., and of the African and Imperial Service Clubs, was born Sept. 20, 1855, in London. He was educated privately, and entered into business with a firm of diamond and precious stone cutters. In 1881 the freedom of the City of London was conferred upon him, and later he received the Livery of the Worshipful Company of Turners. In 1886 he managed the Diamond Washing, Cutting, and Polishing Works in the Cape Court of the Colonial and Indian Exhibition; had charge of the diamond industries at the Glasgow Exhibition in 1888, and in 1889 was manager of the Diamond Cutting Works at the Glasgow Exhibition. He took charge of the De Beers and Cape Govt. exhibits at the Paris Exhibition in 1900, and afterwards took over the curatorship of the Cape Colony and Bechuanaland at the Imperial Institute, until 1904. Meanwhile (in 1902) he was appointed Emigration Officer to the Cape Govt. in London, and (in 1905) Commercial Agent to the Cape Govt.

AVEBURY, The Rt. Hon. Baron, Bart., P.C., F.R.S., D.C.L., LL.D. Camb., Edin., and Dubl., and M.D. Wurzburg, of High Elms, Down, Kent; Kingsgate Castle, Kingsgate, Thanet; 6, St. James' Sq.; and of the Athenaeum, National Liberal, and

City Liberal Clubs; born April 30, 1834, at 29, Eaton Place, educ. at Eton, represented the constituency of Maidstone 1870-80, and the Univ. of London in the Liberal and afterwards in the Unionist interest 1880-1900. He is the head of the great banking house of Robarts, Lubbock and Co., and was second Pres. of the African Society. Lord Avebury is known in the literary world as the author of *The Scenery of England*, *The Scenery of Switzerland*, *The Use of Life*, *The Beauties of Nature*, *The Pleasures of Life*, (Parts I. and II), *British Wild Flowers Considered in Relation to Insects, Flowers, Fruit, and Leaves*, *The Origin and Metamorphoses of Insects*, *On Seedlings, Ants, Bees, and Wasps*, *On the Senses, Instincts, and Intelligence of Animals*, *Chapters in Popular Natural History*, *Monograph on the Collembola and Thysanura*, *Prehistoric Times*, *The Origin of Civilisation and the Primitive Condition of Man*, *On Representation*, *On Buds and Stipules*, *La Vie des Plantes*, *Free Trade*, *Coins and Currency*, *Scientific Lectures*, and *Fifty Years of Science*, being the Address delivered to the British Association in 1881. Many of these works are translated into foreign languages, including Russian, Polish, Bohemian, Estonian, Greek, Arabic, Hindustani, Gujerati, Mahrattee, and Japanese, but more popularly he will be remembered, when he was simply Sir John Lubbock (the 4th Bart.), as having selected the 'hundred best books' published by Messrs. Harmsworth. He is also the author of over 100 Memoirs published by the Royal and other scientific societies. He is Pres. of the Soc. of Antiquaries, a Trustee of the British Museum, and Foreign Secretary of the Royal Academy. The German Order *Pour le Merité* was conferred upon him in 1902. He is also a Commander of the Legion of Honour. Lord Avebury has been twice married : first, in 1856 to Miss Hordern, dau. of the Rev. P. Hordern; and second, in 1881, to Miss Fox-Pitt-Rivers, dau. of Gen.. Fox-Pitt-Rivers.

AYLMER, Colonel Fenton John, V.C., was born April 5, 1862, and entered the Royal Engineers as Lieutenant in 1880, becoming Colonel in 1901. He took part in the Burmese Expedition in 1886-8 (despatches, medal with clasp); the Hazara Expedition in 1891 (despatches and clasp); the Hunza Nagar Expedition in 1891-2, commanding the Royal Engineers (despatches, V.C., and Brevet of Major); the Isazai Expedition in 1892; and the operations in Chitral in 1895 with the Relief Force, being present at the storming of the Malakand Pass, the action near Khar on the descent into the Swat Valley, the Passage of the Swat River, and the actions at Panjkora River and Mamazai (despatches, Brevet of Lieut.-Col., and medal with clasp).

BADENHORST, F. H., M.L.A., sits in the Cape House of Assembly as member for Swellendam. He belongs to the S. African Party, and was last elected in Feb., 1904.

BADENHORST, J. F., M.L.A., represents the constituency of Riversdale in the Cape House, of Assembly, and is a supporter of the Bond. He was returned unopposed at the general election in 1904.

BADEN-POWELL, Major-Gen. Robert Stephenson Smyth, C.B., F.R.G.S., of 32, Prince's Gate, London, and of the Cavalry, Naval and Military, and Beefsteak Clubs, is son of Prof. Baden-Powell, his mother being dau. of Admiral Smyth. Gen. R. S. S. Baden-Powell was born in London, Feb. 22, 1857, was educated at Charterhouse, and joined the 13th Hussars in 1876, being Adjt. from 1882 to 1886, Capt. in 1883, Major in 1892, and Brev. Lt.-Col. in 1896. He transferred to the 5th Dragoon Guards in 1897, shortly afterwards receiving the brevet rank of Colonel. His promotion to Major-Gen. dates from May, 1900.

Gen. Baden-Powell was A.D.C. and Asst. Military Secretary to the General Officer commanding in Cape Colony in 1888, taking part in the operations in Zululand in that year. From 1890 to 1893 he served in a similar capacity at Malta, and in 1895-6 was honourably mentioned in connection with the Ashanti Expedition, receiving the brevet rank of Lt.-Col. and the Star. He was employed on special service in the second Matabele War in 1896-7, when he rendered invaluable services as C.S.O. to Col. Plumer. During the operations in the Matopos he commanded the advanced force during its attacks on Babyaan's stronghold, July 20, 1896; performed excellent service in risky scouting work by night and day in the Matopos, and commanded successful patrols in clearing the Shangani, Wedza, and Belingwe districts. (Despatches, brev. of Colonel and Medal.)

In the great South African War he gained great popularity by his gallant defence of Mafeking and was promoted Maj.-Gen. in recognition of his distinguished services in the field. Later he raised and commanded the S.A.C., a corps which at one time numbered 10,000 strong (Queen's medal with three clasps, King's medal with two clasps, and the C.B.). Relinquishing this command in 1903, he was appointed Inspector-Gen. of Cavalry in Great Britain and Ireland. Gen. Baden-Powell takes his profession seriously and enthusiastically. He has written a useful text book on scouting, which is also regarded as a text book by, the German Army; he is a clever sketcher and has considerable theatrical talent. In 1884 he won the Kadir Cup for pig-sticking in India, and he plays polo and golf. Unmarried.

BAGOT, Major the Hon. Walter Lewis, D.S.O., of the Guards', Travellers', and Pratts' (London), Rand and Athenaeum (Johannesburg), and Durban Clubs; was born April 22, 1864, at Blithfield, Rugeley, Staffs; and is younger son of William, Third Lord Bagot. He was educated at Eton and Royal Military College, Sandhurst. Entered the Grenadier Guards as Lieut. in 1884; was A.D.C. to the Governor of South Australia, 1890; took part with the lst Battalion in the Sudan Campaign, 1898; including the battle of Omdurman (British medal, Khedive's medal and clasp). Retired Dec., 1898; assisted Lord Chesham in raising the Imperial Yeomanry in Dec., 1899; recalled to active service as D.A.A.G., I.Y., and took part in the Boer War from Feb., 1900. On reaching Pretoria he was appointed Administrator of Civil Posts to reconstitute the P.O. Department of the Transvaal. He joined Col. Sir Henry Rawlinson's force as Chief Staff Officer April, 1901 (mentioned in despatches, Queen's medal, three clasps, D.S.O., King's medal, two clasps, brevet of Major), and served as such until the conclusion of the war. He organised the Chamber of Mines Labour Importation Agency for the importation of Chinese labour for the Witwatersrand mines, of which Agency he is general manager. He married Feb., 1891, Margaret, youngest dau. of the late Hon. Fredk. Cadogan.

BAILEY, Amos, M.L.A., represents the constituency of Woodstock in the Progressive interest in the Cape House of Assembly, and was last elected in Feb., 1904.

BAILEY, Abe, J.P. (Sussex), D.L. (City of London), Capt. Sussex Imp. Yeomanry, of Yewhurst, East Grinstead; Summerstone Lodge, Pateley Bridge, Yorks; Ruste en Vrede, Muizenberg; Clewer House, Johannesburg; and of the Raleigh, Wellington, Rand, Kimberley, and Civil Service (C.T.) Clubs; was born in Cape Colony in 1864. He is the only son of T. Bailey (q.v.), was educated in England, and proceeded first to Barberton and then to Johannesburg in the early days where he soon acquired large mining interests. He was an active member of the Reform Committee; was tried for high treason against the Govt. of the late S.A.R.; was imprisoned, and only released on payment of the generally imposed fine of £2,000.

At the commencement of the S.A. War he served as Intelligence Officer with Lord Roberts, and took a prominent part in the formation and organisation of Roberts' Horse and the S.A. Light Horse, largely contributing to the expense of their equipment, and afterwards proceeded to the front with the rank of Major as second in command with Gorringe's Flying Column, which he was also partly instrumental in raising. After the war (in Oct., 1902) he was appointed to the command of Kitchener's Fighting Scouts. Mr. Bailey entered the arena of Cape Colonial politics in 1902, when he was elected unopposed in the Progressive interest for Barkly West, the only constituency which the late Cecil Rhodes ever represented in the Cape Legislative Assembly. He was Whip of the Progressive Party, and was re-elected at the general election in Feb., 1904, retiring in 1905 with a view to devoting himself to Transvaal politics. In the summer of 1906 he came to England to lay the views of the Transvaal Progressive party as regards the new Constitution before the British Government.

He is a keen patron of all forms of sport, racing in both S. Africa and England, and indulges particularly in shooting and cricket. He was elected Pres. of the Wanderers' Club (Johannesburg) in 1902, and is a member of the M.C.C. and many other sporting clubs. He married Caroline, elder dau. of John Paddon, who died in 1902, leaving him with two children: John Milner (godson of Lord Milner) and Cecil Marguerite Sidwell (godchild of the late Cecil Rhodes).

BAILEY, Captain William Edward, was born Feb. 7, 1858, and received his first commission in the Army in 1896, becoming Captain in 1900. He took part in the Nile Expedition in 1884-5 (medal with clasp and bronze star); the operations in the Sudan in 1889, being present at the action of Toski (clasp); the Dongola Expedition in 1896 (despatches, promoted 2nd Lieut., medal and Egyptian medal with two clasps), and the Nile Expeditions of 1897-8, as Staff Officer in the Egyptian Army at the Base (4th class Medjidie). Captain Bailey retired from the East Yorkshire Regt. in Feb., 1903.

BAIN, Charles Alfred Oliver, of the Constitutional Club, London, and of the Rand and New Clubs, Johannesburg, was born at Port Elizabeth, Aug. 12, 1864. He is son of Samuel Bain, whose father Thomas Bain (of the East India Co.'s Service), settled in 1850 at Port Elizabeth, where he was a prominent citizen and Councillor and was Mayor (twice) and District Grand Master of the Eastern Province Masonic Lodge. Mr. C. A. O. Bain was educated at Grey Institute, Port Elizabeth, and at Driffield Coll., Yorks. In 1886 he made an attempt to open up the Millwood Goldfields at Knysna, but recognising that those fields were doomed to failure, went to the Transvaal in Dec., 1887, and became associated with the African Estates group in 1894. In 1898, with the intention of retiring from business, he returned to England, but became Chairman of the Estate Finance and Mines Corporation in London, finally returning in 1893 to S.A. as Managing Director of that company in Johannesburg.

Mr. Bain used to be prominent in football and gymnastics, and was one of the founders of the Olympic F.C., the most important in the Eastern Province. He was Pres. of the Musical Section of the Wanderers' Club, 1888-9, and Acting-Pres. of the Transvaal Game Protection Society. He married, Feb. 2, 1887, Jane Treadwell, youngest dau. of D. G. de Villiers, of Beaufort West, C.C.

BAIN, T. H., of Tarkastad, Cape Colony, joined the Cape Colonial Civil Service some years ago, and is now Assistant Resident Magistrate for the Tarka District. He is keen on sport, and the principal supporter of local polo. Married.

BAINBRIDGE, John, M.L.A., F.G.S., son of Geo. Peacock Bainbridge, of Dutton Hall, Yorks, was educated at St. Peter's Gram. Sch., York, and at Rathbury Gram. Sch., Northumberland. He served in the lst Batt. of the West York Rifle Volunteers, and shot for the Silver medal, Queen's Prize, at Wimbledon, in 1860. He went to Natal in 1870; engaged in farming; was elected to a seat on the Legislative Council in 1884, which he resigned four years later. He was re-elected in 1890, and represents the Klip River Division in the Natal Assembly.

BAINES, Eustace Henry Melville Talbot, of Johannesburg, was appointed Asst. Resident Magistrate at Johannesburg in 1902, having previously held the post of Public Prosecutor at Krugersdorp, Asst. Resident Magistrate at Vereeniging, and was a member of the Special Criminal Court at Pretoria.

BALDWIN, Capt., succeeded Capt. FitzCrowe as British Consul-Gen. at Delagoa Bay in 1902.

BALE, Sir Henry, K.C.M.G. (1901), K.C., (1897), of Ingleside, Maritzburg; Craigellachie, Hilton Road; and the Victoria Club, Maritzburg, Natal, was born Jan. 12, 1854; is the son of W. E. Bale, J.P., formerly Mayor of Pietermaritzburg, and was educated at the High Sch., P.M.B., and the Gram. Sch., Exeter, England. Sir Henry practised as Attorney at the Supreme Court of Natal from 1875, and as Advocate from 1878; was member of the Committee of the Zulu War Relief Fund, 1879; member of the late Council of Education, 1886-93; member of the Council of the Cape of Good Hope University, 1902; nominee member of the Legislative Council, 1890; and M.L.A. for Pietermaritzburg City, 1893-1901. He was twice sent for to form a Ministry, but declined. However, he acted as Attorney-General and Minister of Education from 1897 to 1901. During the late Boer War he acted as Procurator-General, for which he received the thanks of the Secy. of State. He was also Chairman of the Natal Volunteer and War Relief Fund 1899-1902; Chairman of the Pietermaritzburg Assoc. for Aid to Sick and Wounded for the same period, and received his knighthood for services rendered to, the Imperial Govt. during the war. He became Chief Justice of Natal in 1901; acted as Administrator of that Colony during the illness of the Governor, June and July, 1903, and again from Jan. to Sept., 1904. Sir Henry married in 1887 Eliza (d. 1890), dau. of W. B. Wood of Edinburgh; and in 1904 Margaret, dau. of W. F. Berning, of Maritzburg.

BALFOUR, Dr. Andrew, M.D., C.M., B.Sc. (Public Health), Edin., M.R.C.P.E., D.P.H. (Camb.); of Khartoum, and of the Drumsheugh Baths Club, Edin., the Turf Club, Cairo, and the Sudan Club, Khartoum, was born at Edinburgh in 1873. He is the son of T. A. G. Balfour, M.D., F.R.C.P.E., etc., Curator of the Museum of the Royal College of Physicians, Edin., who married Miss Margaret Christall, of Elgin, Morayshire, Dr. A. Balfour was educated at George Watson's Coll., Edinburgh, Edinburgh University, and Caius Coll., Cambridge, graduating M.B., C.M., Edinburgh, 1894. After practising privately and at the Fever Hospital, Edinburgh, where he was Asst. Physician, he went to Cambridge, taking D.P.H. in 1897, M.D. (gold medal thesis) 1898, and B.Sc. in Public Health 1900. He went to S. Africa as Surgeon in April of that year, being attached to the No. 7 General Hospital at Estcourt and Pretoria, and afterwards in charge of the British Garrison and Boer Laagers at Kaapsche Hoop, E. Transvaal (medal and clasps). He returned in April, 1901, and took his M.R.C.P.E. in 1902. In the same year he was appointed Director of Govt. Research Laboratories, Gordon Memorial College, Khartoum. He is also Med. Officer of Health, Khartoum, and Sanitary Adviser to the Sudan Civil Medical Service.

Dr. Balfour collaborated in the production of a book on Public Health, and is the author of *By Stroke of Sword*, *To Arms*, *Vengeance is Mine*, *Cashiered; and Other War Tales*, and *The Golden Kingdom*. He also wrote a war play, *The Camp Catch*.
Dr. Balfour was a Scottish International Rugby football player, a Cambridge 'Blue', and captained

the Watsonian XV and the Edinburgh XV against the Paris team recently. He is a swimmer, and is fond of shooting. He married, Sept., 1902, Grace, dau. of G. Nutter, of Sidcup, Kent.

BAM, Christian Jacobus, of Carnarvon, Cape Colony, acted as Clerk to the Special Commissioner of the Northern Border in 1887; was appointed Civil Commissioner and Resident Magistrate at Kuruman in 1889; at Van Rhyn's Dorp in 1897, and at Carnarvon in 1902, which position he still holds.

BAM, Capt. Sir Pieter Cauzius van Blommestein, M.L.A., J.P. for Cape Town and District, of Sea Point, Cape Town, and of the Sports (Lond.), City and Junior City Clubs (C. T.), was born at Cape Town July 29, 1869; is eldest surviving son of the late J. A. Bam (formerly M.L.A. for Cape Town), and was educated at the Normal Coll. (C. T.), the Diocesan Coll., Rondebosch, the S. African Coll. (C. T.), and Cheltenham Coll., England. He entered the Cape Garrison Artillery in 1892, from which he resigned in Aug., 1901, and served through the greater part of the S. African War, for which he holds the medal. Sir Pieter probably holds a record in having fought three Parliamentary elections in six months. In Jan., 1904, he stood as an Independent Progressive for Cape Town, and was beaten by a small majority. In March of the same year he unsuccessfully contested Victoria West against the Bond leader (Hon. J. X. Merriman), but in the following July at the election for the two new seats for Cape Town, he was elected at the top of the poll by a large majority. He belongs to an old Dutch family, and is the youngest member returned to the House of Assembly for Cape Town.

BANGOR, Viscount, of Castle Ward, Co. Down, was born in 1828. Henry William Crosbie Ward, Viscount Bangor and Baron Bangor, is one of Ireland's representative peers. The Wards have been settled in county Down for over three hundred years. Sir Robert Ward was Surveyor-General of Ireland in 1570. The head of the family was elevated to the peerage of Ireland in 1770, when Mr. Ward, for many years M.P. for county Down, was created Baron Bangor of Ward Castle, and eleven years later was made Viscount Bangor.

The present Viscount was educated at Rugby and entered the 43rd Light Infantry in 1846. He served through the Kaffir war in 1851-3 (medal), and retired from the Army in 1854. He married, first, in 1854 Mary, dau. of Henry King, and secondly, in 1874, Elizabeth, dau. of Hugh Eccles, of Co. Wicklow.

BANNATINE-ALLASON, Brigadier General Richard, C.B., of Logan, Cumnock, N.B., and of the Naval and Military and Ayr County Clubs, was born at Glaisnock, Cumnock, N.B., Sept. 22, 1855, and is son of Richard Cunninghame Bannatine, of Glaisnock, descended from the Bannatynes of Kames. He was educated at Wellington College and the Royal Military Academy, Woolwich, and entered the Royal Artillery in 1875; served in the Afghan War in 1879-80, including the action of Shajui, the battle of Ahmed Khel, the action of Auzoo, and the famous march from Kabul to Kandahar (despatches, medal with two clasps and bronze star); the Sudan Expedition in 1885 as Brigade Major to the Royal, Artillery, present at the action of Hasheen and the advance on Tamai (despatches, medal With clasp and bronze star); and the South African War in 1899-1902, including the advance on Kimberley and the action at Magersfontein, and the operations in the Orange River Colony (despatches and brevet of Colonel) . Unmarried.

BANNERMAN, Capt. Sir Alexander, R.E., 11th Bart., of Brackley, Northants, where he was born Dec. 16, 1870, was educated at Wellington Coll., and succeeded to the baronetcy Dec. 3, 1901. He served for 32 years in Hong Kong and through the whole of the S.A. War, being mentioned in Lord Roberts' despatches. He left England in 1903 on a special mission for the War Office to Japan.

BARCLAY, President Arthur, of Liberia, West Africa, is the second President of the Republic of Liberia, which received the recognition of all the Powers in 1847, with the exception of the United States of America, which was withheld only until 1862. Pres. Barclay is a West Indian born negro, who conducts the government of the country on sound and liberal lines, endeavouring to maintain the African character of his Republic. The approximate coast population of civilised (mostly Christian) Liberians is between 40,000 and 50,000, while the indigenous population is something like two millions. Mainly owing to the exertions of the American Methodist Bishop of Africa, Bishop Joseph Hartzell, ample provision appears to exist for religious teaching and education, there being no fewer than forty-eight ministers, forty lay teachers, with fifty-nine Sunday schools, attended by 2,700 scholars, under this denomination alone. Pres. Barclay draws a salary of £700 per annum. He is self educated and deeply read, and Sir Harry Johnston (q.v.), in his address on Liberia to the African Society, said that Mr. Barclay was one of the most remarkable men of African blood he had ever met, having done a great deal in recent years to restore the finances of Liberia from the chaos into which they had fallen.

BARLOW, Alfred, J.P., F.R.C.I., of Kelvedon, Bloemfontein, and the Bloemfontein and Rand Clubs, 3rd son of Nathaniel Barlow, M.R.C.S., and grandson of Dr. Wm. Barlow, who raised and commanded the Writtle (Essex) Volunteers in 1805, was born at Blackmore, near Chelmsford, Essex, Aug. 15, 1836; was educated at Ongar Grammar School, and went to the Orange Free State in the year 1859, where he has resided practically ever since. He was a Director of the Bloemfontein Bank from 1872 to 1887, and represented the town of Smithfield in the O.F.S. Volksraad from 1887 to 1890. He edited the *Friend of the Free State* from 1866 to 1899, and is now Chairman of the National Bank of the O.R.C., Chairman of the Bloemfontein Board of Executors, and J.P. for the whole of the O.R.C. He married, April 30, 1874, Kate, dau. of John Brereton, of Cheshire, England.

BARKER, Captain .J., of the Royal Lancs. Regt., served in the South African War in 1899-1902 as Railway Staff Officer (King's medal with two clasps).

BARNATO, Henry Isaac, of Johannesburg; of 23, Upper Hamilton Terrace, London, N.W., and of 10 and 11, Austin Friars, London, E.C., is a partner in the firm of Barnato Bros., founded by his popular but ill-fated brother, 'Barney' Barnato. He is a permanent director in Johannesburg of the Barnato Consolidated. Mines, and is on the Board of the Johannesburg Consolidated Investment Co., Ltd. His main recreation appears to be horseracing, but he has the family fondness for the drama. (See S. B. Joel.)

BARNES, John Frederick Evelyn, C.M.G., M.Inst. C.E., M.Inst.C.E.Id., F.R.C.I., of Pietermaritzburg, Natal, and of the Victoria Club, P.M.B., was born in Co. Kilkenny, Jan. 21, 1851. He is the son of the late F. P. Barnes, C.E., and of Matilda, dau. of the late Rev. Leo. Armstrong, of Listerlyn, Co. Kilkenny, and was educated privately and at Trinity Coll., Dublin. In 1871, having completed his term of pupillage, as also his second or senior Freshman year in Trinity Coll., Dublin, he began his career as an engineer under the County Surveyor of Antrim. In 1872, and for six years subsequently, he held the post of engineer and surveyor on the Irish estates of the Duke of Abercorn, also practising privately. He engineered the Flood Protection works on the Mourne at Strabane, the Strabane Waterworks, as also large sub-soil drainage and plantation schemes under the Public Works Loans Act. The land troubles of 1877-8 caused him to turn his attention to other fields of labour, with the result that in Feb., 1880, he landed in Natal, passed the examination, and obtained the licence to practise as a Govt. Land Surveyor in that Colony.

In 1882 Mr. Barnes was appointed Bore Engineer of Durban, and held that post for six years. He carried out the Umbilo Waterworks, many town improvements, and constructed over thirty miles of Streets and footpaths. At the Natal Exhibition of 1883 he was awarded a silver medal for specialities in concrete work, and prior to his entering the service of the Natal Govt. the Corporation voted him a bonus of £500 as a token of appreciation of his services. In Jan., 1888, he received the appointment of Asst. Colonial Engineer and Surveyor-General of Natal, and throughout the six years following he held frequent appointments as Acting Colonial Engineer, with seats on the Executive and Legislative Councils of the Colony. With the first responsible Govt. of Natal, Mr. Barnes was entrusted with the charge of the Public Works Dept. That appointment he still holds under the title of Chief Engineer Public Works Dept.

Throughout the late Boer War his dept. lent valuable assistance to the military co-operating with the G.O.C. lines of communication, the R.E., the R.A.M.C., and other branches of the -service. His dept. raised and supervised a Pioneer Corps of Artisans for the building of bridges, forts, buildings, and such like; a Native Labour Corps of 3,000 Kaffirs for unskilled work, and an Indian Ambulance Corps of 1,200 Indian coolie stretcher-hearer. For these services Mr. Barnes and the staff of his dept. were thanked publicly, and in despatches by Lord Roberts and by Gen. Buller, while, on the recommendation of Governor Sir Henry McCullum, Gen. Hildyard, and the Natal Ministry, of which Col. Sir A. H. Hime was Premier, he received the Order of C.M.G. at the hands of H.R.H. the Duke of York. In 1904 he attended the St. Louis Exposition as Commissioner for Natal, as a result of which the Natal Govt. published his *Notes of a Visit Paid to the World's Fair, 1904*. He married, in 1879, Mary Sanbach, dau. of the late E. E. Graves.

BARNETT, Percy Arthur, M.A., of Heatherleigh, Isleworth, Eng., Burnt Hill House, Bradfield, Reading, Eng., and of the Savile Club, London, was born in 1858, and was educated at the City of London Sch. and at Trinity Coll., Oxford. He was Scholar of Trinity, 1877; Prof. of English at the University Coll., Sheffield, 1881; Principal of Isleworth Training Coll., 1888; H.M. Inspector of Schools, 1892; H.M. Asst. Inspector of Training Colleges, 1893, Superintendent of Education for Natal, 1903 to 1905. He returned to the Board of Education, England, and was appointed by the Marquis of Londonderry Chief Inspector for the Training of Teachers, 1905. He represented Natal on the Council of the Cape University. In addition to this he has spent some time in Egypt, and advised Lord Cromer on certain matters of educational organisation. He also assisted in the selection of the English teachers engaged for service in the Boer Concentration Camps. Mr. Barnett edited and contributed to *Teaching and Organisation*, and is the author of *Common Sense in Education*, *The Little Book of Health and Courtesy*, and various magazine articles and reviews. He also produced, as joint author with Mr. G. W. Sweeney, *Natal—the State and the Citizen*.

BARNETT, Major William Alexander, D.S.O., of Johannesburg, Transvaal, was born in 1866. He joined the North Staffs. Regt. in 1885, serving in Zululand in 1888 and in the S. African War in 1899-1902, including the operations in the Orange Free State, actions at Karee Siding, Vet River, and Zand River, and the operations in the Transvaal (despatches, D.S.O. and King's and Queen's medals with five clasps). In 1890 Major Barnett was attached to the Swaziland Police Force; was specially employed in Rhodesia from 1891-2, subsequently acting Resident Magistrate of the Tuli Dist. in 1892. From 1894-7 he acted as Staff Officer for Volunteers, Cape Colony; was appointed personal assistant to the Military Commissioner of Police at Johannesburg in 1901, and in the following year he became Deputy-Commissioner of Police at Johannesburg. He married, in 1894, Eloise, dau. of Henry Orpen, C.M.S., of Wynberg, Cape Colony.

BARRETT, Robert John, of 54, Wool Exchange, London, E.C., and of the City Athenaeum Club, was born in 1861, and was educated privately. For some twenty years he has been connected with the London and Provincial Press, and was one of the earliest sub-editors of the *Financial Times* and the *Africa Review*. He was subsequently proprietor of the *Times of Africa*, and is now a director and editor of the *Financier and Bullionist*, journal which has done a great deal to encourage the introduction of capital for developing African enterprises. But Mr. Barrett has not confined his energies to Africa. He is well known as a writer upon Canada, and probably no journalist in London has a keener grasp of the commercial possibilities of the Dominion than he. His articles in the *Financier*, embodying his experiences of an extensive trip from the Atlantic to the Pacific, have excited wide spread interest, and have unquestionably don much to bring the possibilities of that country before the attention of English investor: He has written from time to time several stories, including an historic romance, called *Friends and Foes*, and was formerly part proprietor and joint editor with W. H. Wills of the *Anglo-African Who's Who*. Mr. Barrett has always been very keen on sport of all kinds. He was an active playing member of the once well-known Pontefract Football Club; was secy. of the Sandown Bay Rowing Club, and during many years of

volunteering in the Middlesex and Hampshire regiments of Yeomanry Cavalry he carried off numerous prizes for military sports. Latterly he has devoted his leisure to photography and yachting. He was one of the founders of the flourishing Westcliff Yacht Club, of which he was commodore for two years, his cutter, *Doris*, having been successfully sailed by him in club racing in the Thames Estuary. He was also on the racing committee of the Alexandra Yacht Club.

BARRETT, William Herbert, J.P., of the Bloemfontein Club, was born Dec. 10, 1860, at Crumlin, Mon. He was educated at Abergavenny Grammar Sch., and joined the staff of the London and N.W. Railway in 1875, but in 1879 he transferred to the Cape Govt. Railways and in Sept., 1900, to the Imperial Military, Railways. He is now traffic manager of the Central South African Railways at Bloemfontein and a J.P. for the O.R.C. Mr. Barrett served with the Duke of Edinburgh's Own Volunteer Rifles in the Basuto War in 1880-81 (medal), and also won the medal with clasps for Cape Colony, O.R.C., and the Transvaal in the South African War, 1899-1902.

BARROW, General Sir Edmund George, K.C.B., of the Junior United Service Club, was born in 1852, and is son of Major-Gen. Barrow, C.B. He was educated at Marlborough and Sandhurst, and entered the Army in 1871; served in the Afghan War in 1878-9; the Egyptian campaign in 1882; the Tirah expedition in 1897-8, and in the China Expeditionary Force in 1900. In 1901 he acted as Secretary to the Military. Department of the Government of India, and since 1904 he has commanded the Peshawar Dist. He married in 1882 Marion, dau. of the Rev. W. Story, of Tyrone.

BARRY, Maj. James David, of Scribblestown Park, Castlerock, Co. Dublin, and of Kildare Street Club, Dublin, was born in Dublin Apr. 12, 1858, is eldest son of the late Rt. Hon. C. R. Barry, and was educated at Woolwich. He served in the R.H.A. from 1877 to 1899, retiring in the latter year with captain's rank. In the interim he served as A.D.C. to the Lord-Lieutenant of Ireland (1880-84). When the S. African War broke out he rejoined his regt. (Jan., 1900); commanded a mixed battery, received the Queen's medal and three clasps, was mentioned in despatches, and was promoted Major. He married June 6, 1895, the Hon. Florence Madeline, 2nd dau. of the late Lord Clanmorris.

BARTER, Colonel Charles St. Leger, C.B., of Chatham, and of the United Service Club, was born Oct. 8, 1856, and is son of the Rev. J. T. Barter. He was educated abroad, and received his first commission in the Army in 1875; acted as instructor at the Royal Military College from 1884-9, and from then until 1894 was employed at the War Office as D.A.A.G. In the following year he was appointed Military Secretary to the Governor of Cape Colony and High Commissioner of South Africa. He served in the Ashanti Expedition in 1895-6, with the Special Service Corps (Star); the operations on the North-West Frontier of India in 1897-8; with the Tirah Expeditionary Force (despatches, and medal with two clasps); and the South African War in 1899-1902, in command of 2nd Battn. Yorks Light Infantry; took part in the advance on Kimberley, including the actions at Belmont, Enslin, Modder River, and Magersfontein; the operations in the Transvaal and Orange River Colony, including the actions at Lindley, Bethlehem, and Wittehergen. He commanded the troops at Rietfontein, and acted as Station Commandant there (despatches, Queen's medal with four clasps, King's Medal with two clasps, and C.B.). Unmarried.

BARTON, Folliott Cyril Montgomery, of the Royal Colonial Institute and the United Sporting Club, was born June 4, 1875, at Grahamstown, S. Africa, and is of Irish parentage. He was educated at St. Paul's Sch., Lond. and was appointed Clerk in the Colonial Audit Branch of the Exchequer and Audit Dept., Lond., in 1895; Assist. Local Auditor British Central Africa Protectorate in 1899, and in June of the same year he became Acting Local Auditor remaining so until June, 1900. He was subsequently appointed to the Audit Office in the Transvaal Civil Service.

BATEMAN, Walter Slade, J.P., served in the S. African War in 1899-1902 (medal). He served in the Convict and Prisons branch of the Cape Govt. Service from 1894-1901, was Secretary to the

Board of Management of the Somerset Hospital, Cape Town, from 1897-1901, and was a member of the Transvaal Tender Board from Nov., 1902, till Jan., 1903. In June, 1903, he was appointed Acting-Inspector of Prisons in the Transvaal, previously having held the post of Chief Clerk of the Prisons Department.

BATTERSEA, Lord, of Aston Clinton, Tring, Herts; 7, Marble Arch, W.; and of the Devonshire and Brooks' Clubs, was born in 1843, and is son of P. W. Flower, of Streatham. He was educated at Harrow and Trinity College, Cambridge. In 1880 he entered Parliament as Member for Brecon, which he retained until after the Reform Bill. Three times he has sat for South Bedfordshire, rose to be Lord of the Treasury under Mr. Gladstone's last Administration, and in 1889 won the House of Commons Steeplechase. He is President of the Recreative Evening School Association, and is a director of A. Goerz and Co., Ltd., and the Alliance Assurance Co., Ltd.; is also the possessor of many valuable paintings. He married in 1877 Constance, dau. of Sir Anthony de Rothschild.

BAXTER, Ernest Charles, J.P., of Bulawayo, and the Bulawayo Club, was educated at the Royal High Sch., Edinburgh, and Padcroft Coll. He went to Natal in 1879, and to Cape Town in the following year, where he remained in private accounting work' for five years. Subsequently he occupied several Civil Service appointments in Bechuanaland, receiving in 1892 the thanks of the Secy. of State for the Colonies for services rendered. On the annexation of British Bechuanaland to the Cape Colony, he retired on pension (1896), and practised as an accountant at Mafeking and Bulawayo for three years, when he joined the Civil Service of S. Rhodesia to inaugurate and control the Customs Dept. (July 1, 1899). Whilst residing in Cape Town Mr. Baxter took an active part in the management of the Y.M.C.A. He holds a licence as Lay Reader for the Dioceses of Cape Town, Bloemfontein, and Mashonaland, and is treasurer of the latter diocese. He has also assisted in the founding and management of Church Schools. In Freemasonry he is known as a Founder and P.M. of Lodges in Mafeking Bulawayo, as P.Z. of the Bulawayo R.A. Chapter) and as Treasurer of the Rhodesia Masonic

Education Fund. He married in 1883 Emma Anne, dau. of the late Rev. Dr. Robertson, of Cape Town.

BAYLY, Col. Hon. L. S., M.L.C., is member of the Cape Legislative Council for the Eastern Circle, having been last re-elected in 1904.

BAYNES, Joseph, C.M.G. (1902), M.L.A., J.P., of Nel's Rust, near Maritzburg, Natal, and the Victoria Club, P.M.B., is the son of the late Richard Baynes, and was born at Austwick, near Settle, Yorks, on March 2, 1842. He arrived in Natal in 1850, and commenced farming on Lawkland, near York, and since 1862 has farmed at Nel's Rust. He has acted as a member of several Govt. Commissions; has been a member of the Indian Immigration Board since 1887, and was Chairman in 1891-2; is J.P. for the County of Pietermaritzburg; Pres. of the Richmond Agricultural Soc.; member of the Legislative Council for the Ixopo Division 1890-3, when under the new constitution he was elected to the House of Assembly. He is a sound protectionist, and has worked hard for the agricultural and industrial development of Natal. He strongly supported the movement in the Assembly in 1897 which led to the Customs Convention between the Cape Colony, Orange Free State, and Natal; he moved also in that House the resolution approving and supporting the action of the Imperial Govt. in its endeavours to obtain equal rights for all civilised people in S.A. He afterwards became Minister of Lands and Works in the Natal Ministry. He married: lst, in 1874, Maria H., second dau. of Paul Hermanus Zietsman, J.P.; and 2nd, in 1878, Sarah A., elder dau. of Ed. Tomlinson, who was four times Mayor of Maritzburg.

BAYNES, William, M.L.A., J.P., of Settle, near Pietermaritzburg; Glen Dushie, P.M.B., 316, Longmarket St., P.M.B., and the Victoria Club, P.M.B., was born at Austwick, Yorks, May 22, 1840. He is son of the late Richard Baynes, of Settle and Nel's Rust, Natal; was educated at Lancaster and Giggleswick Gram. Schools, and settled in Natal as a farmer in 1860. He was twice elected to the Legislative Council as member for Lion's River Division (1890-1893) as an opponent of Responsible Government, but on this being granted to the Colony he was elected to represent Umgeni in the Natal House of Assembly. Mr. Baynes married, Aug. 2, 1870, Ellen, third dau. of Richard Stone, of Faversham, Kent.

BEAL, Lieut.-Col. Robert, C.M.G., J.P., of Beira, E. Africa; and of the Thatched House (London) and the Beira, Salisbury, Bulawayo and Umtali Clubs, is the son of John Beal, a master mariner of Sunderland, and was born in the north country in 1858. Robert Beal went to South Africa in 1875, where he started farming. He served in the Gaika-Galeka Wars in 1878-9 (medal and clasp), and then became Clerk in the P.W.D. in Cape Colony, being stationed at E. London from 1881-3. In the following year he was employed with Fairbank and Pauling on the Queenstown-Aliwal North Railway. In 1884-5 he served in Sir C. Warren's Bechuanaland Exped., at first as trooper, afterwards being promoted Lieut., and Acting Adjutant of the right wing of the 3rd Mounted Rifles under Lieut.-Col. Hugh S. Gough. In Aug., 1885, he enrolled in the B.B.P. as a trooper, leaving that regt. in April, 1890, as R.S.M. to join the Pioneer Corps for the occupation of Mashonaland, commencing with the same rank; was promoted Lieut. and Acting Adjutant, June 10, 1890, the corps being disbanded in the following October. In 1891 he was appointed Inspector of Public Works for Mashonaland. He was elected Senior Lieut. in the Mashonaland Horse, and served with the Victoria Column through the Matabele War in 1893 as Lieut., afterwards returning in command the column (medal). On the formation of the Rhodesia Horse Vols., he was elected Senior Captain, being promoted Lieut.-Col commanding in 1896. In that year he commanded a column from Salisbury and Gwelo for the relief of Bulawayo, and was second in command under Col. Spreckle at the celebrated action of Umguza Drift on June 6, when 400 of the rebellious Matabele were left dead on the field-an action which practically broke the back of the rebellion. Col. Beal commanded the Mashonaland Forces in the Mashonaland Rebellion in 1896-7, and on the arrival of Col. Alderson, was placed in charge of the lines of communication, transport and supply from Beira to Salisbury, which was probably the most difficult part of the operations, owing to the guerrilla tactics employed by the rebels (mentioned in despatches, C.M.G.

and two clasps). In 1897 he was appointed Chief Inspector of Public Works for Rhodesia; J.P. for Mashonaland in 1898; was appointed Acting Manager of the Beira and Mashonaland Rlys. in 1901, and on the appointment of Mr. Webberley as Manager, Col. Beal became Asst. General Manager of the Beira and Mashonaland Rlys. and of the Rhodesia Rlys. (Northern extension), and Agent for the B.S.A. Co. in Beira. In the late S. African War in 1899-1902, he organised the transport for the Rhodesia Field Force as Director of Transport with the rank of Lieut.-Col. (mentioned in despatches, and medal and clasp for Rhodesia). He still holds the hon. rank of Lieut.-Col. Col. Beal bears the reputation of being a man who will go anywhere and do anything, seemingly quite unable to recognise difficulties. His chief sports are big game shooting and yachting. Col. Beal is not married.

BEATTY, Hazlitt Michael, C.M.G., of Salt River, Cape Colony, was engaged in England as draughtsman in 1874, and became District Locomotive Superintendent at Worcester in 1877. Subsequently he was transferred to the Salt River, Cape Colony, in 1884, and in the following year was appointed Assistant Locomotive Superintendent of the western system, and Manager of the Salt River Locomotive works. In 1896 he was appointed Chief Locomotive Superintendent.

BEAUFORT, Judge; was formerly Governor and Commander-in-Chief of the Colony of Labuan and the State of North Borneo, 1895-1900. He is now in charge of the High Court of North-Eastern Rhodesia established at Fort Jameson.

BEAUMONT, Hon. William Henry, of 10, Burgher St., Maritzburg, Natal, and the Victoria Club, Maritzburg, was born in India, Feb. 24, 1851; is the son of the late Lieut.-Col. W. Beaumont, of the 23rd Madras Light Infantry; was educated at Sherborne and Sandhurst, and joined the 75th (Stirlingshire) Regt: as Ensign in Aug. 1870; Lieut. 1870, and retired in Aug. 1875. He became Private Secy. to Lieut.-Governor Sir Benjamin Pine, and Clerk to the Executive Council of Natal in 1873; acting R.M. Umlazi Divn., 1874; Governor's Clerk and Clerk to the Executive

Council, Oct., 1875; Magistrate, 1878; Acting Puisne Judge of the Supreme Court for various periods from Feb. 1895 to Oct. 1902; Judge of the Special Treason Court, Oct. 1901; 2nd Puisne Judge of the Supreme Court of Natal, Nov. 1, 1902, and Senior Puisne Judge, 1904. Judge Beaumont served with the Langalibalele Expedition, 1873; was Colonial Commandant of No. 1 District, Natal, at the commencement of the Zulu War. Jan. 1879, when he raised native levies for the defence of the border, and a troop of mounted natives called the Newcastle Scouts (medal). He also served as Commandant of the Pietermaritzburg Town Guard during the late Boer War (medal). He has always been an enthusiastic sportsman, and has during the last few years been Capt. of the Maritzburg Golf Club. He was married, 1876, to Alice, dau. of the late Hon. John Millar, M.L.C., of Durban.

BECK, Arthur Andrews, of Cape Town, entered the Cape Civil Service in 1893; was employed in the Colonial Secretary's Office as Assistant Bookkeeper in 1894; acted as Assistant Accountant there in 1899, and as Inspector of Books and Stores. In 1902 he was appointed Accountant, and Accounting Officer in 1903.

BECK, Dr. Johannes Hendricus Meiring, M.L.A., has represented the electoral division of Worcester in-the Cape Legislative Assembly for some years. He is a member of the Bond, and was last returned unopposed at the General Election in 1904.

BECK, Walter Francis Lockhart, of Cape Colony, entered the Cape Civil Service as Clerk in the Control and Audit Office in 1871; Examiner of Accounts in the Revenue branch in 1876, and Inspector there in 1896.

BECKER, George Ferdinand, B.A. Harvard, Ph.D. Heidelberg; of 1,700, Rhode Island Avenue, Washington, D.C., and of the Metropolitan (Washington), Chevy Chase, (Maryland), and the Mount Vernon Ducking Assn. Clubs; was born Jan. 5, 1847. He was educated at Harvard and Cambridge (Mass.) Universities, also at Heidelberg and Berlin, and was a graduate of the Royal Mining Academy, Berlin, in 1871. He is a member of the National Academy of Sciences, American Institute:

of Mining Engineers, &c., hon. member of the Witwatersrand Chamber of Mines, and of the Geological Society of S. Africa. Mr. Becker has been Geologist-in-Charge in the United States since 1879; acted as special agent for the, 10th census in 1880, and has been Geophysicist of the Carnegie Institution of Washington since 1903. He was attached to the American army of occupation in the Philippine, Islands in, 1898, as official geologist (mentioned in despatches), and was awarded a medal by the State of Montana for participating with the Montana Regt: in the capture of Caloocan in 1899. His writings include the *Geology of the Comstock Lode, Statistics and Technology of the Precious Metals* (with S. F. Emmons), *Geology of the Quick-silver Deposits of the Pacific Slope*, and has contributed to the Annual Reports of the United States Geological Survey on *Goldfields of the Southern Appalachians*, *Goldfields of Southern Alaska*, *The Witwatersrand Banket*, and *Geology of the Philippine Islands*; and has also contributed *The Revolt of the Uitlanders, Rights and Wrongs in S. Africa, Are the Philippines Worth Having?* and *Conditions Requisite to Our Success in the Philippine Islands*, &c., in magazines. He married in 1902 Florence Deakins.

BECKETT, Percy, is a partner in the firm of Beckett, Son, and Morton. He married, Jan. 11, 1905, Gladys, dau. of Dr. and Mrs. Cook, of Nottingham Terrace., W.

BEDFORD, Duke of, has seen active service in Egypt, and was A.D.C. to Lord Dufferin when he was Viceroy of India. The Duchess, who is one of the keenest sportswomen in England, is a dau. of an Archdeacon of Lahore:, while the Duke's relative, Lord Ampthill, has acted temporarily as Viceroy in the absence of Lord Curzon.

BEGG, Alexander James, was formerly engaged in the Resident Engineer's dept. at Cape Town. Subsequently he was promoted to Grootfontein as District Clerk and Cashier, and in 1881 he joined the Surveyor General's dept., Cape Colony.

BEGLEY, David Charles, of Port Alfred, Cape Colony, was employed as Telegraphist at Wellington in 1876; Durban Road in 1878; Worcester in 1879, and Telegraphist and Postmaster at Victoria West in 1881; acted as Postmaster at Rondebosch in 1896; Colesberg in 1898; Fort Beaufort in 1902, and at Port Alfred in 1904.

BEHANZIN, ex-King of Dahomey, took up his residence at Blida, Algiers, in 1906, having been exiled by the French Government. He is accompanied in his involuntary retirement by his four wives, three daughters, and three grandchildren.

BEHR, H. C., Consulting Mechanical Engineer to the Consolidated Goldfields of S.A. He was the first winner of the gold medal and premium of 50 guineas for the best paper contributed on Deep Level Mining questions to the Institution of Mining and Metallurgy. His subject was *Winding Plants for Great Depths*.

BEIT, Otto, of 49, Belgrave Square, London, S.W., and Tewin Water, Herts., is brother to the late Alfred Beit (see Obituaries), and is one of the executors of his will, the others being Sir Julius Wernher and Mr. Franz Voelklein. Mr. Otto Beit is a Director of the Geneva Tramways Co., Ltd.

BELFIELD, Brigadier-General Herbert Eversley, C.B., D.S.O., of Aldershot, and the Army and Navy Club, was born at Dover Sept. 25, 1857; is son of Capt. W. Belfield, J.P., of Malmains, Gloucestershire, and was educated at Wellington Coll., passing into the Army in 1876, rising to the substantive rank of Col. on Dec. 18, 1899. After serving as Brig.-Maj, and D.A.A.G. at Aldershot, he was on special service in Ashanti in 1895-6 as C.S.O., being honourably mentioned and receiving the Brev. of Lieut.-Col. and the Star. In the late S.A. War he acted as A.A.G., S.A., from Dec. 1899, until Jan. 1902, when he became Inspector-Gen. of I.Y. in S.A., taking part in the operations in the O.R.C., Transvaal, and later in the Cape Colony, including the actions at Venterskroon, Lindley, and Rhenoster River. He was twice mentioned in despatches; received the King's medal with two clasps, and was decorated with the C.B. and D.S.O. Col. Belfield was appointed A.A.G. of the lst Army Corps at Aldershot Dec. 11, 1902, and Brigadier-General, 4th Infantry Brigade, Dec. 8, 1903. He married 1st, in 1882, Emily Mary, dau. of the Rt. Rev. Hibbert Binney,

Bishop of Nova Scotia; and 2nd, in 1888, Evelyn Mary, dau. of Albon Taylor, of Barnes.

BELL, Charles George Harland, C.M.G., of East London, Cape Colony, was employed as Clerk to the Resident Magistrate at Leribe, Basutoland, in 1871; acted as Resident Magistrate at Berea, in charge of the Basuto Chief Masupha in 1878; commandant of the Leribe levy from 1880-1; was appointed Resident Magistrate at Idutywa, Transkei, in 1882; Civil Commissioner and Resident Magistrate at Victoria East in 1893, and at Barkly West in 1895. In 1896 he acted as Fencing Commissioner; was appointed Resident Magistrate and Civil Commissioner at Mafeking in 1897, and Special Commissioner during the Langberg Rebellion in 1897. In 1900 he was appointed Resident Magistrate at Uitenhage. He was a member of the Treason Court and of the War Losses Commission in 1903, and was appointed Resident Magistrate at East London in 1904.

BELL, Lieut.-Col. Edward, of White's Club, was born at Gibraltar April 5, 1866, and is the eldest son of the late Maj.-Gen. C. W. D. Bell, V.C., C.B. He joined the Worcestershire Regt. in 1886; acted as Adjt. of the 1st. Vol. Batt. of the Middlesex Regt., also as Adjt. of the C.I.V. Mounted Inf. on their formation in 1900, being present with them at the operations in the O.F.S. and Transvaal, including the actions at Paardeburg, Poplar Grove, Driefontein, Karree Siding, Johannesburg, Pretoria, Diamond Hill, and Wittebergen (despatches, Brevet of Lt.-Col., and Queen's medal with six clasps). Recreations, hunting, shooting, and fishing. He married, Nov. 27, 1898, Dorothy, dau. of the late Capt. W. Hartopp.

BELL, Lieut.-Col. John William, C.M.G., V.D., J.P., M.R.C.I., of Pretoria, Transvaal, and of the Imperial Service and Pretoria Clubs; is the son of William Bell, of Dumfries, Scotland, late of Grahamstown, Cape Colony, Advocate and M.L.A. He was born at Edinburgh, 1848, and was educated at the High Sch., Edin. Col. Bell originally practised as a solicitor at Queenstown, Cape Colony, and is now Master of the Supreme Court of the Transvaal. He is Deputy Chairman of the Transvaal Tender Board, and was a member of the

recent Municipal Commission which sat at Pretoria. He has been a member of the Queenstown Rifle Volunteers since the formation of the corps in 1873, and was in command from 1881 to 1901. He holds the S.A. War medal (1877-78), and was granted the Long Service medal in 1898. He holds the Volunteer Officers' Decoration, and. was decorated for services in the South African campaign 1899-1901 (mentioned in despatches, medal with three clasps, C.M.G.). He married in 1873 Eliza Jane Bradfield, 4th dau. of Edward Mortimer Turvey, one of the British settlers of 1820.

BELL, William Henry Somerset, of Johannesburg, and the, Rand, Pretoria, Grahamstown and Albany (Grahamstown) Clubs, was born near Fort Beaufort, Eastern Province, Aug. 1, 1856. He is second son of Col. Charles Bell, and grandson of Geo. Jarvis, solicitor, of Grahamstown. He was educated at Douglas, Isle of Man, and at St. Andrew's Coll., Grahamstown. At the early age of fourteen he, in conjunction with an elder brother, aged 16, printed and published a small weekly newspaper called the *Kariega News*, which ran for a year, much of the plant being made by these two boys. In 1877 Mr. W. H. S. Bell served with the Albany Mounted Volunteers in the Galeka Campaign. He was admitted as an Attorney of the Supreme Court, Cape Colony, in 1879, and a Notary of the same Court in 1878. In 1884 he founded and became editor of the *Cape Law Journal*, of which he continued editor until 1896, when he went to England on account of ill-health; he resumed the editorship in the beginning of 1900, and still continues to occupy that position. He was a member of the Reform Committee in Dec., 1895; was arrested for high treason against the S.A.R. on Jan. 9, 1896, and lodged in the Pretoria gaol with some 63 other Reformers; was tried in April, 1896, and with 59 others was convicted of the minor offence of *Laesae majestatis*, and sentenced to two years' imprisonment, £2,000 fine, and three years' banishment. After serving about one month's imprisonment his sentence was commuted to a fine of £2,000. Towards the end of 1896 he gave up business in Johannesburg, and went to England for rest and change. In 1898 he became Chairman of the Estate Finance and Mines Corporation, Ltd., in London, which position he resigned at the end of

1899, and went back to S.A., and devoted himself to improving the *Cape Law Journal*, and also compiled his *Digest of the Cape Law Journal*, a work of about 600 pages, published 1901. In that year he altered the name of the *Cape Law Journal* to the *South African Law Journal*, and in June of the same year he resumed in Johannesburg his practice as a solicitor. He joined the Rand Rifles, and was a captain in the force at the time it was disbanded. In 1902 he, in conjunction with Mr. Manfred Nathan, LL.D., compiled and published the *Legal Handbook of British South Africa* (about 750 pp.). He was one of the representatives of the O.R.C. in the Inter-Colonial conference on the Companies' Law. He was a member of the firm of Ayliff, Bell & Hutton, and later of Bell & Hutton, in Grahamstown; of Caldicott & Bell, in Kimberley; of Bell & Mullins, in Johannesburg; and since 1901 he has been a member of the firm of Bell & Tancred, of Johannesburg. He has been a member of the Council of the Incorporated Law Society of the Transvaal for many years; he is also a member of the Council of the Incorporated Law Society of the Cape: Colony. He is a director of several companies, and Chairman of the African Book Co., Ltd. He married Aug. 3, 1880, Charlotte Elizabeth, dau. of the late Geo. Wood, junr., of Grahamstown.

BELL, William Reid, M.I.C.E., served in the Tasmanian Public Works Dept. as Railway Surveyor from 1883-5, and from 1887-8 acted as Inspecting and Superintending Engineer of the lighthouse there. He served in the late S. African War (two medals and three clasps); was appointed Irrigation Engineer to the Transvaal Land Board in 1902, and is a member of the Institute of Engineers and Shipbuilders, and a Fellow of the Royal Meteorological Society.

BELLAIRS, Capt. Norman Edward Breton, R.A., of the United Service Club, London, was born Nov. 12, 1869, at Gibraltar. He is son of Lieut.-Gen. Sir William Bellairs (q.v.); was educated at Clifton Coll.; served in the S.A. War 1901-2, commanding the R.G.A. in the O.R.C. towards the end of the war. He subsequently was appointed Adjt. of the Cape Garrison Artillery.

BELLAIRS, Lieut.-General Sir William,

K.C.M.G., C.B., Knight of the Legion of Honour, and Order of the Medjidieh, of Clevedon, Somersetshires and of the National Liberal Club, was born August 28, 1828, at Honfleur. He is descended from the ancient family of De Beler, Bellers, or Bellars (as formerly variously spelt), of Melton Mowbray, and Kirby Bellars, Leicestershire, in which churches are still to be seen effigies of his ancestors. He is a son of Sir William Bellairs (d. 1863), a distinguished officer of the 15th King's Hussars, who saw much service during the Peninsular and at Waterloo, and was afterwards Exon of the Yeomen of the Guard at the Court of Queen Victoria. Sir William was educated privately, and entered the Army in 1846, retiring as a Lieut.-Gen. in 1887. As Adjt. of the 49th (now the Royal Berkshire) Regt., he was present at the battle of the Alma; as Capt. at the Inkerman combat of the 26th October, and at the battle of Inkerman, where he led a charge with only three attenuated companies which overthrew and dispersed a strong Russian column-an episode related in Kinglake's brilliant pages. Later, when on the Q.M.-Gen.'s staff, he was present at the attacks on the Redan and fall of Sebastopol, being then rewarded with a brevet majority, French and Turkish honours, medals and clasps. He was one of the comparative few (about 100) combatant officers who fought through the Crimea from first to last. He subsequently served on the staff of the Adjutant and Q.M.-Gen.'s departments in the West Indies, Ireland, Gibraltar and South Africa; throughout the Kaffir and Zulu campaigns (S. African medal, 1877-9, and distinguished service reward); then, as Brig.-Gen. Commanding the troops which successfully defended their seven isolated posts in the Transvaal-Pretoria, Potchefstroom, Rustenburg, Marabastad, Lydenburg, Standerton, and Wakkerstroom-surrounded as they were, for three months, by greater Boer forces. Sir William has likewise acted in various civil capacities-as Inspector-Gen. of Police, Barbados, 1857; Local Inspector of Army Schools, Gibraltar, 1868-73; Col. Secretary, Gibraltar, 1872; Administrator, Natal, 1880; Member of Executive Council, Transvaal, 1880-1 and Administrator, Transvaal, 1881, after the war. Sir William wrote *The Transvaal War, 1880-1*, published in 1885 (Blackwood), *The Military Career*, and has contributed to reviews, &c. In 1902 the King selected him for the Colonelcy of the Sherwood Foresters (Nottinghamshire and Derbyshire Regt.). Sir William was married: first,, in 1857, to Emily Craven, daughter of Wm. Barton Gibbons, J.P., and second, in 1867, to Blanche St. John, daughter of F. A. Moschzisker, Ph.D. Sir William's eldest son, William G. Bellairs (q.v.) is a C.C. and R.M. in the Cape, Colony. He has another son, Capt. N. E. B. Bellairs, R.A., who took part in the S.A. War, and a daughter, widow of the late Sir David Tennant, late Speaker of the Cape House of Assembly.

BELLAIRS, William G., eldest son of Lieut.-Gen. Sir Wm. Bellairs (q.v.), is C.C. and R.M. in the Cape Colony. He married in 1901 Augusta Chiappini, dau. of a former member of the Cape Legislative Assembly.

BELLINGHAM, Hon. Philipus Solomon, M.L.C., was born in 1834 at Uitenhage, which he represented for many years on the Divisional Council. He was an office-bearer in the D.R. Church, and a prominent Bond leader in his division. He was returned at the head of the poll in 1891 for the South-Eastern Province in the Cape Legislative Council. Mr. Bellingham still represents this division.

BELLIS, Thomas K., of Croydon, Surrey, and of Bury St., London E.C. was born in Liverpool in 1841, and educated at the Liverpool Coll. At the age of fifteen he entered the Liverpool office of Messrs. Forties, Forties and Co., East India merchants, of London, and shortly afterwards came to London, where he entered seriously upon a business career. For eighteen years he remained with a West Indian firm, and rose from the lowest position to that of manager. On the dissolution of the firm in the West India trade, he started for himself in 1874, and foreseeing the great future of the turtle trade, he kept it well before him in the midst of his other undertakings. To a man of his character and business capacity, a scheme for the importation of the living animal, upon a scale never before attempted, was no sooner thought of than he made extensive arrangements to carry it out. Mr. Bellis has earned the sobriquet of 'Turtle King'. That title is beyond dispute, for throughout the length and breadth of the land there is not another

merchant dealing on the same colossal scale, as a visit to the present offices in Bury Street, St. Mary Axe, will quickly prove. Every fortnight the West India Royal Mail brings a supply, dealers throughout the country looking to Mr. Bellis for the fulfilment of their orders. Not only is he acknowledged as the head of the business in England, but his fame is equally recognised throughout Europe, and he controls the schooners which catch the turtles from amongst the coral islands in the Mexican Gulf. With the energy and enterprise characteristic to him, Mr. Bellis has not limited his efforts to one branch of trade. He is now taking a keenly active part in opening a trade with Tarkwa, on the Gold Coast, and the results up to the present time have amply justified his foresight. He has also for the past seventeen years been engaged in importing Turkish leaf tobacco, at first only on a small scale, but it has developed very considerably, and is now quite an important business. He is promoter and director of the Tarkwa Gold Coast Trading Co., now a successful company. His name is also well known in connection with the exploitation of the Welsbath Incandescent Light. Many other minor inventions were also brought out by him, including the Fleets Tubeless Tyre, the original syndicate proving a great success, as was the case with all the ventures to which he has lent his name and given his consideration. Mr. Bellis has resided for many years in Croydon, and has taken an active part in the local life of the town, but has never been persuaded to accept public office in Croydon or elsewhere.

BELLOC, Hilaire Joseph Peter, M.P., for the South Div. of Salford; of Courthill, Slindon, Arundel, and of the Reform Club, was born in 1870, and is son of Louis S. Belloc. He was educated at The Oratory School, Edgbaston, and Balliol College, Oxford, served as a driver in the 8th Regt. of French Artillery at Toul Meurthe-et-Moselle, and is author of many publications, including *The Bad Child's Book of Beasts*, *More Beasts for Worse Children*, *The Modern Traveller*, *The Moral Alphabet*, *Danton*, *Lambkin's Remains*, *Paris*, *Robespierre*, *Path to Rome*, *Caliban's Guide to Letters*, *Avril*, *Mr. Burden*, *The Old Road*, and *Esto Perpetua*, a book of Algerian studies and impressions. Mr. Hilaire Belloc was returned to Parliament as Liberal member for the S. Division of Salford at the general election in 1906, defeating M. J. G. Groves, the Conservative candidate, by 852 votes. He married in 1896 Elodie A. Hogan, of California.

BEMIESTER, Inspector J. W., of Cape Town, joined the service of the Cape Government Railways in 1865, and took a prominent part in doubling the Wynberg line under Cress well Clark (q.v.). For eleven years he was in charge of the Cape Government Railway Traffic Department, Cape Town Docks, and for the last two years has been attached to the Staff of the Goods Department, Cape Town. He retired in 1906.

BENCOUGH, Captain Douglas Henry Victor, of the Royal Warwickshire Regt., was born in 1878 and entered the Army in 1898. He served in the South African War in 1899-1901, including the operations in the Orange Free State and the actions at Vet River and Zand River, the operations in the Transvaal, including the actions near Johannesburg, Pretoria, and Diamond Hill, and the action at Belfast (Queen's medal with five clasps).

BENDER, Rev. A. P., M.A., of the S. African College, Cape Town, where he is Professor of Hebrew, is a well-known figure in the public life of Cape Town, and is the first Minister of the Hebrew Congregation there.

BENNET, Brevet Colonel F. W., late of the Royal Engineers, served in the Egyptian Expedition in 1882 (medal and bronze star); the Sudan Expedition in 1884-5, on the Nile with the Telegraph Dept. (Despatches, clasp, and Brevet of Major), and the South African War in 1899-1900, on the Staff (despatches, and Queen's medal with two clasps).

BENT, Mrs. Mabel Virginia Anna, of 13, Great Cumberland Place, W., and of the Ladies' Empire Club, is a daughter of Robert Westley Hall-Dare, D.L., of Theydon Bois, Wennington Hall, Essex, and Newtownbarry House, Co. Wexford. She was married Aug. 2, 1877, to the late Theodore Bent, of Baildon House, Yorks. Mrs. Bent accompanied her husband in all his explorations , and took part in the excavations with which he was associated in the Greek and Turkish Islands, Asia Minor, Abyssinia, the Great Zimbabwe (Mashonaland),

Persia, and elsewhere. She is the authoress of *Southern Arabia, Sudan, and Sokotra*, compiled from her own and Mr. Theodore Bent's notes.

BENTINCK, Major Walter Guy, D.S.O., of Wakkerstroom, Transvaal, served in the S. African war in 1899-1902, being present at the relief of Ladysmith, including the actions at Colenso and Vaal Kranz, the operations on Tugela Heights and in Natal and the Transvaal (despatches, King's medal with two clasps and D.S.O.). In 1900 he was appointed Assistant District Commissioner at Vereeniging, and in 1901 he was appointed Resident Magistrate at Wakkerstroom.

BERESFORD, Lord Charles, G.C.V.O. (1906), is second son of the fourth Marquis of Waterford. For three centuries Beresfords have played a conspicuous part in the history of Ireland, but for five centuries before Tristram Beresford crossed St. George's Channel the family had its local habitation and a name in England. Lord Charles Beresford served in Egypt at Abu-Klea, up the Nile, Metemmeh, and Alexandria. Lord Charles Beresford was Lord Commissioner at the Admiralty, and subsequently commanded the Channel Squadron. In 1905 he assumed the command of the Mediterranean Squadron. He has a cool head, infinite resource, and a well-justified self-confidence.

BERNSTORFF, Count John, of the German Consulate, Cairo, was born in London, November 14, 1862. He is the youngest son of the late Baron Albrecht Bernstorff, who, for some years was Prussian Ambassador—afterwards Imperial German Ambassador—to the Court of St. James's, and who died in London in 1873. Count John was educated at Dresden, and in due course entered the army, serving for a time as a captain of the first regiment of Artillery Guards. In 1889 he made his debut in diplomacy as Attaché to the German Embassy at Constantinople. He acted as Secretary successively in Belgrade, Dresden, and St. Petersburg, and was then appointed Councillor of Legation at Munich. From Munich he came to London in 1902 as Councillor of the German Embassy, and on several occasions he has acted as Charge d'Affaires. He has been at once a vigilant guardian of German interests in this country and a *persona gratissima* in official circles. In 1906 he was appointed German Consul-General at Cairo. Count Bernstorff married in 1887 Fraulein Jeanne Luckemeyer, and has two children, a daughter and a son.

BERRANGE, Major Christian Anthony Lawson, C.M.G., joined the Cape Mounted Police in 1883, having previously taken part in the Galeka War in 1879 (medal and clasp), and the Basuto War in 1881. He also served in the Bechuanaland Expedition in 1896-7, and the South African War in 1899-1902, as Second in Command of Col. Scobell's column; took part in the defence of Kimberley and the relief of Mafeking (Queen's medal with four clasps and King's medal with two clasps). He commanded a detachment of Cape Police at the Coronation of King Edward in 1902 (medal); was appointed District Inspector of the Cape Police in 1903, and Commissioner in 1904.

BERRANGE, Pieter Hendrik, entered the Cape Civil Service as Clerk to the Civil Commissioner and Resident Magistrate at Somerset East in 1875, and was appointed to the General Management Dept. of the Customs in 1878. In 1879 he saw three months' active service in Transkei, and was appointed Inspector of Baggage and Examining Officer at Cape Town in 1897.

BERRINGTON, Evelyn Delahay, A.I.M.M., F.R.C.I., F.S.A., is the son of A. D. Berrington, late Secretary of Fisheries. He was born March 6, 1861, at Pant-y-goitre, near Abergavenny, and was educated at Clifton Coll. and Geneva Univ. Mr. Berrington has been connected with gold mining since 1882 in various parts of the world. He was in Venezuela 1882-3, in Florida, U.S.A., 1884-6, and in Johannesburg 1887-8. He joined the pioneer force into Mashonaland in 1890, and was in Johannesburg and Matabeleland from 1894 to 1899. He acted as manager to the Lomagunda Reefs, Ltd., and the Ayrshire Mine in Mashonaland from 1899 to 1903. He married, June 2, 1894, Miss Eleanor A. Witterton.

BERRY, Hon. Sir William Bisset, Knt., M.L.A., M.A., M.D., of Speaker's Chambers, Parliament House, Cape Town; Ebden Street, Queenstown, and the Civil Service Club (C.T.), was born at

Aberdeen, Scotland, 1839. He had a public school and university education, and followed the medical profession from 1864 for many years at Queenstown, Cape Colony, which he was elected to represent in the Cape Parliament in 1893, being last re-elected at the general election in 1904. In politics he is an ardent Liberal, an occasional speaker, and is identified with every movement for the betterment of the people. He has been Speaker of the Cape House of Assembly since 1898, and is on the Council of the Cape University. He has contributed largely to the medical press, and married in 1864 a dau. of Wm. Beale.

BESTER, A. J., of Bethlehem, O.R.C., was formerly a member of the Orange Free State Volksraad.

BETHUNE, Brig.-General Edward Cecil, C.B., was born in 1855, and joined the 92nd Foot (the Gordon Highlanders) in 1875, exchanging to the 6th Dragoon Guards in 1887. He was subsequently Major in the 16th Lancers; served in the Afghan War in 1878-80, including the affairs around Kabul and Sherpur (medal with clasp), the South African War in 1881, and the South African War in 1899-1902, on the Staff, and as Special Service Officer, and he also raised and commanded Bethune's Mounted Horse; present at the relief of Ladysmith (despatches, Queen's medal with six clasps, and King's medal with two clasps). General Bethune commanded the Cavalry Brigade in South Africa in 1901, subsequently commanding the Eastern Sub District of Cape Colony. He is at present acting as Chief of the Staff, Southern Command.

BEVERIDGE, Mrs. Kuhne, sculptor. (See Mrs. Kuhne Branson.)

BEWICKE-COPLEY, Col. Robert Cleverly Arlington, C.B., J.P., D.L., of Sprotborough Hall, Doncaster, Eng., Coulby Manor, Marton, and of the Naval and Military Club, Lond., was born at Durham, Apr. 8, 1855, was educated at Rugby and Merton Coll., Oxon., and was gazetted Sub-Lieut. in the 1st Royals in 1876; transferred to the 60th Rifles 1877; A.D.C. to the Lieut.-Governor of Bengal 1880; took part in the Nile Expedition (medal, clasp, Khedive's star) 1884; Capt. K.R.R. 1886; p.s.c. 1888; D.A.A.G. Barbados, and

Intelligence, Officer, West Indies, 1889-92; D.A.A.G. Ireland, and Military Attaché to special mission to Morocco, 1892-5; took part with the Chitral Relief Force (medal and clasp) 1895; A.M.S. to Sir Baker Russell, 1896; D.A.Q.M.G. Kurram, Kohat Field Force (clasp) 1897; Sainana Relief Force (clasp) and Tirah Expeditionary Force as C.S.O. 2nd Division (clasp) 1898. In the S. African War he commanded (1899) the 3rd Battn. of the K.R.R. in the operations which culminated in the relief of Ladysmith, and in 1900-02 he commanded columns in the Eastern Transvaal, Orange River Colony, and Cape Colony (medals with eight clasps, C.B.). From 1902 to 1904 he commanded the lst Battn. of the King's Royal Rifles. He married in 1886 Selina Frances, dau. of Sir Charles Watson-Copley, of Sprotborough Hall, Doncaster.

BEYERS, General, is on the governing council of the newly formed Boer organisation, *Het Volk* (the People), and is one of the Transvaal representatives of extreme anti-British feeling, his recent utterances especially having been marked by threatening tirades against the British regime.

BIGHAM, William R., of White City, Morris County, Kansas, U.S.A., the U.S. Consulate-General, Cape Town, and the City Club, Cape Town, was born at Hamilton, Ohio, U.S.A., April 12, 1841; is of Scotch origin on both his father's and mother's side, and was educated at Hamilton, Ohio. He acted as Mayor of the city of El Porso, Ill., for three terms; completed three years and three months in the 4th Regt. of Ill. Cavalry; served as representative for the 60th district of Kansas two terms; Alderman in the city of White City two terms; and was on the Education Board of that city for a similar period; was a director of Badger Lumber, Kansas City, Mo., for eleven years. In the year 1887-8 he travelled in S. America, Europe, and the U.K., and was appointed U.S. Consul-General in Cape Town in Aug., 1901, by Pres. McKinley. Mr. Bigham has the Masonic Orders Blue Lodge, Chapter, Comandry and Shrine; also the Grand Army of the Republic and the Ancient Order of United Workmen, the latter being an insurance order. He married Miss Elizabeth H. Bingham, Sept. 1, 1868.

BIKANIR, His Highness the Maharaja of, (See Singh, Sir Ganga.)

BINNS, Percy, of Durban, is a member of the firm of Shepstone, Wylie, and Binns, and was selected as Chief Magistrate of Durban in 1905.

BIRCHENOUGH, Henry, C.M.G., J.P., M.A., of 79, Eccleston Square, London, S.W., and of the Reform and City of London Clubs, was born at Macclesfield, March 7, 1853, and is son of John Birchenough, J.P., of The Elms, Macclesfield. He was educated at the University College, London; Oxford University, and at Paris; is a member of the Council of the Royal Statistical Society and the Executive Committee of the National Service League. In 1903 he acted as Government Special Trade Commissioner to S. Africa, for which he received the C.M.G. in 1905. Mr. Birchenough was a member of the Tariff Commission in 1904; he is everywhere regarded as a great authority on politico economic questions; he enjoys great personal popularity, and takes a very leading part in the affairs of the British South Africa (Chartered) Company, of which he is a director. He is also a director of the Rhodesia Railways, Ltd., the African Concessions Syndicate, Ltd. (see H. Wilson Fox), the Victoria Falls Power Company, Limited, and the Continental Union Gas Company. He is the author of many articles on political and economic questions in the *Nineteenth Century* and other reviews, and is also the writer of the *Official Report on the Present Position and Future Prospects of British Trade in S. Africa*. He is a J.P. for the county of Cheshire, and married in Dec., 1886, Mabel Charlotte, third dau. of the Very Rev. George G. Bradley, C.V.O., Dean of Westminster.

BIRD, Christopher John, C.M.G. (1901), J.P., of Pietermaritzburg, Natal, and of the Victoria Club, P.M.B., was born at Maritzburg Dec. 30, 1855, and is son of the late John Bird, C.M.G., formerly Treasurer of Natal, whose father, Lieut.-Col. C. Bird, was formerly Colonial Secy. of the Cape Colony. Mr. C. J. Bird was educated in Maritzburg, and entered the Natal Civil Service in 1874. He was appointed Asst. Col. Secy. in 1888, and on the establishment of responsible government in 1893 was made Principal Under-Secretary. He is also Chairman of the Civil Service

Board, and J.P. for Natal. He held a commission in the Maritzburg Rifles from 1885 to 1887, and received the S. African war medal for assistance rendered by the civil administration to the military in Natal in 1899-1902. He married in 1887 Edith, dau. of the late Win. Armstrong, M.R.C.S. Eng.

BIRD, Sidney James, A.M.I.C.E., J.P., of Johannesburg, was attached to the Royal Engineers' Civil Staff at the War Office from 1888-1892, subsequently acting as Civil Engineer to H.M. Prison at Portland, and as Surveyor to the Royal Engineers' Dept., Newcastle-on-Tyne. He is a J.P. for the Witwatersrand District, and since 1902 has acted as Governor of the Johannesburg Prison.

BIRDWOOD, Herbert Mills, C.S.I. (1893), J.P. for Middlesex, Barrister-at-Law, of Dalkeith House, Cambridge Park, Twickenham, and 1, Brick Court, Temple, E.C.; the National Liberal, Mid-Surrey Golf, and various Indian Clubs, was born at Belgaum, Bombay Presidency, May 29, 1837, and is son of the late Gen. Christopher Birdwood, Bombay Army. He was educated at Plymouth New Gram. Sch., Mount Radford Sch., Exeter, Edin. University, and Peterhouse, Camb., where he took his M.A. and LL.D. He is also Hon. Fellow of Peterhouse. He entered the Indian Civil Service (Bombay Establishment) Dec. 26, 18-58; retired April 24, 1897; held office as Asst. Collector and Magistrate, 1859-62; Asst. Judge, 1862-3; Under-Secy. to the Bombay Govt., 1863-6; Political Assistant in Kathiawar, 1866-7; Registrar of the High Court, Bombay, 1867-71; District Judge and Sessions Judge in various districts, 1871-80; Judicial Commissioner in Sind and Judge of the Sadar Court, 1881-85; Judge of the High Court, Bombay, 1885-92; Vice-Chancellor of the Bombay University, 1891-92; and Member of the Executive Council of the Governor of Bombay and of the Bombay Legislative Council, 1892-97, during which period he was appointed Acting-Governor of Bombay, Feb. 17, 1895.

Mr. Birdwood is a Commissioner of Richmond Bridge, and for some years was a director of the Consolidated Exploration and Development (Rhodesia) Co. and the Morven (Rhodesia) Co. He edited certain vols. of the Laws and Regulations in

force in the Bombay Presidency, and is the author of various papers and articles on subjects connected with Indian administration and Indian Botany. He married, Jan. 29, 1861, Edith Marian Sidonie, dau. of the late Surgeon-Maj. Elijah Impey, Bombay Army, some time P.M.G. of Bombay.

BIRKENSTOCK, Coenraad J. A., M.L.C., of Vryheid, Natal, was born in Maritzburg in 1853. In 1876 he was selected by the Transvaal Govt. to accompany G. M. Rudolph and G. van Staden on the last mission to Cetewayo. He acted as Secy. to C. Joubert and Rudolph on the visit to Swaziland to crown Umbandine as king in 1875. He joined the opposition during the annexation of the Transvaal, and fought at Laing's Nek in the War of Independence. In 1884 he trekked to Zululand. He assisted in establishing the New Republic, and was Chairman of the Volksraad of twelve till shortly before its incorporation with the Transvaal. He was elected in 1890 to represent Vryheid in the First Volksraad, of which he was one of the most progressive members, and has since become member of the Natal Legislative Council for the N. Districts.

BIRT, Howard Hawkins, of Barberton, Transvaal, was born at London, Aug. 17, 1875, and is the descendant of an old Baptist family. He was educated at Devizes, Wilts., and lost no time in turning his talents in the direction of journalism. For some years connected with the London Press, he subsequently became editor of the *Bloemfontein Post*, and then, in 1904, of the *Goldfields News*. He has also published various short stories, articles, and pamphlets, mainly in connection with criminal identification, the work of the London Police, and the investigations of the Theosophical Society. He married, in 1897, Emily, dau. of H. Becker, of London.

BIRTWHISTLE, C. A., of Lagos, W. Africa, was formerly general manager of the Lagos Stores, Ltd., a trading company of Liverpool and Lagos. In 1905 he was appointed Commercial Adviser to the Govt. of the Lagos and S. Nigeria Colonies—an entirely new office, created in the interests of commerce.

BLACK, Stephen Cope, of Johannesburg, and the

Rand Club, is descended on the paternal side from a Scottish family who settled early in the 19th century in the Cape, where Mr. S. C. Black was born. He left the Western Province in 1889, attracted by the prospects of the Rand, where he has resided ever since. He is a member of the Johannesburg Stock Exchange; an executive mem. of the Chamber of Mines, and director of the Henry Nourse, New Modderfontein, Jumpers, Wolhuter, and other mining and industrial companies, besides being joint manager in S.A. of the Transvaal Gold Fields, Ltd.

BLACKBEARD, Charles Alexander, J.P., of Posno Street, Beaconsfield, Cape Colony, and of the Kimberley Club, was born at Grahamstown, Dec. 19, 1848, his grandparents having settled in the Colony in 1820. He is an old resident on the Diamond Fields, has for many years taken a prominent interest in the municipal affairs of Beaconsfield, for which town he was several times elected Mayor. He was re-elected in 1902. He is also Chairman of the local Public School, the local branch of the S.A. League, and of the Kroonstad Coal and Estate Co., and Director of the Griqualand West D.M. Co. In Freemasonry he is D.D.G.M. of Central South Africa, and Eminent Preceptor 'Diamond of the Desert'. He served as a trooper in the D.F.H. in the Kaffir War of 1877-8, became capt. in that corps in 1889, and served as capt. and adjt. in the Beaconsfield Town Guard during the siege in the S.A. War, and was mentioned in Col. Kekewich's despatches. He married, Dec. 8, 1875, Miss Annie Robinson McKay.

BLACKBURN, Douglas, of Loteni Valley, via Fort Nottingham, Natal; eldest son of the Rev. Geo. Blackburn, was born at Aix, Savoy, Aug. 6, 1857. He was educated at Wylde's King Edward Gram. Sch., Lowestoft, and read for the Bar. He has been connected with journalism since 1892, and is founder of *The Sentinel*, a Progressive Boer journal, and has incidentally been engaged in numerous criminal and civil actions for libel brought by the Transvaal Govt. officials. He is author of two books which have gained him a very favourable notoriety, *Prinsloo of Prinsloosdorp*, and *A Burgher Quixote* (Blackwood), and he has now in the press *Richard Hartley, Prospector*. Mr. Blackburn has travelled

considerably. He has written about sailing subjects, and has performed several unusually long single-handed voyages in small boats in British and Continental waters. Unmarried.

BLACKETT, Capt. Ralph, of the Army and Navy and Cavalry Clubs, was born at Wimborne, Dorset, Sept 19, 1877, and is the son of Maj.-Gen. Sir E. Blackett, Bart. He was educated at Clifton and Sandhurst, and joined the Army in Feb., 1897, served in the S.A. War with the 14th Hussars under Sir Redvers Buller until the relief of Ladysmith. He was with Gen. French's Cavalry Div. in the Orange Free State, and with Gen. Elliott's columns in O.R.C., 1902 (Queen's medal with five clasps, King's medal with two clasps). Capt. Blackett was appointed capt. in the Royal Inniskilling Fus. in Egypt, 1905.

BLACKWOOD, Lord Basil Temple, of Bloemfontein, O.R.C., was educated at Harrow and Balliol College, Oxford, and was called to the Bar at the Inner Temple in 1897. In 1900-1 he acted as Deputy Judge Advocate in South Africa, and from 1901-3 acted as Secretary to the Governor of the Orange River Colony; Acting Colonial Secretary there from May to Sept., 1902; Assistant Colonial Secretary in 1903, and again Acting Colonial Secretary for the Orange River Colony from April to Aug., 1903.

BLAINE, Sir Charles Frederick, Kt., of Jetty Street, Port Elizabeth, Cape Colony, is the eldest son of Benjamin Blame, M.D., of Natal. Sir Charles received his knighthood in 1889, in recognition of his services in promoting the South African Customs Union. He is a partner in the firm of Blaine and Co. of Cape Colony, and married Helen, dau. of Thomas Howie.

BLAINE, George, M.L.A., represents the electoral division of Cathcart in the Cape Legislative Assembly, and votes with the Progressive party.

BLAINE, Herbert Francis, M.L.C., K.C., of Bloemfontein, O.R.C., sits on the Executive and Legislative Councils of the Orange River Colony as Attorney-Gen., and was a member of the Inter-Colonial Council, but resigned his seat in 1904.

BLAKELEY, Robert Henry, of Johannesburg, was born at Harbury, Yorks, Nov. 8, 1867, is the son of Wm. Blakeley, J.P., was educated at Repton, and served with Roberts' Horse during the S.A. War, when he was taken prisoner at Sanna's Post (Queen's and King's medals, five clasps). He is very fond of cricket, football, and hockey; is an authority on the Rugby game, and was for seven years hon. secy. of the Transvaal Rugby Football Union.

BLAKEWAY, H. M., has been Resident Magistrate of Tarkastad, Cape Colony, for some years, and in the latter part of the South African War (Dec. 1, 1901) took over the administration of martial law in his district. Married.

BLAKEWAY, Oswald Munson, of Uitvlugt, Cape Colony, was employed in the Chief Magistrate's Office at Umtata in 1893, and acted Chief Clerk to the Chief Magistrate at Tembuland in 1897. He served as Military Secretary, with the rank of captain, to the officer commanding the Transkeian Territories Forces from 1899-1902, and on the amalgamation of the territories he was transferred to Butterworth as Asst. Magistrate in 1902, subsequently being appointed Asst. Magistrate at Uitvlugt in 1900, which position he still holds.

BLANCKENBERG, Reginald Andrew, of Pretoria, Transvaal, was employed in the B.S.A. Co.'s Cape Office in 1895, and in the Administrator's Office, Bulawayo, in 1896, acted as Private Secretary to the Administrator of Matabeleland in 1899, Private Secretary to the Administrator of Southern Rhodesia in 1901, Acting Secretary to the Lands Dept. and Accounting Officer in the Surveyor-General's Dept. in the same year, and Private Secretary to the Acting Administrator in 1902. Subsequently he was transferred from the Rhodesian service, and was appointed confidential clerk to the Lieut.-Governor of the Transvaal, shortly after becoming private secretary to him.

BLANE, William, F.R.C.I., of 31, Karl Street, Jeppestown, Johannesburg, and of the New Club and Rand Club, Johannesburg, is the eldest son of Robert Blane, of Galston, Ayrshire, and grandson of William Blane, of Ayr, who was the first engineer for William Baird and Co., and one of the

most successful engineers of his time. He was born May 28, 1858, at Galston, and trained in mining and engineering with Boyd, Gilmour, and Co., Kilmarnock. After taking various distinctions and prizes for scientific studies he went to S. Africa in 1883. After being in various parts of the country he went to Johannesburg in March, 1890, and was gen. manager of various gold mining companies to the end of 1893. From that year until 1899 he was senior partner of the firm of Blane and Co., engineers, Johannesburg. From 1899 till 1903 he was managing director of Blane and Co., Ltd. In 1901 he was selected by the Govt. of Queensland to inspect the goldfields of that country and to report on the conditions and mode of working them. He is director of several companies, and is a member of the Institute of Mechanical Engineers, London; of the Federated Institute of Mining Engineers, England; of the S.A. Association of Engineers; and of the Mechanical Engineers' Association of the Witwatersrand. He is also a member of the Rand Pioneers Association. Under the nom de plume of 'Beta' he was a frequent contributor of verses to *Excalibur* in the eighties. About this period a volume of his verses was published in Scotland under the title of *Lays of Life and Hope*, and he is the author of *The Silent Land and Other Poems* (1906). He is also the author of a number of technical articles on mining and engineering subjects for various publications, but still occasionally devotes a spare hour to the Muses. He married: first, Miss Jane Kerr, of Corshill, Kelwinning, in December 1879; and in April 1902 he married Bertha, third dau. of W. H. Roberts, of Somerset House, London, and sister to Morley Roberts, author.

BLELOCH, William Edwin, F.R.C.L, of Hazleyshaw, Albemarle St., Kensington, Johannesburg, and of the New Rand, and Athenaeum (London) Clubs, was born in London, Oct. 2, 1863; is son of Robert Bleloch, of Hazleyshaw, Clackmannanshire, Scotland, and was educated at Saline Public Sch., Fifeshire. He entered commercial life at Glasgow in 1879; went to S.A. in 1889, spent five years travelling in Cape Colony, Orangia, and the Transvaal; settled in Johannesburg in 1894, and engaged in mining. On outbreak of war in 1899 he acted as war correspondent for the *Standard* with Lord

Methuen's Kimberley Relief Column, then with Lord Roberts' Army to Bloemfontein and Pretoria. He was present at Graspan, Modder River, Magersfontein, Paardeberg, Poplar Grove, Driefontein, and all the fights up to Pretoria. He became Special Correspondent for the *Morning Post*, Sept., 1900, continuing to the end of the war. He wrote *The New South Africa*, published by Heinemann (1901). In 1902 he served on the Commission appointed to inquire into the Gold Laws of the Transvaal, and in May, 1902, became Joint Manager in Johannesburg of the United South Africa Association, Ltd. He is a Director of the Federation Syndicate, Ltd., Orangia Main Reef, Ltd., New Transvaal Coy., Ltd., Jooste Claims Syndicate, Ltd., New Options Syndicate, Ltd., East Rand Gold Mine, and Alternate Director of The Premier Transvaal Diamond Mining Coy., Ltd. His recreations are the study of geology and economics. Mr. Bleloch was married on July 11, 1901.

BLENKINS, William Bazett Goodwin, of The Residency, King Williamstown, and of the Civil Service (Cape Town) and Senior (K.W.T.) Clubs,. was born at. Bombay July 4, 1852, his father being Brev.-Major W. B. G. Blenkins, C.B., and his mother a dau. of H. C. Jarvis, formerly M.L.C. Mr. Blenkins was educated at the South African Coll. and entered the Civil Service in 1871; was appointed R.M. at Mount Frere in 1880, additional R.M. for Kimberley at Du Toit's Pan and Member of Special Court 1882; was thereafter C.C. and R.M. at Murraysburg, Hay, and Herschel; became Divisional Inspector in the Attorney-General's Dept. in 1895; was appointed C.C. and R.M. at Cradock in 1897, and C.C. and R.M. and Registrar of Deeds at King William's Town in Aug., 1900. Incidentally Mr. Blenkins has held various other appointments, including Secy. to Special Commissioner with the Transkeian tribes in 1875; has acted as Chief of Police at Cape Town; was Special Commissioner on Agricultural Distress, Northern Districts, in 1899; Sub-Commissioner, War Losses Compensation Board, 1902, and Commissioner in 1903. He has also acted as visiting magistrate at the Convict Stations at East London and Cape Town. Recreations: walking, shooting, and fishing. He married, Nov. 14, 1883, Mary, dau. of Rev. Geo. Chapman, some time Governor of Heald Town Training Institute.

BLENKINSOP, Lt.-Col. Layton John, A.V.D., D.S.O., M.R.C.V.S., of the Junior United Service Club, Lond., was born June 27, 1862, and is son of Col. Wm. Blenkinsop. He was educated at King's School, Canterbury, and Royal Veterinary Coll., Lond. He joined the Army Vet. Dept., Sept., 1883; Senior Vet. Officer, Army of Occupation in Egypt 1896-9 (medal with Khartoum clasp and Egyptian medal, D.S.O.). He also served in the S.A. War, 1899-1902, as S.V.O. to the Cavalry Div. under Sir John French, and afterwards as S.V.O. Remount Dept., S. Africa (promoted Major, medal with six clasps, King's medal with two clasps). Col. Blenkinsop is at present P.V.O. in Ireland.

BLOMFIELD, Col. (local Brig-Gen.) Charles James, C.B., D.S.O., of Harrismith, O.R.C., and of the Army and Navy Club, was born in Devonshire, May 26, 1855, and is son of Rev. Geo. Blomfield by a dau. of Chas. Jas. Blomfield, Bishop of London. Gen. Blomfield was educated at Haileybury, where he played in the 1st Cricket XI., and at Sandhurst, whence he passed into the Army as Sub-Lieut. in 1875. He was Adjt. of the Lancashire Fusiliers 1880-1883, and was given the brevet rank of Colonel in 1900. Gen. Blomfield's staff services include five years (1884-89) as Adjt. of Auxiliary Forces, D.A.A.G. at Bombay, 1892-6, A.A.G. India, 1897, Colonel on Staff commanding sub-district in S. Africa, 1900-02, and Brig.-Gen. in South Africa, 1902-6. His war service includes the Sudan campaign of 1898, when he was present at the battle of Khartoum, in recognition of which he received the D.S.O., the Egyptian medal with clasp, and the Queen's medal, besides being mentioned in despatches. In the South African War, 1899-1902, he commanded the 2nd Lancashire Fusiliers until Oct., 1900, taking part in the relief of Ladysmith and the operations of Jan 17 to 24, 1900, and the action at Spion Kop, where he was severely wounded. Later in 1900 he operated in the Eastern Transvaal, afterwards serving on the Staff and in command of columns in the Transvaal and the Zululand frontier of Natal, being mentioned in despatches and receiving the brevet rank of Colonel, the Queen's medal with four clasps, and the King's medal with two clasps. Gen. Blomfield now commands the Harrismith district of the O.R.C. He married in 1881 Henriette Elizabeth, only dau. of the late Maj. Ed. Briscoe, formerly of the 20th Regt.

BLOMFIELD, Rear-Admiral Richard Massie, R.N., Orders of the Osmanieh (3rd class) and Medjidieh (3rd class); of Alexandria, Egypt; 5, Stanley Pl., Chester; and of the United Service and Pall Mall Clubs, was born at Stevenage, Herts, Mch. 3, 1835. He is son of the late Rev. G. B. Blomfield, Rector of Stevenage and Canon of Chester Cathedral, whose brother was Bishop of London from 1828 to 1856, his mother having been Frances Maria, dau, of the Rev. Richard Massie, of Coddington, Cheshire. The present admiral was educated at the Rev. Jn. Seager's Private Classical Sch., at Stevenage, and entering the R.N. served throughout the Crimea as Mid-Mate and Lieut, of H.M.S. *Agamemnon* and *Royal Albert*, flagship of Sir Edmund Lyons; was Mate of 1st launch of the *Royal Albert*, in the Azoff Expedition in 1855; and Capt. W. R. Mends, who commanded both these ships from 1853 to 1857, on giving up the command, certified that "Lieut. Blomfield is distinguished for patience and coolness in a moment of trial. I have had a good opportunity of judging of the qualifications of officers during the war, and Lieut. Blomfield's are of a high order". (Crimean medals, Sebastopol and Azoff clasps). Lieut. Blomfield was on board H.M.S. *Hero* conveying his present Majesty, when Prince of Wales, representing the Queen, to the British American Colonies and U.S.A. and back to Eng. in 1860. He was selected as Commander of H.M.S. *Agincourt* when the Admiralty flag was first hoisted; in executive command of the Channel and Reserve Squadrons in Apr., 1869; was mem. of the Admiralty Confidential Torpedo Committee from May 23, 1873, to July 28, 1876. As Capt., at the request of Khedive Ismail, the Admiralty appointed him Controller of the Port of Alexandria in Aug., 1878, and he held that post from May 19, 1879, to July 1, 1901, since which date he has been Controller-Gen. of Egyptian Ports and Lighthouses. The Order of the Medjidieh (3rd cl.) was conferred upon him in Aug., 1883, and he received the Egyptian war medal, with Alexandria clasp, and the Egyptian star for services rendered to the British and Egyptian Govts. during the events of 1882. He was present during the bombardment of Alexandria on board

H.M.S. *Invincible*, by invitation of the C.I.C., Sir B. Seymour, and landed with the party under the commander of H.M.S. *Monarch* to take possession of the forts and town on the morning of July 13. Adm. Blomfield received an official letter from H.M. Principal Secy. of State for Foreign Affairs, expressing the appreciation of H.M. Govt. for the valuable services rendered by him to the Expeditionary Force in Egypt during the campaign of 1882, and for the zeal and ability with which he served his country during the operations. He married, July 3, 1877, Rosamond Selina, dau. of the late. Rt. Rev. C. Graves, D.D., Bishop of Limerick, by whom he has two sons, Capt. C. G. Massie Blomfield, 6th R. Warwickshire Regt. (b. 1878), and H. Massie Blomfield, B.A., of Oriel Coll., Oxon (born 1881).

BLONDEL, André E., of Paris; was born in Burgundy in 1863, and studied at the *Ecole Polytechnique* of Paris, and later on at the *Ecole des Pouts et Chaussées*. At the same time he graduated for Mathematical and Physical Sciences at the University. In his earlier professional days he was connected with French public works, and while acting as engineer in the Central Lighthouse service experimented considerably in electric lighting. Amongst other things he planned the lenses and the electric machinery of many important lighthouses.

Meanwhile, M. Blondel was actively employed in writing upon electrical and optical subjects, mainly on alternators, synchronous and asynchronous and collector motors, rotary converters, alternating currents, impedance of lines, photometry, the arc light, and wireless telegraphy, in connection with which he invented new apparatus, such as oscillographs, which opened a new field for the study of alternate currents, lumenometers, a new hysteresis meter, a universal photometer, holophane globes, new sensitive coherers, a method of compounding alternators, a system of arc lighting with mineralised carbons, a system of acoustically syntonic wireless telegraphy, &c.

M. Blondel was the first to explain in 1893 the effect of inertia in the hunting of alternators, and is the author of the 'Two reaction Theory' of alternators, and other works which have made him name famous as an electrical engineer, especially in connection with power transmission. The French Academy of Sciences awarded him the Gaston-Planté prize in 1897 and the Castner-Boursault prize in the following year. He has lectured on electricity at the French National School of Mines, and was selected as the first occupant of the Chair of Applied Electricity in the *Ecole Nationale Des Ponts et Chaussées* of Paris. He is a Chevalier of the Legion of Honour, and member of the Advisory Board of Engineers to the Victoria Falls Power Company.

BLUMLEIN, S. J., of Johannesburg; of the Swaziland Corporation, and formerly Manager for many years of the Bourke Trust and Estate Co., of Pretoria, joined the firm of Lewis and Marks (see Isaac Lewis, Samuel Marks, and C. F. Rowsell) in May, 1906.

BLUNT, Captain Osmond Donald, was born Nov. 17, 1870, and entered the Connaught Rangers in 1898, exchanging to the Lancashire Fusiliers in 1900. He served in the Dongola Expedition in 1896 (despatches, medal, 4th Class Medjidie, and Egyptian medal with two clasps) the Expedition against the Mpezeni, British Central Africa, in 1898 (medal with clasp), and the South African War in 1899-1900 as special service officer, and serving with the Rhodesian Protectorate Regt. (Queen's medal with three clasps).

BLYDEN, Dr. Edward W., of Sierra Leone, was born in 1832 in St. Thomas, Danish West Indies. He is of pure negro blood, and went to the United States at the age of seventeen to improve his education. Being a coloured man he found racial feeling too strong, and accordingly he went to the black republic of Liberia, where he studied further and became a Presbyterian preacher. Dr. Blyden interested Mr. Gladstone in his schemes in 1859, and two years later was sent by the Liberian Govt. to the West Indies to encourage a return of negroes to West Africa. He was accredited Minister for Liberia at the Court of St. James in 1877, and again in 1892. He has travelled in Syria and Egypt, has made two journeys in the hinterland of Sierra Leone on behalf of the British Govt., and has lectured in the U.S.A. on Liberian affairs. He is opposed to the idea of the Christian faith being suitable for African negroes, as is shown in his book *Christianity, Islam, and the Negro Races* (1886), and

has since preached the Muhammedan doctrine amongst natives. In 1895 he was appointed Agent for Native Affairs in Lagos. He then occupied a similar position in Old Calabar, and in 1899 opened up Muhammedan schools in Sierra Leone. The year 1900 he spent as professor of languages (of which he speaks four) in Liberia, and in Aug., 1901, he was appointed Director of Muhammedan Education for Sierra Leone by Mr. J. Chamberlain, with the object of opening up further Moslem schools in that colony. Dr. Blyden visited England in 1903, and was entertained there at a large negro banquet.

BODEN, Captain Athoney Drummond, was born Sept. 24, 1872, and joined the Rifle Brigade in 1892. He served in the South African War in 1900-2, including the operations in Natal and the Transvaal east of Pretoria (Queen's medal with two clasps, and the King's medal with two clasps).

BOGER, Major R. W., R.F.A., served in the S.A. War, his services being several times mentioned in despatches. He was subsequently employed at the Staff Coll., and in 1905 was attached to the Japanese Army in Manchuria.

BOGGIE, Alexander, F.R.C.I., of Old Meldrum, Aberdeenshire, and Bulawayo, Rhodesia, and of the Caledonian (Lond.) and Bulawayo Clubs, is the eldest son of the late Alexander Boggie, of Liverpool and Aberdeen. He was born May 8, 1861, at Liverpool, and was educated privately and at various public schools in Aberdeen, Edinburgh, and London. Mr. Boggie went to S.A. in 1869 with his parents. He was at the Diamond Fields with his father in 1871, when the Kimberley Mine was discovered. He returned to Scotland with his mother on the death of his father in 1875, and went back to S.A. in 1883. He joined in the rush to the Kaap Gold Fields in 1884; visited Swaziland in 1886, and opened negotiations with Umbandine, the Swazi King, with a view to getting a gold concession in his country. This he succeeded in doing, and as soon as this became publicly known the rush for concessions to Swaziland took place. In 1888 he visited the King of the Matabele on a similar errand. He was through the Matabele Rebellion, and during the late S.A. War acted as Special Correspondent for the Rhodesian Press in the Natal Campaign. Ever since the occupation of Rhodesia he has taken an interest in its affairs, both commercial and otherwise. He is on the local board of several gold mining, land, and other companies in Bulawayo, and is also on the Town Council and on the board of most of the local public bodies of that town. At various times he has taken part in hunting and exploring expeditions to various parts of S.A.

BOGGIE, Capt. William James, of Gwelo, Rhodesia, and the Junior Naval and Military Club, Lond., was born at Edinburgh, and is second son of the late Alex. Boggie, of Liverpool and Natal. After some slight banking experience he joined the Queensland Defence Force, serving as Capt. in the Queensland Artillery, and compiled the *Gunners' Handbook*. He also served during the Matabele War, 1896, commanding C Troop B.F.F., and being present at the storming of Thabas Amamba and with the Shangani, Wedzas, and Belingwe patrols (medal). During the last South African War he was recruiting officer for the 2nd Scottish Horse, and he also served in various operations in the Transvaal, O.R.C., and Cape Colony; served subsequently with the 5th Manchester Regt.; was comdt. at Karreefontein and Riet Spruit at close of hostilities in 1902 (Queen's medal, four clasps, King's medal, two clasps) He commands the Southern Rhodesia Volunteers at Gwelo; is member of the Rhodesia Pioneer Assn., Director of the Gwelo Board of Executors and Building Sec., and Ed. of the Gwelo *Times*.

BOLUS, Gillham, of Maldivia, Wynberg, Cape Colony, and of the City and Civil Service Clubs (C. T.), and the Rand Club, is eldest son of Walter Bolus of Bournemouth, Hants. He was born at Port Elizabeth, Oct. 11, 1863, and was educated at King's Sch., Canterbury. He married, July 23, 1889, Maud Constance, 4th dau. of Arthur Gates, J.P. for Cape Colony.

BOND, Lieut.-Colonel Francis George, C.B., R.E., of the United Service Club, was born in 1856, and is son of the late Rev. F. H. Bond. He was educated at Marlborough Coll. and the Royal Military Academy; entered the Royal Engineers in 1876, and served in the Zulu Campaign in 1879 (medal with clasp); the Egyptian Expedition in

1882, being present at the actions at Kassassin, the battle of Tel-el-Kebir, and the march to and occupation of Cairo (medal with clasp and bronze star); the Hazara Expedition in 1891 (despatches, medal with clasp); operations on the North-West Frontier of India in 1897-8, with the Tirah Expeditionary Force (medal with two clasps); and the South African War in 1901-2, on the Staff, including the operations in the Transvaal (Queen's medal with three clasps and C.B.). Colonel Bond is at present A.Q.M.G. in the Punjab. He married, in 1881, Alice, dau. of W. Vivian.

BOND, Major Reginald Copleston, D.S.O., of Crete, was born in 1866, and is son of the late Rev. F. H. Bond, and brother to Lieut.-Col. F. G. Bond (q.v.). He joined the Yorks. Light Infantry as 2nd Lieut. in 1888, and served in the operations of the Zhob Field Force in 1890. From 1895-6 he acted as A.D.C. to the G.O.C. the Poona District; took part in the operations on the North-West Frontier of India in 1897-8, with the Tirah Expeditionary Force (medal with two clasps), and the South African War in 1899-1902, including the advance on Kimberley and the actions at Belmont, Enslin, Modder River, Magersfontein, Lindley, Bethlehem, and Wittebergen (despatches, Queen's medal with four clasps and D.S.O.). He married, in 1897, Isabel, dau. of Major-Gen. Tyler.

BONHAM-CARTER, Edgar, Order of the Osmanieh (3rd class) of Khartoum, of 5, Hyde Park Square, London, and of the United University Club; was born in London, Apr. 2, 1870. He is son of Henry Bonham-Carter and Sibella, dau. of Geo. Warde Norman. He was educated at Clifton Coll. and New Coll., Oxon., where he distinguished himself at football, having been a member of the Oxford University Rugby Football XV. in 1890 and 1891, whilst in 1890 he played in the English Rugby team v. Scotland. Mr. Bonham-Carter is a Barrister of Lincoln's Inn; was appointed Legal Secy. to the Sudan Govt, and Judicial Commissioner in 1899, and is the author of a note on the History of Legislation in Great Britain relating to Alcoholic Liquors, published in the Report of Lord Peel's Commission. Unmarried.

BONUS, Major William, D.S.O., of Clapton Court, Somersetshire, and of the Naval and

Military Club, Lond., was born at Kurrachee, 1864, and is son of Gen. Bonus, J.P. He was educated at Harrow and Sandhurst, and joined the Dorsetshire Regt. in 1883; has served in India and Egypt; A.D.C. 1895; D.A.A.G., Scottish Dist., 1899; served with his regt. in S. Africa until the relief of Ladysmith; afterwards acting as D.A.A.G., 4th Div. (Queen's medal with five clasps, King's medal with two I clasps). Decorated for services in the Transvaal. Unmarried.

BOSHOF, Frederick, of the Waterberg District, Transvaal, was born at Philippolis, O.R.C., in 1848. His father fought at Boomplaats, and then trekked across the Vaal to the northernmost corner of the Waterberg, where young Boshof was brought up amongst only semi-civilized surroundings. He served the Hervormde Church for eight years as deacon, and for four years as elder, and in 1891 was elected to the Second Volksraad of the S.A.R. as member for Waterberg, in which he sat as an uncompromising supporter of the Govt.

BOTHA, Revd. J. B., a wavering minister of the Dutch Reformed Church, who apologised to the Afrikander Bond for having urged the people to accept British rule and declaring that the continued resistance of the Boers was a crime. This action caused such bitter feeling among his congregation that Mr. Botha wrote a recantation to the newspaper *Ons Land*. The feeling, however, continued, but on the matter being referred to the Church Council, that body finally exonerated Mr. Botha.

BOTHA, J. N. P., was senior member of the Cape Legislative Assembly for Aliwal North until the general election of 1904, when he did not seek re-election.

BOTHA, General Louis, was born in 1863, and was a member of the First Volksraad of the South African Republic, representing Vryheid, in which district he farmed and acted as Field Cornet. He was opposed to Mr. Kruger's ante-war policy, but when active hostilities commenced he saw service from the beginning of the war, and on the death of Gen. Joubert became Commandant-General of the Boer forces, fighting on until the ultimate

surrender, when he naturally took a prominent part in the settlement of the Transvaal question. While in the field Gen. Botha kept a watchful eye on the utterances of pro-Boers and public men in England, and it was a direct consequence of the Liberal Federation at Derby in Dec., 1901, that he sent messages to all his Commandants telling them to continue fighting, because the English people were so tired of the war that Parliament would refuse further money for carrying it on.

During the Conference at Vereeniging the General advocated making peace, recognising that it was futile to hope for foreign help, and that Britain would never tolerate the intervention of any foreign Power whatsoever. The conditions of peace being settled, the generals publicly stated that they intended to co-operate with their new fellow-subjects. It is impossible to say what their real sentiments were, but the Boer party in Europe interpreted them to mean that they would wait and educate their children for revenge.

On July 30, 1902, Generals Botha, De la Rey, and De Wet sailed for Europe to collect gifts for the maintenance of those who were widowed and wounded through the war, and to provide for the housing and education of orphans, &c. The feeling towards the trio in England was most cordial, and the Colonial Secretary hoped for a conference with the generals, but the Leyds party on the Continent were preparing a plan for Mr. Fischer to intercept them at Southampton and prevent them responding, as the late Gen. Lucas Meyer had done, to the friendly advances of the English people. They went, however, on board the *Nigeria* to exchange a few wards with Lord Kitchener, Lord Roberts, and Mr. Chamberlain, and on the following day were received by the King on H.M. yacht, after which they visited the fleet at Spithead. Avoiding the welcome which the British had prepared for the generals, they immediately passed to their more serious business on the Continent, where Gen. Botha had to meet Mr. Kruger and his clique, who were intriguing so busily to estrange the generals from an amiable understanding with the British. As to what happened at the Boer councils nothing is definitely known, but it is believed that the generals refused to act in concert with the irreconcilables in supporting their two-fold policy of maintaining an agitation against Great Britain on the Continent and interfering with the settlement in South Africa. A few days later, however, the generals contradicted the suspicion that any differences of opinion had arisen during their conferences.

Meanwhile, in September, 1902, a meeting was arranged between the three generals and Mr. Chamberlain at the Colonial Office. The Boer delegates expressing disappointment that a general amnesty had not been granted at the time of the King's coronation, it was pointed out that this decision had, as a matter of fact, been left entirely to the decision of the Cape and Natal Governments. With regard to the prisoners of war, Mr. Chamberlain pointed out that every assistance would be offered to enable these to return on taking the oath of allegiance, or on making a simple declaration. (See F. W. Reitz.) The generals then asked that certain farms which had been confiscated under the proclamation of Aug. 7, 1901, should be given back to the burghers, and received the assurance that this should be done in any practicable cases. That practically closed the conference, which Mr. Chamberlain concluded with the following words: "We want S. Africa to be a happy abiding place for all who live in it, not for one class alone, not for one section, for one race, or for one political party, but for all, and our duty is to regard the interests of all, and we desire that no section should be entirely unrepresented. I am sure that if you meet us half way you will find us to be in the future quite as good friends as we have been, I hope, loyal enemies in the past."

The generals were disappointed, and, returning to the Continent, the next move (though whether prompted by themselves or by the Leyds clique was difficult to determine) was the 'Appeal of the Boer Generals to the Civilised World', which appeared in the *Nieuwe Rotterdamsche Courant*, the trend of which was to hold England up to the execration of the world, representing her as leaving callously to their fate the inhabitants whose lands had been desolated by the war. Continental countries, however, found good reasons for not appreciably assisting the generals in a financial way, and thus the tour collapsed after much British sympathy had been alienated by the methods employed by the Boer emissaries.

General Botha is a man of strong character, with a powerful following among the Transvaal Boers, and is a prominent leader of the new Boer organisation in the Transvaal known as *Het Volk*. Gen. Botha has hopes of regaining for the Transvaal Afrikanders the power which they lost in the stricken field by means of the Liberal majority of 1906. Although he publicly counsels moderation, he loses no opportunity of condemning Lord Milner's work in Africa and the mining 'clique' headed by Wernher, Beit, and Co.

A son of Gen. Botha's, a high-spirited lad of twelve, went through the last part of the war with his father, and it was stated that he had, like Hannibal, sworn an eternal hatred to his father's enemies. Gen. Botha also has several other children, the youngest boy having been born during the war.

BOTHA, P. M., a farmer of the Kroonstad District, O.R.C. was elected member of the Free State Volksraad in May, 1879.

BOTHA, Hon. R. P., was born in the Swellendam dist., C.C.; was elected member of the Cape Legislative Council in 1883; was returned to the House of Assembly in 1895; and subsequently represented the Midland Province in the Cape Legislative Council. He is an ardent Afrikander of independent views, and was once Pres. of the Bond.

BOULENGER, George Albert, F.R.S., V.P.Z.S., of 8, Courtfield Road, S.W., was born at Brussels, Oct. 19, 1858, and is a naturalised British subject. He is in charge of the collection of reptiles and fishes in the British Museum, having devoted special attention to African fishes, and is the author of many works on zoology. He presided over the zoological section of the British Association on their tour in S. Africa in 1905.

BOULBY, Dr. Anthony Alfred. C.M.G. F.R.C.S. Eng., served in the South African War in 1900, when he was in charge of the Portland Hospital; is surgeon and lecturer on surgery at St. Bartholomew's Hospital, London, and was appointed Surgeon to the King's Household in

1904. He is the author of many works on surgical subjects.

BOULGER, Demetrius Charles, of 11 Edwardes Square, Kensington, W., was born in London, July 14, 1853, and is of Irish parentage, and almost exclusively Irish ancestry. The name Boulger or Bolger—until the surrender of the Leinster Septs in the 16th century, O'Bolger—is that of one of the oldest Septs or clans in Wexford and the adjoining counties. William O'Bolger, in 1463, was the first Irishman allowed to hold lands within the Pale. He began writing in the London Press in 1875, and has since contributed to, practically speaking, all the leading newspapers and reviews on Imperial and Colonial questions. His principal published works are *The History of China*, *The Life of Gordon* (of both of which several editions have been published), *The Life of Sir Stamford Raffles*, *England and Russia in Central Asia*, *India in the XIXth Century*, *The Congo State*, *History of Belgium*, He founded in 1886 (in conjunction with Sir Lepel Griffin) *The Asiatic Quarterly Review*, which he edited for over four years, and assisted Sir George Birdwood in giving practical effect to his idea for the adoption of Primrose Day.

BOULNOIS, Major W. A., R.A., of the Egyptian Army, is commandant of the first class military district of Bahrel-Gha-Zal, Egypt, and was in the winter of 1904-5 in charge of an expedition sent to punish the cannibal Niam-Niams of the Upper Nile, in which he was entirely successful. The Sultan of Yambie was captured, but subsequently died of his wounds. The country was pacified, and order assured.

BOURKE, Edmund Francis, M.L.C., of Barton Keep, Pretoria, and of the Pretoria, Durban, and City (Cape Town) Clubs, is the eldest son of John Bourke, one of the early colonists of Natal. He was educated at private schools, and at Maritzburg High School. He received his business training in Natal, and went to the Transvaal early in 1887, before annexation; returned to Natal for a short time in 1878, and settled finally in Pretoria in 1879. Immediately taking an interest in municipal affairs, he was elected a member of the first Pretoria Municipality. This election was cancelled upon the retrocession of the Transvaal in 1881. In spite of

taking an active part in the mercantile business of Bourke & Co. and other commercial undertakings, and of being an active Director on the Board of the National Bank prior to the war, he devoted himself to public and philanthropic institutions. Before the occupation of the British he interested himself very largely in the hospitals and nursing homes, where his administrative and business abilities were of value. During some months of the war he served as Acting Burgomaster of Pretoria under Gen. Sir J. G. Maxwell, and was appointed to a seat in the Legislative Council of the Transvaal after the war. He is now Chm. of the Pretoria Chamber of Commerce, Pres. of the Irish Association, Chm. of the Bourke Trust & Estate Co., and of several mercantile concerns, and was elected Mayor of Pretoria at the end of 1903. In 1905 he surprised the British section by appearing on the Committee of the newly formed Boer organisation, called *Het Volk* (The People). Mr. Bourke has also been associated prominently with all athletic sports. It was mainly through his efforts that the visits of the English Professionals, Brockwell, Trott, and Braund, to Pretoria took place. Mr. Bourke married, May 18, 1881, Eleanor, third dau. of Henry Griffin, of Woodford, Maritzburg, Natal.

BOURNE, Capt. Henry Roland Murray, of Pretoria; of Cowarne Court, Ledbury, Herefordshire; and of the Bath (Lond.) and Pretoria Clubs, was born in Worcestershire, June 18, 1874, and is son of Lt.-Col. R. Bourne, J.P., D.L., of Cowarne Court, Herefordshire. He was educated at Radley and New Coll., Oxon., entered the Royal Scots as 2nd Lieut. in 1896, and obtained his captaincy in Nov., 1902. He was seconded for service under the Colonial Office in June, 1902, when he was appointed Under-Secretary in the Colonial Secretary's Office, Transvaal. Unmarried.

BOUSFIELD, Lieut.-Col. Henry Hitchins, C.M.G., J.P., of St. Andrew's St., Durban, the United Empire, Durban, Natal Civil Service, and Royal Natal Yacht Clubs, was born at Winchester, Hants, May 3, 1863, and is the eldest son of the late Rt. Rev. Henry Brougham Bousfield, D.D., Bishop of Pretoria; was educated at All Hallowes, Honiton, and Sherborne. He was attached to H.M. Ordnance Dept., Transvaal, 1879-80 (Zulu and Sekukuni wars); joined the Transvaal Civil Service

(Col. Secy.'s Dept.), 1880, and was employed on staff duties during the siege of Pretoria in the Boer War of 1880-1; attached Acct.-Gen.'s Dept. of the Army at Pretoria, Aug., 1881, and was appointed to the Natal Civil Service in the following Sept. Subsequently he became Chief Clerk to the R.M., Durban, and Registrar of the Circuit Court; J.P. for the County, 1886; and acting Magistrate in Durban in 1889. He resigned the Natal Civil Service in Oct., 1890, and was called to the Bar of the Inner Temple in Nov., 1892. He was admitted Advocate of the Supreme Courts of Natal (1893), and the Cape of Good Hope (1899), and a Commissioner in Natal of the Supreme Court of the Transvaal in 1902. He joined the Royal Durban Rifles as Lieut. in 1886, was Capt. in Natal Royal Rifles, 1888, receiving his majority and the command of the Durban Light Infantry in 1893, and transferred to the Reserve, Natal Volunteers, 1895. During the S.A. War he acted as Station Staff Officer at Durban, 1899-1900, being mentioned in despatches and receiving the medal and C.M.G., 1902. Col. Bousfield retired from the Service early in 1902 with the hon. rank of Lt.-Col., and in Feb., 1905, rejoined the Natal Militia Staff (Supernumerary List) as Lt.-Col. He married, Apr. 22, 1890, Coral, second dau. of the late Rt. Hon. Harry Escombe, P.C., Q.C., LL.D., M.L.A., late Premier of Natal.

BOVILL, Edward M., of Norcott Court, Berkhampstead, is Chairman of the Kaapsche Hoop Gold Mines, Ltd., and the Vryheid Exploration Co., Ltd., and is director of the Crown Collieries (1903), Ltd., Natal Coal Trust, Ltd., Newcastle (Natal) Steam Coal Collieries, Ltd, and the Peel River Land and Mineral Co., Ltd.

BOWER, Major Robert Lister, C.M.G., of Northallerton, Yorks., and of the Naval and Military and Yorkshire Clubs, was born in 1860, and is son of the late Robert Bower. He was educated at Harrow, and joined the 60th Rifles in 1881; served in the Egyptian Expedition in 1882-4, including the reconnaissance at Ramleh, the affair at Tel-el-Mahuta, the action at Kassassin, and the battle of Tel-el-Kebir (medal with clasp and bronze star), and was employed on Transport duties during the Sudan Expedition, including the battles of Teb and Tamai (despatches and two clasps); and the

Nile Expedition in 1884-5, with the Mounted Infantry (despatches and clasp). He married Annette, dau. of Henry Head.

BOWKER, Major Charles Allan, J.P., M..B., C.M., of the Bungalow, Port Shepstone, Natal, was born at Tarrington, July 14, 1871. He was educated at Edinburgh Univ., and was captain of the Rugby team and cricket, and rowing member of the Avon Rowing Club. At Edinburgh he took first-class honours in anatomy, and was second prizeman in surgery. On graduating in 1896, he took a sea voyage to S. Africa on account of health, and was acting Dist. Surg. for Alfred County, Natal, until 1897, when he was appointed Dist. Surg. and Indian Medical Officer at Lower Umzimkulu, and health officer at Port Shepstone; was gazetted Lieut.-Surg. in the Border Mounted Rifles, and received his majority in 1904, in recognition of his services during the siege of Ladysmith, at Intombi Volunteer Hospital Camp. J.P. for Alfred County in 1897. He married Oct. 13, 1894, Christina Mackay.

BOWMAN-MANIFOLD, Captain Michael Graham Egerton, D.SO., was born June 9, 1871, and joined the Royal Engineers in 1891; served in the Dongola Expedition in 1896 as Staff Officer of Telegraphs (despatches 4th Class Medjidie and Egyptian medal with two clasps); the Nile Expedition in 1897, as Staff Officer of Telegraphs (clasp to Egyptian medal); the Nile Expedition in 1898 as Staff Officer of Telegraphs on the Headquarter Staff, present at the battles of the Athara and Khartoum (despatches, 4th Class Osmanieh, medal, and two clasps to Egyptian medal), and the South African War in 1899-1901, on the Staff (despatches, Queen's medal with three clasps, and D.S.O.).

BOWRING, Charles Calvert, of Mombasa, E. Africa Protectorate; and of the Union Club; is son of J. L. Bowring, of Forest Farm, Windsor Forest; was educated at Clifton Coll., and joined the Colonial Audit Branch of Exchequer and Audit Dept., Jan. 20, 1890; was sent to Hong Kong, Dec. 12, 1892; Local Auditor British Central Africa, Sept. 7, 1895; Local Auditor East African Protectorate and Uganda Railway, June 5, 1899; and was appointed Treasurer of the East African

Protectorate, Oct. 1, 1901. Mr. Bowring was awarded the Hong Kong Gold Plague Medal, 1894.

BOYCE, Merwanji Rustomji, of Zanzibar. practised as a pleader in H.B.M.'s Courts at Zanzibar from 1884 to 1895; was called to the English Bar in 1900, and is now a leading member of the Bar in H.B.M.'s Courts in Zanzibar.

BOYD, Bryce, of 8, Deanery Lane, Maritzburg; son of William Boyd, Greenock, Scotland; was born at Greenock, March 11, 1863, and was educated at Highlanders' Academy there, and Edinburgh University. He received his first newspaper training on the staff of the *Greenock Telegraph*, afterwards on the *Edinburgh Courant*; and went to South Africa twenty years ago as sub-editor of the *Natal Advertiser*. He soon after proceeded to Barberton, and sub-edited the *Gold Fields Times*; ran a newspaper of his own called *The North Kaap Telegraph* during the alluvial rush; was subsequently in Swaziland when Umbandine was King, and later on with Mr. W. P. Taylor and Mr. J. C. A. Henderson in the Transvaal. At the time of the Jameson Raid he was sub-editor for the *Johannesburg Times*; has been employed on the literary staffs of the *Cape Times*, *Rand Daily Mail*, and *Natal Witness*. Before the end of the war he returned from England to Pretoria as secretary to Major-Gen. Sir John Ardagh, K.C.M.G., and was afterwards Chief Clerk of the Repatriation Department. He married Florence, dau. of William Essame, of Peterborough.

BOYD, Charles Walter, C.M.G., of 1. Whitehall Gardens, Lond., S.W., and of the Garrick and National Clubs, is son of the late Very Rev. A. K. H. Boyd, D.D., of St. Andrew's N.B., where he was born Apr. 11, 1869. Educated at Fettes Coll., Edin., and at Edinburgh University, he read for the Scottish Bar, but drifted into journalism, contributing articles to the *Saturday Review*, *Times*, and various other journals and magazines. From 1895-97 he was Priv. Secy. to the Rt. Hon. G. Wyndham, M.P., and from 1897-98 he acted in a similar capacity to Dr. L. S. Jameson. He was also for some time Political Secy. to the late Rt. Hon. C. J. Rhodes. He is now Joint Secy. of the Rhodes Trust, Mem. of the Executive of the Imperial S.A. Association, and Mem. of the Committee of the

S.A. Colonization Soc., and of the Victoria League. Unmarried.

BOYD, Henry Crawford, of the Rand Club, Johannesburg, and of the Caledonian and National Clubs, London, is 5th and youngest son of the late Very Rev. A. K. H. Boyd, D.D., of St. Andrews, N.B., where he was born Sept. 26, 1870. He was educated at Fettes Coll., Edin., and is at present on the staff of Messrs. H. Eckstein & Co., Johannesburg.

BOYD-CARPENTER, Henry John, M.A. of Sharia, Kasr-el-Nil, Cairo; and of the Junior Carlton, Royal Societies, and Turf (Cairo) Clubs, was born at Tetsworth, Oxon., in 1865, and is eldest son of the Bishop of Ripon. He was educated at Westminster and King's Coll., Camb., where he took a History Tripos in 1887; was Pres. of the Camb. University Union in 1886, and was called to the Bar in 1892. Mr. Boyd-Carpenter was University Extension lecturer till 1897; H.M. Inspector of Schools, Education Dept. at Whitehall; and was appointed Chief Inspector to Ministry of Public Instruction, Egypt, in 1902. He married, in 1902, Ethel, youngest dau. of Francis Ley, J.P., of Epperstene, Notts.

BOYES, Major-Gen. J. E., C.B., took part in the Egyptian Expedition in 1882-4, including the battles of Tel-el-Kebir, El Teb, and Tamai (medal with clasp, bronze star, Brevet-Lieut.-Col., and 4th class Osmanieh, two clasps); the Sudan expedition in 1884-5 (clasp), and the S. African War in 1899-1902, commanding the 17th Brigade, and taking part, under Sir Leslie Rundle, in the operations mainly in the Eastern portion of the O.R.C. (despatches, Queen's medal and three clasps, and C.B.).

BOYLE, Sir Cavendish, K.C.M.G., A.I.C.E., of Government House, Port Louis and Le Reduit, Mauritius; 100, Piccadilly, London, W., and of the Marlborough and Badminton Clubs, was born May 29, 1849, and is the youngest and only surviving son of the late Captain Cavendish Spencer Boyle. He was educated at Charterhouse; acted as Magistrate at Leeward Islands in 1879 was Colonial Secretary and Registrar General, and member of the Executive and Legislative Councils of Bermuda from 1882-7; Colonial Secretary at Gibraltar from 1888-93 (C.M.G.); Government Secretary at British Guiana from 1894-1900 (K.C.M.G.), and acted as Chairman for some time of the British Guiana Bank. He acted as Commissioner to Washington and Canada for the reciprocity treaty arrangements between the U.S.A. and Canada and Guiana and Bermuda in 1899; and was Governor and Commander-in-Chief of Newfoundland from 1901-4, when he was appointed Governor of Mauritius. He is the author of *Newfoundland*, the national hymn of the Colony, and other poems and articles, and received the thanks of the Italian Government (medal and certificate) and of the British Board of Trade and vellum certificate of the Royal Humane Society for services in connection with the wreck of the *Utopia* off Gibraltar in March, 1891.

BOYLE, Colonel Lionel Richard Cavendish M.V.O., of Stansted House, Essex, and of the Army and Navy and Naval and Military Clubs, was born at the Cape of Good Hope Nov. 24, 1851; is son of Chas. J. Boyle, of Kent, and grandson of Edmund, 7th Earl of Cork and Kerry. Col. Boyle joined the Royal Navy in 1864, from which he retired some eleven years later. He commanded the Hon. Artillery Company with rank of Lieut.-Col. from 1896 to 1903, being promoted full Colonel a year before his retirement. He was previously manager of the South African Trust, and managing director of the Oceans Company, and is at present a director of the Beira Railway Co. and the New Colonies Synd. Col. Boyle married, in 1883, Alice, dau. of the Rev. Richard T. Pulteney, of Ashley, Northants.

BOYLES, George J., of Bulawayo; originally came from Lady Frere, Cape Colony; joined the Border Horse in the late S.A. War; was taken prisoner and released after four months' captivity by Gen. French at Nooitgedacht. He then continued fighting on the British side, and gained a Lieutenant's Commission.

BOYS, Captain Reginald Harvey Henderson, D.S.O., R.E., of the War Office, London, S.W., was born Oct. 17, 1867, and entered the Royal Engineers as Lieutenant in 1886. He served in the S. African War in 1899-1902, taking part in the operations in Natal, the defence of Ladysmith, and the operations in the Transvaal east of Pretoria. He also acted as Asst. Director of Army Telegraphs in Cape Colony (despatches, Queen's medal with five clasps, King's medal with two clasps, and D.S.O.) Since 1903 he has been an Associate Member of the Royal Engineers' Committee.

BRABANT, Captain Guy Alfred, D.S.O., of Gonnubie Park, East London, Cape Colony, was born in 1873, and is son of the late Major General Sir Edward Yewd Brabant, M.L.A., K.C.B., C.M.G. (see Obituaries). Captain Brabant served in the South African War in 1900-1902 with the South African Irregular Forces, receiving the D.S.O.

BRABAZON, Maj.-Gen. John Palmer, C.B., C.V.O., of 10, Wilton Crescent, London, S.W. was born Feb. 13, 1843, and is son of the late Major Brabazon, of Co. Mayo. He has seen considerable service against the Ashantis, Afghans, Sudanese and Boers. He took part in the famous march from Kabul to Kandahar, and was wounded at El Teb. Gen. Brabazon is now a Gentleman-Usher to the King, and is unmarried.

BRADFIELD, Hon. John Linden, M.L.C., J.P., of Dordrecht, Cape Colony; was born in 1838. He is senior partner in the firm of Bradfield & Bro., law agents, of Dordrecht, and a deputy sheriff for the Wodehouse Division. He was member of the Tembuland Commission in 1882; represented Wodehouse in the House of Assembly from 1873 to 1883, and was elected to the Legislative Council as member for the Eastern Province in 1891. Mr. Bradfield is a widower.

BRADFORD, Thomas, was born in 1877. He is a professional hunter who has been in some of the wildest parts of Africa. In six months with two guns he shot 2,780 of heavy game, including elephants, lions, hippopotami, giraffes, leopards, rhinoceroses, etc. At his headquarters in Africa he has the carcase of an elephant that stands 15ft. 6in, high-said to be the largest elephant ever shot. Mr. Bradford served throughout the S.A. War (1899-02) in a Colonial corps.

BRADY, John Banks, of Bloemfontein, O.R.C., served in the late S. African War with the Imperial Yeomanry and as Lieutenant in Kitchener's Fighting Scouts. He was appointed Headmaster of Grey Coll. School, Bloemfontein, in 1901, and Inspector of Schools in the Orange River Colony in 1904.

BRAILSFORD, Stanley, of Kemnal Manor, Chislehurst, is a director of Rezende, Ltd., and is on the London Committee of the Anglo-French Land Co., of the Transvaal, Ltd., Anglo French (Transvaal) Navigation Coal Estates, Ltd., Apex Mines, Ltd., Benoni Gold Mines, Ltd., Boksburg Gold Mines, Ltd. (Chairman), Chimes West, Ltd., New Kleinfontein Co., Ltd., and the Rand Klipfontein Co., Ltd.

BRAINE, Charles Dimond Horatio, Assoc. M. Inst. C.E., is son of the Rev. G. T. Braine-Hartnell, B.A. He was educated at the Merchant Taylors School and St. Paul's. From 1885-93 he was employed in Mexico, chiefly in railway construction. In 1898 he was engaged in irrigation work in the Public Works Dept., Cape Colony; appointed engineer for the new water supply for Port Elizabeth in 1900; employed on the Drainage Works at Mowbray, Cape Colony, in 1902. The same year he was awarded the Crampton Prize by the Institute of Civil Engineers for a paper on the *Reclamation of Drift-Sands in Cape Colony*. He has also contributed articles to various magazines. In 1904 he was appointed Executive Engineer, Irrigation Dept., Transvaal, which position he still holds, and in 1905 was appointed Secretary to the Inter-Colonial Irrigation Commission. He read a paper entitled *Notes on S. African Irrigation* before the British Association at their meeting in Johannesburg in 1905. He married in 1894 Norah Mary, a sister of Prof. Conway.

BRAKHAN, Amandus, 20, Bishopsgate Street, London, E.C., is chairman and joint managing director of A. Goerz & Co., Ltd. The group of companies associated with A. Goerz and Co., Ltd., which the late Mr. Adolf Goerz successfully founded and established on a sound basis, includes several well-known and very profitable mining undertakings, as well as a number of mines still in the developing stage, and extensive properties on the East and West Rand, the possibilities of which,

owing to their contiguity to proved areas, are enormous. The controlling company of the group is A. Goerz & Co., Ltd., which has done and is still doing an immense amount of work in extending our knowledge of, and developing, neglected sections of the Rand, and which has been the means of adding very considerably to the workable areas of that celebrated goldfield. Messrs. A. Goerz & Co., Ltd., of which Messrs. Amandus Brakhan and Henry Strakosch are the managing directors, has an issued capital of £1,400,000, and large share interests in the companies included in the Goerz Group, and holdings in many other concerns.

Other well-known companies in the group are the Geduld Proprietary Mines, Lancaster West, May Consolidated, Roodepoort Central Deep, Tudor, Modderfontein Deep, Princess Estate, Geldenhuis Estate, and Lancaster G.M. Companies, the Klerksdorp Exploration Land and Estate Co., and the Rand Central Electric Works, Ltd.

BRAMSTON, Sir John, Knt., G.C.M.G., C.B., of 18, Berkeley Place, Wimbledon, and of the Travellers' Club, is descended from Sir John Bramston, Knt., Chief Justice of England in the time of Charles I., and is the second son of T. W. Bramston, of Skreens, M.P. for South Essex. He was born at Skreens, Nov. 14, 1832; was educated at Winchester and Balliol Coll., Oxon., Fell. of All Souls' Coll., 1855. Sir John Bramston has had a distinguished career. He was Private Sec. to the Governor of Queensland, 1860-1; M.L.C. Queensland, 1863-9; M.L.A. Queensland, 1871-3; Attorney-Gen. of Queensland, 1870-3; Attorney-Gen. of Hong Kong, 1874-6; and Assistant Under Secy. of State, Colonial Office, 1876-97. In July, 1886, he was employed on a mission to Berlin in relation to the Angra Pequeña negotiations with the German Government; and in 1898 he went to Newfoundland in company with Adm. Sir James Erskine, K.C.B., as Royal Commissioner to inquire into matters connected with French Treaty rights. He was appointed Registrar of the Order of St. Michael and St. George, 1892. Sir John married, Dec. 14, 1872, Eliza Isabella, dau. of the Rev. Harry Vane Russell.

BRANSON, Mrs. Kuhne, the well-known sculptor, better known as Mrs. Beveridge, of 89, Park

Street, Mayfair, is the dau. of Phils Judson Beveridge and Ella Beveridge, now Baroness von Wrede. She was born at Governor's Mansions, Ill., U.S.A., on Oct. 31, 1878, and was educated at Dresden, New York, and Paris. Her works include a monument of Rough Riders charging San Juan, and she has executed statues of Grover Cleveland, Sarah Bernhardt, Cecil Rhodes, Major Ricarde-Seaver, E. Windsor Richards, Hon. M. W. Elphinstone, Tom L. Johnson, William Jennings Bryan, H. H. Marks, M.P., Buffalo Bill, and many others. Her statue of Rhodesia is considered a very fine work of art. She married William Branson, of Johannesburg, Aug. 25, 1903.

BRAY, Edward, of Tarkwa, W. Africa, and of Palmerston House, London, E.C., is founder of the firm of Bray Bros., Mining and General Contractors, of Palmerston House. He has travelled considerably, and most of the little-known country adjacent to Lakes Tanganyika, Nyassa, Bangweolo, and Mwero, and the sources of the Congo and Zambezi, is as familiar to him as the Transvaal, Cape Colony, Natal, the South Sea Islands, Fiji, California, New Zealand, and his native colony of New South Wales. He has had an extensive experience of the working of diamond drills on the Rand and the coalfields of Natal.

BRAY, Rex, of Palmerston House, London, E.C., and Tarkwa, W. Africa, is a member of the firm of Bray Bros.; is an Engineer, and has visited most of the ports on the globe open to steam traffic, and has also taken part in an Arctic expedition with a steam whaler.

BREBNER, John; is the eldest son of the Rev. John Brebner (died Nov., 1902), at one time Minister of Education for the O.F.S. He was Minister of Finance for the late S.A.R., and was one of the signatories of the Peace Convention. He afterwards visited Europe with Generals Botha, De la Rey, and De Wet as their secretary.

BRECKER, B. G.; was born in Namaqualand; was educated at the S. A. Coll., and went to the S.A.R. in 1875, trekking through the Kalahari, Kimberley and the Free States, and settling in Utrecht Dist. He served in the Zulu War 'for money', and in the Transvaal War for his adopted country. In 1884 he

joined the filibusters who founded the New Republic, afterwards incorporated with the Transvaal, and recently tacked on to Natal. He was elected for Vryheid in the Transvaal Second Volksraad; was balloted out of the Raad in 1891, but was afterwards re-elected by a large majority.

BRETTON, Lord Monk- (See Lord Monk-Bretton).

BREWSTER, Alfred Berry, Bey, of Cairo, and Alexandria, Egypt, and of the Mohamed Ali Club; was born in London, Nov. 7, 1856, and belongs to an old Essex family, the Brewsters of Wrentham being traced back to 1375, a later ancestor, William Brewster, having been the ruling Elder and Chief Pastor of the Pilgrim Fathers in 1620. Brewster Bey entered the service of the Egyptian Govt. in 1877, in the Customs Administration and Coastguard Service. In 1879 he was appointed Director of Customs at Suakin by the late Gen. Gordon. This post he held till 1882, when he served in the Egyptian campaign on the Commissariat staff (medal and bronze star). He returned to Suakin in 1883, and served under Gen. Valentine Baker Pasha in the Intelligence Department in 1884, and was subsequently appointed by the late Admiral Sir W. Hewitt as Sub Governor, in addition to his duties at the Customs. In 1885 he was lent by the Egyptian Government to the Intelligence Staff of the British Govt. during Gen. Graham's expedition. He took part in several engagements was mentioned in despatches, and on one occasion went out alone to the Dervish camp during the preparations for the attack on Suakin, and persuaded some thousands of Arabs to come in as friendlies, these same men afterwards capturing Tamai from the Dervishes under Gen. Kitchener. Brewster Bey remained in Suakin as Director of Customs until 1890, when he was transferred to the Coastguard Service at Alexandria as Secretary and Controller. In 1891 he was selected by the Khedive Mohamed Tewfik as his Private Secy., and acts now in the same capacity to the present Khedive, Abbas II. He holds the rank of Bey of the first class, and is a Grand Officer of the Imperial Order of Medjidieh, Commander of the Imperial Order of Osmanieh (Turkey), Franz Joseph (Austria), and Imptiaz (Turkey). besides wearing the English war medal, 1882, with two clasps, and the Khedivial Bronze Star. He married in 1886, Marie Cecile, widow of Mons. Paul Sudreau.

BREWSTER, T. A., of Port Elizabeth, Cape Colony, is brother to Brewster Bey (q.v.), and is the proprietor of the *Port Elizabeth Advertiser*.

BREYTENBACH, Isaac Johann, sat in the Second Volksraad as member for Lydenburg, Transvaal. He almost invariably voted with the Conservatives.

BRIDGE, Albert Thomas Vivian, of Cape Town, was in change of the Frontier Armed and Mounted Police Recruiting Office from 1871. He joined the Cape Town Shipping Office in 1874, and was appointed Shipping Master in 1892, which position he still holds.

BRIGHT, Capt. (Brev.-Major) Richard George Tyndall, C.M.G., of the Wyndham and Naval and Military Clubs, was born in 1872, and is son of C. E. Bright, C.M.G., and the Hon. Mrs. Bright. He entered the Rifle Brigade in 1892, and has seen service in Uganda in 1897-8 (despatches, medal and clasp), Juba Expedition, 1898-9 (despatches, brevet majority, and 3rd class Brilliant Star of Zanzibar), Anglo-Sudan and Abyssinian Boundary Expedition in 1899-1900, and the Anglo-Sudan, Uganda and Abyssinian Boundary Expedition in 1900-2 (C.M.G.), Since 1902 Major Bright has been 2nd British Commissioner on the Anglo-German Boundary Comm. between Uganda, British East Africa, and German East Africa. Unmarried.

BRINDLE, Right Rev. Robert, D.S.O., was born in 1837. He was formerly Assistant Bishop of Westminster and Domestic Chaplain to the Pope and Acting Roman Catholic Chaplain the 5th Vol. Batt. Liverpool Regiment; served in Egypt in 1882-4; the Sudan in 1884-6 the Dongola Expedition in 1896, and the Nile Expedition in 1898 (D.S.O.). From 1901-6 he acted as Roman Catholic Bishop of Nottingham, and was then offered an honorary position in the Queen of Spain's household.

BRINK, Johannes Cornelis, M.L.C., was formerly Landdrost of Rustenburg under the Boer regime. In 1903 he became a nominee member of the Transvaal Legislative Council.

BRINTON, John, D.L., J.P., of Moor Hall, Stourport, is a member of the Council of the Union-Castle Mail Steamship Co., Ltd. (see Sir Donald Currie) Chairman of Brinton's, Ltd.; a director of the Durban-Roodepoort Gold Mining Co., Ltd.; and is on the Yorkshire local Board of the Union of London and Smiths Bank, Ltd.

BRINTON, Capt. Oswald Walter, of the 21st Lancers, was present at Omdurman in Sept., 1898, under the command of Col. Martin, when his corps, with a strength of 300, made the historic but mistaken charge through 3,000 Dervishes, who stubbornly held their ground. He married, April 18, 1906, Miss Hope Johnstone.

BRISTOWE, Lindsay William, of the Gold Coast Colony, is grandson of S. E. Bristowe, of Bersthorpe Hall, Notts; was educated privately, and entered the Colonial service in British Honduras in 1880 as clerk; qualified as land surveyor, and was appointed secy. to the Comm. of Inquiry into the Survey Dept. in 1883; promoted clerk in the Supreme Court and Record Office and clerk of the Summary Court in 1884; acted as clerk of the Legislative Council, 1885; Registrar of the Vice-Admiralty Court, 1886; Provost-Marshal, 1887; Registrar of the Supreme Court and Keeper of the Records, 1887-1890; Official Administrator, 1890; Notary and Commissioner of the Supreme Court, 1891; Dist. Commissioner, Toledo, 1892; ditto Belize, 1893. He was promoted a Commissioner of the Gold Coast in 1893, and was attached to the Treasury in 1894; acted as Asst. Treasurer and then Chief Asst. till January, 1895; Commissioner at Accra, 1894; at Elmina, 1895-6; attached to the Secretariat, 1896; Comr. at Chama and Secondi, 1898; at Saltpond, 1899; and Winneba, 1900; afterwards being graded 3rd, 2nd, and lst Asst. Colonial Secretary in 1903. He has published a *Guide to the Records of British Honduras*, edited a *Handbook of British Honduras* for 1888-93, wrote *An Historical Sketch of the Currency of B. Honduras*, and is the author of several short stories and articles on West African subjects.

BROADWOOD, Col. (Temp. Brig.-Gen.) Robert George, C.B. (Military), 4th Class Osmanieh, of the Naval and Military Club; was born in London, Mar. 14, 1862; is son of Thos. Broadwood, of

Holmbush, Crawley, and was educated at Charterhouse and Sandhurst, passing into the 12th Lancers in 1881. He joined the Egyptian Army in 1892, and served through the Dongola Expedition in 1896 (despatches, Brev. of Lt.-Col., Egyptian medal with 2 clasps and medal). In the Nile Expedition of 1897 and 1898 he commanded the Egyptian Cavalry, and was present at the battles of the Atbara and Khartoum (despatches, Osmanieh, 4 clasps to Egyptian medal, and medal). In S. Africa, 1899-1902, after raising Roberts' Horse he commanded the 2nd Cavalry Brigade with rank of Brig.-Gen. He was several times mentioned in despatches; was appointed A.D.C. to the King, and received the King's medal with 2 clasps, and the C.B. Col. Broadwood commanded the troops in Natal from Dec., 1902, to May, 1904, since which date he has been in command of the Orange River Colony district with the rank of Brigadier-General.

BRODIE, Douglas Edward, of 2, London Wall Buildings, Lond. , and of the Bachelors, Club, Lond., was born in Aug., 1873; was educated at Winchester, and entered the service of the B.S.A. Co. in 1897. He was appointed Joint Asst. Secy. of the Chartered Co. and Joint Secy. to the Rhodes Trust in 1902, and on the death of J. F. Jones (q.v.) he was appointed Secy. to the Company, of which he is one of the most suave and popular officials. Unmarried.

BRODIE, Capt. Harry Cunningham, M.P. of Shrubhurst, Oxted, Surrey; Lorne House Redhill, Surrey; 9, Little Stanhope Street London, W., and of the Union, City of London Cavalry, National Liberal, Eighty, and the Hurlingham Clubs, was born at Victoria British Columbia, Jan. 18, 1875, and is son of John Henry Brodie, of Shrubhurst, Oxted. He was educated at Winchester College and abroad and is a partner in the firm of Findlay, Durham and Brodie, South African and Colonial merchants, of Cannon Street House, London, E.C. He successfully contested the Reigate Division of Surrey, in the Free Trade and Liberal interest, at the General Election in 1906; is an imperialist in Foreign and Colonial policy; an advocate of Housing and Land Law Reform and is on the Council of the National Housing Reform Association. He is also on the Book Committee of the Victoria League, which Committee carries on

the work of the Transvaal Libraries Fund, organised by Capt. Brodie in 1903, with a view to encouraging the study of British History and Literature in the elementary schools of the Transvaal.

BROMLEY-DAVENPORT, Lieut.-Col. William, D.S.O., J.P., D.L., of 1, Belgrave Place, London, S.W., is eldest son of the late Lieut.-Col. W. Bromley-Davenport, was born in 1863, and was educated at Eton and Oxford, both of which he represented in the cricket and football teams. He represented the Macclesfield Div. of Cheshire as a Conservative from 1886 until the general election in 1906, when he was defeated, and took a prominent part in representing Lord Penrhyn's case when the Bethesda quarries dispute was brought before the House. He also championed the cause of Col. Kinloch (whose brother-in-law he is) in connection with the 'ragging incident' in the Grenadier Guards, For a couple of years he acted as Parliamentary Secy. to Sir Matthew White Ridley when he was Home Secy., and he succeeded Lord Stanley as Financial Secy. to the War Office. During the S.A. War Mr. Bromley-Davenport commanded the 4th Batt. Imp. Yeo., being mentioned in despatches, and receiving the medal and the D.S.O.

BROMWICH, Alfred, of 2, London Wall buildings, E.C., was for some years connected with Stanford's Geographical Institute, London subsequently entering the Chartered Company's service with a special knowledge of Rhodesia and the southern part of the African Continent, editing and designing all maps and other geographical publications for the company; designing the British South Africa Company's Museum, of which he is Curator; promoting the various exhibitions, and acting as the company's representative in connection with Rhodesia in Great Britain, the United States, and the Continent. Mr. Bromwich designed and carried out the Greater Britain Exhibition at Earl's Court in 1899, when he was awarded diplomas for the Chartered Company's exhibits. He was also connected with the Salvation Army Exhibition in 1899 at the Agricultural Hall, London; Glasgow International Exhibition in 1901, awarded diploma of high merit; the World's Fair at St. Louis, U.S.A., in 1902, awarded the gold silver, and bronze medals; the Exhibition at the Imperial Institute, the Alexandra Palace Colonial Exhibition, Reading Exhibition, and the Royal Exchange Colonial Exhibition in 1902, in which year he had the honour of describing the Rhodesian Exhibits to the Queen and Royal Family; also made an extensive tour in the United States and Canada; designed and carried out the Cirencester Industrial Exhibition in 1904; Liverpool Colonial Products Exhibition in 1904-5, and the Colonial Fruit Exhibitions in 1904-5, besides several minor exhibitions, lectures, conversaziones, and public functions, at all of which he represented the Chartered Company. In 1906 he made tours through Rhodesia, collecting material and information, and in 1907 served on the Executive Committee of the South African Products Exhibition.

BROOK, Major-Gen. E. S., C.B., of Cape Town, served through the Zulu War in 1879; the Boer War of 1880-1; commanded the 2nd Brigade of the Tochi Field Force in India in 1897-8, and was employed on special service during the S. African War. In 1904 Gen. Brook succeeded Major-Gen. Miles in the command of the Cape Colony district, and acted as Administrator during the absence of Sir W. Hely-Hutchinson.

BROOKE, Lord, of Easton Lodge, Dunmow, Essex, is elder son of the Earl (q.v.) and Countess of Warwick, and was born in 1882. He entered the lst Life Guards, and served in the S. African War with his Militia battalion of the King's Royal Rifle Corps, also being employed on the staff as A.D.C. to Lord Milner. During the Russo-Japanese War he acted as one of Reuters's correspondents with the Russian Army in Manchuria for nine months, and has since recorded his experiences in a book. He is decorated by the Mikado and by King Edward.

BROOKFIELD, Col. Arthur Montagu, J.P., of the British Consulate, Danzig, Germany, was born March 18, 1853, and is son of the late Rev. Prebendary Brookfield and of Jane, dau. of the late Sir C. Elton. He was educated at Rugby and Jesus Coll., Camb., afterwards serving with the 13th Hussars from 1873 to 1880. From 1884 to 1900 he was Lieut.-Col. and Hon. Col. in the lst Cinque Ports Volunteers, and in the latter year, as Lieut.-

Col., commanded the 14th Battn. of I.Y. in the S. African War. He commanded a Brigade at Kroonstad, and was in command of the convoy in the actions on June 25-27 between Kroonstad and Lindley, for which he was mentioned in Lord Roberts' despatch. He also relieved the garrisons of Katbasch and Honigspruit on June 22, and was mentioned in Gen. Kelly-Kenny's despatch; was afterwards present at the actions at Retief's Nek, and the subsequent occupation of Fouriesburg (medal and 3 clasps). Col. Brookfield sat in Parliament from 1885-1903 for East Sussex, during which period he initiated and carried the Uniforms Act. He was Chairman of the Committee on Civil Employment for Discharged Soldiers and Sailors, and wrote *The Speaker's A B C* (1894). He was appointed H.M. Consul for Danzig July 27, 1903, is a J.P. for E. Sussex, and a Knt. of the Order of St. John of Jerusalem. He married in 1877 Olive, dau. of the late J. Murray Hamilton, of Dumfries and Buffalo, U.S.A.

BROOKS, F. G., was educated at Bedford Gram. Sch. He is a well-known athlete, and has played in international football. He went to S.A. in Oct., 1902, to take up an appointment in the Rhodesian Civil Service.

BROUN, Alfred Forbes, of Khartoum, and of the East India, United Service, and the Alpine Clubs, was born at Trivandrum, Travancore India, Apr. 27, 1858. He is youngest son of the late John Allan Broun, F.R.S., late , Director of Observatories, Travancore, and was educated at Lausanne, Stuttgart, Paris, at University Coll. and Sch., London, and at the French Forest Sch., Nancy. Passing into the Indian Forest Service in Nov., 1877, he was appointed to the N.W. Provinces, Oudh, Dec., 1880, as Asst. Conservator of Forests. In July, 1888, his services were lent to the Burmese Govt., and he was again lent in Dec. of that year to the Govt. of Ceylon. In Dec., 1891, he was appointed Conservator of Forests, Ceylon, and in Dec., 1901, he became Director of Woods and Forests under the Sudan Govt. He has also acted as Director of Agriculture and Lands since Jan. 1, 1904. His sports are big game shooting, mountaineering, and lawn tennis. He Married, Oct. 4, 1892, Emily Hilda Mahala, youngest dau. of the late James Howard, J.P., of Clapham Park,

Beds, at times M.P. for Beds and Bedford.

BROWN, John, C.M.G., of the Thatch, Rondebosch, C.C.; and of the Civil Service (C.T.) and Kimberley Clubs; was born Apr. 27, 1844; is eldest son of the late John Brown, of Marlborough, Wilts; was educated at Streatham, and was articled as pupil to the late Sir John Coode at Portland Breakwater, and served under him as Engineer in charge of the River Bann Navigation Works in Ireland. He was for some time engaged on the Bristol and Exeter Railway under Mr. Francis Fox, and for the last 30 years has been engaged on the Cape Govt. Railways. He married, Dec. 3, 1867, Miss Augusta Sarah Rhodes.

BROWN, J. Ellis, of Durban, Natal, was Mayor of Durban in 1903-4, and was re-elected Mayor for 1904-5.

BROWN, J. Frank, formerly of Pietermaritzburg, was appointed Postmaster-Gen. of the Transvaal under the British Administration.

BROWN, John Louis Mitchell, of Cape Town, was born at Cape Town in 1835; was educated at the Normal Public Sch. and at J. Gillard's Academy. Since 1860 he has taken an interest in all matters political and social. He was Town Councillor in 1880-1, unsuccessfully contested Cape Town in 1884, but was elected for that constituency in 1894. He was for many years an active member of the Cape Town Chamber of Commerce.

BROWN, Nicol, F.G.S., of 4, The Grove, Highgate, and the Gresham Club, Lond., was born in Ayrshire in 1842, and was educated at Glasgow Academy. In 1869 he became associated with mining in Andalusia in Spain and has, more or less, remained connected with mining until the present time. In 1883 he undertook the Directorship of the old Transvaal Gold Exploration and Land Co., Ltd., which, after varying fortunes, was finally amalgamated with the Lydenburg Mining Estates Co. in 1896, the new Company being called The Transvaal Gold Mining Estates, Ltd. He is now the Chairman of the Rezende, Ltd., in Rhodesia, in which Company the Farrar Group recently acquired a large interest. Outside of South Africa he is largely identified with the Copper Mining Industry, and is a Director of the Pena Copper Mines, Limited, which are situated in Spain; the Tyee Copper Company, Limited, British Columbia; the Copiapo Mining Company, Limited, Chile. Mr. Nicol Brown is the author of *The Organisation of Gold Mining Business*, published by Messrs. Spon, London, and in collaboration with Mr. C. C. Turnbull he recently produced *A Century of Copper*, which deals with this metal, of which Mr. Nicol Brown has made an exhaustive study, in all its aspects-commercial, technical, and statistical. On similar lines he has also written a paper entitled *The Profit and Loss of Gold Mining*, originally published separately, but now included in the second edition of *The Organisation of Gold Mining Business*.

BROWN, Sir William Richmond, Bart., J.P, D.L., of Astrop Park, King's Sutton, Banbury, was born in 1840. He is a member of the Council of the Union-Castle Mail Steamship Co., Ltd. (see Sir Donald Currie); and married in 1862 Emily, dau. of General Mountsleven.

BROWNE, Major John William, D.S.O., of the Cape Mounted Police, served in the Griqualand West Constabulary from 1881-82, when he joined the Griqualand West Border Police. In 1892 he acted as Sub-Inspector of the Cape Police; served in the Bechuanaland Campaign in 1890-7, and was appointed District Inspector in Bechuanaland in 1900. He also served in the South African War in 1900-2, being wounded at the defence of Mafeking, and commanded the sub-district of Kuruman from Jan., 1902, to the end of the campaign.

BROWNLEE, William Thomson, of Butterworth, Cape Colony, was employed in the Chief Magistrate's office in Fingoland in 1876, and during the Galeka War he had charge of the whole district, and also served in the field. In 1877 he was appointed to the Chief Magistrate's office at Transkei, and was twice appointed Resident Magistrate of the Tsomo district and once at Willowvale. He superintended the removal of Galekas from Bomvanaland into the Willowvale district. During the Tembu rebellion in 1880 he had charge of a section of the Tembu-Fingo border, and was on active service in command of a Fingo levy; also acted as Staff Officer to the officer commanding the Colonial Forces in Transkei (

MR. NICOL BROWN

Photo Elliott & Fry

MR. ABE BAILEY

MR. W. BRYSON BUTLER

Photos Elliott & Fry

MR. GEO. CAWSTON

medal and clasp). In 1882 he was appointed Resident Magistrate at Qumbu; appointed Resident Magistrate at Idutywa in 1893, and at Butterworth in 1896. In the late S. African War in 1899-1902 he was Lieut. Col. commanding the Fingo levies, subsequently commanding the Tembuland Field Force and the Tembu and Fingo levies.

BROWNLOW, Major-General William Vesey, C.B., of the Army and Navy, New (Edinburgh) and Kildare St. (Dublin) Clubs, was born in 1841, and is son of William Brownlow, of Queen's County, Ireland. He was educated privately; served in the Zulu War in 1879 with the 1st Dragoon Guards (medal and clasp, Brevet-Major); and in the S. African War in 1880-1, as Brig.-Major of Cavalry, being present at the actions at Laing's Nek and Ingogo (despatches and brevet of Lieut.-Col.). From 1882 to 1901 he held several regimental appointments, and retired from the service in 1901. He married first, in 1881, Lady Anne, a dau. of the 10th Earl of Stair, and secondly, in 1904, Lady Kathleen Bligh, sister of the Earl of Darnley.

BRUCE, Col. David, C.B., F.R.S., R.A.M.C., of 68, Victoria Street, London, S.W., was born at Melbourne, Victoria, Australia, May 29, 1855. Col. Bruce was educated at the High School, Stirling, N.B., and Edin. University, where he took his M.B. C.M., in 1881. He entered the R.A.M.C. in Aug., 1883; served in Malta from 1884-9, and while there worked at Malta fever, discovering its cause in the *Micrococcus melitensis*. He taught pathology and bacteriology in the Army Med. Sch., Netley, from 1889-94; served in S. Africa from 1894-1901, two years of which (1895-6) he spent in Zululand investigating the *Nagana* or tsetse fly disease. He discovered the cause of this disease to be a protozoon since named *Trypanosoma Brucei*, and showed that this parasite lived normally in the blood of the wild animals, whence the tsetse fly conveyed it to the domestic animals. For this addition to natural knowledge he was made F.R.S., and awarded the Cameron Prize of the Edinburgh University. In the S. African War he was at the siege of Ladysmith, and with Gen. Buller in his march to Belfast. He was member of the Commission to investigate the cause of dysentery and enteric fever in the Army. He received special promotion (medal, 7 clasps); was appointed

member of the Advisory Board, War Office, 1901, and Director of the Sleeping Sickness Comm., Royal Society, Uganda, 1903. He proceeded to Uganda and showed that sleeping sickness is a human tsetse fly disease, caused by *Trypanosoma gambiense* and carried by *Glossina palpalis*. For this he was awarded a Royal Medal by the Royal Society and made Brevet.-Colonel, Dec. 10, 1903. In 1904 he was appointed Chairman of the Mediterranean Fever Commission of the Royal Society to direct investigation of Mediterranean fever. Col. Bruce was married in 1883 to Miss Mary Elizabeth Steele, of Reigate, Surrey.

BRUNNER, Ernest August, J.P., M.L.A., of Eshowe, Zululand, Natal, and of the Victoria (P.M.B.) and Eshowe Clubs, was born in the Netherlands, his father having been a clergyman of the Dutch Reformed Church. He was educated at Leiden, and went to Natal in 1872, travelling into Zululand, where he visited Cetewayo at his Royal Kraal. He served through the Zulu War as a Volunteer in the Natal Guides attached to Major Barrow's M.I., with the coast columns (medal and clasp), and was subsequently appointed administrator of native law under the Chief John Dunn, by whom Mr. Brunner was sent home in 1882 to try and influence the authorities against the return to Zululand of the exiled Cetewayo. In 1883 he settled in business in Eshowe; was elected to the Natal House of Assembly in 1898 as member for the Eshowe district, and has retained the seat continuously since then. He married, in 1879, Miss Louise Cornelie Colenbrander.

BRUNYATE, William Edwin, 2nd Class Osmanieh, of Cairo, late Fellow of Trinity Coll., Camb., is a Barrister-at-Law, of Lincoln's Inn, and a Khedivial Councillor.

BRYCE, Right Hon. James, P.C., D.C.L., LL.D., F.R.S., M.P. for Aberdeen, of 54, Portland Place, London, and Hindleap, Sussex, and of the Athenaeum and National Liberal Clubs; is the son of James Bryce, LL.D., and Margaret, dau. of James Young, was born at Belfast, March 10, 1838, and was educated at High Sch. and Univ. of Glasgow, Trinity Coll., Oxon, and became Fel. of Oriel Coll., Oxon, graduating D.C.L. of Oxon., Hon. Litt.D. of Camb. and of Victoria Univ., and

Hon. LL.D. of Edin., Glasgow, St. Andrews, and Michigan Universities; Doctor of Political Science of Univ. of Budapest. Prof. Bryce was called to the Bar of Lincoln's Inn in 1867, and practised as barrister for several years. He has had a distinguished political career, entering Parliament in 1880 as member for Tower Hamlets, and has represented Aberdeen in the Liberal interest since 1885, being last re-elected at the general election in 1906. He was Under-Secy. at the Foreign Office (1886), and thereafter Chancellor of the Duchy of Lancaster in Mr. Gladstone's Cabinet of 1892; was Pres. of the Board of Trade, 1894, and Chairman of the Royal Commission on Secondary Education in 1894. In Sir Henry Campbell-Bannerman's Cabinet formed in the early part of 1906, Mr. Bryce again took office as Chief Secretary for Ireland. In 1895 he made a hurried tour of South Africa, including a trip through Rhodesia, and recorded his *Impressions of South Africa* in 1897. He has also written books on a variety of different subjects, one of his last works being *Studies in Contemporary Biographies* (1903). In 1904 he was unanimously elected to the French Academy in the place of the late Prof. Lecky. He married, July 23, 1889, Elizabeth Marion, dau. of Thomas Ashton, of Fordbank, near Manchester.

BRYDEN, Henry Anderson, of Down View, Gore Park Road, Eastbourne, and the Constitutional Club, S.W., son of the late Wm. Anderson Bryden, of Surbiton, Surrey, and Maria, dau. of the late Wm. Cowper, of Boddington, Northants, was born in Oxfordshire in 1854, and educated at Cheltenham Coll. and at the Rev. Drackenbury's, Wimbledon. In his younger days he was well known as an athlete, representing England against Scotland in Rugby football, and winning some forty prizes, chiefly for long-distance running. He first visited S.A. in 1876, when he resided in some remote and wild mountain country near the eastern extremity of the Great Karroo, interesting himself much in sport and natural history. Has since visited many other parts of S.A., mainly in search of sport, nature, and wild life. Has resided in British Bechuanaland, traversed the Protectorate and Khama's country, crossed and shot through the Northern Kalahari, and hunted big game in Ngamiland, where he had much success. Has travelled in the Transvaal, O.R.C., and many parts

of Cape Colony. His Travels in Ngamiland and the Kalahari were utilised by the War Office, and various desert waters, places and roads, now found in the maps of the Intelligence Department, are the results of his observations. Is a keen angler, and has fished much in Norway and elsewhere. Was a member of the South African Committee, formed during the Bechuanaland troubles in the eighties, and served thereon in company with Mr. Chamberlain, Mr. H. Arnold-Forster, Sir Thomas Fowell Buxton, the late Rev. John Mackenzie, and others. When Khama came to England in 1895 to protest against his country being dismembered and handed over to the Chartered Company, Mr. Bryden lent the aid of his pen towards the objects of the Chief's visit. In the result, Khama's Country remains-as the Chief and his people desired-under direct Imperial control. Mr. Bryden has written much on S.A. Among his books are to be mentioned *Kloof and Karoo* (1889), *Gun and Camera in Southern Africa* (1893), *Tales of South Africa* (1896), *Nature and Sport in South Africa* (1897), *The Victorian Era in South Africa* (1897), *An Exiled Scot* (1899), *Great and Small Game of Africa*, editor and part author (1899), *From Veldt Camp-Fires* (1900), *Animals of Africa* (1901), *Don Duarte's Treasure* (1904), and *Big Game Shooting* (African section), 1905. Mr. Bryden is greatly interested in all kinds of field sports, and has published, in addition, *Hare Hunting and Harriers* (1903), and *Nature and Sport in Britain* (1904). His main recreations are natural history, shooting, fishing, hunting, lawn tennis, and cycling. He married, 1881, Julia, daughter of the late J. P. Wright, of Priors Marston, Warwickshire.

BUCHAN, Lieut. Ernest Norman, D.S.O., was born in 1879, and entered the Manchester Regiment in 1901. He served in the South African War in 1899-1902 as Transport Officer, being present at the operations in the Orange Free State, and the Transvaal and Orange River Colonies (despatches, Queen's medal with two clasps, King's medal with two clasps, and D.S.O.).

BUCHAN, John, of 3, Temple Gardens, London, E.C., and of the Bachelors', Union, and Vincent's (Oxford) Clubs, is the eldest son of the Rev. John Buchan and Helen, dau. of John Masterton, of Broughton Green, Peeblesshire. He was born at

Perth, N.B., on Aug. 26, 1875, and was educated at Glasgow Univ. and at Brasenose Coll., Oxford, where he graduated B.A., and took the Stanhope Prize, the Newdigate Prize, lst class Lit. Hum., and was Pres. of the Oxford Union. When he left Oxford he acted for some time as Asst. Ed. of the *Spectator*. He had then the good fortune to become Asst. Private Sec., to Lord Milner in 1901, and retained the position until 1903. In the latter year he was appointed Acting Commissioner of Lands in the Transvaal, and Acting Sec. to the Inter-Colonial Council of the Transvaal and O.R.C. Amongst his published works are several novels, *A Monograph on Sir Walter Raleigh* (1897), a *History of Brasenose College* (1898), and *The African Colony: Studies in the Reconstruction* (1903). His recreations are shooting, fishing, mountaineering, and travel.

BUCHANAN, Hon. Sir Ebenezer John, Kt., of Clareinch, Claremont, Cape Town, was born in 1844. He was called to the Bar at the Inner Temple in 1873, and in the same year was admitted Advocate of the Supreme and Vice-Admiralty Courts of the Cape Colony; was appointed member of the House of Assembly for Worcester in 1877, subsequently becoming judge, being assigned to the Eastern Districts Court. In 1887 he was promoted to the Supreme Court, and acted as Chief Justice on and off from 1894-1901. For some time he acted as President of the Legislative Council Sessions and President of the Special Tribunal (Treason Court). Sir John Buchanan served with the Duke of Edinburgh's Own Vol. Rifles in the Basuto War in 1879; is editor of the Reports of the Supreme Court, Appeal Court, and the Court of the Eastern District. Since 1888 he has been a member of the Council of the Cape of Good Hope University, and Vice-Chancellor from 1901. He was made a Knight of Grace of the Order of St. John of Jerusalem in England in 1901. He married, in 1878, Mary, dau. of D. Mudie, of Cape Town.

BUCHANAN, James Macdonald, son of the late Justice Buchanan, of Griqualand West; married Elizabeth, eldest dau. of Sir Pieter Faure (1902).

BUCKNILL, John Alexander Strachey M.L.C., M.A., J.P., of the Pretoria and Athenaeum (Johannesburg) Clubs, was born at Clifton, Bristol, Sept. 14, 1873; was educated at Charterhouse and

Keble Coll., Oxon, and is a Barrister-at-Law of the Inner Temple. He has filled the appointments of Commissioner of Patents, Registrar of Trade Marks, and Registrar of Companies for the Transvaal, June, 1902; was appointed J.P. for the Transvaal and Advocate of the Supreme Court in 1902, and member of the Committee of the Transvaal Museum and Zoological Gardens in the same year. In 1904 he was appointed an official member of the Transvaal Legislative Council. He is the author of *Birds of Surrey*, and other ornithological publications, and is joint editor of the *Journal of the South African Ornithologists' Union*. He married, Sept. 18, 1901, Alice Mary, youngest dau. of the late Admiral Sir Geo. Richards, K.C.B.

BUISSERET, Count, was one of the Belgian Plenipotentiaries at the Moroccan Conference at Algeçiras in 1900.

BULLOCK, Col. George Mackworth, C.B., of the Junior United Service Club, is son of T. H. Bullock, Deputy Commissioner at Berar, India, where Geo. Bullock was born, Aug, 15, 1850. He was educated at Cheltenham Coll., University Coll, Oxford, and the R.M.C., Sandhurst, passing into the old 11th Foot in 1872. He commanded the 2nd Devons from Jan., 1897, to Nov., 1900, and arrived in S.A. from India, where he held several staff appointments, in time to take part in the relief of Ladysmith and battle of Colenso. He afterwards commanded the Sub-Dist. of Volksrust, and from April, 1901, until the end of the war he commanded a column (despatches, brev. of Col., Queen's medal with 3 clasps, King's medal with 2 clasps, C.B.). Proceeding to Egypt, Col. Bullock acted as A.A.G. from Nov., 1902, to Mar. 31, 1903, when he was appointed C.S.O., Egypt. He married, June 5, 1884, Amy Isabel, dau. of Jas. Fred Thomson.

BURDON, Brev.-Major John Alder, C.M.G., F.R.G.S., of the Junior Naval and Military and Sports Clubs, was born at Pekin, Aug. 23, 1866, and is son of the Right Rev. J. S. Burdon, late Bishop of Victoria, Hong Kong. He was educated at King Edward VI. Sch., Norwich, and Corpus Christi Coll., Camb., where he graduated B.A. Classical Tripos in 1888. In the same year he enlisted in the Manchester Regt., receiving a 2nd

Lieut.'s commission in the Royal N. Lancs. Regt. in 1893. He was on special service with the Royal Niger Company's Constabulary from Dec., 1896, taking part in the expeditions against Bida and Ilorin in Jan. and Feb., 1897 (despatches, medal with clasp); was in charge of the Jubilee contingent of the R. Niger Constabulary in June, 1897; Adjt. in Oct., 1897; and then saw further active service in the expeditions against Kaffi (Ingara country) in Nov., 1897 (despatches), against Ibuza and Oponam, Jan. and Feb., 1898, and against Lapai in June, 1898. He was acting commandant of the R. N. Constabulary in Aug., 1898, and in the following Dec. commanded the expedition against tribes round Asaba (despatches, clasp, and promotion to Capt. and Brev.-Major in the Queen's Own Cameron Highlanders, from which he has since retired). Major Burden commanded three small but successful expeditions during 1899. In Aug. of that year he was appointed the last commandant of the R. Niger Constabulary, which regt., on the transfer of the Company's territories to the Imperial Govt. in Jan., 1900, he handed over, some 1,100 strong, to the West African Frontier Force. He then joined the Political Dept. of N. Nigeria as Assist. Resident, Benue Province; accompanied the expedition against the Munchi tribes Jan. and Feb., 1900, as Political Officer (despatches and clasp); was in charge of Lower Benue Prov., July, 1900; Resident Bida Prov., July, 1901; promoted lst Class Resident, June, 1902; accompanied Sokoto expedition as Political Officer, Feb. and March, 1903 (despatches, medal with clasp), and has been Resident, Sokoto Province, since March, 1903. Major Burdon qualified as interpreter in the Army in Arabic in 1896; was Hausa scholar of Christ's Coll., Camb., 1901-2; was awarded the Cuthbert Peek grant of the R. Geographical Soc. in 1903 for mapping work in N. Nigeria, and is joint-author with Canon C. H. Robinson of a revised edition of the latter's *Hausa Grammar* (1905). Unmarried.

BURGER, W. Schalk-. (See Schalk-Burger.)

BURGHER, Jacobus Johannes, was born in Lydenburg, Transvaal, in 1848, his father having been a prominent man in the old Republic of Lydenburg. At the time of the annexation he was one of the Committee who kept the spirit of 'passive resistance' alive until the time for striking a blow arrived. In the war of independence he fought as Field Cornet at Majuba and Laing's Nek. In 1882 he was elected to the Raad for Lydenburg, and when the Second Raad was formed in 1891 he was returned for Ermelo, and was unanimously elected Chairman of the New Chamber. 'Oom Kootje', as he is called, is a member of the United Dutch Reformed Church.

BURKE, Henry Lardner, K.C., of Grahamstown, Cape Colony, was educated at Lincoln College, Oxford. He was admitted as an Advocate of the Eastern Districts Court, Cape Colony, in 1880, and of the Supreme Court in 1886; was Examiner in Literature at the Cape University in 1888-90, and acted as Solicitor General on various occasions between 1895-7. He was appointed Crown Prosecutor for Griqualand West in 1897, and in the following year was appointed Queen's Counsel. Since 1903 he has held the post of Solicitor General at the High Court of Griqualand.

BURLEIGH, Bennet, of 95, North Side, Clapham Common, S.W., was born in Glasgow. He took part in the American Civil War, and was twice sentenced to be shot by the Federals; acted as correspondent for the *Central News* during the Egyptian campaign in 1882; present at the action at Tel-el-Kebir; went through the French campaign in Madagascar as correspondent; and in 1884 he accompanied the desert column from Korti to Metemmeh as correspondent of the *Daily Telegraph*. He also served in the Ashanti Expedition, the Athara Expedition, the second Egyptian War, in 1894, when he was present at Omdurman, the S. African War in 1899-1902, in all of which he acted as correspondent for the *Daily Telegraph*. He is the author of *Empire of the East*. Unmarried.

BURMESTER, Charles Mansel, was educated at Dulwich College, and entered the service of the Norddeutscher Lloyd Steamship Co. at Bremen in 1898. He resigned his position in 1899 and joined the Imperial Yeomanry, serving with them in the South African War in 1900-1 (Queen's medal and four clasps). In 1901 he acted as Clerk to the Secretary of the Orange River Colony Administration, and as Clerk to the Colonial

Secretary in 1902; acted as Chief Clerk in 1904, and again in 1905.

BURNABY, Capt. Hugo Beaumont, D.S.O., of Wendover, Bucks, was born in London in 1874, and is the youngest son of the Rev. Sherrard B. Burnaby. He was educated at Uppingham, and was engaged in ranching in British Columbia from 1893-99. He served in the S. African War in 1900-2, at first in the ranks, receiving his commission in 1901; Capt. in June, 1901, of the 1st Battn. of I.Y. (despatches). Recreations: shooting and fishing.

BURNHAM, Major Frederick Russell, D.S.O., of Pasadena, California, was born in Minnesota, U.S.A., in 1861, and was educated in the States, spending his youth in the Indian wars on the American frontier. He took part in the first Matabele War as a scout under Dr. Jameson (1893), and was one of the only two who escaped from Allan Wilson's fatal Shangani patrol. In 1895 he took charge of an expedition to N. Rhodesia. He rendered some fine scouting services during the second Matabele War (1896), when he was credited with having shot the M'Limo, and he served as a scout under Lord Roberts in the Boer War in 1900. In 1899 he visited Klondyke, and is now representing the East African Synd., of which he is Managing Director, near the Anglo-German frontier line on Lake Victoria. His recreations are exploration and shooting, and he married in 1884 Miss Blanche B. Blick, and has a son in the U.S. Army.

BURNS, Leonard Balfour, of Parrock Wood, Coleman's Hatch, Tunbridge Wells, and the Royal Thames Yacht Club, was born in 1854. He visited Natal, the Rand, and Kimberley in 1889, and subsequently became associated with Sir Charles Metcalfe, Mr. B. B. Trench and others in the formation of the S.A. Trust and Finance Coy., Ltd., of which he remained a director until its absorption by the Johannesburg Consolidated Invest. Co. He has been a director of the Van Ryn Gold Mines for many years, is on the Board of the Wassau and other W. African Cos., and is interested in some Rhodesian enterprises.

BURNS-THOMPSON, W., of Harrismith, Orange River Colony, is a member of the Inter-Colonial

Council of the Transvaal and O.R.C., and was elected Mayor of Harrismith for 1905.

BURROWS, Thomas W., the Champion Club Swinger of the World, was born in Australia; joined the Army, seeing service in Egypt, and early in 1900 volunteered for service with the 35th Co. I.Y. in the S.A. War, going out as Corporal. On Feb. 15-17, 1905, he performed the unique feat at the Canterbury Music Hall, London, of swinging clubs for forty-six hours without ceasing. The average speed of his intricate revolutions was 150 per minute, and he made nearly half a million whirls to secure the record.

BURTON, A., R.E. late Editor of the *Cape Government Agricultural Journal*, was appointed (1902) editor of the *Agricultural Journal*, a journal started under the auspices of the Transvaal Agricultural Department. He has written an account of the Cape Colony's urban and rural industries, entitled *Cape Colony for Settlers* (P. S. King & Son).

BURTON, Lieut. Col. Francis Henry Merceron, R.A.M.C., M.R.C.S., Eng., of the Military Hospital, Standerton, Transvaal, was born in London, April 20, 1859, and is eldest son of Reginald Burton, of Regent's Park, N.W. He was educated at St. Bartholomew's Hospital, Lond. He married, in 1893, Margaret, only dau. of Lt. Col. G. Simon, M.D., A.M.S.

BURTON, Henry, M.L.A., represents Albert in the Cape Legislative Assembly, for which constituency he was returned unopposed in the Bond interest in Nov., 1902, and again in Feb., 1904.

BUSH, J. Paul, C.M.G., M.R.C.S., of Vyvyan House, Clifton Park, Bristol, and of the Constitutional (Lond.) and Clifton Clubs, was born June 30, 1857, and is son of the late Major Robt. Bush, 96th Regt. He was educated at Clifton Coll. and the Univ. Coll., London. He served during the S. African War as Senior Surgeon of the Princess Christian Hospital, Natal Field Force (medal and clasps, mentioned in despatches, C.M.G.); and as P.M.O. on H.M. Hospital ship *Lismore Castle* in 1899-1900. He is the author of numerous surgical papers. He married, in 1887, Laura, eldest dau. of the late John Robertson, of Victoria, Australia.

BUSTON, Colonel Philip Thomas, D.S.O., was born in 1853. He entered the R.E. in 1872 and six years later served through the second Afghan War, being present at the action of Charasiah, the operations round Kabul, and storming of the Asmai Heights. He also rendered excellent service during the late S. African War in command of the R.E. Infantry Div., and was present at the relief of Kimberley and the battles of Paardeberg and Driefontein (King's and Queen's medals with clasps, D.S.O.).

BUTCHER, Very Rev. Charles Henry, D.D., of Cairo, was formerly Dean of Shanghai Cathedral, and is now Chaplain at Cairo. He is author of *The Oriflamme in Egypt*, a story of Egypt at the time of the Crusaders.

BUTLER, William Bryson, of 3, Grace church Street, London, E.C., and of the Caledonian Junior Constitutional and Scottish Conservative (Edinburgh) Clubs, is son of the late Thomas Bryson Butler, a prominent merchant chant citizen of Glasgow and one of the pioneers of the Volunteer Movement in the West of Scotland. He was born at Bellahouston, near Glasgow, in Sept., 1865, and was educated at Glasgow Academy and Dollar Academy, afterwards pursuing the study of the law at Edinburgh University. Mr. Butler is qualified as a solicitor of Scotland, but has never practised professionally. He, however, acted as private secretary to the late John Morris, the famous lawyer, for six years, later on associating himself with the Henderson group of companies, having been for some time Managing Director of Henderson's Transvaal Estates, Ltd., and a Director of the Daggafontein Gold Mining Co., Ltd., Daggafontein Prospecting Syndicate, Ltd., Delagoa Bay Development Corporation, Ltd., Henderson's Nigel, Ltd., and the Tyne Valley Colliery, Ltd. The present capital of Henderson's Transvaal Estates is £2,000,000, to which it was raised from £300,000 in 1898 in order to purchase two million shares in Henderson's Consolidated for £1,250,000. This latter company controls about 4,574,599 acres of land. The Henderson's Tvl. direct holdings total about 52,000 acres, in addition

to which it has various shareholdings in the Daggafontein G.M. Co. and Daggafontein Prospecting Synd., Henderson's Nigel, Tyne Valley Colliery, and Delagoa Bay Development Companies. The total issued share and debenture capital of this powerful group is considerably over £3,000,000 sterling. In spite of the depression which has prevailed during the last few years Henderson's Transvaal Estates succeeded, according to the last published accounts, in adding nearly £25,000 to the balance of profit brought forward from the previous year, viz., £97,404, while the balance-sheet of the company also showed assets in the shape of stocks and shares, at or below cost, £536,888; debtors, £14,866; bills receivable, £13,552; loans, £8,238; and cash, £75,301—a financial position which should allow the directors ample scope to take advantage of any favourable opportunities for profitable outlay which the peaceful development of South Africa may offer. The Daggafontein G.M. Co. also enjoys a sound financial position, showing holdings of Consols and cash of considerably over fifty thousand pounds. The Delagoa Bay Development Corporation is a commercial venture interested in waterworks, tramways, telephones, and similar enterprises, which promise to expand with the growth of the port.

In addition to Mr. Butler's faith in the prospective value of the gold, coal, copper, tin, and other mineral deposits on the vast areas under the control of his different companies, he also places much reliance upon the development of other industries which he anticipates will grow up with the Transvaal and Portuguese Southeast Africa, and which should form a permanent source of revenue. He is especially impressed with the possibilities of exploiting commercially the cultivation of rubber and various vegetable products, in addition to extending the market for South African-grown tobacco and cereals, all of which, with adequate labour, may flourish in one part or another of the broad acres owned by this important group. As an instance it may be stated that one of the concessions in which Henderson's Transvaal Estates Co. is interested is a plantation in Swaziland, which is reported to have all the natural conditions requisite for successfully growing cotton, castor oil, tobacco, and such semi-tropical products.

Notwithstanding the fact that Mr. Butler was one of the original members of the Rosebery Club at Edinburgh University, which marked him as a Radical, he has since become an ardent Unionist. In his younger days he took an active interest in politics, and had considerable experience in Scotch County Elections. He also held a commission for some years as Lieutenant in the Edinburgh City Artillery Volunteers. Mr. Butler is a good extempore speaker, with an impressive delivery, and a very quick grasp of essential points in debate. For many years he was a familiar figure in the Rugby football field, but latterly his engrossing business interests have only allowed him to indulge his river hobby of punting. He married, in 1897, Edith Gertrude, dau. of the late Dr. Robert Shuttleworth, L.R.C.P.

BUTLER, Lieut.-Gen. Sir William Francis, K.C.B., was born Oct. 31, 1838. He has had a brilliant military career, including many years' service in different parts of the African Continent, since he joined the 69th Foot in 1858. His first active service was with the field force which repelled the incursion of the Fenians into Canada in 1870-1, and he was later employed as Special Commissioner to the Saskatchewan Indians. Sir William served throughout the Ashanti War, 1873-4; served in Natal in 1875, was D.A.Q M.G. to Army Headquarters, 1875-9, A.A.G. and Q.M.G. South Africa, 1879-89; held the same appointments in the Western Dist., 1880-2; with the Egyptian Expeditionary Force in 1882, and served in a similar capacity in the Nile Expedition in 1884-5. He commanded a brigade of the Egyptian Frontier Field Force in 1885-6, and held other appointments in Egypt till late in 1893. In Nov., 1898, he was appointed to the command of the Cape forces. It was during this command that he made the report as to the improbability of the available forces of the Cape being sufficient to successfully withstand an invasion of the Boers—a report or warning which was not well received at headquarters. Gen. Butler took over the command of the Western Dist. (Eng.) in Sept., 1899, and in 1905 took temporary charge of the Second Army Corps during the absence of Sir Ian Hamilton in the East during the Russo-Japanese War. In the same year he relinquished his command. Sir Wm. Butler is a

Liberal in politics, and a prospective candidate for East Leeds at the next election. Sir William Butler has written a considerable number of books, including *The Great Lone Land*—one result of his services in 1870—*The Campaign of the Cataracts* and the lives of Gen. Gordon, Sir Chas. Napier, and Sir Geo. Colley. He married Miss Elizabeth Thompson, the distinguished painter of military subjects.

BUXTON, Alfred Fowell, B.A., Camb., of Chigwell, Essex, and of the Athenaeum Club, was born in 1854, and is grandson of Sir F. F. Buxton, Bart., who was well known for his efforts on behalf of the slaves in the British Colonies and of Criminal Law Reform. He was educated at Rugby, and was formerly a partner in the banking firm of Prescott, Cave, Buxton, Loder and Co., now merged with the Union of London and Smiths Bank, of which he is a local director. He was a member of the L.C.C. in 1892-5, and is now an Alderman and a Director of the Uganda Co., Ltd. He married, in 1885, Violet, dau. of the Rev. T. W. Jex-Blake, Headmaster of Rugby.

BYRON, John, of Wyefield, Beckenham, Kent, is a partner in the South African firm of John T. Rennie, Son and Co., the well-known ship-owners, of 4, East India Avenue, London, E.C., and of Durban. He is also a Director of the Natal Land and Colonisation Co., Ltd., and a London Director of the Elandslaagte Collieries, Ltd., of Durban.

CALDECOTT, Harry Stratford, F.R.G.S., F.R.C.I., of Johannesburg and the Rand Club, was born at Port Elizabeth, Nov. 24, 1846; is 3rd son of the late Hon. Chas. Henry Caldecott, M.L.C., of Grahamstown, and was educated at the Diocesan Coll., Rondebosch, and St. Andrew's Coll., Grahamstown. He is a Director of the Johannesburg Consolidated Investment Co., Johannesburg Estate Co., Glynn's Lydenburg, and other Cos. He is also Chairman of the Witwatersrand Council of Education, and Member of the Technical Institute recently appointed by Govt. During the late S.A. War, Mr. Caldecott rendered good service in many ways, especially as Chairman of the Uitlander Committee in Natal, and later as Commandant of the Boer Refugee Women's Camp at Howick, for whose comfort as well as for the physical and mental education of their children he worked indefatigably. He married, Mch., 1876, Martha Johanna, dau. of the late J. J. Saner, of Aliwal North.

CALDER, William Menzies Grant, was educated at Wellington College, and leaving there at the age of twenty he went to South Africa, where he joined the Rhodesia Horse and served through the Matabele rebellion. On the outbreak of the Boer War he joined Colonel Plumer's irregular force, and was wounded in the hip at Eland River in June, 1900, returning invalided to England in November of the same year.

CALVERLEY, Joseph Ernest Goodfellow, C.M.G. (1901), of 10, Earl's Avenue, Folkestone, was born in London in March, 1872, He was educated at Dulwich Coll. and received his medical training at St. Bartholomew's Hospital, graduating M.D., B.S. Lond., M.R.C.S. Eng., and L.R.C.P. Lond. He served in the S.A. War during 1899-1900, attached to the Portland Hospital, receiving the C.M.G. in connection with services then rendered. He married, July 27, 1901, Miss Evelyn Doneet.

CAMERON, Major G. E. E. G. entered the Gordon Highlanders in 1892, and took part with the Relief Force in the operations in Chitral in 1895 (medal and clasp); the operations on the N.W. Frontier of India with the Tirah Exped. Force in 1897-8, including the action of Dargai (despatches and two clasps); the South African War in 1899-1900 as a Special Service Officer taking part in the advance on Kimberley, including the action at Enslin; operations in the Orange Free State, and at Paardeberg; present at the actions at Poplar Grove, Driefontein, Houtnek (Thaba Mountain), Vet River and Zand River, and the operations in the Transvaal and Cape Colony (despatches, Brevet-Major and Queen's medal with four clasps). Subsequently he was appointed Adjutant of the Royal Hospital at Chelsea in succession to Major A. E. O. Congdon.

CAMPBELL, Rear-Admiral Sir Charles, C.B., K.C.M.G., of the Senior United Service and Marlborough Clubs, was born in 1847. He was educated at the Royal Naval Academy, Gosport, and was employed in Transport service during the Egyptian War in 1882, and in the Benin Expedition

in 1897. He was A.D.C. to Queen Victoria from 1899 to 1901, and to King Edward in 1901. He was engaged in the work of settling the French claims in Newfoundland. He was made Commander of the Bath in 1894, and was created K.C.M.G. on the occasion of the King's birthday, 1905.

CAMPBELL, Marshall, M.L.C., J.P., of Mount Edgecombe, Natal, and of the Durban Club; is the son of William Campbell, of Muckleneuk. He was born July 10, 1848, and was educated in Natal. Mr. Campbell landed in Natal when eighteen months old. His father was one of the first to start the sugar industry in the Colony of Natal, which he has successfully continued to the present time. He built the Natal Refinery, and the Tongaat Central Sugar Co.'s Estate, of which at one time he was half owner. Mr. Marshall Campbell was M.L.C. when Natal was a Crown Colony. On Natal being given Responsible Government, he was nominated for the Upper House for Victoria County, which seat he holds to the present day. He was asked by Gen. Buller to collect Indian stretcher-bearers during the war, and sent 600 to Colenso and 700 to Spion Kop. Mr. Campbell was appointed as the Natal Commissioner on the Natal-Transvaal Boundary Delimitation Commission. For the excellent work he did while on this Commission he received the thanks of Lord Milner and the Govt. He has been appointed as one of the two Natal Commissioners on the South African Native Commission. He is largely interested in the Natal Estates Co., Ltd., holding the position of Managing Director; he is also acting Chairman of the Tongaat Central Sugar Co., Ltd., and the Molassine Meal Co., Ltd., and is Director of the Elandslaagte, Ltd. Mr. Campbell has travelled largely in S.A., and in 1871 left the Cape for the Victoria Falls, but just failed to reach them through fever and scarcity of water. In the early days he shot a great deal over Zululand, and won the cup given by the Natal Gun Club for the best shot in 1871. He married, in 1877, Ellen Blarney.

CAMPBELL, Major the Hon. Ralph Alexander, was born Feb. 18, 1877, and is third son of the third Earl Cawdor. He entered the Cameron Highlanders in 1896, and served in the Nile Expedition in 1898, being present at the Battle of

Khartoum (medal, and Egyptian medal with clasp), and the South African War in 1899-1902, on the Staff, and as A.D.C. to the Lieut.-General of the Infantry Division; present at operations in the Transvaal and Cape Colon (despatches, Brevet of Major, Queen's medal with three clasps and King's medal with two clasps). At present he holds the appointment of Adjutant to Lovat's Scouts.

CAMPBELL, Capt. Samuel George. Natal Vol. Med. Corps, J.P., of Carndonagh, Musgrave Road, Durban, and the Durban Club, was born at Muckle Neuk, Victoria Co., Natal, July 25, 1861. He is the son of William Campbell, of Muckle Neuk, a Natal sugar planter, and was educated at Hermansberg, and Bishop's Coll., Natal, and at Edinburgh and Vienna Universities, graduating M.D. Edin., F.R.C.S. Edin., M.R.C.S. Lond., and D.P.H. Edin. He served in the Natal Civil Service as Dist. Surgeon and Indian Med. Officer 1883-5; was Med. Officer of Health, Durban, 1890-1902, and served with the Natal Volunteer Med. Corps during the Boer War (Siege of Ladysmith). He is member of the Durban Hospital Board, and J.P. (Natal).

Captain Campbell played in the Rugby Fifteen at Edin. University in 1879, and was elected Capt. of the Durban Polo Club, 1903. He married, in 1886, Margaret W., dau. of Jas. Dunnachie, J.P., of Glenboig, Scotland.

CANNELL, Cameron Corlett, F.R.G.S., M.R.C.I., of Heatherdene, Bagshot, of Blomfield House, London, E.C., and of the Blenheim, Sunningdale Golf, and other Clubs, was born at Grahamstown, Cape Colony, in 1862, and was educated at Grahamstown and Port Alfred. Mr. Cannell was one of the early pioneers of the Rand, where he joined the Johannesburg firm of B. M. Woollan & Co. Coming to England, Mr. Cannell took up the London Agency of several companies controlled by the Woollan group, and very soon entered a larger sphere of usefulness, greatly extending his interests in the Transvaal and Rhodesia. He is a Director of the Consolidated Rand-Rhodesia Trust, the Bulawayo Estate and Trust, Monastery Diamond Mines, the Rand Investment Corporation, the *African World*, and the Collos Portland Cement Co. In the early days of

the late S.A. War he acted as Hon. Capt. on the H.Q. Staff of the Army Remount Dept. (1899). He is keen on shooting, hunting, and motoring, and married, in 1891, Miss Eva Bright.

CANTLIE, Dr. James, M.A., M.B., C.M. Aberdeen, M.R.C.S. and F.R.C.S. Eng., D.P.H., of 140, Harley Street, London, and The Kennels, Cotterell, Buntingford, Herts; is son of Wm. Cantlie, of Keithmore, Dufftown, Banffshire, Scotland, where he was born Jan. 17, 1851. He was educated at Milne's Institution, Fochabers, at Aberdeen Univ., where he graduated with honours in Natural Science, and took his M.B., C.M., with honours in Surgery; at Charing Cross Hosp., Lond., and at Bonn. He was Demonstrator of Anatomy at Charing Cross Hosp., 1872-87; and also occupied the positions there of House Surgeon and Surgical Registrar, and Assist. and Surgeon (1877-87). Dr. Cantlie was in Hong Kong from 1887 till 1896, during which time he founded the Coll. of Medicine for Chinese, Hong Kong (1887); was Dean of the Coll., 1889-97, and Surgeon Chinese Imperial Maritime Customs. On returning to London in 1897 he was appointed Lecturer on Applied Anatomy at Charing Cross Hosp., Surgeon to the West End Hosp. for Paralysis, Surgeon to the Seamen's Hosp., and Lecturer on Surgery at the Lond. Sch. of Tropical Medicine. In 1883 Dr. Cantlie went to Egypt as member of the Cholera Expedition; has travelled in Judea, China, Japan, Korea, W. Siberia, America, and Canada, and is the author of many works on Anatomy, Surgery, Tropical Medicine, and Hygiene. He married, July 30, 1884, Mabel Barclay Brown, of Barnes, London.

CANTWELL, Lieut.-Colonel Robert Francis, joined the F.A.M.P. as a trooper in 1877. He took part in several of the local wars, including the Gaika and Galeka Campaigns in 1877-8, being present at the capture of Moirosi's Mountain in Nov., 1879 (Kaffir War medal). In 1880 he proceeded to Basutoland with the Cape Mounted Riflemen as Regimental Sergeant Major (medal). He was promoted Lieutenant in 1881; Captain, Adjutant, and Musketry-Instructor of the right wing in 1883, and Captain, Adjutant, and Musketry-Instructor in the Cape Mounted Rifles in 1884; promoted Major in 1900, and Brevet Lieut.-Colonel in 1901. In

1903 was seconded as Senior Staff Officer of the Cape Colonial Forces, having previously taken part in the South African War in 1899-1900 (Queen's medal and four clasps, King's medal and two clasps). He also holds the Coronation medal.

CAPETOWN, Archbishop of. (See Most Rev. W. W. Jones.)

CARBUTT, Clive Lancaster, of Bulawayo, and of the Bulawayo Club, was born March 26, 1876, at Ladysmith, and is son of H. L. Carbutt, J.P., of Natal. He was educated at Pietermaritzburg Coll.; was appointed Assist. Native Commissioner under the Chartered Co. in 1897, and recruited the Native Police in Zululand for that Company. In June, 1897, he became Assist. Native Commissioner for the Bubi Dist. of Matabeleland, and Native Commissioner and J.P. for the same district in 1899. He was Native Commissioner for the Wankie, Sebungwe, and Mafungabusi districts in 1900; and has also acted as Inspector of Compounds for the Filabusi, Sebakwe, and other mining areas. He is a special J.P. for Matabeleland, being in charge of the Native Affairs Dept. from June to Dec., 1905, during the absence of the Chief Native Commissioner. Mr. Carbutt was one of the first of the Chartered Co.'s officials to visit the Zambezi Valley, and successfully instituted the collection of the hut tax in the Mafungabusi portion of it in 1898. In 1903 he was selected to inquire into the compound systems of Kimberley and the Rand, and report on them for the information of the Rhodesian Govt. He is a member of the Bulawayo Turf and Polo Clubs, being vice-captain of the latter. He married, Oct. 10, 1901, Frances, dau. of A. M. Anderson, of Pietermaritzburg.

CARDEN, Capt., acted as C.O. and Adjt. of the Rhodesia Horse during the second Matabele War (1896).

CARDEN, John Cecil, of Redhouse and Port Elizabeth, Cape Colony, and of the River Club, is the 2nd son of the late Maj.-Gen. George Carden, who commanded the 2nd Batt. of the Fifth Northumberland Fusiliers. He was born Aug. 3, 1870, at Glasgow, Scotland, and was educated at Llandaff, S. Wales. Mr. Carden is well known in sporting and dramatic circles. In 1892-3 he was

Pres. of the Eastern Province Rugby Football Union, and in the latter year he was President of the South African Swimming Union. He is the stage manager and one of the founders of the Port Elizabeth Amateur Operatic Club. After a successful business career he is now junior partner in the old-established merchant house of Blaine & Co., at Port Elizabeth. He married, Nov. 15, 1894, Amy, dau. of the late William Caldwell Elliot.

CARDIGAN, Lord, is son of Lord Aylesbury, and fought in the recent South African War, winning the D.S.O. while still in his twenties.

CARNWALL, Moses, J.P., Hon. Assoc. of the Order of St. John of Jerusalem, of Erinville, Kimberley, and the Kimberley Club, was born in Dublin, July 6, 1841. He is son of Wm. Carnwall, of Dublin, by his wife May Teresa, dau. of Moses d'Arcy, of Wexford, Ireland. He emigrated to S.A. in 1859, and was one of the early settlers in the Diamond Fields in 1870. He was Mayor of Kimberley in 1881, 1882, and 1893; represented the district of Kimberley in the Cape House of Assembly from 1884 to 1888. He was for many years member of the Borough Council and Divisional Council; is Chairman of the Kimberley Hospital Board, the Public Library, and the Rhodes Memorial Committee. Mr. Carnwall served in the Griqualand West War of 1878 as a Volunteer (medal and clasp), and during the Boer War he served in the Kimberley Town Guard (medal and clasp and Mayor's siege medal). He married, Feb. 29, 1864, Margaret, dau. of Wm. Lundie, of Co. Monaghan, Ireland.

CARRINGTON, Maj.-Gen. Sir Frederick, K.C.B., K.C.M.G., of Perrott's Brook, Cirencester, and of the Naval and Military Club, was born at Cheltenham, Aug. 23, 1844, and is son of Edmund Carrington, J.P., of that town. Sir Frederick was educated at Cheltenham, and passed into the Army at the age of nineteen, and has seen very considerable service in S.A. ever since 1875, when he organised and commanded the Mounted Infantry in the Griqualand West Expedition. In 1877 he raised and commanded the F.L.H. in the Kaffir War, fighting in the battle of Quintana and in the later operations in the Transkei and the Peri Bush (despatches). He also commanded the Transvaal

Volunteer forces against Sekukuni in 1878-9 (despatches, medal with clasp, brevs. of Maj. and Lt.-Col., C.M.G.). During the siege of Mafeteng by the Basutos he was in command of the C.M.R., and later, in the Basuto War, he had command of the Colonial forces, and was severely wounded. Sir Frederick commanded the 2nd Mounted Rifles in 1884-5, and was commandant of Native Levies in Zululand in 1888. He then commanded the B.B.P. until 1893, when he was appointed Military Adviser to the High Commissioner during the first Matabele War. He commanded the Infantry Brigade at Gibraltar from May, 1895, until March, 1899, with a brief interval in '96, when he commanded the troops in the Matabele Rebellion of 1896. With the local rank of Lieut.-Gen., Sir Frederick commanded the Rhodesian Field Force in the S.A. War, Feb., 1900, to April, 1901, taking part in the operations in Rhodesia, Western Transvaal, including the actions at Elands River, the Cape Colony, and the North of the O.R.C. Gen. Carrington married, Nov. 18, 1897, Miss Susan Margaret Elwes.

CARSTENSEN, Captain Herman, of the Cape Mounted Rifles, joined that corps in 1880 and served in the latter part of the Basuto campaign. He also took part in the South African War in 1899-1902 (Queen's medal with three clasps, and King's medal with two clasps).

CARSWELL, R. G., of the Port Elizabeth Swimming Club. In the 1903 S. A. Swimming Championships he was second to E. M. Wearn (q.v.) in both the 500 and 200 yards, his time being 7 min. 24 4-5 secs. for the former. In the latter he was only beaten by a couple of yards.

CARTER, Brev.-Lieut.-Col. Charles Herbert Philip, C.M.G., of the Naval and Military Club, Lond., was born in Aylesbury, Bucks, Feb. 14, 1864; was educated at Cheltenham Coll., and joined H.M.S. *Britannia* as a naval cadet in 1875. In 1885, however, he enlisted in the 4th Dragoon Guards, but received a commission in the Black Watch (Royal Highlanders) in 1888. Col. Carter has had considerable service in Africa, including the Benin City Expedition in 1897; Staff Officer to Gen. Bruce Hamilton (despatches; promoted to Capt. in the Royal Scots, and Brev. majority);

commanded operations against the Kwo Ibos, S. Nigeria, 1899 (Governor's despatches); commanded operations in Benin territories (W. Africa), 1899 (despatches, C.M.G. Brev. of Lieut.-Col.); served with the Ashanti Field Force for the relief of Kumasi in command of the S. Nigeria Regt. (1900) under Maj.-Gen. Sir Jas. Willcocks, and was severely wounded at the battle of Bompodssi. Col. Carter was commandant of S. Nigeria, 1899-1900. He married, in 1899, Kathleen Maud, dau. of Jas. Hartley.

CARTER, Edgar Bonham-. (See E. Bonham Carter.)

CARTER, Colonel Francis Charles, Middelburg, Transvaal, was born Dec. 21, 1858. He entered the Army in 1878, and served in the Afghan War in 1878-80, with the Khyber Line Force at Jellalabad (medal); the Hazara Expedition in 1888, as Field Intelligence Officer (despatches and medal with clasp); the Lushai expedition in 1889, and the Hazara Expedition 1891, as D.A.A.G. (despatches and clasp). In 1894 he joined the Royal Berks Regt., from which he subsequently retired. In 1906 he was appointed to command the Middelburg Sub-District of the Transvaal.

CARTER, Lieut. Herbert Augustine, V.C., of the 6th Indian Mounted Infantry; served in the operations in Somaliland in 1904, receiving the D.S.O., but this distinction was cancelled on the V.C. being conferred upon him for conspicuous bravery under the following circumstances: during a reconnaissance near Jidballi, when a small British force was pursued by a force of Dervishes that outnumbered it by forty to one, Lieutenant Carter rode back alone a distance of 460 yards to the assistance of Private Jai Singh, who had lost his horse. He took the sepoy up behind him and brought him safely away.

CARTER, Rev. James, M.A., was Precentor of Grahamstown Cathedral from 1890 to 1893, after which he was for seven years Rector of St. Paul's, Port Elizabeth, subsequently holding the living of Graaff Reinet. He was appointed to the living of Plymbridge, near Stonehouse, in 1902.

CARTER, Right Rev. William Marlborough,

Bishop of Pretoria, D.D. (Oxon), of Bishop's House, Pretoria, Beechwood House, Hook Street, Johannesburg, and of the Athenaeum Club, Johannesburg, is the son of the Rev. W. A. Carter, late Fellow of Eton Coll. He was born July 11, 1850, at Eton, and educated at Eton and Pembroke Coll., Oxon. He was ordained in 1874 by Bishop Selwyn, of Lichfield, and was appointed curate of Christ Church, West Bromwich. He took charge of the Eton Mission, Hackney Wick, E., from 1880-91, during which time the mission greatly flourished and the name of Bishop Carter became a household word. In 1891 he was appointed Bishop of Zululand, but after eleven years' service in this diocese he received the appointment of Bishop of Pretoria, 1902.

CARTON DE WIART. Leon, D.L., of Kasrel-Dubara, Cairo, and of the Conservative and Junior Athenaeum Clubs, London, was born at Brussels in 1854, and was educated at Stonyhurst Coll. and at Brussels University, where he took his degree as Doctor of Laws. He is an advocate at the Bar of the International Mixed Tribunals of Egypt; is a Knt. of the Order of Leopold of Belgium, and has received the orders of the Osmanieh and Medjidieh. He married Miss May James.

CARTON DE WIART, Lieut.-Col. René, of Joura, near Cairo, and of the Turf and Khedivial Clubs, Cairo, was born at Brussels in 1867. He holds the rank of Kaimakan (Lieut.-Col.) in the Egyptian Army, and is now director of Joura prisons. He married, in 1902, Miss Gabrielle Quisini.

CARTWRIGHT. Albert, of Rosebank, near Cape Town, was born at Manchester, Eng., Dec. 25, 1868, and is the son of a Lancashire bookseller. Educated at Davyhulme Wesleyan Gram. Sch., Lancs., he emigrated to the Cape at the beginning of 1889; served three years on the staff of the *Cape Times*, then founded a weekly paper, *The South African*, now defunct; became sub-ed. and afterwards asst.-ed. of the *Johannesburg Star*, from which paper he resigned in connection with the Raid; then edited the *Kimberley Advertiser*, until in 1898 that paper's pro-Rhodes policy necessitated a change in the editorial direction. In 1889 he became first editor of the *South African News*, and was sentenced during the war to a year's

imprisonment for reproducing from English papers the letter of an anonymous British officer, asserting that he had received orders, should he overtake Gen. de Wet, to take no prisoners. In 1903 Prof. Fremantle (q.v.) became associated with Mr. Cartwright in the editorship of the *South African News*. In 1905 he resigned his connection with the *South African News* and became London editor of the *Rand Daily Mail* cable service. He married, in 1891, Anne, dau. of Christopher H. Robertson, shipbuilder, of Cape Town.

CARTWRIGHT, John Dean, M.L.A., was returned to the Cape Parliament as one of the Progressive representatives of Cape Town at the general election in Feb., 1904.

CASEMENT. Thomas, son of the late Capt. Roger Casement, 3rd Light Dragoons, of Ballycastle, Co. Antrim, Ireland, and of the Athenaeum Club, Johannesburg, was educated privately, and entered the Mercantile Marine at the age of 15. Travelled considerably in Australia, New Zealand, California, and South Sea Islands; went to S. Africa, 1896; joined Imperial Light Horse, 1899, and received commission in Roberts's Horse (medal, and four clasps); was sent to Barberton by Lord Roberts in Oct., 1900, as Commissioner of Mines and Native Affairs to organise Civil Administration, and remained there until 1902. He returned to Johannesburg in 1904 to take up position of Chief Claim Inspector for the Transvaal. In that year, whilst travelling on duty, he received several serious injuries which compelled him to leave the service.

CASSEL, Right Hon. Sir Ernest, G.C. V.O., K.C.M.G., P.C., of 48, Grosvenor Square, London, W., was born in 1852 at Cologne, where he was also educated. He is an engineer by profession, and is the constructor of the wonderful dam at Assouan, which cost two and a-half millions to build, but the storing of the Nile water will, it is estimated, increase, the wealth of Egypt by eighty millions sterling.

CASSILLIS, Earl of, of 1, Moray Place, Edinburgh, and of White's Club, was born May 22, 1872, and is the eldest son of the 3rd Marquis of Ailsa. He was educated at Eton and Trinity Coll., Camb., and was gazetted 2nd Lieut. in the 3rd Royal Scots Fusiliers in April, 1890, obtaining his captaincy in Jan., 1900. Lord Cassillis served with the 2nd Royal Scots Fusiliers in the S. African War, taking part in the operations in the Transvaal west of Pretoria, including the actions at Frederickstad; was a member of the Military Tribunal at Johannesburg; acted as Intelligence Officer from June to Nov., 1901, and was subsequently on the blockhouse lines and at Middelburg (Transvaal) until the end of the war. He was admitted a member of the Faculty of Advocates, Edinburgh, in Dec., 1897, and married, in 1903, Frances Emily, 3rd dau. of Sir Mark John MacTaggart-Stewart, Bart., M.P.

CASSINI, Count, was one of the Russian Plenipotentiaries at the Moroccan Conference at Algeçiras in 1906.

CASTENS, Herbert Hayton, M.L.C., B.A., of the Administrator's Office, Southern Rhodesia, was called to the Bar at the Inner Temple in 1889, and in the following year was admitted to the Supreme Court at Cape Town. He is a member of the Executive and Legislative Councils of Rhodesia. In 1897 he was appointed Public Prosecutor for Southern Rhodesia, and became Chief Secretary to the Administrator there in 1899, which position he still retains.

CATANNA, Catanna Santa Anna, a native of Portuguese extraction, is nominal Chief of the Chukunda in Northern Rhodesia. His headquarters were at Feira on the north bank of the Zambesi and west of its junction with the Loangwa River; but since the Chartered Company took over this territory, Catanna, who did not enjoy an enviable reputation, has been deprived of any real power. The company wished to transfer him to Portuguese territory, but the Portuguese authorities preferred not to accept him as a subject.

CATLIN, Robert Mayo, of Vermont, Nevada, California, of Johannesburg, and the Rand and New Clubs, Johannesburg, was born at Burlington, Vermont, June 8, 1853, and is of English descent. He was educated at the University of Vt. Since 1875 he has been managing mines, including the Navajo, Belle Isle, N. Belle Isle, Commonwealth, Nevada Queen, N. Commonwealth, Del Monte,

Independence and Mardin in America, and since 1895 he has been Gen. Manager for the Deep Level Cos. of the Consolidated Gold Fields of S.A., Ltd., in Johannesburg. He was elected Pres. of the Association of Mine Managers of the Witwatersrand (1903), and Pres. of the Mechanical Engineers Assoc. of the Witwatersrand (1903). Mr. Catlin was married to Miss Ann E. Robertson, June 15, 1882.

CAVE, Basil Shillito, C.B., M.R.A.C., F.R.G.S., of the British Agency, Zanzibar, of 14, Redcliffe Square, London, S.W., and of the St. James's Club and M.C.C., was born at Mill Hill, Middlesex, Nov. 14, 1865; is youngest son of the late Thos. Cave, M.P. for Barnstaple, 1865-80, of Richmond, Surrey; and was educated at Merchant Taylors' Sch. and the Royal Agricultural Coll., Cirencester, of which latter he is a member by examination, as he is also of the Royal Agricultural Society of Ireland. He became Professional Associate of the Surveyors' Institution in 1885; was appointed Vice-Consul for B.E.A., March 20, 1891; Consul for Zanzibar, June 1, 1895; Consul-General for Zanzibar, July 9, 1903; Agent and Consul-General for Zanzibar and Consul-General for German East Africa, July 8, 1904; was member of the Council of the East Africa Protectorate from June, 1896, to Jan., 1897, and from April-Dec., 1899, and was acting Pres. from Oct. to Dec., 1897. Mr. Cave was decorated for service in connection with the attempt of Seyyid Khaled to usurp the Sultanate in 1896, and the subsequent bombardment of the Palace. He also wears the Coronation Medal (1902), and was Pres. of the International Maritime Slave Trade Bureau as Zanzibar in 1903. He married, Feb. 19, 1892, Mary, younger dau. of the Rev. J. B. McClellan, Principal of the Royal Agricultural Coll., Cirencester.

CAWSTON, George, of 56, Upper Brook Street, W., and of the Manor House, Cawston, Norfolk, was born Feb. 13, 1851. He is son of the late S. W. Cawston, and has been a member of the London Stock Exchange since 1872. He is also a member of the Inner Temple, and was called to the Bar in 1881.

Mr. Cawston took an interest in South Africa directly after Sir Hercules Robinson made the so-called treaty with Lobengula on Feb. 11, 1888, by which the latter acknowledged the supremacy of Great Britain in Matabeleland. Mr. J. Scott Keltie, in his book, *The Partition of Africa*, says it would seem that the first person to actually step forward and make proposals to the British Government with regard to obtaining concessions in Matabeleland was Mr. George Cawston, who on May 4, 1888, wrote to the Colonial Office, as printed in the *South African Blue Book*: "It is the intention of myself in conjunction with others to send a representative to Matabeleland to negotiate with Lobengula for a treaty for trading, mining, and general purposes". Further correspondence took place between Lord Knutsford and Mr. George Cawston and his friends, with the result that the Exploring Company was formed for the purpose. But, adds Mr. Keltie, "though Mr. Cawston seems to have been the first to approach the Govt., and although he lost no time, after he had satisfied the Colonial Office, another company, the moving spirit of which was Mr. Rhodes, was already on the spot, and thus had the advantage of him". An arrangement between these companies was subsequently made, and the Exploring Company applied to H.M. Govt. for the grant of the Charter, which was made on. Oct. 31, 1889. Mr. Cawston was one of the signatories of the application for the Charter, and became one of the first directors. He remained on the Board until the directors had met their shareholders after the Raid, and then resigned. He was joint editor with Mr. A. H. Keane (q.v.) of a book on the Early Chartered Companies.

CAYZER, Sir Charles William, Bart., of Gartmore, Perthshire; Ralston, Renfrewshire; Newtyle, Forfarshire; 27, Belgrave Square, London; and of the Carlton and City of London Clubs, was born in London, July 15, 1843, and is eldest son of the late Charles Cayzer, of Hatherleigh, Devon. He is an Hon. Colonel of the lst Lanarkshire Vol. Artillery; was the first Conservative elected for Barrow-in-Furness, and sat as M.P. for that constituency from 1892 until 1906, when he was defeated by a Labour opponent. Sir Charles is head of the S. African shipping firm of Cayzer, Irvine, and Co., and had for some years borne a well-merited knighthood when he received a baronetcy on the occasion of the King's birthday, 1904. Recreations: shooting,

fishing, and golf. He married, in 1868, Agnes, only dau. of William Trickey, of Clifton, Bristol.

CECIL, Lieut. A. W. J., Grenadier Guards, of Johannesburg, was appointed A.D.C. to Lord Selborne, High Commissioner for South Africa, in March, 1905.

CECIL, Brev. Lieut.-Col. Lord Edward H., D.S.O., Gren. Guards, of Khartoum, Sudan, is son of the late Marquess of Salisbury, Prime Minister of England, and brother of the present holder of the title. He fought in the late South African War, and is at present Director of Intelligence and Agent-General in the Sudan Administration.

CHABAUD, Claude Wright, of Robben Island, Cape Colony, was appointed Clerk to the Superintendent of Natives at Bolotwa in 1878; Clerk to the Resident Magistrate at St. Mark's in 1881; held a commission in the native levies from 1880-1; was appointed Clerk to the Resident Magistrate at Xalanga, in 1883; Resident Magistrate at Elliott in 1894; acted Civil Commissioner and Resident Magistrate at Barkly East in 1900; Resident Magistrate at Lusikisiki in March, 1902, and Civil Commissioner and Resident Magistrate at Calvinia in the following Oct. In July, 1904, he was appointed Commissioner of Robben Island and Asst. Magistrate for Cape Town at Robben Island.

CHAKOUR, Joseph Gabriel, Pasha, Grand Officer of the Medjidieh (Turkish), Commander of Sts. Maurice and Lazarus of Italy, Commander of the Grecian Order of the Saviour; of 1, Rue d'Abdine, Cairo, and of the Oriental Club, Cairo, was born at Alexandria, July 7, 1855. He is son of Gabriel Chakour and Assine Dahan, and was educated at Lyons, France, receiving the diploma of the French University. Chakour Pasha entered the Ministry of Finance under the Khedival Govt. on Jan. 1, 1877, and took an active part in the reorganisation of that dept. under the British Administration. He published several works on real estate and the assessment of the land taxes in Egypt. In 1890 he had charge of the organisation of the Municipality of Alexandria, the first and only institution of the kind in Egypt in which the foreign colonies then established in Alexandria were combined with the native element for administering the affairs of the city. In 1892 he was appointed Director-Gen. of the Municipality with the office of Pres. of the Executive. It was under his administration that the town was most fully developed by the opening up of roads and tramways, the installation of the electric light, construction of quays, resulting in the most beautiful promenade of Alexandria, and by the creation of a fine quarter formed on land previously intended for the deposit of town rubbish. He occupied this position for eleven years, during which period he was frequently commended in the reports of Lord Cromer. At the beginning of 1903 Chakour Pasha retired from the service of the Egyptian Govt., since when he has devoted himself to financial and more especially to industrial affairs. He married, Nov. 30, 1879, Sophie von Reinlein von Rautenbough.

CHAMBERLAIN. Right Hon. Joseph, P.C., M.P., F.R.S., J.P., of Highbury, Moor Green, Birmingham; 40, Prince's Gardens, London, S.W., and of the Athenaeum and Devonshire Clubs, was born in Camberwell Grove, London, on July 7, 1836. He is the eldest son of a boot and shoe manufacturer, a man who took no part in politics, but devoted his spare time to his duties as a master cordwainer and as a staunch supporter of the chapels to which he belonged.

Had the course of political events during the past thirty years never brought Mr. Chamberlain into close contact with South Africa, had it never led up to his famous tour throughout the country, had it never caused the names of the, great statesman and the great Continent to be associated, still the echo of notable things done for some part of the Empire must have reached Anglo-African ears. But when we remember those eight years from 1895 to 1903 spent almost entirely in the service of South Africa, with all their record of successful labour, it would be an extraordinary omission if there did not appear in this volume an account of Mr. Chamberlain's career, including details other than those which refer more particularly to his connection with Africa. He is the one man whose actions, whether admired or hated, whose words, whether believed or ridiculed, invariably arouse exceptional interest in every country. His qualities are eminently those that excite simultaneously the dislike and the admiration of the foreigner. Above all, and to this

dictum friend and foe alike subscribe, he is 'the man who knows his own mind'. He is indeed a 'maker of programmes', but he knows how to get them carried out, and he believes that the people are the ultimate judges of right and are in the long run prepared to maintain it at any sacrifice. It was to a great extent from this belief that his inauguration of the Tariff Reform Crusade sprang. It was his belief that the time had come when England had a new duty to perform to her colonies which demanded a change in her business methods, and he felt it his duty to promulgate that belief and to ask for that change. When he has expounded its meaning and demands, the people, he is sure, will accept and obey. In his own words "Governments propose, but the people decide". It is this, his cardinal tenet, that has led him to leave sheep-like parties, and change his own expressed views with an utter callousness of criticism. To him consistency is no cardinal virtue. The needs of the imminent hour, and of that alone, are his care, and weigh upon his conscience. Whether they are coincident with or opportune to the aims of his party is a small thing in his eyes. As a Liberal, as an Imperialist, as the strongest supporter of a Conservative body, he has often held views radically opposed to his leaders. The style of his speech, coldness, pitiless denunciation, sarcasm, the creation of phrases incredibly destructive, the impassiveness of his demeanour-all these things have combined to convince the public that Mr. Chamberlain is all head, no heart. It is a false estimate, formed on a superficial basis, and an utter inability to judge at a comparatively great distance an essentially complex character. It must be remembered that John Bright said of him "Where he is best known he is best appreciated".

Still, it is interesting to note that within a few years of Joseph's birth many of the colonies with which he was in after life to be so intimately connected were annexed, or ceded to the Crown. After all, the times were stirring. Far away, several minor wars in the East were occupying our attention; the Continent was hardly less disturbed. Further events, such as the death of Sir Robert Peel and the lying-in-state of the Duke of Wellington, made a deep impression on the sensitive lad's character. Experiences of City life came early, through his father's connection with the Cordwainers' Hall.

Relating his early life while unveiling a window in that building in 1896 he recalled the fact that this was the scene of his first public speech, when as a very young man he was dining there with his father. Years afterwards, records that remain of his early childhood represent Joseph as a clever, serious boy who was wont to go deeply into things and, as his mother said, used to ask questions that she had great difficulty in answering. His early education was of the simplest character, but in 1845 on the family's removal to Highbury he became a pupil of the Rev. Arthur Johnson at another Church of England school. But in mathematics at least the pupil soon outran his master, and at the age of 14 he was sent to University College School, where the next two years' training completed his school life. The University was closed to him as a dissenter, and he immediately entered upon his business career at the bottom of his father's house. In the workshop he doubtless imbibed his Radical views of politics and learned at first hand many of the thoughts and hopes of the British artisan. His lighter moments were devoted chiefly to indulging his taste in amateur theatricals, at which, both as actor and author, he was remarkably proficient. But his leisure hours were short. The devotion to the work of the day that has characterised his whole life often led him even in those early years to work many hours overtime, and that despite the excellent position and fair amount of capital for a good start in life which were his. For Mr. Chamberlain is by no means the 'self-made' man which it was at one time the fashion to describe him. It was as a young business man that he first gave evidence of the possession of that combination of qualities to which his success as a statesman is greatly due—the power of accurate foresight, of thinking on a big scale and at the same time giving attention to the most minute details of a scheme. In his position as head of the commercial department of the great firm of Nettlefold and Chamberlain, screw manufacturers, he displayed great ability and enterprise, not only in developing the home trade, but in capturing a good deal of the foreign as well. The consequent prosperity of the firm laid them open to certain malicious libels which were not finally put to rest till 1884, when, after they had been revived in the *Daily News*, a complete retraction and apology appeared in the columns of that newspaper. At that time Mr. Chamberlain was

President of the Board of Trade, and there can be little doubt that these slanderous attacks emanated, at least indirectly, from opponents of certain measures that he was then introducing. Within ten years of his becoming a partner in the firm it had produced a substantial fortune, and in 1874 he retired from business permanently.

During Mr. Chamberlain's superintendence of the commercial department of his business, he had inaugurated and often spoken at a debating club for his men; had taught in the night schools connected with his church; had been President of its Mutual Improvement Society, and had spent his leisure in a variety of political and philanthropic work. He had met and learned much of his future colleague, John Bright. He saw men fighting for vital things the right of free speech, the right of franchise, the right of education for their children. He had early much experience of the struggles on the Irish question, and indeed his first speech in Birmingham Town Hall was made as seconder of a resolution declaring that Mr. Gladstone's Irish Church Disestablishment Bill should become law, a resolution that was carried at one of the most turbulent meetings ever held in Birmingham. This was in June, 1869, but though then but thirty-three years old he had already gained a considerable reputation as a debater. It should be remarked that at an even earlier age he had dissented from his leader, John Bright, on the subject of Colonial expansion, which both the latter and Mr. Gladstone opposed and disliked. The wonderful power of suiting his speeches to his audience, which has been perhaps Mr. Chamberlain's most powerful weapon, was certainly acquired in the course of his addresses to nearly every social and political class of people in Birmingham.

Mr. Chamberlain was in great request in Birmingham society, being, as has already been noted, an excellent actor in private theatricals, and he was also a very good dancer. Especially was he intimate with the Kenricks, and in 1861 he married Harriet, daughter of Mr. A. Kenrick, of West Bromwich. His brother-in-law, Mr. W. Kenrick, afterwards M.P. for Birmingham, married Mr. Chamberlain's eldest sister. But Mrs. Chamberlain, unhappily, died very shortly after the birth of her son, Joseph Austen, and her husband threw

THE RIGHT HON. WINSTON CHURCHILL   THE RIGHT HON. J. CHAMBERLAIN

Photos Elliott & Fry

himself, if possible, more eagerly than before into public work.

There are four great periods of Mr. Chamberlain's public work, which may fitly be termed crusades— the first, Education; the second, Municipal; the third, Home Rule; and the fourth, Tariff Reform. Each may be briefly described in its proper order, while it must not be forgotten that he raised the Colonial Office to a dignity and importance which it had never before enjoyed in so eminent a degree. Mr. Chamberlain made his first efforts on behalf of Education as a teacher at the schools connected with the chapels he attended in London and Birmingham, but his first broader attempts bore fruit in the foundation of the Birmingham Education Society, which later was merged in the bigger National Education League, of the executive committee of which he was appointed chairman. The members of the former society gave freely, not only of their money, but, what was more important still, of their spare time in personally visiting the horrible slums of the town, and the experience thus gained was of great value to their subsequent work. The League included forty Members of Parliament, through whose assistance it was hoped to promote a Bill which was to make attendance at schools compulsory. These schools were to be aided by Government grants, subject to Government inspection, and unsectarian. But the education as yet was not to be free. Mr. Forster's Bill of 1870 did not embody these principles, and was strongly opposed by the League. Mr. Chamberlain and eight other Birmingham men each gave £1,000 to carry on the campaign, but then as now he relied chiefly on the support of the working man. It was Education that first brought Mr. Chamberlain into prominence. He spoke frequently, headed deputations to Downing Street, and attracted Mr. Bright's attention by his uncompromising attitude. The Bill was amended, and the Acts of 1891 and 1903, if not fulfilling his ideal scheme, were a great advance towards it. In another direction Mr. Chamberlain's educationary exertions were more successful. To them mainly Birmingham University (of which he was the first Chancellor) owes its existence. Giving largely himself, he persuaded many others to emulate his generosity, chief among the donations being Mr. Carnegie's contribution of £50,000 and Lord Calthorpe's gift of a site for the new buildings. It is easy now in the light of his Tariff Reform Crusade to see why the establishment of a commercial faculty was made a prominent feature of the new University. As always Mr. Chamberlain was looking ahead.

Mr. Chamberlain's first Municipal efforts when he became a member of the Corporation in 1869 were directed to raising the exceedingly low status of that body by inducing men of ability and position to offer themselves for election. In 1873 most of these reformers were returned to office; their majority was large, and they at once elected Mr. Chamberlain as Mayor. The new Mayor's business training immediately showed him how funds could readily be obtained for the carrying out of three imperative reforms-the acquisition of the gas and water supply, and the improvement of a large area of slums. And it was the introduction of one of these reforms which was to pay for itself and the other two. He saw that the gas supply, if managed by the Corporation, would yield it profits far greater than the competing companies could ever make. It was, of course, necessary to increase very largely the borough debt, but he convinced his colleagues of the excellence of the scheme, and no better answer could have been given his opponents than the fact that within five years of the Corporation's acquisition of the works £80,000 had been carried to the relief of the rates, £50,000 to the reserve fund, and £35,000 to the sinking fund, while the gas supplied was both cheaper and better than before. The waterworks were acquired for the town in 1876. To assist in buying up the slum property Mr. Chamberlain and others opened an Improvement Trust fund to which he contributed £10,000. The cost of his scheme would be, he calculated, only £12,000 per annum, as against a yearly loss in wages of £54,000 through sickness and death in the pestilential districts. Besides the huge amount of local work that he performed during his term of mayoralty from 1873 to 1876, Mr. Chamberlain was enthusiastically assisting in the reorganisation of the Liberal Association, and was writing startling articles for John Morley in the *Fortnightly*, including his famous *The Next Page of the Liberal Programme* and *The Right Method with the Publicans*.

In February, 1875, Mr. Chamberlain's second wife

died after only six years of married life, but despite his heavy private troubles, he acceded to the Council's earnest request and continued in office till June, 1876, when, in place of George Dixon, who had resigned, he was elected a Member of Parliament for Birmingham. In his first address to his constituents Mr. Chamberlain told them that he went to Parliament as a representative of the working classes before all others, and as an advocate of a Free Church. A lengthy list of measures passed on behalf of the working classes could be made, with all of which Mr. Chamberlain's name is closely connected. His first speech was on the Education question, his second in defence of the dignity of local government, from whom it was proposed to transfer the financial control of Prisons to the Imperial Government. His third, and first markedly successful, speech embodied a resolution to the effect that municipalities should be empowered to acquire the control of the liquor traffic within their areas. His proposals were based on the Swedish system of licensing, which he had studied during a tour of Sweden and Lapland in company with Mr. Jesse Collings. Soon afterwards, at Mr. Chamberlain's initiative, all the Liberal Associations of the country were combined in the National Liberal Federation. Its object was to urge the leaders to move faster and further. Mr. Gladstone himself attended its first meeting, in every way one of the greatest ever held in Birmingham. In 1880 Mr. Chamberlain accepted Mr. Gladstone's offer of a seat in the Cabinet and the office of President of the Board of Trade. This necessitated his retirement from municipal affairs, and in recognition of his great services a memorial fountain was erected, bearing his medallion. Mr. Chamberlain's Bankruptcy Bill and Patents Bill were welcomed and became law, but his Merchant Shipping Bill he was obliged to abandon in view of the imminence of the great franchise fight. The Franchise Bill, on behalf -of which he spoke and felt very strongly, was passed in December, 1884. The following month came his much-criticised 'Ransom' speech, with its pregnant question, "What ransom, therefore, will property pay for the security it enjoys, what substitute will it find for the natural rights of which the poor have been deprived?" On Mr. Gladstone's return to power, after Lord Salisbury's short 'Stop-Gap' Government, he put aside everything to offer

Ireland Home Rule, and it was with much precautionary reserve that Mr. Chamberlain again accepted office. He was evidently apprehensive of the Premier's intentions, and he expressed his determination "that the integrity of the Empire should be a reality and not an empty phrase". Of Irish reform he approved to an even greater extent than his leader, but it was and has always been his conviction that it must be given under a purely local form of government. The true reason of his opposition to the Home Rule Bills of 1886 and 1893, and of his resignation of office in 1886, was his discovery that in Mr. Gladstone's hands they did undoubtedly tend to the dismemberment of the Empire. By his resignation he certainly threw away his potential grasp of the Premiership. In the autumn of 1887 Mr. Chamberlain accepted Mr. Gladstone's proposal that he should represent Great Britain in a dispute with the United States touching fishery rights off the coasts of Canada and Newfoundland. The Treaty as actually proposed was not ratified, but a temporary modus vivendi was agreed which has successfully taken the place of the Treaty. There is no doubt that during his stay in America Mr. Chamberlain was in continual, danger of his life from members of the Clan-na-Gael. If he failed in settling the public Treaty, he certainly arranged a private one for himself, which resulted in his marriage with Miss Mary Endicott, daughter of an ex-Minister of the United States Government. On his return he was the first to receive the honour of the Freedom of the Borough of Birmingham. In 1892 Mr. Chamberlain's elder son, Austen, entered Parliament as member for East Worcestershire, and met with a reception in the House and a compliment from Mr. Gladstone on his maiden speech which must have been especially gratifying to his father. Although, apart from Home Rule, Mr. Gladstone and Mr. Chamberlain differed essentially on another subject—colonial expansion—it is pleasant to be able to record that before the former's death the two great statesmen renewed their personal friendship at a luncheon at Mr. Gladstone's residence.

Mr. Chamberlain's term of office as Colonial Secretary began in Lord Salisbury's Cabinet in 1895. To Colonists he brought a new relationship with the Mother Country. Whilst giving the off-spring freedom of control from Downing Street, which was as fresh as it was necessary, that policy had the effect of drawing them nearer in spirit and action than had ever been achieved by any former British Cabinet. Mr. Chamberlain had a sympathetic feeling for his kin beyond the seas; they realised and reciprocated the sentiment. That is the secret of it all. In Africa the name of Joseph Chamberlain has been indelibly impressed. West Africa has become another land since he first took up the portfolio, and the characteristics of the east of the Continent are now as pretty well known as an English province. The personality of Mr. Chamberlain kindled a new spirit in the colonist. The old inclination to cut the painter gave place to a desire for closer attachment and the wish to rally to the old country in her hour of trial and need. His trust of the "men on the spot" produced a sense of responsibility, and the knowledge that they would not be thrown over for the exigencies of home politics made them anxious not to do anything which would embarrass their chief. He assumed public servants abroad to be as incapable of unnecessary brutality as the most high-souled home politician, but he recognised that acts of justice which do not accord with what is considered necessary in this country are imperative in lands where only such lessons are taken to heart. Mr. Chamberlain, as Colonial Secretary, did not, however, give every official full play of life and death of the coloured people under him; and it will be remembered, in the House of Commons debate in 1905 on flogging in the Navy, he described how he had restrained the use of the lash in the Crown colonies.

It is convenient to divide Mr. Chamberlain's eight years of strenuous work as Colonial Secretary into two parts-the period of war and the period of peace. All Kruger's subtle contrivances, evasions, lying and secret plans failed to fool Mr. Chamberlain. Though long patient, he never for a moment wavered from his declaration that England must always remain the paramount power in South Africa. Moreover at the time of the War he was quick to thank the Colonies for their offers of assistance and to acknowledge that England's allies were now the sons of the Empire throughout the world. On May 28, 1899, the petition of the Outlanders for redress of their grievances was accepted by the Home Government, and the Bloemfontein Conference was arranged between the British High Commissioner, Sir A. Milner, and President Kruger. Throughout the whole of 1899 tremendous responsibilities rested on the Colonial Secretary. Again and again he impressed upon the House the impossibility of allowing the independence of the Transvaal, unless concessions could be obtained from President Kruger a thousand times more satisfactory than those He offered. They were not forthcoming. On October 9, 1899, the Boer Government sent in their ultimatum, and war was, of course, immediately declared. During the autumn session Mr. Chamberlain had to reply to fierce accusations that the war was the result of his policy. He showed clearly that words having failed, a recourse to arms had been inevitable, that there had been no other alternative. Our early defeats daunted him not a whit. Again he proved that the war was just and necessary, that it must be carried through to the finish, that there should be no second Majuba. At this inopportune moment a section of the House insisted upon a reopening of the Jameson Raid Inquiry. Malicious charges of implication in the Raid were brought against Mr. Chamberlain before a Parliamentary Commission, but were utterly disproved. The war was undoubtedly prolonged by the speeches of the accredited leaders of Her Majesty's Opposition, in particular by that of Sir H. Campbell-Bannerman referring to "methods of barbarism" employed by our Army in the field, and Mr. Chamberlain was called upon to answer every manner of (sometimes malicious) criticisms on its conduct. In short, every difficulty was thrown in his way, and there could have been no happier man than the Colonial Secretary when amid enthusiastic cheering he entered the House on June 2, 1902, the day after the proclamation of peace.

But even then the problems that faced him and Lord Milner in their great task of evolving order out of chaos and of burying animosities of the past were sufficiently difficult. Many of them were solved in the course of Mr. Chamberlain's great tour through South Africa, in which he travelled over 16,000 miles, gained much experience of the local 'atmosphere', went through all the machinery of deputations, conferences, interviews, complaints, petitions, addresses, presentations, banquets, and gave in return the assurance so greatly desired that in the future the mother-country would extend not only consideration, not only help, but the larger necessities of sympathy and understanding. But he spoke strongly against the idea that the existence of a grievance should in any way affect the loyalty of a British subject. In his own words, "it will be a bad day for the Empire when people consider loyalty as an item in the ledger account". Mr. Chamberlain visited all the chief towns and met many prominent Boers. To all he made clear the firmness that characterised the policy of the Imperial Government, that conciliation was only possible so far as it led to union; and this was the text of all his speeches. To petitioners for modification of the terms of peace he was not only adamant, but strongly rebuked them. Moreover immediate self-government was not to be expected. The tour ended at Cape Town. On his return Mr. Chamberlain made some interesting remarks on his tour, and expressed his confidence in a successful future for South Africa, provided that all forces in the Empire should co-operate loyally to that end. He said: "I leave South Africa with the firm conviction that Providence, which out of evil still brings forth good, will evolve some compensation for the suffering and misery that a great war entails. I leave more than ever convinced that the natural forces which are drawing you together are more potent than those evil influences which would tend to separate you."

Mr. Chamberlain strongly dislikes publicity in anything concerning his private life. His Birmingham home, named Highbury after the suburb in London where his boyhood was spent, is a large but by no means palatial residence. Mr. Chamberlain preferred, when he left Southbourne in 1880, to remain in close touch with the town and his relatives at Moor Green, instead of buying, as it was expected he would do, some big seat in the Midlands. It goes without saying that he has a remarkably fine library. It is probable that Mr. Chamberlain might have taken a high place in literature had not politics claimed him for their own. He studied it carefully in his youth, and the articles that he has published all show great literary ability. He has also an excellent and cultured taste in art. In the fine gardens attached to the house are the greenhouses which daily supply the famous orchid for Mr. Chamberlain's button-hole. Not

infrequently the grounds are filled with parties of Mr. Chamberlain's constituents, his working men friends and admirers. The family is remarkably happy and united. Mrs. Chamberlain is her husband's comrade and constant companion. One of the rare occasions on which his self-control has failed him and he has been overcome for the instant by emotion was at the banquet given before his departure for South Africa. In answering the part of Mr. C. E. Matthews's speech which referred to the help and support given him by Mrs. Chamberlain, he faltered and almost broke down.

The wonderful success of the combination of Mr. Chamberlain and Mr. Balfour as leaders was due undoubtedly to their chief qualities being those most needful for successful leader-ship, but which are almost incapable of inclusion in one character. Firmness is Mr. Chamberlain's nature, conciliation Mr. Balfour's. To the union of these was added an equal and unapproached power of speech, and the result was unique, almost perfect. Much they did together, more they would certainly have done, had Mr. Balfour's scruples allowed him to accept completely his colleague's Tariff Reform policy. The present article is intended to recount Mr. Chamberlain's career up till the General Election of the early part of 1906 only, and it may perhaps be fitly closed by a brief exposition of his Imperial scheme. Its end is perhaps at present over-shadowed and apt to be ignored in the magnitude of the means. Yet to gain a full appreciation of Mr. Chamberlain's attitude it must be remembered that Tariff Reform, great though its intrinsic worth be, is yet only the means. The end is Imperial Federation, the consolidation of the greatest Empire the world has ever seen. Imperialism has always held a high place in Mr. Chamberlain's creed; on that point his convictions have never altered, and they have inevitably led him on to the making of this campaign. Commercial union, he is assured, is the one unbreakable tie of Federation, as commercial prosperity is the primal necessity for the well-being of a State. And that commercial prosperity is obtained by dealing with the best customers is almost a truism. Who then are, and-still more important-who in the future will be, the best customers? Obviously young countries-countries with almost unlimited opportunities for development and growth. But the vast majority of these countries are our own colonies, easy to retain as our customers through the strength of the invisible bonds of race, faith, and sentiment. Surely then at any cost these must be retained. And the cost is a preferential tariff in their favour.

There have always been three fundamental propositions underlying Mr. Chamberlain's dream of Imperial Federation. Firstly: the union of the mother-country with all parts of the Empire must become closer. Secondly: the demand for that closer union must come from the colonies themselves. Thirdly: when the demand comes it must be met, and probably at some sacrifice. Now the demand has come. Now change, and perhaps sacrifice, are necessary. Hence has arisen the Tariff Reform Crusade. And in our midst, too, the necessity for change is clearly apparent. The cry for work of thousands of unemployed, of steady, deserving, skilled, or unskilled artisans, not of hypocritical loafers, is a good and sufficient reason out of scores that could be found. Mr. Chamberlain contends that if his proposals are accepted, the increased orders from the colonies would force manufacturers to take on more men, to provide work and wages for the unemployed. Again the increased prosperity of the colonies would enable them to offer greater inducements to the British immigrant, and to find employment for them in greater numbers. Then there is the process known as 'dumping'. We are the dumping ground of the world, and it is a most effectual method of diminishing trade. It throws on to British markets large quantities of foreign-made goods, similar to British-made, which are sold at cost price or even less. The foreign maker does not care; he has made his profit in his own country, and is only anxious to get something for his surplus goods. But these dumped goods compete, of course, with the home-made article, whose makers, owing to our present fiscal system (or lack of one), are unable to retaliate. Mr. Chamberlain has thoroughly expounded his system. Unfortunately only actual trial can prove its merits, and this trial his opponents refuse to give. Until Mr. Chamberlain's ideals find root in the convictions and consciences of his fellow-countrymen, the success of his crusade largely depends on a continuance of his bodily health and powers. But he is hopeful that his great lesson has already been taken to the hearts of the

people. It is a simple lesson. Mr. Chamberlain himself has summed it up in four words, words that touch, perhaps, the key-note of his career: "learn to think Imperially".

CHAMBERLAIN, Colonel Sir Neville Francis Fitzgerald, K.C.B., of Oatlands, Castleknock, Dublin; and of the Kildare St., Dublin, and Naval and Military Clubs, was born in 1856, and is the only son of the late Lieut.-Col. C. F. Falcon Chamberlain, C.B. He joined the Army in 1873, being attached to the Devonshire Regt. until 1876, when he joined the Central India Horse; took part in the Afghan War in 1878-80, on the staff of Sir F. Roberts, being present at the action at Kandahar (medal with four clasps and bronze star); and acted as A.D.C. to Sir F. Roberts from 1881-5, and from then until 1890 he acted as Persian interpreter; served in the Burmese Expedition in 1886-7 (medal and clasp), and acted as Private Secretary to Field Marshal Lord Roberts in the late S. African War. Sir Neville retired in 1900 from the Army, when he was appointed Insp.-Gen. of the Royal Irish Constabulary. He married, in 1886, Mary, dau. of the late Major-Gen. Hay.

CHAMBERS, Charles Roland, J.P. for Richmond (C.C.) and Smithfield (O.R.C.), of Middlemount, Richmond District, Cape Colony, is the son of S. H. Chambers, Barrister-at-Law, Inner Temple, and his mother was one of the family of Hares, of Hurstmonceaux Castle, Sussex. His grandfather was Sir Charles H. Chambers, Puisne Judge, Bombay, and his grandfather on the maternal side was Captain Marcus Hare, R.N., of Court Grange, Newton, Devon. He was born Nov. 1, 1863, in London, and was educated at Tonbridge Sch. and Clifton Coll. He went to Cape Colony in 1889 and purchased the property of Middlemount, in the District of Richmond, and was appointed a J.P. in 1893. On the S.A. War breaking out he served in the Transport Service under General Paget with the 20th Brigade at Lindley, Bethlehem, etc., and subsequently in the Northern Transvaal. He joined the Scouts, and was commissioned in the S. African Irregular Forces as Lieut. He was with the columns in O.R.C. and Western Transvaal, and was finally transferred to the Field Intelligence Department and given the rank of Capt. At the conclusion of hostilities he was appointed Pres. of the

Repatriation Commission for the District of Smithfield, O.R.C., by the Governor of the Colony, and subsequently Administrator of Relief for the same District. He has the Queen's medal and three clasps and the King's medal and two clasps. He married Ruby Mabel Montagu, dau. of John Montagu, and great-granddau. of John Montagu, Colonial Sec. of Cape Colony.

CHAMBERS, Frederick W., of Winchester House London, E.C., is the London Secretary of the General Mining and Finance Corporation Ltd. and is on the London Committee of the Aurora West United G.M. Co., Ltd., Cinderella Deep, Ltd., Rand Collieries, Ltd., Roodeport United Main Reef G.M. Co., Ltd., and the W. Rand Mines, Ltd.

CHAMBERS, Sydney, of Crete Hill, South Nutfield, Surrey, is Chairman of the Pretoria Estates Ltd., South African Hotels, Ltd., and the Winchester G.M. Co., Ltd., Deputy Chairman of the South African Breweries, Ltd., on the London Committee of the Rooderand G.M. Co., Ltd., and on the London Board of the Jubilee Gold Mining Co., Ltd., and the Salisbury G.M. Co., Ltd. Mr. Chambers's son, Sydney H. Chambers, is well known on the Rand, and married a dau. of George Raw (q.v.).

CHAMIER, Major George Daniel, C.M.G., of 64, Inverness Terrace, Hyde Park, W., and of the United Service and Constitutional Clubs, was born in the E. Indies, Sept. 24, 1860, and is son of Lt.-Gen. S. H. E. Chamier, C.B. He was educated at Cheltenham Coll. and the R.M.A.. Woolwich, where he was gymnastic champion in 1879. He has won numerous prizes at tent-pegging, lemon-cutting, etc., and as an amateur rider and owner of horses between 1880-90, including the challenge cup for the best all-round man at games and skill at arms, in 1888. He took up golf in 1890, and won several prizes from the scratch marks, including the championship of the Cape-Peninsular (Robertson trophy) in 1898. He served in the Royal Horse and Field Art. in India, 1880-5, at Gibraltar in the R. Garrison Art. in 1888-90 and 1891-97, and from 1891-6 as Adjt. in the Lanes. Art. He took part in the S. African War, and commanded the Artillery in the defence of Kimberley, with the local rank of Lt.-Col., was commandant of Kimberley (graded as

D.A.A.G.), 1900-01, defended Schweitzer Reinicke, in the Transvaal, and commanded a mobile column in the attack on Petrusburg, O.R.C., in 1901, when the town was captured. Appointed Commandant and Special Commissioner in the Bloemhof Dist., Transvaal, in 1901-2 (Queen's medal with three clasps, King's medal with two clasps, and created C.M.G.). Recreations: cricket, golf, billiards, and hunting. He married, in 1903, Amy St. Leger, widow of the Hon. James Buchanan, and dau. of the late H. J. Bertram, of Queenstown, S. Africa.

CHARLESWORTH, Francis, M.B., C.M. Edin. (1883), of Zanzibar, and of the Badminton and Thatched House Clubs, was born in London, April 6, 1859; is son of T. D. Charlesworth, and was educated at Blair Lodge Sch. and at Edinburgh University. He was appointed Medical Officer to H.M. Agency at Zanzibar in 1897. He married, in 1903, Mary Frances, dau. of the Hon. Mrs. Ram.

CHARRINGTON, Col. Francis, C.M.G., of Pishiobury, Sawbridgeworth, Herts., and of the Union Club, was born Nov. 17, 1858, in Herts., and is son of the late Spencer Charrington, M.P., of Humsden House, Herts. He was educated at Winchester; joined the lst K.O. Staffordshire Militia in 1880, and was appointed to the command of the 4th Battn. South Staffordshire Regt. in 1895, commanding his battn. in the S.A. War in 1899-1901, during which period he was present at the operations about Lindley, Bethlehem, Fouriesburg, and Winburg (despatches, C.M.G., medal and three clasps). Col. Charrington is a director of Charrington and Co., Ltd., brewers. His recreations are hunting and fishing, and he married, in 1885, Alice Maud., dau. of Walter Leith, J.P., of Leicestershire.

CHAUVEL. Lt.-Col. Henry George, C.M.G., of Victoria Barracks, Brisbane, and of the Queensland Club, was born at Tabulam, N.S.W., April 16, 1865. He was educated at Sydney Grammar Sch. and Toowoomba Grammar Sch., Queensland; joined the N.S.W. Cavalry Regt. as 2nd Lt. in 1886, and the Queensland Mounted Inf. in 1890; served in the Queensland Police with temporary rank of Sub-Insp. during the civil troubles in Western Queensland in 1894-5, and in S. Africa with the Q.M.I., afterwards with the 7th Battn. of Australian Commonwealth Horse with the temporary rank of Lt.-Col. Unmarried.

CHESHAM, Major-Gen. Rt. Hon. Lord, K.C.B., J.P., of Latimer House, Chesham, Bucks, and of the Marlborough, Guards', and Turf Clubs, was born in 1850. He was educated at Eton, and entered the Coldstream Guards in 1870, afterwards joining the 10th Hussars in 1873, and the 16th Lancers in 1878, retiring in the following year. He served in South Africa in 1899-1902, as Brig. Gen. on the Staff, in command of a Brigade of Imperial Yeomanry, after wards as Inspector-Gen. of Imperial Yeomanry; present at the operations in the Orange Free State and the Transvaal, including the actions at Venterskroon; the operations in the Orange River Colony, and the actions at Lindley and Rhenoster River, and in Cape Colony, north of the Orange River (despatches, Queen's medal with three clasps, King's medal with two clasps, and K.C.B.)

Lord Chesham is now Hon. Col. of the Royal Bucks Hussars, and since 1901 has been Lord of the Bedchamber to H.R.H. the Prince of Wales. In 1906 he sat as a member of the Committee of the Volunteer Commission. He married, in 1877, Lady Beatrice Grosvenor, dau. of the Duke of Westminster.

CHESTER-MASTER, Lieut.-Col. R. (See Master, Lieut.-Col. R. C.).

CHICHESTER, Lieut. Sir Edward George, Bart., of Youlston, Barnstaple, Devon, was born in 1883, and is son of the late Rear-Admiral Chichester, who died in Sept., 1906. Sir Edward Chichester is a Lieutenant in the Royal Navy, and served in South Africa during the Anglo-Boer War.

CHOLES, Major Frederick John, F.R.G.S., F.I.Inst., F.R.C.I., of Scott St., Pietermaritzburg, third son of Jas. Choles, of Devizes, Wilts, was born at Wolverhampton, Staffordshire, Dec. 24, 1847. He was, educated at the Wolverhampton Gram. Sch., and received a practical training as an engineer in the London and N.-W. Locomotive Engineering Depts. In 1869 he was selected by the late Maj.-Gen. Worgan, R.A., Inspector-Gen. of

Ordnance, Bombay, for special duty in connection with the Powder Mills and Ammunition Factories at Kirkee, India. Subsequently his services were solicited at the Grand Arsenal and Government Dockyards, Bombay, to supervise the erection of the 18-ton guns for H.M. turret ships, *Abyssinia* and *Magdala*, of the Bombay Harbour Defence. In 1874 he was again sent forward on special duty to the arsenals at Mhow and Neemich, Central India. In 1879 he was the successful candidate from among nearly 200 applicants for the post of Ordnance Officer, Natal Volunteer Dept., which he now holds.

Owing to his many years of experience and his natural abilities for the special duties pertaining to Ordnance work, he has brought the Ordnance branch of the Natal Volunteer Dept., of which he is the chief, from its infancy to a state of efficiency, and as far as practicable up to date in all details of military requirements. In 1899 he had the responsibility of equipping the Volunteers, and putting forward the mobilisation stores for the whole of the Natal Force, which were railed at Pietermaritzburg for Ladysmith within 24 hours from the time instructions were received for mobilisation. In Sept. and Oct. of the same year, he equipped those smart Irregular Corps, the Imperial Light Horse, Bethune's M.I., and Thorneycroft's M.I. He was at the base of operations, Pietermaritzburg, during the S.A. War, Sept. 13, 1899, to May 31, 1902 (Queen's and King's medals). He married Johanna Jane, third dau. of Edward and Mary Vale, of Upper Clapton, London, on Sept. 6, 1880.

CHOLMONDELEY-PENNELL, Henry, of Palace Mansions, Kensington, W., and of the Hurlingham, Queen's, Sports, and Fly-fishers' Clubs, was born in London, Feb. 13, 1838; is eldest son of the late Sir Henry Pennell, great grandson of Sir Philip Francis, the inveterate opponent of Warren Hastings, and whose name is so generally associated with the authorship of *Junius*. Mr. Pennell was educated privately, and his official career commenced at the Admiralty, subsequently, from about 1867 to 1875, holding the post of H.M. Inspector of Sea Fisheries under the Board of Trade. In the latter year he became Director of Interior Commerce, Egypt—a new Dept. which he organised, receiving for his services special recognition from the Khedive. Mr. Pennell has penned numerous official reports, and besides contributing to many important periodicals, has published some poems and books on Sport, including two volumes on Fishing in the Badminton Library. In addition to his prowess as an angler, he has been described as one of the straightest shots and straightest riders in England.

CHRISTIE, H. Duncan, of Ordiquhill, Gordon Terrace, Edinburgh, is a director of the Geld Proprietary Mines, Ltd., Montgomerie and Co., Ltd., and the United African Explorations, Ltd.

CHRISTOPHERSON, Stanley, of 47, Prince's Gardens, London, S.W., is a director of the Consolidated Gold Fields of South Africa, Ltd., New Geld Coast Agency, Ltd. and the South African Gold Trust, Ltd.

CHURCHILL, Winston Leonard Spencer, M.P., of 12, Bolton St., London, W., was born Nov. 30, 1874, and is the son of the late Lord Randolph Churchill, and of the clever American lady who is now Mrs. George Cornwallis West. He was educated at Harrow and Sandhurst, whence he passed into a Hussar Regt. in 1895. He took part in Cuba with the Spanish forces; served with the Malakand Field Force; was in the Tirah Expedition, and in the Nile Expedition he was present at the battle and occupation of Khartoum, being attached to the 21st Lancers. In the S. African War Mr. Churchill acted as correspondent of the *Morning Post*, and as such witnessed some of the most thrilling incidents, and was himself taken prisoner to Pretoria, from where he made a sensational escape over the Portuguese frontier. But these adventures were merely the hurried prelude to the more serious affairs of life. In 1900 he contested Oldham as a Conservative, and won the seat. Since then, however, his political views underwent a radical change. Crossing over to the Opposition, he was repudiated by the Oldham Conservative Association, and at the General Election in 1906 he found a seat at N.-W. Manchester, for which he was returned by a large majority as a Liberal and a Free-Trader, having just previously joined Sir Henry Campbell-Bannerman's Ministry as Under-Secretary of State for the Colonies. It will be

recalled that Mr. Wanklyn, when M.P. for Bradford, told his constituents of an alleged plot by which Mr. Winston Churchill sought in 1902 to overthrow the Conservative Govt. in order to let in a weak Radical Ministry, which in turn was to be overthrown by Mr. Churchill and his political allies, who were then to lead back to power a rejuvenated Conservative Unionist party. The story, however, was as resolutely denied by Mr. Churchill as it was stoutly maintained by Mr. Wanklyn. Mr. Churchill's entry into office was marked by his relentless attacks upon Mr. Chamberlain, a partial withdrawal from the Chinese 'slavery' charges, and a general eagerness to support, if not lead, his chief, Lord Elgin, in the disturbing S. African policy pursued by the new Liberal Government-a policy of interference which, amongst other things, led to the resignation of the whole of the Natal Cabinet as a protest against the interference of the home Govt. in matters of colonial domestic affairs. Mr. Churchill has written a considerable number of books, mainly as a result of his observations on active service. He lately produced a life of his father, Lord Randolph Churchill, and those who have not had a surfeit of his views on the fiscal question may read his speeches *For Free Trade*, published in 1906. Unmarried.

CLARK, James A. R., of Suffolk House London, E.C., is a director of Mitchell's Creel Gold Mines, Ltd., and the Northern Nigeria Exploration Syndicate, Ltd.

CLARK, William Henderson, of Salisbury House, London, E.C., is managing director in England of the Anglo-French Exploration Co., Ltd., and is in the London Committee of the Anglo-French Land Co., of the Transvaal, Ltd., Anglo-French (Transvaal) Navigation Coal Estates, Ltd., Chimes West, Ltd., Kleinfontein Deep, Ltd., Klipfontein Estate and G.M. Co., Ltd., and the Van Ryn Deep, Ltd.

CLEMES, H. P., of Sunnyside, Moss Hall Grove, Finchley, N., is a director of the Golden Valley (Mashonaland) Mines, Ltd., Mashonaland Consolidated, Ltd., Rhodesia Consolidated, Ltd., and the Rhodesia Mines Trust, Ltd.

CLIFTON, H. A., of 36, Buckingham Gate, S.W., is a director of the Barberton Exploring and Development Co., Ltd., Jourdie Hills G.M. Co., Ltd., North Sheba Gold and Exploration, Ltd., and the South African Mining Syndicate, Ltd.

CLOETE, Louis Gerald, B.A., was educated at the Cape University. He acted as Clerk to the Colonial Secretary in British Bechuanaland in 1895; to the Res. Magistrate at Vryburg in 1895; to the Attorney General at Cape Town in 1896; to the Resident Magistrate at Wynberg, Cape Colony, in 1897, and at Simonstown and Cape Town in 1898; also acted as Clerk to the Civil Commissioner at Cape Town in 1899. He took part in the South African War in 1899-1900 as Lieutenant in the S. African Light Horse and Roberts's Horse (medal and three clasps); was appointed Resident Magistrate at Winburg, O.R.C., in 1900; also acted as District Commissioner and Superintendent of the Refugee Camp there in 1900; Resident Magistrate at Frankfort in 1902; Chairman of the Repatriation Commission in 1902-3; President of the Ex-Burgher Claims Board in 1902-3, and was appointed with the Military Assessor to hear Protected Burgher claims in 1903, and Special Commissioner to hear claims of British subjects, foreigners, and natives in 1902-3.

COHEN, Arthur W., of 11, Queen Victoria Street, London, E.C., is a director of the Adventurers (Ashanti and Wassau), Ltd., African and General Exploration Co., Ltd., Ashanti Three Rivers Syndicate, Ltd., and the Soowin Concessions, Ltd.

COHEN, Joseph W., of 11, Queen Victoria Street, London, E.C., is managing director of the Adventurers (Ashanti and Wassau), Ltd., African and General Exploration Co:, Ltd., and the Ashanti Three Rivers Syndicate, Ltd., and is director of the Soowin Concessions, Ltd.

COHEN, Samuel F., of Finsbury House, London, E.C., is Chairman of the South Randfontein Deep, Ltd., director of the Arndt Reefs G.M. Co., Ltd., and is on the London Committee of the Angolan Mining and Finance Co., Ltd., Bantjes Deep, Ltd.,

Durban Roodepoort Deep, Ltd., and the South Village Deep, Ltd.

COKE, Viscount, C.M.G., M.V.O., of 67, Grosvenor Street, Grosvenor Square, W., was born in 1845, and is the eldest son of the second Earl of Leicester. He was educated at Harrow; joined the Scots Guards, in which regiment he attained the rank of Colonel; is now Lieut.-Col. commanding the Prince of Wales' Own Norfolk Artillery. He went through the Egyptian War of 1882, taking part in the action of Mahuta and the battle of Tel-el-Kebir, for which he was awarded the medal with clasp and the Khedive's Star. Three years later he accompanied the 2nd Scots Guards in the Expedition to the Sudan, and took part in the engagements at Hasheen and Tamai. Viscount Coke retired from the Army in 1894, subsequently serving in the South African War in 1901-2, during which he officiated as Commandant at Orange River, and took part in several actions, for which he was mentioned in despatches and received the C.M.G. He married, in 1879, the Hen. Alice White, dau. of the second Lord Annaly.

COKE, Hon. Thomas William, of 67, Grosvenor Square, London, W., is eldest son of Viscount Coke (q.v.), and was born July 9, 1850. He entered the Scots Guards as Second Lieut. in 1900, and saw active service in the South African War in 1901-2, taking part in the operations in the Cape Colony from Dec., 1901, to May, 1902. He was promoted Lieut. in Jan., 1902.

COLLEY, Capt. Gerald Henry Pomeroy, 3rd Royal Irish Regt., of Boksburg, Transvaal, and Mount Temple, Clontarf, Co. Dublin, was born at Lucan, Dublin; was educated at Haileybury, and is a member of Inner Temple, London. He was successively A.D.C. to Sir Henry A. Blake, Governor of Jamaica; A.D.C. and Priv. Secy. to Sir Augustus L. Hemming, Governor of Jamaica; and Inspector of Jamaica Constabulary. He served through the S.A. War with the 1st M.I. as Special Service Officer (Queen's and King's medals); was later appointed Military Magistrate at Boksburg, under the Military Governor of Johannesburg, and is at present Asst. R.M. at Boksburg.

COLLYER, Lieut. John Johnston, of the Cape Mounted Rifles, entered the corps in 1889, and served with the Pondoland Field Force in 1894. He also served in the South African War in 1899-1902, as Field Adjutant to the Colonial Division in 1900-1, Adjutant to the C.J.M.R. in 1901, and as Staff Officer for Supplies, Transport and Equipment to No. 1 Division of the Cape Colonial Forces (Queen's medal with three clasps, and King's medal with two clasps). In 1903 he was seconded for service with the Border Light Horse as Captain and Adjutant, and was appointed Staff Officer to the Commandant-Gen. of the C.M.R. in 1904, which position he still holds.

COLNAGHI, Major Dominic Henry, R.E. of the Junior United Service Club, was born at Turin, March 15, 1866, and is son of Sir Dominic E. Colnaghi, formerly H.B.M.'s Consul-Gen. for N. Italy and H.B.M.'s Consul-Gen. at Boston, U.S.A. He was educated at Cheltenham Coll. and the R.M.A., Woolwich; and entered the R.E. in 1885; served in Egypt in 1890-4, and in Malta, 1894-97. He was adjutant in the E. London R.E. Vols. from 1897-99, and took part in the S.A. War as staff officer of R.E. in the eastern part of Cape Colony from 1900 until the close of the war. He was employed in constructing defences for the protection of new naval docks at Simon's Bay, C.C., from 1903 until 1905. He was the winner of a gymnastic competition while a cadet at the R.M.A., and was captain of the Boating Club at Cheltenham Coll. Recreations : Riding, tennis, and cycling.

COLQUHOUN, Archibald Ross, F.R.G. S., F.R.C.L, of 43, Bedford Gardens, London, W., and of the Royal Societies' Club, London, was born at sea, off the Cape of Good Hope, his father having been Dr. Archibald Colquhoun, of the H.E.I.C.S. He was educated in Scotland and Germany, and joined the Indian Pub. Works Dept. in 1871; was attached to the Govt. of India Mission to Siam in 1879; explored Canton-Bhamo through S.-W. China, 1881-2; and was *Times* correspondent in the Far East in 1883-4; visited Siam in connection with railway proposals in 1885; was Deputy Commissioner in Upper Burma, 1885-9; and was Administrator of Mashonaland, 1890-2. In 1893 he travelled in the U.S.A., and went over the

Nicaragua and Panama Canal routes in 1895. The following year found him in China in connection with railway schemes; travelled through Siberia and Mongolia to China in 1898-9, returning via Siberia in 1900-1. Mr. Colquhoun has published *Across Chryse* (1883), *Railway Communication, India and China* (1885), *The Key of the Pacific* (1895), *China in Transformation* (1898), *The Overland to China* (1900), *The Mastery of the Pacific* (1902), *Greater America* (1904), and has contributed to the *Quarterly Review*, *Monthly Review*, *Harper's Mag.*, *North American Review*, and the *Morning Post*. He married, in 1900, Ethel, dau. of S. Cookson, M.D., of Stafford.

COLVILE, Maj.-Gen. Sir Henry Edward, K.C.M.G., C.B., of Lightwater, Bagshot; Lullington, Burton-on-Trent; Grangewood House, Ashby-de-la-Zouch; 80, South Audley Street, W.; and of the Guards', Travellers', Beefsteak, Automobile, and Aero Clubs, and member of the Royal Yacht Squadron, son of the late Col. Chas. R. Colvile, J.P., D.L., and M.P. for S. Derbyshire, and Katherine, dau. of 23rd Baroness de Clifford and Captain Jn. Russell, R.N., was born at Kirkley Hall, Hinckley, Leicestershire, July 10, 1852. He was educated at Eton and privately in Switzerland and France, meanwhile travelling about considerably with his father on yachting cruises. Sir Henry entered the Grenadier Guards in 1870. In 1878 he undertook a journey to Morocco, explored the Riff country, and was the first European to cross from Fez to Algeria, his account of which, *A Ride in Petticoats and Slippers*, was published in 1879. In 1880 he was appointed A.D.C. to Gen. the Hon. Sir Leicester Smythe, who then commanded the British forces at the Cape. He resigned this on attaining his Captaincy, and shortly after took part in an expedition to survey and report upon the country between the Dead Sea and the Gulf of Akabah. This accomplished, he was appointed to Sir F. Stevenson's Intelligence Department at Cairo, joined the Suakim Expedition in 1884, and was present at El Teb and Tamai, receiving medal and clasp, the Khedivial Star, and being twice mentioned in despatches. After returning to England, he was selected for a special mission to survey the Arbain Road and report on the possibility of the Mahdi invading Egypt by this route. Having reported in the negative, he was detailed for further important work in the Sudan before and during Lord Wolseley's expedition, meanwhile being promoted Lieut.-Col. For these services he was mentioned in despatches (clasp and C.B.). He was next Chief of the Intelligence Department of the Frontier Field Force, was present at the action at Gennis (despatches), and attained Colonel's rank. Sir Henry returned home in 1866, was appointed to the Intelligence Department of the War Office, and wrote the official history of the Sudan Campaign. During a term of sick leave he made the tour of South Africa accompanied by Lady Colvile, who subsequently published her book, *Round the Black Man's Garden*. Sir Henry also crossed Madagascar from Antananarivo to Majunga. Early in 1893 he went to India, and subsequently as Intelligence Officer to a British column in Burma. Thence he was placed in charge at Uganda, and established a post on the Albert Nyanza. All this hard work caused a breakdown in Col. Colvile's health, and he returned home, was decorated with the K.C.M.G., Central African medal, and the Star of Zanzibar. He resumed regimental duty, and in 1898 was gazetted Maj.-Gen. In 1899 he was appointed to command the Infantry Brigade in Gibraltar, thence being appointed (March 1900) to command the 9th Division in S.A. (medal and 5 clasps). He was mentioned in despatches four times by Lord Methuen and twice by the C.I.C. in S.A. for services at Paardeberg and Poplar Grove, but it is regretted that his military reputation was not enhanced by the incidents of Sanna's Post and Lindley. He was soon reappointed to Gibraltar by Lord Lansdowne, but in February, 1901, was recalled and placed on retired pay by Mr. Brodrick. Sir Henry has also written a description of his Akabah exploration, entitled *The Accursed Land*, *The History of the Sudan Campaign*, *The Land of the Nile Springs*, describing his Unyoro Expedition, *The Work of the Ninth Division*, and occasional contributions to the Press. Sir Henry married, first, in 1878, Alice Rosa, daughter of the Hon. Robert Daly, who died in 1882; and second, in 1886, Zelie Isabelle, daughter of M. Pierre Richard de Preville, of Basses Pyrenees, France.

COLVIN, Sir Auckland, K.C.S.I., K.C.M.G., C.I.E., Grand Cordon of the Orders of Osmanieh and Medjidieh, of Earl Soham Lodge, Framlingham, Suffolk, and of the Travellers' Club, is the son of the late John R. Colvin, Indian Civil Service. He was born March 8, 1838, in India, and was educated at Eton and the East India Coll., Haileybury, and entered the Indian Civil Service in 1858. He has held with success a number of Govt. secretaryships of importance, was in 1879 appointed British Member of the Caisse de la Dette Publique in Cairo, was made a member of the International Commission for Egyptian Liquidation in 1880, and shortly afterwards became the representative of England under the scheme of Anglo-French control. When the dual control was abolished in 1883 he became Financial Adviser to the Khedive (1882-3), but shortly after he returned to India as Financial member of the Viceroy's Council, in which capacity he introduced and passed an Income-Tax Bill in 1886. In 1887 he was Lieut.-Governor of the North-West Provinces of India and Chief Commissioner of Oudh, retaining that position till 1902. He is Chairman of the Burma Railways, of the Egyptian Delta Light Railways, of the Oriental Telephone Co., of the Khedivial Steamship Co., and a Director of the British and Chinese Corporation. He married, Aug. 4, 1859, Charlotte Elizabeth, dau. of Lieut.-Gen. Herbert. C.B., who died in 1865.

CONGLETON, Major-Gen. Lord, C.B., of Anneville, Mullingar, Co. Westmeath, and the Carlton and United Service Clubs, was born in 1839, and is the second son of the third Baron who was a midshipman on the *Glasgow* at Navarino, and was the officer sent to apologise to the captain of the Russian ship which had been purposely and effectively fired into after accidentally hitting the British vessel. The second Lord Congleton married an Armenian lady, the widow of a merchant named Yoosoof Constantine. This peer was of a serious and missionary turn of mind, and made the widow's acquaintance while travelling in the East. When he converted her to Christianity her friends discarded her, whereupon Lord Congleton married her.

The present Lord Congleton was educated a the Royal Military College, Sandhurst, and formerly commanded the 2nd Batt. of the Buffs took part in the Crimean Campaign in 1855 and the Zulu War in 1879, including the action of Inyezane and the occupation of Eshowe (despatches, medal with clasp, and C.B.). From 1895-1900 he commanded the Infantry Brigade at Gibraltar and also at Malta. He married, in 1885, Elizabeth, dau. of Dugald Dove.

CONYBEARE, Charles Augustus Vansittart, of Oakfield Park, near Dartford, Kent, and the National Liberal and New Reform Clubs, was born at Kew, June 1, 1853; is the eldest son of John Chas. Conybeare, by Katherine Mary Vansittart; was educated at Tonbridge and Christ Church, Oxford, where he took a Junior Studentship by open competition; Lothian Prize Essayist, 1876; published Text Books on the Married Women's Property Acts and the Corrupt Practices at Elections Act; represented Camborne in Parliament 1885-95; and is a Director of the Beira Junction Railway, Oceana Development Co., N. Charterland Exploration Co., etc. He married, Oct. 15, 1896, Florence Annie, eldest dau. of Gustave Strauss, of 2, Bolton Gardens, W. Kensington. Mrs. Conybeare takes an interest in matters of moment. She publicly opposed the Education Act introduced by Mr. Balfour's Govt., and is an active member of the Executive Committee of the Women's Liberal Federation.

CONYBEARE, Henry Grand Madan, of Delmore, Ingatestone, Essex and of the Camera Club, Lond., was born in Surrey, Oct. 26, 1859; is son of Jn. Chas. Conybeare, by his wife, Katherine Mary, dau. of the Rev. W. Vansittart, and was educated at Tonbridge Sch., Sidney Sussex Coll., Camb., and the Crystal Palace Sch. of Engineering. He is now a Director of the North-Western of Uruguay Railway, the Balkis Land Co., the Africa Trust Co., the United Reefs, the New Rand Southern G.M. Co., and the Associated Tamworth Mines, Ltd. His recreations are: Photography and mechanics, and he married, in 1896, Minna, dau. of Sir R. C. Shakespeare, K.C.B.

COOPER, Rev. Alfred Augustus, M.A., of Ibrahamieh, Alexandria, Egypt; was born in Aberdeenshire, N.B., Oct. 1, 1866; was educated at Aberdeen Gram. Sch.; King's Coll., Aberdeen, and New Coll., Edin., graduating M.A., and taking lst class Honours in Classical Literature. He took Holy Orders as a Minister of the Presbyterian Church of Eng.; spent three and a-half years in

Bengal, and is now Agent-Gen. of the B. and F. Bible Soc. for Egypt and Sudan, Syria and Palestine, Cyprus, Aden, Abyssinia, and E. Africa. He is author of The Story of the Turkish Version (B. and F. B. S., 1901), and God's Forget-me-Not (Elliot Stock, 1900), and other addresses to boys and girls. He married, Sept. 28, 1893, Florence, dau. of the late John Howden, of Waterloo, Liverpool.

COOPER, Colonel Harry, C.M.G., of The Red House, Hasberton, Woodbridge, and of the United Service Club, S.W., was born April 14, 1847. He was educated at the R.M.C., Sandhurst; joined the Army in 1865, and served with the 47th Foot in Canada, West Indies, and Ireland, between 1865-70. He took part in the Ashanti Expedition under Sir Garnet Wolseley in 1873-4. In 1881 he served in the Boer War with the mounted Inf. in Natal and on the Transvaal Frontier. He acted as chief staff Officer to the Army of occupation in Egypt from 1896-8. When the S. African War broke out, he raised 10,000 men for Town Guards in the Cape Peninsula in 1901, and in 1902 he commanded the Namaqualand Field Force. He retired in 1904. He married in 1894 a dau. of Commodore H. Caldwell, R.N., C.B.

COPLEY, William Dawn, M.P.S., of Bulawayo, and of the Imperial Colonies and the Rhodesia Clubs, was born June 16, 1871, and is partner in the firm of Smart and Copley, chemists, of Bulawayo, where he has been since the rebellion in 1896. He was a Director of the Rhodesian Club, Ltd., an ex-Town Councillor of Bulawayo, and was for two years Chairman of the local musical and dramatic society. He married in 1900 Florence Mary, eldest dau. of Rev. E. W. Cantrell, of Birmingham.

CORBET, Eustace Kynaston, C.M.G. M.A.; of Cairo, and the New University Club youngest son of the late Rev. Andrew Corbet and of Marianne, dau. of Sir M. W. Ridley (3rd Bart.), of Blagdon, Northumberland, was born at South Willingham Rectory, Linc. June 22, 1854; was educated at Cheltenham Coll. and Balliol Coll., Oxon, where he graduated M.A. He was appointed English Secy. to the late Khedive, Tewfik Pasha, in July, was made Judge in the Native Court of Appeal April, 1891; and became Procureur-Général to Native

Courts in Nov., 1897. He published in 1853 a verse translation of Lessing's *Nathan der Weise*, with critico-historical introduction and notes, and is decorated with the Orders of the Osmanieh (2nd Class) and Medjidieh (3rd Class), and the C.M.G. (1905).

CORBET, Frederick Hugh Mackenzie, of 1 Brick Court, Temple, London, E.C., was born at Barcelona, July 17, 1862, and was Private Secretary to Mr. Justice Lawrie, 1885, 1886, and 1888; Librarian of Colombo Museum, 1886-93; Acting-Secretary of Central Irrigation Board, Ceylon, 1890-91; resigned salaried Government employment, 1893; Honorary Executive Officer and Home Agent of the Ceylon Government at the Imperial Institute, 1893-1904; Hon. Sec. of Ceylon General Committee for Paris Universal Exposition, 1889; Member of Council, and successively Hon. Sec. and Hon. Treas. of Ceylon Branch of Royal Asiatic Society, 1887-93; and Delegate to International Congress of Orientalists, London, 1891. He was called to the Bar at Gray's Inn in 1897, and practises mainly in appeals before the Privy Council; President of Hardwicke Society, 1902-3. Mr. Corbet had some share in securing (in 1896) recognition of status of Ceylon Advocates by the Inns of Court (which led to similar recognition being accorded to Cape Advocates) and in securing the establishment of a Chair of Roman-Dutch Law at University College, London, in 1905. He is Member of Council of Society of Comparative Legislation; Executive Committee of Ceylon Association in London; Committee of Social and Political Education League. He is Chairman of the Gwanda (Rhodesia) Consolidated Co. and the Rhodesian Mining and Finance Co., and is a Director of the Bulawayo Town Stands Synd. and the Whangamata Gold Corp., Ltd. He published the introduction to Ceylon portion of *The Golden Book of India*, 1900; and *The Laws of the Empire* (British Empire Series), 1901. He married, in 1893, Eila Louisa Mary, eldest dau. of Sir G. W. R. Campbell.

CORBETT, Sir Vincent Edwin Henry, K.C.V.O., of Cairo, Egypt, comes of a younger branch of the Corbetts of Elsham, the elder branch of the family being represented by Sir Francis Astley-Corbett, of Elsham, whose father, the late Sir John Astley,

married Miss Eleanor Corbett, the heiress of Elsham. Sir Vincent Corbett formerly served in the Diplomatic Service at Berlin, The Hague, Rome, Constantinople, Copenhagen, and Athens, subsequently becoming Financial Adviser to the Egyptian Government.

The phenomenal progress of Egypt in recent times has been evidenced by the great rise in the value of land, the large amount of capital invested in various commercial enterprises, and the remarkable growth of foreign trade. During the quarter of a century ended in 1906 the revenue expanded from £E9,000,000 to upwards of £E14,000,000; the imports and exports of the country increased by over £E22,000,000; one million additional acres of land were brought under cultivation, and the cotton crop approximated 160,000 tons in excess of that for the year 1880. In the year 1896 the combined totals of imports and exports were £E23,271,000; in 1900 they had reached £E31,236,000; and in 1905 they amounted to no less than £E41,923,000. Of the imports for 1905, which aggregated £E21,564,000, 38.6 per cent. came from the United Kingdom and British colonies, 12.8 per cent. from Turkey, and 10.9 per cent. from France, the remainder being supplied by various countries in much smaller ratios. The United Kingdom and colonies took a little more than one-half of the total exports of £E20,360,000.

Sir Vincent was given the rank of Councillor of Embassy in Dec., 1904, and he was knighted in 1905 in consideration of his services in Egypt, receiving also in the same year from the Khedive the Egyptian Order of the Osmanieh. In the middle nineties he married a sister of Lord Alington, but was left a widower in 1899.

CORNER, Charles, M.Inst.C.E., Assoc. Mem. Am. Soc. C.E., and Member of the S.A. Association for the Advancement of Science; of Agorica, Paignton, Devon; of Bulawayo, Rhodesia, and of the Salisbury Club, Rhodesia, is the son of the Headmaster of Wellington Academy, now West Somerset County School. He was born Nov. 1859, at Wellington, Somerset, and was educated at Wellington Academy. He was Assist. Engineer to the Harrisburg and San Antonio Railway Company (Southern Pacific System), 188t-2-3;

Assist. Engineer to the San Antonio and Aransas Pass Railway of Texas, 1884; Engineer in charge of Graduation, Bridges and Buildings, San Antonio and Aransas Pass Rly., 1885-8; Division Engineer in charge of Location, French Company of Venezuelan Rly., *Compagnie de Fives* Lille, 1889; Div. Engineer for Sub-Contractors, Interoceanic Rly. of Mexico, 1890; Sub. Div. Engineer, with Reed and Campbell, of Lond. and Mexico, Mexican Southern Rly. of Mexico, 1890-1-2; Civil Engineer to the Railroad Commission of Texas, 1893-8, inspecting, valuing and reporting on nearly 10,000 miles of rly.; from 1899 to 1904 he was District Engineer of the Beira and Rhodesia Railways, and in 1904 was appointed Resident Engineer to the Rhodesian Railways., Northern Extension. He married, March 24, 1887, Margaret Muncey, of San Antonia, Texas, U.S.A.

CORNISH, Right Rev. Charles Edward, D.D., Bishop of Grahamstown, of Bishopsbourne, Grahamstown, C. Colony, is the eldest son of the Rev. Charles L. Cornish, formerly Fellow of Exeter Coll., Oxon. He was born in London, Oct. 9, 1842, and was educated at Uppingham and Exeter Coll., Oxon. He is M.A. and D.D. of Oxon, and M.A. Univ. of the Cape of Good Hope. From 1882-9 he was Vicar of St. Mary's, Redcliffe, Bristol. He was also Rural Dean of Bristol and chaplain to the Bishop of Bristol, and still remains Hon. Canon of Bristol. In 1899 he left England for the purpose of taking up the appointment of Bishop of Grahamstown. He is also Moderator and Sub Dean of the Faculty of Divinity of the Province of South Africa; visitor of St. Andrew's College, Grahamstown, the Diocesan School for Girls, and the Grahamstown Training College.

CORSTORPHINE, Dr. George Steuart, B.Sc. (Edin.), Ph.D. (Munich), M.A. *ad eund. grad.* (Cape), of Johannesburg, and of the Rand and Athenaeum Clubs, Johannesburg, was born at. Edinburgh, Nov. 19, 1865; is the eldest son of the late John Corstorphine of that town, where he began his education. He is an eminent geologist who has had much experience in S.A. in the service of the Cape Colonial Government. Dr. Corstorphine was Asst. in the Dept. of Geology and Mineralogy at Edin. Univ., 1892-4; Lecturer on Geology at Heriot-Watt Coll., Edin., 1894; was

appointed first professor of Geology and Mineralogy in the S.A. Coll. and Keeper of Minerals in the S.A. Museum, Cape Town, in 1895; Geologist to the Geological Commission, Cape Col., in 1896; and Director of the Geological Survey, Cape Col., 1901. From 1897 to 1902 he was Member of the Council of the University of the Cape of Good Hope, and in the latter year he was appointed Consulting Geologist to the Consolidated Goldfields of S.A., Ltd. He has published: *Reports of the Geological Survey, Cape Colony, 1896-1901*; *The Massive Rocks of the Southern Portion of Arran, Scotland*, in *Tchermak's geol. u. min. Mitt.*, 1895; *Note on the Age of the Central South African Coalfield*, in *Trans. S.A. Geol. Soc.*, 1903. He married Miss Clara Ursula Hoffman, July 2, 1896.

CORYNDON, Robert Thorne, of Kalomo, N.W. Rhodesia; 2, London Wall Buildings, London, E.C., and of the Devonshire (Lond.) and Salisbury and Bulawayo (Rhodesia) Clubs; was born at Queenstown, Cape Colony, April 2, 1870, and was educated at St. Andrew's Coll., Grahamstown, C.C., and at Cheltenham Coll., Eng. He joined the B.B.P. in Nov., 1889, and the Mashonaland Pioneer Force in June, 1890, serving in the Matabele War of 1893 and the Matabele Rebellion of 1896 (medal and clasp). Prior to this date Mr. Coryndon spent some years hunting big game, and in the office of the Surveyor-Gen. in Salisbury, Mashonaland. In one of his hunting expeditions he shot two specimens of the almost extinct white rhinoceros. In June, 1897, he took charge of the B.S.A. Co.'s expedition to Lealui, Barotseland, and became British Resident with the Barotse chief, Lewanika. He was appointed Administrator of N.W. Rhodesia in 1900. Unmarried.

COSGROVE, Captain Alfred, of the Cape Mounted Riflemen, joined the C.M.R. in 1881 and served in the Matabele War in 1893 (medal) and the South African War in 1899-1902; present at the operations in the Orange Free State, including the defence of Wepener, and in the Transvaal and Orange River Colony, including the actions at Wittebergen (Queen's medal with four clasps, and King's medal with two clasps).

COUPER, William, of Riverslea, Blundellsands, Liverpool, is a director of the African Association,

Ltd., and the Bank of Nigeria, Ltd.

COVENTRY, Capt. Hon. Charles John, of Earl's Croome Court, Worcester, and of White's Club, was born in 1867, and is son of the 9th Earl of Coventry; was formerly attached to the Worcestershire Regiment, and now holds a captaincy in the Queen's Own Worcs. Hussars, Imp. Yeomanry. He was seconded in March, 1889, for service in the Bechuanaland Border Police; took part in the Matabeleland campaign in 1893; and was appointed a magistrate for the Bechuanaland Protectorate in 1894. He was second in command of the contingent of B.B.P which invaded the Transvaal under Dr. Jameson in 1896, when he was severely wounded near Doornkop. For his participation in the raid Capt: Coventry was sentenced to five months' imprisonment, but in Aug., 1896, he was released unconditionally on account of severe illness following his wounds. He married, in 1900, Lily Whitehouse.

COWAN, Commander W. H., D.S.O., was formerly Senior Officer of the Devonport Instructional Flotilla. He was appointed to command the torpedo vessels in commission in reserve at Devonport in 1905. He has served on the coasts of Africa under Admiral Sir Frederick Bedford and Admiral Rawson; served with the gunboats on the Nile in the Khartoum Expedition, and was Staff Officer in the operations against the Khalifa in 1899. He also acted as Naval A.D.C. to Lord Roberts and Lord Kitchener in S. Africa.

COWELL, Temple Theodore, of the firm of Adams and Co., 1, Sise Lane, London, E.C., is a director of the Ashanti Gold Coast Acquisitions Co., Ltd., Tarkwa Main Reef, Ltd., and the Wassau Extended Gold Mines, Ltd.

COWEN. Charles, F.S.A., F.R.C.I., is the only surviving son of Joseph Cowen, of Bryanston Street, Portman Square, London, and of Catherine Louisa, his wife, of Merrion Square, Dublin, was born in 1828, and has been identified with our colonial life from 1853, when he arrived in S.A. Having been, from a very early date, associated with educational organizations in England, and with the Press, he soon found a new sphere for his energies after landing at Cape Town, where he

inaugurated, with others, classes, conducted gratuitously by some of the best members of the community, for elementary instruction, as well as for advanced young men in modern languages the classics, literature and some of the arts. He also occupied himself as a lecturer and journalist, and in 1874 became Secy. of the Port Elizabeth Chamber of Commerce. Broken down in health, about the end of 1886 he left for the newly-opened goldfields, paying visits to the Free State Territories and other parts.

An old M.M. of the British Lodge, co-founder of and P.M. of the Joppa, one of the originators of the D.G.L. of S.A., and a member of its executive until 1875, Bro. Cowen was influential in obtaining the warrant for the first Brit. L. under the Cons. of the G.L. of England for Johannesburg, and was elected its first W.M. When Mr. Rhodes, having passed the Glen Grey Act, decided to visit the Transkeian tribe to explain to them the merits and requirements of it, Mr. Cowen met him at Butterworth as the *Cape Times* representative, and accompanied him on the tour, and then stayed behind to watch the practical working of the new measure. In 1892 he was associated with the Editorship of the *Cape Mercury* for a while. In 1898 he went to the East; later settled in Rome, and came back to England at the close of 1902. He is an hon. life member of the Chamber of Commerce at Port Elizabeth, hon. member of the S.A. Press Association and of the Imperial S.A. Association, F.S.A., and M.R.C.I. He is the author of *The Life of William Schröder, Artist*, The Zingari Series of *Our Public Men*, The *Wynberg Times'* new series *Men of Mark*, *The Laws in Relation to the Farmer*, *Johannesburg the Golden*, and has also published *Eleven Years' Annual Reviews of the Trade and Commerce of S.A.* (for the Chamber of Commerce at Port Elizabeth) and of the Cape of Good Hope. He married: first, the eldest dau. of Wm. Painton, brewer, of Oxford; and, second, a sister of the Right Rev. Jn. Rooney, D.D., of St. Mary's, Cape Town.

COX, Hugh Bertram, C.B., B.C.L., M.A. Oxon., of 25A, Sussex Place, S. Kensington, London, S.W., and of the United University Club, was born in London, April 19, 1861, was educated at Westminster Sch. (Muir Scholar) and Christ Church, Oxford (Junior Student 1879, first-class

Lit. Hum. 1883, B.C.L. 1884). He was called to the Bar in April 1885, and in 1886-7 assisted the then Attorney-General, Sir Richard Webster, in official and party work; was Junior Counsel to H.M. Treasury in Peerage cases, 1892; Junior Counsel to H.M. Customs, 1896; Counsel in Venezuela Boundary Arbitration, 1897; and became Asst. Under-Secy. of State of the Colonies, Nov. 15, 1897. He was the recipient of the Coronation medal in 1902, and in 1896 married Rachel, youngest dau. of Gen. Sir Julius Richard Glyn, K.C.B., of Sherborne House, Sherborne, Dorset.

COX, Captain W. S., took part in the operations against Sekukuni in the Zulu War of 1879-80 (medal with clasp and hon. rank of Captain), and took part in the Bechuanaland Expedition in 1884-5.

COXMOORE, Edward W., of 1, Bloomsbury Square, W.C., is Chairman of the Northern Transvaal Lands Co., Ltd., and director of Read's Drift Land Co., Ltd.

CRAIG, Capt. James, J.P., M.P., A.I.N.A., of Craigavon, Strandtown, Belfast, and of the Ulster, Belfast, and Union (Belfast) clubs, is sixth son of the late James Craig, J.P., of Craigavon and Tyrella, Co. Down, brother of Charles C. Craig, M.P. for South Antrim; was born Jan. 8, 1871, and educated at Merchiston Castle Sch., Edinburgh. On the outbreak of the South African War he volunteered for active service, and was given a lieutenancy in the 46th Company Ulster Imperial Yeomanry, in which he served till its disbandment, when he was appointed R.S.O. and D.A.D.R. at Kroonstad, Orange River Colony, where he did duty for nine months, being at length invalided home. On his recovery he was promoted captain in the Army and commissioned by Lord Longford to raise a squadron of Irish Horse, to which regiment he presented two Colt guns and outfit complete, and with them served in South Africa till the close of the war. (Two medals and five clasps.) He is a captain in the 3rd Royal Irish Rifles and honorary captain in the Army. On the retirement of Mr. E. M. Archdale in 1903 he contested North Fermanagh in the Unionist interests against Mr. Mitchell, the Russellite candidate, being defeated

by the narrow majority of 152. In 1906 he was elected for the E. Division of Co. Down. He has always taken a keen interest in politics, and worked hard in the Unionist interest for many years. A keen yachtsman, he is an Associate of the Institute of Naval Architects, a member of the Yacht Racing Association, the Royal Ulster Yacht Club, and other local clubs, and he is a member of the Council and life member of the Royal Ulster Agricultural Society. He is a Presbyterian and Orangeman, and married, in 1905, Cecil Nowell, only child of Dan Tupper, M.V.O., Asst. Comptroller, Lord Chamberlain's offices.

CRASTER, W. S., of Salisbury, Rhodesia, was born in 1874, and is the youngest son of the late John Craster, J.P., D.L., of Craster, Northumberland. He commenced to shoot at Clifton College. In 1889 he shot at Wimbledon for the Cadets' Trophy, and at the first Bisley meeting in 1890 for the Ashburton Shield for Clifton College. Subsequently he joined the firm of H. and W. Hawthorn, Leslie, and Co., of Newcastle-on-Tyne, receiving a training there as an engineer, and in 1891 he proceeded to Rhodesia, where he practised his profession until 1904, when he became a partner in the Rhodesian Rickshaw Co. In this year he also joined the Salisbury Rifle Club, and shortly afterwards entered the Southern Rhodesia Volunteer Corps. At the Bisley Rifle Meeting in 1906 he scored the second highest number of points in the con test for the King's Prize, the first prize being won by Capt. R. H. Davies, 1st Middlesex V.R.C., with 324 points, Mr. Craster scoring only one point less. Both these scores were records, the previous best having been made in 1904 by Pte. S. T. Perry, of Canada, with a total of 321.

CRAWFORD, Hugh, M.L.C., was born in Scotland, but has made his home for many years in the Transvaal, where he was identified with the well-known firm of Lewis and Marks until his partial retirement from active business in 1905. He is, however, still chairman of the National Bank of South Africa (see E. C. Reynolds), and in the first Transvaal Legislative Council nominated by the High Commissioner under Responsible Government he was selected as President of the Council. He is regarded as a reliable and well esteemed man in connection with the political, social, and industrial affairs of the Transvaal, and one whose voice in the Council will be entirely free from any particular class interest.

CREEWEL, Jacob, of Warnford Court, London, B.C., is on the London Committee of the Buffelsdoorn Consolidated G.M. Co., Ltd., and is a London Agent of the New Transvaal Gold Farms, Ltd.

CRERAR, A., of 50, Wynstay Gardens, London, W., is a director of Acton's Swaziland Concessions, Ltd., Belingwe Gold Reefs, Ltd., and the Vermilion Forks Mining and Development Co., Ltd.

CREWE, Col. Charles Preston, C.B. (1900), J.P. for the Cape of Good Hope, of Cambridge, East London, and of the Civil Service Club, Cape Town; is the son of Capt. Frederick Crewe, 17th Madras Infantry, and is descended from the Crewes of Crewe, Cheshire, of which family he is one of the few male representatives remaining. He was born in London on Jan. 11, 1855, and was educated privately. Col. Crewe has had a varied political and military career. He went to S.A. in March, 1878, and joined the Cape Mounted Riflemen, serving with this regiment through the Kaffir War, receiving for his services medal and clasp, 1878-79. He again saw service in the Basuto War of 1880-81, receiving medal and clasp. In 1881 he retired from the C.M.R. and commenced farming. In 1898 he stood for Aliwal North for the House of Assembly, and was only defeated by two votes. In May of the following year he was returned to the Legislative Assembly for East Griqualand, and devoted himself to the reorganization of the Progressive party. At the general election in Feb. 1904 he succeeded in ousting Mr. J. W. Sauer from the representation of Aliwal North, and on the resignation of Sir Gordon Sprigg's Ministry immediately after the elections he joined Dr. Jameson's Cabinet as Colonial Secy.

On war breaking out in S.A. he raised the Border Horse Regt. (Feb. 1900), and served first as Major commanding and was promoted Lieut.-Col. in May 1900, and full Col. in May 1901. He for many months commanded a mobile column of Colonial troops in the O.R.C., and later on took command of the Western Div. of the Cape Colony from Nov. 1901 to the end of the war. He retired from the C.C.F. Dec. 31, 1902. For his eminent services Col. Crewe was mentioned in despatches, received the C.B., and the medal with clasps for Wepener, Transvaal, and Cape Colony. He married Helen Orpen, dau. of J. M. Orpen, late Surveyor-Gen. of S. Rhodesia, on July 11, 1887.

CRICHTON (Henry William), Viscount, D.S.O., of Crom Castle, Newtown Butler, Ireland, and of the Turf, Marlborough, and Army and Navy clubs, is the eldest son of John Henry, 4th Earl of Erne, K.P., P.C., and of Florence, Countess of Erne. He was born Sept. 30, 1872, and was educated at Eton and the Royal Naval Col. Lord Crichton was Adjt. of the Royal Horse Guards, Dec. 1896 to Oct. 1899; was A.D.C. to Major-Gen. Brocklehurst in the S. African War; and was present during the siege of Ladysmith, and was with General Sir R. Buller during the operations from Ladysmith to Lydenburg May to Oct. 1900, being mentioned in despatcbes. He did excellent work during this war; obtained the D.S.O., and was promoted Capt. in Feb. 1900. He accompanied their Royal Highnesses the Duke and Duchess of Cornwall and York during their Colonial tour in H.M.S. *Ophir* as A.D.C., and was appointed Equerry-in-Waiting to H.R.H. Prince of Wales in Nov. 1901. He married, June 10, 1903, Lady Mary Cavendish Grosvenor, eldest dau. of the 1st Duke of Westminster and Katherine, Duchess of Westminster.

CRISP, Venerable Wm., B.D., was ordained at Bloemfontein in 1868, and was Canon there from 1880 to 1901, being made Archdeacon in 1887. In 1901 he became Diocesan Secy. at Cape Town, and in the following year he was appointed a Canon of St. George's Cathedral, Cape Town. He is author of several treatises, amongst them being a Sechuana Grammar and translations of the New Testament, the Book of Common Prayer, and several other books in the Sechuana language.

CROMER, Right Hon. Earl of, P.C. G.C.B., G.C.M.G., K.C.S.I., C.I.E., 1st Class Medjidieh, of Cairo, and of the Turf, Brooks', Travellers', St. James', and Marlborough Clubs, is son of the late Henry Baring, M.P., and Cecilia Windham. Evelyn

Baring, the first Lord Cromer, was born at Cromer Hall, Norfolk, Feb. 26, 1841, and was educated at The Hethel Hall, Norfolk, the Ordnance Sch., Carshalton, and at Woolwich, and is Hon. D.C.L. of Oxford. At the age of seventeen he joined the Royal Artillery, serving as A.D.C. to Sir H. Storks in the Ionian Islands in 1861, and as Secretary during the inquiry following the outbreak in Jamaica in 1865. He retired from the Army with the rank of Major in 1879 for the purpose of taking up his duties as one of the Controllers-General appointed in Egypt in 1879 by England and France, when Ismail had been deposed by the Sultan, and his son Tewfik had succeeded on the Khedivial throne.

Previously Major Baring had acquired useful experience to fit him for his responsible post. He had acted as private secy. To his cousin, Lord Northbrook, when that nobleman was Governor-General of India, and during this period (1872-6) had obtained a close insight into the practical art of government. While he held a commissionership of the public Debt in Egypt (1877-9) he was enabled to greatly extend his financial knowledge. The powers held by Major Baring and his fellow controller, de Blignières, were very considerable. They were admitted to the Ministerial Council; they had the right to advise in all matters of finance, and they were authorised to appoint resident inspectors. The success of his work of that period in Egypt was borne witness to by Lord Granville in the House of Lords in 1881, when he stated that the system "had undoubtedly worked admirably for the finances and administration of Egypt". Towards the end of 1889 Sir John Strachey's resignation left vacant the post of Finance Minister of India. Major Baring received the appointment under the Marquis of Ripon, who was then Viceroy, and during his tenure of office framed and carried three successful budgets. In 1883 he was made a K.C.S.I., and became and has since remained Consul-General and Minister Plenipotentiary in Egypt. Sir Evelyn Baring had not been many years in Egypt before the financial position, which had been in a critical state since 1876, became still more acute. It had been evident for some time that the finances of the country must again be taken in hand by the Powers. There was the question of meeting the heavy liability of the Alexandrian Indemnity, as well as

the debts due to the rebellion and to the war in the Sudan. The question also of the distribution of the revenue between the Government and the bondholders had assumed an acute phase. The Law of Liquidation under which the Public Creditor "starved the Government" could not be altered without the consent of the Great Powers. To raise a new loan required the consent not only of the Great Powers, but also of Turkey. As an initial step towards procuring these consents the British Government appointed a Committee, of which Sir Evelyn Baring was one, to examine and report. A Conference was held in London for the purpose of discussing the schemes put forward by this Committee, but the Conference broke up without coming to any agreement. After many negotiations an arrangement was come to whereby a loan of £9,000,000 sterling was agreed to, to be issued.

In connection with this transaction Sir Evelyn rendered one of the most valuable of his many important services to the prosperity of Egypt. £8,000,000 of this new loan was applied to the liquidation of the indemnities and to wiping out the deficits of the three previous years. The remaining £1,000,000 was the sum of money which enabled the Consul-General to work such a marvellous change in the economic condition of the country. It was life and death to Egypt to put the great central works upon which the irrigation of the country depended into proper order. This extra million provided the necessary capital to save the irrigation system and with it the finances of Egypt. No sooner was the financial position of the country dealt with than Sir Evelyn Baring entered into his long struggles for reforms. How he has succeeded the present state of prosperity of the country is sufficient proof (see Sir V. Corbett's biography for the further data). In 1892 Sir Evelyn Baring was raised to the peerage, under the title of Baron Cromer, and in the same year occurred the untimely death of Tewfik Pasha and the descent of the Khediviate to his son. It was not long before Lord Cromer's struggles again commenced. In Jan. of the following year Abbas declared war, so to speak, with the British Govt. A sharp but short struggle ensued, but it was followed by the complete victory of the Consul-General. A story had gone the round of the Press that before this was accomplished Lord Cromer had to invite His

MR ABNER COHEN

Photo Elliot & Fry

MR L. EHRLICH

Photo Thos. Fall

THE EARL OF CROMER, O.M. *Photo Elliott & Fry*

Highness to look from a window of the Abdin Palace on a British regiment parading on the square without, but we have Lord Cromer's *ipse dixit* that this was a "pure invention". Unquestionably it was by the Consul-General's firmness at this critical juncture that British prestige and power were not seriously threatened. But the truce was of short duration, for in Jan. 1894 the Khedive complained publicly and pointed out to the Sirdar, Gen. Kitchener, the military inefficiency of the force under his command. The British Consul-General waited on the Khedive and there demanded that he should issue a general order expressing his approval of the discipline and efficiency of the army, and his satisfaction with the officers whose authority he had so deliberately attempted to overthrow. He was also required to remove Maher Pasha from his post at the War Office. These demands were complied with, and from it may be dated a cessation of the struggle of the Khedive to emancipate himself from British control.

Lord Cromer received his K.C.B. in 1887, his G.C.M.G. in 1888, end was raised to the peerage as Baron in 1892, as Viscount in 1898, and Earl in 1901. He married: first, in 1876, Ethel Stanley, dau. of Sir Roland Stanley Errington, Bart. (died Oct. 16, 1898); and second, Lady Catherine Thynne, sister of the present Marquess of Bath.

CRONJE, Andries Petrus Johannes, M.L.C., is a nominated member of the Transvaal Legislative Council, and is very popular among the section of the Transvaal population whose representative he is. Mr. Cronje is brother to the well-known General of that name, who was defeated and captured by the British at Paardeberg during the late S. African War.

CRONJE, Pieter Arnoldus, ex-Commandant of the Potchefstroom District, Transvaal, of Palmietfontein, Schoon Spruit, Klerksdorp, Transvaal. During the War of Independence he commanded the Boer forces at Potchefstroom. At that time he ordered the summary execution of several British subjects who were suspected on wholly insufficient grounds of being spies; he caused prisoners of war to work in the trenches, where they were shot by their own comrades, and refused to allow women in delicate health to leave

the fort to obtain medical aid and food. When the general armistice was declared he treacherously withheld the news from the besieged garrison, until, in order to save the lives of the wounded and the women and children, they were compelled to surrender.

Many years later (Jan. 1896) Comdt. Cronje was in command of the commando which beat Dr. Jameson's forces at Vlakfontein, and received his surrender on condition of sparing the lives of the entire force. This condition when known to Comdt. Malan caused the greatest antagonism, and Cronje was accused of neglect of duty for accepting such a condition. Seeing that Comdt. Cronje stoutly maintained against all opposition that the condition should be loyally recognised, it was probably strong Government pressure which induced him later on to stretch the terms, explaining that the promise to spare the lives was only to hold good until the prisoners were handed over to the Comdt.-General. He succeeded Gen. Joubert as Superintendent of Natives, and was given a seat on the Executive. Comdt. Cronje was married, and no less than thirty-three of his descendants were either killed or died of disease in the field or concentration camps during the last S.A. War. Mrs. Cronje herself died of paralysis at the age of 64 at the latter end of 1903.

CRONWRIGHT-SCHREINER, Samuel Cron, M.L.A., J.P., of Hanover, Cape Colony, is the eldest son of the late S. C. Cronwright, who for many years represented Grahamstown in the Cape Legislature, three of his grandparents having been Scotch, Irish, and English. Mr. Cronwright-Schreiner was educated at St. Andrew's Coll., Grahamstown, and after taking his B.A. started farming, principally with Angora goats, ostriches, and cattle, in 1884, in the Karoo, and then till 1894 at Cradock, afterwards spending four years at Kimberley and one at Johannesburg, until on the outbreak of war he came over to England to lecture and represent the views of the pro-Boers. His tour was a complete failure, however, as no British audience would give him a hearing. He returned to the Cape Colony in 1900, and was detained by the military at Hanover (C.C.), where he made a study of *Arachnidae*, discovering locally over 100 species new to science, a description of which was published in the *Popular Science Monthly* (New York).

He published in 1895, *The Political Situation*, jointly with his wife, Olive Schreiner (q.v.) whose surname he added to his own on the occasion of his marriage in 1894, and he is also the author of *The Angora Goat*, *The Ostrich*, and (in the *Zoologist*), *The Trekbokken*, or migratory springbucks.

Mr. Cronwright-Schreiner is a member of the South African party, and in Dec. 1902 he defeated the Progressive candidate, Mr. Macfarlane, at Colesberg, and at the general election in Feb. 1904 he was elected for Beaufort West. At St. Andrew's Coil, he captained both the cricket and football teams, and was champion athlete of his year.

CRONWRIGHT-SCHREINER, Mrs. Olive, of Hanover, Cape Colony, is the dau. of a German missionary of the L.M.S., and has written a number of interesting stories of South African life, besides frequently using her pen in furtherance of her political sympathies, which are decidedly pro-Boer. She married, in 1894, Mr. S. C. Cronwright, who thereupon adopted the surname of Cronwright-Schreiner (q.v.).

CROOKSHANK, Dr. Harry Maule, Pasha, F.R.C.S. (Edin.), FR.G.S., Grand Cordon of the Order of the Medjidieh, Order of the Osmanieh (2nd class), Knt. of Grace, Order of St. John of Jerusalem; of Cairo; of the Junior Carlton (Lond.) and the Turf and Khedivial Sporting (Cairo) Clubs, was born in Cuddalore, India, in 1849. He is 3rd son of the late Capt. C. Crookshank, 51st Regt., and grandson of Col. A. Crookshank, K.H., 33rd Regt. Dr. Crookshank was educated at Boulogne-sur-M. and at Cheltenham. He served as surgeon to the British Red Cross Soc. during the Franco German (1870-71), Turko-Servian (1876), Turko-Russian (1877) and Sudan (1885) wars; was Inspector-Gen. of Egyptian Prisons Administration from 1883 to 1897; British Controller-Gen. of the Daira Sanieh Administration from 1897; and is Director of the Daira Sanieh Co. and of the Standard Life Insurance Co. He married, in 1891, Emma Walraven, only dau. of Major S. Comfort, of New York, U.S.A.

CROSBIE, R., was senior member of the Cape Legislative Assembly for the Province of Albany until 1903.

CROSBIE, W., M.L.A., represents the electoral division of Vryburg in the Progressive interest in the Cape Legislative Assembly. He was returned unopposed at the election in 1904.

CROSSE, Rev. A. J. W., formerly vicar of Rye, Sussex, was given the living of St. Cypriands, Durban, in 1902, rendered vacant through the resignation of Canon Johnson.

CRUDDAS, Capt. H. W., was appointed Inspector of Chinese in South Africa in 1905.

CULLEN, Rev. S. A., of Christiana, Transvaal, served in Holy Orders in India from 1888 until 1902; was then curate-in-charge of Bedford, Cape Colony, and in 1904 was transferred in a similar capacity to Christiana.

CUMMING, Capt. A. W., M.L.A., is member of the Cape House of Assembly for Barkly West.

CUMMING, Robert Forbes, of King William's Town, Cape Colony, served as Lieut. in the Transkei-Fingo levies in the Galeka War of 1877, and as Lieut. and Adjutant in Streatfield's Fingo levies during the Gaika Rebellion in 1875 (medal); acted as Clerk to the Resident Magistrate at Maclear in 1875, and as Commissioner of the Gatberg Survey in 1880; served as Captain and Field Adjutant of the Maclear Constabulary during the Podomise-Tembu Rebellion in 1880-1 acted as Clerk to the Magistrate at Matabele in 1885; and at Qumbu in 1890. During the late South African War he commanded the Matabele Native Reserves, and was appointed Special Magistrate at Tamacha in 1903.

CUMMINS, Edward R., of 35, Gracechurch Street, B.C., is a director of the Associated Tamworth Mines, Ltd., Cataract G.M. Co., Ltd., Klip River Estate and Gold Mines, Ltd., New Graskop Exploring Co., Ltd., New Lydenburg Minerals Exploring Co., Ltd., Niekerk

Consolidated, Ltd., Niekerk, Ltd., and the Zwartland (Transvaal) Land Co., Ltd.

CUNINGHAME, Captain Sir Thomas Andrew Alexander Montgomery, D.S.O., of Kirkbride, Ayr, N.B., was born in 1877, and is the eldest son of the 9th Baronet, whom he succeeded in 1897. He was educated at Eton and the Royal Military College, Sandhurst, and holds a captaincy in the 4th Batt. Rifle Brigade; served with the Natal Field Force during the late Boer War, being present at the relief of Ladysmith, the actions at Colenso, Vaal Kranz (severely wounded), Laing's Nek, and the operations in the Transvaal, East of Pretoria. He subsequently served on the Staff (despatches, King's Medal with two clasps, and D.S.O. Sir Thomas is the claimant to the dormant earldom of Glencairn. He married, in 1904, Alice, daughter of Sir G. W. des Voeux.

CUNNINGHAM, S. F., of Uganda, Central Africa, and of the Reform Club, was born in Ireland in 1863. He was educated privately and at King's College, London. In 1899 he acted as Chief British Commissioner for the delimitation of the Anglo Portuguese boundary in Central Africa, and acted as secretary to the special mission to Uganda in 1900. He entered the Middle Temple in 1901, and in 1905 was elected Company Commander of the Uganda Volunteers. Author of *Uganda and its Peoples*. He married, in 1901, the Comtesse de Berkel.

CUNNINGHAM, Rev. William, D.Sc., Hon. LL.D. Edin., D.D. of Trinity Coll., Cambridge, and of the Oxford and Cambridge and Albemarle Clubs, was born at Edinburgh, Dec. 29, 1849. He was educated at Edinburgh and Cambridge Universities, and was one of the pioneers of the University extension movement in Leeds, Liverpool, and other places in 1874-8. He has devoted himself to the study of economic history, and is the author of *The Growth of English Industry and Commerce*, *Alien Immigrants to England*, 1897, an essay on Western Civilisation in its Economic Aspects, and other works. He was Lecturer on Economic History at Harvard Univ. in 1899, President of the Economic Section of the British Association at Cardiff in 1891, and again in S. Africa in 1905. He was ordained in 1894, and

appointed Vicar of Gt. St. Mary's, Cambs., in 1887; Proctor in Convocation, 1891, and Hon. Canon of Ely in 1896. He has written numerous theological works, including *Dissertation on the Epistles of St. Barnabas*, 1874; *St. Austin*, 1886; and *Gospel of Work*, 1902. He married, June 1, 1876, Adile R. Dunlop.

CUNNINGTON, William Alfred, Ph.D. (Jena), of 13, The Chase, Clapham Common, Surrey, and of Christ's Coll., Camb., was born Aug. 31, 1877; was educated at Mill Hill Sch., the Royal Coll. of Science, Lond., Jena, and Cambridge. He was appointed Demonstrator of Zoology at the Royal Coll. of Science, Dublin, in 1899; took his Ph.D. degree in 1902; was Research Student at Christ's Coll., Camb., 1902, and left in charge of a scientific expedition to Tanganyika in 1904. Unmarried.

CURLING, Jesse Hancock, of 25, Campden Hill Court, Kensington, W., is a director of Klerksdorp Extended, Ltd., and the Klerksdorp Gold and Diamond Co. (1904), Ltd.

CURREY, L., M.L.A. An advocate by profession, he was returned unopposed to represent George (C.C.) in the Legislative Assembly in the Bond interest in Nov., 1902, and was re-elected at the general election in Feb. 1904.

CURRIE, Sir Donald, G.C.M.G., of 4, Hyde Park Place London, W., and of the Reform and City Clubs, was born at Greenock in 1825, and is son of the late James Currie, of Greenock. He was educated at Belfast, but returned to Greenock in 1839 to enter a shipping firm at that port. A few years later he joined the staff of the Cunard Line, under which company he subsequently held many important positions. In 1862 Mr. Currie himself became a ship-owner, founding a service of sailing ships between Liverpool and Calcutta. Ten years later he substituted a steam service, and transferred his activities to the South African trade. Sir Donald is chief partner in the firm of Donald Currie and Co., managers of the Union Castle Mail S.S. Coy.

Although that company dates only from January, 1900, the two important fleets which were then joined under the one title had individual histories reaching back for half a century. The older firm in the co-partnership was formed in 1853, under the title of the Union Steam Collier Company. The Cape Mail Service was inaugurated by the despatch from Southampton of the R.M.S. *Dane* (530 tons) in Sept. 1857, after which sailings continued at monthly intervals during the continuance of the contract. The *Iceland* was the pioneer steamer of the Castle Line, and started on her first voyage in January, 1872. She was followed by her sister ship, the *Gothland*, both vessels being of about 1,400 tons burthen. In the meantime the Cape Parliament made an allowance to the Castle Line for the carriage of letters, and granted an additional bonus of £100 per diem for delivery of the same within the stipulated period of thirty-seven days, a concession which resulted in a gain to the company of £1,000 per voyage. When the postal contract was renewed in 1876, the mail service was equally divided between the Castle and Union lines. The arrangement was confirmed in 1893 for a period of seven years, from October 1893, the charge for letters being reduced to 2½d. per half ounce, and the contract time to nineteen days. In striking contrast to the modest tonnage of the pioneer mail steamer to the Cape are the latest additions to the fleet of steamers of upwards of 12,000 tons each. Nor is this marvellous increase merely in the number of the ships or in their enlarged dimensions. Speed, comfort, and luxurious environments on board ship show an equally marked development. The fleet of the Union Castle Mail Steamship Company at the present date (1906) consists of forty full powered steamships, with a gross tonnage of about 272,321 tons. In 1897 Sir Donald was created C.M.G. by the late Queen Victoria in connection with the assistance to the Government in the settlement of the Diamond Fields dispute, and the boundaries of the Orange Free State; was made K.C.M.G. in 1881 for the services which he rendered in connection with the relief of Ekowe, and was promoted G.C.M.G. in 1897. He is a Deputy Lieutenant for London, and a Liberal Unionist; was elected to Parliament for the county of Perth in 1880, and was elected for the western division when that county war divided in 1883, and sat for it until 1900. Sir Donald is proprietor of the large estates of Garth, Glenlyon, and Chesthill, in Perthshire, also the Island of Scalpay and neighbouring islands near Skye. He

married, in 1851, Margaret, dau. of John Miller, of Liverpool and Bute.

CURRIE, James, B.A., of Khartoum, of the Turf Club, Cairo, and the Savile Club, London; was born at Edinburgh in 1868; was educated at Fettes Coll., Edin., and at Lincoln Coll., Oxon. He was appointed Director of Education under the Sudan Govt., and Principal of the Gordon Coll., Khartoum, in 1900. Unmarried.

CURRIE, John MacMartin, of 3 and 4, Fenchurch Street, London, E.C., is one of the hardworking partners in the firm of Donald Currie and Co., the managers of the Union S.S. Co. (see Sir Donald Currie), and a director of the African Boating Co., Ltd.

CURRIE, Oswald James, M.B. (Lond.), M.RC.S. (Eng.), of 24 Longmarket Street, Maritzburg, and of the Victoria Club, Maritzburg, is son of Alexander Currie, of the firm of Roxburgh, Currie and Co., London. He was born Mar. 15 1860, at Greenwich, and was educated at the University Coll. Sch. and Guy's Hosp. and graduated M.B. with 1st class honours at London Univ. Dr. Currie was Sen. House Physician at Guy's Hospital, 1882; Sen. House Surgeon, Huddersfield Infirmary, 1883-5; Surgeon at the Yeatman Hospital, Sherborne, and Med. Officer at Sherborne School, 1886-9; Surgeon under the P. and O. S.N. Co., 1889-91, and was Surgeon to the Natal Carbineers, 1894-1902, receiving the Queen's Boer War medal (three clasps). He was in medical charge of the Natal First Field Hospital (Volunteers) during the siege of Ladysmith, arid is at present Major commanding the C Battery, Natal Royal Artillery; Surgeon of Grey's Hospital, Maritzburg, and Medical Officer of Health, Maritzburg. Dr. Currie has written various papers for medical journals. He married, 1896, Sara, dau. of Geo. Gubbins, of Limerick.

CURTIS, Lieut.-Col. Reginald Salmond, D.S.O., of Clunie Lodge, Park Town, Johannesburg. and of the Army and Navy Club, was born Nov. 21, 1863, and is the eldest son of Maj.-Gen. Reginald Curtis, R.A. He was educated at Cheltenham Coll., and the R.M.A., Woolwich, and entered the R.E. in 1883; served in the Egyptian Army from 1890-3 on active service, including the Eastern Sudan in 1891, when he was present at the capture of Tokar (bronze star with clasp, 4th cl. Medjidieh); served in the Ashanti expedition in 1895-6 as Director of Telegraphs (star, bt. of Major, despatches); special service under the Admiralty, Falkland Islands, in 1899. He took part in the S. African War in 1899-1902 as A.D.C. to the Engineer-in-Chief, also as Asst. Director of Telegraphs, and with the S.A.C., of which he is now C.S.O. (D.S.O., Queen's medal and five claps; King's medal and two clasps, bt. of Lt. Col., and despatches). He was nominated a member of the Inter-Colonial Council of the Transvaal and the O.R.C. in 1904-5. He married, in 1894, the Hon. Hilda, youngest dau. of Viscount Barrington.

CUTHBERT, Colonel Gerald James, of Cairo, was born Sept. 12, 1861, and joined the Scots Guards in 1882. He took part in the Sudan Expedition in 1885 (medal with clasp and bronze star); acted as A.D.C. to the Brig. Gen. at Aldershot from 1889-90; and served in the S. African War in 1899-1902, taking part in the advance on Kimberley and the actions at Belmont, Enslin, Modder River, and Magersfontein; the operations in the Orange Free State, including the actions at Poplar Grove, Driefontein, Vet River, and Zand River; operations in the Transvaal, including the actions near Johannesburg, Pretoria, and Diamond Hill, and at Riet Vlei and Belfast (despatches, brevet of Lieut. Col., Queen's medal with six clasps, and Kings medal with two clasps). In 1906 Colonel Cuthbert was appointed A.A.G. on the Staff in Egypt.

CUTHBERT, Capt. James Harold, D.S.O., J.P., of Beaufront Castle, Rexam, Northumberland, and of the Guards' and Carlton Clubs, was born at Melsetter, near Pietermaritzburg, July 21, 1876. He was educated at Eton and Sandhurst, and entered the Scots Guards in 1896. He served with his regt. in the S. African War in 1899-1902; acted as extra A.D.C. to Lord Methuen before the relief of Kimberley; was present at the actions at Belmont, Gras Pan, Modder River, Magersfontein (mentioned in despatches, D. S.O.), Driefontein, Johannesburg, Diamond Hill, Belfast, and subsequent actions. He was also Brigade Signalling Officer to Col. Pulteney's column. Capt. Cuthbert retired from the Guards in 1905. He is the author

of *1st Battalion Scots Guards in S. Africa, 1899-1902*. He won the Army revolver championship in 1904, and is a J.P. for the County of Northumberland. He married, Sept. 24, 1903, Lady Anne D. F. Byng, dau. of the Earl of Strafford.

CUTTEN, Rev, James Alfred, M.A., of Christiana, Transvaal, was born in London in 1869. He was educated at Durham Univ., and was ordained by the Bishop of London in 1895, and from then until 1897 he acted as a missionary at Hing-Hwa, China, also at Hakodak, Japan, from 1898-1900. In 1901 he became curate of Fairlight, Hastings, also held the same position at St. Mark's, Cape Town, in 1902, St. Andrew's, Bedford, Cape Colony, in 1902-3, and St. Philip's, Christiana, Transvaal, from 1904.

DAHOMEY, EX-KING of (see Behanzin).

DALGETY-CAMPBELL, Dalgety Gordon, Hon. Lieut. N.S.W. Forces, of Florida, Western Witwatersrand, Transvaal, and of the Barberton Dist. Club, was born at Sydney, N.S. Wales, Oct. 21, 1877. He comes from an old Argyll and Aberdeenshire family, and is a cousin of Lady Trafalgar, who married the eldest son of the 3rd Earl Nelson in 1879. He is also cousin of Col. Dalgety of Wepener fame. Mr. Dalgety-Campbell was educated at Oxley Coll. and Hawksbury Agricultural Col., N.S. Wales, and has had a varied career in Australia, China, Africa, and other parts of the globe. In early life he was for a short period in the Navy; he spent a short time with an exploring party in China; later on he was bookkeeper in a store in Parkes, N.S.W., and eventually went into the backblocks of Australia as a schoolmaster. A year later saw him as one of the best-known cross-country and steeplechase riders in the colony, at which he earned his living; he, however, abandoned this means of livelihood, and after engaging as a professional cycle rider, milkman, drover, fencer, and miner, he drifted into journalism. He was for some time editor of the Wyalong *Advocate*, published in a small township in N.S. Wales. When the Boer War broke out he went to Sydney, joined the N.S. Wales M.I., and came to Africa as a trooper. He was severely wounded at Vet River, May 1, 1900. When Pretoria fell, he raced with Bennet Burleigh, the war correspondent, to see who would be the first man to enter the capital. He reached the Artillery Barracks first, took possession, and when some hours later the troops entered Mr. Campbell handed the barracks over to Major Marker, D.S.O. of the Coldstream Guards, and A.D.C. to Lord Kitchener. Among the prisoners in the barracks at the time were the famous Lt. Mike Du Toit, Major Erasmus, and Lt. Cordua, who was subsequently executed for being implicated in the attempt to kidnap Lord Roberts. At the hour of Mr. Campbell's entry there were about 4,000 Boers in the town, guns, etc. At Diamond Hill, June 13, he was again severely wounded and invalided to Australia. Six months later be was again in S.A., in command of a squadron of Mounted Rifles, retaining the command until peace was declared; after which he resigned his commission and was appointed as special travelling correspondent to the *Leader*. His articles ran in the *Leader* for weeks, and were noted for their fine descriptive power.

Subsequently Capt. Campbell was appointed to the Central Repatriation Commission sitting in Johannesburg; he resigned this position and took over the editorship of the *Gold Fields News*, Barberton. From here he went to England on journalistic work, returned to the Transvaal to edit the *Transvaal Advertiser*, and since became election agent for Mr. Abe Bailey. He married, in 1906, Miss Carrie Erskine.

DALHOUSIE, Earl of, of Brechin Castle, and Panmure House, Carnoustie, Forfarshire, and of Dalhousie Castle, Bonnyrigg, Midlothian, was born Sept. 4, 1878, and is the son of the 13th Earl and Ida, daughter of the 6th Earl of Tankerville. He was formerly in the Scots Guards, with which he served in the South African War 1901-2. He married in 1903, Lady Mary Adelaide Willoughby, the youngest of the six daughters of the Earl and Countess of Ancaster. Lord Dalhousie has one son, Lord Ramsay, who is heir to the Earldom and the large estates in Forfarshire and Midlothian, and one daughter.

DALRYMPLE, Capt. Viscount, M.P. J.P., of the Guards' (London) and New (Edin.) clubs, is eldest son of the 11th Earl of Stair, was born in London, Feb. 1, 1879. He was educated at Harrow and

Sandhurst, passing into the Scots Guards, Feb., 1898; Lieut., Oct., 1899; Capt. June, 1903. He served in South Africa with the 1st Batt. Scots Guards from Jan., 1900, to July, 1902 (Queen's medal, 5 clasps; King's medal, 2 clasps). He is a member of the King's Bodyguard, Scottish Archers (1903), J.P. for Wigtownshire, and he was elected Conservative M.P. for Wigtownshire at the General Election in Jan., 1906. His recreations are shooting and fishing. He married, in Oct., 1904, Violet, dau. of Col. Harford, of Down Place, late Scots Guards.

DALTON, Llewellyn Chisholm, B.A. of Harrismith, O.R.C., was educated at Marlborough and Trinity College, Cambridge and was called to the Bar at Gray's Inn in 1901; was employed in the Land Settlement Dept., Orange River Colony, in 1901; Clerk and Asst. Resident Magistrate at Bethulie in 1902; Acting Chief Clerk to the Attorney-General in 1904; admitted as Advocate of the High Court, Orange River Colony, in 1904; Acting Asst. Resident Magistrate at Bloemfontein in Jan., 1905; and was appointed Asst. Resident Magistrate at Harrismith in Feb., 1905, which position he still holds in the Orange River Colony.

DAMANT, Lieut.-Col. Frederick Hugh, C.B., D.S.O., of Lydenburg, Transvaal, was born at King Williamstown in 1864. He served in the S. African War in 1899-1902 (D.S.O.), and was employed in the Cape Government Service from 1883 until 1902, when he was appointed Resident Magistrate at Lydenburg.

DANZIEGER, B., of Johannesburg, Transvaal, is President of the Johannesburg Hebrew congregation.

DARLEY, Hon. Sir Frederick Matthew, G.C.M.G., K.C.M.G., K.B., P.C., of Quambi, Albert Street, Sydney, was born in 1830, and was educated at Trinity College, Dublin. He was appointed Chief Justice of New South Wales in 1886 and Lieutenant-Governor in 1891. He was a member of the Legislative Council of the Colony from 1868-86, and Vice-President of the Executive Council from 1881-83. In 1902 he was a member of the South African War Commission. He was created Privy Councillor on the occasion of the

King's birthday, 1905. He married, in 1860, Lucy, dau. of S. Browne.

DARLEY-HARTLEY, William, M.D M.R.C.P., of Cauvin's Gift, Sea Point, Cape Town, and of the Imperial Union Club, Cape Town, was born at Sheffield in 1854. He was educated at Sheffield Grammar School and Guy's Hospital. Settled in Cape Colony since 1879, practising at East London, Cathcart, and Cape Town. He served as Civil Surgeon in Gaika-Galeka and Zulu campaigns (medal and clasp), and as Surgeon Captain with the Kaffrarian Rifles in the Langeberg campaign (medal), and as Civil Surgeon in the Boer War (King's and Queen's medals and clasps); is a life member of the Council of St. John's Ambulance Association. He has also served as Town Councillor, East London, Past District Grand Warden of the Eastern district of the Masonic body; has taken great interest in the work of the English Church. Took part in the formation of the South African League, drafting its constitution and being elected its first President. In that capacity he addressed, in 1896, the huge meeting at Johannesburg which led to the formation of the League in that town; is senior Vice Chairman of the Cape Town Branch of the Imperial Union. Proprietor and editor of the *South African Medical Record*, and a member of the Cape Medical Council; President of the Cape Town Yorkshire and Lancashire Association, and a contributor to various South African papers. Recreation, poultry-keeping. He married, in 1879, Harriet, eldest dau. of the late H. L. Head, first Mayor of King Williamstown.

DARTNELL, Major-Gen. Sir John George, K.C.B., C.M.G., of 13, Cadogan Court, Chelsea, London, S.W., was born in Canada in 1838, and entered the British Army in 1855, from which he retired some fourteen years later, although he still retains hon. rank of Major-General therein. He became lieutenant, 1856; promoted captain, unattached, 1859; brevet major, 1865; appointed to the 2nd Battalion, 16th Regiment, 1859; exchanged to the 27th Regiment, 1862; and retired by sale of commission, 1869. In the course of his career Gen. Dartnell served in the 86th Regiment with the Central India Field Force under Sir Hugh Rose (Lord Strathnairn) in 1857-8, and was present at the storm and capture of Chandaree, and led the

only successful escalade attack on the fortress of Jhansi. He was severely wounded, mentioned in despatches (medal and clasp, captain, unattached, and brevet of major). He served in the Bhootan Expedition in 1865 as aide-de-camp to Major General Sir Henry Thombs, and was present at the recapture of Dewangiri (medal with clasp). He was appointed commandant of the Mounted Police and Volunteer Forces of Natal in 1874; was a member of local Defence Committee, 1887; granted the rank of Colonel Commanding the local forces of Natal, 1888; served through the Zulu War, 1879 (medal with clasp); and in the Transvaal Campaign of 1881, being present at the battle of Laing's Nek; C.M.G., 1881. He became Chief Commissioner of Natal Police, 1894; Justice of the Peace for the Colony; has acted as Secretary for Native Affairs Commissioner of Mines, and Inspector of Prisons. He married, in 1865, a dau. of Judge Steer, of the Calcutta Supreme Court.

DARWIN, Professor Sir George Howard, K.C.B., M.A., F.R.S., LL.D., D.Sc., of Newnham Grange, Cambridge, and of the Athenaeum Club, was born in 1845, and is son of the late Charles R. Darwin. He was educated at Trinity College, Cambridge (Scholar). He acted as President of the British Association in S. Africa in 1905, and in that capacity opened the Victoria Falls railway bridge over the Zambesi. Since 1885 he has been a member of the Council of the Meteorological Office, and is the author of many learned works. He was created K.C.B. on the occasion of the King's birthday in 1905. He married, in 1884, Maud, dau. of Charles du Puy, of Philadelphia.

DAVEL, F. R., M.L.A. A member of the Afrikander Bond, sitting in the Cape Legislative Assembly as the representative of Graaff Reinet.

DAVEY, Thomas Garby, F.G.S., M.I.M.M., M.A.I.M.E., was born in Spain; he was educated in England, and very soon turned his attention to the study of mining, following up his theoretical knowledge with a practical experience commencing in the silver and other mines of Spain and Australia. In the United States he has been retained to report upon the gold and copper of Arizona and elsewhere, and has lately been appointed Consulting Engineer to the Northern Copper

(B.S.A.) Co., Ltd., and the Rhodesian Copper Co., Ltd. In addition to his professional work on behalf of individuals he has found leisure at different times to act as lecturer on mining to the Technical College at Sydney (N.S.W.), where he was the founder and a director of a School of Mines, and in 1895 was appointed Examiner in Metallurgy of the various Schools of Mines in the State of Victoria. He acted as a Shire Councillor for the Bright District of that colony for seven years, during which time he was once President of the Council, and was Justice of the Peace from 1895 until the termination of his residence in Victoria.

DAVIDSON, Alexander, is Chairman and Managing Director of the African City Properties Trust, Ltd., Chairman of the Gaika G.M. Co., Ltd., Luipaard's Vlei Estate and G.M. Co., Ltd., and the Mayfair Development Co., Ltd., director of the Chicago-Gaika Development Co., Ltd., C. Davidson and Sons, Ltd., Rhodesia Sebakwe Development Syndicate, Ltd., Rhodesian Banket Co., Ltd., and the West Rand. Central G.M. Co., Ltd., and is on the London Committee of the Windsor Gold Mines, Ltd.

DAVIDSON, Colonel Arthur, C.V.O., C.B., of the Red House, Warnham, Sussex; is Equerry-in-Waiting to the King. He has seen a good deal of active service, having served in the Afghan War of 1878-80, including Lord Roberts's famous march to Kandahar, the Boer War in 1881, Egyptian War in 1882, and the Bechuanaland Expedition. Subsequently he became Groom-in-Waiting and then Equerry-in-Waiting to Queen Victoria. He was a member of Prince Arthur of Connaught's suite which left for the East early in 1906 in order to invest the Mikado with the Knighthood of the Garter.

DAVIDSON, Walter Edward, M.L.C., C.M.G., *Palmes Academiques* (*en Or.*); of Pretoria; of 62, Brook Street, W., and of the Sports Club, was born at Valetta, Malta, in 1859. He was educated at Christ's Coll., Camb. (Scholar), and entered the Civil Service in 1880; has filled the posts of Magistrate, Judge, and Commissioner, besides which he has been Secy. of the Ceylon Section of the Colonial and Indian Exhibition (1886); Mayor of Colombo, Ceylon, 1896-97; representative of

the Govt. of Ceylon at the Exposition Universelle, Paris (1900), for his services in connection with which he was made *Officer d'Instruction Publique* (France); and special officer to deal with waste lands, Ceylon, 1901. He has also written two books on the resources of Ceylon, 1886 and 1900. He was Colonial Secy. of the Transvaal from 1902 to 1903, and is a member of its Legislative and Executive Councils. Mr. Davidson was married in 1882; is a widower, and has one son at Balliol Coll., Oxon.

DAVIDSON, Col. W. Leslie, C.B., of York, served through the Zulu campaign, being slightly wounded at Ulundi and mentioned in despatches, and was Colonel on the Staff in the recent S.A. War. He was subsequently appointed C.R.A. of the N.E. District.

DAVIES, E. H., F.G.S., M.I.M.M., is the author of *Machinery for Metalliferous Mines: A Practical Treatise for Mining Engineers, Metallurgists, and Managers of Mines.*

DAVIES, Col. W. D., of Johannesburg. 'Karri' Davies (as he is generally called) was one of the two Reform prisoners who, when the question of petitioning for some mitigation of their sentences was raised, consistently refused to sacrifice their self respect by making such a supplication to the Govt. which had treated them in what they deemed to he a dishonest and treacherous manner. Those only who can comprehend the terribly insanitary condition of a Boer gaol, where blacks and whites were huddled together as ordinary felons fed on the worst of fare, and continually subject to the harsh treatment of the gaolers, can appreciate fully such a sacrifice to principle when a word would have effected their release. He took part in the recent S.A. War.

DAVIES, William Thomas Frederick. B.S.C., M.D. (Lond.), M.R.C.S. (Eng.), D.S.O., of Johannesburg, and of the Rand Club, Johannesburg, and the Sports Club, London, was born at Swansea, Aug. 13, 1860. He is son of Dr. E. Davies, Medical Officer of Health, Swansea, and grandson of P. F. Bluett, of Holcombe Court, Holcombe Rogus; was educated privately and at Guy's Hospital. He went to S. Africa to practise in

1889; was a member of the Reform Committee in 1896, for which he underwent trial and imprisonment. In the late S.A. War he served as Surgeon Major in the I.L.H., being present at Elandslaagte, and served in Ladysmith during the siege; was afterwards in medical charge of Col. Mahon's relief column to Mafeking, and was invalided home in Aug., 1900, receiving the D.S.O. Dr. Davies afterwards became Surgeon to the Johannesburg Hospital and Pres. of the Transvaal Medical Council. He married, in 1886, Florence, dau. of T. Dixon, of Kimberley and London.

DAVIS, Alexander, of 73, Brondesbury Road, London, N.W., was born in London; was educated privately and studied in Germany. He has spent the best part of his life in SA., in commerce, travel, prospecting, and journalism. He was one of the early hands at the Lydenburg Goldfield, settling afterwards in Swaziland under King Umbandine, trading and hunting the eastern littoral. After prospecting in Barber ton he settled in the Rand, and eventually followed the stream northwards to Bulawayo, where he was in laager during the siege (1896). There he established the *Bulawayo Sketch*, which he edited and illustrated; afterwards founded the weekly *Rhodesia*, which, however, he closed down in 1902, when he became editor of the *African Review*. This he relinquished in 1905. Mr. Davis is a disciple of Cecil Rhodes, a devotee of art, an amateur sculptor, and a student of philosophy and ethics. He is the author of *The Native Problem*, *Umbandine, a Romance of Swaziland*, and a contributor of articles and reviews to current literature. He married, at Durban, Arabelle, dau. of the late Edwin Selig, of Manchester.

DAVIS, Peter, of Pietermaritzburg, Natal, of the firm of P. Davis and Sons, is proprietor of the *Natal Witness* and of the Durban *Advertiser*. He is also chairman of the old-established Natal Bank, which was founded in 1854, and has for some years maintained a dividend of 14 per cent.

DAWSON, Fred, of Robertson, Cape Colony, was formerly secretary and general manager of the Londonderry and Lough Swilly Rly. Co., agent for the Board of Works, Ireland, for the Letterkenny Rly; and secretary for the Derry Central Railway,

Coleraine. He is now general manager of the New Cape Central Railway.

DEANE, Colonel Thomas, C.B., of Newlands, Surbiton, Surrey, and of the Garrick Club, was born in Dublin in 1841, and is son of S. C. Deane. He served in India with the King's Dragoon Guards, 21st Hussars, and the Viceroy's bodyguard, 16th Bengal Cavalry; he has acted as deputy secretary to the Government of India in the Military Secretariat, in which position he served for 13 years; he acted as Asst. Controller of Transport and Supply during the Afghan War, and was thanked by S. of S. for India for his services in the field; was director of the Army Remount Dept. in India for nearly ten years, and is now employed under the India Office to select and purchase in England horses for the Indian studs, being an authority on the selection of thoroughbred horses for stud purposes. Col. Deane has seen service in S. Africa in 1900-1, with the Imperial Yeomanry, when he commanded the depot of that force at Elandsfontein, and was employed for three years in connection with its organisation. His recommendations on remount organisation during the war were specially called attention to by the War Commissioners, and he has contributed many articles to the Press on military organisation. Recreations: Shooting, fishing, and theatricals. He married, in 1872, Jessie, dau. of Surg. Gen. J. Murray.

DEANE, Hon. William Arthur, M.L.A. for Umvoti County, joined Mr. Moor's Cabinet in Nov. 1906.

DE BEER, M.J., M.L.A., represents Picquetberg in the Bond interest in the Cape House of Assembly. He was elected in Feb., 1904.

DE BUCY, Marquess Sergius Mortimer Emmanuel Rouault de Longueville, of 117, Piccadilly, W., and of the United Forces and Cocoa Tree Clubs, was born in London, March 8, 1865. and is son of the tenth marquess. He was educated at Cambridge Univ. and first went out to S. Africa with Sir Chas. Warren's expedition to Bechuanaland in 1884-5. At the end of that time he proceeded up north on a hunting trip after big game until 1886. He joined the 12th Prince of Wales's Royal Lancers in 1887, took part in the Matabele Rebellion, and remained in Matabeleland attached to the Mounted Police until the outbreak of the Boer War in 1899. He served throughout the campaign as Major in the S.A. Field Force, and at the close of it he accompanied Col. Owen Thomas on a special mission north of the Transvaal to report upon the possibilities of land settlement there. He has travelled and hunted in most parts of S. Africa, from Bechuanaland to the East Coast, and along the Limpopo and Zambesi rivers.

DE JAGER, Dr. A. L., M.L.A., is member of the Cape House of Assembly for the Paarl.

DE KOCK, J. W., M.L.A., represents Mafeking in the Progressive interest in the Cape Legislative Assembly, to which he was elected in 1904.

DELALLE, Right Rev. Henry, Ph.D., D.D., Catholic Bishop of Natal, of Emmanuel Church, Durban, was born at Nancy, France, Dec. 1, 1869; was educated at Pont-a-Mousson, France, and at Rome; was Principal of St. Charles's Coll., Maritzburg, for eight years, and was consecrated Bishop on June 2, 1904.

DE LA MOTTE, Lieutenant Reginald Barker, was born August 19, 1879, and entered the Army Service Corps in 1902. He served in the South African war in 1900-2 with the Imperial Yeomanry, being present at the operations in the Orange River Colony in 1901, and in the Cape Colony in 1902.

DELAP, Captain George Goslett, D.S.O., was born in 1873, and entered the Royal Army Medical Corps in 1899. He served in the South African war in 1899-1902, and took part in the advance on Kimberley, including the action at Magersfontein, and the relief of Kimberley, the operations in the Orange Free State, including the operations at Paardeburg and the actions of Karee Siding, Vet River, and Zand River, and the operations in the Transvaal, including the actions at Johannesburg, Pretoria, Diamond Hill, and Riet Vlei (despatches, King's medal with two clasps, and D.S.O.).

DE LA PASTURE, Lieutenant Charles Edward, was born Sept. 15, 1879, and entered the Derby Regt. in 1900, subsequently changing into the Scots Guards. He served in the South African war in 1901, and was awarded the Queen's medal with clasp.

DE LA POER BERESFORD, Captain Marcus John Barré, was born April 10, 1868, and entered the South Wales Borderers as 2nd Lieut. in 1889. He served in the South African war in 1900-2, employed with the Mounted Infantry, and performed the duties of commandant at Kromellenborg, afterwards acting as Commandant at Rietfontein Bridge. He also took part in the operations in the Transvaal and Orange River Colony. (Queen's medal with four clasps.)

DE LA REY, General Jacobus Hendrick, represented the Lichtenberg Dist. of the Transvaal in the First Read for three years and was regarded as moderate in politics, with a predilection for progress. He served right through the Boer War, and if not the most brilliant from a military point of view of the Boer generals, he followed close on the reputation of Commandant Louis Botha. He was responsible for Lord Methuen's unfortunate defeat at Tweebosch early in March, 1902—practically the last affair of importance in the S.A. War—and took an important part in the peace negotiations, and subsequent efforts to alter the conditions of peace. With this end in view Gen. De La Rey went to Europe with Generals De Wet and Louis Botha after the termination of the war. (For a summary of the three Generals' proceedings in Europe see the biography of Gen. Louis Botha.) Gen. De La Rey's wife is about to publish a book entitled *My Rambles and Experiences During the War*. The General was first Pres. of the Western Transvaal Farmers' Association, the policy of which is said to be to cooperate cordially with the new British Government.

DE LOS MONTEROS, Gen. Espinosa, was exile of the Spanish Plenipotentiaries at the Moroccan Conference at Algéçiras in 1906.

DE MEIRELLES, Viscount Francisco de Menezes, Meirelles do Canto e Castro, K.C.M.G. (Nov. 9, 1902), Knight Commander of the Order of Our Lady of Conception, of Villa Viçosa, and Officer of the Order of Santiago for Literary and Scientific Merit; of Guinta de San Mathens, Dafundo,

Portugal, and Potsdamerstrasse, Berlin, is the son of Senhor Andre Meirelles de Tavora do Canto e Castro, Knight Commander of the Order of Christ, and Dona Anna de Menezes de Lemos e Carvalho. The Meirelles are an old Portuguese family of Northern Portugal a branch of which settled at Terceira (Azores) in the fifteenth century. The male members have the hereditary rank of Knight of the Royal Household (*Fidalgo Cavalleiro da Caza Real*). The present Viscount was born Nov. 21, 1850, at Angra do Hereismo, Terceira Island, Azores. He was Director of the Customs, Mozambique, 1875-79, *idem* at Goa (Portuguese India), 1879-81; Consul and afterwards Consul General in British India, 1883-91, and Governor of Manica e Sofala (Mozambique), 1894-95, 1897 and 1899-1901. The Viscount de Meirelles is best known as the Portuguese Governor who at Beira (chief town of the Manica and Sofala Territories) in 1900 welcomed so warmly the Colonial troops (Canadian and Australian contingents) which landed there on their way to Rhodesia. He was one of the first among his countrymen to perceive that the future relations of Portugal and Great Britain largely depended upon the way the British troops were received at that delicate juncture. His speeches (especially the one he made at the dinner he offered to Gen. Sir Frederick Carrington) were then much commended in the Portuguese Press, and also in the English papers all over the world, including the *Times*. Shortly afterwards the Lisbon Government did not approve of some local measure promulgated at Beira by Governor Meirelles, and he was dismissed in May, 1901. In the Order to the British Army issued by Lord Roberts at the end of that year the Portuguese Governor was referred to as one of the few foreigners who were deserving of honour able mention for his attitude during the war. Later on (May, 1902) Counsellor Meirelles was created a Portuguese Viscount, and in the following Nov., on the birthday of H.M. King Edward VII., he was made a K.C.M.G. At present be is an Attaché for Commercial Affairs to the Portuguese Legation in Berlin. Viscount Meirelles is a Counsellor to H.M. the King of Portugal. He married, April 9, 1875, Dona Maria Carlota da Costa Freitas.

DE MOLEYNS, Lieut. Col. Hon. Frederick Rossmore Wauchope Everleigh, D.S.O. (1897), of

Salisbury, Mashonaland, was born Dec. 11, 1861; is the eldest son and heir of the 4th Lord Ventry. He was educated at Harrow, and entered the 4th Hussars in 1883. In 1889 he was A.D.C. to Lord Hopetoun, when he was seconded from his regt. He rejoined in 1890, acting as Adjt. from 1893 to 1896. In May of that year he obtained leave to proceed to S.A., and was employed on Sir Fred. Carrington's Staff, serving through most of the campaign in Matabeleland, and afterwards in Mashonaland (mentioned in despatches, and D.S.O.), where he was appointed Commissioner of Police. He retired from the service in 1901.

DEMPERS, Hon. H. J., M.L.C., was member of the Cape Legislative Assembly for the province of Caledon until the general election of Feb., 1904, when he was returned to the Legislative Council as representative of the South-Western Circle. He is a member of the Bond.

DENBIGH, Lord (Rudolph Robert Basil Aloysius Augustine), of Newnham Paddox, Lutterworth, and of the Canton, Naval and Military, and Beefsteak Clubs, was born in 1859, and is son of the 8th Earl. He was educated at the R.M.A., Woolwich, and joined the Royal Artillery in 1878, serving in the Egyptian campaign in 1882, being present at the action at Tel-el-Kebir (medal and clasp). Since 1898 he has commanded the Hon. Artillery Co. with the rank of Lieut. Col. He was Parliamentary candidate for the Rugby Division in 1889-92. He married the Hon. Cecilia M. Clifford, dau. of Baron Clifford, in 1884.

DENISON, Lieut. Garnet Wolseley, of the Royal Societies' Club, Lond., was born at Toronto, Sept. 5, 1876, and is son of Lieut.-Col. O. T. Denison. He was educated at Upper Canada Coll. and the R.M.C., Kingston, Canada (diploma with honours and gold medal). He entered the R.E. in 1898, and in 1900 was Asst. British Commissioner to the Anglo-French Boundary Commission in N. Nigeria; was head of the Roads Dept. in British Central Africa in 1902, and in the same year he proceeded again to N. Nigeria as lieut. in the Sapper Co. (R.E.) with the W.A.F.F., when he commanded a company of R.E. with the local rank of capt., and served in that capacity during the Kano-Sokoto Expedition (medal and clasp). In 1903 he was appointed Intelligence Officer on the Staff of the High Commissioner, and returned to England in 1904. He afterwards became a member of the Berbera-Argan Railway Survey in Somaliland. His antelope trophies include twenty species.

DENISON-PENDER, Sir John, K.C.M.G., J.P., of 6, Grosvenor Crescent, S.W., was born in 1855, and is son of the late Sir John Pender. He is one of the pioneers of submarine telegraphy, and is vice chairman and managing director of the Eastern Telegraph Co. and director of the other Associated Telegraph Companies. Their first cable to America lasted only a month, but in that time its use saved the War Office £50,000. During the South African War Sir John arranged for cheaper cable rates for wounded officers. The services rendered in connection with submarine cable telegraphy were recognised by the K.C.M.G. bestowed in Oct., 1901. He has also received Orders from the Governments of Denmark Turkey, and Portugal. Sir John has served in S. Africa and China, and married, in 1879, Beatrice Katherine, only dau. of the late Cuthbert Ellison.

DENMAN, Major Lord, of 16, Carlton House Terrace, London, was born in 1874, and in 1894 succeeded his great-uncle, the second Baron Denman of Dovedale, who in 1887 was in a minority of one in the House of Lords and opposed the third reading of the Law of Evidence Amendment Bill. It was the first Lord Denman, the Solicitor General of Queen Caroline, whose introduction of the case of the woman taken in adultery into the Queen Caroline trial provoked the epigram quoted by Mr. Herbert Paul in the House of Commons:

"Most Gracious Queen, we thee implore
To go away and sin no more;
Or, if that effort be too great,
To go away at any rate."

The present Lord Denman, after leaving Sandhurst, became a lieutenant in the Royal Scots, and afterwards served with the 11th Battalion of Imperial Yeomanry in the South African War in 1900, towards the end of which year he was slightly wounded. Returning to England, he joined the Middlesex I.Y., in which he holds the rank of

Major. When Sir Henry Campbell-Bannerman became Premier in 1906, Lord Den man was appointed a Lord-in-Waiting. He married, in 1903, Gertrude, dau. of Sir W. Pearson. Lady Denman is a busy political hostess on the Liberal side.

DENNE, Major Alured Barkley, R.A., was on the Instructional Staff of the Royal Military Academy from 1892-99; Advanced Class at the Ordnance College from 1899-1901, and was on the Inspection Staff of the Royal Arsenal from 1901 until 1902, when he was appointed Chief Inspector of Explosives for the Transvaal.

DENNY, George Alfred, member of the Australian, American, and North of Eng. Institutes of Mining Engineers, of Yeoville, Johannesburg, and of the Rand Club, was born at Bathurst, New South Wales, Feb. 28, 1868. He was educated at various institutions in New South Wales, and attended science lectures at Ballarat Sch. of Mines. He acted as Asst. Engineer to various mining Cos. in Australia, 1888-90; was Inspecting Engineer in America and Europe for London groups, 1891-92; was engaged in construction work, 1892-95; was Consulting Engineer to the Klerksdorp Prop. Mines from 1895 to 1897, since when he has acted in a similar capacity to the General Mining and Finance Corporation, Ltd. Mr. Denny is the originator of new metallurgical processes principally relating to the continuous and automatic treatment of gold ore slimes; is the author of *Klerksdorp Goldfields*, *Diamond Drilling*, *Deep Level Mines of the Rand*, and frequently contributes to Scientific Societies on technical subjects. He married, Mar. 5, 1903, Winifred, dau. of Fred. Bennett, J.P., of Durban.

DE NORDWALL, Charles Flesch, M.Inst. E.E., A.M.A. Inst. E.E., F.R.C.I., Commander of the Persian Lion and the Sun, of 2, Observatory Gardens, Campden Hill Road, Lond., W., and of the Devonshire Club, Lond., was born in Vienna Oct. 19, 1850, and became a naturalised British subject in 1890. He is son of Privy Councillor August Flesch do Nordwall, of Vienna, and was educated at Vienna and Paris with a view to entering the Diplomatic Service. He, however, took up electrical engineering, with which he has been connected since 1882. Since then he has travelled three times round the world; has spent nearly fifteen years in British Colonies, China, Japan, and the U.S.A., and is well known in S. Africa, being especially interested in the industrial development of the subcontinent. He is a London director of the Allgemeine Electricität-Gesellschaft of Berlin, director of the A.E.G. English Manufacturing Co., Ltd., and of the Electrical Co., Ltd., and is managing director of the A.E.G. Electrical Co., of South Africa, Ltd. The last-named is one of the affiliated companies of the Allgemeine Electricität-Gesellschaft of Berlin, which, together with its affiliated companies, controls a capital of fifty millions sterling. The South African company has agents in all the important business centres in South Africa, including East London, Port Elizabeth, Cape Town, Durban, and Bloemfontein. They keep a large stock in Johannesburg and also at the various towns on the coast, and are contractors for harbour installations, central stations, electric railways and tramways, wireless telegraphy installations, and all kinds of electrical machinery. Amongst others, the following contracts have been carried cut up to the present in South Africa; Table Bay Harbour plant, East London Harbour plant, extension to Pretoria Municipal Electric Lighting Station, winding plant for Village Main Reef, sundry electric light and power installations on the Rand. Mr. De Nordwall married, June 29, 1872, Miss Mario Lallesco.

DENTON, Sir George Chardin, K.C.M.G. C.M.G., of Government House, Gambia, Hilltop, Oxford, and of the Naval and Military Windham, and Grosvenor Clubs, is the only surviving son of the late Rev. Robert A. Denton, rector of Stower Provost, Dorset, where he was born on June 22, 1851. He was educated at Rugby and by private tutors. He entered the Army (57th Regt.), 1869, became lieut., 1871, captain in 1878, and retired in 1878. Joining the Civil Service, he was Chief of Police at St. Vincent in 1880, Col. Secy. at Lagos, 1888, and Lieut.-Gov. Lagos in 1900. He administered the Governments of St. Vincent and Lagos on various occasions for long periods between 1885 and 1900, and in 1901 he was appointed Governor of the Gambia. He married, in 1879, Joan Margaret Alan, dau. of the late Alan Stevenson, C.E., F.R.S., who died in 1900.

DE PAAS, Ernest Simeon, of Naphill, near High Wycombe, Bucks, who made an attempt on his own life in 1905, has served as a Volunteer in five campaigns, including the Zulu War, one of the Sudan expeditions, and the recent S.A. War, when he went out in 1900 as a corporal in the 11th Battn. I.Y., and finished as quartermaster and hon. lieut. in the 50th Battn. I.Y. He is married.

DERNBURG, Bernhard, Chief of the German Colonial Office, of Berlin, was born at Darmstadt, July 16, 1865, and is son of a well known journalist, Friedrich Dernburg, who was once a National Liberal Deputy in the Reichstag; was formerly Editor of the *National Zeitung*; a writer of feuilletons for the *Berliner Tageblatt* ; and in 1906 visited England with a number of German editors at the invitation of a Committee represented by Mr. Leo Weinthal (q.v.) and Mr. W. T. Stead.

Herr Dernburg, as a boy, was employed as a clerk in the *Berlin Handelsgesellschaft* (Trading Company), afterwards spending some years in the United States with the well-known New York house of Ladenburg, Thalman, and Co., learning American methods of business and banking. Returning to the German capital, he was given a good appointment in 1889 at the Deutsche Bank, where by hard work he soon acquired a name as an authority on high financial matters, his talents being mainly employed in the development of the bank's American business. He first came prominently before the public in connection with the German financial crisis in 1900, when he succeeded in restoring order to a number of chaotic banking concerns engaged in real property speculations. It was at this time that he earned the title of *sanitätsrat* (Councillor of Health), because the company over which he presided devoted itself to reorganising and resuscitating tottering financial concerns. One of his most brilliant achievements was perfecting the reorganisation of the Northern Pacific Railway in cooperation with the late George von Siemens. German capital was heavily interested in that hitherto unfortunate venture. About this time Herr Dernburg was also actively engaged in consolidating German interests in South African mining holdings. His success in conducting the Treuhand Gesellsehaft attracted the attention of the management of the *Bank für Handel und Industrie*, commonly known as the Darmstadter Bank, owing to the location of the head office in the Hessian capital. The bank quickly rose under his management to rank among the leading German institutions. Herr Dernburg has been a Director of a dozen of the largest German industrial companies, as well as a Director of the Consolidated Mines Selection Co., a concern holding many mining properties in South Africa. He was interested not only in haute finance, but in matters as various as small arms and chocolate, electrical appliances and mining. From all his Directorates he has now retired, and in order to throw himself wholeheartedly and disinterestedly into the affairs of his new office, it is understood that his Excellency has disposed of all his share interests in German, Colonial, and other enterprises.

Herr Dernburg was a comparatively young man of forty-one when, although he had had no experience of official, political, or Colonial matters, he relinquished an annual income of about £20,000 to become head of the German Colonial Office with a modest salary of £750 and an official residence. For some time past the affairs of this department had been in a desperate state—in fact, the German Colonies were unqualified failures. German East Africa was singularly unproductive of anything but expense to the Home Government, and a tedious and long-drawn-out war in South-West Africa paralysed progress as well as involving large expenditure in life and treasure. The Kaiser determined that the fault lay at home, and on the resignation of Prince Ernest of Hohenlohe-Langenburg (a kinsman of the Kaiser through the Empress's family, and a nephew of King Edward VII), he decided that he could not do better than place a shrewd business man in charge of the Empire's Colonial affairs. One great result is anticipated from Herr Dernburg's appointment, and that is the attraction of much capital to the Kaiser's undeveloped Colonies. Hitherto German capitalists have held aloof from sinking their money in the more or less barren wastes of East and West Africa, the Cameroons, Togo, Samoa, or Kiauchau, largely because they lacked confidence in the bureaucratic Colonial régime; but so soon as Herr Dernburg's control shall have made itself felt it is thought that Germany's captains of finance and industry—men like Ballin, Rathenau, Lowe,

Guilleaume, Wiegand, Friedlander, Thyssen, and Simon—will thenceforth be disposed to look with favour upon Colonial enterprises, not only because they have faith in the new management, but because Herr Dernburg's appointment will be looked upon as an encouragement to the great German commercial classes.

Herr Dernburg is recognised throughout the German business world as a man of relentless energy, force, and daring, and the supposition is that his Imperial master expects him to employ On behalf of the German Colonies the same qualities which have made him so early in life a leader of Teuton industrial affairs. He speaks English fluently, and his motto is said to be "Energy is the greatest virtue". In the City of London, where amongst financial circles he is well known, he is held in the highest esteem, and his general attitude is extremely friendly towards Great Britain.

DE SAUSMAREZ, Sir Walter, has been Judge of his Majesty's Supreme Consular Court for the Ottoman Dominions since 1903. He was Asst. Judge in the Consular Court for Zanzibar 1892-97, and Asst. Judge in the Ottoman Dominions from 1897 to 1903. Sir Walter was created Knight on the occasion of the King's birthday, 1905.

DE SMIDT, Hon. A. G., M.L.C., is a member of the Cape Legislative Council for the South-West Circle, and was last re-elected to the Upper House in Feb. 1904. He holds his seat in the Progressive interest.

DEVENISH, M., of Warnford Court, London, E.C., is the adopted son of Mr. Fred A. English, and is a director of the British Lomagunda Development Co., Ltd., and is on the London Committee of the Consolidated Main Beef Mines and Estate, Ltd., Main Reef Deep, Ltd., and the Main Reef East, Ltd.

DE VILLIERS, Johan Zulch, of Standerton, Transvaal, was born at the Paarl, C.C., July 12, 1845, and is of Huguenot descent. He was educated at the Paarl Gymnasium and privately by Dr. Rose-Innes at Cape Town. After leaving school he was appointed Secy. to the Paarl Wine and Brandy Co., but on the Basuto War breaking out he joined the Free State forces, and after fifteen months' fighting settled in a mercantile house at Fauresmith, shortly afterwards (May, 1868) entering the Civil Service as Public Prosecutor at Boshof, O.F.S. He then became private secy. to the late President, Sir John Brand; then first clerk to the Govt. Secy. and successively Secy. to the Volksraad, Registrar of the High Court, Landdrost of Boshof (1871), Landdrost of Harrismith (1875), which he relinquished (1881) at the request of the triumvirate composed of Kruger, Joubert, and Pretorius, to become Landdrost of Pretoria, during which time he also acted for six months as Attorney General. From July, 1890, to July, 1895, he was Govt. Sec., Treasurer, and Landdrost for Swaziland under the dual Govt. He was later appointed Special Landdrost of the Pilgrim's Rest Gold Fields and Burgomaster of Johannesburg, Oct., 1897, which post he held until the British occupation.

Mr. de Villiers passed under the old law of the Free State as an attorney, which gave him the right to practise as an advocate of the High Court. He is a Masonic Knight of the H. Cross. He married, Nov. 1, 1870, Susanna Margaretha de Villiers, first cousin to Sir Henry de Villiers, Chief Justice of the Cape of Good Hope.

DE VILLIERS, Rt. Hon. Sir John Henry, P.C., K.C.M.G., B.A., of Wynberg House, Wynberg, Cape Colony, was called to the Bar at the Inner Temple in 1865. From 1867-73 he was a member of the House of Assembly for Worcester, Cape of Good Hope, and in 1872-3 became first Attorney General under responsible Government, subsequently Acting Judge of the Vice-Admiralty Court, Chief Justice, and President of the Legislative Council and of the Diamond Law Commission. He has been a member of the Cape Executive Council since 1872, and since 1873 has been a member of the Council of the Cape University. In 1881 he was appointed one of the Royal Commissioners for the settlement of the Transvaal territory, for which he received the K.C.M.G., and was one of the delegates to the Colonial Conference in 1894. He married, in 1871, Aletta, dau. of J. P. Jourdan, of Worcester, Cape of Good Hope.

DE VILLIERS, Melius, B.A. LL.B. of Wynberg,

C.C., is the son of the late C. C. de Villiers of Paarl, C.C. He was born at Paarl, Sept. 5, 1849, and educated at the Paarl Gymnasium and the S.A. Coll., Cape Town, graduating B.A. and LL.B. at the Cape Univ. He was appointed Second then First Puisne Judge, and subsequently Chief Justice of the High Court of the O.F.S. But it is as an Arbitrator in several disputes between the British and Transvaal Govts. that he is principally known. In 1885 he was the Arbitrator between the two Governments regarding the Western Boundary of the Transvaal, and subsequently he was an Arbitrator between the same Govts. as to a question arising under the London Convention with regard to the position of H.B.M. Indian subjects in the Transvaal. He is the author of *The Roman and Roman Dutch Law of Injuries* (1899). He married Miss A. Holmes-Orr, dau. of the Rev. W. Holmes-Orr, of West Lysford Rectory, Somerset, England.

DEVINE, Dr. James Arthur, M.A., B.Ch., B.A.O. (Trinity Coll., Dublin), D.S.O., of Osborne Place, Winnipeg, Man., Canada, and of the Manitoba Club, Winnipeg, was born at Toronto, Nov. 9, 1869; is son of the late Capt. Devine, Surveyor-Gen. of Ontario, and was educated at St. Charles' Coll., Lond., and Trinity Coll., Dublin. Dr. Devine practises as a physician at Winnipeg, and is Prof. of Clinical Medicine and Therapeutics to the Med. Coll. of the University of Manitoba. In the South African War he served with the Canadians: first with the 1st Regt. Canadian Mounted Rifles (1899-1900) in the advance from Bloemfontein under Generals Hutton and French, and afterwards with the 2nd Regt. until the end of the war (1902). He attained the rank of Major on the Canadian Army Med. Staff, is Ron. Major in the R.A.M.C., and was decorated for services at Hart's River, being twice mentioned in despatches (Queen's medal and five clasps). Unmarried.

DE WAAL, David C., M.L.A., of Cape Town, was born at Modder, Stellenbosch, C.C., and comes of an old Colonial stock, his father and grandfather having fought against the British at Blaauwberg. He followed first the calling of farmer, and then became an ironmonger and merchant at Cape Town, which he formerly represented on the Town Council. He was Mayor of Cape Town in 1889-90, when he marked his year of office by planting an avenue of trees in the Street which bears his name. He has for a long time represented Picquetberg in the House of Assembly; is a Protectionist; a member of the Bond; generally accompanied Mr. Rhodes on his journeys in the Cape, and remained his faithful champion during the troubles following on the Raid. He also warmly supported Lord Milner in the House, energetically protesting against the enmity to the British being encouraged and kept alive in the Cape Parliament (Sept. 1902). Mr. de Waal has travelled extensively in Europe as well as in S.A. He was not re-elected at the general election in 1904.

DE WAAL, Nicholas Frederick, M.L.A., is member of the Cape Legislative Assembly for the province of Colesberg, for which constituency he was last elected in Feb., 1904. He is a member of the Bond.

DE WET, Christian Rudolf, of the O.R.C., farmer. Ex-Gen. De Wet fought right through the S.A. War, 1899-1902. Although a man of considerable local influence, he entered the Heilbronn Commando as an ordinary burgher, but was elected Vice-Comdt. on the day the ultimatum expired. The skill and boldness he displayed at Nicholson's Nek attracted Pres. Steyn's attention, and at Magersfontein he found himself in command of the O.FS. contingent with Gen. Cronje, whose second in command he was. His capture of our convoy at Waterval and his gallant attempt to relieve Cronje at Paardeberg were the prelude to his appointment as Commander-in-Chief of the Free State forces. Meanwhile the British successes of that time so demoralised the burghers that the general had to allow them a respite from military service. However, his accidental success at Sanna's Post, and his capture at Reddersburg, gave fresh courage and brought new recruits to his side. Many vicissitudes followed, and Gen. De Wet began to give evidence of his extraordinary resources in evading the British forces and getting out of tight places. At the same time he deputed men of energy to rally those burghers who had already surrendered and taken the oath of neutrality, with great results. Once decided that the condition of the country would not permit of operations on a large scale, he split up his forces into small commandos and adopted the guerrilla style, and his

record now was mainly harassing and running away, but so excellent were his mobility, field intelligence, and dash when occasion prompted, that he still gave the greatest trouble, and every now and then effected a coup, such as the capture of Col. Firman's camp at Tweefontein, soon after which the proclamation of peace relieved us of one of the most resourceful, energetic, and capable leaders that have opposed the British aims in S.A. in the wider aspect of strategy his judgment was somewhat lacking; his scruples were not always over fine. But he was latterly playing a losing game, in a huge country, with no communications, and ever-increasing difficulties in obtaining stores, munitions and horses, upon which his very existence depended. He has written a book called *Three Years of War*, for which he received £10,000, and he is said to be contemplating a work on scouting which would no doubt be a highly useful text book for the British Army. (See General Botha.)

DE WET, Hon. M. J., M.L.C., is member of the Cape Legislative Council for the Eastern Province.

DE WIART. (See Carton De Wiart.)

DE WITTHAMER, Verselewel, ex-member of the Second Raad for Barberton; took part with the Boer forces in the late S.A. War, was captured at Elandslaagte, and sent to St Helena. On his return to the Transvaal he took the oath in the Supreme Court, Pretoria as sworn translator in several languages.

DIBDIN, Robert W., of the firm of Bridges Sawtell and Co., of 23, Red Lion Square, London, W.C., is a director of the Ashanti Goldfields Auxiliary, Ltd., and of the British Law Fire Insurance Co., Ltd.

DICKSON, George Arthur Hamilton F.R.I.B.A., of Johannesburg, and of the Rand Athenaeum (Johannesburg), and Pretoria Clubs was born in London. He is son of the late Rev, Geo. Dickson, M.A., for many years Vicar of St. James the Less, Westminster, and grandson of the late Sir David James Hamilton Dickson, R.N., and of Sir Henry Hunt, C.B., of H.M. Office of Works. He was a pupil of the late Geo. Edmund Street, R.A.,

Architect to the new Law Courts, Strand, and on his death he transferred his articles to the late Sir Arthur Blomfield, A.R.A. He went to S.A. a few years later, and has since practised in Johannesburg and Pretoria. Mr. Dickson is a Fellow of the Royal Institute of British Architects; Pres. of the Transvaal Institute of Architects; member of the S.A. Association of Engineers; Diocesan Surveyor of Pretoria; member of the Johannesburg Town Council; Chairman of the Rand Public Monuments Committee; and is also on the Committee of the Rand Club. He was at one time in the 1st Derbyshire Militia, but resigned his commission in 1890, on deciding to settle in S.A. On the outbreak of the S.A. War he was appointed Capt. in Bethune's M.I., and commanded C Squadron in the field throughout the war, with the exception of a short period from Dec. 1900 to May 1901, when he was invalided home. For some time he acted as second in command of his regiment (Queen's and King's medals and eight clasps), and he is now Pres. of the B.M.I. permanent committee. Mr. Dickson has for years been an enthusiastic polo player. He popularised the game in Pretoria, and was for some time Capt. of the Rand Polo Club, for which he still plays.

DICKSON, Thomas, of Bloemfontein, O.R.C. was educated at Fettes College, Edinburgh. He served in the South African War in 1900-01 with the 1st Contingent Ceylon Mounted Infantry and with the S.A.C. (Queen's medal and three clasps, and King's medal with two clasps). In 1901 he was appointed Chief Clerk in the Land Settlement Dept., Orange River Colony, Assistant Secretary there in 1903, and Secretary in 1905.

DIETRICH, Heinrich, J.P., F.R.C.I., of Zeerust, District Marico, Transvaal, is son of the late eminent surgeon, Andreas Friedrich Dietrich, and was born at Altona, Germany, May 18, 1860. He emigrated to S.A. in Oct. 1883, where he has since resided. Although a burgher of the late S.A.R., he rendered excellent services to the British military authorities on their occupying the town of Zeerust, and also took a prominent part in the defence of the town, he having been placed in command of the Zeerust Town Guard by the British. At the conclusion of the war in 1902 he was appointed J.P. and a member of the Health Board for the

town of Zeerust. Recently he has been entrusted with the charge of the Govt. Meteorological Station at Zeerust. In 1892 he married the widow of the late August Griete, of Matabeleland fame, and after her death he married Anne, eldest dau. of the late Advocate Peter Johannsen, of Altona, Germany.

DIETZSCH, Ferdinand, of Salisbury House London, E.C., is a director of the African Gold Dredging and Mining Concessions, Ltd., Clitters United Mines, Ltd., and the Totoral Mining Co., Ltd.

DIGBY, Lord, J.P., of 39, Belgrave Sq., London, S.W.; Minterne House, Cerne Abbas, Dorsetshire; and of the Carlton and Travellers' Clubs; was born in 1846, and is son of the 9th baron, his ancestry stretching as far back as 1461. Lord Digby has maintained the reputation of his family as a race of warriors, having served in the Suakim Expedition in 1885. He is an Irish peer, and has sat in the House of Commons since his accession to the family honours. He married, in 1893, Emily dau. of the Hon. Albert Hood.

DISTANT, William Lucas, of Steine House, Selhurst Road, S. Norwood, S.E., was born near London, Nov. 12, 1845, and is the only surviving son of the late Capt. Alex. Distant. He was a director and Hon. Secretary of the Anthropological Institute in 1878-81; Secretary of the Entomological Society in 1878-80, and Vice President in 1881 and 1900. He travelled during the late sixties in the Malay Peninsula, making natural history collections there, and afterwards writing *Rhopalocera Malayana*, a description of the butterflies of the Malay Peninsula. Recently he passed four years in the Transvaal, wrote *A Naturalist in the Transvaal*, made large zoological collections in that country, and is now writing and publishing *Insecta Transvaaliensia*, a contribution to a knowledge of the entomology of S. Africa. He is also author of a large part of the description of the order *Rhynchota* in Godman and Salvin's *Biologia Centrali Americana*, and is editor of the *Zoologist*. Recreation: Angling.

DIXON, Major Frances Joseph, of Volksrust, Transvaal, was formerly in the Canadian Civil Service, and took part in the North-Western

Campaign in Canada in 1885 (medal). He also served in the late S. African War (two medals and six clasps). He is a J.P. for the Wakkerstroom Dist., Transvaal, where he acted as Asst. Resident Magistrate in 1902, subsequently being appointed Asst. Resident Magistrate at Volksrust.

DIXON, John, of Harewood House, Cross hills, Keighley, is Chairman of the Bulawayo Commonage Claims, Ltd., and the Kamfersdam Mines, Ltd., director of the Elands Drift Diamond Mines Estates, Ltd., and the Diamond Exploration and Finance Syndicate, Ltd., of which concern he is also a life governor, and is on the London Committee of Knights Pietersburg Gold Mines, Ltd.

DOBSON, Professor Joseph Henry, M.Sc., B.Eng., A.M.I.C.E., A.M.J.E.E., of the Transvaal University College, Hall of Residence, Saratoga Avenue, Doornfontein, South Africa, and of the New and Golf Clubs, Johannesburg, was born at Crewe, Cheshire, Oct. 12, 1878, and is son of John Dobson, of Crewe. He was educated at Crewe, Manchester, and Liverpool, and was apprenticed to engineering in the London and North-Western Railway Works at Crewe from 1892-1899; Senior Cheshire County Council Scholar, 1899-1902; Whitworth Exhibitioner in 1900; Sir Richard Moon Scholar in 1901-1903, and Silver Medallist for mechanical engineering at the London City and Guilds Technological Institute, 1900; was appointed Asst. Professor of Mathematics and Electrical Engineering in 1904, and Professor of Electrical Engineering at the Transvaal University College in 1905. He is a member of the Council of the South African Association of Engineers; Member of the Transvaal Institute of Mechanical Engineers; Associate Member of the Institution of Civil Engineers, and Associate Member of the Institution of Electrical Engineers. He is the author of *The Measurement of Three Phase Electrical Power and Energy* (1906) and *The Mathematical Investigation of the Stresses in Winding Drums and Ropes* (1906). Recreations: golf and tennis.

DODD, Thomas R., was arrested early in 1899 for having organised a public meeting for the purpose of presenting a petition to the British Vice-Consul on the subject of the murder of Edgar by a Boer policeman.

DOLLEY, Hon. John Frederick, M.L.C., was born at Witney, Oxon, in 1852, and went with his parents to Uitenhage six years later. He was for many years a member of the Uitenhage Divisional and Town Councils. He was elected to the Cape Legislative Council in 1891, as member for the S.E. Province, and in his first season carried a resolution recommending the imposition of a royalty on diamonds. He still retains his seat in the Council.

DONALDSON, Lieut. Col. James, D.S.O., of Johannesburg and Delagoa Bay, and of the Rand and New Clubs (Johannesburg), is the son of a London banker, and was born in London, Feb. 28, 1863. He was educated at Edinburgh, went to S.A. when quite young, and was well known as one of the old hands at Pilgrim's Rest and Lydenburg. He is now a member of the firm of Donaldson and Sivewright, of Delagoa Bay and Johannesburg, and is interested in several commercial undertakings. In 1896 he was tried for high treason against the S.A.R. as one of the Reform Committee, and was mulcted in the generally imposed fine of £2,000. At the outbreak of the Boer War he joined the 1st Regt. of I.L.H. as Capt. and Qr.-Master, and it was largely owing to his efforts and business aptitude that the regiment was equipped sufficiently quickly to enable it to take part in the action of Elandslaagte. He was amongst the besieged in Ladysmith, and took part in the relief of Mafeking, after which he was appointed to the command of A Squadron I.L.H. He was twice mentioned in despatches, and his services were recognised by the D.S.O. He was severely wounded near Klerksdorp; and declared unfit for further active service. He obtained his majority just before the disbandment of the corps, and he was subsequently given the command of the right wing of the Volunteer Regiment of the I.L.H. lately formed in Johannesburg. Col. Donaldson was a member of the Native Labour Commission lately sitting in Johannesburg. He is a keen sportsman; has imported some good racing stock, and just before the war he won the Johannesburg Handicap. He married, Aug. 5, 1903, Miss N. Newton, of New Zealand.

DONALDSON, Kenneth Macleay, of Johannesburg (where he is popularly known as 'Ken'), was born in London, Aug. 27, 1864. He is the younger brother Of Lieut. Col. James Donaldson, D.S.O. (q.v.), and saw active service in the Sudan, 1884-5, during which time he acted as War Correspondent and Artist for the late *Pictorial World*. He was subsequently decorated with the Egyptian medal, Suakim clasp, and bronze star. He went to S.A. in 1889, and was well known in Barberton and district till 1893. Early in 1894 he arrived in Johannesburg and in conjunction with his present partner, Mr. S. W. H. Hill, originated and successfully developed Donaldson and Hill's *South African Directories*. On the day of the great dynamite explosion in Johannesburg (Feb. 19, 1896) he married Miss Violet Helen Brereton, a granddaughter of the late Canon Brereton, of Bedford, England, by whom he has one son.

DONNE, Colonel Benjamin Donisthorpe A., C.B., commanding the 35th Regimental Dist. Chichester; of the United Service Club; was born in London, Oct. 4, 1856, and is the eldest son of B. J. M. Donne, of Crewkerne, Somerset. He was educated at Wellington College and abroad, and joined the 35th (Royal Sussex Regt. in 1875, and served in the West Indies and the Mediterranean, and under the Colonial Office as Local Commandant in the Cyprus Pioneer and Military Police from 1880-2; joined the Egyptian Army in 1883 under Sir E. Wood and Sir F. Grenfell, serving in it until 1893 in various campaigns and capacities. He organised the Camel Corps in 1885, and raised the 10th Sudanese Battn. in 1886; was Comdt. of Egyptian Military Sch. at Cairo, 1890-3, and commanded the Egyptian troops at Alexandria in 1892 (3rd cl. Osmanieh). For his war services in 1882 he was awarded medal and Khedive's Star; clasp for the Nile Exped., 1884-5, and 4th cl. Medjidieh; Suakin Campaign, 1888, clasp and Brevet Major (despatches); Nile Campaign, 1889, 3rd cl. Medjidieh and clasp (despatches); N.W. Front. India, 1897-8, with the 2nd Battn. Royal Sussex Regt. (medal and two clasps). Col. Donne took part in the S.A. War in 1900-2, in command of the 1st Royal Sussex Regt., including the march from Bloemfontein to Pretoria, the actions at Houtnek, Welkom Farm, Zand River, Dornkop, the capture of Johannesburg and Pretoria, and the battle at Diamond Hill. He was in command of the detached column at Retief's Nek, and was present at the surrender of the Boer forces at Golden Gate; commanded at the investment of Lindley (despatches, C.B., medal and four clasps, King's medal and two clasps). He married, in 1886, Cecil, dau. of the late Rev. Robert Hughes.

DORMER, Francis J., of 33, Collingham Road, London, S.W., and of 28-31, Bishopsgate Street Within, is one of the many Anglo-Africans who have made journalism a stepping stone to a prominent position in S. African financial circles, having been one of the first editors of the Johannesburg *Star*, which post he resigned to come to London. He was an early and strenuous assailant of Krugerism, and is familiar with the varied conditions and difficult questions affecting S. Africa and its chief industry. He is now Chairman of the Transvaal Estates and Development Co., Ltd. (see C. F. Rowsell), the Siberian Proprietary Mines, Ltd., and a Director of Siberian Timber, Ltd.

DOUGLAS, Rev. R. O., of Rondebosch, Cape Colony, formerly Vicar of North Nibley, was appointed Rector of Rondebosch in 1905.

DOWNE, Viscount, C.B., K.C.V.O., C.I.E., M.A., of Wykeham Abbey, Yorks; Dingley,. Market Harborough; Danby Lodge, Grosmont, York, and of the Carlton, Turf, Marlborough, and United Service Clubs, was born in 1844 and is son of the 7th Viscount. He was educated at Eton and Christ Church, Oxford, and joined the 2nd Life Guards in 1865, subsequently entering the 10th Hussars as Lieut. Colonel in 1886, having previously served in the Zulu War with that regt. in 1879, and also acted as A.D.C. to H.R.H. the Duke of Connaught, and commanding the Meerut Division in India from 1883-5; acted as A.D.C. to H.R.H. the Duke of Cambridge from 1892-5, and commanded the Cavalry Brigade at the Curragh from 1897-9. He served throughout the South African War in 1899-1902 (despatches), and represented H.M. the King as Special Envoy to the Shah of Persia in 1903. Viscount Downe retired from the Army in 1901 with the rank of Major-General. He married, in 1889, Cecilia, dau. of the 3rd Earl of Sefton.

DOWNER, Alfred William, F.R.C.I., of Georgetown, Demerara, British Guiana, and of the Cape Coast Castle Reading Club, was born Demerara, April 21, 1874, and is son of Stephen and Emily Downer. He was educated at Emmore Primary School, British Guiana. He was formerly teacher at the Wilberforce Congregational School there, and Sergeant Major of the British Guiana Police. At the present time he is Senior Superintendent of Police, Gold Coast Colony. He married, April 13, 1899, Susan Braimer, of Georgetown, British Guiana.

DRAKE, Francis Martin, of Del Norte, Houghton Estate, Johannesburg, and of the Land, New, and Athenaeum Clubs, Johannesburg, was born at Campo Seco, California, Feb. 1858, his father being a Californian mining man whose ancestors migrated from Devonshire to America early in the 19th century, while his mother belonged to an old family of New Brunswick, British North America. Mr. F. W. Drake was educated at public schools at San Francisco, afterwards studying privately. At he age of 17 he made his first acquaintance with nines in the U.S.A., where he remained until 1883, when he left for Australia. In that year he put up the first silver lead smelting water jacketed furnace in Australia, which was the pioneer of many others. Returning to S.A., he became in 1896 Consulting Mining Engineer to the *Compagnie Française de Mines d'Or et de L'Afrique du Sud*, and is at present the principal manager of the company's affairs in S.A. He is also a director of the Rand Mines, Ltd., the East Rand Proprietary Mines, and other leading Witwatersrand Cos. He is also on the Pretoria Board of the National Bank of S.A., and on the Executive Committee of the Chamber of Mines (Johannesburg). He married, in 1888, Miss Agnes Matilda Mackey, of Bendigo, Victoria.

DREW, Rev. Dewdney W., first became famous in Johannesburg for his rabid attacks on Mr. Kruger's regime. Latterly he became the champion and apologist of the Cape Colonial rebels. In 1902 he joined the staff of the *South African News*. Ed. *The Friend*, 1904.

DUBY, N. (See Ndube.)

DUCK, Vet.-Col. Francis, C.B., A.V.D., P.R.C.V.S., of Surbiton, Surrey, and of the Junior Constitutional Club, was born in 1845. He was educated at Stonyhurst Coll., and entered the A.V.D. in 1867, served in S. Africa in the Old Colony, Sekukuni, and the Zulu Wars in 1877-8-9-81, and was present at the battles of Hlobana, Kambula, and Ulundi (mentioned in despatches, medal and clasp). He also took part in the first Boer War and the Bechuanaland Expedition in 1884-5 (honourably mentioned); appointed Principal Vet. Officer in India from 1894-7, and was afterwards Dir.-Gen. of the A.V.D. from 1897-1902. He married Miss Edith Garrett, of Maritzburg, Natal.

DUFF, Major-General Sir Beauchamp, K.C.B., C.I.E., of Simla, India, and of the United Service Club, was born in 1855, and is son of the late G. W. Duff He was educated at Trinity College, Perthshire, and the Royal Military Academy, Woolwich, and entered the Royal Artillery in 1874; served in the Afghan War in 1875-80, and was transferred to the Indian Staff Corps in 1881. In 1892 he acted as Brigade Major in the Izazai Expedition, and as D.A.A.G. in the Waziristan Expedition in 1894-5. In the latter year Sir Beauchamp became Military Secretary to the Commander-in-Chief in India, and in 1899 he was appointed Assistant Military Secretary for Indian Affairs at the War Office. He served in South Africa in 1899-1901 (despatches, medal with five clasps and C.B.). Subsequently he was appointed Brigadier General commanding the Allahabad District, and since 1903 has acted as Adjutant General in India. He married, in 1877, Grace, dau. of the late Oswald Wood.

DUFFUS, Capt. F. F., of the Army Service Corps, served throughout the S. African War in 1899-1902, being afterwards quartered in Egypt. He appeared as a witness before the S. African Sales of War Stores Commission in 1905.

DUGMORE, G. E., M.L.A., sits in the Cape House of Assembly in the Progressive interest as the representative of the electoral division of Wodehouse.

DUNCAN, James Denoon, J.P., was born at

Greenock, Sept. 30, 1861. He arrived at Kimberley in 1881; was admitted Conveyancer of the High Court of Griqualand in 1887, and became Attorney-at-Law and Notary Public at the Supreme Court, Cape Colony, in 1888. He is a member of Kimberley School Board and Library Committee, and Chairman of the Kimberley Branch of the S. African Imperial Union, the Progressive Party organisation in Cape Colony. Mr. Duncan takes a great interest in public affairs, and has rendered services to the Imperial cause and that of the loyalist population of S. Africa. On the outbreak of war he volunteered his services to the military, who appointed him their legal adviser, subsequently being appointed Military Crown Prosecutor during the siege of Kimberley, rendering special services in connection with the regulating of supplies and a scheme for the removal of the inhabitants, being mentioned in despatches by Gen. H. G. Kekewich and Lord Methuen. In 1890 he visited England as one of the Cape Colony delegates appointed by the Vigilance Conference of S. Africa to interview the Government on questions affecting the settlement in S. Africa. He was President of the Diamond Fields Scottish Assn. in 1902, and presided at the ceremony at Magersfontein on the third anniversary of the battle, when H.E. the High Commissioner unveiled the Scottish memorial to the Highland Brigade. Recreation, bowling, having played in most of the Cape Colony tournament matches, and is an ex-President of the Kimberley Bowling Green Club.

DUNCAN, John Scarlett, of Cairnsmore, Purley Downs, Surrey, and of the City Liberal Club, was born at Edinburgh, Nov. 9, 1849. He has been in the service of the Natal Bank, Ltd., since 1886, and when the London office was opened in 1890 Mr. Duncan was appointed, and has since remained, the manager of the branch. He has been twice married.

DUNCAN, Patrick, C.M.G., of Pretoria, Transvaal, was born in Banffshire, Scotland, in 1870, and was educated at Edinburgh Univ. and Balliol Coll., Oxford, graduating M.A. (1st class classical moderations and final classical scholar). Mr. Duncan entered the Inland Revenue Department in 1894, was appointed Colonial Treasurer for the Transvaal in 1901, and Colonial Secretary for the Transvaal in 1903. Unmarried.

DUNLOP, William, of 148, Jorissen Street, Johannesburg, and of the Rand and Athenaeum (Johannesburg) Clubs, was born at Glasgow, March 17, 1864. He was educated in the same city, and has had considerable banking experience since he joined the Union Bank of Scotland in 1880. Since then he has served with the Natal Bank at Johannesburg, the National Bank of S. Africa at Pretoria and Germiston, and in 1897 he was transferred to the Johannesburg office of the bank as sub manager, in which position he remained until Nov. 1901, when he was appointed manager of the new Eloff Street branch. In Dec. 1904 he was appointed manager of the chief Johannesburg office of the bank. He married, in 1894, Miss Sarah Rainsford.

DUNN, Sir William, 1st Bart., J.P., F.R.G.S., of 34, Phillimore Gardens, Kensington, W., and of The Retreat, Lakenheath, Brandon, Suffolk, was born in 1833, and is son of the late John Dunn, of Paisley. Sir William left Paisley in 1852 for Algoa Bay, and entered the firm of Messrs. Mackin and Co., of Port Elizabeth. Aft two years he was given a partnership in the business, and six years later, on the death of Mr. Mackie, he became the sole proprietor. He then took up his residence in London, and opened a business house there owing to the growth of the Port Elizabeth branch, subsequently establishing the firms of Messrs. Dunn and Co., in East London; W. Dunn and Co., in Durban, Natal; and Mackie, Dunn and Co., in Johannesburg, in all of which Sir William is the senior partner. He is chairman of the S. African section or the London Cham her of Commerce, a director of the Royal Exchange Assurance Co., and of the Union Discount Co., chairman of the Home and Foreign Insurance Co., and a member of the Executive Council of the London Chamber of Commerce, and formerly acted as Hon. Consul-Gen. in Great Britain for the Orange Free State. He was a Liberal M.P. for Paisley from 1891 until the dissolution in 1906. Sir William married, in 1859, Sarah Elizabeth, dau. of the late James Howse, of Grahamstown, Cape Colony, who was murdered by Kaffirs in 1851.

DUNNE, Col. Walter Alphonsus, C.B., of 28, Victoria St., S.W., and of the Junior United Service

Club, son of the late Jas. Dunne of Dublin, was born Feb. 10, 1853; was educated at Queen's Univ., Ireland; joined the Army in 1873, and has seen active service in the Kaffir War of 1877-8; the Zulu War (being present at Rorke's Drift and Ulundi); the Sekukuni Expedition of 1880 (despatches), the Boer War 1880-1 (siege of Potchefstroom; dies patches); the Egyptian Campaign, 1882 (present at Tel-el-Kebir); and the Suakin Expedition, 1885. Col. Dunne has been Asst. Q.M.G. at Army Headquarters since Jan., 1900, and represents the War Office on the Army Med. Advisory Board. He married, July 23, 1885, Winifred, dau. of the late John Bird, C.M.G., Treasurer of Natal.

DUNNING, Sir Edwin Harris, of Easterlands, and Stoodlight Court, near Tiverton, Devon, was one of the earliest miners on the Witwatersrand, working properties on tribute, until he made a considerable fortune out of the flotation of the Rietfontein mine, whose shares went to a large premium, at which Sir Edwin Dunning was wise enough to sell out and retire. He was subsequently associated with Messrs. Lewis and Marks, and became Managing Director of the African and European Investment Co., and a Director of the Evancon G. M. Co. He was Mayor of Tiverton in 1891. He owns large estates in Devonshire, where he interests himself in horse and cattle breeding. He was knighted on the King's birthday (1904), and married, in 1881, Hannah Louise, dau. of Richard Freeman.

DUNTON, Henry, son of the late Rev. C. Dunton, of Bedford, England, who proceeded to S.A. when quite young, is a member of the firm of Dunton Bros., wholesale merchants, having branches in many parts of S.A. For many years, until the beginning of the late war, he was the managing partner in Johannesburg, where there was a large wholesale branch of the firm. He was married, in 1901, to a daughter of late Capt. Gayer, R.N.

DU PLESSIS, Andreas Stephanus, M.L.A., represents the constituency of Albert in the Cape Legislative Assembly; is a good speaker, and takes a special interest in coal. He was elected in Feb., 1904, and is a member of the S.A. party.

DU PLESSIS, Casper Jan Hendrik, was born at Rustenburg in 1845, and was a near relative of the late Pres. Kruger. He was said to enjoy a native war, and in 1891 was prevailed upon to stand for his native town in the Second Volksraad. He is a member of the Gerefomeerde Church.

DU PLESSIS, David Jacobus, was member of the Cape Legislative Assembly for Middelburg, for which division he was last returned opposed in 1904. He belongs to the S. African party.

DU PLESSIS, Revd. H., formerly minister of the Dutch Reformed Church at Lindley, was always opposed to the war which broke out in 1899. He became chaplain of the Refugee Camp at Kronstad, and earned the gratitude of both sides by his impartial care of sick and wounded at Lindley. His strong British sympathies led to a boycott which resulted in his resigning his ministry, and he was then appointed Inspector of Schools in the Transvaal under the British Administration (1902-3).

DU PLESSIS, Johannes Petrus, J.P., was born at Gorstland Kloof, Cradock, C.C., where he still resides and farms. He served as a burgher in the Kaffir War of 1852; served as Capt. of the Cradock burghers in the Kaffir War of 1878, and in the Basuto War of 1880. He has acted as an Asst.-Field-Cornet since 1873, and has been a member of the Cradock Divisional Council since 1876. He was made a J.P. in 1885. He has also served as member of the School Committee at Cradock; deacon of the D. R. Church, of which he is now an elder; member of the Licensing Court, and of the Land Commission. He was elected to the Cape House of Assembly in 1887, re-elected for Cradock at the head of the poll in 1888, and again in 1894,

DU PLESSIS, Matthew Jacobus, M.L.A., is member of the Cape Legislative Assembly for the Province of Cradock, and was last re-elected in 1904. He belongs to the S.A. party.

DU TOIT, Hon. J. F., M.L.C., is member of the Cape Legislative Council for the Midland Province.

DU TOIT, P. J., was originally a schoolmaster;

subsequently a storekeeper; member of the Cape Legislative Assembly for Richmond, and Pres. of the Afrikander Bond. He was a member of the Jameson Raid Committee, but no longer represents Richmond in the House.

DYER, Bertram L., Librarian of Kimberley, S. Africa, was born May 20, 1868; he was educated at King's Coll., London; entered the War Dept. as clerk; became asst. librarian at Toynbee Hall and Kensington in 1888, and Librarian of Kimberley in 1900. He was also founder and first editor of the *Library Assistant*, and has published *The Public Library Systems of Great Britain, America, and S. Africa*, &c. He married, Sept. 20, 1901, Alice Cornish Watkins, of Kensington.

DYER, Major Stewart Barton Bythesea, D.S.O. (1903), of White's, Cavalry, Marlborough, St. James's, Ranelagh, Roehampton and Prince's Clubs, was born. Nov. 26, 1875, and is only son of Capt. Stewart Dyer, of Westcroft Park, Surrey, and grandson of the late Sir Swinnerton Dyer, 9th Baronet. He was educated privately and at Balliol Coll., Oxford, for which he played football, and joined 2nd Life Guards in 1899 as 2nd lieut. He served with the West African Frontier Force on the Kaduna Expedition in 1900, being present at the actions at Lemo and in the Kaje Hills, and the occupation of Zaria (despatches, West African medal and clasp, 1900); as staff officer to Col. Festing in Ashanti, 1901; on the Bornu Expedition, 1902; with Col. Morland's column to Lake Chad; was present at the action against the rebel chief, Mallum Jibrella, and captured him after riding sixty miles in a night, with nine men (despatches); present at the operations against the Bassama, and in the Wurkum Hills (wounded). In the Kano-Sokoto Expedition in 1903 he led the storming party at Kano (twice wounded), and was present at the action of Tokoto (despatches); commanded small expedition into the Dakakeri country, Northern Nigeria, Feb.-March, 1904, being thanked in Brigade Orders by the High Commissioner, and receiving the African General Service Medal with two clasps for N. Nigeria, 1902 and 1903. He was attached to the Egyptian Army with rank of Bimbashi (Major), March, 1905, and commands the Mounted Infantry Company of the Camel Corps in Kordofan. Recreations: Big game shooting, fox hunting, and polo. Unmarried.

EARP, C. J., formerly held the position of Mayor of Rondebosch. He is a member of the firm of Maxwell and Earp, general merchants and importers, of Cape Town.

EATON, Capt. William Arnold, of Middelburg Cape Colony, and of the Sports Club, London, was born at Lapworth, Warwickshire, April 7, 1870; is son of Canon Eaton, and was educated at Marlborough Coll., entering 'The Buffs' in 1890, since when he has served with the relief force in Chitral in 1895 (medal and clasp); the operations in the N.W. Frontier of India, 1897-8, including the action of Landakai (clasp); Northern Nigeria in 1900, when he served with the Munshi Expedition (wounded, despatches; medal and clasp); and the S. African War, 1900-02, as D.A.A.G. (Queen's and King's medals and two clasps). He was appointed Staff Capt., Middelburg, Sub. District, Cape Colony, May 27, 1904. Capt. Eaton's recreations are racing and polo, and he is a member of the Jockey Club of S. Africa. He married, in 1904, Miss P. M. Douglas, dau, of the late Andrew Douglas.

ECKSTEIN, Friedrich, of 18 Park Lane, London, W. and of 1, London Wall Buildings, was born in Germany in 1857, and was educated at Stuttgart. He is brother of the late Hermann Eckstein, founder of the great Johannesburg house of H. Eckstein and Co., and has always taken a leading part in matters affecting the main industry of the Transvaal. After Mr. Lionel Phillips came to England to join the firm of Wernher, Beit and Co., Mr. F. Eckstein became the virtual head of the Johannesburg community. In 1902 however, he was himself taken into partnership with that firm. He is a Director of the Central Mining and Investment Corp, Ltd., and is on the London Committee of the South Knights, Ltd. He married, April, 1890, in Johannesburg, Miss Catherine Mitchell.

EDGAR, Clifford Blackburn, J.P., of Wedderlie, Queen's Road, Richmond, Surrey and of the Royal Societies and Richmond Clubs, is the elder son of the late John Edgar, of Richmond Hill; was born in

1857, and was educated at Owens College, Manchester; has taken a Mus. Bac. (Lond. Univ.), and B.Sc. (Manchester). He is an original and still an active Director of the Niger Co., Ltd., and a Director of the Bank of Nigeria. In 1898-9 and again in 1903-4 he was Mayor of Richmond; is an Alderman of Richmond and a Member of the Surrey County Council; takes much interest in Educational work, being Vice Chairman of the Surrey Education Committee, Chairman of the Richmond Education Committee, and a Senator of the University of London. He is also Ron. Treasurer of the Musical Association (Incorporated), a Member of the Worshipful Company of Musicians, and Fees, of the Richmond Philharmonic Soc. His recreations are music and travel. He married, in 1883, Miss Fowden.

EDGCUMBE, Sir Edward Robert Pearce, Knt. Bachelor, J.P., LL.D., Deputy Lieut.; of 4, Queen's Gate Gardens, S.W.; of Newquay, Cornwall; and of the Reform, Newquay, and Eighty Clubs, was born at Fordington, Dorset, March 13, 1851, and is the representative of the Lamerton branch of the Edgcumbes of Edgcumbe, near Tavistock, Devon, of whom the Earl of Mount Edgcumbe's family is another branch. He was educated at Cambridge Univ., B.A. 1874 (Queen's Prizeman, S. Kensington, 1868); obtained a studentship at the Royal Academy in 1874, and was called to the Bar at Lincoln's Inn in 1877. Sir Robert was appointed official examiner to the High Court in 1883; contested S. Dorset in 1891 and 1892, and was again a parliamentary candidate, this time for Hereford City, in 1895. He became High Sheriff of Cornwall in 1896. He has travelled considerably, and has published *Zephyrus, a Holiday in Brazil and the River Plate* (1887), *Bastiat's Economic Fallacies* (last edition, 1888), *Popular Fallacies regarding Bimetallism* (1896), *Parentage and Kinsfolk of Sir Joshua Reynolds* (1901), *Works of A. C. Hilton* (1904), and numerous magazine articles. In England he was the pioneer of the small-holdings movement, creating many in Dorsetshire in 1888 (see Rider Haggard's *Rural England*). Sir Robert is a Director of the N.W. Uruguay Railway, the Nyassa Co., Balkis Co., Africa Trust Co., Consolidated Rand Rhodesia Co., and Estates, Mines, and Finance Co. His recreations are boating, cycling, and travel He married first, in 1884, Clara Jane

Constance Conybeare, who died Sept. 22, 1888; and, second, Aug. 6, 1891, Frances, dau. of Admiral F. A. C. Foley.

EDINGTON, Dr., bacteriological specialist, went to Mauritius (1902) at the request of the government to investigate into the cattle disease prevailing there.

EDWARDS, E. J., of Johannesburg, Transvaal began a busy life of journalism and newspaper control on the staff of the *Birmingham Daily Mail* and the *Daily Times*, proceeding to Cape Town in 1888 as sub-editor of the *Cape Argus*. In the following year the Argus Co. acquired the Johannesburg *Star*, and Mr. Edwards was then transferred to the Golden City as editor *pro tem.* of that important paper. In 1891 he returned to Cape Town to join the staff of the *Cape Times*, frequently acting as editor-in-charge, and eventually becoming managing editor. During his association with that journal he represented it is special correspondent at the conferences between the Governors of the C.C. and the Pres. if the S.A.R. and O.F.S. In 1902 Mr. Edwards negotiated, on behalf of the proprietors of the *Cape Times*, the purchase of the Johannesburg *Transvaal Leader*, of which he is now Managing Director, being also Resident Director of the *Cape Times*, Ltd., in the Transvaal Colony.

EDWARDS, Frederic Georges Henry, M.D., F.R.C.I., of Florida Road, Durban, Natal, is the second son of the Hon. W. A. Edwards, M.D., C.M.G., member of the Executive and Legislative Councils of Mauritius, and grandson of the late Hon. A. Edwards, Mayor of Port Louis, and member of the Legislative Council of Mauritius, and great-grandson of Brig. Gen. W. T. Edwards, who was killed in 1820 at the siege of Bhurtpore, India. He was born Nov. 14, 1871, in Mauritius, and was educated at the Royal Coll., Mauritius, and was a student at the Univ. of Paris, and at the Royal Colls. of Physicians and Surgeons, London, graduating M.D., B.A., B.Sc. (Univ. of Paris), M.R.C.S. Eng., L.R.C.P. Lond. He is the author of several well-known works on Sociology, Philosophy and Medicine, amongst which is the noted thesis on *Acute Paralysis of the Spinal Cord in Adults*, published in 1898 by G. Carre and C. Naud, edit. Paris. He has held several appointments as house surgeon, house physician, and house *accoucheur* in hospitals in Paris. He has studied Bacteriology at the Pasteur Institute in Paris, and at King's Coll., Lond. At present he is a general practitioner at Durban, Natal. He married, Sept. S 1898, Marie Vincente Costar, of Paris.

EGERTON, Maj.-Gen. Sir Charles Comyn, G.C.B., D.S.O., A.D.C. to the King, was born in 1848; entered the Army as second lieut. in June 1867, and obtained his first step in Oct. 1869, and his captaincy in 1879. He took part in the Afghan War in 1879-80, accompanied Lord (then Sir F.) Roberts in his march to Kandahar, and was present at the battle of Kandahar, for his services in which he was mentioned in despatches and received the medal with clasp and the bronze star. He was gazetted Maj. on June 5, 1887, and served with the Hazara Expedition in 1888 as A.A.G. (despatches, medal with clasp). In 1891 he took part in the two Miranzai Expeditions under Sir William Lockhart as A.A.G., was severely wounded, and received the brevet of Lieut. Col. and the D.S.O. His war services also include the Waziri Campaign of 1894-5, when he commanded the Bannu column, and received the C.B.; the Sudan operations, 1890, when he commanded the Suakin force; the operations in the Toohi Valley, when he commanded the brigade; and the operations against the Darwesh Kheyl Waziris in 1902, when he was in command of the troops. The order of K.C.B. was conferred on Gen. Egerton on Jan. 1, 1903, and he was invested with the insignia by the Duke of Connaught at Delhi. Gem Egerton superseded Gen. Manning in the command of the Somaliland Expeditionary Force in 1903, and inflicted severe punishment on the Dervishes at Jidballi on Jan. 10, 1904, and by April following the operations were considered practically at an end, the Mullah having disappeared.

EGERTON, Sir Walter, K.C.M.G., of Lagos, W. Africa, has been in the Colonial service since 1880, and has occupied many positions in the Straits Settlements. He arrived in Lagos in Sept., 1904, as Governor of the Colony, and High Commissioner of Southern Nigeria. In 1906 the name of the colony of Lagos was designated Southern Nigeria, and Sir Walter was appointed Governor and Commander-in-Chief thereof. He was created

K.C.M.G. on the occasion of the King's birthday, 1905.

EGLINGTON, William, of Raylands, Maidenhead, is the son of Henry Eglington, newspaper proprietor. Educated privately, he read for the Bar, but subsequently forsook the law for journalism. Was editor-proprietor of the *New Age* and other well-known publications; he resuscitated *The Tatler* in 1888, and in 1892 founded the *British and South African Export Gazette*, of which he is editor and proprietor, and which is one of the leading and most successful commercial journals published. He has also been a prolific contributor to the magazines and the Press on S.A. affairs, and is the author of a number of books which have been widely read. These include *The Sportsman in South Africa*. He has travelled extensively and has shot practically everything there is to shoot in S.A. His collection of trophies is most complete, and numbers upwards of seventy varieties of antelope, including every S.A. species. He was the vice chairman of the Anglo African Writers' Club in 1895 and chairman in 1896. His recreations are shooting golf, cycling, yachting. He married, on April 28, 1887, Lile, only daughter of Edward Chambers Connolly, of Clifton.

EGYPT, Khedive of (see Abbas II.).

EHRLICH, Ludwig, of 10-11, Austin Friars, London, E.C., was born at Bad Kissingen (Bavaria), in 1863; commenced his business career in 1878, with the banking firm of Sulzbach, at Frankfurt, and entered their Paris house some ten years later. In 1890 Mr. Ehrlich went to Johannesburg to join Mr. Carl Hanau in the representation of Mr. S. Neumann, and as such became a Director of the Ferreira, Modderfontein, Knights, Wolhuter, Main Reef, and other Transvaal companies of the Neumann group, from which Directorships he, however, retired in 1894. In 1894 Mr. Ehrlich started for himself in business in Johannesburg. He floated (with the assistance of the Consolidated Goldfields Co.). the Klipfontein Estate and G. M. Co., the Sub Nigel, Ltd., the Midas Deep, Ltd., also the Pretoria Market and Estate Co., the Fordsburg Market and Estate Co. etc. Transferring the centre of his activities to London in 1896, He joined the Exploration Co. in the flotation of the

Consolidated Goldfields of New Zealand. Since Mr. F. H. Hamilton (q.v.) became a partner in 1900, the firm of L. Ehrlich and Co. has been concerned with the flotation of the H. E. Proprietary Ltd., the East Rand Deep Ltd., and the New Districts Development Co., Ltd. The firm is also largely interested in the Modderfontein Est., and G. M. Co., the Luipaard's Vlei Estate and G. M. Co., and the Pigg's Peak Development Co., and further, apart from South African enterprises, in the Corporation called the Spassky Copper Mine (in Siberia), the Siberian Syndicate the Australian Commonwealth Trust, Ltd. (for Deep Leads mining in Victoria), the Oxnam Prospecting Co., Ltd. (in Mexico), the Gold Creek Placers (in Montana), the Manchu Syndicate, &c.

The firm of L. Ehrlich and Co. is represented in Johannesburg by Mr. C. F. Tainton (q.v.); their consulting engineer in London is Mr. E. T. McCarthy. Mr. Ehrlich is a Conservative Free trader in politics. He married, in 1903, Miss Vera de Mosenthal. Mr. Ehrlich is a member of the Automobile Club.

EIFFE, Lieut. Franz Ferdinand, 9th Sharpshooters (Landwehr), Knt. Commander of the Mecklenburg Order of the Falcon, Turkish Order of the Medjidieh, Red Cross Medal (Prussia), Long Service Order, of Adolphstrasse 45, Hamburg; of the Harmonie Club, Hamburg, and the German Club, Lourenço Marques, was born in Hamburg, Nov. 24, 1860. He is son of Senator F. F. Eiffe, of that city, by his wife Susan, née Godeffroy, of London; was educated in Hamburg, and after being for a few years with a banking and import firm, served his year with the 14th Batt. at Schwerin (Mecklenburg) 1882-3. After several years in various offices in England and Germany he started at Hamburg a business on his own account in 1887; opened business relations with S.A. three years later, becoming a partner in the firm of Seemann & Eiffe, of Hamburg and Delagoa Bay, to which latter place he went in 1895 and bought the so-called Catembe Concession in Delagoa Bay, eventually taking over the whole business himself, and continuing it from 1896 under the name of F. F. Eiffe & Co. He is on the Board of the Central African Lakes Co., the S.W. African *Schäferei Gesellsehaft*, the *Deutsches Schauspielhaus* Co., the

Hamburger Nachrichten journal, and on the committees of the German Red Cross Society, the German Colonial Society, etc. He is hon. life member of the Thames Rowing Club, a life member of the S. London Harriers, and held for many years the German running records for several distances, notably the mile. His recreations now are yachting, riding, and driving. He married, May 7, 1892, Miss Mariquita Oetling, of Hamburg.

EISSLER, M., A.I.M.E., M.J.M.M., is the author of many standard works of reference on gold and its metallurgy, including *The Cyanide Process for the Extraction of Gold and its Practical Application on the Witwatersrand Gold fields and Elsewhere*, and *The Metallurgy of Gold*.

ELGIN AND KINCARDINE, Earl of, K.G., G.C.S.I., G.C.I.E., P.C., of 18, Ennismore Gardens, London, S.W., Broomhall, Dunfermline, Fifeshire, and of the Travellers' and Brooks' Clubs, was born in Canada, near Montreal, May 10, 1849. Victor Alexander Bruce is the 9th Earl of a creation of 1633, and also bears the titles of Baron Bruce, Earl of Kincardine, and Baron Bruce of Tory. Lord Elgin's grandfather was Ambassador at Constantinople, and collected the world-famous Elgin marbles, while the next holder of the title was Plenipotentiary to China, and a most successful Viceroy of India. The present peer was educated at Eton and Balliol Coll., Oxford, where he graduated M.A., and he also holds the degrees of LL.D. and D.C.L. He succeeded to the family titles in 1803, and has held offices as Treasurer of the Household and First Commissioner of Works. He was also, from 1894 to 1899, a most tactful and popular Viceroy of India, and when Sir Henry Campbell-Bannerman formed his Ministry in Dec., 1905, Lord Elgin joined the Cabinet as Secretary of State for the Colonies. In this high office Lord Elgin found himself embarrassed as regards South African affairs by the Liberal and Radical crusade, leading up to the General Election, against the so called 'Chinese slavery' in South Africa. The Colonial Secretary's views, however, on this question were not apparently so pronounced as those generally expressed by his Under-Secretary and by the rank and file of the party. But during the first few months of his holding office Lord Elgin twice had to appear in the unenviable position of 'climbing

SIR C. B. ELLIOTT   THE EARL OF ELGIN

Photos Elliott & Fry

down' from the attitude which the Government had adopted. In the first case he caused an outburst of popular indignation, not only in Natal but in the whole of South Africa, by ordering the suspension of the executions of natives implicated in the murder of Natal police. This blunder, which might and probably did, revive the subsequent unrest among the native tribes, immediately led to the resignation of Mr. Smythe's Ministry being handed to the Governor. The home Government thereupon contrived to shift the burden of responsibility upon Sir Henry McCallum (q.v.), and, having gained his point, Mr. Smythe withdrew his resignation. it was very shortly after this that the Colonial Office had to acknowledge that the condition of the Chinese labourers on the Rand bore no resemblance to the 'slavery' so much talked of in the election campaign. It is gratifying to find, however, that Lord Elgin's attitude has since ended to conciliate colonial feeling, and he is convinced that the mother country must look sore than anything else to secure sympathy and support to 'the man on the spot'. A further sign of this was shown in Lord Elgin's firm refusal to question the action of the Governor of British Guiana during the serious disturbances which took place there in the early part of 1906. There had been something approaching a rebellion amongst the local coloured races, and the resident Europeans were in serious danger. That part of the Empire, however, had not become a pawn in the political game, and instead of interference the Governor's action met with staunch support at the Colonial Office.

The most momentous event during Lord Elgin's tenure of office was the announcement of the Constitution granted to the Transvaal in July, 1906. The Constitution allowed for suffrage for all males over 21 years of age (exclusive of the British garrison) who had resided in the Transvaal for six months; one vote would have one value, voting to be by ballot; and the representatives would be as follows: The Rand to elect thirty-four members, Pretoria six, and the rest of the country twenty-nine, the old magisterial districts being reverted to as the basis of the electoral areas. The members were to be paid about £200 per annum. English or Dutch would be spoken in the Assembly and the Speaker would vacate his seat on election. A Second Chamber was to be provisionally nominated

for five years, after which arrangements would be made for an elective Upper House. A Land Board would deal with settlers, and as regards labour a clause was inserted abrogating the Chinese Ordinance "after reasonable time", but no law which would sanction any condition of service or residence of a servile character would be assented to.

Legislation relating to the native franchise was postponed. Swaziland was reserved for direct administration under the High Commissioner. The Government were not yet prepared to grant a Constitution to the O.R. Colony, but it was announced that no unnecessary delay would take place in inaugurating a system which would secure "the effective will of the majority," which meant approximately a majority of nine Boers to one Briton.

Although a Commission had visited South Africa for the purpose of enquiring into the subject of Constitutions for the Transvaal and Orange River Colonies, the complete Report of the Commission was only received at the Colonial Office on the very day that the details of the Transvaal Constitution were to be discussed in Parliament. There was, therefore, little opportunity for the Government to make use of the Report, and none whatever for the general public to consult it before the debate took place.

The terms of the Constitution were received with something like dismay by the members of the late Conservative Government and their following in Britain, who regarded the Constitution as a surrender of the Transvaal to those who had four years before been in arms against the British. in South Africa the Government's announcement did not seem to be altogether pleasing to either party, but was regarded as a compromise, and possibly a workable one, the general feeling being that anything was better than the prolongation of the uncertain state of affairs which had been existent since the Liberal Government bad come into power. The only concession to the British community was the basis of representation being the number of voters and not the total population, but this was largely neutralised by the decision to grant manhood suffrage instead of requiring a property qualification—a state of political development which has not yet been reached in Great Britain itself.

Lord Elgin married, in 1876, Constance, second daughter of the 9th Earl of Southesk, K.T.

ELIN, Henry Dyne, of 18, Sumner Place, South Kensington, S.W., and of the Isthmian, Roehampton, and Royal Cruising Clubs, is third son of the late George Elin, J.P., of Leahoe, Hertford, where he was born in 1867. He was educated at Rugby School, and has since had varied experiences in the backwoods of Queensland, the orange groves of Florida, and in Rhodesia, where he served with the Chartered Company's forces in 1890-91 during the occupation of Mashonaland. He also saw active service with Paget's Horse in the South African War (medal), and is now a director of the Sudan Mines, Ltd. He is a keen sportsman, and especially fond of shooting, yachting, and croquet.

ELIOT, Sir Charles Norton Edgcumbe, K.C.M.G. (1900), C.B. (1898), M.A., of Brockwell Triangle, Halifax, and of the St. James's Club, son of the late Rev. Ed. Eliot, formerly vicar of Norton Bavant, was born in 1864, was educated at Cheltenham Coll., Scholar of Balliol Coll., Oxon, and Fellow of Trinity Coll., Oxon. He entered the diplomatic service as an attaché in Oct., 1886. He was Third Secy. at St. Petersburg, Second Secy. at Constantinople and Washington; Chargé d'Affaires in Morocco, 1892-3, Bulgaria in 1895, and Servia in 1897. Sir Charles was British High Commissioner in Samoa in 1899, and was appointed H.M. Commissioner, Commander-in-Chief, and Consul-Gen. for the British East African Protectorate, and R.M. Agent and Consul-Gen. at Zanzibar, Oct. 27, 1900. He resigned these offices in 1904 owing to differences with the Foreign Secretary, who ordered him to refuse grants of land to private persons while giving a monopoly of land on advantageous terms to the East African Syndicate. He is the author of *A Finnish Grammar* (1890), *Turkey in Europe, by Odysseus* (1900), and *The British East Africa Protectorate* (1905), as well as several papers or marine zoology. He is a Fellow of the African Geographical and Zoological Societies.

ELIOT, Edward Canyon, of Fairmont, Brockenhurst, Hants, and of the Sports Club, was born Apr. 18, 1870, and is brother of Sir Charles Eliot (q.v.). He was educated at Bradfield Coll., and Uppingham Sch., and went to Argentina in 1888, where he was engaged upon ranching and railway construction. In 1893 he went to British Guiana, and after two years sugar planting entered the Civil Service. He transferred to the Gold Coast Colony in 1900 as paymaster of the Hausa force, and was subsequently promoted Senior Assistant Treasurer of the Gold Coast, 1902, and District Commissioner of the Gold Coast in 1905. He was appointed lieut. in the Gold Coast Volunteers in 1903, and commanded the Axim detachment in 1905. His recreations are shooting, fishing, polo, etc. He married, in 1899, Clara Frances, dau. of Col. Paterson, late of the 19th Infantry.

ELLENBOROUGH, Commander Lord, R.N., of 65, George St., Portman Sq., London, W., and of the Naval and Military and Alpine Clubs, was born in 1841, and is eldest son of the Hon. H. S. Law. He was educated at Charterhouse, and in the Royal Navy. In 1871 he commanded the *Coquette* in the Ashanti War. He also served with the Earl of Glasgow both in the Baltic during the Crimean War, and in the Chinese Expedition a few years later. Recreations: riding, shooting, and travelling. Unmarried.

ELLERMAN, Sir John Reeves, Knt, is a leading S. African ship-owner, who assisted the Government in providing transports for the troops at the time of the S. African War. He was created Knight on the occasion of the king's birthday, 1905.

ELLIOTT, Arthur A., B.A. (Cape), M.A. (Oxford), is fourth son of Sir Charles Elliott, ex-gen. manager of the Cape railways, and now fills the office of Assistant Registrar of the Cape University, in place of Mr. C. S. Edgar, M.A., recently appointed to the Professorship of Greek in the Victoria College, Stellenbosch,

ELLIOTT, Sir Charles Bletterman, K.C.M.G. (1901), LL.B. (Cape University), of The Knoll, 5, Chichester Road, E. Croydon, was born May 5, 1841, at Uitenhage, Cape Colony, and is son of the Rev. William Elliott. He was educated at the Boys'

SIR CHARLES N. E ELIOT

Photo Elliott & Fry

SIR GEORGE FARRAR

MR. H WILSON FOX

Photo Elliott & Fry

SIR J. G FRASER

Mission School, Hampstead, and the S. African College, Cape Town. In 1859 he entered the Colonial Office, Cape Town; was secretary to the Board of Public Examinations in Literature and Science, subsequently becoming a member of the Cape University Council, and Moderator of Examiners in Science. He acted at one time as Registrar of Circuit, under Mr. Justice Cloete, and subsequently under Mr. Justice Watermeyer. Among his numerous appointments, he has acted as Clerk of the Peace, chief clerk to the Attorney-Gen. and to the Commissioner of Crown Lands and Public Works, Resident Magistrate, Supt.-Gen. of Education, Asst. Commissioner of Crown Lands and Public Works, Advocate of the Supreme Court in 1875, general manager of the Cape Govt. Railways from 1880-91, Commissioner of Table Bay Harbour Board and Tender Board, Civil Service Commissioner, special Railway Commissioner for the Cape Govt. Hallways and now acting hon. Special Commissioner; was also Actuary to the Cape Govt. and Actuary to the S. African Mutual Insurance Society. He married, first, Aug. 9, 1865, Julia C. Home (died June 1, 1895); and secondly, March 26, 1905, Ida G. Brune.

ELLIOTT, Sir Henry, of Durban, was for many years Chief Magistrate of Tembuland, Transkei, and Pondoland, from which he recently retired through ill health, and settled down in Natal.

ELTON, Edward Hallam, of East London, S.A., and of the East London and Panmure Clubs (S.A.), was born at Stoke, near Wareham, Dorsetshire, in 1860. He is second son of the Rev. H. G. T. Elton, youngest son of Sir Chas. Elton, Bart., of Clevedon, Somersetshire, and was educated at St. Edward's Sch., Oxford. He sat as Town Councillor, East London, from 1896 to 1899, and is chairman of the Seamen's Institute (E. London), a branch of the Mission to Seamen of London. He married, Feb. 7, 1887, Ada Constance, dau. of J. H. Webb, J.P., late of the Crown Lands Dept., Cape Town.

ELWELL, Frederick, of Abchurch House, Sherborne Lane, London, E.C., and of Clovelly, Charlton Hoad, Shepperton, was born at Wednesbury, Feb. 12, 1847, He was educated at

Leamington Coll, and at Paris. He has visited Australia and S. Africa, having resided in Johannesburg for two years.

ELWES, Capt. H. C., late of the 3rd Batt. Scots Guards, served in the S.A. War, and was severely wounded at Modder River. He is now on the retired list.

EMMOTT, Alfred, M.P., B.A., of 30, Ennismore Gardens, S.W., and of the National Liberal and Reform Clubs, is son of the late Thomas Emmott, and has been Liberal Member for Oldham since 1899, and has taken a leading part in politics in the House of Commons. He has repeatedly attacked the administration of the Congo State, and became Chairman of Committee in the House of Commons in 1906. He is Chairman of Emmott and Wallshaw, cotton spinners, a decided Free Trader, and an "impenitent Home Ruler." He married Mary, dau. of the late John Lees.

ENGLAND, Rev. Thomas Samuel, of Mombasa, British E. Africa, was born at Guernsey, Dec. 20, 1861. He was ordained by Bishop Tucker in 1894, and is a missionary of the Church Missionary Society and Diocesan Inspector of Schools. He married, Aug. 23, 1898, Clarice E. Bridgewater.

ENGLISH, Robert, of Scatwell, Rossshire, resided for many years at Kimberley, where he was prominently connected with the De Beers Consolidated Mines. He is also largely interested in Transvaal and Rhodesian gold-mining undertakings.

EPLER, Adolphe, Knight of the Imperial Royal Austrian Franz Joseph's Order, of Johannesburg, and of the Rand and New Clubs, is the son of a well-known Austrian Govt. official who at one time was chief inspector of Northern Railway System of Austria, and an Imperial Austrian Councillor. Educated in Vienna, he commenced business in that city in and remained there until 1889, when he left for S.A., and proceeded to Johannesburg, remaining there during the whole time of the war.

In conjunction with A. Brakhan and E. Boucher, he formed the Official Police for the protection of the mines, holding the rank of Capt. In May, 1901, he was appointed by Lord Milner as a Town

Councillor for Johannesburg, having the unique distinction of being at the time the only non-British subject on the Council. As a representative of Austro-Hungarian capital he is a director of several gold mining companies. He has been president of the Austro-Hungarian Benefit and Patriotic Society in Johannesburg since 1891, and was decorated by the Emperor of Austria in 1900. Since 1897 he has acted continuously on the Executive Committee of the Transvaal Chamber of Mines.

ERASMUS, Commandant, after service with the Boers in the late S.A. War, visited Madagascar (1902) and Argentina, with a view to finding a suitable country for the settlement of Boer irreconcilables.

ERROLL, Earl of, of Slaines Castle, Aberdeenshire, and of the Marlborough Club, was born in Canada in 1852, and is son of the 18th Earl. He was educated at Harrow, and became a cornet in the Royal Horse Guards in 1869, rising to the command of the regt. in 1891. He took part in the late S. African War, and did some good work on Lord Roberts's staff, throwing up a good appointment at the War Office in order to go out to the front. In 1875 he married Mary, dau. of Edmund and Lady Harriett l'Estrange.

ESPEUT, Claude Vyvian Armit, F.R.C.I., Member of the Society of Engineers, of 77, Sinclair Road, Kensington, was born at Spring Gardens, Jamaica, Oct. 3, 1875. He is the son of the late Hen. Wm. Bancroft Espeut, F.L.S., M.L.C., of Jamaica, and grandson of the late Peter Alexander Espeut, Custos of Kingston, Jamaica. Mr. Claude Espeut was educated at St. Paul's Sch. and the Crystal Palace Engineering Sch., and from 1894 to 1900 he was employed in public works in Jamaica. From 1900-04 he was engaged in railway construction in West Africa, and from 1905 he has been employed in the Public Works Dept. of British East Africa. Unmarried.

ESSELEN, Ewald, is of German parentage, and was born in Cape Colony. He was educated in Edinburgh. At the time of the War of Independence he was studying medicine, and volunteered for medical service, subsequently joining the President's staff. On completing his legal education he was appointed Judge of the High Court of the Transvaal, but relinquishing his seat on the Bench after some years of honourable service he returned to the Bar, and took an active part in politics. He withdrew his strong support from Mr. Kruger and became the dominant factor in the opposition under the nominal leadership of Gen. Joubert.

At the general elections of 1893 Mr. Esselen was elected member for Potchefstroom, but the Krugerite polling officer stayed at nothing to obtain a reversal of the election. Dead and absent men recorded their votes, and Mr. Esselen was declared to have lost his seat by seven votes. Mr. Esselen's defeat was the worst blow to Gen. Joubert's candidature for the Presidency. Subsequently Mr. Esselen was prevailed upon to accept, the office of State Attorney, he stipulating that he should have a free hand in reorganising the detective and police forces, which were at that time in a very depraved condition. The many reforms which he worked, with the assistance of his chief detective, Mr. Trimble, especially as regards the illicit liquor traffic, raised such opposition that Mr. Esselen at length resigned. He was admitted to practise at the Bar of the Supreme Court of the Transvaal Colony, Dec. 18, 1902.

ESSER, J., ex-Judge of the High Court of the late S.A.R., was admitted as an Advocate of the Supreme Court of the Transvaal in 1902.

EUAN-SMITH, Col. Sir Charles Bean, K.C.B., C.S.I., of the United Service Club, is a man who has played many parts, and has gained no little distinction. He began his military career in the Indian Army in 1859, and served in the Abyssinian War of 1867-8, when he was present at the capture of Magdala (medal). In 1879-80 Sir Charles saw further service in the Afghan War, taking part in the action of Ahmed Khel, the affair at Urzoo, the march from Kabul to Kandahar, and the battle of Sept. 1. He was several times mentioned in despatches, and received the brev. of Lieut. Col., the medal with two clasps, and bronze star. Col. Euan-Smith retired from the Indian Army in 1889; subsequently joined the diplomatic service, and was Minister Resident at Bogota in 1898-9. In 1890 he was created a Civil K.C.B., and was Consul-Gen.

at Zanzibar, and Minister at Tangier, 1891-3. Sir Charles Euan-Smith is well known in African circles in the City. He is Chairman and Director of several South and West African mining companies, in which capacities his abilities and experience are highly appreciated by his colleagues. Sir Charles is Chairman of the Abosso G.M. Co. and of the Taquah and Abosso G.M. Co. (1900), and a Director of the New African, New Egyptian, Oceana Consolidated, Rhodesia, Ltd., and the Sudan Development and Exploration Cos. He is also a Trustee for the debenture holders of the French Rand G.M. Co., the Vogelstruis Consolidated Deep, and the Witwatersrand Deep. He married, in 1877, a dau. of the late Gen. Alexander, R.A.

EVANS, Sir Francis Henry, Bart., K.C.M.G., M.P., of 40, Grosvenor Place, S.W., of Tubbendens, Orpington, Kent, and of the Reform Club, was educated at Manchester, New Coll., and at Neuweid. He was in early life a pupil of the eminent engineer, Sir Jas. Brunlees. He is a partner in the firm of Donald Currie and Co., and Director of the Union Castle Line, Thames and Mersey Marine Insurance Co., and the International Sleeping Car Co. His parliamentary career commenced in 1888, when he was elected for Southampton, which constituency he retained until 1895. Defeated at the general election, he regained the seat in a by-election in 1896. He has represented Maidstone in the Liberal interest since 1901. He married, in 1872, Marie, dau. of the late Hon. Samuel Stevens, Attorney-General of New York. (See Sir Donald Currie).

EVANS, John Emrys, C.M.G., of Johannesburg, and of the Northumberland and Northern Counties Club, the Rand and Athenaeum (Johannesburg), Civil Service (C.T.), and the Durban, Kimberley, and Pretoria Clubs, was born at Abergele, Denbighshire, Aug. 18, 1853, and is eldest son of the late Emrys Evans, of Cotton Hall, Denbigh. Educated at the Liverpool Institute and the Denbigh Grammar Sch., he joined the National Provincial Bank of England in 1870, and in 1882 transferred his services to the Standard Bank of South Africa. Mr. Evans was British Vice-Consul at Johannesburg from Aug., 1897, until the declaration of war, Oct. 11, 1899; was Financial Adviser at Bloemfontein,

March, 1900; Financial Adviser to Lord Roberts, June, 1900; Controller of the Treasury, Transvaal, Aug., 1900, and Auditor General in the Transvaal from April to December 31, 1901. Lord Milner nominated him a member of the Johannesburg Town Council in June, 1902, and he became an elected member in Nov., 1903. He is also a Director (and Vice Chairman) of the National Bank of South Africa the Johannesburg Consolidated Investment Co., Henderson's Consolidated Corporation, the Vereeniging Estates, Sheba G.M., add other companies. His recreations are fishing shooting, and golf. Mr. Evans married, in 1893, Johanna Margareta, dau. of the late P. G. Leeb, of Wynberg, near Cape Town.

EVANS, Maurice Smethurst, C.M.G., of Crest, Berea, Durban, Natal, was born in 1854; was Chairman for the Invasion Losses Inquiry Commission, and was formerly Member of the Natal Legislative Council.

EVANS, Samuel, of Rhos, near Ruabon, and of Johannesburg, started life as a journalist; went to Egypt as Sir Edgar Vincent's private secretary, and afterwards entered the Khedivial service. Later on he went to Constantinople where he became Controller of the Imperial Tobacco Régie. For some years Evans has taken an active interest in finance in Johannesburg, and he was admitted partner in the firm of H. Eckstein and Co., in the autumn of 1902. Incidentally he had charge of the recent libel action of Messrs. Wernher, Beit and Co. against Mr. Markham, (q.v.). After the occupation of Johannesburg Mr. Evans acted for a short time as Lord Roberts's Financial Adviser. He was a member of the recent Labour Commission and has a seat in the Witwatersrand Chamber of Mines. He married, Dec. 24, 1903, Katherine, elder dau. of Richard Hous Mabson, editor of the *Statist*.

EVANS, W., formerly Protector of Chinese in the Straits Settlements, was appointed to take charge of the department for the regulation of Chinese Labour in the Transvaal in 1905. He had been continuously connected with the Chinese Protectorate of the Straits Settlements for the previous twenty-one years, and has served in Singapore, Penang, and Malacca.

EVERARD, Thomas, M.L.C., J.P., of Leeuwpoort, Carolina, Transvaal, is the son of Thomas Everard, of New Hall Parks, Thurlston, Leicestershire, where he was born in 1850. He was educated at Leicester, and went to S.A. in 1872, and settled in the Lydenburg district of the S.A.R. in the following year, where he traded at the Macamae Alluvial Gold Fields for several years. In 1876 he removed to the part now known as the Carolina district, where he has been trading and farming ever since. He has bred horses for the last twenty years, and has been successful in breeding many winners on the Turf, both locally and at principal racing centres in S.A., and also numerous prize winners at the large agricultural shows. During the first Sekukuni War assisted his Boer neighbours against the marauding Kaffirs, and the expedition was the first one to successfully drive back the native cattle looters during the outbreak. He has gone through various troublesome times under many Govts., viz., under President Burgers, Sir T. Shepstone, Sir Owen Lanyon, and President Kruger. During the late war, as in the one in 1880, Mr. Everard was allowed to remain on his farm without taking an active part against his own countrymen. After peace he was nominated a Member of the Ermelo-Carolina Repatriation Commission. He was appointed a J.P. for the district, and on the formation of the Legislative Council was asked by the High Commissioner, Lord Milner, to become a nominee member of that body. He married, in 1893, Ella Christie, dau. of the Rev. John Christie, D.D., Professor of Church History, Aberdeen Univ.

EWING, William, of 137, West George Street, Glasgow, and of the New (Glasgow), City Liberal (London), and the Royal Clyde Yacht Clubs, was born in Glasgow, Jan. 16, 1852, and is son of William Ewing, a manufacturer of Glasgow. He was educated at the High School, Glasgow; Orthez, near Pau; and Glasgow University. Mr. Ewing has been identified with African development for many years, chiefly in connection with the African Lakes Corporation, of which he is a Director. Unmarried.

EYLES, Frederick, of Bulawayo, Rhodesia, and of the Bulawayo Club, and Member of the Anthropological Institute, Folk Lore Society, S.A.

Philosophical Society, and Rhodesia Scientific Association (formerly Hon. Sec.), was born at Wick, near Bath, May 10, 1864; is the author of a work on Zulu Grammar, *Zulu Self-Taught* (Juta and Co., 1900), and is the editor and founder of the *Bulawayo Observer*. Mr. Eyles was married May 17, 1893.

FAIRBRIDGE, William Ernest, J.P., of Salisbury, Mashonaland, and the New Club, London, and the Salisbury and Rand Clubs, son of the late W. A. Fairbridge, of Port Elizabeth, and grandson of Dr. Jas. Fairbridge, of Cape Town, was born at Port Elizabeth in 1863, and was educated at Bedford, Eng. He has long been connected with journalism. On the occupation of Rhodesia he represented the *Johannesburg Star* and the *Cape Argus*, subsequently establishing and editing the *Rhodesia Herald*. He is a Director of the Argus Company, controlling a large group of papers in S.A. On a municipality being formed in Salisbury he was twice elected Mayor of that town, and he unsuccessfully contested a seat in the Rhodesian Legislative Council. Mr. Fairbridge is unmarried.

FALCK, David George Anosi, M.L.C., J.P., of the Bloemfontein and United Service Clubs, was born June 3, 1856, at Swellendam, Cape Colony, and is of Dutch parentage. He was educated privately and at Swellendam Grammar School. For some years he served in the Cape Colony Postal Service, serving under the late Free State Govt., where he held the appointments of Postmaster, Magistrate's Clerk, and Magistrate. He occupied the position of Secretary to the Post Office when that office was first created in the O.F.S., and in Jan., 1895, he was appointed to the Postmaster-Generalship, on the retirement of the late George Hurford, which office he still retains under the British Govt. He is a J.P. for the Orange River Colony, and a nominated member of the Legislative Council of that Colony. He married, in March, 1880, Cornelia Sophia, dau. of the late Vincent Rice, M.L.A., of Beaufort West, Cape Colony.

FALMOUTH, Lord, of Tregothnan, near Truro, Cornwall, holds, though the fact has been disputed, the premier barony of England, that of Le Despencer, a barony by writ, dated Christmas Eve, 1264. His titular viscounty, of which he is the seventh holder, dates only to 1720. He is twenty-fourth baron Le Despencer by reason of his father's marriage with Baroness Le Despencer, who died two years after Lord Falmouth had succeeded to the viscounty. The present Lord Falmouth's father was one of the most famous of racing men, owning the finest horses, which he ran for pure sport, and never betted. He had won £300,000 in stakes when he sold off his stud for 110,000gs. The present peer at one time commanded the Coldstream Guards, and took part in the actions at Tel-el-Kebir, Abu-Klea, Abu-Kru, and Metemmeh (medals and clasps), where he commanded the Guards' Camel Corps. Lord Falmouth retired from the service with the rank of Major-Gen., and has been for some years a member of the Jockey Club. He was created K.C.V.O. on the occasion of the King's birthday, 1905. Lady Falmouth is known as one of the best lady skaters in England, and is also a good croquet player.

FARLER, John Prediger, M.A. (Cantab), J.P., F.R.G.S., 20, Pall Mall, London, Government House, Pemba, Zanzibar, and of the Cocoa Tree, Sports, Royal Societies, Grosvenor, and English (Zanzibar) clubs, was born in Somersetshire, May 24, 1855; is son of John Reed Farler and Anne Prediger von Cassel, and was educated privately and at St. John's Coll., Camb. He has been Commissioner for the Sultan of Zanzibar for the Island of Pemba since March, 1897, and was appointed British Judge and Magistrate for the Island, Sept. 10, 1897; Acting Vice-Consul for Pemba from May 10, 1901, to Jan. 1, 1903; Treasurer of Pemba, 1901, and Collector and Administrator of Pemba, 1903. Mr. Farler successfully carried Pemba from slavery to freedom without friction with the Arabs, and has read papers before the Royal Geographical Society on exploration in Africa. He has shot big game on the Rovuma River, and in his younger days was keen on rowing and football.

FARQUHAR, Capt. Francis Douglas, D.S.O., of Gilmilnscroft, Mauchline, N.B., and of White's and Guards' Clubs, was born in Lond. Sept. 17, 1874, and is the son of Sir Henry Farquhar, 4th Bart. He was educated at Eton, and joined the Coldstream Guards in 1896. He served in the Remount Dept. under Major (now Gen.) Scobell,

1899, and in the S.A. War with his regt., being subsequently A.D.C. to Maj. Gen. Sir R. Pole-Carew, 1899-1900 (mentioned in despatches, medal and clasps, D.S.O.). From May, 1901, to July, 1902, he served with the first Chinese Regt. at Wei-hei-Wei, and later he took part in the Somaliland Campaign, 1903-4, as Special Service Officer, with the Somali Mounted Inf. (medal and one clasp). He married, April 27, 1905, Lady Evelyn Hely-Hutchinson. Recreations: Hunting and shooting.

FARRAR, Col. Sir George Herbert, Knt., D.S.O., M.L.C., of Chicheley Hall, Newport Pagnell, Bucks, of 4, London Wall Buildings, London, E.C., of Bedford Farm, Johannesburg, and of White's and Boodle's Clubs, was born June 17, 1859. He is the second of three sons of the late Charles Farrar, M.D., of Chatteris, Cambridgeshire, and was educated at Bedford Grammar Sch. Sir George began his business career in the engineering firm of his uncles, the famous agricultural implement makers at Bedford, and early in life went out to join his brother, Mr. Sidney Farrar, at Port Elizabeth, where the firm of Howard Farrar and Co. had established itself. But the discoveries on the Rand soon attracted him thither. Sir George and his brother and partner, Mr. Sidney Farrar (q.v.), took full advantage of the opportunities that offered, and eventually he became the head of one of the principal groups of mining companies. The operations of the Farrar group are mainly confined to the East Rand, chiefly in the district of which the town of Boksburg is the centre, and it has done more to exploit and develop that section of the Witwatersrand Goldfields than any other corporation. The principal undertaking of the group is the East Rand Proprietary Mines, Ltd., with the fortunes of which Sir George Farrar and Mr. Sidney Farrar (q.v.) have been prominently identified from its inception, and it is to their administrative ability and untiring energy that the enormous success of the Company and its numerous subsidiaries is largely due. The producing companies of the East Rand Proprietary Mines contain ore of higher value than the average for the Rand, and the whole of this corporation's subsidiaries are so well laid out and developed that, under normal conditions, they cannot fail to yield large profits.

The companies controlled, or partly controlled, by the group are the Driefontein Consolidated, Angelo, New Comet, Cason, Cinderella, New Blue Sky, H. F. Co., Limited, G. F. Co., Limited, the Benoni, Kleinfontein Estates, Boksburg Gold, Rand Klipfontein, New Kleinfontein, Anglo-French Land Co., Anglo-French (Transvaal) Navigation Coal Estates, Chimes West, Apex, Klipfontein Estate, and Penhalonga Proprietary Mines, the last being, of course, a Rhodesian property. Of many of these companies Sir George Farrar is the Johannesburg Chairman.

Always an energetic opponent of the narrow anti-British policy of the Boer Govt., Sir George joined the leaders of the Reform Party a few weeks after the movement started, and he was one of the four who, pleading guilty to the charge of high treason against the late South African Republic, were condemned to death. This sentence was commuted, and after a few months he was liberated (1896) in payment of a fine of £25,000, and on his undertaking not to intervene in the politics of the State for fifteen years. When the Boer War broke out in 1899 he and his brother, Capt. Percy Farrar, joined the Colonial Division under Gen. Brabant, and Sir George took an active part in raising colonial corps, to the expense of which his firm contributed very large amounts. Sir George, who attained the rank of Major on the Staff of the Colonial Division, accompanied Gen. Brabant as chief of his Intel. Dept., and saw a great deal of fighting. He was afterwards at the relief of Wepener, and at the surrender of Gen. Prinsloo in the Brandwater Basin, campaigning in the Cape Colony, O.F.S., and Transvaal. He retired with the rank of Major and with the right to wear the uniform of his regt.; was mentioned in despatches, receiving the medal with three clasps, the D.S.O. (1900), and afterwards (in 1902) having the dignity of Knight Bachelor conferred upon him in recognition of his good services on the recommendation of the War Office.

Sir George is a Member of the Transvaal Legislative Council, through which, in Dec., 1903, he successfully piloted a resolution in favour of importing alien coloured labour for unskilled work in the mines. He was Pres. of the Transvaal

Chamber of Mines for 1903, and in 1905 was elected first Pres. of the Transvaal Progressive Association. Sir George Farrar is perhaps the best trusted man among the British community in South Africa, with a really keen insight into the requirements of the Transvaal, and a sound all-round record. In the electoral campaign leading up to the elections for the first Transvaal Legislative Assembly in February, 1907, Sir George Farrar played a leading part in the Progressive interest. He intends to contest the East Boksburg Division of the East Rand against the Labour candidate, Mr. W. B. Madeley.

He has always been a keen patron of sport, both in South Africa and in England; he was formerly sprinting champion of South Africa, and even now is a fine point-to-point rider. He also takes a considerable interest in horse breeding, horseracing, and in pedigree stock. He married, June 3, 1892, Ella Mabel, dau. of the late Dr. Charles Waylen, Ind. Med. Service.

FARRAR, Captain John Percy, D.S.O., of Brayfield House, Cold Brayfield, Newport Pagnell, Bucks, and of the Alpine Club, was born in 1857, and is son of the late Charles Farrar, M.D., and brother to Sir George Farrar (q.v.) and Sidney Farrar (q.v.). Capt. Farrar served in the South African War (medal with four clasps and D.S.O.), and is now attached to the Kaffrarian Rifles. He married, in 1886, Mary, dau. of F. Beswick, of Queenstown.

FARRAR, Sidney Howard, M.I.C.E., F.G.S., of 4, London Wall Buildings, London, and of Johannesburg (P.O. Box 455), is son of the late Dr. Chas. Farrar, of Chatteris, Cambs., and brother of Sir Geo. Farrar, D.S.O. (q.v.), with whom he is in partnership under the style of Farrar Bros., of London and Johannesburg, the firm controlling a very large section of the East Rand, chiefly in the Boksburg District. Mr. Sidney Farrar himself represents his firm's interests on the London Committees of the Anglo-French (Transvaal) Navigation Coal Estates (Chairman), the H.F. Co. (Chairman), the Angelo, Anglo-French Land, Apex Mines, Benoni, Cason, Driefontein Consolidated, Eastern Rand Exploration, East Rand Proprietary (European Committee), Kleinfontein Deep, New

Comet, New Kleinfontein, and Rand Klipfontein Cos,, and he is also a Director of Kleinfontein Estates and Township, Ltd., and the Witwatersrand (Knights) Co. Mr. Sidney Farrar married the youngest daughter of the late Joseph Simpson, one of Port Elizabeth's most esteemed pioneer citizens. Mr. Farrar lost his wife in May, 1906, a sad event, which was followed in the following August by the marriage of one of his daughters, Miss Violet Helen Farrar, with her father's expert chauffeur, John Henry Fellows, of Thames Ditton.

FARRER, Baron, is a nephew of the Dowager Countess of Iddesleigh and of Lady Hobhouse, and is the second baron of the creation which was originally bestowed on Sir Thomas Henry Farrer in acknowledgment of his six and thirty years' work at the Board of Trade, of which he became in 1850 Assistant Marine Secretary and was subsequently appointed Permanent Secretary. The present baron, though he has not been conspicuous in public life, is a man of very sound qualities and great abilities, and proceeded in the latter end of 1904 to report with Mr. Oliver Bury on the administration of Egyptian State railways.

FAURE, Hon. .J. A., was formerly senior member of the Cape Legislative Council for the Western Circle.

FAURE, L. S. de V., of Pretoria, Transvaal, passed the cape Civil Service Exam, in 1888, and in the following year was appointed Clerk in the Surveyor General's Office, which position he held until 1891, when he entered the Mashonaland Civil Service. In 1893 he took part in the Matabele War, and returned to the Cape Civil Service in 1894 as Clerk to the Civil Commissioner and Magistrate at East London. He served in the Matabele Rebellion in 1896, in the same year entering the Rhodesia Civil Service in the Civil Commissioner's Office and the Deeds Office Registry, Bulawayo. His active service also includes the S. African War in 1899-1902, and during that time he was appointed Magistrate at Rustenburg. He was employed in the Military Service until 1903, when he became Clerk in the Lieut.-Governor's Office at Pretoria, being promoted to Chief Clerk in 1904.

FAURE, Hon. Sir Pieter Hendrik, K.C.M.G.,

M.L.A., of Cape Town, is son of Jacobus Faure, of Eerste River fame, and brother of John A. Faure, the famous horse breeder of that place. Pieter Faure was brought up for the law, but joined Mr. A. B. de Villiers in the firm of De Villiers, Faure and Co., auctioneers and general agents, taking a special interest in agricultural matters. Entering the Cape Parliament, he became Secy. for Native Affairs on the formation of the Rhodes' Ministry in 1890. He weathered the Ministerial crisis in 1893, and joined Mr. Rhodes' second Cabinet as Colonial Secy. In Sir G. Sprigg's third and fourth Ministries he resumed the offices of Secy. for Agriculture and Colonial Secy. Sir Pieter Faure was last re-elected for the division of Namaqualand in 1904, and is a member of the Progressive party. He married Miss Johanna Susanna van der Byl.

FAWCETT, Mrs. Millicent Garrett, Hon. LL.D., of St. Andrews Univ., of 2, Gower Street, London, and of the Lyceum and Alexandra Clubs, London, was born June 11, 1847, is dau. of Newson Garrett, J.P., of Aldeburgh, Suffolk, and was educated privately. She paid an official visit to S. Africa in connection with the Concentration Camps, and afterwards took a journey through the Cape and the Transvaal, delivering on behalf of the Victoria League during the trip some thirty lectures to Britons and Boers, with the object of healing the wounds of war and creating harmony with the Mother Country. Mrs. Fawcett has written many notable books and essays. She married, April 23, 1867, the late Rt. Hon. H. Fawcett, M.P., F.R.S., formerly P.M.G.

FAWKES, Stephen Hawkesworth, of Ladybrand, O.R.C., served in the South African War in 1900 with the 13th Batt. Imperial Yeomanry. Subsequently, in Sept., 1902, he became Registrar to the Hon. Mr. Justice Fawkes, and was appointed Chief Clerk and Asst. Resident Magistrate al Ladybrand, O.R.C., in 1904.

FEAR, B. G., for several years a subeditor of the *Western Daily Mercury*, joined the staff of the *Midland News*, C.C., in 1902.

FELKIN, Robert William, M.D., L.R.C.P. and S. Edin., F.R.S.E., F.R.G.S., Member Anthropological Institute; Fellow of the Berlin,

Munich, and Tyneside Geographical Societies; of 12 Oxford Gardens, London, W., and of the Royal Societies Club, was born March 13, 1853; son of the late Robert Felkin, and was educated at Wolverhampton Grammar School, Edinburgh University, and at Marburg. Dr. Felkin went to Uganda, via the Nile, in 1878, returning via Bahrel-Gha-Zal, Darfour, and Kordofan with Mtesa's envoys to Queen Victoria in 1880. He was on the East Coast of Africa in 1880, having meanwhile mapped the route from Lado to Dara (1879); joint author of *Uganda and the Egyptian Sudan* (1882); Lecturer on Diseases of the Tropics and Climatology at Edin. Medical School (1886-98); was the first to start special instruction in Tropical Diseases in Medical Schools, and from 1880 advocated the construction of railways from Suakim to Berber and from Mombasa to the Victoria Lake. He has written many papers on Geography of C. Africa, Anthropology, Medicine, on the Geographical Distribution of Disease (1889), and Tropical Diseases in Africa (1895); was Consulting Physician to the Imperial British East Africa Co., is now Consulting Physician to the British Tropical Africa Co., and Anglo-Belgian Africa Co., in addition to his ordinary practice as a physician in London. He married, in 1882, Mary Jane, dau. of the late S. S. Mander, of Wolverhampton (died Jan. 18, 1903).

FELL, Henry, M.L.A., has represented Umgeni in the Natal Legislative Assembly since 1883.

FELL, T. E., joined the Gold Coast Service in 1897, and became Travelling Commissioner of the Colony in 1903, being appointed District Commissioner of Ashanti in 1905. He has also acted as Commissioner for Native Affairs.

FELTHAM, John Alric Percy, D.S.O., B.A., of Stellenberg, Kenilworth, and of the Civil Service Club, Cape Town, was born in England May 12, 1862. He was educated at Trinity Hall, Cambs., and the Diocesan Coll., Cape Town; served as Lieut. with the Rhodesia Horse Artillery in the Matabele War and the Mashona Rebellion (thrice wounded, despatches twice, and medal with clasp); also took part in the S. African War in 1899-1902, when he was present at the siege of Mafeking (wounded, despatches, Queen's medal with four

clasps, King's medal and D.S.O.). He is Attorney-at-Law in Cape Colony, Rhodesia, and the Transvaal. He married, Nov. 16, 1903, Beatrice, dau. of F. W. Good, and widow of A. Pynsent Scott, of Adelaide.

FERGUSSON, Malcolm, J.P., A.R.S.M., F.R.G.S., of Oaklands, Johannesburg, and of the Sports and Rand Clubs, was born at Brettenham, Shetford, March 5, 1874, and is son of the late John Fergusson. He was educated at Bedford Grammar Sch. and the Royal Sch. of Mines, Lond., and went out to S. Africa in 1895, where he was engaged in mining in the Transvaal until the latter end of 1898; he then returned to England and joined a scientific expedition under Mr. Moore, as geographer, geologist, and surveyor. This expedition started from Chinde in June, 1899, and proceeded up the Zambesi and Shire Rivers, across Lakes Nyassa and Tanganyika, and thence northwards through the little known volcanic country around Kiva and Albert Edward to Ruwenzori and the Albert, returning via Mombasa in July, 1900. From his survey notes the position of Lake Tanganyika was readjusted. From Jan. to Nov., 1901, he was engaged in mining in Ashanti; in 1902 he was appointed Asst. Insp. of Mines in the Transvaal, and in 1903 was given the post Dep. Insp. of Mines, which position he still holds. He married, in 1906, Miss Olive Grace Hill.

FERRAS, Count Martens, was one of the Portuguese Plenipotentiaries at the Moroccan Conference at Algeçiras in 1906.

FERREIRA, Capt. Sir Cornelius do Costa, K.C.M.G., was formerly Governor-Gen. of the Province of Mozambique, and was created a K.C.M.G. on the King's birthday (1902).

FESTING, Capt. and Brevet-Maj. Arthur Hoskyns, C.M.G., D.S.O., F.R.G.S., the Royal Irish Rifles, son of the late Henry Blathway Festing, of Bois Hall, Addlestone, Surrey, and grandson of the late Benjamin Morton Festing, Captain R.N., Knight of Hanover, of the Naval and Military, St. James's, Royal Societies, and Bath Clubs, London, was born in 1870, and educated on the Continent, and came to England, 1886, and joined Royal Military Coll., Sandhurst, in 1887. He was extra regimentally employed with the Royal Niger Co., 1895-98. During this period he took part in the operations in the Niger, 1896-7; he was with the expeditions to the Katshella Town Stockade, Egbom, Bida Illorin, receiving for his services medal and clasp and a brevet majority. Later he was in command at Ibonsa and Anam; was on Col. Pilcher's Staff at Lapai and Argeyah (despatches and D.S.O.). He served in S.A., 1900-1, in command of the 11th M.I. and on Gen. Carrington's Staff (medal and four clasps). From 1901-5 he was again in West Africa as Second in Command of the W.A. Frontier Force (N. Nigeria Regt.), his services including Aro Field Force, 1901-2 (despatches, C.M.G.); Kano Expeditionary Force, 1902-3 as O.C. Lines of Communication (despatches). Major Festing holds three records of African big game, according to Rowland War's measurements—notably *Kobus kob*, 19 11-16ins.

FIDDES, George Vandeleur, C.B. (1901), B.A., of St. Stephen's Club, Lond., was educated at Dulwich Coll., and was subsequently a scholar of Brasenose Coll., Oxen., where he took a second-class in Classical Moderations in 1879. He was appointed a Clerk in the Colonial Office in 1881, after competitive examination, and served as Private Secy. to Lord Onslow (1887), Baron H. de Worms (1882-92), and Sir Robert Meade, March, 1896. In that year he was promoted to a first-class Clerkship in the Colonial Office, and in 1897 was appointed Secy. to the High Commissioner, Cape Colony; was appointed Political Secretary to the Commander in Chief in South Africa in June, 1900, and Secretary to the Transvaal Administration in Dee., 1900; Chairman of the Rand Water Board Commission, 1901-2; and Principal Clerk, Sept., 1902.

FIENNES, Hon. Eustace, Capt. Oxfordshire Yeomanry, of 8, Cromwell Place, London, S.W., and of the Orleans, Cavalry, Prince's and S.A. Clubs, is the second son of the 14th Baron Saye and Sole, of Broughton Castle, Banbury. He was educated at Malvern Coll. In addition to serving with distinction in the North-West Rebellion, Egypt (medal and clasp, and Khedive's Star), he served in the Pioneer Expedition to Rhodesia in 1890 in the B. S.A. Police, and also during the recent S.A. War (medal and three clasps). In 1900

he contested North Oxford shire in the Liberal interest, and was defeated by 733 votes. He was elected for the Banbury Division of Oxfordshire at the election in 1906. He married, Nov. 6, 1894, Florence Agnes, widow of Arthur Fletcher, and dau. of John Bathfelden, Belleombre, Constantia, Cape Town.

FINCASTLE, Viscount, Major 16th Lancers, V.C., of South Harris, Invernessshire, and of the Carlton, Marlborough, Cavalry, and Automobile Clubs, was born April 22, 1871, and is the eldest son of the Earl of Dunmore. He was educated at Eton, and joined the 16th Lancers in 1891, serving for nearly nine years in India. His active services include the Sudan Campaign in 1896, as Special Service Officer with the Egyptian Cavalry, the Indian Frontier Campaign in 1897, and with the Guides' Cavalry in the Malakand Expedition, when he was awarded the V.C. for his pluck at the action of Nowagi, in the Swat Valley. He acted as A.D.C. to Sir Bindon Blood in the Buner Expedition in 1898, and took part in the S.A War with the Inniskilling Dragoons in 1899; subsequently with the 16th Lancers. He afterwards raised and commanded a regt. of Yeomanry (Fincastle's Horse) with the rank of Lt. Col., and took part in the fighting around Colesburg, in the relief of Kimberley, the battle of Paardeburg, and the subsequent fighting in the Orange Free State. Viscount Fincastle has travelled and shot all over India, including elephant shooting in Mysore. He played polo in the 16th Lancers Regt. team in several tournaments in India. He married, Jan 10, 1904, Miss Dorothy Kemble.

FINLAYSON, Lieut. Col. Robert Alexander, C.M.G., of Kimberley and the Kimberley Club, was born Oct. 11, 1857, at Edinburgh, where he received his education. He went to SA. in 1875. In 1882 he was in the service of the Railway Dept., and joined the Hon. J. D. Logan in business in 1884, remaining with him until 1892. He joined the Kimberley Volunteers as a Lieut. in 1890, and received his majority in 1895. He commanded the Infantry in the Bechuanaland Rebellion of 1896-7, and became Lieut. Col. in '98. In the late S.A. War he commanded the Kimberley Regt. and a section of the Defence Force during the siege of Kimberley, 1900 (despatches, C.M.G.), afterwards being in command of Infantry on columns operating in the Cape Colony, O.H.C., and the Transvaal (1900-2).

Col. Finlayson identifies himself with all forms of sport, and was for some years Pres. of the Diamond Fields Scottish Association. His chief recreations are shooting and golf. He married, in 1887, Miss Emily Bees, of Kimberley.

FINNEMORE, Robert Isaac J.P., of Westhury House, Loop St., Maritzburg, was born at Addington Park, Surrey, Oct. 28, 1842. He is eldest son of the late Isaac Powell Finnemore, of Co. Wicklow, and his wife Jane (born Clarke). He was educated at the Church of England Gram. Sch. and Bishopstowe Mission Station, where he was a pupil teacher, and entered the Natal Civil Service Aug. 4, 1858, as Pupil-Asst. to the Surveyor-Gen., being appointed Second Clerk in March, 1859. He passed the exam. in the theory and practice of land surveying in 1863; was Chief Clerk, Draughtsman, and Examiner of Surveyor's Work in 1864; was transferred to the Law Dept. at his own request in 1865, and was called to the Bar in 1868; has acted as Surveyor-General, acted as Clerk of the Peace, Magistrate, and Master and Registrar of the Supreme Court at various times in 1872-4. He was Postmaster-Gen., 1876-7; Acting Col. Treasurer in 1877; Magistrate at Maritzburg, 1877-8; Master and Registrar of the Supreme Court and Registrar of the Vice-Admiralty Court, 1878-81. He was appointed J.P. for Natal in 1881, and was Magistrate at Durban from that year until 1889; was acting Puisne Judge in 1883; Marriage Officer at Durban, 1887-9; Collector of Customs, Registrar of Shipping, Emigration Officer and Harbour Commissioner, 1889-94; has served on numerous commissions and boards; was Deputy Chairman of the Harbour Board, 1881-89; Chairman of the Zulu War Relief Fund; Pres. of the Pietermaritzburg Collegiate Institution; Crown Solicitor and Parliamentary Draughtsman, 1894-6; was appointed Puisne Judge Nov. 1, 1896; Senior Puisne Judge from 1902, and has acted as Chief Justice of Natal. Retired on pension of £1,000 per annum Dec. 1, 1904, after 46 years' public service, conspicuously marked by ability and devotion to his work; and receiving, in recognition of those services, an official letter of thanks, expressing the Government's warm appreciation.

He edited the *Natal Almanac and Register*, 1876-8; published *Digests of Decisions of the Supreme Court* for 1860-3 and 1866-7, and is author of *Natal Law Reports* for 1872, 1873, 1879, 1881, etc. In Freemasonry he is Past Dist. Grand Master; Past Dist. Grand Mark Master; Past Grand Superintendent Royal Arch; Past Provincial Prior of the Temple and Malta; Sovereign Grand Inspector-General, 33 deg.; Intendant General Knights of Rome and Constantine, Knt. of the Royal Order of Scotland, Knt. Commander of the Temple, etc. He has worked in the temperance cause; was Past Grand Vice-Templar; hon. member of Rechabites, and Pres. of various religious and temperance organisations. For the public libraries and many other institutions of Maritzburg and Durban he has done good service as Pres. and otherwise. He formerly gave lectures on the most varied topics; was Lay Reader, Churchwarden, and occasional Preacher (C. of E.). He was long connected with the Royal Agricultural Society of Natal, and was constituted, *honoris causa*, a life member of the Society and of its managing committee. He is life member of the St. John Ambulance Assoc., and of the chief Masonic institutions. He is also F.R.A.S., F.R.G.S., F.Z.S., F.A.I., F.R.Met.S., F.H.Hist.S,, F.S.S., M.S.A., F.R.C.I., F.I.I., Hon. Corr. Mem. V.I., Mem. Amer. Aced. Polit. and Soc. Sc., Mem. Astron. S. of Pacific, Mem. of Brit. Astron. Assoc., Mem. Selden Soc., and of numerous other Societies. He married, June 7, 1887, Catherine Augusta, dau. of John Russom, J.P., sometime Mayor of Maritzburg, and has issue surviving, one son and three daughters. (Mr. Finnemore died in 1906.)

FINNIE, John Pulsford, F.R.C.I., of 'Bon Accord', Gwelo, Rhodesia, and the Gwelo Club, is the eldest son of John Finnie, a Scotch lawyer, and was born in 1860 at Aberdeen. He was educated at Fortrose Acad. and King's Coll., Aberdeen, and went to S.A. in 1885. After a short residence in Natal and the Transvaal, he became one of the early pioneers of Rhodesia. In 1890 he was taken prisoner by the Portuguese at Beira, at the time that Sir John Willoughby tried to force the East Coast Route to Salisbury. From 1891 to 1893 he was shooting big game between the Pungwe and Zambesi rivers. In 1892 he spent some little time with Selous in the vicinity of Sacramento, and in 1893 was obliged to return to Natal owing to having been severely mauled by a lion. In 1894 he was again in Matabeleland, and took an active part in the Rebellion of '96. In '97 he lectured throughout the North of Scotland on Rhodesia and S.A. generally.

He is senior partner of the firm of Finnie & Finnie, agents and brokers of Gwelo, and is interested in many mining ventures.

FIRMAN, Lieut.-Col. R. B., was originally in the Royal Welsh Fusiliers, of which he acted as adjutant. On the outbreak of the S. African War he volunteered his services, and went out as Capt. of the 35th Co. of Imperial Yeomanry in the early part of 1900. He was soon promoted Lieut. Col., with ultimate command of a mobile column operating under Sir Leslie Rundle mainly in the eastern portion of the Orange River Colony. He was at one time well known as an amateur jockey, and still rides a good race.

FISCHER, Abraham, of the Orange River Colony, was formerly a member of the Free State Volksraad with a seat on the Executive Council. Shortly after the relief of Kimberley he was one of the Boer delegates who arrived at the *Chancellerie de la Republique Sud-Africaine* in Brussels to stir up anti-British feeling. He was sent to intercept the three Generals, Botha (q.v.), De la Rey, and De Wet when they arrived after the war at Southampton, and was largely responsible for their avoiding the preparations of the British to welcome them. Mr. Fischer afterwards accompanied the Generals to Rotterdam, returning with them to London for the conference at the Colonial Office, but Mr. Fischer was not received by Mr. Chamberlain. Permission for his return to South Africa was for a long time withheld, but he was eventually allowed to resettle in the Colony. In 1906 he was elected by the Central Committee Chairman of the Orangia Union.

FISHER, Edward Montague, served in the 10th Royal Hussars from 1887 till 1889, and from 1889 till 1891 in the 2nd Vol. Batt. of the Suffolk Regt. In 1892 he joined the Cape Police; served in the Bechuanaland Rebellion in 1896-7 (medal with clasp). He was appointed Sub Inspector of the Cape Police in 1899; served in the South African War in 1899-1902 (medal with clasps), and was appointed Inspector in the Corps in 1902.

FITZGERALD, Admiral Charles Cooper Penrose, of Claret Rock, Mount Pleasant, Co. Lough, and of the United Service Club, was born in 1841. He became a cadet on board the *Victory* in 1854, and served as a midshipman of the *Colossus* in the Baltic during the Russian War (medal); was present in the *Retribution* at the bombardment of Nankin in 1858 (medal); and was Flag-Captain to Sir Francis Sullivan in the *Inconstant* during the Egyptian Campaign in 1882 (Egyptian modal, Khedive's Star, and Third Class Medjidieh). Admiral Fitzgerald acted as A.D.C. to the late Queen for three years, and in 1897 was appointed second in command of the China Station. He married, in 1882, Henrietta, dau. of the late Rev. F. Hewson.

FITZGERALD, Francis, M.A., LL.B., of Wroxton, Oxfordshire, and of the Travellers' and Marlborough clubs, was born at Melbourne in 1864, and is the eldest son of the Hon. Nicholas FitzGerald, M.L:C., of Victoria. He was educated at Oscott and Trinity Coll., Dublin; was called to the Bar in 1886, and joined the Oxford Circuit. In 1896 he was appointed a Revising Barrister, and became Recorder of Newbury in 1904. He is a director of the Anglo-Belgian Co., of Egypt, Ltd. He married, in 1889, Mina, eldest dau. of the eleventh Lord North, of Wroxton Abbey, Banbury.

FITZGERALD, William Walter Augustine, J.P., D.L., of Carrigoran, Newmarket-on-Fergus, Co. Clare, 26, Ashley Gardens, S.W., and of the Carlton, Wellington and Kildare Street (Dublin) clubs, was born at Worthing Nov. 24, 1852, and is the only surviving son of Field Marshal Sir John Foster FitzGerald G.C.B. After spending eighteen years in Southern India Mr. FitzGerald was sent out by the Imperial British East Africa Company on a two years' special mission to report on the agricultural capabilities of the coast lands of the British sphere of influence in South Africa, and also with a view to the opening out of new districts for English trade and commerce. He was the first European to explore the coast regions lying between Lamu and Port Durnford, and he explored and reported upon an area of coast land 300 miles in length. Amongst his various reports was one upon the spice and other cultivations of the islands of Zanzibar and Pemba for the Zanzibar Government, made at the personal request of Sir Gerald Portal, a report for which Mr. FitzGerald received the thanks of H.M. Government. He returned to England in 1894, and in January, 1S95, delivered an address at the Imperial Institute on the subject of the agricultural resources of the coastline of British East Africa. Mr. FitzGerald is an Irish landlord, a magistrate, and Deputy Lieutenant of County Clare. In 1899 he was invited by the Egyptian Government to visit the Sudan and report on its agricultural and commercial capacities; but, as he was at that time standing for Parliament, he declined. He is the author of *Travels in British East Africa, Zanzibar, and Pemba*. He married, Oct. 30, 1904, Clara, Lady FitzGerald, widow of the late Sir Augustine FitzGerald, fourth baronet.

FITZPATRICK, Sir James Percy, Knight Bachelor, M.L.C., of Hohenheim, Johannesburg, and of Buckland Downs, Harrismith, O.R.C., was born at King William's Town, July 24, 1862. He is the son of the Hon. James Coleman FitzPatrick, an Irish barrister, who supported the political fortunes of Daniel O'Connell in his declining years, as well as those of the Liberator's son, John O'Connell, and who afterwards became Judge of the Supreme Court of the C.C. Sir Percy was educated at St. Gregory's Coll., Downside, near Bath, and went to the Transvaal in 1884, where he has resided practically ever since, either on the alluvial diggings, or trading, hunting, or prospecting. In 1886 he settled at Barberton, leaving three years later for the Witwatersrand. He accompanied the Randolph Churchill expedition through Mashonaland in 1891, and in 1892, on returning to Johannesburg, took charge of the intelligence department of the firm of H. Eckstein & Co., of which he became a partner in 1898, representing the firm on the boards of many of the premier mining companies of the Rand. Few men are more conversant with all the details of the mining industry or with the general affairs of the Transvaal than Sir Percy, as those will know who remember his evidence before the Industrial Commission in 1897, and subsequently before the Concessions Commission. He was one of the first to become

associated with the Reform Committee in 1895, to which he acted as an indefatigable hon. secretary. For his participation in that movement he was arrested in January, 1896, and, with other ringleaders, was refused bail. He was put on trial in April for high treason against the Government of the S.A.R., and was condemned to suffer two years' imprisonment, to pay a fine of £2,000, or as an alternative another year's imprisonment, and thereafter to be banished from the State for a period of three years. This sentence was reduced to one year's imprisonment in the following May, but he was released during the same month.

In 1897, when everybody thought (and rightly) that the Industrial Commission was intended merely as a farce, Sir Percy nevertheless pressed hard for the Uitlanders to take it seriously, if only for the purpose of once more putting their ease on record. In Feb., 1899, although this fact is not generally known, it was he who suggested to the Transvaal Govt. a conference between Mr. Kruger and Lord Milner, and another between the Govt. and the people of Johannesburg. This was a most earnest and sincere effort to avert a war, as Sir Percy plainly stated, and his suggestions resulted in the Bloemfontein Conference and the 'Capitalist Negotiations'. However, these meetings were turned by the Boer Govt. to purposes other than peace. As evidence of his party's sincerity, he proposed, in order to remove causes of constant friction, that the mining people should forego their *Bewaarplaatsen* Rights, and buy them at a valuation instead of going to law and to the Raad for restitution in tote, and should also acquiesce in the Dynamite Monopoly, "Provided the profits, as originally intended, should go to the Govt."; in fact that the terms of the original concession should be enforced if the Govt. would introduce the reforms in administration of the Liquor and other laws, as recommended by the Industrial Commission, and make some equitable concession of political rights to the Uitlanders. When the Capitalist Negotiations came about the Govt., at first through Mr. Lippert, and afterwards through Dr. Leyds and Mr. Reitz, refused to allow Sir Percy (although a partner in the leading house of Eckstein) to take part. He was the one barred. As soon, however, as the Government tried to introduce the Franchise question, the other representatives of the Capitalists refused to take part until Sir Percy FitzPatrick and some other representatives of the Uitlanders were admitted. After some delay the Govt. gave way, but Sir Percy would not participate in the negotiations without a written invitation which would release him from the condition of three years' silence which had been imposed on him in connection with the Reformers' sentences. This was given, and Sir Percy, having been authorised by the representatives of all classes to voice their case, went into the matter heart and soul, incidentally proving step by step how the Govt. had authorised the negotiations, and showing the devices by which they had sought to inveigle the negotiators into a false move. Sir Percy drew up the five years' franchise memorandum which was embodied in the Capitalist Negotiations documents (published in March or April, 1899), and which afterwards served as the basis of Lord Milner's Bloemfontein proposals. Before sending this memo. in, he showed it to the State Secy. and State Attorney in Pretoria, who both said that it was absolutely just, but that Mr. Kruger would never be induced to agree to it. Sir Percy's answer to this was, "Well, let us try. Let it be a basis for discussion, to bring us together and avert trouble."

Sir Percy, as spokesman for the guarantors of the War Loan and representative of the public committee, took a principal part in the War Debt negotiations with Mr. Chamberlain. He is one of the nonofficial members of the first Transvaal Legislative Council, and was elected by that body as one of the two Transvaal Representatives on the Inter-Colonial Council of the Transvaal and O.R.C., from which he resigned in 1904. He was Pres. of the Witwatersrand Chamber of Mines in 1902.

Sir Percy has a facile pen. He was, years ago, editor of the *Barberton Herald*, and besides many able contributions to the Press on questions of the moment, he has published an account of his Mashonaland trip, *Through Mashonaland with Pick and Pen*, and a charming volume of short stories under the name of *The Outspan*. But in England he will be more generally known as the author of *The Transvaal from Within*—a work which is everywhere regarded as the textbook upon the events which led up to the inception of the Reform movement, and eventually culminated in raid and war. Sir Percy was made a Knight Bachelor in 1902 in recognition of his great services in connection with S.A. He married, February 16, 1889, Elizabeth Lillian, dau. of John Cubitt, of Pretoria.

FITZWILLIAM, Earl, of 4, Grosvenor Square, London, W., is the representative of an old family which traces its descent to a Sir William Fitzwilliam, a Knight of the Conqueror's time, who married a daughter of Sir John Elmley, and so acquired the lordships of Elmley and Spothurgh. A later Fitzwilliam married the daughter of Hameline Plantagenet, Earl of Surrey, and in 1506 there was that famous Sheriff of London and Alderman of Bread Street Ward who, refusing to forsake his old friend Cardinal Wolsey after his fall, was sent for by the King, and, instead of losing his head, left the royal presence knighted as Sir William Fitzwilliam and a Privy Councillor.

The present Earl, who succeeded to the title in 1902, was born in 1872, in Canada, where his father lost his life in saving his family from their burning home.

Lord Fitzwilliam served in the South African War, when he gained the D.S.O.; is one of the richest peers in the kingdom, is an expert on mining engineering, and in 1904-5 undertook an expedition to Cocas Island, where the party searched for lost treasure, the hunt being productive of nothing worse than somewhat severe injuries to Lord Fitzwilliam and some members of his crew during blasting operations. He married, in 1896, Lady Maud Dundas, dau. of the Marquess of Zetland.

FLEMING, Andrew Milroy, C.M.G. (1898), of Salisbury, Rhodesia, and of the Badminton Club, was born at Edinburgh, Jan. 28, 1871. He is son of Rev. John Fleming, of Edinburgh; was educated at Durham Sch. and Edinburgh Univ., and holds the degrees M.B., C.M., F.R.C.S.E., and D.P.H. Camb. He has been for many years in S.A.; served in the Mashonaland Rebellion in 1896-97; is Medical Director and Inspector of Hospitals for Rhodesia, and P.M.O. of the B.S.A. Police. He married, in 1896 Philadelphia Alice, dau. of the late Wm. Fisher, of British Columbia.

FLEMING, Charles David J.P., of Gwelo,

Rhodesia, is son of Rev. John Fleming, of Edinburgh, where he was born Sept. 15, 1869; was educated at the Edinburgh Acad. and Univ. and joined the B.S.A. Co.'s service, Oct. 28, 1895. He served throughout the Matabele Rebellion in 1896 (medal), and was appointed Mining Commissioner at Gwelo April 1, 1899. He married, June 3, 1903, Lily, youngest dau. of the late Donald Mackenzie, J.P., of Gaisloch, Rossshire.

FLEMING, Thomas, J.P. for the county of Maritzburg, of Good Hope, Boston, Natal, was born in Natal, March 29, 1855. He has devoted many years to farming, and is chairman of the Boston Farmers' Association, also President of the Impendhle Rifle Association, and is a member of the Licensing and Road Board for Impendhle. He married, Aug. 27, 1886, Jeanie, dau. of Major John Granger, of Glasgow.

FLINT, Rev. William, D.D., of Wolmunster Park, Rosebank, C.C., was born at Stand bridge, Bedford, and educated at Leighton Buzzard and Headingley Coll.; entered the ministry of the Wesleyan Methodist Church in 1879; was ordained at Hull in 1882, and received appointments at Torquay, Williton, Weston-super-Mare, and Bournemouth. His health failing, he visited S. Africa in 1889, where he travelled for two years, and in 1892 joined the Conference of the Wesleyan Methodist Church of S.A., and was appointed successively to Maritzburg and Cape Town. He founded and was the first editor of *The Methodist Churchman*, and later became a minister without pastoral charge. In 1899 he was elected second Pres. of the Cape Peninsula Church Council. In 1901 he was appointed Librarian of the Cape Parliament. He is a Doctor of Divinity of the Wesleyan Theological Coll, of the McGill Univ., Montreal, a member of the Council of the University of the Cape of Good Hope, of the Council of the S.A. Philosophical Society, and also of the S.A. Association for the Advancement of Science, being appointed editor of the first volume of the proceedings of the latter association. He is chairman of the Rondebosch and Mowbray Hospital Board, and also of the Christian Endeavour Executive for S.A. Has contributed extensively to reviews, magazines, and journals, and is co-editor of *Science in South Africa: a Handbook and Review*. He

married, in 1892, Margaret, dau. of Alexander McGregor, of Rondebosch, formerly Mayor of Kimberley.

FLOWERS, Sergt., R.M.L.I., served in the Somaliland Campaign, and in Feb., 1905, was presented with the Conspicuous Gallantry Medal for bravery in the capture of Illig, under the following circumstances: the vessels of the fleet shelled the rebel camp from the sea, and when the ships' crews landed they found the rebels had taken refuge in some caves. In routing them out the officer in command of Sergeant Flowers' party from H.M.S. *Fox* was stricken down. Flowers took the sword from the fallen man's band, and, leading his men, rushed into the cave at the risk of death from an unseen hand.

FLOYER, Ernest Ayscoghe, of Skidbrook, near Louth, Lincs., and of the Oriental Club, was born in Lincolnshire, July 4, 1852; was educated at Charterhouse; joined the Bengal Civil Service (uncovenanted) in 1869; was called to Egypt to assist in reforms in connection with the Railways and Telegraphs in 1878, and has remained there ever since, taking part in the campaign of 1882 (Egyptian medal and clasp, bronze star). He is the author of *Unexplored Baluchistan*, *Etude sur le Nord Etbai*, and certain scientific papers in Arabic. He married, Sept. 1, 1887, Miss Mary Louisa Watson.

FOADEN, George Pearse, Secretary-General to the Khedivial Agricultural Society, was the recipient in 1905 of the Insignia of the Second Class of the Imperial Order of the Osmanieh, conferred by the Khedive in recognition of valuable services rendered to his Highness.

FORBES, Gordon Stewart Drummond, M.L.C., D.S.O., of the Bulawayo Club, Rhodesia, and of the Junior Carlton and Welling ton Clubs, was born in 1868, and is son of Gen. Sir J. Forbes, G.C.B. He was formerly attached to Thorneycroft's Mounted Infantry, and served in the Matabele War in 1896, taking part in the battle of the Umgusa, and in the South African War he was present at the action at Spion Kop (D.S.O.). Mr. Forbes is a member of the Legislative Council of S. Rhodesia; is Managing Director of the Antenior (Matabele) Gold Mines, Ltd., Forbes Rhodesia

Syndicate, Ltd., and Hartley and Sebakwe Development Co., and is on the Committee of the Rhodesia Chamber of Mines. Unmarried.

FORBES, Major Patrick William, of Salisbury, Rhodesia, is son of the late A. C. Forbes, of Whitchurch, Oxon. He was formerly Capt. in the 6th (Inniskilling) Dragoons, and served in the operations in Zululand in 1888. He was the first officer to command the Mashonaland Volunteer Regt., and took part in the Matabele War of 1893 in command of the Salisbury column, contributing a long account of the operations to *The Downfall of Lobengula*, by W. A. Wills and L. T. Collingridge. He married, Jan. 21, 1903, Beatrice, dau. of Robert Grey, Treasurer of the Foundling Hospital.

FORBES-LEITH, Baron, of Fyvie Castle, Fyvie, Aberdeenshire, was born in 1847, and is the eldest son of the late Rear Admiral John J. Leith. He served in the Royal Navy, retiring with the rank of Lieut., and is a Deputy-Lieut. of Aberdeenshire. He was created Baron on the occasion of the King's birthday, 1905; and married, in 1871, Marie, dau. of Derrick January, of St. Louis.

FORD, Lieut. John Everard Hugo, of Brereton Lodge, Wokingham, Berks., was born at Southport, Dec. 14, 1873, and is son of Lt. Col. J. Ford, late R.A. He was educated at Wellington Coll., and was in S. Africa when the war broke out in 1899. He went on active service as a Serjeant in Prince Albert's Own Cape Vol. Batt. (S. African medal and four clasps), subsequently receiving a commission as Lieut. in the H.F.A. in 1901, and embarked with his Batt. for India at the end of that year. He served at Kamptee until May, 1902, when he was seconded for the purpose of joining the Gold Coast Regt., serving with that until he retired from the Army in 1905, and went out to British E. Africa exploring. Unmarried.

FORD, Lewis Peter, of Burton Tower, Gresford, N. Wales, was born Jan. 26, 1846. He studied law under Advocate Brand, who afterwards became Pros. of the O.F.S., and was admitted to practice in S.A., in 1865. He was Deputy Sheriff of Richmond (C.C.) and Murraysburg from 1866-71; was the first Attorney-Gen. appointed under British rule in the Transvaal in 1877 under Sir Theophilus Shepstone; Legal Adviser in the Transvaal to the Imperial Govt., 1878-88; was also Chancellor of the Diocese of Pretoria, 1879-89. Since then Mr. Ford has resided in England, and has gradually liquidated his S. African interests, and taken up other enterprises. He is Chairman of the Limni Copper Mining Synd., and has devoted much time to the development of 'Ford Stone', now in the hands of a syndicate, the Silicate of Lime Stone, Ltd., of which he is also chairman. He married twice: first, in 1866, Miss E. Utting, dau. of a former editor of the *Cape Argus*; and secondly, Miss E. Tanner, dau. of Sir Henry Tanner, of H.M. Office of Works.

FORESTER-WALKER, Major G. J., R.A., (local Lieut. Col.), entered the Royal Artillery as Lieut. in 1894; obtained his Captaincy in 1895, and became Major in 1900. In the late Anglo Boer War he served on Lord Methuen's Staff in the advance on Kimberley, and was subsequently with Lord Roberts's army up to the capture of Pretoria and the operations to the east of that place.

With the local rank of Lieut. Col. he took part in the operations against the Mullah in Somaliland in 1903-04, and was slightly wounded at Jidballi.

FORRESTER, Thomas Paul Wallace, of 48, Kensington Mansions, London, was born at Gravesend, England, in 1853; is the eldest son of William Alexander Forrester, of Juniper Green, Edinburgh, and was educated at the Albion House Acad., Woolwich. He has been connected with the South African trade nearly all his life with the shipping house of Houlder Brothers and Co. Ltd., of which he is now managing director, and he is also a director of the Houlder Line, Ltd. During this time he has made many visits to S. Africa. He has had nearly 23 years' service as an officer in the Essex Volunteer Artillery, joining as Second Lieut. and retiring in 1899 with the rank of Lieut. Col. and the Volunteer Decoration (1898), since when he has continued to render service on the Council of the National Artillery Association. His principal recreations are boating and walking. Mr. Forrester was married, in 1880, to Mary, dau. of Henry Mills, of London.

FORT, George Seymour, B.A., of 2, Little

Stanhope Street, Mayfair, and of the Bath Club, is the son of the Rev. H. Fort, Hector of Coopersale, Essex; was born at Coopersale in 1860, and was educated at Uppingham and Hertford Coll:, Oxford, where he graduated BA. He was private secy. to Maj. Gen. Sir Peter Scratchley, first High Commissioner of New Guinea and the Western Pacific, 1885-86, in which latter year he wrote the report of the Administration; private secy. to the Right Hon. Lord Loch, Governor of Victoria, 1887-9. In the latter year he proceeded to Cape Town, where he remained until 1891. He was appointed Magistrate in Umtali, Manicaland, in 1893. Mr. Fort is a Captain in the King's Colonials, and was formerly well known in the rowing world, having taken part in the Oxford and Cambridge races in 1883-4. He is the author of various articles on Australia and S. Africa, which at the time of publication excited great interest.

FOSTER, Edward William Perceval, C.M.G., Second Class Order of the Osmanieh, Second Class Order of the Medjidieh, of 7, Rue des Ptolemées, Alexandria, Egypt, was born in Mauritius, Dec. 26, 1850. He is son of the late Major-Gen. E. H. H. Foster, of the 12th Regt. and the 18th Regimental District, his mother being youngest dau. of Capt. G. Fairbairn Dick, late Colonial Secy., Mauritius. He was educated privately and at the Thomason Engineering Coll, Roorkee, India. He joined the Irrigation Branch of the Indian Public Works Dept. in 1871, and was selected for employment in the Irrigation Service of Egypt in 1884. He resigned his office under Govt. ten year later to take n the managing direction of the Bahera Company which is largely interested in land reclamation.

He married, Feb. 24, 1875, Annie, youngest dau. of the late Christopher Strachan, of Inverness.

FOSTER, J., M.L.A., is a member of the S.A. party, and was elected to represent the division of Oudtshoorn at the general election in Feb., 1904.

FOURIE, Gen. Christian, was one of the most progressive and broad-minded of the Boers, and when the last South African War broke out, was one of the best-known fighting officers in the Boer ranks in the Eastern Transvaal.

FOWLE, Capt. Henry Walter Hamilton, J.P., served in the S. African War, 1899-1900, with Roberts's Horse, subsequently being seconded for service under the Military Governor at Pretoria; acted as Military Commissioner of Police and Asst. Prov. Marshal for Heidelberg and district in 1900-1; was Asst. Commissioner of Police at Pretoria in 1901; and from that time until 1902 he held various positions, including Political Officer to the Military Commissioner of Police at Johannesburg, Military Intelligence Officer for Johannesburg and district, and Asst. to the Director of Military Intelligence, Army Headquarters, and to the Prov. Marshal (two medals and six clasps). He is a J.P. for the Transvaal; was Chief Secy. for Permits under the Peace Preservation Ordinance in 1902, and in 1903 was appointed Registrar of Asiatics in the Transvaal.

FOWLE, Col. J., 21st Lancers, served in the Nile Expedition in 1884 with the Light Camel Regiment. He was in the Sudan with Lord Kitchener in 1898, and took part in the battle of Khartoum, and in that gallant but useless charge of the 21st Lancers which was said to have freshened up the reputation of a regiment with a rather poor record.

FOWLER, Lieut. William Edward Nesfidel, of Woodthorp Hall, Derbyshire, and Kalomo, NW. Rhodesia; served through the South African War in the Imperial Yeomanry (Queen's medal with four clasps and King's medal). He is now on the Reserve of Officers, and became a Lieut. in the Barotse Native Police in 1904. Unmarried.

FOX, Captain Arthur Maxwell, D.S.O., R.A., was born in 1875. He served in the South African War in 1899-1902 (despatches, Queen's medal with four clasps, King's medal with two clasps, and D.S.O.).

FOX Sir Charles Douglas, Knt. Bachelor (1886), of 12, Queen's Gate Gardens, S.W., and the St. Stephen's and National Clubs, was born in Smethwick, May 14, 1840; is the eldest surviving son of the late Sir Charles Fox; was educated at Cholmondeley Sch., Highgate, and King's Coll., London, of which he is a Fellow. He is a Past

Master of the Furness Company, County Alderman of Surrey, and J.P. or London and Surrey. He has been in practice in Westminster since 1861 as a civil, mechanical, and electrical engineer, and is senior partner of the firm of Sir Douglas Fox and Partners; Past Pres. of the Institution of Civil Engineers, member of the Institution of Mechanical and of Electrical Engineers, and Hon, member of the American Societies of Civil and Mechanical Engineers. Sir Douglas has been prominently identified with railway enterprise in South Africa and elsewhere, especially in North and South America, and India. During his early training he assisted his father in the engineering details of the Cape Town and Wellington and Wynberg Railways, which were the first lines in South Africa. He is Joint Consulting Engineer with Sir Charles Metcalfe of the Rhodesian and Mashonaland Railways see J. R. Maguire), the Cape Govt. Railways, the Benguela Railway, the British South Africa Chartered Co., the British Central Africa Co., and the African Concessions Syndicate, which Last named Company holds the concession for the use of the water power of the Victoria Falls (see H. Wilson Fox). Sir Douglas was knighted in 1886 in connection with his work as engineer of the Mersey Railway tunnel. He married, May 26, 1863, Mary, dau. of the late Francis Wright, of Osmaston Manor, Derby.

FOX, Henry Wilson, B.A., of 4, Halkin Street, London, S.W., and of the Junior Carlton, Wellington, and Prince's Clubs, was born at Cavendish Square, London, Aug. 18, 1863. He is the son of Wilson Fox, M.D., Physician in Ordinary to her late Majesty Queen Victoria was educated at Charterhouse, Marlborough Coll., Univ. Coll., Lond., and Trinity Coll. Camb., of which he was Exhibitioner and Scholar; B.A., Natural Science Tripos. He was called to the Bar, Nov. 29, 1888, and was Equity Scholar of Lincoln's Inn (1888). He was admitted Advocate of the Supreme Court of the Colony of the Cape of Good Hope and Advocate of the High Court of Southern Rhodesia in 1894.

Mr. Wilson Fox, after leaving the Cambridge University, spent some time in the office of the late Sir Charles Mills, then Agent-Gen. to Cape Colony. In 1889 he went out to Johannesburg on

the Johannesburg staff of the Consolidated Gold Fields of South Africa. In 1892 he took to journalism, and immediately came to the front as the editor of the *South African Mining Journal* of Johannesburg. In this capacity he assisted Mr. John Hays Hammond in drafting the Rhodesian Mining Laws. This brought him into touch with the late Mr. Cecil Rhodes, and ultimately led to his being appointed Public Prosecutor of Rhodesia in the same year. When the rebellion broke out in 1896-7 in Matabeleland and Mashonaland he carried out the duties of Director of Transport and Commissariat for the Salisbury force with quite exceptional success, under, of course, quite exceptional difficulties, being mentioned in despatches, and wears the medal with clasp. In May, 1897, he returned to England for a holiday, and was unexpectedly offered the appointment in June, 1898, of manager of the Chartered Company, a responsible and arduous position which he still fills, and for which his all round knowledge of mining, finance, law, and South African politics gives him exceptional authority. He took a prominent part in the extraordinarily successful flotation of the Charter Trust and Agency, and represents the Chartered Company on most of the principal Rhodesian directorates, including the following: African Concessions Syndicate, Ltd.; Antenior (Matabele) Gold Mines, Ltd.; Ayrshire Gold Mine and Lomagunda Railway Co., Ltd.; Beatrice (Rhodesia) Co., Ltd.; Bonsor Gold Mining Co., Ltd.; Charter Trust and Agency, Ltd.; Clark's Consolidated, Ltd.; Jumbo Gold Mining Co., Ltd.; Mashonaland Agency, Ltd.; New Rhodesia District Development Co., Ltd. Northern Copper (B.S.A.) Co., Ltd.; Penhalonga Proprietary Mines, Ltd.; Rhodesia Broken Hill Development Co., Ltd.; Rhodesia Copper Co., Ltd.; Selukwe Gold Mining Co., Ltd.; Surprise Gold Mining Co., Ltd.; Wanderer (Selukwe) Gold Mines, Ltd.; Wankie (Rhodesia) Coal, Railway, and Exploration Co., Ltd.; and Willoughby's Consolidated Co., Ltd. Mr. Wilson Fox has recently come into further public prominence in connection with his great scheme for harnessing the Victoria Falls in the Zambesi for the transmission of power to the Witwatersrand Gold Fields. As the distance is 600 miles as the crow flies, this project on completion will mark an epochal stride in the practice of long-distance transmission of electrical power. The project is supported by some of the greatest minds known to electrical science, among whom may be mentioned Sir Douglas Fox, Sir Charles Metcalfe, Bart., Lord Kelvin, and Mr. Arthur Wright, of London; Mr. Ralph D. Mershon, of New York; Professor Dr. G. Klingenberg, of the *Allgemeine Elektricitäts-Gesellschaft*, of Berlin; Mons. Andre Blondel, of Paris; Dr. Edouard Tissot, of Basle; and other names of worldwide distinction. In financing this vast undertaking the Chartered Company are, it is understood, allied with the powerful electrical and financial groups headed by the Allgemeine Elektricitäts-Gesellschaft and the Dresdner Bank. When completed, the transmission of power at low price to Johannesburg should very greatly modify and improve the state of the mining industry on the Rand, as at present the cost of power constitutes the second largest item in the bill of working costs.

Mr. Wilson Fox has invented and patented a system of hydraulic storage, which, according to the opinions of several of the greatest electrical experts in the world, will revolutionise the practice of long-distance transmission, partly by effecting numerous economies, partly by enabling the transmission lines to run a constant load, and partly by allowing a much larger sale of power from the same supply under the ordinary load factors.

Mr. Fox is a fervid supporter of the Imperialistic ideals of the late Mr. Cecil Rhodes, and is a fine speaker either on political or commercial subjects, with an unusual hold over public meetings. He is a most popular man in South African circles, and a good sportsman. He represented Cambridge University at lawn tennis in 1885-6, was the chief exponent of the game in South Africa for several years, and still plays for the English championship every year. Golf and shooting are his other principal recreations. He married, on July 19, 1898, the Hon Eleanor B. Sclater-Booth, sister of the present Lord Basing, and has a son, born in 1900.

FRANKLAND, Sir Frederick, 10th Bart., of 3, Queen's Gardens, Windsor, and of the Carlton and White's Clubs, was born Sept. 2, 1868, and was educated at Cheltenham Coll. He was formerly Capt. in the 3rd Batt. Bedfordshire Regt., from which he was seconded for service with the B.S.A.

Co., serving from 1893 till 1900 in the Mines Department as Asst. Mining Commissioner at Bulawayo. Sir Frederick took part in the Matabele Rebellion in 1896 (medal) and in the S. African War in 1899-1900 (medal and four clasps). He is on the London Committee of the Brakpan Mines and the North Geduld G.M. Co. He married Miss Mary Cecil Curzon in 1901, and has one son.

FRANKS, Sir Kendal Matthew St. John, Kt., C.B., M.D., F.R.C.S.I., of Kilmurry Hospital Hill, Johannesburg, was born in 1851, and is son of the late R. F. Franks. He served in S. Africa during the war in 1899-1902 as Consulting Surgeon to the Forces (mentioned in despatches). He married, first, in 1879, and secondly in 1885, Gertrude (died, 1896), dau. of Lieut. Col. T. B. Butt.

FRASER, Miss Agnes (Frances MacNab), of the Vicarage, South Weald, Brentwood, Essex, is dau. of the Rev. Duncan Fraser, M.A. She travelled in S. Africa in 1894, and in Morocco in 1901-2, besides having been in Canada and Anatolia. She is the author of *No Reply*, *Relics*, *On Veldt and Farm*, *British Colombia for Settlers*, and *A Ride in Morocco*.

FRASER, Sir John George, Knt. Bachelor (1905), M.L.C., of Beaufort House, Bloemfontein, O.R.C., and of the Bloemfontein Club, was born at Beaufort West, Cape Colony, Dec. 17, 1840. He is son of the Rev. Colin Mackenzie Fraser, a minister of the Scotch Church, and afterwards of the Dutch Reformed Church at Beaufort West, his mother having been a Miss Sieberhagen. Sir John was educated at the Free Church Institution, Inverness, and at Marischal and King's Colleges, Aberdeen. He returned to South Africa in 1860, and settled in the Free State three years later, serving on Line Commando in 1864, and then as Field Cornet of Philippolis in the Basuto War of 1865-6. Soon afterwards he entered the Civil Service of the O.F.S., and was appointed priv. secy. to Sir John Brand in 1871; Secy. to the Volksraad and Registrar of the Higher Courts in 1872; and Master of the Orphan and Insolvent Chambers in 1875. He qualified as practitioner of the High Court of the O.F.S. in 1877, and retired from the Civil Service in order to follow the profession of Law. He was elected member of the Volksraad for Knapzariver in 1879, and as member for Bloemfontein in the following year, since which he continued to represent the capital up to the Anglo Boer War in 1899. During that long period he was Chairman of the Raad from 1884 to 1896, and represented the State at various important conferences including one at Pretoria with Pres. Kruger on inter-Republic interests in 1887, on Customs and Railways at Cape Town in 1888, with Pres. Kruger at Potchefstroom in 1889, Natal Railway Conference at Harrismith, and Conference with the Cape Govt. for establishment of a Customs Union at Bloemfontein in the same year, in 1890 a further Conference with the Cape Govt. for extending the Railway to the Vaal River, and in 1895 a Railway Conference of all African Governments at Pretoria. In the Presidential Election of 1897 he unsuccessfully contested the Presidency against Mr. Steyn, and in the same year attended yet another Conference for a Customs Union with Cape Colony and Natal.

Sir John was ever a consistent supporter of the late President, Sir John Brand, and his Liberal policy, and as strenuously opposed a closer union with the Transvaal and Pres. Kruger's reactionary policy. It was only natural, therefore, that at the close of the S. African War he was nominated an unofficial member of the Legislative Council of the O.R.C. and elected a member of the Inter-Colonial Council. He was also Chairman of the Central Repatriation Board of the O.R.C., 1902-3; member of the Conference for General Customs union in S.A. in 1902; and Chairman of Conference for Settlement of Railway Employees' Differences. He was for many years Government director of the National Bank of the O.R.C., director of the S.A. Mutual Life Assurance Society (O.R.C. branch), chairman of the Board of the National Hospital, and also held various other public positions. He married, in 1866, Dorothea, second dau. of A. A. Ortlepp, of Colesberg, Cape Colony.

FRASER, William Percy, of Johannesburg, and of the Pretoria and Rand Clubs, was born Ipswich, Oct. 26, 1849. He is son of Wm. Fraser, of Grimdisburgh Hall, near Woodbridge, Suffolk; was educated at the Gram. Sch., Ipswich, and went to S.A. in 1879, serving as a Volunteer during the siege of Pretoria, 1880-1. In conjunction with the late Advocate, H. W. A. Cooper, of Pretoria, he

formulated the Gold Law No. 1 of 1883; was a member of the first Diggers' Committee of the Witwatersrand throughout its existence; was a member of the National Union at Johannesburg prior to the S.A. War of 1899, and was afterwards a member of the Uitlander Committee at Durban. Mr. Fraser has been on the Witwatersrand Council of Education since its inception, and is a member of the governing body of the Technical Institute for the Transvaal. He married Miss Ellen Maud Cook, of Estcourt, Natal.

FREMANTLE, Admiral Hon. Sir Edmund Robert, G.C.B., K.C.B., C.M.G., F.R.G.S., J.P., of 44, Lower Sloane Street, S.W., and of the United Service, Royal Naval, and Portsmouth Clubs, was born in London, June 15, 1836, and is the fourth son of the 1st Baron Cottesloe. He entered the Navy in 1849, and served in the Burmese War in 1852; took part in the New Zealand War in 1864-6, and as Senior Naval Officer in the Ashanti War in 1873-4 (C.B., C.M.G.). He also served on the East Coast of Africa in 1888-9. He is the author of a Prize Essay on Naval Tactics, for which he was awarded a gold medal by the Royal United Service Institution, in 1880; and lives of Hawke and Boscawen in *From Howard to Nelson*. Admiral Fremantle still indulges by way of pastime in shooting, boating, swimming, and cycling. He married Barbarina, eldest dau. of Robert M. Issacs, LL.D., of New S. Wales.

FREMANTLE, Professor Henry Eardly Stephen, M.L.A., M.A., F.S.S., of Bedwell Cottage, Rosebank, C.C.; Swanbourne, Muizenberg, Cape Colony, and the Civil Service Club, Cape Town, was born at Bedwell Park, Hatfield, Herts, Aug. 6, 1874; is the son of the Hon. and Very Rev. W. H. Fremantle, Dean of Ripon, who was son of the first Lord Cottesloe and the Hon. Mrs. W. H. Fremantle. He was educated at Eton and Oriel Coll., Oxen.; First Class Classics, Oxen., 1895-7; Lecturer in Greek at University Coll., Aberystwyth, 1897-8; Lecturer, Worcester Coll., Oxen., 1898-9; Professor of English and Philosophy at the S. African Coll., Cape Town, 1899; Member of the University Council, 1899; Professor of Philosophy alone at the S. African Coll., 1903. In 1903 he was Secy. of Section D of the South African Assn. for the advancement of

Science, and Mem. of the Council of the Assn., and proceeded to England in that year to collect funds in aid of the Prince of Wales' Professorship of History at the S. African Coll. Prof. Fremantle published in 1899 *Oxford, a Retrospect from South Africa*; he edited the *South African Educator* in 1902, and in 1903 he resigned his professorship at the S. African Coll. to become joint editor of the Bond paper, the *South African News*, and director of the S. African Newspaper Co. In politics, he was a Progressive until the split in that party on the question of Suspension, when he went over to the new S. African party. In view of the changes in parties which have recently taken place in S. Africa he is careful to define himself further as not of the Old S. African party, or of the New Progressive party. He was unsuccessful Bond candidate at the general election in Cape Colony in 1904, and in 1906 was returned to the Cape Parliament as member for Uitenhage. He married, April 20, 1899, Margaret Elizabeth, youngest dau. of Alexander MacDonald, Keeper of the University Galleries, Oxon.

FRENCH, Sir Somerset Richard, K.C.M.G., of Erritt Lodge, Kenilworth, Cape Town, was born in 1849, was director of postal services during the S. African War, and is now Postmaster-General of Cape Colony. He arrived in London in 1906 in route for Rome to attend the meetings of the International Postal Conference, where he will represent the Cape Colony, Natal, the Bechuanaland Protectorate, and Rhodesia at the Conference.

FRENCH-SHELDON, Mrs., F.R.G.S., of 36, Pembroke Square, W, was born in U.S.A., and is dau. of the late Col. J. French. She has lectured in U.S.A. and Europe, and is a distinguished traveller and explorer. In 1901 she conducted an expedition to Africa, and in 1904 travelled on the Congo. She has also journeyed three times round the world. Formerly she was engaged in editorial work, and conducted Messrs. Saxon and Co.'s publishing house for many years. Recreations, hunting and walking. She married Eli L. Sheldon.

FRERE, Major Sir Bartle Compton Arthur, Bart., D.SO., B.A., of 22, Bryanston Square, London, W., and of the Athenaeum, Bachelors', and City of London Clubs, was born in London, Oct. 24, 1854, and is sort of the Rt. Hon. Sir Bartle Frere. He was educated at Eton and Trinity College, Cambridge. Sir Bartle served in the Zulu War in 1879, the Bechuanaland Expedition in 1884-5, and in Burma in 1886-8. He formerly belonged to the Rifle Brigade, and was in 1906 the moving spirit in the National Address to Lord Milner.

FRIPP, Sir Alfred D., Kt. Bach. C.V.O., C.B., of 19, Portland Place, W., and the Bath Club, was born Sept. 12, 1862, at Blandford, Dorset, and is son of the late Alfred D. Fripp, R.W.S. He was educated at the Merchant Taylors' School and Guy's Hospital, graduating M.S., M.B. Lond. Univ., and F.R.C.S. Eng. He organised and took out to S. Africa the I.Y. Hospital, which during the Boer War did such good service at Deelfontein, C.C., being mentioned in despatches by Lord Roberts, and receiving the medal with two clasps and C.B. (civil). Served upon Mr. Brodrick's Committee for reorganisation of the Army Medical Services and for three years upon the Advisory Board, for which work he was knighted in June, 1903. Sir Alfred is surgeon-in-ordinary to H.M. the King; surgeon to, and lecturer upon anatomy and operative surgery at, Guy's Hosp., and surgeon to King Edward VII's Hospital for Officers. He married, in 1898, Margaret Haywood, of Woodhatch, Reigate. (R.R.C. for services rendered to sick and wounded in S. African War.)

FROST, Hon. Sir John, M.L.A., K.C.M.G., of Rondebosch, Cape Town, and of Thibet Park, Queenstown, Cape Colony, was born in 1828, and is a progressive farmer in the Queenstown division. He served as Commandant of Volunteers in the frontier wars of 1877-78, receiving the thanks of Parliament and the C.M.G. for his services. He entered the Cape Parliament as member for Queenstown as far back as 1874, and has represented that division ever since, being last re-elected in 1904. He took office in the second Rhodes Ministry in 1893, first as Secy. for Native Affairs and then as Secy. for Agriculture, going out in the great Rhodes smash in 1896. In 1900, however, he entered Sir G. Sprigg's Cabinet as Minister without portfolio, but in June, 1902, he became Secy. for Agriculture. He was not included in Dr. Jameson's Cabinet in 1904, although he is a supporter of his party. Sir John was knighted in 1904, having previously been made a C.M.G.

FULLER, Hon. Arthur John, M.L.A., a merchant and farmer of the Eastern Province of the Cape Colony. He is a strong supporter of the Progressive cause in the Colony; was re-elected member of the Legislative Assembly for Tembuland at the general election in Feb., 1904, and joined Dr. Jameson's first Ministry as Secy. for Agriculture in the same month.

FULLER, Claude, of Pietermaritzburg, Natal, and of the Victoria Club, P.M.B., was born Oct 1, 1872. He is a Fellow of the Entomological Society (Lond.), formerly member of the U.S. Association of Economic Entomologists, and has held the post of Asst. Govt. Entomologist in N.S.W., Western Australia, and Cape Colony, and has been Govt. Entomologist in Natal since 1899. He has written several books, including *Some* Coccidae *of W. Australia*, *Handbook of Injurious Insects and Plant Diseases of Natal*, *Fruitmen's Handbook and Guide*, and numerous pamphlets and articles entomology in its relation to agriculture.

FULLER, Lieut. Col. S. W., formerly Chief Inspector commanding the Southern Rhodesia Constabulary, was appointed Chief Staff Officer of the British S. Africa Police, with the local military rank of Lieut. Col., in 1906.

FULLER, Sir Thomas Ekins, K.C.M.G., Agent-Gen. for Cape of Good Hope, of 100, Victoria Street, S.W., 39, Hyde Park Gate, S.W., and of St. Stephen's Club, Westminster, was born at West Drayton, Middlesex, in August, 1831, is the son of the Rev. Andrew Gunton Fuller, and was educated at Bristol Coll. He became Baptist Minister at Melksham (Wilts.), Lewes, and Luton in the early part of his career, and contributed to the London Press until Aug., 1864, when he proceeded to Cape Town, there to become editor of the *Cape Argus*. He was Cape Govt. Emigration Agent London from 1873 to 1875, when he resigned the office to accept the general managership of Union Steamship Co. in South Africa. This latter office he held until Dec., 1898, when he resigned it and became a director of De Beer's Consolidated Mines, Ltd., in the Colony. He elected a member of the House of Assembly Cape Town in 1878, 1884, and 1888, and was his Parliamentary days deemed one of the best speakers in the Assembly. He resigned his seat therein in Jan., 1902, on being offered the office of Agent-Gen. for the Cape of Good Hope in London, the duties of which he assumed on Jan. 1, 1902. In his capacity as Agent-Gen. Thomas has worked assiduously in the interests of the Colony, while from a social point view he and Lady Fuller have made their residence a Mecca for the hosts of Anglo-Africans who so constantly visit England. Sir Thomas received the honour of knighthood on the King's birthday, 1904. He married: first, 1855, Mary Playne, dau. of Isaac Hillier, of Nailsworth, Glos.; and second, in 1875, Elizabeth, dau. of the Rev. Thos. Mann, of Cowes, I.W.

FULLER, William Henry, of East London, S.A., and of the E. London and King William's Town Clubs, is the son of Sir T. E. Fuller, C.M.G (q.v.), Agent-Gen. for the Colony of Cape of Good Hope. He was born July 6, 1858, at Melksham, Wiltshire, and was educated at the S.A. Coll., Cape Town, and the London Univ. Sch. He has the medal for the Kaffir War 1877, and during the Boer War, 1899-1902, he commanded as Lieut.-Col. the East London Town Guard. At the present he is director of Dyer & Dyer, Ltd., chairman of the East London Harbour Board, and Consular Agent for the U.S.A. He takes a great interest in athletic sports, and is president of the East London Rowing Association.

GALLWEY, Lieut. Col. (retired) Henry Lionel, C.M.G., D.S.O., F.R.G.I., of Government House, St. Helena; 30, Enys Road, Easthourne; and of the Naval and Military, Sports, and Ranelagh Clubs, was born at Gosport, Sept. 25, 1859, and is son of Lieut. Gen. Sir T. L. Gallwey, K.C.M.G., R.E. He was educated at Cheltenham Coll, and the R.M.C., Sandhurst, and was racquet champion at Cheltenham Coll. in 1877. He joined the 58th Foot Regt. in 1878, and was transferred to the 30th Foot in the latter end of that year; served in India in 1880-2, and was A.D.C. to the Governor of Bermuda from 1882-9; Vice-Consul, Oil Rivers and Niger Coast Protectorate, 1891-7; Consul, Niger Coast Protectorate, 1897-8; Divisional Commissioner in S. Nigeria in 1899-03; Acting Consul-Gen. on three occasions in the Niger Coast Protectorate between 1896-9; Acting High

Commissioner in S. Nigeria in 1900; and Governor and Commander-in-Chief of St. Helena in 1903. His war services include the Brass Expedition in 1895, when he commanded the Houssas (mentioned in despatches, D.S.O., and medal with clasp), the Benin City Expedition in 1897 (brevet-major, despatches, and clasp), the Aro Expedition in 1901-2, as Chief Political Officer (medal and clasp, despatches), and present in many expeditions against the Delta tribes. He concluded the treaty with the King of Benin at Benin City in 1892. Recreations: All field sports. Unmarried.

GALTON, Francis, F.R.S., was born Feb. 16, 1822, and is the youngest child of S. T. Galton, of Duddeston and Claverdon, Warwickshire. He was educated at King's Coll, and Cambridge University. He travelled through Egypt to Khartoum and the White Nile in 1846, and in 1850-2 he made an expedition to S.W. Africa with Mr. Charles Andersson, and explored Damara and Ovambo lands. For the results of this journey he was awarded the gold medal of the Royal Geographical Society, and he was elected to its council, on which he served for many years. He became hon. secy. of the British Association in 1863, but resigned in 1867 owing to a breakdown of health. He has also held numerous other offices, and has published numerous books and memoirs.

GAMBLE, Major Richard Warrien, D.S.O., of Trent Park, New Barnet, and of the United Service Club, was born March 10, 1860, at Edinburgh, and is son of the late Lieut. Gen. D. J. Gamble, C.B. He was educated at Blaerlodge, N.B., and the R.M.C., Sandhurst, passed the Staff Coll., 1890-1, and joined the 10th (Royal Berks) Regt. in Aug., 1879; served in the Bechuanaland Expedition, under Sir Chas. Warren, K.C.B., as adjutant, in the Mounted Rifles; was A.D.C. to the G.O.C. the Scottish Dist. in 1893-95; D.A.A.G. in Cork Dist., 1896-97; and was in the Egyptian Army in 1898-99, including the 1898 campaign. Major Gamble took part in the S. African War, 1899-1900; his orders include the D.S.O., 4th class Medjidieh, British medal Sudan Campaign 1898-9, Egyptian medal Sudan Campaign 1898-9, and S.A. medal and four clasps. He married, Oct. 8, 1901, Audrey, second dau. of Frank Bevan, D.L., J.P.

GARDINER, Edward Bennett, M.A., of 4 Bickenhall Mansions, Portman Square, London, W., of Carse Grange, Errol, Perthshire, Scotland, and of the City (C.T.), Rand (Johannesburg), and Gresham (Lond.) Clubs, was born in Ireland, March 25, 1845; is the eldest son of the late Geo. Gardiner, of Dublin, and is descended from an old Perthshire family, the late Geo. Gardiner having been one of the first managers of the National Bank of Ireland. Mr. E. B. Gardiner resided for five years in Bohemia, Austria, where he represented the London Board of directors of a large colliery company carrying on business in Bohemia. He then entered the service of the Standard Bank of S. Africa, where he remained for over thirty years, retiring there from in Jan., 1902. During Mr. Gardiner's period of service in the Standard Bank he held for a considerable time the post of manager at the Johannesburg branch, and from this position he was promoted asst. general manager of the Bank in S. Africa, which office he held until his retirement. Mr. Gardiner is now on the Boards of the Johannesburg Consolidated Investment Co., the Carlton Hotels (S.A.), Ltd., the Cobra Gold Mines, Ltd., the Swaziland Corporation, Ltd., and is on the London committee of the Hercules Deep, Ltd. He married, in 1868, Sidonia, only dau. of the late Capt. Fred. von Doeringk, of the Austrian Army, by whom he had issue: Frederick Geo., B.A. Oxen., barrister of the Middle Temple and the Cape Bar; and two daughters, Madeline Louisa Sidonia, wife of E. M. Clarke, and Esther Amabel, married to Capt. J. H. R. Winder, R.A.M.C.

GARDINER, Frederick George, B.A., of Hillside, Bower Read, Wynburg, Cape Town, and of the Civil Service Club (C.T.), was born in London April 19, 1874. He is only son of E. B. Gardiner (q.v.); was educated at the Diocesan Coll., Rondebosch, and at Keble Coll., Oxen., and graduated B.A. at the Cape Univ. and at Oxford. He was called to the Bar of the Middle Temple about the year 1895, and practices at the Cape Bar. He has already been senior counsel in several important cases, and amongst ether causes celebres he conducted the defences of Gen. Kritzinger and Judge Koch, both of whom were acquitted. He was also engaged in the famous Princess Radziwill case and in the Cape 'ragging' case, Stamford v. certain officers. Mr. Gardiner is a member of the Council of the Diocesan Coll., Rondebosch, and married, Jan. 6, 1901, Stella Clare Brailey, dau. of an English bank manager.

GARDNER, Lieut. Col. Alan, M.P., J.P., of Clearwell Castle, Glos.; 5, Grosvenor Crescent, Belgrave Square; and of the Turf, White's, and St. James's Clubs, was born Nov. 19, 1846; is son of the late Alan Legge, Lord Gardner, was in the 11th and 14th Hussars, and passed Staff Coll. (1872). He served in the Zulu Campaign in 1879, being present at the battles of Isandhlwana, Z'lobane Mountain (horse killed), and Kambula, where he was severely wounded. He was twice mentioned in despatches and received the medal with clasp and promotion to a brevet majority. In 1880 he was A.D.C. to the Viceroy of Ireland. He served in the Boer War of 1881, and contested E. Marylebone as Liberal candidate in 1895, and in 1906 was elected for the Ross Division of Herefordshire. Col. Gardner has shot big game in nearly every quarter, accompanied by Mrs. Gardner (q.v.). He married, in 1885, Nora Beatrice, eldest dau. of Sir James Blyth, Bart., of Blythswood, Stansted, and 33, Portland Place, W.

GARDNER, Mrs. Nora Beatrice, of Clearwell Castle, Gloucestershire, and Newton Hall, Dunmore, Essex, in which county she was born, is the eldest dau. of Sir James Blyth, Bart., and is a famous sportswoman, having shot bears, lions tigers, and all kinds of big and small game in Northern India, Assam, Nepaui, N. America, Australia, Abyssinia, and Somaliland. She also hunts, fishes, sketches, is an excellent horsewoman, and is fond of photography and needlework. In the course of her travels she has explored many comparatively unknown countries, Mrs. Gardner is absolutely fearless and apparently quite indifferent to the extremes of heat and cold which she has had to endure.

Mrs. Gardner also finds time to interest herself in many public capacities, being president of the Marylebone Women's Liberal Association, president of the Clearwell Reading Rooms, vice president of the Liberal Federation of Eng., vice-president of the Children's Happy Hours Association, vice-president of the Essex Needlework Guild, and vice-president of the Social League. She was married, in 1885, to Col. Alan Gardner (q.v.).

GARLICK, John, M.L.A., was formerly member for the Western Province of Cape Colony in the Legislative Council. He now represents Cape Town in the Progressive interest in the Cape Parliament, to which he was returned in Feb., 1904.

GARRETT, F. Edmund. While editor of the *Cape Times* in 1896 he rendered much assistance to Sir James (then Mr.) Rose-Innes in promoting the monster petitions throughout S.A. which were a considerable factor in hastening the release of the Reform prisoners. Of sound views, political stability, and independence of thought, he rendered great services to the Progressive party, and represented Victoria East in the Cape Legislative Assembly. He returned to England Sept., 1902, and although still contributing occasional clever contributions in verse and prose to the leading London journals, is in very delicate health, and obliged to live very quietly in Devon.

GARSTANG, Professor John, M.A., B.Litt., F.S.A., of the University (Liverpool) and Royal Societies Clubs, was born in 1876, and is the son of the late Dr. Walter Garstang, M.R.C.P. He was educated at Blackburn Grammar School and Jesus College, Oxford, and has been engaged in Archeological research since 1897. He has conducted excavations in Great Britain, and in Egypt at Bet Khallâf, Abydos, Regagneh, Mahâsna, Beni Hasan, Esna, and Negâdeh, resulting in the discovery of the tomb of Zeser, 3rd Dynasty, the missing part of the inscribed tablet of Mena, the first Egyptian King, and the necropolis of Beni Hasan with 800 tombs of official classes. He is also the author of numerous publications on archeology.

GARSTIN, Col. Alfred Allan, C.M.G., of 36, Eaton Terrace, S.W., and of the Army and Navy Club, was born Aug. 30, 1850, at Edinburgh, and is son of Charles Garstin, of the Bengal Civil Service. He was educated at Cheltenham Coll, and R.M.C., Sandhurst, and joined the 57th Regt. in 1871. He commanded the 2nd Battn. of the Middlesex Regt. from 1893-98, and a Regimental Dist. from 1898-1900. Col. Garstin's war services include the Zulu War in 1879, when he was present at the action of Gingindhlovu and the relief of Eshowe. He also took part in the pursuit of Cetewayo after Ulundi, and served in the operations of Clarke's Column (medal with clasp), the Egyptian Campaign in 1885, as D.A.A.G. of Lines of Communications with Sir Gerald Graham's Expeditionary Force (medal with clasp and Khedive's Star), and the S.A. Campaign in 1900-02, when he went out on special service in Feb., 1900. He acted as A.A.G. of 2nd Div. from the relief of Ladysmith until Dec., 1900, and shared in the operations of the 2nd Div., A.I.G. Western (Mafeking Kimberley line), Jan. to March, 1901. He was Commandant of Port Elizabeth from March to Aug., 1901, and commanded the Kimberley Dist. in succession to Major-Gen. Pretyman, from Aug., 1901, to July, 1902 (twice mentioned in despatches, Queen's medal with four clasps, King's medal with two clasps, C.M.G.). Col. Garstin retired from the Army in 1903. Recreations: Shooting, fishing, and sketching. He married, Sept. 13, 1904, Isabel, dau. of Col. Chas. Noble.

GARSTIN, Sir William Edmund, G.C.M.G., Grand Cordon of the Osmanieh and Grand Cordon of the Medjidieh, of Cairo, Egypt, and of Brooks' and the St. James's Clubs, is the son of the late Charles Garstin, of the Bengal Civil Service. He was born in India, Jan. 29, 1849, and educated at Cheltenham Coll. He was appointed to the Indian Public Works Dept. in Oct., 1872, and is one of the many Indian public servants whose services were lent to Egypt and who have done so much in the civil administration of that country. He left India for Egypt in 1885, and was appointed Inspector-Gen. of Irrigation in May, 1892, and Under-Secy. of State for Public Works in Nov., 1893. It was for services in connection with the Assouan Dam that he gained his G.C.M.G. In 1899 he made trips down the White and Blue Niles, his journeys ending respectively 200 and 700 miles south of Khartoum. Recently he lies returned to Cairo after a journey of 7,000 miles for the purpose of investigating the sources of the Nile. Sir William Garstin has rendered many eminent services to Egypt.

GAUGHREN, Right Rev. Matthew, Bishop of Tentyra, Vicar Apostolic of Kimberley, and Administrator Apostolic of the Transvaal; of Bishop's House, 80, Dutoitspan Road, Kimberley, and of 32, Gold St. (Box 32), Johannesburg, was born in Dublin, April 7, 1843; commenced his education at a couple of Dublin schools, and received his theological training chiefly in France. He received orders to a Deaconship from the Bishop of Autun, was ordained priest by the late Cardinal Cullen on April 29, 1867, and was employed thereafter for many years in parochial work in Liverpool and in the East End of London. He spent a few years in missionary work in S. America, and afterwards in Australia For six years he was stationed in Leith, Scotland, where, on March 16, 1902, he was consecrated Bishop to succeed his brother, who died during the late S.A. War, as Vicar Apostolic of Kimberley, with spiritual charge of the O.R.C. To that was added the ecclesiastical administration of the Transvaal.

GAUL, Right Rev. William Thomas, Lord Bishop of Mashonaland, D.D., of Bishop's Rooms, Salisbury, Mashonaland, was educated at Trinity Coll., Dublin, and went to S.A. in 1874. In 1877 he became Vicar of Bloemfontein, O.F.S., subsequently Rector of All Saints', Dutoitspan, and afterwards Rector and Archdeacon of Kimberley. He was consecrated Bishop of Mashonaland in 1895.

GAUNT, Commander, R.N., C.M.G., of H.M.S. *Mohawk*, was born in Australia, and is a brother of Capt. Guy Gaunt, who received a sword of honour from the King of Samoa for gallantry some years ago. He received the C.M.G. for services rendered in the Far East, and the Italian silver medal for gallantry in action was bestowed upon him in recognition of his generous initiative and gallant conduct in rescuing an Italian comrade during the operations in Somaliland in 1903.

GAUSSEN, Alfred, of 88, Eaton Place, S.W.; 3, Walpole Street, Chelsea; Southwold, Suffolk; 97, Gresham Street, London, E.C.; and of the Union Club, London, was born March 9, 1855; is eldest son of Frederick Gaussen, barrister-at-law, and was educated at Eton and Christ Church, Oxon. Mr. Gaussen was formerly Lieut. in the 25th Regt. (King's Own Borderers) and is now a director of Henderson's Transvaal Estates and Henderson's

Consolidated Corporation (see J. C. A. Henderson and W. B. Butler). He married Lady Kathleen Bernard youngest dau. of James, 6th Earl of Bandon, K.P.

GELL, Philip Lyttelton, J.P., M.A., of Hopton Hall, Derbyshire; of Langley Lodge, near Oxford; and of Brooks', Athenaeum, and the City of London Clubs, was born in Lower Seymour Street, London, W., April 29, 1852. He is the elder surviving son of Rev. John Philip Gell, Rector of Buxted, of Kirk Langley, Derby, and of Eleanor Isabella Franklin, sole issue of Admiral Sir John Franklin K.C.B., the Arctic navigator. Mr. P. Lyttelton Gell was educated privately, and at Balliol Coll., Oxon, where he graduated M.A. He is director of the British S.A. Co., the Foreign. and Colonial Investment Trust Co., and the Westminster and General Life Assurance Association. He married, in 1889, Hon. Edith Brodrick, dau. of Viscount Lord Midleton, Lieut. of Surrey, and sister of the Right Hon. St. John Brodrick, M.P.

GIBBONS, Major Alfred St. Hill, of Cull Cottage, Bude, and of the Sports Club, was born Nov. 9, 1858. He was educated privately and at Christ's Coll., Camb., and took a commission as Lieut. in the 3rd East Kent Regt. in 1882. he served in the B.B.P. from 1890 to 1893, being present at Rhodes' Drift at the time of the threatened Boer trek into Mashonaland. In 1894 he originated a movement in favour of the preservation of big game, which has since had far-reaching effects in the desired direction. He explored a large district in the Upper Zambesi basin in 1895-96, and from 1898 to 1900 led an important expedition into the interior of Africa in the interests of Imperial advancement and geography. He compiled a map of Barotseland as far as the Congo-Zambesi watershed in the north and the Kwito River in the west. He was the first to navigate the Middle Zambesi from the Kebrabasa Rapids to the Gwaai confluence, in the pioneer steamer *Constance*. He discovered the source of the Zambesi in 1899, and has followed the whole course of that river. The combined routes of his various expeditions represent a mileage of upwards of 20,000, and included the journey from Cape Town to Cairo, and from the mouth of the Zambesi to Benguela.

Major Gibbons commanded a squadron of Younghusband's Horse during the late S. African War, and he was afterwards (1905) sent to examine the territory offered by the British Govt. in Uganda for the establishment of a Zionist Colony. He is the author of *Exploration and Hunting in Central Africa*, and has since completed *Africa from South to North through Barotseland* (1904). He married, in 1898, Constance, dau. of the Rev. Henry Wood.

GIBBS, George A., M.P., was educated at Eton and Oxford; is a son-in-law of the Right Hon. Walter Long, and served with the Imperial Yeomanry in the South African War, receiving the Queen's medal with four clasps. He was first returned to the House of Commons at the general election in Jan., 1906, as Unionist member for West Bristol, defeating the Liberal candidate, Mr. T. J. Lennard, by 365 votes.

GIBSON, Harry, J.P. for Cape Town, of Stains Avenue, Kenilworth, near Cape Town, and of the City and Civil Service Clubs, C.T., is the son of Henry Thomas Gibson, who was the son of the Rev. John Gibson, Vicar of Sheffield, and of the dau. of John Drewitt, of Houghton, Sussex. He was born April 27, 1863, at Haslemere, Surrey, and was educated at Reigate Gram. Sch. and Dulwich Coll. He is Hon. corresponding secy. of the Royal Colonial Inst., Fellow and hon. member of the Society of Accountants and Auditors, and hon. secy. of the S. African Committee since its formation in 1893. For five years—from Jan., 1879— he served with the late Charles Frewer, Public accountant; then from 1884-89 chief accountant to the S.A. Loan Mortgage Mercantile Agency, Ltd., of Cape Town (for same time acting as gen. manager); 1889-1903 gen. manager and secy. of the S.A. Association for the administration and Settlement of Estates, which he resigned June 30, 1903, and is now practising in own name at 92, Adderley Street, Cape Town. In 1904 he was selected as a member of the Commission appointed by the Governor of Cape Colony to inquire into the administration of the public service, and to suggest improvements herein. Mr. Gibson takes considerable interest in technical education and philanthropic Work. He had a large share in organising and rebuilding both the All Saints' House for Orphans and the School of Industry, Cape Town. He married, Oct. 3, 1899, Henrietta Louisa, eldest dau. of James Hewlett Collard, J.P., of Sea Point, near Cape Town.

GIFFORD, Major, Lord, V.C., of Old Park, Chichester, Sussex, and of Salisbury House, London Wall, E.C., was born July 5, 1849. Edric Frederick Gifford is son of the 2nd Baron Gifford, whom he succeeded in the title in 1872. He was educated at Harrow. In 1869 he entered the Army, and in 1873-4 Lieut. Gifford saw his first active service in the Ashanti War, taking part in the repulse of the Ashantis at Abrakampa, Amoaful, and Becquah (where he was wounded). He was with the advance guard before the Prah, and, after crossing it, commanded the scouting party up to Coomassie, and was present at the capture of that town. As a result of this campaign he was mentioned in despatches, received the V.C., medal and clasp, and was promoted Capt. In the Zulu War Lord Gifford joined in the pursuit of Cetewayo, and at the end of the operations carried home the despatches (mentioned in despatches, Queen's medal and clasp, and brevet of Major).

He retired from the service in July, 1880, and from that year until 1883 acted as Colonial Secy. for West Australia, and sat in the Legislative Council. From 1883 to 1888 he was Colonial Secy of Gibraltar. He has been a director of the B.S.A. Co. since its inception, and is chairman of the Bechuanaland Exploration Co., Charterland Goldfields, Northern Copper (B.S.A.) Co., Rhodesia Copper Co., and is a director of some other 5 African companies. Lord Gifford married, April 22, 1880, Sophie Catherine (q.v.), dau. of Gen. J. A. Street, C.B.

GIFFORD, Lady (Sophie Catherine), of Old Park, Chichester, is dau. of Gen. J. A. Street, C.B. During the S. African War (1900-2) she served as an Army nursing sister, receiving the Queen's S.A. medal. She is an Hon. Serving Sister of the Order of St. John of Jerusalem in England, and married, in 1880, Lord Gifford (q.v.).

GIFFORD, Hon. Maurice Raymond, Q.M.G., of Boothby Hall, Grantham, and of Arthur's and the

Orleans Clubs, was born in 1859, and is younger brother of Lord Gifford, V.C. (q.v.). He was educated at Worcester, and served in the mercantile marine from 1876 to 1882, and has since seen considerable fighting in the Egyptian Campaign of 1882; with French's Scouts in the Riel rebellion in Canada in 1885 (medal and clasp); in the Matabele War of 1893 as scout with the Salisbury column (medal), and in the Matabele Rebellion of 1896, when he commanded Gifford's Horse, and lost an arm (clasp and C.M.G.). He commanded the Rhodesian contingent in the Jubilee procession in 1897 (medal), and in the S. African War served with the Kimberley Horse at the relief of Mafeking (medal and three clasps). He is a director of the British Columbia Electric Railway Co., British Empire Trust, Selukwe G.M. Co., and the Rhodesia Copper Co. He married, in 1897, Marguerite, dau. of Capt. Cecil Thorold.

GILES, Charles Tyrrell, M.A., J.P., of 2, Hare Court, Temple, E.C., and of Copse Hill House, Wimbledon, is a member of the Council of the Union Castle Mail Steamship Co., Ltd. (see Sir Donald Currie). He held a seat in the Conservative interest for the Wisbech Division of Cambridge from 1895-1900, and married Isabella, dau. of The late J. Colman.

GILL, Sir David, K.C.B. (1900), Order of the Medjidieh (1875); of 34, De Vere Gardens, London, W., and the Athenaeum and Caledonian Clubs; was born at Aberdeen, Scotland, June 12, 1843. He is the eldest son of David Gill, of Blairythan, Aberdeenshire; was educated at Marischall Coll, and Univ., Aberdeen, erected a private observatory in that city, and applied himself to the study of astronomy and its allied sciences. He undertook the direction of Lord Lindsay's private observatory at Dunecht, near Aberdeen (1872-76); organised Lord Lindsay's Transit of Venus Expedition to Mauritius; made a series of heliometer observations there of the opposition of the minor planet Juno (a new and original method of determining the Solar Parallax), connected the longitudes of Berlin, Malta, Alexandria, Suez, Aden, Seychelles, Mauritius, and Rodriguez, and measured a baseline for the Geodetic Survey of Egypt. In 1877 he organised an expedition to Ascension for determining the Solar Parallax by heliometer observations of the planet Mars. In 1879 he was appointed H.M. Astronomer at the Cape, and was identified with the well-known work of that institution and the Geodetic Survey of Natal and C.C., the latter work alone,, begun in 1883, taking eleven years to accomplish. The accurately determined longitudes on the East and West Coasts of Africa, as well as the longitudes of Mauritius, Reunion, and Seychelles, were established on the initiative and authority of Sir David Gill. In 1885 he commenced the work of photographing all the stars to the 10th magnitude from 18 deg. S. to the S. Pole, and, with the cooperation of Prof. J. C. Kapteyn, of Groningen, published three large volumes of Annals of the Cape Observatory showing the places and magnitudes of 454,875 stars. In 1887, in conjunction with Admiral Mouchez, he carried through, an international scheme for photographing the whole sky and cataloguing all stars to the 11th order of magnitude, and Sir David became senior member of the permanent committee, whose reunions he attended at Paris in 1887, 1891, 1896, and 1900. In 1881-83 he conducted a series of determinations of Stellar Parallax, and later another series with the same object—these together form the only determinations of Stellar Parallax in the Southern Hemisphere. In 1888-90 he organised a series of observations of the Minor Planets Iris, Victoria, and Sappho for the determination of the Solar Parallax, all the principal observatories of the world cooperating, and the conclusions as derived by Sir David in his final discussion of the whole series were adopted for use in the nautical almanacs and astronomical ephemerides of all nations at the Paris International Congress in 1896. In that year Sir David Gill was entrusted by the British and German Govts. with the direction of the operations to determine the boundary between British Bechuanaland and German S.W. Africa, and the necessary survey operations, begun in 1897, are now completed and the results published in a separate volume. He took the initiative in interesting Earl Grey and Mr. Rhodes in a Geodetic Survey of Rhodesia, and the project of carrying the work along the 30th meridian from the south to the Mediterranean is already being extended towards Tanganyika under his direction. The execution of the Great African Arc of Meridian is perhaps the pet scheme of Sir David's life. Meanwhile, owing to the munificence of Mr. Frank McClean, the Cape Observatory has been fitted with a complete equipment for astrophysical research, and Sir David has been able to greatly extend the scope of his operations and the volume of his work, and under his direction the observatory has become by far the most important one in the Southern Hemisphere.

Sir David Gill is Hon. LL.D. of Aberdeen and Edinburgh, Hon. D.Sc. of Oxford, Cambridge, and Cape of Good Hope, a F.R.S.—one of the twenty Hon. F.R.S., Edin.; correspondent of the Inst. of France (*Acad. des Sciences*); corresponding member of the Academies of Science of Berlin, St. Petersburg, Bureau des Longitudes, Paris, of the Spectroscopic Soc. of Rome, and member of the Academies of Science of Amsterdam, Washington, New York, as also of many other scientific bodies. He is a gold medalist of the Royal Astronomical Soc., London (1882), Valse Medalist of the Inst. of France (1882), and in 1900 received the Watson Gold Medal of the Nat. Acad. of Sciences, Washington, and the Bruce Gold Medal of the Astronomical Soc. of the Pacific for distinguished services to astronomy, and the Royal Medal of the Royal Society of London. He has been Pres. of the S.A. Philosophical Soc. and of the S.A. Assoc. for the Advancement of Science, and he originated the invitation extended to the British Assoc. to visit S.A. in 1905. He was one of the three trustees of the SA. Museum, a member of the Cape Geological Commission, and is J.P. for the county of Aberdeen, Scotland, and for the Cape Division.

He has published *A Determination of the Solar Parallax from Observations of Mars at the Island of Ascension*, *Heliometer Determinations of Stellar Parallax in the Southern Hemisphere*; Catalogues of Stars for the Equinoxes, 1850, 1860, 1865, 1885, 1890, and 1900 (in the press), from observations made at the Royal Observatory, Cape Town; *The Cape Photographic* Durchmusterung (in conjunction with Prof. J. G. Kapteyn); *Determination of the solar Parallax and Mass of the Moon from heliometer Observations of Victoria and Sappho*; *The Geodetic Survey of South Africa*, vols. 1, 2, and 3, and many other papers and memoirs.

Sir David is fond of shooting, especially spring buck, and when opportunity occurs of deerstalking.

He also takes up golf moderately. He married, July 7, 1870, Isobel, dau. of John Black, of Linhead, Aberdeenshire. He retired from his post as H.M. Astronomer Lt the Cape on Feb. 20, 1907. He is still occupied in scientific work, and is President-elect of the British Association for 1907-8.

GILSON, Capt. C. Hugh, D.S.O., is third son of Alexander D. Gilson, R.M., at Greytown, Natal, and formerly of the Cheshire Regt. He won the D.S.O. in Mashonaland, and is now Commandant of the S.A.C. in Swaziland.

GINSBERG, F., M.L.A., is member of the Cape House of Assembly for King William's Town.

GIROUARD, Lieut. Col. Sir Edouard Percy Cranwill, K.C.M.G., D.S.O., R.E., is the son of a French Canadian, who is a Judge of the supreme Court of Canada, the highest appellate Court for the whole Dominion. He was born in 1867, and educated at the Canadian Royal Military Coll., from which he graduated, proceeding at once to an appointment on the engineering staff of the Canadian Pacific Railway. Here he had that splendid training which fitted the young student for the great work which he was destined to do in the service of his country. He entered the Royal Engineers in 1888 and proceeded to Woolwich, where his great knowledge of practical railway work led so rapid promotion. At the age of 23 he was appointed Traffic Manager of the Royal Arsenal Railways, and it was here that the keen eyes of Lord Kitchener discerned in young Girouard the very man to undertake the construction of the railway across the Sudan which was to enable Lord Kitchener to push forward his advance from Dongola to Khartoum. Col. Girouard carried out this work as Director of Sudan Railways, and afterwards was appointed Pres. of the Egyptian Railway Board. In 1889 he accompanied Sir Redvers Buller to the Cape as Director of Military Railways. He married, Sept. 10, 1903, Mary Gwendolen, only child of the Hon. Sir Richard Solomon, K.C.M.G., C.B., K.C., Attorney-Gen. of the Transvaal, and Lady Solomon, Governor N. Nigeria, 1907.

GLEICHEN, Lieut. Col., Count, C.V.O., C.M.G., D.S.O., of the British Embassy, Washington, and of the Guards', Beefsteak, Marlborough, and Turf Clubs, was born in London, Jan. 15, 1863, and is son of H.S.H. the late Prince Victor of Hohenlohe, G.C.B. He was educated at Charterhouse and Sandhurst, and joined the Grenadier Guards in 1881. He served with the Guards' Camel Regt. in the Gordon Relief Expedition in 1884-5, being present at the actions of Abu Klea and Abu Kru (medal and two clasps, Khedive's Star). He was attached to the Intelligence Dept. at the War Office in 1886-8. In 1893 he served with Sir W. Ridgeway's Mission to Morocco; travelled in Tunis and Algeria in 1893, and in Bulgaria in 1894; took part in the Dongola Expedition in 1896, also went on special service to Suakim and Massawa (medals); acted as Intelligence Officer in Sir R. Rodd's Mission to the Emperor Menelik in 1897 (C.M.G. and Star of Ethiopia); served in S. Africa with the Grenadier Guards in 1899-1900, present at the actions of Modder River, Paardeburg, occupation of Bloemfontein, Sauna's Post, Winburg and Heilbronn (medal and five clasps, D.S.O. He was recalled to the Egyptian Army in 1900. Count Gleichen is the author of *With the Camel Corps Up the Nile, With the Mission to Menelik, The Armies of Europe* (translated), and edited the *Anglo Egyptian Sudan* in 1905. Recreations: Shooting, yachting, and travelling.

GLOSSOP, Capt. Bertram Robert Mitford, was born Sept. 30, 1870, and entered the Dragoon Guards in 1891. He served in West Africa in 1897-8, including the operations on the Niger and in Borgu (despatches, medal with clasp), and in the South African War in 1899-1900 as Special Service Officer and as Adjutant of the Imperial Light Horse (Queen's medal with four clasps). Capt. Glossop has had considerable big game shooting in Africa and India, and has recorded his experiences in *Sporting Trips of a Subaltern*.

GLYNN, Henry Thomas, J.P., F.E.C. Inst., of Sabie, District of Lydenburg, Transvaal, was born at Cape Town, Nov. 30, 1857. He is son of the late Henry Glynn, a well-known S.A. hunter, traveller, and rifle shot, who won the first gold medal shot for in S.A., and who was one of the first few to start the Cape Town Royal Volunteer Rifles, and finally died, in 1894, of fever while on a hunting expedition. Mr. H. T. Glynn was educated at the

S.A. Coll.; spent his early days on the River Diggings; then, after some success on the Kimberley fields, settled down in the Cape for two years. In 1875 he went north and stayed in the Transvaal up to a year before the great Boer War, with the exception of occasional hunting trips through the low-lying country extending up to the Zambesi. He returned to Lydenburg in Aug., 1902, and is a Director of Glynn's Lydenburg, Ltd. Mr. Glynn married, in Oct., 1896, Miss G. G. Wales.

GOCH, George, of Johannesburg, was in Kimberley in the early seventies, and came prominently before the public in connection with the Black Flag incident. In 1878, when the new municipality of Kimberley came into existence, he was invited to become one of its representatives. Shortly afterwards the much-debated question of the annexation of Griqualand West to the Cape Colony arose. Mr. Goch was a strenuous supporter of the annexation, which was only accomplished in 1S83. In 1884 the General Election resulted in his return as second member for Kimberley. Retiring from the Municipal Council in 1885, he assisted in the formulation of a railway construction and extension policy, for which the support of the Government and the eventual sanction of Parliament were obtained, with the result that Kimberley was connected by rail with Cape Town. His next effort was directed to securing some understanding with the Transvaal and Orange Free State Governments with regard to Inter-Colonial Free Trade. His object was to establish common ground with the Boers on railway matters and to simplify the vexed railway question. Unfortunately the Cape Parliament of the day did not share Mr. Goch's views. The Lands and Stands question was another problem which Mr. Goch took in hand, and he succeeded in getting the law reconstructed for the benefit of shareholders in such undertakings.

When the gold discoveries on the Rand were first made, Mr. Goch decided to make that neighbourhood the scene of his future operations, and established himself there, and acquired interests in such properties as the Bantjes and Wemmer. His interest in the first named was afterwards joined to those of Messrs. J. B. Robinson and H. Eckstein, but he himself floated the Wemmer and the George Goch Companies. He resigned his seat in the Cape Parliament and became a member of the newly formed Chamber of Mines. He was a reformer from the beginning; and when in a few years political questions began to arouse apprehension, he advocated the franchise being extended to all who could prove a £100 wage-earning or property qualification and a residence of two years in the country. Mr. Goch was a member of the first Johannesburg Municipality, and, after acting as Deputy Mayor, was elected Mayor at the latter end of 1904, in succession to Mr. St. John Carr.

GODLEY, Godfrey Archibald, of the Native Affairs Dept., Transvaal, acted as Clerk to the Secretary for Zululand at Maritzburg in 1895; was Clerk to the Deputy Commissioner of Mines at Mondweni in 1896, and to the Treasurer there in 1896-7. In 1898 he became Clerk to the Accounting Officer and Registrar of Deeds for the Prov. of Zululand, in Natal; was appointed Clerk in the Audit Office at Maritzburg in 1899 and Asst. Inspector there in 1901. He acted as first-class Clerk in the Native Affairs Dept. in the Transvaal, and was appointed Private Secretary to the Commissioner for Native Affairs in 1902.

GODLONTON, Burt Glanville, of Bloemfontein, O.R.C., was educated at Totteridge Park, Herts. He took part in the South African War in 1899-1901, with Brabant's Horse (Queen's medal and five clasps); subsequently acting as Clerk to the Editor of the O.R.C. *Government Gazette*, of which he became Editor in July, 1904.

GOLDIE, Right Hon. Sir George Dashwood Taubman, K.C.M.G., P.C. (See Taubman-Goldie, Right Hon. Sir George Dashwood.)

GOLDIE-TAUBMAN, Capt. Ernest Harcourt, of the Junior United Service Club, was born at Edinburgh, Dec. 26, 1868, and is son of Sir John Goldie-Taubman, of the Nunnery, I. of Man. He was educated at Cheltenham Coll., served in the E. African Coast (Mbaruk) Rebellion in 1895-6 (Queen's medal); and is 2nd in command of the Sultan of Zanzibar's forces (medal, 2nd cl. Said and 3rd cl. Hamoudieh). Recreations: Golf and shooting.

GOLDMANN, Charles Sydney, of 34, Queen Anne's Gate, Westminster, S.W., of Salisbury House London, E.C., and of White's and Pratt's Clubs was born at Burghersdorp, C.C. For many years Mr. C. S. Goldmann had been identified with the firm of S. Neumann and Co., one of the most powerful of the S.A. mining and financial groups, when in 1895 he was admitted to partnership in the firm, from which he has since retired. Mr. Goldmann is a man of enormous energy and concentration; he has an almost encyclopedic knowledge of the requirements of the Rand industry, and devoted himself entirely to the gold mining branch of his firm's business. He is Chairman of the Lingham Timber and Trading Co., and a director of the Langlaagte Block B Deep, the Alexandra Estate and G.M. Co., the Knight Central, the Marievale Nigel, the Riekuil Co., Consolidated Main Reef, Main Reef Deep, Main Reef East, New Modderfontein, Treasury, Vogelstruis Consolidated, Deep, Witwatersrand Deep, Wolhuter, Bantjes Consolidated Mines, Cloverfield Mines, Hercules Co., Main Reef West, Randfontein Deep, West Rand Consolidated Mines, West Rand Trust, Withank Colliery, and York G.M. Co., Ltd.

Mr. Goldmann is the author of *The Witwatersrand Goldfields*, *Goldmann's South African Mining and Finance*, and *Goldmann's Map of the Witwatersrand*— all invaluable works for those who aspire to complete knowledge of the Transvaal Fields. In the late S.A. War he acted as war correspondent of the *Argus* and *Standard*, and at its close he brought out a book on the cavalry operations, entitled With *General French in South Africa*. He is Pres. of the S.A. Football Assoc., and has a cultivated artistic taste. He married, Feb. 11, 1899, Hon. Agnes Mary, younger dau. of the Right Hon. Viscount Peel, of the Lodge, Sandy, Beds., late Speaker of the House of Commons, and granddau. of Sir Robert Peel, the great Prime Minister.

GOLDRING, A. R., of Salisbury House, London Wall, E.C., was born in London in the late fifties, and was little more than a youth when, in 1876, he left England for Cape Colony. On arriving at Kimberley he devoted himself to the mining industry. In 1882 he took to journalism, and became associated with the old *Daily Independent*, then the leading organ of the diamond fields, and remained on that journal until 1889, when he went up to Johannesburg, where he again turned his attention to mining. Three years later he was appointed Secy. of the Transvaal Chamber of Mines, a position which, he retained until very recently, when he was transferred to London as Secy. to the London Committee of the Chamber.

GOLDSMID, L. Lionel, is editor of the *S. African Jewish Chronicle*.

GOLDSWORTHY, Captain Charles Leycester Johnson, served in the F.A.M. Police from 1876-8; acted as Lieutenant in Pulleine's Rangers from Jan. to Aug., 1878, when he rejoined the F.A.M. Police. He took part in the Kaffir War in 1877-9, including the attack on Moirosi's Mountain and the capture of the stronghold (medal with clasp); the operations in the Transkei and in Basutoland in 1880-1 (medal with two clasps), and the South African War in 1899-1900, being present at the operations in the Orange Free State, including the defence of Wepener and the operations in the Cape Colony south of Orange River (Queen's medal with two clasps and King's medal with two clasps). For some months in 1902 he was in command of district Colonial troops at Dordrecht and King William's Town.

GOODALL, Captain Sidney Goodall, D.S.O., was born in 1874. He served in the South African War in 1899-1902, including the operations in Natal; present at the relief of Ladysmith and the actions at Colenso, Spion Kop, and Vaal Kranz; the operations on the Tugela Heights, and the actions at Pieters Hill and Laings Nek; also took part in the operations in the Transvaal, east and west of Pretoria (despatches, Queen's medal with five clasps, and D.S.O.)

GOOLD-ADAMS, Major Sir Hamilton John, K.C.M.G., C.B. (Civil), of Bloemfontein, O.R.C., and the Army and Navy Club, was born in Co. Cork, Ireland, on June 27, 1858. He is son of Richard Wallis Goold-Adams, of Jamesbrook, Co. Cork, and was educated privately and on the training ship *Conway*. He joined the Army in Jan., 1878, receiving his Captaincy seven years later, and his Majority in 1895. In Sir Charles Warren's Bechuanaland Expedition in 1884-5 he served under that officer; he commanded the B.B.P. in the Matabele War of 1893, and in the S.A. War he served during 1899 and 1900, first as Resident Commissioner in Bechuanaland, afterwards having command of the Kimberley Town Guard during the latter half of the siege (twice mentioned in despatches). Major Goold-Adams retired from his regt., the Royal Scots, in March, 1901, when he was appointed Lieut.-Governor of the O.R.C., which important position he still occupies, but from which he is expected to shortly retire. He is not married.

GORDON, Lieut.-Colonel Alexander Weston, was born July 9, 1859, and entered the Army in 1878. He served in the Afghan War in 1880 (medal), and in the South African War in 1899-1902, present at the Relief of Ladysmith, including the action at Colenso and the operations in the Transvaal east of Pretoria, acting Commandant at Potchefstroom (dispatches Brev. of Lieut. Col., Queen's medal with two clasps, and King's medal with two clasps). In 1906 he succeeded Col. Bird, D.S.O., in the command of the 1st Dublin Fusiliers.

GORDON, Webster B., A.M.I.C.E.; formerly Superintending Engineer in the Public Works Dept. of India, was appointed late in 1903 expert adviser to the High Commissioner for S.A. on matters of irrigation, to which subject he had devoted much attention during his service in India.

GORGÃO, General Sir Raphael, K.C.B., Governor-General of the Province of Mozambique, was honoured with a K.C.B. (Military Division) on the occasion of the King's Birthday, 1902.

GORGES, Lieut-Colonel Edmund Howard D.S.O., of the Manchester Regt., was born Nov. 23, 1868, and entered the Manchester Regt. as second Lieutenant in 1887; served in the Maluka Expedition in British East Africa in 1898; the Uganda Mutiny in 1898-9; the South African War in 1900 as Special Service Officer employed with the Mounted Infantry (medal with two clasps) and served in Uganda in 1901, commanding a force in the operations against the Suk, Turkana, and other

hostile tribes (despatches, medal with clasp and D.S.O.). Since 1902 Lieut.-Col. Gorges has been serving with the King's African Rifles, Uganda. He was promoted Lieut. Col. in 1906 for services rendered in connection with the quelling of the Nandi rebellion in E. Africa.

GORRINGE, Brev. Lieut. Col. George Frederick, R.E., C.M.G., D.S.O., was born at Southwick, Sussex, Feb. 10, 1868; is second son of Hugh Gorringe, of Kingston-by-Sea, and was educated at Lee's Sch., Brighton, and Wellington Coll., passing in to the Royal Engineers at Chatham in 1888. He transferred to the Egyptian Army in 1893, and became D.A.A.G., Headquarters Staff, two years later. He served in the Dongola Expedition in 1896, receiving the D.S.O., and medal and clasps for Firket and Hafir. In 1897 he was on the staff of the G.O.C., commanding at the actions of Abu Hamed and Athara, gaining a brevet majority and clasps for 1897, Abu Hamed and Athara. He was again D.A.A.G. on the Headquarters Staff of the Khartoum Expeditionary Force in 1898 (clasp, fourth class Medjidieh and British medal), and later in that year advanced with the Gedaref Relief Column (clasp). Col. Gorringe commanded Irregulars at the actions of Abu Adel and Om Debriket—death of the Khalifa—(2 clasps, brev. Lieut. Col.), after which he was specially employed in charge of the reconstruction of Khartoum (1899). During the S. African War (1900) he was first of all A.D.C. to Lord Kitchener, and D.A.A.G. on the Headquarters Staff, taking part in the relief of Kimberley and the capture at Paardeberg, and afterwards commanded a flying column in Cape Colony, Jan. to Oct., 1901 (despatches, Queen's medal and 5 clasps). Unmarried.

GORST, Sir Eldon, K.C.B., Grand Cordon of the Orders of the Medjidieh and Osmanieh, of the Turf, Carlton, and St. James's Clubs, is the son of the Right Hon. Sir John Gorst, M.P., and Mary, dau. of the Rev. Lorenzo Moore. He was born in New Zealand, Juno 25, 1861, and was educated at Eton and Trinity Coll., Camb., where he graduated M.A. (20th Wrangler). He entered the Diplomatic Service in 1885, becoming Attaché; in 1887 he was Third Secy.; in 1892 Second Secy.; and in 1901 Secy. of Legation. In 1890 he was appointed

Controller of Direct Taxes to the Egyptian Govt. and in 1892 Under-Secy. of State for Finance; in 1894 he was appointed Adviser to the Ministry of the Interior; in 1898 he became Financial Adviser to the Egyptian Govt. (See Sir Vincent Edwin Henry Corbett, K.C.V.O.) He subsequently was appointed to succeed the Right Hon. Sir Francis Bertie as Asst. Under-Secy. at the Foreign Office. Sir Eldon Gorst has rendered eminent services to the cause of reform in Egypt. He married, June 25, 1903, Evelyn, dau. of C. D. Rudd (q.v.), of Ardnamurchan, N.B.

GOTTSTEIN, Hermann Hans, of 19, Clifton Gardens, Maida Vale, London, W., and of the New Club, Johannesburg, Transvaal, was born in Germany, and was educated at the University towns of Breslau and Leipzig. Since 1894 he has been associated with S. Africa in the mining industry. He took part in the Jameson raid in 1895 as officer under Col. Wollaston. In 1899 he was in Germany and Austria in connection with an industrial concession, granted him by the Boer Govt., which was to be taken up by the Prince Henckel Donersmarck group. During the late S. African War he acted as special war correspondent for the Berlin *Lokalanzeiger* and *Die Woche* with Gen. Buller's column, holding that appointment until the beginning of 1901. At the close of war he gave a course of lectures in Germany. Subsequently he was connected with Laffans, and did special work for the *Daily Express*, *Daily Mail*, *Times*, *New York Herald*, and *Süd Africa* (formerly *Burenfreund*) and now represents in London the journals *Plutus*, the *International Economist* (*Volkswirt*), and other Continental papers. He is the author of a book on the *Mines of the Transvaal*, and *S. African Tales and Sketches* (under the pseudonym of Hans Hermann).

GOUGH, Lieut. Col. S. E., V.C., was born in 1874, and has served in the Rifle Brigade since 1892. He first saw active service in British Central Africa in the expeditions against Chikusi and Chilwa in 1896-7. In 1898 he took part in the Nile Expedition, and served throughout the S. African War in 1899-1902, being present at the actions at Lombard's Kop, Ladysmith, Laing's Nek, Belfast, and Lydenburg. He also took part in the operations in Somaliland in 1903, for which he was promoted

Lieut. Col., and received the Victoria Cross for gallantry at the action at Dartoleh.

GOULD, Edward Blencowe, I.S.O., of H B M. Consulate, Alexandria, and of the Conservative Club, Lond., was born, Aug. 9, 1847; is the eldest surviving son of Rev. J. M. Gould, whose wife was a dau. of Gen. J. P. Grant, C.B.; was educated at Uffculme, Devon; entered the consular service as Student Interpreter in Siam in 1868; was Vice-Consul in the Siamese Shan States in 1883; Consul in Siam in 1885; Acting Chargé d'Affaires in Siam in 1886, and again from 1887 to 1889; became H.B.M. Consul at Port Said in 1891, and has been Consul with personal rank of Consul-Gen. at Alexandria since 1897. He married, in 1895, Alice Elizabeth, dau. of Geo. Gordon, of Melbourne.

GOULBURN, Lieut.-Col. Cuthbert Edward, D.S.O. of Grundisburgh Hall, Woodridge, Suffolk, and of the Travellers', Bachelors', and Naval and Military Clubs, was born at Betchworth House, Surrey, Feb. 8, 1860, and is son of the late Col. Goulburn, Gren. Gds. He was educated at Cheltenham and the R.M.A., Woolwich; and served in the S. African War in command of the 42nd Battery of R.F.A. from the commencement of the war until May, 1900; for his services in S. Africa, including the siege of Ladysmith, and the actions at Elandslaagte and Belfast, he received the D.S.O. and medal with two clasps; has since commanded the B Battery of R.H.A. until he was promoted Lieut. Col. in Dec., 1904; he retired from the R.A. in March, 1905. Lieut.-Col. Goulburn was appointed Master of the Albrighton Hounds in Shropshire, Mat, 1905. He married, Feb. 8, 1902, Grace, eldest dau. of W. H. Foster, of Apley Park, Salop.

GOWER-POOLE, Percy, F.R.G.S., M.I.M.E., M.F.I.M.E., F.R.C.I., of Klerksdorp, Transvaal, was born at Gravesend, Kent; is son of the late Rev. Samuel Gower-Poole, Chaplain to Hon. Trinity House, London; was educated privately, and was a cadet on H.M.S. *Worcester*. He spent some years in Canada in the Engineers Dept. of the G.W.R.; served in the Canadian Militia; afterwards studied in Venice, and went to S.A. in '73; took part in the Zulu War as Lieut., being present at the taking of Morosi's Mountain, Nov. 19, 1879 (medal and clasp). In the late Boer War he served with Rimington's Guides and Scouts for 27 months, and with the 16th Brigade as Transport Officer for three months (medal and clasps). He has had experience of the Gold and Diamond Fields in Kimberley, De Kaap, Klerksdorp, Swaziland, Orangia, and the Rand; and practises now as Civil and Mining Engineer at Klerksdorp. He married, May 5, 1887, Fanny Burnett, eldest dau. of J. F. Wood, of Stonehare, Scotland.

GRAAF, Johannes Jacobus Arnoldus, M.L.A., is member of the Cape Legislative Assembly for the Province of Worcester, having been last re-elected in Feb., 1904. He is a member of the Bond Party.

GRACE, Amy, professional name of Mrs. Leonard Rayne (q.v.).

GRAHAM, Frederick, C.B. (1899), of Kincairney, Weybridge, and of the St. Stephen's Club, was born in 1848 at Cherry Bank, Newhaven, N.B. He is the son of Frederick Graham, of East Ferry Cottage, Dunkeld, N.B., and Marjorie, dau. of the Rev. Alex. Niven, D.D., of Dunkeld. He was educated at Edinburgh, and entered the Colonial Office in 1870; became principal clerk in 1896, and subsequently Asst. Under-Secy. of State, Colonial Office.

GRAHAM (James), Marquis of, D.L., of Buchanan Castle, Drymen, Glasgow, and of the Carlton (London) and the Western (Glasgow) Clubs, and of the Royal Institution of Naval Architects and the Royal United Service Institution, is the eldest son of the 5th Duke of Montrose, K.T., A.D.C., Lord Clerk Registrar of Scotland, his mother being the second dau. of Sir Frederick Graham, Bart., of Netherby Hall, Cumberland. He was born May 1, 1878, and was educated at Eton Coll. The marquis takes a great interest in all Imperial and maritime affairs; served in the Mercantile Marine, and possesses a Board of Trade master's certificate. He saw service in S. Africa as Lieut. attached to the Army Service Corps, and also with the Doris Naval Brigade, and was Assist. Press Censor at Cape Town (S.A. medal, three bars). He visited Cape Town a second time on a wireless telegraphy mission for the Corporation of Lloyds, London, and again in Dec., 1902, to study questions

affecting the resettlement of the land. Lord Graham assisted Lord Brassey in the navigation of the Sunbeam to Montreal in 1903, and has travelled all over the world, visiting fourteen countries, and all the British Colonies excepting Canada and New Zealand. He commands the Clyde Division of the Royal Naval Volunteer Reserve, and in 1905 acted, as Asst. Priv. Secy. to the Chancellor of the Exchequer, the Right Hon. Austen Chamberlain, P.C., M.P. Lord Graham unsuccessfully contested the Eye Division of Suffolk at a by-election in 1906 as a Conservative, reducing the Liberal majority to 197. He is fond of all sports, particularly yachting, fishing, and shooting; and married, in June, 1906, Lady Mary Hamilton.

GRAHAM, Hon. T. L., M.L.C., K.C., Attorney-Gen. in Sir Gordon Sprigg's Ministry; has had a varied experience of political parties, having started under the Bond. At the commencement of the Boer War (1899) he was a bitter and uncompromising opponent of that organisation; but as Attorney-Gen. he caused great consternation by refusing to place papers relating to alleged treasonable practices by Dr. Te Water before the House, while admitting the existence of such documents being in possession of the Govt. and the military authorities. Finally, on the approach of the elections for the Legislative Council, he offered himself as a Progressive candidate for the Western Circle of the C.C., and was elected, Nov., 1903, second on the poll, with 12,530 votes. He formerly sat as the representative of the same constituency in the Council.

GRAHAMSTOWN, Bishop of. (See Right Rev. C. E. Cornish.)

GRAHAMSTOWN, Canon of. (See Rev. A. T. Wirgman.)

GRANARD, Earl of, J.P., D.L., of Castle Forbes, Longford, was born in 1874, and is son of the 7th Earl, succeeding his father In 1889. He became a Lieut. in the Scots Guards in 1899, serving with them in the S. African War in 1900-2 (Queen's medal and three clasps; King's medal and two clasps). He formerly belonged to the Gordon Highlanders, and acted as A.D.C. to Earl Cadogan, when Lord Lieutenant of Ireland from 1896-9. Unmarried.

GRANT, Brev.-Major Alexander George William, was born Aug. 13, 1868, and entered the Duke of Cornwall's Light Infantry in 1890. He served in the South African War in 1899-1901 as Commandant at Elands River, subsequently being employed with the Rand Rifles; present at the operations in the Orange Free State and at Paardeberg, including the actions at Poplar Grove, Driefontein, Houtnek (Thoba Mountain) and Vet River and Zand River (despatches, brev. of Major, Queen's medal with four clasps and King's medal with two clasps).

GRANT, Lieutenant Arthur, D.S.O., was born Sept. 14, 1879, and entered the 12th Lancers in 1899. He served in the South African War in 1899-1902, being present at the operations in the Transvaal and Cape Colonies (despatches, Queen's medal with five clasps, and D.S.O.).

GRANT, Lieut. Col. Edward James, C.B., of the Royal Scots Regt., served in the Egyptian Expedition in 1888, including the battle of Tel-el-Kebir (medal with clasp and bronze star), and the South African War in 1899-1902, as Commandant at Kaffir River Bridge; present at the operations in the Orange Free State and the Transvaal, including the action at Venterskroon, and the operations in the Orange River and Cape Colonies (despatches, Queen's medal with three clasps, King's medal with two clasps and C.B.).

GRANT, Major-General Henry Fane, C.B., was born May 4, 1848, and entered the 4th Hussars in 1869. He served in Egypt in 1884 and quelled a mutiny of Turkish soldiers serving in the Egyptian Army, capturing the mutineers (brevet of Lieut.-Col.), and the Sudan Expedition in 1884-5, in command of Mounted Infantry (despatches, medal with two clasps, bronze star, and C.B.).

GRANT, Captain James Murray, joined the Cape Mounted Riflemen in 1887, and served with the Pondoland Field Force in 1894, and also saw further service in the South African War in 1899-1902 (Queen's medal and three clasps. and King's medal with two clasps).

GRANT, Brevet-Lieut.-Col. Ronald Charles, D.S.O., joined the Cape Mounted Riflemen in 1880, and served through the Basuto Campaign in 1880-1 (medal); passed through long course of gunnery at Woolwich and Shoeburyness in 1897, and received a course of mounted infantry instruction at Aldershot in 1898. He also served in the South African War in 1899-1902, including the defence of Wepener (Queen's medal and four clasps, King's medal and two clasps, and D.S.O.).

GRANT-DALTON, Alan, J.P., of Shanks House, Wincanton, Somerset; Arundel, Rondebosch, Cape Colony, and of the Civil Service Club, Cape, Town, was born in Dorsetshire, June 10, 1850; is son of Dalton Foster Grant Dalton, late of Shanks House, and Alice, dau. of John Chas. Bettersworth Trevanion, of Caerhayes Castle, Cornwall. He was educated at Marlborough Coll., and commenced his career at the Liverpool Docks under Geo. Fosbery Lyster, Engineer-in-Chief of the Mersey Docks and Harbour Board. In 1872 he joined the Madeira and Mamori Railway Co.'s staff in Brazil, and was employed surveying and exploring, including a canoe trip up the Madeira rapids into Bolivia. Owing to the Company's financial difficulties he returned to England in 1874, and in the following year was appointed to the engineering staff of the C.G.R., mainly on survey and construction work until March, 1901, when he was appointed Chief Resident Engineer (construction). In June, 1901, he became Asst. Engineer-in-Chief, open lines and construction, and was promoted to Engineer-in-Chief in July, 1904. Mr. Grant-Dalton is a Member of the Institution of Civil Engineers, Lond., J.P. for the Cape Colony, and married, in 1878, Emma, dau. of Geo. Brehm, of Uitenhage, Cape Colony.

GRAUER, Rudolf, of the Austrian Alpine Club, made four attempts at the end of December, 1905, and during January, 1906, accompanied by the Rev. W. Tegart and Mr. H. Maddox, of the Church Missionary Society, to climb the Mountains of the Moon on the Uganda border. In their fourth attempt, on January 18, they climbed through a thick mist and a heavy snowfall to the top of a peak 15,030 ft. high. The flow from a glacier near the summit of the watershed was towards the Congo

Free State. Herr Grauer named the peak 'King Edward's Rock', exercising a privilege he had obtained before he started his expedition.

GRAY, Robert Kaye, of 106, Cannon Street, London, E.C., is Chairman of the Spanish National Submarine Telegraph Co., Ltd., and is on the Board of the West African Telegraph Co., Ltd., Cuba Submarine Telegraph Co., Ltd., and the South American Cable Co., Ltd.

GRAYDON, Newenham Arthur Eustace, was born at Dundalk in 1863; is the eldest son of the late Arthur P. Graydon, of Dublin, and great-grandson of the late Right Hon. Sir Edward Newenham, M.P. for Dublin County. He was educated at the Dundalk Inst. and the Univ. of Oxford; was formerly a Lieut. in the 3rd Batt. the Queen's (Royal West Surrey) Regt., and for several years in the Civil Service, which he entered by open competitive examination, passing first of 150 candidates for eight places. In 1885 he became Ed. of the *Civil Service Gazette*, and was officially connected with the first and famous Conference of Colonial Premiers in 1887. After spending some years as Asst. Ed. and Acting-Ed. of the journal *South Africa*, he became Ed. of the *African Review*. In 1896 he was appointed Ed.-in-Chief of the *Johannesburg Times* and *The Times of Africa*, of which, latter he subsequently became proprietor. He was afterwards on the staff of the *Financial News*, and also contributed mining and financial articles to the *Economist* and other journals. He is now on Reuter's Indian staff. His *Limited Liability Laws of the South African Republic* ran into a third edition, and among other works from his pen are *In Saintly Stamboul* and a volume of Moliere's and Racine's comedies translated and adapted from the French. He has written a good deal on travel subjects in *Blackwood's Magazine* etc., being also joint author with Mr. Joseph Kitchen of a Map of the Witwatersrand Goldfields which achieved a considerable popularity. He is F.R.G.S., M.R.A.S., possesses the Freedom of the City of London, is a Livery man of the Fruiterers' Company, and a Freemason. He married Mary, eldest dau. of the late Thomas Southwell, of Bridgnorth, a kinswoman of Viscount Southwell.

GREEN, Edward Graham, Civil Commissioner and Resident Magistrate of Mafeking, Cape Colony was born at Northampton, June 24, 1865 and is the fifth son of the Rev. E. P. Green, MA. He was educated at Leatherhead, Surrey; went out to Cape Colony in 1882; became a Master at St. Andrew's Coll., Grahamstown, in 1884, and entered the Cape Civil Service in 1887. He married, Dec. 4, 1894, Eugenie, dau. of Thomas Warren, of Chalumna, Cape Colony.

GREEN, Frederick W., is connected with the firm of A. Dunkelsbühler and Co., of 1, St. Andrew's Street, London, E.C., and is a director of the Anglo-Klondyke Mining Co., Ltd., Consolidated Mines Selection Co., Ltd., and the National Discount Co., Ltd., on the London Committee of the Brakpan Mines, Ltd., Driefontein Deep, Ltd., Geduld Proprietary Mines, Ltd., Geygerle, Ltd., Jubilee G.M. Co., Ltd., New Era Consolidated, Ltd., and the Wemmer G.M. Co., Ltd., and is on the London Board of the Transvaal Coal Trust, Ltd.

GREEN, Henry Edward Owen, J.P., F.R.C.I., of Johannesburg, and of the New (Johannesburg), Victoria (P.M.B.), Bloemfontein, and the Johannesburg Golf Clubs, was born at Queenstown, Cape Colony, Aug. 1, 1860, and is son of the Rev. E. P. Green, M.A. Oxon. He was educated privately at the Hartley Institute, Southampton. For five years he was employed at the Standard Bank, and in the Cape Govt. Service for six and a half years; subsequently serving in the Transvaal Chamber of Mines and the Rhodesia Chamber of Mines for ten and three years respectively. He holds the Basuto War medal with two clasps for 1881; and on the outbreak of the S. African War in 1899, he joined Thorneycroft's Mtd. Infantry. He received his commission in April, 1900, from the ranks; was present at the actions of Colenso, Tugela Heights, Relief of Ladysmith, Laing's Nek, and the operations in the Transvaal, Orange Free State, and Rhodesia (medal and six clasps). Mr. Green is a J.P. for the Bulawayo District, Matabeleland, and is a Rand pioneer. He holds many golf prizes. He married, Jan. 5, 1886, Annie, youngest dau. of Major Scott-Waring, of Crossbeck Hall, Durham.

GREEN, John Dampier, F.R.G.S., M.Inst. J.E., of Johannesburg, is a descendant of William Dampier, one of the earliest circumnavigators of the world, and was born in London March 23, 1850. He was educated at Chester Coll., of which he is an old King's Scholar. He commenced his engineering career on the Dee (Chester) Reclamation Works on the Dee Estates, of which he was a part owner; was owner of copper, lead, and coal mines and lime smelting works in North Wales, and left England in 1886 to assist in the construction of the Cape Central Railways. On completion thereof he fitted out an expedition to Malmani Gold fields. While there, in conjunction with others, he organised an expedition for the taking of Matabeleland. Some members of the O.F. State and Transvaal Boers expressed a desire to join the enterprise, but the Home Govt. sent word that 'Her Majesty would look with grave displeasure upon any armed force leaving Bechuanaland to molest the natives,' and in deference thereto the undertaking was abandoned. Mr. Dampier Green is Hon. Curator of the Mineralogical and Geological Dept. of the Transvaal Chamber of Mines, and Hon. Treas. and Secy. of the Geological Society of S.A., Johannesburg.

GREEN, Maurice John, of the Junior Civil Service Club, was born Aug. 31, 1878, at Cape Town. He was educated at the S. African College, Cape Town; served as Secretary and Shorthand Writer to the Stockenström Boedel Erven Commission in 1903; as Shorthand Writer to the Civil Service Commission in 1904, and the Agricultural Commission in 1904-5. He is at the present time Committee Clerk and Clerk of the Papers of the Legislative Council, Cape Town. Unmarried.

GREEN, Samuel, of 4, Chester Place, London, S.W., is Chairman of the London Cemetery Co., Niekerk, Ltd., Town Properties of West Australia (1905), Ltd., and the Victoria Consolidated Gold Fields, Ltd., Chairman of the London Board of the Transvaal Coal Trust Co., Ltd., and is a director of the Hampton Plains Estate, Ltd.

GREENACRE, Sir Benjamin Wesley, Knt. Bachelor, of Caister House, Durban, was born in 1832, and is well known in Natal as one of the partners in the large drapery firm which bears his name. He was at one time Mayor of Durban, and a Member of the Natal House of Assembly. Sir

Benjamin, who was created Knt Bachelor in 1901, married Mary, dau. of the Rev. Ralph Stott, in 1863.

GREENE, Frederick, of Rydinghurst, Cranleigh, is a director of the Standard Bank of South Africa, Ltd., and the Atlas Assurance Co., Ltd.

GREENE, Henry, of 22, Martin's Lane, London, E.C., is a partner in the firm of Henry Greene and Co., and is Chairman of the Belingwe Gold Reefs, Ltd., and the Belingwe Development Syndicate, Ltd., and is director of Acton's Swaziland Concession, Ltd.

GREENE, Sir William Conyngham, C.B. (1897), K.C.B. (1900), of the British Legation, Berne; Glencarrig, Glenealy, Co. Wicklow, and of the Travellers', St. James', and Royal St. George Yacht Clubs, is the son of Richard J. Greene, Barrister-at-Law, and the Hon. Louisa Plunket, fourth dau. of the third Baron Plunket. He was born Oct. 29, 1854, in Ireland, and educated at Harrow and Oxford where he graduated M.A. (1880). He entered the Foreign Office in 1877, and the Diplomatic Service in 1887; served as Secy. to H.M. Legations at Athens, Stuttgart, Darmstadt, The Hague, and Brussels; as Secy. of Legation and Chargé d'Affaires at Teheran 1893-96, but it was when he was appointed Agent at Pretoria in Aug., 1896, with the rank of Chargé d'Affaires in H.M. Diplomatic Service that he first came prominently before public attention. It will be remembered that Mr. Steyn roundly accused him of 'decoying' the Transvaal Govt. into making a conditional offer of the five years' franchise. It was Sir Conyngham who told Mr. Kruger that, whether he said 'suzerainty' or not, suzerainty there would have to be; but that "if the present were a *bona fide* endeavour to settle the political rights of our people for good and all, we should neither wish, nor have cause, for interference with the internal affairs of the Transvaal". At 5 p.m. on Oct. 11, 1899, Sir W. C. Greene's official duties at Pretoria came to an end. He received the ultimatum of the Transvaal Govt., and having asked for and received his passports left Pretoria on Oct. 12 for England. For his services he was made K.C.B., May 24, 1900, and promoted to be an Envoy Extraordinary and Minister Plenipotentiary in H.M. Diplomatic service in

1901. He married, in 1884, Lady Lily Stopford, fifth dau. of the Earl of Courtown.

GREENER, Lt. Col. Herbert, D.S.O., of Bucharest, and of the Athenaeum Club, was born in 1862, and is son of the late Thomas Greener, of London. He entered the Cape Civil Service in 1884, joined the staff of the Administrator of British Bechuanaland in 1888, and was acting as Postmaster General and Receiver of Revenue for Bechuanaland in 1889: was Accountant to the High Commissioner at Cape Town in 1890, and in 1891 was sent to the Northern Bechuanaland Protectorate to reorganise the pay and accounts of the Bechuanaland Border Police, and was retained as Paymaster with the rank of Captain. In 1895 he took over control of the Customs Dept. of the Bechuanaland Protectorate, as Principal Customs Officer in conjunction with his duties as Paymaster. On the outbreak of the Boer War he volunteered his services on the staff of Maj. Gen. Baden-Powell during the siege of Mafeking, and on the siege becoming prolonged, he took over the local finances and instituted the garrison savings bank, being responsible for the paper currency, which was of so much use when the supply of cash was exhausted (mentioned in despatches, and awarded the D.S.O.). Soon after the relief of Mafeking he was appointed Financial Asst. to the Military Governor at Bloemfontein. In Oct., 1900, he was employed in organising the pay and accounts of the S.A.C., involving an expenditure during the first eighteen months of more than three millions; was transferred from the Bechuanaland Service as Chief Paymaster and Accountant-Gen. with the rank of Major, and promoted to Lieut. Col. in 1901. He subsequently went to Berne until 1905, and is now Minister at Bucharest, Rumania. He married, in 1898, Helen, dau. of C. Bennett, late of the Isle of Wight.

GREENLEES, James Neilson, late Capt. S.A.M.I.F., of Johannesburg, and the Rand, New (Johannesburg), and Durban Clubs, was born at Glasgow, June 22, 1852. He is son of Matthew Greenlees, of Campbeltown, N.B., by Elizabeth Jack, of Paisley, N.B., and was educated at Blair Lodge Sch. and Edinburgh Univ. Arriving in S.A. in 1871, he worked on the Diamond Fields for over a year without success. For the next eight years he was farming and storekeeping in the Free State, making two hunting trips into what was then considered the far interior north of Bechuanaland. In 1881 he had a wholesale mercantile business in Newcastle, Natal, where he was head of the Municipality in 1883. He was in business at Wakkerstroom, Transvaal, from 1884-89, when he went to Johannesburg and started stockbroking. At the beginning of the late war Mr. Greenlees was appointed War Correspondent to the *Times*, and was with Gen. French in the Colesburg District. He joined the Colonial Division under Gen. Brabant in Dec., 1899, and was through all the Division's fighting, including the siege of Wepener, up till Aug., 1900, when he was with Gen. Clements from Senekal to Bethlehem. In Aug. Capt. Greenlees was appointed A.D.C. to Gen. Brabant and remained (with him until Jan., 1902, when, on the reorganisation of the C.D.F., he retired and returned to Johannesburg. His services were brought to the notice of the CJ.C. by Sir E. Y. Brabant, but as these were deemed to have been rendered to the Cape Colonial Govt. no notice was taken of the recommendation by Lord Kitchener. In Johannesburg he is a Director of several Cos.; he was for years on the Committee of the Stock Exchange, and has taken an interest in local politics. He married, in 1893, Miss Ethel Maud Gittings, of Birmingham.

GREENLEES, Thomas Duncan, M.D., (Edin.), F.R.S.E., J.P., of the Residency, Grahamstown, and the Albany Club, Grahamstown, was born at Kilmarnock, Scotland, Sept. 29, 1858, and belongs to a Campbeltown (Argyllshire) family. He was educated at Glasgow and Edinburgh Univ. Dr. Greenlees was Asst. Med. Officer at Carlisle Asylum from 1884-87, and held a similar appointment at the City of London Asylum from 1887-90. He is now Medical Supt. of the Grahamstown Asylum, the Chronic Sick Hospital, Grahamstown, and of the Institute for Imbeciles, Grahamstown. He is the author of many papers on medical and psychological subjects, and was lately Surg.-Capt. in the 1st City Volunteers. He married, Oct. 17, 1894, Edith, dau. of the late R. White, of Norwich.

GREGOROWSKI, Judge, formerly a Judge of the O.F.S., was in 1896 State Attorney to that

Republic when invited to preside over the trial of the Reform prisoners at Pretoria, although having no status in the Transvaal. He was accordingly provisionally appointed to a seat on the Transvaal Bench. He was noted for the peculiar severity of his sentences of all except Boers, and it is asserted that he came to the trial of the Reformers with the full intent of stretching the law to its utmost against the prisoners. In summing up he stated that he held the signatories of the letter of invitation to Dr. Jameson to be directly responsible for the shedding of the burghers' blood at Doornkop. Notwithstanding that the Committee had offered to guarantee with their persons that if the Govt. would allow Dr. Jameson to come into Johannesburg unmolested, he would leave again peacefully as soon as possible, and setting aside the special statutes of the State, he passed the death sentence upon them under Roman Dutch law. The Judge then passed sentence on the other prisoners, the rank and file of the Reform Committee, condemning them to two years' imprisonment, to pay fines of £2,000 each, or as an alternative to suffer another year's imprisonment, and thereafter to be banished from the State for a period of three years. Mr. Gregorowski resigned his judgeship to fill the post of State Attorney vacated by Dr. Coster. When a law was passed (No. 1 of 1897) empowering the Govt. to exact assurances from the judges that they would respect all resolutions of the Volksraad as having the force of law and declare themselves not entitled to test the validity of a law by its agreement or conflict with the Constitution, and empowering the President to summarily dismiss the judges Mr. Gregorowski emphatically stated that no honourable man could possibly sit upon the Transvaal Bench so long as that law remained upon the Statute Book. Nevertheless, on having to decide the question of costs which was referred to him in the case of Brown v. the State, he gave a judgment which practically brought the case under the operation of the obnoxious law. Furthermore, when Chief Justice Kotze was dismissed by the President under the summary powers of Law 1 of 1897, Mr. Gregorowski did not find it inconsistent to accept the office of Chief Justice.

GREGORY, John Walter, F.R.S., D.Sc., of 4, Park Quadrant, Glasgow, was born in London, Jan. 27, 1864. He became a member of the staff in the Zoological Dept. of the British Museum in 1887, and held that position until 1899, when he was appointed Professor of Geology and Mineralogy at the Melbourne Univ. He was also Director of the Geological Survey of Victoria from 1902-4, when he resigned both appointments on his election as Prof. of Geology at the Univ. of Glasgow. In 1901 he was appointed Scientific Director of the National Antarctic Expedition, but owing to a disagreement with the Committee as to the plan of the expedition, he resigned in 1902. He has travelled for scientific research in various parts of the world, including the Rocky Mountains in 1891, British R. Africa in 1892-3; was one of the three members of Sir Martin Conway's expedition which first crossed Spitsbergen in 1896; West Indies in 1899; S. Africa in 1903, and led an expedition in 1901-2 around Lake Eyre, in Central Australia; has also travelled in New Zealand in 1904. He explored much new country on his expedition to British E. Africa in 1892, discovering the glaciers and the geological structure of Mount Kenya, and the volcanic country along the higher part of the Great Rift Valley, which extends across E. Africa to Lake Nyassa. He is the author of *The Great Rift Valley* (in which he describes the expedition, and over one hundred other books or papers; he has in recent years given special attention to mining geology and has written several papers on the subject, including a book on the Mt. Lyell Mining Field. Recreations: Mountaineering, walking, and canoeing. He married, in 1895, Audrey, dau. of the Rev. Ayrton Chaplin, of Bassetts, Chelmsford.

GRENFELL, Bernard Pyne, M.A., D.Litt. (Oxon.), Hon. Litt.D. (Dublin), Ron. Ph.D. (Königsberg); of Queen's Coll., Oxford, Cairo, Egypt, and of the Royal Societies' Club, was born at Birmingham, Dec. 16, 1869, and is son of the late J. G. Grenfell, master at Clifton Coll. He was educated at Clifton and Queen's Colleges, and obtained the Craven Travelling Fellowship at Oxford in 1894. Since then he has been engaged in the discovery and publication of Greek Papyri in Egypt, being joined in 1896 by Mr. A. S. Hunt (q.v.). He has excavated for the Greco-Roman branch of the Egypt Exploration Fund at Oxyrhynchus, Fayum, and Hibeh, and for the Univ. of California at Tebtunis. He is the author of *Revenue Laws of Ptolemy Philadelphus, An Alexandrian*

Erotic Fragment, etc., and in collaboration with A. S. Hunt, *Sayings of our Lord from an early Greek Papyrus*, *New Sayings of Jesus*, *The Geneva Fragment of Menander*, *New Classical Fragments, and other Greek and Latin Papyri*, *The Oxyrhynchus Papyri*, parts I.-IV., *Fayum Towns and their Papyri*, *The Amherst Papyri*, and the *Tebtunis Papyri*, part I.

GRESSON, Capt. Thomas Tinning, D.S.O., of the York and Lancaster Regt., Mhow, Central India, and of the Army and Navy and Pall Mall Clubs, was born, April 29, 1870, and is son of Major W. H. Gresson. He was educated at St. Paul's and Bedford Grammar Schools, and was gazetted to the Yorks Regt. in 1889. He saw special service in S. Africa in 1899, and rejoined his Regt. in 1900. He also served with the 5th Div. of Mtd. Inf. in Zululand (D.S.O., Queen's medal with six clasps, and King's medal with two clasps). Unmarried.

GREY, The Right Hon. Earl, LL.M., J.P., of Government House, Ottawa, Canada; 22. South St., Park Lane, W,, of Howick House, Lesbury, Northumberland, and of Brooks' Club, is the only surviving son of Gen. the Hon. Chas. Grey, who brought Prince Albert over from Coburg, and was Queen Victoria's Private Secretary, and nephew of the 3rd Earl Grey, K.G., P.C., who was the eldest son of the youngest of the accusers who impeached Warren Hastings at the Bar of the House in 1788 and the six following years. Albert Henry George Grey, who is now the 4th Earl, was born Nov. 28, 1851, and was educated at Harrow and at Cambridge, where he greatly distinguished himself. He began his political career under curious circumstances. It was in 1878 that at a by-election in South Northumberland the Liberal party selected Mr. Albert Grey (as he then was) to contest what was generally regarded as a safe Conservative seat. However, Mr. Grey's popularity won him a majority of two at the poll over his rival, Mr. E. Ridley, Q.C., but as the extra couple of voting papers were found to be irregular, the High Sheriff decided to reject them, and made a double return, each opponent being returned to the House of Commons without having the right to speak or vote. As the Parliament was nearly at an end, the Liberals resolved not to incur the expense of a scrutiny, and the Conservative member was allowed to keep the seat until the dissolution in

1880, when the present Peer was elected by a large majority. In 1885-6 he represented the Tyneside Division of his native county as a Liberal Unionist, but in the latter year he was defeated by a Gladstonian candidate, and did not subsequently seek parliamentary honours.

Earl Grey succeeded to the title in 1894. He was one of the original Directors of the B.S.A Co., and in 1896 he went to Rhodesia as Administrator, filling this high office with considerable success during a troublous period which saw, amongst other things, the settlement of the peace terms with the Matabele chiefs, which put an end to the rebellion of 1896. Lord Grey for a time took an active part in the field against the Matabele, and it is not generally known that he was very nearly cut off by the rebels at the battle of Sepula's Kraal in the Matopos. He returned to England in 1897, and soon after became Vice-Pres. of the Chartered Co., a post which he filled until 1904. He was also Lieutenant of the county of Northumberland, one of the Trustees for the Debenture Holders of the B.S.A. Co., and Chairman of the Charter Trust and Agency, Ltd. He not only devoted himself to the more important affairs of the Chartered Co., but took also a very genuine interest in the personal interests of Rhodesians. Among other popular movements he interested himself in having the remains of four prominent Rhodesians who ware killed in the late S. A. War, viz., Jack Spreckley, Fred Crewe, Claude Grenfell, and C. J. Knapp, removed to Charterland for re-interment hard by the tomb of Cecil Rhodes in the Matopos. But the great philanthropic movement with which Lord Grey has been identified from the commencement is the formation and organisation at home and abroad of the Central Public House Trust Association, the chief aims of which are to promote the higher temperance by the conversion, wherever possible, of the public house from a drinking bar into a house of refreshment for the supply of wholesome food and nonalcoholic liquors as well as of beer and spirits, and to provide such an organisation as will enable the licensing authorities to secure that all new licenses, with their high monopoly values, shall be administered as a trust in the interests of the public, and not by private individuals for their personal gain. In Dec., 1904, Lord Grey left England to occupy a still more important position as Governor-General of Canada in succession to the Earl of Minto. Here his personal charm and sympathetic interest in all those with whom he came in contact, combined with a farseeing appreciation of the requirements of the British Colonies, made him a popular figure, and even in the United States Lord Grey has acquired a popularity which cannot fail to add to the good understanding which has been growing up of recent years between the two great branches of the Anglo-Saxon race. It is an open secret, however, that Lord Grey, as Governor-General, occasionally finds some difficulty in suppressing his strong private views on various public questions, and on one occasion he animadverted so forcibly on the drink evil that the newspapers were asked to omit his remarks with reference thereto. Lord Grey is possessed of a fine gift of speech, and his phraseology is, on occasion, ornate and picturesque. The following brief reference to an after dinner speech on Paardeberg Day at Government House, Ottawa, goes far to explain the secret of his success with Colonials: He wished to avoid the possibility of the celebration of Paardeberg Day being misunderstood. They met on Paardeberg Day not to celebrate any vulgar triumph of race over race. He had lived in Africa and had many Boer friends. Men who slept under the stars, not by necessity but by choice, and who had continual communion with the elemental forces of nature in the silent places of the earth, were generally more interesting than dwellers in cities, whose finer sensibilities were often smothered, and sometimes destroyed, by the dust, hurry, and worry of the Streets.

In 1877 Lord Grey married Alice, youngest dau. of the late R. S. Helford, of Western Brit, Gloucestershire. His son and heir, Lord Howick, has acted as A.D.C. to Lord Milner, and in June, 1906, married the dau. of the present High Commissioner for South Africa, while his eldest dau., Lady Victoria Grenfell, is also well known in South Africa, which she visited with her father during the second Matabele War.

GREY, Col. Raleigh, C.M.G., of Salisbury, Rhodesia, was formerly in the 6th Inniskilling Dragoons, from which he was seconded for service with the B.B.P. He took part in the Raid as Maj. in command of the Mafeking column which combined with Dr. Jameson's forces. He was wounded in the foot, but gallantly insisted on carrying on his duties until the close of the action. As an Imperial officer, Col. Grey was handed over to the British Govt. for trial, and was sentenced to five month's imprisonment for taking part in the Raid. Col. Grey is a Director of the Jumbo G.M. Co.

GREY-WILSON, Sir William, K.C.M.G., of Government House, Nassau, Bahamas; and of the Junior Carlton and Isthmian Clubs, was born April 7, 1852, and is son of the late Andrew Wilson, H.E.I.C.S. He was educated at Cheltenham Coll., and was sometime Private Secretary to the Governor of Jamaica. He acted as Clerk of the Executive and Legislative Councils of British Honduras in 1878; Acting Magistrate at Orange Walk in 1879-81; Asst. Colonial Secy. and Treasurer of Sierra Leone, 1884, and from then until 1886 he acted as Asst. Colonial Secy. on the Gold Coast. He became Colonial Secy. at St. Helena in 1886; Administrator thereof in 1887-9, and Governor, Commander-in-Chief, and Acting Chief Justice from 1890-7. He was appointed to his present position as Governor, Commander-in-Chief, and Vice Admiral of Bahamas in 1904. He married, in 1884, Margaret, only dau. of Robert G. Brown.

GRIFFIN, C. J., was called to the Irish Bar in 1898, and three years later was appointed Crown Prosecutor of British Central Africa. He has already acted as Judge of the High Court, as well as Vice-Consul, and was formerly Attorney-Gen. of the British Central Africa Protectorate until he succeeded Mr. J. J. Nunan as Judge of the High Court of British Central Africa in March, 1906.

GRIFFIN, Townshead, of Blenheim Mansions, Queen Anne's Gate, London, S.W., was formerly a Govt. official in Kimberley, and subsequently Chief Commissioner of Mines in Rhodesia, where he resided for some years. He has now relinquished that appointment, and was a trustee for the Debenture holders of the Rhodesian Railways, a Director of the Eurafrican Co., and some other undertakings, but now serves only on the Board of the Shashi and Macloutsie Exploration and Mining Co.

GRIFFITH, Charles, Native Commissioner for the Western Transvaal, was formerly employed in the Cape Civil Service as Clerk in the office of the Chief Magistrate at Transkei, in 1883; acted as Sub.-Inspector of the Basutoland Mounted Police from 1884-1893, when he was appointed Asst.-Commissioner for Basutoland. He served with the Bechuanaland Border Police during the Matabele War in 1893-4; acted as Asst.-Commissioner for Basutoland on and off during 1894-6, and in 1897 was appointed Asst. Commissioner for Maseru. He has held his present appointment of Native Commissioner for the Western Transvaal since 1902.

GRIFFITH, Horace Major Brandford, C.M.G. (1902), J.P. of Bathurst, Gambia, W. Africa, and of the Constitutional and Grosvenor Clubs, is the youngest son of the late Sir W. Brandford Griffith, K.C.M.G., of Windsor, Barbados, W. Indies. He was born in 1863; was educated at Harrison's Coll., Barbados, and now occupies the position of senior member of the Executive and Legislative Councils of the Gambia, for which Colony he is also J.P. He married, in 1897, Margaret Elizabeth, dau. of the late S. A. Sewell, of Ealing.

GRIFFITH, Sir William Brandford, Knight Bachelor (1898), B.A., Lond., of Accra, Gold Coast; Iver Cottage, Claremont Road, Tunbridge Wells; and the Constitutional Club, London, was born at Stone Court, Stone, Gloucestershire, Feb. 9, 1858. He is a son of the late Sir W. Brandford Griffith, K.C.M.G., by his wife, Mary Eliza, dau. of George Thornton Metcalfe, of Antigua, and previously of Kirkby Lonsdale, Westmorland. He was educated in Jersey, at Harrison's Coll., Barbados, at Univ. Coll., London, and was called to the Bar of the Middle Temple in 1881. In 1885 he was appointed District Commissioner of the Gold Coast Colony, and acted as Queen's Advocate and Puisne Judge of the Gold Coast frequently between 1884 and 1888. He was R.M. at Jamaica from 1889 to 1895; Acting Attorney-Gen., Jamaica, 1892; and received his present appointment as Chief Justice of the Gold Coast in 1895. He administered the Govt. of Lagos in 1896; and was Deputy Governor of the Gold Coast in 1897. Sir Brandford revised the Ordinances of the Gold Coast in 1887, in 1897, and again in 1903, and he now holds a dormant commission to administer the Govt. of the Gold Coast in the absence of the Governor and the Colonial Sec. He married, Feb. 7, 1884, Eveline Florence Elizabeth, dau. of Penrose Nevins, of Settle, Yorks.

GRIFFITHS, Harry Denis, of Johannesburg (P.O. Box 2146), and of the Blenheim (Lond.), and Rand (Johannesburg) Clubs, was born at Manchester in 1866. He is second son of John Griffiths, at one time champion of the Nemesis Rowing Club. He was educated at Dieppe Coll. and at the Royal Sch. of Mines, Lond.; graduated B.Sc.; was Bronze, Silver, and Gold Medallist of Cardiff Technical Schools, and secured the Ware and Cardiff Scholarships. He is also Associate of the Royal Sch. of Mines, 1st Class in Mining, a Whitworth Scholar and Medalist, and member of various technical and scientific societies. He has occupied the following positions: Mine manager, Kimberley D.M. Co., 1890; chief engineer Kimberley Exhibition, 1892; consulting engineer to the Geldenhuis East., Simmer and Jack, and East Rand Prop. Cos., and is now consulting engineer to several important Cos. on the East Rand, Coronation and Heidelberg sections. In 1897 Mr. Griffiths went to New Zealand, spending two years converting dry crushing to wet crushing plants. He was also chief engineer to the Auckland Exhibition. During the S.A. War he went to Rhodesia, resuming his practice in Johannesburg on the declaration of peace. He was a member of the Patents Committee of the Witwatersrand Chamber of Mines; has served on the Auckland (N.Z.) and Rhodesian Chambers of Mines; has written many scientific papers, and has issued a map of the Coronation line of reef. Mr. Griffiths formerly played for the London Welsh F.C.; was vice-capt. of the Sch. of Mines Rowing Club, and captained the winning pair and fours in 1889. He married, in 1895, Florence Maud, second dau. of the late E. Clements, C.E., R.N.

GRIMSTON, Rt. Hon. James Walter. (See Earl of Verulam.)

GRIMWADE, Charles Walter, of Johannesburg, is a director of Hudson's Consolidated, Ltd., and is on the London Committee of Transvaal Banket, Ltd.

GROGAN, Capt. Ewart Scott, 4th Royal Munster Fusiliers, of Good Hope Farm, Middelburg, Transvaal, and the Savage, Alpine, New Oxford and Camb. and Rand Clubs, is the son of the late William Grogan, of 97, Queen's Gate, South Kensington. He was born Dec. 12, 1874, at Eaton Square, London, and was educated at Winchester and Jesus Coll., Camb. Capt. Grogan fought as Gunner in the Second Matabele War and made the first journey from the Cape to Cairo. During this journey he discovered new species of antelope and elephant, and shot 33 elephants and 13 lions. He was appointed on the Johannesburg Town Council by Lord Milner in 1903. He has taken a leading part in the fight for the introduction of Chinese labourers to work the Transvaal Mines. He is now experimenting in agriculture in S.A., and is a Director of the African Farms Co., Ltd. Capt. Grogan has travelled much and studied economics of Australasia, the South leas, and N. and S. America. Besides being an explorer and hunter, he is a writer of some note, and has written a stirring account of his journey through Africa, entitled, *From the Cape to Cairo*, in collaboration with Arthur H. Sharp Hurst and Blackett). He married, Oct. 11, 1900, Miss G. Watt, of Napier, New Zealand.

GROVE, Col. Edward Aickin, C.B., of Belgrave Mansions, S.W., and of Whites and the Wellington Clubs, was born at Dolguog, Machynlleth. He was educated at Bedford Sch. and joined the 2nd Royal Cheshire Militia in 1873, transferring to the 97th Regt. in the same year. He passed Staff Coll. in 1883; was D.A.A.G. and Q.M.G. Canada from 1885 to 1887; D.A.A.G. Eastern Dist. 1881-88; commanded the 2nd Batt. of the Queen's Own (Royal West Kent) Regt. 1896-1901, receiving the brevet rank of Col. in 1900, and was A.A.G. and C.S.O. Scotland in 1902.

Col. Grove has seen much active service, commencing with the Transvaal War in 1881. He was all through the Egyptian Expedition of 1882, being present at Kassassin and Tel-el-Kebir, and acting as Asst. Provost Marshal to the 2nd Division (medal with clasp, Khedive's star, and brevet majority). He served in the Sudan Expedition of

1884-85 as D.A.A.G. and Q.M.G. (clasp), and in the S.A. War commanded his regt. from 1899 to 1901, and afterwards commanded the sub-district of Krugersdorp (mentioned in despatches, C.B., and medal with 4 clasps). He married, in 1887, Georgina, dau. of the late Rev. George Atkinson of Kettlethorpe, Lincs.

GUBBINS, Hon. Charles O'Grady, M.L.A., of Natal, represents the Newcastle Division of the County of Klip River in the Natal Legislative Assembly. On the resignation of Mr. Smythe's Ministry in November, 1906, Mr. Gubbins joined Mr. F. R. Moor's Cabinet as Colonial Secretary.

GUGGISBERG, Capt. Frederick Gordon, R.E., of the Sports Club; was born July 20, 1869, and is son of Frederick Guggisberg. He was educated at 'Burney's', Hampshire, and the R.M.A., Woolwich; was gazetted to the Royal Engineers in 1889; served at Chatham from then until 1893, and at Singapore from 1893-6. From 1896 until 1902 he acted as Instructor in Fortification at the R.M.A., Woolwich. In 1902 he was appointed Asst. Director of the Gold Coast Mines Surveys, under Major A. E. G. Watherston, C.M.G., R.E., succeeding him in that appointment in March, 1905. He is the author of *The Shop* (a history of the R.M.A.), *Modern Warfare* (published under the nom de plume of Ubique), and other publications. Recreations: Golf, racquets, and tennis; has played Association football for the R.E., the Casuals, and Chatham, and also plays cricket for the R.E., Free Foresters, M.C.C., and the Band of Brothers. He married, Aug. 15, 1905, Lilian Decima Moore.

GUILLEMARD, Dr. Francis Henry Hill, M.A., M.D., of Old Mill House, Trumpington, Cambridge, was born Sept. 12, 1852. He was educated at Caius Coll., Cambs.; on leaving there he travelled in the interior of S. Africa, 1877-8, working at its ornithology, afterwards describing his collections and writing a short monograph on Bilharzia, haematobia, and the diseases caused by this parasite in man in Africa. He went out to the Boer War in 1881, but returned to accompany the yacht *Marchesa* in her voyage of exploration in 1881-4, traversing Kamchatka, and investigating the zoology of the Malay Archipelago. *The Provisional List of the Birds of the Suhe Archipelago* was the result of his ornithological exploration of that group. Later on Dutch New Guinea was visited, yielding very large zoological collections. *The Cruise of the Marchesa*, 1886, gave the, account of this voyage, and the scientific work was for the most part published in the Proc. Zoological Soc. In 1887-8, Dr. Guillemard spent a year and a half in Cyprus, publishing a descriptive catalogue of its birds with the late Lord Lilford, and also engaging in archeological work on the island. Returning to England he initiated the Cyprus Exploration Fund, which resulted in the excavation of the temple at Paphos, and other sites. In 1889 he was elected to the Readership in Geography at Cambridge, but relinquished it the same year. He accompanied Sir Chas. Euan-Smith's mission to the Court of Morocco in 1892, and has travelled frequently in all the European countries, and in most of those of the Old World. He is a member of the Council of the Royal Geographical and the Hakluyt Societies, and is Geographical Editor of the Cambridge Univ. Press. He is also author of *Australasia* (Stanford's Compendium) in conjunction with Dr. Alfred R. Wallace, and the *Life of Magellan*. He edited Miss Mary Kingsley's two first African books, Stadling's *Through Siberia*, H. U. Traill's *Egypt*, Beccari's *Nelle Foreste di Borneo*, Clemow's *The Geography of Disease*, A. F. Keane's *Man, Past and Present*, and many other books. He married, in 1890, Katherine, dau. of the Rev. W. H. Guillemard, D.D., of Cambridge.

GUINNESS, Hon. Rupert, C.M.G., L.C.C., was born in 1874, and is eldest son of Lord Iveagh. He won the Diamond Sculls twice, and the Wingfield Sculls; served with the Irish Hospital in the South African War, in connection with which he received the C.M.G. in 1901; was elected to the L.C.C. in 1904, and contested Haggerston at the Parliamentary election in 1906.

GUINNESS, Hon. Walter, is the younger son of the great Irish brewer, Viscount Iveagh, and served with the Imperial Yeomanry in the South African War. He married, in 1903, a dau. of the Earl of Buchan.

GUNN, H. Hamilton, of Kimberley, graduated at the Royal Sch of Mines, passing out in 1876. Since then he has been associated with phosphate of lime and manganese deposits in Germany, iron ore in

Belgium, lead and quicksilver in Austria, tin in Cornwall, copper in Ireland and Arizona, sulphur and borax in Ireland, silver, lead, and gold in the States, and gold and tin in Borneo, the Malay Peninsula and Siam. He has spent some time in special chemical research with Dr. Squire, and has acted as lecturer on mining at the Edinburgh Coll. of Science and Technology. In 1903 he was appointed Professor at the Kimberley Sch. of Mines. Mr. Gunn is a Knight of the Order of the Crown of Italy.

GUNZBURG, Robert, of Electra House, Finsbury Pavement, London, E.C., went out to S.A. in 1893, and was instrumental in forming the S.A. Contracting Assn., Ltd., the Technical and Commercial Corp., Ltd., the Siemens, Ltd., and the Arthur Koppel, Ltd. He returned to Europe in 1901, and later on resigned the directorship in these Cos. He has been associated with the Eastern Gold Farms Synd., Ltd., the Bethal Synd., Ltd., and several other Companies, and is now Representative of the *Banque Française pour le Commerce et l'Industrie* for Great Britain and Ireland.

GUPPY, Robert, of 3, St. George's Mansions, Bessborough Gardens, S.W., and of the Cocoa Tree Club; was born Nov. 17, 1872, at Melbury, near Dorchester. He was educated at Sherborne and appointed to the Imperial Post Office in March, 1890, and to the Colonial Civil Service, Aug. 24, 1900. He is now Accountant of the Post and Telegraph Dept. Gold Coast Colony.

GWYNNE-EVANS, William, of Penlan Hall, Fordham, near Colchester, is a director of the Real Estate Corp. of South Africa, Ltd., and is on the London Committee of the Grootvlei Proprietary Mines, Ltd.

HAARHOFF, Daniel Johannes, M.L.A., of Kimberley, was born at Graaff Reinet in 1846, and was educated at the public sch. in that town. He served his articles with D. J. van Ryneveld, attorney, in 1863; was admitted in 1868, and practised at Graaff Reinet until 1877, when he left for the Diamond Fields. He was engaged for some time in the Kimberley and De Beers mines, and then joined Mr. J. J. Michau in an attorney's business in Kimberley. He was elected Mayor of

Kimberley in 1884, and was returned to the Cape House of Assembly as Progressive member for Kimberley in 1894, and again in Feb., 1904. He is Grand Master of Central S.A. Freemasons.

HACKBLOCK, William H., J.P., of the Manor House, Coltishall, Norwich, is Chairman of the South African Breweries, Ltd., and director of the South African Hotels, Ltd., Elijah Eyre's Brewery, Ltd., and Morgan's Brewery Co., Ltd.

HACKER, Rev. William John, of Maritzburg, Natal, was born at Keinton Mandeville, Somersetshire, April 16, 1853. He was educated at Yeovil and Sherborne Schs. and received his training for the Church at Richmond Coll. He acted as Naval Chaplain at Simonstown from 1876-83, when he went to Butterworth, where he established upwards of fifty schools and churches, in addition to assisting in the foundation of the Lamplough Training Institution and the building of the Ayliff Memorial Church, one of the finest native churches in South Africa. From Butterworth he went to East London (C.C.) in 1896 and to Pietermaritzburg in 1901. He has been Superintendent of the Maritzburg Circuit from that time, and Chairman of the Natal District Synod from 1903. At the Conference held in Grahamstown in April, 1905, he was elected by a practically unanimous vote to the position of General Treasurer of the Church Sustentation Funds, as successor to the Rev. Robert Lamplough. He married, July 28, 1881, Grace, dau. of Thos. H. Lawton, of Cape Town.

HADDON-SMITH, George Basil, C.M.G., of the Secretariat, Sierra Leone, and of the Junior Athenaeum Club, was born Nov. 25, 1861. He is son of the late H. B. Haddon-Smith, C.E. his grandfather having been a Major in the 73rd Regt. Mr. George Haddon-Smith was educated at Victoria Coll., Jersey. He served with the Houssa Force; took part in the expedition against the Jebus (W. Africa) in 1892 (dispatches, medal, and clasp); and was Political officer on Sir Gilbert Carter's mission to Jorubaland in 1893, for which service he received the thanks of the Secy. of State. He was subsequently Asst. Colonial Secy. at Lagos; Priv. Secy. to Sir Francis Scott in the Ashanti Expedition in 1895-6 (dispatches and Star); Chief Asst. Col.

Secy. at the Gold Coast, 1896, and Political Officer on Sir James Willcocks' staff during the Ashanti Expedition in 1900, for which service he was mentioned in despatches, received the medal and clasp and also the C.M.G. He was Acting Gov. of the Gambia in 1901, and received his present appointment as Colonial Secy. of Sierra Leone, 1901. He married Ivy Constance, dau. of the late Col. B. Hodson.

HADEIJA, Emir of, is the most powerful ruler in Northern Nigeria, and has persistently resented British Administration. His town, which is as strongly walled as Kano, although not quite so large, is in the newly formed province of Katagum, and is about 120 miles to the east of Kano, in the direction of Lake Chad. In the summer of 1905 the Emir's demeanour became so insolent and threatening that a force of men was got in readiness at Kano to proceed against him, but when the advance guard reached Hadeija the Emir's attitude changed, and he received the British Resident and submitted.

Since that time a garrison of 240 troops has been camped outside the city walls; but, as the headquarters of the Resident are at Katagum, thirty miles distant, no European has actually been stationed in the town. In the spring of 1906 the Emir again became truculent, and the Government prepared an expedition against him. Hadeija is renowned for the bravery of its fight men; and, although it is not improbable that news of the fate of the Sokoto Mahdi will have a salutary effect, and may even result in the Emir really giving in, yet there is no intention relying upon this, and a strong expedition is therefore being despatched against him from Kano, whence Hadeija is a six days' march over open country.

HAGGARD, Lieut.-Col. Andrew Charles Parker, D.S.O., of the Hurlingham Club, was born in 1854, and is son of the late William Haggard. He was educated at Westminster, and joined the King's Own Borderers in 1873; served in the Egyptian Expedition in 1884, being employed on transport duties; present at the battle of Tamai and the advance on Tamanieb (despatches, medal with clasp, bronze star and 4th class Osmanieh); the Suakim Campaign in 1885, in command of the

THE RIGHT HON EARL GREY

Photo Elliott & Fry

MR H RIDER HAGGARD

Photo Elliott & Fry

MR S. B. JOEL

Egyptian Infantry Battn. (despatches and clasp), and the Sudan Expedition in 1885-6, with the Frontier Field Force and the Egyptian Army; present at the action of Giniss (despatches and D.S.O.). He is the author of numerous publications, his latest one bearing the title of *A Persian Rose Leaf*.

HAGGARD, Major Edward Arthur, B.A., of Cathcart Road, Redcliffe Gardens, S.W, and the Army and Navy, Junior Naval and Military, and Authors' Clubs, was born Nov. 5, 1860, and is the youngest son of the late Wm. M. Rider Haggard, of Bradenham Hall, Norfolk. He was educated at Cambridge, and the R.M.C., Sandhurst; joined the 1st Batt. King's Shropshire Light Inf. in 1884 at Malta; served in the Suakim campaign in 1885, including the march to Tamai, and throughout the British occupation (Egyptian medal and clasp and star), subsequently serving in Egypt and Malta. He was appointed to the Army Service Corps in 1889, but retired in 1892 and joined the 3rd Batt. Beds. Regt. (Mil.), from which he retired in 1904. He saw special service in S. Africa in 1900-1 as D.A.A.G., attached to the A.S.C., and acted as Supply Officer to the 11th Divisional Troops during the advance of Lord Roberts from Bloemfontein to Pretoria; was present at the British entry into Pretoria, when he was appointed Officer-in-Charge of Supplies at Johannesburg, which post he held until 1901 (Queen's medal and four clasps). Major Haggard has been Secy. of the Union Jack Club (a national memorial to the sailors, soldiers, and marines who lost their lives in S. Africa and China) since its inauguration in 1902. He is the author (under the pseudonym of Arthur Amyand) of *Only a Drummer Boy*, *Sidelights on Soldier Life*, *Comrades in Arms*, and *The Kiss of Isis*. He is deeply interested in all questions tending to the improvement of the conditions of the sailor on the lower deck, and the soldier in the ranks, and to the raising of their social level in the eyes of the general public. Recreations: Fishing, hunting, shooting, and travelling. He married, July, 1887, Emily, dau. of the late Edmund Calvert, of Walton-le-Dale, Lanes.

HAGGARD, Henry Rider, J.P., of Ditchingham House, Norfolk, and of the Athenaeum, Savile, and Authors' Clubs, was born at Bradenham, Norfolk,

June 22, 1856; is the sixth son of Wm. M. Rider Haggard, of Bradenham Hall, and was educated at Ipswich and privately. He resided for a considerable time in Natal on a farm which is well known as the supposed home of 'Jess'. He was Secy. to Sir Hy. Bulwer, Governor of Natal, in 1875, and in 1877 he joined the staff of Sir T. Shepstone, and was one of the "handful of individuals" concerned in the annexation of the Transvaal in that year, where he hoisted the British Flag in 1877. In 1878 he was appointed Master of the High Court of the Transvaal, and the following year was given a Lieut.'s commission in the Pretoria Horse at the time of the Zulu War. He was called to the Bar of Lincoln's Inn in 1884, and unsuccessfully contested the Eastern Division of Norfolk in the Conservative interest in 1895.

Mr. Haggard is famous as the author of a number of charming romances, besides which he has published several books on rural life, known as *A Farmer's Year*, *A Gardener's Year*, and *Rural England* (2 vols.), in connection with which latter he made a prolonged tour of the country to acquire at first hand such data as were necessary to make his work a valuable book of reference and rural and social research. In addition to this, he constantly finds occasion to inform the public in the Press on questions connected with Africa and country life, on which subjects his large and varied knowledge always procures him a ready hearing. For many years he was one of the proprietors of the *African Review*, and recently he was appointed by H.M.'s Govt. a Commissioner to investigate the Salvation Army Land Settlements in the United States and for other purposes. He takes a considerable interest in Egyptology, but his main hobbies (though he takes them quite seriously) are farming, gardening, and cycling. He married, in 1880, Mariana Louisa, dau. of the late Maj. Margitson, of Ditchingham.

HALDON, Baron, is a son of the second Lord Haldon, who married, in 1868, the eldest dau. of the seventh Viscount Barrington. Lawrence William Palk, 3rd Baron Haldon, is descended from the Palks of Ambrooke of Henry the Seventh's time. One Robert Palk, Governor of Madras, was created a Baronet in 1782, and his son, who was for many years M.P. for Devon, married, firstly, Lady Mary Bligh, dau. of the third

Earl of Darnley, and, secondly, Lady Dorothy Vaughan, dau. of the first Earl of Lisburne. It was to a grandson of the second marriage, Sir Lawrence Palk, who for more than a quarter of a century represented first South and then East Devon in the House of Commons, that the barony of Haldon came in 1880. The present Lord Haldon was formerly Capt. in the 3rd Batt. Royal Fusiliers, and served with the I.Y. in the South African War. He succeeded to the barony hi 1903. He married, in 1893, Miss Lidiana Amalia Crezencia Maichlé, dau. of an officer in the Russian Army. Lady Haldon made a reputation on the stage as Mlle. Miska, and is a talented musician, good horsewoman, and shot, and an amateur artist.

HALES, Alfred Arthur Greenwood, of Leigh-on-Sea, Essex, and the Press Club, was born July 21, 1860. He has visited and reported upon most of the principal mines in Australia, Africa, America, and England. He went out to S. Africa as a war correspondent during the late war for the London *Daily News* (medal), and also in the same capacity to Macedonia, Japan, and Russia; has lectured in England, Australia, Africa, and America. He is the author of many books, including *Campaign Pictures*, *Driscoll*, *King of Scouts*, *Jair the Apostate*, *McGlusky*, *Angel Jim*, *Molly Mickleden*, *Campfire Sketches*, *Little Blue Pigeon*, and *The Viking Strain*. He married Emmaline Pritchard, of Adelaide.

HALL, Rev. Alfred, F.R.C.I., of Baydonfield, Rosebery Avenue, Port Elizabeth, was born at Newbury, Berks, in 1860; was educated at St. Bartholomew's Gram. Sch., Newbury, and at the Metropolitan Baptist Coll., London, and exercised his home ministry at Ashley, Lymington, Hampton Court, St. Leonards-on-Sea, and Merthyr Tydfil, S. Wales. He was formerly a member of the Hastings School Board, and was appointed Minister of Queen Street Baptist Church, Port Elizabeth, in 1898, and has founded, in that town and at Mossel Bay, missions to Dutch speaking coloured persons. He is editor of the *S.A. Baptist*, the official organ of the Baptist Union for the S.A. Colonies, and President of the S.A. Baptist Union (1904).

HALL, John, Junr., of 3, Brick Court, Temple, E.C., and the Constitutional Club, London, was born in London, Sept. 28, 1870; is the second son

of John Hall, banker, of 1, Fleet St., E.C.; was educated at St. Paul's Sch. and privately in Germany and France; was Private Secy. to the Governor of the Gold Coast Colony, 1894-5, in which capacity he visited Ashanti before the outbreak of the Ashanti War. He was called to the Bar in 1899, and collaborated with W. H. Wills in the editing of *Bulawayo Up to Date, a Handbook of Rhodesia*, 1899. He is associated with T. A. Edison's inventions in ore crushing machinery. His chief recreation is golf.

HALL, Miss Mary, is an intrepid explorer who left Chinde, on the coast of Portuguese East Africa, in June, 1905, making her way up the Zambesi to Port Herald. Thence she struck northward, carried in a hammock by natives, to Lake Nyassa, which she crossed, and continued her journey to Fort Abercorn, where she had to wait six weeks for a boat to carry her across Lake Tanganyika. Thence she entered German East Africa in November of the same year, and travelled by an almost unused route to Lake Victoria Nyanza. This stage lasted twenty-eight days, during which time white men were only twice. Two German native soldiers and a number of servants accompanied her on this journey through the mountains, the natives on the route bringing in offerings of food and native products. Though the lake country was practically closed to whites by a native rising, Miss Hall traversed it and reached British East Africa, where all kinds of big game were encountered. Miss Hall's route then lay through Kampala, in Uganda, Nimale by the Nile, Gondokoro, and on to Khartoum, where she arrived in Feb., 1906.

HALL, Richard Nicklin, F.R.G.S., Fellow of the Anthropological Institute of Great Britain, was born in 1853, and is the son of Joseph Hall, J.P., of Dudley, Worcestershire. He was educated at Birmingham and Kinver, Staffs, is elicitor of the High Court of Judicature, and was formerly Political Agent to Hy. Brinsley Sheridan, M.P., the late W. H. Gladstone, M.P., Sir Lewis McIver, M.P., and Sir Edward Reed, K.C.B., M.P. for Cardiff. In 1897 he acted as secretary to the Rhodesian Landowners' and Farmers' Association and the Bulawayo Chamber of Commerce, also as editor of the *Matabele Times*, and as correspondent in Rhodesia of several London papers. He was

Commissioner for Rhodesia at the Greater Britain Exhibition, London, 1899, and also filled a similar position on behalf of the Rhodesian Government at the Glasgow Exhibition, 1901. In 1902 he was engaged in exploring the ancient ruins of the Great Zimbabwe on behalf of the Rhodesian Government, which operations extended over two years, and was co-author with Mr. W. G. Neal of *The Ancient Ruins of Rhodesia* (Methuen), and is the solo author of *Great Zimbabwe*. In 1904-5 he lectured on the archaeological remains of Rhodesia before the British Association, at Cambridge, the Royal Geographical society, and many of the leading scientific associations in the United Kingdom. He married the sister of the Rev. C. Silvester Horne M.A., London.

HALLIBURTON, Professor William D., M.D., B.Sc., F.R.C.P., F.R.S., of Church Cottage, 17, Marylebone Road, N.W., was born in London in 1860. He was educated at the Univ. Coll., Lond., at which he was formerly Asst. Professor of Physiology, and obtained the Chair in that subject at King's Coll., Lond., in 1889. He was selected by the Royal College of physicians, Lond., to deliver the Goulstonian lectures in 1893, and the Croonian lectures in 1901; has also published numerous scientific memoirs (dealing with original investigations) in the *Journal of Physiology* and the *Proceedings and Transactions of the Royal Society*. He has always taken an active interest in the work of the British Association, and was President of the Physiological Section in 1902. He accompanied the Association in their visits to Canada in 1897 and S. Africa in 1905. He is the author of the following works: *Text Book of Chemical Physiology and Pathology* (1890), *Essentials of Chemical Physiology*, 5th Ed. (1904), *Handbook of Physiology*, 7th Ed. (1905), *The Biochemistry of Muscle and Nerve* (1904), a series of lectures delivered at the Lond. Univ. and the Bellevue Hosp. Med. Coll., New York. He married, in 1886, Ann, dau. of the late James Dawe, of Cornwall.

HALLIWELL, E. A., of the Wanderers' Club, Johannesburg, is perhaps the best-known S.A. cricketer. He is a good bat, and is said to be the best wicketkeeper of the day. He accompanied the S.A. teams to England in 1894, 1901, and 1904, fully sustaining his reputation in the latter tour. He

is also the official starter for the Turf Club and the Pony and Galloway Club of Johannesburg.

HALSWELL, Lieutenant Wyndham, was born in 1882, and joined the 2nd Battalion Highland Light Infantry in 1901, with which regiment he served in the South African war in 1902 (Queen's medal with four clasps). He is the amateur quarter mile and Army half mile champion, and won the officers' quarter at the Army Athletic Meeting at Aldershot in 1906.

HALTON, Herbert Welch, LL.D., 3rd Class Orders of the Medjidieh and the Osmanieh, of Cairo, and of the Turf (Cairo) and Royal Societies' (Lond.) Clubs, was born in London, July 26, 1863, and is eldest surviving son of Walter Fox Halton, of London. He was educated at University Coll., Lond., and the University of Paris, where he graduated LL.D. in 1897, becoming a barrister of the Middle Temple in 1890. He was formerly Inspector attached to the Committee of Judicial Control of the Ministry of Justice, Cairo; was for some time a lecturer at the Khedival School of Law, Cairo, and was appointed a Judge of the Court of Appeal, Cairo, in 1897. He has published, in French, *L'Instruction Criminelle en France et en Angleterre* (1897), and in English *Treatise on the Egyptian Civil Codes* (1904). Unmarried.

HAMILTON, Frederick Howard, of 10 and 11, Austin Friars, E.C., and of the Rand, Devonshire, City University; and Eighty Clubs, was born in London in 1865; was educated at Mill Hill Sch. and Caius Coll., Camb., graduating B.A., LL.B. After reading for the Bar at the Inner Temple, he went to S.A. in 1889, where his scholarly attainments and grasp of affairs inclined him to journalism. He owned and edited the *Zoutpansberg Review*, and was editor of the Johannesburg *Star* from 1894 until 1896, when on account of his active participation in the Reform movement as member of the Committee the paper was suppressed, and he himself was put on his trial for high treason, ultimately getting off with a fine of £2,000. On returning to England he became editor of the *African Review*, an appointment which he relinquished in 1899 to join the firm of L. Ehrlich & Co. He is Chairman of the East Rand Deep, Elmina Concessions, and the H.E. Proprietary; on the

London Committee of Midas Deep, and the New Districts Development Co., and Director of the Australian Commonwealth Trust, Great Fingal Consolidated, Luipaard's Vlei Estate and G.M. Co., and the Spassky Copper Mine, Ltd.

HAMILTON, Lieut.-General Sir Ian, K.C B., D.S.O., of 3, Chesterfield Street, London, W., was born in 1853, and, entering the Army twenty years later, has seen active service in the Afghan War, Boer War of 1881, Nile Expedition of 1884-5, Burmese Expedition, was with the Chitral Relief Force, and finally served during 1899-1902 in the S. African War. During these years he acted as Chief of the Staff in Natal, on the Staff commanding the Mounted Infantry Division, and on special duty at the Army Headquarters. He was present at the operations in Natal, including the actions at Elandslaagte, Rietfontein, and Lombard's Kop, and the defence of Ladysmith; the operations in the Orange Free State, including the actions at Hout Nek (Thoba Mountain), Vet River, and Zand River; the operations in the Transvaal, and the actions near Johannesburg, Pretoria, Diamond Hill, and Lydenburg; and the operations in the Transvaal, west of Pretoria; being present at the action at Silicate's Nek. He subsequently acted as Chief of the Staff in S. Africa, taking part in the operations in the Transvaal, Orange River and Cape Colonies (despatches, promoted Major-Gen. and Lieut.-Gen., Queen's medal with six clasps, King's medal with two clasps, and K.C.B.). Sir Ian Hamilton was referred to by Sir George White as the "indispensable" Hamilton—as much a tribute to his military genius as to distinguish him from the other generals of that name then in S. Africa. Gen. Hamilton was attached to the Japanese Army in Manchuria until the beginning of 1905, when he was recalled to assume command of the 2nd Army Corps. He is the author of *A Staff Officer's Scrap Book during the Russo-Japanese War.*

HAMILTON, Robert William, of Mombasa, E. Africa, and of the Devonshire Club, was born at Temple Sheen, Aug. 26, 1867; is son of the late Sir R. G. C. Hamilton, K.C.B., and was educated at St. Paul's Sch. and Trinity Hall, Camb.; Classical Scholar, B.A., 1899 (honours), M.A., 1892. He was Secy. of the Commission of Inquiry in Dominica 1893-4; was a student at the Inner

Temple in 1893, and was called to the Bar in 1895. From 1895 to 1897 he was District Commissioner at Lagos; was Registrar, East Africa Protectorate, 1897; Acting Judicial Officer, Apr. to Nov., 1898; Town Magistrate, 1899; Asst. Judge and Administrator-Gen., 1900; Acting Judge from June, 1901 to March, 1902; Acting Asst. Judge at Zanzibar, July, 1902; a Judge of the High Court of East Africa, Aug., 1902, and Principal Judge, April, 1905.

HAMPSON, Charles, was appointed first Consul of St. Pierre, Newfoundland, in 1905. He was formerly Vice-Consul at Moush during the Armenian massacres, and in 1900 he acted as British Consul at Zaila in Somaliland.

HANAU, Carl, of Victoria West, C.C., Johannesburg, Berlin, and London, is son of T. Hanau of the firm of Hanau and Hoffe. He was born at Freiberg, Germany, on July 3, 1855, and was educated at Frankfort-on-Main. Mr. Hanau was one of the pioneers of the Rand, and very early in its history began to take a leading part in the building up of its (and incidentally his own) fortunes. He was formerly a partner of S. Neumann and Co., and a Director of the Rand Mines, Ferreira, Crown Reef, Wolhuter, Consolidated Main Reef and Modderfontein Cos. Later he represented the firm of Barnato Bros. in S.A.; was Chairman of the Coronation Synd. (which he founded), Barnato Consolidated Mines (Acting), Johannesburg Consolidated Investment (local), and Randfontein Deep, and was also on the Boards of the African Farms, Ltd., Ginsberg, Glencairn, Kleinfontein Deep, Langlaagte Royal, New Primrose, New Rietfontein, New Spes Bona, New Unified, Rietfontein, B Roodepoort, South Cinderella Deep, Van Ryn, Western Rand Synd., and the Witwatersrand (Knights) G.M. Cos. He is no longer connected with the Barnato group. Mr. Hanau acted as Pres. of the Chamber of Mines in Johannesburg during the absence of Mr. Lionel Phillips, and was for many years a Steward of the Johannesburg Turf Club, and a member of the Committee of the Wanderers' Club of Johannesburg. He married, Jan. 19, 1886, Miss Sophie Baumann.

HANBURY-WILLIAMS, Lieut.-Col. John,

C.M.G., of 79, Eccleston Square, S.W., and of The Army and Navy Club; son of the late Ferdinand Hanbury-Williams, of Coldbrook Park, Mon.; was educated at Wellington Coll. and passed into the 43rd L.I. in 1878. He acted as A.D.C. to Sir E. Hamley in the Egyptian Campaign of 1882, when he was present at Tel-el-Kebir, where his horse was shot under him, being mentioned in despatches, medal, clasp, star, and 5th class Medjidieh; he was extra A.D.C. to Sir M. Grant Duff during his Governorship of Madras, 1884-5; was extra A.D.C. to Sir H. Macpherson in Burma in 1886, and was in 1892 appointed Adjt. of the 3rd (Militia) Batt. of the Oxfordshire L.I., attending the German Army manoeuvres in 1894. He relinquished this appointment in 1897 to join Lord Milner in S.A. as his Military Secy.; he received the C.M.G. in 1899, and was appointed secy. to the Secy. of State for War in 1900. He married, in 1888, Anne Emily, dau. of Emil Reiss.

HARARI, Victor, Pasha, C.M.G. (1905), had rendered yeoman service while in the service of the Egyptian Govt., and when he retired in Dec., 1904, from the post of Director General of Accounts, he was accorded quite an ovation by his subordinates.

HARDCASTLE, Capt. Richard Newman, D.S.O., was born Nov. 5, 1876, at Wakefield and is son of the late John W. Hardcastle. He joined the 1st Batt. of the Manchester Regt. in Dec., 1897, and was stationed at Gibraltar. In Aug., 1899, he proceeded to Natal with his Regt. and was present at the battle of Elandslaagte, he siege of Ladysmith, and held with his Co. part of Cesar's Camp in Jan., 1900, when the Boers made their first attack, and where the losses were heaviest (awarded D.S.O.) Subsequently he took part in Gen. Buller's operations in the Eastern Transvaal in 1900 (mentioned in despatches), and was present in the actions round Lydenburg, in 1900-02 (mentioned in despatches). He commanded a depot of the 7th Inf. Brig. at Maritzburg, 1901; and was Commandant of the Waterval Onder in June, 1902. Recreations: Shooting and yachting.

HARDING, Col. Colin, C.M.G., commandant of Barotse Native Police, of White's, Sports, and Bulawayo Clubs; is the son of the late Charles

Harding, of Montacute Abbey, Somerset, where he was born Aug. 15, 1863. He was educated privately, and went to S.A., where he served in Mashonaland during the rebellion. For some time he was galloper to Col. Alderson. He received his commission in the B.S.A. Police in the same year, and raised and commanded the Mashonaland Native Police. He was mentioned three times in despatches, and received his C.M.G. for services during the Mashona Rebellion. He proceeded to British Central Africa in 1898 and raised the Native Police Force for North Eastern Rhodesia. In 1899 he went to North Western Rhodesia as Acting Administrator, and later raised a force of Native Police for North Western Rhodesia. Col. Harding was sent on special service to explore the boundaries of Lewanika's kingdom, and during his expedition went to the source of the Zambesi River. In 1902 he escorted Lewanika to England for the Coronation, returning in Aug. of the same year to act as Administrator of Barotse Land during the absence of. Mr. R. T. Coryndon. He married, June 28, 1899, Margaret, youngest dau. of Robert Porter, of Lyncombe, Bath.

HARDINGE, Sir Arthur Henry, K.C.B., K.C.M.G., of the British Legation, Teheran, Bencombe, Dursley, Glos., and of the Travellers', Marlborough, and St. James's Clubs, was born in London, Oct. 12, 1859, and is the eldest son of Gen. the Hon. Sir Arthur E. Hardinge, K.C.B. He was educated at Eton, Balliol Coll., Oxon (fellow of All Souls' Coll.). From 1872-6 he acted as Page of Honour to Queen Victoria; passed a competitive exam., and was appointed to a Clerkship in the Foreign Office in 1880, Acting Second Secy. at Madrid in 1883; précis writer to the late Marquess of Salisbury, 1885-6; Second Secy. at St. Petersburg, and Private Secy. to the late Sir V. Muir, British Ambassador at the Court of Russia from 1886-88. He was transferred to Constantinople in 1888; acted as Chargé d'Affaires at Bucharest in 1890; was selected to accompany the Emperor of Russia when he visited India in 1890-1; transferred to Cairo in 1891; and acted as Agent and Consul General in Egypt several times between 1891-3; was appointed Agent and Consul General in Zanzibar, and Consul General for British East Africa in 1894; also Commissioner for the British E. Africa Protectorate in 1895. He was appointed Minister in Tunis in 1901, and accompanied the Viceroy on his tour in the Persian Gulf in 1903. Sir Arthur received the E. Africa military medal for taking part in the operations against the Mazrui in the Arab rebellion in 1895-6, also the Uganda medal and clasp, for services rendered during the Uganda mutiny in 1897. He married, Nov. 4, 1899, Alexandra, dau. of Major-Gen. Sir Arthur Ellis, G.C.V.O.

HARDWICKE, Edward Arthur, L.R.C.P., (Edin.) L.S.A. (Lond. 1873), and L.S.A. Lond. (Triple Diploma 1889), of Havermere, Howick Falls, Natal; of Burcote Vale, Bulwer, Natal, and of the Royal Colonial Institute, is the eldest son of Junius Hardwicke, M.D., F.R.C.S. Eng. (claiming descent from St. Joscelyn Havermere de Hardwicke, temp. Edward Confessor), and Ellen Jane his first wife, second dau. of Thos. Wright, J.P., of Mespil House, Co. Dublin. He was born 1847 at Rotherham, Yorks, and was educated at the Royal High Sch., Edin., King's Coll., Lond., and Charing Cross Hospital, London. Dr. Hardwicke was appointed in 1877 a Surgeon Superintendent in the Govt. Emigration Service of the Emigration Commissioners, and subsequently transferred to the Department of the Crown Agents for the Colonies in 1897 as a branch of the Colonial Office régime. He retained this position until 1897, when the gloomy outlook of the service, dependent as it was upon the prosperity of the sugar industry in the West Indies, decided him to resign and seek more definitely settled employment in one of the newer Colonies. Natal was selected, and after a very considerable travelling record and armed with credentials from the British Colonial Office, and letters of introduction to some of the most influential citizens of the Colony including the late Premier, Sir Henry Escombe, He was selected by the last-named gentleman for the post of District Surgeon to the Division of Polela, at the extreme S.E. corner of the Colony. Here he remained until Jan., 1902, when he was offered and accepted a similar appointment in Lion's River, the District Health Officership being conferred upon him at the same time. An ardent antiquary and archeologist, Dr. Hardwicke has devoted much of his spare time to the study of genealogy and kindred pursuits, for which his grandfather, William Hardwicke, of Bridgnorth, Shropshire, was celebrated; and he is a member of the Harleian and Yorkshire Parish Register Societies. He is the possessor of what is probably the largest collection of Midland Counties Genealogies in S.A. In 1888 he was elected a Resident Fellow of the Royal Colonial Institute, becoming a nonresident Fellow on his departure for Natal in 1897. He has also been a Fellow of the Imperial Institute from its opening. He is the author of the following pamphlets and books, *The Religion of Agnostic Philosophy*, 1892; *Epidemic Cerebrospinal Fever*, 1891; *The Decalogue as a Code of Morality*, 1890; *Annals of the Perton Family*, 1896; *Bulwer and Consumptives*, 1900; and also of numerous contributions to magazines and newspapers in England and the Colonies. Dr. Hardwicke has been twice married; first, to Margaret, third dau. of William Calvert, of Braddup House, in Craven, Yorkshire, who was the mother of his one son and five daus., and who died in 1889; and secondly to Louisa Annie, 3rd dau. of Benjamin Charles Branch, of Warwick Road, Kensington, formerly Asst. Librarian at the British Museum, by whom he has no issue.

HARE, Capt. Robert William, D.S.O., Norfolk Regt., served with the Rhodesian Protectorate Regt., and on the Staff as D.A.A.G. in the S.A. War; was appointed (1902) A.D.C. to the Lieut. Governor of the O.R.C.

HARE, W., is member of the Cape Legislative Assembly for Woodstock. He sits with the Progressives.

HARE-BOWERS, Lieut. Dillon Aldworth D.S.O. of the Cape Mounted Rifles, entered the corps in 1886. He served in the Bechuanaland Rebellion in 1897 (medal with clasp), and the S. African War in 1899-1902, including the defence of Wepener (Queen's medal with four clasps and King's medal with two clasps). He was appointed Adjutant in Prince Alfred's Volunteer Guard with temporary rank of Captain in the Colonial Forces in 1904.

HARGREAVES, E. S., of Butterworth, Cape Colony, was formerly Clerk to the Resident Magistrate of Butterworth, Cape Colony, and was promoted Assistant Resident Magistrate of that District in place of Mr. E. Barrett in 1906.

HARMAN, Sir C. A. King. (See King-Harman.)

HARRINGTON, Lieut. Col. Sir John Lane, K.C.V.O., C.B., of the British Legation, Addis Ababa, Abyssinia, and of the Marlborough and St. James's Clubs, was born in 1864. He was educated at Stonyhurst College; acted as Vice Consul at Zalla from 1895-8, and as Consul in 1898. In that year also he was appointed Agent at the Court of the Emperor Menelik of Ethiopia; appointed Agent and Consul General there in 1900, and in 1903 he was appointed Minister Plenipotentiary at the Court,, Col. Harrington accompanied the late Ras Makonnen (see *Obituaries*) to the Coronation of King Edward in 1902, when the distinguished Ethiopian acted as Envoy of the Emperor Menelik. His perseverance, tact, and courage were warmly eulogised by Lord Lansdowne for the able manner in which he recently paved the way for the settlement of the boundary between British Africa and the land of the Negus, a work which is now proceeding.

HARRIS, 4th Baron (George Robert Canning), G.C.S.I., G.C.I.E., of Belmont, Faversham; 6, Oxford Square, London, and of the Carlton and Cavalry Clubs, is the son of the third holder of the title, who was Governor of Trinidad and Madras, and played an important part in the Indian Mutiny. He was born at St. Ann's, Trinidad, March 2, 1851. He was educated at Eton and Oxford, where he graduated E.A. Lord Harris after filling several important Ministerial positions, including Under Secy. of the India Office, 1885-86, and Under Secy. at the War Office, 1886-90, received the appointment of Governor of Bombay in 1890, which office he retained until 1895. From that year he was Lord-in-Waiting to Queen Victoria until 1900. In the City Lord Harris has made a name for himself in connection with the important mining corporations over which he presides, and he is rightly regarded as an authority on the various questions which perplex the majority of those interested in the industry of the Transvaal. Lord Harris is Chairman of the Consolidated Goldfields of S.A., Chairman of the S.A. Gold Trust, Chairman of the New Gold Coast Agency, and a member of the Board of the National Telephone Co. and the Wondalli (Deccan) Gold Mines, Ltd.

He is also Vice-President of the Clergy Mutual Assurance Society. He is a cricketer of renown, and an all-round sportsman, having won the walking race, swimming, foils, and single-sticks at Eton, and was Capt. of the Kent Cricket Eleven, 1875-85, and Captain of the England Eleven v. Australia, 1878-80-84. Lord Harris commands the Royal East Kent Yeomanry, and was Acting Adjt. Gen. for the Imperial Yeomanry in England, 1900, and in S.A., 1901. He is also Chairman of the East Kent Quarter Sessions. He married, July 8, 1874, the Hon. Lucy Ada Jervis, dau. of the 3rd Viscount St. Vincent.

HARRIS, Charles Alexander, C.B., C.M.G., of The Homestead, Cuddington, Surrey, was born at Wrexham, N. Wales, June 28, 1855; is son of Rev. Geo. Poulett Harris, Vicar of Hawes, Yorks., and grandson of Capt. Poulett Harris, well known as a great linguist, who married a dau. of Van Stont, one of the last men to leave New York in the War of Independence, who was afterwards Chief Magistrate of Nova Scotia. Mr. C. A. Harris received his education at Richmond Sch., Yorks.; Christ's Coll., Camb. (1874-8); and at Lincoln's Inn. At college he was specially noticed for the Bell University Scholarship, and took a First Class in the Classical Tripos, while at his Inn he took the Tancred Studentship. He entered the Colonial Office by open competition in 1879; was Secy. to the West India Royal Commission of 1882-3, and was in the W. Indies from Dec., 1882, to May, 1883, visiting nearly every island; was Assistant Secy. to the Sugar Bounties' Conference in 1887-8; attached to the Attorney Gen.'s staff in the Venezuela Boundary Arbitration in Paris in 1899, and has been on Service Missions to Madrid (1897 and 1902), Lisbon (1902), and elsewhere.

After many years' service in the West India Dept. of the Col. Office, he was transferred to the North American and Australasian Dept.; became head of the W. Africa Dept. in 1898, and after a period of special work on the Brazilian Boundary Arbitration, was appointed head of the dept. which deals with the British Central Africa Protectorate, the B.S.A. Company's territories, etc. He wrote the lives of the late Lord Rosmead, President Brand, and others for the Dictionary of National Biography; he also has written a good deal on economics, and represents the Colonial Office on the Advisory

Committee of the Board of Trade (Commercial Intelligence).

At Cambridge Mr. Harris was capt. of his college boat, and pres. of the Athletic Club. He is still a good all-round athlete, and is the father of the football international, S. S. Harris. He married, in 1879, Constance Maria dau. of John Shute, of Glenavon House, Clifton, Glos.

HARRIS, Col. David, M.L.A., C.M.G., of Kimberley, and of the Kimberley and Civil Service (C.T.) Clubs, was born in London, July 12, 1852. He is son of Woolf and Phoebe Harris, and was educated at Coxford's Coll., London. He arrived in the C.C. in 1871, served in the Diamond Fields Horse through the Gaika-Galeka War, 1877-8 (mentioned in despatches medal and clasp); took part in the Griqua War of 1878; commanded the Field Force in the Bechuanaland Rebellion in 1896, receiving the thanks of Govt., and the Colonial General Service medal and clasp. During the siege of Kimberley he commanded the Town Guard, 1899 (mentioned in despatches, medal and clasp, and C.M.G.). Col. Harris has also received the Volunteer Decoration, and has won several medals, cups, and team trophies for rifle shooting. He entered the Cape Parliament as a Progressive in 1897 as member for Kimberley; was last re-elected for Barkly West in Feb., 1904; is a director of De Beers Diamond Mines, and of several ether mining cos. His recreations are hunting and shooting. He married, Nov. 12, 1873, Miss Rosa Gabriel, of Pomerania, Prussia.

HARRIS, Dr. F. Rutherford, M.D., Edin., is a great-grandson of a former Commander in Chief of the Madras Presidency (who received a peerage); is a kinsman of Lord Harris (q.v.), and son of the late G. A. Harris. He was born in 1856; was educated at Leatherhead Gram. Sch., matriculated at Edinburgh, and graduated at the Royal Coll, of Surgeons. He proceeded to S. Africa in 1882, and became associated with the late Cecil Rhodes, becoming his confidential Agent, and also the first Secy. in S.A. of the B.S.A. Co. He entered the Cape Parliament as member for Kimberley, and became one of the Whips of the Progressive party. He then came to England; was associated with some few finance Cos., including the Rand

Rhodesia Exploration Co., and .entered the arena of British politics in 1900 as Conservative M.P. for the Monmouth Burghs, but he lost his seat on a technical point. He subsequently entered Parliament as member for Dulwich, defeating Mr. C. F. G. Masterman by 1,437 votes, and he was re-elected in 1906 by a majority of 357, but he resigned soon after as he was unable to find time to devote to parliamentary affairs in consequence of several business matters requiring attention, chiefly in Japan. Dr. Harris is a keen dog fancier, and is very popular in South Wales, where he spends most of his time.

HARRIS, Rev. J. H., a missionary in the Congo Free State, who gave much evidence before the Belgian Commission of Inquiry, sitting at Baringa in 1905, notably against Mons. Longtin (q.v.), of the Anglo-Belgian India Rubber Co.

HARRISON, C. W. Francis, of Natal, youngest son of David Harrison, of Nottingham, was born, Dec. 7, 1874, at Grantham, Lines. After serving in the G.N.R. Co's chief offices he joined the Natal Railway service (Dec., 1898), becoming personal assist. to Sir David Hunter, and later Acting Chief Clerk to the Gen. Manager. He was appointed Secy. to the Special Commission in Railways, 1902, and Secy. to the Railway Employees' Inquiry Board, 1904. Mr. Harrison directed the preparation of the art albums and souvenirs presented to the Royal visitors to Natal, 1901-2; was joint compiler of the Official Birdseye Map of the War District in Natal; compiled also the *Official Railway Guide and General Handbook to Natal* (1903), *Guide to Port Natal*, and other Governmental publications.

HART, Edward Aubrey, of Spencer House, Surbiton, and of the Constitutional Club, is the son of Thomas Gray Hart, artist, was born, March 12, 1842, at Southampton, and was educated at the Rev. Eldred Woodland's Sch. at Southampton. He joined the Union Steamship Co., Ltd., in Sept., 1857, when the first mail steamer sailed for Cape Town, and was appointed Secy. of the Co. on January 1, 1870, and Manager and Secy. in 1893. This position he retained until the amalgamation of the Union with the Castle S.S. Co., in 1900; and he retired from the Co. in 1903. During these thirty years he was frequently consulted by the various Govt. Depts., especially by the Transport Dept. of the Admiralty, for whom he arranged the conveyance of many thousands of troops in the late S.A. War. In 1884 he was instrumental in providing Her Majesty's Govt. with two of the then fastest steamers, the *Moor* and *Mexican*, as armed cruisers. The former was the only merchant ship at that time which flew the pennant; she was commanded by Royal Naval officers, carried a naval crew, and was armed with heavy guns. It was likewise his good fortune to he called upon to make all arrangements for the journey to Africa of the ill-fated Prince Imperial at the time of the Zulu War, and when the body of the dead Prince was interred at Chislehurst Mr. Hart was one of the very few Englishmen, outside the Royal family, who were invited into the chapel. Subsequently Mr. Hart was requested to carry through all the arrangements for the journey out and home to Natal of the Empress Eugenie, and on her return to England he was specially thanked by Her Majesty. Mr. Hart married, Oct., 1868, Harriette Steele, dau. of John Dotterill, of Gosport.

HARTLEY, Col. Edmund, Baron, V.C., C.M.G., Hon. Assoc. Order of St. John of Jerusalem, M.R.C.S. Eng., L.R.C.P. Edin., of Rondebosch, C.T., and of the Civil Service Club, C.T., was born May 6, 1847; is son of the late Dr. Edmund Hartley, of S. Devon, and was educated privately at Plymouth. He joined the C.M.R. Nov. 4, 1877; served through the Gaika-Galeka and Marotsi rebellions, 1877-8-9 medal); Basuto and Tembuland, 1880-1; Langberg, 1897 (medal and three clasps); and the S.A. War (Queen's medal, three clasps, and King's medal, two clasps). Col. Hartley commands the Cape Med. Corps, and is P.M.O. of the C.C. Forces. He married Ellen, 2nd dau. of J. Rose-Innes, C.M.G., late Under-Secy. for native Affairs.

HARVEY, Major William Lueg, D.S.O, of Tredarvah, Penzance, was born in 1858, and is son of the late Nicholas Harvey. he entered the Army in 1878, and served in the Egyptian Expedition in 1882, present at the battle of Tel-el-Kebir (medal with clasp and bronze star); the Sudan Expedition in 1884-5, with the Nile River Column (clasp), and the South African War in 1899-1902, as

Commandant at Kaapminden, present at the operations in the Orange Free State, including the operations at Paardeberg, and the actions at Poplar Grove, Driefontein, Houtnek (Thoba Mountain), Vet River and Zand River, and the operations in the Transvaal, including the actions near Johannesburg and Pretoria (despatches, Queen's medal with four clasps, King's medal with two clasps, and D.S.O.). He married, in 1893, Florence, dau. of the late Captain F. C. Hooper.

HASLER, Lieut. Col. Julian, was born October 16, 1868, and entered the East Kent Regt. in 1888. He took part in the operations in Chitral with the Relief Force in 1895 (medal with clasp); the operations on the N.W. frontier of India in 1897-8, with the Malakand Field Force (clasp), and the South African War in 1899-02, in which he was severely wounded (despatches, King's medal with two clasps and brevet of Major) He was promoted Lieut. Col. in 1906 in recognition of his services during the Munshi Expedition.

HATCHELL, Lieut.-General Henry Melville, D.S.O., of Halifax, Nova Scotia, was born in 1852, and entered the Army in 1874. He served in the Afghan War in 1880 (medal); the Egyptian Expedition in 1882, present at the battle of Tel-el-Kebir (medal with clasp and bronze star), and the South African War in 1899-1900, in command of a regiment of Mounted Infantry (despatches, Queen's medal with three clasps, and D.S.O.).

HATHORN. M., was a member of the S. African cricket team which visited England in 1904. The Colonials played twenty-two first class matches, being defeated only twice, and Mr. Hathorn scored 1,167 runs, with an average 37. He was also one of the successful members of the team which opposed the M.C.C. in Africa in 1905-6.

HAWKESBURY, Baron, is eldest son of Lady Selina and George Savile Foljambe, and grandson of the third and last Earl of Liverpool. The present Baron Hawkesbury—Cecil George Savile Foljambe, as he then was—began his career in the Navy, and served with the Naval Brigade in the Zulu War of 1863. Giving up the sea, he entered Parliament as one of the members for

Nottinghamshire, which he represented for twelve years. He was created Baron Hawkesbury in 1893.

HAWKSLEY, Bourchier F., of the well known firm of Hollams, Sons, Coward, and Hawksley, who is the solicitor to the Victoria Falls Power Co., is a warm believer in and supporter of that company's project. He was the personal adviser of Mr. Cecil Rhodes and Mr. Alfred Beit, and is also solicitor to the Chartered Company, since the date of inception of which he has been closely associated with Rhodesian affairs.

Mr. Hawksley was a firm believer in and friend of Mr. Rhodes, and is a strong supporter of that statesman's Imperialistic ideas in South Africa.

HAWKSLEY, I. A. Douglas, J.P., of Kalomo, North Western Rhodesia, and of the Salisbury (Mashonaland), and Bulawayo Clubs, was born in 1875, and is the eldest son of Rev. T. E. Hawksley, of Dorchester. He was educated at Leatherhead, Surrey, and went to Rhodesia in 1895 and joined the Civil Service. He as at various times acted as Mining Commissioner for several districts of Southern Rhodesia, and in 1903 was sent to N.W. Rhodesia to organise a Mines Department for that Administration, and afterwards remained there in charge of the Mines and Lands Departments. He is a J.P. for North Western Rhodesia; and served in the Matabele Rebellion in 1896 (medal). Recreation: big game shooting. Unmarried.

HAWTAYNE, Major Thomas Montgomery, was born June 28, 1859, and entered the Army in 1879. He served in the Sudan Expedition in 1884-5, with the Egyptian Army (medal with clasp and bronze star); the Expedition up the Gambia against the native chief, Fodey Kabba, in 1891-2, as Superintendent of the Gambia Police Force (medal with clasp), and the South African War in 1901-2, in command of the Wakkerstroom Section, Volksrust Sub District, being present at the operations in the Transvaal (Queen's medal and clasp).

HAY, Maj. Gen. Edward Owen, C.B., of the United Service Club, was born at Ryde, Oct. 24, 1846, and is son of the late Admiral J. B. Hay. He was educated at Rugby, Clifton, and the R.M.A.,

Woolwich; entered the R.A. in 1867, and served in Egypt in 1882, including the battles of Kassassin and Tel-el-Kebir (mentioned in despatches, brevet of Major, medal and clasp. 4th Cl. Medjidieh and Khedive's star). He commanded troops at Ladysmith in 1897-9; and was appointed A.A.G., R.A., at the War Office, 1899-1903; was Maj.-Gen. on the Staff, commanding R.A. of the 2nd Army Corps in 1903, and Administrative Gen. of the Southern Command in 1905. He married, in 1870, Helena, dau. of the late Admiral Sir J. Crawford Caffin, K.C.B.

HEANY, Maurice, of Bulawayo, Rhodesia, was born in America, and has been pioneering in Africa for a number of years. He took part in the Mashonaland Pioneer Expedition, and in the expedition for the occupation of Matabeleland. He is associated as managing director with a number of mining cos.—those composing the Matabele Gold Reefs Group:

HEATH, James, M.P., of Ashorne Hill, Leamington, 54, Cadogan Square, London, and of the Carlton, Junior Carlton, Cavalry, St. Stephen's, and Atlantic Clubs, was born at Kidsgrove, Staffs., Jan., 1852. He is third son of Robert Heath, of Biddulph Grange, Congleton, and was educated at Clifton Coll. He has sat in the House of Commons for N.W. Staffordshire since 1892; was Col. of the Staffordshire Yeomanry from 1897-1902; and is a director of Robert Heath and Sons, the Birchenwood Colliery Co., and the South Rand Exploration Co. He married Euphemia Célena, dau. of P. G. van der Byl, of Cape Town, in 1881.

HELLIER, J. G., M.L.A., sits as Member for East London in the Cape Parliament, having been elected in the Progressive interest in Feb., 1904.

HELY-HUTCHINSON, the Hon. Sir Walter Francis, G.C.M.G., B.A., of Government House, Cape Town, is son of the 4th Earl of Donoughmore, and was born in the Irish capital, Aug. 22, 1849. Commencing his education at Cheam Sch., he afterwards went to Harrow and Trinity Coll., Camb., where he graduated B.A. He is also a Barrister of the Inner Temple. At the age of 25 he went to Fiji as attaché on Lord Rosmead's (then Sir Hercules Robinson) staff, becoming Priv.

Secy. for Fiji Affairs, and the following year Priv. Secy. for New South Wales Affairs. After acting in this capacity for a couple of years he went to Barbados as Colonial Secy., leaving the West Indies in 1883 to take up an appointment as Chief Secy. at Malta. In 1884 he became Lieut. Governor of the Island, remaining there until 1889, when he was appointed Governor of the Windward Islands. Sir Walter Hely-Hutchinson's connection with S.A. dates from 1893, when he represented the Crown in handing over responsible government to Natal, of which Colony he was Governor from 1893-1901, his public services being meanwhile recognised by the Grand Cross of St. Michael and St. George, conferred upon him in 1897. Since 1901 Sir Waiter has been Governor and C.I.C. of the C.C. He married, in 1881, May, eldest dau. of Major.-Gen. Wm. Clive Justice, C.M.G.

HENDERSON, Captain Harold, is son of Sir Alexander Henderson. He was formerly in the 1st Life Guards, and served throughout the S. African War in 1899-1902. He unsuccessfully contested a seat in Parliament at the General Election in 1906. He married Lady Violet Dalzell, dau. of Lord Carnwath.

HENDERSON, S. C. A., of 120, Bishopsgate St., London, E.C., is one of the oldest pioneers of mining in the Transvaal; and although he is connected with many other companies it is with Henderson's Transvaal Estates Co. with which he is mainly identified. The interests and holdings of this company in the Transvaal and other parts of South Africa place it in the front rank of land owners in that country. Henderson's Transvaal Estates, besides carrying on operations on some of its own properties in various parts of the Transvaal for the purpose of proving the existence of and developing gold or other ore bodies, controls several companies, and, generally speaking, as far as present conditions will allow, it is doing its share to advance the material interests of the country. The capital of the company is £2,000,000, and the directors include Messrs. J. C. A. Henderson, W. Bryson Butler (the able managing director) (q.v.), Alfred Gaussen, Geo. Lawson Johnston, and Roger C. Richards. The local committee at Johannesburg is composed of Messrs. Emrys Evans, C.M.G., Samuel Thomson, Leopold Kessler, Richard

Currie, and William Pott. The companies under the control of Henderson's Transvaal Estates are: Consolidated South Rand Mines Deep. Ltd.; Daggafontein Gold Mining Co., Ltd.; Tyne Valley Colliery, Ltd.; and the Delagoa Bay Devel. Corporation.

HENDERSON, Robert Hugh, C.M.G., of Armagh House, Kimberley, and of the Kimberley Club, was born at Armagh in 1862. He was Mayor of Kimberley when the Diamond Fields were invested by the Boers in 1899, and took part in the S. African War, for which he was awarded the C.M.G.

HENNIKER-MAJOR, Col. Hon. Arthur Henry, C.B., of 13, Stratford Place, W., and the Guards', Travellers', Carlton, and Turf Clubs, was born in London, April 3, 1855; is the third son of the 4th Lord Henniker; was educated at Eton and Camb. (B.A.); entered the Coldstream Guards in 1875, the 2nd Batt. of which he has commanded since Nov. 29, 1902. He served in Egypt in 1882 (medal and bronze star), and in the S.A. War, 1899-1902, with brevet rank of Col. (Queen's medal and six clasps, and King's medal and two clasps). He married the second dau. of Lord Houghton.

HENSHALL, Thomas, of Port Elizabeth, and the St. George's Club (P.E.), was born at Adswood, Cheshire, March 28, 1867; was educated at the National School, Stockport, Cheshire, and entered the British and Irish Magnetic Telegraph Co.'s service in 1868. He transferred to the Imperial Post Office two years later, and was for two or three years an instructor in telegraphy, opening up offices in Cheshire, Derbyshire, and Staffordshire. After serving in several important centres, he was transferred to the Cape Telegraphs in 1881. He has since held appointments in Fauresmith, Queenstown, Kokstad, Grahamstown, and Port Elizabeth, to which he was appointed Postmaster in July 1898.

HERBERT, Col. Ivan John Caradoc, C.B., C.M.G., of Llanarth Court, Raglan; Triowen, Monmouth; and of the Guards', Marlborough, Travellers', Pratt's, and Hurlingham Clubs; was born at Llanarth Court, July 16, 1851, and he traces his descent to Hubert, Count of Vermandois, who came over at the Norman Conquest, the family possessions in S. Wales having been held in unbroken male succession from the 12th century. Col. Herbert is the eldest son of the late J. A. E. Herbert and his wife, the Hon. Augusta Charlotte Elizabeth, dau. of the 1st Baron Llanover. He was educated at St. Mary's Coll., Oscott, and entered the Grenadier Guards in 1870, reaching the rank of Colonel in 1889. He entered the Staff Coll. in 1879, and in 1882 was appointed Brigade Major of the Brigade of Guards, and served in that capacity through the campaign against Arabi Pasha in Egypt (medal and two clasps, Khedivial star, and 4th class Medjidieh). He subsequently served in the Camel Corps in the Sudan Campaign of 1884-5; was Adjt. of the Guards Camel Regt., and took part in all the actions on the Nile and in the Bayuda Desert. Returning in 1885, he was appointed commandant of the School of Instruction for Auxiliary Forces, and in 1886 was sent to St. Petersburg as Military Attaché—a post which he occupied till 1890. He acted as Military Adviser to the Ambassador, Sir R. Morier, in the negotiations which led to a delimitation of the Russo Afghan Frontier in 1887, and in 1890 was given the command of the Canadian Local Forces with the rank of Major-Gen., occupying this post for five years. In1897 he had command of all the Colonial troops assembled in London for the Jubilee of her late Majesty Queen Victoria; commanded the 3rd Batt. Grenadier Guards in 1897-8, and was appointed A.A.G. for the Home Dist. in the latter year. Col. Herbert having devoted much attention to the study of foreign languages, of which he speaks five, he was placed charge of the foreign representatives with the army in S Africa in 1899. He also served as .A.G. on the Staff of Lord Roberts, and was for a time Inspector-Gen. of the Lines of Communication. In addition to the orders already mentioned, he is decorated with the Egyptian medal with three clasps, the S. African medal with four clasps, the Order of the Red Eagle and class); is a Commander of the Order of the Crown of Italy, and an Officer of the Legion of Honour. At the General Election in 1906 he was returned as Liberal M.P. for S. Monmouthshire. In the field of sport Col. Herbert has found time for steeplechasing, polo, and hunting. He married, in 1873, the Hon. Abertina Agnes Mary, dau. of the 1st Baron Londesborough.

HERHOLDT, Hon. Albertus Johannes, M.L.C., J.P., was born in the Murraysburg Dist., C.C., in 1846; was educated at Murraysburg, where he was for many years a member of the Divisional and Municipal Councils and a member of the Licensing Court. He has been member of the Cape Legislative Council for as Midland Province since 1889, and sits as an Independent member.

HERMON-HODGE, Lieut.-Col. Sir Robert M.P., commanded the Imp. Yeo. Depot at Oxford at the outbreak of the S.A. War, in which two of his sons served. He was appointed to the command of the Queen's Own Oxfordshire Hussars (Yeomanry) in Jan., 1905.

HERTZOG, Ex-Judge, was formerly a Judge of the O.F.S. He was a Commandant of Boer forces in the late S. African War, and was admitted to practice at the Bar of the Supreme Court of the Transvaal Colony, Dec. 18, 1902.

HESS, Henry, of Tugvor House, Kew Gardens, Surrey, and Beach Haven, St. Margaret's Bay, Dover, Kent, was born July 19, 1864, at Homburg; is the youngest son of the late Joseph Chas. Hess and Lina Hess (née Schottenfels); was educated at Frankfort-on-Maine. He was admitted solicitor and Notary Public of the Cape of Good Hope, 1885. He was Ed. of the *Critic* (London, Johannesburg, and Pretoria), and of the *Critic Black Book*, and has published songs and dance music. The *Critic* ceased to exist early in 1905, and Mr. Hess's affairs subsequently went before the Bankruptcy Court. He married, Nov. 6, 1895, Miss Maude Marion Lyons.

HETHERWICK, Rev. Alexander, M.A., hon. D.D. (Aberdeen), F.R.G.S., of the Manse, Blantyre, British Central Africa, was born Apr. 12, 1860; was educated at King's Coll., Aberdeen, and graduated with first class honours in Mathematics at Aberdeen Univ. (1880), Simpson Mathematical Prizeman (1880); Neil Arnott Prizeman in Physics (1880); ordained Missionary of the Church of Scotland to Central Africa, May 8, 1883; arrived at Blantyre, Central Africa, in 1883; founded Domasi Mission Station, 1884; appointed head of Blantyre Mission, 1898; contributed papers to *Journal of*

Royal Geographical Society (1888) on *A Journey to the Country North of Lake Sherwa*; and to the *Journal of the Anthropological Society* on *Some Animistic Beliefs of the Yao Tribe*; editor of *Life and Work in British Central Africa*; Translator of *New Testament* in the Yao language (1888-1898), published by the British and Foreign Bible Society; Chairman of Nyanja Bible Translation Board; author of *Handbook of Yao Language* (1889) and *A Practical Manual of the Nyanja Language* (1902), both published by the Society for Promoting Christian Knowledge. He married, in 1893, Elizabeth Barclay, dau. of the late Jas. Pithie, of Aberdeen.

HEWAT, Dr. John, M.L.A., represents Woodstock in the Cape House of Assembly. He is a Progressive, and was returned to the House in Feb., 1904.

HICKMAN, Col. Thomas Edgcomb, C.B., D.S.O., 4th class Osmanieh and Medjidieh, of Wightwick, near Wolverhampton, 22, Kensington Palace Gardens Lond., and of the Naval and Military, Prince's, and Hurlingham Clubs, was born July 25, 1859, is son of Sir Alfred Hickman Bart. M.P., was educated at Cheltenham Coll., and joined the 36th Regt. of Foot in 1881. He served on the Staff of the Egyptian Army from 1884 to 1894, taking part in the Sudan Expedition of 1884-5, action of Kirbekan (medal and clasp, Khedive's star), the operations around Suakin, 1886-8 (4th class Medjidieh), action of Handoub as Brigade Major and O.C. Mounted Troops, action of Gemaizeh as D.A.A.G. to Gen. Grenfell (clasp, 4th class Osmanieh, despatches), Nile Frontier (1889) as D.A.A.G. to Col. Wodehouse in command, actions of Arguin and Toski (despatches, two clasps, D.S.O., 4th class Osmanieh); served as Governor of Tokai on the Red Sea in 1893; Adjt. of 2nd Worcestershire Regt., 1894-6; Campaign of Dongola as A.A.G. to Gen. Hunter (despatches, Egyptian medal, clasp, brev. of Major); operations on Nile, 1897-8, during which he commanded the Infantry to Shendy, and was present at the battles of Athara and Khartoum (despatches, brev. of Lieut. Col., clasp), and in the operations for the relief of Gedaref he commanded the 12th Sudanese Infantry (clasp and medal). In 1899 he served in Kordofan in the final operations for the capture of the Khalifa as C.S.O. to Gen. Wingate's flying column

(despatches, two clasps, bray, of Col.). He subsequently commanded the 1st Class Military Dist. of Dongola, and was Governor of Dongola Province from June, 1899, to Apr., 1900. In the South African War Col. Hickman commanded a column in the Transvaal, including the actions at Rhenoster Kop and Mozillikaats Nek; took part in the De Wet hunt in Cape Colony and the O.R.C.; acted as A.I.G. to the C.D.F. in 1901, and commanded columns operating against Scheepers and Theron in Cape Colony later in 1901. He also commanded the Western Dist. of Cape Colony, including lines of communication Cape Town to Orange River, and columns under Gen. French from Dec., 1901, to end of war (despatches, C.B., two medals and five clasps). After the close of the War he was still employed on special service in South Africa.

Col. Hickman plays polo, cricket, and golf and hunts with the Albrighton hounds when at home. He is also fond of fishing and shooting, and has won several horse races in the Cape during 1903-5. His imported Galloway 'Chiffon' won twelve races and twelve seconds from March, 1904, to March, 1905. Unmarried.

HICKS, Col. Henry Tempest, C.B., of Gladsmuir, Monken Hadley, Herts., Eng., Hillgrove, Wells, Somerset, and of the Army and Navy Club, Lond., was born in Essex in 1852, is son of Geo. H. Tempest Hicks, of Hillgrove, Wells, and was educated at Harrow and Cambridge. He served through the S. African War in command of the 2nd Royal Dublin Fusiliers from March, 1900, and was in command of columns of three arms on several occasions, being three times mentioned in despatches, and receiving the C.B. Subsequently Col. Hicks served in the Aden Hinterland. He married, in 1885, Anne Clara Georgina, dau. of Chas. Hemery, of Monken Hadley, Herts.

HIERN, William Philip, J.P., F.R.S., F.L.S., of The Castle, Barnstaple, Devon, Eng., and the New University Club, was born at Stafford, Jan. 19, 1839, and is only surviving son of the late James Gay Hiern, who was of Swedish extraction. He was educated at St. John's Coll., Camb., of which he was a Fellow (1863-8), and graduated B.A., Camb, (1861), M.A., Camb. (1864), and M.A., Oxon.

(1868). Mr. Hiern is Foreign Corresponding member of the Academy of Lisbon, and is the author of contributions to the *Flora of Tropical Africa*, vol. ii. (1871), nat. ord. *Lythraceae*, vol. iii. (1877), *Umbelliferae, Arialicae, Rubiaceae, Valerianeae, Dipsaceae, Compositiae* (jointly with Prof. D. Oliver), *Goodenovieae*, and *Ebenaceae* and to the *Flora Capensis*, vol. iv (1904), *Scrophulariaceae*; also of the *Catalogue of the African Plants collected by Dr. Friedrich Welwitsch in 1853-61, Dicotyledons* (1896-1900); of *African Species of the Genus* Coffea *Linn*. (1876); of *Central African Plants collected by Major Serpa Pinto*, jointly with Prof. Count Ficalho (1881); and of other botanical or mathematical papers and works, some relating to the African flora. He married, in 1868, Martha, dau. of the late Chas. Bamford, of Cottingham Hall, Yorks.

HIGGS, Henry, LL.B., of R.M. Treasury, London, of 68, Curzon Street, W., and the Savile Club, was born in 1864, and was called to the Bar at the Middle Temple, 1890. He is secy. to the Royal Economic Society, and joint editor of the *Economic Journal*; author of *The Physiocrats*, a treatise on the French Economists of the 18th Century; and edited *Jevons's Principles of Economics*, 1905. He has travelled in Canada, the United States, Egypt and South Africa, and was Special Commissioner to Natal, 1902-3, to report upon the pay, organisation, and working of the Natal Civil Service. His report, strongly criticising nearly every section of the administration, was adopted by the Government.

HILDER, Capt. Frank, of 20, Copthall Avenue, London, E.C., is a member of the London Stock Exchange firm of Hilder and Paul, and is largely interested in the South African, and particularly the Northern Rhodesian market. He is an officer in the Essex Imperial Yeomanry, and very keen on hunting.

HILDYARD, Lieut. Gen. Sir Henry John Thoroton, K.C.B. (1900), Order of the Osmanieh, of Pretoria, and of the United Service Club, was born July 5, 1846. He was educated at the Royal Naval Acad., Gosport, and served in the Navy for five years before entering the Army in 1867, when he joined the 71st Highland Light infantry, of which battalion he was Adjt. from 1868 to 1875. He was

Brig. Maj. at Cyprus, Aug.-Nov., 1878; Brig. Major at Gibraltar from at date till Aug., 1882; and served in the Egyptian Expeditionary Force in 1882 as D.A.A. and Q.M.G. of the 1st Division, being resent in the engagements at El Magfar and Tel-el-Mahuta, at the action at Kassassin, and t the battle of Tel-el-Kebir (mentioned in despatches, brevet of Lieut. Col., medal with clasp, 4th Class of the Osmanieh, and Khedive's star). After again occupying his Staff appointment at Gibraltar, Sir Henry became D.A.A.G. on the H.Q. Staff, Dec., 1883, to March, 1889; A.A.G., Aldershot, Oct., 1889, to March, 1891; A.A.G, at Army Headquarters, Apr., 1891, to Aug., 1893; Comdt. Staff Coll. till Feb., 1898; Major-Gen. Commanding Infantry Brigade Aldershot, until Oct. 8, 1899, when he took command in S.A. first of an Infantry Brigade, afterwards commanding an Infantry Div. with local rank of Lieut.-Gen., and from Oct. 19, 1900, to Oct. 24, 1901, he had the command of the Natal District. Gen. Hildyard took part in the relief of Ladysmith, including the action at Colenso; the operations of Jan. 17 to 24, 1900, and the action at Spion Kop; of Feb. 5 to 7, 1900, and the action at Vaal Kranz; on Tugela Heights, Feb. 14 to 27, and the action at Pieters Hill; and in Natal, March to June, 1900, and the action at Laing's Nek (four times mentioned in despatches, K.C.B., medal with five clasps). On Oct. 25, 1901, Sir Henry Hildyard was appointed temporarily to the command of the First Army Corps; Director of Military Education and Training at Army Headquarters, Jan. 15, 1903; and in March, 1904, he was promoted to the rank of Lieut. Gen., and appointed to the command of the Forces in S.A. in succession to Sir Neville Lyttelton. He married, in 1871,. Annette, dau. of the late Admiral J. C. Prevost.

HILL, Archibald Oakley, of Kimberley, Cape Colony, entered the Royal Navy in 1860, and retired in 1878. He was appointed Record Clerk in the Civil Commissioner's Office at Kimberley in 1882; acted as Ordnance Storekeeper from 1884-96; and in 1897 was appointed Secretary to the Kimberley Board of Health.

HILL, Clem, was born in Australia, where he was an engineer on the South Australian railways. He was the champion left-hander bat of Australia, and visited England with the Australian cricket team in 1902, with the reputation of being the best bat in the eleven. He went to South Africa with the Australian team later in 1902, scoring 76 and 142 against All South Africa at Johannesburg. Mr. Hill remained in that town as a stockbroker, but in 1904-5 he was again playing in Australia, completing in that season over 2,000 runs in interstate matches, with an average (at the end of 1904) of 62. He was married in Jan., 1905.

HILL, Sir Clement Lloyd, K.C.B., K.C.M.G., of 2, Whitehall Court, S.W., and of the St. James' Club, was born May 5, 1845, and comes of a family which has served the country in Army, Navy, Church, and Diplomacy, and is a grand-nephew of Gen. Sir Rowland Hill, whose distinguished service at Waterloo and in the Peninsular War brought him the title of Lord Hill, of Almarez and Hardwicke, and subsequently a viscounty. Sir Clement is son of the Rev. John Hill, of Shrewsbury. He was educated at Marlborough Coll., and served in the Foreign Office from 1867-1905. During that period he acted as Secy. to Sir Bartle Frere's Mission to Zanzibar in 1872-3, and as Private Secy. to the Rt. Hon. Robert Bourke in 1885-6. He was attached to the Sultan of Zanzibar's suite, when he visited England in 1875; acted as Chargé d'Affaires in Bavaria in 1876; was a member of the Commission for the revision of Slave Trade Instructions in 1881-91; special Commissioner in Haiti in 1886-7; and was a Member of the Uganda Railway Committee in 1896. He represented the British Protectorates under the Foreign Office at the conference in London on Postage within the British Empire in 1898, and was one of the British Plenipotentiaries at the International Conference in London for the Protection of Wild Animals in Africa, 1900. He was appointed Supt. of African Protectorates under the Foreign Office, and visited E. Africa, Uganda, and Somaliland in 1900, but retired in 1905 when the Protectorates were transferred to the Colonial Office. Sir Clement was returned to Parliament in Jan., 1906, as Unionist Member for Shrewsbury. His principal sport is shooting; having shot in various parts of the world, including Africa, and has fished in Norway. He married a dau. of Sir G. Denys in 1889.

HILL, William Henry, B.A., of Cairo, and the Turf Club, Cairo; was born at Swindon, Wilts., where his father, Henry Hill, resided; and was educated at King's Sch., Worcester, and Lincoln Coll., Oxon. (Exhibitioner). Formerly an Asst. Master in the Khedivial Sch., Cairo, under the Ministry of Public Instruction; he is now Law Lecturer at the Khedivial Sch. of Law, Cairo. Mr. Hill is *licencié en Droit*, Paris. He married, in 1902, Mary Agnes, only dau. of Rev. F. W. Quilter, D.D.

HILLIER, Dr. Alfred Peter, of 30, Wimpole Street, London, W., and of the Junior Carlton Club and Royal Institution of Great Britain, also Member of the Council of the Royal Colonial Institute, is the son of the late P. Playne Hillier of Shortwood, Glos., where he was born in 1858. He was educated at King William's Coll., Isle of Man, and Edinburgh Univ. Dr. Hillier first went to S. Africa as a boy, and was ostrich farming in 1875-8. He took his B.A. degree at the Cape Univ. in 1878, and served in that year in the Gaika-Galeka War (medal and clasp). After the war he went to Edinburgh Univ., taking his M.B. and C.M. in 1882 and his M.D. in 1884. After practising for a couple of years in East London, C.C., he proceeded to Kimberley as Resident Surgeon to the hospital there, and afterwards entered into medical partnership with Dr. L. S. Jameson. He was Pres. of the S.A. Medical Congress in 1892. In 1893 Dr. Hillier went up to Johannesburg, and found time to take an active part in the politics of the Transvaal, being a prominent member of the Reform Committee, for which he was lodged in Pretoria gaol, until in May, 1896, he was liberated on payment of the £2,000 fine. In 1897 he returned to England. Dr. Hillier was Secy. to the National Association (of Great Britain) for the Prevention of Consumption, and is now on the Council of that body, and Consulting Physician to the London Open Air Sanatorium, and was nominated by H.R.H. the Prince of Wales in 1899 as one of its representatives, at the Tuberculosis Congress in Berlin. He was successful in inducing the National Conference of British Friendly Societies to send an important deputation (which he himself accompanied) to Germany to inspect sanatoria and other institutions established and controlled by the German State Workmen's Insurance Dept., and was received by the Empress of Germany as an English delegate to the International Tuberculosis

Conference. He is also a Member of the Council of the International Bureau for the Prevention of Tuberculosis, which has its headquarters at Berlin, and Vice Chairman of the Allied Colonial Universities Conference (1903).

Dr. Hillier is the author of *South African Studies*, and of the historical articles on South Africa, Transvaal, Orange River Colony, Cape Colony, and others in the *Encyclopedia Britannica* (new volumes, recently published by the *Times*), and has contributed largely to our knowledge of S.A. by lectures and articles in newspapers and reviews. At the General Election in 1900 he unsuccessfully stood as Unionist candidate for Stockport, but in March 1904, he was adopted as Unionist candidate for South Beds., being defeated at the 1906 election by some 1,850 votes. He has retired from practice, and is on the London Committees of the Robinson, Crown Reef, Ferreira, Crown Deep, and several other well-known Rand Cos. When in Johannesburg he was a frequent player in the Rand Polo Club team, of which he was Vice Capt. His recreations are now shooting, hunting, and golf. Dr. Hillier was married, in 1885, to Ethel, dau. of F. B. Brown, of Queenstown, Cape Colony.

HIME, Lieut. Col. The Right Hon. Sir Albert Henry, P.C., K.C.M.G., late R.E., served as a Subaltern in the West Indies, and was then appointed by Lord, Knutsford (the then Colonial Secy.), Colonial Engineer to Natal, in which position he rendered an excellent account of himself: In the Zulu War he held a small command, and a few years after Responsible Govt. was granted to Natal, he entered the House of Assembly, becoming Minister of Lands and Works in Sir Henry Binn's Ministry from 1897 until June, 1899, when he formed his own Cabinet, retaining his last portfolio. He resigned the Premiership in Aug., 1903, and his seat in the Assembly as Member for Maritzburg City early in 1905

HINCKS, Capt. Thomas Cowper, F.R.G.S., of Barons Down, Dulverton, and Govt. House, Accra, G.C.C., and of the Army and Navy Club, was born at Thirsk, Yorks., Jan. 31, 1875, and is son of the late Capt. Thos. C. Hincks. He was educated at King's Sch., Canterbury, and the R.M. Coll., Sandhurst. Gazetted to the 1st Batt. Royal

Berks. Regt., Feb., 1895. He was seconded as Adjutant in the Malay States Guides, Feb., 1901; and was appointed A.D.C. to the Governor of the Gold Coast, Jan., 1904. His captaincy dates from May 8, 1904. Unmarried.

HINDE, Mrs. Hildegarde, of Fort Hall, via Mombasa, E.A.P. 3rd dau. of C. D. Ginsburg, JL.D., J.P., published in collaboration with her husband in 1901 The Last of the Masai. She married, in 1897, Dr. S. L. Hinde (q.v.).

HINDE, Sidney Langford, L.S.A., of Fort Hall, via Mombasa, E. Africa, and of the Savage, Sports, and Camera Clubs, was born at Niagara, Canada, in 1863, and is eldest son of Surgeon-Gen. G. L. Hinde, C.B. He was educated in Germany and France, and at Clare Coll., Camb., and qualified in medicine at St. Bartholomew's Hospital, afterwards becoming House Surgeon and House Physician at the London Temperance Hosp. and at the North Stafford Hosp. In 1890 he was appointed Med. Officer in the service of the Congo Free State, and in the same year was given a Lieut.'s Commission in the Belgian Colonial Force. He served through the Arab campaigns of 1892-4; was promoted Capt., mentioned in despatches, received medal and star, and was made a Chevalier of the Royal Order of the Lion. He retired in 1894, and in the following year was appointed Med. Officer to the E. Africa Protectorate under the Foreign Office, serving in the Mbaruk Rebellion in 1895-6 (medal). He transferred to the Administrative Dept. as Collector in 1896, and was promoted Sub Commissioner for the Kenya Province, E.A.P., in 1902. Mr. Hinde published *The Fall of the Congo Arabs* in 1897, and (in collaboration with his wife) *The Last of the Masai* in 1901, besides geographical and other scientific papers. He has presented large natural history collections to the British Museum, which included many previously unknown species of mammals, birds, fish, and insects. He married, in 1897, Hildegarde, 3rd dau. of C. P. Ginsburg, LL.D., J.P.

HINDLIP, Baron (Charles Allsopp), F.R.G.S., F.Z.S., of Hindlip Hall, Worcester; of Alsop-en-le-Dale, Derbyshire; and of the Turf and Bachelors' Clubs, is the son of the 2nd Baron Hindlip. He was born Sept. 22, 1877 was educated at Eton and

Trinity Coll., Cambridge, and obtained his B.A. in 1898. Baron Hindlip was A.D.C. to the late Governor of Victoria, Baron Brassey, K.C.B. He was Capt. in the 5th Worcester Regt., and served in the 8th Hussars in 8.A., 1900-1. He has travelled extensively, principally in Abyssinia, in 1902, and British East Africa in 1903-4, his expeditions being mainly for the purpose of sport. On the latter trip after visiting Obbia Lord Hindlip proceeded to Mombassa, and thence travelled by the Uganda Railway to Londiani. From that point he marched north to Lake Baringo, and after spending some months there and in the country to the west worked his way back to the Eldoma Ravine. As a result of these journeys, he wrote a book entitled, *Sports and Travel*. He married, April 19, 1904, Agatha Lilian, second dau. of Mr. and Mrs. John Thynne.

HINE, Right Rev. John Edward, M.D., Lond., M.A., Oxford, Hon. D.D., Oxford, M.R.C.S., Eng., Bishop of Zanzibar, of Mkimazini, Zanzibar; was born in England, April 10, 1857. He was educated at the University College School and Hospital, London, and Oxford University. He was formerly Resident Medical Officer at the Radcliffe Infirmary, Oxford. After his ordination he became Curate of Richmond, Surrey, and since 1899 has been a Missionary in Central Africa, first in Nyassaland and afterwards in the Yao Country. He was appointed Bishop of Likoma, Nyassa, in 1896, and Bishop of Zanzibar in 1901.

HINKS, Arthur Robert, M.A., of the Observatory, Cambridge, was born in London, May 26, 1873. He was educated at Trinity Coll., Cambs.; appointed Asst. Astronomer at Cambridge Observatory in 1895, and became Chief Asst. in 1903. Since 1902 he has acted as Secy. of Section A of the British Association, and as a Member of the Council of the Royal Astronomical Society from 1903. He accompanied the British Association on their visit to S. Africa in 1905, delivering the evening lecture at Bloemfontein on 'The Milky Way and the Clouds of Magellan'. He married, in 1899, Lily, dau. of Jonathan Packman, M.I.C.E., of Croydon.

HIPWELL, Brev. Col. Alfred George, C.B. M.A., care of Sir C. R. McGrigor, Bart., and Co., 25,

Charles St., St. James' Sq., S.W., was born in Dublin, March 16, 1863, and is the only son of the late George B. Hipwell. He was educated at Trinity Coll., Dublin; was called to the Bar at the Middle Temple in 1883, and joined the Army Service Corps in 1873; was D.A.A.G. of the late Thames Dist. 1895-8; served in the S.A. War, 1899-1902 (mentioned in despatches, Queen's medal with clasp, King's medal and two clasps, C.B.). He was Col. on the Staff as Director of Supplies, 1902-4. He married, Nov. 24, 1886, Annie, only dau. of the Rev. W. R. C. Cockill.

HIRSCHLER, Isidore Henry, 61, Queensborough Terrace, Lancaster Gate, London, W., and of Bulawayo, Rhodesia, and of the Badminton Club, was born at Vienna, Nov. 15, 1855, and was educated in that city. He went to S.A. in the eighties for the purpose of representing English and French capital invested in the Rand. In 1893 he went to Rhodesia, and was elected the first Mayor of Bulawayo in 1897. He is Chairman of Empress (Rhodesia) Mines, Ltd., Sneddon Concessions, Ltd., South African Gold Dredging Co., and Wareleigh (Rhodesia) Development Co., and Director of African Concessions Synd. (see H. Wilson Fox), Manica Copper Development Co., Rhodesia, Ltd., Rice-Hamilton Explor. Synd., and Theta G.M. Co. He went through the Matabele Rebellion in 1896, and held the rank of Capt. in the Rhodesia Horse. He married, May 8, 1900, Miss Jeanne Goldstuecker, of Frankfort-on-Main.

HOARE, Edward Brodie, M.A., of Tenchleys, Limpsfield, and of the Carlton Club, was born in Surrey, Oct. 30, 1841, and is son of the Rev. Edward Hoare, Hon. Canon of Canterbnry. He was educated at Trinity Coll., Cambs., and is a partner in Messrs. Barretts, Hoares, and Co., bankers, also a Director of Lloyds Bank, the Standard Bank of S. Africa, and the Colonial Bank. He contested the Attercliffe division of Sheffield in 1886, and the central division of Bradford in 1887; was M.P. for Hampstead in 1888-1902. He married, July 1, 1868, Katherine, dau. of Sir William Edward Parry.

HOBART, Capt. Claud Vere Cavendish, D.S.O., F.R.G.S., of Shipley Place, Horsham, Sussex; West Cliffe Hall, Hythe, Hants; 19, Ashley Place, S.W.;

and of the Guards' and Travellers' Clubs; was born March 12, 1870; is only son of Sir Robert Henry Hobart, K.C.V.O., C.B., and Julia, eldest dau. of the 1st Baron Kesteven; great grandson of John, 3rd Earl of Buckinghamshire; and a descendant of John Hampden, the Patriot. He was educated at Eton and Sandhurst; joined Grenadier Guards in 1890; served as a Military Officer in the Uganda Protectorate, 1897-99; took part in the operations against the Waganda rebels in the province of Buddu under Col. Ternan in July and Aug., 1897, being present at the engagement of Kabawoko and the action near Marengo; was left with three companies of Sudanese to maintain order in Budda and Koki on the withdrawal of the remainder of the troops for the Macdonald Expedition in Sept. of that year, and had shortly afterwards to take the field against a combined force of Waganda rebels and Wahima tribesmen, who made a raid from the adjoining native kingdom of Ankole. With the aid of some hastily collected local levies Lieut. Hobart and his Sudanese defeated the enemy in a decisive encounter at Nyendo, and subsequently pursued the rebels and their allies into the remoter fastnesses of Ankole. Whilst so engaged he traversed a quantity of hitherto unexplored territory lying to the eastward of Stanley's route in 1889, and discovered a lake in lat. 0.60 deg. S., and long. 31.10 deg. E., now known as Lake Hobart. On returning from Ankole he received intelligence of the mutiny of the Sudanese who had been sent to join Major Macdonald's expedition, and for many months had a difficult and anxious task in keeping his own troops to their allegiance. In this, however, he was successful, and his loyal Sudanese, who rejected all overtures of both mutineers and rebels, were subsequently rewarded by being sent to garrison the Nile Province, whence they had originally come. Lieut. Hobart, who had meanwhile mastered the Luganda language and taken over the Political Administration of Buddu and Koki, was next deputed to raise regular companies of Waganda troops, who proved in all respects equal, if not superior, to the Sudanese, as the Waganda rebels discovered to their cost, on once more endeavoring to try conclusions.

In 1899, peace having been finally restored throughout the Protectorate, Capt. Hobart returned to England. He had been several times mentioned in despatches, and had received the D.S.O. in recognition of his services. On the outbreak of hostilities in South Africa, he was dispatched to Port Elizabeth as Staff Officer on the Lines of Communications under Lt. Col. Fairholme, R.E. With the local rank of Major he assisted in reorganising the Volunteer Forces of Port Elizabeth, Grahamstown, and Uitenhage, and with these the Midland Line of Railway to Naauwpoort was held. Capt. Hobart then fell ill with enteric fever and had to be invalided home in 1902. He acted as a Gold Staff Officer at the Coronation, and was specially deputed to look after Apolo Kagwa, the Regent of Uganda, who came over to England for the occasion, and whom he accompanied and interpreted for when he had an audience of His Majesty. Capt. Hobart can speak Arabic, Swahili, and Luganda, besides several European languages; he is a keen rider, rifle shot, and takes great interest in horse breeding and agriculture. He was at one time an enthusiastic yachtsman, and was one of the founders of the Hythe Yacht Club on the Southampton Water. Whilst serving in Uganda he converted a war canoe into a sailing boat and made several voyages with her on the Victoria Nyanza to the no small astonishment of the natives. He married, Dec. 10, 1900, Violet Verve, 2nd dau. of the late John Wyhe, of West Cliff Hall, Hants.

HOBSON, George Andrew, M.Inst.C.E., of 28 Victoria Street, Westminster, S.W., Coverdale Lodge, Richmond, Surrey, and of the Constitutional Club, is a member of the firm of Sir Douglas Fox and Partners (see Sir Douglas Fox). He was born in Leeds, March 29, 1854, and belongs to an old Yorkshire family which has been settled in the dales of the North Riding for some five hundred years; was educated at King James's School, Knaresborough, and the Watt Institution, Edinburgh. He is the inventor of Hobson's patent flooring—a system of steel construction for the purpose of carrying heavy loads, of which it is estimated there are upwards of 100,000 tons now in use in bridges, piers, and warehouses in various parts of the world. In 1900, on the completion of the extension to London of the Great Central Railway, Mr. Hobson contributed to the proceedings of the Institution of Civil Engineers a paper on the Metropolitan Terminus of that line, and was awarded a Telford premium and gold medal. His chief work in the last fifteen years has been in the development of Rhodesia. The firm, in conjunction with Sir Charles Metcalfe (q.v.) have engineered over 2000 miles of railway and allied works in that country. To Mr. Hobson is chiefly due the design of the Victoria Falls bridge. As an expert on steel construction he has been much consulted by owners and architects for the internal frame work of theatres. Recently (in 1905) Mr. Hobson was commissioned to proceed to the Victoria Falls to investigate and report upon the hydrodynamic value of the cataract. He also made a detailed study of the Zambesi River immediately above and below the falls, with a view to the selection of the most suitable site for the Power House. He has expressed the opinion that the formation of the ground at the Falls is admirably fitted by Nature for the economical construction of hydroelectric works of enormous capacity. Though his work confines him almost entirely to London, he has found opportunities to travel through all the South African colonies and Mozambique, and through much of the territories of the United States, Canada, and Russia. He is a member of two of the Engineering Standard Committees, an occasional contributor to the technical Press, and author of the life of Sir James Falshaw, Bart., C.E., his maternal uncle. He married, April 13, 1882, Annie Jean, only dau. of Thomas Addyman, of Harrogate, and has an only daughter.

HOFMEYR, San Hendrik, of 'Avond Rust', Stephen Street, Cape Town, and of the City Club, Cape Town, was born in the capital of the Colony, July 4, 1845, his father, Jan Hendrik Hofmeyr, of Cape Town, having been the descendant of an ancestor of exactly the same name, who left Eppenburen to settle in the Cape Colony early in the eighteenth century. The subject of our sketch was educated at the S. African Coll., and began his career as a journalist on the staff of the *Volksvriend*, of which he afterwards became proprietor. In 1871 he purchased the *Zuid Afrikaan*, amalgamated the two papers, and thus became the controller of a very powerful Press organ. Seven years later he founded the Boeren Vereeniging (Farmers' Association), starting with purely local aims, mainly to combat the Excise, but eventually, in 1883, after an evidently impending rivalry, this

association joined forces with the Afrikander Bond, which at first had been supposed to be hostile to British rule. But Mr. Hofmeyr rapidly became the virtual controller of the Bond, and from that time it was not at any rate officially disloyal, though he has been suspected of a desire to constitute S.A. an independent Republic. Mr. Hofmeyr entered the Cape Legislative Assembly as member for Stellenbosch in 1879. He was for a short time a member of Sir Thomas Scanlen's Ministry without portfolio. He was offered the Premiership in 1884, but declined. In 1887 he was one of the Cape delegates to the first Colonial Conference in London and again at Ottawa in 1894. He was a member of the Customs Union Conferences at Cape Town in 1888, and at Bloemfontein in the following year. In 1890 he acted as H.M. Special Agent to Pretoria, to induce the Transvaal Govt. to sign the Swaziland Convention, his success in the matter at the time having been thought to have averted war. Though he had retired from active political life in 1894, he, at the time of the Raid, exercised considerable influence over Lord Rosmead, at that time High Commissioner.

He also endeavoured to act as arbiter during the crisis preceding the late war, and while retaining the nominal leadership of the Dutch Afrikander party, who are devoted to him and believe and trust him implicitly, he was at one time the hope of the Moderates and persona grata with the Colonial Office. He is chairman of the Afrikander Bond Committee on Elections, and on the occasion of Mr. Chamberlain's visit to South Africa he issued an appeal in favour of reconciliation between the English and Dutch after the War. He is president of various Cape Town and Stellenbosch cricket and football clubs. Mr. Hofmeyr married, Sept. 1, 1900, Johanna Hendriksz. of Somerset West.

HOLE, Hugh Marshall, B.A., of Bulawayo, and the Bulawayo and Salisbury Clubs, was born at Tiverton, Devon, May 16, 1865. He is son of Charles Marshall-Hole, of Tiverton, and grandson of the late Dr. Medhurst, pioneer missionary in China. He was educated at Blundell's Sch., and Balliol Coll., Oxon., where he graduated B.A., and took Honours in Final Sch. of Law in 1887. He joined the service of the B.S.A. Co. in April, 1890; was transferred to Mashonaland in 1891, and has served in various civil capacities in S. Rhodesia from that time. During the Matabele Rebellion of 1896 he served as Lieut. in the Rhodesia Horse (medal), and he also served as Capt. in the S. Rhodesia Volunteers during the late S.A. War (medal and clasp). In 1901 he was sent on a special mission to Arabia to report on and organise Arab labour for Rhodesian mines. He now occupies the position of Civil Commissioner, Bulawayo, and Government Representative in Matabeleland, and in 1903 and 1904 acted as Administrator of N.W. Rhodesia in the absence of Mr. R. T. Coryndon. He married, in 1890, Ethel, dau. of the late T. Rick man, of Poole, Dorset.

HOLLAND, Arthur Herbert, of Salisbury, Rhodesia, was born at Grahamstown, Oct. 11, 1873; is son of Ben. H. Holland, late Registrar of Deeds for Cape Colony; was educated at St. Andrew's Coll., Grahamstown, and joined the Cape Civil Service as Clerk, King Williamstown, in 1892; Queenstown, 1892; Acting Chief Clerk, Cathcart, 1893; returned to Queenstown, 1893; Treasury, 1893, and Prime Minister's Office, 1895. He transferred to Rhodesia Civil Service as a clerk in the Administrator's Office, Jan. 1, 1897; Private Secretary to his Honour, Sir William Milton, Jan. 1, 1900; acted as Clerk of Councils from July to Dec., 1904. He is now also Editor of the Rhodesia Civil Service List, and married, in 1901, Madeleine, youngest dau. of J. M. Orpen (q.v.).

HOLLAND, Frederick Catesby, of Palace Chambers, Westminster; Watchers, Haslemere; and of the St. Stephen's and South African Clubs; is third son of Rev. C. Holland, Prebendary of Chichester, and for thirty-five years Rector of Petworth. He was educated at Haileybury; has travelled in S.A., and on one occasion in Rhodesia shot a wounded lion which had already chased and knocked over Cecil Bisset. He was a Director of the St. Helen's Development Synd., Ltd., and is now associated with a few Transvaal Cos. He married, in 1881, Frances, dau. of Ed. Livesey, M.D.

HOLLAND, William S., LL.D., F.Z.S., of Pittsburg, Pennsylvania, U.S.A., and of the University and Union (Pittsburg), Cosmos (Washington), and Authors' (New York) Clubs,

was born near Kingston, Jamaica, Aug. 16, 1848, and is descended from John Holland, an early settler of N. Carolina. He graduated at Amherst Coll. and Princeton, holding the degrees A.B., A.M., Ph.D., D.D., Dc.D., and LL.D., of St. Andrews, Scotland (1905). He was on the active clergy list from 1874 to 1891; Chancellor of the Western University of Pennsylvania, 1891 1901; Director of the Carnegie Museum, Pittsburg, 1898; and is now Director of the Chamber of Commerce of Pittsburg (since 1894) Vice-Pres. and Chairman of the Executive Committee of the Carnegie Herd Fund Commission. He was Naturalist on the U.S. Eclipse Expedition to Japan in 1887; was in W. Africa in 1889, and is regarded as one of the leading zoologists and authorities upon the biological sciences in America. Dr. Holland has published over thirty papers upon the insect fauna of Africa, in which he has named and described over 800 species new to science, and over 200 papers on entomology, paleontology, and the natural sciences in general. He also discovered and set up reproductions of the skeleton of the Diplodocus in the British Museum and the Natural History Museum, S. Kensington. His recreations are fishing, shooting, mountaineering, and painting in oils and water colours. He married, in 1879, Carrie, dau. of John Moorhead, iron manufacturer and banker, of Pittsburg, Pa.

HOLLIS, Alfred Claud, F.R.C.I., of Mombasa, E. Africa, second son of Geo. Hollis, of the Inner Temple, was educated at Highgate, and St. Leonards, in Switzerland and Germany. He was appointed Asst. Collector, East Africa, Protectorate, in March, 1897; became Collector in June, 1900; Acting British Vice-Consul for German East Africa from Apr., 1900, to Feb., 1901; Acting Secy. to the Administration, East African Protectorate, from then until Apr., 1903, and Secy. to the Administration Apr., 1903. He published *The Masai; their Language and Folklore* (1905).

HONEY, Thomas, of 131, Maida Vale, London, W., and of the Constitutional Club, London was born at Portsmouth, and, though he is still comparatively young, he has been of many years identified with the Barnato group companies as the popular secretary of the Johannesburg Consolidated

Investment Co. (see S. B. Joel), being also on the London Committee of the Buffelsdoorn Estate, Consolidate Langlaagte, Ginsberg, Glencairn, Main Reef, New Primrose, New Rietfontein, New Spes Bona, New Unified Main Reef, and Roodepoort companies. Mr. Honey is also connected with some Rhodesian groups outside the aegis of the House of Barnato, being a director of the Tanganyika Concessions and Zambesia Exploring Co. (see Robert Williams), and of Clark's Consolidated, the Bulawayo Syndicate, and the Gwanda Mines, Ltd.

HOOD, Samuel S., of Lagos, W. Africa, started his career in the Gov. service at British Honduras; was transferred to the Gold Coast as Supervisor of Customs in 1894; was Asst. Collector at Sierra Leone in 1901; became Asst. Comptroller of Customs of the Gold Coast Colony later in 1901, and in 1904 was appointed Collector of Customs at Lagos.

HOPCRAFT, S. D., spent five months in the Civil Supply Office at Kimberley, whence be was transferred to Johannesburg. In 1902 he was appointed Chief Director of Supplies for the O.R.C.

HOPKINSON, Dr. Emilius, D.S.O., L.R.C.P., M.R.C.S., of 45, Sussex Sq., Brighton, was born in 1869. He served in the S. African War as Medical Officer with the Imperial Yeomanry. In 1905 he was appointed a Medical Officer in the Gambia.

HOPKINSON, Capt. S. F., was formerly in the 6th Dragoon Guards, and was appointed Asst. Superintendent of Civil Police, Northern Nigeria, in 1906.

HOPWOOD, Sir Francis John Stephens, K.C.B., C.M.G., of 13, Hornton Street, Kensington, W., and of the Reform and Wellington Clubs, was born in 1860, and is son of J. T. Hopwood, of Lincoln's Inn. Since 1891 he has been Permanent Secretary to the Board of Trade. He was a member of the Royal Commission on London Traffic, and acted as Hon. Secretary to the Chairman of the Select Committee of the House of Commons to inquire into the Jameson Raid. In 1906 he was a member of the S. African Committee of Inquiry. He married

first, Alice (died in 1888), dau. of Capt. Smith-Neill, R.A., and secondly, in 1892, Florence, dau., of Lieut. Gen. S. Black, C.S.I., C.I.E.

HORNBY, Major Montagu Leyland, D.S.O., of the Army and Navy Club, was born in 1870, and entered the Army in 1889; took part in the Waziristan Expedition in 1894-5 as Orderly Officer to the Gen. Officer Commanding the Waziristan Delimitation Escort (despatches, medal with clasp, and D.S.O.); the Tirah Expedition in 1897-8; operations in the Barra Valley (medal with two clasps); the operations in British East Africa in 1898 against Ogaden Somalis, with the 1st Uganda Rifles (medal with clasp); operations in Uganda in 1898-9 against Kabarega (clasp); and in the Nandi Expedition in 1900 (despatches). He married, in 1902, Harriet, dau. of Major C. Winder.

HOSKEN, William, M.L.C., of 'Entabene', Berea, Johannesburg, and of the National Liberal and Rand Clubs, was born at Hayle, Cornwall, July 6, 1851, and is the son of Richard and Caroline Hosken. He was educated at Hayle and had his commercial training with Wm. Hosken and Son, a well-known firm in Cornwall, now merged in Hosken, Trevithick, and Polkinghorn, Ltd. He went to S.A. early in 1874; became a digger at Pilgrim's Rest; subsequently went to Natal, and was engaged in merchant business there until 1889; then went to Johannesburg as Managing Director of the City and Suburban, Heriot, Nigel, and other Natal directed mines; became Foundation Executive Committee Member of the Chamber of Mines; established the merchant business of Wm. Hosken and Co., and joined the Chamber of Commerce, having been six times elected Pres. of that Chamber; is Lloyd's Agent for Johannesburg and Chairman of the Committee of Management of the British S.A. Explosives Co., Ltd. He has for years taken a large interest in politics. He assisted in establishing the National Union in 1892, and was elected to the Executive Committee; was member of the Reform Committee in 1896, and sentenced to two years' imprisonment and fined, as in the case of the other prisoners. He was Chairman of the mass meetings and political demonstrations in 1899, and was unanimously elected Pres. of the Uitlander Council formed that year. He was also Chairman of Committee which in 1899 raised Thorneycroft's and Bethune's Mounted Infantry, and subsequently raised the Imperial Light Infantry. All these corps were raised without expense to the Govt. He has served on various Govt. Commissions during and since the war; was a Transvaal delegate at the Bloemfontein Customs Union Conference in March, 1903, and became a member of the Legislative Council which commenced its sitting at Pretoria in May, 1903. In 1904 he was elected a member of the Inter-Colonial Council, and was re-elected in 1905. He is President of the Associated Chambers of Commerce of South Africa. In the Transvaal and Inter-Colonial Councils he is a vigorous critic of Government finance, and succeeded at the last Session of the Inter-Colonial Council in carrying through a scheme for light railways to develop agricultural districts, in place of the Government proposal to build heavy standard gauge lines. Mr. Hosken had the locally unenviable distinction of being the only non-official member of the Council in favour of granting the municipal franchise to coloured persons. He married, Oct. 16, 1877, Miss Clara James, of Maritzburg.

HOTSON, S. H., B.A. (Oxon.), of Thaba Nchu, O.R.C., was admitted to practise as a solicitor in England iii 1898. He served at Lieut. with the Volunteer Co. of the Norfolk Regt. in the South African War in 1901-2 (Queen's medal and five clasps), and was appointed Asst. Resident Magistrate at Thaba Nchu in 1904.

HOWARD, Esme William, M.V.O., Officer of the Italian Order of St. Maurice; H.M. Consul General for Crete, of Canea, Crete, Ravenstone, Keswick, Cumberland, and of the Travellers' Club, was born at Greystoke Castle, Penrith, Sept. 15, 1863, and is son of the late Henry Howard, of Greystoke. He was educated at Harrow, and passed a competitive examination for Diplomatic Service in 1885; acted as Private Secretary to the Lord Lieut. of Ireland in 1885-6, subsequently being appointed Attaché to the Embassy at Home. In 1887 he was promoted to be third Secy., and was transferred to the Embassy at Berlin in 1888. He resigned in 1892; was Asst. Private Secy. to the Earl of Kimberley, Secy. of State for Foreign Affairs in 1894-5. During 1900 he served in the S. African War with the Imperial Yeomanry (medal with four clasps), and received the Coronation medal in 1902. He became Hon.

Second Secy. to the Embassy at Rome in 1903, and has held his present position since then. He married, Nov. 17, 1898, Lady Isabella, dau. of Prince Giustiniani-Bandini, Earl of Newburgh.

HOWARD, Maj. Gen. Sir Francis, K.C.B. (1900), C.M.G. (1899), Commander of the Star of Romania (1892), Commander of the Bavarian Order of Michael; of Godwyn, Painswick, Glos., and of the Army and Navy Club, was born at Berlin, March 26, 1848; is 2nd son of the late Sir H. F. Howard, G.C.B., and Baroness M. E. van der Schulenburg, and was educated privately and at the R.M.C., Sandhurst. He joined the Rifle Brigade in 1866, since which he has seen much active service, including the Jowaki Expedition in 1878 (medal and clasp), Afghan War, Bazaar Valley and Lughman Expeditions, 1878-9 (medal and clasp for Ali Musjid); operations in Upper Burma, 1887-89 (despatches, brev. of Lieut. Col. for Burma); commanded the 2nd Batt. Rifle Brigade, 1894-98; A.D.C. to the Queen, 1895; C.B. and Jubilee decorations, 1897; Sudan Campaign, 1898 (despatches, two medals and clasp for Omdurman, and Distinguished Service Reward); saw active service in Crete in 1898; half-pay in Dec., 1898; commanded the 8th Brigade in the South African War, 1899-1900, including the defence of Ladysmith (despatches, medal and four clasps); Coronation medal and A.D.C. to the King, 1901; Maj. Gen. and Inspector-Gen. of Recruiting at the War Office, 1903; commanded the N.W. District in 1904; and in 1905 became Acting General Officer Commanding-in-Chief of the Welsh and Midland command. Sir Francis married, in 1895, Gertrude, dau. of Hugh Conyngham Boyd.

HOWARD, John William, F.R.C.I., of Durban, Natal; was born at Eaton Socon in 1867, and was educated privately and at the Royal Univ., Ireland. He went to S.A. for the Argus Co. in 1889, as editor of the weekly edition of the *Cape Argus*. Early in 1893 he travelled to Fort Salisbury, Mashonaland, and took the first printing plant into Rhodesia. In 1894 he went to Bulawayo, and founded the *Bulawayo Chronicle*. He is now on the staff of the *Natal Mercury*, Durban. During the Matabele rising (1896) he acted as Correspondent for Reuter's Agency, *Pall Mall Gazette*, and Dalzell's Agency. He holds the medal as war correspondent for the Matabele War (1896). He was one of the founders of the first Masonic lodges in Mashonaland and in Matabeleland. He has been married twice: first, in 1895, to Evelyn Lydia, only dau. of the late Mr. Glendinnen, of Stafford, England; and second, to Agnes, eldest dau. of the late Geo. Pike Hannaford, of Newton Abbot, Devon.

HOWICK, Lord, was born, Dec. 14, 1879, and is the only son and heir of the fourth Earl Grey (q.v.). Lord Howick left Cambridge with a Bachelor's hood in 1901; entered the 1st Life Guards, and subsequently joined Lord Milner's Staff in South Africa. He married, in 1906, Lady Mabel Laura Georgiana Palmer, dau. of Lord and Lady Selborne, and granddau. of the late Marquis of Salisbury.

HULETT, Hon. Sir James Leigh, M.L.A., J.P., Knt. Bachelor, of Kearnsey, Victoria County, Natal; Blenheim Place, Pietermaritzburg; the Manor House, Mentone Road, Durban, and of the Durban and Victoria (P.M.B.) Clubs, was born at Sheffield, Yorks, May 17, 1838, and was educated at Gillingham House Sch., in Kent. He arrived in Natal in 1857, and in the following year decided to settle in Victoria County as a planter. He gave his principal attention to the cultivation of coffee until its complete failure was established, and he then went in for tea planting, and after many years floated the estates, under the style of J. L. Hulett and Son, Ltd., of which he has since been Managing Director. Sir James had not been in the Colony long before he turned his attention to politics, entering the Legislative Council as member for Victoria County in 1883. Meanwhile, in 1888, he was given a seat on the Executive Council, which he held until responsible government was granted in 1893. Although he led the Opposition to this from 1890 to 1893, he was returned as M.L.A. at the first general election for Victoria County. He held the portfolio of Native Affairs in Sir Henry Binns' Cabinet, and at Sir Henry's death was elected Speaker of the Assembly. In 1902, however, he resigned this in order to lead the Opposition to Sir Albert Hime's Ministry, which he succeeded in overthrowing in the following year. Thereupon, Sir James was called upon to form a fresh Administration, but he requested the Governor to send for Mr. (now Sir George) Sutton. Sir James, who was knighted on the occasion of King Edward's Coronation, was a delegate to the Bloemfontein Conference in 1903; is a Fellow of the Royal Colonial Inst., and of the Royal Geographical Society of Australia. He married, in 1860, Mary Ann, only dau. of B. Balcomb, of Umhlali, Natal.

HULL, Henry Charles, M.L.C., was born at Caledon, C.C., on Nov. 21, 1860. He went to Kimberley in 1879; was in the Civil Service for a short period, and then became admitted and practised there as a solicitor until 1889, when he removed to Johannesburg. He was one of the members of the Reform Committee, and with his comrades was sentenced to two years' imprisonment, to pay a fine of £2,000, and in default of payment to a further year's imprisonment, and to banishment for three years. After undergoing imprisonment for a short period, the sentence was commuted to the payment of the fine. He assisted Lord Milner at the Bloemfontein Conference, and shortly before the war took a prominent part in the Franchise agitation in Johannesburg. During the war he assisted in recruiting the S.A. Light Horse, Marshall's Horse, and the Eastern Province Horse, and took part in the column which under Gen. Brabant relieved Wepener. He was appointed one of the unofficial members of the Legislative Council of the Transvaal in May, 1903, and was one of the small minority of four who opposed Sir Geo. Farrar (q.v.) in his motion in the Council to import Chinese or other alien labour.

HULLEY, Thomas Benjamin, J.P., of Umtali, Rhodesia, and of the Umtali and Salisbury Sporting Clubs, is the son of Edward and Mary Hulley, and grandson of Richard Hulley, one of the British settlers of 1820. He was born May 15, 1860, at Somerset East, CM., and was educated at Grey Coll., Bloemfontein, holding the Free State Bursary for two years. In 1881 he served with the Cradock Volunteer Rifles, and during this period he saw active service in Basutoland, receiving medal and clasp. During a portion of this time he was ostrich farming in C.C. In 1883 he commenced trading in East Griqualand, and continued until 1886, when he left for the Barberton Gold Fields and he remained with the Sheba Gold Mining Co. till 1895. In April of that year he joined the B.S.A. Co.

as Native Commissioner, and has held this office at Mazoe, Lomagunda, Melsetter, again at Umtali, Inyanga, and once more at Umtali. From Nov., 1902, to Feb., 1903, he acted as Chief Native Commissioner for Mashonaland, and has on several occasions acted as magistrate for the Umtali District. He was appointed Asst. Magistrate for Umtali and J.P. for Southern Rhodesia in 1900. Mr. Hulley saw active service again as Capt. of the Umtali Volunteers in the Mashonaland Rebellion in 1896. He represented the district of Umtali at the funeral of the late Hon. Cecil Rhodes in the Matopos. He was detailed for duty with the Anglo Portuguese Boundary Commission in 1896, and on war breaking out in the Transvaal he volunteered for service. He married, Oct. 13, 1897, Georgina, third dau. of Edward Coleman.

HUNEBERG, Joseph, of the Public Works Department, Transvaal, joined the Cape Mil. Forces in 1878; acted as Capt. in command of the Northern Border Horse in 1879, and served in the hostilities in Cape Colony, Griqualand West, Bechuanaland, Koranaland, Namaqualand, and in the Transvaal between 1878-9; the first Boer War in 1881, and the S. African War in 1899-1902 (two medals and seven clasps). In 1879 he was Landdrost Clerk at Standerton, and held a similar position at Pretoria in 1880, and at Waterberg in 1880-1. He was transferred to the Natal Civil Service Customs Dept. in 1881, but owing to an engagement in the Colonial Secretary's Office in Natal he did not take up his duties until 1882; was employed in the Natal Treasury in 1883, became second Clerk in the Treasury in 1884, and was Acting Chief Clerk and Accountant there in 1886 and 1889. In 1890 he held a similar appointment in the Colonial Engineer's Department; acted as Chief Accountant in the Public Works Dept. in 1896, and was one of the Committee to draft new regulations for the keeping of accounts in the Natal Service in 1898. He became Chief Clerk and Accountant in the Transvaal Public Works Department in Sept., 1901, and in the following year he was nominated Secretary to the Central Judicial Commission, appointed under Article 10 of the Terms of Surrender.

HUNT, Arthur Surridge, D.Litt., M.A., Ph.D., Königsberg; of Queen's Coll., Oxford, Romford Hall, Essex, and of Cairo; was born, March 1, 1871, and is son of the late Alfred H. Hunt, of Romford, Essex. He was educated at Eastbourne Coll., and Queen's Call., Oxford (Aubrey Moore student, 1894, Senior Demy of Magdalen Coll., 1896-1900, Fellow of Lincoln Coll., 1901). In 1895 he made some researches in Spanish libraries, and first went to Egypt in 1896. Since then he has been regularly engaged in the discovery and publication of Greek papyri from that source. He is the author (with B. P. Grenfell, q.v.) of *New Classical Fragments and other Papyri, Logia Jesu, Sayings of Our Lord, Menander's Georgos, The Oxyrhynchus Papyri*, vols. i.-iv., *The Amherst Papyri* (Greek), vols. i. and ii., *Payûm Towns and their Papyri, The Tebtunis Papyri*, vol. i., *Catalogue General du Musée du Caire, Greek Papyri*, and *New Sayings of Jesus*. Recreations: Shooting, lawn tennis, and photography. Unmarried.

HUNTER, Lieut. Gen. Sir Archibald, K.C.B., D.S.O., of Bombay, and of the United Service and Naval and Military Clubs; was born in 1856, and is son of the late Archibald Hunter. He was educated at Sandhurst, and joined the King's Own Lancaster Regt. in 1874, the record of his promotion having been phenomenal—Sub-Lieutenant 1874, Lieutenant 1874, Captain 1882, Major 1885, Lieut. Col. 1889, Col. 1894, Major-Gen. 1896, Lieut. Gen. 1900, and full General 1905. Gen. Hunter has fought with Lord Kitchener in many campaigns, and was accounted one of his most trusted officers. His active service includes the Sudan Expedition of 1884-5, when he served in the Egyptian Army (despatches, medal, and clasp, bronze star, and 4th Class Osmanieh). He again fought in the Sudan in 1885-6-9, taking part in the actions at Giniss, where he was severely wounded, Arguin and Toski, where he was again wounded (D.S.O., 3rd Class Medjidie, despatches); the Dongola Expedition in 1896, in command of the Egyptian Infantry Div. (Egyptian medal, two clasps); the Nile Expeditions of 1897-8, in command of columns, being present at the action of Abu Hamed, the occupation of Berber, and the battles of Atbara and Khartoum, for which services he was thanked by both Houses of Parliament, and received the K.C.B., and two clasps. Sir Archibald was with the besieged forces in Ladysmith during the S. African War in 1899-1900, in connection with which he was the hero of one of the most sensational episodes of the war—the raid on Gun Hill from Ladysmith, which ended in the blowing up of the damaging gun 'the Stinker'. He only obtained Sir George White's halfhearted consent to the venture after a long argument, and went out in inky darkness with 200 men. As the little force stole along a wild fire broke out from above. General Hunter realised that the moment had come when success and failure were balanced on a razor's edge. He seized a trumpet, and probably for the first time in the history of the British Army a general sounded the 'Cease fire'. The firing dropped. The hill was rushed, and Sir Archibald Hunter returned to Ladysmith, his men carrying the breech of the obnoxious gun slung on a pole. For this and other distinguished services he was promoted Lieut. Gen., and received the Queen's medal with four clasps. In 1905 he was given the command of the Madras Army. Unmarried.

HUNTER, Charles Hastings, I.S.O., of Holmhurst, Reigate, Surrey, and of the Sports and Imperial Colonies Clubs, is the son of Col. Charles Hunter, Royal (Bengal) Artillery. He was born at Allahabad, India, Sept. 7, 1864, and joined the Colonial Civil Service in Nov., 1883; served in various capacities in St. Lucia and Grenada, West Indies, from that time until Oct., 1891; in that year he was transferred to the Gold Coast Service. In Nov., 1896, he was appointed Asst. Colonial Secy. of Sierra Leone and a J.P. for that Colony. In 1897 he was retransferred on promotion in a similar capacity to the Gold Coast, where he held numerous appointments, including those of Colonial Secy. and Deputy Governor, and member of the Executive and Legislative Councils of the Colony. For his services in connection with the Ashanti Expedition of 1900 he was, mentioned in despatches, and appointed a Companion of the I.S.O. (May, 1903). He was appointed Chief Asst. Colonial Secy. for the Gold Coast Colony, Oct., 1901.

HUNTER, Sir David, K.C.M.G. (1901), C.M.G. (1898), of Colinton, Durban, Natal, and of the Durban Club is the son of David Hunter, of Broxburn, Linlithgowshire, Scotland. He was born, Jan. 24 1841, at Broxburn, and was educated at the Parish and Free Church Schs., Kirkliston,

Linlithgowshire. He entered the service of the North British Railway Co., Edinburgh, as an apprentice in the Accountants' Dept., 1853 and served successively in the Stores, General Superintendent's, and General Manager's Depts. till 1879, when he was appointed by the Secy. of State for the Colonies to the office of General Manager of Natal Govt. Railways at their inception. In 1881 and 1882 his services to the military authorities during the Boer War were noticed in despatches by Gen. Sir Evelyn Wood, and he received the thanks of the Secy. of State. In the same year he was appointed by the Governor a Commissioner of the Natal Harbour Board. In 1883 he was elected first President of the Natal Caledonian Society. In 1890 he was created a member of the Executive Council of the Colony under Royal Sign Manual, and was a member of the Harrismith Hallway Conference. In 1892-3-4 he was a delegate of the Natal Govt. to the Govt. of the (late) S.A.R. on Railway Extension to Johannesburg, which ultimately was arranged under agreement, the construction of the line being carried out by Natal in 1894-5, he representing the Govt. as contractor. He represented Natal in various conferences on Railway and Harbour questions at Cape Town, Pretoria, East London, Johannesburg, and Bloemfontein. He originated and was the first Chairman of the S.A. Railway Officers' Conference, Pietermaritzburg, 1897. Elected Chairman of Port Advisory Board, 1898, and was a member of Coal Industry Commission, appointed by Govt. in same year. He was first Pres. of Durban Church Council, 1899; was elected Chairman of Colonial Reception Committee in connection with Royal visit to Natal, 1901. Sir David's services during the Boer War (1899-1902) were mentioned in the despatches by Genls. Sir George White, Sir Redvers Buller, Field Marshal Lord Roberts, and Lord Kitchener. He was Chairman of the S.A. Congregational Union in 1903, and Chairman of the Technical Education Commission, 1904-5. He married, Oct. 5, 1865, Margaret Gordon Laing, second dau. of Robert Laing, of Mossy Mill. Colinton, near Edinburgh.

HUSSEY-WALSH, Major William, of Indian House, Kenilworth, Cape Town; 81, Onslow Gardens, S.W.; and of the Naval and Military Club, was born, Dec. 16, 1863, at Monkstown, Co.

Dublin. He was educated at Sandhurst, and joined the Cheshire Regt in 1884. He served in the Burmese Expedition in 1888, and in the Chin-Lushai Expedition in 1889 as Regimental Officer, also as correspondent of the *Illustrated London News*. He was appointed to the Burma Intelligence Branch in 1890 serving on the Chinese Boundary in the Kachin Expedition in the same year. In 1895 he served as Adjutant in the 1st V.B. Essex Regiment, from which he retired in 1899, subsequently rejoining when the war broke out in South Africa, and serving with then during embodiment. He joined the S.A. Constabulary in 1901 as Troop Commander, being promoted to District Commandant, Middelburg, on conclusion of the war, subsequently being transferred to the Headquarter Staff of the S.A.C. as Recruiting Staff Officer, which position he still holds. Recreations, principally aquatic sports. He married, Feb. 14, 1902, Miss Mary Evered.

HUTCHINS, David Ernest, J.P. for Cape Colony, of Cape Town, is son of the late David Hutchins, of Albert Square, London, and was born Sept. 22, 1850. He passed fifth out of eighty-five candidates for the Indian Forest Service in 1869; was three years at the School of Forests, Nancy, France, and had special course of forestry instruction in Scotland; Assistant Conservator of Forests, India, third grade, 1872; second grade, 1875; first grade, 1878; selected for special duty with the Inspector-Gen. of Forests, and appointed Deputy Conservator of Forests, second grade, 1882; transferred temporarily from India to Cape Colony, June, 1883; awarded a diploma at the International Forestry Exhibition, Edinburgh, 1884; Conservator of Forests, Eastern Division, 1886; Knysna, 1888; selected to visit and report on forests of West Virginia, 1889; accompanied Cooper's Hill students on official tour through South German forests, 1890; Conservator of Forests, Western Division, and Consulting Forest Officer at Headquarters, 1892. In 1889 passed nine weeks at Kew, and was awarded silver medal of Society of Arts for paper on *National Forestry in England*.

He transferred from the Indian to the Cape Forest Department in June, 1883, and has served in his present appointment as Conservator of Forests, Cape Town, since March, 1892. Since 1884, but especially during the last ten years, the work of the Cape Forest Department has grown at a rapid rate. The indigenous forest has been rescued from destruction, demarcated, and administered on the scientific system of forestry followed in France and Germany. The Cape Legislature has passed two Forest Acts to protect the forests. Plantations have been formed of the best exotic timbers drawn chiefly from Australia, the Mediterranean, and California. The measured growth of timber in these plantations is already equal to about one third of all the timber now imported to Cape Colony. These timber plantations in 1905 covered an area of 18,000 acres. There were besides about 4,000 acres of Morram grass and wattles formed for the purpose of arresting sand drifts. Altogether, Cape Colony has spent over £1,000,000 on forestry. This expenditure has been incurred mainly with the object of producing in the Colony the timber now imported at great expense from abroad. It is estimated that the timber bill of Cape Colony amounts, on an average, to £500,000 yearly, and of all South Africa to 14 million pounds sterling yearly. The Cape Forest Department now plants ten million trees yearly in the Govt. forests, and distributes half a million trees yearly to farmers and others, at cost price, to encourage tree planting. Forestry has an important climatic influence, and for many years Mr. Hutchins has made Meteorology his pastime. In 1888 he published a small work, entitled *Cycles of Drought and Good Seasons in South Africa*. Surmising that there might be a connection between the weather of the northern and southern extremities of the Southeast Trade region, he was led to believe in a correspondence between the phases of summer rainfall in South Africa and the Indian monsoon rains. Acting on this belief, in April, 1896, he addressed a warning to the Indian authorities, which was verified, only too sadly, in the subsequent famine of that year. Since then, at the repeated request of the Indian Govt., he has each year sent data on the weather conditions prevailing in South Africa, these data being used in framing the yearly monsoon forecast issued early in June. The relation between the South African summer rains and the Indian monsoon rains was worked out in a paper by Sir J. Eliot read at the meeting of the British Association in 1904. (See also *Nature*, of Aug. 25, 1904). He is the author of the following papers on Forestry and Meteorology: *Cycles of Drought and Good Seasons in South Africa, 1888*; *Journal of a Forest Tour*, 1890; 'Tree planting for Farmers', *Agriculturists' Almanac*, 1890; 'Rainfall of South Africa', *Cape Agric. Journal*, Dec., 1897; 'Agricultural Weather Forecasts in England and in South Africa', *Cape Agric. Jour.*, Feb. and March, 1898; 'National Forests (Cape Colony)', *Cape Agric. Jour.*, Oct., 1898; *Forestry in the British Isles*, 1900; 'A Chat on Tree planting with Farmers', *Agriculturists' Yearbook*, 1900; 'Misuse of Coal and the Use of Forests', *Nature*, reprinted in *Cape Agric. Jour.*, Sept., 1902; 'Some Aspects of South African Forestry', *S.A. Assoc. for the Advancement of Science*, April, 1903; *Transvaal Forest Report*, 1903; *Forestry in Rhodesia*, report to the Rhodes' Trustees, 1903; *The Clusterpine at Genadendal*, 1904; 'Indigenous Timbers of the Cape', *Cape Agric. Jour.*, Feb., 1904, and 'Extratropical Forestry', now appearing in the *Cape Agricultural Journal*. He married, in 1891, Violet Beatrice, dau. of the late Fredk. Jo. Walker, F.R.G.S., of Bath.

HUTCHINSON, Arthur, M.A., Camb., Ph.D., Würzburg; of 3, Belvoir Terrace, Cambridge, and the Royal Societies' Club, was born in London, July 6, 1866, and was educated at Clifton Coll., Christ's Coll., Camb., and at Würzburg, and is a Fellow of Pembroke Coll., Camb., Demonstrator of Mineralogy, and Asst. Curator of the Mineralogical Museum at Cambridge. Dr. Hutchinson has published papers on chemical and mineralogical subjects in various scientific periodicals. He married Miss E. D. Shipley, in 1901.

HUTCHINSON, Capt. Elliot St. Maurice, M.L.C., of Bulawayo; the Redwoods, Johannesburg (P.O. Box, 6434); and the Bulawayo, Rhodesia, and Junior Constitutional Clubs; son of Bury Victor Hutchinson, Solicitor; was born in England; educated at King's Coll. Sch., London, and spent the early part of his life in the redwoods of California and on the plains as a cowboy. Returning to England he became a solicitor and member of the firm of Hutchinson and Sons, Lincoln's Inn Fields. He went to S.A. in 1896 during the Matabele rebellion, and was admitted as a solicitor in Rhodesia, where he practised until the war, when he joined the Rhodesian Frontier Force,

serving as Lieut. in the Rhodesian Volunteers. He was severely wounded at the commencement at Tuli; was sent home as one of the delegates to interview Mr. Chamberlain, on behalf of the S.A. Vigilance Assoc., in connection with the peace terms. On returning to S.A. he took command of G squad of 2nd Kitchener's Fighting Scouts, and saw much fighting with Col. Wilson's column in the N. Transvaal and O.R.C., being mentioned in despatches by Lord Kitchener for conspicuous gallantry at Blaauwkrantz, O.R.C. He was on the Staff and Special Intelligence at Pretoria at the close of the war, when he resumed his practice as a solicitor in the firm of Hutchinson, Sons, and Russell, of Johannesburg and London. Capt. Hutchinson is the author of *Two Years a Cowboy*, which is an account of his early life. He is unmarried.

HUTCHINSON, M., of 14, Rue Taitbout, Paris, is editor of the *Revue Sud Africaine*, a paper dealing with South African matters, which was established about the year 1894.

INNES, Sir James Rose, K.C.M.G., B.A., LL.B., of Park Street, Pretoria; and of the Reform (London), Civil Service and City (C.T.), the Pretoria and Athenaeum (Johannesburg) Clubs, was born in Grahamstown, Jan. 8, 1855. He is son of James Rose Innes, C.M.G., late Under Secy. for Native Affairs for the C.C., and a nephew by marriage of Sir Gordon Sprigg. He was educated at Bedford and at the Gill Coll., Somerset East, and graduated B.A. and LL.B. at the Cape University. Sir James was admitted an advocate of the Supreme Court, Cape Town, in 1878. He sat in the Cape House of Assembly from 1884 as member for Victoria East, and at the General Election in 1888 was elected for the Cape Division, being re-elected in 1894, and retaining his seat until 1902. He was made Q.C. in 1889; was Attorney-Gen. in the first Rhodes Ministry, which he resigned in 1893. He was retained by the Imperial Govt. on behalf of the British, American, and Belgian Reform prisoners, tried for high treason against the S.A.R., but owing to a slight technical objection he was not permitted to address the Court. He was allowed, however, to sit at counsel's table and to advise the barristers defending the prisoners. After the latter were imprisoned Mr. Innes (as he then was) remained in

Pretoria with Mr. (now Sir Richard) Solomon, endeavouriug to obtain some amelioration of their conditions and mitigation of their sentences. He was Attorney-Gen. in the Sprigg Ministry, June, 1900, resigning Feb., 1902, and in the following month he was appointed Chief Justice of the Transvaal Colony under the British Administration, winning the confidence of British and Afrikander alike. He married, Oct. 18, 1881, Jessie, youngest dau. of the late William Dods Pringle, of Lynedoch, Glen Lynden, Bedford District, C.C.

INNES, Robert Thornburn Ayton, of the Observatory, Johannesburg, was born in Edinburgh Nov. 10, 1861. He was formerly Secy. of the Royal Observatory of the Cape of Good Hope, and is now Director of the Transvaal Meteorological Department. He is the author of *Sudden Double Stars* and other scientific papers.

INSKIPP, Frank Warren, of Salisbury, Rhodesia, and of the Salisbury Club, was born in London Nov. 30, 1867; is son of Jas. Inskipp, of Bournemouth; was educated privately, and was for five years in the service of the Union Steamship Co. Going to Mashonaland in 1895 he entered the Surveyor General's Dept., becoming Secy. to Surveyor General in 1898; Secy. to Survey Dept. in 1901, and Secy. to Dept. of Lands for S. Rhodesia Dec. 1, 1903. He married, in 1901, Maud Evelyn, daughter of the late Wm. Pollett, of Horndon, Essex.

IRMANOFF, Miss Warwara, is a British subject, of Russian descent, having been born and educated at the Cape. Her musical abilities showed themselves at an early age, and before her 11th birthday she had announced her intention of devoting herself to the violin-cello. She studied under Herr Gustav Windisch, and under his tuition made rapid progress, as is shown by her record at the Cape of Good Hope University, where she was awarded the higher honours certificates, two advanced honours certificates, and the bursary of the Univ. Besides her skill as an executant, Miss Irmanoff has given evidence of considerable ability in other directions. She has composed songs of considerable merit, and is also an artist.

IRVINE, James, F.R.G.S., of 34, Castle St. Liverpool, was born Feb. 16, 1835. Early in 1858 he went to the West Coast of Africa, since which date he has been associated with various W. African enterprises, two of which have since gone into liquidation. He is now a director of the Anona Mining and Mahogany Co., Ltd., and the Fanashanti Gold Fields, Ltd. He is also Vice Chairman of the Liverpool Geographical Soc. He married, first, a Miss Elizabeth Hickson, and, secondly, Miss Catherine Emma Strong.

ISEMONGER, Francis Maxwell, F.R.C.I., of Masaka, Buddu, Uganda, and of the Imperial Colonies Club, was born at Thou, Switzerland, July 5, 1876; is grandson of Sir Peter Benson Maxwell, and son of the late E. E. Isemonger, Treasurer and Auditor Gen. of the Straits Settlements Civil Service. He was educated at Reading Sch., and, after a couple of years as a schoolmaster at the English Coll. at Bruges, was appointed a cadet in the British North Borneo Service in 1898, serving subsequently as district officer in various centres. He resigned that service in 1904, and became in Aug. of that year Asst. Collector in the Uganda Protectorate: Acting Asst. Secy. Oct., 1904, and acting Collector for the Buddu Dist. in May, 1905. Unmarried.

JA JA, King Frederick S., of Opobo, Nigeria is the son of the late King Ja Ja. He was educated at Glasgow, and his son, Prince Eugene S. Ja Ja, is also receiving his education in the west of Scotland. A pedestal and a statue of the late King were shipped from Glasgow in May, 1906, to be erected in Africa.

JABAVU, Tengo, editor of a native Cape Colonial paper, *Imvo*, which was suppressed under martial law regulations during the S. African War for publishing inflammatory articles against British rule.

JACK, J. N., of the Elsenburg Agric. Sch., was formerly Agric. Inst. and Direc. of the experimental farm of the Cheshire Agric. Coll., and lecturer in the County Work Dept. of the Edinburgh and East of Scotland Coll. of Agric. In 1905 he was appointed Prin. of Elsenburg Agric. Sch.

JACKSON, Capt. Frederick George, of the Royal Societies and Grosvenor Clubs, was born at Alcester Lodge in 1860, and is the eldest son of Geo. F. Jackson, of Cheltenham. He was educated at Edinburgh Univ., and has explored in the central deserts of Australia and in Waigatz. He made a famous journey across the Bolshaia Zemelskija Tundra in midwinter, and was leader of the Jackson-Harmsworth Polar Expedition; served through the S. African War, commanding a company in the 6th Mounted Inf., also on the staff of a column as Provost Marshal (despatches, medal, and five clasps). Publications—*The Great Frozen Land*, *A Thousand Days in the Arctic*, &c., and a paper before the Royal Soc. of London, entitled *An Experimental Enquiry into Scurvy*, in conjunction with Vaughan Harley, M.D., and other papers and articles. He has shot big game in S. Africa, the Arctic Regions, America, Australia, and elsewhere. He married, in 1898, Marjorie, third dau. of Col. R. C. Dalrymple Bruce.

JACKSON, Frederick John, C.B., C.M.G., of Nairobi, East African Protectorate; The Red House, Aldeburgh, Suffolk, and of the Savile and Isthmian Clubs, was born in Yorks. in 1860. He was educated at Shrewsbury Sch. and Jesus Coll., Cambs. He commanded an expedition sent to Uganda in 1889 by the British E. Africa Co. to arrange a treaty with the King of that country. In 1894 he was appointed a 1st class Asst. in Uganda, and British Vice Consul there in 1895; acted as Deputy Commissioner Uganda Protectorate in 1896; and H.M. Acting Commissioner in 1897-8. While holding the latter appointment he served against the Sudanese mutineers (Uganda Mutiny medal and two clasps, C.B.). He also took part in the operations against the Nandi in 1900 as Chief Political Officer (medal and clasp); was transferred to the E. Africa Protectorate as Deputy Commissioner in 1901; H.M. Acting Commissioner 1902. He is the author of *Big Game Shooting in E. Africa*; is well known as a naturalist, and has a very fine collection of the birds of British E. Africa, from the coast to Lake Nairascha, Uganda, and Ruwenzori. He married, in 1904, Alma, dau. of the late William Wallace Cooper, of Dublin.

JACKSON, Lieut. Colonel Herbert William, C.B., of the Turf Club, Cairo, and of the Sudan Club, Khartoum, was born Feb. 5, 1861, and is son of the late W. H. Jackson, of Leicestershire. He was educated at Rugby, and entered the Army in 1881. He took part in the Egyptian Expedition in 1882 (medal and Khedivial star); Suakim Expedition in 1884, being present at the actions of El Teb and Tamai, and the Nile Expedition in 1884-5, when he served with the River Column (clasp). He was seconded for service with the Egyptian Gendarmerie in 1886, and joined the Egyptian Army in 1888. He took part in the operations round Suakim in 1888 (clasp); action of Toski 1889 (clasp, 4th class Medjidieh); was present at the capture of Tokay in 1891 (clasp, 4th class Osmanieh); the Dongola Expedition in 1896 (despatches, Brevet Major, Khedive's medal and two clasps); Nile Expedition in 1897 (despatches, clasp); battle of the Atbara, 1898 (dispatches, clasp); battle of Khartoum (despatches, clasp, British Nile medal). He became Governor of Fashoda, and took command of the forces on the reoccupation of that district in 1898. He commanded the 2nd Inf. Brigade in the White Nile Expedition in 1899 (Brevet Colonel, clasp). He acted as Governor of the Berber Province in 1899-1900 (C.B.), and as deputy Governor-General. of the Sudan, and Civil Secy. in 1900-2, subsequently becoming Governor of the Dongola Province in 1902.

JACKSON, Hugh Marrison Gower, of Fort Usher, Matabeleland, was born at Maritzburg, Sept. 18, 1870, and is son of John Otter Jackson, a former magistrate of Natal. He was educated in England, and in 1889 became student interpreter attached to office of Secy. for Native Affairs, Natal; thereafter, until 1895, filled various posts in Native Dept., Natal; was appointed a Native Comm. in Matabeleland in 1895; took part in suppression of native rising of 1896, as lieutenant in Gifford's Horse; acted on two occasions as Chief Native Commissioner, also as Government nominee on Native Labour Board; is an assistant magistrate for the Bulawayo District, and commands the Matopo troop of the Southern Rhodesia Volunteers. He married, in 1897, Martha Lawson, dau. of T. W. Greer, of Ixopo, Natal.

JACKSON, Lieut. Colonel Hugh Milbourne, RE., M.L.C., served in the Burmese Expedition in 1887-8, and in the S. African War in 1899-1902 on the Staff, including the operations in the Orange Free State, and at Paardeberg, being present at the actions at Poplar Grove, Driefontein, Vet River and Zand River, the operations in the Transvaal, and the actions near Johannesburg and Pretoria (Brevet Lieut. Col., Queen's medal with four clasps, and King's medal with two clasps). In 1902 he was on Special Commission in connection with the Transvaal-Natal boundary, and in 1903 he was appointed Surveyor General for the Transvaal, with a seat on the Legislative Council.

JAGGER, John William, M.L.A., of Wynberg, Cape Town, and of the City Club, Cape Town, is the son of the late William Jagger, of Only House, Northowram. He was born Sept. 20, 1859, at Northowram, Yorks., and was educated at Burnsall Gram. Sch. He went to S.A. in 1880. He is President of the Association of the Chambers of Commerce of S.A., member of the Table Bay Harbour Board, and was elected to represent Cape Town in the Progressive interest in the Legislative Assembly in Nov. 1902, being last re-elected in Feb. 1904. Mr. Jagger is head of the firm of J. W. Jagger and Co., S.A. merchants. He is a Fellow of the Royal Statistical Society and a Fellow of the Society of Arts. He married, in 1885, Mary, only dau. of the late William Hall, of Cape Town.

JAMESON, Dr. Adam, M.L.C., of Pretoria, Transvaal, was born in Scotland in 1860, and was educated at Craigmount Sch. and Edinburgh Univ., graduating as Bachelor of Medicine and Master in Surgery in 1883, and later took the degree of Doctor of Medicine. He sailed for Western Australia in charge of an emigrant ship in 1884, practising his profession and taking some part in the political life of the Colony. Dr. Jameson returned to Europe in 1893, and practised as a physician in Rome until 1897, when, upon the death of his wife, he returned to the Antipodes and entered the Legislative Council of W. Australia in 1900, becoming Minister for Lands and leader of the Council in the following year. He transferred to the Transvaal as Commissioner of Lands and member of the Executive Council in 1903. He married in

1889 a dau. of Mr. Justice Hensman, of Western Australia.

JAMESON, Dr. The Hon. Leander Starr, M.L.A., C.B. (1894), of 2, Down St., Piccadilly, W., and of the Beefsteak Club, was born in Edinburgh Feb. 9, 1853, and is one of many children of the late H. W. Jameson, W.S. He was educated at Godolphin Sch., Hammersmith, and studied medicine at London Univ., graduating M.B. and B.S. 1875, M.R.CS. Eng. 1875, and M.D. 1877. He then went to America, and on his return to England was offered the post of Consulting Physician to the Kimberley Hospital and a partnership in the practice of Dr. Prince of that town. Proceeding there he was soon recognised' as one of the leading members of his profession, with what was probably the best practice in S.A. From this period dates his friendship with the late Cecil Rhodes. In 1881 Dr. Jameson came to Europe on a holiday, and from the time of his return to S.A. began his interest in the historic movement known as the Northern Expansion. He accompanied Dr. F. Rutherfoord Harris and Rochfort Maguire, M.P., on a special mission to Lobengula (whom he treated for gout); and it was perhaps owing to this fact that the mission was successful in accomplishing its objects. On his return to Kimberley Dr. Jameson again returned to the practice of his profession until Sept. 1889, when with Major Maxwell, Major Frank Johnson, and Mr. Denis Doyle he unofficially accompanied another mission to Lobengula. On the occupation of Mashonaland Mr. Colquhoun was administrator of that territory, but Dr. Jameson held Mr. Rhodes' power of attorney. During these early days he had to endure a course of self-denial so severe that nothing but the most single-minded devotion to his self-imposed duties could have carried him through. Long wanderings through the 'flybelt' with Major Johnson in search of the East Coast route, endless troubles with his sorely-tried pioneers, imminent prospects (sometimes realised) of conflicts with Boer trekkers, Matabele and Portuguese—these were some of the propositions which required his infinite patience, tact, courage, and hard work combat.

Eventually reaching Kimberley again, Nov. 15, 1890, he left once more for Mashonaland on Dec. 2 with some officials of the Chartered Co. At

Rhodes' Drift he met the Boer expedition organised by Gen. Joubert to set up a new republic of Banjai in Chartered territory, and with great tact and firmness prevented the Boers from crossing the Crocodile River.

On Sept. 18, 1891, Dr. Jameson succeeded Mr. Colquhoun as Chief Magistrate and Administrator of Mashonaland; he took over also the administration of Matabeleland from Sept., 1894, and in Oct. following was appointed Resident Commissioner of the territories along the western border of the S.A.R., north of Bechuanaland. These posts he relinquished in 1895 in consequence of his complicity in the Raid.

It is difficult to say when Dr. Jameson's connection with the Transvaal Reform movement first originated. He possibly for years had in mind the part which he was to play. However at may be, arrangements were made between the Reform leaders and Dr. Jameson as early as Sept., 1895, that he would maintain a force of some 1,500 mounted men with Maxims and field artillery on the western border of the Transvaal (ostensibly in case of difficulties with the Bechuanaland natives), and the seizure of the Pretoria fort and the railway was planned in conjunction with local levies. That was the original idea, but the arrangements were modified. The Johannesburg leaders appear to have somewhat regretted that they had invited outside aid, and it was agreed with Mr. Rhodes in Nov., 1895, that the B.B.P. and other troops should be kept across the border only as moral support or for assistance in case the Uitlanders found themselves in 'a tight place', for which eventuality an undated letter, signed by the leaders, was handed to Dr. Jameson towards the end of Nov., setting forth the condition of affairs and inviting him to come to their assistance. This letter was mainly to justify the doctor before the British Govt. and the Directors of the Chartered Co. Dates for the invasion were tentatively fixed, but the Secy. of the Reform Committee has recorded that the primary condition of these arrangements was that under no circumstances should Dr. Jameson move without receiving the word from the Johannesburg party. Doubts were then entertained as to whether there was not some underlying intention on the part of Mr. Cecil Rhodes and the doctor to come in under

the British flag, and so strong did these suspicions become that emissaries were sent to Mr. Rhodes (Dec. 25) to get his clear pronouncement that they were cooperating for a reformed and representative republic only, and the next day officers were dispatched to Dr. Jameson to emphatically prohibit any movement on his part, and explaining the flag difficulty and the unpreparedness of the Uitlanders. But the doctor began to reveal an impatience which no protest either from the Committee, from Mr. Rhodes, or from individuals at Johannesburg could restrain. On Dec. 28, 1895, he wired, "I shall start without fail tomorrow night," and he left accordingly with 8 Maxims, two seven-pounders, one twelve-pounder, and about 480 well mounted men. Such was the consternation produced by this act that the first impulse was to repudiate the doctor's interference. But that was of course impossible. Maxims had already been placed in position round Johannesburg, and some 2,000 rifles distributed, and now earth works were thrown up and defensive measures hastily taken. The force left Pitsani at about 5 p.m. on Sunday, and in spite of messages received from the High Commissioner, the British Agent, and the Reform leaders, warning Dr. Jameson to withdraw his troops, he continued to Krugersdorp (150 miles), which he reached at 3 p.m. on Wednesday. Near here, at the Queen's mile, the invaders suffered a small reverse, and withdrew, the firing being carried on until 11 p.m. During the night the Boers were reinforced with guns, Maxims, and men, bringing up their numbers to 1,200 or 1,500 men. Dr. Jameson seemed quite unacquainted with the locality, and relied in the guidance of a local man, who led him into the strong position held by the Boers at Doornkop, Vlakfontein. He made a desperate attempt to break through, his men behaving with great gallantry. But the position was unassailable, and the force surrendered at 9.15 on Thursday morning, conditionally on the lives of all his force being spared. The casualties were 18 killed and about 441 wounded, while the Boers owned to 4 killed and 5 wounded.

Dr. Jameson was handed over by Mr. Kruger's Govt. to the British Govt. for trial in London. Following on the police court proceedings, he was tried at Bar on the charge of having contravened the Foreign Enlistment Act of 1870 by organizing and heading a hostile expedition from Pitsani-Pitlogo against a friendly power. The trial commenced on June 20, 1896, at the High Court of Judicature, and lasted seven days. He was found guilty and sentenced to imprisonment as a first-class misdemeanant for fifteen months. He was, however, released from Holloway in the following Dec. on account of illness.

After a partial retirement for some years, Dr. Jameson returned to S.A., serving in the war (1899-1900), during which time he was besieged in Ladysmith, doing useful work until he was himself laid up with enteric. In 1900 he was elected a member of the Legislative Assembly for Kimberley, and made his maiden speech in the House on Aug. 28, 1902, in which he hoped that the Raid might now be forgotten. Seceding from the Sprigg party, he identified himself with the Suspension movement, and was eventually (June 8, 1903) elected leader of the new Progressive party, which, after a long and difficult struggle, entailing considerable organizing powers, tact, control, and restraint, he lad to victory at the general election in Feb., 1904, himself being returned as member for Grahamstown. The Progressives being in a majority of five in the new assembly, and of one in the Council, and Sir Gordon Sprigg having been defeated at the poll, the resignation of the Ministry followed as a matter of course, and a new Cabinet was immediately formed by Dr. Jameson, consisting of himself as Premier with charge of Native Affairs, Col. Crewe as Colonial Secy., E. H. Walton as Treasurer, Dr. Smart as Commissioner of Crown Lands and Public Works, Victor Sampson as Attorney-Gen., Arthur Fuller as Secy. for Agriculture, and Sir Lewis Michell as Minister without portfolio, all of whom are referred to more particularly in other pages. The Premier will have to exercise all his qualities of leadership to achieve the objects of his party, the immediate task being the passing of an equitable redistribution bill, and the ultimate aim of the Imperial federation of British S. Africa. But in spite of certain limitations, he possesses that knowledge of men and affairs, patience, sobriety of thought and action, imagination, capacity for hard work, and that necessary amount of daring which make for success. If he has not the magnetic power of a commanding personality, he certainly does not fail

in inspiring friendship and zeal, courage, and persistence. He is accessible and suave, well able to bear extremes of fortune, and has never yet forgiven his one great failure. To the department over which Dr. Jameson now presides he brings a close knowledge of native character and a keen appreciation of the necessity of raising the status and usefulness of the native.

Dr. Jameson is a Director of the British S.A. Co., and of the De Beers Consolidated Mines, and by the last codicil of Mr. Cecil Rhodes' will, he was appointed a co executor and trustee thereof. He is not married.

JAMESON, S. W., of 28, Princes Sq., London, W., is a brother of Dr. L. S. Jameson (q.v.)

JAMIESON, James William, F.R.G.S., of Johannesburg, and of the Thatched House Club, was born Sept. 11, 1867. He was appointed a student interpreter in H.M. Consular service in China in 1886; commercial attaché in the diplomatic service 1889; is commercial attaché to H.M. Legation in China, and has acted previously as Consul at several ports; as Consul General at Shanghai, and Chinese Secy. to the British Legation at Pekin. Mr. Jamieson was detached in 1898-9 for service under the Government of India as Chinese adviser to the Burma China Frontier Delimitation Commission; was temporarily attached to Major-Gen. Sir Alfred Gaselee's staff as political officer in North China in 1900; was attached to Sir James Mackay. K.C.M.G., K.C.I.E., during the negotiations for the revision of the commercial treaties with China; and is seconded for service under the Colonial Office as Supt. of Foreign Labour in the Transvaal. Unmarried.

JAMIESON R., is head of the firm of H. Jamieson and Co., the pioneers of the jam-making industry of Natal.

JANSON, Edmund William, M.A. (Camb.), A.M.I.C.E., F.R.G.S., of Eaton Mansions, Eaton Square, London, S.W., and of the New University, City University, Ranelagh, and Whitefriars Clubs, was born at Radwell House, Baldock, Harts., on June 29, 1869, and is son of Edmund Janson, of Etherington Hill, near Tunbridge Wells. Mr. E.

W. Janson was educated at Uppingham and at Jesus College, Cambridge, subsequently becoming associated with the late Mr. Percy Tarbutt in a large number of important companies, mainly West African, of which Mr. Janson is now one of the controlling heads, the other most important head of the group being Mr. Edmund Davis. Mr. Janson married, on August 2, 1900, Dorothy, dau. of the late Percy Tarbutt.

JARVIS, Captain Charles Francis Cracroft, was born in 1875, and entered the Yorks Regt. as 2nd Lieutenant in 1896. He served in the South African War in 1899-1901; present at the Relief of Kimberley and the operations in the Orange Free State, including Paardeberg and the actions at Vet River and Zand River; the operations in the Transvaal and the actions near Pretoria, Johannesburg, and Diamond Hill, and the operations in the Transvaal east of Pretoria, and in Cape Colony, including the actions at Belfast and Colesburg (despatches and Queen's medal with five clasps). Captain Jarvis is acting as Adjutant of the Royal Scots Volunteer Brigade in Edinburgh. He married, in 1906, Mrs. Johnston Stewart, dau. of the late Sir Edward Hunter Blair, Bart., and widow of Captain Johnston Stewart, of Physgill.

JARVIS, Lieut. Col. Alexander Weston, C.M.G. (Apr., 1901), M.V.O. (1901), of 66, Park Street, Grosvenor Square, London, W., and of the Carlton, Marlborough and Bachelors' Clubs, is the eldest son of Sir Lewis Jarvis, of Middleton Towers, King's Lynn, where he was born, Dec. 26, 1855. He was educated at Harrow, and represented King's Lynn as Conservative M.P. from 1886 to 1892.

As a member of the firm of Partridge & Jarvis, he was actively interested in the formation and control of a large number of Rhodesian undertakings. He was in Rhodesia when the Matabele Rebellion of 1896 broke out. He then accompanied the Volunteer forces in an unattached capacity, but took command of a squadron on its leader being mortally wounded (medal). He was again in Rhodesia when the S.A. War opened in 1899, and joined the Rhodesian contingent under Col. Plumer, taking part in the relief of Mafeking. On leaving Plumer's force at the end of 1900, Col.

Jarvis came to England, but returned three months later in command of the 21st Battn. of I.Y. serving with Col. Rimington's and Sir Henry Rawlinson's columns, during which time he took part in the successful drives under Gen. Bruce Hamilton, from the beginning of Nov., 1901, to the end of Jan., 1902. Towards the end of the war Col. Jarvis was employed in putting up the Blockhouse lines from Ermelo to Carolina in the North, and from Ermelo to the Swaziland Border On the East (S.A. medal and four clasps, and King's medal and two clasps). At the conclusion of hostilities his battn. was disbanded, but Col. Jarvis was given the hon. rank of Lieut. Col. in the Army, together with the dignity of C.M.G. On returning to England he exchanged from the Derbyshire Yeomanry Cavalry to take command under Lord Dunraven of the 3rd County of London I.Y.—a regiment which was formed out of the old 18th, 21st, and 23rd Batts. of I.Y. which had served with Col. Jarvis in S.A.

In Nov., 1902, Col. Jarvis proceeded to the Delhi Durbar on the Staff of H.R.H. the Duke of Connaught. Meanwhile the partnership of Partridge and Jarvis had terminated by the effluxion of time, but Col. Jarvis returned to the City to supervise the business of the Willoughby group of companies. He is also a Director of the India Rubber, Gutta Percha, & Telegraph Works, and many Rhodesian Cos. At one time an ardent steeplechaser and cricketer, he now limits his recreations mainly to hunting and shooting. Col. Jarvis is unmarried.

JEFFREYS, Brig. Gen. Henry Byron, C.B., of Pretoria, Transvaal, and of the Naval and Military Club, was born in 1854, and is son of the late Gen. Jeffreys, C.B. He joined the Royal Artillery in 1873, from which he was seconded in 1890 as A.A.G. in the Madras Army until 1894; acted as Brigade Major in the Royal Artillery at Aldershot from 1896-8, and served in the South African War in 1899-1901 in command of a Brigade Division of the Royal Horse Artillery, taking part in the operations in the Transvaal, including the engagements near Johannesburg, Pretoria, and Diamond Hill; in the Transvaal east of Pretoria, including the actions at Riet Vlei and Belfast, and in Cape Colony north and south of the Orange River, in command of a column (despatches, Queen's medal with five clasps, and brevet of Colonel).

From 1901-3 he was in command of the Royal Horse Artillery at Aldershot. He married, in 1888, Marion, dau. of the late Capt. W.. F. Burlton-Bennet.

JENKIN, Thomas Nicol, of Tolgus, Redruth, Cornwall, and 124, Palace Chambers, Westminster, was born Mar. 6, 1865. He is proprietor of the *Cornubian* newspaper, Secy. of the National Industrial Assoc., and Secy. of the S.A. Trade Committee, by whom he was sent out as Special Commissioner to report upon the general trade of S.A. (excluding engineering and textiles). The results of his investigations were published in 1902 by P. S. King and Sons under the title of *South African General Trades*. He married, in 1887, Jessica Frances Lemon, dau. of John Tregenza.

JENKINS, Capt. Edward Vaughan, D.S.O., West Riding Regt., was born in India, Oct. 14, 1879; is son of the late Lieut. Col. Vaughan Jenkins, and was educated at Clifton Coll. He served with the King's African Rifles 1902-5, and married in 1904 Evelyn, eldest dau. of the late Lieut. Col. H. C. H. Germon, J.P., of the Nor folk Regiment.

JENKINS, Rev. W. Owen, M.A., of the Diocesan Coll., Rondebosch, near Cape Town, was educated at Jesus Coll., Oxford. He was chaplain of St. Andrew's Coll., Grahamstown, from 1888-91; became rector of E. London, Cape Colony, in 1891 until 1894, when he was appointed rector and rural dean of Graaff Reinet, which position he held until in 1899 he became Principal of the Diocesan Coll., Rondebosch.

JENNINGS, Hennen, C. E., of 1, London Wall Buildings, E.C., and of the University Club, New York, the Union Club, San Francisco, and the Rand Club, Johannesburg, was born in Hawesville, Kentucky, U.S.A., May 6, 1854, and is son of Jas. R. Jennings, of Norfolk, Virginia, an owner of coal mines in Kentucky, by his wife Katherine Sharpe Hennen, of New Orleans. Mr. Hennen Jennings was educated at Lawrence Scientific Sch., Harvard Univ., where he graduated C.E. in 1877. Since then he has been identified with many mining undertakings, notably with the North Bloomfield Gold Gravel Mining Co. in California, in 1877 and 1880; the New Almaden Quicksilver Mines in California, 1877 to 1880, and 1883 to 1887; the Ruby Gold Gravel Mining Company in California, from 1881 to 1883; and the El Callao Mine, Venezuela, from 1887 to 1889. From December 1889 to June 1898 he was Consulting Engineer to H. Eckstein & Co., Johannesburg, and has been Consulting Engineer for various periods to the following Transvaal Gold Mining Companies: Rand Mines, Robinson, Crown Reef, New Heriot, City & Suburban, Henry Nourse, Nigel, New Modderfontein, and others. From July, 1898, to the present time he has acted as consulting Engineer in London to Messrs. Wernher, Belt, & Co.; in addition to which he was President (1903 and 1904) of the Institution of Mining and Metallurgy.

Mr. Jennings is greatly interested in educational matters; was a member of the Transvaal School Board in 1897 and 1898; Member of two Technical Education Commissions in Transvaal, 1902, 1903, and 1904; Member of the London Advisory Committee of the Transvaal Technical Institute, and Member of the Departmental Committee of the Royal College of Science, etc., etc. Besides which he is a Member of the Institute of Civil Engineers; American Institute of Mining Engineers; South African Association of Engineers; Chemical, Metallurgical and Mining Society of South Africa; Transvaal Institute of Mechanical engineers; Geological Society of South Africa; South African Association for Advancement of Science, and the Society of Arts. He is a keen golf player, and a member of the West Herts and Cinque Ports Golf Clubs. He married, Oct. 7, 1880, Mary L., dau. of John C. Coleman, of San Francisco, California.

JENNINGS, Sidney Johnston, A.I.M.E., M.I.M. and M., S.A.A.E., of Corona House, Mayfair, Johannesburg, and of the Rand and Athenaeum Clubs, Johannesburg, is the son of James R. Jennings, his mother being a dau. of Alfred Hennen, a lawyer of New Orleans. He was born Aug. 13, 1863, in Hancock County, Kentucky, U.S.A., and was educated at Tours, France, Hanover, Germany, and Lawrence Scientific Sch., Harvard Univ. Mr. Jennings acquired a practical knowledge of mining in the quicksilver mines of New Almaden and the Copper Mines of the Anaconda Co. He went to S.A. as Manager of the

Willows Copper (Argentiferous) Synd., Ltd., in 1890, and was appointed Assist. General Manager of De Beers Consolidated Mines, Ltd. Mr. Jennings went to the Rand in 1893 as Manager of the Crown Deep, Ltd., and was appointed Gen. Manager of the Crown Reef G. M. Co. in 1896; he joined H. Eckstein & Co.'s Mining Dept. in 1899, and was appointed Consulting Engineer to that firm in 1900, and is also Consulting Engineer to the Robinson G. M. Co., the Crown Reef, Bonanza, Robinson Central Deep, Ferreira, City and Suburban, Village Deep, New Modderfontein, Henry Nourse, Turf Mines, Ltd., etc. Mr. Jennings was member of the Johannesburg Town Council from December, 1901, to April, 1903, when he did very good service as Chairman of the Works Committee. He has also taken a great interest in education; is a member of the Governing body of the Transvaal Technical Institute, and is also a member of many scientific societies. He married, Aug. 18, 1903, Amy Florence Valby, dau. of Col. Philip Dassie Home, R.H.A.

JEPPE, Carl, of the Rand Club, was born at Rostock, Mecklenburg, Germany, in 1858, and was educated in Germany and Pretoria. He went to the Transvaal in 1870, entering the Govt. service as Public Prosecutor for the Waterberg in 1877. He was admitted to practise as advocate at the Transvaal Bar in 1884, and in the early days of the Rand he became joint owner of the Johannesburg Suburbs—Jeppestown and Fordsburg. He was member of the Diggers' Committee in 1877; Chairman of the Chamber of Mines in 1888, and Member of the Johannesburg Chamber of Mines in the following year. Mr. Jeppe was elected Member of the Second Raad for the Rand Gold Fields in 1891, but was unseated on the ground of informality and declined to stand again. He was, however, returned as Member for Johannesburg to the First Raad in 1893. He was strongly in favour of extending the franchise to the newcomers under certain conditions; advocated a spirited railway policy and the remodeling of the financial system of the State. During the 1894 session he was the mainstay of the Progressives in the Raad, and fought valiantly in the interests of the Uitlanders. His plea for the alien during the Franchise debate was said by the *Argus Annual* to have been recognised as the finest piece of oratory ever heard

in the Raadzaal, and his speech won over several members of his side who were previously undecided. At the conclusion of the session he was publicly thanked for his efforts in the cause of his constituents. Since the South African War Mr. Jeppe retired from the practice of his profession, and has resided in Cape Town.

JEPPE, Julius, J.P., Knight of the Danish Order of Danebrog, and Knight of the Grecian Royal Order of the Saviour, of 68, Shortmarket Street Cape Town, of 'Vredenburg', Rosebank, Cape Town, and of the City Club, C.T., is son of the late Dr. Jeppe, of Rostock. He was born Sept. 22 1855, at Swellendam, Cape Colony, and was educated at the S.A. Coll. He has had a long commercial career, having been connected with shipping, produce, and manufacturing interests in S. Africa since 1880— for fourteen years in the Transvaal, and now in Cape Town. His official positions are Consul for Denmark, Consul for Greece, Justice of the Peace for Cape Town and District, and Member of Cape Town Chamber of Commerce. Recreations: Shooting and riding. He married, Sept. 24, 1884, Julia, eldest dau. of the late Capt. Richard Ellis, ship-owner, of London.

JEPPE, Julius, of Friedenheim, Belgravia, Jeppestown, Johannesburg, and of the Rand and Athenaeum (Johannesburg), City (Cape Town), and Pretoria Clubs, was born at Butzow, Germany, in July, 1859, and is son of Julius Jeppe, of Mecklenburg-Schwerin. He was educated at Butzow and Pretoria. In 1876 he took part in the Secocoeni War, and in the Boer War in 1880, when he held a commission in the Pretoria Carabineers. He also served in the Boer War in 1899, being taken prisoner at Graspan, subsequently doing parole duty. He as a member of the Sanitary Board from 1890-99; Alderman from 1898-9; member of the Town Council from 1893-5; and is a Director of the Rhodesian Exploration and Development Co., Ltd., Rhodesian Banket Co., and West Rhodesian Banket Co. He is also a member of the Executive of the Witwatersrand Chamber of Mines, Member of the Water Board, and of the Witwatersrand Native Labour Association, and figures on the Committee of the Landowners' Association. Mr. Jeppe is Hon. Col. of the Boys' Brigade Cadet Corps, and is connected with nearly every sporting club in Johannesburg. He is steward of the Hockey and the Johannesburg Turf Clubs, and has for many years been chairman, and now vice president, of the Wanderers' Club; and has shot lots of kinds of big game of S. Africa. He married, in April, 1891, Grace, dau. of Charles Owen.

JOEL, J. B., of 34, Grosvenor Square, London, and of Northaw House, Potter's Bar, is son of the late Joel Joel, and a member of the firm of Barnato Bros., whom he represents in Johannesburg as a Permanent Director of the Barnato Consolidated Mines. He is also on the board of the Johannesburg Consolidated Investment Co. Mr. 'Jack' Joel is a fairly successful winner of racehorses, and in 1906 won the City and Suburban Handicap in a canter with his somewhat disappointing horse Dean Swift. He married, in 1904, Olive Coulson, dau of the late Thos. Sopwith, of 83, Cadogan Gardens, London.

JOEL, Solomon Barnato, of Johannesburg, and of 10 and 11, Austin Friars, London, E.C., is son of the late Joel Joel, and a nephew of the late B. I. Barnato. He is one of the chief members of the firm of Barnato Bros., and as such largely assists in the control of the firm's interest in mining and industrial companies in South Africa. He is a Director of the De Beers Consolidated Mines, the New Jagersfontein Mining Company, the Four per Cent. Industrial Dwellings Company, the South African Breweries, and the Witwatersrand Gold Mining Company, and is on the London Committee of the Imperial Cold Storage and Supply Company, the Transvaal Consolidated Gold Mines, and the Van Ryn Deep, Limited. He is also chairman of the Johannesburg Consolidated Investment Company, Limited.

The group of companies under the control of the house of Barnato is very large, and includes several powerful concerns, some of which are producing gold and earning considerable profits, while others that have not yet reached that much desired goal are possessed of great potentialities. The firm of Barnato Bros. wields a powerful influence in South Africa, where it has vast holdings and interests, including very large holdings in the De Beers

Consolidated Mines and New Jagersfontein companies.

The most prominent members of the Barnato group are Messrs. S. B. Joel, J. Joel, Henry Barnato, H. A. Rogers, Harold F. Strange, J. Emrys Evans, J. Friedlander, Isaac Lewis, E. B. Gardiner, Sir John Purcell, K.C.B., and Mr. Thomas Honey, whilst the companies that come under their direction are the Johannesburg Consolidated Investment Company, the Consolidated Langlaagte Mines, the Rand Central Gold Mines, the Ginsberg G.M. Co., the Glencairn Main Reef G.M. Co., the New Primrose G.M. Co., the New Rietfontein Estate Gold Mines, the New Unified Main Reef G.M. Co., the Randfontein Deep, South Cinderella Deep, the Roodepoort G.M. Co., the Johannesburg Estate Co., and the Witwatersrand G.M. Co.

For such a company as the Johannesburg Investment Company, which invests in and lends money to mining and other concerns, and is interested in the development of widespread claim areas with which little or nothing could be done in the absence of labour, the opportunities for business have of late years been necessarily few and far between; and, to emphasise the position during the last twelve months, there was contemporaneous depreciation in investments, necessitating the writing off of £379,610, over and above the £227,024 written off in the previous year.

In the result, including the previous year's balance of £173,736, there was on the year's trading (with a net revenue of £331,643 and total outgoings of £70,071, exclusive of depreciation) a balance of profit of £38,780, which was carried forward. Against the formidable item in the name of depreciation, charged to profit and loss account for the year, there had to be placed the important compensating fact that, at the date of the accounts, the market value of the company's other holdings was largely in excess of the book figures, and that no appreciation on that head had been taken into account. This appreciation amounted on June 30, 1906, to £480,435, or over £100,000 more than was written off for depreciation. With regard to the company's investments in real estate, its

Johannesburg town and suburban properties stand in the accounts at £642,279 but the present municipal valuation of these properties is £1,517,535, or £875,256 above the values in the company's books.

Finally, the position generally of the gold-mining companies in which the Investment Company is interested—roughly speaking, the whole of the Barnato Group—had shown marked improvement during the fiscal period ended June 30, 1906, the working costs in most cases reflecting satisfactory reductions. The New Rietfontein was beginning to yield enhanced profits; the Ginsberg Co., having purchased the adjoining Balmoral property and plant, promised soon to resume its excellent record; satisfactory dividends had been paid by the New Rietfontein, New Primrose, and Witwatersrand companies, all of which were steadily increasing their profits. One has only to bear in mind the substantial nature of the Investment Company's original holdings in Rand real estate and Rand mines, and the potential nature of the assets, interests, and holdings brought in by the Barnato Consolidated Mines, to feel assured that, under favourable conditions, there is ample room for development, for appreciation, for exploitation, and for a rich harvest.

Mr. 'Solly' Joel is the owner of the Madden Erlegh Estate, near Reading, and of Sefton Lodge, Newmarket; he races considerably in Johannesburg and in England; is particularly partial to the drama; and is the owner of the steam yacht *Doris*.

JOHNSON, Capt. Arthur Evans, D.S.O., of Zungeru, Northern Nigeria, and Coolayna, Carbury, Co. Kildare; captain in the Reserve of Officers, and Asst. Commissioner of Police in Northern Nigeria; served throughout the S. African War, 1899-1902, in the Imperial Yeomanry; was wounded, mentioned in despatches , received the D.S.O. and two medals and five clasps.

JOHNSON, El-Lewa Edward Armstrong, Pasha, 2nd Class Medjidieh; of Cairo; of Lilly Ledbury, Herefordshire, and of the Junior United Service and Turf (Cairo) Clubs, was born in Dublin, Aug. 15, 1846. He is son of the Ven. Evans Johnson, Archdeacon of Ferns, and Mary, dau. of William

Henry Heaton Armstrong, of Mount Heaton, and of Forney Castle, Ireland. He was educated at Cheltenham Coll., where he was in the Cricket XI. in 1864-5. He passed for Woolwich in June of that year, and joined the R.A. in Jan., 1868; went to India with the 9th Brigade in 1869, and held charge of the Quetta Arsenal during the second Afghan Campaign and Siege of Kandahar. He was several times thanked for services by resolutions of the Bombay Govt.; was mentioned in despatches, and his services were a second time brought to the notice of the Govt. of India by the Bombay Govt. He bad charge of the Grand Arsenal, Bombay, from the close of the war till invalided in 1882 (Afghan medal 1879-82). He acted temporarily as R.M. in Ireland, but resigned that appointment to join the Staff of Gen. Val. Baker in Egypt in 1883. He served as Deputy Inspector-Gen. of Gendarmerie and Police for several years there, and was made Lewa (Major-Gen.) by Khedivial decree in June, 1885. On the reorganisation of the Ministry of the Interior he joined the Ministry of Justice as Chief Inspector of Native Tribunals, but gave up that position in 1902 to undertake the establishment of model workshops, which were intended to serve as Technical Schools for Egyptian artisans on a system suggested by him.

About the year 1895, Johnson Pasha commenced to devote a portion of his spare time to the revival of the ancient ceramic industries of Egypt, which had been almost abandoned, with such success that several potteries are now doing a fairly profitable trade in glazed pottery, and the industry shows promise of extensive development. The development of the mining industry which has recently taken place in Egypt is also largely due to Johnson Pasha's initiative. Between 1889-95 he spent most of his holidays in visiting the ancient mining centres in the Eastern Desert, which he found to be much more numerous than had been supposed.

As Capt. Johnson, he was Secy. of the Mhow Tent Club from 1873-76, and won the sportsman's contest at the Mhow Rifle Meeting in 1875. He published (1887) a translation of the *Gulshan-i-Raz* in blank verse with some of the *Rubaiyat* of Omar Khayyam. A second publication (1893) contains the *Gulshan-i-Raz*, the introduction to the *Diwan* of Be-

Dil, and a considerable number of the *Rubaiyat* not previously translated. Johnson Pasha married, Feb. 25, 1871, Mary Holroyd, dau. of the late Maj. J. E. Knox-Grogan, formerly of the 68th Regiment.

JOHNSON, Edward Odlum, of Freetown, Sierra Leone, W. Africa, and of the Colonial West Indian Clubs, was born at Montserrat, West Indies, Sept. 8, 1867, and is the younger son of the late Dr. Burdett Johnson, of Montserrat. He was educated at Harrison Coll., Barbados, Epsom Coll., Eng., and entered the Colonial Service as 2nd Clerk in the Montserrat Treasury Dept. in 1884; promoted 1st Clerk, 1886; 1st Clerk, St. Kitts Treasury, 1891; 1st Revenue Officer, St. Kitts, 1895; Acting Treasurer, St. Kitts, Nevis, 1897; Asst. Treasurer, Sierra Leone, 1897; and Colonial Treasurer for that colony, Mar. 1899. Mr. Johnson is *ex officio* Member of the Executive and Legislative Council and Member of the Education Board. He married, March 31, 1902, Ida Mabel, dau. of Fredk. S. Johnston, of Malo les Bains, France.

JOHNSON, Major Frank, of Finsbury Pavement House, London, E.C., and Erin House, Clapham Park, S.W., was born in Norfolk and was educated at King's Lynn Gram. Sch.; came out to S.A. in 1882, and for two years was a member of the Cape Civil Service. In 1884 he led the 2nd Mounted Rifles under Colonel (now Gen.) Sir Frederick Carrington, and took in the Warren Expedition to Bechuanaland, at the close of which he joined the Bechuanaland Border Police, in which corps he met his future partners, Maurice Heany and H. J. Borrow. Drawn north by the reports of wealth in the interior, he left the B.B.P. early in 1886, and at Cape Town formed a small syndicate to obtain concessions in the Protectorate and in Lobengula's country. He was successful in getting a big concession in Khama's territory, which led to the foundation of the Bechuanaland Exploration Company. He then went to Lobengula's kraal, where he was one of the first white men who dared to ask the sable chief for a mineral concession. In 1889 Mr. Rhodes obtained his charter, and in the following year set about the effective occupation of Mashonaland, making, on somewhat original lines, a contract with Frank Johnson to carry out the occupation, in which the latter was assisted by two troops of B.S.A. Police, F. C. Selous acting as

Intelligence Officer and Frank Johnson getting the Colonial rank of Major—in other words he was practically, and came to be known as, the 'Contractor' for Mashonaland. The chief commander of the whole expedition was Col. Pennefather. After the occupation of Mashonaland he settled down in partnership with Heany and Borrow, and acquired a number of mining and landed interests, which ultimately were merged into the United Rhodesia, Ltd. Capt. Borrow was killed at Shangani in the first Matabele War, and Major Heany afterwards associated himself with the Partridge and Jarvis group. From 1890 Maj. Johnson made his headquarters at Cape Town, where he held a commission and took an active interest in the Cape Volunteer Forces.

In 1896 he was one of the two Colonial officers chosen by the Cape Govt. as members of the Commission appointed by Parliament to inquire into the defences and forces of Cape Colony, the other members being Imperial officers. The scheme of defence finally recommended by the Commission was chiefly based on that of Canada. At the end of 1896, at the outbreak of native troubles in Bechuanaland, Maj. Johnson was appointed Staff Officer of the Colonial Forces at the headquarters in Cape Town, and when an expedition was finally dispatched to the Langeberg early in the ensuing year, under Col. Dalgety, of the Cape Mounted Rifles, Maj. Johnson was appointed Chief Staff Officer. At the close of the expedition he was specially thanked by the Cape Government I or his services. For the next three years he resided with his family in Salisbury. Rhodesia, as Managing Director of the Mashonaland Consolidated, Limited. In 1900 he returned to England, and settled down in London as a Rhodesian financier and company director. He is now Chairman of the Rhodesia Consolidated, Ltd., and the Injoka (Rhodesia) Tobacco Company, Ltd., and is on the Boards of the Golden Valley (Mashonaland) Mines, Ltd., the Mashonaland Consolidated, the Rhodesia Cold Storage Co., Ltd., and the Rhodesia Mining and Finance Co., Ltd. He also took a leading part in the formation of the Rhodesian Landowners' Association. He is a good game shot, an habitual motorist, and is married.

JOHNSON, Col. Frederick Francis, C.B., of 78, Belgrave Road, S.W., and of the Army and Navy, United Service, Sandown Park, Ranelagh, and Marylebone Cricket Clubs, was born May 1, 1852, and is the youngest son of the late Ven. John E. Johnson, D.D., Archdeacon of Ferns. He was educated at Cheltenham Coll, and Dublin Univ., entered the Army in 1874, and served in the 69th Foot at Gibraltar.

He was transferred to the 50th Foot in 1878, and was attached to the Commissariat and Transport Staff in 1881. Col. Johnson served in the Egyptian Campaign in 1882 as transport officer in the Cavalry Div. (medal and clasp for Tel-el-Kebir; bronze star, 4th class Medjidieh). He was transferred to the Army Service Corps in 1889, and acted as A.A.G. on the Headquarters Staff, S. Africa, as Asst. Director of Supplies, and Transport to Sir Edward Ward from 1899-1900. In 1900 he was sent on a special mission from Paardeberg by Lord Roberts to Mr. Cecil Rhodes at Kimberley (medal and three clasps, despatches, and C.B.); was A.A.G. of the N.E. District from 1900 to 1903, when he was appointed Director of Supply and Transport to the 4th Army Corps. Since 1905 he has acted as Administrator of the Eastern command. Recreations: Cricket, football, hunting, shooting, and golf. He married Bertha, dau. of the late Henry Gotts, of Newhouse Park, St. Albans.

JOHNSON, Dr. Obadiah, M.D., M.LC., was reappointed an unofficial member of the Legislative Council of Southern Nigeria in 1906.

JOHNSTON, Lieut. Col. David William, F.R.C.S. Edin., D.P.H., of 94, Sherwell Street, Doornfontein, and of the New Club, Johannesburg, was born at Newhaven Oct. 12, 1856. He is principal medical officer to the Transvaal Volunteers, and commands the Vol. Medical Staff Corps.

JOHNSTON, Col. Duncan Alexander, C.B., R.E., is son of Henry Johnston, H.E.I.C.S. He was educated at Trinity College, Glenamond, and entered the Royal Engineers in 1868. From 1899-1905 he acted as Director-Gen., of the Ordnance Survey, and in 1906 he was a member of the South African Committee of Inquiry. He married, in 1883, Clara, dau. of F. H. Mackenzie.

JOHNSTON, George Lawson, of 29, Portman Square, London, W., and of the Devonshire, Hurlingham, Bath, Royal Temple Yacht, and Union des Yacht Française Clubs, is the son of the late John Lawson Johnston and Mrs. Lawson Johnston, of Raynham Hall, Norfolk; was born at Edinburgh in 1873, and was educated in Canada and at Dulwich College, England. he has travelled extensively in Europe, North and South America, and North and South Africa. Commercially his career has been most successful, amongst the great enterprises with which he is connected being Bovril, Ltd. He is now the Vice Chairman of this well-known Co.; he is also a Director of the *Daily Express* newspaper, and a Director of Henderson's Transvaal Estates, Ltd. he is identified with many philanthropic works, and is on the Executive Committees of King Edward's Hospital Fund and the Royal Normal College for the Blind. Having seen so much of the British Empire in different parts of the world, it is not surprising to find that he is an active member of the Council of the British Empire League. He is fond of shooting and riding, and is a supporter of all forms of healthy sport. He married, in 1902, Laura, fifth dau. of the 16th Baron St. John.

JOHNSTON, Sir Harry Hamilton, G.C.M.G. (1901), K.C.B. (1896), of 27, Chester Terrace, Regent's Park, London, and of the Travellers' Club, is the son of John Brooks Johnston and Esther Letitia Hamilton, and was born in London, June 12, 1858. He was educated at King's Coll., London, and studied at the Royal Academy of Arts, Burlington House. He was made a D.Sc. Camb.; is a Gold Medalist of the Royal Geographical Soc. and of the Royal Scottish Geographical Soc., a Gold Medalist of the Zoological Soc. and medalist of the S. Kensington Sch. of Arts. He is also a trustee of the Hunterian Museum of the Royal College of Surgeons, and an hon. mem. of the Royal Water Colour Soc.

A man of infinite variety, of high mental attainments, an artist, naturalist, student of human nature, and an Administrator, Sir Harry has had a career of great distinction, and may fairly be numbered amongst the band of empire builders who have done so much to make the present age illustrious. In 1880 and the two following years he explored Tunis, West Africa, and the Congo River, adding very considerably to our store of knowledge of these countries. He was in command of a scientific expedition sent out by the Royal Soc. to Mount Kilimanjaro in 1884. In 1885 he entered H.M. Consular service as Vice-Consul for the Oil Rivers and the Cameroons; Acting Consul for the Niger Coast Protectorate, 1887; and in 1889 was appointed Consul for Portuguese East Africa. Later in that year (1889) he led an expedition to Lakes Nyassa and Tanganyika. In 1891 he was transferred as H.M. Commissioner and Consul-Gen, for British Central Africa, and received general recognition for the energy, tact, and skill with which he carried out the delicate and difficult mission with which he was entrusted. At the same time he was appointed Imperial Commissioner for Nyassaland and Administrator of the British S.A. Co.'s territory north of the Zambesi. Under his able administration great progress was made, raising Indian police, constructing roads, establishing postal services, inaugurating schemes for the development of the resources of the country, and incidentally checking the slave trade, which at that time was still engaged in about Lake Nyassa. In 1897 he took up the appointment of Consul-Gen. for Tunis, where he remained until 1899, in which year he received the appointment of Special Commissioner, Consul-Gen., and Commander-in-Chief for the Uganda Protectorate, where he served with distinction until 1902. He is a Director of the Liberian Development and Monrovian Rubber Cos., and was President during 1903-5 of the African Society. He contested the constituency of Rochester at a by-election in Sept., 1903, in the Liberal interest, and was defeated by Mr. Charles Tuff by 521 votes. This choice of party by one whose record has been so far removed from Little Englandism was received with keen disappointment by the majority of his Imperialist friends, but Sir Harry justified his action on the grounds of the necessity for Free Trade and the ineptitude shown by the existing Ministry in their conduct of the S. African War; so on the ground of their indifference to matters connected with the physical well-being and education of Englishmen.

Sir Harry is a fellow of many learned activities. He has exhibited pictures at the Royal Academy and other galleries, whilst his sketches have given an additional value to many of his books. He has written Essays on the *Tunisian Question* in the *Globe*, 1880-1; on the *Congo River*, 1884; on *Kilimanjaro*, 1885; *History of a Slave*, 1889; *Life of Livingstone*, 1891; *British Central Africa*, 1897; *A History of the Colonisation of Africa by Alien Races*, 1899; *The Uganda Protectorate*, 1902; *British Mammals*, 1903; *The Nile Quest*, 1904; *Siberia*, 1905; and also a number of Bluebooks and Reports on Central Africa, which may be said to have introduced a style of writing up to his time quite foreign to the prosaic writings of his predecessors. He married, Oct. 15, 1896, the Hon. Winifred Irby, dau. of the 5th Lord Boston, and step-dau. of Sir Percy Anderson, K.C.B., late Asst. Unde-Secy. for Foreign Affairs.

JONES, Sir Alfred Lewis, K.C.M.G., J.P., of Oaklands, Aigburth, Liverpool, was born at Carmarthen in 1845. He received his education at the Liverpool College, and entered the firm of Elder, Dempster, & Co. when quite young, remaining with them until he became the controlling factor. He also acquired the business of the Beaver Line, which was subsequently sold to he Canadian Pacific Railway Co. He is now President of the Liverpool Chamber of Commerce, Chairman of the Liverpool Steamship Owners' Protection Association, Consul in Liverpool for the Congo Free State, President of the Liverpool School for the Study of Tropical Diseases, Chairman of the Elder-Dempster Shipping Co., Ltd., the British & African Steam Navigation Co. (1900), Ltd., Imperial Direct West India Mail Service Co., Ltd., Bank of British W. Africa, and of Elder & Fyffes, Ltd. Sir Alfred was some years ago connected with the West African boom which resulted so unfortunately for the general investing public. He has, however, since retired from his mining directorates. He recently served on the committee appointed by the Admiralty to enquire into the question of our naval reserves, and in 1901 he was decorated with his K.C.M.G., whilst Jesus Coll., Oxford, has conferred on him the degree of Honorary Fellow.

JONES, G. Roderick, General Manager for South Africa for Reuter's Telegram Co., resides at Cape Town, and was born in England in 1875. He proceeded as a youth to Sonth Africa, was educated at Pretoria, and had a remarkably successful journalistic career at the *Pretoria Press*, *Pretoria News*, and *Cape Times* offices, until he joined Reuter's after the war, being called by them to London, and after organising their special South African cable services most effectively, was appointed their general manager for South Africa in Oct., 1905. He is probably the smartest bi-lingual journalist at present in South Africa, and has made a London reputation by a series of clever articles on the native problem (especially the Ethiopian question) in the leading magazines.

JONES, James, F.R.C.I., of Greenhill, Justice St., Cape Town, was born in 1850. Trained as a chemist, he went to S. Africa and settled in Cape Town. In 1882 he was elected one of the first vice-presidents of the Pharmaceutical Society of Cape Colony, and is now President. He served as a captain with the Prince of Wales's Light Horse in the S. African War (Queen's medal), having previously assisted in the formation of the First Mounted Inf. Co. ever raised in S. Africa, a branch of the Army which was immensely augmented during the late war. He married, first, in 1876, Mary, dau. of the late Thos. Harries (died 1890), and, secondly, in 1898, Persis, dau. of W. R. Thomas.

JONES, Colonel Morey Quayle, C.B., of Northgate, Warwick, and of the Army and Navy Club, was born March 5, 1855, and is second son of the Rev. C. W. Jones. He was educated at Wellington Coll. He joined the 6th Royal Regt. in 1873, and was Capt. in the Royal Warwickshire Regt. in 1883; was Major in the 4th Pioneer Bechuanaland Field Force in 1884; Adjutant in the Auxiliary Forces in 1886, and Major in the Royal Warwickshire Regt. in 1890. From 1891-4 he was commandant of the School of Instruction, Aux. Forces, at Aldershot, and Acting A.A.G. for prisoners of war at Bermuda in 1901. His war services include the Bechuanaland Expedition in 1884, the Nile Expedition in 1898, when he was present at the Battle of Atbara (C.B.),

and the S. African Campaign in 1899. He married, in 1888, Isabel, dau. of the late Maitland Dashwood.

JONES, The Hon. Sidney Twentyman, of Oiles, Grahamstown, and Ravensworth, Claremont, and of the Civil Service (C.T.) and Port Elizabeth Clubs, is the son of Thomas Jones, of Stanimore, Rondebosch, by Sarah Elizabeth Head Twentyman, dau. of John Twentyman, of Dwerry House, Lancashire. He was born Jan. 20, 1849, and educated at the Diocesan Coll., Rondebosch, and the S.A. Cull., Cape Town. He took the second-class certificate of the Cape Board of Examiners, graduated B.A. in 1868; entered Trinity Hall, Camb., in 1868, and was Legal Prizeman and Scholar of his year, graduating LL.B. in 1872, LL.M. in 1876, and LL.D. in 1890. He was called to the Bar at the Middle Temple in 1873, and joined the Supreme Court Bar as an Advocate in 1874. In 1878 he entered the Cape Town Cavalry as Sec. Lieut. and later the D.E.O.V.R.

Subsequent to 1881 he was frequently one of the Law Examiners at the Cape Univ. In 1882 he was raised to the Bench of the Supreme Court and assigned as Senior Puisne Judge to the High Court of Griqualand, where he frequently acted as Judge-President. In 1887 he was assigned to the Court of the Eastern Districts, and occasionally acted as Judge-President, which office he has held since the retirement in 1901 of Sir Jacob D. Barry. In 1891, during the absence of the Chief Justice from the Colony, he occupied the position of Senior Puisne Judge in the Supreme Court while Sir John Buchanan was Acting Chief Justice. At Kimberley he was President of the Agricultural Soc., Chairman of the Public Schools, and President of the Boating Club, which, it is interesting to state, rowed their weekly excursion near the scene of the great Modder fight. At Grahamstown for some time he was Chairman of the Public Schools, of the Public Library, and President of the Eastern Province Literary and Scientific Soc. He has had the honour of being the founder of the leading colonial football club (which now holds the championship cup) the Villagers F.C. He married Florence, dau. of Henry M. Arderne of the Hill, Claremont, in 1878.

JONES, The Most Rev. William West, Archbishop of Cape Town and Metropolitan of the Church of S. Africa; of Bishop's Court, Claremont, C. Colony, and of the Royal Colonial Institute, is the son of E. H. Jones; was born at South Hackney, May 11, 1838, and was educated at the Merchant Taylors' Sch. and St. John's Coll., Oxon. He graduated B.A. 1860, M.A. 1864, B.D. 1870, and received the Hon. Degree of D.D. 1874. He was Fellow of St. John's Coll., Oxon., 1859; Hon. Fellow, 1895; from 1861 to 1864 he was Curate of St. Matthew's, City Road, London; Vicar of Summertown, Oxen., 1864-74; Oxford Preacher at Whitehall Chapel, 1870-72; Rural Dean of Oxon. 1871-4; was consecrated in Westminster Abbey, Bishop of Cape Town and Metropolitan, 1874; Archbishop of Cape Town, 1897. He married Emily, dau. of John Allen, of Altrincham, Cheshire, in 1879.

JORDISON, Frank Lloyd, of Bulawayo, and of the Bulawayo and Gwelo Clubs, is the son of Dr. Robert Jordison, of Hornchurch, Essex. He was born July 28, 1866, at Hornchurch, and was educated at the Albert Memorial College, Framingham, Suffolk. He left England for S. Africa in Dec., 1888, and proceeded to Johannesburg, and from there to Bulawayo in 1894. He is one of the pioneers of Rhodesia; served as Lieut. in the '96 Rebellion, and raised the Gwelo Troop of the Southern Rhodesia Volunteers, of which he became Captain, resigning his commission in July, 1903 (medal). Recreations: shooting and all kinds of sports.

JORISSEN, Dr., acted as Justice of the High Court of the S.A.R. during the Kruger régime. He was so violently opposed to the Reform movement that he honestly recognised the impossibility of maintaining an impartial attitude and therefore refused to preside over the Court at the trial of the Reformers. He has since retired.

JOUBERT, Christiaan, was Minister of Mines for the Transvaal under the Govt. of the S.A.R., and was one of the members of the Industrial Commission appointed by the Transvaal Govt. Sworn evidence was adduced that the attempt to 'jump' the Ferreira claims had been suggested by Mr. Joubert himself.

JUDD Captain Bertram Christopher, of East London, Cape Colony, and the East London Club, was born in Essex, Sept. 28, 1873, and was educated at Bedford Grammar Sch. Joining the C.M.R. in 1893, he was appointed Lieut. in 1900, and served through the S. African War with the C.M.R., being severely wounded at Magato Nek in Aug., 1900. He was Supply and Transport Officer in No. 1 Division of the Cape Colony from Jan. 1, 1902, till the end of the war, receiving the Queen's medal with clasps for Wepener, Wittebergen, Cape Colony, and Transvaal, and the King's medal with two clasps. He also received the Jubilee medal in 1897. In Sept., 1904, he was appointed Adjt. of the Kaffrarian Rifles, with rank of Capt. in the C.C.F. Recreations: rowing, golf, and tennis. Unmarried.

JUDD Walter Albert, of Upper Norwood, Surrey, and of the St. Stephen's Club, Weststmnster, and of the Richmond, Cromer, and Le Touquet Golf Clubs, is the second son of late James Judd, J.P., of Upper Norwood, and was born in 1864.For many years Mr. Walter Judd was connected with the *Illustrated London News*, and while in America he published the first American edition of that paper in 1888. He founded the publishing firm Heywood and Co., Ltd., in 1889, a company which owns a large number of important trade papers, including the *Watchmaker and Jeweller*, *The Confectioners' Union*, *The Dyer*, *Grocery*, etc., etc. In 1891 Mr. Judd established the firm now so well known as Walter Judd, Ltd., which has the distinction of having been the first Contractors to H.M. Government for the *Board of Trade Journal* and other Government publications.

Mr. Judd is the proprietor of the *Councils' Journal*, and besides being well known in London, Berlin, and in the South African and other Colonies in connection with many successful public issues, he is joint proprietor with W. H. Wills of the *Anglo-African Who's Who*. He married, in 1888, Flora Adelaide, second daughter of James Sharp, of Bradford, who was one of the founders of the Bradford Dyers' Association.

JURISCH, Carl Heinrich Leopold Max, Surveyor-Gen. of C.C., of Cape Town, is of German parentage, and was born at Jammi, West Prussia. Educated at Orandeny and Berlin. He entered the German Army in 1860, was promoted Capt. in the Royal Artillery in 1871. In the interval he fought in the wars of Prussia against Denmark (1864), against Austria (1866), and against France (1870-1). For his distinguished services he received the decoration of the Iron Cross on the battlefield of Sedan. In 1872 he went to S.A., and obtained (July, 1878) the appointment of Col. Govt. Land Surveyor; was appointed Acting Examiner of Diagrams, April, 1879; Examines of Diagrams, July, 1882; University Examiner in Science, 1891; Second Asst. Surveyor-Gen., July, 1892; First Asst., July, 1897; and Surveyor-Gen., Aug. 10, 1902. He received the thanks of Lord Kitchener for assistance rendered in compiling maps during the S.A. War of 1899-1902. He married, Sept. 2, 1872, the Countess Marie Antoinette de Marillac.

JURITZ, Charles Frederick, M.A., of Villa Marina, Sea Point, Cape Town, and of Lake Cottage, Muizenberg, Cape Town, was educated at the S. African Coll. and the Cape of Good Hope Univ. (Queen's Scholar, S.A. Coll., 1878; matriculated with honours, C.G.H. Univ., 1881; Jamieson Exhibitioner, 1881; University Exhibitioner, 1883; Governor's Prize, S.A. Coll., 1883; graduated B.A., with honours in mathematics and natural science, C.G.H. Univ., 1885; and M.A. in department of chemistry in 1886). He was elected a Fellow of the C.G.H. Univ. in 1886, and was temporarily retained by the Cape Govt. to perform the analysis of Colonial tobaccos and soils, 1886. Appointed Tutor in Science at the Govt. Agricultural Sch., Somerset East, in 1900; but instead of proceeding there he was employed in Cape Town in connection with the establishment of a Public Health Branch of the Colonial Office. While serving in that capacity he conducted an inquiry into the outbreak of enteric fever in the Cape Peninsula; he also codified the municipal regulations of Cape Colony. In 1891 he was appointed Senior Analyst in charge of the Government Analytical Laboratory at Cape Town; established a branch laboratory at Grahamstown in 1902; was examiner to the C.G.H. Univ. in mathematics and chemical science in 1892-6; member of some Govt. Commissions. For many years he acted as judge of fertilisers at the annual

show of the Western Province Agricultural Society of Cape Colony. He is a member and secretary of the S.A. Coll. Union, member of the S.A. Philosophical Society, and of the S.A. Association for the Advancement of Science, and local secretary of the Chemical Section of the British Association. In 1881 he assisted in founding the Sea Point Debating Soc., and acted for upwards of twelve years, first as secretary and afterwards as president. On the death of his father he succeeded, in 1903, to a directorship of the Good Hope Seminary, Cape Town.

Publications: *Chemical Composition of Colonial Fodder Plants and Woods* (1890), *Course of Inorganic Qualitative Chemical Analysis* (1890), *Chemical Composition of the Soils of the S.W. Districts of Cape Colony* (1900), *South African Pharmacology* (1905), and *The Need for Organised Chemical Research in Cape Colony* (1905).

JUST, Hartmann Wolfgang, C.B., C.M.G., son of the late Heinrich Just, of Bristol, was born in 1854. He was educated at Bristol Gram. Sch. and Corpus Christi Coll., Oxon. He was Asst. Private Secy. at the Colonial Office to the late Earl of Derby, to the late Mr. Edward Stanhope, to Sir Henry Holland (now Lord Knutsford), to Sir Gee. Osborne Morgan, and the Marquis of Ripon. He also acted as Asst. Secy. to the Colonial Conference of 1887. He subsequently became a principal clerk in the Colonial Office, and head of the S.A. Dept. In 1902 he accompanied Mr. Chamberlain on his African tour. He married, in 1879, Katherine Francis, dau. of Samuel Rootham.

JUTA, Carl Wilhelm Thalman Biccard, was called to the Bar at the Inner Temple in 1898, and became an advocate of the Supreme Court of the Transvaal in 1899. From 1900-1902 he acted as Registrar of Patents and Trade Marks, part of that time acting as Registrar of Companies. He also served in the Dept. of the State Attorney for the Transvaal under the late Govt. He is now chief clerk to the Commissioner of Patents, and Asst. Registrar of Companies in the Transvaal.

JUTA, Hon. Sir Henry Hubert, M.L.A. for Port Elizabeth, K.C., of Cape Town, was born at Cape Town in 1858, and is of Dutch extraction. He was educated in Cape Colony and in England; was admitted an advocate of the Supreme Court of Cape Colony in 1880, and devoted himself mainly to law reporting and Chamber practice. He was also formerly Law Examiner at the Cape University. He was Judge of the High Court of Griqualand West; was appointed a special Commissioner in the settlement of the Swaziland difficulties in 1890; became Attorney-Gen. on Mr. Schreiner's resignation in 1893, but resigned that office in Sept., 1894. From 1896 to 1898 he was Speaker of the Cape Parliament, and he coalesced with the Progressive Party in the endeavour to persuade the Colonial Secy. to agree to the temporary suspension of the Cape Constitution towards the end of the S. African War. He was last returned to the Cape Parliament in Feb., 1904, and was offered office in Dr. Jameson's Cabinet, which, however, he did not see his way to accept. Sir Henry is a partner in the great publishing firm of Juta & Co., of Cape Town, and married a dau. of Mr. M. M. Tait.

KAGWA, Sir Apolo, K.C.M.G., Prime Minister of Uganda, of Mengo, Uganda, was born in that country in 1864. He is a grandson of Kadumukasa, deputy chief of the county of Budu. He was educated by the Church Missionary Society of Uganda; was formerly page to Kabaka Mutesa. and subsequently steward to Mwanga, Kabaka (or king) of Uganda. He was made Mukwenda, chief of the county of Sirgo, in 1888; took part in the Christian-Mohammedan War in 1888-9, and was the chief agent in inviting the Imperial British E. Africa Co. to Uganda in 1889, and in getting the treaty signed with Capt. Lugard in 1890. He served with the English in the war between the English and French sections of the Bagwanda in 1892, and was the chief instrument in effecting the return of King Mwanga. He took part in the Bukedi Expedition in 1895 (medal), the expedition against the rebel King Mwanga in 1897 (medal), and served in the expedition against the Sudanese mutineers, 1897S (medal and two clasps). He was invited to attend the King's coronation in 1902 (coronation medal), when he toured round the country, visiting the chief manufacturing towns of England. He is the author of *Basekabaka be Baganda* (Kings of Uganda), 1898; *Engero za Baganda* (Uganda Folk Lore), 1902;

and *Ekitabo Kye Kika Kye Nsenene* (History of the Grasshopper Clan), 1905. He was married in 1888.

KANYEMBA, a native chief of Portuguese extraction in North Eastern Rhodesia, whose kraal is situated some six miles south of the Zambesi River and five west of the Mozambique Company's border. Kanyemba is generally hospitable to white men, but is fast losing his authority amongst his own natives owing to his cruelty in what he considers the dispensing of justice.

KEANE, Henry Augustus, F.R.G.S., of Arám-Gáh (Abode of Peace), 79, Broadhurst Gardens, South Hampstead, N.W., is the son of James and Elizabeth Keane, of London. He was born in 1835 at Cork, Ireland, and educated at his native place, Dublin, Jersey, Rome, and Hanover. He has devoted his life chiefly to ethnological, philological, and geographical studies. His principal life work has been the preparation of a scheme of ethnology in three parts. The first part deals with fundamental problems—antiquity, unity, cradle dispersion, physical and mental characters of man—Cambridge University Press, 1896. Part 2, with the main division of mankind—Camb. Univ. Press, 1900. He is now engaged upon Part 3, which comprises a Universal Anthropological A.B.C. with 20,000 entries, of which the American section in MS., 5,000 entries, is completed. His works about Africa include *Africa*, 2 volumes, Stanford Series; *Boer States, Law, and People* (Methuen); *The Gold of Ophir, Whence Brought* (Stanford). His recreations are walking and poetry. He married, May 24, 1874, the dau. of William Hearn Jacobs, of Chale Abbey, Isle of Wight, sister of the late Very Rev. Henry Jacobs, Dean Christchurch, N.Z.

KEARNS, Capt. Thomas Joseph, was born with the colours, and, joining the Army, served fourteen and a half years in the ranks before becoming warrant officer. Eight years later he was appointed riding master of the Army Service Corps at Woolwich with an hon. commision, and in 1904 was elected City Marshal (London) He has the medal and clasp for the 1879 Zulu Campaign, the star for the Ashanti Expedition of 1895, and the Queen's medal with six clasps for the South African War, and has been mentioned in despatches four times. Captain Kearns was one of the founders of the Army Temperance Association, and is Secy. of the Church of England Soldiers' Institute at Woolwich, and has been actively associated with the Military Tournament at Islington.

KEEBLE, George, J.P., of Peterborough, of which he has been twice Mayor, is chairman of the African Farms, Ltd., Saxon Portland Cement Co., Ltd., Norman Cement Co., Ltd., and the Kent Jam Co., Ltd.

KEKEWICH, Major-Gen. Robert George, C.B., of Peamore, Exeter, and of the Naval and Military Club, was born in Devonshire on June 17, 1854, and comes of a family which has produced many notable men, including Sir George and Mr. Justice Kekewich. He was educated at King Edward's Sch., Birmingham, and at Marlborough Coll., and joined the Buffs 1874. Almost immediately he found himself in the tented field, taking part in the Perak Expedition in 1875-6 (medal and clasp); the Sondan Expedition in 1884-5, as D.A.A.G. and D.A.Q.M.G. (despatches, medal with clasp, bronze star, brevet of Maj); the Sudan in 1888, when he was at Suakin as Brig.-Maj. and afterwards D.A.A.G., and was present at the action of Gemaizeh (despatches and 4th class Medjidieh). When the S.A. War (1899-1902) broke out Gen. Kekewich was in command of the 1st Batt. Loyal North Lancashire Regt., and commanded Griqualand West and Bechuanaland, and no man worked harder than the hero of Kimberley in the defence of that town. Lord Roberts was of opinion that the greatest credit was due to Col. Kekewich for the able dispositions which he made for the defence of Kimberley, an unwalled town, spread over a wide area, for his rapid organisation of an auxiliary force which, in conjunction with the regular troops, enabled him to keep the enemy in check, and for the tact, judgment, and resolution which he displayed throughout the siege.

After the relief of Kimberley Gen. Kekewich was given the command of a mobile column, and from Feb., 1902, until the end of the operations he had command of a group of mobile columns. He was severely wounded at the action of Moedwill, and in recognition of his various distinguished services he was several times mentioned in despatches; received the brev. of Col., was afterwards

promoted Maj. Gen., and decorated with the C.B. and the Queen's medal with three clasps and the King's medal with two clasps. But among his most valued souvenirs of the war is a handsome sword presented to him by the inhabitants of Kimberley. The scabbard is emblazoned with uncut Kimberley diamonds and the General's arms, pictures of the conning tower at Kimberley, and the charge of his own regt.—the Loyal North Lancashires. General Kekewich retired from the Army in 1904. He is not married.

KELLY, Major-Gen. Sir William Freeman, K.C.B., of Valetta, Malta, was born in 1847, and is son of the late W. R. Kelly, of Kent. He entered the King's Regiment in 1867, and became a Captain in the Royal Sussex Regt. in 1880; served in the N.W. Frontier Expedition in India in 1876 as Staff Officer in the Peshawar Movable Column; action at Aimall Chabootra; the Egyptian Expedition in 1882-4; present at the battles of El Teb and Tarnai (despatches, two clasps, 4th class Medjidieh and brevet of Lieut. Col.); the Sudan Expedition in 1885 (despatches and two clasps); and the South African War in 1899-1902 as Special Service Officer, afterwards on the Staff; operations in the Orange Free State and the Transvaal; present at the actions at Poplar Grove and Driefontein, and the actions near Johannesburg and Pretoria (despatches, King's medal with two clasps, and K.C.B.). Since 1903 he has been in command of the Infantry Brigade at Malta. He married, in 1889, Mary, dau. of Lieut. Col. C. Russell, of Ockenden, Essex.

KELLYKENNY, General Sir Thomas, GC.B., K.C.B., of Doolough Lodge, Co. Clare, was born in 1840. He served in China in 1860, including the action of Sinho, and the capture of Tangku and Taku Forts (despatches, medal, and clasp), and in Abyssinia in 1867S (despatches, medal). During the late S. African War he commanded the 6th Division, being present at the relief of Kimberley, the operations in the Orange Free State, the actions at Paardeberg, Poplar Grove, and Driefontein, the operations in the Orange River Colony, and the actions at Ladybrand (despatches, Queen's medal with four clasps, and promoted Lieut. Gen.) Since that time he has held various district commands in England. He was a member of Prince Arthur of

Connaught's suite which left for the East early in 1906 in order to invest the Mikado with the Knighthood of the Garter.

KELTIE, John Scott, LL.D., Knight of the North Star (Sweden); of 15, Neville Court, Abbey Road, N.W., and of the Royal Societies, Ravage, and Geographical Clubs, was born in Dundee and was educated at St. Andrews and Edinburgh Universities. He was formerly on the editorial staff of Messrs. W. and R. Chambers; was subeditor of *Nature*, from 1871-84, Inspector of Geographical Education to the Royal Geographical Society in 1884, Librarian of the R.G.S. from 1885-92, and Secretary of the Society since 1892. He has been editor of the *Statesman's Year Book* since 1881, and of the *Geographical Journal* and the *Story of Exploration*; author of *Reports on Geographical Education*, *Applied Geography*, and the *Partition of Africa*. He also contributes in African and other subjects to the *Times* and various magazines He presided over the Geographical Section of the British Assn. at their Toronto meeting in 1897, and is an hon. member of the Geographical Societies of Berlin, Rome, Brussels, Amsterdam, Geneva, Lisbon, Budapest, Philadelphia, &c. Recreation: Golf.

KELVIN, Right Hon. Baron, P.C., O.M., G.C.V.O., M.A, D.C.L., LL.D., of Netherhall, Largs R.S.O., Ayrshire, and of 15, Eaton Place, London, S.W., was born at Belfast in 1824, and, although Irish by birth his parents were of Scotch extraction. William Thomson, Lord Kelvin's baptismal name, is the son of Prof. Jas. Thomson, who occupied the Chair of Mathematics at Glasgow University, and under his father's tutelage showed such extraordinary aptitude as to distinguish him from all the rest of his contemporary students. At St. Peter's College, Cambridge, he graduated as Second Wrangler and First Smith's Prizeman in 1845, and also found time for athletic and aquatic sports, carrying off on one occasion the Colquhoun Silver Sculls. He also interested himself in classics, music, and general literature, but soon devoted himself almost entirely to electrical and mathematical physics. While still a youth, Lord Kelvin was publishing original investigations in mathematics, and at the age of twenty-two became Professor of Natural Philosophy at the University of

Glasgow. Even at that time one of the tutors at St. Peter's recorded that he is regarded here by the most competent judges as the first man of science of the rising generation in this country. From that time Lord Kelvin has been ceaselessly associated with Glasgow University.

Lord Kelvin's main electrical work commenced in connection with the early Atlantic cables, and his inventions, which principally contributed to making submarine telegraphy practically and economically workable, have been many. Among these may be quoted the Mirror galvanometer, an ingenious instrument for the easy reading of electrical signals received through a long cable. However, his siphon recorder improved upon the latter by writing down the message as received. Other of his inventions are a tidal harmonic analyser and tide predictor for calculating the height of future tides at any place; instruments for making electrical measurements; a valuable new compass for marine navigation; the introduction of pianoforte wire for deep-sea sounding—a valuable aid to cable laying; and a navigation sounding machine, largely used in the naval and mercantile marine. In later years Lord Kelvin has devoted much time to the production of measuring instruments for electric light purposes, and his standard balances, his newer electrostatic potential instruments and electromagnetic voltmeter and ampere meter, are in common use. Lord Kelvin has from the early days before mentioned contributed largely to the public knowledge in the way of hooks (not forgetting his great work, in collaboration with Professor Tait, on National Philosophy), addresses, and the published records of his various researches. In 1866 he was knighted by her late Majesty, and he became Baron Kelvin in January, 1892. He is one of the recent recipients of the Order of Merit, Knight of the German Order *Pour le Merité*, Grand Officer of the Legion of Honour, Commander of the Order of Leopold of Belgium, and Foreign Associate of the French Academy. He is also Privy Councillor of Great Britain, Knight Grand Cross of the Royal Victorian Order, Lieutenant of the County of Glasgow, and Chancellor, since 1904, of Glasgow University, having previously resigned his Chair at the University after filling it for fifty-three years.

Some eight years ago Lord Kelvin became a

director of the Eastman Kodak Co., Ltd., and of the Linotype Company, afterwards joining the Board of the British Aluminum Company. He is also President of the Scottish Amicable Life Assurance Society, and one of the Advisory Board of Engineers of the Victoria Falls Power Company. In enlisting the support of a past president of the Institute of Electrical Engineers and of the Royal Society, the sponsor for the Power Company have interested one of the greatest names in electrical engineering and his advice should be of incalculable value in solving any technical difficulty which may possibly present itself.

Lord Kelvin married, first in 1852, Margaret, dau. of the late Walter Crum, and secondly, in 1874, Frances Anna, dau. of Charles R. Blandy, of Madeira.

KEMBALL, Colonel George Vero, C.B., D.S.O., of 3, Cadogan Mansions, S.W., and of the United Service Club, was born in 1859, and is son of Major-Gen. J. S. Kemball. He was educated at Harrow, and entered the Royal Artillery in 1878, and served in the Afghan War in 1878-9 (medal); the operations in Chitral in 1895, with the Relief Force; as D.A.Q.M.G. with the 1st Brigade, and as D.A.A. and Q.M.G. on the line of communications (despatches, brevet of Major); the operations on the N.W. Frontier of India in 1897, with the Tochi Field Force, as D.A.Q.M.G. of Intelligence (despatches); took part in the Kaduna Expedition, N. Nigeria, in 1900 (medal with clasp); commanded the operations against the forces of Bida and Kontagora, N. Nigeria, in 1901 (despatches, medal with clasp, and D.S.O.); and the Kano-Sokoto Expedition in 1903 (despatches, C.B.). From 1901-5 he acted as Inspector-General of the West African Frontier Force. He married, in 1889, Hattie, dau. of Gilbert Elliott.

KEMPTHORNE, Capt. Henry Noel, F.R.G.S., of the Junior Naval and Military and Grosvenor Clubs, as born May 29, 1878, and is son of the Rev. P. H. Kcmpthorne, M.A., F.R.A.S. He was educated at Wellington Coll., and passed out of the Militia by competitive examination into the H. Sects Fusiliers in 1898. After serving in India he was seconded for service under the Colonial Office in April, 1901, and was appointed to the N. Nigeria Regt. (now

known as the West African Frontier Force), serving as Adjt. of the 1st Battn., with local rank of Capt. for three years. He served in the Kano and Sokoto Campaign in 1903 under Gen. Kemball and Col. Morland as Adjt. (despatches, medal and clasp), and was promoted Captain in his own regt. (R.S.F.) in Dec., 1904. Recreations: Polo and shooting. Unmarried.

KEMSLEY, James, of Richmond, Surrey, and recently of Port Elizabeth, and of the Port Elizabeth Club and Royal Colonial Institute, was born at Gillingham, Kent, Jan. 7, 1838, and left with his parents in 1849 for Port Elizabeth, where he received his education. Mr. Kemsley served his apprenticeship to journalism on the staff of the *Eastern Province Herald*, and in 1860 became the proprietor of the *Port Elizabeth Telegraph* (now the *Cape Daily Telegraph*), which he edited and conducted until his retirement from business, after over forty years of active journalistic work. Mr. Kemsley took a general interest in all local affairs, and served the town with appreciation on most of the public Boards, including the Town Council, the Committee of the public Library, the Board of Managers of the Grey Institute, and the Provincial Hospital. He was one of the founders and supporters of the Newspaper Press Union of South Africa, of which he was elected President in 1893, and has now retired. He married, in 1860, Miss Caroline Ann Beal.

KENNA, Col. Paul Aloysius, V.C., D.S.O., at present serving in Somaliland, was born in 1862; is second son of Jas. Kenna; was educated at Stonyhurst, and entered the 21st Lancers. He served in the Sudan in 1898, and throughout the late S.A. Campaign, commanding a column from Dec., 1901, to the end of the war. From Dec, 1902, he has been in command of mounted troops of the Somali Field Force with the local rank of Lieut. Col. Col. Kenna won his V.C. during the famous charge of the 21st Lancers at Omdurman.. In the thick of the mêlée in the Dervish-crowded khor Major Kenna found himself beside Lieutenant Colonel Wyndham, whose horse had been killed; "I'm all right," cried Wyndham, "but give me a revolver." Kenna, however, lifted his comrade from the ground, swung him up behind his saddle, and thus the two officers came out of the fray.

When the regiment formed up after the charge on the far side of the khor, Kenna and the late Captain Montmorency rode back through the Arabs to rescue from mutilation the body of Lieutenant Grenfell. In addition to the V.C. and D.S.O. he possesses the Royal Humane Soc. Certificate for saving life (June, 1895); for several years he headed the list of gentlemen riders in India, and has played in his regimental polo team for 14 years. Colonel Kenna was gazetted to the command of the 21st Lancers in 1906, and married, in 1895, Lady Cecil Bertie third dau. of the Earl of Abingdon.

KERR, Philip, is elder son of Lord Ralph and Lady Anne Kerr, finished his education at Oxford Univ., and in Jan., 1905, was appointed Priv. Secy. to Sir Arthur Lawley, Lieut.-Governor of the Transvaal.

KESSLER, Leopold, of 9, Hanover Square W., and of the Rand Club, Johannesburg, was born in the mining district of Upper Silesia, is the son of a manufacturer and mine owner. He was educated at Berlin and the Royal Saxon Mining Coll., Freiberg, where he graduated as mining engineer. The anti-Semitic feeling in Germany caused him to leave that country. In 1890 he accompanied as mining engineer an expedition through Matabeleland, where he remained until 1892, when he left for the Witwatersrand, acting there as Consulting Engineer for several financial houses. With the exception of some intervals, during which he inspected mines of other countries, and led an exploring expedition through Arabia Petra, he has resided in Johannesburg ever since. Mr. Kessler is Managing Director of the Montrose Diamond Co., and is the author of *Valuation Plans of the Witwatersrand Goldfields* (Edward Stanford, 1902).

KESTELL, Philip, took part in the war of 1899-02 as Chaplain to Gen. de Wet. He was captured by the British, and was detained in their camp during the action at Graspan, when it was alleged by the Continental Press that the British placed Boer women in front as cover to their troops. Mr. Kestell escaped, and attended Mr. Steyn on his wanderings from place to place during the late stages of the war. He also acted as one of the Secretaries at the Peace Conference at Vereeniging. His book *Through Shot and Flame*, needless to say,

contains not even a hint of the Graspan incident referred to above.

KHEDIVE OF EGYPT (see Abbas II.).

KIDGER, Capt. William, of Johannesburg, is son of Wm. Kidger of Tarkastad, Cape Colony. He is a member of the Johannesburg Stock Exchange, and served in the S. African War with Brabant's Horse, latterly being Intelligence Officer for Tarka, C.C., where his knowledge of the surrounding districts was of great local value.

KILPIN, Ernest Fuller, C.M.G. (1901); J.P.; Clerk of the House of Assembly of the Cape of Good Hope; of Linford, Kenilworth, near Cape Town, and of the Civil Service Club, was born in Reading, May 5, 1854, being the only son of the Rev. S. W. Kilpin, who died Aug. 6, of the same year. He was educated at private schools in Weymouth and Reading, and entered the Cape Civil Service in London in 1874, being shortly placed in charge of the West of England and South Wales District for the purpose of obtaining and forwarding to the Cape large numbers of the artisans required for the construction of public works. In 1876 he went to Cape Town as Private Secy. to the late Sir Charles Mills, then Under Colonial Secy., and when Sir Gordon Sprigg first took office (Feb. 5, 1878) during the Kaffir War, he sent for Mr. Kilpin to join him on the frontier as his Private Secy. For some months he resided in King William's Town, and organised and carried on there a Colonial Secy.'s. Office in miniature. During the next two years Mr. Kilpin accompanied Sir Gordon Sprigg on many tours of inspection through the Colony; attended him during the negotiations in Kimberley in regard to the annexation of Griqualand West to the Cape, and was with him at the great Disarmament *Pitso* in Basutoland, and at the siege of Morosi's Mountain. In 1886 he was appointed Clerk Assistant of the House of Assembly, and was elected Clerk of the House in 1897. When Sir Thomas Scanlen was Prime Minister in 1883 he obtained Mr. Kilpin's services as Priv. Secy. for a visit to Basutoland in the effort to secure a satisfactory settlement of that territory, which at that time was annexed to the Cape. He has been Secy. of the following Cape Govt. Commissions: Dorthesia, 1877; War Expenditure, 1881; Liesbeek

Municipality, 1883; Diamond Laws, 1887; Liquor Laws, 1889; Lighthouses, 1890; Fisheries, 1892; Scab, 1893; Defence, 1896. He was Secy. of the Imperial British and German Joint Commission on Angra Pequeña and West Coast Claims in 1885, for which inquiry H.M.S. *Sylvia* was specially detached and fitted up, proceeding up the coast as far as Walfisch Bay. He has been Examiner in Shorthand under the Cape Civil Service Commissioners since that paper was first set in 1889; is proprietor and Editor of the *Cape Civil Service List*, which he instituted in 1885; author of the *Parliamentary Agent's Manual (Cape) 1902*, and is a J.P. for the whole Colony. He married, in 1880, Augusta (Lady of the Royal Red Cross, 1902), dau. of G. W. Pilkington, of Cape Town.

KINDERSLEY, Archibald Ogilvie Lyttelton, of Germiston, Transvaal, served under the Imperial Govt. as Lieutenant in the Highland Light Infantry (Mil.) in 1887, and was seconded for service under the Colonial Office in the Niger Coast Protectorate in 1893, when he commanded an expedition to Ekat; also took part in the expedition to Okurike (despatches), and the Brass River Expedition in 1895 (despatches, medal, and clasp). He acted as Adjt. of the Niger Coast Protectorate Force in 195, subsequently acting Commandant. In 1896 he retired from the service of the Protectorate. Mr. Kindersley also served in the late S. African War, afterwards being appointed Inspector of Native Affairs for the Germiston District in the Transvaal, which position he now occupies.

KING, Godfrey James, of The Northgate, Salisbury, Rhodesia, and of the Salisbury Club, was born at Oxford, Oct. 29, 1870, and is son of the Rev. Canon King. He was educated at Oriel Coll., Oxford, and was Capt. in the 4th Battn. of Sherwood Foresters in 1895-6. He became Registrar of Deeds, Companies, and Patents for S. Rhodesia in 1897, and has also acted as High Sheriff for S. Rhodesia. He received the Mashonaland War medal in 1896. In 1898 he married Mary, dau. of R. H. Capper.

KING, Henry James, of Salisbury House, London Wall, E.C., and Eastwell Park, Kent, was a partner in the firm of Neumann & Co. (see Sigismund Neumann). He is a Director of the Clement's Lane

Estate, Ltd., Haling Down Estate, Ltd., Salisbury House Estate, Ltd., and the Woodcote Grove Estate, Ltd., and is on the London Committee of the Premier (Transvaal) Diamond Mining Co.

KING, Thomas Burnham, was returned unopposed to the Cape Parliament as Progressive Member for Victoria East (C.C.) in Nov., 1902, and was re-elected in Feb., 1904. Late in that year he was appointed by the Baptist Union in S. Africa a delegate to the Pan Baptist Conference in London. He is no longer a member of the House of Assembly.

KING, William Joseph Harding, B.A., F.R.G.S., M.R.A.S., of Wollescote Hall, near Stourbridge, was born at Churchill Court, near Kidderminster, April 28, 1869. He is the eldest son of the late Wm. Hartley King and Louisa, dau. of Benjamin Harding, of Wadhurst Castle, Sussex. He was educated at Newton Abbot Coll. and Jesus Coll, Camb., and at the Middle Temple. In 1900 he made an expedition into the Sahara, publishing in 1903 an account of the journey in a paper to the Royal Geographical Society Journal, and afterwards in book form under the title of *A Search for the Masked Tawareks*.

KING-HARMAN, Sir Charles Anthony, KC.M.G., of Government House, Nikosia, Cyprus, and of the Windham Club, belongs to the distinguished family of which the Earl of Kingston is the titular head. He is son of the late Hon. L. H. King-Harman, was born in 1851, and was educated at Cheltenham Coll., and Trinity Coll., Cambridge, where he graduated M.A. He has seen considerable hard service as a Colonial administrator, mostly in the tropics, and has done much distinguished work for the Empire. In 1874 he acted as Private Secretary to Sir W. Robinson, and to General Sir Robert Biddulph in 1879; acted as Asst. Chief Secretary at Cyprus in 1881; was appointed Auditor General of Barbados in 1883, and Colonial Secretary for Mauritius in 1893. From 1897-1900 he acted as Administrator of St. Lucia, West Indies, and acted as Governor of Sierra Leone from 1900 until 1904, when he was appointed High Commissioner of Cyprus, which position he still holds. Sir Charles was created K.C.M.G. in 1900, in recognition of his Colonial services. He married, in 1888, Constance, dau. of Gen. Sir Robt. Biddulph.

KIMBERLEY, Vicar Apostolic of. (See Right Rev. Matthew Gaughren.)

KIPLING, Rudyard, D.C.L., of Bateman's, Burwash, Sussex; The Woolsack, Rosebank, near Cape Town, and of the Athenaeum and Century (New York) Clubs; was born at Bombay, Dec. 30, 1865, and is son of J. Lockwood Kipling, C.I.E. He was educated at Westward He United Service College, and has travelled in China, Japan, Africa, America, and Australia. From 1882-9 he acted as asst. editor in India of the *Civil and Military Gazette and Pioneer*. He is the author of numerous publications, including *Departmental Ditties*, *Plain Tales from the Hills*, *Soldiers Three*, *In Black and White*, *The Story of the Gadsbys*, *Under the Deodars*, *Phantom Rickshaw*, *Wee Willie Winkie*, *Life's Handicap*, *The Light that Failed*, *Barrack Room Ballads*, *Many Inventions*, *The Jungle Book*, *The Second Jungle Book*, *The Seven Seas*, *Captains Courageous*, *The Day's Work*, *Stalky and Co.*, *From Sea to Sea*, *Kim*, *Just So Stories for Little Children*, and *Traffics and Discoveries*. He married, Jan. 17, 1892, Caroline Starr Balestier.

KIRK, Sir John, G.C.M.G., K.C.B., of Wavertree, Sevenoaks, Kent, and of the Athenaeum Club, is the son of the Rev. John Kirk; was born Nov., 1832, at Barry, Forfarshire, and was educated at the Edinburgh Univ., where he graduated LL.D. He is also D.C.L. Oxon., Sc.D. Camb., and M.D. Edin. Sir John Kirk served during the Crimean War in Asia Minor. He was Chief Officer under the Foreign Office in Dr. Livingstone's second Expedition, and with the great traveller explored and mapped the Zambesi from the coast to the Victoria Falls, and discovered Lake Nyassa, 1858-64. He was appointed H.M. Vice-Consul at Zanzibar in 1866, and Indian Assist. Political Agent at Zanzibar, 1868, Political Agent to the Viceroy of India at Zanzibar, 1873; H.M. Consul-Gen. 1873, and H.M. Agent and Consul-Gen. 1880. He was British Plenipotentiary to the African Conference at Brussels, 1889; British Delegate at Brussels to fix the tariffs under the Brussels Act, 1890; Member of Commission to revise the Slave Trade Instructions, 1891; and H.M. Commissioner to inquire into disturbances on the Niger, 1895. Sir John Kirk is

Chairman of the Uganda Railway Committee, of which he was first appointed a member in 1895. He is also a Director of the Niger Co. He married in 1867, Helen Cooke, Gold Medal list of the Royal Geographical Society.

KIRK, Lieut. J. W. C., B.A. (Camb.), of the Junior United Service Club, was born at Zanzibar; is son of Sir John Kirk, K.C.B. (q.v.); was educated at Marlborough Coll., and King's Coll., Camb. Entering the Duke of Cornwall's L.I. he proceeded to S.A. and served throughout the war; was wounded at Paardeberg (despatches, Queen's medal, four clasps, and King's medal). Transferring to the 6th Batt. King's African Rifles he served in the M.I. in Somaliland (1903). He is the author of a grammar of the Somali Language.

KIRKMAN, Hon. Thomas, M.L.C., F.R.M.S. of Croftlands, Equeefa, Natal, of the Quekett Microscopical Club (Lond.) and the Victoria Club (Maritzburg), is second son of the late Rev. T. P. Kirkman, M.A., P.B.S., of Croft, near Warrington, Lanes., where he was born Dec. 22, 1843. He was educated at Rossall Sch., and went to Natal with his brother John, in 1868, settling on a Govt. land grant in Alexandra County. He was elected to represent his county in the Legislative Assembly on responsible government being granted to the Colony in 1893, and was returned to the Legislative Council in 1898. For fourteen years Mr. Kirkman served in the Volunteer force, seeing active service for eight mouths in the Zulu War, 1878-79. He takes an interest in coffee planting and microscopical studies, and was elected a Fellow of the Royal Microscopical Soc. in 1898. He is unmarried.

KITCHENER, of Khartoum, General Viscount Horatio Herbert, of Simla, India; was born in Ireland in 1850, and is son of the late Lieut-Col. H. H. Kitchener. He received his early military training at the R.M.A., Woolwich, passing thence into the Royal Engineers. In 1882, Lieut. Kitchener, as he then still was, had a command of Egyptian Cavalry. In the following year he got his captaincy, and then promotion came to him rapidly in recognition of his untiring work and frequent active service in Egypt and the Sudan. From that time his war service included the Sudan Expedition in 1884-5, as D.A.A. and Q.M.G. (medal with clasp and bronze star); operations round Suakim in 1888, being in command at the action at Handoub (severely wounded); Sudan in 1888-9, action at Gemaizeh, when he was in command of a Brigade of the Egyptian Army, and took part in the action at Toski (two clasps, C.B.) Dongola Expedition in 1896, in command of the Expeditionary Force; operations of June 7 and Sept. 19 (promoted Major-Gen. for distinguished service; K.C.B.; 1st class Osmanieh, and Egyptian medal with two clasps); the Nile Expeditions in 1897-8, acting as Gen. Officer Commanding-in-Chief the Expeditionary Forces throughout the operations, including the battles of the Atbara and Khartoum (raised to the Peerage; thanked by the Houses of Parliament; medal and two clasps to Egyptian medal). Soon after the S. African War broke out in 1899, Lord Kitchener went out as Chief of the Staff to Lord Roberts, and participated in all the operations in the Orange Free State, Feb.-May, 1900, including the actions at Paardeberg; the operations in the Transvaal in May and June, 1900; present at the actions near Johannesburg and Pretoria; the operations east and west of Pretoria from July-Nov., 1900, and in the Orange River and Cape Colonies. Subsequently in Nov., 1900, Lord Kitchener succeeded Lord Roberts as Commander-in-Chief of the Forces in S. Africa, directing the operations in the Transvaal, Orange River Colony, on the Zululand Frontier of Natal and in Cape Colony. (Despatches, promoted Lt.-Gen. and Gen. for distinguished service; Queen's medal with three clasps, King's medal and two clasps; G.C.M.G.) Having brought the S. African War to a successful conclusion, Lord Kitchener was appointed Commander-in-Chief of the Forces in the E. Indies, in which position he immediately set about the reorganisation of the Indian Army and a redistribution of the troops, in order to effectively resist any possible invasion of the North. These radical changes brought him into frequent conflict with the Viceroy, although it was characteristic of Lord Kitchener's methods that his views received no airing by the aid of an inspired Press crusade. However, with the change of Government in 1906, a modus vivendi by a satisfactory compromise was arranged. The burden of Lord Kitchener's original complaint was that although he was the Commander in Chief in India, the real control of the Army under the Viceroy was not vested in himself, but in a junior General at Simla, who has since been displaced; Lord Kitchener now being directly responsible to the Viceroy. Unmarried.

KITCHIN, Joseph, of Beckenham, Kent, was born at Croydon, Surrey, on Dec. 15, 1870, and from 1885 onwards followed the occupations of shorthand writer, reporter, and journalist. Early in Johannesburg's life he became attracted by the progress of the world's premier goldfield; he made a systematic collection and study of information relating to Rand mining, and prepared much statistical matter, which was published in seven or eight newspapers, one in Johannesburg, another in Paris, and the rest in London. He cooperated with Mr. C. S. Goldmann in his work on *South African Mining and Finance*, a three volume work, which saw the light in Nov., 1895. In September, 1895, he gave up his scattered journalistic contributions in order to become the Mining Editor of the *African Review*, a position which he resigned in May, 1897, in order to enter the service of A. Goerz and Co., Ltd., taking charge of that Company's Intelligence Dept. in London. In 1899 he paid six months' visit to Johannesburg, also visiting Pretoria, Belfast, Barberton, Lourenço Marques, Durban, Cape Town and Kimberley. In Sept., 1899, he was appointed a second Manager of the Company in London, and in the spring of 1901 he became sole Manager in London. He has now served the Goerz Corporation for nine years, at first under the late Mr. Adolf Goerz and latterly under Mr. Henry Strakosch, the two Managing Directors who took up residence in the Metropolis. He is a hard worker, and dabbles a little in science. On January 1, 1892, he married Marianne, dau. of John Henry Davy, of Hastings.

KLIMKE, Joseph, Ex-State Mining Engineer of the late S.A.R., a Knight of the French Legion of Honour; Knight of the Prussian Red Eagle, Third Class; Commander of the Portuguese *Nossa Senhora da Conceicao de Vila Viçosa*, of which latter order he wears the Star; was born Oct. 5, 1849, in Upper Silesia, Germany, and is the son of a small farmer. After tending a nine years course at a college in his native country, he entered at the age of twenty the profession of mining. Left to his own resources he did two years' manual work as a miner and mechanic in coal and metal mines. At the end of this period he obtained two years' instruction at a mining school, and then he received three more years' training in engineering and mine surveying. After being admitted as Govt. Mine Surveyor, he practised a short time and then took up an appointment as captain of a zinc and lead ore mine. In 1880 he was appointed manager of a gold mining company in Guayana, Venezuela. On arriving in S. America he vigorously devoted himself to attaining a knowledge of the Spanish language and the local conditions of the country. Shortly after his arrival he removed to the adjoining El Callao gold field. He acquired from the Univ. of Caracas the diploma of Civil Engineer, and was consequently instructed to draw up the working plans for the once famous El Callao and other adjacent mines. In 1887 he returned to Europe, but after a very brief stay he went on a tour of inspection to the Transvaal, arriving there in Feb., 1889, about the close of the first boom. Anticipating a great future for the Rand, he settled at Johannesburg as Consulting Engineer, and was appointed in Sept., 1891, by the Govt. as State Mining Engineer. At that time the position did not carry much power or responsibility; but seeing that with the rapid development of the mines the number of accidents increased at such a serious rate, he undertook to draw up the necessary rules and regulations for the Govt.'s supervision of all mining operations and over all boilers and machinery, and to establish a proper technical mining department. Hitherto, the Mining Dept. had confined itself to the carrying out of the provisions of the Gold Law, consisting chiefly in the disposal of mineral lands and water rights, and receiving the taxes from the proclaimed gold fields. The conflicting interests, however, of the various parties of the mining public, and the opposition of the Govt. itself and the Volksraad to every new measure from which no direct pecuniary returns were derived, made it a diffiult task to obtain the object in view. After several years of ceaseless effort, however, he succeeded in obtaining the Volksraad's sanction to the Mining Regulations and the Boiler Law in their latest forms, and finally to the Explosives Law and Diamond Law. Since the first two laws came in force the use of the metric system in place of the old measures and weights has been legalised as far as his dept. has been concerned. At the beginning

of the war he was on leave of absence in Europe when all the mines stopped working. Some of these were immediately restarted by officials of his department. When in he early days of Feb., 1900, rumours reached Europe expressing fear that the mines might be blown up by the Boers, he returned immediately to the Transvaal, and it is stated that he arrived just at the time when, with the consent of the Govt. and by the order of his representative, boreholes had been made in some of the working shafts to prepare for their eventual destruction. Being convinced that wanton destruction of this character was very ill-advised, he immediately had these holes filled up. In the meantime as much gold as possible had been extracted. The Govt., however, had failed to pay a portion of the working cost, while indebtedness to an enormous extent had been incurred for supplies with various commercial houses of Johannesburg. He vigorously pressed the Govt. for an immediate settlement of these accounts, and took measures to put the produced gold under proper control. As a result of this he was suspended from service, but permitted to return to Europe. Since that time he has been living in Germany and in London, but, as an ox-burgher of the late Republic, it is understood that he intends to settle at Johannesburg.

KLINGENBERG, Dr. Georg Ernst, was born in Hamburg in 1870, and is engaged in electrical engineering in a theoretical as well as practical manner. His father, Baurat L. Klingenberg, is an architect in Oldenburg. Professor Klingenberg went to college in Osnabruck, where he passed his final examination in 1889. After this he went in for his one year's military service, and was occupied with practical work for another year in the railway shops in Oldenburg and in several other works. He continued his studies at the Royal Technical College in Charlottenburg, under Slaby and Riedler. At Easter, 1894, he became assistant to Professor Slaby in the Laboratory at the Technical College. During this time he obtained the diploma of D.Phil. at the University in Rostock in 1897, and in July of the following year he settled down as private lecturer at the Technical College in Charlottenburg.

In January, 1900, he was nominated Professor. The subjects on which he lectured were the practical application of electrical engineering and engineering in general. He gave theoretical as well as practical lectures on these subjects up to 1902. During this time he also lectured on electromechanical designs, especially for apparatus for heavy currents, a subject which had not been represented till then at any other college. Shortly after he had been nominated Professor—in April, 1900—he also became Professor at the same Institute for the projecting of electrical installations. During this time Dr. Klingenberg had also an extensive practice dealing with projects and the erection of electricity works. Amongst the great number of large and small electricity works laid out by Professor Klingenberg, and the erection of which was partly supervised by him, should be mentioned the following: electricity works in Bredstedt, Marne, Meldorf, Blankenese, Wreschen, Hamborn bei Ruhrort, Potsdam, Schwerin, Tegel, the barracks of the shooting ranges at Juterbog, the Imperial Castle at Urville, Laudonvillers Castle near Metz, the Vulkan Shipyards at Stettin, Gas and Water Works at Stettin the Schonau Mill in Posen, in Charlottenburg and Halts. In addition to these, his Imperial Majesty the Emperor William II. commissioned him to prepare a scheme for the development of the Falls of the Mosel near Metz for the generation of electrical energy. It was due to this practice that Professor Klingenberg was enabled to obtain very extensive information and considerable practical experience in the layout of electrical installations, and this experience was most advantageously made use of for the benefit of the students attending his lectures.

In 1902 Prof. Klingenberg was elected one of the directors of the largest electrical engineer ing establishment, the *Allgemeine Elektricitäts Gesellschaft*, in Berlin, which is supplying the machinery for the Victoria Falls Power Company, and he is now one of the Advisory Board of Engineers of that company. Meanwhile, it became, of course, necessary for him to restrict his lectures at the Technical College, and he confined himself to those dealing with the projecting of electrical installations.

Professor Klingenberg has travelled a great deal both at home and abroad in order to study electrical undertaking and plants. He lends active support to technical societies, being a member of the Academic Club Hutte, the Society of German Engineers (*Verein Deutscher Ingenieure*), the Electrical Society (*Electrotechnischer Verein*), the Society for the Furtherance of Aerial Navigation, the Central European Motorcar Club, and the Society of German Electrical Engineers (*Verband Deutscher Electrotechniker*), in which last-named society Professor Klingenberg is on the committee.

KNAPP, Major George Harvey, of the Cape Mounted Rifles, was gazetted Surgeon Lieutenant to the corps in 1897, having previously taken part in the Langberg Campaign as Medical Officer to the Colonial Forces He also served in the S. African War in 1899-1901, including the operations in the Transvaal and Orange River Colony, and the actions at Bethlehem and Wittebergen. On its formation in 1903 he was transferred to the Medical Dept. of the C.M.R.

KNIGHT, Edward Frederick, B.A., of the Yorick, Savile, Eldon, and Whitefriars Clubs, was born in 1852, and is son of Edward Knight, of Cumberland. He was educated at Westminster and Caius College, Camb., acted as Times correspondent in Matabeleland in 1893-5; the Sudan Campaign in 1896, and again in 1897-8. He also served in the S. African War in 1899-1900, being severely wounded at Belmont, which resulted in the amputation of his right arm. He now acts as special correspondent for the *Morning Post* in the Far East. Mr. Knight is the author of several publications, including *Rhodesia of Today* and *Letters from the Sudan*.

KNIGHT, James Hartley, of Bourne House, Copthall Avenue, E.C., was born in 1868. He was formerly private secretary to the late Sir Walter Besant, and has since had much valuable journalistic experience on the Johannesburg *Star* in the early nineties, and several other Colonial journals. Mr. Knight is one of the most experienced writers on the South African Press, and has acted as editor of the *African World and Cape-Cairo Express* since that well-known weekly was established in 1902 in London, and also compiles, jointly with Mr. Leo Weinthal (q.v.) the very successful Christmas Annual of the *African World*, and other offshoots of that paper which have become such popular productions. Mr. Knight also is a frequent contributor to many of the leading magazines in England and in the United States of America.

KNOX, Major-Gen. Sir Charles Edmund, K.C.B., of the Naval and Military Club, was born in 1846, and is the eldest son of the late Dr. Knox, Archbishop of Armagh. He was educated at Eton, and joined the 85th Foot as Lieutenant in 1865; served in the Bechuanaland Expedition in 1884-5, in command of the 4th Pioneers (brevet of Lieut. Col.). From 1895-99 he was in command of the Regimental District at Bodmin. He served in the South African War in 1899-1902, in command of the 13th Brigade, being present at the relief of Kimberley; operations in the Orange Free State, including the actions at Paardeberg, Poplar Grove, and Driefontein; the operations in the Orange River Colony, present at the actions at Bothaville and Caledon River, and the operations in Cape Colony (despatches, promoted Major-General, King's medal with two clasps, and K.C.B.).

KNOX, General Sir William George, K.C.B., R.A., of Cork, Ireland, and of the United Service and Naval and Military Clubs, was born in 1847, and is son of the late Gen. T. E. Knox, C.B. He was educated at the R.M.A., Woolwich, and in 1867 entered the Royal Artillery, serving in the Abyssinian Campaign in 1867-8 (medal), the Ashanti Campaign in 1874 (medal and clasp); Afghan Campaign in 1878-9 (medal and clasp); the Zulu and Transvaal Campaigns in 1879 (despatches, medal and clasp), and the S. African War in 1899-1902, being present at the siege of Ladysmith and the operations in the Orange River Colony. Gen. Knox was appointed to command the 8th Infantry Division, with headquarters at Cork, in 1905. He married in 1889, Alice, dau. of Sir Robt. Dundas.

KOHLER, Hon. Charles William Henry, M.L.C., J.P., of Riverside, Paarl, C.C., and of the City Club, Cape Town, is grandson of a German gentleman who settled in Ireland and married an Irish woman. Their eldest son William, who married Mary Fletcher Hutchinson, went to the Cape as a govt. architect, and the subject of our sketch was born Oct. 14, 1862, at Calvinia, C.C., and educated at Mr. Close's Sch. and (the Rev.

Hole's) Trinity Coll., C.T. Mr. Kohler was one of the earliest pioneers of Johannesburg; he was Chairman of the Aurora G.M. Co.; Managing Director of the Unified G.M. Co.; Chairman of the Paarl Pretoria Co., and Director of the Langlaagte United Co., 1888-9. He purchased the farm Riverside in the Paarl Dist. in 1890, and has since carried on wine-farming very successfully, being a student of economic questions in other countries, with a very pronounced idea of the line legislation should follow for Cape Colony to keep abreast or ahead of her competitors. Mr. Kohler stood for the Legislative Assembly for Stellenbosch in 1895, but retired on nomination day. He was nominated by Stellenbosch. Somerset West, etc., to contest a seat for the Cape Legislative Council, Aug., 1903, and in 1904 was elected in the Progressive interest to the Legislative Council, as member for the W. Circle of Cape Colony, defeating his opponent, a labour candidate put forward by the Bond, by 3,600 votes. Mr. Kohler has a strong belief in the future of his country, with an equally strong belief in the brilliant destiny of the white races, when fused by the natural healing of time, into one virile nation, for it is his opinion that the present soreness will yield to time. He has himself been a Bondsman, and recognizes the earnestness of purpose of the members of that thorough society, and he is particularly outspoken about the republican tendencies of the extremists, because he holds that straight speaking is the best. In his campaigning tour he encountered many of these extremists, who walked out of the room when the National Anthem was sung, and some of whom made remarks insulting to the King, and rather than ignore these ebullitions he prefers to expose them to the condemnation of public opinion in the belief that it is better to speak openly. He is a Member of the Cape Board of Horticulture, and was a Lieut. in the Paarl D.M.T. in 1901.

KOLBE, Rev. F. C., D.D., is minister of the Roman Catholic Church of the Cape Peninsula, and Chaplain of the Nazareth Orphanage and Asylum for the aged.

KOTZE, John Gilbert, LL.B., K.C., was born at Leeuwenhof, C.T., on Nov. 5, 1849. He is the youngest son of the late P. J. Kotzé, who was Member for C.T. in the House of Assembly and was twice Major of that city. Judge Kotzé was educated at the S.A. Coll. took the degree of LL.B. at the London Univ. in Jan., 1873, and was called to the Bar by the Honourable Society of the Inner Temple on April 30, 1874. He practised at the Bar of the Supreme Court, C.T., and of the Eastern Districts Court at Grahamstown; was appointed Judge of the High Court of the Transvaal Province during the period of British annexation in May 19, 1877, which appointment he held until the retrocession of the country in Aug., 1881; was appointed one of the Commissioners under the Pretoria Convention to investigate and compensate claims for losses and injuries sustained during the first Boer War, and became Chief Justice of the late S.A.R., August 1881. He was Chairman of the Board of Examiners in Literature and Science of that state from 1890-8, and was created a Knight and Cross of the Order of the Immaculate Conception by H.M. the King of Portugal in July, 1896, in recognition of his services in the late Transvaal Republic. In consequence of his judgment in the case of Brown v. Leyds, in which he held that a Volksraad resolution could not override the Grondwet or Constitution of the country, and because he refused to renounce the right of testing the proceedings of the Executive and Volksraad by reference to the Grondwet, he was summarily and illegally dismissed from office as Chief Justice by ex-Pres. Kruger in Feb., 1898. He was appointed Attorney-Gen. of Southern Rhodesia with a seat in the Executive and Legislative Councils of that territory, Aug., 1900; acted as Administrator of Southern Rhodesia during the absence of Sir William Milton, K.C.M.G., from May to Oct., 1902; and was appointed Judge of the Supreme Court of the Colony of the Cape of Good Hope, April 15, 1903. Mr. Kotzé, together with the late Mr. Frederick Jeppe, edited the *Transvaal Statute Book*, 1845-85. He has also edited three volumes of reports of cases decided by the High Court at Pretoria, 1877-88, and has translated into English, from the original Dutch, Simon Van Leeuwen's *Commentaries on Roman Dutch Law* in 2 vols. royal 8vo. He married, in 1872, Mary Aurelia, dau. of the late Daniel Bell of Milton House, Clapham, Surrey.

KRAUSE, Dr., was convicted in 1902 of an attempt to incite Cornelius Broeksma to kill John Douglas Forster at the time of the S.A. War. He is now a leading Advocate at the Witwatersrand.

KRIGE, Gideon Johannes, M.L.A., represents the electoral division of Stellenbosch in the Cape House of Assembly to which he was last re-elected in the Bond interest in Feb., 1904

KRIZINGER, Commandant, was during the South African War leader of the Cape Colonial rebels, styling himself 'Chief Commandant of the Cape Colony', part of which he 'annexed' in 1901. He speaks English fluently.

KUHN, Peter Gysbert, M.L.A., is member of the Cape Legislative Assembly for the province of Victoria West. He sits in the Bond interest, and was last elected in Feb., 1904.

LABISTOUR, Gustave Aristide de Roquefeuil, K.C., was appointed Attorney-General of Natal by Sir Albert Hime in 1901, with the title of Procurator-General.

LABUSCHAGNE, Casper Jeremiah, M.L.C., J.P., of Haasfontein, Colenso, Natal, was born at Weenen County, Natal, Dec. 5, 1854. He is the son of John Hendrik Labuschagne, who fought for the British against Machana and the Basutos, on the occasion of their invasion of Natal, and also against Langalibalele. Mr. C. J. Labuschagne's grandfather was one of the voortrekkers who left Cape Colony for Natal in 1836, and, becoming an officer in the Boer Army, fought against Dingaan in 1837, and afterwards against the British in 1842 at Congella, Durban.

Mr. C. J. Labuschagne was appointed J.P. in 1892 and M.L.C. in Nov., 1898. He is a member of several Rifle Associations; has won several prizes, and on one occasion won a gold medal for the best aggregate score. He married, in 1877, Miss Hatting, the youngest dau. of J. M. Hatting, of Blauwkrans, Natal, on whose farm Lord Roberts' son is buried. Mr. Labuschagne lost his first wife in 1902, and then married Mrs. Pieters, eldest dau. of William Mande, of Dundee, Natal.

LAGDEN, Sir Godfrey Yeatman, K.C.M.G., (1897), C.M.G. (1894), M.L.C., Member of

SIR GODFREY LAGDEN

SIR LEWIS MICHELL

VISCOUNT MILNER

MR. E. P. MATHERS

Photos Elliott & Fry

218

Executive Council, and Commissioner for Native Affairs, Transvaal; of Pretoria, Transvaal, and the Sports Club, London; is the son of the late Rev. Richard Dowse Lagden, Balsham House, Camb., and Sherborne, Dorset. He was born Sept. 1, 1851, and educated at Sherborne Sch. A bare recital of his official appointments shows that he has had a busy as well as a distinguished public career. He entered the Civil Service in the G.P.O., 1869-77; went to South Africa in the latter year; was sent by Sir Bartle Frere to the Transvaal, where he was attached to Sir T. Shepstone's staff after the annexation; was appointed chief assistant to the then Colonial Secy., and Private Secy. to the Administrator, Sir Owen Lanyon, 1875-81, and Secy. to Executive Council. During the Boer War of 1881 he was present at the siege of Pretoria and was employed on the staff of the G.O.C. H.M. forces there. He afterwards became Private Secy. to Administrators Sir Evelyn Wood and Sir Wilham Bellairs; was attached to the Royal Commission that sat in the Transvaal in 1881, and then became Secy. to Transvaal Sub-Royal Commission on Compensation Claims, 1882. Sir Godfrey went to Egypt at the outbreak of war, and served as Special War Correspondent for the *Daily Telegraph* during the Egyptian Campaign, 1882-3, being present at all engagements, including Tel-el-Kebir, charge of Kassassin and occupation of Cairo; was appointed Assist. Colonial Secy., Sierra Leone; employed on Special Financial Mission to Gold Coast, 1883. He accompanied Sir Marshal Clarke at the annexation of Basutoland, 1884, and assumed the offices of Secretary and Accountant of that territory; Asst. Commissioner, 1885; acted as Resident Commissioner, 1890; as British Commissioner, Swaziland, 1892; Resident Commissioner, Basutoland, 1892-1901. Sir Godfrey occupied important positions during the S. African War of 1899-01, and was several times mentioned in civil and military despatches, and was later Chairman of the Inter-Colonial S. African Native Affairs Commission.

It will thus be seen that Sir Godfrey Lagden has represented this country on various missions, but it was as British Resident in Basutoland that he made his reputation. "To use the power and influence of the chief as a means of governing and guiding the nation", was the motto of his rule, and it is claimed that his success has shown how a black population may be moulded and governed with its own consent. No greater evidence exists of Sir Godfrey's remarkable faculties for inducing in the native mind an appreciation of progressive measures than the result of the introduction of a Native Savings Bank and remittance agency established in the Transvaal in Sept., 1902, of which the natives have taken full advantage from its initiation. He indulges in most games and sports, played cricket for his county, and was engaged in first class football, athletics and rowing between 1869 and 1877. He has had considerable experience of big game shooting, and walked from the Cape Coast to Coomassie through the Ashanti country in 1883, shooting and collecting specimens. He married, in 1887, Frances Rebeka, dau. of the Rt. Rev. Henry Brougham Bousfield, Bishop of Pretoria.

LAIDLEY, J. E., of Dashwood House, London, E.C., is a director of the Durban Gold Mines, Ltd., and the Glen Elgin Gold Mines, Ltd.

LAING, J. M., of Maritzburg, Natal, was appointed Controller of Telegraphs at Pietermaritzburg in 1902.

LAING, W. T., was appointed Native Commissioner for the District of Inyanga, Southern Rhodesia, and Assist. Magistrate for the District of Umtali in 1905.

LAIRD, Major Robert Montgomery, was born Aug. 10, 1857, and entered the Royal Artillery as Lieutenant in 1887, having previously served in the ranks for ten years. He took part in the Egyptian Expedition in 1882, including the action at Kassassin, in which he was wounded (despatches, medal and bronze star). He was promoted Captain in the Royal Artillery in 1898, and Major in 1902.

LAMBRECHTS, Alphonse, of Antwerp, is a director of the Transvaal Gold Fields, Ltd.

LAMBTON, Lieut. Colonel Hon. William, C.M.G., D.S.O., of the Guards' and Turf Clubs, was born in London, Dec. 4, 1863, and is son of the second Earl of Durham, and brother to the present Earl. He was educated at Eton and the

R.M.C., Sandhurst, and joined the Coldstream Guards in 1884, and acted as Adjutant of the 2nd Battn. from 1888-1892. In 1898 he passed the Staff College, and served with the Egyptian Army in 1898, being present at the battles of Atbara and Omdurman. Col. Lambton also took part in the South African War in 1899 with the 1st Battn. Coldstream Guards, being present at the actions at Belmont, Modder River, and Magersfontein, being wounded in the latter action. From 1901-4 he acted as Military Secretary to Lord Milner (q.v.), High Commissioner of South Africa, and in 1906 was appointed to the command of the 1st Battn. Coldstream Guards.

LAMBTON, Col. Hon. Charles, D.S.O., of the Naval and Military Club, was born in 1857, and is son of the 2nd Earl of Durham. He was educated at Eton, and entered the Northumberland Fusiliers as Lieutenant in 1877. From 1880-83 he served in India, and acted as A.D.C to the Viceroy of Ireland from 1886-9; was employed in the Straits Settlements in 1895-6. He served in the Nile Expedition in 1895, being present at the battle of Khartoum (despatches, D.S.O., medal, and Egyptian medal with clasp), and the South African War in 1899-1902, in command of the 2nd Battn. Northumberland Fusiliers; took part in the advance on Kimberley, including the actions at Belmont, Enslin, Modder River, and Magersfontein; operations in the Orange Free State, Transvaal, Orange River Colony, and Cape Colony; and acted as Commandant at Dewetsdorp (despatches, Queen's medal with four clasps, King's medal with two clasps, and brev. of Col.).

LAMBTON, Capt. George Charles, D.S.O., of Brownslade, Pembroke, S. Wales, was born Nov. 10, 1872; is fourth son of Lieut.Col. F. W. Lambton, late of the Scots Guards, and of Lady V. Lambton, dau. of the 2nd Earl Cawdor. Capt. Lambton was educated at Wellington Coll., and entered the Worcester Regt. in 1895, gaining his Captaincy in 1900. He served in the S.A. War 1900-02; was present at the occupation of Johannesburg and Pretoria, and took part in the operations which resulted in the surrender of Prinslon in the Brandwater basin. He then continued fighting in the O.R.C. and C.C.; was present at the action at Bothaville, and subseqnentiy

served under Gen. Sir C. Knox until April, 1902 (despatches, D.S.O., Queen's medal with four clasps, King's medal with two clasps). Capt. Lambton is unmarried.

LAMBTON, Rear Admiral Hon. Sir Hedworth K.C.V.O., C.B., of the Naval and Military Club, was born in 1856, and is son of the 2nd Earl of Durham. He entered the Royal Navy in 1870, and took part in the bombardment of Alexandria and the Egyptian War of 1882, receiving the medal and two clasps. In the early days of the late S. African War, Capt. Lambton (as his rank then was) landed a naval brigade of 280 men from the Powerful at Durban, and proceeded to Ladysmith, where he arrived on Oct. 30, 1899, with two Maxims, four long naval 12-pounders, and two 45-pounders, the popular conviction being that the timely arrival of these guns and the fine marksmanship displayed by his men saved Ladysmith from falling into the hands of the Boer forces. Sir George White referred to Capt. Lambton as "the life of the garrison throughout the siege". Admiral Lambton arrived back in England in May, 1900, and since 1901 commanded the King's yacht, until in Nov., 1904, he was appointed Rear Admiral of the Third Cruiser Squadron in the Mediterranean in succession to Sir Baldwin Walker. He is the youngest flag officer in the British Navy, and was promoted K.C.V.O. in 1906.

LANE, Capt. A. H., A.V.D., took part in the Dongola Expedition in 1896 (Egyptian medal); and was S.V.O. and Remount Officer for the 5th Division during the S. African War in 1899-1902.

LANGERMAN, J. W. S., is a well-known leading figure in Rand mining circles. He has represented Mr. J. B. Robinson's vast Transvaal interests for over ten years. He was born in the Cape Colony of a well-known and esteemed Cape Dutch family, and is a typical Afrikander, and regarded as one of the shrewdest and most far seeing of the mining magnates; and one who will be a big factor in political movements in the colony.

LANGERMAN, Max, of Johannesburg, Transvaal, is a well known figure in Witwatersrand mining circles, and is the proprietor of the Kensington Estates, near Johannesburg. He is greatly respected in Johannesburg and takes a considerable interest in everything connected with the social life of the Jewish community there. He is President of the Witwatersrand Old Hebrew Congregation, and Chairman of the Jewish Board of Deputies for the Transvaal and Natal. Mr. Langerman was formerly a member of the Reform Committee, for which privilege he contributed £2,000 to the late President Kruger's Treasury.

LANKESTER, Professor Edwin Ray, M.A., LL.D., F.R.S., of the Savile, Athenaeum, and Arts Clubs, was born in 1847, and is the eldest son of Edwin Lankester, M.D. He was educated at St. Paul's School, Downing College, Cambridge, and Christ Church, Oxford, where he took his degree at the age of twenty-one. In 1870 the Radcliffe Travelling Fellowship sent him abroad to study under biologists and geologists of Continental reputation. Since 1898 he has acted as Director of the Natural History Department of the British Museum, which post he resigned in 1906. He presided over the meeting of the British Association at York in Aug., 1906, and is the author of numerous publications on Natural History, including the article on *Okapia*, a new genus of mammals from Central Africa, for the Transvaal Zoological Society in 1902.

LANSDELL, Rev. Henry, D.D., Chaplain of Morden College, Blackheath, S.E., was born in Kent, Jan 10, 1841. He was educated at St. John's Coll., Highbury; and was ordained in 1867. He founded the Church Homiletical Society in 1873, and also founded and edited the *Clergyman's Magazine* from 1875-86. He has travelled in almost every country in Europe and Asia, and in America, and Canada. In. 1890 he travelled from the North of Egypt, through Tripoli, Tunis, Algiers, and Morocco, and published accounts of his travels in *Through Siberia*, *Russian Central Asia*, *Through Central Asia*, and *Chinese Central Asia*; he is also the author of *The Sacred Tenth*. Recreations: fruit culture and literary composition. He married, Oct. 18, 1892, Mary, dau. of Charles Colyer, of Farningham, Kent.

LATHAM, Robert J., was formerly employed by the Board of Agriculture, and by the Surveyor of Taxes, Inland Revenue, London, afterwards serving as Clerk in the Accountant's Department of the Orange Free State and Cape Government Railways. He took part in the late South African War with the Prince of Wales' Light Horse (King's medal and two clasps); and was appointed Clerk in the Land Settlement Department of the Orange River Colony in 1903.

LAW, Colonel, the Hon. Cecil Henry, C.B., of Montrose, Dorchester; and of the Naval and Military Club, was born in London, Nov. 25, 1849, and is 3rd son of the Hon. H. S. Law. He was educated at Wellington College, and took part in the Afghan War in 1878-9, and served in S. Africa in 1899-02; is fond of sport and has played polo in India. He married, July 22, 1884, Alice, dau. of John H. Astell, of Woodbury Hall, Beds.

LAWLEY, Capt. the Hon. Sir Arthur, K.C.M.G., of Madras, was born in 1860, and is a brother of Lord Wenlock, and a nephew of the late Duke of Westminster. He was at one time in the 10th Hussars, and for five years acted as Private Secy. to the Duke of Westminster. Sir Arthur made his first hit as Secy. to the Administration of S. Rhodesia in 1896, and from 1898 until 1901 he was Administrator of Matabeleland, during which time he earned golden opinions by the happy tact which he exercised between the Chartered Company on the one part and the settlers on the other. The difficult questions of land tenure, native labour, and other matters which were the subject of local agitation owed much to the attention which he gave to them, and to the care with which he endeavoured to reconcile conflicting differences of interest. In the early days of the South African War, he went in person to inform the chiefs of the outbreak of hostilities, and to explain the situation to them. During 1901-2 Sir Arthur Lawley acted as Governor of Western Australia, and he then returned to South Africa to take up the appointment of Lieut.-Governor of the Transvaal, a most difficult post which called for diplomatic ability of no common order. In 1903, during Lord Milner's absence, Sir Arthur acted as High Commissioner in South Africa, and at the latter end of 1905 he was appointed to succeed Lord Ampthill, G.C.S.I., as Governor of Madras. He married, in 1885, a dau. of the late Sir Edward Cunard, Bart.

LAWRENCE, James, M.L.A., J.P., of Kimberley, Muizenberg, and of the Kimberley Club and Civil Service Club of C.T., was born at Georgetown, C.C., in 1852. Educated at C.T. and Cradock, he has represented Kimberley in the Cape Colony House of Assembly since 1894. He is a Progressive Member, and was last re-elected in Feb., 1904. For fourteen years he has been Municipal Councillor, and Mayor of Kimberley in 1889-1903. It will thus be seen that Mr. Lawrence has been prominently associated with the municipal affairs of the great diamond city. His other public positions include that of Chairman of James Lawrence and Co., Ltd., Director of the Board of Executors, Kimberley, and Senior Whip to the Progressive Party in the Cape Parliament. He also served on the Peninsular Commission in 1902-3. His recreations include riding and driving. Married, in 1880, to Miss Kilby, of Somerset East.

LAWTON, Lancelot Francis, is son of Joseph Lawton. He was educated at the Jesuit College of St. Francis Xavier, in Liverpool, and started his journalistic career on the *Daily Mail*. When the Russo-Japanese War broke out, he resigned and went to Tokyo, subsequently becoming attached to the staff of the *Daily Telegraph*. Mr. Lawton served throughout the S. African War in 1899-1902 as a trooper and despatches rider, and was wounded twice.

LEA, Hugh Cecil, M.P., of 60, Cadogan Place, London, S.W., and of 59, Mark Lane, London, E.C., was formerly a Corporal in a cavalry regt. Subsequently he was on the London staff of the *African Review*, afterwards becoming the proprietor of the *Wine and Spirit Trades Record*. At the Parliamentary Election in 1906 he contested and won the seat for East St. Pancras in the Radical interest. In the House of Commons he takes a special interest in military matters, and serves on the Kitchen Committee. Mr. Lea is married.

LEARY, Arthur Ernest, of Harrismith, O.R.C., acted as Clerk to the Resident Magistrate at Umtata, Cape Colony, and also at Mqandule in 1885; Asst. Resident Magistrate at Mqandule in 1886, and Asst. Resident Magistrate at Umtata in 1889. He was appointed Interpreter of native

languages in the Eastern Districts Court, and Relieving Magistrate in 1895; took part in the Tembu and Pondomise Rebellion in 1880-81 (medal); and the South African War in 1899-1901, as Intelligence Officer to Major-Gen. Sir J. T. Maxwell (Queen's and King's medals with seven clasps). Subsequently he was appointed one of the Magistrates of Pretoria on the occupation of that town. He returned to Cape Colony in 1901, and was transferred to the Orange River Colony as Resident Magistrate at Harrismith in the same year.

LEBOMBO, Lord Bishop of. (See Right Rev. W. E. Smyth.)

LECONFIELD, Lord, of Petworth House, Sussex, and of 9, Chesterfield Gardens, London, W., was born in 1872, and is son of the 1st Earl. He is Lieut. Col. of the Sussex Imperial Yeomanry, and was formerly in the 1st Life Guards, serving in the S. African War in 1899-1900. Unmarried.

LEE Charles, M.L.A., is Member of the Cape Legislative Assembly for the Province of Uitenhage, and was last re-elected in Feb., 1904. He sits in the Progressive interest.

LEGGETT, Major Edward Humphrey Manisty D.S.O., F.A.S., M.R.C.I., of Pretoria, S.A., 72, St. James' Street, S.W., and of the Reform and Junior United Service Clubs, was born at Weymouth Dec. 7, 1871, and is son of Maj. G. E. Leggett, of Folkestone. He was educated at Clifton Coll, and R.M.A., Woolwich (Pollock gold medalist). He received his first commission in the R.E. in 1890, and was attached to the staff of the L. & N.W. Railway as pupil of the late Sir Geo. Findlay, in 1892-3, obtaining Board of Trade certificates; was Board of Trade delegate to the International Railway Congress in 1895, and held the War Office appointment of railway traffic man. in 1895-99. He served through the S. African War as special service officer on the Headquarters' Staff, 1899-1902, including special duty on the staff of the Vereeniging Peace Congress in May, 1902 (mentioned in despatches, D.S.O., brevet rank of Major and two S.A. war medals with 6 clasps). From 1902-5 Maj Leggett's services were placed at the disposal of the High Commissioners in S. Africa, by the Imperial Government, and he has been employed as director of the Burgher Camps, and other temporary Govt. departments. Unmarried.

LEIGH, Capt. Chandos, D.S.O., Bimbashi in the Egyptian Army, of the War Office, Khartoum, and the Army and Navy Club, was born at Liverpool in 1873; is son of Sir E. Chandos Leigh, K.C.B., and grandson of the 1st Baron Leigh. He was educated at Harrow, and joined the King's Own Scottish Borderers in 1895, and served in the S. African War in 1900-1, being present at Paardeberg, relief of Kimberley, Poplar Grove, Zand River, Wittebergen, Diamond Hill, and Bothaville (Queen's medal and six clasps). He joined the Egyptian Army in 1902, and served with the Bahr-el-Ghazal Expedition in 1904-5, being appointed Staff Officer, Khartoum Dist., in 1905. Unmarried.

LEIGH, Hon. Rupert, is brother and heir-presumptive to Lord Leigh; he formerly belonged to the 4th Dragoon Guards, serving with them in Egypt and Afghanistan; has acted as A.D.C. to two Governors of New South Wales, and as Military Secy. to Lord Northcote, when Governor of Bombay. He is about to marry Beatrice, dau. of the late Mr. Dudley Smith, M.P., and sister to Lady Moreton.

LEITRIM, Earl of, of Mulroy Milford Co. Donegal, and of 40, Portman Sq., W., was born in 1879, and is the eldest son of the 4th Earl. He served with the Imperial Yeomanry in the S. African War in 1899-1902; and married in 1902, Violet, dau. of the late Robert Henderson, a director of the Bank of England.

LELAND, Capt. Herbert John Collett, D.S.O., of Ballinacorty, Castleconnell, Co. Limerick, and of the Junior United Service Club, was born in Westmorland, Feb. 27, 1873, and is the only son of the late John Smallman Leland. He was educated at Bedford Grammar Sch., and was gazetted to the Royal Munster Fus. in 1900. He served in the Northern Territories, Gold Coast, in 1897-8, in operations against the Sofas and Northern Tribes (medal and clasp), and in Ashanti in 1900 as A.D.C. to Sir James Willcocks; was present at the relief of Kumasi and the action at Obassa (mentioned in despatches, D.S.O., and medal with

clasp). He was appointed to the Gold Coast Constabulary in 1897, and was Commissioner of the Western Gold Coast frontier in 1898-9; was Adjt. in the Gold Coast Constabulary in 1901; Adjt. in the 1st Gold Coast Regt., W.A. Frontier Force in 1902-3, and Adjt. of the 5th Royal Munster Fus. in 1904. He married, Jan. 3, 1902, Lena, dau. of the late Alexander Duncan, of Glencarron.

LENFANT, Major, the French explorer, returned to Paris in April, 1904, after an adventurous journey from the West Coast of Africa, up the Niger, along the Benue (a tributary of the Niger), through the Suburi marsh country, thence along the Shari river to Lake Chad, the return journey only occupying sixty-five days, as against five months by the Congo route. Major Lenfant's white party consisted of ten. They were confronted with innumerable difficulties, hostile natives with poisoned arrows, and much sickness. He made many scientific observations, and discovered a monstrous silk spinning spider, a specimen of which he brought home.

Another expedition left France in Aug., 1906, under Major Lenfant to traverse unknown regions, far from the recognised routes, and peopled with hostile tribes. Between Lake Chad and the Congo basin there is to be seen on all the maps of Africa, between the seventh and ninth parallels to the southeast of the great African lake, a large blank spot which, as far as modern exploration goes, is virgin soil. The explorers Maistre, Nachtigal, Vogel, and Mizon passed to the north of this region, never traversing the ninth parallel. Major Lenfant has his route marked out as far as Carnot, but beyond that point he possesses no data whatever. Starting from Pauillac for Matadi, he will go first to Brazzaville, where the real organisation of the expedition will take place. Thence the mission will proceed to Nola, the point of junction of the Mambere and the Kadei which form the Sangha. At Nola it is probable that the mission will be occupied some time in the study of the immense forest there. From Nola it will ascend the Mambere to Bania. Thus far it will have followed the route recently taken by Major Moll for the delimitation with a German mission of the Cameroon frontier. From Carnot Major Lenfant will plunge into the wilderness. His goal is Lake Laka, which is situated between the Upper Logone and the depression of the Tuburi, which he has already traversed. His object is to trace the various navigable stretches permitting the linking, as far as possible by means of the river routes, of the basin of the Logone to that of the Sangha.

LEONARD, Charles, of Johannesburg, has resided in South Africa for many years, and has always occupied a prominent position in social and political matters. At the time of the Reform movement in the Transvaal he was an active Chairman of the Transvaal National Union.

LEONARD, Hon. James Weston, K.C., of 12, King's Bench Walk, Temple, E.C., was born in Cape Colony. In 1887 he went to the Transvaal to practise, and eventually settled there. He is a member of the Cape Executive Council, and acted as Attorney General for Cape Colony under two Administrations, first in 1881, and again in 1882, subsequently in 1884 returning to private practice. He is a brilliant lawyer, having distinguished himself at the Cape Bar, a practised speaker, and a keen politician.

LETSIE, Paramount Chief of the Basutos, was proclaimed as such by Lord Selborne in Feb., 1906. Letsie's chief town is Maseru, Basutoland.

LEVERSON, Col. Julian John, C.M.G., of 11, Park Lane, London, W., and of the Army and Navy, Naval and Military, and Wellington Clubs, was born in London, May 16, 1853, and is son of G. B. C. Leverson. He was educated at the R.M.A., Woolwich, and the Staff College, Sandhurst. He took part in the Egyptian Expedition in 1882; acted as special service officer with Sir Charles Warren's expedition in Bechuanaland in 1884-5, and was subsequently appointed one of the commissioners to settle the claims to land in British Beehuanaland in 1885-6. He went out to S.E. Africa in 1891-2 as British Commissioner for the delimitation of the boundary between the British and Portuguese spheres of influence; the differences, however, had to be settled by the Manica boundary arbitration, at which Col. Leverson was present as British delegate. He went out to S.E. Africa again in 1898 to continue the

work of frontier delimitation. Col. Leverson has alsc served in other boundary commissions, and in the Intelligence div. of the War Office. Unmarried.

LEVEY, Charles Joseph, of Marico, Transvaal, was employed by the Cape Government Service as Clerk and Interpreter in Fingo land in 1868; was on special service to the Kaffir Chiefs in connection with labour for railways in 1874; and acted as Political Agent with the Tembus in 1875. He commanded the Tembu contingent in the Gaika Rebellion, capturing the rebel chiefs, Edmund and Mantanzima Sandilli. In 1878 he was appointed Resident Magistrate at Southeyville, which town he fortified and successfully defended in 1879 assisted in defending the besieged at Lady Frere; commanded a column in an expedition against the chiefs Mfanta and Stockwe (medal) acted as Political Officer to Colonel Wavell's column during the Tembu War, and removed the farmers who invaded the conquered territory in Tembuland. In 1883 he was appointed resident Magistrate at Xalanga, and Civil Commissioner and Resident Magistrate at Wodehouse in 1900, being transferred to his present position of Resident Magistrate at Marico in 1901.

LEWANIKA, King of Barotseland, of Lealui, Barotseland, N.W. Rhodesia, visited England in 1902, and had an audience with King Edward VII. He was immensely impressed with all he bad seen, and hoped to introduce European ideas in his country. He relies upon England to protect him from encroachments on his territory. It is probable that few people outside North-West Rhodesia are aware that until 1906 slavery existed in Lewanika's kingdom. Some idea of the old order of things may be gleaned from the late Rev. F. Coillard's book *On the Threshold of Central Africa*. For many years M. Coillard and his colleagues on the Paris Mission strove, with no small meason of success, against such appalling social conditions. Lewanika profited by his visit to England at the time of the Coronation to such good effect that on July 16, 1906, slavery was abolished throughout his dominions. For the last few years the Administration of the British South Africa Company had been bringing strong moral pressure to hear upon the Chief and his indunas to better the social status of the Barotse, for in native matters the company has no jurisdiction.

LEWIS, Barnet, of Threadneedle House, Bishopsgate Street Within, London, was born at Neustadt, and is a younger brother of Mr. Isaac Lewis, and a partner in the firm of Lewis & Marks, whose market interests it is his especial role to supervise. (See Isaac Lewis and C. F. Rowsell.) He is also a Director of the East Rand Mining Estates, the Transvaal Farms and Finance Co., and the Vereeniging Estates, Ltd. He has an artistic temperament, and a fine collection of pictures.

LEWIS, Henry D., of 28-31, Bishopsgate Street Within, E.C., is connected with the firm of Lewis and Marks. (See Isaac Lewis, Samuel Marks, and C. F. Rowsell). He is a Director of the African and European Investment Co., National Bank of South Africa, Ltd., and Transvaal Estates and Development Co., and is on the London Committee of Vereeniging Estates, Ltd.

LEWIS, Isaac, of Bedgebury Park, Kent, and of Threadneedle House, Bishopsgate Street Within, E.C., was born in Neustadt in 1849, and went to South Africa in 1870, being one of the first to exploit the Kimberley diamond fields. He is the Johannesburg head of the firm of Lewis and Marks, which also includes in the partnership Samuel Marks and Barnet Lewis, brother of the subject of this sketch. In 1881 the firm began to acquire interests in the Transvaal, exploiting the mineral, industrial, and agricultural resources of that country, to the great material advantage of his firm and the shareholders whose interests they protect.

Today Messrs. Lewis and Marks are as active as ever in exploiting the unbounded resources of the Transvaal, including mining and agriculture, and they are also building up several important industries, which are none the less necessary because they have none of the glamour of gold-seeking about them. Through the group of companies with which they are associated Messrs. Lewis and Marks control enormous land and mining interests, and a prosperous Transvaal will bring them and their co-shareholders profits such as are little dreamt of today. There is hardly any interest or branch of industry in the Transvaal that

can have prosperity without some measure of it falling to the lot of the Lewis and Marks group, and this fact, taken in conjunction with the recently disclosed possibilities of the firm's holdings on the eastern extension of the Rand, augurs well for the future of this comprehensive combination. This is, without doubt, one of the best of the groups operating in the Transvaal, and when the unfavourable labour conditions have passed away from the Rand, great progress will be made with the mining portion of its holdings, and the interests and influence of Messrs. Lewis and Marks will be considerably extended. The property with which Messrs. Lewis and Marks are prominently identified, which is engaging the great attention at present, is that of the East Rand Mining Estates, Limited, which has a very large holding on the eastern extension on the Main Reef, including the farms Groot Vlei and Palmietkuil, situated east of Geduld and south of Welgedacht, and which is taking a leading part in proving the continuation of the Main Reef series eastwards, and the results it has so far achieved lead to the conclusion that it will eventually develop into a huge undertaking, and the parent of many flourishing subsidiary companies.

Of the latest interests with which Messrs. Lewis and Marks are mainly identified, we must refer to the African and European Investment Company and the Transvaal Estates and Development Company. The landed interests of the former company extend to some 726,223 acres, as well as extensive shareholdings in several estate, gold, diamond, and coal mining undertakings in the Transvaal and Orange River Colony, and considerable financial interests in some of the flourishing industrial concerns in Johannesburg and Cape Town. In addition to investments standing at £468,894, there is on loan, secured and at call, the sum of £246,629, which, with cash in hand at the Company's bankers, totals a sum of £718,200. The Transvaal Estates and Development Company owns about 2,000,000 acres of land, stands and buildings in Johannesburg, and various other investments.

Messrs. Lewis and Marks are also greatly interested in the coalmining industry of the Belfast Carolina districts on the main railroad to Delagoa, in the development of which port this enterprising firm is taking a premier place. The great Sheba Mine, the pioneer gold producer of the De Kaap-Barberton fields, along with other local properties, is under the control of the Threadneedle House financiers, whose industrial and mining ramifications literally extend from the Cape to Central Africa. (See Barnet Lewis, C. F. Rowsell, and Samuel Marks.)

Mr. Lewis himself is on the Boards of the East Rand Mining Estates, Groot Vlei Proprietary Mines, Johannesburg Consolidated Investment Co., South Rand Exploration, Sheba G.M., Swaziland Corporation, Transvaal Estates and Development, African and European Investment, and Transvaal Farms and Finance Cos. He is also on the London Committees of the Great Eastern Collieries and the Transvaal Consolidated Coal Mines, Ltd., and is Chairmen in Johannesburg of the Vereeniging Estates. The latter company is an undertaking of vast extent, of great potentialities, and one that is full of promise. There are on the company's estates valuable collieries, the coal in which it is well-nigh impossible to estimate; a recent geological survey has revealed possibilities in regard to the existence of other minerals and metals which cannot fail to have an important bearing on the future of this great enterprise, and the farming and kindred operations, to say nothing of the company's interest in the township of Vereeniging, amounting to over three fourths of the erven, are no mean sources of revenue. With regard to the coal mines, the New Cornelia and the Central are well developed, and are producing satisfactorily.

Without going into details, it may be stated that there are several other profitable industries carried on by the Vereeniging Estates, and that the position and prospects of the company are undoubtedly of the brightest description. Another big coal undertaking with which Messrs. Lewis & Marks are associated is the Great Eastern Collieries.

LEYDS, Dr. Willem Johannes, LL.D., Knight of the Portuguese Order of Villa Viçosa, Commander of the Legion of Honour, Knt. of the Second Class, with Star, of the Prussian Red Eagle, and Commander of the Orders of Jesus Christ, St. Charles, Orange Nassau, and Leopold of Belgium; of 3, Van de Spiegelstraat, The Hague, Holland, and of the Club de la Haye, The Hague; was born at Magelang, Java, on May 1, 1859. He is second son of W. J. Leyds, who was youngest son of the Rev. Leyds, of Veenendaal, Holland, by Nine, second dau. of the Rev. R. van Beuningen van Helsdingen. Dr. Leyds came to Europe at the age of six, and received his education at Haarlem and Amsterdam. His original intention was to become a teacher, and in 1878 he passed the final examination in the Govt. school for the preparation of tutors. In the same year he qualified as a teacher of drawing; took a Govt. diploma for gymnastics, and passed in mathematics in 1879. He graduated LL.B. in 1882, and after a further two years of study took the Doctor's degree *cum laude* at the Univ. of Amsterdam. In 1884 Dr. Leyds went to the Transvaal as Attorney-Gen., and after serving in this capacity for three years, was appointed Govt. Commissioner with the Netherlands Railway Co. in 1887. He was made a J.P. for the whole Republic in 1889, and in the following year was deputed Govt. Syndic with the National Bank of the S.A.R.

Meanwhile Dr. Leyds had given ample evidence of his talent for diplomacy, and in 1890 he relinquished the office of Railway Commissioner for the State Secretaryship, to which he was re-elected in 1894, and again in 1898. The office carried a seat in the Executive Council, and was, after the Presidency, the most onerous and responsible in the service of the Republic. Meanwhile Dr. Leyds had been sent on political missions to Lisbon and Berlin, his skill in the diplomacy bad been tried, and when his withdrawal from the State Secretaryship became a matter of expediency, Mr. Kruger appointed his able and useful Secy. Minister Plenipotentiary in Europe. Dr. Leyds had been for years the President's right-hand man, and it is doubtful if his influence on affairs, so far as concerned the Uitlanders, was as malign as was oft-times stated. His position was a delicate one, and it is not surprising that he created feelings of resentment amongst the British. Dr. Leyds is the author of *De rechtsgrond der schadevergoeding voor preventieve hechtenis* (1884). He married, July 10, 1884, Louisa, second dau. of F. Roeff, Mathematician.

LIBERIA, President of. (See Pres. Arthur Barclay in Addenda.)

LICHTENBERG, Capt. John Wills, D.S.O., was

226

born June 19, 1872, and after serving. in the militia was gazetted second lieutenant in the 18th Hussars Apr. 21, 1900, becoming Lieut. May 1, 1901, and Capt. Nov. 29, 1904. He served with his regt. in the South African War from 1899 to 1900, taking part in the operations in the Transvaal and the O.R.C. from Dec., 1900 to Sept., 1901, and from Nov. of that year until the following May. Meanwhile in Sept. and Oct., 1901 he was fighting on the Zululand frontier of Natal. In the course of the campaign he was severely wounded, and was decorated with the D.S.O. in 1901 for gallantry in the defence of Fort Prospect and Fort Itala. He was mentioned in despatches, and received the Queen's medal with clasp, and the King's medal with two clasps.

LINDUP, Walter, F.R.C.I., of Fairview Tower, Maritzburg, Natal, was born in London, Jan. 3, 1858; was educated at the Philological Sch. Marylebone road, Lond., and studied dentistry under his father. He now practises this profession in Maritzburg. He was formerly a Director of the Stanhope and New Heriot G.M. Cos., and was elected a Town Councillor for Maritzburg in 1902. Mr. Lindup is an amateur architect and painter in oils. He married, in 1902, Elizabeth, dau. of J. D. Holliday, of Maritzburg.

LIPP, Charles, J.P., of the Rand and Kimberley Clubs, was born at Fochabers, Scotland, in 1861; is son of John Lipp, of Fochabers, where he was educated at Milne's Institution. After a bank training in the Aberdeen Town and County Bank he went to S.A. in 1882. He joined the Cape of Good Hope Bank, and rapidly rose to the position of Manager of their Kimberley branch in 1899, in which year he was appointed J.P. for Kimberley. He became Manager of the Kimberley branch of the African Banking Corporation in 1892, and was promoted to the management of the Johannesburg branch in 1898, which position he still fills. He remained in that town during the war, and was appointed J.P. for the Witwatersrand in 1908. He married, in 1890, Miss Harvey, of Aliwal North.

LIPSETT, Capt. L. S., Royal Irish Regiment, late of the Staff. Coll., was appointed in February, 1905, D.A.Q.M.G. in the Transvaal District for three years.

LISTER, Joseph Storr, I.S.O. (1903), J.P. for Cape Colony, of King William's Town, Cape Colony, and of the Civil Service (Cape Town) and King William's Town Clubs, was born at Uitenhage (C.C.) Oct. 1, 1852, and was educated at the Diocesan Coll., Rondebosch. At the age of 17 he went to India under a nomination for a commission in the Military Police, but pending a vacancy became Asst. Manager of the Tukvah Tea Estate, Darjeeling. Six months later he entered the Forest Dept. as Sub-Asst. Conservator at the plantation of Chunga Munga, of which he was later on placed in charge. Subsemuently he coudncted sylvienltural operations at Ihadera, Umballa, and the Forest Khagan was then on special duty in the Kulu Valley in connection with the rafting of timber to the plains, and thereafter had charge of the Nurpur SubDivision in the Kangra fist. In 1875 he was appointed Supt. of Plantations, Cape Colony, and in conjunction with the forestal duties was made custodian of ex-Chief Langalibalile and Cetywayo during their detention at Uitvlugt and Oudemoulon. He established plantations at Worcester, Beaufort West, Tokai, and Kluitjies Kraal; was Secy. to the SubCommittee for Woods and Vegetable Products at the Indian and Colonial Exhibition in 1886 (medal and diploma); was appointed Conservator of Forests in the Eastern Conservancy in 1888; reported on extent and value of Crown Forests of the Transkei in 1893, and on the administration of Transkeian Forests in 1898; twice reported on Johannesburg plantations; organised the Natal and Zululand Forest Dept. in 1902, receiving the thanks of the Natal Govt., and was also thanked by the Govt. of the O.R.C. for similar services in that Colony. He married, in 1885, Georgina Johanna, dau. of the late Thos. Bain, A.M.I.C.E., Cape Irrigation and Geological Surveyor.

LITHMAN, Karl Vilhelm, of Scandia, Rosebank, near Cape Town, and of the City Club (C.T.), was born Oct. 13, 1853, at Gothenburg, Sweden; is youngest son of a Gothenburg merchant, and was educated at the Gothenburg Coll., where he matriculated in 1872. He went to S.A. in 1879 as Secy. to the Swedish and Norwegian Consul-Gen. at Cape Town. In 1881 he became Vice-Consul, and acted as Consul-Gen. in 1885 on the death of his chief, whose business he took over under the style of Karl Lithman & Co. In 1886 he was appointed Agent-Gen. in S.A. to the Norwegian Veritas, and he now holds the general agency of the principal Scandinavian underwriters. He was made Consul for Venezuela in 1887, and in the same year founded the match factory near Cape Town, which he afterwards sold to the Rosebank Match Co., Ltd. Besides his Consular appointment, he carries on a timber, shipping, insurance, and general merchant's business, and is a director of various cos. He married, April 4 1891, Sophia Akerberg, widow of the late Swedish and Norwegian Consul at Cape Town.

LITTLE, James Reginald Upton, M.L.C., of Lagos, W.A.; and of the Park, Hillsborough, Co. Down, Ireland, is son of I. Little, of Hillsborough Park, and was born in Co. Meath in 1873. He is an unofficial member of the Legislative Council at Lagos, besides being Lloyd's agent, Vice-Consul for Belgium, and agent for the African Royal Mail steamers and British & African Line at Lagos. Unmarried.

LITTLE, James Stanley, of the Royal Colonial Institute, W.C., and of the Authors' Club, is a son of the late Thomas Little, of Woodville, Forest Hill. He was educated at King's Coll., London, and went to S.A. as a youth, when he contributed to the *Cape Times* and the *Natal Mercury*. He returned to England with a knowledge of S.A. questions, which he utilised by lecturing on various matters affecting the country and Imperial Federation. He was a member of the S.A. Committee (1886), and served on the Executive Committee of the State Colonisation Association and the Executive Council of the Imperial Federation League. He edited the *African Review* from Dec., 1895, to June, 1897, and from Aug., 1901, to Aug. 1902. Mr. Little's main work has been to popularise the Imperial idea. As early as 1876 he contributed leading articles to the *Natal Mercury* advocating the annexation of the Transvaal. His works especially dealing with Imperial subjects began with *A World's Empire* (1879). This was followed by *South Africa* (1884), *The United States of Britain* (1887), *A Vision of Empire* (1889), *The Enemies of South Africa* (a series of articles in the *New Century Review*, 1897), *Progress of British Empire in Century*, published in Canada (1902)

and in Great Britain and the United States (1903). During the past twenty years he has worked hard for the reform of the Royal Academy. On subjects connected with Imperial, Colonial, South African, artistic and literary matters he has contributed largely to the periodical press and magazines, including the *Nineteenth Century*, *Academy*, *Studio*, *Library Review*, *The Artist*, *The Morning Post*, *The Literary World*, and other publications. He is also the author of some half a dozen novels, viz., *My Royal Father* (1886), *The Day Ghost* (1887), *Doubt* (1888*), Whose Wife Shall She Be* (1888), *A Wealden Tragedy* (1894). He wrote the *Life and Work of W. A. Orchardson, R.A.* (1897); and, besides all this literary activity, has found time to write two plays, which have been presented. He was the first executive secy. of the Society of Authors, and inaugurated the system of annual dinners, with a dinner to American men and women of letters in 1889. He was the hon. secy. of the Shelley Soc. in 1886-7, and, in conjunction with Mr. J. J. Robinson, organised the Shelley Centenary celebration at Horsham, Aug. 4, 1892. His recreations are country walks and genealogical research. He married March, 1895, Fanny Maud Thérèse Lablache, elder dau. of Count Luigi de Lablache.

LITTLEJOHN, Robert, of 8, Cavendish square, London, W., and of the Constitutional, Caledonian, and Gresham Clubs, began his business career in the service of the Bank of Scotland in 1872, and went to S.A. in 1883. He was gen. manager of the African Banking Corporation in S.A. from its start in 1891 to the end of 1900, when he joined the Board of Directors of that bank in London (see G. W. Thomson). He is also a director of other companies connected with S. Africa.

LLEWELLYN, cricketer, was born in S.A. He made his first appearance in important cricket at Pietermaritzburg in 1896 against Lord Hawke's XI. In 1899 he went to England to qualify for Hampshire, for which county against the Australians he scored 90 in his first innings, and took 7 wickets. In 1890 he showed good form against the West Indians, taking 13 wickets and making over 50 runs in one of his innings. In 1902 he displayed good form also against the Australians, clean bowling Clem Hill for 0 and 7. In addition to his lefthander bowling, he is a brilliant field at mid-off and a dashing bat.

LLEWELLYN, Capt. Noel, D.S.O., of Hersham Cottage, Walton-on-Thames, and of White's Club, was born Nov. 24, 1871, at the Court, Langford, East Somerset, and is son of Col. Evan H. Llewellyn. He was educated at sea on H.M.S. *Britannia* (1884), and was midshipman in the Royal Navy from 1888 to 1890, during which period he saw active service on the East Coast of Africa in the suppression of the slave trade (despatches). From the Navy he joined the British S.A. Police, serving as Artillery Officer throughout the Matabele War of 1893-4 (despatches). In 1896 he was appointed J.P. (Rhodesia), and received his Captaincy in the B.S.A. Police, and on the outbreak of the second Matabele War in that year he took command of the company's artillery, greatly distinguishing himself on more than one occasion by his gallantry and presence of mind in tight places, being recommended by Gen. Sir Fred. Carrington for the coveted V.C. He continued fighting through the operations in Mashonaland, which were concluded in 1897. Capt. Llewellyn served through the Anglo-Boer War from the commencement in 1899, commanding the armoured trains north of Mafeking until Jan., 1900 when he took over the command of Col. Plumer's artillery until the relief of Mafeking, in connection with which he was decorated with the D.S.O. Transferring to the S.A. Constabulary, he was appointed Comdt. of the Lichtenburg District (until Dec., 1902) and J.P. for the Transvaal. He married, Oct. 20, 1902, Winifred Lady Ross, youngest dau. of A. Berens, of Castlemead, Windsor.

LLEWELYN, Sir Robert Baxter, K.C.M.G., of Government House, St. George's, Grenada, W. Indies, and of the Junior Carlton Club, was born in 1845. He was formerly employed in the Colonial Office, London, and in the Colonial Secretary's office in Jamaica in 1869; acted as private secy. to Sir J. P. Grant in 1873. He has also served as Administrator in Tobago, St. Vincent, St. Lucia, and on the West Coast of Africa, having received the African War medal for service in the Gambia Colony. In 1900 he was appointed Governor of the Windward Islands, which position he still holds. He

married, in 1873, Theodora, dau. of Charles Harvey, of Campbeltown.

LOCH, Lord, D.S.O., is son of the 1st Lord Loch, formerly High Commissioner for S. Africa, was born in 1873, and is an officer in The Grenadiers. He served in the Sudan with great distinction, was mentioned in despatches, and rewarded with the D.S.O. In South Africa he acted as Divisional Signalling Officer, was dangerously wounded, again mentioned in despatches, and was given the brevet rank of major. He married, in 1905, Lady Margaret Compton, dau. of the Marquess of Northampton.

LOCHVER, Hon. S. A. van Aarde, M.L.C., is a member of the Cape Legislative Council for he North-West Province.

LOCKHART, Col. Sir Simon Macdonald, Bart., C.V.O., of The Lee, Lanark, N.B., and the United Service, Carlton, and St. James's Clubs, was born in 1849. He is head of a very ancient Lowland house, which has played its part for centuries in the history of Scotland, and is a large landowner in Lanarkshire. He was educated at Eton, and took part in the Egyptian campaign in 1882. From 1892-8 he commanded the 1st Life Guards, and he retired under the age limit in 1906. He married, in 1898, Hilda, dau. of Col. Macdonald Moreton, and granddau. of the 5th Earl of Ducie. There is at present no heir, either apparent or presumptive, to the baronetcy, to which Sir Simon succeeded about the time he came of age.

LOEWENTHAL, Leopold, of Edensor, East Molesey, Surrey, was born on Jan. 18, 1865, at Glasgow, and was educated at Hutchinson's Sch., Glasgow, and the Friedrich Wilhelm Univ., Germany. In the early days of Johannesburg he was prominently associated with municipal affairs and exercised very considerable interest. Any candidate for the Town Council or the Volksraad who had his support was invariably elected. Mr. Loewenthal writes trenchantly on financial subjects. He collects 18th century English furniture and old Nankin porcelain, and makes gardening his hobby.

LOGAN, Hon. James Douglas, M.L.C., J.P., of Cape Town; Tweedside Lodge, Matjesfontein, C.C.; Palguise Castle, Perthshire, Scotland; and of the City Club, C.T.; is the son of Mr. James Logan, of Reston, Berwickshire, where he was born Nov. 26, 1857. He was educated at Reston, and started life as a railway clerk on the North British Railway. He then went to sea as an apprentice on a sailing ship, and was wrecked at Simons Town twenty-five years ago. Joining the Cape Govt. Railway service as porter, he came to be stationmaster, at the then new Cape Town Station, and worked through the different grades of the service until he was appointed Dist. Superintendent over the railway from Touws River to Prince Albert Road. Leaving the railway service, he purchased the Frere Hotel, Touws River, started a wholesale wine and spirit store in Cape Town, and soon became refreshment and advertising contractor on the Cape Govt., O.F.S., and Rhodesian Railway systems. Matjesfontein, on the Karoo, he transformed from a state of barrenness to a condition of fertility by means of diamond drilling for water, converting the locality into a charming residential resort. His gardens at Matjesfontein and Tweedside, where he has also been successful in boring for water, now contain orchards unequalled in the Colony.

Mr. Logan was elected member of the Cape Legislative Assembly for Worcester in 1894, and in 1898 was returned as the representative for the N.W. Circle in the Legislative Council, and at the last election (Nov., 1903) he was returned for the Western Circle, which he now represents in the Legislative Council. During the late Boer War he raised and commanded a corps of District Mounted Troops, and was present at the engagements of Belmont, Modder River, Ronsburg, etc. He is a keen sportsman, a first-class shot, and very fond of cricket. He was instrumental in bringing Lord Hawke's cricket teams of 1894 and 1898 to S.A., and conducted at his own expense the tour of the S.A. Amateur Cricket XI. in 1901, which showed up very creditably. Mr. Logan married, Sept. 9, 1878, Emma, dau. of C. H. Haylett, of Cape Town.

LOIR, Dr. A., of the Pasteur Institute, Paris, is a nephew of the late M. Pasteur, and in 1902 established a laboratory at Bulawayo for the treatment of hydrophobia.

LOMAS, John E. H., of 32, Great St. Helen's, London, E.C., was born and educated in the Isle of. Man, and proceeded to South Africa early in life. He is now Chairman of the Sudan Mines, Ltd., and director of the Bulawayo Estate and Trust Co., Ltd. In the Transvaal he captained the Transvaal Association football team, and he is now a well-known croquet and hockey player. He married Sarah Frances, eldest dau. of William Myers Wills, of Selsey, Sussex.

LONG, Alexander John Wakeman; Judge in the Native Tribunals of Egypt, of the Turf (Cairo) and Union (Alexandria) Clubs; was born at Bermuda, Nov. 22, 1869. He is only son of Francis Pigott Wakeman Long, late of the 61st (Glos.) Regt., and of The Graig, Monmouthshire; was educated at Cheltenham Preparatory Sch. and at Malvern College; passed solicitors' final in 1891, and was admitted in the same year. He practised in England till 1901, and in April of that year was inscribed as an advocate in the Court of Appeal of Mixed Tribunals, practising in Alexandria till Jan., 1905, when he was appointed a Judge in the Native Tribunals. His recreations are yachting, golf, tobogganing, and Alpine sports. Unmarried.

LONG, John Bloemendal Spyker, of the Cape Civil Service, was employed in the Native Affairs Dept. in 1880. In the following year he served with the Duke of Edinburgh's Own Vol. Regt. during the Basuto War. He entered the Control and Audit Office in 1881; was appointed Assistant Examiner of Accounts in 1883, and SecondClass Clerk in 1889.

LONGTIN, Mons., a Belgian official in the Congo Free State, against whom charges of murdering natives in connection with the Anglo-Belgian Indiarubber Co., were brought in 1905. M. Longtin admitted that the missionaries' charges were true.

LOTTER, Caspar Jacobus, M.L.A., is member of the Cape Legislative Assembly for the Province of Jansenville, having been last elected in Feb., 1904. He is a member of the Bond.

LOVAT, Lieut. Col. Lord (Simon), C.V.O., C.B., D.S.O., of Beaufort Castle, Inverness, and of the

Carlton Club, was born in 1871. He was educated at Oxford, and formerly belonged to the Cameron Highlanders. During the South African War in 1900-2 he served with Lovat's Scouts, Imperial Yeomanry (despatches, Queen's modal with three clasps, C.B., and D.S.O.). Lord Lovat is in the 1st Vol. Battn. Queen's Own Cameron Highlanders; since 1893 he has been attached to the 1st Life Guards, and now commands the famous scouts bearing his name. Lord Lovat has acquired a large property in S. Africa, which it is his project to stock with Scottish cattle, and to have farmed by Scottish men. Several consignments of shorthorns have already been sent out from his Inverness estate.

LOVEDAY, Richard Kelsey, M.L.C., F.R.G.S., was born at Pietermaritzburg in 1854. Left to his own resources very early in life, and having poor health, he went to Pretoria in 1872, and entered the Deeds Office of the S.A.R. in 1873, becoming Master and Registrar of the High Court under the British Administration after the annexation. In the Boer War of Independence he was second in command of the Pretoria Rifles, who were besieged in Pretoria. On the Transvaal regaining self-government Mr. Loveday's services were dispensed with, though he subsequently held important positions in the Transvaal. He was elected unopposed member of the First Volksraad for the Barberton Goldfields in 1890 and 1891, and was the only member of the Chamber of British descent. He was a strenuous opponent of the Kruger régime and its attendant abuses. In the sessions of 1893 and 1894 he rendered great services to the Progressives, and in the course of the debate on the Franchise in 1895 he dealt exhaustively with the question, and exhorted the Raad to appeal to the country on the matter. He is a member of the First Legislative Council of the Transvaal Colony and director of several public companies.

LOVELL, Edward Alphonse, of Lagos, West Africa; of Storridge Vicarage, Malvern; and of the Junior Athenaeum and Northumberland County Clubs, was born 1857 at Winslow Hall, Buckinghamshire. He was educated at Rugby, and Heidelburg Univ., where he graduated M.A., M.B., and D.C.L. He joined the Govt. service in 1890; was Collector of Customs 1891, and Acting

Treasurer and Colonial Secy. on various occasions. He served on the Boundary Commission in Paris, 1898.

LOWTHER, Claude, M.P., of H.3, the Albany, Piccadilly, W., and of the Carlton, Garrick, St. James', Marlborough, and Bachelors Clubs, is the son of Capt. F. W. Lowther, R.N., and was born in 1870. He was educated at Rugby and Fribourg, and was an Attaché in the Diplomatic Service for some years. He held a Captaincy in the Cumberland and Westmorland Yeomanry in S.A. He was appointed A.D.C. to Sir Charles Warren, who recommended him for the V.C. for saving the life of a comrade at the battle of Fabers Put. He successfully contested the Eskdale Division of Cumberland in 1900. Capt. Lowther is a well-known *littérateur* and dramatist. His play, *The Gordian Knot*, at Her Majesty's, will be well within the public recollection.

LOWTHER, Gerard Augustus, C.B., of Tangier, Morocco, is the younger brother of J. W. Lowther, the Chairman of Ways and Means, and Deputy Speaker of the House of Commons, and a nephew of the third Earl of Lonsdale. He has served in the diplomatic service at Madrid, Paris, Constantinople, Vienna, Sofia, Bucharest, Tokyo, and Budapest. He then became secy. at Washington; went to Chile in 1901 as H.M. Envoy Extraordinary and Minister Plenipotentiary at Santiago, and received the appointment of Envoy Extraordinary and Minister Plenipotentiary at Tangier in Dec., 1904, in succession to Sir Arthur Nicholson. He married, Feb. 28, 1905, Alice, dau. of Atherton Blight, of Philadelphia.

LUDLOW, Frederick, of Horfield Park, Horfield, Glos., was born at Birmingham May 20, 1862, and is the eldest son of the late Thomas Ludlow, of Birmingham. He was educated at the Rev. Isaac Walton's Academy at Sparkbrook, and at Wimberley Coll., London. For some time he acted as Vice and Deputy Consul for the United States of America at Bristol, which post he resigned and came to London, where he wrote *Foreign Competition: Its Evils and its Remedies* in the *Kentish Mercury*, subsequently serving on the staff of the *British and South African Export Gazette*. He next went to the Midlands and wrote *Black Country Tales and*

Sketches. He acted as editor of the *Bristol Guardian* from 1904-5; is an associate of the Incorporated Society of Authors, and hon. secy. and treasurer of the Upper Horfield Mutual Improvement Society, which he was largely instrumental in founding. His publications include *The Habitual Criminal and How to Prevent Him*, *The Voice of a Child*, *Two Christmas Samaritans*, *Told to the Waves*, and a story in connection with the W. African slave trade, entitled *The Death of a Slave* and illustrated by Frank Brangwyn, A.R.A. His latest book, *Tales and Sketches of Old and New Bristol*, is illustrated by many good artists. He married, in 1888, Miss Kate Taylor.

LUEBECK, Martin, of 49A, Pall Mall, London, S.W, and of the German Athenaeum Club, was born and educated at Hamburg. He commenced his banking career in the well-known house of L. Behrens and Sons in Hamburg, and after fourteen years with that firm he transferred to the famous Dresdner Bank in Berlin, where he had supreme control of the department connected with the issue of State loans and similar financial business. This important position led him to many different countries, notably to Mexico in 1893, to Sweden in 1895, where the Wasa Order was conferred upon him for his successful conclusion of a large inter national loan for the Swedish Government, and to the Transvaal later in the same year, where he stayed for three years, being connected with the foundation of the General Mining and Finance Corporation, of which he is still a director. In 1898 he came to London as a director of the Dresdner Bank, which position he still occupies. He is also one of the trustees for the debenture holders of the Victoria Falls Power Co., Ltd.

Mr. Luebeck devotes nearly all his time to his business affairs, but when opportunity offers he likes to indulge in pedestrian tours about odd corners of England, having previously visited practically every European country, as well as Central America, the United States, Canada, and South Africa. He is very fond of art, especially painting and music, and is unmarried.

LUGARD, Major Edward James, D.S.O., of Haslemere, Surrey, was born at Worcester, Mar. 23, 1865, and is the youngest son of the late Rev.

F. G. Lugard, M.A. He joined the 3rd Worcestershire Regt. in 1885, passed first in the military competitive from Militia into Line in 1886; joined the 2nd Northumberland Fus. in 1886, and was transferred to the India Staff Corps. in 1888. He served in the Burma Expedition in 1888-9 (medal with clasp); the Chin-Lushai Expedition in 1889-90 (despatches, clasp, and D.S.O.); and in the Manipur Expedition in 1891 (slightly wounded, clasp). He acted as second-in-command under Major F. D. Lugard in the British W. Charterland Co.'s expedition to Ngamiland, S. Central Africa, in 1896-7; in command of an expedition in 1897-9; and took part in the S. African War as a special service officer 1899-1900 (medal and three clasps). He is now serving as political asst. to the High Commissioner of N. Nigeria. Recreations: Shooting and travel. He married, in 1893, Charlotte, eldest dau. of the Rev. G. B. Howard, B.A., of Bromley, Kent.

LUGARD, Lady (Flora Louise), of Little Parkhurst, Abinger, Surrey, was born at Woolwich, Kent, is the dau. of Major-Gen. George Shaw, C.B., by Marie Adrienne Junot Desfontaines, and was educated privately. She is the author of *Castle Blair* and other books. In 1890 she joined the staff of the *Times*, and was for ten years head of the colonial dept. of that paper, which post she resigned in 1900. Lady Lugard always took a great and active interest in S.A. matters, and was believed to receive a large share of the late Cecil Rhodes' confidence in respect of his political schemes for the development of SA. She gave long and important evidence before the Commission which inquired into the events leading up to the Jameson Raid. She was married, June 11, 1902, to Gen. Sir Frederick Lugard (q.v.).

LUGARD, Brig.Gen. Sir Frederick Dealtry, K.C.M.G., C.B., D.S.O., until 1906 High Commissioner for Northern Nigeria; of Little Parkhurst, Abinger, Surrey; and of the St. James' and the Royal Soc. Clubs, is the son of the Rev. F. G. Lugard, and was born at Fort St. George, Madras. Educated at Rossall and Sandhurst, he entered the Army in 1878, and served with the 9th Foot in the Afghan War of 1879-80, and was present at the engagement of Saidabad, receiving the Afghan medal. He was promoted Capt. in the

Norfolk Regt. in 1885, and served in the Sudan in that year with the Indian Transport, receiving the medal and clasp and bronze star, and with the Burmese Expedition in 1886, when he was mentioned in despatches and received medal and clasp and D.S.O. In 1888 he was again on active service, being in the Nyassaland operations, when he was severely wounded, and with the Imperial East Africa Co.'s Troops in Uganda in 1889-92, obtaining medal for his services. In the years 1894-96 he commanded the expedition sent by the Niger Co. into the interior. Sir Frederick Lugard has done great services to the Empire and to civilization, and as a soldier, administrator and explorer he will be numbered among those who during the Victorian era have done so much to consolidate and extend British influence and power in Africa. Particularly may be instanced his able report to the Administrator of the British East Africa Co. at that critical period in 1892, when Mr. Gladstone's Govt. was about to abandon Uganda. This report did much to strengthen the cause of the Anti-Evacuationist party. Whilst in Nyassaland he was unremitting in his efforts to suppress the Arab slave trade, waging a perpetual war against the traders for that purpose. He was Commissioner in Lagos Hinterland and Comdt. West African Frontier Force in 1897. Sir Frederick resigned his High Commissionership in Sept., 1906. He married, June 11, 1902, Flora (q.v.), dau. of Major-Gen. George Shaw, C.B., and granddau. of the Right Hon. Sir Frederick Shaw, Bart.

LUKIN, Henry Timson, Commandant General Cape Colonial Forces, commanding Cape Mounted Riflemen, C.M.G., D.S.O.; served through Zulu Campaign in native contingent (medal and clasp), severely wounded at Ulundi; joined Cape Mounted Riflemen as Lieutenant, March 23, 1881; served in latter part of Basuto Campaign (medal); promoted Captain and Gunnery Instructor, Feb. 1, 1894; Pondoland Field Force, 1894, Field Adjt. Bechuanaland Field Force, and commanded Maxim guns and Signalling Staff during Langeberg Campaign, 1899 (clasp).

Up to now promotion in this corps d'élite had been slow, but when the South African War broke out, Col. Lukin's soldierly qualities were soon recognised. At first, from Nov., 1899, to Oct.,

1900, he commanded the Artillery of the Colonial Division, taking part in the defence of Wepener. He was then promoted Lieut. Col. in the C.M.R., and in Oct., 1900, was attached to the Imperial Forces. He was then specially chosen for the command of a mixed force of Imperial and Colonial mounted troops (1901), and from Dec. 1, 1901, under the new scheme of Cape Colonial defence he received, and brilliantly sustained, the appointment of Colonel, commanding the Colonial Troops in Eastern District, Cape Colony (Queen's medal and four clasps, and King's medal and two clasps). He became Colonel commanding Cape Mounted Riflemen, Jan. 1, 1903; and Commandant General Cape Colonial Forces, June 1, 1904.

LYNCH, Colonel Arthur Alfred, is of Irish descent, and was born in Australia. After the S. African War broke out he swore allegiance to the S.A.R., and became a burgher of that State. He was appointed to the command of the Irish Brigade, fighting on the Boer side. He was elected M.P. for Galway in Jan., 1900. He subsequently took up his residence in Paris, describing himself as a journalist. In connection with Col. Lynch's fighting in the Boer ranks, he came over to England voluntarily to answer to the charge of high treason, for which crime he was sentenced to death by Mr. Justice Wills on Jan. 23, 1903. The sentence was immediately commuted to penal servitude for life, but he was released after twelve months' imprisonment in Lewes Gaol. He is married.

LYNE, Michael John, of Kuruman, Cape Colony, of the Cape Civil Service, acted as Junior Assistant in the Postal Service in 1884; was appointed Clerk to the Civil Commissioner at Uitenhage in 1889, at Kenhardt in 1892, and at Port Elizabeth in 1895. In 1896 he was appointed Assistant Magistrate at Port Elizabeth, and at Cape Town in 1899. He acted as Secretary to the War Losses Compensation Commission in 1900-1; became Civil Commissioner and Resident Magistrate at Clanwilliam in 1902, and Resident Magistrate at Kuruman in 1902, which position he still holds.

LYNN, Capt., of Tarkastad, Cape Colony, is Chief Constable of Tarkastad, and during the South African War was in command of the Tarkastad Town Guard (medal).

LYONS, Capt. Henry George, F.R.G.S., F G.S. of Gezira, Cairo, and of the Army and Navy Club, was born in London Oct. 11, 1864. He is the son of Gen. T. C. Lyons, C.B., was educated at Wellington Coll., Berks., passing into the Royal Engineers, from which he has now retired. He is Director-Gen. of the Survey Dept. of Egypt; has published reports on the Island and Temples of Philae, and has also contributed articles on Egypt and Cairo in the supplementary volumes of the *Encyclopedia Britannica*. He married, July 5, 1896, Miss Helen Julia Hardwick.

LYSONS, Lieut.-Col. Henry, V.C., of the Naval and Military Club, was born in 1858, and son of the late Gen. Sir D. Lysons, G.C.B. he was educated at Wellington Coll., and entered the 90th Light Infantry at the age of twenty; served in the South African War in 1879 as A.D.C. to Brig. Gen. Wood; present at the actions at Nungen Nek and Inhlobana Mountain, and at the battles of Kambula and Ulundi (despatches, medal with clasp, and V.C.); and the Sudan Expedition in 1884-5, employed with he Egyptian Army (medal with clasp and bronze star). He had only had ten months' service, and was only twenty-one, when he gained the Victoria Cross on the Inhlobana Mountain, charging a cave occupied by hundreds of Zulus. In 1890 he passed the Staff College, and, after holding various staff appointments, he is now soldiering in Jhansi. He married Vanda, dau. of C. B. Treffry.

LYTTELTON, Lieut. Gen. Hon Sir Neville Gerald, K.C.B., of 28, Grosvenor Road, S.W., and of the Army and Navy and Brooks' Clubs, is the third son of the 4th Baron Lyttelton; was born at Hagley, Worcestershire, Oct. 28, 1845, and was educated at Eton, where he played in the Cricket XI. in 1862-3-4, and was senior keeper of the Wall Football in 1863. He won the 100 yards at Eton in 1862, and was second in the 350 yards. Since his schooldays Sir Neville has continued to play cricket for many tears, chiefly regimental and military, and racquets and lawn tennis, and has had a good deal of large and small game shooting. He joined the Rifle Brigade in Jan., 1865, becoming Lieut.-Col. commanding a battalion in Dec., 1892. He has held the following Staff appointments: A.D.C. to Earl Spencer, Lord-Lieut. of Ireland, 1868-73; Private Secy. to Mr. Childers, Secy. of State for War, 1880-2; A.D.C. to Sir John Adye, Chief of Staff, Egyptian Campaign, 1882; Mil. Secy. to Sir John Adye, Governor of Gibraltar, 1883-5; Mil. Secy. to Lord Reay, Governor of Bombay, 1885-90; A.A.G., War Office, 1895-97; Asst. Mil. Secy, 1897-9; Brig.-Gen. Khartoum Campaign, 1898; Major-Gen. Infantry Brigade, Aldershot, 1899; Major-Gen. 4th Infantry Brigade, S.A., 1899-1900; Lieut. Gen 2nd and 4th Divisions in Natal and the N.E. Transvaal, commanding in Natal, 1900-02; Lieut.-Gen. commanding Transvaal and O.R.C. from 1902 to Feb., 1903, and commanded the troops in S. Africa from that date until, under the new Army reorganisation scheme, he returned to England early in 1904 to become one of the three military members of the Army Council and Chief of the General Staff. Gen. Lyttelton saw active service in the Fenian raid in Canada in 1866 (medal and clasp), Jowaki Expedition, 1877 (medal and clasp), Egyptian War, 1882, when he was present at Tel-el-Kebir (medal and clasp, bronze star, 4th class Osmanieh, brevet of Lieut. Col.), Khartoum Expedition, 1898, including the battle of Khartoum (Egyptian medal and clasp and medal, was promoted Major-Gen. and thanked by the Houses of Parliament). His fighting in the S.A. War, 1899-1902, included the campaign in Natal, the operations in Eastern and N.E. Transvaal in the Cape Colony against De Wet, and the operations on the Natal border (medal with clasps for Tugela Heights, Relief of Ladysmith, Laing's Nek, Belfast, C.C. and O.R.C.; also the King's medal and two clasps). He was further promoted to Lieut. Gen. and made K.C.B. He was eight times mentioned in despatches. He has received the Good Service Reward. His other service abroad includes twelve years in India. Sir Neville married, Oct. 1, 1883, Katharine Sara, dau. of the Rt. Hon. James Stuart Wortley.

MAASDORP, G. H., M.L.A., was formerly member of the Cape Legislative Council for the Midland Circle. At the general election in Feb. 1904, he was returned to the Lower House as member for Graaff Reinet. He is a supporter of the Bond.

MABSON, Richard Rous, F.S.S., of 51, Cannon Street, London, E.C., was born in 1846 at Gt.

Yarmouth, and was educated privately. Mr. Mabson is best known as having been associated with the *Statist* since 1880, and in 1905 he completed a quarter of a century as editor of that paper. In connection with South African matters, Mr. Mabson shortly after that year personally, through force of circumstances, took up the subject of mining in South Africa, and he has on four occasions visited the Subcontinent, three times to the Rand, and once passing through Rhodesia as Special Commissioner of the *Statist*. His first trip in 1897 was due to disquieting rumours in London that the Deep Levels were likely to prove disappointing, but the result of a personal investigation of eight Deep Level properties enabled him to cable home at a crucial moment the brief hut reassuring message, "Deep Levels all right".

In 1900 Mr. Mabson appeared as author of the now well-known book, *Mines of the Transvaal*, which has passed through three editions, and the fourth edition is now due. This work deals comprehensively with the history of the important mining companies of the Transvaal, including the Coalfields of Natal and the Diamond Mines of the subcontinent.

Mr. Mabson is married, and his elder daughter is married to Samuel Evans (q.v.), a partner in the well-known firm of H. Eckstein and Co., of Johannesburg.

McBRIDE, Major, who commanded the Irish Brigade with the Boer Forces in the recent S.A. War, intends, it is reported, to again contest South Mayo at the next Parliamentary election. He married an Irish agitator, named Miss Maud Gonne, who recently obtained a divorce from him.

McCALLUM, Sir Henry Edward, R.E., G.C.M.G., of Government House, Pietermaritzburg, Natal, was born in Cornwall, Oct. 28, 1852, his father being a Major in the R.M.L.I. He entered the Royal Military Academy, Woolwich, in 1869, passing first out of 152 cadets in 1871 into the Royal Engineers. A few years afterwards he went to Singapore, where he acted as Private Secy. to the Governor for a couple of years, taking part in the Perak Expedition of 1875-6

(medal with clasp). Then he became Superintendent of Admiralty Works at Hong Kong, Singapore, and Woolwich, returning to the East in 1880 as Deputy Colonial Engineer at Penang, afterwards becoming Colonial Engineer and Surveyor-General for the Straits Settlements, with a seat on the Executive and Legislative Councils. In 1897 Sir Henry went to Lagos as Governor and Commander-in-Chief, and in the following year was dispatched on a mission to the Hinterland on account of French aggression in that region (medal and clasp). From 1898 to 1901 he was Governor of England's oldest colony, Newfoundland, and in the latter year he returned to Africa as Governor of Natal, receiving the South African medal with 4 clasps in connection with his services during the War.

A man who enters the public service, and especially one who has held high office for a number of years under one political party, must be well aware of the treatment to which he may be liable at the moment he finds himself drawn into the vortex of party strife. Whether he be soldier, administrator, or diplomatist, a change of Government may make him a useful scapegoat, and in the recent case of the trial and condemnation of the native murderers of two Natal policemen in March, 1906, no one wondered, though all sympathised, when Sir Henry McCallum was practically held responsible by Sir H. Campbell Bannerman's Government for the deplorable interference of the Colonial Office, which led to the immediate resignation of the Natal Ministry. The Natal Governor, however, tactfully succeeded in inducing the Premier of the Colony to temporarily remain in office, and when the Colonial Secy. "climbed down" (at Sir H. McCallum's expense), Mr. Smythe withdrew his resignation. (See Lord Elgin.) Sir Henry is understood to be about to retire from his post.

Sir Henry was knighted in 1898 for his services in connection with the construction of the fortifications of Singapore. He became G.C.M.G. in 1904, having previously been appointed A.D.C. to the Sovereign. He has been twice married; first to the dau., of the late Admiral Johnson, and afterwards, in 1897, to Maud (Dolly), a dau. of Lieut. Col. Fitzmaurice Creighton, of the R.M.L.I.

Princess Christian was sponsor for Lady McCallum's daughter, born in 1905.

McCARTHY, James Abran, of Freetown, Sierra Leone, is of African parentage, and only son of J. B. McCarthy, J.P., N.J., a merchant of Freetown; was educated at the Grammar Sch., Freetown; at Wesley Coll., Sheffield, Eng.; and is Barrister-at-Law and Common Law Scholar of the Inner Temple (1879). He was appointed Queen's Advocate of Sierra Leone and Mem. of Exec. and Legislative Councils and of the Board of Education of that Colony, 1889-95; was appointed Admiralty Advocate of Sierra Leone by the Lords Commissioners of the Admiralty; Escheator of Sierra Leone, 1893; Acting Chief Justice, May to Sept., 1893, and May to Aug., 1894; Solicitor-Gen. Gold Coast Colony since 1895; and Acting Puisne Judge of the Gold Coast 1895, 1898, and 1902; Acting Attorney-Gen. 1895 and 1899; sole Law Officer of the Crown, 1900 and 1902. When Queen's Advocate he accompanied the Administrator, Maj. Crooks, on a special mission to Monrovia to congratulate Pres. Cheeseman on his inauguration, and received a Knight Commandership of the Liberian Order of African Redemption, but was not permitted to accept it. He married: married: first, Lillie dau. of the late Councillor Vivian, of Hull, and second, Alice Maude, dau. of Surgeon-Major Davies (retired).

McCAUL, Miss Ethel Rosalie Ferrier, of 51, Welbeck St., W., and Windmill Fields, Freshwater, I. of Wight, was born in 1867, and is the second dau. of the Rev. J. B. McCaul, Hon. Canon of Rochester Cathedral. She entered the nursing profession in 1890, being trained at the Radcliffe Infirmary, Oxford. When the S. African War broke out she offered her services and nursed in a Field Hospital with Sir Redvers Buller's column from the Battle of Colenso to the relief of Ladysmith. (Royal Red Cross, Queen's S. African medal). She visited Japan and Manchuria during the Russo-Japanese War, by command of the Queen and by permission of the Japanese Govt., to inspect the working of the Japanese Red Cross Society. She was appointed lady visitor to the King Edward VII. Convalescent Home for Officers of the Army and Navy, at Osborne; and founded the Union Jack Club in 1902. She is the author of an Article on

Army Nursing in the XIXth Century, and *Under the Care of the Japanese War Office* (1904).

McCLINTOCK, Capt. Frederick William, F.S.A., of Krugersdorp, and the West Rand Club, Krugersdorp, was born at Dublin, Aug. 10, 1864. He is the eldest son of the late Lieut. Col. T. E. McClintock, of the Army Pay Dept., and nephew of the famous Arctic explorer, Admiral Sir Leopold McClintock. Capt. McClintock was educated at the Public High Sch., Dublin, and proceeded to S.A. at the ago of 21, joining the Education Dept. of the Natal Civil Service. He subsequently took up an appointment in the Cape Forestry Dept.; went to the Transvaal in 1895, where he acted as Secy. to some mining groups, and became identified with the Krugersdorp branch of the S.A. League. At the outbreak of the late war he joined the Prince Alfred's Guards as Sec.-Lieut., this being the only permanent Colonial Corps which is entitled to carry its colours into action—a privilege obtained for the regt. by the late Duke of Edinburgh, after whom it is named. At the close of hostilities, he retired with the permanent rank of Capt., in recognition of services rendered during the Anglo-Boer War. He then returned to the Transvaal, where he is engaged in secretarial duties in connection with the Commission investigating Burgher Claims upon the Imperial Govt., ultimately taking up an appointment in the Mines Dept., of the Transvaal Civil Service. Capt. McClintock is the author of *Hints: A Handbook for South African Volunteers*. He married, Aug. 10, 1896, Miss F. L. Soundy, dau. of J. T. Soundy, of Cradock, Cape Colony.

McCRACKEN, Col. Frederick William Nicholas, D.S.O., of the United Service Club, was born in Kent, Aug. 18, 1859. He was educated at the R.M.C., Sandhurst; gazetted to the 49th Regt. in 1879, and passed the Staff Coll. in 1889. From 1892-7 he acted as D.A.A.G. at Barbados. He served with the 1st Battn. Berks Regt. throughout the Egyptian Campaign in 1882, being present at the surrender of Kafr-Dawar (medal and Khedive's star); took part in the Suakim Expedition in 1885; present at the actions at Hasheen, M'Neil's Zeriba, etc. (mentioned in despatches, two clasps, brevet of Major); and the Egyptian Frontier Expedition in 1885-6, actions at Ginniss. He also served throughout the S. African War with the 2nd Battn. Berks. Regt. in 1899-1902 (despatches, Queen's medal and three clasps, King's medal and two clasps; D.S.O., and brevet of Lieut.-Col.). He married, Oct. 18, 1887, Ann, dau. of Thomas C. Glover, C.E., of Edinburgh, and Fife.

McEWEN, T. S., of Cape Town, was formerly Assistant Manager of the Cape Government Railways, and succeeded Mr. T. R. Price as General Manager in 1902.

MACFARLANE, Lieut. Col. George James (Natal Carbineers), C.M.G., J.P., of Redlands, Maritzburg, and of the Victoria Club, P.M.B., was born at Maritzburg, June 6, 1855. He is son of John Macfarlane, late R.M. of Natal, and was educated at the High Sch., P.M.B. He served in the Zulu War in 1878-9, and was besieged in Ladysmith in 1900. He was Mayor of Maritzburg, 1898-1902; Deputy Mayor for that town, 1903-4; and was made J.P. in 1902. Col. MacFarlane has taken keen interest in cricket, football and shooting, and possesses a fine collection of S.A. big game. He married, Dec., 1888, Mary Maria, dau. of Walter MacFarlane, late Speaker of the Natal Legislative Council.

McGREGOR, Arthur Wallace, was sent out by the Church Missionary Society for Uganda in 1892, trouble having broken out at Kilimanjaro between the natives and the German Governor, and he was dispatched by Bishop Tucker to join the missionary in charge at Mocki, the headquarters of the rebellion. On the withdrawal of the mission to Varita, B.E. Africa, he was located at the same place. In 1900 he was removed to Kikuya to establish the first C.M.S. station in that county. He commenced C.M.S. work in the Kenya Province of B.E. Africa, at Weithaya, in 1903, and in the same year published the first book in the language of the Wakikuya; viz., the Gospel of St. John; he is also the author of a Kikuya vocabulary of 5,600 words, and a Kikuya Grammar. Unmarried.

MACGREGOR, Sir William, of St. John's, Newfoundland, relinquished the Governorship of Lagos in 1904, and was then appointed Governor of Newfoundland.

MACHADO, Col. K.C.M.G., was formerly Governor-General of the Province of Mozambique, rendering considerable services to the British troops passing through Portuguese E. Africa at the time of the last S. African War. He was the recipient of the honour of K.C.M.G. on the King's Birthday (1902).

McILWAINE, Robert, J.P., M.A., LL.B., Ireland; of Orange Grove, Salisbury, Rhodesia, and of the Salisbury Club, was born in Ireland, Oct. 15, 1871. He was educated at Queen's Coll, at Belfast and Galway, and the Royal University of Ireland; and joined the Cape Colonial Civil Service in 1895. He acted as Secy., Civil Service Commission in 1898; passed a special examination in Dutch language; sometime Examiner for Cape Civil Service Commission; transferred to the British South Africa Company's service, in Oct., 1898, as assistant magistrate, Salisbury; appointed Chief Clerk; Judicial branch, Chief Secy.'s office, 1899; Relieving Magistrate and Civil Commissioner, 1901. He was admitted Advocate of High Court of Southern Rhodesia in 1903; appointed Legal Assistant and Senior Clerk to Attorney General, 1903; has acted as Magistrate, Victoria, Umtali, Enkeldoorn and Salisbury, as Secy. to the Law Dept., and as Inspector of Schools for Southern Rhodesia, and Statist. He is author of *Instructions for Special Justices of the Peace in Southern Rhodesia*. He married, in 1902, Sophie, dau. of Geo. B. Hanna, C.C., J.P., of Ballymena, Ireland.

MACKENZIE, Col. Duncan, C.B., C.M.G., of Cotswold, Nottingham, Natal, and of the Victoria Club, Maritzburg, was born in 1859, and is son of the late D. Mackenzie, of Natal. He is in command of the Natal Carbineers, and during the Zulu rebellion in the early part of 1906 commanded the Natal forces. Col. Mackenzie married, in 1883, Katharine, dau. of the late Alexander Macarthur, of Natal.

MACKENZIE, Sir George Sutherland, K.C.M.G., C.B., of 52, Queen's Gate Gardens S.W., and of the Oriental and Travellers' Club, was born in India, May 5, 1844, and is son of the late Sir Wm, Mackenzie, M.D. Sir George was the first Administrator of the British East Africa Company's territories, and was instrumental in bringing the Uganda and the Nile basin within the British zone. He opened up direct caravan routes between Isfahan and Mahommerah, Persia, in 1875, and also concluded the treaties of the Italian Govt. with Somali Chiefs. In 1899 he settled the dispute between the Arabs and the missionaries, bringing freedom to over a thousand slaves. He married, in 1883, Elma (died 1904), dau. of the late Major W. C. Armstrong.

MACKENZIE, Lieut. Hector Rose, Johannesburg and the Natal Club, P.M.B., is the eldest son of the late Alexander Mackenzie, Highland Clan historian and founder of the *Celtic Magazine* and the *Scottish Highlander*, Inverness, and Emma Sarah, eld. dau. of the late Thomas Whitaker Rose, of Bath. He was born at Ipswich, Feb. 25, 1867 and was educated at the Royal Academy, Raining's Coll., Inverness, and Glasgow Univ. He commenced his business career as private sec to the late Dr. Charles Fraser Mackintosh M.P. for Invernessshire. Passing his final examination as a Scots solicitor in 1899, he joined the clerical staff of the Crofters' Commission for twelve months, commencing practice as a solicitor in Inverness in April, 1890. In 1896 he went S.A. and entered journalism, passing successfully through various stages until he became acting editor of the *South African Telegraph* (Cape Town). His other journalistic position include that of sub-editor and acting editor *The Press of Pretoria*; asst. editor of *The Durban Star*; asst. editor, joint editor, and editor of the *Cape Mercury* (King Williams Town); subeditor *Cape Daily Telegraph* (Port Elizabeth); asst. editor *Cape Register* (Cape Town); subeditor *Times of Natal* (Pietermaritzburg); and, finally, asst. news editor *Rand Daily Mail* (Johannesburg). On the outbreak of war he joined the Cape Town Highlanders as private; and rose to the rank of corporal; he served at Kuils River, Mulder's Vlei, Tulbagh Road, Belmont, Douglas and Modder River. In Sept., 1900, he was appointed Asst. Manager at Mafeking of the Western Division of the Imperial Transport Service. For some time during 1901 he was attached to the Army Service Corps at Army Headquarters at Pretoria as shorthand writer to the Director of Supplies. He is now Lieut. in the Natal Royal Regt. and on the Reserve of Officers, and has the S.A. War (Queen's) medal with three clasps.

He is the author of *Yachting and Electioneering in the Hebrides and Old Inverness*; also of several articles and poems in *Blackwood's Mag.*, *Chambers' Journal*, the *Celtic Mag.*, the *Cape Illustrated Mag.*, and other serial publications. He married, July 19, 1892, Barbara Sutherland, eldest surviving dau. of John Anderson, late of the 71st Regt. of Foot (Highland Light Infantry). Issue, one dau., Janet Dorothy Rose, born June 4, 1894.

MACKENZIE, William Cossar, D.Sc., F.R.S. Edin., Imperial Order of the Osmanieh (3rd class), of Ghizeh, Egypt; the Crescent, Cromer; and the Royal Societies (Lond.), Union (Edin.), and Turf (Cairo) Clubs, was born Feb. 15, 1866. He is third son of A. B. Mackenzie, J.P., of Edinburgh; was educated at George Watson's Coll., Edinburgh, and at the Edinburgh, Strasburg, and Halle a. S. Univs. After leaving Halle Univ. in 1891, he was appointed Lecturer in Agricultural Chemistry at the Durban Coll, of Science, Newcastle-on-Tyne. In Dec., 1891, he was appointed Lecturer in General and Analytical Chemistry at the Ghizeh Agricultural Coll., and became Principal of that institution in June, 1896. In 1902 he was appointed Principal of the Polytechnic Sch. of Engineering under the Egyptian Ministry of Public Instruction. Both these institutions are still under Dr. Mackenzie. He married, June 27, 1902, Marian, younger dau. of Samuel Gurney Sheppard, of Leggatts, Herts.

MACKINDER, Halford John, M.A. (Oxon), *Officier de l'Instruction Publique de France*; of Minster House, St. James's Court, London, S.W., and of the Royal Societies' and Alpine Clubs; was born at Gainsborough, Feb. 15, 1861; is son of Dr. B. Mackinder, and was educated at Epsom Coll. and Christ Church, Oxford. He was Pres of the Oxford Union Society, 1883; Reader in Geography, Oxford University, 1887-1905; Principal of University Coll., Reading, 1892-1903, and Pres. of the Geographical Section British Assoc., 1895. In 1899 he led an exploring expedition in British E. Africa through Kikuyu and Laikipia, and made the first ascent of Mount Kenya. He contested Warwick and Leamington for Parliament in 1900, and in 1904 was appointed Director of the London School of Economies and Political Science, and Senator of the London Univ. Mr. Mackinder is also a Barrister of the Inner Temple, Medalist of the

Royal Scottish Geographical Sec. (1903), corresponding member of the Berlin Geographical Society, and the author of *Britain and the British Seas* (1902), and various magazine articles.

MACKINNON, Maj.-Gen. Wm. Henry, C.V.O., C.B., of 15, Ovington Sq., Lond., S.W., and the Guards', Travellers', and Union Clubs, is the second son of W. A. Mackinnen, 34th Chief of the Clan. He was born in London, Dec. 15, 1852, and educated at Harrow. He joined the Grenadier Guards, Jan. 22, 1870, and was Asst. Military Secy. at Malta, June, 1884, to July, 1885; Private Secy., Madras, July, 1895, to July, 1898. On the formation of the C.I.V., Col. MacKinnon assumed command, which he retained throughout the regiment's service in S.A. He was also in command of troops at the Orange River; took part in the operations in the Orange Free State, including the action at Zand River, and the operations in the Transvaal, including the actions near Johannesburg, Pretoria, and Diamond Hill, and the action at Elands River (despatches, Queen's medal with four clasps, and C.B.). Since 1904 Gen. MacKinnon has acted as Director of Auxiliary Forces, and in 1906 was a member of the Committee of the Volunteer Commission. He married, in 1881, Madeline, dau. of Villiers la Touche Hatton.

MACLAREN, James Paterson, M.A., B.Sc., M.B., C.M., of the Civil Service Club, Cape Town, was educated at Glasgow Univ., graduating M.A., with double honours in Classics and Philosophy, Gold Medalist in Greek, Wm. Hunter Medalist in Anatomy and Zoology, and Luke Prizeman in History. Dr. MacLaren has been House Surgeon in Chesterfield, Leicester, and Moorfields (Royal London Ophthalmic) hospitals; Asst. Eye Surgeon in Middlesex Hospital, and Clinical Asst. in the Chelsea Hospital for Women, Gray's Inn Read, Golden Square Throat Hospital, and Moorfields Eye Hospital. Later he served as Surgeon to H.M.S. *Carthage* (Hospital ship) in the China Expeditionary Force, and on H.M.S. *Nubia*. During the last S.A. War he saw more service as Civil Surgeon with H.M. Forces, and he now holds the appointments of Immigration Officer of Cape Town, Additional Port Health Officer of Cape Town, Additional District Surgeon of Cape Town, and Medical Officer of Health to the Table Bay Harbour Board.

MACLEAN, Capt., of the East Lancashire Regt., was specially selected for service with the West African Frontier Force in 1905.

MACLEAN, Sir Harry Aubrey de Vere, K.C.M.G. (1901), Kaid of Fez, of Tangier, Morocco, was born on June 15, 1848, at Chatham, and is son of Surgeon-Gen. Maclean. In 1869 Sir Harry obtained his commission in the 69th Foot. In 1886 Sir Drummond Hay, then British Minister at the Court of the Sultan, approached him with a view to his joining the service of the Sultan of Morocco as Instructor of Musketry to the Moorish Army. He accepted, and this necessitated the resignation of his commission and residence for some months of every year in Morocco. Sir Harry taught the Moor how to shoot, and, as a master of military matters in a country where the problem of defence is of immense importance a very few years found him standing close to the throne itself. Then, as a high honour, and as a fitting recognition of the services he had rendered to the nation, the Sultan made him a Kaid, and later, when Abdul Aziz came to the throne of Morocco, Maclean became his friend and counsellor, roaming the wild country with the nomadic Court, and so firmly establishing himself in the confidence of the Sultan that the jealous designs of Europeans as well as anti-European intriguers were not able to shake his position. Kaid Maclean accompanied the corpse of the late Sultan, Mulai el Hasan, on that dramatic trek from Marrakesh to Rabat, all the while maintaining the necessary fiction that the Son of Mahomet was still alive until the succession of Mulai Abdul-Aziz might be securely proclaimed in Rabat. The new Sultan, quite ignorant of his country's needs, speedily recognised Kaid Maclean as a strong and resourceful counsellor to lean upon, and Sir Harry still maintained his position as Chief Military Adviser to his Shereefian Majesty In habit the Kaid is practically as much a Moor as a Scot. He is a perfect master of the Moroccan language, short of stature, of great courage, and of commanding ability. In 1874 Sir Harry met Miss Catherine Coe, a lady of Spanish origin, at Gibraltar, and they were married at the British Consulate at Mogador, on Aug. 19, 1882, there being four children of the marriage. Lady Maclean was, however, divorced in 1905.

MACLEAN, L., is the General Manager of the Cape Town branch of the Union Castle Mail Steamship Co., Ltd. (See Sir Donald Currie).

MACLEAN, Ronald, of East London, Cape Colony, entered the Customs Dept. in 1864. He was transferred to the Stores Dept. of the London and Queen's Town Railway in 1875; served in the Gaika-Galeka Campaign in 1877-78; acted as Captain of the East London Fingo Levies in 1879; and was granted leave, at the special request of Lord Chelmsford, to proceed to Zululand, where he served in command of native levies attached to Colonel Pearse's column, and subsequently in command of the Mounted Native Corps under the immediate direction of Lord Chelmsford. He was transferred to the Wharf Dept. of the Eastern System Railways in 1879, and in 1881 commanded a company of Buffalo Volunteer Rifles under Commandant von Linsingen in Tembuland, and subsequently in the Basutoland Campaign. He is Captain of the East Bank Rocket Brigade.

MACLEAR, Capt. and Brevet Major Percy, of the Junior Naval and Military Club, was born Oct. 22, 1875. He was educated at Bedford and Sandhurst; was gazetted as 2nd Lieut. to the Royal Dublin Fus. in 1895, promoted Capt in 1900, Brevet Major in 1901. He served throughout the S. African War, 1899-1902 (mentioned in despatches). He was appointed second in command and Adjt. of the Lagos Battn W.A.F.F. in 1903, and to the full command 1905. Unmarried.

McMICKING, Major Gilbert, M.P., C.M.C of Miltonise, Stranraer, NB., and of the Nay and Military Club, was born in 1862, and is son of the late Gilbert McMicking. He was educated at the R.M.A., Woolwich, and served in the Royal Artillery until 1894. During the African War in 1899-1902, he commanded the C.I.V. Battery, with the rank of Major, and was a Major in the Hon. Artillery Company of London. Major McMicking is Liberal M.P. of Kirkcudbrightshire, having won the seat in 1906. He married, in 1893, Gertrude, dau. of the late Nathaniel Gore.

MACMILLAN, W., an American explorer who having already made one expedition up the Blue Nile, organised a second in 1905 for the purpose of establishing a commercial river route between Abyssinia and the Sudan.

MACMUNN, Major George Fletcher, D.S.O., care of Messrs. Cox and Co., 16, Charing Cross Road, London, W.C., was born Aug. 24, 1869, and is son of the late J. G. MacMunn, R.A., of the Royal Hospital, Chelsea. He was Silver Medalist at the H. Art. Institution in 1896, and Gold Medalist in 1900, also Gold Medalist at the United Service Institution in 1904. Major MacMunn served in Burma with the Irrawaddy column n 1892, including the march to and defence of Sadon (mentioned in despatches, medal and clasp, wounded); the Sima column in 1893 (clasp); W. Frontier of India, 1897-8, as Staff Officer of the Imperial Service Transport (medal and two clasps); and the Tirah Campaign in 1897-8 (clasp). He took part in the S. African War in 1899-02 with the R.A., and as Staff Captain and D.A.A.G. to various mobile columns (despatches, Brevet-Major, Queen's and King's medals). He acted as Inspecting Officer to the Imperial Service Art. in India, 1894-9; and as D.A.A.G. in India, 1904. He married, July 5, 1893, Alice, dau. of Lieut. Col. J. H. Watson, Indian Army.

MACOWAN, Peter, D.Sc. (Cape of Good Hope Univ.), B.A. (Lond.), FL.S. (1885), Deutsche Botanische Gesellsehaft (1888), Acad. Natural Sciences, U.S.A. (1874), Royal Hort. Society (1885), Massachusetts Hort. Soc. (1889), S. A. Philosophical Soc. (1887); of Grahamstown, Cape Colony; was born at Hull, Eng., in 1830. He was Professor of Chemistry and Analyst at Huddersfield Coll, in 1857; Headmaster of Shaw Coll., Grahamstown, 1862; Science Tutor in Gill Coll., Somerset East, 1869; Director of Cape Town Botanical Gardens and Curator of the Govt. Herbarium, 1881; and Govt. Botanist, 1892. Dr. MacOwan, who has been a referee in Cape Botany and Cultural matters for many years, retired from the service of the Cape Agricultural Dept., June 30, 1905.

MACRORIE, Right Rev. William Kenneth, D.D., D.C.L., of the College, Ely, is the son of David Macrorie, M.D. (Edin.), and was born, Feb. 8, 1832, at Liverpool. He was educated at Winchester and Brasenose Coll., Oxon. He graduated M.A. and D.D. of Oxon, D.C.L. of the Univ. of the South Tennessee, and M.A. of the Cape Univ.; Hulmeian Exhibitioner, 1854. From 1855-58 he was Fellow of St. Peter's Coll., Hadley; 1858-60 he was Curate of Deane, Lanes.; from 1860-61 he was Vicar of Wingater; from 1861-66 he was Rector of Wapping; and from 1866-68, Vicar of Accrington. In 1869 he went to S.A. as Bishop of Maritzburg, retaining the appointment until 1892, when he left S.A. to become Canon of Ely. In his early life he was a well-known oarsman and fond of fishing and fives. At the present time his principal outdoor recreation is croquet. On April 9, 1863, he married Agnes, dau. of William Watson, of South Hill, Liverpool. (See Obituaries.)

MACSHERRY, Right Rev. Hugh, Catholic Bishop and Vicar Apostolic of the Eastern Prov. of the Cape of Good Hope, of St. Augustine's Church, Port Elizabeth, and Bishop's House, Beaufort St., Grahamstown; is the son of Arthur MacSherry, of Loughgilly, county Armagh, Ireland. He was born at Loughgilly, Feb. 1, 1852, and was educated at the Diocesan Seminary, Armagh, and at Paris, and took the degree of D.D. He was ordained Feb. 7, 1875, and for twenty-one years laboured in various parishes of his native diocese. In 1893 he was appointed Administrator of Dundalk; and in 1896 was nominated by Pope Leo XIII. Titular Bishop of Justinianopolis, and consecrated by His Eminence Cardinal Logue on Aug. 2 of that year. In December, 1896, he went out to South Africa as successor to the Right Rev. Bishop Strobino and has ever since been actively engaged in the administration and development of the different missions confided to his spiritual care. In his new sphere of labour and of ecclesiastical government those qualities which have endeared him so generally in Ireland quickly made themselves felt. His courtesy, his strength of resolve, and breadth of view, and his contagious zeal for work all have stamped him as eminently fitted to fill with honour to himself and the cause of religion the responsible office he was appointed to occupy by the Holy See. He was mentioned in his last despatches (June 21, 1902) by Lord Kitchener for services to the Army Chaplain's Dept. in S.A. during the Anglo Boer War, and was elected a Fellow of the Royal Colonial Institute in 1902.

MADDOX, H., of the Church Missionary Society, attempted to climb the mountains of the Moon, on the Uganda border, with Herr Rudolf Grauer (q.v.) in 1905-6.

MAGUIRE, James Rochfort, M.A., of 8, Cleveland Square, London, W., was born in 1855, and was educated at Cheltenham and Oxford Univ. He was called to the Bar of the Inner Temple in 1883, and represented N. Donegal in the House of Commons from 1890 to 1892, when he was elected for West Clare. His Parliamentary career closed in 1895, and some years later, at the instigation of Mr. Rhodes, he undertook, in company with Messrs. D. Rudd and F. H. Thompson (q.v.), a mission to Lobengula, and obtained from that chief the concession ceding the mineral rights over the whole of his territories, This concession was ultimately taken over by the Chartered Co., of which Mr. Maguire became a director. He is also on the directorate of the Consolidated Goldfields of South Africa, the Exploration Co., and the Rhodesia Railways, Ltd. In spite of the difficulties of developing a new country so vast and remote as Rhodesia, considerable progress has been made in railway construction during the fourteen years of its history.

There are two railway systems in Rhodesia, the Cape to Cairo Trunk line, and the Eastern system. The Cape to Cairo Trunk line has been constructed by the Rhodesia Railways, Limited, from Vryberg, to which point the railway is the property of the Cape Colony, through Bechuanaland into Rhodesia, and was completed as far as Bulawayo in October, 1897. The construction of the line was then proceeded with to Wankie, and although seriously delayed by the Boer War, the coalfields were reached in Sept., 1903, and was completed to the Victoria Falls on April 25, 1904. The whole line from Bulawayo to the Victoria Falls was opened on June 20, 1904. The next step was the spanning of the Zambesi River by a bridge thrown across the gorge in the immediate vicinity of the Victoria Falls. An aerial cableway was constructed across the river to enable materials to be taken over, and the building of the bridge was carried on from both banks simultaneously. The bridge is the highest in the world and the steel work was erected in the almost record time of six months. The bridge was opened by Professor Darwin, Pres. of the British Assn., on Sept. 12, 1905, the fifteenth anniversary of Occupation Day. The construction of a further ninety-five miles north of the Zambesi to Kalomo, the capital of North Western Rhodesia, has recently been completed, and a further section of 265 miles to the rich copper deposits in the Hook of the Kafue and the Broken Hill country has been commenced by the Mashonaland Railway Company. A branch line leaving the main line at Heany Junction, seventeen miles north of Bulawayo, has been completed, and opened for traffic as far as West Nicholson, in the Gwanda District, a distance of 104 miles. Other lines completed are the Gwelo to Selukwe, twenty-four miles long, opened in August, 1903, and a short line to the Matopos, built by the trustees of late Mr. Rhodes.

The other railway system of Rhodesia, the East Coast Line, was originally built as a light railway from Beira to Umtali. Opened in 1898, it was widened to a 3ft. 6in. gauge, the standard gauge in Rhodesia, in August, 1900, in order to complete a uniform line from Salisbury to the coast, a 3ft. 6in. line having already been opened between Salisbury and Umtali in May 1899. This line was continued from Salisbury westward to Gwelo, 188 miles, to meet a line which had been commenced from Bulawayo eastward, but upon which construction had been suspended owing to the war. The line from Salisbury to Bulawayo was completed and opened for traffic in June, 1902. Mr. Maguire married, in 1895, Julia, eld dau. of the first Lord Peel, late Speaker of the House of Commons.

MAKINS, Dr. George Henry, C.B., F.R.C.S., of 47, Charles St., London, W., and of the Athenaeum, Savile, and Alpine Clubs, born at Surbiton, Nov. 3, 1853; was educated at Gloucester, and received his medical training at St. Thomas's Hosp., Lond., Halle, and Vienna. In 1880-1 he acted as Under-Secy. to the International Medical Congress in London in 1881, and has held numerous posts connected with medical societies since then. In 1899 he was sent out as Consulting Surgeon to the South African Field Force, and served in that capacity during the first ten months of the Boer War (medal with three clasps;

despatches). He has been connected with St. Thomas's Hospital and School in various posts since 1875, and is now Surgeon and Lecturer on Surgery there: also Surgeon to King Edward VII.'s Hospital for Officers, the Convalescent Home for Officers at Osborne, and the Royal Hospital for Incurables, and is member of the Consultation Board, Royal Naval Medical Service. Dr Makins is the author of *Surgical Experiences in South Africa*, and numerous papers on surgical subjects in contemporary medical literature. He married, in 1885, Margaret Angus, dau. of Maj.Gen. Kirkland, and widow of Maj.-Gen. Fellowes.

MAINWARING, Colonel Henry Germain, F.G.S., of Kensington Palace Mansions, S.W., Inverclair, Inverness-shire, and of the Army and Navy and Junior Carlton Clubs, was born at Barrackpore, Bengal, in 1852, and is the son Major Henry G. Mainwaring, late of the 1st Bengal Native Infantry. He was educated privately, and in 1872 was gazetted to the 24th Regt. He served with his regt. in the Kaffir War in 1877-8, including the operations against the Galekas; and also served throughout the Zulu War, afterwards surveying the battlefield of Isandhlwana. He acted as Transport Commissariat and Ordnance Officer, and was on the Camp escort of Lord (then Sir Garnet) Wolseley at Ulundi. Whilst on a big game shooting expedition in Somaliland, he surveyed some hitherto unexplored ground along the southern boundary of Abyssinia. Colonel Mainwaring commanded the 1st Battn. South Wales Borderers (24th Regt.) from 1896-1901. Recreations: Shooting and fishing, having won several prizes at rifle meetings, amongst others, The All Comers at the Caird Rifle Meeting in 1894. He married, Feb. 2, 1889, Henrietta, dau. of the late Henry Wigan.

MAIR, Captain George Tag, D.S.O., of the Royal Artillery, was born April 25, 1873, and entered the Army in 1893. He served in the South African War in 1899-1900, including the operations in the Orange River Colony, and the action at Bothaville, where he was severely wounded (Queen's medal with three clasps). For his services during the native risings in Northern and Southern Nigeria he was awarded the D.S.O. in 1906.

MALAN, Francois Stephanus, M.L.A.

(Malmesbury), of Schoongezicht, Kloof St., Cape Town, is the son of Daniel G. Malan, of Leeuwenjacht, Paarl, and is descended from French Huguenot stock, Jacques Malan, his direct ancestor, having landed in S.A. in 1689. Born March 12, 1871, in the district of the Paarl, he was educated at Paarl; Victoria Coll., Stellenbosch; and Camb., graduating B.A. (Science) Cape Univ.; also LL.B. Camb. Admitted as an Advocate of the Supreme Court, C.C., Aug., 1895. Appointed editor, Nov. 15, 1895, of *Ons Land*, one of the leading Dutch newspapers in C.C. Elected unopposed M.L.A. for Malmesbury in succession to the Hon. W. P. Schreiner, Sept., 1900; re-elected Feb., 1904; was convicted for publishing defamatory libel on Gen. French, April 19, 1901, and sentenced to twelve months' imprisonment without hard labour. He is one of the most prominent politicians of the S.A. party, and commands a very large following among the Dutch. Married to Miss Johanna Brummer, Sept. 21, 1897.

MALCOLM, Dougal Orme, of 1, Princes' Gardens, London, S.W., Halton Manor, Epsom, and Staff Cottage, Sunnyside, Johannesburg; and of the Bachelors' and Union Clubs, London, and the Rand and New Clubs, Johannesburg; was born in Argyllshire, Aug. 6, 1877, and is son of W. R. Malcolm and Georgina, dau. of the late Lord Charles Wellesley. He was educated at Eton and New Coll., Oxford (First Class *Literae Humaniores*, Oxon., 1899), and is a Fellow of All Souls' Coll., Oxford. After serving in the South African Dept. of the Colonial Office, Mr. Malcolm was appointed in 1905 Private Secretary to the High Commissioner for S. Africa and Governor of the Transvaal and Orange River Colony. Unmarried.

MALCOLM, Capt. Neill, D.S.O., of Poltalloch, Lochgilphead, Argyllshire, and of the Naval and Military Club, was born in London, Oct. 8, 1869, and is son of Colonel Malcolm. He was educated at Eton and Sandhurst, and joined the Argyll and Sutherland Highlanders in 1899; took part in a shooting expedition in Ladakh in 1893; and shot in Somaliland in 1894. He accompanied Capt. M. S. Welby across Tibet and China from India to Pekin, 1896, and took part in the Indian Frontier Expedition in 1897. From 1897-99 he served in the Uganda Mutiny, and afterwards in the S. African War, where he was wounded at Paardeberg. He was at the Staff Coll, in 1902-3; took part in the Somaliland Expedition in 1903-4, and accompanied the British Mission to Fez in 1905. Captain Malcolm edited Col. Henderson's essays and lectures *The Science of War*, 1905.

MALET, Sir Edward Baldwin, P.C., G.C.B., G.C.M.G., of 85, Eaton Square, London, S.W., Wilbury Park, Salisbury, and of the Travellers', St. James's, Bachelors', Automobile, , and Queen's Clubs, was born Oct. 10, 1837. He was educated at Eton, and Corpus Christi Coll., Oxford, and began his diplomatic career in 1854. He was in charge of the British Embassy at Paris during the Commune in 1871 (C.B.), and acted as Agent, Consul-Gen., and Minister Plenipotentiary in Egypt in 1881 (K.C.B.). He represented H.M. Govt. at Cairo during the time of the Arabi Rebellion, and after the battle of Tel-el-Kebir he reentered the capital with the Duke of Connaught and Viscount Wolseley (q.v.) in 1882. In 1884 he represented Great Britain at the W. African Conference which confirmed Great Britain in possession of the Niger Territories, and also signed the agreements with Germany which resulted in the Protectorates of Zanzibar, Uganda, and British E. Africa being established. Sir Edward retired in 1895. He is a member of the Court of Arbitration at The Hague, and is a trustee of the Wallace Collection. He married, March 19, 1885, Lady Ermyntrude Sackville Russell, dau. of the 9th Duke of Bedford.

MALMUSI, Signor, was one of the Italian Plenipotentiaries at the Moroccan Conference at Algeçiras in 1906.

MALLESON, Percy Rodbard, of the Willows, Hex River, Cape Colony and of the Civil Service Club, C.T., was born at Wimbledon, Surrey, in 1867; was educated at Univ. Coll. Sch., Lond., and Hertford Coll., Oxon.; was sub-agent in Lord Sudeley's fruit farms in 1889-90; County Council Lecturer on Fruit Growing, 1891-2; went to S.A. in 1892, and assisted in starting the first large fruit farm in C.C., and in inaugurating the fruit export trade to Eng. He is now Managing Director of the Cape Orchard Co., of Hex River; Mem. of

Western Prov. Horticultural Board, the Royal Agricultural Soc. of Eng., the Royal Horticultural Soc. of Eng., and the Royal Colonial Inst. During the late S.A. War he served as an officer of the Hex River D.M.T., and as Colonial Mem. of the Protected Horses Board, W. Dist. He married, in 1896, Beatrice Mary, dau. of H. W. Struben, of Cape Town, and Pretoria.

MANCE, Capt. Harry Osborne, D.S.O., of Old Woodbury, Sandy, Beds., was born at Karachi, Oct. 2, 1875, and is son of Sir Henry C. Mance, C.I.E., LL.D. He was educated at Bedford and the R.M. Academy, Woolwich; gazetted to R.E. as Second Lieut. in March, 1895, and served in the S.A. War, 1899-1902, as Deputy Asst. Dir, of Rlys., and as D.A.D.R. of armoured trains on the Kimberly line. Decorations: Queen's S.A. medal with Belmont clasp, King's S.A. medal with clasps, mentioned in despatches, and D.S.O. He was the winner of the Revolver Aggregate, Transvaal Bisley, 1903-4.

MANLEY, Francis Hubert, of Alexandria; of Spofforth Hall, Yorks., and of the Khedivial Club, Alexandria, is grandson of the 19th Lord Stourton and son of Geo. Manley, of Spofforth Hall, Turks., where he was born in 1872. He was educated at Ampleforth Coll., near York, and acts as Reuter's and Lloyd's Agent at Alexandria. Unmarried.

MANNING, Brigadier-Gen. William Henry, of the Naval and Military Club, was born, July 19, 1863, in England, and was educated at Cambridge, and the Royal Military Coll., Sandhurst. Gen. Manning entered the Army in Aug. of 1886, and served in the Burmese War of 1887-8-9, and in the Miranzai and Hazara Expeditions of 1891. He proceeded to Central Africa in 1893, and was promoted Brevet Major and then Brevet-Lieut.-Col. for the eminent services he rendered in Central Africa and Northern Rhodesia. He was made Deputy Commissioner and Comdt. of the troops in Central Africa, 1897-1901, and acted as Commissioner and Consul-Gen. from Dec., 1897, to Dec. 1898 and from July, 1900, to April, 1901. Gen. Manning was appointed Inspector-Gen. of the King's African Rides, Oct., 1901, and it was undoubtedly owing to the great services he rendered in Central Africa that he soon after was given the command of the

Somaliland Field Force, which post he filled from Nov., 1902, to July, 1903. He had many difficulties to contend with, owing chiefly to want of transport and water. In spite of a serious reverse his subordinate, Col. Plunkett, sustained, his services were retained after Gen. Egerton was appointed to the supreme command. Since then he has been doing good work, and has greatly added to his already high reputation in military circles. General Manning is unmarried.

MANSEL. G., C.M.G., Chief Commissioner of Natal Police.

MARAIS, Eugene, was formerly editor of the Dutch paper *Laud en Volk*, in which he consistently and patriotically raised his voice in support of a pure and enlightened Govt., and spared no one in the exposure of abuses, notably in the Dynamite case, when he accused Mr. J. M. A. Wolmarans of accepting a bribe of 1s. per case (estimated at that time to amount to nearly £10,000 per an.) on dynamite as a consideration for his support in the Executive Council, of which he was a member. This charge was not denied. Then there was the case of his successfully sustaining his alleged libel that Mr. Kruger had defrauded the State by charging heavy travelling expenses for a certain trip on which he was actually the guest of the Cape Colonial Govt. Subsequently (in 1893-4) his exposure of thefts of Govt. stores by Landdrost Kock, a satellite of the Kruger regime, at last forced a private investigation, though the case was not allowed to be brought before the courts of the country. At the time of the Raid, when matters had assumed their most threatening appearance, Mr. Marais and Mr. Malan hastened to Johannesburg fully authorised by the Executive to confer with the Reform Committee and if possible to avert a conflict. These gentlemen were successful in so far as they persuaded the Committee to appoint representatives to treat with a commission in Pretoria having for its object the removal of some of the chief grievances of the Uitlanders.

MARAIS, .Johannes Henock, M.L.A., member of the Cape Legialative Assembly for the electoral division of Stellenbosch, for which he was re-elected in Feb., 1904, in the Bond interest.

MARAIS, Rev. Johannes Isaac, B.A., D.D., of Stellenbosch, Cape Colony, was born at Cape Town, Aug. 23, 1848, of Huguenot parentage. He was educated at the S. African Coll., Cape Town; the Theological Seminary, Stellenbosch; and the Universities of Edinburgh and Utrecht. For some time he was Asst. Minister of the Dutch Reformed Church at Cape Town, subsequently being ordained to the full ministry of the said church at Hanover, Cape Colony. In 1887 he was appointed Professor of Apologetics and Natural Theology at the Theological Seminary, Stellenbosch. Since 1883 he has been a member of the Council of the Cape of Good Hope Univ., and also President of the Council of Victoria Coll., Stellenbosch; and was for many years secretary and treasurer of the Bloemhof Seminary there. He married, Aug. 23, 1870, Hester, dau. of the late Oloff Fehrsen, M.D.

MARAIS, Petrus Johannes, was born in the Cape Colony, and accumulated a considerable fortune by judicious investments in house property in Pretoria. He was the victim of a vitriol outrage in Mar., 1904, by his daughter-in-law, Mrs. Bellfield Marais, and her young daughter, aged fifteen, by which Mr. Marais nearly lost the sight of an eye. He is familiarly known as Long Piet, on account of his six feet five inches of stature.

MARJORIBANKS, Capt. Hon. Dudley Churchill, D.S.O., M.V.O., was born in 1874, and is the only son of the 2nd Baron Tweedmouth. He was educated at Harrow, and entered the Royal Horse Guards in 1895; took part in the South African War in 1899-1902 with the composite regt. of Household Cavalry, being present at the relief of Kimberley and the operations in the Transvaal, Orange River and Cape Colonies (despatches, Queen's medal with six clasps and D.S.O.). Capt. Marjoribanks is now acting A.D.C. to Lord Selborne, and went out to South Africa with him when he took up his appointment. He married, in 1901, Muriel, dau. of the Rt. Hon. St. John Brodrick by his first wife.

MARKHAM, Arthur Basil, M.P., of Stuffynwood Hall, Mansfield. was born in 1867, and has represented Mansfield in the Liberal interest since 1900, having been last returned unopposed at the general election in 1906. He is chiefly notorious for his antagonism to Rand capitalists, and for having in the course of a speech in the House of Commons made charges against Messrs. Wernher, Beit and Co. of criminal misconduct with reference to their financial operations, and declaring that they were nothing more nor less than swindlers. Mr. Markham repeated these statements outside the privileged precincts of the House, whereupon Messrs. Wernher, Belt and Co. instituted libel proceedings. Mr. Markham, however, unreservedly withdrew and apologised for the charges, which he admitted were without foundation. He married, in 1898, a dau. of Capt. Cunningham.

MARKS, Major Claude Laurie, D.S.O., of 11, Curzon Street, Mayfair, and of the Junior Naval and Military Club, is the youngest son of the Rev. Professor D. W. Marks. He was born Dec. 11, 1863, and was educated at University College School. He went out to South Africa at the age of fifteen, and saw service in the Sekukuni War with Ferreira's Horse (1880), in the Basuto War with Dimes' Rifles (1881), and in the Warren Expedition with Carrington's Horse (1884). He assisted in organising a company of the East Kent Yeomanry in 1900, and took them out to the late S. African War as Captain Commanding, being twice mentioned in despatches, and being decorated with the D.S.O. for assisting in saving the guns at Leeuwkop, O.R.C. He is Hon. Major in the Highland Light Infantry (Militia Batt.), and occupies himself as a journalist and financier. Recreations: Shooting and hunting. Major Marks married, Feb. 1, 1887, Carrie, eldest dau. of A. Hoffnung, late Chargé d'Affaires at the Court of St. James's. He has two sons, the elder of whom was educated at Eton and Sandhurst, and was lately gazetted 2nd Lieut. in the Army (Middlesex Regt.).

MARKS, Major Harry Hananel, M.P., J.P., of Callis Court, St. Peter's, Kent; 6, Cavendish Sq., W.; and of the Carlton, Automobile, and Royal Cinque Ports Yacht Clubs, was born in London, April, 1855; is son of the Rev. Prof. Marks, of Univ. Coll., and was educated at that Coll. and at the Athenée Royal of Brussels. Mr. Marks is the founder and editor of the great City daily paper, *The Financial News*; is Chairman of the Argus

Printing Co., and Chm. of the Royal Orthopedic Hosp.

He represented East Marylebone on the London County Council, 1889-92, and St. George's-in-the-East, 1895-8. He contested Northeast Bethnal Green in the Conservative interest in 1892, and represented St. George's Div. of the Tower Hamlets in Parliament from 1895 to 1900. In 1904 he was elected M.P. for Thanet, in succession to the late Rt. Hon. James Lowther, and he was re-elected in Jan., 1906. He is J.P. for the county of Kent, and now commands the Cadet Battn. of the Buffs (East Kent Regt.). He married, in 1884, Annie Estelle, dau. of William Benjamin, of Montreal.

MARKS, Samuel, of Zwartkoppies hall, near Pretoria, Transvaal, and of Threadneedle House, Bishopsgate Street Within, E.C., is one of the chief partners of the firm of Lewis and Marks, of London and Pretoria. From very modest beginnings Mr. Marks established a big position in the Kimberley diamond fields, which, however, he left in 1881 for the Transvaal Republic. From the first he was *persona grata* with Mr. Kruger, and it was no doubt partly owing to his influence with the ex-President, added to his natural endowments, that he was enabled to assist in building up so rapidly the immense interests which the firm now has in S.A. Coal properties were developed on a large scale, agriculture was encouraged, and, of course, mining interests in gold and diamonds, and the possession of real estate swelled the list of the firm's main enterprises. Mr. Marks himself is on the Board of the African and European Investment Co., Ltd. (See Isaac Lewis and C. F. Rowsell).

MARLING, Col. Percival Scrope, V.C., C.B., J.P., D.L., of Sedbury Park, Chepstow, Mon., Stanley Park, Stroud, Glos., and of the Naval and Military, Cavalry, and Ranelagh Clubs, was born in Gloucestershire, March 6, 1861; is eldest son of Sir William Marling, Bart., and was educated at Harrow and the R.M.C., Sandhurst. Col. Marling served in the Boer War, 1880-81, as 2nd Lieut. 3rd Battn. 60th Rifles, being present at the Battles of Laing's Nek and Ingogo; served throughout Egyptian Campaign, 1882; present at the actions round Alexandria, the affair at Tel-el-Mahuta, the

action at Kassassin, and the Battle of Tel-el-Kebir; served with Mounted Infantry in the Suakim Campaign in 1884, when he was present at the Battle of El Teb, and relief of Tokar; the Battle of Tamai, and the affair at Tamanib (mentioned in despatches, London Gazette, awarded Victoria Cross for saving the life of a Private in the Sussex Regt.); served through out the Khartoum Expedition, 1884-85; present at the Battles of Abou Klea and El Gubat, and the reconnaissance before Metemmeh, and in all the Desert operations with the Camel Corps under the late Sir Herbert Stewart; promoted to a Troop in the 18th Hussars for services in Egypt, Dec., 1886. He proceeded to India with the Rest. in Nov., 1889, and was promoted Major in Aug., 1896; served in South Africa, 1899-1902, including Battle of Talana, retirement from Dundee, action at Lombard's Kop, siege of Ladysmith, operations in Transvaal and O.R.C. (twice mentioned in despatches, London Gazette, C.B., Queen's Medal with five clasps, King's medal with two clasps). Owns 5,000 acres. Recreations: Pole, cricket, hunting, shooting, golf. He married, in 1899, Beatrice Caroline, eldest dau. of F. H. Beaumont, of Reigate, and great-grand-dau. of the 5th Duke of Manchester.

MARSH, Major James Reynolds Marshall, is a second son of the Marsh family of Springmount, Queen's County, Ireland, and is a descendent of a Dr. Francis Marsh, Archbishop of Dublin, who married a daughter of the famous Jeremy Taylor. Major Marsh served with the 2nd Lincoln Regt., in the Nile Expedition, and was present at Athara and Khartoum. He also took part in the East African Expedition of 1904.

MARSHALL, Francis, of 2, Chesham Place, W., was formerly in the Russian trade at St. Petersburg, where he lived for fourteen years, and is now a Director of several leading S.A. Cos., including the Estate, Finance and Mines, and the Bulawayo Estate and Trust Cos. He is quite a well-known golfer, and married a sister of the present Lord Basing.

MARSHALL, Hon. John Edwin, Judge of the Egyptian Native Courts of First Instance, Commander of the Order of the Medjidieh; of Kasr-en-Nil Cairo, and the Turf Club, Cairo, is the eldest son of the late William Marshall, Solicitor, of Durham and West Hartlepool, and grandson of the late John Edwin Marshall, of Durham, Solicitor and Registrar of the Sunder land County Court. He was born March 3, 1864 near West Hartlepool, and was educated at the Durham Sch. Judge Marshall was articled in Jan., 1881, to Mr. Thomas Cousins, J.P., Solicitor, of Portsmouth, and passed the solicitors' final examination in July, 1886. He became a member of the Middle Temple on Oct. 26, 1886, and was called to the Bar on Nov. 18 1889. He went to Egypt in Nov., 1890, and was in practice before the British Consular Courts and the International Tribunals for seven years; in Dec., 1897, was appointed a Judge in the Egyptian Native Courts of First Instance, and since Jan. 1, 1905, has been one of the Judges of the Supreme Court of Appeal in Egypt. At the time of the appointment he was a member of the Bar Council of the International Tribunals, and also occupied the position of Treasurer to that body. He was Senior Legal Adviser to the British Chamber of Commerce in Egypt, a correspondent of the London Chamber of Commerce, and was closely identified with the formation of the jurisprudence relating to the protection of Trade Marks and Patents in Egypt. He was appointed in June, 1903, by the Minister of Public Instruction, Examiner in the Law relating to Civil and Commercial Procedure at the School of Law in Cairo. He married, Jan., 1888, the dau. of the late Wm. Best.

MARSHALL, Major William Thomas, VC., was born in 1854. He joined the 19th Hussars in 1873, serving in the Egyptian War in 1882, when he was present at the Battle of Tel-el-Kebir (Khedive's star; medal and clasp); the Sudan Expedition in 1884, present at the Battle of El Teb (V.C., two clasps, despatches), and the S. African War in 1899-1900, taking part in the defence of Ladysmith, and the action at Laing's Nek (medal and four clasps). In 1905 he was appointed Camp Quartermaster to the Aldershot Army Corps.

MARTIN, Dr., who has had a wide experience of tropical diseases, was appointed head of the Mission organised by the Geographical society in conjunction with the Colonial Office and the Pasteur Institute, Paris, which was sent to West Africa in the autumn of 1906 to study the origin of the sleeping sickness.

MARWICK, John Sidney, of the Native Affairs Dept., Transvaal, was employed in the Natal Civil Service from 1892-1895. In 1896 he acted as Zululand Native Agent at Johannesurg, and was thanked by the Cape Govt. for assistance rendered to the Cape Colonial Native Labour Agent in 1898. He planned and conducted the exodus of Natal natives from Johannesburg on the outbreak of hostilities in 1899, and was sent by the Governor of Natal and General Officer commanding the Lines of Communication to the Native Chief Kula, with authority to prevent the natives from looting the town of Pomeroy, after the Boer invasion in 1899; served in the Imperial Guides in the same year, subsequently recruiting a Native Labour Corps, and continued in charge of it until Aug. 1900 (despatches, medal and four clasps). In 1900 he acted as Superintendent of Native Affairs for Pretoria and District; acted as Native Commissioner for Pretoria District in 1902, and in 1903 was appointed Asst. Secy. for Native Affairs in the Transvaal; also acted as Chairman of the Conference on Municipal Native Regulations in 1903.

MASHONALAND, Bishop of. (See Right Rev. William Thom. Gaul).

MASSEREENE and FERRARD, Viscount, D.S.O., of Oriel Temple, Collon, Co. Louth, and of Antrim Castle, Co. Antrim, was born in 1873, and is son of the 11th Viscount. He was educated at Winchester College and the Royal Military College, Sandhurst, end entered the Army in 1895; served in the S. African War in 1900-2 (despatches, Brevet of Major, Queen's medal with four clasps, King's medal with two clasps, and D.S.O.). He married, in 1905, Jean, dau. of John Ainsworth, Liberal M.P. for Argyllshire.

MASTER, Brevet Major (Local Lieut. Col.) Richard Chester, of Salisbury, Rhodesia, the Carlton, and the Army and Navy Clubs, was born at Cirencester, Aug. 29, 1870; is eldest son of Col. T. W. Chester Master, of the Abbey, Cirencester, and of Knole Park, Almondebury, Glos., and was educated at Harrow and Christ Church, Oxon. He served as Lieut. in the 4th Gloucester Militia from 1890 to 1893, when he was gazetted to the King's Royal Rifles. He was A.D.C. to H.E. the High Commissioner for S.A. (then Sir Alfred Milner) from 1898 to 1900, and served in the S.A. War in 1899 and 1900 as Capt. in Rimington's Corps of Guides, afterwards (in 1901) raising and commanding the Western Province Mounted Rifles for the Cape Colonial Defence Force. Capt. Chester Master was mentioned in despatches, received a brevet majority and medal with six clasps. He received his appointment as Commandant-Gen. of the Police Forces of S. Rhodesia with local rank of Lieut. Col. in Sept., 1901, and became Resident Commissioner and Commandant-Gen. in S. Rhodesia on the combination of these two offices in April, 1905. Col. Chester Master is fond of all field sports, and was Master of the Cape Hunt Club Foxhounds from 1897 to 1901. He married, Aug., 1901, Geraldine, eldest dau. of the late John Hungerford Arkwright, Lord-Lieut. of Herefordshire, of Hampton Court, Herefordshire.

MATCHETT, Lieut. Col. Harry Gerald Keith, of Cairo, and of the Army and Navy Club, was born at Stoke Lacey, March 1, 1866, and is the only son of the Rev. Henry H. Matchett, late Chaplain in the R.N. He was educated at Rugby, and joined the Army in 1886. He took part in the Dongola Expedition in 1896, and the Sudan Expedition in 1897, when he was present at the Battle of Khartoum in command of the 18th Battn. of the Egyptian Army (brevet of Major, mentioned in dispatches, Khedive's medal and three clasps, and the Queen's Sudan medal); he also served in the Sudan Expedition in 1898, and is at present in command of the Cairo Dist., and Commandant of the Military Sch. Egyptian Army. He married, July 24, 1902, Mary, eldest dau. of the late Percy Charrington.

MATHERS, Edward P., F.R.G.S., F.G.S., of 6, Queen's Gate Terrace, S.W., and of the Thatched House, Royal Societies, Caledonian, and United Empire Clubs, is the second son of the late David Mathers, printer and publisher, and newspaper proprietor, of Edinburgh. He was born at Edinburgh on Aug. 19, 1850, and was educated at the High Sch., Edinburgh, and Edinburgh

Institution. Mr. Mathers followed the profession of an English journalist until 1878, when he migrated to S.A., where he commenced work on a paper in Durban, and at the same time acted as representative of a London daily paper, and also of *The Scotsman*. He was there at the time of the Zulu campaign and remained in S.A. for ten years. To him is largely due the publicity which has so greatly contributed to the enormous development of the S.A. Gold Fields. It was in 1883 and 1884 that the news of the discoveries of gold in the De Kaap District roused enormous interest throughout S.A. With a small party of explorers he found his way through an unknown and unhealthy region to the new goldfields, proceeding by steamer to Lourenço Marques, whence they plunged into the interior and began their perilous Journey. The difficulties of the task were vividly described in his letters to the *Natal Mercury*, for which he was acting as Special Commissioner. Many of the party died upon the way, but Mr. Mathers retained his good health despite the trials of the journey and the privations it was necessary to undergo. Arrived at the gold fields, Mr. Mathers pursued his busy career in connection with mining and financial journalism, spreading the knowledge of the early discoveries. His letters naturally attracted a large amount of attention, and were subsequently collected and published under the title of a *Trip to Moodie's* in 1884. The rush to the Barberton District continued until 1887. Then, when the Rand began to claim attention, Mr. Mathers revisited De Kaap and the Rand and wrote a further series of letters which have been published in an interesting volume, entitled *The Goldfields Revisited*, 1887. In the following year he left for London. He had come to the conclusion that the Transvaal was going to be a great mining centre, and that as the capital for the development of the mines must come from England, it was necessary to bring London into closer touch with S.A. His chief intention was to organise a newspaper in London in the interests of S.A., and returning to England he started the journal known as South Africa. He has been more than a journalist, however; he has travelled and explored a good deal in S.A., and has shown in a remarkable way the possession of the faculty of foresight. His paper has been very successful; he has written *Golden South Africa* and *Zambesia*; he founded and is Chairman of the Committee of the

South African Dinner, which has proved a useful and popular annual function in London. Mr. Mathers is thoroughly imperialistic, and having a hearty distrust of Boer methods, he foretold long before the war against Kruger the inevitableness of a final and desperate conflict with the Boers. Since the starting of his paper he has paid many visits to S.A., and was there at the outbreak of hostilities, having a narrow escape of being locked up in Ladysmith. He has a fine S.A. library, and at his residence he has some fine pictures of S.A. Among his curiosities is the skull of a hippopotamus which was shot by him on the Pungwe River, and a battleaxe given to him by Umbandine, the Swazi king. He was a Director of the Swaziland Corporation, and in addition to the books already mentioned, he has published South Africa, and How to Reach it (1889), and *The Story of the* South Africa *Newspaper and its Founder* (1903). He married Aug. 6, 1885, Mary Augusta, eldest dau. of R. H. Powys, of Natal.

MATHESON, Greville Ewing, of Tanybryn, Lower Road, Harrow-on-the-Hill, and of the Savage Club, was born at Soham, Cambs. He is the eldest son of the late Rev. D. L. Matheson of Wolverhampton, and great-grandson of the late Rev. Greville Ewing, LL.D., of Glasgow; and was educated at Tattnall Coll., Staffordshire, and privately. He has been on the staff of Donald Currie and Co., managers of the Union Castle Line, since 1883; was Hon. Secy. of the Anglo African Writers' Club since its inception in 1895; Joint Editor of *The Hampstead Annual* since 1899, and has published *About Holland* (1894), and (under nom de plume of M. E. Greville) *From Veld and Street; Rhymes more or less South African* (1899), and numerous articles and verses in various newspapers, etc. His recreations are golf, gardening and novel reading. He married, in 1887, Emily Elizabeth, dau. of the late Thomas Pugh, of Penylan, Oswestry.

MATHEW, Lieut. Col. Charles Massy, D.S.O., of 113, St. James's Court, Buckingham Gate, S.W., and of the Sports Club, was born in 1866, and is the eldest son of the late Surgeon-Major C. B. Mathew. He was educated at Portsmouth Grammar Sch., and in 1884 he joined the 2nd Durham Light Infantry, taking part in the Sudan Campaign in 1885-6, including the action at Giniss (medal and

bronze star); the Ashanti Expedition in 1895-6 (star); Dongola Expedition in 1896 (despatches, Egyptian medal with clasp); the Nile Expedition in 1898, present at the battle of Khartoum (despatches, D.S.O., clasp to Egyptian medal; medal); and the South African War in 1899-1901, including the operations in the Orange River and Cape Colonies (Queen's medal with two clasps). Col. Mathew served in the Army Ordnance Dept. from 1891 to Aug., 1906, when he was appointed Asst.-Director at the War Office, in succession to Col. Moulton-Barrett, C.M.G. Unmarried.

MATHIAS, Capt. George Montague, D.S.O., of Krugersdorp, went up to the Rand in the early days, where he has been associated with the Robinson Crown Reef, and other mines. He served with the Matabeleland Relief Force in 1896 (medal), and in the South African War; distinguished himself as a Squadron Commander of the Imperial Light Horse in the attack on Waggon Hill, Jan. 6, 1900 (medal and D.S.O.). He joined the Transvaal Mines Dept. in 1901, and in 1902 he was appointed Asst. Commissioner of Police for the West Rand.

MATTHEWS, Charles Edward, of the Cape Civil Service, served in the Cape Mounted Rifles from 1876-79 (medal), and as Lieutenant with Strachan's Native Levies, afterwards as Adjutant of the Kokstad Mounted Volunteers in the Podomise and Basuto Rebellion. He acted as Assistant Surveyor General and Examiner of Diagrams in British Bechuanaland upon annexation in 1894, and was appointed Clerk in the Surveyor General's Office in 1895, which position he still holds.

MATTHEWS, Dr. Josiah Wright, F.R.G.S., of Johannesburg, and of the Civil Service (C.T.), Gold Fields (Johannesburg), and Junior Conservative (Lond.) Clubs, was born in 1841 at York, Eng., where he was educated privately, and studied medicine there and at Glasgow. Late in 1864 he sailed to Durban in medical charge of an emigrant ship, and obtained an appointment in the Natal Govt. Med. Service and a lucrative private practice. In 1871, however, he took a trip to India, and returning to England graduated M.D. at Aberdeen. Dr. Matthews shortly returned to Natal, but was attracted by the new El Dorado and practised his profession at Kimberley. When the Cape Legislative Council was constituted he was returned as senior member, becoming Vice-Pres. of the Council. With annexation, Kimberley became an Electoral Division of the C.C., and in 1881 the doctor entered the Cape Assembly, resigning after the special session of 1883. Recovering from a serious accident, he toured the Transvaal; took another trip home; engaged in a visit to America, and went up to the Rand in 1889. He became member of the Johannesburg Sanitary Board in 1892, and took an important part in public and social life.

Dr. Matthews published in America in 1887 *Incwadi Yami* (My Book) or *Twenty Years' Personal Experience in South Africa*. He has lectured considerably before Rand gatherings, and addressed big audiences at the Chicago Exhibition in 1893 on S.A. affairs. He is an enthusiastic collector of curios, objects of vertu, coins, medals, etc., and was awarded a bronze medal by the Kimberley South African and International Exhibition of 1892. He married, in 1867, Lucy Virginia, fifth dau. of Dr. Lindley, an American pioneer missionary in S.A. who gave his name to a town in the O.R.C.

MATTHEWS, Maynard Reginald Nelson, J.P., of The Residency, Dundee, Natal, was born in India, March 1, 1865, and entered the Civil Service of Natal in 1878, rising from a Junior Clerkship in the Durban Court to the office of a Magistrate for the Colony in 1895, being stationed successively at Verulam, Weenen, Durban, Newcastle, and Dundee, where he is at present Magistrate. He served as Intelligence Officer during the S. African War (medal), and takes a keen interest in fishing, golf, and other forms of sport. He married, in 1889, Sadie, eldest dau. of the Rev. J. Goodwin, Vicar of Lower Umgeni, near Durban.

MAUDE, Major Frederick Stanley, C.M.G., D.S.O., of 6, Lower Sloane St., S.W., and of the Guards' Club, was born at Gibraltar, June 24, 1864, and is son of Gen. Sir Fredk. F. Maude, V.O. He was educated at Eton from 1878-82, and was the winner of the School Steeplechase in 1881, and of the Eton Mile in 1882, also winner of the House Fours in 1881-2, and was ninth man of the Eton Eight in 1882. He joined the 1st Battn. of

Coldstream Guards, and took part in the Sudan War in 1885 (medal and clasp and Khedive's star); served in the S. African War in 1899-1901 (mentioned in despatches, medal and six clasps and D.S.O.). He married Cecil, dau. of Col. the Rt. Hon. Edward Taylor.

MAUGHAM, William Fraser, of Fairview, Johannesburg, was born at Grahamstown, in 1877, and is son of the late Thomas Maugham, of Grahamstown. He acted as Correspondent during the S. African War with the Colonial Division, under Gen. Brabant, and was present at the Siege of Wepener. In 1902 he joined Mr. Edgar Wallace when that gentleman organised the *Rand Daily Mail*, and was his news editor for nearly two years, resigning to take up the appointment which he now holds on the Editorial Staff of the *Transvaal Leader*; he also acts as Transvaal Correspondent for several London papers, and watches the Chinese labour experiments on the Rand in the interests of Northern and Southern Chinese papers. He married, Jan. 27, 1904, Ivy, eldest dau. of the late W. Dewey, Mayor of Alice, and Editor of the *Alice Times and Peddie Gazette*.

MAVROGORDATO, Theodore Etienne, J.P., F.R.G.S., of Johannesburg, son of Stephen Mavrogordato and Fanny, née Sarell, was born at Constantinople in 1861, and was educated in Berlin. He joined the Cyprus service in Jan., 1881; Asst.-Inspector of Cyprus Military Police, 1883; Inspector of same, 1884; had charge of Special Police Force, 1895; became Local Commandant, Asst.-Commissioner, Governor of Prison and Deputy Coroner June 7, 1895; Act ing Commissioner, Paphos, 1897; Acting Commissioner, Limassol, 1900; transferred to Transvaal service, Nov. 4, 1901, becoming Asst. Commissioner of Police and J.P., Johannesburg. He married, in 1886, Ethel Constance, eldest dau. of the late Rev. Joseph Kenworthy, Rector of Ackworth, Yorks.

MAXWELL-HIBBERD, Charles, Postmaster-Gen. of Pietermaritzburg, Natal, and of the Victoria Club, Maritzburg, is the son of the late Charles Hibberd, of Ventnor, I.W., and grandson of the late William Hibberd, of Harbridge, Hants; was born at Bryantspuddle, Dorsetshire, and entered the Electric and International Telegraph Co. in 1867; stationed at Ventnor, I.W., he had the advantage of serving under Mr. W. H. Preece (now Sir W. H. Preece) until 1870. Then, when the British Govt. took over the telegraphs, he was engaged in giving instruction in telegraphy at various post offices in England, and during the Franco-German War acted as private telegraphist to the late Lord Granville, then Foreign Minister, at Walmer Castle, Deal. At the close of the war Mr. Maxwell-Hibberd was attached to the Engineering Dept. of the Central Telegraph Office, G.P.O., London, as a Junior Engineering Inspector, where he remained until Jan. 1, 1885, when he was appointed a Second Class Asst.-Surveyor. As an Asst.-Surveyor of the G.P.O., Mr. Maxwell-Hibberd was attached to the South Wales District, where he obtained a thorough knowledge of the organisation of the postal and telegraph services of the country. He revised postal services in various parts of South Wales, and in 1894 was promoted to a First Class Asst.-Surveyorship. This promotion necessitated his transfer to another district, and he then went to North Wales, where he worked until Nov., 1900, when, at his own request, he was transferred to the North Western Postal District of England. He was appointed Postmaster of Reading on June 1, 1901, and in April, 1903, Postmaster General of Natal. He married, Oct., 1876, Mary Jane, dau. of the late Mr. Wm. Sheppard, of Tunbridge Wells.

MAXWELL-LYTE, John Maxwell, F.R.HS., of 3, Portman Square, London, and of the Govt. Experimental Orchard, Potchefstroom, Transvaal, was born May 10, 1875; is son of Sir Henry C. Maxwell-Lyte, K.C.B., and was educated at Radley Coll. and Merton Coll., Oxford. He went to S. Africa in 1898, studying fruit culture on the Cape Colony, and has been since April, 1903, Manager of the Transvaal Govt. Experimental Orchard, under the Colonial Office. When the S. African War broke out he joined Roberts' Horse, transferred as Lieut. in Northumberland Fusiliers in May, 1900, taking part in the Relief of Kimberley, and the operations at Paardeberg, Poplar Grove, Driefontein, Zand River, and Sanna's Post. Lieut. Maxwell-Lyte also filled some Staff appointments, and joined the Reserve of Officers in Aug., 1905. At Oxford he was a member of the Univ.

Swimming team which beat Cambridge in 1896, and he also rowed in the 'Varsity Torpids in that year. Recreation: Photography. Unmarried.

MAXSE, Col. Frederick Ivor, C.B., D.S.O., F.R.G.S., of 2, Gloucester St., Portman Sq., W., was born in London, Dec. 22, 1862, and is the eldest son of Admiral F. A. Maxse, of Dunkley Hill, Dorking. He was educated at Rugby and Sandhurst, and joined the 2nd Battn. of Royal Fus, in India in 1882; exchanged into the Coldstream Guards in 1891; was A.D.C. to the G.O.C. Scotland, and to the Governor of Malta in 1893. He was attached to the Egyptian Army from 1896-99, during the Sudan Campaign; was appointed Brig. Major of the 2nd Sudanese Brig, in 1898, and was Chief Staff Officer to the Military Governor of Omdurman in the same year. He commanded the 13th Sudanese Regt. on active service throughout 1899, and his active services in the Sudan include the Battles of Abu Hamada, Athara, Khartoum, and El Gelid. At the end of 1899 he took part in the S. African War as D.A.A.G. of Transport, and as A.A.G. and Commissioner of Police, Pretoria. He was present at the Relief of Kimberley and the actions at Paardeberg, Johannesburg, and minor engagements (three medals and nine clasps). He raised and commanded the Transvaal Constabulary, which was merged into the S.A.C. in 1901; he also served in the Mobilisation Dept. at the War Office, Load,, and is at present in command of the 2nd Battn, of Coldstream Guards. He married, Dec. 18, 1899, the Hon. Mary Wyndham, dau. of Lord Leconfield.

MAY, Arthur John, of Studdale House, Whitfield, Dover, was born in London, Feb. 27, 1856, is eldest son of the late Baron May, Consul-Gen. for the Netherlands in London, and was educated at Lancing Coll, and Trinity Coll., Dublin. He entered the Colonial Civil Service in the Attorney General's Dept. at Cape Town in 1881, transferring to the Imperial service in the War Office Dept. at Cape Town, Dec., 1881, to Dec., 1882. At the beginning of 1883 he was again employed under the Colonial Civil Service at the High Court at Kimberley, of which he was appointed Asst.-Registrar in March, 1883, resigning in 1886. He married, in 1885, Adelaide, youngest dau. of the late Admiral T. V. Anson, cousin of the 2nd Earl of Lichfield.

MAY, Lieut. John, is son. of the late Staff Commander May, R.N., and brother to Mr. Dan May, of Somerset West, Cape Colony. He was educated in Cape Town at the Rev. Mr. Sutton's Sch., and joined the flagship *St. George* on the Cape Station, as Midshipman, subsequently taking part in the Benin Expedition and the Siege of Zanzibar. In 1905 he was promoted to the command of H.M.S. *Janus*, a torpedo boat attached to the China Station.

MAY, Col. William Allan, R.A.M.C., C.B., of the Army and Navy Club, is the son of the late Joseph May, F.R.C.S., Eng., of Stoke Damerel, Devon. He was born Sept. 18, 1850, at Stoke Damerel, Devon, and was educated at the Gram. Sch., Tavistock, Devon, and Guy's Hospital Med. Sch., London. On Sept. 30, 1874, Col. May joined the Army Medical Service, and was promoted Lieut. Col. Royal Army Medical Corps, Sept. 30, 1894, and Col., March 22, 1903. He was Principal Medical Officer 8th Div. of the Field Force, S.A., from Jan., 1900, to end of campaign, May 31, 1902, with local rank of Col. He was mentioned in despatches, C.B. (1902) and has the Queen 's medal with three clasps (C.C., Wittebergen, Transvaal) and King's medal with two clasps (S.A., 1901, S.A., 1902). He was appointed Principal Medical Officer, Natal, Aug., 1902, with local rank of Col.; Principal Medical Officer, Egypt, May, 1903; Principal Medical Officer, Salisbury Plain District, Jan., 1905, and Acting P.M.O. of the Southern Command, 1905. Col. May. is a M.R.C.S. Eng., and L.S.A. He married, Feb. 3, 1876, Cecilia Adele Aloise, dau. of the late Gustav A. B. C. von Ohlhaffen.

MAYDON, John George, M.L.A., J.P., of Seafield, Lower Muzimkulu, Natal, of Nethuley, Maritzburg, Natal, and of the Durban Victoria (P.M.B.), John Carpenter, and Junior Constitutional Clubs, was born Oct. 14, 1857, is only son of the late John Maydon, of Salden, Bucks; was educated at City of London Sch., and went to Natal in 1878 in order to take part in the Zulu War through which he served with the Coast column. On the establishment of Responsible Govt. in Natal in 1893 he was elected M.L.A. for Durban County.

Visiting England in 1897 he did not seek re-election; spent two years in travel and the study of the racial problem, becoming an ardent advocate of war as the only means of solving the question of British supremacy in S. Africa. On war being declared, he offered his services to the military authorities. These were not accepted, and he became correspondent of the *Daily News*, being first with Lord Methuen. After Magersfontein he joined Gen. French, with whom he was at the relief of Kimberley, and the captures of Cronje and Bloemfontein, receiving a scalp wound at Driefontein. Returning to Natal in April, 1901, he was re-elected to the Assembly as member for Durban Boro', in succession to John Robinson, and worked to secure a more vigorous development of Natal's resources. Upon the resignation of the Home Ministry in 1903, he joined the Sutton Administration as Colonial Secretary, and subsequently was appointed Minister of Railways and Harbours.

Mr. Maydon is the author of a short account of the early operations of the S. African War, entitled *French's Cavalry Campaign*. He married first, a dau. of the late D. King, and second, Dorothy Isabelle, eldest dau of the late I. L. Cope, of Highlands, Natal.

MAYNARD, Henry Whaler, of 3, Grosvenor Hill, Wimbledon, is a member of the Council of the Union Castle Mail Steamship Co., Ltd. (See Sir Donald Currie); Chairman of the Brockie-Pell Arc Lamp, Ltd.; Deputy Chairman of the New Era Assurance Corp., Ltd.; and is a Director of the Employers' Liability Assurance Corp., Ltd., and the Ocean Marine Insurance Ltd.

MEIKLEJOHN, Capt. Ronald Forbes, D.S.O., of the Castle, Cape Town, was born at Rawal Pindi, and is son of Lieut. Col. J. F. Meiklejohn, late of R.H.A. He was educated at Rugby and Sandhurst, and joined the Royal Warwickshire Regt. in 1896; took part in the Nile Expedition in 1898, and was present at the Battles of Athara and Khartoum (Queen's medal and Khedive's medal, with two clasps); served in Natal, during the S.A. War, with the Ladysmith Relief Force, being attached to the 2nd Devonshire Regt., and took part in the Battles of Colenso and Spion Kop (mentioned in despatches Queen's medal and two clasps and D.S.O.). Capt. Meiklejohn was appointed Staff Capt. at Naval Base, C.C. in June, 1904. He married, Jan. 1. 1903, Kathleen, dau. of H. H. Myburgh, late Imp. Ottoman Consul, Cape Town.

MEINTJES, E. P. A., J.P., of Pretoria, formerly member in the second Volksraad of the Transvaal, and one of her most public-spirited citizens, is an Afrikander who is married to an English lady, and who is very popular in all sections of the community.

MEINTJES, L. S., was born in 1868 in Aberdeen, Co., and is descended, as his name indicates, from one of the old Dutch families who originally colonised the Cape Peninsula. He went up to Johannesburg in 1891, and first took to cycling about that time, his first performance on the track being made on the Wanderers' Club ground, when he won the only three open events. His times were so good that the club committee decided to send him to Eng. and America. He arrived in Eng. in April, 1893, and beat all the English records for one and two miles and from seven to twenty-five miles, and from a flying start he held the records for three, four and five miles. He was also the first to cover twenty-four within the hour.

MEIRELLES, Viscount de. (See De Meirelles.)

MEIRING, Johannes Hendricus, M.L.C., J.P., of Northdene, Aliwal St., Bloemfontein, and of the United Service Club, and Ramblers' Club, Bloemfontein, is descended from a French refugee family who fled to Holland after the revocation of the Edict of Nantes in 1684, his direct descendant, Arnoldus Mauritius Meiring, having gone to the Cape as minister of the P.R. Church at Tulbagh, C.C., in 1734. The subject of our sketch is the son of J. W. H. Meiring, Mayor of Worcester, C.C., where Mr. J. H. Meiring was born Oct. 22, 1849. He was educated in that town; was Headmaster of the Govt. Sch. at Murraysdorp, C.C., in 1872, and in 1881 went to the O.F.S. as Secy. to the Mining Board at Jagersfontein, when he subsequently entered the Free State Civil Service as Public Prosecutor to the Special Court for the trial of I.P.B cases, as well as to the Magistrates' Court. In 1886 he became Landdrost Clerk and Public Prosecutor at Harrismith, and in 1889 when the O.F.S. entered into a Customs Union with the C.C., he was appointed Collector of Customs of the State. He attended the Customs Conferences of 1896 and '98. He retained this appointment until the British occupation on March 13, 1900. Seven days later, however, he was reinstated by Lord Roberts, and on the military regime being superseded by Civil Govt., his position as Collector of Customs for the O.R.C. was confirmed by Lord Milner. In 1902 Mr. Meiring was nominated a member of the Legislative Council for the O.R.C., and he took part in the Customs Conference in 1903 as Customs Adviser. From 1883 to 1894 he was J.P. for the respective districts in which he held office, and from the latter year has been a J.P. for the whole Colony. He married, Jan. 30, 1872, Anna C., dau. of J. G. de Wet, of Worcester, C.C.

MEIRING, Rev. Pieter Gerhard Jacobus, Dutch Reformed Minister, of Joubert's Park, Johannesburg, is the youngest son of J. W. H. Meiring, J.P., of C.C., who for a considerable number of years was Mayor of Worcester. He was born Dec. 20, 1866, at Worcester, C.C., and was educated at the Public Sch., Worcester; the Victoria Coll., and the Theological Seminary Stellenbosch, and is a B.A. of the Cape Univ. Cape Town. He is Scriba of the Gen. Assem. of the D.R. Church, Transvaal, and is Joint Editor of the *Vereeniging*, the official organ of the Church; is an able writer, and eloquent preacher, and exercises considerable influence. He married, Nov. 28, 1902, Susanna the, youngest dau. of the late Adrian J. Louw, of the Paarl, every one of whose seven daughters, it is interesting to note, is married to a D.R. minister.

MELLISS, Brevet Lieut.-Col. Charles John, V.C., Indian Army, Brilliant Star of Zanzibar, 2nd class, and Bronze medal of Royal Humane Society, is the son of Lieut.-Gen. G. J. Melliss. He was born on Sept. 12, 1862, and was educated at Wellington Coll. Col. Melliss took part in the Mazeni Rebellion, E. Africa, 1896; Tirah Campaign, 1897-8; and Ashanti Campaign, 1900; and was four times wounded. He is the author of *Lion Hunting in Somaliland*. He married, Aug., 1901, Kathleen, youngest dau. of General Walter, C.B.

MENDELSSOHN, Sydney, J.P., of 21, Kensington Court Gardens, London, and of the Kimberley Club, was born at Exeter, Dec. 31, 1860, and belongs to an old German family. He was educated at Bristol, and is best known as the pioneer of the Vaal River Diamond Estate, upon which he reported during the S. African War. His firm then bought the property and subsequently he laid out the diggings on the estate and founded the township of Sydney, which is situated on the Vaal River about fifteen miles from Barkly West. He also founded the Sydney Public Library, and was one of the founders of the Mendelssohn Lodge, No. 3142, E.C., at Sydney. The Vaal River Estate consists of three large farms, named respectively Than, Mozih, and Droogveld, with a river front age of about twenty-seven miles, on the Vaal River, just at the junction with the Hertz. The extent of the property is 23,793 morgen, or eighty square miles. The company was formed in 1902, and the present capital is £200,000. The diggers have been working on the estate ever since the formation of the company and the throwing open of the diggings, particularly along the banks of the river and in the bed, but the company has recently been prospecting over portions of the farms about eight miles away from the banks of the river, and a number of holes have been put down. The holes are far apart, and cover an extent of something like twelve square miles. The yield and quality of the diamonds found in prospecting are stated to be excellent. Droogveld and Than are the farms on which these latest discoveries have been made. About four square miles on the discoveries have now been allotted to diggers and companies, and water works are being erected. The local directors are Messrs. Maurice Mendelssohn, W. P. Anderson, P. W. Mallett, and Captain Tuckney.

Mr. Mendelssohn retired from active business about three years ago, and his main recreations are the collection of African books and the preparation of a *catalogue raisonné*, descriptive of his library, which contains probably the largest private collection of books on African (mainly South African) subjects in existence. He married Emma, dau. of Moses Blanckensee, merchant, of Bristol.

MENNELL, Frederic Philip, F.G.S., of Jameson St., Bulawayo, and of Pembridge Villas, London, W., was born Feb. 1, 1880. He studied geology at the Royal Coll. of Science in London, and was appointed Curator of the Rhodesian Museum in 1901, which position he still holds. He was Secy. of the Rhodesian Scientific Assn. from 1902-4, and since then been has been a member of the Council. Mr. Mennell has published numerous scientific papers, chiefly on S. African geology and archaeology, the principal being the *Geology of Southern Rhodesia*, and *The Zimbabwe Ruins*, issued by the Rhodesian Museum.

MERRIMAN, Hon. John Xavier, M.L.A., of Schoongezigt, Stellenbosch, C.C., and of the Reform (Lond.) and the Civil Service (C.T.) Clubs, was born at Street, near Glastonbury, Somerset, on March 15, 1841, his father having been the Bishop of Grahamstown. He was educated at Dive Coll., Rondebosch, and at Radley Coll., Oxford. Mr. Merriman is a land surveyor by profession, but he has made politics the principal business of his life. He entered the Cape Parliament in 1869, and has sat continuously from that date until the general election in 1904, when he was defeated at the poll. He was subsequently elected as member for Victoria West. From 1875 to 1878, and again from 1881 to 1884, he sat in the Cabinet as Commissioner for Crown Lands, and from 1890 to 1893 he was Treasurer-Gen.—a portfolio which he subsequently held in 1899-1900.

Mr. Merriman is a good debater and an exceedingly able man, but he is a mass of prejudices, which have inclined him to every extreme—Bond-friend and Anti-Bond, No party, consequently, has felt that it could absolutely depend upon, or trust, him politically. His natural asperity of manner and innate disagreeableness are disadvantages which he appears to cultivate for the express purpose of alienating support and making enemies. In fact, he has been described as an excellent type of a gentleman who has deliberately cast off the manners of one.

As an apologist for rebellion, he urged that Cape Colonials who rebelled during the late S.A. War should receive full compensation for losses caused by the invasion of the Colony. Mr. Merriman is a member of the Council of the Univ. of the Cape of Good Hope as representative of the Colony of

Natal. He married, Sept. 1&, 1874, Agnes, dau. of the Hon. J. Vintcent.

MERSHON, Ralph D., of New York, is a University graduate, and was for years closely identified with the Westinghouse group. He is engineer in the Shawinigan Falls Co., the Ontario Power Co., at Niagara and many other undertakings which are practically the *dernier cri* in electrical science. He is also one of the engineers of the Victoria Falls Power Co. (see H. Wilson Fox), has a worldwide reputation in regard to long-distance transmission, has had considerable experience in power plant, and will have charge of the transmission line from the Victoria Falls to Johannesburg. Mr. Mershon has made exhaustive experiments in high voltages up to 200,000 volts, and has expressed the opinion that the proposed transmission line would be erected with a pressure of 150,000 volts. [t is sufficient to say that the dictum of this famous engineer is generally accepted as final upon questions of transmission of power at high tensions.

METCALFE, Sir Charles, of 28, Victoria Street, S.W., is a partner in the well-known civil, mechanical, and electrical engineering firm of Sir Douglas Fox and Partners. He is jointly with Sir Douglas Fox (q.v.) consulting engineer to the Cape Government Railways, the British South Africa Co., the Chartered Co., the Rhodesia and Mashonaland Railways, the British Central Africa Co., the Benguela Railway Co., and the Company which holds the concession for utilising the power of the Victoria Falls, some description of which appears under the biographical details of H. Wilson Fox. The firm has also designed and supervised the construction of the great bridge over the Zambesi at the Victoria Falls (see J. R. Maguire). Sir Charles is a director of the Rhodesia Railways Trust, Ltd., and the Southern Land Company, Ltd.

MEYER, Carl, of 35, Hill St., London, W., and of Shortgrove, Essex, has been for many years in closest touch with the great banking house of Rothschild, and, in that connection negotiated the first important Transvaal loan, and established the National Bank of South Africa. He wields immense powers as London Chairman of the De Beers Mines and as London Director of the National Bank of

Egypt, and he is also on the Boards of A. Goerz and Co., the Pekin Synd. (Chairman), the Burma Ruby Mines, the Chinese Central Railways, the *Société Egyptienne de la Daira Sanieb*, etc.

Mr. Meyer is an intimate friend of many great Anglo Africans, and, together with Mrs. Carl Meyer, is a well-known figure in social, musical, and artistic circles.

MEYRICK, Colonel Frederick Charlton, C.B., B.A., of Bush, Pembroke, and of the Naval and Military and the Orleans Clubs, was born July 7, 1862, and is the eldest son of Sir Thos. Meyrick, Bart., C.B., of Apley Castle, Shropshire. He was educated at Eton and Cambridge. He stroked the Cambridge Eight against Oxford in 1883; served fifteen and a half years in the 15th (King's) Hussars, and commanded the 5th Regt. of I.Y. during the S. African War, 1900-01, during which time he was once wounded and had his horse shot under him, he also sustained a broken collarbone through his horse falling during action. Colonel Meyrick is now commanding the Pembroke I.Y. He married, in Oct., 1897, Mary E. Cresswell, of Cresswell Hall.

MICHAU, Jan. Johan, M.L.A., J.P., F.R.C.I.. of Bedford Lodge, Rondebosch, near Cape Town, was born at Cradock, Cape Colony, June 9, 1863; is son of the late Hon, W. J. Michau, M.L.C., and was educated at Victoria Coll., Stellenbosch. He is by profession an Attorney at Law and Notary Public. As partner in the firm of Haarhoff and Michau he was for over ten years the legal adviser in Kimberley to the De Beers Company, which he retained until he left Kimberley at the end of 1899. He then commenced practice in Cape Town under the style of Michau and De Villiers. Mr. Michau is a prominent Bondsman; he is, and has been for many years, Assistant Secretary of the Bond; at the general election in 1904 he was returned unopposed as a member of the Legislative Assembly for the Riversdale Division in the Bond interest. He is a true son of the soil, and as such commands great influence among his fellow Africanders. Mr. Michau has always taken a keen interest in municipal matters. For several years he was a member of the Municipal or Borough Council of Kimberley, where he acted as Deputy Mayor; and for three years he was the Mayor of Somerset

Strand, which is about thirty miles by rail from Cape Town, and is one of the best seaside resorts of the Colony. Mr. Michau was the Attorney to the Princess Radziwill (q.v.), and defended her throughout her troubles in connection with the Rhodes forgeries. He married, in 1885, Miss A. M. Oosthuizen.

MICHELL, Sir Lewis, of Queen Anne's Mansions, London, S.W., and of the Imperial Colonies Club, is a descendant of an old Cornish family. He was born at Plymouth in 1842, and was educated at Christ's Hospital and under private tutor. He was for many years, until June 30, 1902, General Manager of the most important banking institution in South Africa, viz., the Standard Bank of S. Africa, Ltd. He represented the Cape Colony at the Mint Conference at Pretoria in 1893, and Rhodesia at the Company Law Conference at Johannesburg in 1902, and at Customs Conference at Bloemfontein in 1903. He was for three years Chairman of the De Beers Consolidated Mines, and is now a Director of the British S. Africa Co., and of the Rhodesia Railways (see J. R. Maguire), in connection with which he undertook a tour through Rhodesia in the autumn of 1902 with Mr. Beit (q.v.), Dr. Jameson, and the late Mr. J. F. Jones—a tour which resulted in many difficulties of the northern settlers being greatly ameliorated. Sir Lewis was elected to fill one of the vacant seats for Cape Town in the Progressive interest in the Cape House of Assembly at the latter end of 1902, and at the general election in Feb., 1904, was returned for the electoral division of Wynberg, entering Dr. Jameson's Ministry without portfolio, but resigned in 1905 to reside in London. He was J.P. for Cape Town and District, Pres. of the S.A. Progressive Association, and a prominent member of various local societies. He was also a frequent lecturer in Cape Town, and closely associated with every movement tending towards political, commercial, and social progress in the colony. During the South African War he acted as Pres. of the Martial Law Board and Treasurer of the Mansion House Relief Committee at Cape Town. He is one of the trustees of the late Cecil Rhodes, and was knighted on the occasion of the King's birthday in 1902. He married, in 1870, Maria Agnes, dau. of the late Edward Philpots, Civil Commissioner of the Cape Service. His eldest son was killed in the Matabele

Rebellion while with the B.S.A. Police, and he also lost a son-in-law, Major Scott-Turner, in the siege of Kimberley.

MILES, Colonel Charles Napier, C.B.. M.V.O., of Burton Hill, Malmesbury, and of the Carlton, Orleans, Pratt's, and Arthur's Clubs, was born in 1854, and is the eldest son of Colonel Miles. He was educated at Eton, and joined in the 1st Life Guards in 1875, succeeding Col. Sir S. M. Lockhart Bart. (q.v.), in the command of that regt. in 1898. Colonel Miles took part in the Egyptian Expedition in 1882, being present at the actions at El Magfar, Mahsameh, Kassassin, and the battle of Tel-el-Kebir; also in the march to and occupation of Cairo (medal and clasp, bronze star); and the S. African War in 1899-1900, being for some time in command of a Composite Regt. of household Cavalry. He took part in the operations in the Transvaal, west of Pretoria; action at Elands River; the operations in the Orange River Colony, including the actions at Bethlehem and Wittebergen (Queen's medal with three clasps and C.B.). Since 1892 he has been High Steward for Malmesbury, and is Lord of the Manor of Burtonhill. Col. Miles retired from the Army in April, 1906. He married, in 1880, Emily, dau. of the late J. W. G. Spicer.

MILLAIS, John Guille, F.Z.S., of Comptons Brow Horsham, Sussex, and of the Royal Societies' Club; fourth son of Sir John E. Millais, Bart., D.C.L., Pres. of the Royal Acad.; was born in London, March 25, 1865; was educated at Marlborough and Trinity Coll., Camb. After leaving Cambridge he served two years in the 3rd Batt. Somerset L.I. (1884-5). During this period he began to illustrate works in sport and natural history, notably for the Badminton Library and for H. Seebohm's books. In 1886 he began his hunting expeditions, and he next spring joined the 1st Batt. Seaforth Highlanders, in which he served for seven years. Since then he has embarked on the following expeditions for the purpose of studying nature at first hand, and making a collection of heads of wild animals, which includes red roe, fallow, mule, and whitetailed deer; grey, common, and Greenland seals; wapiti; moose; bighorn; Caribou; reindeer; elk; waterbuck; sable and rean antelopes, koodoo, hartebeste, sassaby, duiker, steinbuck, klipspringer, whitetailed and brindled gnus, Cape buffalo, pallah, leopard, lion, brown bear, etc. In the process of acquiring this collection he has travelled in W. America (1886), Iceland (1892), S.A. (1893), S. Norway (1898), N. Norway (1899), N. Africa (1900), Newfoundland and Canada (1902), and Newfoundland again (1903). He is also said to have the most complete collection of British birds in any private museum, numbering 4,000 specimens, obtained by his gun in the British Islands.

He is Vice-Pres. of the Anglo African Writers' Club, and is the author of *Game Birds and Shooting Sketches*, 1892; *A Breath from the Veldt*, 1895; *British Deer and their Horns*, 1897; *The Life and Letters of Sir John Everett Millais, Bart. a Biography*, 1890; *The Wild Fowler in Scotland*, 1901; *The Natural History of the Surface Feeding Ducks*, 1902, and *The Mammals of Great Britain and Ireland*, 1904. Besides the study of natural history and the pursuit of big game, his recreations are lawn tennis, shooting, and fishing. He married, Oct. 31, 1894, Frances Margaret, second dau. of P. Skipwith, of Hundleby.

MILLER, Allister Mitchell, J.P., of Mbabane, Swaziland, and of the Pretoria and Barberton Clubs, was born at Singapore, April 30, 1865 is son of Alexander and Agnes Miller, of Wick, Caithness, N.B., and was educated privately and at the Liverpool Coll. After being on the staff of the *Liverpool Mercury*, which he joined in 1884, he went to S.A. in 1887 as sub-ed. of the *Cape Argus* ; became ed. of the *Gold Fields Times* at Barberton, June, 1885, and in the following Aug. was appointed Govt. Secy. to the first White Committee elected under charter in Swaziland, later being appointed Secy. and Agent to King Umbandine, a well as a member of the Committee and Magistrate. On the death of Umbandine, he took up farming until 1891, when he became Manager of the Swaziland Corporation, Ltd. During the late war he served as Secy. to the Resident Commissioner for Swaziland, attached to the 18th Brigade, and was afterwards second in command of a corps of scouts with rank of Lieut. He is a F.R.G.S., F.S.A., F.R.C.I., and Fellow of the Geological Society of S.A. He has written *A Short History of Swaziland*, and numerous papers on that country. He married, Nov. 21, 1891, Beatrice Mary, dau. of John Thorburn.

MILLER, Lieut. Edward Henry, of Bulawayo, was born in London in 1874; is son of Roger Woods Miller, L.C.M., and was educated at the City of London Sch. and at Neuweid, Prussia, and Paris. He served on the Medical Staff of the B.S.A. Police during the Matabele War of 1896, and again saw fighting in the Boer War, 1899-1900, and is an officer of the S. Rhodesia Volunteers. He is librarian of the Bulawayo Public Library; Secy. of the Rhodesia Museum; and Hon. Secy. of the Rhodesia Scientific Assoc. He published papers on entomology, bibliography, etc., and is now compiling a *Bibliography of Rhodesia*, being his section of the *Bibliography of South Africa*. He married, in 1904, Faith, youngest dau. of Thos. Dawson, of Umlilo, Natal.

MILNE, Rear Admiral Sir Archibald Berkeley, Bt., K.C.V.O., R.N., of Inveresk Gate, Musselburgh, N.B., and of the United Service, Marlborough, and Naval and Military Clubs, was born in 1855, and is son of the late Sir Alex. Milne, Admiral of the Fleet. He entered the Navy in 1869, and served in the Transkei War in 1877-8; acted as A.D.C. to Lord Chelmsford during the Zulu War; and took part in the Egyptian Campaign in 1882, being present at the battle of Tel-el-Kebir.

MILNER, the Right Hon. Viscount, G.C.B. (1901), G.C.M.G. (1897), P.C. (1901), of Sturry Court, near Canterbury, Kent, and of Brooks', Reform, Athenaeum, and New University Clubs, was born on March 23rd, 1854, and is the only son of Charles Milner, M.D., and of Mary, dau. of Maj. Gen. Ready, sometime Governor of the Isle of Man. He was educated at Tübingen, in Germany, where his father was for many years resident, and subsequently at King's College, London; and at the age of eighteen was elected to a scholarship at Balliol, where he was more or less contemporary with Mr. Asquith, Mr. St. John Brodrick, Dr. Gore (the Bishop of Birmingham), Sir Thomas Raleigh, and many other men since distinguished in public life. He has been a Fellow of New Coll., Oxford, since 1877. At Oxford he carried off the Hertford, Craven, Eldon, and Derby Scholarships, in addition to obtaining Firsts in Moderations and Greats. He was successively Treasurer and President of the Union Debating Society—then in its palmiest days— and a weighty contributor to its debates. As an undergraduate he was a Liberal tempered with the Imperial sentiment, and was an intimate friend of Arnold Toynbee, of whose career he has written a charming monograph. Following upon his Oxford days, a period of indecision came as to his future. He was called to the Bar at the Inner Temple in 1881, and for three or four years—from 1882 to 1885—was principally engaged in journalism, under such stimulating editors as Mr. John Morley and Mr. W. T. Stead, from whom Lord Milner now differs so completely on political lines of thought. But although journalism attracted him more than the Bar, Milner was altogether too big a man to be bound by the limitations of the Press. At the General Election in 1885 he unsuccessfully contested the Harrow Division as a Liberal, and in Jan., 1887—on the occasion when Lord Randolph Churchill forgot Goschen—he became private secretary to the new Chancellor of the Exchequer, who had heard and admired young Milner as an undergraduate at the Union. The Right Hon. G. J. Goschen, as he then was, was not a man to place his confidence recklessly but when once he did so it was done unreservedly, and in the result he formed the highest opinion of Milner, who, in return, repaid his chief by the most devoted service, in the course of which time the subject of our sketch received many flattering offers of advancement, which he only refused out of loyalty to his chief. During this period Lord Goschen conceived and carried out his famous conversion scheme, which gave the name of 'Goschens' to a large part of the British Public Debt. His health becoming impaired, Lord Milner in 1889 entered the Egyptian service as Under-Secretary of State for Finance. Three years of administrative experience in Egypt supplied him with the material of his well-known book, *England in Egypt*, published at the end of 1892, to the later editions of which his friend Sir Clinton Dawkins, who succeeded him in Egypt, and subsequently Sir Eldon Gorst, contributed appendices. The work went through many editions, and is still regarded as one of the most valuable contributions to Anglo African literature, and one that has completely altered the views of Britons as regards the work of their countrymen on the Nile. It is written in a fine literary style, with a brilliancy of local colouring, and displays a close insight into matters of high politics and finance, with a keen

appreciation of England's mission in what the author called the Land of Paradox, engendering a healthy confidence in the faculty possessed by Englishmen of doing good work under the most untoward circumstances.

In 1892 Mr. Milner (as he still was) was appointed Chairman of the Board of Inland Revenue, in succession to Lord Iddesleigh and Sir Algernon West, and in that important position he rendered valuable assistance to the late Sir William Harcourt, who was then Chancellor of the Exchequer, in rearranging the Death Duties.

In 1897 the Colonial Secretary was called upon to find some one to succeed Lord Rosmead in the dual office of Governor of the Cape of Good Hope and High Commissioner for South Africa—one of the most arduous, responsible, and difficult positions in the gift of the Crown, and a position which demanded sagacity above the average asked of colonial administrators, foresight, courage, tenacity of purpose, and impartiality, tempered with a conciliatory, but at the same time resolute, spirit. These high qualities Mr. Chamberlain found in Sir Alfred Milner, who had been knighted some two years previously. Men of all shades of opinion united at the outset in commending Mr. Chamberlain's choice, and the High Commissioner received a singular proof of his popularity in the shape of a dinner given in his honour under the presidency of Mr. Asquith. Nominally the feast was private and personal, but, to use Mr. Balfour's phrase on another occasion at the Athenaeum, the gathering was one of such undiluted distinction that the light thereof could not be hid under a bushel. There were no fewer than fifteen former Presidents of the Oxford Union present, the guest himself being the sixteenth. Mr. Balfour, Mr. Chamberlain, Lord Curzon of Kedleston, Mr. John Morley, and even Mr. Leonard Courtney—who was afterwards to describe Milner as a lost mind— were there.

The exciting days of the raid were not long passed, and a still more eventful epoch awaited Lord Milner's arrival at Table Bay. A careful study of the S. African problem on the spot led the High Commissioner to arrive at certain conclusions, which were not altogether to the taste of the

Afrikander Bond, or of a section of the Radical party in England. The abortive Bloemfontein Conference with Pres. Kruger took place in the summer of 1899—a time when matters in the Transvaal were particularly complicated. Sir Alfred Milner took a very grave view of the issues which were at stake. The policy of President Kruger appeared to him to threaten the total extinction of British influence in South Africa. He made, however, every effort to secure a peaceful solution, short of surrendering what he regarded as the vital interests of his country. But after four months of ceaseless and harassing negotiations an agreement with the Beer Republic proved impracticable, and in October, 1899, the Transvaal and Orange Free State put an end to further discussion by abruptly presenting Great Britain with an aggressive ultimatum, and after forty-eight hours' notice invading Cape Colony and Natal. During the war which followed Lord Milner's administrative ability was strained to the utmost in dealing with the internal affair of Cape Colony, where a large section of the population were in sympathy with the enemy while some 10,000 of them went into open rebellion. Lord Roberts has borne eloquent testimony to the great assistance which he received from the High Commissioner in the conduct of the war. Early in 1901, while the war was still in progress, Sir Alfred Milner was transferred from the Governorship of Cape Colony to that of the newly annexed Boer States henceforward known as the Transvaal and Orange River Colonies, while retaining the office of High Commissioner. From that time onwards till his departure from South Africa four years later his headquarters were at Johannesburg. During a visit to England in the summer of 1901, which he paid nominally on leave, but mainly in order to confer with the Government on the future conduct of affairs in the newly annexed but not yet completely subdued States, he was raised to the peerage as Baron Milner and made a member of the Privy Council. He returned to Johannesburg in August, 1901, and in the following May he conducted, together with Lord Kitchener, the negotiations with the Boar leaders which resulted in the surrender of all the Boer forces and the termination of the war (May, 1902). In connection with these events he was raised to the rank of Viscount.

No sooner was the war ended than Lord Milner was called upon to undertake the difficult and delicate work, first of repatriation, end then of national reconstruction, in the new colonies. The three years which followed were even more arduous than those immediately preceding. All the threads of administration centered in Lord Milner's hands, and he had at one and the same time to provide for the restoration of the whole Boer population, who had been driven from their homes during the war, and were mostly in a state of complete destitution, for the introduction of British settlers, and for the creation of a completely new system of government on British lines. Finance, public works, education, the reform of the Statute Book, the establishment of Courts of Justice and of a new Civil Service in all its branches, railway development, native administration, the creation of a Customs Union to embrace all the South African States, and a number of other weighty matters, all demanded his constant care. In the teeth of the sullen hostility of the leaders of the conquered people and of much criticism from various sections of the British population, he went doggedly on, and, whatever may be said in derogation of certain aspects of his policy, it is incontrovertible that he displayed extraordinary energy in creating order out of chaos and in establishing the new system on such sure foundations that it was found possible before his departure from South Africa to grant a large measure of self-government to the Transvaal, which the present British Ministry converted, within a year of his resignation, into complete responsible Government. Lord Milner himself declared, after his return to England, that the latter step had been taken too soon. But the mere fact that it was possible even to think of it is a testimony to the success of his work in restoring perfect tranquility and a large measure of prosperity to a country which he had taken over a few years previously as a complete wreck, devastated by war, and devoid even of the rudiments of civil administration and orderly government.

Lord Milner's health suffered severely from the strain of these years of incessant labour. In the autumn of 1903 he had to take a few months' leave to visit a German watering place. It was during this time that Mr. Chamberlain resigned the office of

Colonial Secretary, and Lord Milner was suddenly summoned to England and asked to fill the vacant post. It is recounted of him that he found the greatest difficulty in resisting the persuasiveness with which Mr. Balfour, then Prime Minister, urged him to accept office as his colleague. But, in spite of all the pressure brought to bear upon him, Lord Milner felt bound to return to his unfinished work in South Africa, which he did in November of that year (1903). After another eighteen months of bard work, however, he considered that sufficient progress bed been made to justify his retirement, and, his health still suffering, he succeeded, not without difficulty, in inducing the Govt. to accept his resignation, and left South Africa for good in April, 1905, being replaced as Governor of the Transvaal and the Orange River Colony and High Commissioner by the Earl of Selborne.

Lord Milner's speech at the farewell banquet given to him in Johannesburg struck strongly the chord which was the dominant feature of his character. He may have deliberately bent the Boers to his will for the achievement of a great end, but he is unmeasured in his respect for their sterling qualities. "Neither oppress nor kowtow to the Dutch", was his last word to the Uitlanders. "Politics will divide, but common work in the cause of material prosperity will unite. Do not gird at the Boers for an absence of friendliness which they cannot feel. Absolute sympathy must be the growth of years." These are the words of a strong and broadminded man, and in them may be discerned the perfect round of Lord Milner's policy which aimed at the great ideal of imperial unity, the goal of all our hopes.

Alfred Milner has received almost as many flattering marks of distinction from his country and countrymen who believe in him as he has marks of censure from that section at home and abroad who revile his works. He was made a C.B. in 1894, a K.C.B. a year later. The G.C.M.G. was conferred upon him in 1897, and the G.C.B. in 1901. His advancement to the rank of Baron, Privy Councillor, and Viscount has been referred to above. To few men can it have been vouchsafed from the very out set of their public career to receive so many public and private testimonials of gratitude and admiration. But possibly the one most prized by Lord Milner is the National Address, containing over 370,000 signatures, expressing appreciation of his great services to South Africa and the Empire, which was forwarded to him by the Duke of Somerset as Chairman of the committee appointed for that purpose in July, 1906. The moment was ripe. An amendment moved by Mr. Churchill virtually censuring one of the greatest servants of the Crown for a single (and admitted) error of judgment had been voted by the House of Commons in March, and although Lord Milner's conduct had been approved by the House of Lords, public opinion was aflame at the ingratitude of a Government which, according to long tradition, is bound to support the servants of the State when unjustly attacked. But Lord Milner is not the only great Imperialist whose actions have been condemned when they should have exalted him to a place beside the ablest of Englishmen. The immortal Marlborough, whose descendant was one of the foremost to attack Lord Milner, was dismissed from public employment on a cruel charge, his prosecution being ordered by the House of Commons. Clive was examined by the House as if he had been a sheep stealer, and died by his own hand in disgust at his country's ingratitude. Warren Hastings bravely bore for seven years the persecution of the most eloquent combination of men that Parliament has ever produced at one time, and, later, Sir Bartle Frere broke his heart after serving his country with the single-minded devotion of a knight of romance in South Africa. It is the fame of these men that now remains secure, while the memory of their detractors must still suffer. After all, it is persecution which is the hallmark of commanding capacity—the persecution of the great by the little, who thus avow their impotence to sway the verdict of Time.

And now, having retired from the public service, though his voice is still heard in the House of Lords and occasionally on the public platform, Lord Milner is settled down at the old Kentish house, Sturry Court, which is an historical estate, comprising about 160 acres, and an old Elizabethan farmstead, just outside Canterbury, on the northern bank of the Stour. The property is supposed to have been originally an Augustinian convent, the manor being a gift from King Ethelbert. The abbot, during his residence there, threw a stone bridge across the river. After the

Reformation it was presented by Queen Elizabeth to Thomas Smythe, a noted City merchant and farmer of the Customs, who was grandfather to the first Viscount Strangford.

In 1906 Lord Milner joined the Board of Directors of the London and Joint Stock Bank. He is also a Director of the Northern Assurance Company and of the Bank of Egypt. He is unmarried.

MILLS, John Saxon, M.A., St. John's Coll Camb (Classical Tripos), Associate of the Owens Coll., Manchester, Barrister-at-Law of the Inner Temple, of the Compatriots', Liberal and Unionist Clubs, and of the Royal Colonial Institute, is the son of James and Martha Mills of Ashton, and was born at Ashton-under-Lyne. At the beginning of the South African War he was on editorial staff of the *Daily News* under Mr. E. T. Cook; had been an active worker of the Eighty Club, and took part in organising Liberal Imperialist sentiment in the Liberal party. He was joint founder of the Liberal Imperial Council in opposition to the pro-Boer and little-England section of the party, the Council being ultimately merged into the Liberal League. At the beginning of 1901, the *Daily News* being bought by the pro-Boer section, Mr. Saxon Mills proceeded to South Africa as Editor of the *Cape Times*, a position which he held until several months after the close of the war. He was incidentally one of the party on the train which carried Mr. Rhodes to burial in the Matoppos. On returning to England he joined Mr. Chamberlain's movement in favour of the economic union of the Empire, and wrote and spoke much on the question. Has contributed to *Westminster Gazette*, *Globe*, and many other journals including the *Times*, *Fortnightly*, *National* and *Empire Reviews*. Recreations: Music and most outside sports. He married Miss Grace Keeler in 1901.

MILTHORPE, Bernard Thomas, F.R.C.I. 2nd Assistant of the B.C.A. Protectorate; son of C. H. Milthorpe, J.P., late of Bradford Yorks., where he was born Nov. 10, 1871; was educated at Bedford Gram Sch.; was appointed Asst. Collector in the B.C.A. Protectorate, Dec. 24, 1896; was stationed at Fort Johnson, S. Nyassa, from April 1, 1897, to Nov. 17, 1897, whence he was transferred owing to ill-health to Blantyre, Dec. 31, 1897. From

Aug., 1899, to Jan., 1900, he was stationed at Chiromo, on the Lower Shire River; from then until April, 1901, at Fort Anderson, Mlange; and from there he returned to Blantyre, where he was stationed till April 17, 1902. After a short leave of absence he was stationed at Liwonde (Upper Shire River), Fort Hill (Nyassa Tanganyika Plateau), and Chikwana (W. Shire Dist.), where he is at present in charge, having been promoted from 2nd Asst., Feb. 13, 1902. Unmarried.

MILTON, Sir William Henry, K.C.M.G. (1903), of Govt. House, Salisbury, Rhodesia; on of the Rev. Wm. Milton, of Little Marlow, formerly curate of Newbury; was born Dec. 3, 1854; was educated at Marlborough, and enered the Cape Civil Service in 1878, officiating s Clerk to the Executive Council in 1885; Actg.-Secy. in the Prime Minister's Dept., 1890; Priv. Secy. to the Right Hon. Cecil Rhodes during his Premiership from July 1, 1891; was Chief Clerk and Chief Accountant in the Colonial Secy.'s Office from Dec. 1, 1891; and was made Permanent Head of the Prime Minister's Dept., March 8, 1894. In Aug., 1896, he was detached from the Cape Civil Service to go to Rhodesia, where he became Chief Secy. and Secy. for Native Affairs in Sept., 1896; Acting Administrator of Rhodesia, July, 1897; Administrator of Mashonaland and Senior Administrator of S. Rhodesia, Dec. 3, 1898. He as appointed sole Administrator of S. Rhodesia Dec. 20, 1901, and is also Pres. of the Executive and Legislative Councils of S. Rhodesia. Sir William married, in 1883, Eveline, dau. of A. R. Borcherds, of Wynberg, C.C He as three sons being educated in England, who are all well-known athletes; the 2nd, J. G. Milton, being the possessor of the school athletic championship for 1903.

MIREHOUSE, Colonel Richard Walter Byrd, C.M.G., of The Hall, Angie, Pembroke, was born in 1849. He served in the South African War in 1900-2 as Commandant of the Beaufort West District until Nov., 1900, when he took command of the 4th Batt. North Staffs Regt., took part in the operations in the Cape Colony (Queen's medal with clasp, King's medal with two clasps, and C.M.G.).

MITCHELL, James Alexander, M.B., Ch. B.

Glasgow, of Cape Town, and the Civil Service Club (C.T.), was born in Co. Tyrone in 1876, and was educated at Foyle Coll., Londonderry, completing at Glasgow University (medals for surgery, midwifery, and gynaeocology; Mackintosh Bursar in mental diseases) and Edinburgh University (medallist, tropical diseases). Dr. Mitchell was Acting-Asst. Surgeon in the Army Med. Service, 1898-9, and was then appointed on behalf of the Cape Govt. to the post of Govt. Bacteriologist on Robben's Island for leprosy investigation. He was only a few months there when plague broke out in the Cape Colony, and he was appointed Medical Officer in Charge of the Plague Camp at Saldanha Bay in 1900, and at Izeli, King Williamstown, 1901. During the epidemic in the same year he was made Superintendent of the Govt. Plague Hospital and Contact Camp at Cape Town, and he received his present appointment as Asst. Med. Officer of Health for Cape Colony on July 1, 1901. He is the author of *Report on Leprosy Investigation* (1900), *The Treatment of Plague* (1901), and *Plague in Cape Colony* (1905). Unmarried.

MITFORD, Bertram, F.R.G.S., of the Junior Athenaeum, Savage, Authors', and New Vagabond Clubs, is the third son of B. L. Osbaldeston Mitford, of Mitford Castle, Northumberland, and of Hunmanby Hall, Yorks.; was educated at the Royal Naval Sch., New Cross; Hurstpierpoint Coll., and by Continental tutor. He went to S.A. at the beginning of 1874, where he engaged in stock farming, and at the time of the Kaffir War of 1877-78 he held posts in the Cape Civil Service on the frontier. At the close of the Zulu War, he trekked alone through Zululand, exploring the battlefields and interviewing the principal indunas. On various visits to Africa he has travelled in Matabeleland, and visited Zanzibar, Mozambique and other East Coast ports, and has also travelled in Baluchistan and on the N.W. Border of India. He is also well acquainted with the continent of Europe, and at one time went in for climbing in the High Alps, He is fond of most forms of outdoor sport, principally shooting.

Mr. Mitford was proprietor and part editor of the *East London Advertiser* from 1886 to 1888. In the latter year he took seriously to literature as a profession, and has published the following

volumes :— *Through the Zulu Country, A Romance of the Cape Frontier, 'Tween Snow and Fire, Golden Face, The Gunrunner, The Luck of Gerard Ridgeley, Renshaw Fanning's Quest, The King's Assegai, The White Shield, The Induna's Wife, The Word of the Sorceress, The Curse of Clement Waynflete, A Veldt Official, The Expiation of Wynne Palliser, Fordham's Feud, The Sign of the Spider, The Ruby Sword, The Weird of Deadly Hollow, John Ames: Native Commissioner, Aletta, War—and Arcadia, The Triumph of Hilary Blachland, Dorrien of Cranston, Haviland's Chum, A Veldt Vendetta, The Sirdar's Oath, In the Whirl of the Rising, The Red Derelict*, and *A Frontier Mystery*. All of those except the first named are novels, the scenes of which are mostly laid in S.A.

MITFORD, Lieut. Col. W. Kenyon, C.M.G., served in the Afghan War in 1879-80 (medal), and after leaving the regular service, commanded the Middlesex Reg. of Yeomanry Cavalry for several years. Early in 1900 he took command of the XI. Batt. of Imp. V. for a few months in the S African War, after which he resumed the command of the home regt., from which he has since retired.

MOBERLY, Major Frederick, D.S.O., I.A., was born in 1867. He took part in the Expedition to Manipur in 1891 (medal with clasp); the Burma Expedition in 1891 with the Wuntho Field Force (clasp); the operations in Gilgit in 1893 (despatches, D.S.O.); the operations in Chitral in 1895, took part in the defence of Mustaj (despatches, medal with clasp, promoted Captain); the operations in the N.W. Frontier of India in 1897-8 (clasp), and the South African War in 1899-1900 as Special Service Officer, afterwards on the Staff; present at the operations in the Orange Free State, including the actions at Paardeberg, Poplar Grove, Driefontein, Vet River and Zand River; operations in the Transvaal, including the actions near Johannesburg, Pretoria, and Diamond Hill; and the operations in the Transvaal east of Pretoria, including the actions at Belfast (despatches, Brevet of Major, and Queen's medal with six clasps).

MOCATTA, Ernest George, of 4, Throgmorton Avenue, E.C., is a partner in the firm of Mocatta and Foá, stockbrokers. He is a director of the Penhalonga Proprietary Mines, Ltd., and is on the London Committee of the Angelo Gold Mines,

Ltd., Anglo-French Exploration Co., Ltd., Anglo-French Matabeleland Co., Ltd., Cason Gold Mines, Ltd., Driefontein Consolidated Mines, Ltd., H.F. Co., Ltd., Hercules Co., Ltd., New Comet G.M. Co., Ltd., and is in the European Committee of the East Rand Proprietary Mines, Ltd. (See Sir Geo. Farrar.)

MOCKLER-FERRYMAN, Lieut. Col. Augustus Ferryman, F.R.G.S., Barrister-at-Law, of Broadway House, Sandhurst, and of the Naval end Military Club, was born in Dublin, Dec. 25, 1856. He was educated at Cheltenham Coll. and the R.M.C., Sandhurst; joined the 43rd Light Inf. in 1877; acted as Private Secretary to H.B.M.'s Special Commissioner to the Niger in 1889-90; was appointed Instructor in Fortification at the R.M.C., Sandhurst, from 1892-7; Instructor in Mil. Topography there from 1897-1900, and Professor in 1900-03. He was employed at the War Office from 1903-5 in assisting to write the official history of the S. African War; author of *Up the Niger: a narrative of Major Claude MacDonald's Mission to the Niger and Benue Rivers, W. Africa*; *British W. Africa*, *The Bedfordshire Light Inf. in S. Africa*, *British Nigeria*, *Hemmed In: a tale of the W. Sudan*, and numerous other works. He married, July 14, 1891, Evelyn, dau. of Chas. Whitehead, J.P., D.L, of Barming, Kent.

MOFFAT, John Smith, C.M.G., was born in Bechuanaland, March 10, 1835, and is son of the Rev. Robert Moffat, a South African missionary. He was educated in London and returned to S. Africa in 1858 in the service of the London Missionary Society. He commenced operations with two other missionaries with the chief Umziligaas in Matabeleland under the directions of his father; left there in 1865, and took up work with his father in Kuruman. He came to England on furlough in 1872-4. In 1877 he was transferred to Molipolelo with the Bakwena tribe, and the Chief Sechele; resigned his appointment with the London Missionary Society in 1879, and in 1880 became Native Commissioner for the N.W. border of the Transvaal. This appointment lapsed with the retrocession of the Transvaal 1881. He was Resident Magistrate at Maseru from 1882 until 1884, when the Administration was taken over by the Imperial from the Colonial Govt. He spent a

year in England and published a memoir of Robert and Mary Moffat. In 1885 he was appointed Resident Magistrate at Taungs, British Bechuanaland, and acted as Special Envoy to Lobengula, the Matabele Chief, in 1887; was transferred in 1892 to the Chief Khama's town, Palapye; Resident Magistrate in 1895 at Taungs, and retired in 1896. He travelled in British East and British Central Africa in 1904. He married, Feb. 15, 1858, Emily Unwin, of Brighton.

MOFFAT, Dr. Robert Unwin, C.M.G., of Uganda, and of the Sports Club, was born in 1866 in S. Africa, and is son of the Rev. J. S. Moffat, C.M.G. He was appointed Principal Medical Officer of the East Africa and Uganda Protectorates in 1905. Dr. Moffat has been connected with British East Africa since 1891, and accompanied the late Sir Gerald Portal's mission to Uganda in 1893. He has since been connected with the Medical Department of that country. He married, in 1900, Hilda, dau. of J. Vavasseur, of Knockholt, Kent.

MOIR, Capt., J.P., D.S.O., R.E., of Lagos, left England in Jan., 1905, to take charge of the telegraph construction in S. Nigeria, under the Colonial Office.

MOIR, Herbert, of The Common, Weybridge, is a director of the Colonial Consolidated Finance Corp., Ltd., Cosmopolitan Proprietary, Ltd., Egyptian Options, Ltd., Gold Finance Co., Ltd., Golden Pike and Lake View East Mines, Ltd., Hannan's Proprietary, Ltd., Oroya East (Hannan's) Gold Mine, Ltd., and the West Australian Collieries and Fireclay Co., Ltd.

MOLTENO, James Tennant, M.L.A., is member of the Cape Legislative Assembly for Somerset East. He is a member of the S.A. Party, and was last re-elected in Feb., 1904.

MOLTENO, Percy Alport, M.P., B.A., M.A. LL.M., of 10 Palace Court, London, and of the Eighty, New Reform, Royal Societies and City of London Clubs was born at Edinburgh in 1860 and is 2nd son of the late Sir John C. Molteno, first Premier of the Cape Colony. He was educated at the University of the Cape of Good Hope (Porter Student) and at Trinity Coll., Camb., and is a

Barrister-at-Law of the Inner Temple and an Advocate of the Supreme Court of the Cape of Good Hope. He has ceased practising the Law, however, and is now a partner in the firm of Donald Currie and Co., and was elected Liberal member for Dumfriesshire at the general election in Jan., 1906, defeating his Conservative opponent by 1,383 votes. Mr. Molteno is the author of *A Federal South Africa* and *Life and Times of Sir John Charles Molteno*. He is married to Elizabeth, dau. of Sir Donald Currie (q.v.).

MOLYNEUX, A. J. C., F.G.S., F.R.G.S., of Hillside, Bulawayo, and of the Bulawayo Club, is son of the late Wm. Molyneux, of Burton-on-Trent. He served in the Matabele War in 1893 as Staff Officer of the Victoria Column with Major Wilson (medal), and afterwards commanded a troop in the Rhodesia Horse. He is interested in scientific research; has been President, 1902-3, of the Rhodesia Scientific Association; is a trustee of the Rhodesian Museum, and author of several geological and geographical papers.

MOMBASA, The Lord Bishop of. (See Peel, Right Rev. W. G.)

MONEY, Capt. Charles Francis Lethbridge, of Salisbury, Rhodesia, was born Sept. 26, 1869, and is son of the late Rev. Canon Money. He was educated at Cheltenham Coll, and Corpus Christi Coll., Cambs. In 1892 he went to Canada and joined the North-West Mounted Police, but left in 1895 and went to S. Africa in the following year, arriving at Salisbury a week before the Mashonaland Rebellion broke out, in which he served, first as a burgher in the Salisbury Laager; afterwards as Troop Sergt.-Major in the Salisbury Field Force, and Paymaster-Sergt. to the Volunteer Forces; subsequently being promoted to Lieut. and Paymaster in the same year (medal and clasp). He was appointed to the district Paymastership of the British S. Africa Police for Mashonaland in 1897; and occupied the same position for Rhodesia in 1903. He received his captaincy in 1901; wears the King's and Queen's medals and three clasps for the S. African War, and is a J.P. for S. Rhodesia.

Recreations: Golf and tennis. He played Rugby football and cricket for the College XV. and XI. in

1889-91. He married, Feb. 14, 1900 Lily, dau. of T. Spunner, of Kildare.

MONK-BRETTON, Lord, C.B.; formerly in the service of the Foreign Office, and was attached to the Embassies in Paris and Constantinople before he became Assist. Private Secy. to the late Lord Salisbury. His lordship subsequently occupied an important position in the Colonial Office, and accompanied Mr. Chamberlain as Principal Private Secy. on his S. African tour in 1902. In 1904 he became a director of the De Beers Consolidated Mines, and he is also on the Board of the Rock Life Assurance

MONTAGU OF BEAULIEU, Lord, of Beaulieu, Hampshire, and of the Automobile, Bachelors', Beefsteak, and Carlton Clubs, was born in 1866, and is the eldest son of the first Lord Montagu of Beaulieu. He was educated at Eton and Oxford, and has travelled extensively, including Egypt and South Africa. During the Matabele War in 1896 he acted as *Times* correspondent, was recently a regular contributor to the *Daily Mail*, and has written various magazine articles. He was of formerly a director of several South African companies, but he soon relinquished these directorates to found the first motor paper, *The Car*, of which he is editor. Lord Montagu was formerly M.P. for the New Forest Division of Hants, and is a Major in the 4th Vol. Battn. Hants Regt. He married, in 1889, Cecil, dau. pf the 9th Marquis of Lothian.

MONTEIL, Commandant, left Senegal in Aug., 1890, on a journey to Lake Tchad, reaching Segour on the Upper Nile, the furthest point at which the French had established their authority, on Dec. 20, 1890. Thence he struck out across the bend of the Niger for Say, and on to Argungu, the fortified capital of Kabbi. He then proceeded to Sokoto, Kano (where he received an enthusiastic welcome), and Kuka, eventually reaching Tripoli after a difficult and dangerous journey late in 1892.

MONYPENNY, William Flavelle, B.A., of 2, Queen Anne's Gate, London, S.W., and of the Rand (Johannesburg) and Athenaeum (Johannesburg) Clubs, was born in Co. Armagh, Ireland, Aug. 7, 1866. He is descended from a collateral branch, settled in Ireland, of a Scotch family whose headquarters are at Pitmilly, in Fife. He was educated at the Royal Sch., Duncannon, at Trinity Coll., Dublin, where He graduated B.A., and at Balliol Coll., Oxon. After leaving the Univ. he contributed for a time to the *Spectator*; joined the staff of the *Times* as Asst.-Editor in 1893, and was appointed Editor of the *Johannesburg Star* early in 1899, and in that capacity and as correspondent of the *Times* he incurred the displeasure of the Boer Govt., who, in the beginning of Sept., attempted to arrest him on a charge of high treason, but he escaped to British territory. On the outbreak of the S.A. War he obtained a commission in the I.L.H., and served with that regt. through the siege of Ladysmith. He was afterwards Director of Civil Supplies in Johannesburg during Col. Colin Mackenzie's tenure of office as Military Gov., and he resumed the editorial control of the *Johannesburg Star* when that paper reappeared at the beginning of 1902. Owing to his disagreement with the policy of introducing Chinese labour into South Africa he resigned the editorship of the *Star* in Dec., 1903, and returned to England, where he is now engaged in writing a life of Lord Beaconsfield from the original papers bequeathed to the late Lord Rowton.

MOOR, Hon. Frederick Robert, M.L.A., of Grey Stone House, Estcourt, Natal, and of the Victoria Club, P.M.B., was born in 1853, and received his education in Natal. He was formerly a diamond digger at Kimberley, and was twice elected a member of the Kimberley Mining Board by his fellow diggers. In 1880 he returned to Natal and settled down as a farmer. Six years later he sat in the Natal Legislative Assembly, in which he has held a seat up to the present date. From 1893-97 he acted as Minister for Native Affairs, under the Robinson and Escombe Ministries; declined office under the Binns Ministry in 1897, and was reappointed Minister for Native Affairs in 1899 under Sir Albert Hime (q.v.). In 1898 Mr. Moor acted as one of the Natal Representatives at the Custom's Union Conference at Cape Town, and also at the inaugural festivities of the Australian Commonwealth. He undertook the duties of Prime Minister for Natal, during Sir Albert Hime's absence in England on the coronation of King Edward. He sits in the House of Assembly as Member for Weenen County.

MORCOM, William Boase, K.C. (1888), of 327, Loop St., Maritzburg, and the Victoria Club, P.M.B., was born at Redruth, Cornwall, Oct. 9, 1846. He first entered the Civil Service as Clerk Asst. to the Natal Legislative Council. in 1872, afterwards filling various offices under the Colonial Govt. In 1878 he was admitted to practice as an Advocate of the Supreme Court of Natal. He was Attorney-Gen. for the Transvaal in 1880; was made Q.C. in 1888; became Attorney-Gen. for Natal in 1889, from which he retired when that colony was given responsible govt. in 1893. He was appointed Minister of Justice for Natal in 1903. Mr. Morcom is not married.

MORECROFT, T. L., of South Africa, is a director of the Witkopje Gold Mines, Ltd., and the Thistle Consolidated Mines, Ltd.

MOREL, Edmund D., of Hawarden, Chester, was born in Paris in 1873. He was educated at Bedford, and early turned his attention to a journalistic career. He has contributed for a number of years to many of the leading magazines and newspapers on W. African questions, and as he is regarded as a leading authority his contributions have excited considerable public interest. His exposures of the Congo scandals have particularly done much to bring the whole question of the Congo Administration under the attention of the Govt. He is the Editor of the *West African Mail*, and is the Author of *Affairs of West Africa* (1903), *The British Case in French Congo* (1903), *King Leopold's Rule in Africa* (1904), *The Congo Slave State*, *Trading Monopolies in West Africa*, and other pamphlets too numerous to mention. Mr. Morel was delegated (1904) by the Congo Reform Association, the British and Foreign Antislavery Society, Aborigines Protection, and other Societies to present a Memorial to President Roosevelt on the Congo Question; was one of the British delegates to the last mentioned Peru Congress held at Boston (1904), and addressed it on the Congo question, the Congress ultimately passing unanimously the resolutions he submitted to it. He married, in 1896, Miss Mary F. Y. Richardson.

MORGAN, Benjamin Howell, of Orchard House, Westminster, and the Royal Societies Club, was born, Aug. 24, 1873, at Glenarberth, Cardiganshire, is the fourth son of Benjamin Morgan, of White Castle, and was educated as an engineer. He has since taken a deep interest in general economic and trade questions, and is a well-known authority on such, particularly as affecting S.A. affairs. In 1895 he travelled through the U.S. and Canada, studying the economic conditions prevailing there, and later made a similar journey through Europe, visiting principally engineering and manufacturing establishments. At the age of 23 he was appointed editor of a trade journal, and a few years later became Editor of the *Engineering Times*, a position which he now holds. At the close of the S.A. War in June, 1902, he was appointed Trade Commissioner to S.A. to inquire into and report upon the state of, and openings for, trade in engineering and machinery. The results of his investigations were comprised in a volume published in the following November. This report has been described as a masterly work, and has given rise to much comment and discussion. He is one of the most strenuous opponents of the Shipping Ring, whose methods he exposed in his report and subsequent lectures before the Royal Colonial Institute and elsewhere. With the assistance of the Board of Trade and the Colonial Governments he has successfully organised a scheme of National Engineering and Trade Lectures (illustrated with lantern views) for reading in Colonial and Foreign markets with the object of showing the progress which Great Britain has made in recent years in her manufacturing industries. He is a Vice-Pres. of the Nottingham Society of Engineers, and Fellow of the Royal Colonial Institute, etc., and is the Author of *The Engineering Trades of South Africa*, *The Trade and Industry of South Africa*, *The Prevention of Strikes and Lockouts*, *The Systematic Promotion of British Trade*, *High Speed Steam Engines*, and other technical works. Mr. Morgan married, in Feb., 1904, Rachel, dau. of the late David Cowling, of York.

MORLAND, Lieut.-Col. (local Col.) Thomas Lethbridge Napier, C.B., D.S.O., of the Naval and Military Club, was born in Canada, Aug. 9, 1865; is son of the late Thos. Morland, and was educated at Charterhouse. He joined the King's Royal Rifle Corps, Aug. 23, 1884; was promoted Capt. in April, 1893; was at the Staff Coll. 1891-2; A.D.C. to the Governor and G.O.C., Malta, 1895-98; joined the W. African Frontier Force, Feb. 5, 1898, and was appointed Commandant of the Northern Nigeria Regt. in 1901. Col. Morland married, in 1890, Mabel, eldest dau. of Admiral and Mrs. St. John, of Stokefield, Thornbury, Glos. Mrs. Morland died in 1901.

MORRIS, Bt.-Major Edmund Merritt, was born in Canada in 1868, and was educated at the R.M.C. there. He served with the Devonshire Regt. in Egypt and India, and in the campaign on the N.W. Frontier of India in 1897-8 (medal and two clasps); went to S. Africa with his regt., and was appointed Adjt. to Thorneycroft's M.I., which corps he assisted to raise. He became Sub Divisional Commander in the S. African Constabulary in 1901, and on the continuation of the war he raised and took command of a Mounted Corps of 600 Burghers, known as the Farmers' Guard, which Corps he commanded till the end of the war (Queen's medal and six clasps, King's medal and two clasps, mentioned in despatches). He remained in the S.A.C. until 1904, when he was selected by Lord Milner to raise a Volunteer Force in the O.R.C., and to command it; owing in the lack of funds, however, the movement was postponed. He married a dau. of Major-Gen. Shakespear.

MORRIS, Edward Walter Henry, of Kimberley, Cape Colony, served in the artillery troop of the Frontier Armed and Mounted Police during the Gaika-Galeka and Moirosi campaigns (medal with clasp), and as lieutenant in the Herschel native contingent during the Basuto War. He was temporarily employed in the resident magistrate's office at Grahamstown in 1882; was appointed clerk to the resident magistrate at Kokstad in 1882, and at Tsolo in 1893; acted as clerk to the registrar of native servants at Kimberley in 1895, which position he still holds He was appointed deputy registrar of births and deaths at Kimberley in 1898.

MORRIS, Major William Pollok, D.S.O., of Craig, Kilmarnock, N.B., and of the Naval and Military and Cavalry Clubs, was born at Glasgow, March 12, 1867, and is son of Col. Pollok Morris. He was educated al Harrow and Oxford, and entered the 18th Hussars as Lieut. in 1886. He served in the Chitral Relief Force in 1895, under Sir Robert Low (medal and clasp); took part in the Tirah Expeditionary Force in 1897-8 on the Tamana Range, and was present at the capture of the Sanpaja and Arhunga Passes; was with the expedition to the Warnn Valley and the return march down the Barn Valley (mentioned in despatches, three clasps). Major Morris served in the S. African War in 1899-02, including the action at Talana, and the operations in Eastern and Northern Transvaal, Natal and O.R.C., under Gen. French, Major-Gen. Kitchener, and Sir Bruce Hamilton (mentioned in despatches, Queen's medal and four clasps, King's medal and two clasps, D.S.O.).

MORRIS, Sir John Henry, K.C.S.I, of 88, Queen's Gate, S.W., was born in 1828, and is son of the late Henry Morris, of the Madras Civil Service. He was educated at Reading and Haileybury College; joined the Bengal Civil Service in 1848, and served in the Punjab from 1848-1859. From 1861-63 he acted as Magistrate of Allahabad, and from then until 1868 he acted as Settlement Commissioner in the Central Provinces, and as Chief Commissioner from 1868-83. He is a director of the Gold Coast and Ashanti Explorers, Ltd., Namaqua Copper Co., Ltd., New Colonial Co., Ltd., Ooregum G.M. Co., of India, Ltd., and the St. James' and Pall Mall Electric Light Co., Ltd. He married, in 1854, Anna, dau. of Colonel C. Cheape.

MOSELY, Alfred, C.M.G., of West Lodge, Hadley Wood, Barnet; is a native of Bristol; spent a great part of his life in S. Africa; received C.M.G., and was created Knight of Grace of the Order of St. John of Jerusalem in England for services in connection with the Boer War, 1900. He personally organised and conducted to the United States a Commission of over twenty Trade Unionists to inquire into conditions of wages and labour there; and a Commission of thirty Educational Delegates to the United States and Canada to ascertain and report upon the strong points of American Education. He is a strong Trade Unionist as regards cooperation and organisation of workmen, though not in favour of all that Trade Unionism does. Is a great admirer of the American practical system of education for the masses, and thinks the British have much to learn from that country on both the Educational and Industrial sides. He erected a War memorial on Plymouth Hoe to late Prince Christian Victor and the West Country soldiers who fell in South Africa, and is a member of the Executive of Mr. Chamberlain's Tariff Commission.

MOSELEY, C. H. Harley, C.M.G., late of Lagos; has been in the Colonial Civil Service since 1881, the whole of which time has been spent in West Africa, where he has served in Sierra Leone, the Gambia, and Lagos, in which latter Colony he was Colonial Treasurer, and subsequently Col. Secy. and Acting Administrator on various occasions, during the absence of successivo Governors. Mr. Moseley retired from the service, on a pension early in 1905, at which time he was probably the oldest European official on the Coast.

MOSENTHAL, G. J. S., of 72, Basinghall Street, London, E.C., of the firm of Mosenthal, Sons, and Co., is on the London Board of the Griqualand West Diamond Mining Co., Ltd., and the New Jagersfontein Mining and Exploration Co., Ltd.

MOSENTHAL, Harry, of 72, Basinghall Street, E.C., and of the firm of Mosenthal, Sons, and Co., is a director of the Atlas Assurance Co., Ltd., Consolidated Company, Bultfontein Mine, Ltd., De Beers Consolidated Mines, Ltd., Exploration Co., Ltd., Marine Insurance Co., Ltd., and the Rand Mines, Ltd.

MOSES, William, J.P., M.L.M. and M.E., of Balmoral, Germiston, Transvaal, and of the Athenaeum, (Johannesburg) and Kimberley Clubs, was born at Newcastle-on-Tyne, Ap. 28, 1854, and is the second son of John Moses, of Cumberland. He was educated at Durham Univ., and in 1870 became an articled pupil in the Earl of Durham's collieries; from 1875-81 He was engaged in the management of the same. He acted as Asst.-Manager of the Marquess of Londonderry's collieries from 1881-3; at the end of that time he became Manager of Sir Mark Palmer's Wardley Collieries. He also owned the Hetton and Chatton Collieries in Northumberland from 1881-92. In 1889 he was Mining Engineer to the Chinese Govt.

at Pekin; subsequently becoming Manager of the Kimberley Diamond Mines and Pa Beers Consolidated Mines in 1892. He held the post of General Manager of the Transvaal Coal Trust from 1897-1900, when he became Inspector of Mines for the Transvaal. Recreations: all kinds of sport, and is Pres. of the Germiston Turf and Sporting Club. He married, April 8, 1879, Mary, dau. of John Leith, of London and New York.

MOSS, Capt. E. W., D.S.O., of the Worcestershire Regt.; was appointed Major in the West African Regt. in 1904, with temporary rank of Major in the Army while so employed.

MOULE, Lieut. Louis Horsford D'Oyly, of Eastdale, East Sheen, Surrey, and of the Junior Naval and Military Club; was born in India, Oct. 31, 1876; is son of H. D. Moule, C.S.I., and was educated at Exeter. He served with the C.M.R. in the South African War, being appointed to a Commission in the East Lancashire Regt. in May, 1900 (Queen's medal with three clasps, King's medal with two clasps). He subsequently saw active service with the S. Nigeria Regt., to which he was appointed in 1903 (African General Service medal with one clasp). Unmarried.

MOUNTENEY-JEPHSON, A. J., is the last surviving officer of Sir H. M. Stanley's Expedition for the relief of Emin Pasha. (See Sir H. M. Stanley in Obituaries.)

MOUNTMORRES, Viscount, was nominated by the *Globe* newspaper in 1904 to proceed to the Congo Free State to make a thoroughly independent inquiry into the alleged maladministration of the country. He also acted as correspondent of the *Globe*.

MOUTRIE, Arthur, of 12, Fenchurch Street, London, E.C., is a partner in the firm of A. Moultrie and Co., commission agents. He is Chairman and Managing Director of the Katanga Trading and Cold Storage Co., Ltd., Chairman of the Mines Acquisition Syndicate Ltd., Otto's Kopje Diamond Mines, Ltd., and the Waverley Block Gold Mines, Ltd., and is a director of the Bulawayo and General Exploration Co., Ltd., Nile Development Syndicate, Ltd., Rose of Sharon and

Shamrock Gold Mines, Ltd., Salisbury Building and Estates Co., Ltd., Southern Gold Trust, Ltd., Sutherland Reef, Ltd., and Victoria Proprietary (1903), Ltd.

MOXON, Richard, of 30, Addison Gardens, W., is a director of the Approponsu (Ashanti) Syndicate, Ltd., and the Murchison Proprietary (Transvaal), Ltd.

'MPESENI is Chief of the Angonis in North Eastern Rhodesia, and is directly descended from one of the three sons of Tshaka (generally incorrectly spelt Chaka), the great Chief who, organising the Zulus into a great warlike race, overran huge portions of South Africa including Rhodesia and the Zambesi territories; he also carried his victories as far East as Delagoa Bay, slaughtering men and women alike. Tshaka was finally stabbed to death by his half-brother Dingaan, whose subsequent overthrow by the Boers has since been celebrated by them as a national holiday on every 16th of December. 'Mpeseni migrated with his followers from Zululand in search of new lands to conquer, eventually settling in what has since become part of N.E. Rhodesia.

MUDIE, Charles John, of Balmuies, Loop St., Pietermaritzburg, and of the Victoria Club, P.M.B., was born at Dundee, Scotland, in 1857; is elder son of the late William Ball Mudie, and was educated at the Morgan Hospital (Academy); Dundee High School; Moray House Training College; and Edinburgh University. Junior House Master, Morgan Hospital, Dundee; First Assistant Master, Ladyloan School, Arbroath, and afterwards in Victoria Rd. School, Dundee; Latin and English Master Literary Institution, Dundee, 1880-83; selected by the Crown authorities out of a large number of applicants for the post of First Assistant Master, Boys' Model School, Durban, Natal, 1883-6; Head Master, Estcourt School, 1886-9; Asst. Inspector of Schools, 1890; Inspector of Schools 1898; Chief Inspector of Schools and Acting Superintendent of Education, 1902; seconded for service with the Scotch Education Department as H.M. Inspector of Schools, 1904 is member of Council of University of Cape of Good Hope (1905), and has been Superintendent of Education for Natal since Oct., 1904. He married, in 1892, Miss Adele Marguerite Anderson.

MUIR, James, M.L.C., was appointed to be an unofficial Member of the Legislative Council of the Gold Coast Colony in 1905.

MUIR Thomas, C.M.G., M.A., LL.D. (Hon.), F.R.S., of Mowbray Hall, Rosebank, near Cape Town, and of the Civil Service Club (C.T.), was born at Stonebyres, Lanarkshire, Aug. 25, 1845, and is son of the late Geo. Muir of that place. He was educated at Wishaw Public Sch., Glasgow Univ., and in Germany. In 1868 he was appointed Sub Warden of College Hall, St. Andrews; Asst. Prof. of Mathematics in Glasgow Univ. in 1871; was elected F.R.S.E. in 1874, and became in the same year Head of the Mathematical and Science Depts. of the High Sch. of Glasgow, and member of the London Mathematical Soc. In 1879 he was appointed Examiner in Mathematics and Natural Philosophy for Glasgow Univ., was elected Pres. of the Edinburgh Mathematical Soc. in 1883; was awarded the Keith Medal of the Royal Soc. of Edinburgh for Mathematical Research in 1884; appointed Exam. of Secondary Schools under the Scotch Education Dept. in 1885; Examiner in Mathematics and Natural Philosophy for St. Andrews Univ., 1886; Hon. Fel. Royal Scottish Geographical Soc., 1892; and in the same year was chosen for his present post as Supt.-Gen. of Education for Cape Colony.

Dr. Muir was appointed Vice-Chancellor of the Univ. of the Cape of Good Hope in 1897; was awarded the Keith Medal for the second time in 1899, and was elected P.R.S. in 1900. He is a Trustee of the S.A. Museum; the S.A. Public Library; and of the S.A. Art Gallery, of which latter he is also Chairman. He is member of the Geological Commission,. the Meteorological Commission, and of the Civil Service Commission; Vice-Pres. of the S.A. Assoc. for the Advancement of Science; Vice-Pres. of the Cape Town Musical Soc., and Chairman of the Chamber Music Union. He is author of *A Treatise on the Theory of Determinants*, a *History of Determinants*, and of various other works and contributions to scientific journals, and learned societies' publications. Dr. Muir has taken much interest in the development of musical

taste in the Colony, and besides his more serious geographical and mathematical studies, plays golf and lawn tennis. He married, in 1874, Margaret, youngest dau. of the late Dugald Bell, of Glasgow.

MULDER, Hon. Hendrik Johannes, M.L.A. of Armoed, Oudtshoorn District C.C. was born at Oudtshoorn. He commenced business in 1865, and now carries on a large ostrich farm. He was a member of the Cape Legislative Council for the South-West Province, having been first elected in 1891 at the head of the poll, and was afterwards elected as Bond member of the Legislative Assembly for Oudtshoorn. He is an elder of the D.R. Church, and has a large family.

MULLINS, Major Charles Herbert, V.C., C.M.G., of Johannesburg, served in the South African War in 1900, and was awarded the V.C. for gallantry at Elandslaagte. He was also mentioned in despatches, and created C.M.G. Major Mullins is a director of the National Bank of South Africa. For some time a partner in the late firm of Hudson, Hutchinson, and Mullins, Attorneys, of Johannesburg, he subsequently joined Sir A. Woolls-Sampson in a financial and estate business in that town. In Feb., 1906, he was enrolled as an Advocate of the Witwatersrand High Court. He married, in 1902, Norah, dau. of S. Haslam.

MUNNIK, C. H., son of ex-Landdrost J. H. Munnik (q.v.); was Inspector of Mines under Pres. Kruger's Govt., and during Mr. Klimke's absence in Europe during the early period of the South African War, he acted temporarily as State Mining Engineer.

MUNNIK, J. H., was Landdrost at Boksburg, Transvaal, until he joined the Boers on the outbreak of the War in 1899, remaining in the field until captured by Colenbrander's Scouts in April, 1901. He then spent fifteen months as a prisoner of war in India. Until peace was signed Mr. Munnik was an irreconcilable, but he then determined to accept the inevitable and became a loyal British subject. Mr. Munnik occupied his leisure time as a prisoner in writing a romance of the Boer War, entitled *Major Greville, V.C., D.S.O.*

MURPHY, Edward Robert, of Mwomboshi River, Luangwa Dist., N.W. Rhodesia, Cambridge Lodge, Newlands Park, Sydenham, Eng., and of the Sports Club, was born in Co. Cork, Sept. 12, 1878, and is eldest son of Surgeon Major R. P. Murphy, late of the Indian Medical. He was educated at Wellington Coll., and started ranching in Assinaboia in 1897; in Cassiar district, British Columbia, with Warburton Pike and others, for Cassiar Central Railway Co., in 1878, during the Yukon rush; on continuation of Crow's Nest Pass construction, Arrowhead Lake, Kootenai, B.C., end of 1898, and returned home beginning of 1899; he left for Ceylon end of 1899, and was tea planting on Weyvelhena estate, Uva Province; and the Rothschild estate, Pussellava, in 1900-1; left for South India, where he was engaged on Yellapatty estate. He left India in 1902, and was appointed Asst. Native Commissioner, N.E. Rhodesia, 1903; sent to new district just opened at Mwomboshi in the West, took first census north of Mwomboshi to the Lukanga Swamp, 1904, and transferred to N.W. Rhodesian Administration on Oct. 1, 1905, as Native Commissioner. Recreation: Big game shooting. Unmarried.

MURRAY, Capt. C. A., commanded an Australian section of the Scottish Horse in the South African War, and took charge of the contingent which was entertained in England on the occasion of the Coronation of Edward VII. in 1902.

MURRAY, Hon. Charles Gideon, of Johannesburg, and the Bachelors' Club, London, third son of Lord Elibank (10th Baron), was born Aug. 7, 1877, and was educated at Blairlodge, Polmont, N.B., and abroad. In 1891 he was appointed Asst. Priv. Secy. to the Lieut.-Governor of British New Guinea; was Clerk to the Govt. Secy., British New Guinea, 1899; Resident Magistrate, Western Division, B.N.G., 1900; Priv. Secy. to Sir Godfrey Lagden, Commissioner for Native Affairs for the Transvaal, 1901; and Asst. Native Commissioner for the Zoutpansberg Dist. of the Transvaal in 1902. His recreations are shooting, riding, golf and tennis. Unmarried.

MURRAY, George Alexander, of 85, London Wall, London, E.C., is Chairman of the Dome Oil Co., of Wyoming, Ltd., Exploring Land and Minerals Co., Ltd., Mines and Minerals Exploration Syndicate, Ltd., and Redbone's South African Syndicate, Ltd., and is director of the Heidelberg Estates and Exploration Co., Ltd., and the Lingham Timber and Trading Co., Ltd.

MURRAY, James, D.L., J.P., is a partner in the firm of William Murray and Son, 453-65, George Street, Aberdeen, and is a director of the Inez G.M. Co., Ltd., London and Lancashire Fire Insurance Co., Tanganyika Concessions, Ltd., United Rhodesia Goldfields, Ltd., and the Zambesi Exploring Co., Ltd. (See Robert Williams.)

MURRAY, John R., of 70, Gracechurch Street, E.C., is a director of the Assin Fesu and Gold Coast Syndicate, Ltd., and Oceana Consolidated Co., Ltd., and is on the London Committee of New South Rand, Ltd., Transvaal Nigel, Ltd., Welgedacht Exploration Co., Ltd., and Western Kleinfontein, Ltd.

MURRAY, Hon. Sir Thomas Keir, K.C.M.G., J.P. for Natal, of Cleland, Pietermaritzburg, and of the Victoria Club (P.M.B.), son of A. K. Murray, was born Nov. 6, 1854, in Pine Town, Natal, where he also received his education. Sir Thomas Murray has for over thirty years taken a prominent part in the Military, Political, Commercial, and Sporting interests of Natal. As early as 1873 he was a member of the Natal Frontier Guards, and in 1879 served as second in command of the Ladysmith Defence Force in the Zulu War. In the South African War he raised and commanded Murray's Horse (1899), and was Chief of Murray's Scouts and of Gen. Buller's Intelligence Dept. on the Staff. He took part in the relief of Ladysmith and was three times mentioned in despatche; subsequently he was General Superintendent of Burgher Camps in Natal, and the Transvaal and Natal Governments, Lord Milner, and Mr. Chamberlain specially thanked Mr. Murray for his services, who was then made K.C.M.G.

Sir Thomas Murray's political life has been still more busy. He has sat in the Natal Parliament since 1886, during which period he has been Chairman of Finance, Railway and Harbour Committees Minister of Lands and Works (1893-7), Colonial Secy. (1897), Acting Prime Minister, Chairman of

Govt. Board of Arbitrators on Defective Surveys, Chairman of Stock Commission, Chairman of Utrecht-Vryheid compensation Comm., Commissioner of Census, and member of Magistracies and Crown Lands Commissions. He was delegated to represent Natal at the opening of the Australian Commonwealth Parliament; received the C.M.G. in 1895 in connection with the Natal railway extension to the Transvaal, and was a member of the Railway Conferences at Pretoria and Cape Town, and the Customs Conference at Bloemfontein.

Sir Thomas is a Director of the Natal Bank, the Town Hill Wattle Co., and the Natal Tannery, and incidentally has been Pres. of the Natal Farmers' Congress, Maritzburg Agricultural Society, Caledonian Society, Natal Rugby Union, and the Natal Turf Club. He has also captained the Maritzburg County Cricket Club, and has won prizes for rifle shooting, racing, and athletic sports. He married, in 1877, Annie, dau. of Henry Procter.

NAPIER, Hon. Mark Francis, B.A., of 1, Temple Gardens, E.C., was born in 1852, and is son of the 10th Baron Napier and Ettrick, and was educated at Cambridge. From 1892-5 he was Liberal M.P. for Roxburgh, and is Chairman of the National Mutual Life Assurance Society, and director of the Dareheib and African Syndicate, Ltd., Egypt and Sudan Mining Syndicate, Ltd., Gold Fields of Mysore and General Exploration Co., Ltd., Mysore G.M. Co., Ltd., National Liberal Club Buildings Co., Ltd., New Kempenkote Gold Fields, Ltd., Nine Reefs Co., Ltd., Reuter's Telegram Co., Ltd., Sudan Gold Field, Ltd., and the Tasmania Gold Mining Co., Ltd. He married, in 1878, Emily, dau. of the 7th and last Viscount Ranelagh.

NAPIER of Magdala, Baron, of 9, Lowndes Sq., London, S.W., Lynedale, Isle of Skye, and of the Bachelors' and Carlton Clubs, was born in 1845, and is son of the late Gen. Sir Robert Napier, who brought to a successful conclusion the Abyssinian Campaign in 1868, having been present at the storming and taking of the fortress of Magdala, for which he received a baronetcy. The present Lord Napier succeeded his father, the first Baron, in 1890. He was privately educated, entering the

Army in 1860. From 1861-82 he served in the Bengal Army; taking part in the Umbeyla Campaign in 1864, and the Abyssinian Campaign in 1868, retiring from the Army in 1883. He married, in 1885, Eva, dau. of Lord Macdonald, a widow of Capt. Langham, of the Grenadier Guards.

NARIMAN, Dr. Pestonji Bhicaji, of Zanzibar, E. Africa, and of Fort K. Buildings, Frere Road, Bombay, is youngest son of Ervad Bhicaji Ruttonji Nariman, one of the early promoters of liberal English education in Nowsari, in the Bombay Presidency, and is a brother of Dr. Temulji Bhicaji Nariman, founder of the Parsee Maternity Hospital of Bombay. He was born at Nowsari in the dominion of H.H. the Gaikwar of Baroda; was educated at Grant Medical Coll., and is a graduate in medicine of the Bombay University, and as such holds the degree of Licentiate of Medicine and Surgery, 1884. He was appointed Physician to the Sultan of Zanzibar, Syed Khalifa, in 1888, and to the successive Sultans Syed Ali and Syed Ahmed Bin Thooini. On the formation of the Zanzibar Govt. he was appointed Surgeon to the Military Hospital, and was thanked by Rear-Admiral Sir Harry Rawson, C.I.C. of the Cape station, for assistance rendered in attending to the rebel wounded after the bombardment of he palace at Zanzibar in 1896. Dr. Nariman is decorated with the Orders of the Brilliant Star of Zanzibar (3rd cl. 1893, and 4th cl. 1901); the Order of Hamoudieh, 1897, and the Order of Syedi (3rd cl.). He married Bai Ruttonbai, youngest dau. of Ervad Rustoniji Cowasji Modi.

NATAL, Bishop of (see Right Rev. Henry Delalle).

NATHAN, Emil, J.P., of Johannesburg, Transvaal, and of the Rand and New Clubs (Johannesburg), was (born at Graaff Reinet, C.C., Dec. 23, 1859; is second son of the late Ed. Nathan, merchant, of that town, and was educated at Graaff Reinet Coll. He was Registrar of the Supreme Court, C.C., in 1880-81; was admitted as Solicitor and Notary Public of the Supreme Court in 1881; practised at Port Elizabeth until 1889, and during the last five years of his residence there was Deputy Sheriff of the town. From 1889 he practised at Johannesburg until 1895, when he proceeded to London, joined Gray's Inn, and was called to the Bar in 1898.

Returning to Johannesburg, Mr. Nathan continued his law practice until the war, in which he served as Lieut. and afterwards as Capt. in the J.M.R. Subsequently he was a member of the Permit Committee. He is a Director of a few Rand Cos., and married, Feb. 27, 1884, Lizzie, dau. of the late Henry Godfrey.

NATHAN, Manfred, B.A., LL.D., Advocate of the Supreme Courts of the Cape Colony, and Transvaal, and of the High Court of the late S. African Republic, of Johannesburg, and of the Rand, New, Savage (Johannesburg), and Pretoria Clubs, was born at Hanover, Cape Colony, in 1875, and is son of the late Carl Nathan, J.P. He joined the editorial staff of the *Johannesburg Star* in 1885, remaining with that paper throughout the Jameson Raid and the Reform trial; was on the staff when the paper was suppressed by the Kruger Govt., reappearing the following day under the title of *The Comet*. He obtained his LL.B. in 1897, and his LL.D. in 1901. In 1897 he was called to the Cape Bar, and since then has practised at the Bar of the Transvaal High Court. On the outbreak of the war he went to Cape Town and practised there, but in 1901 he returned to Johannesburg, where he has since maintained a leading position. He is the author of *The Legal Effect of War on Contracts* with Mr. W. H. S. Bell, *The Legal Handbook of British S. Africa*, *The Common Law of S. Africa*, and *The Company and Commercial Law of the Transvaal*, and has also contributed largely to S. African periodicals. Since 1903 he has been law examiner at the Cape Univ.; is President of the Jewish Board of Deputies for the Transvaal and Natal; member of the S.A. League; member of the Council of the Transvaal Philosophical Society, and of the Responsible Govt. Assn. He married, in 1903, Miss Mina Sessel.

NATHAN, Major Sir Matthew, R.E., K.C.M.G., of 11, Pembridge Sq., London, W., and the Army and Navy Clubs, was born in London Jan. 3, 1862. He is son of the late Jonah Nathan, of Pembridge Sq., and was educated privately and at the R.M.A., Woolwich. He entered the Royal Engineers in 1880, becoming Capt. in 1889, and Maj. in 1898. He served in the Nile Expedition in 1885, and in the Lushai Expedition in 1889 (medal with clasp). Sir Matthew acted as Secy. to the Colonial Defence Committee in 1895, administered the Govt. of

Sierra Leone in 1899, became Governor of the Gold Coast in 1900, and Governor and Commander-in-Chief of the Colony of Hong Kong and its Dependencies, Oct., 1903. He is unmarried.

NDUBE, a white Zulu chief, whose original name was N. Duby, was formerly a hooligan in the village of Schupfer, in the Bernese Oberland. After a particularly brutal attack on a cavalryman, in 1893, he was forced to leave the country, and he worked his way to South Africa. After being concerned in some transactions which demanded the attention of the police at Durban, he went into the interior to escape arrest. He mastered the Zulu language and finally married the dau. of the chief of a small tribe. On the death of the chief, Duby was appointed in his place. He fought with the Boers during the late South African War, and when Bambata revolted in the spring of 1906, Duby induced his tribesmen to join the rebel forces.

NEAME, Laurence Elwin, of Johannesburg; is eldest son of L. E. Neame, of Bristol, where he was born in 1875. He has had a varied journalistic experience abroad, and served for three years on the *Times of India* previous to his present appointment as News Editor of the *Rand Daily Mail*. Mr. Neame acts as S. African correspondent for some of the principal Indian journals, and has contributed to the *Empire Review*, *Chambers' Journal*, the *Westminster* and *Pall Mall Gazettes*, etc.

NEAVE, Sheffield, of 7, Great St. Helen's, London, E.C., is a partner in the firm of R. and T. Neave, general merchants. He is Chairman of the Vermilion Forks Mining and Development Co., Ltd., and director of the Gas Lighting Improvement Co., Ltd., Tanganyika Concessions, Ltd., and the Zambesi Exploring Co., Ltd. (See Robert Williams.)

NEEDHAM. Robert R., of Dashwood House, E.C., is Chairman of the Estates and Mining Co., of Rhodesia, Ltd., and the Prospectors of Matabeleland, Ltd., and is director of the Bulawayo and General Exploration Co., Ltd., Gwanda (Rhodesia) Consolidated Developing Co., Ltd., Rose of Sharon and Shamrock Gold Mines, Ltd., and the Waverley Block Gold Mines, Ltd.

NEETHLING, Hon. M. L., M.L.C., of Stellenbosch, Cape Colony comes of an old Prussian family. He was for many years Chairman of the Municipal Commissioners of Stellenbosch and member of the Divisional Council. He was elected Mayor of Robertson, Cape Colony, in 1905, and is a member of the Cape Legislative Council for the Western Province.

NESER, Johannes Adriaan, J.P., F.R.C.I., Mayor of Klerksdorp, Transvaal, was born in the Colesburg Dist. of Cape Colony, July 11, 1880, and is son of Christiaan Petrus Neser, a successful and progressive farmer. He was educated at Colesburg Dist. Sch. and at Victoria Coll., Stellenbosch, and was an undergraduate of the Cape Univ. He was then articled to various attorneys in the Cape Colony; was a partner of Sluiter at Colesburg from 1885-92; went to Klerksdorp and interested himself as far as the repressive policy of the late régime permitted in the interest of progress and in the practice of his profession of Attorney at Law and Notary Public. He is also J.P. for the Potchefstroom Dist. Upon the creation of Klerksdorp as a Municipality in 1903, he was elected Mayor, which office he still holds. He is a member of the Inter-Colonial Irrigation Commission, appointed in 1904 by Lord Milner, to inquire into the laws in force in the Transvaal and Orange River Colonies, regarding Irrigation, and to make recommendations for their amendment; is a patron of many forms of sport. He married, Dec. 11, 1886, Maria Angelina Roehlin, of Colesburg.

NEUMANN, Ludwig, of 11, Grosvenor Square London, W., and of Warnford Court, E.C., is a brother of Sigismund Neumann (q.v.) and a partner in the firm of Leo Hirsch and Co., one of the largest firms of Kaffir Brokers. He is on the London Committees of the S.A. Gold Mines Ltd., and the Witwatersrand Township, Estate and Finance Corporation, Ltd. Mr. L. Neumann races in England, and is a popular figure in Society.

NEUMANN, Sigismund, of Salisbury House, London E.C., of 146, Piccadilly, W., and of Invercauld, N.B., was born in Bavaria in 1856.

Spending most of his youth in Württemberg, he went to S.A., when still young, and founded the firm of S. Neumann and Co., mine owners, diamond buyers and financiers, of London and S.A. of which he is the chief partner. The firm, which included, up till recently, Mr. C. Sydney Goldmann (q.v.) and Mr. H. J. King among its partners, is chiefly identified with the following companies, which have admirable prospects of yielding a long series of dividends when normal conditions in S.A. are restored: Treasury, Wolhuter, New Modderfontein Consolidated M. R., Witwatersrand Deep, Knight Central, Driefontein Deep, African Farms, and Cloverfield Mines. Messrs. S. Neumann and Co. are associated with other large mining and financial groups in the control of the Randfontein Deep and the West Rand Consolidated Gold Mines, and it has representatives on the Boards of the Rand Mines, Rand Mines Deep, the East Rand Proprietary Mines, and its subsidiaries, the City Deep, South City, Wolhuter Deep, Klip Deep, South Wolhuter, Suburban Deep, the Turf Mines, the South African Gold Mines, and other Cos. They are also one of the chief owners of Salisbury House, a huge block of new buildings in London Wall. Mr. Neumann is also on the Board of the African Banking Corporation (see G. W. Thomson).

Mr. S. Neumann has for many years rented Invercauld, where Mrs. Neumann entertains on a large scale, and he has also a country seat near Newmarket. He is a good gun shot, and shows considerable skill at whist and bridge.

NEVILLE, George William, of 18, Sussex Place, Regent's Park; Weybridge, Surrey and of the Constitutional Club; was born June 4, 1852; entered the service of the African S.S. Co. in 1874; became Agent of the Co. at Bonny River in 1876, and Chief Agent for S.S. Cos. at Lagos in 1880. He was founder and first manager of the Bank of British West Africa, M.L.C., for Lagos Colony 1894-9, and was present at the fall of Benin city. He is now director of the Bank of British W. Africa and of the *Compagnie Belge Maritime du Congo*. He married in 1884, Elizabeth, dau. of E. Price-Lewis.

NEWBERRY, Charles, J.P., F.R.C.I., of Prynnsberg, O.R.C., was born at Brampton,

Huntingdon, May 17, 1841. He is son of W. Newberry, of Brampton, and was educated privately. He emigrated to Natal in 1864, and after a seven years' residence there transferred to the Kimberley Diggings, and later to the Basutoland border of the O.R.C., where he commenced tree planting on a large scale. He married Elizabeth Mary, dau. of the Rev. I. Daniel, of Thaba Nchu, O.R.C.

NEWPORT, Viscount, of Lowndes Sq., London, S.W., was born in 1873, and is son of the 4th Earl of Bradford. He was educated at Harrow and Trinity Coll., Cambridge. From 1902-5 he acted as Private Secy. to the Right Hon. Arthur Balfour. Lord Newport served with his regt., the Royal Scots, throughout the S. African War, 1900-02. He married the eldest dau. of Lord Aberdare.

NEWTON, Francis James, C.M.J., Barrister-at-Law, of Salisbury, Rhodesia; Hillingdon House, Uxbridge; and of Arthur's Club, was born at St. Croix, W.I., Sept. 13, 1857. He was educated at Rugby and Univ. Coll., Oxford, where he graduated M.A. He was A.D.C. to Sir Hercules Robinson in 1881, and acted as his Private Secy. from 1883-89. From 1890-95 he was Colonial Secy. and Receiver-Gen. for the Bechuanaland Protectorate, and was Resident Commissioner in Bechuanaland from 1895 until 1897. Later on he went to British Honduras as Colonial Secy., where he served from 1898-1901, occupying a similar position in. the Barbados during 1901-2, when he returned to England with a view to a further appointment in S. Africa. In the latter year he was appointed Treas. of S. Rhodesia and member of the Executive Council. Mr. Newton married, March 12, 1889, Henrietta, eldest dau. of R. Cloete, of Newlands, Cape Town.

NEYLAN, John Nolan, D.S.O., of the Cape Mounted Police, joined the F.A.M. Police in 1877, and served throughout the Gaika-Galeka War in 1877-8. He entered the Cape Mounted Rifles in 1879, and served with that corps during the Morosi campaign (medal and clasp); also throughout the Basuto War, and commanded No. 1 troop of the C.M.R. from 1881-2. In 1882 he resigned his commission in the corps and became clerk in the commissariat department. In the same year he was

appointed an inspector of the Cape Police; served in Bechuanaland in 1896-7 (clasp), and in the South African War in 1899-1902, in command of Neylan's Orange River Scouts; present at the operations in Cape Colony, south of the Orange River (despatches and D.S.O.): He became district inspector of the C.M.P. in 1903, and in 1905 was appointed acting commissioner.

NICHOLSON, Right Hon. Sir Arthur, Bart., G.C.M.G., G.C.V.O., K.C.B., K.C.I.E., of the British Embassy, St. Petersburg; formerly served in Persia; was in Morocco, and acted as the British Plenipotentiary at the Moroccan Conference at Algeçiras in 1906, his services there being rewarded by the Grand Cross of the Order of St. Michael and St. George. Sir Arthur is now Ambassador Extraordinary and Plenipotentiary at St. Petersburg.

NICHOLSON, Lieut. Col. John S., C.B., D.S.O., was born in 1868. He is son of W. Nicholson, of Basing Park, and brother of W. G. Nicholson, M.P. for E. Hants. Obtained his commission in the 7th Hussars in 1884; went to Bulawayo as an Imperial representative to take over the command of the M.M.P. very soon after the outbreak of the Matabele War (1896), rendering conspicuous services till the close of the campaign in Matabeleland. Towards the end of 1896 he was appointed Commandant of the Chartered Co.'s forces north of the Zambesi. Col. Nicholson served in the South African War in 1899-1900, at first in command of the B.S.A. Police, and afterwards in command of the 1st Brigade of the Rhodesian Field Force, being mentioned in despatches and receiving the brevet rank of Lieut. Col. He joined the South African Constabulary in Oct., 1900, and in May, 1903, became Inspector-Gen. of that force. In that capacity he acquired a seat on the Inter-Colonial Council.

NICHOLSON, Lieut.-Gen. Sir William G., K.C.B., R.E. When Lord Roberts left England for South Africa at the end of 1899 he at once telegraphed to Sir William Nicholson offering him employment on his staff, and, the offer being accepted, he reached Cape Town in time to go forward with the main column, and was thus able to take part in the operations in the Orange Free

State (Feb. to May, 1900), the actions at Paardeberg, Poplar Grove, Driefontein, Vet River, Tina River, and those subsequently in the Transvaal, including Johannesburg, Pretoria, and Diamond Hill. He was twice mentioned in despatches, and besides obtaining the Queen's medal with five clasps was specially promoted to the rank of Major-Gen. Subsequently Sir William proceeded to the Far East as Military Attaché with the Japanese Army in Manchuria, and in 1905 was appointed Governor and C.I.C. of Gibraltar in succession to Sir Geo. White.

NICHOLSON, William S., J.P., of Eastmore, Yarmouth, Isle of Wight; is a member of the Council of the Union Castle Mail Steamship Co., Ltd. (See Sir Donald Currie.)

NICOL, A. F., of Uplands, Woldingham, Surrey, is a director of the Anglo-Klondike Mining Co., Ltd., and is on the London Committees of the Clydesdale (Transvaal) Collieries, Ltd., Driefontein Deep, Ltd., Geygerle, Ltd., Home Coal Estates, Ltd., New Era Consolidated, Ltd., and the Roodepoort Central Deep, Ltd.

NIGHTINGALE, Dr. Percy Athelstan, M.B., C.M., M.D., of 5, Hertford St., Mayfair, W., was born at Robertson, Cape Colony, Oct. 7, 1867, and is second son of the late Percy Nightingale, Inspecting Civil Commissioner, Cape Colony. He was educated at Edinburgh Univ. After graduating there and holding the appointment of Resident Physician and Registrar at the City (Fever) Hospital, he was from 1891-4 one of the Medical Officers to the Government of Johore, Malay Peninsular, and in 1893 he travelled through Europe as Physician-in-Ordinary to H.H. the late Sultan of Johore. In 1894 he went to Siam and became Physician to the British Legation, Bangkok, Physician to the Royal Palace, and Surgeon to the Police. He founded the Public Health Dept. in 1897, and was appointed the first Medical Officer of Health in Siam. In 1898 he graduated M.D. at Edinburgh Univ., taking honours for his thesis on Beri Beri; went to India in 1899 and made a special report on the Plague there for H.M. the King of Siam. Subsequently he organised and had charge of the Quarantine Regulations against Plague in Siam. He represented the Siamese Govt. as their Delegate

at the International Medical Congresses held at Brussels in 1902-3, and has written various papers on medical, tropical, and electrical subjects. He married, in 1899, Muriel, dau. of Charles S. Collison, of E. Bilney, Norfolk.

NIGHTINGALE, Thomas Slingsby, of Kneesworth, Limpsfield, Surrey, and 100, Victoria St., Westminster, and of the Royal Societies Club, was born at Bedford, C.C., Jan. 29, 1866. He is eldest son of the late Percy Nightingale, Inspecting Civil Commissioner, C.C. (d. 1895), and great-grandson of Sir Chas. F. Nightingale, 7th Bart., of Kneesworth Hall, Cambridgeshire, and was educated at the Royal Naval Sch., New Cross, and at St. George's Sch., Brampton, Huntingdon. He joined the Cape Civil Service as Clerk, and after filling various minor offices at K. W. Town, Cape Town, P. Elizabeth, and Kimberley, became Acting R.M., Sub Collector of Customs and Port Officer at Port Nolloth in 1891, and first-class Clerk and Asst. Warehouse Keeper Customs Dept. at East London (C.C.) and Port Elizabeth in 1896. In Nov., 1898, he was appointed Chief Clerk in the London office of the Cape Agent-Gen.; became Asst.-Secy. in April, 1902, and Secy. Jan. 1, 1905. He was appointed, under Rule 274, a Commissioner of the Supreme Court of the C.C. Mr. Nightingale married, in 1900, Doris, dau. of Chas. S. Collison, of East Bilney, Norfolk.

NILAND, B., M.L.A., represents the electoral division of Fort Beaufort in the Cape Parliament, to which he was elected in the Progressive interest in Feb., 1904.

NIND, Charles Edward, of the Conservative (London), the Kimberley, Rand, Civil Service (C.T.) and City (C.T.) Clubs, is son of the Rev. P. H. Nind, of Woodcote House, Oxon., where he was born Aug. 24, 1847. He was educated at Marlborough Coll. Originally in business for some years in Bombay and Burma, he went to S.A. in 1881, and has resided in Kimberley mostly since that time. He is a Director of the De Beers Consolidated Mines and various other S.A. Cos.

NIVEN, A. Mackie, of Johannesburg, is one of the oldest members of the Johannesburg Stock Exchange, and represents the Witwatersrand Deep,

Ltd., in the Transvaal Chamber of Mines. He acted as Chairman of the Rand Labour Commission, and is a strict vegetarian.

NOBLE, Major, was born in 1859, and is the eldest son of Sir Andrew Noble, Chairman of the great Elswick works. He was educated at Harrow and Sandhurst, joined the 13th Hussars in 1880, and served with that regiment in Afghanistan, India, and Natal. When the South African War broke out Major Noble volunteered for active service, and went out with the remounts in March, 1900. In 1905 he unsuccessfully contested North Westmorland in the Unionist interest at the by-election.

NORBURY, Insp.-Gen. Sir Henry Frederick, K.C.B., M.D., F.R.C.S., Eng., of St. Margaret's, Eltham, Kent, was born at Wool, Haversham, Dorset. He was educated at St. Bartholomew's Hosp., Lond., and the University, Malta; he is Insp.-Gen. of Hospitals and Fleets in the R.N., and was for several years Director-Gen. of the Med. Dept. at the Admiralty; was Staff Surgeon of the Active Flagship on the Cape of Good Hope and West Coast of Africa stations from 1876-9, and served on shore with the Naval Brigade during the Kaffir War in 1877-8 (twice mentioned in despatches). During the Zulu War in 1879, he was Principal Med. Officer of Sir C. Pearson's column, and of the garrison of Fort Eshowe during the time of its investment by the Zulus, and after its relief by Lord Chelmsford, was P.M.O. of the Naval Brigade and advanced a second time into the Zulu country (several times mentioned in despatches, both naval and military; created a C.B. (military), and promoted to the rank of Fleet Surgeon; medal with three clasps). In 1879 he was awarded the Blane Gold Medal. Gen. Norbury was Insp.-Gen. of the Royal Naval Hosp., Plymouth, from 1895-98, is Honorary Surgeon to H.M. King Edward VII., a Knight of Grace of the Order of St. John of Jerusalem in Eng., and an honorary Fellow of the Royal Coll. of Surgeons, Eng.; he has received the Jubilee and Coronation medals and was created K.C.B. in 1897. He is the author of *The Naval Brigade in S. Africa*, and married in March, 1868, Mina, dau. of E. G. Wade Brown.

NORMAN-LEE, Rev. Frederic Bethune Norman, F.R.G.S., of Alexandria, Egypt, and of the Army and Navy Club, Lond., was born in London, Sept. 14, 1855, and was educated at the City of London Sch. and St. John's Coll., Camb., where he graduated M.A. Mr. Lee (as he was before his father, the Rev. Thos. Lee, prefixed his wife's name of Norman in 1881) joined the Victoria Rifles in 1872, and the Camb. Univ. Volunteers (now attached to the Suffolk Regt.) in 1875, shooting in intervarsity rifle teams in 1876-7, when he won the N.R.A. bronze medal as the best shot in both universities in 1876. He was ordained in 1882 by the Lord Bishop of Rochester, and received a commission to her late Majesty's Land Forces, Jan. 19, 1884, serving variously at home stations, Nova Scotia, and afterwards in the S. African War, 1899-1900, as senior Chaplain to the VI. division, when he was present at the relief of Kimberley, the operations at Paardeberg, and the actions at Poplar Grove and Driefontein (Queen's medal and three clasps). In Aug., 1903, the Rev. Norman-Lee arrived in Alexandria as Senior Chaplain (C. of E.) in Egypt. He is a freeman of the City of London, and took up his freedom by patrimony in the Leathersellers Co. in 1878, and will in due time become its worshipful master, He is an enthusiastic Freemason; has been Grand Chaplain to all the Grand Bodies in England, as well as Past Grand Officer of Canada, and is at present District Grand Chaplain of Egypt and Sudan. Mr. Norman-Lee has travelled in the U.S.A., Canada, Europe, Turkey, and Asia Minor, etc., besides in countries already mentioned, and has taken a great interest in the work of the St. John Ambulance Association, both in Nova Scotia and in England. He married, in 1888, Margaret Corestine, dau. of the Rev. Wm. Coates, MA., of Co. Meath, and granddau. of the late Lt.-Gen. Sir Edmund de Gonville Bromhead, Bart., C.B.

NORRIE, Ebenezer Steven, of the New Club, Johannesburg, was born in New Zealand. He is second son of the Rev. Thos. Norrie, Presbyterian Minister of Papakura, Auckland, N.Z., who married Elizabeth Angus, eldest dau. of the late Ebenezer Steven, of Glasgow. Mr. Norrie joined the staff of the South British Fire and Marine Insurance Co. of New Zealand, in 1884, and arrived in Johannesburg in Feb., 1893, as the

Transvaal Representative of that institution which is there domiciled in its own premises. Mr. Norrie is a non-resident Fellow (for life) of the R.C.I.

NORRIS-NEWMAN, Capt., was appointed Staff Officer in the R.H.V. at the outbreak of the second Matabele War (1896).

NORTH, Frederic William, F.G.S., M.I.M.E., M.I.M.M., of the Junior Conservative Club, Piccadilly, Commissioner for South Staffordshire Mines Drainage Acts, 1873 to 1894, Mining and Civil Engineer; was born at Ballston, in the heart of the South Staffordshire Mining District, where his father, William North, was a Coal Master and Mining Engineer. He was privately educated at Wolverhampton, and in 1860 was articled to his father, who acted as Mining Agent for many colliery proprietors. In 1866 he became a partner with his father, who was then resident at Dudley (of which he was twice Mayor), the firm being William North and Son. At this time they were largely interested as coal masters and mining engineers in their own county, South Wales, and in the Forest of Dean, and the activity of the junior partner, together with his professional knowledge, helped to secure for the firm a wide practice in the development of the new mining enterprises which sprang into existence in the colliery boom of 1873. Amongst these were the Aldridge Colliery Company, near Walsall, at that time the deepest in the county, the Cannock and Wimblebury at Cannock Chase, the important Sandwell Park Colliery enterprise, and also the Cannock and Huntington Colliery upon Lord Hatherton's estate, which resulted in discovering coal there, and in considerably extending the then known Western boundary of the coalfield. In 1876 at this latter colliery, owing to the rush of water discovered by the preliminary borings, Mr. North introduced into England the Kind-Chaudron method of sinking through aqueous strata without pumping. At this time Mr. North was also General Manager and part owner of the Rowley Hail Colliery, which he had superintended from its inception in the year 1864. In April, 1877, he was appointed by the Crown Agents for the Colonies to visit Cape Colony to inspect and report upon the supposed coalfield in the Stormbergen District. During his inspection of the coalfield he made an exhaustive test of the carboniferous deposits at the Indwe River in the Tamboekie native location. Soon afterwards the War with the neighbouring Galeka Chief Krelli broke out, causing his examination to be hastily concluded. In 1878 he visited the Kimberley Diamond Mines, and at the request of Sir Owen Lanyon, K.C.B., the then Administrator of Griqualand West, he examined the whole of the neigbbourhood as to the possibility of either coal or water being found by systematic boring.

Returning to England he was one of the first mining engineers to give information, publicly upon the diamond mine, and read a paper in Sept., 1878, to the Institute of South Staffordshire Mining Engineers, in which he made many interesting forecasts which have since turned out to be astonishingly accurate. In 1879 he took the contract for the construction of the Port Elizabeth Water Works, in which contract he was subsequently joined by Mr. John Mackie, who constructed the pipe line from Port Elizabeth to the Van Standen River. In 1880, at the request of Sir Henry Bulwer, the Governor of Natal, he visited that Colony to inspect and report upon the coal deposits.

He returned to England in 1881, and in June, 1882 upon the death of the senior partner, the whole of the work devolved upon him with the entire management and control of the extensive Rowley Rail Collieries, of which he had now become the predominant partner. In Johannesburg Mr. North subsequently in 1889 joined in taking up a block of claims formerly the South Simmer and Jack Co., and which was ultimately absorbed by the Simmer and Jack G.M. Co.

Returning to England he sold the Rowley Hall Colliery, and devoted himself to his profession in London. In 1895 he became connected with West Australian mining, and was the first Chairman of the Golden Horseshoe G.M. Co. He also became professionally interested in coal mines in Southern Russia, France, and Spain, and still later acted as Consulting Engineer for the Consolidated Kent Collieries Corporation, Limited, whilst the Kind-Chaudron process of sinking was being carried out at that troublesome sinking.

MR. F. W. NORTH

MR. LIONEL PHILLIPS

THE RIGHT HON. LORD PIRRIE

MR. T. R. PRICE

NOTCUTT, Henry Clement, B.A., of Stellenbosch, Cape Colony, and of the Civil Service Club, Cape Town, was born at Cheltenham in 1865. He was educated at the London Univ.; went out to Cape Colony in 1895, and was appointed Asst. Professor at the S. African Coll., Cape Town, which appointment he held for four and a half years, subsequently becoming Headmaster of the Boys' High Sch., Kimberley. During the siege of that town he served in the Cycle Corps of the Town Guard, and published an account of it, entitled *How Kimberley was held for England*. He was elected President of the S. African Teachers' Assn. in 1902; became a member of the Council of the Univ. of the Cape of Good Hope in 1903, and was appointed Professor of English Language and Literature in the same year; has published editions of *Macbeth*, and *England in 1685* (the third chapter of Macaulay's History). He married, in 1904, Lilian, dau. of the late Geo. Healey, of Kimberley.

NOURSE, A. D., who played for S. Africa in 1905-6 against the M.C.C. team, scored an average of 62 runs per innings for the first three Test matches, which won the rubber for the Colonial XI. Mr. Nourse has not played cricket in England.

NOURSE, Henry, of Johannesburg, has been identified with the Golden City since the very early days, his name being especially associated with the Henry Nourse Gold Mining Company, which he represents in the Transvaal Chamber of Mines.

NUNAN, Hon. Joseph John, F.R.C.S., Judge of H.M. High Court of British Central Africa, Judge of H.M. Court of Appeal for East Africa; of the Pilgrims Club; is son of Patrick Lewis Nunan, of Limerick, Ireland, where Judge Nunan was born in 1873. He was educated abroad, and at University Coll., and Trinity Coll., Dublin, graduating B.A. and LL.B. He is Fellow and Scholar of the Royal University Ireland, Blake Scholar and Vice-Chancellor's Prizeman, Dublin Univ., Gold and Silver Medalist, etc., and was called to the Bar in 1898. From 1894 to 1899 he acted as Officer of the High Court of Justice, Ireland, under the Master of the Rolls; was appointed H.B.M. Vice-Consul and Chief Judicial Officer for the B.C.A. Protectorate, Aug. 12, 1899; presiding Judge of the High Court of B.C.A., and Judge of H.M.

Appeal Court for East Africa, Aug. 11, 1902, and Pres. of the Native Land Commission, B.C.A. In Dec., 1905, he was appointed Solicitor-Gen. for British Guiana. He was some time in the 14th Middlesex Volunteers, and in 1902 originated the B.C.A. Volunteer Reserve. He acted as a Protectorate draughtsman from 1900 to 1905, and is author of *Islam before the Turk*.

NUNN, Capt. Thomas Henry Clayton D.S.O., of the Army and Navy Club, was born Aug. 11, 1873, and is son of the Rev. John B. Nunn. He entered the Army in 1891, and joined the West Kent Regt. in 1894; took part in the S. African War in 1900-2, as Adjt. in the 27th Battn. of Mounted Inf. (Queen's medal and five clasps, mentioned in despatches, and D.S.O.); was given a Staff appointment as Adjt. in the Egyptian Mounted Inf. 1902-5. He married, May 8, 1902, Miss Aileen Tatham.

OAKES, Capt. Richard, is son of the late Col. R. F. Oakes, R.E., his mother being dau. of the late Rev. T. J. Trevenen, of St. Austell, Cornwall. Capt. Oakes was born at Torquay, March 12, 1876; was educated at Harrow and the Royal Military Academy, Woolwich; and joined the Royal Engineers, March 21, 1896; promoted Lieutenant, 1899; and Captain, 1905. He served through the Boer War, 1899-1902, being present at the Battles of Belmont and Modder River, and was twice mentioned in despatches, receiving the Queen's medal with four clasps, and the King's medal with two clasps. During the War he was employed on the railway, and since July, 1902, has been employed on the Central South African Railways, as Loco. Supt. of the Pretoria District. Capt. Oakes married, on April, 22, 1908, Mabel Caroline, dau. of Charles Trubshaw, of Derby, who died the following February.

OATS, Francis, M.L.A., of Kimberley and of St. Just, Cornwall, is member of the Cape Legislative Assembly for the electoral division of Namaqualand, for which he was last re-elected in Feb., 1904. He supports the Progressive Party; is a Director of the De Beers and a few other S.A. Cos.

O'BRIEN, A. S. M., formerly Resident Justice of the Bight, San Salvador, Bahamas, was transferred to the West Coast of Africa in 1905.

O'BRIEN, Lieut. Col. Charles Richard Mackey, acted as Pres. of the Military Tribunal at Johannesburg in 1900-1. During 1901-2 he acted as Personal Assistant to the Commissioner of Police, and also served in the late S. African War. In 1901 he was appointed Deputy Commissioner of the Rand and Mounted Police, which post he still retains.

O'CALLAGHAN, Sir Francis Langford, K.C.M.G. (1902), C.I.E. (May, 1883), C.S.I. (Jan., 1888), of Crichmere, Guildford, and of the Royal Societies Club, is the son of the late James O'Callaghan, J.P., of Drisheen, County Cork, and is descended directly from one of the Chiefs of the Clan or Sept of O'Callaghans outlawed by Charles I. in 1642. He was born July 22, 1839, at Kilcornan Rectory, Limerick, and educated at private schools and at Queen's Coll., Cork. He graduated M.E. Royal (formerly Queen's) Univ., Ireland. He is M.I.C.E. since 1872, and F.R.G.S. He entered the service of the Govt. of India in the Public Works Dept. under covenant with the Secy. of State for India in June, 1862. He was posted to the Central Provinces, then governed by the late Sir Richard Temple; was frequently mentioned favourably in the Administration Reports by that and subsequent Governors. He was posted to the State Hallways branch in 1870, when that branch was organised by Lord Mayo, then Viceroy of India. He rose quickly through the various grades of the Dept., and in 1889 succeeded Sir Guildford Molesworth as Consulting Engineer. During this period he was Engineer-in-Chief for the construction of various State Railways, and was several times thanked by the Govt. of India for his services. In 1892 he was appointed Secy. to the Govt. of India, and retired from the service under the age rule in 1894. He was created C.I.E. for construction of the bridge over the Indus at Attock, and C.S.I. for the building of the railway through the Bolan Pass in 1885-86. In Sept., 1895, he was selected as Managing member (or Director) of the Uganda Railway Committee at the Foreign Office, and it was in recognition of his services on that Committee that he received the K.C.M.G. among the Coronation honours in 1902. Sir Francis is now Director of the Burma State Railways Co. and of

the Egyptian Delta Light Railways Co. He married, on Sept. 22, 1875, A. M. Powell, dau of Col. Powell, of Banlahan, County Cork.

OCHS, Albert L., of 34, Clement's Lane London, E.C., is a partner in the firm of Ochs Bros., and is a director of the International Ethiopian Railway Trust and Construction Co. Ltd., London and South African Agency, Ltd. Marconi International Marine Communication Co., Ltd., Marconi's Wireless Telegraph Co. Ltd., Mozambique Co., New African Co., Ltd. and the Oceana Consolidated Co., Ltd.

O'CONNER, Gen., commenced his military career in the Corps of Guides which distinguished itself before Metz. During the second siege of Paris, necessitated by the Commune he was A.D.C. to De Galliffet. He campaigned in Tunis and commanded the Cavalry in Tonking. He is now engaged in active operations in Morocco.

ODDIE, Colonel H., of Beaudesert, Ascot, is on the London Committee of the Alexandra Estate and G. M. Co., Ltd., Knight Central, Ltd., Modderfontein Deep Levels, Ltd., New Modderfontein G. M. Co., Ltd., and the Potchefstroom Exploration G. M. and Estate, Ltd.

O'DWYER, Arthur Williamson, F.A.S. F.R.C.I., of Old Calabar, is the son of Maj. Gage Hall O'Dwyer, late of the 1st Indian Regt. He was born Feb. 21, 1861, at Freetown, Sierra Leone, and was educated at the Roman Catholic and Wesleyan High Schs. at Freetown. Mr. O'Dwyer entered the Public Works Dept. as Clerk in 1878, and was transferred to Customs and Harbour Master's Office, 1879. He relinquished office for mercantile pursuits in 1880, and travelled to the Oil Rivers, now Southern Nigeria, and became Consular Clerk to E. H. Hewett, C.M.G., H.M. Consul-Gen. for Bights of Benin and Biafra, 1888. He saw active service during the blockade of Opobo, 1889 and was mentioned in despatches and received the thanks of H.M.'s Secy. of State for Foreign Affairs. Mr. O'Dwyer served respectively as Store Keeper to the Protectorate Administration, and Paymaster of the Chartered yacht *Whydah*. He was appointed Clerk of the Post Office in 1894, Chief Clerk, 1897, and Postmaster in 1900. He was transferred to Pay and Quartermaster's Office, Southern Nigeria Regt., in 1902. He is unmarried.

OGSTON, Dr. Alexander, M.D., LL.D., of 252, Union St., Aberdeen; Glendavan, Dinnet, Aberdeenshire, and of the Junior Conservative Club, was born April 14, 1844, and is son of Prof. F. Ogston, LL.D. He was educated at Aberdeen and abroad; served as a Volunteer in the Suakin Campaign in 1884-5; part of which time under the Red Cross Society (Queen's medal and clasp, Khedive's medal); and took part in the S. African War as a Volunteer in 1890 (medal and two clasps). He served on Mr. Brodrick's War Office Committee on the reorganisation of the R.A.M.C. in 1901, and was a witness before the S.A. War Commission in 1902. He is an Examiner in Surgery at the R.A.M. Coll, and is a Director of the North of Scotland Bank, Ltd., and author of numerous writings on medical, surgical, and other subjects. He married, first in 1867, Mary, dau. of James Hargrave, of the Hudson Bay service; and, secondly, in 1877, Isabella, dau. of James Matthews, of Springhill, Lord Provost of Aberdeen.

OHLSSEN, A., of Cape Town, is head of the Ohlssen Brewery Company, a prosperous undertaking, which Mr. Ohlssen established many years ago at Cape Town.

OLDFIELD, Frank Stanley, F.R.C.I., of the Durham Club, Natal, was born Sept. 26, 1875, and was educated at the East London Technical Coll., afterwards studying engineering at King's Coll., London. Commencing his professional career with Messrs. Walter A. Hills and Son, Architects and Surveyors in 1893, he went to Natal in 1902 as Sewerage Engineer to the Dublin Corporation. Unmarried.

OLIPHANT, Major-Gen. Sir Laurence James, K.C.V.O., C.B., was born in 1846 He served in the Sudan Campaign in 1885 (Khedive's star, medal and clasp). From 1894-8 he commanded the Grenadier Guards, and subsequently was in command of a brigade at Aldershot. He served in S. Africa in 1901-2 on the Staff of the S. African Field Force; was in command of the Home Dist. and of the Second Guards' Brigade in 1903. and at present commands the London District. He was created KCVO. on the occasion of the King's birthday, 1905.

OLIVER, H. A., M.L.A., is one of the four Progressive members for Namaqualand, for which electoral division he was returned in Feb, 1904. He speaks lucidly and forcibly, and is regarded as a considerable acquisition to the debating power of the House.

O'MEARA, Major Walter Alfred John, C.M.G., late R.E., of Simla Lodge, Sunbury Common, Middlesex, and of the Royal Societies Club, was born Jan. 28, 1863, and is the eldest son of the late Alfred O'Meara, of Simla, India. He was educated at the R.M.A., Woolwich, and the Sch. of Military Engineering, Chatham, and joined the R. Engineers in 1883. He proceeded to India in 1885 and took part with the 5th Co. Bengal Sappers in the hostilities in Upper Burma. He went to S. Africa in 1894, and was in charge of the Table Bay defences for nearly two and a half years. After the Jameson Raid in 1895 he was selected by Gen. Goodenough to accompany Col. Morgan Crofton to Mafeking and Pitsani to take over the arms and ammunition of the Chartered Co. He came to England in 1896 to study at the Staff Coll., and after the failure of the negotiations between Sir A. Milner and President Kruger at Bloemfontein in the early part of 1899 he was one of a party of special service officers sent to S. Africa in that year. He served through the war in 1899-1902 (Queen's medal with five clasps, and C.M.G.), and was appointed Govt. Commissioner of Johannesburg in 1901, which position he resigned in 1902 in order to accept the post of Asst. Engineer-in-Chief, at the General Post Office. He retired from the Army in 1903. He married, Sept., 1892, Annie, dau. of Col. W. Graves.

O'MOLONY, Chidley Kearnan, J.P., of Kiltanon House, Kimberley, is the son of Lieut. Henry Anthony O'Molony, was born at Cawnpore, Jan., 1845, while the first Sikh War was raging, his father being present at the battles of Moodkee, Ferozeshah, Aliwal, and Sobraon. Mr. O'Molony comes of the very ancient Milesian family of Molony, of Kiltanon, Co. Clare, his father was second sun of Lambert Molony, formerly a Judge in the H.E.I.C.S., and again assumed the prefix which was dropped by the head of the family after the Revolution of 1688, the family name still remaining without the prefix. His early years were spent in the Royal Navy, retiring from the service soon after obtaining a first-class certificate fur the rank of Paymaster. He served in Australia and in New Zealand during the closing periods of the Maori War in the sixties; also in the South Sea Islands, including the Samoa and Fiji groups; in the Channel Fleet, and on the West Coast of Africa. Mr. O'Molony was mentioned in despatches by Col. (now Gen.) Kekewich for services in his Civil capacity during the siege of Kimberley by the Boers in 1899-1900.

Mr. O'Molony is Town Clerk and Treas. of the important borough of Kimberley, in which capacity he has served for many years and still holds the appointment. He is a J.P. for the District of Kimberley, of a studious disposition, and fund of shooting. He married, in 1872, Emma, dau. of the late Selwyn Schofield Sugden, formerly Deputy Gov., of H.M. Prison at Gibraltar. Of his four children one son, Chidley Selwyn Anthony, is in the service of the O.R.C., another, Ernest Andrew, is in the Cape Govt. Railway Service, and a third, Frederick Sugden, is at present an undergraduate at the South African College, Cape Town.

OOSTHUIZEN, Okkert Almero, M.L.A., is Bond member of the Cape Legislative Assembly for the electoral division of Jansenville, for which he was re-elected in Feb., 1904.

ORKIN, Abraham, F.R.C.I., of Johannesburg, was born at Riga, Russia, Jan. 6, 1879, and was educated at Riga and Berlin. He arrived in S. Africa when quite young, and settled at first at Philippolis, O.R.C., but left there for East London (CC.), in 1901. After the War he settled in Johannesburg, establishing the timber business of Hillman Bros., of which he is a partner. Unmarried.

ORMSBY, S., a Special Duty Officer under the Sub Commissioner of Kampala, Uganda, with charge of the Kakermiro Station.

O'RORKE, Rev. Benjamin Garnisa, of 9, Magdala Road, Nottingham, and Robert's Heights, Pretoria, S. Africa, was born at Nottingham, April 7, 1875, and is son of William Joseph O'Rorke. He was educated at Nottingham High Sch., and Exeter Coll., Oxford; was ordained Deacon in 1898, and priest in 1899 by the Bishop of Exeter. From 1898-1901 he acted as Curate of St. Peter's, Tiverton, Devon; served with the S. African Field Force in 1901-2 (medal and four clasps). He was stationed at Aldershot from 1902-4; Bloemfontein from 1904-5 when he was transferred to Robert's Heights, Pretoria, which position he still holds. He has travelled in Switzerland, Belgium, E. Africa, and Uganda. Recreations : Tennis, running and cycling. Unmarried.

ORPEN, Joseph Millard, F.R.C.I., of Barkly East, C.C., is son of the late Rev. Charles Edward Herbert Orpen, M.D., F.R.C.P. Lon., F.R.C.S., Dublin, was born in Dublin, Nov. 1828, and educated privately.

Mr. Orpen is probably the oldest of the S. African Parliamentarians, and was until late in 1903 Surveyor-Gen. of Rhodesia, having administered its Dept. of Lands and Agriculture since 1896. He was also a member of its Legislative and Executive Councils.

On Dec. 24, 1846, when just turned seventeen, he arrived with three of his brothers in Table Bay. Thence they went to their elder brother's farm, Taaiboschfontein, in the then Coleberg District, between Nasuwpoort and De Aar. After a few months' study with his father, who arrived in the Colony with his wife and the rest of the family in Jan., 1848, Mr. Orpen, in 1849 passed his theoretical and practical examination for a Cape Govt. Land Surveyorship, and received that appointment as well as a Justiceship of the Peace early in 1851. In the Kafir War of that year, he served as a Lieut. of Volunteers. Early in 1852, he, with his elder brother, F. H. S. Orpen, undertook to survey for the Govt. of the then Orange River Sovereignty the Harrismith or Vaal River District of that Colony. In Aug., 1853, H.M. Minister announced, through a Special Commission sent to Bloemfontein, their intention to abandon the territory immediately, calling upon its European inhabitants to elect delegates and constitute a Republican Govt. Mr. Orpen and his brother were elected delegates at Harrismith and received instructions from their constituents to protest against and resist abandonment. The Assembly of Delegates, of which Mr. J. Orpen is the only surviving member, met on Sept. 5, 1853, and, after a short session, passed a unanimous protest against abandonment, and elected a standing committee to represent the permanently in so doing. Of this committee Mr. Orpen and his brother, who had each taken a prominent part in the Assembly's proceedings, were elected members. The committee supported a public deputation, which proceeded to England to petition the Govt. against abandonment, but on Sept. 23, 1854, H.M. Special Commissioner formally abandoned the territory, removed the troops and Govt. officers, and handed over the administration to those who had, under his encouragement, organised a movement in favour of abandonment. In the Convention which thus created the O.F.S. Republic, it was, however stipulated that an elective constituent and Legislative Council should he called together within three mouths, and Mr. Orpen was at once re-elected by Harrismith to represent it in the first Volksraad of the Free State. He then took a leading part in the framing of the Constitution of that State, which lasted, with little modification, till the recent fall of the two Republics. After the prorogation of the Volksraad (of which Mr. Orpen is, likewise, the sole survivor), he was appointed by the Pres. to conduct negotiations and open up friendly relations with Moshesh, the aged Chief of Basutoland, which had been received under the Queen's sovereignty and then abandoned by H.M. Govt. After Mr. Orpen had successfully opened these negotiations and relations, the Pres. at the public request of the inhabitants of the District of Winburg, induced him to accept the position of Landdrost of that district. To it the District of Harrismith was annexed by a resolution of the Volksraad in its next session. Thus Mr. Orpen was given the fiscal and magisterial administration of two thirds of the Free State, which, being bounded by the Vaal River, then included a considerable territory afterwards comprised in the Transvaal Republic. His position included an ex officio membership both of the Volksraad and of the Supreme Court of Justice and

Appeal, which was called The Court of Combined Landdrosts, and consisted of three of those officials. In this court Mr. Orpen at times presided, being then only twenty four years of age. Within a few months of his appointment (in Sept., 1854), Mr. Orpen had to deal with the first attempt on the part of the adherents of Comdt-.Gen. Marthinus Pretorius, of the Transvaal, to overthrow the Govt. of the O.F.S. By diplomacy, however, Mr. Orpen was successful in frustrating this attempt, though it was renewed, in an armed invasion by Pretorius and Kruger, a few years later. Cooperating with the Paramount Chief of the Basutos, Mr. Orpen produced a satisfactory state of affairs on the whole Basuto border of his District, while he successfully repressed attempts by burghers of the Free State to kidnap native children beyond and within its borders. In connection with this practice of kidnapping, Mr. Orpen was sent on a mission to the territories north of Natal, and so demonstrated the extensive nature of that practice, that legislation against it was passed in the Cape Parliament and the Free State Volksraad. In 1856, Mr. Orpen was deputed by the Pres. to represent him in giving directions on the spot to officers of a Free State Commando, sent to coerce the native chief, Wietzie, and remove him from the Harrismith District, where he was occupying farms granted to whites during the British régime. During this commando, Mr. Orpen (with difficulty and by his own action alone) restored to their mothers a number of native children who had been seized by members of the commando. The first expeditionary force, having broken up without accomplishing its object, the Pres. gave Mr. Orpen authority to raise and take command of another commando, with which he carried the operations to a successful conclusion. In the Presidential speech at the opening of the next session of the Raad, these services were brought to the notice of the Assembly, and at the conclusion of the session a vote of thanks for these and other services was accorded to him. He soon afterwards resigned and retired to the District of Aliwal North, in the C.C., where the Governor, Sir George Grey, entrusted him with extensive surveys. Seeing that a war was imminent between the Free State and the Basutos over a question of disputed frontier, he used his influence with the Paramount Chief, Moshesh, to induce him to propose to the Pres. that all questions at issue should be referred to the arbitration of the Governor of the Cape. This proposal was not accepted, and the Pres., after repulsing an invasion by Pretorius and Kruger, declared war upon Moshesh, but being unsuccessful, eventually proposed to Moshesh the very mediation which he had before declined, also begging Sir George Grey to press it upon Moshesh. The latter at once accepted it, and, acting on Mr. Orpen's advice, commenced a series of petitions to the British Govt. to be again taken under its sovereignty. This, after some years and another war, led to the ultimate annexation of Basutoland to the British dominions.

Mr. Orpen, in 1863, acquired landed property in the District of Aliwal North, upon which he still carries on farming operations on an extensive scale. In Feb., 1872, he was chosen (in a by-election) to represent the division of Queenstown in the Cape House of Assembly. Both before and after his election, he strongly advocated the gradual and steady extension, with the consent of the native tribes, of British authority over the countries lying outside Colonial jurisdiction between the Cape Colony and Natal, where native relations existed, entailing serious responsibilities without practical means of fulfilling them. Murder and intertribal bloodshed were rife, and general misgovernment prevailed. During the sessions of 1872 and 1873, Mr. Orpen pressed his views in the Assembly, and moved for select committees to consider the state of the Colony's native relations, and elicited much information through the reports of those committees. He voted against the introduction of Party Government, on the grounds that it would lead, with disastrous results, to native affairs becoming the football of party politics.
After the dissolution of the Cape Parliament in 1873, Mr. Orpen was asked by the first Ministry of the C.C. to take office as British Resident in the territory between the Umtata and Natal, with the object of developing and extending the authority and jurisdiction of Govt. there. That territory was in a state of war on his arrival in it in Aug., 1873, but before Nov. of that year British authority had so far advanced that on the outbreak of the rebellion of Langalibalele, in Natal, Mr. Orpen was able to raise a native army and take part in the movements for suppressing the outbreak. His services in this

respect were honorably mentioned in 1874, both by the Natal and Cape Govts. in their reports to their respective Parliaments. Without external support Mr. Orpen succeeded in establishing authority, jurisdiction, and just administration as far as the borders of Natal, and was able to punish some of the chiefs in those territories placed under his charge of or murders committed under the pretext that the victims were guilty of witchcraft, and thus to a great extent suppressed that cruel system. Mr. Orpen's administration in the territories mentioned, lasted from Aug. 1873, to June, 1875. The last territory annexed during that time was Griqualand East, at that time governed by Adam Kok. He and his people, the Griquas, had been permitted to occupy it (it being land ceded to Govt.) on the written stipulation that they should eventually be placed under the direct administration of the Govt. Adam Kok in Council now asked, and caused the request to be recorded, that he should be either placed under direct administration or made wholly independent. Governor Sir Henry Barkly thereupon, acting on the advice of his ministers, proceeded to Kokstad, declared the Govt. of Adam Kok at an end, accorded him a retiring pension of £1,000 a year, and placed the administration in the hands of Mr. Orpen. In 1875, after very honourable mention in the Governmental report to Parliament, Mr. Orpen resigned his office and returned to farming and the practice of his profession.

It was while he was engaged in a large survey for Govt. in the District of Bay, in Griqualand West, that a rebellion of the Griquas, Korannas and Kafirs of that territory broke out in 1878. Mr. Orpen was appointed at first Capt. of Corps of Guides, then Chief of the IntelligenceoDept. On the Staff, and afterwards Maj. in command, as well as a C.C. and R.M. over the seat of the rebellion. He held these offices for six months till the close of the rebellion and the Bechuanaland War. He was engaged in several battles and honourably mentioned in despatches by Lieut.-Governor Sir W. O. Lanyon, and Gen. Sir Charles Warren, on whose staffs he had served.

In 1879 Mr. Orpen was re-elected as a member of the Cape House of Assembly for the Division of Aliwal North. He retained that seat till Aug. 1881, when, after the impotent close of the campaign in Basutoland, Col. C. D. Griffiths C.M.G., who had, before the rebellion, been a most successful Governor's Agent and Colonial Magistrate, retired, as he did not consider restoration of authority possible by him, under existing circumstances. He advised that Mr Orpen should succeed him, as he believed that only under his administration was there a possibility of success. In the admittedly difficult task of administering Basutoland without extraneous support, Mr. Orpen met with a considerable measure of success. He collected large amount of Hut Tax, punished the Chiefs Jonathan and Joel, who had fought against each other, and restored authority over a considerable portion of the population, but one of the Basuto chiefs, Masupha, being opposed to the establishment of Colonial authority, the Ministry gave up the attempt to enforce it, withdrew all magisterial jurisdiction, and determined to appeal to the Imperial Govt. to undertake itself the govt. of Basutoland, and all through repeal of the Act annexing it to the Cape. Upon this, Mr. Orpen was retired, in Marc 1883, with expressions of high regard, and shortly afterwards Basutoland reverted to direct rule of the Imperial Govt.

Mr. Orpen then went to reside on his property in what is now the District of Barkly East. In 1889, he was again elected Senior Member for the Electoral Division of Wodehouse to the Cape House of Assembly, was re-elected in the subsequent general election, and held his seat till 1896 when he was called to be Survey Gen. of Rhodesia and Member of its Executive and Legislative Councils. He married, Mar. 1859, Elise Pauline, dau. of the Rev. S. Rolland.

ORPEN, Redmond Newenham Morris, C.M.G. M.L.A., M.R.C.I., of Cape Town, and of the Civil Service Club, C.T., is fourth son of the late Francis H. S. Orpen, Surveyor General of Griqualand West and first member, with the late Rt. Hon. C. J. Rhodes, for Barkly West, in the Cape House of Assembly, and was born at Grahamstown, Cape Colony, on May 22, 1864. He was educated at the Barkly West High School and at St. Andrew's College, Bloemfontein, farming at St. Clair, near Douglas, Division of Herbert, Griqualand West, from 1884. Always interested in politics, and a strong opponent of the Afrikander Bond, he took an active part in the formation of the South African League in May, 1896. On the outbreak of the Boer War he joined Orpen's Horse, 350 strong (raised by his brother, Major Frank Orpen), as Captain and second in command, subsequently commanding the corps, with the rank of Major (upon his brother's retirement through ill health), from June, 1900, to November, 1901 (mentioned in dispatches, C.M.G., medal and clasp). Subsequently, after being on special service for three months, he commanded the Border Scouts, 800 strong, until the end of the war (King's medal and clasps).

At the general election in 1904 he was elected member for Prieska in the Cape House of Assembly, after having been defeated by eleven votes at the by-election in the previous year. In June, 1905, he took over the duties of General Secretary of the South African Imperial Union, and Chief Organising Agent of the Progressive Party in the Cape Colony. He married, May 7, 1906, Dora. Agnes, dau. of the late Abraham Difford, of the Cape Government Railways.

ORR, Major Michael Harrison, D.S.O., of the Royal Portrush Golf Club, was born at Ballymena, and is son of the late William Orr, of Hugomount, Ballymena. He was educated at Trinity Coll., StratfordonAvon, and the R.M.C., Sandhurst. He served in the Nile Expedition of 1884-5, with the 1st Battn. of the Yorks. Regt., on the lines of communication up the Nile, took part in the operations on the Upper Nile, with the Sudan Frontier Field Force, in 1885-6 (medal and Khedive's star). He served in the S.A. War, 1899-1902 with the 1st Battn. York. Regt., and was present at the actions round Colesburg in Jan., 1900, when he was severely wounded (mentioned in despatches), took part in the march from Bloemfontein to Pretoria, including the passage of the Vet and Zand Rivers, the engagements at Brandfort, Kroonstad, and Johannesburg, the occupation of Pretoria, and in the advance to the Eastern Transvaal, including the operations at Diamond Hill and Belfast (mentioned in despatches, D.S.O., medal with five clasps). Unmarried.

ORSMOND, M. C., M.L.A., represents Aliwal

North in the Cape Parliament; was elected in Feb., 1904. and is a Progressive member.

OTTLEY, Capt. Charles Langdale, R.N. M.V.O., of Widcombe Manor, Bath; 2, Whitehall Court, S.W., and of the United Service Club, was born Feb. 8, 1858, at Richmond, York, and is son of the late Canon Ottley, of Ripon. He was educated on board H.M.S. *Britannia* and entered the Navy as a cadet at the age of 13; serving continuously at sea and elsewhere in Naval appointments, including the action against the Peruvian rebel ironclad *Huascar*, in May, 1877; and was present at the bombardment of Alexandria in 1882. He was given the post of Attaché to the Maritime Courts, and served in that capacity in the United States in 1899; in Japan, 1900; Italy, 1901; Russia, 1902; and France, in 1902-4. Capt. Ottley was Unionist candidate for the Pembroke Boroughs in 1904, but relinquished his candidature in order to serve as the Secretariat of the Committee of Imperial defence. He was appointed Director of Naval Intelligence in Feb., 1905. In addition to his being an M.V.O., he is an Officer of the Legion of Honour. He married, in 1892, Kathleen, dau. of the late Col. A. Stewart, R.A.

OWEN, J. Wilson, was appointed Chief Accountant of the Railway Dept. of Sierra Leone in 1905.

PAGE, G. M., was formerly District Commissioner of the Bandajurna Dist. of Sierra Leone, and was appointed District Commissioner of the Sherbro Dist. of that Colony in 1905. He has been connected with the Civil Service of Sierra Leone for over twenty years, acting as Keeper of the Freetown Gaol from 1897 to 1901, when he became a Dist. Commissioner.

PAGET, Commodore Sir Alfred Wyndham, K.C.V.O., was born in 1852, and is son of the late Gen. Lord Alfred Paget, and grandson of the first Marquis of Anglesey. He entered the Royal Navy in 1865, and served in the Egyptian War in 1882 (Egyptian medal and the Khedive's bronze star). Two years later he saw more active service in the Eastern Sudan, and in 1888 he was mentioned in despatches and promoted to the rank of Commander for his services at Suakin. He has since

been Naval Attaché in Paris, St. Petersburg, and Washington and he served in China in 1900-1. As Commodore on the North America Station he took part in the negotiations which resulted in the settlement of the French claims in Newfoundland. Sir Alfred was created K.C.V.O. on the occasion of the King's Birthday, 1905.

PAKES, Dr. Walter Charles Cross, L.R.C.P. (Lond.), M.R.C.S. (Eng.), D.P.H. (Camb.), F.C.S. of the Govt. Laboratories, Johannesburg, was Bacteriologist to Guy's Hosp. from 1895-1902; Demonstrator of Sanitary Science and Bacteriology in Guy's Hosp. Medical Sch. from 1893-1902; and in 1899-1900 was Examiner in Hygiene at the S. Kensington Science and Art Dept. He was a member of the Transvaal Commission on Technical Education, and is on the Council of the Chemical, Metallurgical, and Mining Society of S. Africa; was appointed Govt. Analyst and Bacteriologist for the Transvaal in 1902; and is a member of the S. African Board of Examiners of the Sanitary Institute. He is the author of *The Science of Hygiene*, and joint author of *School Hygiene*; was formerly Professor of Hygiene at the Bedford Coll. for Women, London.

PARK, Maitland Hall, of 17, Mill St., The Gardens, Cape Town, and of the Imperial Colonies (London) and Civil Service and City Clubs (C.T.), is the youngest son of the late Rev. Hugh Park, and was born Oct. 10, 1862, at Cumbernauld, Dumbartonshire, N.B. He was educated at the Glasgow High Sch., and Glasgow Univ., where he headed the list in open Bursary Competitions and graduated in Arts some years later, in 1885. In 1885 he was appointed Sub-editor of the Glasgow Herald, and a year later he joined the staff of the *Pioneer*, Allahabad, N.W.P. India, and remained there as Asst. Editor, Officiating Ed. and Ed.-in-Chief until 1902, when he was appointed Chief Editor of the *Cape Times* in succession to Mr. Saxon Mills (q.v.). He is an able journalist who has made his mark in India, and who bids fair to worthily carry on the high traditions of the *Cape Times*.

PARKER, Sir Gilbert, Knt. M.P., of 20, Carlton House Terrace, London, S.W., was born in Canada in 1862, and represents Gravesend in the House of Commons, and is a strong supporter of tariff reform. He was selected as Chairman of the Imperial South African Association in succession to Mr. Lyttelton when the latter became Secty. of State for the Colonies.

Sir Gilbert has travelled in Australia, and he recently (1904-5) made an extensive tour in Africa, from Cape Town to the Zambezi. He takes a very considerable interest in the question of land settlement in the newest S.A. Colony and is hopeful of the ultimate success of the S.A. farmer. He concluded his tour in Africa with a lecture at Cape Town on Commercial Union of the Empire. Sir Gilbert was until recently best known as a writer of novels, plays, and a volume of poems.

PARKIN, Dr. G. R., C.M.G., resigned post of Principal of Upper Canada Col. except the position of Organiser of the Rhodes Scholarships, a scheme which involved his travelling round the world.

PARKIN, Henry Clarence, F.R.C.I., Fort Jameson, N.E. Rhodesia, and of the Jameson Club, was born at Kimberley, Jul 1874, and was educated in Cape Town. Starting in the offices of the Cape Govt. Railways in 1895, he joined the Civil Service of N.E. Rhodesia in 1899 as Secretary's Clerk; transferred as Priv. Secty. to the Administrator of N.E. Rhodesia, and was appointed Comptroller of Transport and Supplies for N. Rhodesia in 1905. His recreations are hunting, riding, and golf. Unmarried.

PARSONS, Major Harold Daniel Edmund C.M.G., of Southbourne-on-Sea, and the Isthmian Club, is the fourth son of Major C. J. H. B. Parsons, Indian Army, who was fourth son of the late Lieut.-Gen. J. G. Parsons C.B., of the Indian Army, who was great-grandson of Samuel Parsons, of Powerstown, Co. Tipperary. He was born July 3, 1863, in London, and was educated at Dulwich Coll. He joined the Queen's Regt. in 1882 and saw active service in the Burmese Campaign in 1887, receiving medal with two clasps. He joined the Army Ordnance Dept., 1890, and was promoted to Capt. in the following year. He was Chief Ordnance Officer, Straits Settlements, 1894 to 1898, and in the latter year was promoted Maj. He served in the S.A. Campaign in 1899 with distinction. He held the appointment of Chief

Ordnance Officer of various districts, and was mentioned in despatches. He received his C.M.G. in 1901, and the Queen's medal with three clasps and King's medal with two clasps. He is now serving as Chief Ordnance Office the Western District. He married, Feb. 10, Julia second dau. of Thomas Archer, C.M.G., of Grassmere, Queensland, late Agent-Gen Queensland. He has one son, Harold Arthur James, born 1895.

PARTRIDGE, E. T., is a director of the British South African Trust, Ltd., and the Klondyke Estates Corporation, Ltd.

PARTRIDGE, Henry, of 3, Copthall Buildings, London, E.C., was until recently associated with Col. A. Weston Jarvis (q.v.) and Sir John Willoughby (q.v.) in the direction of several Rhodesian flotations, having been Chairman of the British South African Trust, Ltd., Matabele Reefs and Estates Co., Ltd., Rhodesia Concessions, Ltd., and Rhodesia Gold Fields, Ltd., and also a director of the Bembesi District Gold Claims. Ltd., East Gwanda Mines, Ltd., and Willoughby's Consolidated Co., Ltd.

PATERSON, Andrew Burton, of West Hall Woollahia, Sydney, and of the Australian Club, was born in N.S.W. in 1864. He was educated at Sydney Grammar Sch., and acted as correspondent to Reuter's Agency, and to the *Sydney Morning Herald* during the S. African war. He is the author of *The Man from Snowy River*, and *Rio Grande's Lost Race*; also editor of the *Sydney Evening News*. He married Alice, dau. of W. H. Walker, of Tenterfield.

PATTERSON, Lieut.-Col. John Henry, D.S.O., of the Cavalry Club, London, fought in the South African war in 1899-1900 and 1902, being three timies mentioned in despatches, and winning the D.S.O. He is a Major in the Essex I.Y., and has ranked as Hon,, Lieut. Col. in the Army since Feb. 11, 1903. Col. Patterson is a noted big game hunter. At the latter end of 1905 he accompanied the Earl of Warwick on a sporting expedition to Uganda, and some of his many thrilling experiences are shortly to be published in book form. He has a fine collection of trophies from different parts of the world, and his favourite amusements are riding, shooting, and travelling. Married.

PAULING, George, of 26, Victoria St., London, S.W., is senior member of the engineering firm of George Pauling and Company, Ltd., and has aided in constructing almost all the important railways of South Africa, where he is known as the Railway King. He has travelled extensively, and is said to have a very great influence over the African native. He is a Director of the Cape Town Consolidated Tramways and Land Co., the General Trust and Finance Association, and the Monomotapa Development Co., and also acts as the London Agent of the Premier Coal Estates, Ltd.

PEACE, Sir Walter, K.C.M.G., I.S.O., *Chevalier de l'Ordre de Leopold*, of the St. Stephen's, Junior Constitutional, and Durban Clubs, was born at Huddersfield, Oct. 19, 1840. He is second son of James Peace, Professor of Music, of Huddersfield, and was educated at a private academy in that town. Sir Walter went to Natal in 1863, and became head of the firm of Peace, Blandy and Co., merchants. He was Consul for Belgium at Durban, 1870-1879, and Vice-Consul for Portugal, 1870-1878. He was appointed Natal Emigration and Harbour Board agent in London, 1880-1893, and Agent-Gen for Natal in 1893, in which year he was made C.M.G., receiving the honour of Knighthood in 1897. He retired from the Agent Generalship in 1905. He is the author of *Our Colony of Natal* and *Notes on Natal*. Sir Walter is a fellow or member of various Institutes, and Hon. Member of the Institute of Marine Engineers. He was one of the Royal Commissioners for the Paris Exhibition in 1900; was a Commissioner for the Colonial and Indian Exhibition in 1886; is a Member representing South Africa on the Advisory Committee of the Board of Trade in connection with the Imperial Institute, and a member of Mr. Chamberlain's Tariff Commission (1903). In 1905 he joined the Directorate of Wm. Simmons and Co., Ltd., Engineers, of Renfrew. He is also a director of the Natal Land and Colonisation Co., and of the very old established Rock Life Assurance Co. On his retirement from the Natal Agent Generalship, Sir Walter Peace visited Natal as the guest of the Colony, and was entertained by members of both Houses of Parliament. At a banquet in London he was also, on his retirement, presented with his portrait in oils by Mr. A. S. Cope, R.A. He married, April 24, 1869, Caroline, youngest dau. of Wm. Tilbrook, of Woodham Lodge, near Chelmsford.

PEACOCK, John Michael, of Addiscombe, Queenstown, C.C., and of the National Liberal (Lond.) and City (C.T.) Clubs; is son of George Peacock of Manchester, where he was born, Feb. 22, 1831; was educated privately, and proceeding to the Cape became senior partner in the merchant firm of Peacock Bros., of London, Queenstown, and East London (C.C.). He represented King Williamstown in the Cape House of Assembly from 1874 to 1877; was appointed by the Scanlen Ministry a member of the Committee of Advice to Sir Chas. Mills, the first Agent-Gen. for the Cape of Good Hope in 1883; and sat in the Legislative Council for the E. Circle, Co., from 1891 to 1898. Mr. Peacock married, Sept. 25, 1867, a dau. of I. Hincksman, cotton spinner, of Preston, Lancs.

PEAKE, Major (local Lieut. Col.) Malcolm, R.F.A., C.M.G., 4th Class of the Imperial Orders of the Omani (1899) and Medjidieh (1896), of Cairo, and of the Naval and Military, Boodle's, and the Cavalry Clubs; was born in London, March 27, 1865; is youngest son of Frederick Peake, of Burrough, Melton Mowbray, Leicestershire; was educated at Charterhouse, and joined the Egyptian Army in July, 1895. He served in the various campaigns of 1896-97-98-99 for the recovery of the Sudan and the destruction of the Dervish power. He received a brevet majority in 1896, and was subsequently decorated with the Medjidieh, the Osmanieh, and the Queen's medal and the Khedive's medal with clasps for Ferket Hafir Nile (1897), Athara, Khartoum, and Nile (1899). Major Peake commanded a battery of artillery under Lord Kitchener when Comdt. Marchand was encountered at Fashoda in Sept., 1898 and had command of the expedition sent to the Upper Nile in Dec., 1899, to clear the sudd away and open a waterway, which was completed in May, 1900, in which month the first steamer from the north reached Gondokow. For this service he was decorated with the C.M.G. He now commands the artillery of the Egyptian army, and is in charge of all small arms and ammunition connected with the

Egyptian army and the Anglo Egyptian Sudan. He married, June 20, 1900, Louisa, eldest dau. of the late P. H. Osborne, of Currandooley, New South Wales.

PEARCE, Henry, J.P., of Bloemfontein, O.R.C., and of the City, Bloemfontein, Turf, and the United Service Clubs, was born in 1869. He was a well-known traveller, in S. Africa before the Boer War in 1899-1902. On the outbreak of the War he joined the Intelligence Dept. as Special Service Officer. Subsequently he became Commercial Adviser to the Military Governor of the O.R.C. and Director of Supplies for that Colony. He retired from the Civil Service in 1902, and was appointed Managing Director of the Orange River Colony Cold Storage Co.

PEARSE, Samuel Herbert, F.R.C.I., of Lagos, and Old Calabar, W. Africa, was born in the Colony of Lagos, Nov. 20, 1865, and is the only surviving son of the late Rev. S. Pearse, of the C.M.S. He was educated at the C.M.S. Gram. Sch. at Lagos; was trained to commercial pursuits on the West Coast, and entered into a partnership in 1890 with the late I. A. Thompson, trading in Lagos and London. This partnership was dissolved in 1894, when he started on his own account at Lagos and afterwards at Old Calabar. In 1897 he visited Benin city and the adjoining forests, under Govt. auspices, reporting on the rubber resources, etc. He was elected in 1901 a Life Fellow of the R.C.I. He married, in June, 1897, Constance, eldest dau. of J. P. Decker, of Lagos.

PEARSON, Alfred Naylor, of Pietermaritzburg, was born May 17, 1856, at Leeds, Eng., and was educated in his native town and at the Royal Sch. of Mines, London. In 1874 he obtained a Royal Exhibition at that Institution and for two years was at the head of the examinations, thus gaining two additional scholarships. In 1877 he accepted a position in Kutch, India, in connection with the development the mineral resources of the State. After thirteen months' service he resigned and was appointed temporarily Curator of the Victoria and Albert Museum, Bombay, and Acting Prof. of Biology of the Elphinstone Coll. in that city. In 1880 he was appointed Resident Engineer of the Wynand G.M.C., resigning that position in 1882 to assume temporary charge for two and half years of the Meteorological Department in Western India. In 1884 he was made Fellow of the University of Bombay; at the end of that year he left for Australia, and in the following year was appointed Examiner for higher degree in various science subjects at the University of Melbourne. In 1886 he was appointed Chemist to the Dept. of Agriculture, Victoria, and subsequently Chemist of Lands, Agriculture and Water Supply in that Colony. In 1888 he was appointed Member of the Royal Inter-Colonial Commission to report on proposals by Pasteur and others for suppressing the rabbit pest in Australia, After serving on various conferences and receiving a resolution of thanks for splendid services to the Agriculture of the State, he was appointed in 1901 Director of Agriculture in Natal, and subsequently gazetted also as Commissioner of Industries for that Colony.

Under his direction a large experimental farm of 3,600 acres is being laid out. He is the author of many reports, papers, and other writings upon the development of the mineral resources of India, meteorological works on part of India, agricultural subjects connected with Australia, also on various educational scientific and literary matters, and a scheme of agricultural settlement for Natal, which he has written in co authorship with the Surveyor-Gen. R married: first, in 1882, the eldest dau. of Dr R. T. Corbett, M.D,, etc., Glas., and second, ii 1896, the eldest dau. of Richard Harding, a sister of Maj. R. Harding, of Melbourne, Australia.

PEEL, The Right Rev. William George D.D., Lord Bishop of Mombasa, of Bishop's Court, Mombasa, East Africa, and the Mombasa Club, was born in N. India, in 1854. He is son of Capt. Peel, who died in Calcutta of cholera. He was educated at the Blackheath Proprietary Sch., and at the Church Missionary Theological Coll., Islington; was ordained Deacon at St. Paul's, London, in 1879; Priest, 1880; and was consecrated Bishop in 1899. He was Curate, Trowbridge, Wilts, 1879-80; Rugby Fox Master, Noble Coll., Masulipatam, 1880-87 (Acting Principal for three years); Acting Secy. Church Missionary Society, Diocese of Madras, 1888, '89, and '92, and was Secy. of the Church Missionary Society, Diocese of Bombay, 1882-90. He married, Aug. 3, 1880, Agneta Jane,

dau. of the Rev. R. Guy Bryan, late Principal of
Monkton Combe School, nr. Bath.

PEIRSON, Joseph Waldie, F.R.G.S., F.R.C.I., of
Johannesburg (P.O. Box 561), of 2, Mitre Court
Buildings, Temple, B.C., and of the Royal Societies
(London), the Rand, New, Athenaeum and
Wanderers' (Johannesburg) Clubs, and the Jockey
Club of S.A.; was born at Darlington, County
Durham, July 31, 1865. He is eldest son of Joseph
Peirson, of Stokesley, Yorks., and Margaret, dau.
of Thomas Waldie, of Darlington; was educated at
the High Sch., Pietermaritzburg, and at Dr.
Ehrlich's Sch., at Newcastle-on-Tyne. He is a
Barrister of the Inner Temple, and Advocate of the
Supreme Court of the Transvaal. He went to Natal
in 1877, and to Johannesburg in 1889, where he is
on the boards of several G.M. Cos. He has been
member of the Provincial Synod of S.A. and on the
Diocesan Synods of Maritzburg and Pretoria on
several occasions, and is Chancellor of the Diocese
of Pretoria (1903). He is also Vice-Pres. of the
Geological Soc. of S.A.; on the Council of the Soc.
of Accountants and Auditors of Eng. (Transvaal
branch); Fellow of the Chartered Inst. of
Secretaries (Eng.); Member of the Council of the
Witwatersrand Agricultural Soc.; Mem. of the
Johannesburg Chamber of Commerce, and Mem.
of the Transvaal Chamber of Mines. His recreations
are racing and bridge. Unmarried.

PENDER, Sir James. of Donhead House,
Wiltshire, was born in Dumbartonshire, in 1841,
and is son of the late Sir John Pender, G.C.M.G.
He was educated at the University College,
London, where he matriculated and took the first
B.A. In 1860 he joined the King's Own Borderers,
serving in that Regt. at Gibraltar, Ceylon, and in
the Mediterranean. Subsequently he retired from
the Service, and was entrusted by his father with a
mission to S. Africa on behalf of the Eastern
Telegraph Co., to obtain subsidies from Aden,
Zanzibar, and other places about Africa for the new
Cape cable. He afterwards travelled through the
United States for two years. Sir James is a member
of the Royal Yacht Squadron; Vice Commodore of
the Royal Thames Yacht Club, and is on the
Council of the Y.R.A. He married, Mary, dau. of
Mr. Gregg-Hopwood, of Hopwood Hall,
Lancashire.

PENDER, Sir John Denison. (See Denison-Pender,
Sir John.)

PENNEFATHER, Lieut.-Col., 6th Dragoon
Guards, was the first officer to command the
B.S.A. Police, Sir John Willoughby being his
second in command.

PENNELL, Henry Cholmondeley. (See
Cholmondeley-Pennell.)

PENTON, Major (local Lieut. Col.) Richard Hugh,
D.S.O., R.A.M.C., 3rd class Medjidieh, 4th class
Osmanieh, of the War Office, Cairo, Egypt, and
the Junior United Service Club, is the eldest son of
the late Major-Gen. John Fenton. He was born
April 25, 1863, in Norfolk, and was educated at
Norwich. Major Penton is M.R.C.S. and L.R.C.P.
Lond. He joined the R.A.M.C. as Capt. in 1887,
and saw service in the Dongola Expedition in 1896
(despatches, medal, two clasps and D.S.O.), in the
Nile Expedition as S.M.O. of the Infantry Division
of The Egyptian Army (despatches, medal, two
clasps, Order of the Osmanieh) and in the Nile
Expedition of the following year he served as
P.M.O. of the Egyptian Army in the first advance
against the Khalifa (clasp and Egyptian medal and
3rd class Medjidieh.)

PETERS, Dr. Carl Friedrich Hubert, of 68,
Buckingham Gate, London, S.W., is the son of a
Lutheran clergyman of Hanover. He was born at
Neuhaus, Hanover, in 1856, and was educated at
the High Sch. of Held (Hartz Mountains), and at
the Univ. of Gottingen, Tubingen, Berlin, and in
London. He is well known as an African explorer
and administrator, and is the founder of the
German Colonisation Socy. In 1884 he acquired in
S.A. large tracts of land, and obtained for them an
Imperial Protectorate from the German Govt. As
head of the German East Africa Company, he
extended its possessions and organised its stations,
and was instrumental in bringing about a Colonial
Congress in Berlin in 1886. In 1887 he returned to
B. Africa and fought his way through Manicaland
with reckless bloodshed and tried to place Uganda
under German protection. He became
Imperial German High Commissioner in the
Kilimanjaro district, but had to resign his

commission in the German service after an inquiry into his treatment of the natives in German B. Africa, which resulted in a verdict of misuse of official power. He commanded the German Emin Pasha Relief Expedition in 1889-90, and later, in 1899-1901, he embarked on a journey through Portuguese territory south of the Zambesi and along the eastern border of Charter land, spending much time in the Makalango country, on behalf of a gold syndicate which he had formed in England. The results of his trip were published in a book called *The Eldorado of the Ancients*, much of which is devoted to showing that the region between the Lower Zambesi and the Limpopo was the Land of Ophir, and even the Egyptian Punt. He further maintains that Pharaoh kept a Governor in this district, of which Quilimane was at that time the port. Dr. Peters has travelled on foot or horseback about 20,000 miles in the interior of Africa. His hunting trophies include five lion skins, seventeen rhino horns, seven double elephant tusks, and four leopard skins. He has been decorated with the Order of the Prussian Crown, Albrecht Order (King of Saxony), Order of the Falcon (Grand Duke of Saxony), Order of the Lion of the Zuebringens (Baden), etc. In addition to *The Eldorado of the Ancients*, he is the author of several works, including *New Light on Dark Africa*, *King Solomon's Golden Ophir*, *Sun and Soul*, etc., etc. Unmarried.

PETRIE, William Matthew Flinders, F.R.S., Hon. D.C.L., LL.D. Litt.D., Ph.D., of 5, Well Road, Hampstead, N.W., and of the University Coll., London, was born June 3, 1853. Since 1880 he has been engaged in excavating in Egypt, the general results of his work being the settlement of the early stages of civilisation in Egypt, the earliest Israelite connection, and the dating of prehistoric Greek civilisation as early as 6,000 B.C. He married, Nov. 27, 1897, Hilda, dau. of Richard Urlin, of Rustington Grange.

PHILLIPS, Lionel, D.L., J.P., of 33, Grosvenor Square, London, and of Tylney Hall, Winchfield, Eng., was born in London in Aug. 1854. He was on the diamond fields of Kimberley in the early days, but in 1889 he coached up to the Rand, and joined the firm of H. Eckstein and Co., of which he became the chief after the death of Hermann

Eckstein. As a mining engineer he had a very considerable experience, but it required all his knowledge, resolution and energy to combat the difficulties of the early days of the Witwatersrand —not only the economic difficulties which had to be solved, but also the obstacles which a reactionary Govt. placed in the way of progress. These latter bore especially hard on the mining industry, and in those days every captain of industry in the S.A.R. was forced in self-defence to take an active part in local politics. As Pres. of the Johannesburg Chamber of Mines and chief partner in the premier firm of the Rand, Mr. Lionel Phillips exercised the greatest influence in matters mineral and political. The long and bitter fight against Mr. Kruger's Govt. found an ardent champion in Mr. Phillips. He was one of the four leaders of the Reform movement, and after the failure of the ill-starred raiding enterprise, he was tried with Col. Frank Rhodes, J. Hays Hammond, and Sir Geo. Farrar (q.v.), and was condemned to death—a sentence which was afterwards commuted to a fine of £25,000 and banishment, in default of an undertaking, not to meddle in the politics of the State for fifteen years (See also Dr. Coster and Judge Gregorowsky). On returning to England Mr. Phillips became a partner in the firm of Wernher, Beit and Co., in connection with which he takes a highly prominent place in financial circles, although so far as directorships go he sits only on the London Committees of the Angelo Deep, Cason G.M., Main Reef Deep, and Main Reef East Companies, and on the European Committee of the East Rand Proprietary Mines. Mr. Phillips is an able speaker, and whether in his public utterances or with his pen, always expresses himself in adequate and convincing phrases. He takes a more than ordinary interest in Egyptology; is J.P. for Hampshire; a D.L., and a member of the Committee on Commercial Education in connection with the London Chamber of commerce.

When in the Transvaal Mr. and Mrs. Lionel Phillips were at the head of the Uitlander community. In England they entertain considerably, and make capital hosts. Mrs. Phillips, after the Raid, published an interesting history of that period.

PHILLIPS, Major William Henry Boothby, of the Cape Mounted Rifles, joined the F.A.M. Police in

1876, and served in the Gaika-Galeka War in 1877-9, including the final attack on Moirosi's Mountain, and the capture of the Stronghold (medal with clasp); the Basuto Rebellion in 1880-1, including the siege of Mafeking; was promoted lieutenant to the Cape Mounted Riflemen in 1881; served with the Pondoland Field Force in 1894-5, and in the South African War in 1899-1900; present at the operations in the Orange Free State and the defence of Wepener, the operations in the Transvaal and Orange River Colony, including the actions at Wittebergen (Queen's medal with four clasps, and the King's medal with two clasps). He also holds the Diamond Jubilee medal.

PIGOTT, John Robert Wilson, of the British Consulate, Paramaribo, Surinam, was born Nov. 27, 1850, and is son of the late Rev. John Robert Pigott. He entered the service of the British East Africa Company in 1888, and was appointed to the charge of the Coast Dist. at Mombasa. In 1889 he conducted an expedition up the Tana River as far as the Mackenzie River, which he named, returning through Ukambani, and along the Sabaki River. The primary object of this journey was to establish the British claim to the Territory on the north left bank of the Tana River, before Doctor Carl Peters could do so for the Germans. Returning to Mombasa in 1889, he was appointed Asst. Administrator, and acted as Administrator of the territory from 1890-1 and 1892-5, when the territory was taken over from the company by the British Govt. In 1894 he was appointed Judicial Officer in and for Zanzibar, under the administration of the Imperial British East Africa Co. He left E. Africa in 1896, and was appointed H.M. Vice-Consul in Zanzibar for the British sphere on the East Coast of Africa, subsequently becoming Consul for the Island of Sicily, and Consul for Surinam, Dutch Guiana, in 1898 (which position he still holds), and Consul for French Guiana in the same year. He married, at Mombasa, in 1893, Louisa, dau. of the late Richard Y. Bazett, of the E.I.C. Civil Service, Bombay.

PIKE, Lieut. Colonel William Watson, R.A.M.C., D.S.O., F.R.C.S.I., was born Mar. 10, 1860, in Co. Mayo, and is son of the late William Pike, J.P. He was educated at Kingstown Sch., entered the Army Med. Corps in 1882, and served in China, Ceylon, and in S. Africa during the war, being

present at the relief of Kimberley, and the actions at Paardeberg, Driefontein, and Wittebergen (King's medal and two clasps). He played in the Irish fifteen in 1879-83, also in Ulster v. Leinster at hockey in 1898. He married, in 1886, Sarah L. Wheatley.

PILCHER, Captain G., of the North Lancashire Regt., served in the South African War in 1899-1902, as Railway Staff Officer, present at the operations in the Cape Colony (Queen's medal with clasp).

PILKINGTON, Charles William Macdonald, of Port Elizabeth, Cape Colony, was employed in the customs department at Cape Town in 1895. In 1896 he was appointed asst. examining officer at Mossel Bay, and at Knysna in 1897. He served in the South African War in 1899-1901; was appointed second-class clerk at Cape Town in 1901, and second-class examining officer at Port Elizabeth in 1903, which position he still holds.

PILKINGTON, Col. Henry Lionel, C.B., of 1, Bateman St., Cambridge; Tore, Co. Westmeath, Ireland, and Zorg Vleit, Bloemfontein, O.R.C., is the eldest son of the late Henry M. Pilkington, D.L., Q.C. He was educated at Queen's Coll., Cambridge, and the R.M.C., Sandhurst; served on the West Coast of Africa in 1881-2 in the 1st West India Regt., subsequently joining the 21st Hussars, with which Regt. he served in India. His former appointments include: Private Secy. to Sir F. Napier Broome, when Governor of Western Australia; Commandant of Local Forces there; was appointed to the W. Australian Mtd. Inf. for service in S. Africa in 1899, and afterwards was given the command of that Corps. He became Col. and Divisional Commandant of the S.A. Constabulary in 1900, and commanded the S.A.C. in the O.R.C. from 1900 until the end of the War, and subsequently till June, 1904. He married, in 1896, Louisa, dau. of the late Rt. Hon. Sir John Esmonde, Bart.

PIM, Howard, of Johannesburg, was elected Deputy Mayor of Johannesburg in Nov., 1904.

PINK, Lieut.-Col. Francis John, C.M.G., D.S.O., was born in 1857, and is son of the late Charles

Pink. He joined the Royal West Surrey Regt., in 1878, and served in the Afghan War in 1879-80 (medal); the Burmese Expedition in 1886-9 as Orderly Officer and Intelligence Officer to the Brig. Gen., and subsequently as D.A.Q.M.G., 3rd Brigade, and as Staff Officer to the Karen Field Force (despatches, medal with two clasps, and D.S.O.); the Dongola Expedition in 1896 (despatches, and Egyptian medal with two clasps); Nile Expedition in 1897 (despatches and clasp to Egyptian medal); the Nile Expedition in 1898, including the battles of the Athara and Khartoum, in charge of a Battalion of Egyptian Infantry (despatches, brevet of Lieut. Col., two clasps to Egyptian medal, and medal). He also served in the South African War in 1899-1902, in command of 2nd Batt. Royal West Surrey Regt., being present at the relief of Ladysmith and the actions at Colenso, Spion Kop, and Vaal Kranz; the operations on Tugela Heights, and the actions at Pieter's Hill; the operations in Natal, and the action at Laing's Nek (despatches, Queen's medal with five clasps, King's medal with two clasps, and C.M.G.).

PIRRIE, Right Hon. Baron, P.C., D.L., LL.D., D.Sc., of Ormiston, Belfast, Ireland; Downshire House, Belgrave Square, London, S.W. and of the Reform (Lond.), Kildare St. (Dublin), and Ulster (Belfast) Clubs, was born at Quebec, Canada, May 31, 1847, and is the only son of the late James Alexander Pirrie, of Little Clandeboys, Co. Down, Ireland. He was educated at the Royal Belfast Academical Institution, and in 1862 he entered Harland and Wolff's shipbuilding and engineering establishment, Belfast; became partner in 1874, and is now Chairman of that Company. During Lord Pirrie's control of these works his firm has designed and built many of the largest and finest steamers afloat, including the *Oceanic*, 17,000 tons; *Celtic*, 21,000 tons; *Cedric*, 21,000 tons; and *Baltic*, 24,000 tons. In the pursuit of his profession he has travelled much, making himself acquainted with the various conditions and requirements of the main trade routes of the world; and he made a study some years ago of the South African trade, visiting the principal harbours there, and subsequently building not only the largest mail steamers running to the Cape, including the *Norman*, *Briton*, *Saxon*, *Walmer Castle*, and *Kenilworth Castle*, but also

designing and building the smaller vessels known as the G's.

In the steamship connections between the Mother country and her Colonies, including Canada, Australia, and New Zealand, Lord Pirrie's originality and technical knowledge, combined with the enterprise of his ship owning friends, have been the means of remarkable developments that have to some extent transformed the conditions under which our trade is conducted, and have done much to keep the British Mercantile Marine well ahead of its competitors, thereby securing and promoting British and Colonial interests. Since Lord Pirrie's connection with the firm of Harland and Wolff nearly four hundred ships have been built, the aggregate gross tonnage amounting to over 1,500,000 tons, and the indicated horse power to about 1,000,000, a unique record. He is also associated with the shipping trade, being director of several lines, and chairman of the African Steamship Company.

Lord Pirrie is a member of the Institution of Civil Engineers, a member of the Council of the Institution of Naval Architects, and of the Institution of Mechanical Engineers. He is also a Deputy Lieutenant for the City of Belfast, and a J.P. for that city, and for Co. Antrim and Co. Down. He was Lord Mayor of Belfast in 1896 and 1897, during which time the Prince and Princess of Wales visited Belfast, and he is a member of His Majesty's Most Honourable Privy Council in Ireland. He was High Sheriff of Co. Antrim 1898 and Co. Down 1899. The degree of LL.D. was conferred upon him by the Royal University of Ireland in 1899, in recognition of his eminent services in the industrial advancement of his country; the degree of D.Sc. was bestowed by the Dublin University in 1903, and he was created Baron Pirrie of the City of Belfast in 1906. He married in 1879 Margaret Montgomery, dau. of the late John Carlisle, M.A., of Belfast.

PLUMER, Major-General Herbert Charles Onslow, C.B., of the Curragh Camp, Ireland, joined the 65th Foot in 1876, and saw his first active service in the Sudan in 1884, when as captain of the York and Lancaster Regiment he took part in the battles of El Teb and Tamai, being mentioned in despatches, and received the medal and clasp, bronze star, and the 4th Class Medjidjieh. When the Matabele War broke out in 1896 General Plumer organised and commanded a relief corps of mounted rifles, which he marched up country, doing much execution in the strongholds of rebels. But it was in the South African War, 1899-1902, that Gen. Plumer earned the greatest distinction as a soldier, although his services do not appear to have been acknowledged as completely as they deserved, but Gen. Plomer is not one of the advertising generals. Commencing the campaign as a Special Service officer, he was afterwards placed on the Staff, and it was as a natural sequel to his excellent record in the Chartered territory that he was given the command of the Rhodesian contingent. In his march to the relief of Mafeking he was slightly wounded. His subsequent operations took place in the Transvaal, Orange River, and Cape Colony, for which he was promoted to Major-General and was made A.D.C. to the King; he was mentioned in despatches, and received the C.B., two medals and six clasps. In 1902 he took command of the 4th Brigade of the 1st Army Corps at Aldershot, and in March, 1906, he was appointed to command the 7th Division at the Curragh in the place of Lieut.-Gen. Sir G. C. Morton, K.C.I.E.

Rather short and slim of stature, Gen. Plumer suggests in appearance rather the dandy than the soldier. His temper is imperturbable, even in the heat of action, and he enjoys a keen sense of humour.

POISSON, Frederick Cutlar, of Bartholomew House, London, E.C., is a cadet of one of the best families of S. Carolina. He was for some time engaged in mining in California, Texas, and other States. Subsequently went to the De Kaap, where he went through rough times. In 1887, however, he left there for the Witwatersrand, and managed to accumulate a comfortable fortune. Since his marriage Mr. Poisson has resided mainly in England. He is Chairman of the Consolidated Goldfields of Mexico and the Rand Investment Corporation, besides being on the Boards of the Western Rand Estates, and the Saxon Gold Mines (London Committee).

POLE-CAREW, Major-Gen. Sir Reginald, of Antony, Cornwall, and of the Carlton, Marlborough, Guards', Pratt's, United Service, and Turf Clubs, is the head of an old Cornish family, and joined the Coldstream Guards in 1869, and first saw active service under Sir Frederick (now Lord) Roberts in the Afghan War of 1879-80, when he took part in the march to Kandahar, being three times mentioned in despatches. He acted as A.D.C. to the Duke of Connaught in the Egyptian Campaign, and was military secretary to Lord Roberts during the Burmese War of 1886, being again mentioned in despatches, and receiving the C.B. In the South African War he successively had command of the 9th Brigade, the Guards Brigade, and afterwards the 11th Division. He took part in the advance on Kimberley, including the actions at Modder River and Magersfontein; the operations in the Orange Free State, including the actions at Poplar Grove, Driefontein, Vet River, and Zand River; operations in the Transvaal in May and June, 1900, including the actions near Johannesburg, Pretoria, and Diamond Hill, and from July to Nov., 1900, was present at the actions at Belfast and district. During the campaign he distinguished himself repeatedly, as much by his cool courage as by his successful strategy, and he was one of the few general officers who went through the war without any of those regrettable incidents which characterised the campaign. For his services so ably rendered he was promoted to Major-General; was created K.C.B., and received the Queen's medal with five clasps. For three years subsequently Gen. Pole-Carew commanded the 3rd Army Corps, retiring from the army in the summer of 1906. He married, in 1901, Lady Beatrice Butler, eldest dau. of the Marquis of Ormonde, and has one son and two daughters.

POLLOCK, Lieut. Col. Arthur Williamson Alsager, of Wingfield, Godalming, and of the Junior United Service Club, was born July 3, 1853, and is the only son of the late Major William Pollock, R.A. He was educated at Shrewsbury and the B.N.C., Oxford; joined the 13th Somersetshire L.I. in 1875, and served in S. Africa from 1876-9; was present at the annexation of the Transvaal in 1877; served in the operations against Sekukuni in 1878; took part in the Zulu War in 1879, including the actions at Kambula and Ulundi (medal with clasp); the Suakim Expedition in 1885, as transport officer of the 2nd Brigade; present at the actions of Hasheen and Tofrek; and took part in the march to Tamai (medal and two clasps, bronze star). He was a special *Times* correspondent during the Boer War, 1899-1900; and is the author of *Simple Lectures for Company Field Training*, *With Seven Generals in the Boer War*, and various pamphlets, &c. he contributes to the *Nineteenth Century*, *Fortnightly*, *Monthly*, and *Contemporary Reviews*, and edits the *United Service Magazine*. Recreations : Rowing, hunting, and shooting. He married, July 7, 1881, Edith, dau. of the late Copleston Lopes Radcliffe, of Derriford, Devon.

POOLE, Major A. E., rose from the ranks, and served in the 10th. Hussars for upwards of thirty years. In 1884 he took part in the Sudan Campaign, and in the late South African War participated in most of the important engagements. Subsequently he was Camp Quartermaster at Aldershot. He is a Military Knight of Windsor.

POORE, Major Robert Montagu, D.S.O, 7th Hussars, of Old Lodge, Salisbury, and of the Cavalry, Prince's, and Marylebone Cricket Clubs, was born at Blackrock, Dublin, March 20, 1866, and is son of Major R. Poore, late 8th Hussars, his mother having been a dau. of Rear Admiral Sir A. L. Cary, K.C.B. Major Poore was educated privately, and was gazetted to the 3rd Battn. Wilts Regt. in 1883. In 1886 he joined the 1st Battn., and later in that year transferred to his present Regt. He served in India from 1886 to 1895, during which period (June, 1892 to Feb., 1895) he acted as A.D.C. to Lord Harris, Governor of Bombay, and in South Africa from 1895 to 1898, including the Rhodesian Campaign of 1896-7, when he was mentioned in despatches, and received his Brevet Majority and medal and clasps. He returned to service in the Cape in 1899 in time to participate in the South African War as Provost Marshal to the S.A. Field Force, 1899-1902. He was three times mentioned in dispatches, and received the D.S.O., Queen's medal with six clasps, and King's medal with two clasps. Major Poore is a keen all-round sportsman, and is especially devoted to cricket and polo. He married, Sept. 29, 1898, Lady Flora

Douglas Hamilton, sister of the 13th Duke of Hamilton.

POPE, Edward, of St. Stephen's Chambers, Telegraph Street, London, E.C., is Chairman of the Australasian G.M. Co., Ltd., and the Mount Usher Gold Mines, Ltd., deputy Chairman of the Kalgoorlie Electric Power and Lighting Corp., Ltd., Chairman of the London Board of Carrington's Lion P.C. Mining Co., Ltd., and director of the African and Australian Co., Ltd., Cecil Syndicate, Ltd., Brilliant Central G.M. Co., Ltd., New Options Exploration, Ltd., and No. 2, South Great Eastern G.M. Co., Ltd.

POPE-HENNESSY, Major Ladislas Herbert Richard, was born Aug. 18, 1875, and entered the Welsh Regt. in 1895, subsequently changing to the Oxford Light Infantry in 1895. He served in Lagos in 1897-8, being employed in the Hinterland (medal with clasp); took part in the operations against Ogaden Somalis in Jubaland, British East Africa, in 1901 (medal with clasp), and the operations in Somaliland in 1901-3 (despatches). He was promoted Major in 1906 for services rendered in connection with the quelling of the Nandi rebellion in East Africa.

PORGES, Jules, was one of the original pioneers of the Kimberley diamond fields, where, in 1876, he laid the foundation of the firm of Wernher, Beit, and Co. His first big coup was the purchase of the Kimberley mine, which was afterwards floated in conjunction with Messrs. Lewis and Marks into the *Cie. Française des Mines de Diamants Du Kaap*, which was the first limited liability company formed in South Africa to work diamond claims, it being subsequently absorbed by the De Beers Company.

PORTER, Brig.-General Thomas Cole, C.B., J.P., of Trematon Castle, Saltash, Cornwall, and of the Royal Western Yacht and Army and Navy Clubs, was born in 1851, and is son of the Rev. E. J. Porter. He formerly commanded the 6th Dragoon Guards, and served in the Afghan War in 1879-80 with the Khyber Division Kabul Field Force, including the affair against the Mohmunds at Ali Boghan, the expedition against Asmatoola Khan in Lughman Valley against the Waziri Khugiani and the Hissaracs, and the attack on, and destruction of, the villages of Nargozi, Arab Khel, and Yokan (despatches and medal). He also took part in the S. African War in 1899-1900, in command of the 1st Cavalry Brigade (despatches, Queen's medal with five clasps, and C.B.). He married first, in 1878, Minnie (died 1889), dau. of J. W. M'Leod; and secondly, in 1903, Jane, dau. of C. W. Hodge.

POTT, William, of the Rand, New, and Pretoria Clubs, belongs to an old Border family, about which Tancred quotes in his *Annals*, an old document, dated 1821, referring to the Potts, Rutherford's, Dogfishes, and Robsons, who, with their followers, made a raid into England with two sleuthhounds and carried off a number of sheep and about 100 head of cattle. He was born in Roxburghshire, educated at Edinburgh Acad., and went to New Zealand in 1883 to start stock farming, but not satisfied with this, proceeded to the Transvaal in connection with the Oceana Consolidated Co. in 1899.

He took up the property management for Mr J. C. A. Henderson in 1890, and the general management of the Henderson Cos. in 1895, having meanwhile visited Matabeleland (1894) and been on two extended big game shoots between Leydsdorp and Komatipoort (1892-3). He represented South Africa as special correspondent in Natal with Sir G. White's force, and was through Ladysmith in that capacity. Mr. Pott married, in 1906, Ella, dau. of J. C. A. Henderson.

POTTS, George, Ph.D., B.Sc., Lecturer in Natural Science, Gray College, Bloemfontein, was born April 8, 1877. He was appointed Asst. Lecturer in Agriculture at the Armstrong Coll. from 1902-5, since when he has held his present position. He obtained a diploma in Agriculture of the Highland and Agricultural Society of Scotland in 1899, Diploma in Forestry of the same society in 1899, and Diploma in Agriculture of the University of Cambridge in the same year. He also holds an Honours Certificate of the Board of Education, with a bronze medal in the principles of Agriculture; National Diploma in Agriculture with gold medal, 1900; National Diploma in Dairying, 1902; and a Diploma in Dairying of the British

Dairy Farmers' Assn. He is the author of *Mir Physiologie des Dichjostelium Mucoroides* in *Flora*, and *Large and Small Farms in Prussia*. Recreation: Bridge. Unmarried.

POWELL, Hon. Edmund, M.L.C., of Cambria, Harfield Road, Claremont, near Cape Town, and of the City Club, C.T., was born in Worcestershire in 1849. He is son of W. Powell, of Worcester, where he was educated, and commenced his business career. He joined the reporting staff of the *City Press* in 1871, becoming sub-editor of that well-known journal. Transferring to the *Cape Argus*, as sub-editor in 1880, he became editor in the following year, combining with that the Resident Directorship of the Argus P. & P. Co., in 1889. During this time he has taken part in most public movements in the capital of the Colony, including election work and the organisation of the Progressive party. He was elected in 1904 unopposed as Member of the Legislative Council for the Western Circle, is a Vice-President of the Cape Cambrian Society, and is on the executive of the S.A. Newspaper Press Union. Mr. Powell married, in 1876, Ellen Maria, dau. of Thomas Price, of Worcester.

POWRIE, F. W., M.L.A., sits in the Cape Legislative Assembly as Progressive Member for Wodehouse, for which electoral division he was elected in Feb. 1904.

PRETORIA, Bishop of. (See Right Rev. W. M. Carter.)

PRETORIOUS, Hon. M. S., M.L.C., is Member of the Cape Legislative Council for the Northeast Circle, for which electoral division he was re-elected in Feb., 1904. He is a member of the S.A. party.

PRICE, Lieut. Col. Rhys Howell, C.M.C., J.P., of Penworthem, Belgravia, East London, Cape Colony, and of the East London Club, was born in Monmouthshire in 1872; is son of T. R. Price (q.v.); served in the South Africa War, 1899-1902, in the Kaffrarian Rifles and in command of a mobile column, being wounded and mentioned in despatches on several occasion . He is a director of Malcomess and Co Ltd, of East London, and is a

Commissioner of the East London Harbour Board. He married, in 1902, Mary Constance, second dau. of the late John M. Peacock, of Queenstown, Cape Colony.

PRICE, Robert John, M.P., M.R.C.S., was educated at Univ. Coll. Hospital, and has sat in Parliament since 1892 as Liberal Member for the East Norfolk Division. He is a barrister, at law, a doctor (M.R.C.S.), and takes an active interest in some Rhodesian and Egyptian enterprises, being chairman of the Bulawayo an General Exploration Co., Ltd., the Unite African Explorations, Ltd., and many other companies.

PRICE, Thomas Rees, C.M.G., J.P., of Bryn Tirion, The Berea, Johannesburg, and of the Civil Service (C.T.), Rand, Pretoria, Bloemfontein, and East London Clubs, was born at Merthyr Tydfil, South Wales, Feb. 20, 184 He is the son of the late Rhys and Hannah Price, of Carmarthenshire, and was educated at Ballarat, S. Australia, and Swansea. Mr. Price was trained for the railway service, and had varied experience in different depts. of the Great Western Railway until 1880, when he became District Traffic Superintendent of the Cape Govt. Railways at Grahamstown, and acted as Asst. Traffic Manager at Port Elizabeth in 1881; Traffic Manager of the Eastern System in 1882; Traffic Manager of the Northern System in 1892; Cape Govt. Railway Agent in the Transvaal and O.R.C. in the same year; Chief Traffic Manager in 1893, and Asst. General Manager of Railways in 1901. He acted as Sir James Sivewright's adviser on railway matters in the negotiations with the Transvaal in 1890; is Hon. Col. of the Railway and Post Office Batt. of the Cape Peninsula Regt., is J.P. for the Colony of the Cape of Good Hope, and Vice-Pres. of the Cape Cambrian Society. He married, March 28, 1872, Miss Mary Howell, of Neath.

PRICE-DAVIES, Capt. Llewellyn Alberic Emilius, V.C., D.S.O., of Marrington Hall, Chirbury, Salop, was born in 1878, and is son of the late L. H. Price. He was educated at Marlborough and Sandhurst, and entered the King's Royal Rifle Corps as 2nd Lieut. in 1898, taking part in the South African War in 1899-1902, as Adjutant in the 2nd Batt. Mounted Infantry. He was present at the operations in the Transvaal and Orange River

Colonies, and received the V.C. for gallantry in the action at Blood River Poort, in Sept., 1901, under the following circumstances: The Boers had overwhelmed the right of the British column, and some 400 of them were galloping round the flank and rear of the guns, and calling upon the drivers to surrender. Lieut. Price Davies (as he then was) drew his revolver, and dashed in among the charging Boers in a gallant and desperate attempt to save the guns. Capt. Price Davies married, in Aug., 1906, Eileen, dau. of James Wilson, of Currygrane, Co. Longford.

PRIOR, Melton, the famous war correspondent and artist, is well-known in S.A., where he has represented the *Illustrated London News* on many occasions. His services on behalf of that paper have been retained on the following occasions: Ashanti War, 1873; the Carlist Rising, 1874; the Herzegovinian, Servian, Turkish, Basuto, Zulu, and first Boer Wars; Egypt, 1882; the Sudan and Nile Expedition, the Burmese War, the Jameson Raid episode of 1896, the Greco-Turkish War, and the Tuchim rising of 1897. He was besieged in Ladysmith during the Boer War of 1899-1902, and then represented his paper in the Russo-Japanese War. In addition to these services as war artist, Mr. Prior accompanied King Edward's (then Prince of Wales) suite to Athens in 1875, travelled with the Danish King's expedition through Iceland, accompanied the Marquess and Marchioness of Lorne on their first visit to Canada, and was present at the Berlin Conference. In 1902 he left to represent his journal at the Coronation Durbar at Delhi.

PRITCHARD, Percy Hubert, M.A., was attached to the Premier's office at Cape Town in 1899-1900; on the High Commissioner's Staff from 1900 until Feb., 1901, when he was appointed Clerk to the Secretary of the Orange River Colony Administration; acted as Clerk to the Colonial Secretary in June, 1902; subsequently he was appointed Editor of the *Orange River Colony Govt. Gazette*, and, later, Clerk in the Municipal and Native Affairs office in the Orange River Colony in 1904.

PROBYN, Leslie, C.M.G., of Sierra Leone and of 3, Old Court Mansions, W., and of the Orleans

Club, was born Feb. 23, 1862. He was educated at Charterhouse, and was called to the Bar, Middle Temple, in 1884; was captain in the 3rd Battn. of the Gloucestershire Regt. (Mil.) in 1883; is a Liveryman in the Gold and Silver Wire Drawers Co. of London, was a Liberal candidate for the Uxbridge division of Middlesex in 1892, and is now Governor of Sierra Leone. He married, in 1885, Emily Davies.

PURCELL, Major John Francis, D.S.O., of the Cape Mounted Riflemen, joined the force in 1880, and served in the Basuto Rebellion in 1881 (medal with clasp). He served with the Pondoland Field Force in 1894, and took part in the South African War in 1899-1902, including the operations in the Transvaal, Orange River and Cape Colonies (despatches and D.S.O.).

PURLAND, Capt. Thomas Terence Constantine, J.P., F.R.G.S., was employed in the Cape Government Service from 1879-1900; served in the control and audit office of the Treasury and Customs, and in the Divisional Courts in 1884; acted as Asst. Resident Magistrate at Simonstown in 1886, also Examining Officer for the Customs in 1890; Acting Superintendent at Shark's River Convict Station in 1894, and Asst. Superintendent and Accountant at the Breakwater Convict Station in 1895. In 1896 he was appointed Deputy Inspector of Prisons, and became Principal Clerk in the Convict Branch of the Colonial Office in 1899. His services were lent to the Commander-in-Chief to organize the Transvaal prisons, subsequently being appointed Director of Prisons in the Transvaal in 1900, which position he still bolds. He took part in the Basuto Rebellion in 1880-1, as Lieut. and adjt. in Prince Alfred's Guards, being severely wounded at Poqane (medal and clasp), and receiving the honorary rank of Captain. He is a J.P. for Cape Colony and the Transvaal, a member of the Tender Board, and was a member of the late Municipal Commission at Pretoria.

QUILLIAM, William Henry Abdullah, Sheikh-ul-Islam of the British Isles, Bey of the Ottoman Empire, Kahn of Afghanistan, Orders of the Osmanieh (2nd class) and Medjidie (3rd class), Impiaz (Premier Double Class), Iftihar (Turkish), Lion and Sun of Persia (2nd class), Izgat of

Afghanistan, of Fern Bank, Fairfield Crescent, Liverpool, Woodland Towers, Ouchan, Isle of Man, and of Rue Akaret Beshiktache, Constantinople, was born at Liverpool, April 10, 1856, and was admitted as a Solicitor in 1878. He founded the Liverpool Muslim Society in 1887, founded the *Crescent* newspaper in 1892, and the *Islamia World Magazine* in 1903; visited Morocco in 1884 and 1893; was the first Englishman to enter the sacred city of Wazan (March, 1903); went on a special mission to Lagos, as representative of the Sultan of Turkey; appointed Persian Consul at Liverpool in 1901, and Ottoman Consul to the Isle of Man in 1905; was appointed Special Imperial Ottoman Commissioner to Roumelia, and conducted an inquiry in Macedonia and elsewhere until April, 1905. Mr. Quilliam has received from time to time many marks of favour, decorations, and emoluments, from the Shah of Persia, the Sultan of Turkey, the Shahzadè of Afghanistan (Nasrullah Khan), and H.H. Abdur-Rahman Khan, Ameer of Afghanistan. He has published *Faith of Islam*, 1887; *Fanatics and Fanaticism*, 1888; *Religion of Sword*, 1890; *Polly* (a novel), 1892; *Wages of Sin* (a novel), 1894; *Moses, Christ, and Mohammed*, 1897; *Studies in Islam*, 1898; *Manx Antiquities*, 1898; *The Balkan Question*, 1903; *Az-Nahir-ud-deen*, 1904; and another novel, *King Bladud*, in 1904. He married, in 1879, Hannah, dau. of the late William Johnstone, and his wife and several of his children are decorated by the Sultan of Turkey.

RABIE, Dirk de Vos, M.I.A., is Bond Member of the Cape Legislative Assembly for Worcester, for which electoral division he was re-elected in Feb., 1904.

RADEMEYER, Jacobus Michael, M.L.A, of Humansdorp, Cape Colony, is member of the Cape Legislative Assembly for Humansdorp, for which electoral division he was re-elected in Feb., 1904. He belongs to the S African party.

RADFORD, Arthur, J.P., of Bradfield Hall near Reading, is on the London Committee of the Jupiter G. M. Co., Ltd., Nigel Deep, Ltd. Rand Victoria East, Ltd., Rand Victoria Mines Ltd., South Rose Deep, Ltd., and Sub Nigel Ltd.

RADNOR, Earl of, of Longford Castle, near Shrewsbury, was born in 1868. He acted as private secretary to the Rt. Hon. H. Chaplin from 1890-2, and was elected M.P. for the Wilton Division in 1892-1900. Lord Radnor took part in the S. African War in 1900. In 1891 he married Julian, dau. of Charles Balfour.

RADZIWILL, Princess Catherine, of Kenilworth, near Cape Town, was born in 1858; she is descended from a princely Polish family, her father, Count Adam Rzewuski, having been formerly Ambassador at Madrid, and A.D.C to Czar Nicholas I. Her mother was Mdlle Daschkoff. The Princess was a niece of Gen Skobeloff, and also of Mme. de Balzac, wife of the great novelist at whose house in Paris she spent many of her early days. She was educated in the Parisian capital, and was betrothed at the age of fifteen to Prince W. Radziwill, whom she married in 1873. She then resided mostly at Berlin, where she became intimately acquainted with the Emperor William II., the Emperor and Empress Frederick, and the present German Emperor, and moved in the highest Court and diplomatic circles in Germany and Russia.

Taking up journalism, she started a weekly paper in Cape Town called *Greater Britain*. In May, 1902, she was convicted in Cape Town of forging the late Mr. Cecil Rhodes's signature to a bill for £1,000, and was sentenced to two years' detention in a house of correction. She was released however, in Aug. 1903, and in the following Nov. obtained a writ against Mr. Rhodes's trustees in respect of a claim against his estate for £1,400,000 under an alleged agreement dated about June 20, 1899.

Princess Radziwill has published some novels in French and has contributed a good deal to the British and American Press.

RADZIWILL, Lieut. Prince, is son of Princess Catherine Radziwill, and served in the South African War as a trooper in K.F.S., having previously failed to obtain a commission. This, however, he gained eventually, was mentioned in despatches, and on the conclusion of the war returned to Russia.

RAITT, Alexander Seaton, M.L.C., is member for the Witwatersrand Labour Community in the Transvaal Legislative Council. He is a fluent speaker, and has the gift of being capable of putting forward every point for the party whom he represents.

RAMSAY, Charles W., of 62, London Wall, E.C., is Chairman of the Amalgamated Mining and Exploration Co., Ltd., Egyptian Exploration Development Co., Ltd., and Nile Valley Block E, Ltd., and is director of the Mines and Minerals Exploration Syndicate, Ltd.

RANDALL, A. B., of Bryanston, Highfield Mill, Upper Norwood, S.E., is Chairman of White Cliffs Opal Mines, Ltd., director of the Inez G. M. Co., Ltd., Mayo (Rhodesia) Development Co., Ltd., Menzies Mining and Exploration Co., Ltd., and United Rhodesia Gold Fields, Ltd., on the London Committee of the Buffelsdoorn Estate and G. M. Co., Ltd., Consolidated Langlaagte Mines, Ltd., Ginsberg G. M. Co., Ltd., Kleinfontein Deep, Ltd., Langlaagte Royal G. M. Co., Ltd., New Primrose G. M. Co., Ltd., New Rietfontein Estate Gold Mining, Ltd., and the Randfontein Deep, Ltd., and in on the London Board of the Glencairn Main Reef, G. M. Co., Ltd., and the New Unified Main Reef G. M. Co., Ltd.

RANSOME, James Stafford, M.Inst. C.E., M.Inst. Journalists, of 16, Carlisle Mansions, S.W., Sibton, Yorford, Suffolk, and of the Constitutional and Tokyo Clubs, was born in London, Dec. 6, 1860. He was educated at Rugby, and commenced journalistic work about 1880; he has acted as special correspondent for numerous London papers in different parts of the world, and in S. Africa for the *Engineer* and *Pall Mall Gazette* in 1902-3. He is the author of several publications, including *Modern Labour*, 1893; *Japan in Transition*, 1899; *The Nonsense Bluebook*, 1899; *The Engineer in S. Africa*, 1903; and various technical works and pamphlets on economic questions. He is also founder and editor of *African Engineering*. Recreations: shooting, punting, billiards. He married, in 1886, Helena, dau. of the late Major Thomas Cooke, the Indian Army.

RASSAM, Hormuzd, F.R.G.S., of 30, Westbourne Villas, Hove, was born in 1824, and is a naturalised Englishman, but of Chaldean nationality. He was educated at Magdalen Coll., Oxford. For some years he was engaged in research work for the British Museum. He became 1st Asst. Political Resident at Aden in recognition of his services as representative of the British Govt. at the Court of the Imaum of Muscat, when the serious complications arose between the Imaum and the Sultan of Zanzibar. He acted as special envoy to the crazy King, Theodore, of Abyssinia, in 1864, when the latter had imprisoned Consul Cameron and other Europeans. Mr. Rassam succeeded in obtaining their release, but subsequently they were recaptured, together with the whole of the mission, the result being that they were imprisoned for two years; this being the cause of the Abyssinian War. He was thanked by the Govt. for his services. Author of *British Mission to Abyssinia and Asshur*, and the *Land of Nimrod*. Mr. Rassam is a great linguist, and is fond of reading. He married, in 1869, a dau. of Capt. S. C. Price, 72nd Highlanders.

RATHBONE, Edgar Philip, of Johannesburg (P.O. Box 927), and of the Rand, Pretoria, and Barberton Clubs, was born at Liverpool, Sept. 3, 1856. He is the son of the late Mr. Philip H. Rathbone, of Liverpool, was educated at Univ. College, London, the Royal Sch. of Mines, London, and at the Sch. of Mines at Freiberg and Liege. He is a member of the following institutions: Institute of Civil Engineers, Institute of Mining and Metallurgy, S. African Association of Engineers, Chemical, Metallurgical, and Mining Society of S.A., Geological Society of S.A., and is an Associate Member of the Chamber of Mines, Johannesburg. During some twenty-five years Mr. Rathbone has been engaged in active mining operations in S.A., Bolivia, Argentine Republic, the Brazils, Mexico, U.S.A., British Columbia, Klondike, and many of the European mining districts. From the first he showed a firm belief in the deep level properties of the Rand, upon which he made many reports, and did great service to the industry, together with Mr. W. A. Wills, by writing a series of articles drawing attention to the potentialities of the Rand Goldfields, principally through the medium of the *S.A. Mining Journal* and the *African Review*. For several years Mr. Rathbone occupied the position

of Inspector of Mines under the late Transvaal Government. He married Miss Barbara Georges in 1892.

RATHENAU, Geheimrath, Dr. Emil, is the founder of the *Allgemeine Elektricitäts Gesellsehaft* of Berlin, and has been its manager ever since its inception. He has brought the company to such a solid position that it is today probably the largest electrical concern in Europe. Geheimrath Rathenau has carried out huge electrical undertakings all over the world with such success that he has never found the least difficulty in obtaining the necessary financial backing for any new scheme advanced by him. But perhaps the greatest project with which he is connected is the great scheme to supply the Rand with electrical power from the Victoria Falls (see H. Wilson Fox). He is father of the Berlin Electrical Works, which are considered to be amongst the most economically managed in the world. As the leader of the electrical technical industry in Europe he enjoys the confidence of the highest financial circles, and he is received with some favour at the German Court.

RAUBENHEIMER H. J., M.L.A, is the new Bond representative of the electoral division of George, C.C., in the Assembly, having been first elected in Feb., 1904.

RAVENSTEIN, Ernest George, Gold Medallist Royal Geog. Society, of 2, York Mansions, Battersea Park, S.W., and of the Savage Club, was born, Dec. 30, 1834. He was attached to the Topographical and Statistical Depot at the War Office in 1856, first president of the German Gymnastic Society from 1861-72; president of Section E, British Assn., 1891, and professor of geography at Bedford College in 1884-5. He is also honorary Fellow of various geographical societies. He is the author of a map of Eastern Equatorial Africa, published by the R.G.S. in 1881-3, a map of Ibea or British E. Africa, published by the Imperial British E. Africa Co. in 1889, a language map of Africa in 1883, and *The Lake Regions of Central Africa*, 1891. He reported on the Cermatology of Tropical Africa in 1892-1901 to the British Assn.; also on the meteorological observations in British East Africa in 1893, and made climatological observations at Colonial and foreign stations, including Tropical Africa, in 1904. He married, in 1858, Ada S. Parry.

RAW, George H., of 278, Kensington Gore, London, S.W., is Chairman of the Natal-Zululand Railway Co., Ltd., director of the African Saltpetre Co., Ltd., and the South African Breweries, Ltd., is on the London Committees of the Cassel Coal Co., Ltd., May Consolidated G. M. Co., Ltd., Natal Rank, Ltd., and Witwatersrand G. M. Co., Ltd., and is on the London Board of the City and Suburban G. M. and Estate Co., Ltd., Moodie's G. M. and Exploration Co., New Heriot G. M. Co., Ltd., and the Nigel G. M. Co., Ltd.

RAWLINGS, Edward, of 16, Victoria Street, London, S.W., is Chairman of Barrett's Brewery and Bottling Co., Ltd., Barrett's Country Bottling Co., Ltd., Canterbury and Paragon, Ltd., Cataract G. M. Co., Ltd., Hans Crescent Hotel Co., Ltd., New Rand Southern G. M. Co., Ltd., Springfield Breweries, Ltd., Washington Brewery Co., Ltd., and the Woodstock (Transvaal) Gold Mine, Ltd., and director of the British Transvaal Mines, Ltd., Goebel Brewing Co., Ltd., Hyde Park Hotel, Ltd., and the Queen Anne Residential Mansions and Hotel Co., Ltd.

RAWLINSON, John Frederick Peel, K.C., M.P., J.P., of 5, Crown Office Row, Temple, E.C., and of the United University, Prince's, and Isthmian Clubs, was born, Dec. 21, 1860, and is youngest son of the late Sir Christopher Rawlinson. He was educated at Eton and Trinity College, Cambridge was called to the Bar in 1884, joining the South Eastern Circuit, as Q.C., in 1897; represented the Treasury in Inquiry in S. Africa as to circumstances connected with the Jameson Raid in 1896, and took evidence on that occasion it Cape Town, Pretoria, Johannesburg, Kimberley, and Mafeking. He has been a member of the General Council of the Bar since its formation; acted as Recorder of Cambridge in 1898; became Commissary of Cambridge University in 1900, and J.P. for Cambridgeshire in 1901. He contested Ipswich in the Conservative interest in 1900, and was elected member for Cambridge University in 1906. Unmarried.

RAWNSLEY, Col. Claude, D.S.O., was born at Saltash, Aug. 4, 1862, and is the eldest son of the late Lieut. Col. T. J. Rawnsley, Army Ord. Dept. He was educated at Queen Elizabeth's Grammar Sch., Cranbrook, and the R.M.A., Woolwich; joined the Royal Arty. in 1882, and was transferred to the Army Service Corps as Capt. in 1889. He served in the S. African War, 1899-1902, first as D.A.A.G. and afterwards as A.A.G. on the Lines of Communication (mentioned in despatches, D.S.O., Queen's medal with three clasps, and King's medal with two clasps). Recreations: hunting, polo, and racquets. He married, in Aug., 1887, Lilian, dau. of the late Capt. Fredk. Wood, R.M., and Receiver-Gen. of the Gold Coast.

RAWSON, Col. H. E., R.E., F.R.G.S., is son of the late Sir Rawson W. Rawson, K.C.M.G., C.B., a former Colonial Office official and Governor of the Windward Islands from 1868 to 1875. Colonel Rawson is an expert authority on submarine mining; served in the South African war, and in 1905 was appointed Colonel on the Staff for Royal Engineers in South Africa. He is a Freemason; holds the Royal Engineer Fowke medal, and is a member of the Royal Meteorological and Physical Societies. in 1874 Colonel Rawson played cricket in the County XI. for Kent, and was one of the English Association football team.

RAYNE, Leonard, of 36, Albert Mansions, Battersea Park, S.W., and of Johannesburg, has for some years past been a prominent figure as actor and manager in the theatrical world of S. Africa. He is lessee of the Gaiety Theatre, Johannesburg, joint lessee of the Port Elizabeth Opera House, besides running several theatrical ventures in other S.A. towns. He married in 1895 a daughter of J. S. Ham, lately instructor of shipwrights in Portsmouth Dockyard.

RAYNE, Mrs. Leonard (Amy Grace), of 36, Albert Mansions, Battersea Park, London, was born in 1876 at Southsea, where also she was educated privately. As a girl she distinguished herself as an elocutionist, and made her first appearance on the stage at the age of seventeen at the Grand Theatre, Islington. Mrs. Leonard Rayne is particularly well known in S. Africa, where she has toured with her own company, starring as Nell Gwynne, Cigarette,

Wally, Jane, Betsy, Constance (in the *Musketeers*), Dulcie Larondie (in the *Masqueraders*), Minnie (in *A Message from Mars*), etc. She was in Mafeking during the siege, and married in 1895 Leonard Rayne (q.v.).

RAYNER, Sir Thomas Crossley, Kt. Bach., K.C., of 35, Main Street, Georgetown, B. Guiana, 1, Plowden Buildings, Temple, E.C., and of the Royal Societies and Camera Clubs, was born at Manchester, April 19, 1860, and is son of Thomas Rayner, M.D., of Manchester. He was educated at Owens Coll., Manchester, and was called to the Bar, Middle Temple, in the Easter term, 1882, and joined the Northern circuit. He was appointed a District Commissioner of the Gold Coast Colony in 1887, and acted as Queen's Advocate of that colony, and as Puisne Judge in 1889-90; was given the post of Stipendiary Magistrate of San Fernando, Trinidad, in 1891, and acted as a Puisne Judge of the Supreme Court, 1891-93. Sir Thomas was Commissioner of Tobago in 1892, and was also chairman of a commission of enquiry into the Registry of the Supreme Court in the same year. He was appointed Chancellor of the Diocese of Trinidad in 1893, Puisne Judge of the Gold Coast Colony in 1894, and Chief Justice of Lagos in 1895. He acted on three occasions as Deputy Governor of Lagos; was appointed Attorney General of British Guiana in 1902, King's Counsel for that colony, and Chancellor of the Diocese of Guiana in 1903. Sir Thomas prepared a new edition in five vols. of the *Laws of British Guiana* in 1904-5. He married, in 1889, Agnes, younger dau. of William Harrison.

READ, Capt. Beresford Moutray, of 7, Trinity Crescent, Folkestone, and of the Sports Club, was born at Cheltenham, Sept. 16, 1874, and is son of John Moutray Read, of Donnybrook, Ireland. He joined the Lagos Constabulary in 1897, serving in S. Borgu in 1895 (mentioned in despatches, medal, and clasp); served in the Ashanti war in 1900 with the Lagos Contingent, including the siege of Kumara, when he was severely wounded (mentioned in despatches, medal, and clasp). He took part also with the Lagos Contingent in the Aro Expedition in 1901-2 (medal and clasp), and commanded the Lagos Contingent of the W.A.F.F. at the Coronation in 1902 (decoration). He was transferred on promotion to the 2nd Battalion of

the Gold Coast Regiment in 1903, in which he is still serving. Recreations: shooting and fishing. Unmarried.

READY, Capt. Felix Fordati, D.S.O., of the Army and Navy Club, London, was born at the Isle of Man, July 16, 1872; is son of Col. J. L. Ready, of Ellerslie, Hawkhurst, Kent, and was educated at Wellington Coll., passing into the R. Berkshire Regiment. He served with the Egyptian Army in the Nile Expedition in 1898, being present at the battles of Athara and Khartoum (despatches, 4th Class Medjidie, two medals with two clasps) He also served in the South African war in 1889, 1900, and 1902 (despatches, Queen's medal with four clasps, D.S.O.). Captain Ready was at the Staff Coll. in 1901, and is at present employed as D.A.Q.M.G. at Gibraltar. He married in Dec., 1900, Marguerite Violet, dau. of the late William Cotterill, of Jongswood, Hawkhurst.

REED, Rev. George Cullen Harvey, F.R.G.S., F.R.C.I., of the London Mission, Dombadema; of Bulilima, S. Rhodesia, and the Bulawayo Club; was born at St. Leonard's-on-Sea, Eng.; is son of the Rev. Andrew Reed, B.A., and grandson of the Rev. Andrew Reed, D.D., founder of the Earlswood, Reedham, and Putney Asylums. He was educated at the Univ. Coll. Sch., Lond., and Univ. Coll., Lond. He first visited S.A. in 1887, and travelled for five years in Cape Colony and Natal. In 1894 he undertook mission work in Rhodesia under the Lond. Missionary Soc. Unmarried.

REED, Major Hamilton Lyster, V.C., of the Naval and Military Club, Lond.; was born in 1869; is son of Sir Andrew Reed, K.C.B., C.V.O., and entered the R.F.A. in 1888, becoming Captain in 1898, and Major in 1904. He served in the South African war (1899-1902) as Capt. of the 7th Battery, R.F.A., as Adjt., H.F.A., and as D.A.A.G., being decorated with the V.C. for gallantry at Colenso, where he was wounded. He was three times mentioned; despatches, and received the Queen's medal with six clasps, and the King's medal. Unmarried.

REID, Arthur Henry, F.H.C.I., of Mannamead, Kenilworth, Cape Town, and of the City (C.T.) and Rand Clubs; was born at Plymouth Devon, July 5, 1856; was educated at the Gram. Sch.,

Plymouth, and was trained as an engineer. He went to Cape Town in 1877 as Asst. City Engineer; was appointed City Engineer of Grahamstown in 1879, and in 1882 started a private practice in Port Elizabeth. He went to the Rand in 1886, practising as an architect; sat on the Johannesburg Town Council for some years, and took an active part in the foundation of scientific and technical institutions. In 1897 he returned to Cape Town where, in partnership with his brother, Walter Held, he still practises his profession. Mr. A. H. Reid is Fellow of Royal Inst. of British Architects; Fel. Sanitary Inst. of Great Britain; Chairman of Board of Examiners for Sanitary Inst. in S.A.; Past Pres. of S.A. Assoc. of Engineers (Johannesburg); Councillor for City of Cape Town, and F.S.A. He married, June 15, 1884, Miss Victoria Walsh.

REID, James, of Hamiota, The Avenue, Beckenham, is a director of the Albion (Transvaal) Gold Mines, Ltd., Klip River Estate and Geld Mines, Ltd., Mikado G. M. Co., Ltd., Mines and Banking Corp., Ltd., and the Transvaal Mortgage, Loan and Finance Co., Ltd.

REITZ, Dr. Francois Willem, was formerly, in the 'eighties, a Judge of, and subsequently President of, the Orange Free State. Later on he succeeded Dr. Leyds (q.v.) as State Attorney of the South African Republic, becoming eventually Pres. Kruger's State Secretary, and it was in the latter capacity that he penned the ultimatum in Oct. 1899, which immediately preceded the Beer invasion of British territory in South Africa. He was at one time regarded in the Transvaal as having progressive tendencies, though without sufficient strength to influence the President. But his ostensible attitude was probably merely the veil to temporarily obscure that hostility to England which he had expressed more than twenty years before the South African war, when he allowed that he aimed at the expulsion of the British from South Africa. As Secretary of State in the Transvaal Mr. Reitz was deep in Mr. Kruger's confidence, and his previous association with the Free State could not fail to be of the utmost value to the astute Pres. of the S.A.R. in supporting his intrigues with the Orange Colony.

In 1900 Mr. Reitz published a pamphlet which contained an *ex parte* statement of the case for the Boers against Great Britain, in which he prophesied that "Freedom shall rise in South Africa as the sun out of the morning clouds, as freedom rose in the United States of North America. Then shall it be from Zambesi to Simon's Bay, Africa for the Afrikander".

At the Peace Conference at Vereeniging, Mr. Reitz was one of the most difficult of the Boer representatives. He held out for continuing the war as long as possible; then suggested such concessions as ceding the Witwatersrand to Great Britain, or, alternatively, acknowledging a British Protectorate. Ultimately, however, he signed the Articles of Peace, but in the *North American Review* of Nov. 1902, he wrote frankly that he did so in his representative capacity, and not as an individual, apparently retaining a mental reservation that was not morally bound to abide by the terms to which he had affixed his signature.

After the South African war Mr. Reitz joined the Irreconcilables in Europe, and, later on, undertook a lecturing tour through America to raise funds for the Boers. He denounced the British conduct of the campaign, and accused Lord Milner (q.v.), Mr. Chamberlain (q.v.), and other British Ministers of bad faith in their interpretations of the peace terms, particularly on the question of amnesty. At Brussels he complained that the English with their habitual bad faith were spreading false reports designed to show that Generals Botha, De la Rey, and De Wet were not acting in perfect harmony with Mr. Kruger's party, with whose opinions, so ably declared by Mr. Reitz, it was desired to identify the Glorious Trio in the eyes of Europe. So venomous was the attitude of Mr. Reitz that Mr. Chamberlain referred to him when addressing the Boer Generals at the Colonial Office in these words: "We want to be friends, but the friendship must be on both sides, and when anyone gives us reason to believe that he will not be friendly if he returns to South Africa, we will do our best to prevent him from returning".

Mr. Reitz sailed for the United States in his forlorn hope in Sept., 1902, and began his agitation with the article in the *North American Review* previously alluded to. His plan was to embark on a lecturing tour, denouncing Britain and her Ministers, which he did with inexcusable recklessness, and so violent were his denunciations both in the States and in Europe that they called forth remonstrances even in the columns of the pro-Boer journals.

The career of the ex-State Secretary was throughout very much assisted by his mental attainments. Amongst his associates in the Transvaal he shone as a speaker, and as a writer. One of his contributions to Afrikander literature was *Vijftig Uitgesogte Afrikaanse Gedigte*, a volume of fifty songs in the Taal, containing translations from Burns and other British poets. Mr. Reitz was sufficiently astute to understand how much depended upon the question of language in South Africa. The Taal, ungrammatical, and possessed of no literature, could not held its own against the English tongue, and recognising the supreme importance of this question he eloquently advocated at the Congress at Coutrai (Aug., 1902) the adoption of the more polished language of the Hollanders in the curriculum of schools for the Boer children.

It cannot be claimed that Mr. Reitz has advanced the Boer cause in any way since he left Delagoa Bay for Europe. He was eventually allowed to return to his estates in the Orange River Colony. His sons had all studied in Europe, and all fought in the Boer war, one of them being wounded and taken prisoner.

RENNIE, George Hall, of 4, East India Avenue, London, E.C., is a partner in the ship owning firm of John T. Rennie, Son and Co., and is on the London Committee of the Natal Bank, which acts as bankers to the Colony of Natal, and which curiously enough has practically always been managed by Scotchmen.

REVOIL, Mons., was the chief French Plenipotentiary at the Moroccan Conference at Algeçiras in 1906.

REYERSBACH, Louis J., of Welfenheim, Johannesburg, was born in Hanover, Germany, in 1869. He is son of M. M. Reyersbach, and was educated in Hanover. Mr. Reyersbach was for some years in Kimberley and London in charge of the diamond business of the great firm of Wernher,

Beit and Co. He joined the house of H. Eckstein and Co., at the end of 1901, and represents that firm on the Boards of the Rand Mines, Ltd., the Robinson, and other of the premier G.M. Cos. of the Rand. He was in Kimberley during the siege, and is a member of the Executive of the Transvaal Chamber of Mines. Mr. Reyersbach married, in 1897, Miss Martha Wallach, of Aix-la-Chapelle.

REYMESCOLE, Capt. William Elmer, of 20, St. George's Road, Eccleston Square, S.W.; was Assist. Collector in the Uganda Protectorate in 1905; also Assistant Secretary to the Uganda Administration in the same year. Recreations: Fishing and shooting. He is Capt. in the V.B. East Surrey Regt.

REYNOLDS, Edward Charles, of the National Bank of South Africa, Ltd., of Circus Place, London Wall, E.C., was born in London in 1871, and received his banking training at the head offices of the London and Westminster Bank. He joined the National Bank of South Africa in 1891, at which time it was styled the Nat. Bank of the S.A.R., and has since been in charge of a number of upcountry and coast branches, amongst which may be mentioned Krugersdorp, Lydenburg, Port Elizabeth, East London, Durban, Cape Town, and Pretoria, at which latter town he was during the recent S. African war, becoming manager of the National Bank of S.A. in 1903

The bank was established in 1890 with a paid up capital of £502,000. The present capital is £1,100,000, with power to increase to £4,000,000. In its early stages there were very few branches, but now they number over 72, and are established in practically every big town in South Africa. In 1892 and 1894 a dividend of 5 per cent, was declared; in 1895 7 per cent.; 1896, 1897, and 1898 10 per cent., and a like interim dividend was declared in 1899, when, unfortunately, the Boer war broke out, and business was practically at a standstill all over the country. Nevertheless, in 1901 21 per cent. was paid, and in 1902 7 per cent. Since then a regular dividend of 8 per cent, has been maintained. The reserve of the bank has grown to £140,000, and it deposits now reach over £7,650,000. The bank acts as bankers to the

Transvaal Government.

Mr. Reynolds married, in 1895, a dau. of the late C. H. Caldecott. His recreations, when a busy life permits of any, are hunting, shooting, and golf.

RICHARDS, David, of the National Liberal Club, Whitehall, London, S.W., is Chairman of the Tarkwa Main Reef, Ltd., and director of Sons of Gwalia, Ltd.

RICARDE-SEAVER, Major Francis Ignatius. (See Obituaries.)

RICHARDS, Roger Charnock, Barrister at Law, F.S.S., of 14D, Hyde Park Mansions, London, W., of 2, King's Bench Walk, Temple, E.C., and of the City Liberal, National Liberal, and Reform (Manchester) Clubs, is son of John Richards, of Preston, where Mr. B. C. Richards was born, March 15, 1850. He was educated at Kirkham Grammar Sch., and at Bramham Coll., near Leeds, with a view to the Bar, but abandoned this career, as well as a course at Cambridge, owing to temporary deafness. On the death of his uncle, H. C. Richards, J.P., by whom he was adopted, he succeeded with his brother to an extensive business of cotton spinners and manufacturers at Kirkham, Lanes., and chemical manufacturers at St. Helens. During the same period he was also closely identified with agriculture in the Fylde district of Lancashire. Mr. Richards went to Manchester in 1879, where for twenty years he was actively engaged in commercial and political life, becoming incidentally Hon. Secretary of the National Reform Union for some years.

After declining, at Mr. Gladstone's request, to contest Rossendale against Lord Hartington, he unsuccessfully stood for Bolton, together with the late Joseph C. Haslam, in the Liberal interest in 1886.

Mr. Richards retired from his various businesses in 1887, and was called to the Bar, 1891, practising for some years with considerable success on the Northern Circuit. Meanwhile, in 1892, he served in England and Ireland as an assistant commissioner on the agricultural section of the Royal Commission on Labour. Though still practicing in

arbitrations, he is identified in the City with influential South African groups, and is a director of Henderson's Transvaal Estates, Daggafontein G.M. Co., Daggafontein Prospecting Co., Tyne Valley Colliery Co., Henderson's Nigel Co., etc., etc. Mr. Richards has written for the *Fortnightly Review* on Landlords' Preferential Position, and married in 1873. One of his Sons was Craven Scholar at Cambridge, and Vice-Chancellor's medallist. Another son was killed in endeavouring to save life in a mine accident at Johannesburg.

RICHARDS, Acting Commissioner William John, of Cape Town (Post Office Box, 707), was born March 21, 1857, and left his home in Merthyr Tydfil at the age of twenty-three to enter the Salvation Army Training Home, in order to fit himself for officership in the ranks of that organisation. He subsequently held various appointments in England, after which he was in 1898 placed at the head of the Salvation Army in Denmark, a position he held until in Nov. 1904, he was appointed Acting Commissioner and Chief Officer in charge of the Salvation Army work in South Africa.

The work of the Salvation Army in South Africa now extends from Cape Colony to the Zambesi River, and is represented by 200 officers, 63 corps and societies, 24 social institutions, and 10 day schools. The social side of its operations stands out prominently. The 24 Institutions above named include 6 shelters for destitute men, at which during the year 1904 100,686 beds and 203,819 meals were supplied; 7 rescue homes, with accommodation for 162 women; 1 inebriates' home; 3 farms or land colonies; 3 prison-gate homes, the officers in connection with which visit the local prisons regularly and hold from 50 to 60 meetings each month among the prisoners; and 4 workshops, at which during last year employment was given to 3,000 men.

RICKETTS, Arthur, C.M.G., M.B. (Lond.), M.R.C.S., L.R.C.P., of Freshfield, Woodside Park, London, was born at Haywards Heath, Sussex, Aug. 7, 1874. He is son of Wm. Tyler Ricketts, Solicitor, of Chailey, near Lewes, and was educated at Dulwich Coll. He was House Physician at Univ. Coll. Hosp., and served as Civil Surgeon in the S.A. Field Force, 1899 1901, being mentioned in Lord Roberts's despatches, and receiving the C.M.G., medal and clasps for Paardeburg, Driefontein, Relief of Kimberley, Wittebergen, and Transvaal. He returned to S.A. as Surg. Capt. in the Irish Horse, 1902, relinquishing his command in Feb., 1903, with the hon. rank of Capt. in the Army.

RIDER, Rev. William Wilkinson, F.R.C.I., Superintendent Minister of the Wesleyan Methodist Church of S. Africa, Secretary of the Army and Navy Committee of that Church, and Commissioned Chaplain of the Natal Militia; of Dundee, Natal; was born in England April 18, 1861. He became a Wesleyan Minister in 1882, serving for a short period in Newfoundland. In 1883 he went to S. Africa; removed to Port Elizabeth in 1897, and for five years was a member of the Governing Committee of the Govt. Hospital there, also a member of the Board of Management of the many schools on the Grey Foundation. On the outbreak of the S. African War in 1899, he assisted in establishing a Local Refuge Relief Committee, caring for some thousands of fugitives. Of this he was elected Vice-President, assisting in the careful disbursement of the Mansion House Funds at this centre. During the S. African War, also, he was engaged at Modder River in conveying hospital and other stores soon after the disastrous battle at Magersfontein, and at Rensburg, supplying Gen. French's force with numerous gifts when starting on their famous march to the relief of Kimberley and the surrounding of Cronje. He came to England in 1900 on a lecturing tour, dealing with S. African history and the genesis of war, serving for a few months the Imp. S. African Assn. Recreation: writing. He married, Aug. 27, 1891, Elizabeth, dau. of the late Francis Bell, the founder of Stamford Hill, Natal.

RIDGEWAY, Col. Rt. Hon. Sir J. West, P.C., K.C.B., G.C.M.G., K.C.S.I., has had a large and varied experience in Military, Diplomatic, and Governmental affairs. Joining the Bengal Army in 1861, he became a Lieut.-Col. in 1881, during which period he did much good work on the Afghan Frontier, for which he was decorated. From 1880-4 he acted as Under-Secy. to the Govt. of India in the Foreign Dept., and as Commissioner for fixing the frontier between Russia and Afghanistan in 1885; was on special duty in St. Petersburg in 1886-7, and in the latter year he was Under-Secy. for Ireland. Sir West Ridgeway was Envoy Extraordinary to the Sultan of Morocco in 1892-3; Governor of the Isle of Man from 1893-95, and Governor and Commander-in-Chief of Ceylon from 1896-1903. At the General Election in 1906, he was unsuccessful Parliamentary candidate for the City, and he was soon after appointed Chairman of the S. African Committee appointed to advise H.M. Govt. on the subject of the proposed new Constitution of the Transvaal and Orange River Colonies, with special reference to the various questions affecting the franchise and the social and political needs of those Committees. (See Lord Elgin.) He married, in 1881, Line dau. of R. C. Bewicke. of Coulby Manor, Yorks.

RIVERS-WILSON, Sir Charles, G.C.M.G., C.B., of 21, Pont Street, London, S.W., and of the St. James's, Arthur's, and Marlborough Clubs, was born in 1831. He was educated at Eton and Balliol College, Oxford, and entered the Treasury in 1856; acted as Comptroller-Gen. of the National Debt Office from 1874-94, and as Finance Minister in Egypt from 1877-79, receiving the K.C.M.G. (see Sir Vincent Corbett). He was previously on the Council of the Suez Canal Co., and since 1895 has acted as President of the Grand Trunk Railway of Canada. He married, first, Caroline, dau. of R Cook, and secondly, in 1895, the Hon. Violet Mostyn, sister to the 7th Lord Vaux.

ROBERTS OF KANDAHAR, Field Marshal Earl, P.C., K.P., G.C.B., G.C.I.E., V.C., of Englemere, Ascot, and of the United Service and Athenaeum Clubs; was born in India, Sept. 30, 1832; is son of the late Sir Abraham Roberts, G.C.B., was educated at Eton, Sandhurst, and Addiscombe, and received his first commission as Second Lieutenant in the Bengal Artillery at the age of nineteen. He saw his first active service in the Indian Mutiny in 1857-8, taking part in the siege and capture of Delhi, where he was wounded, and in the actions. of Bolundshuhur, Allyghur, Agra, Kunoj, and Bundhera, and being present during the operations connected with the relief of Lucknow; the operations at Cawnpore; the defeat of the Gwalior contingents; the action of Khodagunge;

the reoccupation of Futtehghur; the storming of Meeangunge; the action of Koorsee, and the operations which culminated in the capture of Lucknow. It was at Khodagunge that Lieut. Roberts (as he then was) won his V.C. While following up the retreating enemy he saw a couple of Sepoys escaping with a standard. Galloping after them Roberts overtook them, when the men turned and faced him. Lieut. Roberts seized the standard, cutting down the man from whom he took it. While this struggle was going on the other Sepoy levelled his musket point blank at him and pulled the trigger. Fortunately it missed fire, and the standard and the future Field Marshal were saved. The same day Lord Roberts rode up to the rescue of a Sowar, who was being attacked by a rebel armed with a bayonet. Small of stature though he was, Lord Roberts killed the Sepoy with one blow of his sword and brought the Sowar into safety. For his services Lord Roberts was several times mentioned in despatches; received the thanks of the Governor-General of India; medal with three clasps, and the brevet rank of Major. A few years later Lord Roberts was again actively employed in India in the North-West Frontier Expedition of 1863, being present at the storming of Laloo; the capture of Umbeyla, and the destruction of Mulkah (medal with clasp). He then served through the Abyssinian Expedition in 1868 (medal and brevet of Lieut. Colonel), and the Looshai Expedition of 1871-2, playing his part in the capture of Kholel villages and the attack on the Northlang Range, and commanding the troops engaged at the burning of Taikoom (despatches). The Afghan War of 1878-80 next brought Lord Roberts into prominence, on which occasion he commanded the Kuram Valley Field Force at the capture of Pelwar Kotal. He carried out the reconnaissance to the summit of Shutar Garden Pass; defeated the attack by Mangals in the Sapari Pass; occupied the Khost district, and conducted the reconnaissance up the Kuram River. He then had command of the Kabul Field Force at the occupation of Kabul, his engagements in eluding the battle of Charasiah, and eventually commanded the whole force in the historic march from Kabul to Kandahar, after a series of brilliant victories inflicting a crushing defeat on Ayoob Khan. These splendid services were frequently referred to in despatches. He was thanked by the Government of India and the Governor-General in

Council, and on his return to England at the age of forty-eight, he was loaded with honours; received the thanks of Parliament, and was created a Baronet, K.C.B., and G.C.B., adding another medal with four clasps and the bronze star to his other decorations. In 1883 he was appointed Commander in Chief in India, and in the following year after the capture of Mandalay, Lord Roberts commanded the Army in the Burmese Expedition, for which he was again thanked by the Govt. of India (dispatches and clasp).

The South African War had already been in progress a couple of months or so when Lord Roberts was asked to start on his famous journey which was to end at Pretoria. He arrived at Cape Town and proceeded up country with a sufficient force to necessitate the withdrawal of Boers from Ladysmith to contest his progress through the Orange Free State to the Transvaal, thus in a great measure relieving the opposition which Sir Redvers Buller had found so disastrous in his persistent endeavours to relieve Sir George White's force in Ladysmith. The Commander-in-Chief's operations in the Orange Free State included the capture of Gen. Cronje's forces at Paardeburg, and the actions at Poplar Grove, Driefontein, Vet River, and Zand River. Leaving Bloemfontein, Lord Roberts followed hard in the wake of the fleeing President of the South African Republic. He entered the Transvaal, and engaged the Boer forces about Johannesburg, Pretoria, and Diamond Hill on June 11 and 12, 1900. From July to November of that year Lord Roberts was principally occupied in that part of the Transvaal east of Pretoria, and his last big action was at Belfast on Aug. 267, 1900. By this time the Boer States were apparently subjugated, and Lord Roberts returned home to be created an Earl and a Knight of the Garter, receiving also the Queen's medal with six clasps. The assumption that the War was then practically over was open to question, and the obvious doubt was whether the apparent cessation of hostilities (see Christian de Wet) was not seized upon by the Government as a pretext to appeal to the country for another term of office. But in any case the indications did not point to the Commander-in-Chief being privy to any such merely political move. Since Lord Roberts retired from active participation in the affairs of the Army, he has been adding still more eminent services to his country by throwing all the weight of his authority and experience into an effort to arouse the British public to a sense of the dangerous in efficiency of the land defences of the Empire, and Great Britain has not been backward in recognising his efforts in this as well as in other directions The Crown has bestowed titles; he has received the thanks of the Govt. of India and of both Houses of Parliament; Universities have conferred honorary degrees; cities and boroughs innumerable have given their freedoms, and the Council of the Royal United Service Institution has appointed him their Chairman in succession to Admiral H.S.H. Prince Louis of Battenberg. He was a member of the Committee of the Volunteer Commission in 1906. Lord Roberts published *The Rise of Wellington*, in 1895, and *Forty-one Years in India,* in 1897. He has always led an abstemious life, and has a magnificent constitution, of which he takes the greatest care. He rises every morning about six o'clock, and disposes of a considerable amount of work before breakfast. He is a nonsmoker, and now finds exercise and recreation in horse riding and cycling. Lord Roberts married, in 1859, Nora Henrietta, dau. of Capt. Bews of the 73rd Foot. Lady Roberts, who is considerably taller for a woman than her husband is for a man, takes considerable interest in the Army Nursing Service.

ROBERTSON, Frederick Ewart, C.I.E., of 32, Courtfield Gardens, S.W., and of the Reform Club, was born in London, Feb. 24, 1847. He entered the Indian Public Works Dept. in 1868; served in the Railway Dept. principally on the N.W. Frontier, and joined the E. Indian Rly. as Chief Engineer in 1889. In 1897 he went to Egypt as President of the Board of Administration of Railways, Telegraphs and Port of Alexandria, leaving in 1898 to join Sir A. M. Rendel, K.C.I.E., as Consulting Engineer. He is the author of *A Practical Treatise on Organ Building*, and *An Arabic Vocabulary*. He married, Jan. 7, 1879, Jane, dau. of Mungo Ramsey, of Crieff.

ROBERTSON, Captain James R. D., took part in the Karene Expedition, Sierra Leone in 1898-9 (medal with clasp), and the S. African War in 1902. In 1906 he was appointed Asst. District Commissioner in Southern Nigeria.

ROBERTSON, S. W., of Thaba Nchu, O.R.C. acted as Clerk in the Customs Dept., British Bechuanaland, in 1890, and as Clerk to the Civil Commissioners at Bulawayo, Salisbury, and Umtali from 1895-1899. He took part in the Mashonaland Rebellion in 1896 (medal); joined the Kimberley Light Horse as Lieut. in 1899, and commanded the garrison at Koffyfontein from 1900-1901 (despatches, Queen's medal with four clasps and King's medal). He was appointed Asst. Resident Magistrate at Koffyfontein in 1900; Resident Magistrate at Hoopstad in 1901, and at Thaba Nchu in 1904.

ROBERTSON, James, of Salisbury, Rhodesia, entered the Administrator's Dept., Dec., 1895; acted as Secy., to the Administrator from April, 1896, to Sept., 1897. He served in the Mashonaland Rebellion, 1896-97 (medal); was Acting Under-Secy., April 26-June, 1898; and from Jan. 31 to May 1, 1899, Acting Govt. Representative at Enkeldoorn, June, 1898; and was appointed Clerk to the Legislative and Executive Councils, May 1, 1899.

ROBERTSON, William, R.M., of Bethlehem O.R.C., was born at Swellendam, C.C., Nov 17, 1861. He is of Scotch descent; grandson of the Rev. Dr. Wm. Robertson, of Cape Town, and son of Peter John Robertson. He was educated at Grey Coll., Bloemfontein, and entered the Free State Govt. Service as Clerk to the State Attorney in 1881, subsequently holding the following appointments: Clerk to the Commissioner at Thaba Nchu, 1884; Asst. Registrar of the High Court, 1885; Landdrost Clerk at Kroonstad, 1886; Landdrost Clerk at Bloemfontein, 1890; Postmaster at Bloemfontein, and Landdrost at Ficksburg, 1891; Landdrost at Boshoff, 1894; and Landdrost at Kroonstad, 1895. He was reappointed Magistrate of Kroonstad after the British occupation in May, 1900, and became R.M. of Bethlehem, June, 1902.

Mr. Robertson was considered one of the best target shots in the Free State from 1888 to 1898, and in the latter year secured a badge in the Governor's Prize, being eleventh out of some 300 competitors. He has also won several cups and medals at target shooting. He married, March 14,

1888, Ada Elizabeth, eldest dau. of the late State Attorney C. J. Vels.

ROBINSON, Rev. Charles Henry, M.A. Canon of Ripon since 1897; Editorial Secy. to the Society for the Propagation of the Gospel in Foreign Parts since 1902; Lecturer in Hausa in the University of Cambridge since 1896; of 19, Delahay Street, Westminster, and of Lynwood, Limpsfield, was born at Keynsham, 1861; is son of the Rev. G. Robinson, Monaghan, Ireland, was educated at Liverpool Coll, and Trinity Coll., Cambridge, College and University Prizeman, B.A., 1883, M.A., 1888; ordained Deacon 1884, Priest 1885; Fellow and Tutor of St. Augustine's Coll., Canterbury, 1889; Vice Chancellor of Truro Cathedral, 1890-1893. He travelled in Armenia in order to examine into the condition of the Armenian Church, and to report to Archbishop Benson on the possibility of establishing a school in Armenia for the training of Armenian priests, 1892; conducted Pioneer Expeditions, 1893-1895, to Kano, the commercial centre of Northern Nigeria, starting by way of the Rivers Niger and Binué, after first making an ineffectual attempt to reach Kano by crossing the Great Sahara Desert from the north by way of Tripoli or Tunis. The Expedition, which was partly supported by the English and Scottish Royal Geographical Societies, was organised under the auspices of the Hausa Assn. Its object was to obtain materials for the study of the Hausa language, and to report as to the best means of opening out the country to the influences of Christianity and civilisation.

He has published: *Hausaland, or Fifteen Hundred Miles through the Central Sudan*, 1896; third ed., 1900; *Specimens of Hausa Literature*, 1896; *Grammar of the Hausa Language*, 1897; second ed., 1905; *Mohammedanism, Has it any Future?* 1897; *Dictionary of the Hausa Language*, 1899; *Studies in the Character of Christ*, 1900; second ed., 1905; *Nigeria, our latest Protectorate*, 1900; *Human Nature: A Revelation of the Divine*, 1902. He married, in 1896, Clare, dau. of Joseph Arnold, of Tunbridge Wells.

ROBINSON, Major Ernest Rokeby, F.R.G.S., F.R.C.I.; of Sandown, Isle of Wight; the Green House, Bezuidenhout, Johannesburg; and of the Junior United Service and the Sports Clubs, was born at Brussels, Jan. 30, 1872; is son of Maj. John Robinson, of Lydd, Kent; was educated privately; joined the 4th Royal Irish Rifles, and has seen service in the Niger-Sudan Campaign, 1896-7 (mentioned in Sir Geo. Goldie's Report, medal and clasp); commanded the Artillery in the operations on the Niger, 1895-8 (R. Niger Co.'s medal and clasp); Ebusa-Upinam Expedition, 1898 (clasp); Sierra Leone Rebellion as Adjt. of the S.L.F.R, 1898-9 (medal and clasp); S.A. War as Adjt., Staff Capt. and D.A.A.G. Imp. Yeo. 1900-1902; (two medals with three and two clasps). Maj. Robinson has won several swimming trophies, and has had some big game shooting on the Niger. He married, Jan. 19, 1901, Minnie Edith, dau. of John Crochett, of Wimbledon and Singapore.

ROBINSON, Joseph Benjamin, of Dudley House, Park Lane, was born in Cradock, Eastern Province, C.C., in 1845. Formerly farming in the Colony, he moved to the Vaal River diggings and then to Kimberley, of which he was Mayor in 1880. He was M.L.A. for Griqualand (West) for four years, and went to the Rand in July, 1896. He was one of the first capitalists to sink money in the new fields. Within three days of his arriving he purchased the Langlaagte Estate (which at that time included the Block B) for £7,000, and in the following Sept. he bought a half interest in the De Villiers Mynpacht (now the Robinson G.M. Co.) for £1,100, and two months later was able to buy the remaining moiety for £12,000.

Shortly afterwards, with extraordinary perspicuity, he made up his mind as to the westerly trend of the main reef series, and purchased for the Robinson Synd. the large block of farms constituting the Randfontein group. He controlled the Robinson South African Bank, Ltd., and is Chairman of the large group of Randfontein and Langlaagte Cos., and is perhaps the only financial magnate who always plays a lone hand in regard to his African enterprises. Mr. Robinson served in the Basuto War, and was at other times on commando. He was on intimate terms with ex-Pres. Kruger; takes considerable interest in politics, and is fond of yachting. He is married, has a large family, and entertains on a lavish scale at Dudley House, where the services of Melba, Kubelik, Réjane, Clara Butt,

Plançon, and Sassoli have been engaged.

ROBINSON, Leo George, J.P., of Bulawayo; was appointed Clerk in the Chief Native Commissioner's Office, Bulawayo, Feb. 1, 1897; Asst. Native Commissioner, July 1, 1897.

ROBINSON, Lieut. Col. Macleod Bawtree, C.M.G., of Wychwood, Silwood Road, Rondebosch, Cape Colony, and of the Civil Service Club, C. Town, was born at Grahamstown (C.C.), Jan. 12, 1858; and is the eldest son of the late Edward A. Robinson. He joined the Cape Civil Service in 1875, in which he held various appointments. In May, 1904, he was appointed Chief of the Detective Dept. in Kimberley, and Commissioner of the Cape Police, Dist. No. 2, in April, 1904. On the amalgamation of the Cape Police, under the title of the Cape Mounted Police, he was appointed Commissioner in command at headquarters, Cape Town. He served with the Queenstown Volunteer Rifles in the Gaika and Galeka War, 1877-8 (medal and clasp), and was Capt. of Nesbitt's Light Horse in the Transkei Rebellion in 1880-1; commanded a force of Mounted Police and Volunteers at Phokwani, in the Bechuanaland Rebellion in 1896-7 (Cape of Good Hope general service medal and clasps for Transkei and Bechuanaland); appointed Commandant of Colonial Forces in 1899 in Griqualand West and Bechuanaland, with the local rank of Lieut.-Col. He served in the S. African War, 1899-1902, as Town Commandant during the siege of Kimberley, and took part in the defence of that town (mentioned in despatches, medal and clasp); commanded the 2nd Div. of the Cape Colonial Forces from July to Sept., 1902. In recognition of his services during the War, he was authorised by the Govt. to retain the rank of Lieut.-Col. He married, first, in 1887, Annie, dau. of James Ayliff (died in 1891), and, secondly, in 1896, Theodora, dau. of the late Laurence Dahl.

RODD, Sir James Rennell, K.C.M.G., C.V.O., C.B., of the British Legation, Stockholm; 17, Stratford Place, W., and of the Travellers', Athenaeum, St. James's, Beefsteak, Authors', and Cosmopolitan Clubs, was born Nov. 9, 1858. He is son of the late Major Jas. Rennell Rodd, and was educated at Haileybury Coll., and at Balliol Coll.,

Oxon, where, in 1880, he gained the Newdigate Prize with a poem on Sir Walter Raleigh. He joined the Diplomatic Service, and after serving in Berlin, Athens, Rome, and Paris, he went to Zanzibar, where he acted as Agent and Consul-Gen. for some months. Took part in second Witu Expedition (medal with clasp). In 1894 he was transferred to Cairo, becoming Second Secy. to the British Agency, and Secy. of Legation in 1898. Meanwhile, he acted on various occasions as Agent and Consul-Gen. In 1897 he was selected to leave on a special mission to the Emperor Menelik in Abyssinia. On his return he resumed his duties at Cairo, until in 1901 he was appointed Secy. of Embassy at Rome. In 1904 he was appointed H.M.'s Envoy Extraordinary and Minister Plenipotentiary at Stockholm. In addition to several volumes of poems he has published a biographical sketch of the Emperor Frederick, *Customs and Lore of Modern Greece* and *Sir Walter Raleigh*. He married, in 1895, Lilias, dau. of the late. Jas Guthrie, of Craigie, Forfarshire.

RODGER, Sir John Pickersgill, K.C.M.G. (1904), of Accra, Gold Coast, W. Africa, Governor and Commander-in-Chief of the Gold Coast Colony, was born in 1851. He served for over twenty years in the Malay Native States, and was afterwards employed successively as British Resident of Sengalor, Pahang, and Perak. He received his present appointment in Oct., 1903. Sir John is a Barrister-at-Law, and married in 1872, Maria, dau. of the late Geo. D. Tyser.

ROGERS, Alexander Stuart, of Zanzibar, is British Vice-Consul in the East African Protectorate, and Prime Minister of the Zanzibar Govt. On the death of the late Sultan, Mr. Rogers was appointed Regent during the minority of the Seyyid Ali bin Hamoud, an old Harrovian.

ROGERS, Lieut.-Col. Sir John Godfrey, K.C.M.G., D.S.O., R.A.M.C., Grand Cordon of the Medjidieh, 2nd class Osmanieh, of Cairo, Egypt, and the Turf (Cairo) and Junior United Service (Lond.) Clubs, is the second son of the late G. F. H. Rogers, and Frances, youngest dau. of the late Richard Phillips, of Gaile, Co. Tipperary. He was born April 11, 1850, in Dublin, and was educated at Trinity Coll., Dublin, where he graduated B.A., M.B., M.Ch. Sir John entered the Army Medical Dept. in 1871, and was made Surg. in 1873, Surg. Maj. in 1882, and Surg. Lieut. Col. in 1891. He served in the Afghan War in 1878 to 1881 (medal). He accompanied the Egyptian Expedition in 1882, and was present at Kassassin and Tel-el-Kebir (despatches, medal with clasp, and bronze star, promoted Surg.-Maj.). He was appointed temporarily P.M.O. of the Egyptian Army during the cholera epidemic of 1883, and was later appointed permanently to that post. Sir John organised the Medical Corps of the Egyptian Army, and went through the Nile Expedition as P.M.O. in 1884-85 (despatches, clasp, and 3rd class Osmanieh). He served with the Sudan Frontier Field Force in 1885-86, and was present at the action of Giniss (despatches, D.S.O.). With the Suakin Field Force in 1885, as P.M.O. of the Force, he took part in the action of Gemaizeh (despatches, clasp, 2nd class Medjidieh). While he was Director-Gen. of the Sanitary Dept., Ministry of Interior, 1892-99, he introduced various legislative Acts dealing with the sanitation of the country and the outbreaks of cholera and plague. He retired from the Egyptian service Nov., 1899, and was appointed Local Manager of the New Egyptian Co., Ltd., 1899. He is also Local Manager of the Sudan Development and Exploration Co., Ltd.; Chairman of the Anglo-American Nile Steamer and Hotel Co., Ltd.; Director of the Agricultural Bank of Egypt; is a member of the *Conseil d'Administration of La Société de la Daira Sanieh*; Vice Chairman of the Gresham Assurance Co.; Chairman of the Menzaleh Canal and Navigation Co., Ltd. His recreations are fishing and shooting, and he has travelled in Canada, Iceland, Finland, and Russia in search of sport. He married, Sept. 26, 1883, Edith Louisa Julia, dau. of the late Major W. F. H. Sykes, of the Bombay Cavalry.

ROLLAND, Capt. George Murray, V.C. 1st Bombay Grenadiers, Indian Army, is the son of the late Major Patrick Murray Rolland, H.A. He was born at Wellington, India, May 12, 1869; was educated at Harrow and Sandhurst, and on Nov. 9, 1889, joined the 2nd Batt. Bedfordshire Regt. as 2nd Lieut., became 1st Lieut. in 1891, Capt. Nov. 9, 1900, and in Aug. of the following year joined the Indian Army. He was Adjt. of the 1st Bombay Grenadiers from 1894 to 1901, and was with the

Somaliland Field Force from Oct., 1902, to June, 1903, acting as Intelligence Officer to the Berbera-Bohotle Flying Column, and Staff Officer to Maj. J. E. Gough's Column. It was while in Somaliland that Capt. Rolland won the coveted distinction of the Victoria Cross, under circumstances related in the biographical sketch of Maj. W. G. Walker (q.v.).

ROLLER, Major George Conrad, of Tadley, Basingstoke, and the Arts Club, was born in London in 1856. He is son of Frederick Wm. Holler, and was educated at Westminster Sch., afterwards studying hard for three years in Paris under Bougereau. He then travelled for some years in Australia, New Zealand, Peru, and Argentina. He is an artist by profession, and was made a Fellow of the Royal Soc. of Painter Etchers in 1887. He rode for many years as a qualified gentleman rider under National Hunt Rules, until a severe accident made him relinquish this form of sport. He was appointed to the Surrey Bench in 1888, and to the London County Bench in the following year. When the S.A. War broke out he volunteered and went out with the Middlesex Yeomanry as Col.-Sergt., soon obtaining his Commission, and medal for distinguished conduct in the Field. On returning home in 1900 he took up a commission in the I.Y. in G. Britain. He married, in 1884, Mary, dau. of W. Halliday, of Thames, New Zealand.

ROLLESTON, Dr. Humphrey Davy, M.A., M.D., F.H.C.P., of 55, Upper Brook Street, W., and of the Athenaeum Club, was born June 21, 1862, at Oxford, and is son of the late Dr. G. Rolleston F.H.S. He was educated at Marlborough, St. John's Coll., Cambs., and St. Bartholomew's Hosp. In 1893 he was elected Assistant Physician, and in 1898, Physician to St. George's Hosp., Lond.; went out to S. Africa in 1901, and acted as Consulting Physician to the Imperial Yeomanry Hosp. in Pretoria (medal). He is a member of the Consultative Board to the Medical Dept. of the Navy, and has acted as Examiner in medical subjects to the Cambridge and Durham Universities. Dr. Rolleston is the author of a book on *Diseases of the Liver*, and formerly edited the English translation of the late Professor Nothnagel's

Diseases of the Intestines and Peritoneum. He married, Jan. 15, 1894, Eila dau. of F. M. Ogilvy.

ROMILLY, Capt. Bertram Henry Samuel, D.S.O., of 56, Eccleston Square, W., and of the Guards' Club, was born in London, Nov. 6, 1878, and is son of Samuel H. Romilly, D.L., J.P. He was educated at Charterhouse, and the R.M.C., Sandhurst, and entered the Scots Guards in 1898; served in the S. African campaign from 1900-02 (twice mentioned in despatches, medal with five clasps and D.S.O.); he was attached to the Egyptian Army in 1902, first in the 9th Sudanese Regt., and in 1903 in the Camel Corps, where he is at the present time. Recreations: hunting, shooting, and polo. Unmarried.

RONAN, Barry, F.A.S., of 61, Braid St., Maritzburg, Natal, was born in Dublin, May 3, 1863; joined the R.A. at the age of sixteen, passing a number of Artillery College examinations. He abandoned the Service for journalism in 1881, and has since been on the staff of most of the leading S. African journals, being at present sub-editor of the *Natal Witness*. He is also known as a cartoonist, and besides several short stories has published *The Passing of the Boer*, and *The Kingdom of Kruger*. He acted as Secretary to Sir F. Carrington in Bechuanaland during the formation of the Rhodesian Pioneers, and in a similar capacity under Sir Thomas Tancred on the Delagoa Bay Railway, and during the last Boer war he was on the Intelligence Dept. He married, in 1904. Miss Frances Kennedy, of Kokstad.

ROSADO, Major, was Portuguese Governor-General of Mozambique, until the beginning of 1905, when he relinquished his appointment and returned to Portugal.

ROSE, F. Horace, Editor of the *Natal Witness* (Maritzburg), was born July 7, 1876, at Port Alfred, Cape Colony, which place, under the name of Barmouth, figures in his novel of that name, published serially in South Africa in 1905. He is the youngest surviving son of the late Rev. G. A. Rose, Wesleyan Methodist minister, and descends on the maternal side from the family of Impey, for generations past well known in Yorkshire and the West of England. Mr. Rose was engaged in legal work in Johannesburg under Mr. Charles Leonard in 1895, an subsequently under Mr. (now Sir) William Van Hulsteyn (1896-99). He left the Rand on the outbreak of the war, and in 1902-03 visited England, embodying his impressions in a series of articles to the South African Press, afterwards republished in book form by Messrs. J. M. Dent and Co. (1904), under the title of *An Impressionist in England*. On returning to South Africa in 1903, Mr. Rose was engaged as a writer of specials on the staff of the *Natal Witness*, and within a year he rose to the occupancy of the editorial chair. Under his management numerous important innovations were introduced, and the paper was twice enlarged. Mr. Rose takes a keen interest in the subject of Penology and Prison Reform, an articles from his pen have drawn the attention of the Natal Parliament to the matter with the result that a special Commission is to go into the whole subject.

ROSS, Archar Russell, J.P., of Rusape, Makoni District, S. Rhodesia, was born a Queenstown, Cape Colony, Oct. 23, 1863, and was educated at Lovedale, C.C. He went up to the newly discovered Rand goldfields in 1886; returned to the Cape Colony in 1893, and commenced sheep farming, but two years later was appointed Native Commissioner for the Makoni District. He served as Lieut. in the Umtali Volunteers during the 1896-7 rebellion in Rhodesia, and in 1900 was sent to Australia by the Rhodesian Government to bring 1,000 head of cattle for Rhodesia. He was appointed a Lieut in the S. Rhodesia Volunteers in 1903, and a Special J.P. for the Makoni District, as well a J.P. for S. Rhodesia. He married, in 1898 Louisa Jane, dau. of the late Thomas Laxton.

ROSS, Mrs. Janet Anne, of Poggio, Gherardo Settignano, Florence, Italy, was born in London, Feb. 24, 1842, and is the eldest dau of Sir Alex. Cornewall Duff Gordon, Bart. She lived for six years in Egypt, during part of which time she acted as Times correspondent. She is the author of the following publications: *The History and Literature of the Crusades*, 1861; *Essays on the Political History of the XV., XVI., and XVII. Centuries*, 1868; *Italian Sketches* in 1887; *Three Generations of English Women*, 1888; *The Land of Manfred*, 1889; *Early Days Recalled*, 1891; *Leaves from our Tuscan Kitchen*, 1899; *Florentine Villas*, 1901; *Old Florence and Modern Tuscany*, 1904,

MR. BARRY RONAN

MR. C. F. ROWSELL

Photo Elliott & Fry.

MAJOR F. A. SAUNDERS

COL. J. A. M. STUART

and many magazine articles. She also edited *Letters from the East*, by Henry J. Ross, and *Letters from Egypt*, by Lady Duff Gordon, in 1902. She married, Dec. 5, 1860, the late Henry J. Ross, banker, at Alexandria, Egypt.

ROSS, Major Ronald, C.B., F.R.S., F.R.C.S., of The University, Liverpool; the Lodge, Aigburth Vale, Liverpool, and of the University Club, Liverpool, was born in India, May 13, 1857, and is son of Gen. Sir C. C. G. Ross, K.C.B. He was educated at Southampton, and St. Bartholomew's Hosp., Lond., entered the Indian Medical Service in 1881, and ten years later he commenced the special study of malaria, and in 1897-8 he demonstrated the lifecycle of malaria parasites in mosquitoes, for which he was awarded the Nobel Medical Prize in 1902; was appointed Lecturer and Professor of Tropical Medicine at Liverpool Univ. in 1899. He travelled to W. Africa in connection with anti-malarial sanitation in 1899-01-02, to Ismailia, Egypt, in 1902, and Panama in 1904. He is the author of several literary, mathematical, and medical publications. He married, in 1889, Rosa B. Bloxam.

ROSS, Hon. William, M.L.C., was born at Stranraer, Scotland, in 1850. He was for many years Manager of the Oriental Bank Corporation, and is now head of the firms of Ross, Priest and Page, of Kimberley, and Ross, Page and O'Reilly, of Johannesburg. He has been member of the Cape Legislative Council for Griqualand West since 1883. He is fond of sport, a well-known boxer, and married a dau. of the late Geo. Page, of Bloemfontein.

ROSSLYN (James Erskine), Earl of, is a descendant of John Erskine, Earl of Mar, and of the first Duke of Lennox. Lord Rosslyn has had a varied career, having been a Guardsman, an actor, editor of Scottish Life, and a war correspondent; was present at the relief of Ladysmith, and was for nine weeks a prisoner of war in Pretoria. His career on the stage commenced in a very obscure part; in fact, as a super at fifteen shillings a week, but his talent soon asserted itself, and, he coming to London, made a distinct hit in Trelawny of the
Wells. In 1904 Lord Rosslyn became unpaid Priv. Secty. to the Secretary for Scotland.

ROULIOT, George, Knt. of the Legion of Honour, was born in France, Aug. 15, 1861. He was educated in Paris, and at the Univ. of Bonn, Germany. He took an engineering degree in Paris, and went to S.A. in 1882 as General Manager of the *Cie. Generale des Mines de Diamants* in Kimberley, where the Cape Govt. appointed him to the Dutoitspan Mining Board and the Board for the Protection of Mining Interests. After the De Beers Amalgamation in 1890 he left Kimberley and joined Mr. Beit and Lord Randolph Churchill in their expedition through Mashonaland, returning via Beira. Mr. Rouliot joined the firm of Eckstein in 1892, and was admitted a partner two years later. He was one of the early believers in the Deep Levels, and was associated with the Rand Mines, Ltd., from the inception of the Company. He has been on the Executive Committee of the Chamber of Mines since 1894, and was Pres. of the Chamber from 1897 until 1902. Mr. Rouliot worked assiduously for the reopening of the mines during the latter part of the war period, and his services in this connection were acknowledged in Lord Kitchener's despatches.

ROWLAND, Frederick, of Parktown West, Johannesburg (Box 4375), and of the Athenaeum Club, Johannesburg, was born April 13, 1871; was educated privately, and went to S.A. in June, 1889, engaging in commercial pursuits in Cape Town, Durban, Lindley, Bloemfontein and Johannesburg. He acted as Secy. of the Chemical and Metallurgical Soc. in 1896; was secy. of companies from 1897 to 1899; became Secy. of the Uitlander Council on its inception in 1889, and remained such until the outbreak of the war; was secy. of the committee formed for the purpose of raising Irregular Corps in Natal; became Lieut. of Bethune's M.I. on formation; Capt. and Quartermaster in Nov., 1900; resigned April, 1902, to take up appointment in the Mines Dept. of the Transvaal. This he vacated in the following Nov. to enter the service of H. Eckstein and Co. He is also Secy. to the Chemical, Metallurgical and Mining Soc. of S.A., and Associate of the Chartered Institute of Secretaries, Eng. While on active service he married, Aug. 6, 1900, Maud Mary Peutney, a nurse in the Natal Volunteer service through the siege of Ladysmith.

ROWLANDS, General Sir Hugh, V.C., K.C.B., of Plas Tiron, Llanrud, R.S.O., Carnarvonshire was born in 1829, and entered the Army in 1849. He served in the Crimean war in 1854-5, being present at the battles of Alma and Inkerman (severely wounded); the siege and fall of Sevastopol; assault on the Redan, and the attack on the Quarries (despatches, medal, and clasps, V.C., Knight of Legion of Honour, 5th class Medjidie, Turkish medal, and C.B.) and the Kaffir War in 1877-9, when he was on special service at Lueneberg, and commanded the troops at the action of Tolako Mountain (despatches, medal, and clasp). General Rowlands commanded the 1st Class District in India from 1884-9; acted as Lieutenant of the Tower of London in 1893, and commanded the Scottish District from 1893-6. Since 1897 he has been Colonel of the Duke of Wellington's (W. Riding Regt.). He married, in 1867, Isabelle J. Barrow.

ROWLATT, Frederick Terry, of Cairo, and of the Turf Club, Cairo, was born at Alexandria, Feb. 10, 1865; is son of the late A. H. Rowlatt, banker, of Egypt; was educated at Fettes Coll., Edin., where he won swimming prizes; entered the Bank of Egypt in London in 1885; transferred to the Egyptian branch, of which he acted as Manager. He left this to take up the sub governorship of the National Bank of Egypt in Cairo, and he became Governor of that Bank after the death of Sir E. Palmer (q.v.). He became a Fellow of the Institute of Bankers, London, in 1902. He married, May 14, 1903, Edith May, dau. of T. E. Cornish, C.M.G., of Alexandria.

ROWSELL, Charles Frederick, of Ridge Green House, South Nutfield, Eng., was born in London, June 21, 1864. He was originally a solicitor, and practised as such for a good many years, and then joined the old established and well-known South African firm of Messrs. Lewis and Marks, of Threadneedle House, Bishopsgate Street Within, London, a firm which has been the means of founding several prosperous industries in the Transvaal, and has materially assisted in developing the various resources of that colony. (See Isaac Lewis.)

Although the firm with which he is connected is not interested in Rhodesian undertakings, Mr. Rowsell himself has a considerable stake in the prosperity of Charterland, and is Chairman of the United Rhodesia Goldfields, the Jumbo G.M. and the Mayo Rhodesia Development Co., besides being on the Boards of the. Tanganyika Concessions and the Zambesia Exploring Co. He also represents his firm as Chairman of the Grootvlei Prospecting Synd., and Director of the East Rand Mining Estates Swaziland Corporation, Transvaal Estates and Development Co., Transvaal Farms and Finance Co., Transvaal Proprietary, and the African and European Investment Co.

Mr. Rowsell has been the sole architect of his own fortunes, having come to London in 1890 without literally a single acquaintance in the great metropolis. It is needless to say that he has raised his structure in a remarkably able manner. He married, in 1903, Miss Olive C. Wright.

ROYLE, Charles, of Cairo, and of the Khedivial (Cairo), and of the Junior Athenaeum (London) Clubs, was born at Lymington, Hants, Dec. 24, 1838; is fourth son of Wm. Royle, solicitor; was educated at Queenswood Coll., Hants, and served as an officer in the Royal Navy from 1854 to 1863. Mr. Royle is a Barrister-at-Law, having been called to the Bar at Lincoln's Inn, Nov., 1865, and is Judge of the Egyptian Court of Appeal. He is author of *The Egyptian Campaigns*, published by Hurst and Blackett. Unmarried.

ROYLE, George, of Gezireh, Cairo and Port Said; of 11, De Vere Gardens, London; and of the Khedivial Sporting Club, Cairo, and Constitutional Club, London; is the fifth son of the late William Royle, solicitor of Lymington, Hants, and was born, July 5, 1841, at Lymington. He was educated at Queenwood Coll and Southampton Coll. Mr. Royle was present at the taking of Peiho Forts, 1860, and with the Naval Brigade on the March to Pekin, and was engaged with Flotilla on the Pei He and Wen He Rivers during the continuance of hostilities. He was subsequently on H.M.S. *Havock* when that vessel successfully attacked the pirate town of Foo Shan on the Yangtze, and captured many Imperial war junks later on, up the Yangtze

River. He left the Royal Navy, 1863 or 1864, and was called to the Bar at Lincoln's Inn, Jan., 1870. He went to Egypt (Port Said) in 1871, and was appointed P. and O. Agent in 1875. He has been Manager of the Port Said and Suez Coal Co. since 1872, and is a Director of the Egyptian Salt and Soda Co., the Nungovich Hotels Co., etc., etc. Orders: China War medal, 1860; Chevalier of the Crown of Italy; Medjidieh, 3rd class. His recreations are yachting and sculling, and formerly Alpine climbing. He married, in 1878, Fanny Longueville, eldest dau. of Thomas Snow, Barrister-at-Law,

ROZIEBRODZKI, Count, was one of the Austrian Plenipotentiaries at the Moroccan Conference at Algeçiras in 1906.

RUBE, C., of 17, Hill Street, Mayfair, London; 1, London Wall Buildings, E.C., and of 29-30, Holborn Viaduct, E.G., was born in Germany in 1852. Proceeding to South Africa in 1876 with Mr. Jules Porges, he managed in Kimberley for some time the Cie. Française des Mines de Diamants du Kaap, eventually becoming a partner in the firm of Wernher, Beit, and Co., with whom are associated the well-known firm of H. Eckstein and Co., and the Rand Mines, Limited. This powerful combination has unquestionably done more than any other to open up the resources of the Rand, especially the deep level areas, and it has enormous interests in other properties the development of which will be proceeded with whenever the conditions are favourable. This group includes a considerable number of important Rand outcrop mines, but their deep level holdings are by far the most important. The parent company of the producing deep levels belonging to the Wernher Beit group is the Rand Mines, Ltd., which has numerous subsidiary companies in which its share holdings are enormous, ranging from 20 per cent. to 80 per cent. Among these subsidiary companies are the Glen Deep, Ltd., Rose Deep, Ltd., Geldenhuis Deep, Ltd., Jumpers Deep, Ltd., Nourse Mines, Ltd., South Nourse, Ltd., Ferreira Deep, Ltd., Crown Deep, Ltd., Langlaagte Deep, Ltd., Wolhuter G.M., Ltd., Wolhuter Deep, Ltd., City Deep, Ltd., Village Deep, Ltd., Robinson Central Deep, Ltd., Paarl Central G.M., and Exploration Co., Ltd., and many others, some

forty in all, upon the London Committees of which Mr. Rube represents his partners' interests. His only daughter married, in 1904, Mr. Leopold Canning, son and heir of Lord Garvagh.

RUBIDGE, W., M.L.A., of Dalham, Graaff Reinet, represents Vryburg in the Cape Parliament, to which he was returned in Feb., 1904. He supports the Progressive party.

RUDD, Charles Dunell, of 23, Hyde Park Gardens, London; Ardnamurchan, Argyllshire; and of the Union and United University Clubs, and Rear Commodore of Royal Highland Yacht Club; was born at Hanworth Hall, Norfolk, Oct. 22, 1844. He was educated at Harrow and Cambridge, at both of which he distinguished himself in athletics. He won the Harrow mile, quarter mile, hurdle race, and throwing the cricket ball in '62; carried off the Interuniversity Racquet trophies for Camb. in '65, and owing to a breakdown through overtraining at Camb., he sailed to the Cape in 1866 for the benefit of his health, and there occupied some few years mainly in shooting expeditions in Zululand and Swaziland together with the famous John Dunn and others. He joined the first rush to Kimberley, where he and Mr. Cecil Rhodes each purchased a quarter claim in De Beers, which they subsequently amalgamated and worked in partnership (1871), thus forming the nucleus which, after a long series of purchases, amalgamations, and absorptions, taking up many years of patient effort, eventually led to the formation of the De Beers Consolidated Mines. The foundations of the Rhodes and Rudd partnership were laid by a series of profit able pumping contracts in the De Beers and Du Toit's Pan mines, and were further strengthened by the acquisition of various diamond pro parties. From 1883 to 1888 Mr. Rudd represented Kimberley in the Cape Parliament, with the main object of introducing legislation bearing on the questions of the compound system, and the I.D.B. and the liquor laws. These ends being attained he did not seek re-election.

The year 1886 witnessed the inception of the Gold Fields of S.A., Ltd., from which the existing colossal corporation in its Consolidated form was developed under the joint managing direction of

Messrs. Rudd & Rhodes. Mr. Rudd was also instrumental in obtaining the mineral and land concessions from Lobengula in 1888, on which the Charter to the British S.A. Co. was based. He has now retired from his directorships and all active business in the City. He married: first in 1886, Miss Chiappini; and second, in 1898, Miss Wallace.

RUFFER, Dr. Marc Armand, M.A., M.D. C.M.G. (1905) (Oxon), B.S., F.L.S., F.S.S. F.R.M.S., 2nd class Medjidieh, 2nd class Osmanieh, Commander of the Orders of the Saviour of Greece, and St Anne of Russia; of Ramleh, Egypt, and of the Royal Societies (Lond.), Turf (Cairo), and Khedivial (Alexandria) Clubs, was born at Lyons, France, Aug. 29, 1859; is third son of the late Baron A. de Ruffer, late Consul of Switzerland; was educated privately, and at Brasenose Coll., Oxon, Univ. Coll., Lond., the Sch. of Medicine and Institut Pasteur, Paris, From 1886 to 1888 he was Medical House Physician and Obstetric Assistant of Univ. Coll, Hospital; he was Medical Registrar at the Victoria Park Hosp., 1890; Director of the British Institute of Preventive Medicine, 1892-96; Prof. of Bacteriology, Cairo Medical Sch., 1896-8. He was appointed Pres. of the Sanitary Maritime and Quarantine Council of Egypt, 1897; Member of the Indian Plague Commission, 1899-1900; and Egyptian Delegate to the International Sanitary Conference, Paris, 1903, and has done sterling work in successfully organising the campaigns against the epidemics which have infested Egypt. The practical immunity of the country from these scourges is largely due to the thoroughness of his measures. He is a member of many scientific associations, and is the author of a number of scientific works. He married, Nov. 11, 1900, Alice Mary, eldest dau. of Capt. John Tyndale Greenfield, R.A.

RUNCIMAN, William, M.L.A., J.P., of The Highlands, Simonstown, C.C., and of the Royal Naval Club (Simonstown), and City Club (C.T.); was born at Shields, Eng., in Apr., 1855. He is the eldest son of the late Capt. Wm. Runciman of the Merchant Service. He was educated at Leith and Dunbar, Scotland, and migrated with his family in 1873 to Cape Town, where his father held for some time the position of Dock Master. Soon after arrival in Cape Town Mr. Runciman joined the well known firm of W. Anderson & Co., Merchants and Mail Steamship Agents. At the age of 19 years he was promoted to fill the place of Manager to the Simonstown Branch of the business. From manager he was soon promoted to junior partner, and is now senior partner, the name of the firm being changed to Wm. Runciman & Co. Since his advent in Simonstown Mr. Runciman has devoted a great deal of time to public affairs; from the inauguration of Municipal Government he has sat in the Council Chamber, and he has been repeatedly and is still Mayor. To his untiring energy the town owes much of its present prosperity. The railway extension from Kalk Bay, the sanitation, the water supply, the fine public schools, the town lighting, and public library are all mementos of his assiduous perseverance and skilful policy. He has also done good service in the Simonstown District as Divisional Councillor for the Cape Division, of which body he has been Member of the Legislative Assembly of the Cape Parliament for some five or six years; sits as a strong Progressive; has rendered good service in educational matters already, and bids fair to fill a prominent place in Cape politics in the not distant future. He married, in 1883, Elizabeth Sarah, eldest dau. of A. N. Black, of Simonstown, by whom he has two sons and a daughter.

RUNDLE, Major-Gen. Sir Henry Macleod Leslie, K.C.B., K.C.M.G., D.S.O., second son of the late Capt. J. S. Rundle, R.N., was born at Newton Abbot, N. Devon, Jan. 6, 1856. He was educated at the Royal Mil. Acad.; entered the Royal Artillery in 1876, and first saw service in the Zulu War in 1879, afterwards taking part in the Boer War of 1881. Subsequently he proceeded to Egypt, where he acted for about fourteen years as Chief Staff Officer to the Sirdar and Adjt.Gen. to the Egyptian Army. Sir Leslie was second in command to Lord Kitchener at the battle of Omdurman. In the South African War, 1899-02, he commanded the 8th Division. He latterly also acted as Military Governor of the Eastern O.R.C., with headquarters at Harrismith. On returning to England he was given the command of the South Eastern District at Dover in succession to William Butler, afterwards commanding the Northern District. He married, in 1887, Eleanor Georgina, dau. of the late Capt. J. H. Campbell, R.A.

RUSSELL. Robert, I.S.O., of 33, Prince of Wales
Mansions, Battersea Park, London, was born at
Edinburgh in 1843; was educated at the Church of
Scotland Training Coll. and the Univ. of
Edinburgh, and has had a long and useful public
career mainly devoted to educational matters in
Natal. In 1865 he was appointed Headmaster of
Durban High Sch and became Supt. of Education
and Secy. to the Council of Education in 1878. He
was for some years Chairman of the Survey Board
and Member of the Civil Service Board, and was
appointed to represent Natal on the Council of the
Cape Univ. in 1896. He was mainly instrumental in
establishing the Cadet system in vogue in Natal.
Mr. Russell retired from the Civil Service of the
Colony in 1903 on full salary specially voted by the
Natal Parliament. The same year he was created a
Companion of the Imperial Service Order. He is
the author of *Natal; the Land and its Story* (1903).

RUSSELL, Robert, Junr., M.A., B.C.L., of 26,
Victoria St., London, S.W., and of the New
Vagabonds' Club, was born, Aug. 13, 1867, at
Durban. He is son of Robert Russell, ex-Supt. of
Education for Natal (q.v.), and was educated at
Pietermaritzburg High Sch., and, Merton Coll.,
Oxon, where he graduated with honours in law.
He is now about to enter of the higher degree of
D.C.L. While at Oxford he played in his college
cricket and Associate football teams from 1886 to
1888. Returning to Natal he was an Acting
Inspector of Schools of the Colony in 1891-2; was
called to the Bar of the Inner Temple in 1893; and
received his present appointment as Secy. to the
Natal Govt. Agency in the same year. Mr. Russell
contributes verse to the *Westminster Gazette*, *Sketch*,
and *Pall Mall Gazette*. He married, May 5, 1895,
May, dau. of the late A. S. Smith, of Tudor Hill
House, Sutton Coldfield.

SADLER, Lieut. Col. James Hayes, C.B., of
Government House, Mombasa, East Africa
Protectorate, was British Commissioner in the
Uganda Protectorate from April 1, 1902, until at
the latter end of 1905 he was appointed
Commissioner and Commander-in-Chief in the
British East Africa Protectorate in succession to the
late Sir Donald Stewart.

ST. AUBYN, Hon. L., was Secretary to the English
Plenipotentiary at the Moroccan Conference at
Algeçiras in 1906.

ST. JOHN'S (Kaffraria), Bishop of. (See Right Rev.
J. W. Williams, D.D.)

ST. LEGER, F. L., is son of the late F. Y. St.
Leger, who first edited and helped to found the
Cape Times, of which Mr. St. Leger is now
Managing Director. He is also a Director of the
Transvaal Leader and of the Central News Agency.
He formerly held the position of Bank Manager at
Barkley West, which post he resigned in 1883, and
returned to Cape Town to take up his present
appointment. In 1908 he was re-elected a Member
of the Cape Town Municipal Council. He is a
Member of the South African Turf Club, and is a
keen sportsman.

SALISBURY, Right Hon. the Marquis of was born
in Oct., 1861, and is the descendant of a family of
statesmen and politicians, ranging from the Sir
William Cecil of Queen Mary's time, and the
famous Lord Burleigh of Queen Elizabeth's reign,
to the late Marquis and Premier, whose eldest son
the present Lord Salisbury is. He was M.P. for the
Darwen Division of Lancashire from 1885 to 1892,
and represented Rochester from 1893 until he
succeeded to the Peerage. While in the Commons
Lord Cranborne, to give him his then courtesy
title, was a constant attendant, a hard working
Member of many Committees, a regular supporter
of the Conservative Government, and a good,
though sometimes blunt, speaker. He identified
himself mainly with Church matters, and was
appointed chairman of the Church Parliamentary
Committee in 1893, a post which he occupied until
he became Under-Secretary for Foreign Affairs in
1900; he also showed great Parliamentary interest
in agricultural and Volunteer questions. In 1903 he
went to South Africa as Col. of the 4th Battalion
Bedfordshire Regt., his services being mentioned in
despatches. Returning to England, he became Lord
Privy Seal, and in March, 1905, he succeeded Mr.
Gerald Balfour as President of the Board of Trade.

SALMON, Charles, one of the early deep level
kings, went up to the Witwatersrand in the early

days, where he engaged in business as a tailor. He, however, distinguished himself by his belief in the deep levels long before their value was understood even by the leading mining magnates of the day. Holding on to his claims with a tenacity which neither the ridicule of experts nor the depression of the times affected, their immense worth was at last appreciated, and Mr. Salmon realised a large fortune, which he now enjoys in retirement.

SAMPSON, Col. Sir Aubrey Wools. (See Wools Sampson.)

SAMPSON, Victor, K.C., M.L.A., of Kimberley, and of the Civil Service and Kimberley Clubs, was born at Cape Town in 1855. He was educated privately, and in 1871 entered the Civil Service under the Imp. Govt.; served for eight years in the Control and Audit Office; Accountant for East Griqualand to 1881. He passed BA. and LL.B. while in the Civil Service, and obtained the Cape Univ. Chancellor's Gold Medal for an essay on the native question in 1877. He was called to the Cape Bar in Dec., 1881; was made Q.C. in 1896; is the leader of the Kimberley Bar, and was a Director of De Beers Mines from 1902 to 1904. Mr. Sampson is a sound Progressive, and was returned to the Cape Legislative Assembly for the electoral division of Albany in 1895, being re-elected at the general election in Feb., 1904. In the same month he joined Dr. Jameson's Cabinet as Attorney-Gen.

SANDBACH, Col. Arthur Edmund, D.S.O., of Bryngwyn, Oswestry, and of the Naval and Military and Bachelors' Clubs, was born July 30, 1859, and is son of Henry R. Sandbach, D.L., J.P., of Abergele, N. Wales. He was educated at Eton, and the R.M.A., Woolwich; became a Lieut. in the R.E., in 1879, and served in Egypt in 1882, Suakim in 1885, Burma in 1886-7, Sikkim in 1888, Hazara Expedition in 1891 as A.D.C. to Major-Gen. Elles, commanding the Rawal Pindi Dist., on the Gilgit Frontier in 1892-3, Khartoum in 1898, and S. Africa in 1899-1900. He was quartered at the Staff Coll. in 1896-7, and acted as Military Secretary to Lord Curzon of Kedleston in 1898-9, also served in the Egyptian Army in 1895. He was A.A.G. in the Natal Army in 1900, and now commands the 1st Suppers and Miners at Roorkee. He married in

1902, the Hon. Ina Douglas-Pennant, dau. of the 2nd Baron Penrhyn.

SANDHURST, Lord, of 60, Eaton Sq., Lou don, S.W., and of the Garrick, Brooks', and Turf Clubs, was born in 1855, and is son of the first Baron Sandhurst. He was educated at Rugby, and began his official career as a Lord in Waiting to Queen Victoria in 1880-5 In 1886 he became Under-Secretary for War, and again from 1892-4. He acted as Governor of Bombay from 1895-1900, and in 1906 was a member of the S. African Committee of Inquiry. He married in 1881, Lady Victoria Spencer, C.I., dau. of the 4th Earl Spencer.

SANDWITH, Dr. Fleming Mant, Knt. of Grace of the Order of St. John of Jerusalem, 3rd cl. Orders of Osmanieh, Medjidieh, and the Takova; of 31, Cavendish Sq., London, W., and of the Savile (Lond.) and Turf (Cairo) Clubs, is second son of late Col. J. W. F. Sandwith, Bombay Staff Corps; was born near Bombay, Oct. 11, 1853; was educated at Charterhouse, and studied medicine at St. Thomas's Hosp. (M. D. Durham, F.R.C.P. Lond., M.R.C.S. Eng.). Dr. Sandwith was attached in 1876 to the Servian Army as National Aid Soc. Surgeon in the Turko-Servian war, and received special gold medal for services after the battle of Zaitchar. In 1877-8 he was attached to the Turkish Army as Stafford House Surgeon in the Russo Turkish campaign; was present at the six days' fighting at the Shipka Pass, and was on Gen. Val Baker's staff during his retreat from Tashkessen, across the Rhodope mountains (Turkish medal). Proceeding to Egypt for the cholera epidemic in 1883, he became Vice Director of the Sanitary Dept. of the Egyptian Govt., being the first Englishman appointed to that service. At that time lunatics in the Govt. Asylum were kept in iron chains, and were subjected to much ill-usage, which Dr. Sandwith was instrumental in removing. He was Prof. of Medicine and Senior Physician to Kasr-el-ainy Hospital until 1903, and on retirement became a consulting physician, and also was made Consulting Physician to the Khedive. Meanwhile, in 1900, he was Senior Physician of the I.Y. Hospital at Pretoria during the war (medal with three clasps). He is now lecturer at the London Sch. of Tropical Medicine, Corresponding Member of the Imperial Soc. of Medicine, Constantinople, and of the American Climatological Assn., and *Membre de l'Institut Egyptien*. Dr. Sandwith is author of *Egypt as a Winter Resort*, *History of the Kasr el Amy, 1466-1900*, *The Earliest Known Physician*, and *The Medical Diseases of Egypt*. He married, in 1891, Gladys, dau. of the late Humphrey Sandwith, C.B., D.C.L., M.D.

SANDYS, Lord, of Ombersley Court, Droitwich, and of Percy House, Great Portland Street, W., was born in 1855, and is son of the third baron. He succeeded his brother in 1904; is a director of Bipposu Mines, Ltd., Nanwa Gold Mines, Ltd., Obbuassi Mines, Ltd., Obo Syndicate, Ltd., and the West African Exploring Co., Ltd. Lord Sandys married, in 1856, Marjorie Clara Pentreath, dau. of the late John Morgan

SARGANT, Edmund Beale, M.A., of the Oxford and Cambridge Club, London, and the Athenaeum Club, Johannesburg, was born in London in 1855. He is son of Henry Sargant, Barrister-at-Law, of Lincoln's Inn, and was educated at Rugby Sch., University Coll., and Trinity Coll., Camb. He fills the position of Director of Education for the Transvaal.

SARTORIS, Lionel C. G., of High Hall, Wickham Bishops, Witham, Essex, is a director of the British South African Explosives Co., Ltd., and Rio Tinto Co., Ltd., and is on the London Committee of the City Deep, Ltd., Geldenhuis Deep, Ltd., Jumpers Deep, Ltd., Klip Deep, Ltd., Rose Deep, Ltd., South City, Ltd., South Wolhuter, Ltd., and Wolhuter Deep, Ltd.

SAUER, Hon. S. W., M.L.A., of Uitkyk, Stellenbosch, Cape Colony, is son of an O.F.S. Landdrost; was educated at the S. African Coll., after which he was articled to Fairbridge & Arderne, Attorneys, of Cape Town, and practised for many years in conjunction, first with Mr. H. S. Caldecott (q.v.), and after with Mr. Orsmond at Aliwal North. He entered the Cape Parliament as member for that constituency, for which he has since been re-elected on many occasions. Formerly associated with Sir Gordon Sprigg, he broke with him in 1876 on questions of native policy. From 1881 to 1884, he was a member of the Scanlen Ministry as Secy. for Native Affairs, and became

Colonial Secy. in Mr. Rhodes's Ministry, in 1890, but was one of the three who wrecked it three years later. Although not a member of the Afrikander Bond, he is one of its most effective supporters, and makes no secret of his belief that the latter day Imperialism is inimical to the best interests of South Africa. Mr. Sauer has declined a knighthood. He was Commissioner of Public Works in the Schreiner Ministry, and was defeated at the general elections in Feb., 1904, but was elected later for the constituency of George, for which he now sits, and is one of the two Leaders of the Parliamentary Opposition to the Jameson Ministry. He will probably succeed Mr. J. N. Merriman as the Leader of the South African Party. He married a dau. of Henry Cloete, of Constantia, C.C.

SAUNDERS, Captain Frederick John, D.S.O., R.M.L.I., of the Junior Naval and Military Club, was born Sept. 18, 1876, and is son of William Saunders, of Sydenham. He served with the Naval Brigade in the S. African War, 1899-1900 (despatches, medal with four clasps, D.S.O.). He married, July 31, 1902, Muriel, only dau. of A. Maxwell Ted.

SAUNDERS, Major Frederick Anastasius, 3rd West Yorks Regt., J.P. for Grahamstown, F.R.C.S., L.R.C.P.Edin., F.R.G. S., F.R.C.I., F.S.A., Fel. Obstetrical Soc., of Lancing House, Hill St., Grahamstown, and of the Scottish Conservative Club, Edin., and the Junior Conservative Club, Lond., was born in London, June 12, 1859; and was educated at King Edward VI. Sch., Gt. Berkhampstead, Herts. He commanded the second detachment of the First City (Grahamstown) Volunteers at Langeberg, Bechuanaland, in 1897 (medal), and during the late S. African War acted as Station Staff Officer, as Adjt. of Marshall's Horse, and as Adjt. of the 1st City Volunteers, Grahamstown, which he now commands (Queen's and King's medals, three clasps). Major Saunders married: first, in 1882, Cissy, only dau. of Col. Barnes, St. Helena Regt., and stepdau. of the 11th Earl Lindsay; and second, in 1893, Lucy Anderson, dau. of Prof. J. Meiklejohn, of St. Andrews Univ., Scotland.

SAWERSHAL, Henry George Emanuel Julius

Edward, was draughtsman in the Public Works Dept. at Queenstown, C.C., May, 1882; was Asst. Surveyor in Tembuland Commission, Aug., 1882; Computer at the Royal Observatory, C.C., July, 1885; Asst. Surveyor, Bechuanaland railway extension, Aug., 1890; became Asst. to the Surveyor-Gen. in Mashonaland, Sept., 1891; acted as the B.S.A. Co.'s representative at Umtali June to Aug., 1896; Acting Asst. Surveyor-Gen., Jan., 1897, and has twice acted as Surveyor-Gen. He was Acting Examiner of Diagrams, Feb. 28, 1901.

SAYCE, Rev. Archibald Henry, M.A., Hon. LL.D. (Dublin), Hon. D.D. (Edin.); of Cairo; 5, Chalmers Crescent, Edinburgh, and of the Athenaeum (Lond.), and University (Edin.) Clubs, was born in 1846. After gaining two first classes at Oxford, he was elected to a Fellowship at Queen's Coll. in 1869, and made Tutor of the College in 1870; was ordained Priest in 1871; elected Deputy Professor of Comparative Philology in 1876 on Max Muller s retirement; Prof. of Assyriology in 1891; appointed Member of the Old Testament Revision Co. in 1874; Pres. of the Anthropological Section of the British Association in 1887, and of the Assyrian Section of the Oriental Congress in 1892; was Hibbert Lecturer in 1887, and Gifford Lecturer at Aberdeen in 1900-2. Dr. Sayce was tried and threatened with execution on the charge of being a spy at Nantes during the Franco German War; acted as correspondent during the Carlist War in 1873; assisted in the organisation of the movement for the endowment of research, and the appointment of the last University Commission, and in the foundation of the Hellenic Society; has made archeological journeys in the East; and assisted Dr. Schliemann in his excavations at Orchomenos (1881), and elsewhere. In 1890 Prof. Sayce resigned most of his appointments at Oxford and settled in Egypt, where, after excavating for some years with Mr. Somers Clarke at El Nab, Upper Egypt, he excavated a large Twelfth Dynasty Cemetery near Esna in 1904-5. His publications include: *Outlines of Accadian Grammar*, 1870; *Assyrian Grammar for Comparative Purposes*, 1872; *Principles of Comparative Philology*, 1874; *Elementary Assyrian Grammar*, 1875; *Lectures on the Assyrian Syllabary*, 1877; *Babylonian Literature*, 1877; *Introduction to the Science of Language*, 1879; *Monuments of the Hittites*, 1881; *Decipherment of the Inscriptions of Van*, 1882;

Herodotus, 1883; *Fresh Light from the Monuments*, 1883; *Ancient Empires of the East*, 1884; *Introduction to Ezra and Esther*, 1885; *Babylonian Religion*, 1887; *The Hittites*, 1889; *Races of the Old Testament*, 1891; *Higher Criticism*, 1894; *Prince of Assyriology*, 1894; *Patriarchal Palestine*, 1895; *Egypt of the Hebrews and Herodotus*, 1895; *Early History of the Hebrews*, 1896; *Israel and Surrounding Nations*, 1898; *Genesis*, 1901; *Egyptian and Babylonian Religion*, 1903; *Commentary on Tobit, &c.*, 1903. Edited G. Smith's *Babylonia, Sennacherib, and Chaldean Genesis*, the 2nd series of *Records of the Past* (1888-92), and Murray's *Handbook to Egypt* (1896).

SCAIFE, Thomas Earle, A.M. Inst., C.E., of Burnholme, Robertson, Cape Colony; was born at York, England, Sept. 28, 1867, and is the eldest son of George Scaife, of Huttons Ambo, Yorks. He was educated privately, and served as a pupil under Mr. J. H. Rhodes, M.I.C.E., of Leeds. Subsequently he was engaged upon the construction of railways in various parts of England, and upon the construction of dock and Harbour works. He joined the Public Works Department, Cape Colony, in 1897, having since been engaged upon the construction of Irrigation Works, and the reconnaissance of Irrigation Projects. At the present time he is Resident Engineer for the Irrigation Dept. in the Breede River Valley, where extensive irrigation works are in course of construction. He married, in Sept., 1891, Clara Alice, fourth dau. of the late T. W. Brown, of Leeds.

SCANLEN, Hon. Sir Thomas Charles, K.C.M.G., M.L.C., of Salisbury, Rhodesia; and of the Civil Service (C.T.) and Salisbury Clubs; was born in the district of Albany, near Grahamstown, July 9, 1834. He is son of the late Chas. Scanlen, who formerly represented Cradock Dist. in the Cape House of Assembly. Sir Thomas was educated in the Eastern Province until war in 1850 interrupted his studies. He resided at Cradock from 1845 for over 30 years, where he was a member of the Divisional Council and Chairman of the Municipality, besides which he represented that constituency in the Cape Parliament continuously from 1870 to 1896. He was J.P. for the Cape and Cradock Districts; became Prime Minister and Attorney-Gen. of Cape Colony in 1881, and

Premier and Colonial Secy. in 1882-1884. He was appointed Legal Adviser to the B.S.A. Co., Oct. 1894; member of the Executive Council of S. Rhodesia, Jan. 1896, becoming senior member, Dec. 20, 1896; Acting Public Prosecutor, Apr. 1896; Pres. of the Compensation Board, Sept. 1896; was appointed Acting Administrator of S. Rhodesia in Dec. 1898, and again in Jan. 1903, Oct. 1904, Dec. 1904, and June 1905. He has also acted as the Company's representative on several occasions. Sir Thomas was appointed M.L.C. in May, 1899, and was last reappointed in 1905, with precedence of nominated members. He is also Chairman of Committee in the Legislative Council. In July, 1902, he became senior member of the Farming and Transport Aid Board. Sir Thomas was twice married: first, to Emma Thackeray (d. 1862); and second, to Sarah Dennison (d. Feb. 1903).

SCHALCH, Colonel (Miralai) Thomas Andrew Arthur; Orders of the Osmanieh (3rd class) and Medjidieh (4th class); of Port Said, Egypt, The Court, Charmontle, and the Junior Constitutional (Lond.) and Turf (Cairo) Clubs, was born in Bengal, June 8, 1861, and is son of Vernon Hugh Schalch, C.S.I., of the Bengal Civil Service. Col. Schalch was educated at Bradfield Coll., and joined the 4th Battalion of the Norfolk Regt. in 1880, transferring to the Egyptian Gendarmerie in 1884. He is at present Commandant of the Suez Canal Police.

SCHALK-BURGER, W., was member of the Volksraad for Lydenburg, and member of the Executive Council of the late S.A.R. He was Chairman of the Industrial Commission appointed to inquire into conditions of the mining industry. The report was a general condemnation of evils under which the prosperity of the country languished, and many progressive recommendations were made. The President characterised Mr. Burger as a traitor to his country for having signed such a report, which was no doubt framed with an honest desire to remove abuses and to introduce concessions which would benefit both the mining industry and the State. He became Acting-President of the S.A.R. after Mr. Kruger's flight to Europe.

SCHOELLER, Dr. Max, Member of the German Colonial Council; of Zelten 21A, Berlin; of Rittergat Bingel bei Düren (Rheinland) and of the Union Club, Berlin; was born at Düren, July 28, 1865. He is son of Alexander Schoeller by his wife Adele Casstargeis, and received a liberal education at Duren, Cologne, Aix-la-Chapelle, Munich, and Freiburg-i-Br. Dr. Schoeller travelled through Northern Abyssinia in 1894, afterwards publishing *Mitteilungen über meine Reise in der Colonie Eritrea (Nord Abessinien)*, 1894. The years 1896 and 1897 he spent in German and British East Africa and Uganda, publishing three volumes entitled *Mitteilungen über meine Reise nach Aequatorial Ost Africa und Uganda 1896-97*. Throughout 1897 he travelled in S.A. He married, Nov. 28, 1903, Elizabeth Wessel. Dr. Schoeller's merits have been recognised by the following Orders conferred upon him: Roter Adler of the IV. class, Friedrichs III. el., Ernestiner IV. cl., Eiserne Krone III. cl., Italienische Krone IV. el., Medjidieh II. cl., Villa Vicosa II. el., Sonnen und Löwen II cl., and Erlöser IV. cl.

SCHOEMAN, Johannes Hendrick, M.L.A., is Bond Member of the Cape Legislative Assembly for Oudtshoorn, for which electoral division he was re-elected in Feb., 1904.

SCHOFIELD, Major Harry Morton, V.C., of the Army and Navy, White's and Cavalry Clubs, was born Jan. 29, 1865, and was educated at the Royal Military Academy, Woolwich, entering the Artillery in 1884, and receiving his promotion to Capt. in 1893 and Major in 1900. Major Schofield served in the South African War in 1899-1900, taking part in the relief of Ladysmith, including the actions at Colenso, Spion Hop, Vaal Krantz, Tugela Heights, Pieter's Hill, and Laing's Nek. Afterwards he was operating in the Eastern Transvaal, including the actions at Belfast and Lydenburg. During the Natal campaign he served as A.D.C. to Sir Redvers Buller (despatches, Queen's medal with six clasps, V.C.).

SCHOOLING, Edward, of Sutton, Surrey, and of 3, Throgmorton Avenue, London, E.C., was born at Gravesend in 1860, and was educated privately. He is a Goldsmith by patrimony, a Freeman of the City of London, and one of the partners in the firm of Lockwood and Co. This firm—which has just completed its twentieth year, thus establishing a precedence over most similar institutions in point of age—enjoys much support and confidence amongst Stock Exchange investors and operators throughout the United Kingdom, as well. as upon the Continent, the German clientele of the firm being especially important. The net system of dealing, which Messrs. Lockwood and Co. were amongst the first to initiate, is so well known that it only needs a passing allusion here, but it may briefly he said that by this system purchasers and sellers alike undoubtedly escape more or less onerous commission charges. A tribute to the standing and reputation of Messrs. Lockwood and Co. was afforded when Mr. E. Schooling was requested to contribute some notes entitled *Twenty Years of Share Dealing* for the anniversary number of the *Financial News*. This article was generally appreciated as containing a great deal of sound advice and as indicating the real nature of the duties of a stock and share dealer. The concluding passage may not inaptly be quoted here: "The dealer must be an active and a busy man if he attempts to keep abreast of the stock markets, and if he fails to do this he cannot hope to retain the support and confidence of his clients. After many years' arduous experience one fact is borne in on me more than any other, and that is that the man who wants to understand stocks and shares must never leave off studying them and learning about them in a thoroughly impartial spirit. He should store his mind with maxims that have been put successfully to the proof, and yet on occasion he must be able to act decisively quite outside them. He should steer a middle course between doggedness and impulsiveness, seeking, in brief, to move alertly with the times, yet taking excellent heed all the while that he does not outstrip them".

Lockwood's London Letter, published weekly, has become a recognised institution of the financial world, and, besides being of great service to the clients of the firm, is, of course, read by numbers of general investors, who act upon its shrewd suggestions through other channels, of which, it goes without saying, the firm need not, and does not, complain. A comparatively new feature, and undoubtedly an enterprising one, is the weekly issue, at the request of a large body of German clients, of *Lockwood's Londoner Stimmungs-Bericht*. This is a free paraphrase of the *London Letter* and is especially designed by Messrs. Lockwood to keep their Continental friends in the closest touch possible with all sections of the London stock markets, and more particularly, perhaps, with the South African department, in which the firm, both in Kaffirs and Rhodesians, have dealt very largely for many years past. The brochure issued by this enterprising house, it may be added, gives occasionally details of South African Industrial and Commercial stocks, which should prove really valuable to Colonial investors.

SCHREINER, Olive. (See Mrs. Cronwright-Schreiner.)

SCHREINER, Hon. William Philip, K.O., C.M.G., was born in the Wittebergen Native Reserve, new part of the Herschel District of the Cape Colony, in 1857. He is the youngest son of the late Rev. Gottlieb Schreiner, a German missionary of the L.M.S., and brother of the celebrated S. African novelist, Olive Schreiner, now Mrs. Cronwright Schreiner (q.v.). Mr. Schreiner received his preliminary education at Healdtown, in the Fort Beaufort District, Cradock, Bedford, and Grahamstown, proceeding thence to the Universities of Cape Town, Cambridge, and London, where he distinguished himself in scholarly attainments. He took a Senior in Law Tripos and the Chancellor's Legal Medal in 1881 and was called to the Bar of the Inner Temple in the following year, when he was also admitted an Advocate of the Supreme Court of the Cape Colony. In 1885, he was appointed Parliamentary Draughtsman; became Legal Adviser to the High Commissioner in 1887, filling this appointment until 1893, when he joined the late Cecil Rhodes' second Ministry as Attorney-Gen., having in that year been elected as member for Kimberley in the Cape House of Assembly. He resigned the Attorney Generalship later in 1893; was elected member for Barkly West by the aid of the Bond vote in 1894, and again became Attorney-Gen. in Sept. of that year. His relations with Mr. Rhodes, which had been for many years of a cordial nature, were reluctantly broken off by the Jameson Raid, and he left the Cabinet, declining to accept the same portfolio in the new Ministry under Sir Gordon

THE EARL OF SELBORNE THE HON. W. P. SCHREINER

Photos Elliott & Fry

Sprigg. He became, however, Premier in 1898, retaining that position until June, 1900, the country receiving, under his Premiership, its first taste of Bond rule. How disastrous it proved to the Colony and all S. Africa during those two years history painfully records. In the general election in Feb., 1904, rejected by his Bond friends, he failed to be re-elected to the House of Assembly, and he has since given up the idea of re-seeking election, on the grounds that the party organisation is rigidly on racial lines, and he cannot honestly pledge himself to either party, or feel confidence in their leaders.

A South African to his heart's core, honest in his own views; and of an unsuspecting nature, he probably believed unreservedly in the integrity of those who used him, until he found how not only the members of his Cabinet were betraying his confidence, but his trusted friend, the Pres. of the O.F.S., was deliberately contriving the ruin of the Colony. To his own want of suspicion of the motives of those around him is traceable the odium which followed his action—or inaction—at critical moments. He blindly dismissed the possibility of invasion, until his brother-in-law, ex-Pres. Reitz, and his friend Pres. Steyn rudely awakened him to the reality, and their burghers were within the Cape Colonial border. Duped on all sides from within and without, and nauseated by the Afrikander Party, Mr. Schreiner resolutely retired from the political arena.

To the student of South African politics, it has not always been clear whether Mr. Schreiner's attitude was pro-Boer or pro-British. His tendency seemed to waver between the two extremes. Without being an actual member of the Afrikander Bond, he has on occasions been a supporter of and supported by that organisation; in fact, he has in some quarters been suspected of an inclination to follow the extremists in their desire to constitute South Africa an independent Republic. However that may be, it may be said that during his Premiership he neither prevented nor promoted the South African War, though a strong man in his official position might possibly have done either He is said to have resisted British measures of coercion, and to have given no encouragement to anti-British aims. He neither stopped arms going into the

Transvaal through Cape Colony, nor permitted an early organised defence of Kimberley and the Cape Colonial frontier, nor did he, by a display of resolution, appear to aim at convincing Pres. Kruger that the Colony would tolerate no disloyal actions on the part of British subjects in the event of his issuing an ultimatum. In short, his halting methods of conciliation in the prewar period stood a very good chance of being misinterpreted by a large section of the British. Generally, he is looked upon as a man of high attainments and character (somewhat hampered as a politician by a crossbench habit of mind), with a racial bias towards the Dutch propaganda, and an intellectual sympathy with British methods and characteristics.

Mr. Schreiner has been delegated at various times to conferences between South African Govts.; was a member of the Jameson Raid Committee, and gave evidence before the B.S.A. Committee of the House of Commons in 1897: He is a man of the keenest intellect, of brilliant parts, a practised speaker, and a successful lawyer. In fact, he is far better adapted to the business of the Bar and Beech than to the polemics and anxieties of administration. For the former nature and training have admirably qualified him, but for the latter he has neither temper nor tact. As a lawyer he conducted his cases with judicial discrimination, close argument, faultless logic, rich illustration and convincing clearness.

Mr. Schreiner combines a pleasing appearance with a charming personality, and is *persona grata* with all who know him, however they may differ from him politically. He is married to a sister of Mr. Frank William Reitz (q.v.), ex-Pres. of the Orange Free State.

SCHREINER, Theophilus, M.L.A., represents Tembuland in the Cape Legislative Assembly. He has for many years been a prominent politician, and sits as a supporter of the Progressive party. He was last re-elected at the general election in 1904.

SCHULLER, Oscar H., of Johannesburg, is son of Wilhelm Christian Schuller (q.v.).

SCHULLER, Wilhelm Christiaan, of Johannesburg, S.A., and 2b, Paulinen Strasse, Stuttgart, Germany, and of the Royal Colonial Institute, was born Jan. 18, 1842, at Stuttgart, and was educated in his native city and in London. In 1889 he went to SA. and proceeded direct to Johannesburg. It is claimed that he and his son, Oscar H. Schuller, were the discoverers and pioneers of the notorious Pretoria Diamond Fields. In April, 1897, father and son took up and prospected the Farm Rietfontein 351 (District Pretoria). On Aug. 2 his son discovered the first diamond, and a company was floated and named after the discoverers, The Schuller Diamond Mines, Ltd., of which Mr. Schuller was a director. The mine has since shut down. Mr. Schuller has done much to promote gymnastic exercises, and has given many prizes and trophies to the Wanderers' Gymnastic Soc. His health has now quite broken down.

SCHUMACHER, Raymond William, of Pallinghurst, Johannesburg, second son of Mr. and Mrs. Erwin A. Schumacher, of Porchester Terrace, W., was born in London in 1871. He was educated at Eastbourne under Mr. F. Schreiner, brother of the ex-Premier of the Cape, and at Harrow. He studied banking and finance in London, and for some years on the Continent before going to Johannesburg in 1894, where he entered the employment of the firm of Eckstein soon after his arrival, and he came a partner of that firm, together with Sir Percy Fitzpatrick, in 1898. Although not one of the Reformers, he gave evidence at Pretoria at the trial of the Committee in Feb., 1896, and was imprisoned for a few hours for refusing to divulge his thoughts! In 1899, before the war, he became Chairman of the Johannesburg Relief Committee. One of the last to leave Johannesburg when war broke out, he quickly returned, and served with the Rand Rifles as Capt., taking an active interest in encouraging rifle shooting among the British population on the Rand, and in the Transvaal Volunteer movement. He is now Maj. in command of the T.L.I. He also takes an interest in most forms of sport. He is Chairman of a large number of leading gold mining Cos., and Director of several more. Politically he holds Imperialistic views, and hopes to see an intelligent effort made to protect British trade within the Empire. Mr. Schumacher married, June 8, 1903, Hope, youngest dau. of Mr. and Mrs. Ed. L. Weigall, of 40, Holland Park, W.

SCHUSTER, Hans, of Berlin, is son of a prominent Swiss financier, who was a member of the banking firm of Von Speyr and Co., of Basle, president of the Gothard Railway, and other important institutions. Mr. Hans Schuster was born and educated at Basle, and, inheriting his late father's aptitude for finance, also became a partner in Von Speyr and Co. When, later on, the latter firm was converted into a limited liability company, in which the Dresdner Bank was interested, Mr. Schuster went to Berlin as manager of the Dresdner Bank, an important position, which carries more responsibility than the office of a bank manager generally implies in England. He is also on the directorate of a number of other banking and industrial enterprises. Recently the great German banking house became interested with the Chartered Company in the now power scheme on the Zambesi (see H. Wilson Fox).

Mr. Schuster is first of all a man of business, but at heart he is a sportsman, being particularly partial to shooting, and playing a good game of lawn tennis, as well as a good hand of bridge. He is also very fond of music, the opera, and art, and possesses a fine collection of pictures, which he has gathered together in to course of his rambles in different European cities. His duties mainly keep him occupied in Germany, but he has quite an exceptional admiration for the British and their institutions, whether political or social, and he is always very glad when he is enabled to spend some time in England. Mr. Schuster is a great linguist, and speaks French, English, German, and Italian with great fluency. He has travelled extensively all over the world, and married a daughter of Consul Guttmann, who is also a director of the Dresdner Bank.

SCHWARTZ, R. C., was educated at St. Paul's Sch., Lond., and was a member of the last S.A. cricket team.

SCOBLE, John, of Pretoria (P.O. Box 384), Transvaal, was born in London, March 11, 1826, his father having been Secy. of the Anti-Slavery Society, and afterwards M.P. for the county of Elgin, Canada. He was educated privately, and at the age of 20 joined the staff of the *Morning Herald*,

Lond., becoming City Editor of that paper in 1849, subsequently occupying a similar position on the *Morning Post*. In 1860 he went to Natal; was appointed J.P. for Newcastle Div in 1872; was a member of the Newcastle and Zulu Border Defence Commission; went to Transvaal Goldfields in 1873; was appointed Gold Commissioner and Special Landdrost in 1875, and Landdrost at Middelburg from 1877 to 1879. In 1880 he once more adopted journalism, and edited the *Transvaal Argus*, until publication ceased with the first Boer War, in which he served as a Volunteer in the Pretoria Rifles in the defence of Pretoria. On conclusion of peace he went to the Jagersfontein diamond fields; established the *Free State Argus*, and a daily paper called the *Breakfast Table*. In 1882 he became Editor of the *Transvaal Advertiser*, and advocated British interests of the House of Commons in 1897. He is a man of the keenest intellect, of brilliant parts, a practised speaker, and a successful lawyer. He married a sister of Mr. Reitz, at one time Pres. of the O.F.S.

SCOTT, Baliol, B.A., of The Pines, Weybridge, Surrey, was born at Sydney, N.S.W., on June 17, 1873, is son of Captain L. H. Scott, of the XI. Regt., and was educated at Bath College and University College, Oxford (3rd class Litt. Hum., 1896). Mr. Scott was called to the Bar at the Middle Temple in 1897, and, adopting journalism, was appointed editor in 1901 of the old established *Mining Journal*, the doyen of mining and trade newspapers. Familiar as that journal has always been to mining interests in South Africa, its voice has been widely heard in support of the establishment of an English-speaking administration in the Transvaal, and in connection with the specialised questions of mine labour, sanitation, and finance, its influence since the war has been generally acknowledged. Mr. Scott married, in 1902, Gladys Agnes, dau. of W. C. P. Grant, Paymaster-in-Chief, R.N.

SCOTT, John E., of Bulawayo, practised as a Solicitor in Johannesburg, afterwards going to Bulawayo, where he was the first to follow that profession. He was a member of the first Sanitary Board, and has always taken a leading interest in local affairs. He was elected Mayor of Bulawayo in 1902, and he is a member of the Bulawayo Chamber of Mines.

SCOTT, Rear Admiral Percy, C.V.O., C.B., LL.D., A.D.C., R.N., of the United Service Club, was born in 1853. He entered the Royal Navy in 1866, and took part in the Ashanti War in 1873-4; the Congo Expedition in 1875, and the Egyptian War in 1882. During the late S. African War he rendered excellent service to the State in creating and forwarding guncarriages in time to save Ladysmith. He became Rear Admiral on the death of Vice Admiral Hammet, on Feb. 24, 1905, and relinquished the command of Whale Island Gunnery School, Portsmouth, to become Director of Target Practice at the Admiralty. He married Roma, dau. of Sir F. D. Hartland.

SCOTT, William Edward Edwards, of Hartley, Rhodesia, was appointed Asst. Native Commissioner at Umtali in May, 1896, and became Native Commissioner for the Hartley District, April 1, 1897.

SCULLY, William Charles, of The Residency, Bridasdorp, Cape Colony, and the Civil Service Club, Cape Town, was born in Dublin, Oct. 29, 1855; went to the Diamond fields in 1870, thence to the Northern Transvaal and S.E. Africa, prospecting and hunting; entered the Cape Colonial Civil Service in 1876, and spent several years as Magistrate in Native territories, and became a Special Magistrate for the Northern border, subsequently receiving his present appointment as Civil Commissioner and R,M. at Bridasdorp. Mr. Scully held a commission in Nesbitt's Light Horse in the Tembu and Basuto Wars (1880-81), and has written on the Native question. He is also the author of *Poems*, *Kaffir Stories*, *The White Hecatomb*, *Between Sun and Sand*, *A Vendetta of the Desert*, etc. He married, first, in 1885, Ellen Theodora, dau. of the late Commander Barnes, R.N. (d. in 1887), and, second, in 1890, Honoria Emily, dau. of John Richards, of King Williamatown, Cape Colony.

SEARLE, Charles, M.L.A., is Member of the Cape Legislative Assembly for the electoral division of George; is a supporter of the Bond, and was last returned to the House in Feb., 1904.

SEARLE, James, M.L.A., is Member of the Cape Legislative Assembly for Port Elizabeth, for which constituency he successfully sought reelection at the general election in 1904. He is a member of the Progressive party.

SEAVER, Maj. F. J. Ricardé. (See Ricarde-Seaver.)

SEEAR, John, of The Quarry, Cheam, Surrey, and of Warnford Court, London, E.C., was formerly a partner in the firm of Seear, Hasluck and Co., accountants, of which he afterwards became a sleeping partner, until its liquidation. During the last ten years Mr. Seear has been associated as Chairman or Director of a large number of companies, including Matabeleland Exploration Syndicate, Ltd., Tigerfontein Gold Mines, Ltd., Betsilea Exploring Co., Ltd., Bulawayo Market and Offices Co., Ltd., Crewe's Rhodesia Development Co., Ltd. (since in liquidation), Davies' Selukwe Development Co., Ltd., Warnford Exploration Co., Ltd. (in liquidation), Ibo Investment Trust, Ltd. (in liquidation), and the Lomagunda Reefs, Ltd. He has also been Director of the Van Ryn West Mining Co., British Columbia Agency, Estate, Finance and Mines Corporation, Ltd., African British Columbia Corporation, Ltd., Exploring Lands and Minerals Co., Ltd., Consolidated Rand Rhodesia Trust and General Exploration Co., Ltd., and has served on the London Committee of the Lancaster Gold Mining Co., Ltd., Midas East Estate and Gold Mining Co., Ltd., Molyneux Mines Consolidated, Ltd., Western Molyneux Mines, Ltd., East Rand Gold, Coal and Estate, Ltd., Ginsberg Gold Mining Co., Ltd., and Rand Mines Deep, Ltd. Mr. Seear's connection, however, has since been severed from these companies.

He is now Chairman and Managing Director of the Gold Fields of Matabeleland, and the Rhodesia Exploration and Development Co., Ltd., Chairman of Crescens (Matabele) Mines and Land Co., Ltd., Koffyfontein Mines, Ltd., Lomagunda Development Co., Ltd., and Rhodesia Matabeleland Development Co., Ltd., and a Director of General Trust and Finance Corporation, Ltd., Geneva Tramways Co., Ltd., Nyassa Co., Ltd., Oceana Consolidated Co., Ltd., Transvaal Goldfields, Ltd., and Van Ryn Gold Mines Estates Co., Ltd. He is also on the London Committee of the Wolhuter Gold Mines, Ltd., and of the Nyassa Co.

SEEL, Thomas Joice, of 5, Copthall Buildings, London, E.C., is a director of the Alice Proprietary Mines (Rhodesia), Ltd., Appantoo Mines, Ltd. , Bechuanaland Exploration Co., Ltd., Bechuanaland Trading Assoc., Ltd., Bernheim (Mazoe) G. M., Ltd., Matabele Proprietary Mines, Ltd., Moonie Creek Development Co., Ltd., Prestea Mines, Ltd., Umniati Development Co., Ltd., and the Wanderer (Selukwe) G. M., Ltd.

SEELY, Major John E. B., M.P., D.S.O. of Brooke House, Isle of Wight, served with the Hampshire Imp. Yeo in the South African War in 1900-01, receiving the Queen's medal with five clasps and the D.S.O. He sat in Parliament from 1900 to 1904 as Conservative member for the Isle of Wight, and then in consequence of his opposition to the party, he voluntary resigned, and was re-elected as a Liberal. At the general election in Jan., 1906, he was returned as Liberal M.P. for the Abercromby Division of Liverpool. Major Seely was a member of the Committee of the Volunteer Commission in 1906.

SEIMERT, Benno C. G., of 652-5, Salisbury House, London, E.C., is Vice Chairman of the Cape Asbestos Co., Ltd., Chairman of the Cort Development Syndicate, Ltd., and director of the African Gold Dredging and Mining Concessions, Ltd., Clitters United Mines, Ltd., Cosmopolitan Proprietary, Ltd., Sika Exploring Syndicate, Ltd., White Feather Main Reefs, Ltd., and White Feather Reward, Ltd.

SELBORNE, Right Hon. the Earl of, P.C., G.C.M.G., of Pretoria, Transvaal; Blackmoor, Liss, Hampshire, England, and of Brooks' Club, London, is the only son of the distinguished jurist and statesman who was thrice Lord Chancellor, formerly known as Sir Roundell Palmer, and afterwards the first Earl of Selborne. William Waldegrave Palmer, the present Lord Selborne, was born Oct. 17, 1859, and was educated at Winchester and University Coll., Oxford, where he graduated a first-class in Modern History in 1882. He began his public career as Private Secy. to his father when Lord Chancellor, and then served in the same capacity to Mr. Childers at the War Office, and subsequently at the Exchequer in Mr. Gladstone's second Ministry. In 1885 he entered the House of Commons as Liberal Member for the Petersfield Division of Hampshire, but when Mr. Gladstone brought forward his Home Rule scheme Lord Wolmer (as the present Earl Selborne then was) joined the Liberal Unionists, and became the first Whip of the newly formed party. He entered Parliament in 1885, holding his seat until he succeeded his father (1895) in the Upper House, and rendering yeoman service, not only to the Union, but also to the cause of the Established Church when these were threatened by Mr. Gladstone's Govt.

It was during the course of the same Parliament (1892-5) that he backed Mr. George Curzon's Peers' Disabilities Removal Bill, which was to offer to all peers' eldest sons sitting in the House of Commons the right to elect whether they would go to another place or remain where they were. Indeed, so determined were the supporters of this measure to cling to the Commons that they are popularly supposed to have sworn a secret oath that the first heir apparent implicated who would be summoned to the House of Lords was to be offered up as a test case. The victim proved to be Lord Selborne, and nothing but the Report of a Select Committee would induce him to enter the Upper Chamber.

In 1895 Lord Selborne was appointed Und Sec. for the Colonies under England's great Colonial Sec., Mr. Chamberlain, and retained that office until 1900—a period the most momentous in the history of South Africa, covering the Jameson raid, the Transvaal reform negotiations, and the first year of the S. African War. It was a period of hard work and of great responsibility, but Lord Selborne was more than equal to it, and he seconded Mr Chamberlain's strenuous efforts to awaken true interest for the Colonies in the Motherland with conspicuous success, both in the country and in Parliament.

In 1900 Lord Selborne became First Lord of the Admiralty, in which position he has quickened promotion in the senior service, organised naval education, and most recently increased the power of the Fleet by its redistribution, and its efficiency by weeding out the obsolete ships of war.

In March, 1905, Lord Selborne succeeded Lord Milner as High Commissioner for South Africa and Governor of the Transvaal and Orange River Colonies, and in the same month he was appointed an ordinary member of the First Class of the Knights Grand Cross of St. Michael and St. George. That a statesman who has occupied such high office in the Home Govt., and who has given so many proofs of administrative ability, impartiality, and moderation should have succeeded to this arduous post, has given the deepest satisfaction to loyal South Africa and to all those who have Imperial interests heart. From the moment of his arrival in Africa Lord Selborne has shown a laudable desire not only to study the problems of the country with the greatest care, but also to get in close touch with the people of every shade of opinion.

In his younger days Lord Selborne was keen on cricket and football. He is a good shot, enthusiastic angler, and fond of the hunt. In 1883 he married Lady Beatrix Maud Cecil, eldest dau. of the Marquis of Salisbury.

SELBY, Philip H., was appointed District Commissioner and Magistrate of the Luangwa District of North-Western Rhodesia in 1906.

SELOUS, Frederick Courteney, of Heatherside, Worplesdon, Surrey, was born near Regent's Park, London, Dec. 31, 1851, and is mixed Huguenot and English descent on his father's side, and of English and Scottish descent in the maternal line. He was educated at Bruce Castle (Tottenham), Rugby, Neuchatel, and Wiesbaden, and when still a boy went to S.A., landing at Algoa Bay on Sept. 4, 1871, with the intention of going to the diamond fields. But instead of this he started on a trading expedition through Griqualand. In the following year he set out for Matabeleland, meeting on the way Mr. G. A. Phillips, with whom he made the acquaintance of Lobengula, who granted Mr. Selous permission to shoot elephants because he was only a boy. In 1877, after a trip to England, he again visited the Zambesi. From 1882 to 1892 Mr. Selous was constantly travelling over the Mashona plateau, and during that time roughly mapped out the country by taking compass bearings wherever possible from bill to bill, and sketching the courses of the rivers and streams from the tops of hills. Mr. Selous was associated with Maj. Johnson as guide and intelligence officer in the work of opening up Mashonaland with the early pioneers, and it was in this connection that he prepared the track known as the Selous Road from Tuli to Fort Salisbury, 400 miles long, as well as various other roads connecting the mining centres. He commanded a troop of R.H.V. in the second Matabele War (1896), and was afterwards for a short period associated with the Partridge and Jarvis group. During the last few seasons Mr. Selous has been hunting in Asia Minor, in North America, and in E. Africa again. His museum at Worplesdon contains many magnificent trophies of the chase in different parts of the world. He has written a good number of interesting books on travel and sport; has lectured considerably, and was awarded in 1893 the Founders' Medal of the Royal Geographical Society in recognition of his extensive explorations and surveys in B.S.A. He married, April 4, 1894, Marie Catharine Gladys, eldest dau. of the Rev. Canon Middy, Rector of Down Hatherleigh, Glos.

SEME, Peka Isaka, is the son of a Zulu Chieftain, and won the George William Curtis Medal for honours in Oratory at Columbia University in 1906. The subject of his address was *The Regeneration of Africa*. Mr. Seme had three competitors, but the decision of the judges was given unanimously in his favour. After graduating B.A. at Columbia University, he will begin a course of law at Oxford, and ultimately hopes to become a legal representative of his people. He is a loyal British subject, and has high hopes of the development of Zululand under British rule.

SENIOR, Bernard, M.L.C., Auditor-Gen. of the O.R.C.; of Bloemfontein, S.A., and of the Royal Societies' Club, London, and the United Service Club, Bloemfontein; son of the late John Senior, Solicitor, of 2, New Inn, London, was born at Wimbledon, Surrey, June 23, 1865. He entered the Home Civil Service as Clerk to the Boundary Commission under the Redistribution of Seats Act, in Dec., 1884. He was attached to the Scotch Education Dept. in 1885, and again in 1888. In

1887 he was selected as Private Secy. to the late Rt. Hon. Sir Francis Sandford (afterwards Lord Sandford), Under-Secy. of State for Scotland. In May, 1888, he was appointed First-Class Clerk in the Colonial Secy.'s Office on the Gold Coast. He was appointed Local Auditor of the Colony of Lagos in 1889, and held a similar position on the Gold Coast from Dec., 1889, to Feb., 1894. For the next two years he was Local Auditor of British Bechuanaland, and when that Colony was incorporated with the C.C. in Nov., 1895, he was transferred to the Island of Cyprus as Local Auditor, which position he held until Oct. 1, 1902, when he was appointed Auditor-Gen. of the O.R.C. He was a member of the Commission appointed to enquire into the Law relating to Mining and Prospecting for Diamonds and Precious Stones in the O.R.C. in 1903, and in 1904 was the O.R.C. Delegate at a Conference of all the South African Colonies appointed to consider the charges for Ocean Freights (The South African Freights Conference). He was appointed a member of the Legislative Council of the O.R.C. in 1904, and is a Director of the National Bank of the O.R.C., and is Chairman of the Govt. Tender Board. He married, March 31, 1891, Florence Mary, youngest dau. of the late Dr. S. B. Parr, of Andover, Hants.

SERJEANT, Col. William Charles Litton, C.B., F.R.G.S., of 1, Plowden Buildings, Temple, E.C., St. Benet's Abbey, near Bodmin, Cornwall, and of the Active Service Club, was born at St. Benet's Abbey in 1857, and is the eldest son of the late Capt. Charles E. Serjeant, 74th Highlanders. He was educated privately, and at Nelson House Grammar School, Devonport. From 1874-82 he served in the 2nd Devon Rifle Volunteers, and during that time raised and commanded a Cadet Corps. He also held a commission in the 4th Batt. Royal Fusiliers from 1882-8. In 1884 he commanded the 1st Detachment of Methuen's Horse, and in the following year he took part in the Bechuanaland Expedition, serving with the Pioneer Regt., Bechuanaland Field Force. He was second in command of the Cape Boys' Corps, Matabeleland Relief Force, in 1896, and commanded the attack on Babiyan's and Sikombo's strongholds, and at the action at Inyanda's Mountain (medal, and thanked by the Board of Directors of the British South Africa Co.). Since 1890 he has commanded the 5th

Batt. Rifle Brigade, and during the late S. African war he commanded that Regt. He acted as commandant of No. 3 section, Northern Division, on the Lines of Communication, and the Lace Mines, Valsch River Blockhouse Line from Jan., 1902, until the conclusion of war (Queen's medal and three clasps, C.B.). He was standing counsel of the London Cab Trades Union in 1894, and is Vice-President of the London Cornish Association. Col. Serjeant is the author of several military pamphlets and articles, including *The Complete Guide to Company Drill in Close and Extended Order*, *Guide to the School of Instruction, Aldershot*, *Problems of Militia Service*, and *Hygienic Machinery of Infantry*. He has shot much game, and has also fished a great deal; has invented improvements connected with sporting firearms, and has acted as expert adviser to several firms and companies. As a cyclist he takes a practical interest in military cycling, and is Standing Counsel to the National Cyclist Union of Great Britain.

SETON-KARR, Sir Henry, Knt., C.M.G., J.P., and D.L. for Roxburghshire, of Kippilaw, St. Boswells, N.B.; of 47, Chester Square, S.W., and of the Carlton and New (Edinburgh) Clubs; is the son of G. Berkeley Seton-Karr, of the Madras Civil Service, who was Resident Commissioner at Belgaum, Southern Mahratta, during the great Mutiny. He was born Feb. 5, 1853, in India, and educated at Harrow and Oxford, where he took honours in law and graduated M.A. In 1879 he was called to the bar, and practised on the Northern Circuit. He was elected to Parliament for St. Helens, Lancs, in 1885, and has held his seat through five contested elections, increasing his majority from 57 to 1,878, until Jan., 1906, when he was defeated at the general election. He is greatly interested in State colonisation and the national food supply in time of war. He was elected as a member of the Royal Commission appointed to consider this subject in 1903, and originated the Sharpshooters' Corps for service in S.A. in 1899. During the years 1900-01-02 he acted as Vice Chairman and Hon. Secy. of the Sharpshooters' Committee, who sent out three and a half battalions (18th, 21st, 23rd I.Y.) for service during the war. For this he received his C.M.G. He is Chairman of the Liverpool, St. Helens, and S. Lancashire Railway Co.; Vice Chairman of the

Widnes and Runcorn Bridge Co., and a Director of various other companies. Sir Henry is widely known as a keen sportsman, having shot big game in S.A., Western America, Norway, British Columbia, and Scotland. He has a very fine collection of big game spurting trophies, including wapiti, moose, buffalo, antelope, red-deer, grizzly, black bear and mountain lion, and has an elk forest in Norway. His publications include *The Call to Arms* (1901), *My Sporting Holidays* (1904), and many sporting articles and reviews. He married: first, in Nov., 1880, Edith, dau. of the late W. Pilkington, D.L., of Roby Hall, Liverpool, who died in 1884; and second, in 1886, Janie, eldest dau. of W. Tharburn, of Edinburgh.

SEWELL, Cyril Otto Hudson, of Cirencester, Glos., was born at Pietermaritzburg, Natal, Dec. 19, 1874; is eldest surviving son of J. J. Sewell, late of the Colonial Office, Natal. He was educated at Maritzburg Coll., and accompanied the first S.A. cricket team to England in 1894. He was the youngest player in the XI., headed the batting averages, and was the only member of the team to complete 1,000 runs during the tour. He took up law as a profession, and has practised for some years at Cirencester. Qualified by residence there, he has played in the Gloucester County XI. every year since 1895, with the exception of 1897, when he was called to S.A. on the death of his father. For the 1906 season he was tenth on the list of batting averages in first-class cricket, scoring 409 runs in nine innings, with an average of 45.44 runs. His highest score in an innings was 107. Mr. Sewell married, Feb. 21, 1903, Maud Evelyn, eldest dau. of Mrs. Maunsell-Collins, of Carlyle Gardens, London.

SEYMOUR, Admiral Sir Edward, G.C.B., is principal Naval A.D.C. to the King. He entered the Navy in 1852, and served in the Crimean war, in the China war 1857-62, and in the Egyptian war in 1882. He was appointed to the command of the China Station in 1898, and took part in the Allied Expedition against the Boxers in 1900. Admiral Seymour was a member of Prince Arthur of Connaught's suite which left for the East early in 1906 in order to invest the Mikado with the Knighthood of the Garter.

SEYMOUR, Lord Henry Charles, of Ragley Hall Alcester, and of the Guards' Club, is the second son of the 6th Marquis of Hertford; was born in London in 1878, and was educated at Cowley Coll. He entered the Grenadier Guards in 1898; was A.D.C. to Gen. Kenyon-Slaney in 1900; A.D.C. to H.E. Viscount Milner in 1901, and is now Inspector in the Barotseland Native Police. He served in the S. African war, receiving the medal and clasps. Unmarried.

SEYMOUR, General Lord Wm., K.C.V.O., of 1, Chesham St., London, S.W., and of the United Service Club; was born in London in 1838. Whilst in the Royal Navy he served in the Baltic, subsequently joining the Coldstream Guards, and taking part in the Crimea. He also served in the Egyptian War. Lord Seymour was appointed to command the troops in Canada from 1898-1900, subsequently being appointed Lieutenant of the Tower, which position he resigned in 1905. Recreations: Shooting and riding. He married, in 1871, a dau. of the first Lord Penrhyn.

SHAND, William Robertson, formerly Clerk at Knysna and Swellendam, was appointed Asst Magistrate at Willowmore Aug. 1, 1890; at Glen Grey, April 2, 1893; joined the Chartered Co.'s service as Asst. Magistrate at Gwelo, Oct. 1, 1898; has acted as Civil Commissioner and R.M. in the C.C. on various occasions, and also as Asst. Magistrate at Enkeldoorn and Bulawayo, and as Magistrate at Gwelo.

SHARP, Ernest Chappel, J.P. for S. Rhodesia, of Salisbury, Rhodesia; joined the Chartered Co.'s service as Clerk in the Surveyor General's Office, April 1, 1894; was Acting Asst. Registrar of the High Court, Feb. 18, 1896; served in the Matabeleland and Mashonaland Rebellions until Sept. 1, 1896; was Secy. to the Assessment of Compensation Board, Sept. 7, 1896; Acting High Sheriff and Chief Clerk to Public Prosecutor, Sept. 7, 1896; Asst. Statist, March, 1897; and Clerk to Civil Commissioner, Salisbury, April 4, 1900.

SHARPE, Montagu, D.L., J.P., of Brent Lodge, Hanwell, W.; 3, Elm Court, Temple, E.C., and the Junior Carlton Club; only son of Commander Benjamin Sharps, J.P. for Middlesex (who died in

1883), by Marianne Fanny, dau. of the late Rev. Geo. Montagu; was born in Oct., 1856; was educated at Felstead, and was for some years in the Civil Service, from which he retired in 1883. He was appointed D.L. in 1888, and was called to the Bar of Gray's Inn in 1889. He was placed on the Commission of the Peace for Middlesex in 1883; is an Alderman of that county, and has been Vice-Chairman of the first Middlesex County Council since 1889. He has also been Deputy Chairman of the Middlesex Quarter Sessions since 1896, and is Chairman of the Petty Sessions and Commissioner of Taxes for Brentford Dist.; has been Chairman of the Hanwell Conservative Assoc. since 1883, and was admitted to the Order of Mercy in 1904.

Mr. Sharps is Chairman of John Birch and Co., Ltd., engineers, trading in India, Japan, S. America, and Egypt, in which latter country the company received from the Govt. a concession for establishing a system of light railways in the provinces of Beherah and Garbieh. This concession was taken over by the Egyptian Delta Light Railway Co., Ltd., of which Mr. Sharpe. is a Director. He is also on the Board of the Tendring Hundred Water Co.

In Freemasonry he is P.G.D. Grand Lodge, Eng., and is a member of the Council of the League of Mercy, and Pres. of the Brentford Div. He was winner of the Civil Service Mile Challenge Cup for three years, and of other races. His recreations are now photography, boating, workshop, hunting, and shooting. He married, July, 1888, Mary Annie, only dau. of Capt. John Parsons, R.N.

SHARPE, Major Wilfred Stanley, C.M.G., of Northern Nigeria; Byfleet, Surrey, and of the Sports Club; was born in 1860, and is son of J. C. Sharpe, and cousin to Montagu Sharpe (q.v.). He was educated at Oxford, and served with the 9th Lancers in India in 1883; joined the 4th Bttn. Royal Irish Rifles in 1893. From 1894-1900 he acted as District Commissioner for Sierra Leone, and served in the Karen Expedition, Sierra Leone, in 1898-99 (despatches, medal with clasp, and C.M.G.). He is now Acting Resident in Northern Nigeria. Unmarried.

SHARWOOD, Albert James, of Queen's Road, Park Town, Johannesburg, and of the Rand and Athenaeum Clubs, Johannesburg; was born in London, and is son of Albert Sharwood, journalist and stockbroker. He was educated at King's Coll., London, with the idea of entering the Indian Civil Service, but after passing various qualifying exams., was rejected on medical test. He went up to the Rand in 1893, serving under John Hays Hammond, at that time consulting engineer to Barnato Bros., and afterwards to the Consolidated Goldfields Co. and the Chartered Co. He subsequently joined the firm of Albu, and became manager in Johannesburg of the General Mining and Finance Corporation, Ltd., representing that group on the Executive Committee of the Chamber of Mines, the Native Labour Association, Labour Importation (Chinese) Association, and the Rand Water Board. In the course of his career Mr. Sharwood has done much journalistic work, both in London and on the Rand. He is a member of the Johannesburg Stock Exchange; is on the Committee of the Progressive Association; has been an aspirant for municipal honours, and is a likely candidate for election to the Transvaal Legislative Assembly. He married Miss Elsie Gordon Greatbatch.

SHAW, Charles Courtenay, of 34, Sloane Court, S.W., of Oaklands, Johannesburg, and of the Pretoria Club; was born in London Aug. 15, 1878, and is son of Charles Bousfield Shaw, of London. He was educated abroad, and in 1901 he was appointed to a clerkship in the office of the Secy. to the Transvaal Admn.; acted as private secy. to the Acting Secy. Transvaal Admn. in. 1902; in the same year he was private secy. to the Colonial Secy. in the Transvaal, and in 1904 was Acting Secy. to the Transvaal Immigration Dept. He translated into Dutch language the *Times* pamphlet, *Great Britain and the Dutch Republic of S. Africa*, in 1900.

SHAW, Flora Louise, maiden name of Lady Lugard (q.v.).

SHAW, Frederick George, F.G.S., A.M. Inst. C.E., of Neville Court, Abbey Road, NW., and of the Royal Societies' Club; was born in Essex in 1856, and is a member of a talented family, one of his brothers being Dr. P. Egerton Shaw, D.Sc., of

Worthingham Coll., another being Prof. H. S. Hele Shaw, lately in charge of technical education in the Transvaal. Mr. F. G. Shaw has acquired notoriety in science, engineering, letters, sport, and travel. His connection with the St. Helens Development Co., of which he was manager, is still fresh in the memories of Anglo-Rhodesians, and he has also managed many other mining enterprises in different parts of the world. He originated the idea, which was rejected by our Admiralty, but which developed into the system of submarine signalling since adopted by the Italian and American navies, and invented a process for the pneumatic carriage of dry ore Mr. Shaw's pen is very seldom idle. Besides contributing to the Press on various matters of the moment, he is the author of *The Pseudomorthic Theory of the Witwatersrand Conglomerates*, *The Use of Cement for Cyanide Tanks*, *The Pneumatic Carriage of Ore in the Dry Crushing Process*, *The Mines of Matabeleland (Ancient and Modern)*, *Comets and their Tails*, *The Gegenschein Light*, *The Zodiacal Light*, *The Empires' Salvation*, *Fiscal Facts and Fictions*, *How to Cast Trout Fly*, *Salmon in Fresh Water*, *The Science of Dry Fly Fishing*, etc. He was one of the first members and speakers of the Tariff Reform League, and in 1903 advocated a subsidy of 30s. per acre in favour of home wheat growers, and the subsidising of our Mercantile Marine, the funds so paid to be obtained by the taxation of manufactured imports. He was also successfully opposed to the introduction of the Chinese into Matabeleland in 1900. He is an advocate of agricultural reform for Great Britain, and edited *Our Country Programme* in *Land and Water*. Mr. Shaw has done well in nearly every branch of sport in many countries. He has shot almost every class of animal, and caught most kinds of fish. He won the amateur champion ship in trout fly-casting at the International Tournament in 1904, and has established the first school for salmon and trout fly-casting in England. Among his trophies is a 50lb. salmon, caught in Norway in 1897. He married, in 1903, Augusta, dau. of Andrew Saunders, Downes House, Ealing, and Lord of the Manor of Marchwood.

SHELDON, Mrs. French-. (See French. Sheldon.)

SHELFORD, Frederic, M.Inst. CE., B. Sc. (Lond.), of 35A, Great George St., Westminster;

34, Argyll Rd., Kensington, and of the St. Stephen's and Royal Cruising Clubs, was born Nov. 14, 1871; is son of Sir William Shelford, K.C.M.G., and was educated at Westminster Sch., and Dulwich Coll. He has been engaged upon the design and construction of various engineering works under contractors and as engineer, and has visited on behalf of Government British Honduras, Sierra Leone, Cyprus, Gold Coast, Ashanti, Lagos, United States, and Egypt. He is now acting as responsible engineer on railway construction work in the Colonies and elsewhere in connection with Sir Benjamin Baker. Recreations: yachting, shooting, rowing, tennis, and golf. He married, in 1899, Mildred Alice, dau. of Sir Montagu F. Ommanney, G.C.M.G., K.C.B., I.S.O.

SHERWELL, Percy W., was formerly a student at Camborne Mining School, and assisted the county of Cornwall at both Rugby football and cricket. He went to S. Africa in 1902, and was champion tennis player of South Africa in that year. He also took part in the test matches against the M.C.C. XI. in the Cape Colony.

SHIPWAY, Lieut., of the Gloucester Regt., was specially selected for service with the West African Frontier Force in 1905.

SHORT, George, served as Sergt. on the Mount Darwin patrol in 1897. He then entered the Chartered Company's service, March 7, 1898.

SHORT, Captain Percy Henry, D.S.O., of the Gloucester Regt., was born April 15, 1874, and entered the Army in 1895. He served in the South African War in 1899-1900, including the operations in Natal and the actions at Rietfontein and Lombard's Kop, being slightly wounded (Queen's medal with three clasps). For his service in connection with the quelling of the native risings in Northern and Southern Nigeria he was awarded the D.S.O. in 1906.

SHUTE, Colonel Henry Gwynn Dease, D.S.O., of 9, West Halkin St., S.W., and of the Guards' and Travellers' Clubs, was born in India, Dec. 4, 1860, and is son of the late Gen. Sir Charles Cameron Shute. He was educated at Wellington Coll., his active service includes the Egyptian Expedition in 1882, when he was present at the action of Mehuta and the battle of Tel-el-Kebir (medal with clasp, bronze star); the Sudan Expedition in 1885 (clasp), and the S. African War in 1899-1902, when he took part in the march on Kimberley and the actions at Belmont, Enslin, Modder River, and Magersfontein, the operations in the Orange Free State, and the actions at Poplar Grove, Driefontein, Vet River, and Zand River, the operations in Cape Colony and in the Transvaal in 1900, in command of a mobile column, and as Commndt. at Graaff Reinet, afterwards as Administrator, No. 5 Martial Law Area, Cape Colony Dist. (despatches, bt. of Lieut. Col., Queen's medal with six clasps, King's medal with two clasps, and D.S.O.).

SILBERBAUER, C. Christian, of C.C., was born in S.A. Although he claims to be an Independent representative member of the Cape Legislative Assembly, he has leanings towards the Bond, and was supported by that organisation in his candidature for Tembuland, for which he was elected unopposed in Nov., 1902.

SILBERBAUER, W., M.L.A., represents the electoral division of Richmond in the Cape House of Assembly. He is a member of the S. African party, and was last returned in that interest in Feb., 1904.

SILBURN, Major Percy Arthur, D.S.O., of Mitchell Park, Durban, Natal, was born in 1874, and is son of A. Silburn, of Durban. He was late Staff Officer and Gunnery Instructor of the Natal Forces, joined the Cape Mounted Rifles in 1889, and was present at the annexation of Pondoland in 1894; appointed to the Permanent Staff, Natal Forces, in 1896, passed the school of Gunnery at Woolwich and Shoeburyness, 1895; returned to S. Africa at the out break of the war, and served with Gough's composite regt. in the relief of Ladysmith; also as Staff Officer to Generals Sir J. Dartnell and G. Hamilton, in the Transvaal and Orange Free State (medals, seven clasps, dispatches, and D.S.O.). He was appointed secretary to the Natal Defence Commission, which resulted in the Militia Act of 1903; secretary to the Local Defence Committee in 1903; retired in Feb., 1904. He has written pamphlets on Imperial and Colonial defence and contributions on the same to the *Service* and other English reviews and magazines. He married, in 1901, Marie, dau. of the late J. R. Hartley, of Durban.

SIM, Thomas Robertson, F.L.S., F.R.H.S., of Natal, is the son of a well-known Aberdeenshire botanist and fruit grower. He was born at Aberdeen, Scotland, in 1858, and was educated at the old Aberdeen Gram. Sch. and at the Univ. of that town. He has always been closely connected with economic horticulture, botany, and sylvicultnre. After a thorough training in these subjects in many of the best horticultural schools of England and America, including the Hort. Society's Gardens, Chiswick; the Royal Gardens; Kew; Harvard Univ. Botanic Gardens, and a few years of active connection with fruit growing and nursery work in Scotland, he emigrated in 1888 to S.A., where, after being a short time Curator of the Botanic Gardens of King Williamstown, he joined the Civil Service of C.C., passing through various grades in the Forest Department up to District Forest Officer in the Eastern Conservancy, where also he was occasionally utilised as lecturer on Forestry and Fruit Culture. In 1902, when the reorganisation of the Forest Service of Natal was proposed, he was selected to carry that out, and was transferred as Conservator of Forests of Natal, with which appointment was also conjoined that of fruit expert. Besides numerous contributions to magazine literature, he is the author of *The Ferns of Kaffraria*, *Check List of the Flora of Kaffraria*, *The Ferns of South Africa*, *Tree planting in Natal*, and the *Forest Flora of Cape Colony*.

SINGH, Major Sir Ganga, K.C.S.I., K.C.I.E., A.D.C., Maharaja of Bikanir, was the host of the Prince and Princess of Wales, when they visited Bikanir during their Indian tour. He is a Major in the British Army, and served with the British in China and Somaliland.

SINGLETON, Capt. Henry Townsend Corbet, D.S.O., of Hillside, Banchory, N.B., and of the Isthmian Club, was born at Dover Jan. 27, 1874, and is the eldest son of the late Major L. C. Singleton. He was educated at Wellington Coll. and Sandhurst; joined the 1st Battn. of Highland Light Inf. at Malta in 1895, and served in Crete in

1898-99, being employed there under the Foreign Office as Chief of Police, Dist. Malevezi. He saw active service in S. Africa in 1899, when he served through the siege of Mafeking as Adjt. in the Protectorate Regt. (slightly wounded). He afterwards served on the Staff (despatches, D.S.O., Queen's medal and three clasps, King's medal and two clasps). He married, Nov. 26, 1902, Evelyn, youngest dau. of Gen. Harris, C.B.

SIVEWRIGHT, , The Hon. Sir James, K.C.M.G., M.A., LL.D., of Tulliallan, Fifeshire, N.B., and of Lourensford, Cape Colony, was born at Fochabers, Elginshire, in Dec., 1848. He entered Aberdeen Univ. in 1862 as a Bursar, and graduated MA. in 1866. He adopted telegraphic engineering as a profession, and after passing first in the competitive examination of 1869 for the Indian Telegraph Service, he was appointed upon the acquisition of the British Telegraphs by the State a Superintending Engineer of the Southern Division of England in 1870. He was Secy. to the Society of Telegraph Engineers, and was appointed gen. Manager of S. African Telegraphs in 1877, from which he retired on a pension in 1885. He received the C.M.G. on the conclusion of the Zulu War, and also earned the South African General Service medal with clasp for the three years 1877-78-79. After a short rest in England he returned to the Cape, and entered the political arena in 1888 as first member for Griqualand E., defeating Mr. Zietsman by a large majority. On July 17, 1860, Sir James joined the first Rhodes Ministry without portfolio, but subsequently (Sept. 1890) was appointed Commissioner of Crown Lands and Public Works and energetically supported his chief in the extension of the Cape railway and telegraphic systems northwards. His negotiation with the Transvaal Executive for the construction of the Bloemfontein-Johannesburg-Pretoria section railway was considered a diplomatic achievement of no slight merit. He received the K.C.M.G. on completion of railway communication with the Transvaal. Sir James went out of office in the disruption of 1893, but immediately after the Jameson raid was prevailed upon to return as Commissioner of Public Works in the Sprigg Ministry of 1896.

He was one of the founders of the Johannesburg

Waterworks Co.; was largely responsible for the reduction of the S.A. cable rates, in worked hard for a high level of efficiency in departmental affairs, as well as in all business undertakings with which he has been connected. He was the pioneer of Cold Storage in the Cape and having decided to remain in his British home is devoting his energies to the development of the coal and iron measures of the East of Scotland. Sir James married, in 1880 Jennie, dau. of George Page, of Bloemfontein.

SKINNER, Col. Edmund Grey, C.B. (1908) of Holly House, Haywards Heath, Eng., and of the Grosvenor (Lond.) and Union (Brighton Clubs, was born at Patna, Bengal, Jan. 29 1850, and is son of Russell Morland Skinner, of the Bengal Civil Service. He was educated at Wimbledon Sch. and at Sandhurst, and joined the A.O.D. in 1867; accompanied the Perak Expedition in 1876 (medal with clasp) took part in the Egyptian campaign in 1882 being present at Kassassin and Tel-el-Kebir (medal with clasp, Medjidieh, despatches); and was Chief Ordnance Officer at Suakim in 1885 (despatches, medal with clasp, brev. Lt. Col.) Col. Skinner retired in Oct., 1901, and was employed with the Remount Commission, U.S.A. from March to July, 1902. He married first, in 1878, Alice, dau. of F. Gilliat Smith (d. 1902) and second, in Nov., 1904, Amy, dau. of T. B Foreman, of Breadsell, Battle.

SKINNER, H. Ross, of Johannesburg. Was delegated by the Transvaal Chamber of Mine to proceed to the East in order to investigate and report upon the labour supply there for the S.A. mines.

SLADE, Major-Gen. John Ramsay, C.B. of 8 Lowndes St., London, S.W., and of the St. James's and United Service Clubs, was born in 1843, and is son of the late Gen. Sir Marcus Slade. He was educated at the Royal Military Academy, Woolwich, and entered the Royal Artillery in 1861; served in the Afghan War in 1878-9, taking part in the operations of the 1st Div. of the Peshawar Valley Field Force, and being present at the action of Girishk; second Bazar Valley Expedition, the battle of Maiwand and the defence of Kandahar (despatches, medal with clasp, and brevet of Major); the S. African War in 1881, as

A.D.C. to the G.O. Commanding the Lines of Communication, and the Italian Campaign in Africa in 1895-6, being attached to the Italian Army Headquarters in Eritrea (Italian War medal). From 1903-5 he commanded the British Troops in Egypt. He married, first, in 1871, Lucia (died 1872), dau. of Signor Vincenzo Ramos; and, secondly, in 1882, Janet, dau. of Gen. B. Wood, C.B.

SLADEN, Thomas Oliver Ramsay, of Lydenburg, Transvaal, served in the S. African War in 1899-1902, in the Royal Artillery, and the 6th Mounted Infantry (medal and five clasps). He was appointed Clerk to the Resident Magistrate at Zeerust in 1902, subsequently becoming Public Prosecutor at Lydenburg, which post he now occupies.

SLATER, Josiah, M.L.A., represents Victoria East in the Cape House of Assembly in the Progressive interest. He was elected at the general election in Feb., 1904, and in 1905 was appointed by the Cape Govt. a member of the Council of the University of the Cape of Good Hope, in the Room of the Rev. Canon Espin, M.A., D.D., resigned.

SLOLEY, Herbert Cecil, of the Residency, Maseru, Basutoland, was born at Calcutta, Feb. 4, 1855. He is son of the late Robert Hugh Sloley, of Calcutta; was educated at the Greenwich Proprietary Sch., and proceeding to S.A. served with the Cape Mounted Riflemen and various Colonial Forces until 1884, when he was appointed Sub Inspector of Basutoland Police. He was promoted Inspector, 1886; Asst. Commissioner in Basutoland, 1888; Govt. Secy. in Basutoland, 1895; and Resident Commissioner in Basutoland in 1901. He has seen considerable service in the field, and wears the war medal with clasp, 1877-8-9; medal with clasp for 1880-1, and the S.A. War medal for 1899-1900. He married, Nov. 18, 1886, Charlotte, dau. of the late John Dick, of C.C. and Scotland.

SMARTT, Dr. Thomas William, M.L.A., of C.T., is an Irishman by birth, and trained for the medical profession, which he abandoned to take a more prominent role in Colonial polities. He was formerly a political adherent of Sir Gordon Sprigg, whose Ministry he joined from May to Oct., 1895, as Colonial Secy.; afterwards in June, 1900, becoming Commissioner of Public Works in Sir

Gordon Sprigg's fourth Administration. Ever a staunch Progressive, he seceded from the Govt. on the Suspension movement, taking with him the main body of the Progressive party. Dr. Smartt then for a long time bore the brunt of the hard work on behalf of the Progressives until, in June, 1908, Dr. Jameson became the recognised leader of the party. In the general election in Feb., 1904, Dr. Smartt defeated Sir Gordon Sprigg at East London (C.C.), and took office under Dr. Jameson as Commissioner for Crown Lands and Public Works in the same month. Dr. Smartt is a capable administrator, a fluent speaker, and possesses a youthful appearance.

SMITH, Hon. Sir Charles Abercrombie, Knt. Bachelor, J.P., of St. Cyrus, Wynberg, Cape Colony, and of the Civil Service Club, Cape Town, was born at St. Cyrus, Kincardineshire, Scotland, May 12, 1834. He is son of Andrew Smith, of St. Cyrus, and of Helen, dau. at the Rev. J. Taylor, of Lethnot; was educated at Glasgow and Cambridge Universities, graduating M.A. with highest honours at Glasgow (Breadalbane Scholar) in 1858, and M.A. Cantab, Second Wrangler and Second Smith's Prizeman, 1855; was Fellow of St. Peter's Coll., Camb., 1860-97, and Hon. Fellow since then. He became a member of the Legislative Council of the Cape Colony in 1866, and has been a member of the Executive Council since 1872. In that year he joined the Cabinet as Commissioner of Crown Lands and Public Works. This portfolio he held until 1875, when he became Controller and Auditor-Gen., a post which he held until 1903, when he retired on full pay. Meanwhile, Sir Abercrombie had served on a large number of Govt. Committees and temporary Commissions, etc., including the Federation Committee, 1871; Commission for Reduction of Public Debt, 1872-4; Chairman of the Tender Board, 1875-1903; Chairman of the War Expenditure Commission, in 1881; member of the Civil Service Commission, 1882; Chairman of the Permanent Civil Service Examining Commission, since 1886; and was a member of the Sinking Fund Commissions, from 1897-1903. He has been Chairman of the Meteorological Commission since 1874; member of the University Council since 1873; Vice Chancellor of the Cape University, 1877-79, where he was Science Examiner for twenty-five years, and

he is now serving on a Civil Service Enquiry Commission appointed in 1904. In his official position he has been responsible for a number of annual bluebooks and volumes of Financial, Public Debt, and other regulations. He married, in 1897, Christina Caroline, dau. of H. Remington Home, of Wynberg.

SMITH, Charles Aubrey, B.A., of the Avenue House, West Drayton, and the Sports and Green Room Clubs and the M.C.C., was born in London, July 21, 1863, and was educated at Charterhouse and Cambridge. Since his Charterhouse days, when he played in the School XI. (1880-1), he has been a keen wielder of the willow. He played for Cambridge Univ. 1882-3-4-5, for Sussex County from 1882-92, captained the English team in Australia 1887-8, and was also Capt. of the English XI. in S.A. in 1888-9. For some little time he then settled down in Johannesburg, but returned to England, and adopted the theatrical profession with a success which is well-known to the theatregoing public. He married, Aug. 15, 1896, Isabella, dau. of the late Major Wood, of Abbey Wood, Kent.

SMITH, Col. Sir Chas. Bean Euan-. (See Euan-Smith.)

SMITH, Right Rev. Charles Spencer, D.D., late of Detroit, Michigan, U.S.A., was in 1904 appointed by the General Conference of the S. African Methodist Episcopal Church to the office of Resident Bishop of the A.M.E. Church, embracing the 13th Episcopal Dist. and all their other Church interests in S. Africa.

SMITH, Edward Duffus, of Salisbury, Rhodesia, entered the Chartered Co.'s service as Clerk in the Pay Office Bulawayo, June 1, 196; transferred to Controller's Office, Salisbury, May 1, 1897, of which he became Accountant, April 1, 1895; was appointed Clerk-in-Charge, Stores Dept., Salisbury, July 1, 1901.

SMITH, Frank Braybrooke, M.L.C., Director of Agriculture in the Transvaal; of Pretoria and of the Savile and Pretoria Clubs, was born in Huntingdonshire, and is son of Wm. Cuxton Smith, a prominent agriculturist. He was educated at Downing College, Cambridge, with a view to occupying a position in an agricultural college. After leaving there he was articled to a firm of Land and Estate Agent and also spent several years on farms in various parts of England. He coached students for the Surveyors' Institution exams.; was appointed Professor of Agriculture and Estate Management at the Wye Agricultural Coll. of 1894, which was then being established by the County Councils of Kent and Surrey, assisted, by the Board of Agriculture, and became Vice President in 1895. He undertook a tour in the U.S.A. and Canada to investigate the system of agricultural administration and education in vogue there, the results of which were embodied in a work entitled *Agriculture in the New World*. On the reconstruction of the London Univ. he was placed upon the Board of Agricultural Studies. In 1902 he was appointed Agricultural Adviser to the Governor of the Transvaal, and after inspecting the country, prepared a scheme for the establishment of a Department of Agriculture, which was approved by Lord Milner, and thus formed the basis of the present Department. He became Director of Agriculture in 1902, and is a member of the Council of the Transvaal Technical Institute. Unmarried.

SMITH, Frederick William, J.P., of Bulawayo, joined the Cape Govt. service June 10, 1881; Cape Mounted Police, Jan. 16, 1883; won the first prize essay on Colonial Police Administration, June, 1885, and was appointed Chief Constable at King Williamstown, Nov. 19, 1885; became Supt. of the King Williamstown Borough Police, March 5, 1888; was made J.P, Dec. 20, 1889, and was selected by the Cape Govt. to reorganise the Port Elizabeth Police Dept., Jan. 1, 1895; afterwards returning to King Williamstown. He was seconded for service in Matabeleland to reorganise the Municipal Police, July 1, 1895; was made J.P. for Rhodesia, July 27, 1895; and was appointed Inspector commanding the Municipal Police and head of the Detective Dept. for Matabeleland, Nov. 24, 1895.

SMITH, Hon. G. D., M.L.C., is member of the Cape Legislative Council for British Bechuanaland. He is a Progressive, and was last elected in 1904.

SMITH, George Douglas, C.M.G. (1905), of

Entebbe Uganda, was born at St. Kitts, W. Indies, Feb. 8, 1865, and is son of the late Charles A. Smith. He was educated at Glasgow Academy; was employed by the Imperial British East Africa Co. in 1890; and was appointed Treasurer of the Uganda Protectorate in 1894. He has received the East and Central African medal with clasp for Uganda for 1897-8. He married, Sept. 29, 1908, Anna, dau. of the late James Leitch, of Glasgow.

SMITH, Capt. George Edward, R.E., of the United Service and Fencing Clubs, Lond., and of the St. George's Golf Club, Sandwich, is son of Archibald Smith, of Jordanhill, N.E. He was educated at Winchester, Woolwich, and Chatham; and assisted the British Commissioner on the Anglo-German Boundary in British East Africa in 1892-3. He took part with Capt. B. L. Sclater in making the road from the Coast to Victoria Nyanza Lake in 1887, and published the results in the R.G.S. paper, *Roadmaking and Survey in British E. Africa*. Capt. Smith is at the present time British Commissioner on the Anglo-German Boundary, from Victoria Nyanza to Kilimanjaro, with the local rank of Lieut.-Col.

SMITH, G. Gordon, is an old Camborne mining student. He played centre three quarter in the Blackheath Football XV., and represented England in International matches in 1902. A recent attack of rheumatic fever has caused his retirement from Rugby football.

SMITH, Harry, J.P. for County of Durban, of the Civil Service Club, was born in 1864, and settled in Natal in the early part of 1879. He joined the staff of the Secretary Natal Harbour Board in 1882; was transferred to the permanent Civil Service, Natal, on the dissolution of the Board in 1894; appointed Secretary of the Natal Harbour Department in 1895; holds numerous subsidiary appointments, and has acted as Secretary to two Commissions (one of which sat at East London) on harbour matters. On the passing of the Immigration Restriction Act by the Natal Parliament in 1897, he was, at the instance of the late Rt. Hon. Harry Escombe, P.C., selected to administer that measure at the Port of Durban. He was instrumental in securing the repeal of that Act in favour of the existing Act (No. 80 of 1903), which is a more comprehensive one. On the passage of the new Act he was appointed principal administrative officer thereunder for the whole Colony. He takes a close interest in Fisheries matters, and has worked for the Colony in procuring the adoption of much needed protective measures. He is Honorary Secretary of the Durban Branch of the Navy League, and a member of the Society of Arts, and married, in 1885, Alice Mary, third dau. of R. L. Colborne.

SMITH, Sir John Smalman, Knt. Bachelor, M.A., J.P., of Courtfield, Chiswick, and the St. Stephen's Club, was born at the Chauntry, Quatford, Salop, Aug. 23, 1847; is eldest son of the late S. Pountney Smith, J.P., of Shrewsbury, and was educated at Shrewsbury Sch., and St. John's Coll., Camb., where he graduated M.A. He went to the Gold Coast as Puisne Judge of the Supreme Court in 1883; was transferred to Lagos as sole Judge of the Supreme Court in 1886, and was Chief Justice from 1889 to 1895, when he was invalided, retiring from the service in the following year.

Sir Smalman is a Vice-Pres. of the African Soc., founded in memory of Mary Kingsley, and is J.P. for Middlesex.

SMITH, Percy George, of Gwelo, Rhodesia, was Clerk in the Chief Accountant's Office, C.G.R., Jan., 1889; Clerk to the Engineer-in-Chief, C.G.R., 1889; Magistrates' Clerk at Kimberley, 1902; Asst. Magistrate, Douglass, 1893; Additional Magistrate, Bulawayo, July, 1894; Magistrate at Bulawayo, July, 1896; and became C.C. and R.M., Gwelo, in July, 1897.

SMITH, Robert Tottenham, J.P., F.R.C.I., of Clareen, Berea, Johannesburg, and of the Rand Club, was born Dec. 5, 1857, in King's County, Ireland, where his father, Ralph Smith, was on the Commission of the Peace. He went to South Africa in 1876, and after about two years in the Cape Civil Service joined the Standard Bank of South Africa, and has held the position of Branch Manager of that institution since 1883. He is J.P. for the Witwatersrand Dist.; Associate of the Institute of Bankers in South Africa, and married, in 1892, Katherine Margaret, dau. of H. J. Newberry.

SMITHERS, H. Langworthy Hampden, of Koffyfontein, O.R.C., and Uppertown, Johannesburg, whose mother is a cousin of Robert Browning, was born on March 19, 1857, at Brussels. He arrived in Natal in 1867 with his parents, when he devoted his attention to learning farming. He went to the diamond fields in 1870, and to Pretoria in 1874. He was commandeered by the Boers in 1875, and served on commando. He joined the Transvaal Civil Service in 1870, and was appointed to the special service of the Postal Dept. by Sir Owen Lanyon. In 1880-81 he took part in the defence of Pretoria and was present at the engagements near that town. In 1881 he returned to the diamond fields, and went to Koffyfontein in 1892, where he was very successful as a digger. On war breaking out he was commandeered by the Boers to fight against the English, but he fled the country, passing through the Boer lines to the Gordon Highlanders' camp at Graspan. He returned later, and took a prominent part in the defence of Koffyfontein, becoming O.C., Koffyfontein Defence Force, on the retirement of Major Robertson, K.L.H. He was elected Mayor of Koffyfontein, and made J.P. for Fauresmith by the British Govt. He did much good work on the Hospital Board, etc. Mr. Smithers is an old footballer and lawn tennis player. He is a fair rifle shot, and very interested in music. He married, June 5, 1884, Elsa, eldest dau. of the late Mr. Dietrich, of Sea Point, near Cape Town. He has five children. His eldest son served 19 months against the Boers.

SMITHSON, Lieut. Col. Walter Charles, D.S.O., of the Army and Navy Club, was born Jan. 26, 1860 is son of Samuel Smithson, J.P., of Lentram, Inverness, and was educated privately, in 1880 entering the 18th Hussars, of which he was Adjt. from 1887 to 1891. Lieut. (as he then was) Smithson accompanied his regt. to Kandahar in 1880, and to Natal in 1884, and was A.D.C. to Field Marshal Lord Wolseley when Commander of the Forces in Ireland, from 1891 to 1895. He went with his regt. to Natal in 1899, and served under Sir R. Buller, being present at Colenso, Spion Kop, Pieter's Hill, relief of Ladysmith, etc., and towards the close of the S. African War served under Sir Bruce Hamilton in the Transvaal. He was severely wounded on Aug. 22, 1900, near Newcastle, Natal; was several times mentioned in despatches, and received the Queen's medal and five clasps, and the King's medal and two clasps, as well as the D.S.O. He was promoted to the command of his regt. in 1901; is fond of pig sticking, shooting, and polo, and married, in 1901, Anne Charlotte le Gendre, eldest dau. of John Piers Chamberlain Starkie, of Ashton Hall, Lancaster.

SMITH-WRIGHT, Edward Henry, of Salisbury, Rhodesia; joined the Chartered Co.'s service in July, 1895, as Clerk, passing through various grades until, in Oct., 1897, he was appointed Examiner of Accounts, Audit Dept.; Secy. to the Tender Board at Salisbury, Nov., 1895; and Acting Chief Examiner of Accounts, Feb. 15, 1901.

SMUTS, Johannes, of Pretoria, and of the Civil Service (Cape Town), and the Pretoria Clubs, was born at Sea Point, near Cape Town Oct. 1, 1865, and is son of the late Joseph P. Smuts, of Cape Town. He was educated at the S. African Coll., and entered the Cape Civil Service in 1882. He acted as Private Secy. to Sir Gordon Sprigg (q.v.); was transferred to the Governor's Staff in 1886; acted as Private Secy. to Lord Loch, Sir H. A. Smyth, Sir W. Cameron, and Sir W. Goodenough; and a Clerk of the Executive Council of the Cape Colony. In 1890 he became Secy. to the Special British Agent at Pretoria in connection with Swaziland Affairs; acted as H.M. Consul for Swaziland from 1895-99; from then until 1901 he served on Sir C. Warren's Staff in Natal. Since 1902 he has acted as Registrar of Deeds of the Transvaal, and acted as President of the Swaziland Concessions Commission in 1904. He married, Nov. 19, 1904, Winifred E. Butterworth, of Tiverton, Devonshire.

SMUTS, Jacobus Abraham, M.L.A., is Bond Member of the Cape Legislative Assembly for Malmesbury, for which electoral division he was last elected at the general election in 1904.

SMUTS, J. C., is son of J. A. Smuts, M.L.A. for Malmesbury, and was born in 1870, near Cape Town. He was educated at the Victoria Coll., Stellenbosch, whence he graduated double B.A. in the Cape Univ. in 1891, and went as Ebden Scholar

to Christ's Coll., Cambridge. He took a double first in the Law Tripos in 1894, and returned to the Cape Colony in the following year, practising at the Cape Town Bar till the end of 1896, when he settled at Johannesburg. In 1898 he was appointed State Attorney to the Transvaal Republic—an appointment which gave great satisfaction to the Progressives, with whom he was accounted an able and zealous worker for reform and purity of administration. He was strongly opposed to the policy which led to the S. African War, and ultimately induced Pres. Kruger (to accept the five years' franchise proposals of Lord Milner, but matters had then gone too far. Mr. Smuts served through the Boer War, at first under Gen. Joubert in the Natal Campaign, and after the fall of Pretoria went with De la Rey to the Western Transvaal, where he took part in all the severe fighting. In 1901 he was given the supreme command of the burgher and rebel forces in Cape Colony, and marched with a comparatively small force to the extreme west of the Colony in one of the most arduous and romantic undertakings of the whole war. He reorganised the commandos in the Cape Colony, and maintained a stout resistance against Sir John French till peace was declared. Since then Mr. Smuts has practised at the Pretoria Bar. He was offered, but declined, a seat on the Transvaal Legislative Council, and is now a member of the head committee of the Boer organisation *Het Volk*.

SMYTH, Herbert Warington, M.L.C., M.A., LL.M., F.G.S., F.H.G.S., Barrister at law; of Rosemary, St. Andrew's Road, Parktown, Johannesburg, 5, Inverness Terrace, Hyde Park, W., and of the Rand, Leander Rowing, Royal Cornwall, and Royal Thames Yacht Clubs, was born in London, in 1867, and is the eldest son of Sir W. Warington Smyth, F.R.S. he was educated at Westminster and at Trinity Coll., Cambs., where he captained Third Trinity's boat in 1889-90, when she was Head of the River; was unpaid Asst. to the Mineral Adviser to the Office of Woods in 1890-1; Secy. to the Dept. of Mines, Siam, from 1891-5, Director-Gen. from 1895-7, and acted as Secy. of the Siamese Legation in London in 1898-1901. He was awarded the Order of the White Elephant of Siam, 3rd class, in 1897, for services to the Siamese Govt.; also the Murchison Grant by the R.G.S. for journeys in

Siam; was a member of the Council of the R.G.S. from 1898-1901; was called to the Bar in 1899; acted as Delegate or Siam to the Paris Exhibition International Congress in 1900. He was appointed Secy. of the Mines Dept., Transvaal, in 1901, which position he still holds, and in the same year he was awarded the Royal Society of Arts' medal. In 1906 he was appointed a member of the Transvaal Legislative Council. Publications: *A Journey on the Upper Me Kong*, 1895, *Five Years in Siam* (2 vols.), 1898, *Mast and Sail in Europe and Asia*, 1905, and Papers on Indochina, Malay boatbuilding, etc. Recreations: travel, hunting, and sailing. He married, in 1900, Amabel, dau. of Henry Sutton.

SMYTH, Major Nevill Maskelyne, V.C., of Bangalore, India, and of the Cavalry Club, was born in 1868, and is a son of the late Sir Warington Smyth, of Marazion, Cornwall, and brother to Herbert Warington Smyth (q.v.) Secy. of the Mines Dept. at Johannesburg. He was educated at the Royal Military College, and entered the Queen's Bays in 1888; served in the Zhob Valley Expedition in 1890-91; the Dongola expedition in 1896, attached to the Intelligence Dept. (despatches, 4th class Medjidie and Egyptian medal with two clasps); the Nile Expedition in 1897 (clasp); Nile Expedition in 1899 as Orderly Officer to the G.O.C. Infantry Division of the Egyptian Army; present at the battles of the Athara and Khartoum (despatches, medal, two clasps to Egyptian medal, and Y.C.); also took part in the Nile Expedition in 1899 as Intelligence Officer to the Flying Column; took part in the operations at Shukaba, Blue Nile, and the operations which resulted in the final defeat of Khalifa; actions at Abu Aadel and Om Dubriekat (despatches, two clasps to Egyptian medal, and 4th class Osmanieh). Major Smyth served in the S. African War in 1902. including the operations in the Transvaal and Orange River Colonies (brevet of Major). He was promoted Major to the Carabineers in 1903.

SMYTH, Capt. Robert Napier, D.S.O., of the Naval and Military and Cavalry Clubs, was born at Frimley, Surrey, June 25, 1868, and is son of the late Maj.-Gen. J. H. Smyth, C.B., R.A. He was educated at Wellington Coll., and joined the Queen's R.W. Surrey Regt. in 1885, afterwards

transferring to the Cavalry. In 1899 he was a Capt. in the 21st Lancers; acted A.D.C. to G.O.C. Scotland in 1896-98. Served in the Nile campaign in 1898, and was present at the battle of Khartoum (despatches and two medals). He was Garrison Adjutant at Abbassiyeh, 1898-99; took part in the S. African War in 1899-1902 as D.A.A.G. Intelligence (four times mentioned in despatches, brevet of Major, and D.S.O.); was Divisional Staff Officer of the S.A.C. in the O.R.C. 1903-05; and O.C. Squadron of the 21st Lancers in 1905.

SMYTH, Right Rev. William Edmund, Lord Bishop of Lebombo, was educated at Eton and King's Coll., Camb. (Carus Prize; 1st cl. Theological tripos, 1882; M.A., 1883; M.B., 1888). He was ordained in 1882, and from that year till 1886 was curate of St. Mary the Less, Camb. From 1887-8 he was curate of St. Peter's, London Docks; was appointed Chaplain to the Bishop of Zululand, 1889, and was Theological Tutor at Isandhlwana, 1888-92. He was consecrated Bishop of Lebombo on Nov. 5, 1893, by the Bishops of Cape Town, Grahamstown, Pretoria, Kaffraria, Zululand, and Bloemfontein.

SMYTHE, Hon. Charles John J.P., M.L.A., of Strathearn, Nottingham Road, Natal, and of the Victoria Club, Pietermaritzburg, Natal; was born in Scotland in 1852, and is second son of the late William Smythe, of Methven Castle, Perthshire. He was educated at Trinity College, Glenalmond, and went to Natal in 1872, starting farming in the Nottingham Road district three years later. In 1888 he was placed on the Commission of the Peace, and when responsible government was established in the Garden Colony in 1893 Mr. Smythe was returned as M.L.A. for the Lions River Division. From 1897 to 1899 he was Speaker of the Assembly and in June of the latter year he joined Sir Albert Hime's Ministry as Colonial Secretary, and Minister of Education. These portfolios he relinquished in July, 1903, and in May, 1905, he became Prime Minister of Natal. In the spring of 1906 he tendered his resignation as a protest against the interference of the English Colonial Office in ordering the suspension of the execution of Natal natives, convicted of the murder of two members of the Natal police, but this was soon afterwards with drawn. (See Lord Elgin and Sir Henry

McCallum.) He married, in Aug., 1876, Margaret, dau. of the late John King, of Lynedoch.

SNOW, El-Kaimakam (Lieut. Col.) Cecil Longueville, Bey, 4th class Medjidieh, and 4th class Osmanieh; of Port Said, and the Turf Club, Cairo; was born at Kensington, Aug. 5, 1863; was educated privately at Boulogne-s.-M., and at Merchant Taylors' Sch., Crosby, Liverpool. He joined the N.W. Mounted Police of Canada in 1885, taking part in the suppression of the Riel Rebellion. In 1891 he joined the Egyptian Coastguard Service; received the Order of the Medjidieh (4th class) in 1901, and Osmanieh in 1905, and was promoted Kaimakam (Lieut.-Col.) in 1903. He is now Director of the Suez Canal and Red Sea districts. He married, Aug. 10, 1900, Miss U. B. Valiance.

SOISSONS, Gus Raoul de Savoie-Carignan, Earl of, Count de Dreux, Viscount de Busancy, Baron de Dompmard, Baron de la Fère; of 20, Edwardes Sq., W., was born in 1860 at Aubigny Castle, and is son of Philippe Humbert de Savoie-Carignan, Count de Soissons. The present Earl of Soissons has travelled extensively in Europe, and in Egypt and America, studying art, literature, and languages. He was the first to speak in his literary articles to the Anglo-Saxons about Henryk Sienkiewioz, and was also first to introduce to the English-speaking people Arthur Rimbaud and Maxim Gorky through the medium of his essays in the *Contemporary Review*. The Earl of Soissons is the author of *In the Path of the Soul*, *Fancies*, *The Modern German Novel*, *Maeterlinck as a Reformer of the Drama*, *The New French Idealism*, *Modern German Lyric Poetry*, *Dilettantism in French Literature*, *The New Trend of Russian Thoughts*, *The History of Russian Censure*, and *Mysticism in Modern Literature*. His name also appears on sixteen vols. of novels, translated by him into English from other languages. He has contributed articles on art and literature to the *Contemporary*, *Fortnightly*, *Nineteenth Century*, and *North American Reviews*. Recreations: travel, riding, lawn tennis, and walking. He married, in 1885, the Countess Poniatowska Rozanski, great grandniece of the last King of Poland.

SOISSONS, Pierre Amédée, Viscount de, of 20, Edwardes Sq., London, S.W., and of the Royalist

Club, was born in Montreal, Canada, and is son of the Earl of Soissons (q.v.). For some time he went to St. Paul's School, afterwards being educated privately. When sixteen years of age he exhibited about a hundred pictures, and is the author of *The Saga of Hjalmar of the Thonder-Schall*, *Tales of the Coloured Lanterns*, *Crossed Eyes Mascot*, *The Comedy of Courtship*, and *Under the Little Corporal*. Recreations: travel, cricket, lawn tennis, and walking. Unmarried.

SOLOMON, Edward P., of Johannesburg, is President of the Responsible Government Association in the Transvaal, the programme of which is the federation of South Africa on British lines, and the repatriation of the Chinese on the expiry of their contracts.

SOLOMON, Harry, M.L.C., was appointed a member of the Transvaal Legislative Council by the Lieutenant Governor. He was appointed one of the aldermen under the old Town Council when the management of the Municipal Council of Johannesburg was controlled by President Kruger's Government.

SOLOMON, Hon. Sir Richard, KG, K.C.B., K.C.M.G., C.B, M.L.C., of Zasm House, Pretoria, and of the Reform Club, London, was born at Cape Town, Oct. 18, 1850. He is son of the late Rev. E. Solomon, a missionary in the Transkei territories. He was educated at the S.A. Coll., and at St. Peter's Coll., Camb. (23rd Wrangler), and was called to the Bar of the Inner Temple in 1879. He accompanied Lord Rosmead as Legal Adviser to Mauritius on the Commission of Enquiry in 1886; was Chairman of the Mining Commission; and Member of the Native Law Commission. He entered the Cape Parliament in 1893, as member for Kimberley and Tembuland. In 1896 he was retained with Advocate Wessels to defend the Reform prisoners. He was Attorney-Gen. of the Cape Colony from 1898 to 1900, in which year he received his knighthood.

Sir Richard was appointed Legal Adviser to Lord Kitchener, C.LC. in S.A., and to the Transvaal Administration from 1901 to the end of the Boer War, for which services he received the C.B. He was then appointed Legal Adviser to the Transvaal

Administration (1901-2). He represented S. Africa at the Delhi Durbar in 1902-3 (gold and silver medals), and has been a member of the Executive and Legislative Councils and Attorney-Gen. of the Transvaal since 1902, in which capacity he has had an onerous task to perform in the framing and adapting the laws to the new conditions. Sir Richard will probably at an early date succeed Sir H. Gould-Adams as Lieut.-Governor of the O.R.C. He is extremely able, but is a negrophile, and has Afrikander sympathies. He married Mary Elizabeth, dau. of the Rev. J. Walton, and sister of Sir Lawson Walton, K.C., M.P. Their only child, Mary Gwendoline is married to Sir E. P. C. Girouard (q.v.).

SOLOMON, W. E. Gladstone, artist, is third son of the late Saul Solomon, M.L.A., and was born at Sea Point, Cape Town, on Mch. 24, 1882. It is now some little time since Mr. Solomon carried off the British Institute scholarship of £50 and a silver medal for his oil painting of Abraham offering up Isaac, and in 1903 the greatest technical prize offered by the Council of the Royal Academy was awarded to him. It consisted of £50 and a silver medal for a set of six full-sized figure drawings from the life. He also won the prize of £25 and a silver medal for his oil painting. That year also, Mr. Solomon's decorative painting of Dawn—an allegory, which had already brought him the first prize of £40 and a silver medal, was hung at the Royal Academy Annual Exhibition. In 1904 he exhibited two paintings in the Royal Academy exhibition—one being a portrait of a lady, and the other a subject painting of a group, entitled *Alexander the Great meeting Diogenes the philosopher*. For three years in succession he as chief prizeman at the Royal Academy schools for painting, and he subsequently won a Armytage prize of £30, and a bronze medal, for the best original design in black and white of a subject given by the Council— Cain and Abel. He also took the first prize for the best-painted figure from life.

SOPER, William Garland, J.P., WA., of Caterham, Surrey, and of 54, St. Mary Axe, London, E.C., was educated at St. Austell, Cornwall, and the Cheshunt Coll., afterwards graduating B.A. with a first-class at the University of London. In 1859 he became a partner with his father-in-law, Mr. Davis, a South African merchant. In 1865 Mr. Soper became sole member of the firm, whose interests he continued to direct for nearly a quarter of a century, when his son joined him in partnership, but the style of Davis & Soper is still retained. Mr. Garland Soper has been associated with the introduction of tramways into South Africa, the City of Cape Town and the Green Point line being the work of his firm, who are also the agents of the Cape Town and some other municipalities. Mr. Garland Soper is chairman of the London Board of the Johannesburg Waterworks, Estate and Exploration Co., and a London Director of the Johannesburg Estate Co., and the Union Marine Insurance Co. He is an alderman of the Surrey County Council, and is J.P. for Surrey and also for the County of London. He is the oldest member of the Fruiterers' Co., and was for over eighteen years chairman of the Caterham School Board, and is chairman of the Caterham Urban Council. He is a Liberal Unionist in politics.

SPEED, Edward Armey, M.A., LL.B., of 1, Temple Gardens, London, E.C., was born at Nottingham, March 11, 1869, and is son of R. H. Speed. He was educated at Rugby and Trinity Coll., Camb., Major Scholar of Rugby in 1882, Senior Exhibitioner in 1887, Major Scholar of Trinity College in 1888, first-class classical Tripos, second-class Law Tripos, Part 1; called to the Bar at the Inner Temple in 1893; appointed a Dist. Commissioner, Gold Coast Colony, in 1899, and Attorney General of Lagos in 1900. He has on numerous occasions acted as Chief Justice and Colonial Secretary, and has twice held a commission as Deputy Governor; in 1901 he published a revised edition of the laws of the Colony. He married in June 1901, Ada, only dau. of the late Rev. Wm. Ross, late chaplain to the Royal Highlanders.

SPEIGHT, Arthur Edwin, J.P., of Gwelo, S. Rhodesia, is son of the late Ed. Speight, of Bradford, Yorks, where he was born July 10, 1877, and was educated at Yorkshire Coll., Leeds. After holding various Clerkships under the Imperial and Cape Colonial Govts., he transferred to the S. Rhodesian Customs in 1899; acted as C.C. and Magistrate for Tuli Dist., 1904-5; and became Chief Clerk and Distributor of Stamps, Gwelo,

April, 1905. He passed the Cape Civil Service Law exam. in 1899; is J.P. for S. Rhodesia, and married, in 1905, Margaret, eldest dau. of the late W. T. Gel, of Tavistock, Devon, and Wellington, Somerset.

SPIRO, Socrates Bey (Sanieh); Orders of the Osmanieh and Medjidieh) 4th class); of Ramleh, Alexandria, was born in Cairo, Aug. 24, 1860. He is of Greek origin, his father having been a noted Greek scholar. He was educated at the American Mission Sch., Cairo; entered the Egyptian Govt. service in 1883; was Priv. Secy. to Lord (then Mr.) Milner, Under Secy. for Finance, during his last tour of inspection of the Provinces of Up. Egypt in 1892; was Priv. Secy. to Sir Clinton (then Mr.) Dawkins, Under-Secy. for Finance, from 1895 to 1899 and became Director of the Central Ad ministration of Egyptian Ports and Lighthouses in June, 1899. He is author of *Arabic-English* and *English-Arabic Dictionaries of Modern Egyptian Arabic* (published in 1895 and 1897) and of *Note on the Italian words used in the Modern Spoken Arabic of Egypt* (published in 1904); has contributed many articles and reviews to English papers on modern Arabic, as well as many articles on literary subjects to Arabic periodicals. He is fond of travel and the study of modern Arabic. He married, in 1882, Rose, dau. of H. G. Tarpinian.

SPONG, Major Charles Stuart, DS.O., F.R.C.S., B.Sc., late R.A.M.C., of Cairo, and of the Army and Navy Club; third son of the late Wm. Nash Spong, F.R.C.S, was born June 12, 1859; was educated at Epsom Coll. and Guy's Hosp., and entered the Army in 1887. He was seconded for service with the Egyptian Army in 1890, and acted as S.M.O. in the Sudan Campaign, 1896-98, receiving the D.S.O. and the Order of the Medjidieh. Major Spong retired from the service in 1899 to take the post of Medical Adviser to the Egyptian State Railways. He married, Oct. 4, 1900, Mary Barnsley Pickering, of Newtown, Pennsylvania, U.S.A.

SPRECKLEY, Harry Unwin, after serving as Clerk to the C.C. and R.M. at Mazoe and Salisbury (1895-8), entered the Mines Dept. under the B.S.A. Co. in 1897.

SPRIGG, Major Howard, of Berry St., Queenstown, Cape Colony, was born at Ipswich, Eng., June 26, 1845, and is younger brother of Sir J. Gordon Sprigg (q.v.), whom he joined on his farm on the Cape frontier in 1863. He was farming and teaching until 1882, except during his campaigning periods. In 1873 he raised a troop of Kaffrarian Volunteers at Maclean, and was appointed to the command with rank of Lieut., becoming captain in 1876; transferred to Frontier Mounted Rifles in 1877, and to 1st Cape Yeomanry in Sept., 1878 served in these corps through all the native wars of 1877-8-9, and Basuto War of 1880-1, with local rank of Major during last few months; was mentioned in despatches several times by Comdt. (now Gen.) Brabant and Gen. C. M. Clarke, and held many staff appointments during these wars. The Yeomanry being disbanded at end of 1881, he was gazetted as Captain Cape Infantry in 1882, and served in that regiment and Cape Mounted Riflemen till 1894, all the time in the Native Territories. On the latter date was transferred to Civil Service, and appointed R.M. of Bizana, Pondoland, where he remained till February, 1905, when he had to retire on account of ill health, being specially thanked by the Govt. for services. Major Sprigg has no particular recreations, and has been a local preacher (not connected with any particular denomination) for more than twenty years. He married in 1874 Elizabeth Jane, eldest dau. of J. O. Bate, of East London, Cape Colony.

SPRIGG, Right. Hon. Sir John Gordon, G.C.M.G. (1902), P.C. (1897), of Wynberg, near Cape Town, was born at Ipswich, Eng., in 1830; is grandson of Jas. Sprigg, ironware manufacturer, of Birmingham, and son of the late Rev. Jas. Sprigg, Baptist Minister of Dublin, Ipswich, Margate, and Westbury, his mother having been a Miss Christopherson, of Ipswich. Sir Gordon started business in a shipbuilder's office, afterwards joined Gurney's shorthand staff, and in 1858 went to S. Africa for the benefit of his health. He settled in the Division of East London (C.C.), and entered the Cape Parliament as member for East London in 1873. He was appointed Colonial Secy. and Premier on the dismissal of Sir J. C. Molteno in 1878, and resigned in 1881 on the Basuto question.

In 1884 he became Treas.-Gen. in Sir Thomas Upington's Ministry, and succeeded him as Premier in 1886. In the following year Mr. Sprigg, as he then was, was made K.C.M.G., and soon after was appointed Privy Couocillor. Sir Gordon resigned in 1890, but on the recoustrnction of the Rhodes Ministry in 1893 he joined it as Treas., and was practically Acting Premier. On Mr. Rhodes' retirement in Jan. 1896, he became actual Premier until Oct. 1898. In June, 1900, he succeeded Mr. W. P. Schreiner as Premier, also combining the office of Treas. In the general election in Feb., 1904, Sir Gordon was defeated by Dr. Smartt at East London (C.C.) by a majority of 954, and the Progressives being in a majority in the new House of 50 against the Bond 45, he tendered his resignation of the Premiership, Dr. Jameson being called upon to form a new Ministry.

Formerly the political chief of the Progressives, he was throughout the difficult times following the Boer War accused of pandering to the Bond party, whose tolerance only enabled him to maintain a majority, he being repudiated by five sixths of the Progressives, who seceded on the Suspension question. It is certainly on record that Sir Gordon and his entire Ministry voted with the Bond on more than one occasion. This alliance, however, was simply a makeshift, and although it suited the Bond party to keep Sir Gordon in power, it did not deter that organisation from assisting in four Govt. defeats on divisions during the last short session of 1902. He created much dissatisfaction amongst his earlier followers by his refusal to sanction a fresh registration of voters in view of the fact that in many districts hundreds of disfranchised voters were still on the register as late as Sept 1902 On the occasion of his defeat (Nov. 8, 1902) on the question of increasing the Cape Colonial Forces, however, Sir Gordon Sprigg's appeal to the Bond caused their withdrawal of the amendment and the passing of the vote as originally printed; and elicited the Premier's thanks to the Bond for its generosity. Since then Sir Gordon has been wavering in his allegiance between the Bond and the Progressives, and has thus not been a source of strength to the Loyalists in Cape Colony, although his dogged adhesion to office in the face of many real difficulties may have saved them from still greater dangers.

Sir Gordon is a practised and effective Parliamentary debater, and has cultivated a leas aggressive manner than marked the parliamentary methods of his earlier political days. His range of ideas cannot be said to be broad, but his devotion to the business of the Colony has always been most exemplary.

He was created G.C.M.G. on the occasion of the King's Coronation; he is D.C.L. of Oxford, and Hon. LL.D. of Edin. Univ. He is a widower, having married a dau. of Mr. J. Fleischer. Lady Sprigg died in 1900.

SPRIGG, Will Gordon, J.P, for Witwatersrand District, F.R.G.S., F.R.GS. of Australia, F.R.C.I.; of Johannesburg, Transvaal, was born Aug 14, 1866, at Melbourne, where he was educated. He is a nephew of Sir J. Gordon Sprigg (q.v), and commenced business in Melbourne; afterwards (in 1888) travelling to the Cape, where he entered the Cape Civil Service. After five years he resigned this service and returned to Melbourne, where he became associated with the Y.M.C.A. In 1894 he was appointed gen. Secy. to the Cape Town Branch of the Association, and in 1902 took charge of the Y.M.C.A. work at Johannesburg, which position he still occupies. He is also Secy. of the S.A. Council of Y.M.C.A.s, Travelling and Organising Secy. for South Africa, and a member of the Executive Committee of the Witwatersrand Church Council. During the last. South African War he worked hard in connection with the Y.M.C.A. to provide comforts for the forces in the Transvaal. He married, in 1905, May Jeanette, dau. James S. Goch, of Johannesburg.

SPRINGFIELD, Capt. Joseph, 2nd Dragoon Guards, is son of T. O. Springfield, a well known Norfolk sportsman. Capt. Springfield was originally an indigo planter in Behar, India; went to South Africa to serve in the ranks of Lumsden's Horse, and at the close of the war was given a commission in the Bays. In India he was a first-rate gentleman rider across country and on the flat.

SPURRIER, Dr. Alfred Henry, L.R.C.P. Lond., F.R.G. S., F.R.C.I., Physician-in-Extraordinary to H.H. the Sultan of Zanzibar and medical superintendent of Prison Island, Sanitary Station, Zanzibar, was born Oct. 20, 1862, at Colyford, Devon. He was educated at the Gregorian Univ., Rome, and the London Hospital; was formerly medical officer on the E.T.C.'s cable ships, *John Pender*, *Great Northern*, and *Duplex*, in 1890-3; acted Resident Medical Officer to the E.T.C. Station in Zanzibar in 1894-5, and assisted in the despatch of Sir Gerald Portal's Expedition to Uganda, starting from Mombasa in 1893. He was present at the bombardment of Zanzibar in 1896; deputed by the Govt. to convey to German territory Seyyid Khalid, the usurper's mother, son, and household in 1897. Dr. Spurrier conducted the present Sultan of Zanzibar on a four months' tour through S. Africa, when he was Prince Seyyid Ali, 1898, and was appointed Special Plague Medical Officer in epidemic on the Uganda Rly. in 1902. Since 1895 he has been editor of the *Govt. Zanzibar Gazette*. Orders: Hamoudieh, 3rd class, 1897; Saidi, star of the 2nd class, 1905.

STAIRS, Capt. (brevet Major) Henry Bartram, D.S.O., B.A, LL.B., of Halifax, N.S., and of the Halifax Club, was born April 29, 1871. He was educated at the Collegiate Sch., Windsor, and Dalhousie Univ., Halifax. He served in the S. African War in 1899-1900 as Capt. commanding H Co. of the Royal Canadian Regt., and was present at the actions at Paardeberg, Driefontein, Haut Nek, Sand River and Johannesburg. He married, April 16, 1903, Judith Henderson.

STALLARD, Advocate, C. F., was born in 1871, and was educated at St. Edward's School and at Oxford, being called to the Bar in 1895. He first came before the public in 1895 as a candidate for the London County Council, but being unsuccessful at the poll went to South Africa with the C.I.V., and afterwards joined Paget's Horse. Subsequently, during the South African War, he was for a short time in the Government service, and commenced to practice as an advocate in 1902. At the General Elections for the Transvaal Legislative Assembly in 1907 Mr. Stallard stood for Turffontein as an Independent.

STANLEY, Right Hon. Lord, P.C., K.C.V.O., C.B., D.L., of 36, Great Cumberland Place, London, W., was born in 1865, and comes of a family of politicians, his grandfather, Lord Derby, having been thrice Premier, while his uncle, his father, and Lord Stanley himself all attained Cabinet rank while still under forty years of age. But the Stanleys have been men of mark in public life for centuries. It was the grandson of Sir John Stanley, the warlike Treasurer of the Household of Henry IV., who became the first Lord Stanley in 1456. Two of his sons were among the most famous men of their day. One was said to be the richest and most rapacious subject in the kingdom, and the other was the brave soldier who fought at Bosworth and became the first Earl of Derby. The present Lord Stanley was educated at Wellington College, and at the age of twenty became a Lieutenant in the Grenadier Guards. Four years later he was appointed A.D.C. to his father, who, as Lord Stanley of Preston, was then Governor-General of Canada. Returning home he began his Parliamentary career in 1892 as Member for the Westhoughton division of Lancashire. He was re-elected in 1895, and was for four years one of the Parliamentary Whips. In 1899, however, he accompanied Lord Roberts to S. Africa as Chief Press Censor, later on combining with this office the duties of private secretary to the C.i.C. It was here that his tact stood him in such good stead. Impatient war correspondents, spurred on by relentless competition, hummed round him demanding that their cables should be immediately passed. Lord Stanley was urbane yet firm, stern at times, but always courteous. It is an interesting commentary on the ability with which he discharged his duties that, although loud complaints were heard in England as to the rigour of the censorship, in South Africa he was on good terms with almost all the correspondents, whose duty to their journals and their country he was successful in reconciling. During his absence in S. Africa Lord Stanley was again re-elected for Westhoughton. On relinquishing his duties in the Transvaal he was recommended by Lord Roberts for the important post of Financial Secretary to the War Office, which he only left in 1903 to take up the more important office in succession to Mr. Austen Chamberlain of Postmaster General. In this Dept. he inaugurated two great policies— the settlement of the telephone question and the wireless telegraphy contract. Recently he came into conflict with the staff of the G.P.O. and his firm attitude of resistance gained him at any rate, the approval of ratepayers. At the General Election in 1906 Lord Stanley was defeated by the Labour candidate, Mr. W. T. Wilson, by over 3,000 votes. On his return from Canada Lord Stanley married Lady Alice Montagu, dau. of the seventh Duke of Manchester. Lady Alice shares with her husband his political instincts and ambitions, and if they are realised Lord Stanley may yet follow in the footsteps of his famous grandparent, and become Prime Minister of Great Britain.

STANTON, Lieut.-Col. Edward Alexander, Order of the Medjidieh (3rd class); of Khartoum, and of the Army and Navy, the Sudan (Khartoum), and Turf (Cairo) Clubs, was born at York, Nov. 15, 1867. He is eldest son of Gen. Sir Ed. Stanton, K.C.M.G., C.B., and was educated at Marlborough and Sandhurst passing into the Oxfordshire L.I. in Feb., 1887 He received his Captaincy in 1894, and brevet majority in 1898. Col. Stanton has seen much active service in N. Africa, beginning with the Dongola Expedition in 1896, being present at Firket and Hafir (despatches, medal with two clasps); the Nile Expedition in 1897 (despatches and clasp); the Nile Expedition in 1898, taking part in the battles of Athara and Omdurman (twice mentioned in despatches, brevet majority two clasps, and English medal); and again in the Nile Expedition in 1899 (clasp and Medjidieh). He was employed surveying the navigable channels of the Bahr el Zeraf and Bahr Ghazal in 1898, and was at Fashoda during the Marchand affair. He joined the Sudan Civil Administration in 1899, and received his present appointment as Governor of Khartoum in 1900. In 1901 he was given the local rank of Lieut.-Col. Col. Stanton married Isabel Mary, second dau. of Capt. H. C. Willes, late Royal Welsh Fusiliers.

STAPLEY, Sir Harry, Bart., F.E.A. (Ireland) of Melbourne, and of the Sports, Royal Cork Yacht, and the Queenstown Clubs, was born in 1856, and is the eldest son of the 6th baronet. He has travelled in America, Canada, S. Africa, Algiers, and Morocco, &c. Sir Harry was formerly Lieut. in the 2nd Vol. Batt. of the Royal Fusiliers. Recreations: yachting and travelling.

STEAD, Arthur, M.L.A., is one of the Progressive representatives of Kimberley in the Cape House of Assembly. He was last elected in Feb., 1904.

STEBBING, Rev. Thomas Roscoe Rede, B.A. (Lond.), M.A. (Oxon.), F.L.S., F.R.S., F.Z.S., of Ephraim Lodge, The Common, Tunbridge Wells, Kent, was born in London, Feb. 6, 1835, and was educated at King's Coll. Sch. and King's Coll., Lond. He is the author of numerous essays and reviews on literary and scientific subjects, including *Essays on Darwinism*, *The Naturalist of Cumbrae*, *A History of Crustacea*, *The Ampbipoda of H.M.S. Challenger*, *On Crustacea from the South Seas*, *Crustacea* in the *Encyclopedia Britannica*, *Gregarious Crustacea from Ceylon*, and *South African Crustacea* in Gilchrist's *Marine Investigations of South Africa*, Parts 1, 2, and 3 of which are already published. In middle life Mr. Stebbing keenly enjoyed various forms of sport, but now he finds his pleasure in reading, writing, and research in connection with natural history diversified by the facts and fables of the human story in literature generally. He married, in 1867, Mary Anne (now F.L.S.), dau. of W. Wilson Saunders, F.R.S.

STEELE, Colonel Samuel Benfield, C.B., M.V.O., of Pretoria, Transvaal, was born in Canada in 1849, and is son of Capt. E. Steele, R.N. He took part in the Fenian Raids in Canada in 1866-70, and served with the Canadian Regular Artillery in the Red River Expedition in 1870 under Viscount Wolseley (q.v.). In 1873 he joined the North-West Mounted Police, and took part in the North-West Campaign in 1885; also commanded the D Division of that force in an expedition to Kootenay, British Columbia, and commanded the corps in the Yukon territory during the latter's organisation in 1898-99, and was a member of the Council (*ex officio*) for the Government of the territory; also *ex officio* Stipendiary Magistrate for the Yukon territory, and collector of Royalty and Customs for the North-West territory and Yukon. He also acted as Commissioner of Police and of Peace for British Columbia. Subsequently he was seconded from the North-West Mounted Police, and took part with Lord Strathcona's Corps in the late South African War (despatches, King's medal and two clasps). Since 1901 Colonel Steele has commanded the B Division of the South African Constabulary.

STEEVENS, Col. Sir John, K.C.B., Order of the Medjidie (4th Class), entered the Army in 1873, and gradually worked his way to the highest rank possible to an officer of the Ordnance Department, viz., Principal Ordnance Officer, ranking as Major-General. Sir John Steevens took part in the Zulu War of 1879, gaining a reward in the shape of a step in promotion. He also took part in the Egyptian Campaign of 1882, and was mentioned in despatches, and gained further promotion, in addition to the Order of the Medjidie, conferred by the Khedive. He received a CB. at the time of the Jubilee honours in June, 1897, and a K.C.B. at the time of the Coronation honours in June, 1902.

STEINAECKER, Lieut. Col. Baron Francis Christian Ludwig v., D.S.O., of Mansfield, Alfred County, Natal, was born at Berlin in 1854, and was educated in the Royal Cadet Corps at Wahlstatt and Berlin, and subsequently received a commission in the German Army. In 1879 he resigned his commission and accompanied Prince Alexander of Battenberg to Bulgaria, commanding at Plevna during the Bulgarian Revolution. Some time afterwards he undertook an expedition into the interior of German Southwest Africa, visited Pondoland in 1889 and two years later settled in Port Shepstone, Natal, becoming President of the political association there. He served in the late S. African War with the Colonial Scouts, subsequently raising Steinaecker's Horse (King's medal with two clasps and D.S.O.). He is the author of various articles on politics, phylloxera, and agriculture. Married.

STEPHEN, Capt. Albert Alexander Leslie, D.S.O., of Studham House, Dunstable, and of the Guards' Club, was born in London, Feb. 3, 1879, and is son of Major Stephen. He was educated at Eton, and joined the Scots Guards in 1899; served in S. Africa in 1899-1902, including the actions at Belmont, Graspan, Modder River, Magersfontein, the relief of Kimberley, Poplar Grove, Johannesburg, Diamond Hill, and Bergendal; and was Asst. Provost Marshal to Col. Pulteney's column in 1901-2; acted as Intelligence Officer to Col. Garratt's Force in 1902 (twice mentioned in despatches D.S.O., Queen's medal with six clasps, King's medal with two clasps).

STEPHEN, J. M., is a partner in the firm of Messrs. J. M. Stephen and Co., and is President of the Cape Town Chamber of Commerce, having succeeded Mr. Watson at the close of the 1902-3 session.

STEPHENSON, Admiral Sir Harry, of 18, Lowndes Street, London, S.W., entered the Royal Navy at the age of thirteen; served in Canadian waters in 1866, and nine years later went out with the Arctic Expedition. In 1881 he served in the Egyptian Expedition, and after being Naval A.D.C. to Queen Victoria and Equerry to King Edward, when Prince of Wales, had command of the Pacific station, and afterwards the Channel Squadron. He retired in 1904, and became principal Naval A.D.C. to the King, and Gentleman Usher of the Black Rod.

STEPHENSON, Maj.-Gen. Theodore Edward, C.B., of 43, Bryanston Sq., W., Headquarters Transvaal Dist., Pretoria, and of the United Service Club, was born Mar; 28, 1856; and is the only surviving son of the late Canon John Stephenson, of Weymonth. He was educated at Marlborough Coll., p.s.c., is interpreter to the Army in Turkish, and has passed language examinations in Urdu, Hindu, Pushtu, and Persian. He joined the 56th (2nd Essex) regt. in 1874, and served on the Staff from 1883-90 as D.A.A.G. at Gibraltar and York, went out to S. Africa in 1899, in command of the 1st Battn. of the Essex regt.; gazetted in. Feb., 1900, as Maj.-Gen. on the staff commanding the 18th Brigade, and held the same rank while commanding the Barberton Dist. and Portuguese Frontier Depot in 1900. Gen. Stephenson commanded mobile columns in Cape Colony for the last year of the war; commanded the Bloemfontein Dist. at the conclusion of peace, and was later appointed commander of the troops in the Transvaal, which position he still holds. Decorations : Queen's medal and six clasps King's medal and two clasps, Queen's Jubilee medal (1897), and he was four times mentioned in despatches. He married, in 1889, Philippa, only dau. of Col. Gordon Watson.

STERRY, Wasey, M.A., of Khartoum; of Chapel Cleeve, Washford, Taunton, and of the Savile

(Lond.), Turf (Cairo), and Sudan (Khartoum) Clubs, was born in Devonshire July 26, 1866. He is eldest son of the Rev. Francis Sterry, of Chapel Cleeve, and Augusta Emily, dau. of the late Hastings N. Middleton. He was educated at Eton and Merton Coll., Oxon, and was called to the Bar in Nov., 1892. He was appointed the first Civil Judge in the Sudan in May, 1901, and Chief Judge in 1903. He is the author of *Annals of Eton*. Unmarried.

STEVENS, John Alfred, of Cape Town, and the City Club, Cape Town, is eldest son of the late Dr. Robert Ingram Stevens; was born at Herts, Eng., and was educated privately in England and Belgium. After London office training he joined the staff of London and South African Exploration Company in Kimberley in 1881; accompanied mission to South West Africa in 1890; and went on special mission to Gazaland during latter part of 1890, returning at the beginning of 1891. He entered the Cape Town office of the Chartered Company in March, 1891; acted as Secretary from October, 1894, to April, 1895; was appointed Acting Secretary, January, 1895; is Government Agent for the Rhodesia Government in Cape Town, and also Secretary of the Rhodesia Railways, Limited, in that town.

STEVENSON, Capt. Alexander Gavin D.S.O., joined the Royal Engineers as 2nd Lieutenant in 1891, becoming Captain in Oct. 1901. He served with the Dongola Expedition in 1896, being mentioned in despatches, receiving the 4th class Medjidieh. He then served in the Nile Expeditions of 1897-8, taking part in the battle of Khartoum, and receiving the D.SO., and medal with two clasps. In the S. African War in 1899-1901 he was graded as Staff Captain on the Central South African Railways, and afterwards served as Locomotive Superintendent (graded as D.A.A.G.) (despatches, and Queen's medal with three clasps).

In July, 1901, he was extra-regimentally employed by the Railway Administration, and in the autumn of 1904 he was engaged under the Foreign Office on a detailed survey for a railway in Somaliland from Berbera to Argan.

STEVENSON, Sir Edmund Sinclair, Kt. Bach. J.P.,

M.D., D.Ch., F.R.C.S., of St. Clair, Strathallan, Rondebosch, C.C., and of the Civil Service Club, C.T.; was born at Geneva, July, 1850, and is son of W. Ford Stevenson, F.R.S. He was educated at London, Edinburgh, and abroad; served in the Kaffir War in 1879-80 as medical officer in charge of troops (medal), and in the S. African War; late Physician-in-Ordinary to the High Commissioner, and was formerly President of the Medical Council for the Colony, and of the British Med. Ass. and South African Med. Congress. He married, in 1882, Emmy, dau. of John Easton, and great-granddaughter of Sir Benjamin Durban.

STEWART, Dudley Warren, after serving in the North-West Mounted Police, Canada, from July 1, 1890, joined the C.M.R. May 10, 1894; joined the Mashonaland Mounted Police Nov. 25, 1895, and transferred into the Mashonaland Municipal Police Nov. 18, 1896, serving in the rebellion of that year (medal). He was appointed sub-inspector Aug. 21, 1898, and afterwards transferred into the Matabeleland division.

STEWART, Dr. John Storer Percy, L.R.C.S.L. of the Pretoria Hospital, Transvaal, was formerly House Physician at the House of Industry, Government Hospitals, Dublin. He was attached to the Irish Hospital in the South African War in 1900, and is a Lieutenant in the Transvaal Volunteer Medical Staff Corps. Since 1901 he has acted as Assistant Medical Officer at the Pretoria Hospital.

STEWART, Major-Gen. Robert Grosse, C.B., of 25, Palmeira Mansions, Hove, and of the United Service Club, was born in 1825, and is son of the late Major Archibald Stewart (of Appin), Rifle Brigade. He was gazetted to the 84th Regt. in 1842. In 1845 he passed as interpreter in Hindustani at the Madras Coll., and was appointed interpreter to his regt. During 1854-6 he was Asst. Exec. Engineer at Rangoon, and also acted as Asst. in the Telegraph Dept. and Asst. of Topographical Survey, Burma. He exchanged to the Rifle Brigade in 1856, and on the reduction in the Army after the Crimea was posted to the 35th Regt. General Stewart took part in the Indian Mutiny, and was present at the siege and capture of Lucknow (despatches, medal with clasp, and brevet major).

He passed the Staff Coll. in 1861, and since then has held various appointments, being A.D.C. to Sir David Russell at Aldershot in 1863-4; acted as D.A.A.G. at Headquarters from 1865-70; Asst. Military Secy. at Ceylon, 1870-2; Adjt. Gen. of the Madras Army from 1872-7, and represented the Madras Army at the Imperial Assemblage at Delhi in 1877. He also acted as Governor and Commdt. of the Royal Victoria Hospital, Netley, in 1878-80, and received the late Queen when she visited the wounded from S. Africa. In 1880 he was appointed Brig. Gen. commanding the E. Diet. Madras. Recreations: science, and French and Italian literature. He married, in 1860, Fanny, eldest dau. of the late Capt. T. Davison, of Sedgefield, Durham.

STEYN, ex-President Martinus Theunis, of Kroonstad, O.R.C., was born in the Orange Free State in 1857, three years after the Republic had come into existence. He received little systematic education until, at the age of twelve, he was sent to Grey College at Bloemfontein. Later on, through the influence of Judge Buchanan, he went to Holland to study law, afterwards proceeding to London, where he was called to the Bar of the Inner Temple. Returning to South Africa he practised for a few years in the Free State; became Attorney-Gen., and was raised to the Bench in 1889, where he remained until 1895, discharging his judicial functions in a careful and conscientious manner, and holding himself aloof from politics. In that year Mr. Reitz (q.v.) resigned the Presidency, and Mr. Steyn offered himself as a candidate, defeating his opponent, Mr. J. G. Fraser (at that time Chairman of the Volksraad) by an overwhelming majority.

For many years the Orange Free State had been rightly regarded as a model Republic, with liberal laws, and quite sufficiently progressive for the needs of the burghers. Public questions were really only matters of domestic policy until Pres. Kruger began to inspire the Free Staters with his ambitions schemes to weave all South Africa into one whole Afrikander nation. Mr. Steyn could not resist participating in such a dream, and in accordance with an understanding come to with the Transvaal before the Bloemfontein Conference of May, 1899, when the Presidents of both Republics met Lord

Milner, Mr. Steyn threw himself wholly into the conflict which Mr. Kruger had precipitated, and with the Free State forces remained in the field long after his leader had fled to Europe. After the capture of Bloemfontein and the destruction of the Waterworks Mr. Steyn fled with his commandos, shifting his capital to Kroonstad, Heilbron, and other places. In May, 1901, his burghers were losing heart, and thought it was time to consider a better means of attaining their ends than by the arbitrament of the Mauser. But Mr. Kruger and the Boer delegates in Europe conveyed great hopes of a satisfactory end of the long struggle, and Mr. Steyn, although not relying upon foreign intervention, gave orders for the war to continue.

Meanwhile Mr. Steyn had joined Gen. De Wet (q.v.), and in his flight before the British forces he was taken prisoner, having seriously injured his spine. In consideration of this, and also as he was suffering from his eyes, he was allowed to proceed to Europe to join his wife, who was a Scotch lady, and his children. But already his health had completely broken down under the hardships of war, and he was so weak as to be unable to walk. The fortitude with which he had faced the dangers of the field, the enormous sacrifices he had made, and his firm adherence to Mr. Kruger's policy combined to make him very nearly an object of adoration amongst the Boers in Holland and the Hollanders themselves. Messrs. Fischer and Wessels met the ex-President at Southampton, and induced him to trans-ship at once for the Hook of Holland, in order that he might avoid the friendly welcome that the British were ready to extend to one who was so recently a brave and gallant fee. Arriving in Holland Mr. Steyn was conveyed at once to Scheveningen, where Pres. Kruger visited his faithful ally—or, as some might say, his victim. But so weak was Mr. Steyn that his doctor would only countenance a very brief interview. He expressed the belief that the Boers would recover politically what they had lest for the time being, but his health did net permit of his being actively associated with such a consummation. On the other hand, he eventually returned to the Orange River Colony to devote himself to the mere peaceful pursuit of farming near Kroonstad.

STIGLINGH, J. H., M.L.A., was elected as Bond

Member for Picquetberg at the general election in the Cape Colony, Feb., 1904.

STIRLING, Capt. George Murray Home, D.S.O., of Glorat, Milton of Campsie, N.B., was born in London, Sept. 4, 1869, and is the only son of Sir Charles E. F. Stirling, Bart. He was educated at Eton and the R.M.C., Sandhurst; was gazetted to the 2nd Battn. Essex Regt. in 1889, and took part in the Chitral Campaign in 1895 under Sir Robert Ford (medal and clasp); and the Tirah campaign in 1897-8 under Sir William Lockhart (two clasps). He was selected for the adjutancy of the Burma Mtd. Inf. in 1899, and went with them from Burma to S. Africa in 1900. He took part in the operations in the Orange Free State, being present at the actions at Poplar Grove, Driefontein, Honigspruit, Hout Nek, Vet River, and Zand River; also in the Transvaal and O.R.C.; acted as Staff Officer at the Mounted Inf. Headquarters, 1900-2; and as officer commanding transports, Bloemfontein, 1902 (Queen's medal, four clasps, King's medal and two clasps, D.S.O.). He also served on special service in Somaliland in 1903-4. He married, Nov. 15, 1904, Mabel, dau. of Col. A. Sprot, of Lanarkstown.

STOCKENSTRÖM, Andries, of Pretoria, Transvaal, is an advocate by profession.

STOCKENSTRÖM, Hon. Sir Gysbert H., Bart., M.L.C., is senior member of the Cape Legislative Council for the North-East Province.

STOEHR, Frederick Otto, M.B., of N.E. Rhodesia, was born in 1871. He was educated at Trinity Coll., Oxford, and Guy's Hospital, where he acted as clinical asst. and asst. house surgeon to Sir Downing Fripp in 1899-1901. For two years he served as Civil Surgeon to the S. African Field Force, and is at the present time medical officer to the Geodetic Survey of N.E. Rhodesia.

STOKES, Herbert Leslie, of 59, Cadogan Square, S.W., The Grove, Stalham, and the Junior Carlton Club, was born in London, Feb. 28, 1853; was educated at King's Coll., and after a special training as engineer spent ten years (1879-89) on the West Coast of S. America, being connected with various engineering works in Chile, as well as with the gold

and silver mines of Peru and Bolivia, in which countries he has travelled extensively. In 1891 he went out as Manager in charge of the Mashonaland Agency Expedition to Rhodesia, and since then has been connected with that company and its subsidiaries. He married, Oct. 30, 1899, Marie Carandini (Mrs. Robert Wilson), youngest dau. of the late Marchese de Sarzano, of Modena, Italy.

STOPFORD, Major-Gen. Hon. Sir Fredk. William, K.C.M.G., C.B., of 1, York Terrace. Regent's Park, N.W., and of the Guards' Club, was born in 1854, and is son of the fourth Earl of Courtown. He joined the Grenadier Guards in 1871 and served in the Egyptian Expedition in 1882 as A.D.C. to Sir John Adye, Chief of Staff; present at the battle of Tel-el-Kebir (despatches, medal with clasp, bronze star, and 5th class Medjidieh); the Sudan Expedition in 1884-5 as A.D.C. to Major-Gen. Fremantle, Brigade of Guards, and afterwards as Brigade Major (despatches, clasp, and brevet of Major); the Ashanti Expedition in 1895-6, in command of a composite half battalion (brev. of Colonel and star); and the South African War in 1899-1900, as Military Secretary to Sir Redvers Buller; present at the relief of Ladysmith, including the actions at Colenso, Spion Kop, and Vaal Kranz; the operations on Tugela Heights, and the action at Pieter's Hill; operations in Natal including the action at Laing's Nek, and the operations in the Transvaal, east of Pretoria, including the actions at Belfast and Lydenburg (despatches, Queen's medal with six clasps and K.C.M.G.). In 1904 Gen. Stopford was appointed Director of Military Training, which post he held until 1906 when he succeeded Lt.-Gen. Sir L. J. Oliphant, K.C.V.O., in command of the London District.

STOPFORD, Hon. James Richard Neville, of Pretoria, and of the St. James's Club, was born in 1877, and is son of the Earl of Courtown. He acted as Private Secretary to Sir W. Conyngham-Green, K.C.B., British Agent at Pretoria; clerk in the Imp. Secretary's office from 1899 1900, when he was appointed Private Secretary to the Political Secretary, and from June, 1900, till Feb., 1902, he was Private Secretary to the Secretary of the Transvaal Administration. In Feb., 1902, he acted as clerk in the Colonial Secretary's Office, Transvaal, and as second clerk in Sept., 1902, which position he still holds. He married, in 1905, Cicely, dau. of the late John A. Birch.

STRACHAN, Dr. William Henry Williams, M.L.C., C.M.G., of Lagos, W. Africa, and of the Junior Constitutional, W. Indian, and Corona Clubs, was born in 1859. He is eldest son of the late Col. W. H. P. FitzM. Strachan, and was educated privately and at Guy's Hos., graduating L.R.C.P. (Lond.), M.R.C.S. (Eng.). He is F.L.S. and M.S.A. Dr. Strachan is P.M.O. of Lagos, and is a member of the Legislative Council of the Colony. Unmarried.

STRAKOSCH, Henry, of 9, King St., St. James', was born at Hohenau, Austria, May 10, 1871. He is the son of Ed. Strakosch, of Hohenau, a pioneer of the Austrian beet-sugar industry. After a Continental banking experience he went to S.A. as Manager of the African Mining and Financial Assoc. He joined the firm of A. Goerz and Co. in Aug., 1896, and afterwards (April, 1902) became Managing Director of A. Goerz and Co., Ltd. He is also a director of many other important S.A. Cos., mainly gold mining. During the war he was a member of the Committee appointed by the Governor to advise him on matters affecting the Uitlander population of the Transvaal. He was also a member of the Central Registration Committee. Mr. Strakosch is keen on polo, an inveterate motorist, and a bachelor.

STRANGE, Harold Fairbrother, J.P. for Pretoria, of the Rand and Athenaeum Clubs, Johannesburg, was born at Kingston-on-Thames, June 7, 1861, and has occupied a prominent position in the public affairs of the Transvaal ever since he became Manager of the Mining Dept. of the Johannesburg Consolidated Investment Co., and member of the Executive of the Chamber of Mines in Johannesburg in 1896. He was Vice-President of the Chamber in 1902-3, and Pres. in 1904-5; Chairman of the Council of the Transvaal Technical Institute, 1904-5; member of the Rand Water Board, 1905; and Consul for Greece at Johannesburg since 1899. Mr. Strange was a member of the Reform Committee in 1896, in connection with which he was sentenced, like the other members, to two years' imprisonment, and a fine of £2,000, or in default a further year's

imprisonment, and to banishment for two years. He was, however, released after a few months. He served on Lord Milner's Consultative Committee at Cape Town in 190-01; was Chairman of the Central Registration Committee (Refugees'), 1900-2; Technical Education Comm., 1903; Municipal Boundaries' Comm., 1903; South African Shipping Freights' Conference, 1904-5; Rand Plague Comm., 1904-5; and the Inter-Colonial Railway Conference in 1905, while as the representative of the Barnato Group in Johannesburg he is a director of numerous mining and other companies. Mr. Strange was Chairman of the Wanderers' Club, Johannesburg in 1901 and 1905; is a member of the Governing Body of Johannesburg College; steward of the Johannesburg Turf Club, and member of the Johannesburg Stock Exchange. He married, in 1889, Flora, only dau. of the late Henry Anthony Meredith.

STRANGE, Laurence, was at one time Mayor of Waterford, Ireland, where he bad an extensive practice as a solicitor. He was appointed Public Prosecutor at Klerksdorp in 1902.

STRONGE, Walter Cecil, of 316-19, Winchester House, London, E.C., is a partner in the firm of W. Cecil Stronge and Co., and is Chairman of the South African Co., Ltd., and the Taitapu Gold Estates, Ltd., and director of the Akropong G.M. and Exploration Co., Ltd., North Charterland Exploration Co., Ltd., and the South West Randt Mines, Ltd.

STROYAN, John, D.L. J.P. of Kirkchrist, Wigtownshire; Lanrick Castle, Perthshire; Saxon Hall, Palace Court, London, W.; and of the Carlton, Conservative and Caledonian Clubs, was born in 1856, and is eldest son of the late John Stroyan, of Kirkchrist. Mr. Stroyan is Hon. President of the Scottish Chamber of Agriculture. He was formerly associated with South African commerce and mining, and was Conservative M.P. for West Perthshire, until he was defeated at the general election in 1906 by a majority of 503.

STRUTT, Capt. Charles Brownlow, of the Junior United Service, and the United Forces' Clubs, was born at Dhurumsala, India, Aug. 24, 1872, and is son of Major C. Strutt, R.A. He was educated at

Bedford Grammar School. In 1889 he went to Mogok, Upper Burmah, to take up an appointment under the Burmah Ruby Mine Company, subsequently being invalided home. In the following year he went to S. Africa, serving three years in the Cape Mounted Rifles; returning to England at the end of 1893. He received a commission in the Royal Irish Rifles in 1894, and gained the Ordinary and Extra Certificates of Musketry at Hythe, 1905. Subsequently he returned to S. Africa, and took part in the Jameson Raid. On being released he served throughout the Matabele campaign in 1896, on the Staff of General Carrington, and was present at the fight at Insiza under Col. Maurice Gifford (medal and clasp). He was seconded for service with the B.S.A. Police, and transferred to the S. African Constabulary in 1900. Capt. Strutt also served in the S. African War in 1900-2, being present at the relief of Mafeking and the operations in the Transvaal and Orange River Colony (King's and Queen's medals). He is at present acting as Paymaster to the S. African Constabulary, Orange River Colony. He married, Nov. 27, 1902, Miss C. Flanagan.

STRUBEN, Frederick P. T., of Spitchwick Manor, Ashburton, South Devon, is Chairman of the African Saltpetre Co., Ltd., and is director of the Pilaya Gold Syndicate, Ltd., and the Vogelstruis Estates and Gold Mines, Ltd.

STUART, Col. John Alexander Man, C.B., C.M.G., Knight of Justice of the Order of St. John of Jerusalem and Coronation Decoration; of Dessford, Ceylon; Dalvenie, Kincardineshire; and of the United Service, New (Edinburgh), and Royal Northern (Aberdeen) Clubs, was born in 1841; is son of the late William Man (Stuart), and resumed the ancient name of his family by Royal Warrant in 1898. He served in China, Formosa, and Manchuria, in Egypt, the Sudan, W. Africa, and the West Indies, and was appointed Adjutant of the Royal Archer Body Guard in 1902. In the course of his military career he was A.D.C. to Lieut.-Gen. Valentine Baker Pacha in Egypt in 1886-7, and commanded at base and on line of communications during the Ashanti campaign of 1900; has been three times mentioned in despatches, and—in addition to his British honours and four war medals—has the Turkish Order of the Osmanieh,

the Chinese Precious Star, and the Order of the Italian Crown. He is on the Retired List as a Lieut. Colonel in the Army and Colonel in the Militia, and holds also the ranks of Colonel in the Imperial Chinese Army (with the Red Button of the Mandarinate) and Lieut. Colonel (Bey) in Egypt. Colonel Stuart is a Fellow of the Royal Geographical Society and of the Imperial and Royal Colonial Institutes; and he has at various times contributed articles and reports to official publications and to magazines and journals. He married, in 1885, Helen, a Lady of Grace of the Order of St. John of Jerusalem, and dau. of J. H. Lang. He is a J.P. and C.C. for Kincardineshire and J.P. and D.L. for Aberdeenshire.

STUDD, Capt. Herbert William, D.S.O., of the Guards' and Bachelors' Clubs, was born at Marlborough Dec. 26, 1870, and is son of Edward Studd. He was educated at Eton, and Trinity Coll., Cambs.; joined the Coldstream Guards in 1891, and served in the S. African War, 1899-02 (mentioned in despatches, Queen's medal and six clasps and King's medal with two clasps, and D.S.O.). He played in the Eton cricket eleven in 1885-9; also played racquets for Eton, and cricket for Hampshire in 1892 and 1895; entered the Staff College in 1904. He married, April 19, 1894, Mary, dau. of the late Major F. H. de Vere.

STUTTAFORD, Richard, of Lidcote, Kenilworth, C.T.; of the City Club (C.T.), and the Rand Club (Johannesburg); was born in C.T. in 1870. He was educated at Amersham Sch., near Reading. He is Managing Director of Stuttaford and Co., Ltd., and a Director of the *Cape Times*, Ltd. He married in 1903.

SUMMERS, Frank James, whose affairs were ordered to be wound up in bankruptcy in 1905, was formerly engaged in editing a newspaper at Bulawayo and in prospecting for mines in Rhodesia. He afterwards studied for the Bar, and during 1900 served as a Lieutenant in the East Kent Yeomanry. For two and a half years before March, 1904, he was acting as secretary to the Imperial Service Club.

SUPPLE, Henry Guy, was employed on the Orange Free State Railways from 1897-1899. He served in the South African War in 1899-1900 with Remington's Guides, and was on Major-Gen. Pretyman's Staff from April, 1900, until Feb. 1901, when he was appointed Assistant Director and Chief Clerk in the Prisons' Department, Orange River Colony, and became Asst. Director of Prisons there in 1903.

SUTTON, Hon. Sir George Morris, M.L.C., K.C.M.G. (1904), of Fair Fell, Howick, Natal, and of the Victoria Club (P.M.B.), was born in Lincolnshire, July 8, 1834, and is son of Joseph Sutton, of Crowland, Lincs., where the future Premier of Natal received his education at a private school. Sir George entered the arena of politics in Natal in 1875, when he was elected to the Legislative Council as member for Pietermaritzburg County, which he represented until 1888. In that year he became a member of the Executive Council. He was returned as the member for Weenen County in 1885, but in 1893 he was re-elected for Maritzburg County, which he has since continued to represent in the Upper House. He accompanied Sir John Robinson as delegate to England with reference to responsible government for Natal in 1892, and on this being granted to the Colony he joined the first Ministry under Sir John Robin son as Colonial Treasurer in 1893, retaining this portfolio in the following Cabinet formed by Mr. (afterwards Sir) Harry Escombe in Feb., 1897. The latter resigned in the following October, and Sir George did not again occupy office until he formed his own Ministry, with himself as Treasurer, in Aug., 1903, his Administration lasting until May, 1905. Sir George Sutton is a farmer by occupation, and as far back as 1883 he started the wattle bark industry in the colony, which has now assumed important dimensions. He was also connected with the formation of the Dundee Coal Co., which was the pioneer of coal enterprise in Natal, and still produces. He married, first, in 1859, Harriet Heneage, dau. of Joseph Burkitt, of Alford, Lincs., who died in 1879, and in 1881 he married Mrs. Mary Aire Pascoe (who was a Miss Ritchie), of Edinburgh.

SWAINE, Major-General Leopold Victor C.B., C.M.G., F.R.G.S., of 14, Queen's Gate, London, S.W., and of the Army and Navy and Marlborough Clubs, was born in 1840, and is son of Robert Swaine, of Hamburg. He entered the Army in 1859, and acted as Civil Commissioner for Famagusta in 1878; served in the Egyptian Expedition in 1882 as Military Secretary to the G.O.C., being present at the capture of Mahsameh, the action at Mabuta, and the battle of Tel-el-Kebir (despatches, medal with clasp, bronze star, brevet of Lt. Col., 3rd class Medjidieh and C.B.), and as Military Secretary to the G.O.C., the Sudan Expedition in 1884-5 (despatches , clasp, and promoted Colonel). Gen. Swaine has acted as Military Attaché in St. Petersburg, Constantinople, and Berlin. In 1906 the First Class of the Order of the Red Eagle was conferred on him by the Emperor of Germany.

SWANN, Alfred James, F.R.G.S., was born at New Shoreham, Sussex, Sept. 14, 1856. He is the son of John Swann, and was educated at a Protestant Gram. Sch., and afterwards in London, twice taking honours at Board of Trade examinations. The spirit of the traveller was aglow in him in early life, and there are few districts in the East of which he has not some acquaintance. He first visited Africa in 1882, when he was specially engaged by the London Missionary Soc. to assist in the transport from Zanzibar to Tanganyika of the *Morning Star* lifeboat. During a residence at Ujiji (the meeting place of Stanley and Livingstone) he assisted in the survey of Tanganyika, capturing and preserving some unique specimens of freshwater *Medusae*. During the Arab uprising he was at Ujiji, and succeeded in maintaining communications by the extra ordinary means of Pitman's shorthand written backwards with a quill pen. The claims of Tippoo Tib and Rumaliza (who caused the Belgians so much trouble on the upper reaches of the Congoagainst Stanley were placed by them in Mr. Swann's bands, with the result that they were considerably reduced. The first correct report of the murder of Emin Pacha was brought to England by Mr. Swann, who, after succeeding in establishing marine communication around Tanganyika and diverting a large portion of the Eastern trade to Zanzibar via Blantyre, visited England, conveying in route the Arab's communications to Maj. Von Weissmann, his consultation with whom resulted in peaceful tactics with Ujiji, and consequent uninterruption of trade through German E.A. He later became Political

Officer in Sir H. H. Johnston's Administration; succeeded in stopping the Angonis raids in the N.W. District; discovered a rich deposit of carbonate of lime; unearthed flint (up to that time unknown in Equatorial Africa) and a collection of fossil shells in excellent condition. In 1895 Sir H. Johnston appointed him to the historic country of the late Sultan Jumbo, whose hordes of slavers formerly reigned supreme towards the Luapola River. Having discovered a system of intrigue which was paralysing trade through Kota-Kota, with the aid of Major Edwardes he utterly routed the forces concentrated against him, numbering 20,000, captured the long-wanted Saide Mwazunga, and opened up the way S. and W. towards the Zambesi.

SWANZY, Francis, J.P., of Heathfield, Sevenoaks, Kent, and of the National Liberal and Gresham Clubs, was born at Kennington, Surrey, July 7, 1854; was educated at Rugby; is J.P. for Kent, and a Director of the Wassau (Gold Coast) Mining Co., the Gold Coast Amalgamate Mines, Ltd., the New Gold Coast Agency, and the United Gold Coast Mining Properties. He married, in 1879, Mary Nina, eldest dau. of the late Robert Stephen Patry.

SWEENEY, George William, of Pietermaritzburg, and of the Victoria Club, Pietermaritzburg, is the son of Robert Sweeney, Prof. of Music, of Pietermaritzburg. He was born at Dublin Jan. 24, 1868, and was educated at the College of the Sacred Heart, Limerick, and the Pietermaritzburg High Sch. He obtained his B.A. and LL.D. at the Cape of Good Hope Univ. He was a House Master at Maritzburg Coll. 1888-1895, and Clerk in the Attorney Gen.'s Office at Natal, 1896-1900. In Feb., 1901, he was appointed Clerk of the Legislative Assembly at Natal. During this period he has acted as Secretary to the Law Dept. and Assistant Under-Secy., Natal. In 1900 he compiled a new edition of the *Laws of Natal*, after the manner of Chitty's *Statutes*, in conjunction with R. L. Hitchins. Mr. Sweeney is a keen football, tennis, golf, and cricket player. On several occasions he has represented Natal in the latter game, and was Captain of the Colonial Team against W. W. Read's English Eleven. He married Miss A. J.

Chapman, dau. of J. J. Chapman, J.P. (three times Mayor of Pietermaritzburg), in Sept., 1899.

SWINBURNE, Umfreville Percy, J.P., of the Commission of Mines Dept., Transvaal, took part in the Matabele War in 1893-4 and the Matabele Rebellion in 1896. From 1897-99 he was a J.P. for Western Australia, and special J.P. for the Tati District in 1899-1902; also acted District Commandant of the British South African Police and Controller of Civil Supplies in 1900-02. He took part in the late South African War (despatches and medal with three clasps). He is a member of the Royal School of Mines, London, and in 1902 was appointed Inspector of Mines for the Transvaal which position he still holds.

SWINHOE-PHELAN, Lieut. Wilfred, at present stationed with the 4th Batt. King's African Rifles at Mbarara, Ankole Dist., Uganda, was born Jan. 28, 1877, and is son of A. B. Phelan of the Public Works Dept., Punjab. He was educated at Wimbledon Coll., and was gazetted to the Royal Anglesey R.E. (Mil.) in 1900 served with them in Gibraltar in 1901, and was seconded for service with the King's African Rifles in 1905. Recreations: shooting, football, and hockey.

SYED, His Highness Ali. (See Zanzibar, Sultan of.)

SYKES, Arthur A., B.A., of 10, Edith Road, W. Kensington, and of the Junior Constitutional and the New Vagabonds' Clubs, is the son of the Rev. T. B. Sykes. He was educated at Westminster and Cambridge, and went out to S. Africa in 1898 as a special correspondent for *Black and White*, and on behalf of that paper he visited the leading towns, and interviewed the late Cecil Rhodes, President Kruger, Lord Milner, and other prominent people, and described his journeys in a series in *Punch*, entitled *Flittings*. Mr. Sykes acted as correspondent in Egypt and the East in 1898 and attended the coronation of Nicholas II. and Queen Wilhelmina for Black and White and other papers. He has written several books, including a translation from the Russian of Gogol's comedy, *The Inspector General*, and edited three volumes of reprints from *Punch*; is an Army and University coach; on the outside staff of *Punch* since 1893; on *Renter's* in 1895-6, and asst. editor of Henry Blackburn's *Art*

Handbooks, 1891-1903. He married, in 1897, Nellie, youngest dau. of the late R. D. Ganthony, of Richmond.

SYKES, Francis William of Livingstone, Victoria Falls, N.W. Rhodesia, was born May 21, 1864 at Bishopton, and is the son of the Rev. John H. Sykes. He served in the Matabeleland Relief Force in 1896 (medal), also in the S. Rhodesia Volunteers in the S. African War, 1900-1 (medal and two bars). He entered the Native Dept. Matabeleland, in 1899, and was transferred to N.W. Rhodesia as District Commissioner of the Falls Dist. in Aug., 1901. He is the author of *A History of the Morgan Gold Mine* (Queensland), 1892; *With Plumer in Matabeleland*, 1897, and was the editor of the *Mount Morgan Chronicle and Mining Gazette* from 1889-92. He married, in April, 1905, Beatrice, younger dau. of Edward Webb, Chairman of the African Banking Corporation.

SYMONS, David, of Warnford Court, London, E.C., is a partner in the firm of Symons and Moses, merchants. He is on the London Committee of the Main Reef West, Ltd., on the London Board of the Eastern Corporation, and Klerksdorp Proprietary Mines, Ltd., and on the Johannesburg Board of the New Transvaal Gold Farms, Ltd.

TAINTON, Clifton F., of Johannesburg, is well known on the Rand, where he was a member of the original Diggers' Committee. He was for many years editor of the *South African Mining Journal*, and from that paper he was appointed editor of the *Comet*, which rose from the ashes of the suppressed *Star* (Johannesburg). After the Raid he returned to England, and became financial editor of the *African Review*, of which paper he was appointed chief editor in 1899. He was also the representative of the Argus Printing and Publishing Co. in London. He resigned these appointments to join the firm of Ehrlich and Co., whom he represents on the Transvaal Chamber of Mines. He was a member of the Commission appointed to inquire into the Native Labour question.

TALBOT, Percy Alfred, B.A. (Oxen), F.R.A.S., F.R.G.S., F.Ant.I., of 67, Cambridge Mansions, Battersea Park, S.W.; The Cottage, Abbots

Morton, Worcestershire, and of the Royal Societies' Club, was born in 1877. He was Gunsley exhibitor at University College, Oxford, where he took an Honours Degree in 1901. He went to West Africa as Assistant Commissioner on the Anglo-Liberian Boundary Commission of 1902-1903; accompanied the Alexander-Gosling Expedition to Lake Chad in 1904-1905, and was appointed Assistant District Commissioner, Southern Nigeria, in the latter year. He married, in 1904, Dorothea, dau. of Thomas Bell-Dixon, of Frideswide's Hall, Oxen.

TALLAND, Captain F., served in the Sudan in 1885-6, with the Frontier Field Force, present at the action at Giniss (medal and bronze star).

TANCRED, L. J., has been for years one of the best-known cricketers in S. Africa. When the South African team visited England in 1904, he scored an aggregate of 1,217 runs, with a batting average of 41, compiled against the cream of English bowling. He was also wonderfully successful against the M.C.C. team in South Africa in 1905-6.

TANNOCK, John Porter, J.P., F.R.C.I., M.B., C.M., D.P.H., of St. James's Road, Southernwood, E. London, Cape Colony, and of the East London and Pannure Clubs, was born in 1867 at Greenock. He was educated at Glasgow and Edinburgh Universities, and is now Visiting Medical Officer to the Frere Hospital, E. London.

TATCHELL, Captain Edward, was born Aug. 17, 1870, and entered the Lincolnshire Regt., in 1893. He served in the Nile Expedition in 1895, being present at the battles of the Athara and Khartoum (despatches, medal, and Egyptian medal with two clasps), and the South African War in 1899, where he was employed with the Mounted Infantry, taking part in the operations in the Orange Free State, including the actions at Poplar Grove, Driefontein, Houtnek (Thoba Mountain), Vet River, and Zand River; the operations in the Transvaal, including the actions near Johannesburg and Pretoria and Diamond Hill, and the operations in the Orange River Colony, including the actions at Wittebergen (despatches).

TATHAM, Lieut. Col. Frederic Spence, K.C.,

M.L.A., of Pine Street, Pietermaritzburg, Natal, was born in the capital of the Garden Colony in 1865; is son of the late R. Tatham, and was educated at Bishop's Coll. He saw his first active service in the Basuto War of 1881 (medal and clasp), and again served in the Boer War during the years 1899-1902, when he won the Queen's medal and five clasps and was mentioned in despatches. But Col. Tatham's record has not been confined to soldiering. Since 1893 he has sat in the Natal Legislative Assembly and has been Chairman of Ways and Means since 1897. He was appointed K.C. in 1902; is a member of the Port Advisory Board; member of the Board of Examiners for Bar Appointments; is President of the South African Expansion League; and founded the S.A. League in Natal. In the crisis of 1899 he took an active part in shaping the policy of Natal, and raised and commanded the Natal Royal Regiment, consisting of Artillery, Infantry, and Mounted Infantry. He brought the great railway strike in Natal to a close in 1901 on intervening between the strikers and the Government at the latter's request. He was also largely responsible for the South African action against the objectionable shipping ring, takes great interest in educational matters, and is a member of the Board of Governors of Michaelhouse Diocesan Coll. He married, in 1887, Ada, third dau. of the late William Molyneux.

TATTENBACH, Count, was one of the German Plenipotentiaries at the Moroccan Conference at Algeçiras in 1906.

TAUBMAN-GOLDIE, Right Hon Sir George Dashwood, P.C., K.C.M.G., F.R.S., D.C.L. (Hon.) Oxon, LL.D. (Hon.) Camb., President of the Royal Geographical Society, of 11, Queen's Gate Gardens, S.W., and of the Naval and Military and Athenaeum Clubs, and member of the Royal Yacht Squadron, was born at The Nunnery, Isle of Man, May 20, 1846, his father having been Col. in the Scots Guards and Speaker of the House of Keys. He was educated at the R.M.A., Woolwich, and was a Lieut. in the Royal Engineers. He has travelled extensively in most parts of the world, and was the founder of Nigeria, by which about a twentieth was added to the population and area of the Empire.

TAYLOR, Captain Arthur Henry Mendle, D.S.O., was born Jan. 11, 1870, and joined the 21st Hussars in 1890, exchanging to the 13th Hussars with the rank of Captain in 1899. He served in the Nile Expedition in 1895, including the battle of Khartoum (despatches, medal, and Egyptian medal with clasps); and the South African War in 1899-1902, present at the relief of Ladysmith, including the actions at Colenso, Spion Kop, and Vaal Kranz; the operations on. the Tugela Heights, and the action at Pieters Hill; and the operations in the Transvaal and Orange River Colony (despatches , Queen's medal, with three clasps, King's medal with two clasps, and D.S.O.).

TAYLOR, James Benjamin, of Sherfield Manor, Basingstoke; Salzcraggie Lodge, Helmsdale, N.B. and of the Junior Carlton, Boodle's, and Hurlingham Clubs, is the son of Isaac Rowland Taylor, who was well known in the Cape Colony and Transvaal; was born in Cape Town, Dec. 20, 1860; was educated at Hermannsburg Coll., in Natal, and at an early age commenced his commercial career in the Kimberley office of the firm of E. W. Tarry and Co., Ltd. After a time he went into business as a diamond broker with his brother, W. P. Taylor. In 1882 the two brothers went to the Lydenburg District to exploit the Morgenzon Concession. Here Mr. J. B. Taylor obtained his first experience of practical mining. Two years later he went to the Barberton fields as a broker and as the representative of Wernher, Beit and Co., and some other Kimberley firms. In 1886 Mr. Taylor went to the newly discovered Rand, and became a foundation member of the firm of H. Eckstein and Co., from which he has now retired. Mr. Taylor is Vice-President of the National Bank of South Africa (see E. C. Reynolds). He was one of the founders of, and sat on the Executive Committee of, the Transvaal Chamber of Mines, and during his residence in Johannesburg was Vice-Pres. of the Wanderers' Club, the leading S.A. athletic club. He was a Steward of the Johannesburg Turf Club, a crack shot with either gun or rifle, and he served through the Griqua War of 1876. He married, in 1891, Mary, darn of Charles Gordon, M.D., of Pietermaritzburg, Natal.

TAYLOR, John William, J.P., of 72, Queen's Gate, London, S.W., is Chairman of the Newcastle

(Natal) Steam Coal Collieries, Ltd., and is a director of the Natal Coal Trust, Ltd., and the United Gold Mines of West Africa, Ltd.

TAYLOR, Robert, of 6, Queen Street Place, London, E.C., is a partner in the firm of John Taylor and Sons, and is a director of the Australasian G.M. Co., Ltd., Dareheib and African Syndicate, Ltd., Dharwar Gold Mines, Ltd., Egypt and Sudan Mining Syndicate Ltd., Gibraltar Consolidated Gold Mines, Ltd., Gold Fields of Mysore and General Exploration Co., Ltd., Indian Mines Development Syndicate, Ltd., Mount Boppy G.M. Co., Ltd., Mysore G.M. Co., Ltd., Mysore Reefs (1905) and Explorers, Ltd., New Kempinkote Gold Field, Ltd., New Options Explorations, Ltd., Nine Reefs Co., Ltd., Nundydroog, Co., Ltd., Redruth and Chacewater Railway Co., Sudan Gold Field, Ltd., Tasmania G.M. Co., Ltd., and the Um Rus Gold Mines of Egypt, Ltd.

TECK, H.S.H. Prince Alexander George of, Capt. Royal Horse Guards, G.C.V.O., D.S.O., of Henry III. Tower, Windsor Castle, and of the Bachelors', Marlborough, Army and Navy, and Cavalry Clubs, was born at Kensington Palace, April 14, 1874, and is the third son of the late Duke of Teck and H.R.H. Princess Mary Adelaide, Duchess of Teck. Prince Alexander was educated at Eton and Sandhurst, and joined the 7th Hussars in 1894. He took part in the Matabele Campaign in 1896-7 (medal), and served in the S. African War in 1899-00 (medal and clasps and D.S.O.). He married, Feb. 10, 1904, H.R.H. Princess Alice of Albany.

TEGART, Rev. W., of the Church Missionary Society, attempted to climb the Mountains of the Moon, on the Uganda border, with Herr Rudolf Grauer (q.v.), in 1905-6.

TEMPEST-HICKS, Col. Henry, C.B., of Gladsmuir, Barnet; Hillgrove, Wells, Somerset; and of the Army and Navy Club, was born in 1852, and is son of the late G. H. Tempest Hicks. He was educated at Harrow and Cambridge Univ., where he won the Freshmen's hurdles and the 100 yards' race in 1872. He served in the S. African War in 1899-1902, and during that time he commanded several columns, on one occasion capturing

Commdt. Geo. Hall and twenty of his commando (despatches, Queen's medal and five clasps, King's medal and two clasps, and C.B.). He also served in the Aden Hinterland in 1902, and retired with the brevet of Colonel in 1903. He married, in 1885, Anne, dau. of the late Charles Hemery, of Gladsmuir, Herts.

TEMPLER, Lieut. Col. S. L. B., late 7th Batt. King's Royal Rifles; served for many years as head of the Balloon Dept. of the Army under the Duke of Connaught, Sir Evelyn Wood, and Sir Redvers Buller. He took part in the Egyptian War of 1882, and commanded the balloon detachment in the Sudan Campaign in 1885. In the last Boer War he acted as Director of Steam Road Transports. He retired from the Army in 1892, after 32 years' service.

TENNANT, Hercules, M.L.C., of Pretoria, and of the Civil Service (C.T.), Pretoria, Rand, and Athenaeum (Johannesburg) Clubs, was born at Cape Town, March 3, 1850. He is the eldest son of the Hon. Sir David Tennant, K.C.M.G., a former Speaker of the Cape House of Assembly, and was educated at St. George's Gram. Sch., Cape Town, and the High Sch., Edin. He is a Barrister-at-Law of the Inner Temple, and Advocate of the Supreme Courts of the Cape Colony and Transvaal. He represented the division of Caledon in the Cape House of Assembly, 1879-81; was Extra A.D.C. to H.E. the Governor and C.I.C. in 1879; served in the Basuto War, 1880-81 (medal) with rank of Capt. in the Duke of Edinburgh's Own Volunteer Rifles as C.S.O. to the G.O.C.; was Secy. to the Chief Justice and Librarian of the Supreme Court of the Cape, 1882; was Asst. Registrar of the Supreme Court, 1884; Taxing Officer Cap Supreme Court, 1884; High Sheriff (Cape), Registrar of Deeds, Acting Master, and Registrar of the Supreme Court of the Cape Colony, 1889-1901; and was transferred to the Transvaal as Secy. to the Law Dept. of the Govt., June 1, 1901. In 1906 he was appointed a member of the Transvaal Legislative Council. He married, Sept. 2, 1874, Mary Cathcart, dau. of Robert Graham.

TENTYRA, Bishop of. (See Right Rev. Matthew Gaughren.)

TERNAN, Brig. General Trevor Patrick Breffney, C.M.G., D.S.O., of Standerton, Transvaal, and of the St. James's, Sports, and Army and Navy Clubs, was born in 1860, and is son of the late Gen. Ternan, I.S.C. He was educated at Sandhurst, and entered the Army in 1879; served in the Afghan War in 1879-80 (medal); the Egyptian Expedition in 1882 (medal and bronze star); and the Sudan Expedition in 1884-5 (clasp); served in the Sudan in 1885-6-89, including the action at Giniss, the attack in Fort Khor Mousa, and the action of Toski (despatches, 4th class Osmanieh, clasp, and D.S.O.); the Unyoro Expedition in 1895 (despatches, medal); acted as Commissioner and Consul General for the Uganda Protectorate in 1897, and commanded the operations against King Mwanga in 1897-8, present at the action of Kabowoko (despatches, Brevet-Col., and medal with clasp); acted as Commissioner and Consul-General for the Uganda Protectorate in 1899 (C.M.G.), and for British East Africa in 1900. He served as Special Service Officer in the South African War in 1900; took command of the operations in British East Africa in 1901 against the Ogaden Somalis in Jubaland (medal with clasp), and afterwards served as Special Service Officer during the rest of the Boer war in 1901-2 (Queen's medal with clasp). He married, in 1906, Dorothy, dau. of the late George Alsop, of Teignmouth, Devon.

TERRY, Lionel, was born in Kent, and after receiving a University education, passed into the Royal Horse Guards. He served as a trooper in the Matabele War of 1893, afterwards returning to London. Subsequently he travelled through Australia and New Zealand, where he became imbued with an extraordinary fear of the so-called yellow peril. This he embodied in a book called *The Shadow of the Empire*, which foretold all sorts of dangers from the Chinese influx. As a protest against this, he shot an aged Chinaman in the streets of Wellington (N.Z.) in Nov., 1905, affirming that he was perfectly sane. He was subsequently tried and sentenced to death at Christchurch.

TE WATER, Hon. Dr. Thomas G. N., M.L.A., M.D., of Graaff Reinet, C.C.; was born in 1857. He is son of F. Te Water, formerly M.L.A. for Graaff Reinet for 15 years, and grandson of T. Muller, who represented that division in the first parliament of the Colony. He was educated at Graaff Reinet Coll.; graduated B.A. in 1875; studied at Cambridge Univ., and afterwards attended the medical classes at Edinburgh Univ., where he took the degrees of C.M. in 1879 and M.D. in 1881, spending two years also at the Universities of Berlin, Vienna, and Strasburg, and in walking the London hospitals. He returned to Graaff Reinet to practise, and was returned to the House of Assembly by a large majority as a member of the Afrikander party, becoming one of the party whips. He joined the Sprigg Ministry in 1896 as Colonial Secy. It was admitted by the Attorney-General for Cape Colony that papers were in the possession of the Govt. and of the military authorities implicating Dr. Te Water in treasonable practices in connection with the S.A. War (refer Graham, Hon. T. K.). Dr. Te Water was seized with a paralytic stroke in the House of Assembly in Sept., 1902.

TEYNHAM, The Right. Hon. Lord, J.P., D.L., of Lynstead Lodge, Teynham; Ravensdale House, Ascot; and of the Wellington Club, was born in London, May 27, 1867. He was educated at Eton, and succeeded his father, the 17th Baron, in 1892. The present Lord Teynham was late Capt. in the Royal E. Kent I.Y., and is now a director of the Rand Victoria Mines, of which he is also chairman, the Rand Mines Deep (Chairman of London Committee), the Rhodesia Broken Hill Development Co., the Fanti Consolidated Mines (Chairman), and the Porto Alegre and New Hamburg Ely. Co. He married, in 1895, Mabel, dau. of Col. Henry Green-Wilkinson, Scots Guards.

THACKTHWAITE, T. M., of 15, Austin Friars, London, E.C., is Chairman of the Davies Selukwe Development Co., Ltd., Monomotapa Development Co., Ltd., Monomotapa Gold Dredging Co., Ltd., and the Premier Tati Monarch Reef Co., Ltd., and is director of the Channel Tunnel Co., Ltd., Rhodesia Exploration and Development Co., Ltd., South African Gold Dredging Co., Ltd., Tall Concessions, Ltd., Wareleigh (Rhodesia) Development Co., Ltd., and the West Rhodesian Banket Co., Ltd.

THEAL, Dr. George McCall, LL.D., of the Queen's Univ., Kingston, Canada, and Litt. D. of the S.A. Univ., eldest son of Dr. William Young Theal, of a United Empire Loyalist family, originally from Rye, in Sussex, that settled in Canada after the American Revolution, was born at St. John's, New Brunswick, April 11, 1837, and was educated at the Gram. Sch., in St. John's. The first fifteen years of his life in S.A. were spent as a teacher in public schools at Knysna, Dale College, in King Williamstown, and Lovedale Missionary Institution, and in journalistic work. Having made a close study of Bantu customs, traditions, folklore, etc., when war broke out in 1877 he was requested by the Government to undertake a diplomatic duty which Sir Bartle Frere and his Ministers considered of great importance. Having succeeded in this, he was invited to enter the public service permanently, and did so. But his inclination was towards literary work, in which the Government gratified him to a large extent, though until 1896 he was required also to fill an office in the Native Affairs Dept. The late Mr. Rhodes, when Prime Minister, instructed him to make a collection of Portuguese records and printed books upon S.A., which he continued under Sir Gordon Sprigg. . Dr. Theal proceeded to Europe in 1896, and has been engaged in this duty ever since. He has written a *History of South Africa*, of which the second edition is now being published in seven volumes, *South Africa*, in the Story of the Nations series, *South Africa*, in the Nineteenth Century series, and many smaller volumes. He has also edited nine volumes of Portuguese records, with English translations, fifteen volumes of English records of the Cape Colony, three volumes of records of Basutoland, and three volumes (in Dutch) of genealogical registers of old Cape families. These volumes have all been printed for the Cape Government, and have been so minutely indexed as to make reference easy. Dr. Theal is married to Miss Stewart, of Argyllshire, Scotland.

THEILER, Dr. Arnold, of the Commissioner of Lands Department, Transvaal, was Director of Lymph-form at Johannesburg in 1893, and Veterinary Surgeon to the Sanitary Board and Mine Sanitation Dept. at Johannesburg in 1894-5. In 1896 he served on a special mission to Rhodesia on the outbreak of Rinderpest, and from that time until 1900 acted as Veterinary Surgeon to the late Government, acted as Veterinary Surgeon to the Transvaal Artillery in 1898, and also Director of the Bacteriological Laboratory and the Vaccine Institute of the late South African Republic. In 1899 he was on a special mission to Europe to represent the Transvaal and Natal Governments at the International Congress of Veterinary Surgeons at Baden-Baden, on a special mission to Basutoland on the outbreak of rinderpest in 1901, and on a special mission to Rhodesia in connection with the Rhodesian tick fever in 1902. Dr. Theiler was appointed Government Veterinary Bacteriologist for the Transvaal in 1900, which position he still holds.

THERON, Thomas Philippus, M.L.A., of Britstown, Cape Colony, was born at Tulbagh in 1839, was educated at Wellington (C.C.), and started life as a carpenter's apprentice. From 1864 to 1869 he was a teacher in Richmond (C.C.), then became a sheep farmer, was first elected member of the House of Assembly for Richmond in 1884 and was elected Chairman of Committees in 1894. He is an ardent member of the Afrikander Bond, of which he is now Chairman, and was last returned to the Cape Parliament by the Richmond electors in Feb., 1904.

THOMAS, Lieut. Col. Owen, J.P. of Henblas, Rhosgoch, Anglesey, is the son of Owen Thomas and Eleanor, née Jones-Roberts, of Henblas and Peibrou, Anglesey. He was born Dec. 7, 1858, at Henblas, and was educated a Liverpool Coll. He was appointed Lieut, 3rd Batt. Manchester Regt. in 1884, and Capt. 3rd Batt. Royal Welsh Fusiliers, 1887, and Maj. in 1897. He served as Maj. of the 1st Regt. of Brabant's Horse in S.A. from Nov., 1899, and he raised and commanded as Lieut. Col. the Prince of Wales' Light Horse, 1900 to 1902. Col Thomas was Chief Officer of the Government Life-Saving Apparatus (Cemaes, Anglesey), 1871-1899. He is J.P. for the county of Anglesey was High Sheriff of Anglesey, 1895-1896; is on the County Council of Anglesey; was member of the late Royal Commission on Agriculture (Great Britain), 1895-1898 President of Anglesey Agricultural Show, and has been awarded first prize for the best cultivated farm, and also for the best stocked farm. He was also breeder and exhibitor of the heaviest ox at the Royal Islington Show in 1882. He reported privately after the declaration of war, on the agricultural and pastoral prospects of the Transvaal, and hi is at present writing on the agricultural and pastoral prospects of S.A. Col. Owen Thomas unsuccessfully contested the Oswestry Division of Shropshire in the agricultural interest at the Parliamentary Election in 1895. He married Aug. 13, 1887, Frederica Wilhelmina Skelton only dau. of Frederick Pershouse and Mina Darby, of Pen Hall, Staffordshire, and step dau. of Robt. Newton Jackson, of Blackbrooke Herefordshire.

THOMAS, William, M.L.A., is one of the Progressive representatives of the electoral division of Albany in the Cape House of Assembly to which he was returned at the General Election in 1904.

THOMPSON, E. G. was formerly editor of the *Natal Witness*, and joined the staff of the *Rand Daily Mail* in 1902.

THOMPSON, Francis R., is son of a former member of the Cape Legislative Council. At the age of thirteen, moved by the spirit of adventure, he went up to the diamond fields, working for three years on the Klipdrift diggings. He then started farming on land which formed the nucleus of his Hart's River ranch. In 1878, when the war broke out in the Northern Territories, his father was brutally murdered, and young Thompson, after receiving a wound which cost him part of a rib, and very nearly his life, escaped in a miraculous manner to a neighbour's farm, which he and the owner defended for couple of days and nights, until relieved by a contingent of the old 24th Regt. A few weeks later he joined Sir Charles Warren, and remained with him until the expedition of 1878 was over, when he became, at the age of twenty, Inspector of Natives, with power to settle disputes between the various chiefs. He served as Special Commissioner of Bechuanaland throughout the Stellaland and Goshen troubles; again with Sir Charles Warren when he turned the Boers out of Rooigrond; and then on the Frontier Commission defining the Griqualand West Boundary. Then at Mr. Rhodes' request he undertook the organising of the Compound system at Kimberley, which

proved a wonderful success for the mines. After a short stay in Johannesburg, and just after he was appointed Protector of Natives and Govt. Inspector of Compounds, he undertook for Mr. Rhodes to accomplish the first step towards opening up the northern route by obtaining the concession from Lobengula which formed the basis of the charter.

Mr. Thompson—or Matabele Thompson, as he came to be called familiarly—remained in Bulawayo for two years. He then entered at Oxford, and gave three years to study. On his return to S.A. he was elected to the Cape Parliament member for Georgetown, and served on the rinderpest Commission. Mr. Thompson was married in 1893, his father-in-law having been one of the British Commissioners in the Venezuelan Arbitration in the forties.

THOMSON, George William, of 26, Oakwood Court, Kensington, London, W., of Mayfield, Essex, and of the Savile and Gresham clubs, was born at Aberdeen March 11, 1845, and was educated at the Aberdeen Grammar School and University. From 1870 until 1883 Thomson was in the service of the Oriental Bank in China, Japan, and India. He is the author of *Verses from Japan*, and has contributed to various periodicals. In his early years he travelled extensively in the East and in America, and has visited every capital in Europe. He founded the first European Bank in Persia in 1887, and also in 1891 founded the African Banking Corporation, an important and flourishing institution, with an authorised capital of £2,000,000, with power to increase to t5,000,000. Eighty thousand £10 shares are issued, £6 being paid up on each share. Taking into account the eventful period through which the bank has passed since its inception, there is every reason to be satisfied with its progress. Including the Head Office, London, and the New York Agency, the Bank has thirty-nine branches spread throughout South Africa. Since 1902 a dividend of 6 per cent. per annum has been maintained, and the Reserve Fund now amounts to £140,000. Mr. Thomson is decorated with the Persian Order of the Lion and the Sun. He married, first, in 1878, Ellen Augusta (d. 1879), dau. of A. W. Gadesden, of Ewell Castle, Surrey, and secondly, in 1888, Coralie Louise, dau. of Ed. Woollett, of Paris and Brussels.

THOMSON, James Stuart, F.L.S., of Courtfield, Cape Town, and of the Junior Civil Service Club (C. T.), was born in Scotland, July 21, 1869, and was educated at the High School and George Watson's Coll., Edinburgh, afterwards receiving a training in natural science at the universities of Edinburgh and Freiburg-i-B. After working for a year in the Challenge Expedition office under Sir John Murray, he was for five years Demonstrator and Assistant in Zoology at the Extramural School of Medicine, Edin., and for three years Lecturer on Natural Science at the Municipal Science, Art and Technical Schools at Plymouth, and for the same period carried out original research on fishery subjects at the Marine Biological Laborory at Plymouth. He was appointed Asst. Govt. Biologist to the Cape Colony in Sept., 1903, and in May, 1905, was temporarily transferred to the Colonial Govt. to act as Interim Professor of Zoology at the South African Coll. He is the author of various scientific papers, the most noteworthy being *The Scales of Godidae as an Index of Age*. Unmarried.

THOMSON, William, M.A., B.Sc., LL.D., F.R.S.E., of the Cape of Good Hope University, was educated at Perth Academy and Edinburgh University, medallist in Natural Philosophy, Chemistry, and Zoology, and graduated M.A. with Honours in Mathematics and Natural Philosophy, and B.So. 1878. After being Asst. to the Professor of Mathematics at Edinburh Univ., and Asst. Secy. to the Edinburgh Univ. Local Examination Board, he was Professor of Mathematics and Mathematical Physics at Victoria Coll., Stellenbosch, from 1883 to 1887, when he resigned, being re-elected in 1888. Meanwhile, he was appointed additional Examiner in Mathematics and Science at Edinburgh Univ., and in 1885 became member of the Council of the Cape University, and in 1895 Registrar to the University. He was a member of the Civil Service Comm. of the Cape Colony in 1902, and in 1904 the hon. degree of LL.D. was conferred upon him by Edin. Univ. He has published several mathematical works.

THORBURN, J. S., of Lagos, W. Africa, was formerly Principal Asst. Colonial Secy. of Ceylon, and was in 1905 selected for the office of Senior Provincial Commissioner for the combined Colonies of Lagos and Southern Nigeria with, it is understood, a dormant commission to administer the Government in the absence of the Governor.

THORNE, Sir William, M.L.A., Kt. Bach., of Rusdon, Rondebosch, Cape Town, and of the Junior Civil Service and City Clubs, Cape Town, was born Jan. 27, 1839, at Llansledwell, Pembrokeshire, and is son of John Thorne. He was educated privately, and went to Cape Town in 1859. Since then he has devoted many years to the municipal government of that city, and enjoys the distinction of having been three times Mayor of Cape Town. Sir William is a prominent S. African merchant, and sits in the Cape House of Assembly as one of the Progressive Members for the capital. He is a director of the merchant firm of Stuttaford and Co., Cape Town and Johannesburg, and married, March 31, 1863, Ellen Lane, of Chichester.

THORNEYCROFT, Col. Alexander Whitelaw, C.B., of the Curragh Camp, Kildare, and of the Naval and Military and Princes' Clubs, was born at Tettenhall, Jan. 19, 1859. He is son of the late Lieut. Col. I. Thorneycroft, of Tettenhall Towers, Wolverhampton, and Hadley Park, Salop, was educated at Wellington Coll., and joined the 2nd Battn. Royal Scots Fusiliers, Feb. 22, 1879, becoming Capt. in 1887, Maj. in 1899, Lieut. Col. in 1900, and full Col. in 1902. He acted as D.A.A.G. in Natal from Sept. 16, 1899, to Oct. 16, 1899, when he was selected for special service until the end of 1901. Colonel Thorneycroft has seen much active service in S.A., beginning with the operations in 1879-81, including the Zulu Campaign, attack and capture of Sekukuni's kraal (medal with clasp), and the first Transvaal Campaign and siege of Pretoria. In the S.A. War of 1899-1902 he raised and commanded that smart body of men known a Thorneycroft's Mounted Infantry, who rendered such a good account of themselves. He tool part in the relief of Ladysmith, the actions a Colenso, Spion Kop, Vaal Kranz, Tugela Heights, Pieter's Hill, and Laing's Nek. In the latter half of 1900 he operated in the Eastern Transvaal, and subsequently commanded mobile column and group of columns in the Transvaal, O.R.C. and C.C. (despatches, medals, and clasps, and C.B.). Col. Thorneycroft He received his present appointment as A.A.G., 7th Div. of the 3rd Army Corps, Nov. 12, 1902.

He is fond of shooting and racquets, and married, on June 20, 1903, Mrs. Burrard Crozier, dau. of the late Major J. W. Percy, and cousin of Sir Maurice FitzGerald, Bart., Knt. of Kerry.

THORNTON, Dr. George, M.D., M.R.C.P., D.P.H. (Oxford), of the Pretoria Hospital, Transvaal, was for six years under the Local Government Board in England, as Medical Officer in the Metropolitan Asylums Board Fever Hospitals. Subsequently he served for a year as Civil Surgeon attached to the British Forces in South Africa, and was appointed Medical Superintendent at the Pretoria Hospital in 1900.

THURSFIELD, John George Howard, of Kroonstad, O.R.C., was educated at Christ's Hospital, London. He served in the South African War with the Second Provisional Regt. of Hussars until the Declaration of Peace; acted as Clerk to the Claims Commission in 1903, Clerk to the Resident Magistrate at Smithfield, O.R.C., in 1903, and to the Resident Magistrate at Kroonstad in 1904.

THYNNE, Lord Alexander George, of 15, Manchester Sq., London, W., and of White's and the Bachelors' Clubs, was born Feb. 17, 1873, and is son of the late Marquess of Bath. He was educated at Eton and Balliol Coll., Oxon. From 1895-8 he travelled extensively in the Balkan Peninsula, Albania, Macedonia, Asia Minor, and Montenegro; took part in a shooting expedition in the East Coast Protectorate and Uganda in 1899, and from that year he represented the Corp. of London on the L.C.C. until 1900 when he served in S. Africa with I.Y. and on the Staff (Queen's medal and three clasps King's medal and two clasps). He acted as secretary to the Lieut.-Governor of the O.R.C. from 1902-5, and accompanied the Somaliland Field Force as Reuter's correspondent in 1903-4 (medal and clasp). Lord Alexander Thynne contested the Frome Div. of Somerset in the Unionist interest in 1896.

TIDSWELL, Maj. Edward Cecil, D.S.O., of the Army and Navy Club, is the son of the late

Benjamin Kaye Tidswell. He was born Sept. 13, 1862, at Birkdale, Lancashire, and was educated at Harrow. Entering the 2nd Lancashire Fusiliers in 1882, he was promoted Capt. in 1891, and Maj. in 1900. He served with the Nile Expedition in 1898, being present at the battle of Khartoum, receiving the Queen's and Khedive's medals with clasp. On the Boer War breaking out he went to S.A., serving from 1899 to 1902, receiving the Queen's medal with five clasps, and the King's medal with two clasps. He was also mentioned in despatches, and obtained the D.S.O. In 1903 he was appointed Commander of the Lagos Batt. West African Frontier Force, and now commands the 1st Batt. of the Gold Coast Regt. with local rank of Lieut. Col. He married, in 1902, Miss Ella Pilcher, dau. of the late Thomas Webb Pilcher, of Harrow and Rome.

TILLARD, Richard, J.P., of Fort Beaufort, Cape Colony, is son of the Rev. I. A. Tillard, Rector of Connington, Cambs. He was educated at Marlborough Coll., acted as Resident Magistrate and Sub. Collector of Customs at Port Nolloth; Civil Commissioner and Resident Magistrate at Mafeking in 1886; Supt. of Telegraphs, C.C., and R.M. at Vryburg in 1889, and again in 1899, when he was expelled by the Boers; Master of the Chief Magistrate's Court; Acting Postmaster General under the British Bechuanaland Govt., C.C., and R.M. at Fort Beaufort in 1898; acted as C.C. and R.M, at Aliwal North and King Williamstown. He served as an officer of Volunteers in the Gaika and Basutoland Wars (two medals). He married Amy, dau. of William Ogilvie, of Grahamstown.

TISSOT, Dr. Edouard, of Basle, was born in 1864, and was educated at the Zurich Polytechnic from 1882-5, where he obtained his diploma as Mechanical Engineer. He then made a special study of physics and electricity at Zurich until 1888, receiving the degree of Doctor. In the same year he was appointed engineer to the factory of Electrical Apparatus at Uster. From 1890 to 1899 he was Engineer, subsequently Chief, of the Scientific Department, and Sub-Manager of the Industrial Electrical and Mechanical Company. The principal enterprises with which Dr. Tissot has been actively associated are the Niagara scheme, the reorganisation of the Popp Sector at Paris, the conveyance of power by direct current at

Steinamanger (Hungary), Chaux-de-Fonds-Locle, Grand-Eau, Val de Travers in Switzerland, &c., also in various conveyances of power by alternating current, in particular that at Christiania in Norway.

In 1899 Dr. Tissot was appointed Assistant-Director of the Swiss Industrial and Electrical Company at Basle (paid-up capital, 40,000,000 francs), and was subsequently made Director, and has supervised numerous conveyances of power by high tension three-phase current, central power stations, tramways, &c.

Dr. Tissot is Chairman of the Electrical Union of Paris, a Director of several French electrical companies, deputy-manager of the Electrical Joint Stock Company for Northern Italy, and director of the Piedmontese Electrical company of Turin. In 1901 he founded and subsequently became Vice-President of the Swiss Scientific Committee for Electrical Traction on e Swiss standard full-gauge railways, &c, and he is now one of the Advisory Board of Engineers to the Victoria Falls Power Company. (See H. Wilson Fox.)

TOD, C. E., M.L.A., represents the electoral division of Griqualand East in the Progressive interest in the Cape House of Assembly, to which he was returned in 1904.

TODD, John Spencer Brydges, C.M.G. (1878), I.S.O. (1905), of 24, Cathcart Road, S. Kensington, and the Royal Societies' Club, was born at Dresden, Aug. 28, 1840, is the youngest son of the late Col. Geo. Todd (3rd Dragoon Guards) by daughter of the late Sir Egerton Brydges, Bart., was educated at Blochmann's Gymnasium, Dresden, and at the Imperial Lyceum, Saint-Omer. He accompanied the late Rt. Hon. Sir Geo. Grey, K.C.B. to the Cape of Good Hope in 1860, and entered the Civil Service there. Served in the Colonial Secy.'s office, C.T., and in the C.C. and R.M.'s offices at Swellendam and Robertson, and again at Swellendam until 1874, when he returned to Cape Town, where he successively served in the Colonial Railway Engineer's office, the G.P.O., and the Treasury, in which he, as Secy. to a Special Commission, detected a deficiency of over £50,000. On the introduction of the Appropriation Audit he became Accountant in the

Prime Minister's Dept., and subsequently acted as Accounting Officer thereof. In 1875 was sent as the Colony's Executive Commissioner to the Universal Exhibition in Paris, and there served on the International Jury. On his return to the Cape he served with Sir Henry White and Messrs. Gordon and Lawson on a mixed committee to determine the division between the Imperial and Colonial Govts. of the Transkei War expenditure of 1877-8. In 1881 he proceeded on special service to Kimberley, to adjust the accounts of the then recently annexed province of Griqualand West. This accomplished, he was there detained till the end of the year to act as C.C. of Kimberley and Provincial Registrar of Deeds, and to report on the state of the several Public Departments there. On his return to Cape Town he acted as Asst. Comr. and Permanent Head of the Dept. of Crown Lands and Public Works; and, on the return of the incumbent of that office, was retained in the Dept. as Financial Secy. till the end of Aug., 1882, when he was selected to fill the post of Secy. to the newly created Cape of Good Hope Agency in London, from which he retired on a pension Dec. 31, 1904.

Mr. Todd was by Commission authorised to act as Agent General in the event of the death, disability, or absence of the incumbent for the time being, and very repeatedly so acted, notably during the late Sir Charles Mills' absence at the Ottawa Conference in 1894, and after his death, from March, 1895, to March, 1896. He was one of the Cape of Good Hope delegates at the Universal Postal Conference, held at Washington in 1897, and between 1879 and 1882 was French Examiner to the Cape of Good Hope University. He is author of *The Resident Magistrate at the Cape of Good Hope* (1882), and of a *Handy Guide to Laws and Regulations at the Cape of Good Hope*, published in London in 1887. Mr. Todd married, March 13, 1865, Susan Margaret, eldest dau. of the late Baron Goert van Reede van Oudtshoorn, some time C.C. and R.M. of Swellendam, and later of Stellenbosch, Cape Colony.

TOLLEMACHE, Baron Bentley Lyonel John, of Manton, Oakham, is grandson of the Right Hon. Wilbraham Frederic Tollemache, 2nd Baron, whom he succeeded in Dec., 1904, his mother being the only dau. and heiress of the 7th Earl of

Kingston. The present Lord Tollemache was born in 1883, and served in the recent South African War. He married, in 1902, Wynford Rose, dau. of Gen. Sir Arnold B. Kemball, K.C.B.

TOLLEMACHE, Hon. John Richard Delap, of Tycoed, Bournemouth, and of The Club, Bournemouth, is the third son of the first Baron Tollemache, and was born at his father's Cheshire seat, Peckforton Castle, Oct. 22, 1850. He is a cousin of the present Earl Dysart (an Irish creation dating as far back as 1643), who has been Lord-Lieutenant of Rutland for a quarter of a century, and is on the Commission of the Peace for the Counties of Leicestershire and Lincolnshire. Mr. Tollemache, after leaving school, finished his education on the old *Britannia*, and passed into the Navy as a middy, being posted on the Pacific station. Retiring from the senior service, he then spent ten years in Canada, and subsequently voyaged to Australia and South Africa to gain a more intimate knowledge of Greater Britain. He has been a director of the African Concessions Syndicate for two years, and is on the Board of the Victoria Falls Power Company. (See H. Wilson Fox.)

TOOTH, Dr. Howard Henry, C.M.G., M.A., M.D., F.R.C.P., of 34, Harley St., W., and of the Arts Club, was born at Brighton in 1856. He was educated at Rugby and St. John's Coll., Cambridge. He is Consulting Physician to the Metropolitan Hospital, Physician to St. Bartholomew's Hospital and the National Hospital for the Paralysed and Epileptic. He served in the S. African War in 1900 as Physician to the Portland Hospital (mentioned in despatches, C.M.G.). He is the author of many contributions to medical literature. He married, in 1881, Mary, dau. of the late Edward Price, of Highgate.

TOQUE, Mons., a Government official, formerly occupying a post in the French Congo, who was arrested in 1905 on a charge of using violence towards the natives. The crimes of which he was accused were so monstrous that the Colonial annals of France were said to contain no previous record of such an abuse of power.

TOWNSEND, Edward Ross, M.L.C., J.P., of

Salisbury, Rhodesia, and of the Bulawayo and Salisbury Clubs, was born at Bedford, Cape Colony, Dec. 19, 1863. He entered the Civil Service in Bechuanaland in 1889, serving in the Postmaster-General's Dept. and the Deeds Office (1891). He was appointed Asst. Magistrate and Clerk to Civil Commissioner at Mafeking and J.P. for Bechuanaland in 1894, and in June, 1895, joined the Rhodesian Civil Service as Registrar of Deeds and Companies at Bulawayo, being made a J.P. for Matabeleland later in the same year. In 1896 he was appointed Civil Commissioner at Bulawayo, Secretary to the Departments of Land and Agriculture, April, 1901, Secretary for Agriculture, July, 1903, and Member of the Legislative Council of Southern Rhodesia in 1903. He married, in 1895, Mary, dau. of H. Mallet Veale, J.P.

TREDGOLD, Clarkson Henry, M.L.C., is a member both of the Executive and Legislative Councils of Rhodesia, for the Southern Province of which he acts as Attorney General, having succeeded Mr. John G. Kotzé, K.C., when the gentleman was promoted Judge of the Cap Colony. Mr. Tredgold formerly acted as Solicitor-General for Southern Rhodesia.

TREGARTHEN, William Coulson, Mus. Bac., F.R.C.I., of The Hermitage, Queenstown, Cape Colony, was born at Penzance, Sept. 17 1856, and educated at Penzance Grammar Sch. At the age of eleven he acted as organist of the church of which General Booth (founder of the Salvation Army) was pastor; articled pupil of George Riseley (organist of the Cathedral and Colston Hall, Bristol) from 1873-78, also a pupil of Dr. S. S. Wesley, of Gloucester Cathedral 1875-76, during which time he was organist of St. John's and St. Paul's, Clifton, and acted a deputy to his master at the Cathedral, Bristol and All Saints, Clifton. From there he proceeded to the Collegiate Church of St. Mary's Port Elizabeth, Cape Colony, since which time he has resided in S. Africa, doing much to raise the public taste for the art of organ playing. He was the first to introduce the examination of Trinity College, London. He has contributed largely to the musical literature of the Colony and his *South African March* (dedicated to H.E. the Governor, Sir H. G. R. Robinson, K.C.M.G.), a copy of which was accepted by Her Majesty the late Queen Victoria, is very popular. In 1891 he read a paper on Music before the Teachers' Conference at Kimberley, and in 1892 he graduated as Bachelor of Music of Trinity College, Toronto. During the Anglo Boer War he retired to Cape Town, and whilst there acted as organist of St. Barnabas and St. Andrew's churches of that city. In the presence of the Governor, he opened the organ presented by the Australian Volunteers to the Cape Town branch of the Y.M.C.A. He also edited the *Hymnal Life and Service* for the South African Mission, for which he composed several tunes, and at the Cape Town Eisteddfod held in 1901 he won the gold medal offered for the best composition of a hymn tune. Visiting the Australian Colonies at the time of Mr. Cecil Rhodes' death he took over with him some acorns from the oaks at Groote Schuur, which he presented to the public Botanic Gardens at Adelaide, Melbourne and Sydney, to be known henceforth as the Rhodes Oaks. His *Imperial Grand March* is, by special permission, dedicated to Field Marshal Lord Roberts. At the request of Pres. Kruger he wrote an arrangement of the Transvaal *Volkslied*, published by Novello, Ewer and Co. London. His fine collection of horns and Basuto and Zulu curios he presented to the Trinity College, Toronto, which is known as the Tregarthen Collection. He is a Member of the Incorporated Society of Musicians of Great Britain, Trinity College, London, and the ex-libris Society of England. He married, in 1880, Clementina Moorah Francoise, dau. of Andre Stégere, M.D., Geneva.

TRENCH, Col. F. J. A., D.S.O., of the British Embassy, Berlin, is a kinsman of the present Lord Ashtown, and was born in 1858. Entering the B. Artillery, he saw his first active service in the Zulu War of 1879, taking part in the battle of Ulundi. He also served in the last S. African War, being mentioned in despatches. In 1905 he was attached to the staff of the C.I.C. of the German Forces in Damaraland, and in 1906 he was appointed Military Attaché at Berlin. He married, in 1900, a daughter of John N. Craddock, of Tuscaloosa, Alabama, U.S.A.

TRENCHARD, Captain Hugh Montague, D.S.O., was born Feb. 3, 1873, and entered the Royal Scots Fusiliers in 1893. He served in the South African war in 1899-1902, employed with the Imperial Yeomanry, Bushman Corps, and afterwards with the Canadian Scouts; was dangerously wounded; took part in the operations in the Transvaal, west of Pretoria, and the operations in the Orange. River and Cape Colonies (Queen's medal with three clasps, and King's medal with two clasps). For his services during the native risings in Northern and Southern Nigeria he was awarded the D.S.O. in 1906.

TREVES, Sir Frederick, 1st Bart., K.C.V.O., G.E., LL.D., F.R.C.S., of 6, Wimpole St., London, W., and of the Ranelagh, Reform, and Hurlingham Clubs, was born in 1853, and was educated at the Merchant Taylors Sch. In 1900 he acted as Consulting Surgeon to the Forces in S. Africa, and served in the Ladysmith relief column (medal and clasps) . He was appointed in 1903 Hon. Staff Surgeon to the Royal Naval Volunteer Reserve. Sir Frederick has written numerous papers on surgery and anatomy, and is the author of *Manual of Operative Surgery*, *Manual of Surgery*, *Physical Education*, *System of Surgery*, and several others. He married, in 1877, Annie, dau. of A. S. Mason, of Dorchester.

TREVITHICK, Frederick Harvey, M.I.C.E., of Cairo, and of the Isthmian (Lond.), Khedivial, Sporting, and Turf (Cairo) Clubs, was born Feb. 21, 1852. He is son of Francis Trevithick (Chief Mechanical Engineer of the L. and N.W. Railway) and of Mary Ewart, and grandson of Richard Trevithick, the inventor; was educated at Cheltenham Coll. and received his early training on the G.W. Railway. In 1883 he was appointed Chief Mechanical Engineer to the Egyptian State Railways, and in the following year was sent by the Govt. to Russia to report on the petroleum industry. In 1896 he went to India to report on the railway system there, and n 1900 he was sent to Canada and U.S.A. for the same purpose. His reports have in each ease been published. Mr. Trevithick has been decorated with the Orders of the Osmanieh (3rd class) and the Medjidieh (2nd and 3rd class). He married, Nov. 19, 1896, Henrietta Kate Cornford, M.D. Brux., L.R.C.P. Edin., L.R.C.S. Edin., L.F.P. and S. Glasgow, A.A. Oxford, dau. of the Rev. E. Cornford, M.A.

TROLLOPE, Capt. A. G., of Smithfield, O.R.C., took part with his regiment (the Buffs) in the Chitral Relief Expedition in 1895 (medal with clasp), and in the late S. African War (despatches , Queen's and King's medals). He is a sworn translator in Dutch, and passed the Lower Standard in Hindustani and Pushtu, acted as Staff Capt. on Major-Gen. Pretyman's Staff in 1900-1, and was Chief Superintendent of the Refugee Camps in Feb., 1901. He was appointed Resident Magistrate at Smithfield in 1902.

TUCKER, The Rt. Rev. Alfred Robert, Bishop of Uganda, of Mengo, Uganda, and of Bookham, Surrey, was born April 1, 1849, and is son of the late Edward Tucker of Windermere. He was educated at Christchurch, Oxford, graduating B.A. in 1882, and M.A. four years later, while in 1891 he was made Hon. D.D. of Oxford and Durham. Bishop Tucker acted as curate of St. Andrew-the-Less, Bristol, in 1882-5, and curate of St. Nicholas, Durham, from 1885-90. He became Bishop of Eastern Equatorial Africa in 1890, which position he held until 1899, when he was appointed Bishop of Uganda. He married, in 1882, Hannah, dau. of the late W. F. Sim, of Southport.

TUCKER, Charles, of Enquabeni, near Harding, Natal, where he is a native labour agent, was well known as a sprinter until in 1903 he was accidentally shot in the groin so badly as to preclude his continuing to run.

TUGMAN, Herbert St. John, F.R.C.I., of the New Club, Johannesburg, was born at Birkenhead, June 24, 1860, and is son of the late J. E. Tugman, merchant, of Lisbon and London. He was a civilian combatant in Lady smith during the siege, being present at the Lombaard's Kop, Bester's Farm, and Caesar's Camp engagements; Lieut. in Valentine's Heidelberg Horse (1901). He is the author of *Siege of Ladysmith* (Newnes). Unmarried.

TULLIBARDINE, Lieut. Colonel the Marquis of, M.V.O., D.S.O., of Blair Castle, Blair Atholl, N.B., 84, Eaton Place, London, S.W., and of the Cavalry, Marlborough, Turf, and Caledonian Clubs, was born in 1871, and is son of this 7th Duke of Atholl. He was educated at Eton, and

entered the Royal Horse Guards as 2nd Lieutenant in 1892; served in the Nile Expedition in 1898 as Staff Officer to Colonel Broadwood, and took part in the battles of Athara and Khartoum (despatches , D.S.O., and Egyptian medal with two clasps), and the South African War in 1899-1901, on the Staff; present at the relief of Ladysmith, including the actions at Colenso, Spion Hop, and Vaal Kranz; the operations on Tugela Heights, and the action at Pieters Hill, afterwards taking command of the Scottish Horse (despatches, Brevet of Major and Queen's medal with three clasps). He was a member of the Committee of the Volunteer Commission in 1906, and married, in 1899 Katharine, dau. of Sir James Ramsay, Bart.

TURNER, Hon. George, M.L.C., J.P., of Fletching, Sussex; Arundel, Sussex; Warley, Common, Highlands, Natal; and of the Royal Colonial Institute and Victoria Club, Maritzburg; was born at Fletching, July 29, 1884; and was educated at Christ's Hospital and at Dr. Butler's Sch., Brighton. He married, Feb. 15, 1866, Harriette Julia, younger dau. of Rev. Chas. W. Stocker, D.D., of. Draycott Rectory, near Cheadle, Staffs.

TURNER, Dr. George Albert, P.M.O. of Health for the Transvaal, was for a short time Acting Medical Officer of Health at Johannesburg. He was appointed Additional District Surgeon and Additional Port Health Officer for Cape Town in 1902.

TURNER, Skinner, Judge of H.B.M. Court for Siam; of Bangkok, Siam, and of St. Stephen's (Lond.), Mombasa, British (Bangkok), and English (Zanzibar) Clubs, was born near Tonbridge, June 2, 1865; is fourth son of the late Frederic Turner, and was educated at King's Coll. Sch., Lond. He was called to the Bar at the Middle Temple in 1890, and joined the Western Circuit and Hampshire Sessions. Subsequently he served under the Foreign Office in the following capacities: Registrar, East Africa Protectorate Court, 1900; Magistrate, Mombasa, 1902; Second Asst. Judge, Zanzibar, and a member of H.B.M. Court of Appeal for Eastern Africa, 1902; Asst. Judge, Zanzibar, 1904; and Judge at H.B.M. Court for Siam, March, 1905. Incidentally he has acted as

Legal Vice-Consul for the Uganda Protectorate, 1901-2, and Asst. Judge at Zanzibar in 1902-3. His recreations are lawn tennis, golf and cricket. He married, in 1902, Millicent H., second dau. of the late Rev. W. H. Hewett.

TWEEDIE, Capt. Henry Carmichael, D.S.O., of Mooltan, India, and of the Junior Naval and Military Club, was born in Kent, Jan. 25, 1876, and is son of Major-Gen. Tweedie, late R.A. He was educated at Sandhurst, and joined the 2nd North Staffs. Regt. in 1896; served in S. Africa in 1900-2, with the 8th Mounted Inf.; present at the actions at Paardeburg and Driefontein, and the smaller engagements at Waterval Drift, Poplar Grove, and Zand River.

TWEEDY, Edward Herbert, L.R.C.P.I., L.R.C.S.I., and L.M. Rotunda Hospital; S.M.O. of the Gold Coast Colony; of the Rotunda Hospital, Dublin; and of the Friendly Brothers and Sports Club, was born at Dublin in 1856; is the youngest son of John Johnston Tweedy, Solicitor, of Dublin; was educated at Wesley Coll., Dublin, and the Carmichael Sch. of Medicine. After serving from 1892 to 1896 as Surgeon under the Cunard SS. Co., he became House Surgeon at St. Mark's Ophthalmic Hospital in 1896; joined the W. African Medical Service in 1897, and served with Lieut. Col. Northcott in the Northern Territories, being mentioned in despatches and receiving the medal and clasp. He was also present during the siege of Kumasi in 1901 (despatches, medal and clasp). Unmarried.

TYLER, Robert Emeric, of 11, Pancras Lane, London, E.C., is Chairman of Field's Reward Gold Mines, Ltd., South African Gold Fields, Ltd., Tokatea Trust, Ltd., and Zechan, South Comstock, Ltd., and director of the Murchison Associated Gold Mines, Ltd.

TYMMS, E. R., of 15, St. Swithin's Lane, London, E.C., is the London Secretary of the De Beers Consolidated Mines, Ltd., and is a director of the Consolidated African Copper Trust, Ltd., on the London Committee of the Imperial Cold Storage and Supply Co., Ltd., and on the London Board of the Consolidated Co., Bultfontein Mine, Ltd., and

the Griqualand West Diamond Mining Co., Dutoitspan Mine, Ltd.

TYNDALL, Capt. William Ernest Marriott D.S.O., of the R.M. Coll., Camberley, was born Feb. 2, 1875. He was educated at Bradfield Coll.; joined the Duke of Wellington's Regt. in 1895, and served through the S. African War, 1899-1902 (mentioned in despatches).

UGANDA, Bishop of (see Rt. Rev. Alfred Robert Tucker).

UNIACKE, Capt. Andrew Gore, D.S.O., of 4 Alhambra Rd., Southsea, served throughout the late S. African War with the Colonial Forces and with the City of London Imperial Yeomanry. He was appointed District Superintendent of Police in Northern Nigeria in 1905.

VAILE, H. B., of The Avenue, Cliftonville, Northampton, is a director of the Crescens (Matabele) Mines and Land Co., Ltd., and the French Guinea and Sudan Mining Co., Ltd.

VALDEZ Joachim Travassos; has had a distinguished record as a diplomat, especially as Portuguese Consul at Shanghai. He succeeded Senhor Cinatta as Consul General for Portugal in the Transvaal in 1902.

VAN CAMPEN, Capt., joined Bethune's Mounted Infantry as a trooper, and went all through the Boer War with that Regt., having reached the rank of Capt. on its disbandment. He was appointed Supt. of the Repatriation Department at Middleburg in 1902.

VAN DEN HEEVER, Hon. D.P., of Karreefontein, Venterstad, C.C., was born in 1838. He was for over ten years member of the Divisional Council, was until recently a member of the Cape Legislative Council for the North East Circle, and was leader of the Anti-Scab Act agitation in 1895.

VAN DER MERWE, Franz Johannes, M.L.A., represents the electoral division of Clanwilliam in the Cape Parliament, to which he was last re-elected in 1904. He is a member of the Afrikander Bond.

VAN DER MERWE, J. S., was the first mining commissioner of Johannesburg.

VAN EEDEN, Hon. Frederick Jacobus, was born in the Swellendam Division in 1846, and is a successful agriculturist and stock farmer, owning nearly 30,000 morgen. He was a member of the Cape Legislative Assembly in 1887-8 for Swellendam, and from 1891 until recently sat in the Legislative Council as member for the South-West circle. He is an elder of the D.R. Church, and member of the Divisional Council.

VANES, Dr. Arthur Bayley, M.L.A., is member of the Cape Legislative Assembly for Uitenhage, for which electoral division he was last returned in Feb., 1904. He supports the Progressive party.

VAN HEERDEN, Hercules Christian, M.L.A., of Tarkastad, C.C., is a prominent and progressive farmer in the Eastern Province. He has been for many years a representative for Cradock in the Cape Legislative Assembly, to which he was last returned in 1904. He supports the Bond party, but preserves a moderate and conciliatory attitude.

VAN HULSTEYN, Sir William, was born in 1865, and is strongly identified with mining interests on the Rand, his Directorates being many and influential. He received his accolade for services as Legal Adviser to the C.I.C. during the recent S. African War.

VAN LAUN, Henry Theodore, of 1, St. Helens Place, London, E.C., Government Contractor, and Merchant, is son of the famous author and grammarian, and was himself educated at Cheltenham and Edinburgh, and is a scholar of no small attainments. He is a member of the Inner Temple. He is considerably interested in South African enterprises, being a Chairman of the Beira Railway Company; Ltd., the Beira Junction Railway Company, Ltd., and the Sterkfontein Estates Company, Ltd. He is a keen Conservative politician, a tariff reformer, and recently issued, with Mr. W. H. Wills, a pamphlet on the South African Native Labour problem. He was the chosen Tariff Reform candidate for the constituency of

Saffron Walden in 1906, but withdrew his candidature before the election took place.

VAN MAASDIJK, A. C. J., of Durban, was appointed Consul for the Netherlands at Durban in 1905.

VAN RENSBURG, Hendrik Petrus Francois Janse, M.L.C., formerly represented Heidelberg, in the second Volksraad, and at the same time acted as President of the Burgerwacht, a Boer society. He fought against the British during the Boer War in 1881, and again in the S. African War in 1899-1902. Subsequently he accepted a seat in the Transvaal Legislative Council under the new Government in the Progressive interest.

VAN RHYN, Hon. P. B., of Van Rhynsdorp, Clanwilliam, Co., was born in 1827; was Field Cornet in 1848; was elected to the Cape House of Assembly for Clanwilliam in 1868, and was a member of the Legislative Council for the North-West Circle from 1884 until recently. He is an elder of the D.R. Church.

VAN ROOY, A. C. A., M.L.A., is a member of the Cape House of Assembly for Steynsberg.

VAN ZYL, C. H., M.L.C., formerly Law Lecturer at the S. African Coll., is the compiler of a standard work of reference to the S. African legal profession, *The Theory of the Judicial Practice of the Colony of the Cape of Good Hope and of South Africa Generally*. At the election in 1904 Mr. Van Zyl was elected to the Legislative Council as Bond representative of the South-Western Circle.

VAN ZYL, Dirk Jacobus Albertus, M.L.A., is member of the Cape Legislative Assembly for Clanwilliam, for which electorate he was last returned in 1904 in the Bond interest.

VAN ZYL, H. S., is a member of the Cape House of Assembly for Cape Town, which he represents as a Progressive.

VAN ZYL, I. J., M.L.C., is one of the Bond representatives of the North-Western Circle in the Cape Legislative Council, to which he was elected at the general election in 1904.

VENOSTA, Marquis Visconti, was one of the Italian Plenipotentiaries at the Moroccan Conference at Algeçiras in 1906.

VENTER, M. M., represented the electoral division of Colesburg in the Cape House of Assembly, to which he was returned in Feb., 1904, as a supporter of the Bond. In 1906 he resigned his seat.

VERULAM, Rt. Hon. the Earl of, of Gorhambury, St. Albans, Herts, and of the Carlton and Bachelors' Clubs, was born in London in 1852, The first Earl of Verulam was created in 1815, and the titles held by the present representative are Baron Forrester of Corstorphine, Midlothian, a creation of 1633, Viscount Grimston and Baron Dunboyne, Co. Meath, 1719, and Baron Verulam of Gorhambury, Herts, 1815. He is also a Baronet of England and Nova Scotia. The family is descended from Silvester de Grymestone, who carried the Standard of William the Conqueror at the Battle of Hastings. The present Earl was educated at Harrow; served in the 1st Life Guards in 1870-5, and also in the Herts Yeomanry Cavalry and the Herts Militia. He was first M.P. for St. Albans in 1885-92, has been a County Councillor on the Herts C.C. since its formation, and is a J.P. for that county. He is Chairman of the Abbontiakoon (Wassau) Mine, Ltd., E. Africa Syndicate, Ltd., Effuenta (Wassau) Mines, Ltd., Fanti Mines, Ltd., W. African Gold Trust, Ltd., and Director of the Alliance Assurance Co., Ltd., New Gold Coast Agency, Ltd., and the S. African Gold Trust, Ltd. He married, in 1875, Margaret, eldest dau. of Sir Frederick and Lady Graham, of Netherby, Cumberland.

VIGORS, Major Philip Urban Walter, D.S.O., of Slewton, Whimple, near Exeter, was born in the E. Indies, Feb. 8, 1868, and is son of the late Thomas Mercer Vigors, of Co. Carlow, ,Ireland. He served in Burma in 1891 (medal with clasp); and in S. Africa in 1899-1902, when he took part in the operations in the Transvaal and Orange Free State; present at the actions at Tugela Heights, the Relief of Ladysmith, and Laing's Nek (King's medal and two clasps, and D.S.O.). He retired from the Army in 1902, and acted as Brigade Major in the Devon

Volunteers Inf. Brig. in 1903-5. He married, Oct. 21, 1891, Anna L. H. D'Arcy.

VILJOEN, Dr. Anthony Gysbert, M.B., M.L.A., formerly sat in the Cape Legislative Council as member for the South-Western Circle. At the general election in 1904 he was returned to the Lower House as Bond member for Caledon.

VILJOEN, Gen. Ben. J. of Krugersdorp, Transvaal, is of French Huguenot extraction, and was born in 1860. He served through the early part of the S. African War, and was present at Elandslaagte, where two thirds of the Boers were killed, wounded, or captured, he himself narrowly escaping. He also took part in the operations against Ladysmith, and was present at Spion Kop. He was captured eventually, and sent to St. Helena. Ex-Gen. Viljoen is a genial character, a loyal friend, and a frank opponent. He was careful not to associate himself with the tour undertaken by the three Boer Generals on the Continent after the termination of the War, but he came to England and lectured at Queen's Hall, and afterwards in the States. His book, *My Reminiscences of the Anglo Boer War*, is full of good reading, and throws a strong and unprejudiced light upon the stirring events of the War period. In 1904 he took part in the St. Louis Exhibition, in connection with a display reminiscent of episodes in the S. African War. He is now settled in Mexico.

VILJOEN, E. J., M.L.A., is the member of the Cape Legislative Assembly for the electoral division of Caledon, in succession to Mr. M. M. Venter, a member of the S. African (Bond) party.

VILLIERS, Major Charles Hyde, of 1, Gt. Cumberland Place, London, W., and of the Marlborough, Turf, Bachelors', and Liberal Union Clubs, was born in Essex, Sept. 21, 1862, and is son of the Rev. Charles Villiers. He was educated at Marlborough, Oxford, and Sandhurst, taking honours in History at Oxford; entered the Army in 1887, and served in 1893 as A.D.C. to Sir Gerald Portal on a mission to Uganda (mentioned in despatches); also served under Gen. Macdonald during the Muhammedan Rebellion in Uganda, and in the Unyow Campaign, under Gen. Colvile (mentioned in despatches); served in Matabeleland in 1895-6, as second in command of the Rhodesia Horse; took part in the Raid under Dr. Jameson; and in the S. African War in 1899-1900 (mentioned in despatches). He joined the I.Y., 3rd City of London (Rough Riders) after being fifteen years in the Army. Decorations: the Central African medal, S. African medal with three clasps, and the Star of Zanzibar. Major Villiers contested, unsuccessfully, S. Wolverhampton in the Unionist interest in 1906; is Chairman of the Wassau West Amalgamated Mines, Ltd.; Director of the Berehaven Copper Mines, Ltd.; Brazilian Diamond and Exploration Co., Ltd.; E. Africa Syndicate, Ltd.; Fanti Consolidated Mines, Ltd.; Fanti Mines, Ltd.; Rhodesia Broken Hill Development Co., Ltd.; Rhodesia Copper Co., Ltd.; and the Sebakwe and District Mines, Ltd., and is on the London Committee of the Bushveld Tin Mines, Ltd., East Rand Extension Gold Mining Co., Ltd., and the Lydenburg Land and Exploration Co., Ltd. He married, Aug. 17, 1901, Lady Victoria A. Innes-Ker, dau. of the seventh Duke of Roxburghe.

VINCENT, Rev. D. B., the assumed name of Mojola Agbebi (q.v.).

VINCENT, Sir Edgar, M.P., of Esher Place, Esher, was originally in the Coldstream Guards, and afterwards went to Turkey to assist in the reorganisation of the Ottoman Public Debt. He subsequently became Financial Adviser to the Egyptian Govt., and for seventeen years he worked hard with Lord Cromer (q.v.) to put the financial affairs of Egypt on a sound basis. (See also Sir Vincent Corbett, K.C.V.O.) Sir Edgar's wife, Lady Helen Vincent, enjoys the distinction of being one of the loveliest women in England. She is a sister of the late Duchess of Leinster, and a dau. of Lord Faversham.

VINCENT, Colonel Sir Charles Edward Howard, K.C.M.G., Kt. Bach., C.B., V.C., M.P., A.D.C., of 1, Grosvenor Square, London, W., Villa Flora, Cannes, and of the Carlton, Marlborough, and Naval and Military Clubs, was born May 31, 1849, at Slinfold, Sussex, and is the second surviving son of the late Rev. Sir Frederick Vincent, Bart. He was educated at Westminster, and the Royal Military College, Sandhurst, and served in the Royal Welsh Fusiliers from 1868-73, and from then until 1875

as Captain in the Royal Berks Militia, afterwards commanding the Central London Rangers until 1878, when he became Director of Criminal Investigation in the Metropolitan Police; acted as Colonel commanding the Queen's Westminster Volunteers from 1884-1904, when he was appointed Honorary Colonel, which position he still holds. He suggested the employment of Volunteers in South Africa in 1899, and took a leading part in the formation of the City Imperial Volunteers. During the War in South Africa he served for a considerable part of the campaign, being present at the operations before Ladysmith and the surrender of Paardeberg, writing two treatises on the War. Sir Howard has sat in Parliament for Central Sheffield since 1885, and is a Director of Hadfield's Steel Foundry Co., Bucknall Steamship Lines, and the New Eastern Investment Co.; is a Commander of the Legion of Honour of France, of the German Crown, and the Crown of Italy; Barrister at Law of the Inner Temple; *Bachelier des Lettres et des Sciences*, and Member of the *Faculte de Droit* of Paris. He is the author of numerous publications, including, *The Police Code*, *Russia's Advance Eastward*, *Elementary Military Drawing and Reconnoitering*, *The Imperial Parliament*, *Procedure of Extradition*, and numerous addresses on Foreign Armies and British Trade. In 1887 he initiated the Probation of First Offenders Act; the Merchant Shipping (Life-Saving Appliances) Act, in 1888; Reformatory and Industrial Schools Act, in 1891; Judicial Trustees Act, in 1896; Aliens Act, in 1905; and the Public Trustee Act, in 1906; was also the Founder of the United Empire Trade League in 1891, and has acted as Chairman of the Publication Committee of the Unionist Party since 1895. He married, Oct. 26, 1882, Ethel Gwendoline, dau. and co-heiress of the late George Moffatt, M.P., of Goodrich Court, Herefordshire.

VINCENT, Capt. Louis Leon, of King Williamstown, Cape Colony, is of French parentage, and was originally intended for the Church. But he entered the French Navy as a Middy; served through the Crimea (medal), and since going to S. Africa has seen considerable active service in Colonial warfare. Although advanced in years he joined Brabant's Horse in the S. African War, and was latterly Commandant for the District of Tarka, Cape Colony (medal).

VINE, Sir John Richard Somers, K.C.M.G., B.A., F.R.G.S., of York Road, Brighton, Eng., of Bank Buildings, Johannesburg, and of the Devonshire, National Liberal, and Athenaeum (Johannesburg) Clubs, comes of an old Somerset family and was born under the shadow of Wells Cathedral, Dec. 10, 1847. Sir Somers received his early education at the Grammar School, Spalding, proceeding to Cam bridge as a non-collegiate student, from where he ultimately found his way into the Gallery A at Westminster and subsequently filled every post that offers in a newspaper office, including that of a War Correspondent, his first experience in that capacity being the Franco-German War of 1870-71. He subsequently attracted the attention of Sir Sydney Waterlow, to whom he became Private Secretary when he was elected Lord Mayor, and obtained some prominence under several of his successors in connection with historic City functions and with the Bengal Famine Relief Fund, the Fund for the Relief of the Inundated Departments of the South of France and Hungary, etc. He is a prominent Freemason, ranking as Past Grand Deacon of the English Constitution of Freemasons. Sir Somers was the first elected Master of the Savage Club Lodge, and was for some years Hon. Secretary of the Savage Club. He has interpolated his life with wide travel; has circumnavigated the globe several times, and has more than once visited South Africa, south of the Zambesi. He acted as Hon. Secretary of the National Leprosy Fund, a Society that has done so much, not only to ameliorate but to discover the primary cause of leprosy, and of which the present King was the active President.

In connection with this Fund he was made a Knight of Grace of the Order of St. John of Jerusalem, and he is also a C.M.G.; a Queen's Medalist with clasps; a Commissioner of Lieutenancy for London; a Knight Commander of the Grand Ducal Order Ernestine (Saxe Coburg and Gotha); Knight Commander of the Order of Kalakos of Hawaii; Knight of the Orders of Franz Joseph of Austria and Leopold of Belgium, etc. He is the practical exponent of the adaptation of phonetic communication between civilised and savage races by means of expressive signs, and in his travels adopted a unique system of getting at the root of aboriginal languages by the utilising of phonograph to recount sounds of speech. He is a Fellow of the Royal Statistical Society, and an author of Standard works on English Municipal Laws and Government. He married, in 1870, Eliza, dau. of Wm. Porter, of Pinner.

VINTCENT, Joseph, B.A., LL.B. (Camb.), Senior Judge of the High Court of Southern Rhodesia; of Bulawayo, and of the Civil Service (C.T.) and Bulawayo Clubs, is the eldest son of the late L. A. Vintcent, M.L.A. (C.C.). He was born Nov. 12, 1861, at Mossel Bay, C.C., and was educated at the Diocesan Coll., Rondebosch (C.T.), at Charterhouse (England), and at Cambridge Univ. Mr. Vintcent was called to the Bar, Middle Temple, Jan., 1885, and was admitted Advocate of Supreme Court of C.C. in March in the same year. He was appointed Crown Prosecutor for the Crown Colony of British Bechuanaland March, 1886, and held that office till June, 1894. In Jan., 1892, he was appointed Crown Prosecutor for the Bechuanaland Protectorate, which office he held in conjunction with the Crown Prosecutorship of British Bechuanaland. In Jan., 1893, he was appointed a member of the Concession Commission for the Bechuanaland Protectorate. In 1894 he was appointed Judge of the High Court of Matabeleland, and was President of the Land Commission appointed under the Matabeleland Order in Council, 1894; and was a member of the Council under such Order. He acted as Administrator to Southern Rhodesia from Nov., 1895, to Nov., 1896. In Dec., 1898, he was appointed Senior Judge of the High Court of Southern Rhodesia, He was nominated a member of the Legislative Council of Southern Rhodesia in 1899-1900. He was a member of the Old Carthusian Football team which won the Association Challenge Cup in the season of 1880-81, and was in the Camb. Univ. Football Assoc. XI. in the season of 1882-3. He married, Oct. 14, 1891, Hester Elizabeth, second dau. of the late Henry Myburgh, of Wynberg, Cape Town.

VISSER, A. G., represented the electoral division of Victoria West in the Cape House of Assembly, to which he was returned at the general election in 1904. He was a member of the S.A. party, but subsequently resigned his seat.

VIVIAN, Lord, of Glynn, Bodmin, and of Brooks's and the Bachelors' Clubs, was born in 1878, and is son of the 3rd Baron. He was educated at Eton, and formerly belonged to the 17th Lancers, serving in the S. African War, in which he was severely wounded. He married, in 1903, Barbara, dau. of William F. Fanning.

VLOK, Rev., Pastor of the Dutch Reformed Church at Picquetburg, Co. He tried to keep his people loyal during the Boer War (1899-02) and took his turn in the trenches when his town was attacked. His loyalty brought upon him the displeasure of his congregation. He was boycotted by his brethren of the D.R.C., and was compelled to give up his ministry, after twenty-one years' service, on a pension (Nov., 1902).

VOELKLEIN, Franz, of London Wall Buildings, London, is a cousin of the late Alfred Beit (q.v.) and one of his executors. Mr. Voelklein is a partner in the firm of Messrs. Wernher, Beit and Co. (see Sir Julius Wernher), is a London agent of the Jumpers G.M. Co., Ltd., and the Transvaal Consolidated Land and Exploration Co., Ltd.

VON BUCH, Carl, of 4, Sun Court, Cornhill, London, E.C., is Chairman and Managing Director of the Quasie G.M. Co., Ltd., West African Prospectors, Ltd., Chairman of the Kumassi Exploration Co., Ltd., and director of the United African Lands, Ltd.

VON HESSERT, Karl Friedrich, of 64, Heerdweg, Darmstadt, Germany, and of the Rand and Turf Clubs (Johannesburg); is son of Lieut-Col. von Hessert, of Darmstadt, where he was born Oct. 26, 1855, and educated. He went to S.A. in the service of the French D.M. Co., late in 1880, and took over the management of part of that Co.'s works until 1889, when the property was absorbed by the De Beers group. Mr. von Hessert then proceeded to Johannesburg; took an active part in the development of the Witwatersrand fields, and was for many years a Director of the Crown Reef, Champ d'Or, Ferreira, Geldenhuis Estate, Main Reef, New Modderfontein, Wemmer, Wolhuter, Bantjes, Driefontein, and Village G.M. Cos., and of the Transvaal Coal Trust, City and Suburban Trams, the Alexander Estate, and several other less important concerns. He retired from active business in 1902, and has since settled in Darmstadt. During a visit to Europe Mr. von Hessert took part in the Bulgarian-Servian War, and received for his services then rendered the Order of St. Alexander and the Bulgarian War medal. He married, Nov. 9, 1895, Victoria, dau. of Col. Adolf von Herff, of Darmstadt.

VON PUTTKAMER, Jesko, late Governor of the Cameroons; was recalled by the German Colonial Office in order that a minute investigation might be made into cruelties towards native chiefs and others in South-West Africa, for which Herr von Puttkamer is alleged to be responsible. The matter was to be dealt with in the Reichstag as early as possible in 1906. (See King Aqua.)

VON RADOWITZ was one of the German Plenipotentiaries at the Moroccan Conference at Algeçiras in 1906.

VON RADOWITZ, junior, was Secretary to the German Plenipotentiary at the Moroccan Conference at Algeçiras in 1906.

VON RECHENBERG, Baron, of Dar-es-Salaam, German East Africa, was appointed Governor of German E. Africa in 1906. He had previously taken part in the joint deliberations of the British and German Boundary Commissions which had led to a settlement completely satisfactory to the German Colonial Office.

VON RICHTHOFEN, Baron, LL.D.. of Berlin was born at Jassy, Roumania, in 1847, and saw a good deal of the world as a child, his father having been a diplomatist. He served in the German-Austrian and Franco-German wars; was in the Imperial Civil Service in Alsace-Lorraine from 1871 to 1876; went into the Foreign Office in the latter year, and in 1885 was sent to Cairo as first German member of the *Caisse de la Dette*, assisting not a little in bringing about the present excellent state of Egyptian finances. In 1887 he was in Constantinople while Sir H. Drummond Wolff was carrying on his negotiations with Turkey. In 1889 he and Sir E. Vincent made the necessary preparations for the conversion of the Egyptian Preference Loan, and at the request of the Egyptian Govt. he led the expedition of 1891 with a view to the construction of a railway from the Nile to the Red Sea. During his twelve years' stay in Egypt he greatly assisted his countrymen in the fitting out of their exploring expedition. In 1896 he succeeded Dr. Kayser as head of the German Colonial Council at Berlin, and was Under-Secy. of State for Foreign Affairs from 1897 to 1900.

VOSLOO, A., M.L.A., represents the electoral division of Somerset East in the Cape House of Assembly, to which he was elected in the Bond interest in 1904.

VYVYAN, Col., is eldest son of the Rev. Sir Vyell Vyvyan, of Trelowarren, Cornwall, and served on the Staff in the Matabele Campaign of 1896. He was besieged in Mafeking in the S. African War, and was appointed to the 1st Battn. of the East Kent Regt. in 1902.

VYVYAN, Rt. Rev. Wilmot Lushington, B.A., M.A., Bishop of Zululand, of Vryheid, Natal, and of Isandhlwana, Zululand, was born in England, Aug. 12, 1861, and is third son of the Rev. Sir Vyell Vyvyan, Bart., of Cornwall. He was educated at Charterhouse, Trinity Coll., Cambs., and the Wells Theological Coll. Ordained Deacon in 1888, and Priest in the diocese of Rochester in 1889. From 1888-92, he was Asst. Missioner to the Charterhouse Mission, Southwark, and Missioner from 1892-1900. He was appointed a Missionary in the diocese of Zululand in 1900, until 1902, when he became Bishop. He was consecrated in St. Saviour's Cathedral, Maritzburg, in May, 1903, by the Bishop of Pretoria (Acting Metropolitan). The Bishop is not married.

Following on the Zulu rising in 1906, Bishop Vyvyan wrote to the Natal Govt. alleging that Col. Royston's column early in July took stock belonging to loyal natives, entered kraals, robbing loyal natives of clothes and money, and tearing clothes off women's backs. The Bishop characterised the conduct of the column as a deep disgrace to Englishmen. Further charges were that certain natives found hiding were brought to camp on July 5, five of them being shot the same afternoon, and the bodies thrown into a donga to rot; that the father of three of them who had not taken up arms was forcibly compelled to look on whilst his sons were shot. The Bishop said his object in writing was to endeavour to ensure that if the troops should enter the district again there would be no repetition of such treatment. Col. Royston, on hearing the charges, appointed a Court of Inquiry, consisting of Major Smallie, Major Fraser, and Capt. Dickson. The Court found the charges of robbery not proven. Five native prisoners were undoubtedly shot in attempting to escape near the camp at Rorke's Drift, but the Court considered the shooting justifiable.

Judge Beaumont afterwards held a formal inquiry into the matter, with the result that the Judge's report acquitted Royston's Horse, and considered that the allegations of cruelty were not proved, although the Bishop was justified in bringing the information he received before the notice of the Government.

WAGE, Pieter Gerhard, J.P., F.R.C.I., of Clonane, Indian Road, Wynberg, was born at Stellenbosch, Dec. 3, 1854, and is of Dutch descent. He was destined for the Church, but abandoned it to carry on a legal business at Calvinia, where he served as member of the divisional Council and other local bodies. He was elected M.L.A. for the electoral division of Clanwilliam in 1889, and again in 1893 but in the general election in 1904 he failed to be re-elected to the House of Assembly. He is a J.P. for Cape Town and Wynberg, and takes a great interest in educational matters, being a Director of several institutions in Cape Town. He married, in 1880, Martha S. Wrensch.

WAGER, Harold W. T., F.R.S., F.L.S., H.M. Inspector of Secondary Schools for the Board of Education, Lond., of Hendre, West Park, Far Headingly, Leeds, was born in Gloucestershire in 1863. He was educated at the Royal Coll. of Science, Lond., and has taken a keen interest in local natural History Societies. He was President of the Leeds Nationalists' Club and Scientific Assn., and Chairman of the botanical section of the Yorks. Naturalists' Union; has acted as Secretary of the Biological and Botanical Sections of the British

Assn., and presided over the Botanical Section of the Assn. on their meeting in S. Africa in 1905; also Secretary of the Committee appointed by them to consider the teaching of botany in schools. He is the author of numerous papers and addresses on the methods of teaching Botany and Nature Study, and has written memoirs on the cytology and reproduction of the lower organisms. Formerly he was Lecturer in Botany at Victoria Univ., Deputy Reader in Botany at Cambridge Univ., and was Examiner in the subject at Cambridge, Durham, and Victoria Universities. He married, in 1894, Winifred, dau. of Prof. L. C Miall, D.Sc., F.R.S., of Leeds Univ.

WAGNER, L., of Messrs. Wernher, Beit and Co., 1, London Wall Buildings, E.C. (see Sir Julius Wernher), is a director of the Beira Junction Railway (Port Beira to Fontesvilla), Ltd., Beira Railway Co., Ltd., Lisbon Electric Tramways, Ltd., London Wall Estates, Ltd., and the Nigel G.M. Co., Ltd., and is on the London Committee of Bonanza, Ltd., City and Suburban G.M. Co., Ltd., Durban Roodepoort Deep, Ltd., Ferreira Deep, Ltd., Geldenhuis Deep, Ltd., Glen Deep, Ltd., Glyn's Lydenburg, Ltd., Hercules Co., Ltd., Jumpers Deep, Ltd., Langlaagte Deep, Ltd., Modderfontein Extension, Ltd., New Heriot G.M. Co., Ltd., Nourse Mines, Ltd., Rose Deep, Ltd., Transvaal G.M. Estates, Ltd., West Roodeport Deep, Ltd., and the Witwatersrand Deep, Ltd.

WAKE, Capt. Hereward, D.S.O., of Courtenhall, Northampton, was born in London Feb. 11, 1876, and is the eldest son of Sir Hereward Wake, Bart. He was educated at Eton and Sandhurst, and joined the 60th King's Royal Rifles in 1897 he served in the S. African Wax in 1899-1902.

WALEFFE, Fernand, of the Congo Free State, first arrived at the Congo in 1896, and carried out in succession the duties of Judge and substitute at Matadi, and State Assistant Attorney. He has hold the position of State Attorney since Aug. 24, 1900; is a Knight of the Royal Order of the Lion, and is decorated with the Star of Service with two stripes.

WALKER, Dr., of St. John, New Brunswick, is a coloured barrister who is promoting a scheme to establish in Africa a British Colony of English-speaking educated negroes, with the object of ultimately bringing the whole of the African continent into Christian civilisation. Dr. Walker inaugurated his propaganda in Canada and U.S.A. in order to give publicity to his ideas. His plan is then to proceed to Africa, to select land for the proposed colony, and afterwards to visit England with a view to completing arrangements with the Imperial Govt. for establishing the Colony.

WALKER, Major Henry Alexander, was born Oct. 20, 1874, and entered the Royal Fusiliers in 1894. Since 1901 he has been employed with the King's African Rifles, and served in the operations in Somaliland in 1903. He was promoted Major in 1906 for services rendered in connection with the Nandi rebellion.

WALKER, Capt. John Douglas Glen, D.S.O., the Black Watch; of the Compatriots', Caledonian, and Prince's Clubs, was born Nov. 15, 1874, and is son of Col. Selby Walker. He was educated at Wellington Coll. and the R.M.C., and served in S. Africa in 1894-5, in India in 1896-9, and the S. African War in 1899-02, when he was present at the siege of Ladysmith, as Signalling Officer with Sir George White, and afterwards with M.I. in Lord Dundonald's Brigade. He took part also with the 11th Div. to Komati Poort, and was with Col. Garrett's column in Free State and Transvaal drives at the end of the war (S. African medal, King's medal, DS.O, and nine clasps). He was Unionist Parliamentary candidate for the Central Div. of Edinburgh, but was defeated at the election in Jan, 1906.

WALKER, Dr Philip C., B.A., M.B., B.Ch., B.A.O. (Trinity Coll., Dublin); of Potchefstroom, Transvaal, was late Resident Medical Officer at the Liverpool Fever Hospital and the City Hospital, Parkhill, Liverpool; was late Medical Officer of Health for the Fermon Electrical Division, Co. Cavan; late Medical Officer at Farney Baronial Fever Hospital, Carrickmacross; Asst. Medical Officer of Health, Paisley, and Asst. Physician at the Paisley Fever and Smallpox Hospitals. He was appointed District Medical Officer of Health for the Western Transvaal in 1902.

WALKER, Brev. Lieut.-Col. William George,

V.C., 4th Goorkha Rifles, of the East India United Service Club, is the son of Depy.-Surgeon William Walker, LL.D., and Hon. Physician to the Queen. He was born at Naini Tal, India, May 29, 1863, and was educated at Haileybury, St. John's Coll., where he graduated M.A., and at Sandhurst. In 1885 he joined the Suffolk Regt. in India, and in May, 1887, he transferred to the 4th Goorkhas. He was in 1891 with the Miranzai Expedition, receiving the medal with clasp. He was also with the 1895 Waziristan Expedition, receiving the clasp. In Aug., 1896, he received his Captaincy. In 1898 to 1903 he was seconded with Imperial Service Troops, and in Jan. of the latter year joined the Somaliland Field Force, being granted, in Aug., 1903, the Victoria Cross, the coveted Cross also going to Capt. Holland (q.v.), Indian Army. The story of their heroism is told as follows: during the return of Major Gough's column to Danop on April 22, 1903, after the action at Daratoleh, the rearguard got considerably in rear of the column, owing to the thick bush and to having to hold their ground while wounded men were being placed on camels. At this time Captain Bruce was shot through the body from a distance of about twenty yards, and fell on the path, unable to move. Captains Walker and Holland, two men of the 2nd Batt. King's African Rifles, one Sikh, and one Somali of the Camel Corps, were with him when he fell. In the meantime the column, being unaware of what had happened, were getting further away. Captain Holland then ran back some 500 yards and returned with assistance to bring off Captain Bruce, while Captain Walker and the men remained with that officer, endeavouring to keep off the enemy, who were all around in the thick bush. This they succeeded in doing, though not before Captain Bruce was hit a second time, and the Sikh wounded. But for the gallant conduct displayed by these officers and men, Captain Bruce must have fallen into the hands of the enemy.

WALL, Benson, P., M.I.C.E., of St. Luke's, Parktown, Johannesburg, and of the Athenaeum Club, Johannesburg, was born at Lucknow, Aug. 14, 1865. He began his career on the Indian Midland Rly. as an Asst. Engineer under Mr. Crelin Cregeen, M.I.C.E., and after completing a large dam for the Jhansi Station Waterworks, was placed in charge of the Naraim Bridge. In 1899 he joined

the Staff of the Delhi-Umballar Rly. Co., and later on was transferred to the East Coast Rly. between Madras and Calcutta; was employed for ten years on heavy constructional work, including the plate-laying and maintenance of 350 miles of railway. He came to England in 1902, and was appointed Chief Engineer of the Central S. African Rly. in 1903, and since then has been engaged in the construction and survey of over 1,000 miles of new railways in the Transvaal and O.R.C. He married, Feb 4, 1889, the dau. of J. W. Wilson, of Dehra Doon, India.

WALLACE, William, C.M.G. (1897), of Northern Nigeria, and of the Royal Societies Club, was born in 1850, and is son of James Wallace, of Aberbrothick. He has been chiefly occupied during his long service in Nigeria, dating from 1882, in acquiring and consolidating British interests, and gaining political influence for the Royal Niger Co., of whose territories he became Administrator, concluding numerous treaties with native potentates, one being with the Sultan of Sokoto (1894). Mr. Wallace was appointed Deputy High Commissioner for Northern Nigeria in 1900, and besides the C.M.G. is decorated with three West African medals with clasps, and the Coronation medal. He married, in 1891, Christine Baillie, dau. of Joseph Richard, of Dundee.

WALLACH, B., of the Wanderers' Club, Johannesburg, played in the Cricket XI. for London County several times during 1903, and is generally considered to be nearly the equal of E. A. Halliwell (q.v.) behind the wickets. He accompanied the South African XI. to England in 1904.

WALLIS, Capt. Charles Braithwaite, J.P., F.G.S., F.R.G.S., F.R.C.I., of the British Consulate, Monrovia, Liberia, and of the Royal Societies' and United Forces Clubs, is the son of Charles Woodward Wallis M.A., B.L., of the Middle Temple. He was born June 25, 1873, and was educated at Shrewsbury School, and the Military College, Oxford. He joined the 4th Battn. Manchester Regt. as Second Lieut. in 1894 became Lieutenant and Instructor of Musketry, 1896, and Captain in 1895. He was appointed to the West African Frontier Force in Sierra Leone in 1895; took part in the Mendi and Sherbro Expeditions, and the Protectorate Expedition in 1899, when he was in command of a column, and received the thanks of the Governor-in-Chief (despatches, medal and clasps). During the rising in Sierra Leone, Captain Wallis was attacked and surrounded on April 27, 1898, by great numbers of the insurgents at Gambi, on the Small Boom River. The attacks of the natives, who had already committed most horrible atrocities, were continued with fury for four days and three nights, Capt. Wallis having only twenty-seven native soldiers at his disposal, and a limited supply of ammunition. During the evening of the third night, having succeeded in saying most of the women and children in the place, Capt. Wallis and his small force managed to reach a spot of temporary safety thirteen miles away, after rowing the whole night down the river in an open boat. In 1899 Capt. Wallis was transferred to the Cameronians, and served in India with the regiment until 1901, when, under the Colonial Office, he was appointed Asst.-Commissioner in the Sierra Leone Protectorate. He acted as Commissioner during 1901-3. From January to July, 1904, he was made Acting Commissioner, Coroner, Sub Collector of Customs, Commissioner of the Court of Requests, and Hon. Inspector of Police of Sherbro. In 1905 he was promoted to be Commissioner in the Protectorate of Sierra Leone. In the same year he was sent by the Foreign Office to Monrovia at an important crisis to act as H.M. Consul for Liberia. He took part in the military operations against the Gissis, when a British column entered Liberia to punish the raiding chief Kaffura. During the same year he was admitted to study law at the Middle Temple, and was again sent to Liberia by the Foreign Office, being appointed H.M. Consul at Monrovia in 1906. In 1901 Capt. Wallis received the silver medal and diploma of the Royal Humane Society for saving the life of a soldier in West Africa. He is a member of the African Society, and has published *The Advance of our West African Empire* (1903). Unmarried.

WALTERS, Rev. Frederick Wilfrid, J.P., of Winchester, was born at Winchester, Oct. 11, 1863, and was educated at Hamilton House Sch. and at Exeter Coll., Oxen, of which he was Hasker Scholar. He graduated B.A. with 2nd class theological honours in 1886, and M.A. in 1890, and about the same period was a student at the London Hospital, taking his M.R.C.S. Eng., and L.R.C.P., Lond. (1892) degrees. After some years of Church work in and about London he became Principal of the Native College and Priest-in-charge of Isandhlwana and Nondweni, Zululand (Jan., 1893). He was appointed District Surgeon and Missionary at Nongoma, Zululand, in Apr., 1894, and a J.P. in 1897. He married, in 1888, Helen Millicent, dau. of the Rev. Ed. Mansfield.

WALTERS, Hugh, of 6, Tokenhouse Yard, London, E.C., is on the London Committee of the Lace Diamond Mining Co., Ltd., Lydenburg Gold Farms Co., Ltd., and the Natal Navigation Collieries, Ltd.

WALTON, Edgar Harris, M.L.A., of Port Elizabeth, C.C., is son of the Rev. J. M Walton, M.A., formerly Pres. of the Wesleyan Conference for Great Britain and S. Africa, and is brother of the eminent K.C., Sir Lawson Walton. He went out to the Cape in the lat seventies, and became associated with the firm of Richards, Glanville and Co. He has been long identified with Port Elizabeth, and has represented that Constituency in the House of Assembly since 1895, having been re-elected in Feb., 1904. Originally opposed to Mr. Cecil Rhodes' alliance with the Bond, he became reconciled with him after the rupture following on the Jameson Raid. He became Treasurer Gen. in Dr. Jameson's first Ministry (Feb. 1904). Mr. Walton is the proprietor and editor of the *Eastern Province Herald*, of P.E.

WANNENBURG, P. S., was formerly one of the most esteemed judicial officials of the late Boer Government in his position as Fourth Criminal Magistrate of Johannesburg. The served throughout the late S. African War a Chief Staff Officer to the late General Louis Meyer, and since the declaration of peace he has been studying law in London, being called to the Bar at the Middle Temple in the middle of 1906, afterwards returning to South Africa.

WARD, A. E. N., of 65, London Wall, London, E.C., is a well-known solicitor, and represents the interests of Mr. Abe Bailey (q.v.) it the City. Mr. Ward is Chairman of the London and Johannesburg Trust Co. and on the London Committee of the

Witwatersrand Township Estate and Finance Corporation, and is a director of the African Farms, the South African Gold Mines, the Voorspoed Diamond, the Witbank Colliery, and several other important companies.

WARBURG, Oscar, E., of 2, Craven Hill, London, W., is a director of Charles Butters and Co., Ltd., Exploration Assets Co., Ltd., Exploration Co., Ltd., and the United South African Association, Ltd.

WARD Rev. Canon Algernon, M.A., of 5, Rue du Musée, Alexandria, Egypt, The Limes, Hagworthingham, Lincs., and of the Union Club, Alexandria, was born in 1868. He is only son of Rev. Rob. Ward, B,A., Mathematical Scholar of Christ's Coll., Camb. Canon Ward was educated at the Clergy Sch., Camb., and Cambridge Univ., and is MA. of Durham and Cambridge Universities. He played in the University Lacrosse team, 1888-1890; and was Scholar, Sizar, Divinity Prizeman, and Sub-Librarian of Corpus Christi Coll., Camb., 1887-1890. Subsequently he was Curate of St. Michael's, Coventry; Senior Curate of St. Augustine's, Edgbaston; Curate in sole charge of St. Augustine's Mission Districts; Sub Warden, Tutor, and Divinity Lecturer of Queen's Coll., Birmingham; and he is now Chaplain of St. Mark's, Alexandria, Chaplain of All Saints, Ramleh, and Hon. Canon of St. George's Cathedral Church in Jerusalem. He is author of *Guide to the Study of the Book of Common Prayer*, *Psalmi Poenitentiales*, and has contributed various articles in theological papers. He married, Nov. 10, 1896, Elizabeth Mary, eldest dau. of David Waters, merchant and artist, of Coventry.

WARD, Daniel, K.C., M.A., LL.D., was called to the Bar at the Middle Temple in 1881. He acted as Crown Prosecutor for British Bechuanaland in 1894, Asst. Legal Adviser in the Attorney General's Office, Cape Colony, in 1898, and held the same position in the Transvaal in 1902. He became Legal Adviser in the Transvaal and a member of the Legislative Council there in 1903; is author of Practice at Parliamentary Elections, The Marriage Laws of the Cape Colony, and Digest of the Criminal Law. He was appointed Second Puisne Judge of the Orange River Colony in 1904.

WARD, John, M.P., began work as a labourer at the age of twelve, and fought in the Sudan under Graham in 1885, receiving the Khedive's Star and medal with clasps for Suakin. He takes credit for discovering sewer construction scandals in London, is the founder of the Navvies' Union, and was returned to the House of Commons as Labour Member for Stoke-On-Trent at the General Election in Jan., 1906, having defeated the Conservative candidate, Mr. D. H. Coghill, by 3372 votes.

WARE, Fabian Arthur Goulstone, M.L.C., of Pretoria, is the sixth son of Charles and Amy Carew Ware (née Goulstone). He was born at Clifton, Bristol, 1869, and after being educated privately, proceeded to the Univ. of Paris, where he graduated *Bachelier des Sciences* (Paris). From 1889-99 he was Asst.-Master in Secondary Schools (Bradford Gram. Sch. 1895-1899). From 1900-1901 he was a representative of the Education Committee of the British Royal Commission at the Paris Exhibition. He has been Occasional Inspector of Secondary Schools to the Board of Education in England, and Occasional Examiner to the Civil Service Commission in England. In June, 1901, he joined the staff of the Transvaal Educational Department; became Asst. Director of Education in Sept., 1901, and from Jan. to June, 1903, he was Acting Director of Education for the Transvaal and O.R.C. In May, 1903, he was appointed Member of the Transvaal Legislative Council, and Director of Education, Transvaal, in July, 1903. Mr. Ware has written many works on education. These in elude a translation of *The New Testament* (Père Hyacinthe), 1895, *Teaching of Modern Languages in Prussia*, and *Training of Modern Language Teachers in Prussia*. He has also written a number of special reports of the Board of Education, England; a work on Educational Reform: *The Past of the Board of Education* (Methuen and Co., 1900). He is the author of *Educational Foundations of Trade and Industry* (Harper Bros., 1901), and during 1900 and 1901 wrote a number of leading articles in the *Morning Post*. In 1895 he married Anna Margaret, elder dau. of E. W. Phibbs, of Clifton.

WARNER, Clarence Jenkins, of the Umtata Club, Tembuland, S. Africa, was born at Queenstown

(Cape Colony), Aug. 7, 1860; is eldest son of the Rev. E. J. Warner, Wesleyan Missionary; was educated at Lesseyton Collegiate Sch., Lesseyton, Cape Colony, and entered Cape Civil Service (Native Department) in 1878; was appointed A.R.M. for the district of Nqamakwe, 1885 Chief Clerk to the Chief Magistrate of the territories of Tembuland and Transkei, 1892 promoted to office of Resident Magistrate for the district of Engcobo, 1894; appointed R.M. for the district of Nqamakwe, 1899. Recreations: lawn tennis, quoits, chess. He married, in 1894, Jessie, second dau. of Rev. W. Shaw Caldecott.

WARNER, Pelham Francis, B.A., of 15, Tedworth Sq., Chelsea, S.W., and of the M.C. Club, was born Oct. 2, 1873, and is son of the late C. W. Warner, C.B. He was educated at Rugby and Oriel Coll., Oxford, and was called to the Bar at the Inner Temple in 1900. He acts as cricket correspondent to the *Westminster Gazette* and *Rand Daily Mail*, is athletic editor of the *Captain*, and has written articles in various magazines and newspapers, chiefly on cricket. Mr. Warner has played cricket all over the world, captaining elevens in S. Africa, Australia, New Zealand, and the United States; was a member of Lord Hawke's team to the W. Indies and S. Africa, and in 1903-4 captained the M.C.C. team in Australia which recovered the ashes. He also captained the M.C.C. team in S. Africa in 1905-6. This team suffered its third successive defeat in the Test Matches at Johannesburg in March, 1906, thus losing the rubber. The first was the best game of the three. It was played at Johannesburg, where South Africa, chiefly owing to some plucky batting by White (81) and Nourse (93), when the Colonial chance of victory seemed very slight, pulled the match out of the fire, and won by one wicket. The second match was a rather one sided affair, South Africa winning by nine wickets. The third ended in a victory for the Colonials by 243 runs.

Mr. Warner has played frequently for the Gentlemen at Lords, and is a member of the Marylebone Club Committee. He is the author of *Cricket in Many Climes*, *Cricket Across the Seas*, and *How we recovered the Ashes*. He married, June 7, 1904, Agnes, dau. of the late Henry A. Blyth.

WARNER, Robert, of 10, Walbrook, London, E.C., is Chairman and Managing Director of the Kaffirs Consolidated Investment and Land Co., Ltd., and Westralian Consolidated Investment Co., Ltd., Chairman of the Phoenix Land Society, Ltd., Salisbury Land Corp., Ltd., and the United Kingdom Land Society, Ltd., and is a director of the British South Africa Tobacco Plantations, Ltd., Brockie-Pell Arc Lamp, Ltd., Industrial Union, Ltd., Sheba Crown, Ltd., and the Yan and Axim Exploration Syndicate, Ltd.

WARREN, Gen. Sir Charles, Colonel-Commandant R.E., G.C.M.G., K.C.B., Knight of Justice of the Order of the Hospital of St. John of Jerusalem; of the Athenaeum and United Service Clubs; is the son of Major-Gen. Sir Charles Warren, K.C.B., Col. of the 96th Regiment. He was born Feb. 7, 1840, at Bangor, N. Wales, was educated at Bridgnorth Gram. Sch., Cheltenham Coll., Royal Military Coll., Sandhurst, and the Royal Military Acad., Woolwich, and passed into the Royal Engineers in 1857. He conducted excavations at Jerusalem and reconnaissance work in Palestine, 1867 to 1870; and began his long career of usefulness in S.A. as Special Commissioner in the Griqualand West and O.F.S. Boundary Line in 1876-7 (C.M.G.). He was also Special Commissioner in connection with the land question of Griqualand West in 1877. He commanded the Diamond Fields Horse in the Transkei War of 1875 (brevet Lieut. Col.); was Chief of Staff during the Griqualand West Rebellion in 1875; and commanded the Field Force against the Bechuanas and Korannas in 1878-79. He was appointed Administrator of Griqualand West in 1879, and went to Chatham in the same year as Instructor in Surveying, S.M.E. In 1882 he was employed under the Admiralty in the desert of Arabia Petraea to secure the murderers of Prof. Palmer (K.C.M.G.), and he commanded the Bechuanaland Expedition with the rank of Major-Gen. in 1884-5 (G.C.M.G.). Sir Chas. Warren successfully contested a Parliamentary seat in the Liberal interest in 1885. He was in command of the troops at Suakin with rank of Major-Gen., and was Governor-Gen. of the Red Sea Littoral in 1886; was Commissioner of Metropolitan Police from 1886-89 (K.C.B.); commanded the troops in the Straits Settlements from 1889-96; and had command of the Thames District, 1895-8. In the recent S. African War he commanded the 5th Division, taking part in the relief of Ladysmith, 1899-1900, and in the latter year he once more went to Griqualand West and Bechuanaland as Military Governor.

Sir Charles is the author of *Orientation of Ancient Temples*, *The Temple or the Tomb*, *Underground Jerusalem*, *On the Veldt in the Seventies*, and *The Ancient Cubit and Our Weights and Measures*. He married Sept. 1, 1864, Fanny Margaretta, dau. of Samuel Haydon, of Millmead, Guildford.

WARU, Comte Jacques de, of Paris, is a director of the North Witwatersrand Gold Mines, Ltd., and Waru's Exploration Syndicate, Ltd.

WARWICK, Earl of, of Warwick Castle, Warwickshire, and Easton Lodge, Dunmow Essex, was born in 1853, and is the fifth Earl of the line. The Barony of Brooke, assumed by the eldest sons of the Earls of Warwick, is one which long antedates that of the present earldom. The Barony was conferred upon the third Sir Fulke Greville, the biographer of Sir Philip Sidney, together with a grant of Warwick Castle, in 1620, but the earldom was created in 1759 in favour of the eighth baron to whom was also given the right to use the arms of the ancient Earls of Warwick. The last of the first line of Warwicks fell at the battle of Barnet in 1471; the last of the second line was beheaded, and his son, to whom the title was subsequently restored, died childless in 1589. Then for twenty-nine years there was no Earl of Warwick, but in 1618 the third line came in existence and lasted till the death of the eighth earl without heirs once more extinguished the title.

The present Lord Warwick was educated at Oxford University, and entered the House of Commons in 1879 as Conservative member for East Somerset, afterwards representing Colchester from 1888 to 1892. He is Lord Lieutenant of Essex, and was Mayor of the city Warwick for a couple of years. Lord Warwick has leanings towards agriculture and freemasonry, and towards the end of 1905 he went to Uganda, bent on big game shooting. His bag included lions, hippopotami, and rhinoceroses. In

1881 he married a dau. of Col. the Hon. C. H. Maynard.

Lady Warwick, who is one of the most handsome women in the peerage, has recently become famous in another direction by a vigorous campaign as a leader of socialism and a reformer.

WATERMEYER, Captain Joubert Henry Hutton, D.S.O., of Middelburg, Transvaal, was born in South Africa, and is son of C. F. J. Watermeyer. He was educated at the South African College, and in 1889 was admitted Government Land Surveyor in Cape Colony. In 1893 he joined the Cape Town Highlanders, with whom he served in the Bechuanaland Expedition in 1897 (medal with clasp), and he also saw service in the South African War in 1899-1902, as A.D.C. to the Commander-in-Chief, afterwards as District Commandant; present at the operations in the Orange Free State, including the operations at Paardeberg, the action at Driefontein, the operations in the Transvaal, the action near Johannesburg, and the operations in the Transvaal east of Pretoria, including the action at Belfast (despatches and D.S.O.). Captain Watermeyer is President of the National Sporting Club of South Africa. He married, in 1906, Miss Henrietta Perkins, of Worcester.

WATHERSTON, Major A. E. G., formerly of the Survey Dept. of the Gold Coast Colony, where he was Chief Boundary Commissioner, was transferred to Egypt in 1904 for duty in the Survey Dept. there.

WATKEYS, William David Eustace, of Bloemfontein, and of the Bloemfontein Club, was born at Brecon, S. Wales, July 15, 1871; was educated at St. Andrew's Coll., Grahamstown and at Grey Coll., Bloemfontein, where he follows the profession of law.

WATKINS-PITCHFORD, Lieut. Colonel Herbert, J.P., F.R.C.V.S., of the Laboratory, Maritzburg, and of the Victoria Club, P.M.B., was born in England, June 3, 1866, and is son of the Rev. J. Watkins-Pitchford, M.A., of Shropshire. He was appointed as Principal Veterinary Surgeon to the Natal Govt. in 1896, and was successful in devising the immunisation against the disease rinderpest which has since been universally adopted under the name of the serum system. He served throughout the S. African War, including the siege of Ladysmith, as P.V.O. on the staff of the Natal Commandant, with the rank of Major. In 1902 he was appointed Bacteriologist to the Govt. of Natal and Director of the Natal Laboratory. He is a J.P. for the county of Maritzburg. He married May, dau. of Henry Willson, M.D. of Weybridge.

WATSON, Major James Kiero, C.M.G., D.S.O., of Cairo, and of the Naval and Military Club, was born in 1865, and is son of the late Major-Gen. J. K. Watson. He was educated at Clifton Coll, and Sandhurst. In 1885 he entered the Ring's Royal Rifles, and served with them in Burma. He was attached to the Egyptian Army in 1894-99, acting as A.D.C. to the Sirdar in the Khartoum and Dongola expeditions (despatches; 4th class Medjidieh and Osmanieh; D.S.O.). He acted as A.D.C. to Lord Kitchener in the S. African War in 1899-1901 (C.M.G., despatches), and in 1901 he returned to the Egyptian Army. In 1905 Major Watson was appointed Resident A.D.C. to His Highness the Khedive, being the first British officer to act as such to the present Khedive.
He married, in 1902, Katharine, dau. of H. C. Nisbet, of Wimbledon.

WATSON, Septimus Wooler, of Palmerston House, London, E.C., is a director of the African Estates and Mining Co., Ltd., and the Union Jack Consolidated Mines, Ltd.

WATT, the Hon. Thomas, C.M.G., M.L.A., of Newcastle, Natal, and Pietermaritzburg, Natal, was born at Glasgow, Jan. 20, 1857, and is the son of Thos. Watt, of Orkney, Scotland. He was educated primarily at a private school, afterwards going to Glasgow University. He was admitted as a Scotch solicitor in 1883, and in the same year went out to Natal, where he became managing clerk to Sir Henry Bale. Since 1886 he practised as an advocate and solicitor at Durban, and latterly at Newcastle. The electors of Newcastle returned Mr. Watt to the House of Assembly in 1901, and he became a member of the Natal Defence Commission in 1902, and thereafter of the permanent Local Defence Committee, of which he is now president. He served during part of the South African War of

1899-02 as Lieut. in the I.L.H., and later as Captain of the Newcastle Town Guard (despatches). Mr. Watt was appointed Minister of Justice for Natal in Sir George Sutton's cabinet from July, 1903, until May, 1905, when he joined Mr. Smyth's coalition Ministry with the same portfolio. He married, in 1886, Mary, dau. of the late G. Lindup.

WAY, Captain Alfred Cotton, of the Old Manor House, West Molesey, Surrey, is a director of the Bibiani Gold Fields, Ltd., Human Copper Mines, Ltd., and the West African Hinterland Consolidated, Ltd.

WEARIN, E. M., of the Green Point and Sea Point Swimming Clubs, C.T., holds the 500 and 200 yards South African Swimming Championship, his time in the 1903 contests being 7 min. 24 1-5 sec. for the former, and 2 min. 58 3-5 sec. for the latter. He also held the championship over these two distances in 1902.

WEBB, Clement Davies, of Johannesburg, and the Rand Club, was born in King Williamstown. He is son of Frederick C. Webb, a farmer who settled in S.A. in 1820. He was educated at the Diocesan Coll., Rondebosch, and served in the native wars of 1879 and 1880. Clem Webb, as he is popularly called, has resided most of his life in Queenstown, C.C., where he was known as an athlete, gymnast, and boxer. Between the years 1880-1885 he won a number of trophies for these sports, and was capt. of the Swifts Football Club (Queenstown) for two years—a club which won every match in 1885 and 1887. He was one of the original committee of the long-famous Wanderers' Sporting Club in Johannesburg, and for two years he won the heavyweight amateur boxing competition, and was never once beaten. Short sight, however, compelled him to give up this form of sport.

Mr. Webb was sent by the Cape Govt. as one of the representatives of the Cape Court to the Colonial and Indian Exhibition in 1886 (held in London). The discovery of goldfields at Johannesburg so attracted him that he returned to S.A., and shortly afterwards took up his residence in Johannesburg. After the Jameson Raid, and during the imprisonment of the Reformers, Mr.

Webb and a few others formed a secret society, which afterwards developed itself into a branch of the S.A. League. Mr. Webb was the first President, and became a marked man in the Transvaal. He was arrested by the Boers early in 1899, with the late Major Tom Dodd, for having organised a meeting for the purpose of presenting a petition to the British Vice-Consul on the subject of the murder of Edgar by a Boer policeman; and was tried for high treason against the S.A.R. (see Koch, Advocate). Up to the time of the late S.A. War he took a keen interest in political affairs; spoke at most of the League meetings, and proved himself a good organiser. On the outbreak of the S.A. War he joined the T.L.H. as Lieut. in F squad, and was amongst the besieged in Ladysmith. He was then promoted to the command of B squad, and went with the regt. to the relief of Mafeking; was taken ill with typhoid and pneumonia, and afterwards detached by Lord Roberts for special duty in Johannesburg, where he was for some time senior officer of the mounted battn. of the Rand Rifles. Mr. Webb has now retired from taking any active part in politics or public affairs. He has started a weekly paper, called *South African Mines*, which is a resurrection of the old *South African Mining Journal*, and devotes himself entirely to the interests of this paper and the practice of his profession of solicitor and Notary public. He married a Colonial lady in May, 1890.

WEBB, Edward, of Durrington House, Harlow, is Chairman of the African Banking Corp., Ltd. (see W. J. Thompson), and the New Belgium (Transvaal) Land and Development Co., Ltd., and is a director of the Commercial Union Assurance Co., Ltd., and the Transvaal Mortgage, Loan and Finance Co., Ltd.

WEBB, Harry Howard, Ph.B., M.Inst.C.E., M.I.M.M., M.A.I.M.E, of Johannesburg, of the Rand and New Clubs, Johannesburg, and of the University Club, San Francisco, was born at 'Frisco, Cal., Aug. 15, 1853. He is son of Christopher C. Webb, of Cal., whose ancestors settled in America from England in 1702. He was educated in the Univ. of California, at the Royal Sch. of Mines, London, and at the Royal Saxon Sch. of Mines, Vreiberg, Saxony. He went to S.A. in 1895 as Consulting Mining Engineer to several

groups of Rhodesian Cos. of 1896 he succeeded John Hays Hammond (then on trial in Pretoria) as Consulting Engineer to the Cos. of the Consolidated Gold Fields. Mr. Webb is Past Pres. of the S.A. Association of Engineers. He married, March 9, 1887, Miss Virginia Martin.

WEEBER, Pieter Jacobus, M.L.A., is member of the Cape Legislative Assembly for Beaufort West, for which electoral division he was last re-elected in 1904. He is a member of the Bond.

WEIL, Julius, of 1, Gresham Buildings, London E.C., and of the firm of Julius Weil and Co., is a director of the Empress (Rhodesia) Mines, Ltd., Enterprise G.M. and Estates Co., Ltd., Imperial Cold Storage and Supply Co., Ltd., South Rand Exploration Co., Ltd., and the Theta G.M. Co., Ltd. Mr. Weil and his firm bore a great deal of the onus of supplying Commissariat and transport to the troops on the Western side during the South African War.

WEIL, Samuel, J.P., of 8, Kensington Garden Terr., London, was born in 1862; was educated privately, and went on to Eton when quite young. He settled in Bechuanaland after the close of the Bechuanaland Expedition, 1885, joined the firm of Julius Weil, and assisted in the opening up of the trade route to the north by the establishment of stores and transport. He was appointed J.P. in 1896. He took part in the Matabele War of 1898, and organised the transport; carried despatches from Inkwesi, narrowly escaping capture by the enemy, and was reported killed. On the outbreak of rinderpest in 1896, which put an end to the transport machinery upon which the entire country north of Mafeking depended for their food supplies, with his firm he organised mule transport service, thereby saving the country from famine. He took part in the Matabele Rebellion in 1896, and organised the transport and food supplies in the face of great difficulties; organised the whole of the transport service outside of Natal in the late Boer War, 1899-1994 given the rank of Major in Col. Mahon's staff, took part in the relief of Mafeking, and was mentioned in Lord Roberts' despatches.

WEINTHAL, Leo, F.R.G.S., of the Aspens, Sunbury-on-Thames, and 84, Copthall Avenue,

E.C., Managing Director of *The African World and Cape-Cairo Express*, and Editor of the *Anglo-German Courier*, founded in 1901 to foster good relations between the two countries concerned, a direct result of which was the successful visit of the German Editors to England in 1906. Mr. Weinthal was born at Graaff Reinet, C.C., in 1865, and was educated at Hamburg starting business for himself in 1884 at Port Elizabeth. Proceeding to the Transvaal in 1887, he established a State lithographic department for the Govt., and was for some years General Manager for Mr. J. B. Robinson's Transvaal newspapers, and representative of the interests of his group at Pretoria. He was Reuter's Agent at Pretoria from 1888 to 1897, and acted at various times as Special Correspondent in the Transvaal for the *Times* and *Daily Telegraph*. During the Anglo Boer War Mr. Weinthal was Special War Correspondent for Laffans News Bureau, the New York *Sun*, and the Chicago *Record*. After the British occupation he left for Europe, and spent some time on the East Coast of Africa in order to write and compile a popular English handbook for the German Line, entitled *Round Africa by the D.O.A. Line*, which had a good reception. On his return he decided to remain in England, and in 1902 established *The African World*, the only London weekly dealing regularly with important developments in all parts of the dark Continent. *The African World* has since absorbed the *African Review*, and the *Anglo-African Argus*, and has made a reputation for itself by publishing a voluminous Annual issue, and occasional special editions, which are admitted to be quite unique both for their artistic, literary, and pictorial contents.

WEISER, Benito, of Gresham House, London, E.C., is a director of the Kit Tin Mines, Ltd., and the Rietfontein Deep, Ltd.

WELDON, Horace, M.L.C., of Oaklands, Johannesburg, and of the Rand and Pretoria Clubs, was born at Camb., Eng., July 1, 1867, is son of the late Rev. Geo. W. Weldon, Vicar of Bickley, Kent. He was educated in SwitzerLand, King's Coll., London, and the Royal Sch. of Mines, London. He proceeded to the Transvaal in 1893; was Manager of the Consol. Main Reef, Van Ryn, and George Goch Mines; he then managed the

Rietfontein A, and the New Rietfontein Estate Cos. until his appointment as Transvaal Govt. Mining Engineer, April 12, 1901, with a seat in the Legislative Council. He served throughout the Natal Campaign in the Field Force Intelligence under Col. Sandbach. Mr. Weldon is unmarried.

WEMYSS, M. W., Colchester, D.L., J.P., of Westbury Court, Westbury-on-Severn, is Chairman of Burbank's Main Lode (1904), Ltd., Cherokee (Mexican) Proprietary, Ltd., Stroud . Brewery Co., Ltd., and the West Rand Central G.M. Co., Ltd., and director of Klerksdorp Extended, Ltd., Klerksdorp Gold and Diamond Co. (1904), Ltd., Mines and Banking Corp., Ltd., Potosi Consolidated, Ltd., and South East Africa, Ltd.

WELSERSHEIMB, Count, was one of the Austrian Plenipotentiaries at the Moroccan Conference at Algeçiras in 1906.

WENTZEL, Charles Augustus, Chief Magistrate of Johannesburg and the Witwatersrand district; of Charlton Terrace, Johannesburg, and the Rand and Athenaeum Clubs (Johannesburg), was born Jan. 29, 1866, and was educated at the S.A. Coll., C.T., and took the Advocates' Degree (Law) with Honours in 1903 (Transvaal). He practised as Prof. of Law first in C.C. and subsequently in Johannesburg from 1889 to the outbreak of war. On the occupation of Johannesburg by Lord Roberts he was appointed a member of the Judicial Investigation Committee. From July, 1900, to March 1901 he was Legal Adviser to the Military Governor of Pretoria (Gen. Sir John Grenfell Maxwell) and Acting Legal Adviser to the Commander-in-Chief during part of that time, in the absence of Mr. (now Justice) Wessels. In April, 1901, upon the abolition of Military Courts, he was appointed the first Resident Magistrate of Johannesburg. He was senior member of the Special Criminal Court, which sat at Johannesburg from April, 1901, to March, 1903, when trial by judge and jury was resumed. This Court had plenary powers over all offences in the S.E. portion of the Transvaal. He married, Feb. 13, 1895, and has two children. His recreations are golf and lawn tennis.

WERNHER, Sir Julius, Bart., of Bath House, Piccadilly, London, of Luton Hoo, Luton, Beds., and of the Carlton and Arts Clubs, was born at Darmstadt, April 9, 1850, and was educated at Frankfort-on-Maine. Proceeding to S. Africa, he spent ten years in Kimberley, and became chief partner of the great mining and financial firm of Wernher, Beit and Co. (see A. Beit). Sir Julius is in appearance and temperament the very antithesis of his late partner, Mr. Alfred Beit. He is physically strong and exceptionally tall, reflecting in his reposeful look an apparent freedom from nerves and worries which few men with huge responsibilities enjoy, though he has rather felt the strain of the last few years. He is extremely level-headed, and is said to be the best judge of diamonds in London. He takes no active interest in politics, and may be shortly described as a plain merchant prince, sound in views, liberal in charities, and a popular host. Sir Julius is a Fellow of the Zoological Society of London, and his baronetcy was conferred upon him in 1905. He married, June 12, 1888, Miss Alice S. Mankiewicz.

WESSELS, Johannes, Wilhelmus, Second Puisne Judge of the Supreme Court of the Transvaal; of Pretoria, and of the Pretoria, Rand, and Civil Service Clubs; is son of J. B. Wessels, of Green Point, C.T. He was born at Cape Town, March 7, 1862, and was educated at the S.A. Coll.; at the Cape of Good Hope Univ., where he took B.A. and was a Jamieson Scholar; and at Downing Coll., Camb., where he graduated B.A., LL.B. (1st Class Tripos and George Long Scholar). He was called to the Bar at the Middle Temple, where he took a Scholarship, in 1886, and returning to the Cape, practised as an Advocate at the Cape Bar, and afterwards, in 1887, joined the Transvaal Bar. He conducted the defence of the Reform prisoners in 1896, and in 1900 he became Legal Adviser to Lord Roberts and Lord Kitchener, and he received his present appointment in 1902. He married Helen Mary, dau. of Benjamin Duff, I.S.O.

WESTMINSTER, Duke of, of Eaton, Chester, and of Grosvenor House, Upper Grosvenor Street, London, W., is descended from Gilbert le Grosvenour, who came over with the Conqueror. Since then the Grosvenors have mounted the titular ladder until in the seventies the dukedom of Westminster was created, and later still a nuptial alliance was made with the royal family. In another branch, the descent is traced from a Welsh lawyer practising in the 17th century, in London, named Alexander Davis, whose clients were mainly Welsh dairymen, who entrusted Davis with the management of their affairs. The terrifying plague came down upon London, its foetid breath killing most of the clients and their families, so that when the great fire had purged London clean, Davis found himself with many valuable leases in his possession for which there were no claimants. This fortune was afterwards increased in William III's time by the marriage of Mary, Alexander's winsome daughter, to a Grosvenor with an already fat rent-roll.

Hugh Richard Grosvenor, the present Duke, was born March 19, 1879. He succeeded his grandfather, the first Duke, in 1899, and was at one time in the Royal Horse Guards. He acted as A.D.C. to Lord Milner (then Sir Alfred) at the age of twenty, taking part in the Bloemfontein Conference, and in the early days of the S. African War became A.D.C. to Lord Roberts, and hoisted the British flag at Pretoria. But the Duke's connection with S. Africa did not end with the War. In 1905 he purchased an estate of about 18,000 acres, near Ladybrand, some sixty miles from Bloemfontein, in what is known as the conquered territory, and as the most fertile farming country in the Orange River or Transvaal colonies. Here he is settling married farmers from his Cheshire estates, and other home counties. His tenants pay no rent for a year or so, but when they have made sufficient progress, they will pay rent in the shape of a percentage of profits, thus both landlord and tenants will benefit in good years or suffer mutually when times are indifferent. The Duke of Westminster is a Tariff Reformer, with sound views as to the needs of the Empire. He owns some 30,000 acres in Cheshire, but derives an incalculably greater income from his 600 in London, the greater part of Belgravia being built upon his land, which was once a useless swamp. So great is the estate to which he succeeded that the duties paid on the death of the late Duke amounted to £1,200,000, and when the present leases terminate, about 1935, the present head of the

Grosvenor family will be one of the richest men in the country. In Feb., 1901, he married Shelagh, the beautiful daughter of Col. and Mrs. Cornwallis West, of Ruthin Castle, which was built by Edward I late in the thirteenth century. The young Duchess is a sister of Princess Henry of Pless; is a fine horsewoman, and has inherited her mother's musical accomplishments.

WESTON, Henry James, of 62, London Wall, London, E.C., is a director of the Amalgamated Mining and Exploration Co., Ltd., Egyptian Exploration. and Development Co., Ltd., Egyptian Trust and Investment Co., Ltd., United Gold Mines of West Africa, Ltd., and the Vryheid Exploration Co., Ltd.

WETZLAR, J. S., of 27, Daleham Gardens, London, N.W., is Managing Director of the Consolidated Mines Section Co., Ltd., and on the London Board of the Transvaal Coal Trust, Ltd.

WHEELWRIGHT, Charles Apthorpe, C.M.G., of Zoutpansberg, Transvaal, acted as Clerk and Zulu Interpreter in Zululand in 1890; Registrar and Master in the Chief Magistrate's Court, Zululand, in 1894; Resident Magistrate for the Ingwavuma District in 1897, and Resident Magistrate at Mahlabatini in 1898. He was appointed Native Commissioner for the Zoutpansberg District, Transvaal, in 1902, which position he still occupies.

WHELER, .Aubrey Stewart, of Johannesburg, is son of Col. Charles Wheler, I.S.C., and practises as a Consulting Engineer in Johannesburg. He married, Nov. 3, 1904, Blanche Christina, only dau. of S. W. Jameson, and niece of the Cape Premier.

WHIGHAM, H. J., acted as one of the correspondents of the *Morning Post* during the S. African War in 1899-1902. He also served in China on the occasion of the Boxer outbreak. Subsequently he made a tour of the Persian Gulf, writing a series of articles on international interests in that quarter of the globe, and since then he has acted as Special Correspondent to the *Morning Post* in Macedonia.

WHITAKER, George, M.L.A., is one of the new members for King Williamstown in the Cape House of Assembly, to which he was elected in the Progressive interest in 1904.

WHITE, Capt. Hon. Charles James, of the Naval and Military Club, is the son of Lord Annaly, K.P. He was born June 14, 1860, at Rabeny, Co. Dublin, and was educated at Eton. He joined the Royal Fusiliers, 1881, and served at home and in India till 1890, when he proceeded to S.A., and was appointed to the B.S.A. Co.'s Police with several Extra Service Officers, at the time when Col. Ferreira and a commando of Boers attempted to cross the Limpopo and occupy Banjailand. From this they were dissuaded by Dr. Jameson. From 1891 to Jan., 1892, he was in command of the Depot and Remounts at Tuli, Matabeleland. On the reduction of the Police Force, he was appointed Asst. Mining Commissioner and then Mining Commissioner at Hartley Hill. He also served as Resident Magistrate and Chief Commissioner of Police, retaining the latter appointment from Nov., 1892, to Sept., 1895. He reorganised the police from their former military position into a civil body. Capt. White took part in the expedition to Matabeleland in 1893. He was in command of the combined scouts of the Victoria and Salisbury Columns, and was present in all actions until the occupation of Bulawayo (medal and clasp). He retired from the regular army in 1894. He took part in the suppression of the Matabele Rebellion first as Staff Officer to Col. Spreckley, C.M.G., and then in command of White's Flying Column at the reliefs of Salisbury, Hartley Hill, and Enkeldoorn (medal and clasp). Since 1895 Capt. White has been connected with several business undertakings in Rhodesia. He married, Dec. 11, 1901, Evelyn, dau. of F. B. Bulkeley Johnson.

WHITE, G. C., was a member of the South African cricket team which visited England in 1904, having a batting average of 29 inns for thirty innings. He was also one of the best bats in the teams which opposed the M.C.C. in S. Africa in 1905-6.

WHITE, Hetherington, of 9, Mincing Lane, London, E.C., is a partner in the firm of White, Palmer, and Co., Ltd., and is Chairman of the Gold Coast (Wassau) Deep Levels Syndicate, Ltd., and Menzies United Mines, Ltd., and director of the

British Borneo Exploration Co., Ltd., Dagwin Syndicate, Ltd., Fanti Mines, Ltd., Gwyn Mines (Merioneth), Ltd., and the Umniati Development Co., Ltd.

WHITE, Major Hon. Robert, of 16, Stratton St., Piccadilly, and of the Turf, Travellers', and Naval and Military Clubs, is the son of the second Baron Annaly, K.P.; was born Oct. 26, 1861, at Kirkmichael, Dumfriesshire, and was educated at Eton, Sandhurst, and Trinity Coll., Camb. In 1882 he joined the Royal Welsh Fusiliers, and served in the Nile Campaign, receiving the Egyptian medal (1884-5) and the Khedive's star. He was on the Staff of the Cork Dist. 1886-89; on the Staff of the York Dist. 1890-91, and attended the Staff Coll. 1891-92. He was appointed on the Staff of the Rhodesia Horse in 1895, and was one of the British officers who took part in the Jameson Raid, and for this he was imprisoned in Holloway for seven months in 1896-97. He served on the Staff as A.D.C. to Gen. Kelly-Kenny with the 6th Div. in S. Africa in 1900, during the pursuit of Gen. Cronje, and was present at the battles of Paardeberg and Driefontein, at the relief of Kimberley, Lord Roberts's advance to Pretoria, and at Diamond Hill. He was promoted Maj. by Lord Roberts and gazetted in 1901 (despatches, and medal with six clasps). Major White is a partner in the stockbroking firm of Govett and Sons, of 6, Throgmorton Street, E.C., and is not married.

WHITE, Tyndale, J.P., of Stondon Place, Stondon, Brentwood, is Chairman of the Central Egypt Exploration. Co., Ltd., Egyptian Mines Exploration Co., Ltd., Fatira (Egypt) Exploring Co., Ltd., Gas Lighting Improvement Co., Ltd., Gwanda Mines, Ltd., Tanganyika Concessions, and the Zambesi Exploring Co., Ltd., and is director of the Ivanhoe Gold Corporation, Ltd., Lake View Consols, Ltd., and the Warwick Estates Co., Ltd. (See Robert Williams.)

WHITE, Wallis Harry Brinsley, served in the late South African War with Brabant's Horse (Queen's medal and four clasps). He was appointed Inspector of Schools in the Orange River Colony in 1901, and Chief Inspector in 1904.

WHITELEY, Frank, C.M.G., of Oakville, Ilkley,

Yorks, was born at Bradford, Jan. 3, 1856, and went to Natal in 1872, engaging up country in the ivory and ostrich feather trade. He visited the Zambesi, Lake Ngami, and Matabeleland in the 'seventies, and in 1890 started business in Mafeking under the style of Whiteley, Walker and Co., and subsequently opened branches in Bulawayo, Palapye, and other places. Mr. Whiteley was President of the Mafeking Chamber of Commerce for several years, and was Mayor of the town during the siege, being several times mentioned in despatches, and receiving the C.M.C. in 1901. He is now a Director of the Buttermere Green Slate Co. (Cumberland). His recreations are golf and shooting, and he married, in 1892, Sarah Emily, dau. of John Walker, J.P.

WHITFIELD, C. A., of 18, Bishopsgate Street Within, London, E.C., is a director of Hannan's Main Reef G.M. Co., Ltd., Hannan's North Gold Mines, Ltd., Malaria Exploration Co., Ltd., North White Feather Gold Mines, Ltd., and the South Rhodesia Gold Fields, Ltd.

WHYTE, Alexander, was Director of the Scientific and Agricultural Dept. of the East African Protectorate, from which position he retired in 1905. He has been connected with the three Protectorates of Central Africa, Uganda, and E. Africa for the past fourteen years, and has established gardens in all three.

WHYTE, Hon. John Blair, of 45, Redcliffe Gardens, London, S.W., is Chairman of the Transvaal Claims Syndicate, Ltd., and director of the Coronation Extension Syndicate (Transvaal), Ltd., Nile Valley Block E., Ltd., and the United Gold Mines of West Africa, Ltd.

WHYTE, R., of 2, Bury Court, St. Mary Axe, E.C., is a partner in the firm of Robert Whyte and Co., and is on the London Committee of the New Goch Gold Mines, Ltd., New Steyn Estate Gold Mines, Ltd., Sacke Estates and Mining Co., Ltd., Wemmer G.M. Co., Ltd., and the Witwatersrand G.M. Co., Ltd., and is on the London Board of the Johannesburg Estates Co., Ltd.

WIENER, Ludwig, of the Retreat, Newlands, near Cape Town, of the City Club (C.T.), and of the

National Liberal Club, comes from a long-lived stock on his mother's side, she having lived to the age of ninety-four years. He was born in Berlin in 1838, and emigrated to America in 1850. He was educated in Berlin and New York. He left America for S.A. in 1855, and for fifteen years he was in business at Tulbagh and Ceres. Proceeding to C.T. in 1870, he became a partner of Van der Byl and Co., and retired from the firm as senior partner Dec. 31, 1895. In 1899 he started a new business as general merchants under the style and firm of Wiener and Co., Ltd. of which coy. he was appointed chairman for life. For fifteen years he represented C.T. in the House of Assembly, and during this time always fought for cheap food and dear brandy. He was Commissioner for the C.C. at the Chicago World's Fair in 1893. For many years he has been Chairman of the Table Bay Harbour Board, and for a considerable time Pres. of the Chamber of Commerce at C.T. He was also formerly Pres. of the Associated Chambers of Commerce of S.A. He is the Chairman of the Colonial Mutual Life Assurance and the Manchester Assurance Co. Among other philanthropic works, he has been Pres. of the Somerset Hospital. In 1858 he married Miss Barker, niece of M. M. Tate, of Cape Town.

WIGAN, Frederick William, of 15, Southwark Street, S.E., is a partner in the firm of Wigan, Richardson, and Co., and is a director of Eastwood and Co., Ltd., and the South African Breweries, Ltd.

WILCKEN, Anton F., F.R.G.S., of Greffham Court, near Petworth, Sussex, was formerly a well-known resident of Delagoa Bay, and is viewed as one of the most reliable authorities on the Portuguese Province of Mozambique; especially the Lourenço Marques district, where he has still large interests.

WILKINS, Thomas, of 21, Great St. Helen's, London, E.C., is Chairman of the Abassi (Wassan) Gold Mines, Ltd., African Estates and Mining Co., Ltd., and Rosemont Lydenburg Estates, Ltd., and is director of the South African General Syndicate, Ltd., Stratford-on-Avon, Towcester, and Midland, &c., Railway Co., and W. J. Robson and Co., Ltd.

WILKIE, David, of Bloemfontein, O.R.C., served in the S. African Campaign in 1900-1 (Queen's medal with four clasps). He was employed in the Pay Department of the S. African Constabulary from 1902-3, when he was appointed Clerk to the Lieut.-Governor of the Orange River Colony.

WILKIN, Commander Henry Douglas, R.N., D.S.O., of the United Service Club, and of the Royal Naval Club, Portsmouth, was born in India, March 27, 1862, and is son of the late Major Henry J. Wilkin. He entered the *Britannia* as Naval Cadet, June, 1875; was Midshipman in H.M.S. *Serpent* at the bombardment of Alexandria in 1882 and during the Egyptian War; landed with the Naval Brigade during the occupation of Alexandria and Ramleh (Egyptian medal, Alexandria clasp, Khedive's bronze star); Lieut. and Commander of H.M.S. *Widgeon* during Gambia River Expedition, Vintany Creek, 1891-2 landed with Naval Brigade. Senior Lieut. of H.M.S. *Racer* during second Gambia Expedition in 1892; landed in command of the Naval Brigade from H.M.S. *Racer*, *Sparrow*, and *Alecto*, in conjunction with 1st Battn. West India Regt. under Colonel Ellis, C.B., resulting in storming and capture of Fort Toniataba (mentioned in despatches, West Africa medal 1891-92, clasp, D.S.O.). While Acting Lieutenant in H.M.S. *Rapid* he gained the bronze medal of the Royal Humane Society for assisting to save a Marine who had fallen overboard off the W. coast of Africa, the place being infested with sharks. He was in command of H.M.S. *Sparrow*, Cape Station, from 1896 to 1899 (S.A. medal). While in command of H.M.S. *Otter*, torpedo boat destroyer, in Hong Kong Harbour, he went to the rescue of the crew of H.M.S. *Sandpiper* in a typhoon on Nov. 10, 1900, and saved the crew before the *Sandpiper* foundered, and was promoted to Commander for this service. While in command of H.M.S. *Clio* he received the thanks of the New Zealand Govt. for work performed in the Pacific Islands, and received the thanks of the Colonial Office for services in conjunction with the High Commissioner of the Western Pacific at the Tongan Islands in 1904 and 1905.

WILKINSON, Right Rev. Thomas Edward, D.D., Bishop of Northern and Central Europe, was born in 1837, and is the youngest son of the late Hooper

Wilkinson, of Walsham Hall, Suffolk. He was educated at Bury St. Edmunds Sch., and Jesus Coll., Cambridge; was ordained in 1861, and in 1870 was appointed Bishop of Zululand, carrying the work of the Church northward to the Amaswazi country, which lay within the limits marked out for him by the Provincial Synod of S. Africa. In 1874, at Bishop Webb's request, he visited the Transvaal, and travelled through every township and settlement, in order to report upon its condition to the Church at home. In these journeys he went almost as far North-West as Koloberg, Dr. Livingstone's old mission station, on the edge of the Kalahari Desert. His report led to the foundation of a Bishopric for the Transvaal. He resigned the See of Zululand just before the Zulu War broke out, and returned to England. Bishop Wilkinson is an authority on the Transvaal, residing at one time in Pretoria. He is the author of *A Lady's Life in Zululand and the Transvaal* and *Twenty Years of Continental Work and Travel*. He married, in Aug., 1864, Anne, only dau. of T. A. Green, of Felmersham Grange, Beds.

WILLIAMS, Christopher Alexander Sapara, M.L.C., Barrister-at-Law, was reappointed an unofficial member of the Legislative Council for Southern Nigeria in 1906.

WILLIAMS, Capt. Edward Ernest, D.S.O., of the Army and Navy Club, was born Dec. 4, 1875, and is son of Sir Hartley Williams, late of Melbourne, Victoria. He was educated at Melbourne, and the R.M.C., Sandhurst, joined the Northumberland Fus. in 1896, and served at Singapore, the Malay States, and at Portland, Eng. He served with the WA. Frontier Force from 1899 to 1904, and took part in the Kaduna Expedition from Jan. to Oct., 1901 (mentioned in despatches, medal and clasp). He was specially mentioned in despatches in the Kano-Sokoto Campaign, 1903-4 (medal and clasp), and took part in the Okpolo Expedition in 1903-4 (mentioned in despatches, clasp and D.S.O.). He rejoined his regt. in 1904. Recreations: shooting, polo, and golf. Unmarried.

WILLIAMS, Gardner, F., M.A., of Kimberley, General Manager of the De Beers Consolidated Mines, was born in the United States of America, where he is well known as an authority on mining.

He is author of *The Diamond Mines of South Africa — an account of their rise and development* (1902).

WILLIAMS, George Blackstone, J.P., of Wynberg, C.C., was born in Dorset June 22, 1856; is second son of the late Rev. H. B. Williams, Rector of Bradford Peverell, Dorset; Fellow of Winchester Coll., and Hon. Canon of Salisbury Cathedral. He was educated at Marlborough Coll. He entered the Cape Civil Service in 1879; was Asst. R.M. at Kimberley, 1882; at C.T. 1895; and was appointed R.M. at Wynberg in 1902. He married, March 10, 1885, Elizabeth Mary, eldest dau. of the late Nathaniel Cock, of Kimberley, and granddau. of the Hon. Wm. Cock, M.L.C.

WILLIAMS, H. Sylvester, is a native of Bermuda, and a member of Gray's Inn. In Oct., 1903, he was admitted to practice at the Supreme Court of the Transvaal. of which he is the first and only coloured member.

WILLIAMS, John Richard, M.I.M.M., M.Am.I.M.E., of Park Lane, Parktown, Johannesburg (Box 149), and of the New Club, Johannesburg, was born at Anglesey, N. Wales, Nov. 24, 1862. He is eldest son of James Michell Williams, of Gwennap, Cornwall, and was educated privately. Himself the son of a mining engineer and metallurgist, he was trained in a metallurgical works at Swansea, S. Wales, and proceeded to S.A. as Chief Chemist and Metallurgist to the Cape Copper Co. at Ookiep, Namaqualand. For the past 13 years he has been engaged in metallurgical work on the Rand, and since 1895 has acted as Consulting Chemist and Metallurgist to the Eckstein and other mining groups. During this period he has been largely instrumental in bringing the profitable treatment of slimes to a successful issue.

From 1899 to 1903 he was Pres. of the Chemical and Metallurgical Society of S.A., which during his term of office enlarged its sphere of usefulness by including mining in its scope and title. In 1903 Mr. Williams was elected a member of the Council of the Institution of Mining and Metallurgy, London. He was appointed by Lord Milner a member of the Commission on Miners' Phthisis, and served on the Technical Education Commission nominated by the

Transvaal Govt. He takes a keen interest in scientific work and education, and married, Dec. 4, 1894, Mary Annie, eldest dau. of H. A. Bradley, engineer and architect, of London.

WILLIAMS, Right Rev. Joseph Watkin, D.D., Bishop of St. John's, Kaffraria, of Bishopsmead, Umtata, C.C.; was born at Birmingham, Oct. 15, 1857, is eldest son of Thos Watkin Williams, F.R.C.S.; was educated at Winchester, Oxford, and Cuddesdon; was ordained in 1881; was Domestic Chaplain to the Archbishop of Cape Town from 1892 till 1901, when he was appointed to the Bishopric of St. John's.

WILLIAMS, Ralph Champneys, C.M.G. (1901), of Head Quarter House, Mafeking, and of the St. James's Club, is the son of the Rev. T. N. Williams, of Treffos, Anglesey, and was educated at Rossall. He explored in Patagonia in 1873-4, and was in Central Africa in 188-34. He was head of the Civil Intelligence of the Bechuanaland Expedition in 1884-5. He was British Consular Officer in the South African Republic in 1887, and was appointed first British Agent in the South African Republic, with Letter of Credence, 1888. He was appointed Colonial Treasurer of Gibraltar, 1890, and also Captain of the Port of Gibraltar, 1895. He received the Silver Medal and Vellum Certificate from the Italian Government for services in connection with the wreck of the *Utopia* in 1891. He was appointed Colonial Secy. of Barbados in 1897, and twice acted as Governor of Barbados. He was appointed Resident Commissioner of the Bechuanaland Protectorate in 1901, and still holds that post. He is the author of *The British Lion in Bechuanaland*, and was Special Correspondent of the *Standard*, 1884-5. He married, in 1875, Jessie, dau. of Samuel Dean.

WILLIAMS, Robert, of 30 and 31, Clement's Lane, London, FC., and of 69, Albert Hall Mansions, Kensington Gore, London, was born at Aberdeen, Scotland, and was formerly engineer for the Bultfontein Mine, and afterwards went to the Transvaal and Rhodesia, but it was as a financier in London that he made his chief mark, devoting his energies mainly to the development of the territories about and above the Zambesi. He is Managing Director of the Tanganyika Concessions, Ltd., the Katanga Railway Co., and the Zambesi

Exploring Co., besides exercising considerable influence over other large concerns. The Tanganyika Concessions Co. is an immense concern, holding sway over large tracts of N. Rhodesia and Katangaland. It holds for joint account with the Katanga Co. the prospecting rights over about 60,000 square miles in the Congo district, with the right to work all mines which may be discovered for 89 years, and there are said to be tin and copper deposits exceeding many millions in value, besides gold reefs, cobalt and nickel. The Tanganyika Co also owns a half interest in the Benguela Concession, with the sole right to prospect over about 120,000 square miles for ten years and to work all mines found in perpetuity. But one of the greatest schemes with which Mr. Williams is identified is the construction of the railway from Lobito Bay, under the Benguela Concession, to open up the mineral areas, and eventually probably connect with the Cape to Cairo Railway system, and if he succeeds in satisfactorily financing this, the line should absorb nine-tenths of the S. African passenger traffic to and from Europe. But in view of Mr. Williams' previous success in carry ing out his projects it is not probable that this scheme will fail for want of support in the proper quarters. Mr. Robert Williams is a man of enormous enterprise, who has worked wonders with the aid of such small opportunities as have presented themselves, a small syndicate of his with a capital of but £5,000 having been gradually developed into the Zambesia Exploring Co., from which ultimately sprang the Tanganyika Concessions. A protégé of Cecil Rhodes, who strongly supported his daring and ambitious schemes, he has also received great assistance from the King of the Belgians and the King of Portugal. He was further seconded by the well-known firm of Hilder and Paul. Given a sufficiency of financial support, we may yet see Mr. Robert Williams figuring as the Cecil Rhodes of Northern Zambesia. He is personally very popular, and fond of shooting and yachting, and was formerly the owner of the yacht *Rosabelle*. He drives a double tonneau Panhard motor, and still plays a good game of cricket, and it will be remembered that he captained the team at Bal-na-Coil which played and beat. the S. African XI. in 1901. He married Margaret, dau. of Mr. Bayne, of Kimberley.

WILLMORE, John Selden, M.A., of Seaton, Cairo, and of the Athenaeum Club, was born at Neuilly, France, in 1856; he is younger son of the late Graham Wilmore, Q.C., Judge of the Somersetshire County Court and Recorder of Bath and Wells, by his wife Josephine Selden, of Virginia. He was educated at King's Coll., Camb., where he graduated MA. in 1886; is a Barrister of the Inner Temple, and was appointed a Student Interpreter at Constantinople in 1879. He was Acting Consul-Gen. at Philippopolis, 1885; Vice-Consul at Angora, 1885-7, and at Alexandria, 1887-9, when he was appointed to his present position as a Judge of the Native Egyptian Court of Appeal. He is a Lecturer at the Khedivial School of Law, and has published *The Spoken Arabic of Egypt* (1901) and *Handbook of Spoken Egyptian Arabic* (1903). In his earlier days he won prizes for running and jumping; his recreations are now lawn tennis and swimming. He married, in 1890, Edith Mabel, eldest dau. of the late Alfred Caillard, Director of Customs, Egypt.

WILLOUGHBY, Sir John Christopher, Bart., of 2, Down Street, London, W., was born in 1859, and entered the Royal Horse Guards in 1890. He served in Egypt in 1882, and again in the Nile Expedition three years later. He also went through the first Matabele War as Military Adviser to the Administrator, and was seconded for service in the B.B.P. in May, 1895. He took command, with rank of Lieut-Col., of Dr. Jameson's forces at the time of the Raid, for his connection with which he was sentenced to ten months' imprisonment, and allowed to retire from the Army. He also took part in the S. African War in 1899-1900. For several years he has been connected with several Rhodesian companies, of which he is a director. Sir John was mainly responsible for the discovery of diamond deposits in Gwelo, Rhodesia, and he was given by the Chartered Co. a concession under which he was at liberty to prospect and mine over a certain area, retaining all diamonds without accounting to the company up to Dec. 31, 1909. At the end of that time terms will have to be arranged with them as to the future working of the ground. The whole position with regard to diamonds was somewhat complicated by the company's agreement with the De Beers Company, with which they have a working arrangement. Probably steps will shortly be taken to determine the exact effect of that agreement. Sir John is the 5th Baronet of a creation of 1794, and has no heir.

WILLS, John Trenwith, Order of the Medjidieh, of Formby, Lancashire, fifth and youngest son of the late John Wills, merchant, of Liverpool, his grandfather being Francis Wills, Headmaster of the then great Quaker Sch. at Newton-in-Bolland, Yorks., was born at Olive Mount, Wavertree, near Liverpool, in 1844, and was educated at the Merchant Taylors' Sch, and afterwards in Italy. About the year 1861 he went to Alexandria, Egypt, and joined the firm of the Egyptian Commercial and Trading Co, Ltd, and later, that of Messrs. Robt. Corkling and Co., Ltd., of Alexandria and Mansourah. At the latter place he was for some time Acting British Vice-Consul.

In 1870 he started the well-known firm of Wills, Manché and Co., steamship agents at Port Said and Suez, now called Wills and Co., Ltd. His firm, besides representing many of the principal British and foreign steamship companies, also acted as coal contractors to the British Govt. for some seven consecutive years, and especially during the eventful time of the Arabi Pasha revolt. During this time they had to supply the coal to the immense fleet of hired transports on their way through the Canal with the troops, etc., to Ismailia, just prior to the Battle of Tel-el-Kebir, when the power of Arabi was broken once and for all. Later on they had to supply all the coal to the fleet of hired transports taking out railway material for the projected Suakim-Berber Railway for the relief of Gordon Pasha at Khartoum, which, however, was abandoned, and the ships with their cargoes returned to England by order of the Gladstone Govt. Mr. Wills was for about twelve years Hon. Vice-Consul at Port Said to H.M. King Oscar of Sweden and Norway. One of the interesting events during his term of office was the return of Prof. Nordenskjold's expedition to the Polar regions. Capt. Pallander, R.N. (Norwegian), the Commander of the Expedition, during a visit to the Vice Consular Office gave a very graphic *viva voce* outline of the journey in English, from the time the expedition left home until its arrival at Port Said. This the subject of our sketch translated verbatim into French as the narrative proceeded, and it was taken down on the spot by the representative of the local French paper and duly appeared *in extenso* in the next day's issue. This was the first authentic account that appeared in the public Press, and it made interesting reading.

During the years 1882-3, when the great cholera plague raged in Egypt, Mr. Wills was one of the few Englishmen (another notable one being Mr. James Finney, of Messrs. Carver Bros.) who remained at Alexandria to see it through, nearly all the other Europeans having sealed up their premises and fled. In about 1884 the epidemic raged again, but not so fiercely, and Mr. Wills was one of the committee appointed to ward off the encroaching disease at Port Said, and their combined efforts were so successful that not a single fatal case occurred. For these services he received the decoration from the Khedive of the Imperial Order of the Medjidieh.

He retired from the firm of Wills and Co., Ltd., in 1859. He occasionally acted during the Arabi Pasha revolt as the *Times* correspondent at Port Said, and is now the Liverpool commercial representative of the Press Assoc., Ltd., of Lond., and is also connected with the well-known firm of Sim and Coventry, of Liverpool. He married first, in 1874, Louisa Jane, dau. of Richard Clarke, Solicitor and Clerk of the Peace, of Shrewsbury, by whom he had one dau., Mary Adelaide; and second, in 1890, Florence Elizabeth, dau. of the late Geo. Lovering, of West Norwood, by whom he has two Sons, Trenwith Lovering and John Godfrey.

WILLS-LICHTENBERG, Capt. John, D.S.O. (See Capt. J. W. Lichtenberg).

WILLSON, Maj.-Gen. Mildmay Willson, K.C.B., of Rauceby, Grantham, and of the Guards', Arthurs', and R.Y.S. Clubs, was born at Rauceby, July 13, 1847, and is the eldest son of the late Anthony Willson, formerly M.P. for S. Lincolnshire. We was educated at Eton, and served in the Nile Expedition in 1885, and as Maj.-Gen. commanding the district west of Johannesburg in the S. African War. Unmarried.

WILMOT, Hon. Alexander, M.L.C., F.R.G.S.,

Knight of St. Gregory, and Hon. Chamberlain to the Pope, of Cape Town and Grahamstown, C.C., and of the Civil Service (C.T.) and Port Elizabeth Clubs, was born at Edinburgh, April 9, 1886, and received his education at the Univs. of Glasgow and Edinburgh. After spending some time in the Cape Colonial Civil Service, Mr. Wilmot entered the Cape Parliament in 1889, and has sat ever since in the Legislative Council (on Upper House), and has during his Parliamentary career been sponsor for many useful social measures. He is President of the Temperance Alliance, and is a supporter of the Progressive Party. His constituency, the South-Eastern Electoral Province, comprises Port Elizabeth, Grahamstown, and Uitenhage. Mr. Wilmot is the author of a *History of South Africa*, *History of the Zulu War*, *History of Our Own Time in South Africa*, and *Life and Times of Sir Richard Southey*. He married, Jan. 17, 1860, Miss Alice Mary Slater, belonging to one of the British settler families of 1820.

WILSON, Lieut. Col. A. E., D.S.O., was born in Australia, and migrated to Rhodesia. He served in the S. African War in 1900-02, in command of the 2nd Batt. Kitchener's Fighting Scouts (despatches, Queen's medal and four clasps; King's medal with two clasps and D.S.O.).

WILSON, Admiral Sir Arthur Knyvet, served in the Crimea, the Chinese War, the Egyptian Campaign, and the Sudan Expedition. His other service includes four years as Comptroller of the Navy, and he has been in command of the Home Fleet since 1901. By the death of Vice Admiral Hammet, and the retirement of Admiral of the Fleet Sir Nowell Salmon, and of Admiral Ernest Rice, Sir A. K. Wilson reached the substantive rank of Admiral in 1905.

WILSON, Henry Francis, M.A., C.M.G., of Bloemfontein, O.R.C., was educated at Rugby and Trinity College, Cambridge. He was called to the Ban at Lincoln's Inn in 1888; acted as Secy. to the Trinidad Judicial Inquiry Commission in 1892, and was sent to Malta to collect evidence for the Protestant Communities in connection with the Marriages Case in 1893; was private secy. to the Rt. Hon. J. Chamberlain, Secy. of State for the Colonies, in 1895; Legal Assistant in the Colonial

MR. J. B TAYLOR

SIR WILLIAM THORNE

SIR J SOMERS VINE

THE MARQUESS OF WINCHESTER

Office in 1897; went to South Africa as Legal Assistant on the High Commissioner's Staff in 1900; acted as Secy. to the Administration of the Orange River Colony, 1901; Colonial Secy. in 1902, and Acting Lieut.-Governor of the Orange River Colony in 1903-4.

WILSON, J. P., was transferred from the Imperial British East Africa Company's service to the Uganda Protectorate as Assistant Collector in 1893, and became Sub-Commissioner six years later, retiring on a pension in 1906.

WILSON, Capt. Leslie Orme, D.S.O., State Government House, Sydney N.S.W., and of the Junior Naval and Military Club, was born Aug. 1, 1876, and is a son of Henry Wilson of Stanhope Street, W. He was educated at St. Paul's Sch., and joined the R.M.L.I. in 1895 took part in the S.A. War in 1899-1900 and was severely wounded (mentioned in despatches, D.S.O., and medal with five clasps). He was appointed A.D.C. to the Governor of N.S.W. in May, 1903. Recreations: cricket, shooting, and golf.

WINCHESTER, Marquess of, of Amport St. Mary's, Andover, Hants, is a Director of the British South Africa Co. and President of the Victoria Falls Power Company, and before his succession to the title in 1899 he resided in Rhodesia, where he interested himself in the development of the mining industry. Lord Winchester, who is the premier Marquess of England, and Hereditary Bearer of the Cap of Maintenance, is descended from the Sir John Paulet who fought under the Duke of Gloucester about the year 1350. Another Sir John, four generations later, took part in the suppression of the Cornish rebellion in 1497, and his son became the first Marquess and held the high office of Lord Treasurer under Edward VI., Mary, and Elizabeth. The fifth Marquess made stubborn defence in his stronghold at Basing in support of Charles I. during the Civil War, and the next holder of the title was created the first Duke of Bolton, the second Duke being Viceroy of Ireland, and the third Duke being Constable of the Tower of London. The Dukedom became extinct on the death of the sixth Duke, and the Marquessate passed to a descendant of the fifth holder of that title.

The present Marquess of Winchester, who also bears the titles of Baron St. John and Earl of Wiltshire, which were bestowed originally in the sixteenth century, was born in 1862, and succeeded his brother, the fifteenth Marquess (who was killed in action at Magersfontein) in 1899. He was formerly Capt. in the Hants I.Y., and is now Lord Lieut. of Hampshire (where he has his seat and owns about 4,500 acres) and Chairman of the Hants County Council.

WINDHAM, William, J.P., M.L.C., of Pretoria; son of Ashe Windham, of Wawne Hall, Yorks.; was born at Greytown, Nov. 12, 1864 and was educated at the Diocesan Coll., Cap Town. He was appointed Clerk to the Resident Commissioner, Zululand, in 1882; Student Interpreter, Native Affairs Dept, Natal, 1884; Registrar to H.E. the Special Commissioner for Zulu Affairs, Oct., 1885; Clerk and Interpreter to Resident Commissioner and Chief Magistrate, Zululand, June, 1887; Secy. to the same in Jan., 1889; Clerk to the Executive Council, Natal, Sept., 1889; Priv. Secy. to the Governor of Natal, Oct., 1889; Secy. for Zululand, Dec., 1889; Govt. Secy. for Zululand, Feb., 1894; Asst. Under-Secy. for Zululand Affairs, Natal, Jan., 1897; Registrar of Deeds and Registrar-Gen., Natal, March, 1898; Asst. Secy. Mines Dept. of the Transvaal, July 1, 1901; Secy. for Native Affairs of the Transvaal, Sept. 23, 1901; acted as Commissioner for Native Affairs with a seat in the Executive Council in 1904 and 1905; Member of the Transvaal Legislative Council, 1905; J.P. for the Transvaal. He married, July 10, 1894, Blanche, dau. of A. E. Titren, of Durban.

WINDSOR, Viscount, was born Oct. 23, 1884, and is the eldest son of the 14th Baron Windsor, in whose favour the Earldom of Plymouth was revived by the Conservative Govt. shortly before it quitted office in 1905. Lord Windsor is a 2nd Lieutenant in the Worcester Imperial Yeomanry, and in 1906 he left for South Africa to take up an appointment on Lord Selborne's staff.

WINGATE, Maj.-Gen. Sir Francis Reginald, K.C.B. K.C.M.G., C.B. (Civil), D.S.O., F.R.G.S. (late A.D.C. to the King); Grand Cordons of Osmanieh and Medjidieh, 2nd Class Iron Crown of

Austria, 2nd Class Star of Ethiopia; of the Palace, Khartoum; War Office, Cairo; Stafford House, Dunbar, N.B. and of the Army and Navy, Beefsteak, Turf (Cairo). and Sudan (Khartoum) Clubs; is the son of Andrew Wingate, of Glasgow. He was born June 25, 1861, at Broadfield, Port Glasgow, Renfrewshire, and was educated at Dr. Thompson's Sch., Jersey, and the Royal Military Acad., Woolwich. Gen. Wingate entered the R.A. in 1880, and has been employed with the Egyptian Army since 1882. He acted as A.D.C. and Military Secy. to Sir Evelyn Wood in the Sudan Expedition of 1884-5 (despatches, medal with clasp, bronze star, brev. of Maj.). He again served in the Sudan in 1889-91, being present at the action of Toski (despatches, D.S.O., clasp) and at the capture of Tokar (3rd Class Medjidieh, and clasp to bronze star). In 1895 he was appointed Director of Military Intelligence in the Egyptian Army, and served in this capacity through the Dongola Expedition in 1896 (despatches, brev. of Lieut. Col., Egyptian medal, two clasps), and in the Nile Expedition of the following year (appointed A.D.C. to the Queen, brev. of Col., clasp and Egyptian medal). He also took part in the Nile Expedition of 1895, being present at the battles of Athara and Khartoum, being mentioned in despatches, receiving the K.C.M.G. and the thanks of both Houses of Parliament (two clasps and Egyptian medal). In the Nile Expedition of 1899 Sir Reginald commanded the Infantry Division in the first advance against the Khalifa, and took command in the subsequent operations, which resulted in the final defeat of the Khalifa, being present at the actions of Abu Aadel and Om Dubriekat (despatches, K.C.B., 2nd Class Osmanieh, two clasps and Egyptian medal). Gen. Wingate succeeded Lord Kitchener as Sirdar of the Egyptian Army and Governor Gen. of the Sudan. He is an honorary D.C.L. of Oxford, and was captain of the Dunbar Golf Club for 1904-5. He married, June 15, 1888, Catherine Leslie, dau. of Capt. Joseph Sparkhall Rundle, R.N., of Newton Abbot, Devon.

WINSLOW, Rev. William Copley, Hon. M.A., D.D., Ph. D., Sc.D. Litt.D. D.C.L. LL.D., B.A., of 525, Beacon Street; Boston, Mass, and of the University, Clerical, and Boston Clubs, was born in Boston, Jan. 13, 1840, and is son of the Rev.

Hubbard Winslow, D.D. He was educated at Hamilton Coll., Clinton, New York (B.A.), and the General Theological Seminary in New York City (B.D.). He is an hon. member of various foreign bodies and State Historical Societies, has been on the editorial staff of the *University Quarterly*, *American Antiquarian*, and the *Christian Times*, etc., and is on the regular staff of writers for *Biblia*, a monthly magazine devoted to Oriental research. In 1880 he spent some time studying in Egypt, and in 1883 he founded the American branch of the Egypt Exploration Fund, acting as its head official until 1903. He was with Capt. Gorringe at Alexandria when the obelisk was taken down for removal to New York, and was officially connected with the Exposition at Chicago in 1893 in Egyptological matters, etc. He is an authority on exploration in Egypt and in New England Colonial history, is the author of *A Greek City in Egypt*, *Explorations at Zoan*, *Egypt at Home*, *Pilgrim Fathers in Holland*, *Gov. Edward Winslow and Plymouth Colony*, and numerous articles and papers relating to Egyptian exploration and New England history. He married, in June 20, 1867, Harriet, dau. of the Hon. Joseph Hayward.

WINTER, Hon. Henry Daniel, M.L.A., J.P., of Loch Sloy, Estcourt, Natal, is son of J. E. F. Winter, of Maritzburg, was born Oct. 26, 1851, was educated at Maritzburg, and took up farming in Weenen County in 1875. With the advent of Responsible Government in 1893, Mr. Winter was elected a member of the Legislative Assembly for Weenen County. Under the Binns Ministry he became Minister of Agriculture in February, 1899, and four months later he accepted the same portfolio under Sir Albert Hime. He resigned with Sir Albert Hime's Ministry in 1903, after having made himself responsible for the initiation of the Experimental Farms of the colony, but on May 16, 1905, was offered and accepted the portfolio of Minister for Native Affairs and Public Works in the Coalition Ministry formed by the Hon. C. J. Smythe, who assumed the position of Prime Minister in succession to Sir George Sutton. He married Janet, dau. of William Leslie, of Campsie Glen, Estcourt, Natal.

WIRGMAN, Rev. Augustus Theodore, D.D., D.C.L., F.R.C.I., Canon of Grahamstown, and Vice Provost of St. Mary's Collegiate Church, Port

Elizabeth, Cape Colony, of St. Mary's Rectory, Port Elizabeth, was born Sept. 22, 1846, and is the eldest son of the Rev. A. Wirgman, M.A. He was educated at Rossall Sch. and Magdalen Coll., Cambridge (B.A. Classical Tripos, Theological Honours, 2nd Class, and M.A.). In 1874 he went to S. Africa as Vice Principal of St. Andrew's Coll., Grahamstown, became Rector of St. Mary's, Port Elizabeth, in 1875; Rural Dean of Port Elizabeth in 1884-96; Canon of Grahamstown in 1899, and Hon. Chaplain to the King in 1905. Canon Wirgman is also Senior Chaplain of the Cape Colonial Forces, and holds the General Service medal, 1877-81, Queen's medal and clasp for the Boer War, 1900, and the Imperial Long Service (officers') Decoration, 1896. Canon Wirgman is in Examiner and Member of the Executive of the Divinity Faculty of the S. African Church, and Examining Chaplain to the Bishop of Mashonaland. He is the author of *The Prayer-book with Historical Notes*, *The Beatitudes and the Lord's Prayer*, *The Sevenfold Gifts*, *The Church and the Civil Power*, *The Spirit of Liberty*, *The English Reformation*, *History of the English Church and People in S. Africa*, *The Doctrine of Confirmation*, *The Constitutional Authority of Bishops*, *The Blessed Virgin and the Company of Heaven*, and has written articles in the *Nineteenth Century* on the Boer War. He married, Jan. 13, 1874, Rose, dau. of Andrew J. Worthington, of Staffs.

WISSE, Wilhelm Johannes, of Amsterdam, is a director of the British South-West African Land and Mining Co., Ltd., and Tasmanian Consols, Ltd.

WOLFAARDT, George Sebastian, M.L.A., is member of the Cape Legislative Assembly for Swellendam, for which electoral division he was re-elected in Feb., 1904. He supports the Bond party.

WOLFF, Capt. Cecil Harry, of the Sports Club, London, was born at Port Elizabeth, Jan., 1882; is second son of Victor Wolff, whose father was a doctor in the British Army (M.D., M.R.C.S., London). Capt. Wolff was educated at St. Paul's Sch., and Univ. Coll., London. He won the Public Schools Boxing Championship in 1898 and 1899. Entered the 4th Batt. Bedford Regt. Oct. 16, 1901; served in the South African War Dec., 1901-Oct., 1902 (medal and four clasps), and was gazetted Captain in Oct., 1904. Unmarried.

WOLFF, Charles Ernest, B.Sc., A.M.Inst.C.E., of Hale, nr. Altrincham, Cheshire, the Turf Club, Cairo, and the Khedivial Sporting Club, Gezireh, was born in Cheshire, Jan. 23, 1872, was educated at Bowdon Coll., Cheshire, and Owens College, Manchester, of which he is an Associate. From 1891 to 1899 he was in the Locomotive Dept. of the Midland Railway at Derby; 1899-1901, Chief Asst. in the Mechanical Engineering Dept. to W. H. Allen, Son and Co., Bedford; 1901-3, Professor of Engineering at the Polytechnic Sch., Cairo. He has published books on *Modern Locomotive Practice* and *Diagrams for Egyptian Engineers*, the latter in English and Arabic. He is a member of the Executive Committee of the British Rifle Club, Cairo.

WOLFF, Gustav William, M.P., of 90, Piccadilly, London, W., and of The Den, Belfast was born in 1834, and was educated at Liverpool College Institute and at Hamburg. He is partner in the shipbuilding and engineering firm of Harland and Wolff; is a member of the Council of the Union-Castle Mail Steamship Co. Ltd. (see Sir Donald Currie); and director of the Belfast Rope Work Co., Ltd., Harland and Wolff, Ltd., Ocean Transport Co., Ltd., and Oxychlorides, Ltd. He has been Conservative M.P. for E. Belfast since 1892.

WOLLASTON, Lieut. Col. Charlton Frederick Bromley, J.P., of the Kimberley, Rand and New (Johannesburg) Clubs, was born at Walton on Trent, Derbyshire, Nov. 5, 1849, and is the eldest son of Charlton Wollaston, a civil and electrical engineer who laid the first submarine cable between Dover and Calais. Col. Wollaston was educated at Derby and the Diocesan Coll., Rondebosch, and in 1868 joined the service of the Cape of Good Hope Telegraph Co But in 1870 he turned his attention to diamond and afterwards gold mining, being successively: manager of the Adamant Diamond Mining Co. Consolidated Bultfontein Mine, Premier Mine (Wesselton), Barnato Consolidated Mines, Lace Diamond Mine, and the Montrose Diamond Mine in the Pretoria district. From 1895 to 1899 he was also a director of the Ginsberg, Balmoral, Consolidated Main

Reef, Heidelberg Roodepoort, and Buffelsdoorn Estate Companies.

Col. Wollaston, was arrested and imprisoned at the beginning of 1896 in connection with the Transvaal Reform movement, and has had very many years of military service with the Volunteers, dating from when he was a sergeant in the Dutoitspan Hussars in 1876. In 1877-8 he served in the Kaffir wars (medal and clasp), and in the latter year became a Lieut. in the Diamond Fields Horse, rising to the rank of Lieut.-Col. in 1893. He commanded the regiment for seven years, and during the S. African War served on Lord Roberts's Staff till after the occupation of Bloemfontein, and subsequently as Base Officer to the Railway Pioneer Regt. for fourteen months, receiving the Queen's medal with three clasps. He also wears the Long Service medal.

WOLMARANS, J. M. L., was a member of the Executive Council under the Kruger régime. He was accused by the Dutch paper *Land in Volk* of receiving a commission of one shilling per case of dynamite sold (equal to about £10,000 per annum) as a bribe to secure his support in the Executive Council on the vote as to the renewal of the Dynamite Concession. Mn. Wolmarans always declined to notice the allegation.

WOLSELEY, Field-Marshal Viscount, K.P., P.C., G.C.B., etc., of Hampton Court Palace, Middlesex, was born in 1833, his father having been Major Garnet Joseph Wolseley. The younger Wolseley, christened with the same names, entered the Army in 1852, and during the first twenty years he was almost continuously on active service, participating in the Burmese War in 1852-3, when he led the storming party at the capture of a breastwork at Donabew (severely wounded, medal); the Crimea, in 1854-5, when he served in the trenches at Sevastopol, and was twice wounded and much decorated; the Indian Mutiny, in 1857-9, when he was at the relief of Lucknow, defence of Alum Bagh, action at Sheorajpore, siege and capture of Lucknow, and with the Oode Field Force in the actions at Baree, Nawabgunge, Simree, Fyzabad, Sultanpore, at the passage of the Goomtee, and in the Byswarra, Trans-Gogra, and Trans-Raptee Campaigns; the China War, in 1860-1, in which he took part in the landing at Pehtang

Ho, assault and capture of Tangku, battle of Sinho, assault and capture of the Peiho Forts, battle of Palichau, and the advance on Pekin. After a brief respite, Brevet-Col. Wolseley (as he then was) took part in the suppression of the Fenian Raids in Canada of 1866 and 1870, having, meanwhile, reached the supernumerary rank of Maj.Gen. He commanded the Red River Expeditionary Force in 1870 (K.C.M.G., C.B.). In 1873 Sir Garnet Wolseley was appointed Governor and C.I.C. of the Gold Coast, and when the Ashanti War broke out he received another opportunity of attaining distinction, being thanked by both Houses of Parliament for his successful conduct of the campaign in which he commanded up to the capture of Coomassie. For some months in 1875 he was on the Staff in Natal, and in 1879-80 he was Governor of that Colony, with local rank of General. During this period (1879) he commanded the troops during the closing operations of the Zulu War, including the capture of Cetewayo, and during the attack on Sekukuni's stronghold. (Medal with clasp; G.C.B.). In 1882 Sir Garnet commended-in-chief the Army in the Egyptian Expedition, when he was present at the capture of Mahsameh, the action at Mahuta, and the Battle of Tel-el-Kebir. As a fitting reward for these services he was thanked by both Houses of Parliament; was raised to the Peerage, and further decorated with the 1st class of the Osmanieh. Lord Wolseley was again in Egypt for thirteen months in 1884-5, commanding-in-chief the Expeditionary Forces for the relief of Gordon in the Sudan, and was once more thanked by both Houses, and created a Viscount (1885). During intervening periods Lord Wolseley was mainly occupied with Staff duties at Army Headquarters. He succeeded the Duke of Cambridge as Commander-in-Chief of the Army in 1895, and retired, Nov. 30, 1900. He has published a few books, is a member of the Council of the UnionCastle Mail Steamship Co., Ltd. (see Sir Donald Currie), and married, in 1867, a dau. of Mr. A. Erskine. He has only one child, the Hon. Frances, to whom the title will eventually pass by special remainder.

WOOD, Major-Gen. Sir Elliott, K.C.B., of the United Service Club, was born in 1844. He entered the Royal Engineers in 1864, serving with them during the Egyptian War in 1882; present at the actions at Kassassin and Telel Kebir; the Sudan Expedition in 1884, being attached to the Intelligence Dept., and participating in the victories at El Teb and Tamai. During the following year he saw further fight ing in the Sudan at Suakim, Hasheen and Tofrek. He also served in the S. African War in 1899-1902, in command of the R.E. (K.C.B., Queen's medal and five clasps, King's medal and two clasps).

WOOD, Field-Marshal Sir Evelyn, V.C., G.C.B., G.C.M.G., Grand Cross of the Legion of Honour; of Salisbury, and of the United Service Club, is the youngest son of the late Rev. Sir John Page Wood, Bart., and Emma, dau. of Admiral Mitchell. He was born Feb. 9, 1838, at Cressing, Essex, and was educated at Marlborough. Sir Evelyn Wood has had a long and brilliant career extending over half a century. He entered the Royal Navy in 1852, and was severely wounded while serving with the Naval Brigade in the Crimean War. It was certainly not an unfortunate decision which induced him to resign the service in which, young as he was, his personal gallantry had made him conspicuous, and to enter the Army in which he has done such splendid work. After serving in a Light Dragoon Regt. he joined the 17th Lancers in the Indian Mutiny Campaign, where he gained the V.C. for having on Oct. 19, 1858, during an action at Sindwayo, when in command of a troop of the 3rd Light Cavalry, attacked with much gallantry, almost singlehanded, a body of rebels, and also for subsequently rescuing an Indian from a band of robbers. At this time he was serving as Brigade-Maj. with Beetson's Horse. He also raised and commanded Mayne's Horse, and was present in five actions. He served with greet distinction in the Ashanti and Kaflir Wars, and while engaged in campaigning against the Zulus, was in command of one of the four columns dispatched against Cetewayo. He also went through the first and ill-fated Boer War, and assumed command after Sir G. Colley was killed at Majuba. He afterwards commanded the Second Brigade (2nd Div.) in the Expedition in Egypt in 1882; raised the Egyptian Army in 1883, and took part in the Nile Expedition in 1894-95. It was Mr. Kruger's firm conviction that when the late war broke out the command of the British forces would he given to Sir Evelyn Wood, whom he regarded as the most formidable adversary that General Joubert was likely to meet in the field. As we know, the choice fell upon General Buller, though after the early reverses, and before Lord Roberts was sent out, Sir Evelyn offered to go out to serve under Sir Redvers. He has, at various times, been in command of the Chetham and Eastern Dists. of the Aldershot Div. He has also been Adjt.-Gen. and Quartermaster-Gen. to the Forces, and prior to his retirement commanded the 2nd Army Corps. Sir Evelyn Wood was called to the Bar at the Middle Temple in 1874. He is a well-known writer on military subjects, his book on the Crimea being regarded as a standard work of those stirring times. He married, Sept. 19, 1867, the Hon. Pauline Southwell, who died in 1891.

WOOD, Major Evelyn Fitzgerald Mitchel, D.S.O., of the Army and Navy Club, was born in 1869, and is the eldest son of Field-Marshal Sir Evelyn Wood (q.v.). He joined the Devonshire Regt. in 1889, and served in the Ashanti War in 1895 (star), and was on Special Service during the S. African War in 1899-1901, being present at the actions at Belmont, Graspan, Modder Riven, and Magersfontein (medal and three clasps; D.S.O.), also as A.D.C. and A.M.S. to Sir F. Forestier Walker. In May, 1906, Major Wood was promoted to the Royal Dragoons from the Devonshire Regt. He married, in 1893, Lilian, dau. of the late C. E. Hutton.

WOOD, Henry R., M.L.A., was returned unopposed as Progressive member for Grahamstown in the Cape House of Assembly in No, 1902, and was re-elected in 1904. He is a supporter of the Progressives.

WOOD, Sir Lindsay, J.P., D.L., of the Hermitage, Chester-Le-Street, N. Durham, and of the Carlton and Junior Carlton Clubs, was born in 1834, and is son of the late Nicholas Wood. He was educated at the Royal Kepier Grammar School, Houghton-le-Spring, and at King's College, London. In 1879 and 1886 he was a member of the Royal Commission on Accidents in Mines, and is Vice-Chairman of John Bowes and Partners, Ltd., Chairman of the West African Hinterland Consolidated, Ltd., director of the County of Durham Electric Power Distribution Co., Ltd., Rarton Coal Co., Ltd., Newcastle-on-Tyne Electric Supply Co., Ltd., and the North Eastern Railway Co., Ltd., and is on the Newcastle Board of the North British and Mercantile Insurance Co. He married, in 1873, Emma, dau. of Samuel Gooden Barrett.

WOOD, Rev. Michael Henry Mansel, M.A. of Bishopscourt, Claremont, Cape Town, was born at Prestwood, Bucks; is second son of the Rev. Canon Wood, D.D., Rector of Rotherfield Greys, Oxon, and was educated at Eton, Trinity Coll., Oxon, and Cuddesdon Theological Coll. He was elected Scholar of Eton, 1879; Scholar of Trinity, 1883; 2nd Class Mod., 1884 Gaisford Greek Prose Prize, 1886; B.A. (2n Class Lit. Hum.), 1887; 2nd Class Theol. Sch. 1888; M.A., 1890; and M.A., Cape Univ., 1892 Cuddesdon Coll., 1888; Deacon, 1889; Priest 1890; and Domestic and Examining Chaplain to the Archbishop of Cape Town, 1902. He was formerly Curate of Wantage, 1889-91; Rondebosch, 1891-96; and Monk's Risborough, Bucks., 1898-9. He compiled and edited the *South African Provincial Church Directory,* 1905. Unmarried.

WOOD, Reginald Newcome, J.P., of Bignall End, Staffordshire, is a director of Holbrooks, Ltd., and the South African Venture Syndicate, Ltd.

WOODFORD, Edwin B., of 10-11, Austin Friars, London, B.C., is a director of the Bulawayo and General Exploration Co., Ltd., Eaglehawk Consolidated G.M. Co., Ltd., Ottos Kopje Diamond Mines (1908), Ltd., Prospectors Matabeleland, Ltd., and the Rose of Sharon and Shamrock Gold Mines, Ltd.

WOOLASTON, Dr., of the British Museum Ruwenzori Expedition, together with Mr. Woosman (q.v.), succeeded in 1906 in reaching the summits of the two highest peaks. On May 1 they climbed the Runvoni Peak, 15,89 feet high, and on May 3 the Kiangu Peak, 10,37 feet high. There are said to be no higher peaks in the Congo territory.

WOOLLAN, Benjamin Minors, J.P., of Sherwood Park, Tunbridge Wells, was born in 1857. He went to S.A. in 1882, and after five years spent on the Kimberley Diamond Fields he was attracted by the budding promise of the Transvaal Goldfields, and the year 1887 saw him established in Johannesburg. With great energy and ability he soon built up a

large and prosperous business, and amongst other joint stock ventures founded the Johannesburg Stock Exchange, of which Committee he was the first Chairman. He was also a member of the Transvaal National Union. He returned to England in 1895, and retired from business a few years later. Besides being a Justice of the Peace, Mr. Woollan was elected Mayor of Tunbridge Wells in 1906. He is very fond of shooting, and is married.

WOOLS-SAMPSON, Colonel Sir Aubrey K.C.B., of Johannesburg. In the early 'seventies, at the age of fifteen, he shouldered a rifle in the Diamond Fields Revolt, led by the Fenian Aylward, who singled out young Sampson as one who did not know what fear meant. In 1896 he was one of the two Reform prisoners (*vide* W. D. Davies) who, rather than join in the petition to the Executive, elected to complete their terms of imprisonment in Pretoria gaol. He founded the Imperial Light Horse at the beginning of the S.A. War, through which he served from 1899 to 1902, participating in the operations in Natal, including the action at Elandslaagte, and doing further excellent service, especially on the Intelligence Staff. He was severely wounded at Elandslaagte, and was several times mentioned in despatches. He has been since March 19, 1903, Hon. Col. of the Right Wing of the I.L.H., with hon. rank in the British Army (dating from June 26, 1902); was made C.B., Nov. 29, 1900, and K.C.B., June 26, 1902. At the conclusion of the War he joined Major Mullins, V.C., in a partnership as financial and estate agents in Johannesburg.

WOOSNAM, J. B.,, of the British Museum Ruwenzori Expedition, accompanied Dr. Woolaston (q.v.) on his expedition in 1906, and succeeded in reaching the summits of the highest peaks in the Congo territory.

WREY, Philip Bourchier Sherard, of Bulawayo, and the Union Club, London, was born June 28, 1858. He is son of Sir Henry Bourchier Wrey, Bart., and of the Hon. Lady Wrey, dau. of Baron Sherard. He was educated privately, and served his articles as Civil and Mining Engineer with Jas. Henderson, M.I.C.E., of Truro, Cornwall, 1876-79. In the latter year he went to S.A., practising in Kimberley as a Mining Engineer, 1880-81. He was employed as Cape Govt. Surveyor, 1883-85, during which time he surveyed and reported upon the Walfisch Bay territory. From 1886 to 1891 he was occupied as Mining Engineer in Johannesburg. From then until 1899 he was Consulting Engineer to the Mashonaland Agency and its subsidiaries, and he then became Gen. Manager of that group. He was Pres. of the Rhodesian Chamber of Mines for 1901-2. Mr. Wrey married, Aug. 14, 1889, Alice Mary, dau. of the late Col. Borton, R.H.A.

WRIGHT, Arthur, A.M.I.C.E., M.I.E.E. of 3, Addison Road, Kensington, W., and of the Devonshire Club, is the well-known Consulting Engineer to the Boroughs of Brighton, Marylebone, and Stepney, and Director and Consulting Engineer of the Rosario Electric Co., and one of the Electrical Engineers to the Victoria Falls Power Company. He was born June 24 1855, and is son of Edward Wright; was educated at University College School, Ste. Barbe Paris, and at Marlborough College, after leaving which he had some six years' commercial experience in a London warehouse. He then studied at an electrical engineering institution and was articled to the late Mr. Cromwell Varley, and in 1881 received his first commission to put down a small 'Brush' electric plant at Brighton, which constituted the first generating station for the public supply of electricity in Great Britain, and the forerunner of many other large and successful supply businesses. In 1889 he was asked by Mr. Ferranti to assist him in the large power scheme he had on hand for the supply of electricity to London. In the same year he was sent out to South America to investigate the probable market for electricity in that continent. In 1891 he was invited by the Brighton Corporation to take over the management of their electricity undertaking, and subsequently was appointed their retained Consulting Engineer. In 1902 he was appointed in a similar capacity to the Marylebone Borough Council's electricity undertaking and also to the Borough of Stepney. He has installed 15,000 h.p of plant at Brighton, 15,000 h.p. at Marylebone, 4,000 h.p. at Stepney, 3,000 at Rosario and has been the responsible engineer for about £2,000,000 worth of electrical work during the last fifteen years. Mr. Wright has visited the United States three times, and has been round the world on an engineering tour through Australia,

Japan, and Canada, and has lately been associated with Sir Douglas Fox and Partner (see Sir Douglas Fox), Mr. Mershon and Mr Wilson Fox (q.v.), investigating the commercial feasibility of the Victoria Falls Power Scheme. He married, in 1889, Miss Edith Wassell.

WRIGHT, Lee, of 7, Oakwood Court, Kensington, W., is a director of the Craggiemor Proprietary, Ltd., and the Durban Roodepoort G.M. Co., Ltd.

WRIGHT, Capt. Wallace Duffield, V.C., of the 2nd Queen's Regt., was born at Gibraltar in 1875; was educated at Cranbrook Sch., Kent, and joined the Militia in 1893. Transferring to the Regular Army in 1896, he proceeded to India, taking part in the N.W. Frontier Campaign of 1897-98, in which he was severely wounded. He went to N. Nigeria in 1901, and served with the M.I. in the Kano and Sokoto affairs of 1903 with distinction, being mentioned in despatches and receiving the coveted V.C. He was also slightly wounded. His Captaincy dates from 1903. Unmarried.

WYBERG, Wilfred, of Johannesburg, was well-known for his extreme advocacy of the Uitlander cause before the South African War. Under the British Govt. he became Commissioner of Mines, but he resigned this position two years later, according to the *Times* correspondent, for reasons of which nothing need be said, except that even Mr. Wyberg himself has never dreamed that they involved any question of policy or principles. Mr. Wyberg's fiscal policy is to reduce customs, duties, and railway rates, and to increase the tax on the profits of the mining industry. He advocates the repatriation of the Chinese, although he has no alternative scheme to suggest for unskilled labour to keep the Transvaal mines in the productive stage. His ideal programme, to quote again the *Times* correspondent, is "to make a nation, a white nation, a British nation, or at any rate a nation with British traditions and British institutions." That is an ideal which no one, and least of all the Boers, would venture to disavow in public; but it is hardly open to question that the practical fulfillment of Mr. Wyberg's destructive proposals would be to hasten a very different result. Mr. Wyberg hopes to inaugurate a new political Reform Club.

WYNDHAM, Right Hon. George, M.P., of 35, Park Lane, W., was born in 1863. He has Irish blood in his veins, and is a descendant of Lord Edward Fitzgerald. He joined the Coldstream Gds. when just out of his teens, and saw active service before he was twenty-two in the Suakin Expedition, gaining the medal and star. At the age of twenty-four he became Priv. Secy. to Mr. Balfour when he was Chief Secy. for Ireland. In the following year he entered the House of Commons as member for Dover, which seat he has held ever since. Parliament was ready to greet this new representative of a race of politicians, but Mr. Wyndham was not an early success. His opportunity soon came, however. His talents received recognition, and in 1898 he became Under-Secy. for War, an unenviable office which he held during the S.A. War, in the course of which he had so often to justify the blunders of his department before an angry House. In 1902 at the early age of thirty-nine, he entered the Cabinet as Chief Secy. for Ireland. Himself of Irish descent, with strong sympathies for the people, he was anxious to render Ireland contented and prosperous. With that object in view, in 1902 he approached a distinguished Indian civilian of pronounced Nationalist leanings, Sir Antony MacDonnell, who temporarily accepted the office of Under-Secretary on the understanding that he was to maintain order, solve the land question by voluntary purchase, settle the education question on Mr. Balfour's lines, and generally pursue a policy of material improvement and administrative conciliation. The situation was thus a very peculiar one. The Under-Secretary practically dictated the policy, and was granted greater freedom of action and greater opportunities of initiative than fall to the ordinary subordinate official. The outcome of the policy was Lord Dunraven's Devolution Scheme, in the preparation of which Sir Antony had taken an active part. This was practically Home Rule in disguise, and had to be repudiated by Mr. Wyndham, who had allowed himself to be nominally responsible for an impossible situation. He had apparently let the control of affairs in his department slip from his hands, and become the mere shield of a subordinate who carried out his own interpretation of an impossible agreement. The climax was reached in March, 1905, when Mr.

Wyndham, being of the opinion that the controversy which his action had given rise to had greatly impaired, if not wholly destroyed, the value of the work which he had to do in the office that he had so long held, he resigned the Chief Secretaryship.

WYNNE, Major-General Arthur Singleton, C.B., of Government House, Coichester, was born in 1846, and is son of the late Captain Wynne, of the Royal Artillery. He entered the Army in 1863, and served in the Jowaki Expedition in 1877, as Superintendent of Army Signalling (despatches, medal with clasp), the Afghan War in 1875-9, as Superintendent of Field Telegraphs, and in charge of Army Signalling with the Kurum Valley Field Force, at the capture of the Peiwar Kotal, also present at the actions in the Mungiar Pass and Matun Khost (despatches, medal with clasp and brevet of Major); the South African War in 1881, with the Natal Field Force as D.A.A. and Q.M.G. for signalling; and the Sudan Expedition in 1884-5, employed on the Lines of Communication (despatches, medal with clasp, bronze star and brevet of Lieut. Col.). From 1886-1891 he acted at D.A.A.G. at the Army Headquarters; acted as A.A.G. for the Curragh District from 1891-4; was D.A.G. at Malta from 1894-8, and at Aldershot from 1895-9. He served in the South African War in 1899-1901, on the staff, including service as Chief of Staff in South Africa (afterwards in Natal), and in command of the 11th Brigade at Standerton; present at the relief of Ladysmith, and the actions at Spion Kop and Vaal Kranz, and the operations on Tugela Heights; the operations in Natal, including the action at Laing's Nek, and the operations in the Transvaal and Cape Colony (despatches, Queen's medal with seven clasps; promoted Maj.Gen. for distinguished service). From 1902-4 he acted as D.A.G. to the Forces. He has also acted as Asst. Military Secretary to the Minister of War, and commanded the 6th Division, Eastern Command, until 1906, when he succeeded Col. J. S. Ewart as Military Secretary to the Minister of War. He married in 1886, Emily, dau. of the late Charles Turner.

WYNNE, James, M.L.A., is one of the Progressive members of the Cape Legislative Assembly for Port

Elizabeth, for which constituency he was re-elected at the general election in 1904.

YATES, Rev. John R., M.A., of Belfast, near Pretoria, is a graduate of Christ's Coll., Camb., has been in Holy Orders since 1894, and Rector of St. George, Abbey Hey, Gorton, near Manchester, from 1899 until his appointment in 1904 as Priest in Charge of Belfast.

YOUNG, Frank M. H., S.S.C., of 98, Hanover Street, Edinburgh, is a director of the Anglo-Columbian Investment, Ltd., Gold Proprietary Mines, Ltd., Idaho-Alamo Consolidated Mines, Ltd., Scottish Colonial Gold Fields, Ltd., and the United African Explorations, Ltd.

YOUNG, James, of Krugersdorp, Transvaal; formerly Acting Asst. R.M. at Johannesburg, was appointed Asst. RM. for the Witwatersrand District at Krugersdorp in 1904.

YOUNG, Sir William Lawrence, Bart., of 35, Lower Seymour Street, London, W., was born in 1864, and is son of the late Sir Charles Lawrence. He was educated at Charterhouse, and succeeded his father in 1887. Sir William is Chairman of the Ashanti Goldfields Auxiliary, Ltd., and Midland Uruguay Railway Co., Ltd., deputy chairman of the Cuban Central Railways, Ltd., and the Western Railway of Havana, Ltd., director of the Anglo-Sicilian Sulphur Co., Ltd., Economic Life Assurance Society, and the Grand Trunk Railway of Canada; trustee of the Hawaiian Commercial and Sugar Co., and is on the London Committee of the Grand Trunk Pacific Railway Co. He married, in 1887, Helen, dau. of the Hon. R. William Petre.

YOUNGHUSBAND, Major (Temp. Col.) Sir Francis Edward, C.I.E., of the Army and Navy Club; second son of Major-Gen. J. W. Younghusband, C.S.I., began his military career in the 1st Dragoon Guards in 1882, subsequently transferring to the Indian Staff Corps. He has travelled considerably in China, Chinese Turkestan and India, and has on various occasion served as Political Officer. Perhaps no man in the service of the Indian Govt. is regarded with so much fear by Russia, whose agents have persistently shadowed his movements during his journeys in the Far East.

Col. Younghusband acted as Special Correspondent of the *Times* during the campaign in Chitral, and also during the Rhodesian Rebellion in 1896. In 1903-4 he set out as Commissioner on a Mission to Thibet for negotiating a settlement of the relations between India and that country. The expedition after being delayed on the frontier, arrived at Khambajong, in the Thibetan territory, in July 1903, and remained there on account of the hostility of the Thibetans until Nov. of that year, when an advance of a further ninety miles to Gyangtse, an important centre some 150 miles from Lhassa, was ordered. Gyangtse was reached, after some fighting in which the Thibetans lost heavily, in April, 1904, and Lhassa was entered on Aug. 3, 1904. In the negotiations which followed, friction arose between the Home Govt. and that of India, which latter, Sir Francis appeared to support. It was stated in a Govt. despatch that "Colonel Younghusband has carried out the instructions of his Majesty's Govt. as to the treaty in a manner which enables them to give their general approval to the convention he has negotiated; but in regard to the indemnity his convention has been framed in defiance of express instructions. These were that the indemnity should be limited to a sum which the Thibetans could pay within three years, and that our occupation of the Chumbi Valley should terminate when the indemnity had been paid and the trade marts opened effectually for three years. But Colonel Younghusband, by accepting the proposal made by the Thibetans for the payment of the indemnity by instalments spread over a long period, has contravened our instructions in a most important particular. In the meanwhile we cannot accept the situation created for us by our representative's disobedience of orders." In a memorandum forwarded by the Indian Government to the India Office Colonel Younghusband thus justified his action: "I should have incurred a very heavy responsibility in refusing the Thibetan proposal. It was quite possible that if 1 had refused, the Regent would have fled from Lhassa rather than sign the convention, and, in any case, I would have left him there in a very precarious position. Whereas, by accepting the proposal, I satisfied the Thibetans."
Notwithstanding the strained relations between Colonel Younghusband and the British Govt., the Secretary of State for India in a telegram to the

Viceroy showed that he appreciated the services which the Colonel had rendered.

Col. Younghusband was decorated in 1901, and holds two gold medals, one the Kaisar-i-Hind for Public Service in India, and the other that of the Royal Geographical Society for general exploration work. He is the author of *South Africa of Today*, published in 1895, and of other works. He married, in 1897, a daughter of the late Chas. Magniac, M.P.

ZANZIBAR, Bishop of. (See Rt. Rev. J. K Hine.)

ZANZIBAR, Sultan of, His Highness Ali Syed, is son of the late Syed Hamoud, and succeeded his father in 1902. He was educated at Harrow and Oxford, and has travelled all over Europe and Africa, and in 1903 he made the pilgrimage to Mecca. He represented his father at the Coronation of King Edward in 1902.

ZERVUDACHI, Ambrose, of Alexandria, Egypt, is a director of the Egyptian Salt and Soda Co., Ltd., and the Port Said Salt Association, Ltd.

ZIETSMAN, Louis Frederick, M.L.A., was born on a farm in the District of Humansdorp, in the Eastern Province, Cape Colony, where his father Jacob Frederick Zietsman carried on successful farming for many years. He was partly educated in a public undenominational school at Humansdorp, and towards the end of 1877 he went to Cape Town to pursue his studies. In 1879 he joined a volunteer force to serve in the Transkeian Kaffir Wars. Returning to Cape Town he completed his studies, and was admitted an Attorney of the Supreme Court and Notary Public, starting business in East-Griqualand, taking an active part in establishing the Govt. in the conquered native territories on a satisfactory basis. In 1885 he accompanied (as legal adviser) a deputation of Pondo chiefs to Cape Town to settle some boundary dispute with the Colonial Govt., and on his return accompanied the chief magistrate to the Pondo Paramount Chief's kraal to finally fix up some political disputes. He took an active part in establishing system of public education in the territories, became a committee member of the first public school started under the Educational

Acts, and afterwards Chairman of the School Board, and he was mainly instrumental in starting the first political association (of which he was President for many years), which first obtained representation for East Griqualand in the Cape Parliament. He unsuccessfully contested the first election with Sir James Sivewright, but in 1898 he was returned as member for East Griqualand. When the war broke out with the Republics, he took up a strong stand on the British side, and influenced a number of his own countrymen to remain loyal. In 1899 a Congress was held in Cape Town, representative of all parts of South Africa, this Congress sent a deputation to England to assist in the general erection there, and Mr. Zietsman was chosen to represent the loyal Dutch, and addressed a number of meetings in England and Scotland. In the general election for Cape Colony in 1904 Mr. Zietsman was returned unopposed for his old constituency in the Progressive cause. He is especially interested in railway extension and the encouragement of Colonial industries.

ZOEPPRITZ, H., of 1, Orsett Terrace, London, W., is on the London Committee of the Bantjes Consolidated Mines, Durban Roodepoort Deep, Ferreira G.M. Co., French Rand G.M. Co., Geldenhuis Estate and G.M. Co., Glynn's Lydenburg, Langlaagte Deep, Modderfontein Extension, Nourse Mines, Transvaal G.M. Estates, and the West Roodepoort Deep, and is a London agent of the Jumpers G.M. Co., and the Transvaal Consolidated Land and Exploration Co.

ZULULAND, Bishop of. (See Rt. Rev. Wilmot Lushington Vyvyan.)

Obituaries

AKERMAN, Hon. Sir John William, K.C.M.G., who died in London June 24, 1905, was born in 1825, and was son of the Rev. J. Akerman. He went to S. Africa in 1850, and settled in Natal. In 1859 he acted as Mayor of Pietermaritzburg, and for twelve years he was Speaker for the Natal Legislative Council. He was twice married.

AMESHOF, Judge, was formerly Judge of the High Court of the S.A.H. He was one of the Commission of three appointed by the Government of the S.A.R. to confer with a deputation of the Reformers with a view to an amicable settlement of differences being arrived at. In giving evidence subsequently at the preliminary examination of the Reformers he refused to say anything which might be to the advantage of the prisoners, on the ground that the meeting was privileged. His objection was sustained by the Court, who ruled that the interview was privileged as far as the Government was concerned, but not in so far as it could benefit the Reformers.

Judge Ameshof, in common with the Chief Justice and Mr. Gregorowski, made a stand against the provisions of Law I. of 1897 (*vide* particulars under Gregorowski), in consequence of which he was summarily dismissed. He died in 1905.

ANDOE, Admiral Sir Hilary, who died suddenly at Plymouth on February 11, 1905, took part as a naval cadet in the bombardment of Sveaborg in 1855, and eight years later, as Commander of the *Vigilant*, he was engaged in the suppression of the slave trade on the East Coast of Africa. Subsequently he served as principal transport officer in the Boer War of 1881, and also during the first Sudan Expedition in the Red Sea.

ANSLIGN, Mons., who died in Feb., 1905, was a member of the Administrative Council of the Suez Canal.

BAILEY, Hon. Thomas, of Queenstown, Cape Colony, was born in the parish of Keighley, Yorks, Jan. 80, 1836, where he was educated. He went to the Cape in 1855, and settled in Cradock, subsequently removing to the Albany District, to Bailey Junction, and finally to Queen's town, where he established a large wholesale general business.

He was returned to the Cape Legislative Council as senior member of the Eastern Circle at the general election in 1888, and was Mayor of Queenstown in 1887-89. Mr. Bailey married Annie dau. of Peter McEwen, of Methill, Crieff, Perthshire, by whom he had one son. The Hon. Thos. Bailey died in 1904.

BAKER, Major-Gen. Charles, Pasha, V.C. who died at Southbourne-on-Sea, Hants, on Feb. 19, 1906, was for some years in the service of the P. and O. Steam Navigation Co., the directors of which company conferred upon him a highly valued testimonial for effecting the rescue of the passengers and crew of the S.S. *Duro*, which was wrecked on the Paracel's shoal in 1854, under most difficult conditions. Accompanied by six other volunteers, Mr. Baker made a perilous voyage of over 500 miles in a small open boat in order to obtain assistance, and although they were molested by Chinese pirates, short of water and provisions, and troubled with heavy seas, the party was successful in their mission for succour. Soon afterwards Mr. Baker joined the Bengal Police, and commanded the left wing of the irregular cavalry corps known as Rattray's Sikhs in the Indian Mutiny, receiving the coveted V.C. for gallantry at Suhejnee, near Peero, Shahabad, when with a small mounted force he routed a mixed body of rebels numbering over a thousand men. This feat was described by the C.I.C. as deserving of the highest encomiums on account of both conception and execution. Lieut. Baker served with further distinction in the Sikkim Expedition of 1861 under Col. Gawlor, and two years later he was appointed Officiating Deputy Inspector-Gen. of Military Police for the Dacca Circle of Bengal. He next saw fighting in the Russo-Turkish War, serving under Maj.-Gen. Val. Baker, and being for some time a prisoner in the Russian lines. Subsequently he accompanied Gen. Val. Baker to Egypt, and eventually succeeded his chief as commandant of the Egyptian Police, ranking as Maj.-Gen. He also became Chief of the Public Security Department of the Egyptian Ministry of the Interior until 1885, when he retired from the service.

BALD, Major A. Campbell, D.S.O. (1902), who died. on April 4, 1905, entered the Army in 1882, and served in the Sudan in 1884 (medal and clasp and Khedive's Star), the Nile Expedition in 1884-5, and served with the Black Watch through the South African War in 1899-1901, participating in the operations in the Orange River Colony from Feb. to May, 1900, including the actions at Vet River, Rhenoster River, Wittebergen, and Witpoort. In this campaign the deceased officer was attached to the Army Service Corps. He was mentioned in despatches, was promoted Major on the Reserve of Officers, and received the Queen's medal with two clasps and the D.S.O.

BARRY, Sir Jacob Dirk, who died in 1905, was a well-known Cape Colony judge. He was born at Swellendam in 1832, and received his early education in that place. Subsequently he proceeded to England, and studied at Cheltenham and Cambridge. On being called to the Bar he returned to the Cape and practised in the Supreme Court at Cape Town from 1859 till 1865, when he removed to Grahamstown to practise before the new court which had been established there. Sir Jacob was the leading lawyer of the Eastern Circuit until 1871, when he was appointed to the Recordership of Griqualand West. He entered the old Cape Parliament as representative for Cape Town in 1864, but subsequently sat for Aliwal North. In 1871 he was made official member of the Legislature and senior member of the Executive Council of Griqualand West. He received his knighthood in 1878, and was appointed to the bench of the Supreme Court. Sir Jacob retired in 1901.

BARTER, Charles, an old and respected Natalian, died near Maritzburg in the middle of 1905. He was educated at Westminster, and was a Fellow of New College, Oxford. In 1852 he settled in Durban, and in 1865 he became a member of the Legislative Council. He took command of the Carbineers in 1878, and accompanied Sir Theophilus Shepstone on his coronation visit to Cetewayo For some years he edited the *Natal Times*, subsequently becoming magistrate at Inanda, and, in 1880, at Maritzburg.

BEAL, Colonel Robert, C.M.G., died of heart failure in Rhodesia in Jan., 1907. (See Biographical section.)

BEHANZIN, Ex-King of Dahomey, whose full title was Bedoazin Boaidjere Hossu Bowele, Emperor of Dahomey, Lord of Ahomey, Son of Requin, and Egg of the Universe, died at Blidah, near Algiers, Dec. 10, 1906, surrounded by his wives and sons, who shared his captivity. For two centuries Dahomey had been counted one of the great Powers of Africa, but Behanzin had only enjoyed his rule for six months when a French expedition entered his country, the King being soon driven back on his city of Abomey, where he awaited the final onslaught. From time immemorial the daughter of the chiefs had defended the kingdom in the last emergency, but when the French came in view Behanzin and his famous Amazons fled leaving their city in flames. Two years late the King was captured, and exiled to Martinique, where he was at the time of the great eruption, but in June, 1906, he was removed to Algiers. Death was due to nephritis. (See Biographies)

BEIT, Alfred, late of 26, Park Lane, W., of Tewin Water, near Welwyn, Herts, and of London Wall Buildings, E.C., who died in the early morning of July 16, 1906, a sudden termination to a prolonged state of ill-health—was born in Hamburg in 1858, and after receiving a sound commercial education went with a few thousand pounds to Kimberley, where the great firm of Wernher, Beit, and Co. was originally founded. But the discovery of the Rand Goldfields greatly increased the sphere of the firm's operations. Already exercising the greatest influence over the destinies of the De Beers Mines, of which he was a life governor Mr. Beit soon began to acquire the control of a large proportion of the pick of the Rand outcrop claims, supplementing these holdings with a more or less continuous line of deep level claims along the main reef series, which were soon merged in the huge mining corporation known as the Rand Mines, Limited, of which Mr. Beit was a Johannesburg director, with a seat on the London Committee. To mention the other mining undertakings which come entirely or partly under the aegis of Mr. Beit's firm would be to name some sixty or more of the most prosperous and best managed of the and properties. At the time of his death Mr. Beit was Vice-President of the British South Africa Co., since 1904; life governor of the De Beers Consolidated Mines, Limited; a director of the Beira Railway Co., Limited; Central Mining and Investment Corporation, Limited; Mashonaland Railway Co., Limited; Rand Mines Limited; Rhodesia Railways, Limited (see J. R Maguire); Rhodesia Railways Trust, Limited and was on the London Board of the Consolidated Company Bultfontein Mine, Limited, and the H.F. Co., Limited.

But Mr. Beit's interests were not limited to gold and diamonds, for few men have done more to extend the British Empire in South Africa than this great naturalised Englishman, who had been from the beginning one of Mr. Rhodes' staunchest supporters in opening up the Northern Territory and preserving the road thereto for Great Britain. From the inception of the Chartered Co. his brains and influence had always been at the service of the company; he had been for nearly the whole period a director of the company, although the unfortunate Raid made it desirable for Mr. Beit to remain away from the councils of the board until he was re-elected by the shareholders a couple of years later. However, the death of Mr. Rhodes made it more essential that such a man as Mr. Beit should take a still more active part in the great colonising company, and he became its vice-president in 1904. His earnest desire to carry out the partially completed projects of his late friend and colleague had led him previously (in 1902) to make an extended tour through Rhodesia, the result being immediately reflected in the removal of most of the drawbacks under which the colonisers had been suffering. The old mining law was amended, the 50

per cent. lien clause being reduced to 30 per cent., and such important reforms as throwing open the country to diamond prospecting, reducing the post and telegraph rates, instituting departments for Native Affairs and Agriculture, and, above all, the decision to hurry on railway construction, were decided upon. Mr. Beit became Vice-President of the Chartered Co. in 1904, thus very greatly diminishing the loss which fell to Rhodesia on the death of Mr. Rhodes, and the transference of Earl Grey to Canada.

A man with such responsibilities and interests needs to be something more than a financial genius, and perhaps one of his most fortunate attributes was his perspicuity in judging character and associating himself with the right people. Thus it is safe to say that no other firm contains such a combination of men of brains and financial probity as the firm of Wernher, Beit, and Co. and the allied firm of H. Eckstein and Co., who act as their Transvaal representatives, and between them they are perhaps second only to the house of Rothschild in the magnitude of their operations and the amplitude of their financial resources. Mr. Beit's firm is, of course, not free from those attacks which are periodically directed against the great financial houses. In the case of the libel uttered by Mr. A. B. Markham, M.P. (q.v.), which was so unreservedly withdrawn, it is characteristic of the firm that they abstained from asking for the costs in the case.

Mr. Beit himself was reserved and was for many years somewhat delicate, as most men are who develop their intellectual strength at the expense of their physical force. Nevertheless, he had an extraordinary capacity for hard work, and while he commonly calculated in millions he had that grasp of detail which ensured his schemes being successfully carried through. Although German by birth, he was a naturalised Englishman, and apart from the huge tract of country which he helped to bring under the British flag, he had large ideas on such questions of national importance as technical education, to advance which he and his firm have contributed in princely fashion. Mr. Beit's gifts for public or charitable purposes have been numerous and large. During the late S.A. War he was a munificent supporter of the I.L.H., and it was owing to his generous financial aid that the regiment was, after the relief of Ladysmith, re-horsed in time for it to take part in the relief of Mafeking.

Braamfontein Forest, Parktown, near Johannesburg, consisting of about 200 acres of free hold ground, valued at £200,000, was recently presented to the Johannesburg Town Council by Messrs. Wernher, Beit, & Co. and Mr. Max Michaelis (a former partner in the firm) for the purposes of a public park, which is now known as the Hermann Eckstein Park. In Sept., 1904, Mr. Beit presented the magnificent Frankenwald model estate of 3000 acres, situated close to the dynamite factory, laid out for Messrs. Eckstein at a cost of over £100,000 by Mr. Genth (Prince Bismarck's Chief Forester, who planted the Sachsenwald forests adjoining Johannesburg), to the Transvaal Government for educational purposes. Following hard on this came the announcement of his offer to Oxford University to found a Professorship of Colonial History. The terms of the offer were that Mr. Beit would contribute the sum of £1310 per annum for seven years for the maintenance of a resident professor and assistant lecturers; a prize of £50 for an annual essay on the Advantages of Imperial Citizenship, and the payment of examiners' fees; the purchase of books on the subject, the amount annually expended not to exceed £50. At the expiration of the seven years, if the Hebdomadal Council so desired, Mr. Beit was to make the endowment permanent, and he had already given £350 to the Bodleian Library for the purchase of books and documents required in the study of Imperial History.

Mr. Beit was a great lover of pictures, and possessed an art collection which was amongst the most valuable in England. A year before his death he presented a Gainsborough worth £8000 to the National Gallery in Berlin, in addition to having given at least one large donation to help save a valuable picture from being sold out of England, whilst amongst his treasures bequeathed in his will were Reynolds's *Lady Cockburn and her Children* to the National Gallery; Reynolds's *Mrs. Boone and her Daughter, afterwards Lady Drummond* to the Imperial Museum, Berlin; Polajuolo's bronze statuette of Hercules to the same museum; and Majolica plate

from the service of Isabella Gonzaga d'Este to the Art and Industrial Museum, Hamburg.

In his lifetime Mr. Beit had ceaselessly been depicted by the extremist Press as the typical 'Randlord'—a callous bloodsucker, battening on the prosperity of South Africa from no other motive than a vicious propensity to evil. His will, however, showed the greatness of the man's ideas. It breathed a practical spirit of humanity, which stood as its maker's best defence. As Cecil Rhodes left his money to unite the Anglo-Saxon world in bonds of educational brotherhood, Alfred Beit bequeathed a sum of £1,200,000 for developing Africa's means of communication. "I believe", said the testator, "that by the promotion, construction, and furtherance generally of railways, telegraphs (including wireless telegraphy), and telephones, and kindred or other methods of transmission of persons, goods, and messages, civilisation will be best advanced and expedited in Africa for the benefit of the inhabitants thereof, whether native or immigrant, and I know from experience how difficult it is at times to find the funds for the construction of such methods of transmission in new and undeveloped countries." His educational bequests included £200,000 for the Johannesburg University, a similar sum for Rhodesia, cash and shares worth nearly £140,000 for the College of Technology, London University; £25,000 to the Institute of Medical Sciences Fund, London University; £25,000 to Rhodes University, Grahamstown; £20,000 for educational and charitable purposes in the Transvaal; £15,000 for same purposes in or near Kimberley; and £15,000 for same purposes in Cape Colony (excluding Kimberley); besides which £10,000 went to the Rhodes Memorial Fund, Cape Town; £20,090 to King Edward VII. Hospital Fund; £20,000 to Guy's Hospital; £20,090 for charitable purposes in London; £20,000 for charitable purposes in Hamburg; and £10,000 to the Union Jack Club, London.

It must be remembered that this will was drawn at a time when Mr. Beit was still being constantly attacked by those who have made it their business to hold him up to the working man as the very type of unscrupulous financier who is supposed to be the curse of South Africa. But it is not by such attacks that he will be remembered. Long after they are forgotten the people of Great and Greater Britain will benefit by the farsighted philanthropy of Alfred Beit.

The executors named in the will were Mr. Otto Beit, brother of the deceased, Mr. Franz Voelklein, cousin, and Sir Julius Wernher, one of his partners. Other trustees were also named for carrying out certain definite objects. Mr. Alfred Beit was not married. He was survived by his mother, who lives in Hamburg, of whom he was intensely fond.

BELLORD, Right. Rev. Charles Waldegrave Sandford, DD., Bishop of Gibraltar, who died at Nazareth House, Southend-On-Sea, on June 11, 1905, was an old Rugby boy and a student of Christ Church, Oxford, where he was subsequently a tutor, senior censor, and praetor; was for twenty-six years a British military chaplain, serving in the Zulu War and the Egyptian Expedition under Lord Wolseley. He was present at the battle of Tel-el-Kebir, and, although wounded, was carried round on an ambulance to minister to the dying soldiers of his flock. He was also Bishop of British Congregations in Malta, S. and E. Europe, Anatolia, the northern seaboard of Africa, and Hon. Canon of Canterbury.

BIRCHALL, Charles, late of Liverpool; was born in 1842, and entered the service of the London and North-Western Railway Company at a very early age, and the business training he received in the few years he remained with that concern stood him in such good stead that the intricacies of commercial life thereafter came extremely easy. At the end of twenty years' faithful work in the service of the founder of the *Journal of Commerce*, he became sole proprietor of this well-known organ.

In a quiet and unobtrusive way he did a great deal towards the improvement of South and West Africa, for as proprietor of the Liverpool and Manchester *Journal of Commerce* and Chairman of the company which owns the *Financier and Bullionist*, all the weight of his influence had for many years past been exerted in the direction of promoting a better knowledge of the Dark Continent on the part of Englishmen, and a greater development of the vast resources of Africa by the aid of British capital. At a time when Western Africa was a *terra incognita* to the vast mass of the people of this country, the newspapers which Mr. Birchall so ably controlled in the North of England loudly proclaimed its great possibilities, arid boldly asked for railways, better government, and more general recognition, an advocacy which can claim to have been the chief means of the wonderful latter-day development of such places as Ashanti and the Gold Coast. As one of the principal personages who regulated the policy of the *Financier and Bullionist*, both South and West Africa have to thank him for the uncompromising and unflinching manner in which the interests of that country have always been placed before the public, whilst his belief in the future of Africa has ever been very practically demonstrated by the possession of large financial interests in many of the concerns at present engaged in gold production and general development. Mr. Birchall was one of the most popular and influential men in the city of Liverpool, where, besides producing the *Journal of Commerce*, he conducted a large advertising and printing business. The whole of his commercial career was spent in the great city on the Mersey, and a nearly equally long residential connection with the Wirral Peninsula on the other side of the river led to his taking quite a number of public duties, including that of County Councillor for Cheshire and Chairman of the School Attendance Committee of the local School Board. Perhaps Mr. Birchall's later reputation rested more on his philanthropic work than on anything else, for in establishing the famous Christmas 'hot pots' at Liverpool, he founded a benevolent scheme whose fame has travelled all over the world. In almost every plan for helping the poor and the needy in Liverpool and in Wirral he took the keenest interest, and on the School Board and the County Council, with which he was so long associated, there was no harder worker.

Latterly Mr. Birchall had suffered from a complication of diseases which necessitated his wintering in Jamaica and Madeira, and after much acute suffering he passed away at his residence, The Laurels, Egremont, on July 14, 1905.

BOK, W. E., late of Jeppestown, Johannesburg, who died at the latter end of 1904, was state

Secretary of the S.A. Republic from the time of the retrocession up to 1890, when he was succeeded by Dr. Leyds. Then for three years he served as a member of the Executive Council, and subsequently was appointed Government Commissioner at Johannesburg, an appointment which entailed attendance at the meetings of the *Gezondheids Comite.*

BONAR, Frederick, who died at the latter end of 1905, was British Vice-Consul at Pensacola. He was employed at the Consulate at Tamatave, Madagascar, in 1887-5, and was Acting-Consul at Brest in 1889-90, subsequently being appointed Vice-Consul. In recognition of his services in connection with the loss of the *Drummond Castle* in June, 1896 Mr. Bonar received the Queen's commemorative medal.

BONHAM, Lieut. Colonel Walter Floyd, D.S.O., late of the Essex Regt., who died in May, 1905, was the eldest son of the late Edward W. Bonham, H.B.M.'s Consul at Calais. He was born Jan. 3, 1869, at Naples, Italy, and was educated at Charterhouse and the Royal Military Coll., Sandhurst. Col. Bonham entered the Army in 1899, and graduated at the Staff Coll. 1899. He served throughout the S. African War, and was twice mentioned in despatches and awarded the D.S.O. In Dec., 1902, He was selected to raise and command 100 Boers for service in Somaliland. The Boer Contingent under his command sailed from Durban on Jan., 15, 1903, then landed at Obbia, in Italian Somaliland, on Jan. 22. The Contingent formed part of the advanced flying column throughout Gen. Manning's operations, being present at the occupation of Galkaya Wells on March 4; Dudub, March 29; and the capture of Galadi, March 81. On the night of the Gumburru disaster, April 17, sixty of the Boer Contingent, under Capt. Bonham, formed part of a small mounted force which made a successful march to the relief of Col. Cobbe. The Contingent, at the conclusion of their six months' engagement, returned to S. Africa in July, 1908. For his services with the Contingent Capt. Bonham was promoted to the rank of Brevet Major. At the time of his death he held the post of Military Attaché at the British Embassy in Paris. He was unmarried.

BRABANT, Brig. Gen., Sir Edward Yewd, M.L.A., K.C.B., C.M.G., of Gonubie Park, East London, Cape Colony, who died quite recently, was born in 1839, and had had a long and distinguished career in politics and arms, He entered the 2nd Derby Militia as Ensign in 1855, and joined the Cape Mounted Rifles with similar rank in 1855, from which he retired on half pay with Captain's rank in 1870. He entered the arena of politics as M.L.A. for East London in 1873, and was re-elected in the following year. In 1875 he was appointed Field Commandant of the Cape Colonial Forces; became Colonel of the 1st Cape Yeomanry in 1879; was made C.M.G. in 1880; was re-elected member for East London in 1882, and again in 1885. He was a member of the Defence Commission in 1896, and in 1897 was Pres. of the South African League. Gen. Brabant served through the S.A. War, at first in command of the Colonial Division and subsequently as Inspector-General of the Colonial Defence Force, until the end of 1901, when he retired under the new scheme of Colonial Defence (despatches, medal, and clasps). He resumed his duties in the Cape Parliament, and soon after seceded from his old political leader, Sir Gordon Sprigg, and joined the new Progressive party under Dr. Smaart, with whom he was associated in connection with the Suspension movement. He resigned his seat in Parliament on his reappointment in Dec., 1902, to the command of the Cape Colonial Forces, from which He retired in 1904. Subsequently he re-entered the Cape Assembly as member for East London. He was a keen sympathiser with the loyalists who suffered from the effects of the war, and marked his departure from England after the Coronation by the public declaration that "Loyalty does not pay". Gen. Brabant married Mary Burnet, dau. of the Rev. Canon Robertson, of Canterbury. (See Capt. G. A. Brabant.)

BRAZZA, Pierre Paul François Camille de, Count de Savorgnan, a naturalised Frenchman, who died at Dakar, French West Africa, in Sept., 1905, while on a journey to the Ivory Coast to investigate allegations of cruelty to natives by French officials, was born in 1852. His lifework consisted of exploring Africa, and through his energy and skill the foundations were laid of France's dominion over an immense tract of the African continent. In 1875 he set out to explore the basin of the River Ogowe in West Africa; and in 1879 he made his famous expedition to open up communication between the Upper Congo and the sea by way of Alima and Ogowe. It was during this expedition that he founded the towns of Franchville and Brazzaville, and in 1886 he was made Commissary General of the new settlements. In 1891 he led another expedition, and returned to France in 1897.

BROWN, Major Sir Robert Hanbury, K.C.M.G., of Newlands, Crawley Down, Sussex, was born in 1849. He formerly belonged to the Royal Engineers, from which he retired in 1893. Sir Robert served in Afghanistan in 1878-80, afterwards in the Bengal Irrigation Department. Later on he became Inspector-General in Egypt in connection with the Nile Reservoir. In 1906 the Spanish Government engaged his services to advise on the utilisation of the waters of the Guadalquivir for purposes of irrigation. He married, in 1875, Marian, dau. of the Rev. Edwin Meyrick.

BURNEY, Lieut. Col. Ernest Henry, C.B., formerly of the Royal Berks Regt., who died at Neuilly, France, in the summer of 1905 aged forty-four, was present at the surrender of Kafr Dowar in the Egyptian Expedition of 1882 (medal, bronze star). In the S. African War (1899-02) he commanded the 2nd. Battn. of the R. Berks for twelve months, afterwards commanding a section of the lines of communication and a mobile column, taking part in the operations in the Transvaal and Cape Colony (Queen's medal with three clasps, King's medal with two clasps).

BUTTERY, J. A., who died of appendicitis in Aug., 1906, was formerly chief subeditor of the *Standard and Diggers' News* in Johannesburg during the most exciting period of the diplomatic struggle between London, Cape Town, and Pretoria. He was the anther of *Why Kruger made War; or, Behind the Boer Scenes*. At the time of his death he was conducting the football and cricket department of the *Daily Mail*.

CAMPBELL, Sir George Wm. Robert, K.C.M.G., who died at Wimbledon, Jan. 10, 1905, was the

son of John Campbell, of the Hon. East India Co.'s service. He began his career as a subaltern in the Argyll Militia; afterwards became head of various corps of the Indian Police, and served in the Indian Mutiny. He was Inspector-General of Police in Ceylon from 1866 to 1891, during which time he acted (1872-3) as Lieut.-Governor of Penang. In 1891 he was in charge of Arabi Pasha and other Egyptian exiles in Ceylon, and repeatedly received the thanks of the Secretary of State and Indian Govts. for special services. Sir George married, first, a dau. of Dr. John Moyle, head of the Bombay Med. Service, and, second, Mary Gertrude, dau. of Andrew Murray, W.S., of Edinburgh.

CHELMSFORD, General Lord, G.C.B., G.C.V.O., who died on April 9, 1905, was born in 1827, and succeeded his father, the first Baron, in 1879. He was educated at Eton, and joined the Army in 1844. In 1867-8 he took part in the Abyssinian Campaign, and commanded the forces in the Kaffir War in 1878. In the same year he became Commander of the Forces and Lieut.-Governor of Cape Colony. He also served in the Zulu War in 1879. Lord Chelmsford was appointed Lieutenant of the Tower of London in 1884, which post he held until 1889. He married, in 1867, Adria, dau. of Major.-Gen. Heath, of the Bombay Army.

CHICHESTER, Rear-Admiral Sir Edward, Bart., C.M.O., C.B., late of Youlston, Barnstaple, who died in Sept., 1906, was born in 1849, and was son of the 5th Bart., whom he succeeded in 1898. He entered the Royal Navy in 1864 as a cadet, and was gazetted Commander in 1882, Captain in 1889, and Rear-Admiral in 1902. He acted as Naval Transport Officer in Natal during the South African War in 1881-2, and was Lieutenant of the *Thalia* during the Egyptian War in 1882 (Egyptian medal and Khedive's bronze star); served in the Sudan Expedition in 1884-5 as Transport Officer, and was thanked by the Admiralty for the prompt manner in which the forces for the Nile Expedition were landed. In 1887 he was further thanked by the Admiralty and the Board of Trade for his valuable services on the Board of Trade Committee of Inquiry on British Drift Net Fisheries, and a year later was thanked by the Admiralty and the Board of Trade for judgment and tact displayed when he was employed as senior officer in protecting the North Sea Fisheries. In 1891 he again elicited the thanks of the Board of Trade for services rendered while serving on a Committee on Fishing Boats' Lights. Sir Edward Chichester acted as A.D.C. to Queen Victoria in 1899, and served in the South African War in 1899-1900 as Naval Transport Officer at Cape Town (despatches and C.B.). In 1901-2 he acted as A.D.C. to King Edward VII. Rear-Admiral Chichester is succeeded by his son, Lieut. Edward George Chichester, R.N. (q.v.). He married, in 1880 Catharina, dau. of Commander R. C. White R.N.

CLARKE, Lieut.-Col. H. W., late of the Royal (Bengal) Engineers, died in the latter part of 1905. He was born in 1842, and entered the Bengal Engineers in 1860. During the Abyssinian Campaign he served in the Water Supply Department from Senafe to Addigerut (medal), and in the Nile Expedition as Asst. Adjutant General and Director of Railways (medal and clasp and bronze star).

CLEVERLY, John James, who died in the middle of 1906, at Elliott, Tembuland, where he was Acting Resident Magistrate, was well known in Port Elizabeth, where he resided for many years. He entered the Cape Civil Service in 1876, acting fourth Examining Officer for Customs at East London in 1875, acted as Second Clerk of the Customs at Port Elizabeth in 1884, and as Chief Clerk and Warehouse keeper there until 1885. He was transferred to Walfisch Bay as Resident Magistrate and Customs Officer in 1889; was appointed Collector of Customs and Registrar of Shipping for East London in 1901, and Sub Collector of Customs, Civil Commissioner, and Resident Magistrate at Walfisch Bay in 1903.

COSTER, Dr. Hermanus Jacob, was born in Holland. He was State Attorney of the late S.A.R. and *ex officio* J.P. He prosecuted on behalf of the State in the case of the Reformers. There were originally four indictments against the whole of the prisoners, but negotiations between Dr. Coster and Advocate Wessels (the latter representing the accused) resulted as follows: that the leaders, Col. Rhodes and Messrs. L. Phillips, Hays Hammond, and Geo. Farrar, should plead guilty to count 1

(conspiring with Dr. Jameson to make a hostile invasion), and that the rank and file of the committee should plead guilty to counts 3 (distributing arms, guns, erecting defences, etc.) and 4 (arrogating the functions of Government in Johannesburg, arming their own Police Corps, etc.); that counts 2, 3 and 4 should be withdrawn against the latter. Dr. Coster admitted that the effect of this would be making the charge against the rank and file purely nominal, while in the case of the four leaders he undertook not to press for exemplary punishment. Nevertheless, at the trial Dr. Coster, in a violent speech, depicted in the blackest terms the action of those men, and claimed that the Court should apply the Roman Dutch Law in preference to the statutes of the S.A.R., and demanded the severest penalty that could be imposed under that law and under the Thirty-three Articles and the Gold Law. Dr. Custer resigned the State Attorneyship in consequence of an insulting reference of President Kruger's to his countrymen. He took part in the S. African War, and was killed in action at Elandslaagte.

COSTERMANS,. Mons., one of the Vice-Governors-General of the Congo; died at Banana early in 1905.

CRABBE, Brig. Gen. E. M. S., C.B., who died suddenly at the Headquarters Office, Aldershot, on March 5, 1905, formerly belonged to the Grenadier Guards. His active service included the Egyptian War in 1882, and the Nile Expedition two year later. He also served in S. Africa from 1899 to 1902, and was twice severely wounded. For his services in S. Africa he was mentioned in despatches , received the C.B., and a medal with five clasps, as well as the King's medal with two clasps. At the time of his death Gen. Crabbe was employed as C.S.O. to Gen. Sir John French. He was popularly credited with having the most powerful voice in the British Army, and was highly esteemed by all ranks.

CUPELLI, Count, who died in the early part of 1905 at Shinkakassa of haematuric fever, belonged to one of the great Italian families, and had served in the Army of his country as a Captain of Artillery.

DAELMANS, Jules, was attached to the Special

Committee of the Katanga. He died on Jan. 28, 1905, at Buli, through an attack of fever.

DAUMAS, Dr. F. C., formerly of Natal, who died in Paris on April 24, 1906, was the eldest son of a French Missionary who worked amongst the natives of Basutoland for many years, and it was in that country that his son (the late doctor) was born.

DAVENPORT, Lieut. Talbot Neville Fawsett, late of the Royal Irish Rifles, who died in his twenty-seventh year in 1905, served in the S. African Campaign with the M.I.

DAVIS, Robert G., who died in the summer of 1906, was the London Manager and Secretary of the Bank of Africa, with which institution he had been connected for upwards of twenty five years.

DAWKINS, Sir Clinton Edward, K.C.B., who died on Dec. 2, 1905, was born in 1859, and was the son of the late Clinton G. A. Dawkins, of the Foreign Office. He was educated at Cheltenham and at Balliol College, Oxford. In 1886 he was appointed Private Secretary to Lord Cross, Secretary of State, and three years later he succeeded Lord (then Mr.) Milner as Private Secretary to Lord Goschen, Chancellor of the Exchequer. He represented the Peruvian Corporation in S. America in 1891, and a few years later was appointed Under-Secretary for Finance in Egypt. Having performed that duty successfully, he was promoted to the post of Indian Minister of Finance. In 1900 he became a partner in the firm of J. S. Morgan and Co., and in the year following he became Chairman of the Committee of War Office Reorganisation; for his services in that capacity he was created a C.B., and in the following year he received his knighthood. Sir Clinton Dawkins wrote an Appendix to Lord Milner's *England in Egypt*. He married, in 1885, Louise, dau. of Charles Johnston, and cousin of Mr. Eustis, the first American who bore the title of Ambassador in Paris.

DIXIE, Lady Florence, late of Glen Stuart, Scotland, and of the Lyceum Club, died on Nov. 7, 1905. She was born in London in 1857, and was the dau. of the 7th Marquis of Queensberry. In 1879-80 she travelled in Patagonia and the Andes.

On the outbreak of the Boer War in 1880, she went to S. Africa as War Correspondent for the *Morning Post* ; and was present with Sir Evelyn Wood at the famous meeting of Zulu Chiefs under the shadow of the Inhlazatzo Mountain in Zululand. Lady Florence Dixie was a fine shot and a splendid swimmer and horsewoman. She was a staunch Socialist, and held strong views on the woman question; was the author of many books, including *Ijain, Isola, or the Disinherited, Eilabelle, or the Redeemed* (written in the Drakensburg Mountains in S. Africa); *In the Land of Misfortune (Africa)*; *A Defence of Zululand and its King*, and many others. She married, in 1875, Sir B. Dixie, Bart.

DOUGLASS, Hon. Arthur, late of Grahamstown, Cape Colony, was born at Market Harborough, Leicestershire, Jan., 1843, was fifth son of L. Douglass, Solicitor, Market Harborough; was educated at the Leicester Collegiate Sch., and served as a Midshipman in the Royal Navy. He went to the Cape as a Land Surveyor in 1864, and started farming and the domestication of ostriches. He was Capt. of the 'Rovers' in the Kaffir War of 1878, when he was present at the Pen Bush engagement; in the Morosi Campaign of 1879 was Capt. in the 1st Cape Yeomanry Regt., and served in the Boer War as Major and O.C. of the Albany Mounted Troops. He entered the Cape Assembly as member for Grahamstown at the general election in 1884, and represented that constituency with slight intermission from that time until, in Feb., 1904, the Progressives rejected him at the general election. Failing there he put up unsuccessfully for Woodstock. He went out of the Govt. with Sir Gordon Sprigg's resignation following the result of the elections. Mr. Douglass was a Moderate in politics; was associated with the Anti-Suspensionist party; and joined Sir Gordon Sprigg's Cabinet as Minister for Railways and Commissioner of Public Works. During Sir Gordon's absence in England, in the summer of 1902, he acted as Premier of the Colony, and later in the year (Sept.) made a violent attack upon the High Commissioner for making unreasonable demands upon the Govt. railways.

He published a work, entitled *Ostrich Farming in South Africa*, and married, in 1867, Martha Emily, second dau. of Joseph Perkins, of Laughton, Leicestershire. He died Oct. 12, 1905.

411

ELWES, Richard Gervase, M.Inst.C.E., of 35, Baring Road, Lee, S.E., who died on Aug. 14, 1906, was born Feb. 25, 1841, and was the eldest son of T. H. Elwes, of Ipswich. He was educated at King's Coll., London, where he obtained a scholarship in applied sciences. From 1860-73 he served in the Bengal Public Works Dept., being engaged as engineer on the Hindustan and Thibet and the Kooloo and Ladak roads. He accompanied Lord Elgin on his fatal journey over the Rohtang Pass, was acting secretary to the Resident at Hyderabad, and also officiated as Deputy Controller and Auditor, Public Wks. Accounts, Hyderabad. Since 1888 he had been engaged chiefly in mining and metallurgical work. He was a director of Lisbon Berlyn, Ltd., and the Lydenburg (Transvaal) Gold Exploration Co., Ltd.; and was consulting engineer to Rezende Ltd., Mozambique Macequece, Ltd., Bartissol Gold Mining Co., Ltd., and other mining companies. He had contributed to the *Pioneer* (Allahabad), *Calcutta Observer*, *Calcutta Quarterly Review*, *Financial News*, *Mining World*, and *Nineteenth Century and After*. Married.

EVETTS, Lieut. Col. S. M., late of the 16th (Queen's) Lancers, and of the 2nd Batt. Cameronians (Scottish Rifles), died on March 9, 1905, at Woodstock, at the age of fifty-six. He served in the S. African War (1899-1902) as District Commandant and with the Imperial Yeomanry, receiving the medal with two clasps.

EWART, Captain Frank Rowland, D.S.O., who died at Las Palmas on the homeward voyage from West Africa, in June, 1906 was born in 1874. He was attached to the Liverpool Regt., and served in S. Africa in 1899-1902, taking part in the operations in Natal, including the actions at Rietfontein and Lombard's Kop and the defence of Ladysmith; the operations in the Transvaal, east of Pretoria, including the actions at Belfast, and the operations in the Orange River and Cape Colonies (despatches, Queen's medal with three clasps, and D.S.O.). In 1903 he was appointed second in command of the West African Frontier Force, which post he held at the time of his death.

FARRAR, Mrs. Sidney H., who died on May 9, 1906, was the wife of Sidney Farrar (q.v.). She was the youngest daughter of the late Mr. Joseph Simpson, one of Port Elizabeth's most esteemed pioneer citizens.

FEILDING, Hon. Very Rev. Basil, who met his death through the capsizing of a canoe in which he was touring the Rhine, in July, 1906, was brother to the Earl of Denbigh. He had pursued an active career in the Roman Catholic Church, and spent a year in S. Africa as Roman Catholic chaplain to the British Forces during the Anglo Boer War. Latterly he had been studying Canon Law at the Scots College, Home.

FINCH, Major John Seymour Wynne, late of 105, Mount Street, Grosvenor Square, London, W., who died at the age of fifty-nine, was formerly in the 60th Rifles and afterwards with the Royal Horse Guards. He was a director of the African Banking Corporation and of numerous Joint Stock Companies.

FOLLETT, Col. S. W., who was one of the victims of the wreck of the S.S. *Hilda* off St. Malo on Nov. 18, 1905, joined the 9th Lancers as a subaltern in 1875; was brevetted as a Lieut. Col. in 1902, and retired in 1904. He commanded his regiment of Lancers in the S. African War, receiving the Queen's medal with seven clasps and the King's medal with two clasps.

FROUDE, Thomas, who died, poverty stricken, in March, 1906, served through the first Egyptian War in the 2nd Life Guards, taking part in the actions at Mahuta, Mahsameh, Kassassin, and Tel-el-Kebir, and took part in the flying march to Cairo to intercept Asahi Pasha. He had a great gift for making verse, the result being that he received a visit from Queen Victoria, and letters from many noted people. While lying in hospital at Windsor, he composed some verses in the midnight charge of his regiment at Kassassin. These were read at a regimental dinner when Prince Christian was present, the result being that the poem was printed and published, the composer receiving some sixty pounds profit and the honour of being congratulated by Queen Victoria.

GATACRE, General Sir William Forbes K.C.B., D.S.O., who died at Gambela, Abyssinia, in

March, 1906, while on a mission to report on the Abyssinian rubber forests for the Kordofan Trading Company, of London, was born in 1843, and was son of Edward L. Gatacre, of Shropshire. He entered the Army in 1862. From 1875-79 he acted as Instructor in Surveying to the Royal Military College, Sandhurst, and in 1888 he took part in the Hazara Expedition (medal and clasp, D.S.O.). In 1889-90 he was in command of the Mandalay Brigade, and served in Burmah, including the Tinhorn Expedition (clasp); served in Chitral in 1895 (medal and clasp, despatches, and C.B.). He commanded the British troops in the Sudan in 1898, and was in command of the British Division during the advance on Omdurman and Khartoum (Order of Medjidie, 2nd class, despatches, K.C.B.). The late general also served in S. Africa in 1899-1900 in command of the 3rd Div. S. African Field Force (Queen's medal and two clasps). He retired in 1904. In 1895 he married Beatrice, dau. of Baron Davey.

GLYN, Gen. Sir Julius R., C.B., who died in London, June 16, 1905, at the age of eighty three, served in S. Africa in 1848 as Field Adjt. of the Force at the action against the Boers at Boomplaats (despatches), took part in the Kaffir War, 1852-3 (medal), and in the Crimea (1854-6), being present at Alma, Inkerman, and the siege of Sevastopol (despatches, medal and three clasps, Knt. of the Legion of Honour, 5th Cl. Medjidie; Turkish medal, and brevets of Maj. and Lieut. Col.). He also saw service in 1857-9 in the Indian Mutiny, taking part in the defeat of the Gwalior contingent at Cawnpore, the final capture of Lucknow, and the action of Nawabgunge (despatches, medal with clasp, C.B.).

GORDON, Admiral William Everard Alphonso, R.N., C.B., late of 42, Carlisle Road, Eastbourne, who died in the summer of 1906, was born in 1817, and entered the Royal Navy in 1830. He served in Jamaica in 1832, and in Alexandria in 1841; took part in the Kaffir War in 1852-3 and the Crimean War in 1854 (medals and clasp and C.B.).

GOSLING, Major Audley Vaughan, who died on June 7, at St. Martin's, Guernsey, formerly belonged to the Rifle Brigade. For several years he was attached to the British South Africa Police,

subsequently joining Dr. Jameson (q.v.) and taking part in the Raid, and afterwards standing his trial with his leader and brother officers at Bow Street, and at the High Court of Judicature in June, 1896. Major Gosling also served in the South African War in 1900-2; present at the operations in the Transvaal and the Orange River and Cape Colonies (Queen's medal)). He married, in 1895, Ella, only dau. of the late Sir Sidney Shippard, Administrator of Bechuanaland, and granddau. of the late Lady Stockenström, of Grahamstown, Cape Colony.

GOSLING, Captain G. B., who died of blackwater fever in Central Africa in 1906, was a son of the late Robert Gosling, M.F.H. He joined the Rifle Brigade in 1892, and served on the N.W. Frontier of India in 1897-8 (medal and clasp). and in the late South African War. He had been engaged on the Nigerian Expedition for the last two years, together with Lieut. B. Alexander (q.v.).

GRENFELL, Rev. George, F.R.G.S., who died of blackwater fever at Bassoko, West Africa, in 1906, was born near Penzance in 1849, and was educated at Birmingham and Bristol. In 1874 he was sent to the Cameroons by the Baptist Missionary Society, and made his first journey to the Congo in 1878. In 1884 he discovered the Mobangi River, and was awarded the gold medal of the Royal Geographical Society. He acted as Royal Commissioner for the delimitation of the Lunda Frontier between the territory of the Congo State and that of the Portuguese Colony in 1891-3.

GRENFELL, Rear Admiral Sir Harry Tremenheere, R.N., K.C.B., C.M.G., who died early in 1906, was born in 1845, and entered the Navy in 1858. He served in the Egyptian War in 1882 as Commander of the *Cockatrice* (Egyptian medal and Khedive's bronze star). In 1901 he was appointed to succeed Sir James Bruce in command of the China Squadron, and was made K.C.B. and C.M.G. on his return.

HAICALIS, Pasha, who died at Alexandria in 1905, was of Greek nationality; was educated at Turin, and qualified as a barrister. As Counsel to Govt. he was leader of the Egyptian Bar, but he abandoned his profession to take up journalism, being entrusted by Khedive Ismail with the task of founding a newspaper which would raise the tone of the Egyptian Press, which was then a hotbed of corruption and blackmail. The paper, a French journal, was founded in Alexandria, supported throughout Ismail's reign by a liberal Government subvention, which was withdrawn after the abdication. But the paper had taken a hold in the country, which it still enjoys.

Haicalis Pasha is believed to have been the man who inspired Mr. Cook, the founder of the great tourist firm, with the idea of developing Egypt as a field of travel. The meeting of the two men took place by accident in Venice, whither M. Haicalis himself had gone to initiate a regular steamship service between the Italian port and Alexandria.

HARMAN, Frederick Edwin, who died in Sept., 1904, was the son of Edward Harman and his wife Caroline. He was born at the Manor House, Malden, Surrey, Jan. 3, 1849, and educated at the Brighton Coll., the Royal Agricultural Coll., Cirencester, and at the Royal Sch. of Mines, London. From 1875-80 he managed the Govt. Experimental Farm, Bangalore, and acted as Professor of Natural Science at the Sch. of Engineering and Natural Science. From 1880-3 he managed coffee, tea, and cinchona and gold estates in the Wynaad, and acted as Hon. Magistrate for the Govt. of Madras. In 1884-5 he reported on the estate of the Sante Fé Land Co., Argentine Republic, for colonisation purposes. From that time until his death he was engaged in reporting on mining properties in various parts of the world, and acted as Advisory Director for sundry mining cos. He married, in 1880, Miss Hicks, sister of H. G. Hicks, of Oudtshoorn.

HEPBURN, James S., who died in the early part of 1905, belonged to the legal firm of Hepburn, Son, and Cutcliffe, of London. He took a great interest in all S. African matters, and for several years acted as Chairman of the Transvaal Exploring Land and Minerals Company.

HERBERT, Right Hon. Sir Robert George Wyndham, G.C.B., LL.D., D.C.L., late of 3, Whitehall Court, London, S.W., died on May 5, 1905. He was born June 12, 1831; was the only son of the late Ron. Algernon Herbert; and was educated at Eton and Balliol Coll., Oxford. After gradating there, he was elected a Fellow of All Souls' Coll. and Eldon Law Scholar. In 1855-6 he acted as Private Secretary to Mr. Gladstone when Chancellor of the Exchequer; was called to the Bar in 1858, and in the following year he started an independent official career as Colonial Secretary of Queensland. From 1860-5 he was Premier of that Colony and a leading member of its Legislative Assembly. In 1865 he was nominated one of the Assistant Secretaries of the Board of Trade, which position he held until 1870, when he was appointed Asst. Under-Secretary of State for the Colonies, subsequently being promoted to the Under-Secretaryship, a post which he retained until his retirement from the public service in 1892, when he was created a G.C.B., having previously been decorated with a K.C.B. From 1893-6 he acted as Agent-General for Tasmania in England, and in 1899-1900 was High Sheriff of the County of London. He was Secretary of the Order of St. Michael and St. George from 1877 until 1892, when he became Chancellor of the Order. Sir Robert was Chairman of the Telegraph Construction and Maintenance Company; and a Director of the Eastern and South African Telegraph Company; the Union Castle Mail Steamship Company (see Sir Donald Currie); the P. and O. Steam Navigation Company; and the Union Bank of Australia. He was also Chairman of Mr. Chamberlain's Tariff Commission of 1904.

HOFFMAN, Dr. Jonas Matthias, at the time of his death was Member of the Cape House of Assembly for the Paarl, and one of the leaders of the Bond. He was with the Boer forces in the S.A. War (1899-1902), and he openly referred to the British forces in the Cape House of Assembly as 'the enemy'. He was last returned to the House in Feb., 1904.

HOLLARD, William Emil, who died at Pretoria in the early part of 1906, first went to S. Africa as a private in the German Legion, and was in the company of Lieut. Schermbrucker. On the disbandment of the Legion, Mr. Hollard resigned his position and established himself in business as a Law Agent in Pretoria. He became an Attorney of the Court, and was subsequently admitted as an advocate of the High Court. Apart from his importance as a lawyer (he rose to be the Acting State Attorney of the Republic) he was the Legal and Political Adviser of the Boer Government, and was a personal friend of the late President Kruger. The late Mr. Hollard was the real author of the Concession Policy which proved so ruinous to the Transvaal. In Johannesburg he was well known as one of the earliest land owners, and as partner with Mr. Sam Fox in the Government Square and Marshall's Township. He was a great advocate of the opening up of the country, and materially assisted in influencing the construction of railways, as well as of developing industry and trade in all directions.

HOLMES, Right Rev. John Garraway, Bishop of St. Helena, who died at Worthing in Sept., 1904, in his sixty-fifth year, was educated at University Coll., Oxford, where he held the Gunsley Exhibition, and graduated B.A. in 1862. In the following year he was ordained to the curacy of Lutterworth, in the diocese of Peterborough, and, after serving other curacies at Reading, Reigate, and Wandsworth Common, was preferred to the vicarage of St. Philip, Sydenham, in 1883. During the six years he held this benefice he won general esteem and respect, and in 1888 was elected a member of the London School Board. In 1889 Mr. Holmes determined to throw in his lot with the Church of South Africa, and accepted the office of Dean of Grahamstown and rector of the cathedral parish. To these offices he subsequently added those of Archdeacon and Vicar-General, and for four years edited the *Southern Cross*. His arduous labours in Grahamstown were much valued, and he did a great deal towards allaying the controversies which had arisen in connection with the cathedral. On the death of Dr. Welby, Bishop of St. Helena, in 1899, Dr. Holmes was consecrated by the Archbishop of Cape Town in St. George's Cathedral.

HOOK, Sergt. Henry, V.C., late of Gloucester. where he died of consumption on March 12, 1905, aged 54, was one of the survivors of the ill-fated second battalion of the old 24th—the South Wales Borderers—which was cut up so terribly by the Zulus at Isandhlwana in January, 1879. After the fight the savages made a rush for Rorke's Drift, where the hospital was defended by four men,

Private Hook being one. With the calmness of the parade ground, Rook told off his comrades to remove the wounded from the blazing hut, for the Zulus had fired the fragile structure, while he kept the hordes of Cetewayo, disciplined as they were, and armed with assegai and shield, at bay with a deadly rifle fire. Reinforcements arrived in the nick of time, and the heroic little garrison was relieved. A retreat in good order was effected, the sick and wounded were saved, and Hook was rewarded with a V.C. He was then given the task of taking a share in looking after the umbrellas of the readers at the British Museum, and he became a Sergt.-Instructor to one of the London Volunteer corps.

HORNBY, G., whose death took place at Heidelberg, S. Africa, was the third son of Mr. A. N. Hornby, the well-known Lancashire cricketer. The late Mr. Hornby served in the S. African War as Lieut. in the 2nd Cheshire Regt. He was well known in Cheshire hunting circles.

HORNIMAN, Paymaster-in-Chief W., who died at Southsea, Aug. 17, 1905, was one of the oldest officers in the British Navy. He was born in 1823, and was one of the few survivors of the bombardment of Acre, where he served as a Volunteer. He also served in the China War in 1842 was in several engagements against the Russians as Paymaster under Sir Charles Napier, subsequently being present at the surrender of Sebastopol; and took part in the Zulu Campaign in 1879. He retired from the Navy in 1883.

HOWE, Lady, who died in the early part of 1906, was the wife of Lord Rowe, G.C.V.O. During the S. African War in 1899-1902 she founded the Imperial Yeomanry Hospital, whose medical staff surpassed the Government Hospitals in efficiency. She was also associated with the Mafeking Relief Fund, £27,000 being subscribed in response to her appeal for funds.

JEPPE, Mrs. Julius, who died at Johannesburg on Oct. 2, 1905, was the wife of Mr. Julius Jeppe (q.v.). She was born at the Paarl in 1864, being the second dau. of Mr. Charles Cowen. Mrs. Jeppe was connected with numerous charitable organisations, not the least of which is the Children's League, which she established.

JERNINGHAM, Sir Hubert Edward Henry, who died in 1905, greatly lamented by the community, was a descendant of that Sir Hubert who was in insurrection against King John, but reconciled his differences in the early days of the 13th century when that monarch was succeeded by Henry III. Sir Hubert was a cousin of the present Lord Stafford. In 1881 he entered Parliament as member for Berwick, occupying the unique position of being the only Roman Catholic to represent a Protestant constituency. In 1887 he became Colonial Secy. at Honduras; thence he transferred to Mauritius, of which island he became Governor in succession to Sir J. Pope Hennessy. From 1897 to 1900 he was Governor of Trinidad.

JONES, John Frank, C.M.G., late of 41, Hatfield Road, St. Albans, and of the New Club, was born July 29, 1861. He joined the staff of the British S.A. Co. upon its formation. In 1896 he was appointed Asst.-Secy., and when Mr. Herbert Canning resigned, in 1898, he succeeded him as Secy. In addition to that post he was made Joint Manager with Mr. Wilson Fox in 1902. He also represented the large interests of the Chartered Co. on the Boards of several Rhodesian undertakings. Although Mr. Jones's knowledge of Rhodesia was exceedingly extensive, he had never been to that country until, at the latter end of 1902, he accompanied Mr. Beit, Dr. Jameson, and Sir Lewis Mitchell on a trip extending right through Matabeleland and Mashonaland, where he acquired a practical acquaintance with the country's conditions of the greatest advantage to him in the interests of the Company he so ably served. In recognition of his services to the Govt. in connection with the S.A. War he was made a C.M.G. in Oct., 1902.

At the latter end of 1904 Mr. Jones's health began to fail, and, although he rallied in a satisfactory manner, a relapse took place, and he died at Sidmouth on Feb. 5, 1905, of septic thrombosis.

KEITH-FRASER, Captain Hugh Craufurd, who died in June, 1906, was born April 3, 1869, and entered the 1st Life Guards in 1890. He served in the South African War in 1899-1900 as Adjutant in the S. African Light Horse, being present at the relief of Ladysmith and the action at Colenso (Queen's medal with two clasps).

KOCK, Antonie Francois, was the son of the late Gen. J. H. M. Kock, and grandson of Com. J. H. L. Kock. His grandfather, who was one of the Boer pioneers (*Voortrekkers*), fought against the English under Warren at Boomplaats. His father, Gen. Kock, acted, before the annexation of the Transvaal to the British in 1877, as Member of the Volksraad, and in the war of 1880-81 he acted as Vecht-Gen. over the District of Potchefstroom. Advocate Kock was born at Bronkhorstfontein District, Potchefstroom, Sept. 20, 1869. He was educated at Potchefstroom and Pretoria. In 1885 he took the Republican Scholarship at Pretoria, and was sent to the Netherlands, where he attended the Gymnasium at Doetinchem. As the scholarship was subject to certain restrictions his father renounced it, giving his son a free hand. In 1891 he went to Scotland, and during his stay there he revived the S.A. Union at Edinburgh. At that time he was endeavouring to establish a Union of all South Africans in Europe. After remaining seven months in Edinburgh he went to London, where, in 1892, he was admitted as a student of the Middle Temple. He was called to the English Bar, and after a short visit to Paris he went to Delagoa Bay in June, 1895, and attended the inauguration of the Delagoa Bay Railway as Member of the Festivities Committee. He was admitted as Advocate, after an examination in the Local Laws of the Transvaal, to the High Court of the S.A.R. On June 8, 1897, he was appointed a Puisne Judge of the S.A.R. Among other well-known oases, he defended Col. Ferreira, who was tried for having maliciously, wrongfully, and illegally pegged off the property of J. B. Robinson at Randfontein. He secured the acquittal of the colonel. He made himself notorious at the trial of Constable Jones (over which he presided) for the murder of the Englishman Edgar, by declaring when he discharged the prisoner with a verdict of not guilty that he hoped that the police under difficult circumstances would always know how to do their duty. In the troublesome political times before the war he showed himself an uncompromising opponent of the British. At the meeting of burghers at Paardekraal, Krugersdorp, to discuss the coming war, he addressed the burghers, urging them to maintain their rights as an independent Republic against Great Britain. At the outbreak of the war he accompanied his father, who was appointed Assist.-Comdt. Gen., and was present at Elandslaagte, and with him when he was mortally wounded. A few months later he joined Assist.-Comdt. Lucas Meyer. After being with the Boers before Ladysmith for some time, He went with Gen. Meyer to Colenso, and during the battle of Spion Kop he was in command at Colenso, reinforcing the Spion Kop position with about 1,500 burghers, and at the same time kept the British at bay at Colenso and the lower part of the Tugela River. After remaining three months, he left Colenso on leave for Pretoria, and was in that city during the retreat of the burgher forces from Colenso and Ladysmith. He there arranged, in conjunction, it is said, with State Secy. Reitz, to destroy the mines and meet the British on their ruins. He was prevented from doing this, and was arrested by Dr. Krause on June 2, who, in making the arrest, asserted that he acted under instructions of Commndt.-Gen. Louis Botha. After being confined in a fort he was taken under armed escort to Pretoria, and was lodged in a room on the racecourse amongst about 5,000 English prisoners of war. He was released after narrowly falling into the hands of Lord Roberts, and went to join the forces round Pretoria, where he was slightly wounded in the leg. Retreating with the burghers he arrived at Machadodorp, where as President of Courts-Martial he tried the Cooper case, at Machadodorp, where the prisoner was sentenced to be shot for having blown up a railway bridge with dynamite on the Delagoa line, causing the death of a night watch; and the case of Pienaar, a Boer Comdt., who was sentenced to six months' imprisonment with hard labour at Nelspruit, for attempted fraud on the Transvaal Govt. Proceeding to Delagoa Bay, after an attempt upon his life, he was arrested by the Portuguese authorities, lodged in a fort for three days, and then requested to leave the bay for Europe. He went to Paris and met Pres. Kruger. He then visited the Boer prisoners of war at Portugal, and subsequently made several attempts to got back to the scene of war in S.A., and finally succeeded. He was, however, captured by the British and looked up for ten weeks, when he was tried as a rebel spy. He was found guilty and sentenced to be shot, but acquitted on a legal point

raised by him and upheld by the State Attorney at Pretoria. He was thereupon banished for life, but succeeded in escaping and making his way up country as far as Estcourt. He then went to Pretoria and surrendered himself under the terms of surrender, but he was again arrested and lodged in the Artillery Camp. He finally took the oath of allegiance and was liberated. He afterwards practised as an Advocate in Johannesburg and edited the newspaper *De Transvaaler*.

KOOPMANS, Mrs. de Wet, late of Cape Town, South Africa, who died in the summer of 1906, was the dau. of H. de Wet, a member of one of the most aristocratic old Dutch families, who assisted in the framing of the Constitution of the Cape, and who was the first President of the Legislative Council. Mrs. Koopmans reigned in years gone by as the social queen in Cape Town. She formed a warm friendship with the Empress Eugénie at the time of the Prince Imperial's death, and with other Royalties and distinguished strangers who visited the Cape. At the outbreak of the South African War Mrs. Koopmans gave, her support to the friends of the Republics, and her drawing room became the rendezvous of the leaders of the Dutch party. Her influence in the country was far-reaching, but in spite of her alienation from the policy of the Imperial Government, she was a staunch supporter of Sir Bartle Frere, and formed intimate friendships with the late Lord Loch, the late Lord Rosmead, and General Baden-Powell, whom, however, she refused to receive when he returned from defending Mafeking, saying, "He has shed the blood of my people and I cannot receive him".

KRUGER, Stephanus Johannes Paulus, ex-Pres. of the S.A.R., was born Oct. 10, 1825, in the Colesberg district of the Cape Colony. He was reared in a hard school, his rough training on the veldt, during which his life often depended on his readiness of resource, presence of mind and physical strength, early in life endowed him with those qualities of self-reliance and resource which wore to prove so useful to him in his later years. His boyhood was spent in the manner familiar to the Boers of the early days— farming, hunting, and trekking. There wore no facilities for his receiving any scholastic training, nor did he afterwards add much to his natural sagacity by book reading. Such as it was, however, Paul Kruger's early training only encouraged those characteristics which enabled him to load the movement which wrested the control of the Transvaal from the most formidable empire the world has yet soon, and to hold his own for years in the face of opposition before which the boldest might well have quailed. At the age of ten he accompanied his father on the great trek in search of a new country where they might settle untrammeled by the restrictions of civilised government. At that time the territory lying between the Vaal and the Limpopo rivers was being raided by Mosilikatsi, a Zulu sub-chief who had seceded from the main body of his nation with a large number of followers, and young Kruger— then a lad of twelve years—saw his first active service under Comdt. Potgeiter. Soon after Mr. Kruger served under Comdt. Pretorius in the operations against Dingaan, and was present at the desperate fight which took place at the Blood River on Dec. 16, 1838, where the few Boers gained a great victory which it has been their custom to celebrate every year since then. He also took part in the punitive expedition against Mosilikatsi in 1839.

In 1841 Mr. Kruger became a Field Cornet. In 1852 he was appointed Comdt. of the Districts of Pretoria and Potchefstroom, and in 1856 he began to make for himself a position in local politics, associating himself with Gen. Pretorius in his attempt to join the three independent communities of Lydenburg, Zoutpansberg, and Potchefstroom under one Govt., with a new Volksraad, constitution, and capital in Potchefstroom. Pretorius also sought to absorb the O.F.S., and demanded in the Volksraad at Bloemfontein that the administration of the O.F.S. should be handed over to him. Being ordered to leave the country, however, he returned to the Transvaal, collected an Army, and marched with it back to the Free State, but was met on the banks of the Rhenoster River by Free State forces. A conference was afterwards held, and Pretorius bound himself not again to enter the O.F.S. without permission of its Govt. Many Free Staters who had joined the northern invaders were then tried for high treason, and it is on record how their sentences were reduced to nominal fines owing to the solicitations of Messrs. Kruger and Steyn. As a matter of interest in

showing the trend of Mr. Kruger's character in those first days of his public career, the Pres. of the Free State, referring to this invasion, stated in the Raad that he had proof that the raiders had made a hideous complot with the Basutos under Moshesh to join in the attack against the Orange Republic.

In 1862 Mr. Kruger became Comdt.-Gen., and was elected a member of the Executive Council. Some years later (1877) he promised Pres. Burgers his support on the question of the inevitable annexation of the Transvaal, but Mr. Kruger secretly prompted the resistance of the irreconcilables, and eventually (May, 1877) left for England with Dr. Jorissen to protest against the measure. But it was not thought that either member of the commission really wished the Act of Annexation to be annulled. In fact, on returning to the Transvaal, they both took office under the British Govt., Mr. Kruger only relinquishing his post owing to the refusal of the Govt. to increase his remuneration.

After the Convention of 1881 Mr. Kruger as Vice-Pres. formed one of the triumvirate in whom the Govt. was vested, but in 1882 the old form was restored and he was elected Pres. of the Transvaal State. From this time until the S. African War Mr. Kruger's history is the history of the Transvaal. His policy soon began to declare itself. In that year the first of many laws was passed extending the term of residence for aliens to qualify for natnralisation from one to five years. Soon followed the granting of monopolies, the agitation for the removal of the Suzerainty and freedom in their external relations, whilst he also looked around for new countries to he acquired. Thus Mr. Kruger's Govt. annexed Mafeking and part of Bechuanaland until the Warren Expedition caused a retreat; part of Zululand was taken over, and hungry eyes were turned towards Swaziland (the cession of which we ultimately permitted). In 1890-91 an expedition was sent to Chartered territory, but was appropriately turned back at Rhodes' Drift. Tongaland was also coveted. Meanwhile in 1884 the Pres. and Mr. Smit proceeded to Europe to endeavour to obtain some modification of the Convention and to raise much needed funds, in both of which they were only partially successful. But the discovery of gold at Moodies in 1885-6, and on the Witwatersrand later, brought revenue to the country, which enabled Mr. Kruger to pursue his schemes without remedying the ill condition of the Govt., or providing for the large population which began to flock into the country, and without allowing it, after reasonable residence, a participation in the management of State or even Municipal affairs. Political agitation for reforms, improved ways of communication, remission of taxes, security of titles, etc., gave birth to the Transvaal Republican Union of Johannesburg. The Witwatersrand Chamber of Mines was also formed partly to protect shareholders' interests, and for eight years this Chamber pleaded to the Volksraad for reforms and representation. But Mr. Kruger remained obdurate. Legislation was passed making this practically an impossibility to the then living generation of Uitlanders who had taken up their residence in the Republic. Railways were kept out of the country as long as possible, and then construction was only permitted under such terms as were granted under the Netherlands Railway and Selati Railway concessions, in which connection it may be mentioned that the Selati Railway Co., in order to obtain its concession, had to pay bribes or make presents to many members and officials of the First Volksraad. The dynamite concession was another iniquitous burden upon the industry which had built up the fortunes of the country. Pres. Kruger resolutely set himself against mitigating the abuses which these concerns imposed upon the legitimate industries on the Transvaal. It is true that he secured the Raad's cancellation of the latter concession, but in a few months it was renewed in a still more obnoxious form.

In 1888 Mr. Kruger was re-elected Pres. without much opposition, Gen. Joubert receiving but few votes, but in 1893 he only defeated the General by 7,551 votes to 7,009. About this time Mr. Kruger's control over affairs appeared to be none too sure. Accordingly, in defiance of the *Grondwet* (Constitution) he appointed Mr. Koch, the *Landdrost* and Polling Officer of Potchefstroom who had contrived the defeat of Mr. Esselen at the late election, Minute Keeper to the Executive with the right to vote, which with the President's casting vote, assured the latter the predominant voice in the council. His position thus strengthened, the Pres. turned his attention to other matters,

endeavoring, not without some success, to subordinate justice in the courts to the requirements of his government, curtailing the liberty of the Press, and withholding the right of public meetings and political organisation. However, the attempt to wrest from the High Court the decision in the cyanide case while still *sub judice* miscarried; the endeavour to deprive the mines of their *Bewaarplaatsen* rights only failed after the Minister of Mines had, on his own responsibility, issued the claim licences, and so forced the Volksraad to face the issue of confirming or reversing his action—an alternative which the Government cared not to afford.

Meanwhile Mr. Esselen had accepted the State Attorneyship for a short period, during which he brought about great reforms in the detective and police departments, and his activity in putting down the illicit liquor traffic amongst the natives was so pronounced that backdoor influence was not long in making his office untenable. Dr. Coster, a Hollander, succeeded him and was found more amenable to the Pretorian oligarchy. Laws were passed in defiance of the provisions of the *Grondwet*, and were made retroactive, and on several occasions the Pres. and Executive forced reversals of the decisions of the High Court. Affairs were in this condition when, late in 1895, reform was despaired of by ordinary methods, and a resort to force was freely talked of as a last resource. A Reform party was organised, under the presidency of Mr. Charles Leonard, and eventually the active assistance of the capitalist element was won over to the movement. Dr. Jameson was detained on the western border of the Republic by Mr. Rhodes's orders as moral support, and to come to assistance in case of urgent necessity, but so quiet were the preparations that even Mr. Kruger did not realise the length to which matters had gone. When at length old Hans Botha warned the Pres. of the danger, he replied in his characteristic way that if they wanted to kill a tortoise they must wait until he put his head out of the shell. Meanwhile he received several deputations to induce him to make reasonable concessions, and then Mr. Kruger's plan of procrastination began to reach a height which had never previously been attained. He would promise nothing, but said that he would do his best to see that duties on food stuffs were removed pending confirmation by the Volksraad; that equal subsidies would be granted to English as to Dutch schools, and that the Netherlands Railway would be approached with a view to the reduction of rates, but that it was impossible to grant the franchise to the Uitlander. The leaders, however, could have no faith in these assurances, and matters were hastened by Dr. Jameson (q.v.) crossing the border, on Dec. 29, notwithstanding his distinct orders to the contrary. The following night Pres. Kruger, recognising that the breaking point was nearly reached, issued a proclamation warning persons from disturbing the peace, and stating that the Govt. was prepared to consider grievances without delay. Delegates of both parties met, in fact, in Pretoria, but their deliberations resulted in nothing further than the Boer members having procured a full list of members of the Committee; the Uitlander delegates were handed copy of a resolution stating that the High Commissioner's intervention had been accepted, and that the grievances would be earnestly considered. The surrender of Dr. Jameson's force followed hard upon this, but the Pres. thought that he had still to reckon with 20,000 armed Uitlanders in Johannesburg, and although the doctor's surrender was accepted conditionally upon all lives being spared, he proceeded to let it be known that the doctor's life depended absolutely upon all arms being laid down in Johannesburg, at the same time stating to the High Commissioner that disarmament must be precedent to any discussion of grievances. Accordingly all arms were surrendered in good faith from Jan. 6 to 5, and on the following day Pres. Kruger's 'Forgive and Forget' policy was inaugurated by the Reformers to the number of over sixty being arrested, tried, and found guilty of high treason, the four leaders being condemned to death and the others to fines of £2,000 each, two years' imprisonment and three years' banishment. Soon after these sentences were pronounced Govt. agents were at work trying to persuade the Committee to petition in humiliating terms to the proved magnanimity of the Govt.; and to make statements implicating one another for their complicity in the revolutionary movement, and so on. Meanwhile the gaol treatment was telling severely upon the prisoners, one of whom had already died by his own hand. On May 20, ten were liberated, and most of the other sentences

were commuted to lesser terms of imprisonment, but so great was the feeling growing throughout the country against Mr. Kruger's 'Cat and Mouse' treatment that monster petitions, headed by two hundred S. African mayors, at last (May 30) effected the release of all the prisoners (with the exception of Messrs. Woolls-Sampson and Davies and the four leaders) conditionally on the fines being paid and each binding himself not to meddle in the internal or external politics of the State for three years. After much bargaining with the leaders, Mr. Kruger liberated the latter on payment of a fine of £25,000 each and an undertaking not to meddle in politics for fifteen years.

Negotiations went on in a desultory way. An Industrial Commission of Inquiry was appointed by the Executive at the President's request, and a mass of sworn evidence was taken. In the report which followed, numerous recommendations were made with the end in view of prospering the industries of the State and benefiting the country as a whole, but Mr. Kruger declined to adopt the recommendations, and even charged the chairman of the committee, Mr. Schalk Burger, with being a traitor to his country for having put his name to such a report. Ultimately nothing was done of any benefit to the Uitlander interests involved, and it became apparent that little was to be gained by British diplomacy. Mr. Kruger, who was elected Pres. of the S.A.R. for the fourth and last time in Feb., 1895, was hurrying armaments into the Transvaal to such an extent that it was necessary to reinforce the British garrison in South Africa. The climax was reached when the Pres. delivered the ultimatum in Oct., 1899, which brought on the S.A. War, through the early part of which he remained in the country, urging and encouraging his people to victory, but when this seemed at length a remote possibility, his flight to Europe was rapidly decided upon, and the ex-President's energies were devoted unsuccessfully to obtaining foreign intervention and successfully to stir ring up Anglophobia on the Continent. But Mr. Kruger was already an old man, and this final blow—the defeat of his people and the loss of his country— marked practically the end of his public life.

Strong, fanatical, obstinate, shrewd, and autocratic, Mr. Kruger never concealed his dislike to, and mistrust of, the Uitlanders. When the Barberton rush brought comparative affluence to the country he never once visited the town, and only on three occasions did he visit Johannesburg during nine years, although the law of the land prescribed that the Pres. should visit every town and district yearly. As evidence of this dislike it is remembered that in addressing a mixed crowd at Krugersdorp, where some detested aliens might be present, he began "Burghers, friends, thieves, murderers, newcomers, and others". Nevertheless he did not scruple to commandeer their services for the war against Malaboch, until diplomatic representations from Lord (then Sir Henry) Loch secured exemption for them. Nor did he scruple to fill lucrative posts with relatives who were quite unfit for the public service, nor to appropriate the public revenues for improvements on his personal estates, for which purposes he had little difficulty in obtaining the sanction of the Volksraad. There is on record the case of the editor of *Land in Volk* successfully sustaining an alleged libel charging the Pres. with fraud against the State. He is also generally believed to have brought away with him from the Transvaal the State and Trust funds, variously estimated at from £250,000 to £700,000, of which no satisfactory account has been obtained.

Mr. Kruger employed part of his exile in writing his *Memoirs*, for which he is supposed to have received £30,000. They were dictated to Mr. A. Schowalter, the editor of the *Burenfreund*, afterwards taken over by *Süd Afrika*, a paper now incorporated with *Plutus*. His latter days were spent in almost complete retirement; in a country far removed from his native, but forbidden, veld; with very indifferent health; but with recollections of a long and arduous career of stirring adventure and continual political strife, from which he could scarcely regret being released—even in lonely but peaceful exile.

On July 14, 1904, he expired at his villa at Clarens, Switzerland, death being due to senile decay, hastened by an attack of pneumonia. For three months the ex-Pres. had been only kept alive by continuous massage. But at last he felt the end coming. Five days before his death he took to his bed and Bible, and surrounded by relatives and friends he bade them all farewell, a Dutch pastor

administering the sacrament. Two days later he breathed his last. He had previously made a piteous but ineffectual appeal to the British Govt. to be allowed to end his days in the Transvaal. But his desire to be buried in Pretoria by the side of his wife met with a ready acquiescence from the Govt. It is curious that the British Minister through whom his last appeal was made was Sir W. Conyngham Greene (q.v.), who received from Mr. Kruger, under far different circumstances, the ultimatum of the Transvaal Govt. before the great Boer War.

LECKIE, Major Norman Houston, who died in the spring of 1905, was formerly in the Queen's Own (Royal West Kent) Regt., from which he retired in 1889. He served in the Boer War of 1881 with the Natal Field Force.

LESLIE, William, of Weenen County, Natal, was born in 1830 in Paisley, and when only 20 years of age left his birthplace for Natal, arriving there in 1850. Mr. Leslie was a short time in Maritzburg, and the following year he went to Weenen County. He was one of the founders of the Weenen Agricultural Society, being closely associated with Messrs. Wheeler, Ralfe, Moore, Nickson, Wilkes, and Macfarlane. In the year 1860, when the late Duke of Edinburgh visited Africa, a prize gun was presented by the Royal visitor for the best target shot in Natal, and was won by the deceased gentleman, who was also one of the original members of the Weenen County Rifle Association, and for years was a successful competitor. He died at the latter end of 1904.

LIGHTFOOT, Ven. Thomas Fothergill, B.D., late Archdeacon of Cape Town, was born at Nottingham in March, 1831, and was son of Robert Lightfoot, a lace manufacturer of that town. There also he was educated at the old Grammar School, and was afterwards engaged in journalistic pursuits. In 1854 he entered St. Augustine's Coll., Canterbury, to be prepared for service in the Colonial Church. He was ordained Deacon by Dr. Tait, at that time Bishop of London, in 1857, and went to S.A. as Missionary Curate of St. George's Cathedral, Cape Town, and in 1855 was advanced to the priesthood by Dr. Gray, then Bishop of Cape Town. In the year 1870 Bishop Gray appointed him Missionary Canon of St. George's. In 1879

Archbishop Tait conferred upon him the Lambeth degree of B.D., and he became Archdeacon of the Cape in 1885. Archdeacon Lightfoot has been an hon. Fellow of St. Augustine's Coll., Canterbury, since 1883, and has acted as Vicar General of the Diocese of Cape Town on several occasions during the absence of the Archbishop.

In the formation of a Synod, in the Colenso troubles, in the many difficulties of the S. A. Church, and during the late S. A. War his advice was eagerly sought. His name was a household word in the Colony, and the late Mr. Cecil Rhodes had a high opinion of him. He was a frequent contributor to the English Church Press.

LOCKIE, John, J.P., formerly of Stonehall, Stonehouse, Devon; Boston Hall, Lesbury, R.S.O., Northumberland; and of the Royal Societies Club; was son of John Lockie and his wife Elizabeth Laidlaw Smythe; was born the July 30, 1863, and was educated at George Watson's Coll., Edinburgh, afterwards commencing his commercial career with a Glasgow ship-owner's firm. In 1892 he established works at Jarrow-on-Tyne for the manufacture of brass and copper tubes and engineering accessories. He was part owner of the Planet line of shipping; Chairman of the National Industrial Assoc., and of the S. A. Trade Committee, of which he guaranteed the expenses. He was elected Conservative M.P. for Devonport, Oct. 22, 1902, and was, in 1905, charged on four summonses with having fraudulently taken and applied for his own use the sum of over £86,000, the property of the Venus, Jupiter, and Ceres S.S. Companies. His death occurred suddenly in Court while the case was proceeding in 1906. He married, in 1893, Annie, dau. of John Farrell.

LOWREY, Francis, B.A., late of 16, Cheyne Walk, Chelsea, whose death took place on March 12, 1906, was born at Barmoor, Northumberland in 1856; was educated at Rugby and New Coll. Oxon. (1st Class Modern History Scholar an B.A. 1878). He was called to the Bar, Inner Temple, in 1880, and was for some time a member of the North-Eastern Circuit. He was subsequently a partner in the publishing firm of Swan, Sonnenschein, & Co., and afterwards went to Johannesburg in 1889, where he was one of the first representatives of the Consolidated Goldfields of S. Africa, Ltd. He joined the Reform Committee in 1895-6 and was arrested for his participation in that movement, but did not undergo trial or imprisonment. He was a director of the Consolidated Goldfields of S. Africa, Ltd., Antenior (Matabele) Gold Mines, Central Nigel Deep, Copper Fields of Namaqualand, Dumbleton Gold Mining Federation Syndicate, Forbes' Rhodesia Synd., Giant Mines of Rhodesia Gwanda Mines, Hartley and Sebakwe Reef, Killarney Hibernia Gold Mining, Jupiter Gold Mining, Knight's Deep, Luipaard's Vlei Estate and Gold Mining, Morven (Rhodesia), Murchison Proprietary (Transvaal), New Rand Southern Gold Mining, Nigel Deep, Simmer and Jack East, Simmer and Jack Proprietary Mines, Transvaal Coal Trust, and the United S. Africa Association. He was also connected with the New Gold Coast Agency.

Though so intimately associated with many of the leading groups, he was hardly a foremost figure in Kaffir finance; in fact, he scarcely found his métier in City life. Such success as he achieved, while by no means inconsiderable, was hardly what one would have expected of his high abilities and from his rather special personal standing in his particular world. Mr. Lowrey was a keen lover of literature and a qualified critic of the arts in which his tastes were fully shared by Mrs. Lowrey. He was a keen golfer, and was always glad to slip away from the City to his favourite links at Deal. Under all circumstances, though far from being a perfect mortal, he left one the impression of being a man and a gentleman, and of the South Africans who have passed away during late years few, excepting Cecil Rhodes and Hermann Eckstein, have left behind them such genuine feelings of regret amongst so wide a circle of friends and acquaintances.

MACRORIE, Right Rev. William Kenneth, D.D., D.C.L., who died at the College, Ely, on Sept. 24, 1905, was the son of David Macrorie, M.D. (Edin.), and was born Feb. 5, 1831, at Liverpool. He was educated at Winchester and Brasenose Coll., Oxon. He graduated M.A. and D.D of Oxon, D.C.L. of the Univ. of the South, Tennessee, and M.A. of the Cape Univ.; Hulmeian Exhibitioner, 1854. From 1855-58 he was Fellow of St. Peter's Coll., Radley; 1855-60 he was Curate of Deane, Lancs.; from 1860-61 he was Vicar of Wingates; from 1861-66 he was rector of Wapping; and from 1866-68, Vicar of Accrington. In 1869 he went to S. Africa as Bishop of Maritzburg, retaining the appointment until 1892, when he left S Africa to become Canon of Ely. In his early life he was a well-known oarsman and fond of fishing and fives, afterwards making croquet his principal outdoor recreation. On April 9, 1863, he married Agnes, dau. of William Watson, of South Hill, Liverpool.

MAKONNEN, Ras, K.C.M.G., late Governor of the Abyssinian province of Harrar, was born in 1866, and died on March 23, 1906. He came to England in 1902 as Envoy of the Emperor Menelik for King Edward's Coronation, and made a tour of the country, inspecting our chief cities and industries. He was considered Menelik's probable successor to the throne, and lived in a great white palace at Harrar, which had been built for him chiefly by the labour of Italian soldiers, who were captured at the battle Of Adowa on March 1, 1896.

MARSDEN, Lieut. Cyril, late of Royston's Horse, who died from wounds received during the action of June 9 in the Zulu rising in 1906 was born in 1882, and first went to S. Africa with the Scottish Horse at the time of the Boer War, at the conclusion of which he returned to England. Subsequently, however, he again went out to South Africa, and settled there, and at the time of his death was acting as Lieutenant in Royston's Horse.

MEAKIN, Budgett, late of 21, Heath Hurst Road, Hampstead Heath, was born, Aug. 8, 1866, and was son of the late Edward E. Meakin. From 1884-93 he travelled in Morocco, studying people and conditions, also acting as Editor of the *Times of Morocco*. For comparative study he visited nearly all the Mohammedan countries of the world, including Java, China, Central Asia, Siberia, etc.; received Order of Medjidieh from the Sultan of Turkey for studies of Islam. He was greatly interested in the questions of social service, and in 1902-4 established the British Institute of Social Service, of which Council he was a member; also a member of the Executive Council of the Christian Union for Social Service, and the Garden City Assn. He was

the author of *An Introduction to the Arabic of Morocco*, *The Moors*, *The Land of the Moors*, *The Moorish Empire*, *Life in Morocco*, and *Model Factories and Villages*. He married, June 15, 1900, Kate, dau. of C. J. Hellwell, and died in the summer of 1906.

MELVILL, Commander Francis W., R.N., who lost his life at sea, presumably washed over board, on Oct. 2. 1904, joined the Navy as a cadet in July, 1880. Whilst a midshipman of the *Minotaur* he saw service in the Egyptian War of 1882, receiving the Egyptian Medal and Khedive's Bronze Star. As Lieutenant of the *Forte* he served with the Natal Naval Brigade during the war in South Africa, being in charge of two 12-pounders. He was mentioned in despatches, and in November, 1900, was promoted to the rank of Commander for services during the war.

MERRYWEATHER, James, late of Durban, Natal, who died in May, 1906, was one of the oldest of the Natal Colonists, being one of the pioneers who went to that Colony in the *Haidee* in 1850. The late Mr. Merryweather established the well-known firm of Merryweather and Sons at Maritzburg.

MIDDLETON, Capt. R. W. E., who died on Feb. 26, 1905, served in the Navy for seventeen years, reaching the rank of navigating Lieut., and was for a time engaged in suppressing the slave trade on the East Coast of Africa. On retiring from the Navy he became Secy. to the West Kent Conservative Association and to the Greenwich Conservative Club. Capt. Middleton took up the reins of Party organisation when the Conservative Party were a negligible quantity, and held them for eighteen years, for fifteen of which that dispirited minority developed into a large and united majority, supporting several Unionist Administrations. He retired from the position of Chief Organiser of the Conservative Party in 1903, being succeeded by Captain Wells. Mr. Middleton then accepted an important managerial position in the firm of Messrs. Maple.

MILLER, Sir James Percy, Bart., D.S.O., late of Manderston, Duns, Berwickshire, who died of pneumonia on Jan. 21, 1905, was born in 1864, and was son of the late Sir William Miller, on whom Mr. Gladstone conferred the title in 1874.

Sir James was a Major in the Lothian and Berwickshire Imperial Yeomanry, and served with them in South Africa. He devoted himself largely to the Turf, and in 1903 he was elected to the Jockey Club. Sir James married, in 1893, the Hon. Eveline Curzon, sister to Lord Curzon of Kedleston.

MONTAGU OF BEAULIEU, Lord, who died of heart failure on Nov. 4, 1905, was the second son of the fifth Duke of Buccleuch and Queensberry, and was born Nov. 5, 1832. He was educated at Eton; was M.P. for Selkirkshire from 1861-1868, when he contested and won South Hants, which seat he retained until he was made Baron Montagu of Beaulieu by the late Queen Victoria. He was an intimate friend of Lord Beaconsfield and of Lord Salisbury, and travelled with the latter in the Colonies. Lord Montagu was a keen student of Egypt and Egyptian politics, and had been up the Nile numerous times. He was Chairman of the Westminster Conservative Association when Mr. W. H. Smith was selected as Parliamentary candidate, Chairman of the Hampshire Quarter Sessions, and honorary colonel of the Hampshire Volunteer Battalion.

MONTAGUE, Major-Gen. W. E., C.B., who died in June, 1905, was born in 1835. He served in the Zulu War in 1879 as Brigade Major, 2nd Brigade, 2nd Div. (medal and clasp), and the Boer War in 1880-1, when he was in command at Standerton, which he held during a long investment.

MOORE-LANE, Colonel George Howard, C.M.G., who died on June 11, 1905, was born in 1844, and entered the Army twenty years later. He served in the late S. African War as chief paymaster at Cape Town. At the time of his death he was acting chief paymaster of the South-Eastern District.

MYERS, Julius, who died at East London, Cape Colony, from heart failure, in the middle part of 1906, was head of the firm of Myers Brothers, jewellers. He was born in 1858, and first went to South Africa in 1883.

O'REILLY, John, late of Taungs, Bechuanaland, where he died of cancer towards the end of 1904, was a son of a Colonel in the British Army, whose regiment went to the Cape Colony early in the 19th century. Mr. O'Reilly was a trader in Bechuanaland, but it was his connection with the discovery of diamonds in the Colony that he was better known. Though not the actual discoverer, the first stone came into his possession in 1867, and it was due to Mr. O'Reilly that it was sent to Dr. Atherstone, who pronounced it to be a diamond weighing 21 carats odd. Mr. O'Reilly recently made two unsuccessful petitions to the Cape House of Assembly praying for a pension in consideration of his alleged discovery.

PAGET, Colonel Arthur Leopold, late of Highfield House, near Cirencester, died on March 1, 1906. He was formerly second in command of the 4th Gloucester Regt., and served under Colonel Earl Bathurst at St. Helena in guarding the Boer prisoners of war. The late Colonel was head of the firm of Paget, Rylands, and Co.

PAKENHAM, Major Henry F., who died under tragic circumstances in Feb., 1905, served with his regt., the 60th Rifles, in the South African War in 1901, during which he suffered from enteric. Rejoining in 1902 he again served with his regt. in Malta until Aug., 1903, when he returned to England on leave. He then had a prolonged attack of fever, became convalescent and was married in Feb., 1905. A few days afterwards he disappeared while on his honeymoon at Folkestone, and his body was subsequently washed ashore.

PALMER, Sir Elwin Mitford, K.C.B., K.C.M.G.; 1st class Osmanieh, 1st class Medjidieh, 1st class St. Saviour (Greece); late of Cairo, Egypt, and Park Mansions, Albert Gate, London, was the son of Edward Palmer. He was born March 3, 1852, and was educated at Lancing. Col. Sir Elwin served in the Indian Financial Dept. from 1870-1885, and occupied the position of Acct.General in Egypt, 1885-89, and was Financial Adviser to H.H. the Khedive, 1889-98. (See Sir Vincent Corbett.) Since 1898 he had been Gov. of the National Bank of Egypt and Pres. of the Agricultural Bank of Egypt. He married, Mary Augusta Lynch, dau. of Maj. Clogstown, V.C. Sir Edwin died on Jan. 28, 1906.

PARSONS, Harold G., late of the Colonial Service, who died in Sept., 1905, was born in Australia. He matriculated at Oxford in 1886, and after a spell of journalism he went out to Western Australia on the discovery of the mines. Subsequently he served with distinction in the Boer War, being awarded the medal with five clasps. In 1902 he was appointed District Commissioner at Lagos, and at the time of his death he was occupying an important position on the Governor's Staff.

PIETERS, Isidor, who died at the Memorial Hospital, Bulawayo, Rhodesia, from blackwater fever, was born in 1863. He was connected with the firm of A. and I. Pieters, of Rhodesia, and had been engaged in business at Kalomo since 1904 At the outbreak of the Boer War Mr. Pieters had a store at Siguana, in Bechuanaland, which was attacked by a number of Boers, who killed his wife.

REEVE-TUCKER, Major William R., late of the Hants and Isle of Wight Royal Garrison Artillery (Mil.), who died in June, 1906, from blackwater fever in Southern Nigeria, was born in 1863, and at the time of his death was acting as Travelling Commissioner in Lagos. He served in the Ashanti Expedition in 1895-6 under Sir Francis Scott (despatches, star).

RHODES, Cecil John, P.C., late of Groote Schuur, near Cape Town, came from a stock which records some two hundred years old state to have belonged to the yeoman class. The first of Mr. Rhodes' ancestors who can be traced with any certainty was a man of some substance flourishing at the beginning of the eighteenth century. He acquired an estate in Bloomsbury, where he had considerable flocks. By the time the late Cecil Rhodes' grandfather appeared on the scene the family had already attained to a prosperous position. Samuel Rhodes, great-grandfather of the great Englishman whose death has left so serious a void, founded two county families in the persons of his sons Thomas and William. William Rhodes was succeeded in his estate by his son, the Rev. Francis William Rhodes, Vicar of Bishop's Stortford, Herts, and Cecil John Rhodes was born at the Vicarage on July 5, 1853, within a couple of years of the time when the Transvaal State was accorded its full independence under the Sand River Convention, and a few months after the British Govt. decided to abandon the sovereignty of the O.F.S. For eight years he

attended the Bishop's Stortford Grammar School, pursuing his studies with that diligence and dogged determination which was one of his most striking characteristics, and, in spite of some physical weakness, taking part in field sports. He left school at the end of 1869, and shortly afterwards developed a serious lung affection, which was responsible for Mr. Rhodes taking a long sea trip to South Africa. On Sept. 1, 1870, three years after the discovery of the first diamond, which led to the opening up of the Diamond Fields, in the subsequent exploitation of which he was destined to play such an important part, he landed at Durban, Natal, and joined his eldest brother Herbert, who was a cotton planter in the southern part of the Colony. Here, thanks to the favourable climatic influences, before many months had passed he was restored to health and vigour. Having tired of the prosaic life of cotton planting, the elder brother in 1871 went to the Diamond Fields, where he engaged in the more exciting occupation of diamond digging, and a few months later Cecil Rhodes journeyed to Kimberley for the purpose of seeking his fortune in the same industry. The brothers worked a claim between them for a time, when, in 1874, Herbert left the Diamond Fields on a hunting and exploring expedition in the interior, in the course of which he met with an untimely and terrible death, near the Shire River, through the burning of his hut during the night.

Between the years 1873 and 1881 Mr. Rhodes was very successful on the diamond diggings, and it was during that period that he laid the foundation of the great wealth he subsequently acquired and so liberally spent for the purpose of promoting and carrying out those schemes of Imperial expansion which have made his name a household word even to the most distant parts of the Empire. But Mr. Rhodes was more than a diamond digger. With one eye on his work and the other on his books he managed to complete that education which had been begun at Bishop's Stortford, and from 1873 to 1881 he put in a portion of each year at Oriel Coll., Oxon., where he graduated B.A. and M.A., and where he became acquainted with Mr. Rochfort Maguire (q.v.), who subsequently became associated with his political and commercial enterprises. At the same time he stored up that intimate knowledge of Colonial politics and questions affecting British interests in South Africa, which in later years proved to be of such immense practical value to him.

When he first began to take an interest in South African politics Mr. Rhodes recognised the importance of British expansion northwards, and of the eventual federation of the various Colonies and States in S. Africa, and he determined to devote his powers and his energies to the attainment of those objects. Influences were at work, the aim of which was practically to confine Great Britain in S. Africa to Cape Colony and Natal; and it was in the hope of being able to circumvent the enemies of his country, and to secure the lion's share of Africa for the British, that Mr. Rhodes resolved to attain such a position as would enable him to carry out his aims. For this not only parliamentary power was necessary, but, what was even more important, great wealth. Fortune, in the early days in Kimberley, had smiled somewhat liberally upon him, and he was making money and building up a reputation as a young man possessed of more than ordinary foresight and ability, when, in the latter part of 1880, he was elected to represent the district of Barkly West in the House of Assembly.

He continued to represent Barkly West to the day of his death, the large majority of the electors in spite of strenuous opposition and misrepresentation at election times, loyally supporting their distinguished member, in whom they took more than an ordinary interest. After the death of his brother in 1877 Mr. Rhodes entered into partnership with Mr. C. D. Rudd (q.v.), who, like himself, had gone out to S. Africa in search of health as well as fortune. In addition to working hard in their diamond claims and carrying on their business as diamond merchants, the partners engaged in a variety of schemes, nothing coming amiss which promised a profit. About the same time Mr. Rhodes formed that friendship with Dr. Jameson which was destined to have such remarkable consequences. In those earlier years of scheming and money getting Mr. Rhodes never lost sight of the idea of northern expansion, and his friends knew how intensely he longed to see the British flag carried forward to the Zambesi.

His principal confidant in politics seems to have been Dr. Jameson (q.v.), and while these two were discussing this question of British Expansion in Africa, the late Mr. Kruger was dreaming dreams of an equally ambitious nature. There were thus two prominent expansionists in S. Africa in those early days—the one aiming at securing the hinterland for Great Britain, and the other seeking to extend the Boer flag as far as the Zambesi. Very early in his political career, therefore, Mr. Rhodes realised that he was confronted with considerable diffioulties, as the Cape Dutch strongly sympathised with the aspirations of the Boers of the north, and he recognised that extreme caution was necessary, and that particularly he would have to show the Cape Dutch that their self-interest was being served by supporting his efforts at expansion.

Mr. Rhodes took his seat in the Cape Legislative Assembly in 1881, and he was soon recoguisod as a man of extraordinary promise who was destined to attain a high place amongst S. African politicians. His maiden speech was against the proposal to disarm the Basutos, and it was while serving as a member of a commission to compensate the natives of that country who had not taken up arms against the Cape of Good Hope that Mr. Ehodes formed that friendship with Gen. Gordon which endured until the latter's death. One of the first importaut occasions in which Mr. Rhodes pitted himself against the ex-Pres. of the S.A.R. was in connection with the Stellaland Commission, of which he (Mr. Rhodes) was a member. A number of Transvaal adventurers had set up some small republics in parts of Bechuanaland, more or less with the connivance of Mr. Kruger, with the intention of barring British progress northwards and expanding the border of the Trausvaal in a westerly direction. This was the interpretation which Mr. Rhodes placed upon the presence of the freebooting Boers in Stellaland and Goshen, and subsequent events showed that he was right. After much negotiation, the freebooters were cleared out by a bloodless expedition under Sir Charles Warren, and the first step in the direction of northern expansion was gained. This helped to bring the question of a Protectorate over Bechuanaland to an acute stage, Mr. Rhodes being assisted in this by precipitate action on the part of Germany. The ambition of that Power to obtain a foothold in S. Africa—an ambition foreshadowing a possible German-Boer alliance—stirred the Colonial Office into activity. The Protectorate was authorised at the time when the London Convention of 1884 had been granted to the Transvaal, and mainly at the instance of Mr. Rhodes; but it was almost too late. Mr. Kruger boldly annexed Montsoia's country. The Imperial Government, however, refused to rcognise this action, the boundaries of the Republic having been fixed by the new Convention, and demanded the withdrawal of the proclamation. To strengthen the demand Sir Charles Warren's troops were moved northwards, and Mr. Kruger was immediately brought to his bearings. He came to Fourteen Streams to discuss matters with Sir Charles Warren and Mr. Rhodes.

Mr. Rhodes' share in clearing the Boers out of Bechuanaland directed attention to his expansion scheme, and the ideas which influenced his conduct in this affair were set forth in one of his speeches at the time. He said, "Do you think that if the Transvaal had Bechnanaland it would be allowed to keep it? Would not Bismarck have some quarrel with the Transvaal, and without resources (financial collapse in Pretoria was then imminent), without men, what could they do? Germany would come across from her settlement at Angra Pequeña. There would be some excuse to pick a quarrel— some question of brandy, or guns, or something— and then Germany would stretch from Angra Pequeña to Delagoa Bay. I was never more satisfied with my own views than when I saw the recent development of the policy of Germany. What was the bar in Germany's way? Bechuanaland. What was the use to her of a few sand heaps at Angra Pequeña? And what was the use of the arid deserts between Angra Pequeña and the interior with this English and Colonial bar between her and the Transvaal? If we were to stop at Griqualand West, the ambitious objects of Germany would be attained."

Bechuanaland was, in fact, the key to the question of British supremacy in S. Africa, and Mr. Kruger having been defeated in his endeavours to extend the borders of his Republic, and Germany's ambition for empire in Africa having been curtailed, the road was opened for the northern expansion, which had for years been Mr. Rhodes' high ideal. In pursuing his policy he did not lose sight of the fact that he could only be successful by having the cooperation of the Dutch in Cape Colony, and by cultivating good political relations with the Transvaal; but although the Bond was all-powerful, he resolutely refused to work in subservience to it. He never for a moment turned aside from his plan of extending the Empire to the north, and of establishing a United South Africa under the British flag; but this could only be done by welding the two white races together, by sinking all differences, so that the native question might be dealt with independently of the friction between Dutch nnd British, and on uniform principles throughout the States of S. Africa. The part Mr. Rhodes played in check-mating Kruger's designs in Bechuanaland was his first conspicuous service to the Empire; it was the first of a long series of splendid successes in a direction which continued without intermission down to that date at the end of 1895, when his direct power for usefulness was checked by the fact that he associated himself with the movement for the relief of the Uitlanders, which resulted in failure.

Mr. Rhodes first attained Cabinet rank on March 20, 1884, when he joined Sir Thomas Scanlan's Ministry as Treasurer of the Cape Colony. This Cabinet, however, only lasted until May 12 of the same year. On July 17, 1890, he became Premier and Commissioner of Crown Lands and Public Works. He relinquished that portfolio on Sept. 23, 1890, but retained the Premiership until May 3, 1898, when he formed his second Ministry without portfolio. This lasted until Jan. 12, 1896, when the raid made his resignation necessary.

The success which attended Mr. Rhodes' efforts to bar the ambition of Mr. Kruger to draw a cordon across the British advance to the northwards spurred him to continue in the path he had marked out for himself, and strengthened his resolve to keep open the road for the Empire. It was not only the Dutch he had to fear; Germany had shown that, given a favourable opportunity, she would swoop down upon Mashonaland and Matabeleland. At that time the mineral resources of these countries were not suspected. The desire of the ultra-Colonial party at Berlin to possess themselves of this territory was largely due to those ulterior motives Mr. Rhodes so clearly foreshadowed in the speech already quoted. All the time he was bending his energies to acquire money he was thinking of the main purposes for which he desired it, and maturing his schemes for bringing those purposes to maturity. It would occupy too much space to attempt to give here the history of all the movements which led up to the occupation of Lobengula's territory. Suffice it to say he succeeded in check-mating the designs both of Mr. Kruger and his satellites and of the powerful Berlin Syndicate, secretly backed by a great firm of German bankers. He decided upon applying British red to that portion of the S. African map lying between the Limpopo on the south, Lake Tanganyika on the north, and the Portuguese possessions on the east and west.

Meantime, however, a similar idea had occurred to Mr. George Cawston (q.v.). A few months later Mr. Rhodes induced Mr. C. D. Rudd (q.v.) to make a journey to Bulawayo, with the object of obtaining a concession over those regions ruled by Lobengula. In this he was successful, and obtained from the Matabele chief a concession embracing the whole of Matabeleland and Mashonaland. Subsequent treaties with other native chieftains, and absorption of ether concessions, increased this area to about 750,000 square miles. The romantic story of the occupation of Mashonaland by Major Johnson's Pioneer Force, guided by Mr. Selous (q.v.), is too familiar to need repetition here. The terrible privations endured by the settlers in the new country have been referred to in the lives of Dr. Jameson (q.v.) and Major Frank Johnson (q.v.). But the *African Review* has recorded how, in the face of much discouragement and great difficulties, the gold districts were opened up, townships were built, agriculture was initiated, and law and order established in a land which had been made hideous during the preceding half century by scenes of Matabele rapine and bloodshed. In the settlement of Rhodesia Mr. Rhodes carried the Cape Dutch with him, at all events in a large measure. He had previously conciliated them. He had shown himself in the Cape Parliament extremely mindful of the interests of the Dutch farmers. It took him a considerable time to bring the Dutch to his side, but he succeeded in the end.

Having gained the concession from Lobengula, the next step—procuring a charter from the Imperial Govt.—was fraught with considerable difficulties; but twenty months after the original concession was granted the charter of the British S.A. Co. came into existence. Then followed a period of active pioneering; the settlers, when the pioneer force was disbanded, spread themselves all over the land. However, the greater difficulties were till to come. The Matabele War of 1893 was a small matter compared with the rebellion of 1896. But the way in which Mr. Rhodes grasped the fact that the game of war was not worth the candle, and, recognising this, the readiness with which he completely changed his plan from fighting to dealing, are telling examples of his resourcefulness and judgment. The plucky way in which he went unarmed into the Matopo Hills to treat with the indunas will ever be a subject of admiration to the Anglo-Saxon race. Mr. Rhodes' next move was the acquisition of Barotseland, which was another step in the direction of hemming in the Transvaal with British territory, and keeping open the northern route for the great Cape-to-Cairo Railway which it was his aim should run through all British country. The Afrikander Bond tried to make a condition of their support the stipulation that any further extension northwards should be by way of the railway from the Cape through the Boer Republics. But it was not in Rhodes' scheme of things to give these Republics the control of the interior trade. Presently he got the line extended as far as Mafeking. The Bechuanaland Railway Co. was formed, and, notwithstanding all the obstacles presented by the Matabele Rebellion and the rinderpest, Bulawayo was reached in due season. Concurrently telegraphic communication was pushed on, going in front as the harbinger of the rail way. All manner of evil predictions were adventured, but none of these prophecies have been fulfilled. In constructing the telegraph line Mr. Rhodes' chief concern was to make it the advance guard of the railway, that great linking agency between man and man of modern civilisation; but he also had an eye to the fact that as a commercial enterprise it would prove an extremely remunerative affair. In the prosecution of this work, Sir Charles Metcalfe (q.v.) rendered Mr. Rhodes effective service. It may be said here parenthetically that Mr. Rhodes had to the full that peculiar instinct which enabled him to choose his friends and co-workers with unerring judgment, and that his magnificent successes are almost as much due to this faculty as to any other cause. He was not destined to see the accomplishment of this great scheme, the Cape-to-Cairo Railway; but he lived long enough to be assured that he left it in hands which might be counted upon to bring it to a successful issue. The greatest difficulty Mr. Rhodes had to contend with in the prosecution of this great design confronted him when he found that in the various inter national arrangements made with Belgium and Germany the British Govt. failed to make provision—at whatever cost, it should have been made—for the retention or acquisition by Great Britain of a strip of territory, however slender, which would connect her possessions in Central Africa with the territory under her protection in North Africa. In order to get over this obstacle, Mr. Rhodes came to an arrangement with the authorities of the Congo Free State; but, to make assurance doubly sure, he sought and was accorded an interview with the Kaiser, and so impressed the German Emperor with the soundness of his case that, while guarding to the full all German interests and rights, he gave Mr. Rhodes permission to carry his line through German territory.

There are innumerable aspects of the varied and complex personality of the subject of this memoir which it is impossible to deal with at length. It would, in fact, be interesting to follow Mr. Rhodes' career as a Cape Colonial, in contradistinction to an Imperial, politician; but obviously the only part of his career which has any particular general interest outside narrow limits, seeing that such details are quite uninteresting as concerning the giants of the Imperial Parliament, is that part of it which has to do with those great Imperial problems which temporarily were localized in Cape Colony. It may be noted, however, that his policy was to disarm effective opposition by splitting his opponents into groups when he could not convert them to his views. By hook or by crook he eliminated his political enemies. Indeed, he achieved some success, employing similar tactics, in regard to the statesmen and politicians of the Old Country.

Eminently practical in all that he did, he bent himself to the task of conciliating the Dutch, and endeavouring to bring them to a sound appreciation of their own interests. Witness the Scab Act, which afterwards, vitiated by per missive clauses, has failed to exercise the beneficent influence it would have exercised but for those later amendments. The provisions of the Scab Act in its purity would have saved the Dutch and English farmers—and as the farmers are mostly Dutch, this was a measure especially concerning the Afrikanders—from the cruel loss which the prevalence of disease among the sheep of the country inflicted upon them. Then, as regards the natives, Mr. Rhodes approached them with sympathy shorn of sentimentality. The Glen Grey Act, a masterpiece of constructive statesmanship, though primarily designed—that is to say, on the face of it—in the interests of the white settlers, and especially the employers of labour, was really a measure pregnant with happy auguries for the natives themselves If the natives continue to increase and multiply in idleness in their kraals, discontent must inevitably result, and discontent must breed the poison of sedition and rebellion. In the rupture between whites and blacks which would inevitably follow, the blacks would be the greater and the final sufferers. The Glen Grey Act, and indeed all Mr. Rhodes' legislative and philanthropic actions in regard to the natives, were based on sound common sense, infused with sympathy and sustained by knowledge. Like all Mr. Rhodes' public and private acts his attitude toward the native question was tinctured with imagination. Mr. Rhodes in this, as in all things, looked not merely to the requirements of the immediate moment; he was never content to patch up a convenient *modus vivendi* which left out of account the future. On the contrary, he discounted that future, and his policy was always conceived and carried out with a view to its ultimate effect.

As we understand political parties in England, Mr. Rhodes was a Liberal. He believed in the policy of according the various component sections of the British race the fullest measure of local self-government possible, so long as this liberty did not in any way impinge upon the Imperial unity he desired so fervently to further and did so much to conserve. He had, of course, an ulterior political motive in giving those much debated cheques to

Mr. Parnell and Mr. Schnadhorst. But he was primarily influenced by his prepossession in favour of the idea of local decentralisation plus Imperial centralisation. In this, as in one or two other matters, Mr. Rhodes allowed the proleptic quality he possessed of projecting himself into the future to carry him away. Home Rule for Ireland in conjunction with a general scheme for the readjustment of the local and Imperial government of the Empire is an exceedingly sound proposition. As detached therefrom it is a political impossibility. This Mr. Rhodes would have been the first to allow. Unfortunately, he permitted his sanguine spirit to make him for the moment too previous.

It will always be a difficult matter to understand Mr. Rhodes' true connection with the Reform Movement in the Transvaal. As Managing Director of the Consolidated Gold fields Co. his interference was as justifiable as that of any other member of the Committee, but in his capacity as Premier of the Cape Colony and Managing Director of the Chartered Co. his position was extremely difficult. Mr. Rhodes, who was represented on the Reform Committee by his brother, Col. Frank Rhodes, avowed that his intentions were merely to obtain such amelioration of the conditions a he was entitled to claim as representing an enormous amount of capital invested in the Transvaal. He also aimed at Free Trade in S. African products. Other matters there were—Customs Union, Railway Convention, &c.—but they, he said, would follow in time. He stated that if these objects were obtained the expense of keeping Jameson's men on the border would be amply repaid. Some people averred that it was Mr. Rhodes' intention to seize and annex the Transvaal to Rhodesia, but it was never seriously credited. However, there was evidently considerable suspicion, even among the Reform leaders, that Mr. Rhodes was utilising the Reform Committee and the Rhodesian troops to ultimately plant the Union Jack in Pretoria in the place of the Transvaal flag. This, however, was the one point upon which Johannesburg was united. The Republic must be maintained, but under wider constitutional powers which should give representation and good government to all subjects. So strong was this feeling on the question of the flag that special emissaries were sent to Cape Town to obtain assurances from Mr. Rhodes on the

point. These assurances were given, and Mr. Rhodes telegraphed to Dr. Jameson to restrain him from taking that independent action which his impatience had threatened (see Dr. Jameson's *Life*). But little is to be gained now by dwelling at length on that unhappy business. The provocation must not be forgotten. To a man of Mr. Rhodes' temperament and power of looking into the future it was well-nigh impossible to sit down quietly, while successive Imperial Governments and Cape Ministers paltered with the situation in S. Africa. Mr. Kruger and his friends and myrmidons were leaving no stone unturned to make the position of the British, and, indeed, of all aliens other than their own allies, impossible in the Transvaal, and to eliminate the Imperial factor in S. Africa generally. All efforts at redress in the S.A.R. proving abortive, the Uitlanders repeatedly told from this side that if they wanted relief they must take steps to secure it from within, Mr. Rhodes ultimately determined to lend them a helping hand. Arms were smuggled into Johannesburg, and Dr. Jameson's armed force was stationed on the border. It is impossible to say whether, given fair luck instead of rank bad luck, given discreet subordinates, this ill-judged attempt would or could have proved successful. In any ease, it resulted in dire failure, and it is not too much to say the event itself, and what grew out of it, must have had the effect of shortening by many years the most useful life in South Africa. In dismissing it, it is sufficient to quote and endorse Mr. Chamberlain's famous statement in the House of Commons, which, while recognising the political fault, asserted that nothing existed which affected Mr. Rhodes' personal character as a man of honour.

A man of honour Mr. Rhodes undoubtedly was. The *African Review*, in an excellent appreciative memoir of this great man, has recorded in words which we cannot attempt to improve upon, how loyal he was to his friends, and just to his enemies. He always set before him a high standard of conduct, the standard set up by Aristotle, which he was so fond of quoting. He aimed for himself, and, so far as lay in his power, set the ideal before his fellow men, to achieve that realisation of the highest spiritual good that was in him through the systematic and strenuous training of the best qualities of his manhood. His statesmanship was conceived on these lines. He desired to see the British Empire great and prosperous, not in a merely material and sordid way, but great and prosperous by reason of the aggregated greatness and wellbeing of its individual citizens. He worked unceasingly to this end, sparing himself nothing, and to this noble ambition he sacrificed his life. Almost his last public service to the country he loved so dearly was rendered during the recent war. Those who were with him during the Kimberley siege know with what singleness of purpose he threw himself into the defence of the town. There, as on so many other occasions, he displayed the true nobility and altruism of his nature. For, strongly individual as Mr. Rhodes was, he was in no sense, save the purely superficial one, an egotist. He lived for his race. He knew that his race needed him, and this nerved him to make a splendid struggle with death when he became conscious of its near approach. There is so much to be done, were almost his last words. Nevertheless, he met the spectre with resignation and with the fortitude of a pagan hero. "When I am dead," he once said, "let there be no fuss! Lay me in my grave. Tread down the earth and pass on; I shall have done my work!"

Though not a brilliant orator, he was a most convincing speaker; excelled in knowing what to say and when to say it, and always carried his audience with him. He won the confidence of the Cape Dutch under the leadership of Mr. Hofmeyr, and did not despair of ultimately winning over the Transvaalers, until the unfortunate raid made his temporary withdrawal from S. African politics necessary. Few Englishmen have had a larger following of hero worshippers, and it is fortunate for our predominance in the Cape that he had not to encounter such opposition from British Ministers as might seriously have impeded the fruition of his schemes. This was largely due to his almost hypnotic power of impressing his ideas upon all with whom he came in contact.

We have previously referred to that earlier period in Mr. Rhodes' career when he was first building up a place amongst the mining and financial magnates. The small diamond claims at Kimberley were becoming unworkable owing to thousands of tons of debris falling from the walls, and Mr.

Rhodes quickly perceived that the only possible Way to continue working was by amalgamating the holdings into one workable concern. This process was initiated and followed up until the Kimberley claims were controlled by four companies, and eventually, in 1888, the great De Beers Consolidated Co. was formed to absorb even these. It was not without encountering exceeding difficulties that Mr. Rhodes carried through this great scheme, meeting with much opposition from the late Mr. B. I. Barnato, who, however, ultimately came to terms with the colossus, Messrs. Rhodes and Barnato each being one of the four life governors of the company. In addition to the extraordinary financial energy displayed by so young a man in building up this gigantic diamond corporation, his ability must also be recognised in such details as the compound system diminishing thefts by workers, and the syndicate controlling the price of diamonds.

During the final years in which Mr. Rhodes was working on the diamond combine, his great and initial scheme, his attention was also attracted by the opening of the goldfields in the Transvaal. There is no doubt that, immersed as he was in his De Beers and northern ideas, he did not devote so much attention to the Rand as his financial genius, with so stupendous an opportunity, would have desired. But, in conjunction with C. P. Rudd, he formed the great Consolidated Goldfields of S.A., in 1887, with a capital of £250,000. Mr. Rhodes' personal supervision was, of course, not prominent, and the properties at first acquired were, from subsequent Transvaal mining experience, not first-rate. But the Company quickly found its true footing, and the Consolidated Goldfields of today ranks with the Rand Mines as having for years held the pick of the coming mining areas on the Rand. As evidence of the manner in which, in all Mr. Rhodes' schemes, the success of one was made to hasten the success of another, all on the road to the acquisition of Rhodesia, one may mention the well-known financial share which the De Beers Co. has had in the backing up of the Chartered Co.; while the Consolidated Goldfields of S.A. gave similar assistance. In 1889 it acquired a half interest in the Rudd Concessions, presently represented by eight and a half units out of thirty in a consolidated company, merged once more into a company with a very large share capital, and to be absorbed by the Chartered Co. Under this arrangement the Goldfields company was to receive more than a quarter of a million shares. In addition, the Goldfields took 102,500 shares in the Chartered Co. Then the capital was increased by 130,000 shares to acquire the Johnson, Heany, and Borrow rights in Mazoe, Hartley, &c., in Mashonaland. It was in this way that the astute genius of Mr. Rhodes, working its way stubbornly through a maze of financial intrigues, used the unrivalled financial power of his earlier companies in a country where financial opposition was not to be feared—for those men who had already attained financial importance in the earliest gold and diamond days he had arrayed beside himself—in carrying through the vast schemes which, had he stood alone, would have been too weighty even for himself, while his political power also played an important part in the matter.

So far, however, as the personal finance of Mr. Rhodes is concerned, in 1892, on an amalgamation with other companies, and on the raising of the capital of the Goldfields to £1,250,000, the founders (Messrs. Rudd and Rhodes) received 50,000 shares, while in 1894 their rights to two-fifteenths of the net profits were extinguished by the payment to them of 100,000 shares. From this point onward it may be said that the career of Mr. Rhodes, so far as the building of his personal fortune was concerned, was finished. Thenceforward his schemes concern the provision of ways and means for the great Northern undertaking. His hand was ever in his pocket, and it will probably never be known how much, from his private means, he has contributed towards the exigencies of the infant territories. Especially was this the case in regard to the northern extension of the railway towards Rhodesia, and on its way to Cairo, and on the preliminary telegraph line which is already so far advanced.

In October, 1901, Mr. Rhodes' health, which had been in a precarious state for a year previously, began to show a serious turn for the worse. Acting on medical advice, he started for a trip in the Mediterranean, accompanied by Mr. Beit and Dr. Jameson. He then visited the land of the Pharaohs; returned to England, still an invalid, and soon left the English winter for Muizenberg, a favourite watering place near Cape Town. Here Mr. Rhodes developed heart trouble, and eventually he had to lay aside all business, although no serious result was anticipated, the medical attendants hoping that the patient's vitality would prevail sufficiently to enable him to undertake a voyage to England, arrangements for which were actually made in one of the mail steamers sailing from Cape Town. Mr. Rhodes, too, was anxious to proceed to England, but his condition was such that travelling under the circumstances was absolutely out of the question. During the last few days of his illness it was patent that he was growing weaker and weaker, and although there was a slight improvement occasionally, Mr. Rhodes' friends prepared themselves for the worst. From the Sunday before his death he took little or no interest in matters which before then he freely discussed; but he was constantly dozing, and the continually increasing dropsy working upwards showed only too plainly that the end was not far off. On Tuesday, March 25, 1902, the first serious crisis was surmounted; but it left the patient so weak that, when he had another severe attack on the following day, it was evident the struggle was almost over. Death, which was perfectly painless, occurred at three minutes to six, consciousness being retained till within three minutes of the end. A few minutes previous to passing away Mr. Rhodes faintly muttered the names of his brother and some of the others around him, evidently meaning to say goodbye. Dr. Jameson, Dr. Smartt (Commissioner of Public Works), Sir Charles Metcalfe, Colonel Elmhurst Rhodes, and Mr. J. Walton (member of the House of Assembly for Port Elizabeth) were by his bedside, while all his attendants and boys were also present. Of all those who attended Mr. Rhodes during his illness Dr. Stevenson was the only one absent at the end. Among Mr. Rhodes' last utterances were the words, "So little done. So much to do." A post-mortem examination of the body revealed an extensive aneurism of the heart. The place of Mr. Rhodes' burial was not ill-chosen. In a solid tomb in the Matopo Hills, known now as the World's View, the remains of the founder of Rhodesia lie at rest.

Mr. Rhodes' will and codicils were characteristic of the man. He made large provision for scholarships for the advantage of American, German, S. African, and other students, and set aside ample sums for experimental farming, irrigation, forestry, &c., and for the endowment of an agricultural college. His executors were Lord Milner, Lord Rosebery, Sir Lewis Michell, Lord Grey, Mr. Beit, Mr. B. F. Hawksley, and Dr. Jameson, the latter name having been added in the last codicil. Mr. W. T. Stead had been named previously as an executor, but that gentleman's extraordinary eccentricities led to his being removed from such a responsible post.

RHODES, Col. Francis William, D.S.O., who died of Bright's disease on Sept. 21, 1905, was born in 1851, and was the son of the late Rev. F. W. Rhodes, Vicar of Bishop's Stortford, and elder brother of the late Right Hon. Cecil J. Rhodes. He was educated at Eton, and entered the 1st (Royal). Dragoons in 1873, obtaining Col.'s rank in 1889. He took part in the Sudan campaign in 1884, and was present at El Teb and Tamai, for which he received the Egyptian medal with clasp and the Khedive's Star. Later Col. Rhodes served in the Nile Expedition under Gen. Sir Herbert Stewart, who described him as the best A.D.C. a General was ever fortunate enough to have. He took part in the actions of Abu Klea and El Gubat. In 1888 he was employed at Suakin, being present at the action of Gemaizeh. He acted as correspondent of the *Times* in the Athara campaign, and was wounded at Omdurman. He was Military Secy. to the Governor of Bombay, and acted as Chief Staff Officer to Sir Gerald Portal's Uganda Mission, when he suffered severely from blackwater fever. He returned home in 1893, and subsequently acted as administrator in Rhodesia during Dr. Jameson's absence in Europe.

Col. Rhodes represented the Consolidated Goldfields of S. Africa in Johannesburg, and took a leading part in the Uitlanders' Reform movement of 1895-6, for which he was condemned to suffer death by hanging. This sentence was commuted on the same terms as Messrs. Hays Hammond, Lionel Phillips, and Sir Geo. Farrar (q.v.), but on being liberated from Pretoria Gaol with a fine of £25,000, he refused to give his undertaking not to meddle in the politics of the State, and was put across the border. He immediately proceeded to Matabeleland to take part in the suppression of the rebellion. He attended the Delhi Durbar as the guest of Lord Kitchener. The gross value of Col. Rhodes' estate was returned at £116,993, with net personally £102,139.

RICARDE-SEAVER, Major Francis Ignatius, Knight Commander of the Royal Military Order of Christ, Knight Commander of the Order of Isabella the Catholic, Knight Officer of the Imperial Order of the Rose; Officer of the French Academy; late of 365, Salisbury House, London Wall, E.C., said of the Athenaeum Club, who died at Ventnor, I.W., on July 15, 1906, was born in 1836 at Hand Park, Rush, in the County of Dublin. He was early intended for the law, but his inclination being in the direction of Natural Science the idea of a legal career was abandoned, and he applied himself to the study of chemistry, electricity, geology, mining, and engineering. At the age of twenty he proceeded with the late Prof. Forbes, F.R.S., to the Andes and adjacent territories in S. America, for the purpose of studying the geological conditions, and to ascertain, if possible, the probable mineral wealth of the country. At the conclusion of the mission he was appointed Govt. Assayer at Valparaiso, a position which he retained for some time, until at the age of twenty-six he accepted the position of Inspector-Gen. of Mines to the Argentine Republic. For twelve years he laboured to open up the country by means of railways and telegraphs, with such success that in 1874 1,500 miles of rails were in regular traffic, and 3,000 more were in course of construction, while 5000 miles of telegraph wires were available for communication between the various parts of the Republic. He also initiated the laying of the Transatlantic Cable via Brazil to Europe. These twelve years of his life were how ever not spent entirely in peaceful pursuits, for when war broke out with Paraguay he was created a Major in the Argentine Army, and served with distinction through that long and severe campaign. During this period he made several business visits to Europe for the purpose of conducting important negotiations more or less of a financial character on behalf of the Republic. In 1871 he raised in London a loan of £6,000,000 for the Argentine Govt., the whole of which sum was devoted to the construction of railways, telegraphs, and other public works. In 1874 he returned to Europe in a Consular capacity.

He then devoted himself to science and literature for some time, publishing, amongst other works, what is still a standard work of reference, *The Mineral and other Resources of the Argentine Republic.* He also acted as Special Correspondent for the *Times* and various papers in South Africa. In 1881 he assumed by Royal Licence the name of Seaver (that of his mother), in addition to his former name of Ricarde.

Maj. Ricarde-Seaver was a strong Imperialist and in the year 1888 he took up the subject of S. African development. The expansion of our Empire north and west of the Transvaal was due in some measure to his foresight and energy. He acquired a concession of 400 square miles granted by Khama in Bechuanaland and succeeded in obtaining the financial support of Lord Rothschild and other capitalists, who subscribed £50,000 to carry out explorations right up to the Zambesia and beyond. In conjunction with Lord Gifford, V.C., and others he organised an expedition to proceed to Bulawayo and obtain from King Lobengula the right to prospect and work gold and other mines in Matabeleland and Mashonaland. It was at this period that he was brought into contact with the great Imperialist, Cecil Rhodes, and on the suggestion of Lord Rothschild it was arranged that their efforts should be devoted to obtaining from H.M. Govt. the charter to administer that great territory known as Rhodesia.

At one time Maj. Ricarde-Seaver was a director of as many as twenty-five companies, mostly operating in the Transvaal and Rhodesia, but owing to ill health in the past few years, the number of his directorates gradually diminished, but at the time of his death he was still on the board of sixteen companies, including those of Bechuanaland Exploration Company and the Bechuanaland Trading Association, while he was also a director of the French Rand Gold Mining Company and the Village Main Reef, in both of which the Wernher-Beit element is predominant. His knowledge of scientific mining was profound and varied, extending over close upon half a century.

The deceased gentleman was a Fellow of the Royal Soc. of Edin., of the Geographical Soc. of London, of the Royal Geographical Soc., a member of the Royal Institution of Great Britain, and an associate of the Institute of Civil Engineers. Major Ricarde-Seaver married first, in 1863, an English wife, whom he lost in 1875, leaving an only son; secondly, he married H.S.H. the Princess Marie Louise de Looz et Corswarem, née Princess Godoy do Bassano of Spain. The Princess died in 1880, and in 1891 Major Ricarde-Seaver married the Marquise de la Lanrencie-Charras, of Paris and Château de Charras.

ROMILLY, Lord, who died on June 23, 1905, was the only child of the 2nd Baron, and was born in 1860. From 1886-8 he was attached to the 7th Battn. King's Royal Rifle Corps, and served in S. Africa in 1900-1. He married, in 1897, Violet, sister of Sir Philip Grey-Egerton.

SCHERMBRUCKER, Col. the Hon. Frederic, M.L.A., of Friedrichs Ruh, Wynberg, C.C., who died in April, 1904, was born at Schweinfurth, Bavaria, in 1832, and was son of the Hon. Christopher Schermbrucker, one of the Judges of the Appellate Court of the Province of the Palatinate. He was educated at the Jesuit Institute of Nenburg, on the Danube, was a Latin prizeman at that academy, and entered the ranks of the Bavarian army as a private, but with the privileges of a gentleman cadet. He fought on the Royal side in the disturbances of 1850-2, and was made a Sub-Lieut. in recognition of services in the field; he volunteered to serve in the Crimea with the German Legion. He went to the Cape in 1857 with the rank of Ensign; was for some time a teacher of German before being appointed German Interpreter in the office of the R.M. at King Williamstown. Later he started as an auctioneer, and from 1859 to 1866 took an active part in opposing the annexation of Kaffraria to the Cape Colony. He was one of the accused in the famous Calabash case, and was fined £100 for shooting a Kafir sheep stealer. He was elected a member of the Cape Assembly in 1865. In 1872 he failed in business and went to the diamond fields, to Lydenburg, the Limpopo, and Matabeleland, eventually becoming editor of the *Bloemfontein Express.* He left Bloemfontein (having been burned in effigy there), and returned to King Williamstown; volunteered for service in the Frontier War; was appointed Comdt. of the

Amatola Division; volunteered for service in the Zulu War, and commanded at Luneberg, being present at the engagements of Zlobane and Kambula, and distinguishing himself at the Pemvani River. In 1880 he accompanied Sir Gordon Sprigg to Basutoland to raise a police force, but retired when the Sprigg Ministry was overturned. In 1882 he was elected M.L.C. for the Eastern Circle; was re-elected two years later, and in the same year joined Sir Thomas Uppington's Cabinet as Commissioner of Crown Lands and Public Works, and continued this office in the second Sprigg Ministry. He successfully contested King Williamstown at the General Elections for the Cape House of Assembly in 1885, 1894, and 1904, and was also a life member of the Executive Council of the Cape of Good Hope. Col. Schermbrucker was a keen Imperialist, a clever speaker, a great admirer of Cecil Rhodes, a loyal supporter of Dr. Jameson, and a tower of strength to the Progressive party. He was decorated with the Pope's Order, *Pro Pontifice et Ecclesia*, and wore the medals for the Gaika War, the Basutoland Rebellion, and the Zulu War. He married Lucy, second dau. of the late Patrick Egan and has had a large family of children.

SCHIEL, Colonel, had a long experience of S.A. He was a Native Commissioner in the Zoutpansberg, and Organiser of the Staats Artillerie of the S.A.R., and in the late Boer War (1899) was appointed to the command of the German Brigade. He was captured at Elandslaagte, and during his captivity at St. Helena wrote a book, *Twenty-three Years of Storm and Sunshine in South Africa*.

SPENCER, Richard Stacey, formerly of Birchanger, Essex, who died in South Africa recently at the age of fifty-six, was educated at Bishop's Stortford High School with Mr. Cecil Rhodes, and subsequently became associated with him in South Africa. He was a noted cricketer, and played for Herts County.

STANLEY, Sir Henry Morton, G.C.B., D.C.L., of Oxford, Camb., and Durham, LL.D. of Edin., Ph.D. of Halle; late of 2, Richmond Terrace, Whitehall, London, and of Furze Hill, Pirbright, was born about the year 1841 in Denbighshire, so far as is known, for his early years are clouded by much obscurity. But it is understood that he spent many years of his childhood in the workhouse, and at the age of fourteen shipped as a cabin boy for New Orleans, where he found a generous patron in the person of a Mr. Stanley, whose name he adopted. On the outbreak of the American War in 1861 Henry Morton Stanley joined the Confederate forces, but afterwards fought on the Federal side. In 1867 young Stanley went as correspondent of the *New York Herald* with the British troops in Abyssinia, and after the fall of Magdala he represented that journal in Span. It was while he was there that a telegram summoned him to Paris in October, 1869, and he was commissioned to go and find Dr. Livingstone. He started on this vague enterprise immediately, attending, *en route*, the opening of the Suez Canal, visiting Sir Samuel Baker in Upper Egypt, running over to see Capt. Warren in Jerusalem, visiting Stamboul, going over the old Crimean battle fields, visiting Trebizond, Tiflis, and other places, and eventually journeying through Persia, and finding his way overland to Bombay, where he embarked in Oct., 1870, for Mauritius. Thence he procured a passage to Zanzibar, and began in Jan., 1871, his inland journey in search of the great missionary. In the following November the intrepid party found themelves on the eastern shores of Tanganyika, and here, at a village called Ujiji, they encountered Dr. Livingstone. Upon his return to England, the bearer of Livingstone's diary, Mr. Stanley (not yet knighted) was universally lionised. The Queen presented him with a gold snuffbox with the V.R. in brilliants. The King (then Prince of Wales) gave him an audience; King Humbert of Italy presented a portrait of himself, while from Victor Emmanuel he received a gold medal. Learned societies and illustrious personages showered addresses, gifts, and invitations upon him, Mr. Stanley realised to the full the meaning of fame, and enjoyed the nation's reward for long months of danger, fever, toil, and privations endured for the succour of a fellow man. A year or two later he returned to Africa to represent the *New York Herald* in the Ashanti War, and on his return the ever enterprising *Daily Telegraph* joined with the *New York Herald* in sending Stanley back to complete the discoveries of Speke, Sir R. Burton, and Livingstone (who was now dead). As a result of the liberal means supplied by Mr. J. M. Levy and Mr.

Edward L. Lawson of the *Telegraph*, and Mr. James Gordon Bennett of the *Herald*, Mr. Stanley's expedition resulted in the accomplishment of three great achievements, each one of which would have made the lifelong reputation of any ordinary explorer. The Victoria Nyanza was for the first time circumnavigated and its shores accurately mapped out. The Tanganyika was also circumnavigated, and the result of the expedition showed, what before had been unknown, that these two great inland seas were not in any way connected with each other. But the greatest of his African exploits remains to be chronicled. Striking due west, Stanley met the River Lualaba, followed the mysterious stream northward along its banks, and ultimately embarked on its waters, finally emerging by it on the Atlantic Ocean at the mouth of the Congo. No more momentous geographical discovery has ever been made in modern days than the proof thus given that the Lualaba and the Congo were the same river, and that the latter was almost continuously navigable, and certainly capable of being utilised as a high road for future African commerce. During a great part of the journey through Central Africa Stanley was accompanied by the great slave trader, Tippoo Tib, and many conflicts with natives took place; but, although they met with censure in some quarters, they could only be regarded as part of the price of the advantages to science, civilisation, religion, and empire which ultimately accrued.

In 1879 Mr. Stanley (as he still was) was deputed by the newly formed African International Association, of which King Leopold II was the founder, to establish trading stations and open up the land bordering on the Congo, with the main object of promoting commerce. In 1884 was founded the Congo Free State, referred to in Mr. Stanley's *The Congo, and the Founding of the Free State* (1885), and the first Governorship of this territory was offered to, but declined by, the explorer and pioneer of commerce in West Africa.

In Jan., 1887, the Egyptian Treasury placed £10,000 at Stanley's disposal for the relief of Emin Pasha, upon which he set out from the Congo with many able lieutenants, pushing on to the Aruwimi River, where he established a base. Stanley then took the greater part of his force northwards, and

after seemingly endless obstacles—death, disease, hunger, desperate conflicts with natives, struggles through virgin forests, &c., he at length met Emin, and brought him back in triumph.

But many and fatiguing journeys through the worst parts of Africa, punctuated with over a hundred attacks of fever, were telling upon the explorer's health. Many tempting offers of profitable employment were made, but he resolved to settle down in England. He married Dorothy, a dau. of Mr. C. Tennant, of Cadoxton Lodge, Vale of Neath, Glamorganshire, in 1880, and after one unsuccessful attempt to enter Parliament was elected in the Liberal Unionist interest as member for North Lambeth at the general election in 1895, retiring in 1900, a year after receiving the honour of knighthood. In 1898 he paid one more visit to Africa on the occasion of the opening of the railway to Bulawayo. Sir Henry died on May 10, 1904, and was buried at Pirbright, lamented by numberless friends, and honoured by all. Beside the book already referred to, he was the author of *Coomassie and Magdala*, *How I Found Livingstone*, *In Darkest Africa*, *Through the Dark Continent*, and *Through South Africa*.

STEPHAN, H. R., late of Brighton Castle, Mouille Point, Cape Town, who died in July, 1906, at Vredenburg, was the head of the house of Stephan Bros., Cape Town, and elsewhere in South Africa. The firm has been largely instrumental in opening up Saldanha Bay and the South-West Territory. They own a considerable number of steam and sailing ships, and are largely engaged in the grain trade.

STEWART, Sir Donald William, K.C.M.G., late of Government House, Mombasa, who died of pneumonia at Nairobi on Oct. 1, 1905, was born in 1860. He was son of the late Field Marshal Sir Donald Stewart, Bart., Governor of Chelsea Hospital, and younger brother of the present Bart. Sir Donald was formerly Capt. in the 2nd Battn. of the Gordon Highlanders, and fought in the Afghan War, receiving the star for the march to Kandahar. He took part in the first Boer War; was A.D.C. to his father when he was Commander-in-Chief in India, and served in the Egyptian Campaign in 1885 (medal, clasp, and star). He was political officer with the Ashanti Expedition in 1895-6; served with the Gold Coast Police; became British Resident at Kumasi; and in 1904 succeeded Sir Chas. Eliot as Commissioner and Commander-in-Chief in the E. African Protectorate.

TENNANT, Hon. Sir David, K.C.M.G., who died in 1905, was born in 1829. He was a member of the Legislative Assembly, Cape Colony, from 1860-1896, and acted as Speaker from 1874-1896. From 1896 till 1902 he was Agent General in London of Cape Colony, and was formerly Chairman of the Council of the South African College. He was also a member of the University Council. He married, first, in 1849, Josina (died 1877), daughter of J. du Toit, of Cape Colony, and secondly, in 1885, Amye, dau. of Lieut.-Gen. Sir W. Bellairs (q.v.).

THORPE, T. R., one of the early pioneers of the Rand, died in June, 1906, at the Robinson mine. He held the position of assayer, and was the oldest employee in point of service, having been connected with the mine for seventeen years.

TIPPOO TIB, or Hamra Bin Mohamed al Marjebi, the famous Arab merchant and slave trader of the Upper Congo, died at Zanzibar, June 14, 1905. He was nominally a vassal of the Sultan of Zanzibar, but actually he ruled the country lying between Tanganyika and Stanley Falls, and was a formidable rival to the Sultan himself. In 1883 Tippoo seized upon the Stanley Falls country, whither Sir H. M. Stanley, as the agent of the International African Assoc., the forerunner of the Congo Free State, was despatched to treat with or square the daring slave-raiding adventurer. The result of their negotiations was a tentative agreement, soon afterwards broken by the destruction of the Congo Fort. In 1887 Stanley again fell in with Tippoo at Zanzibar, the Arab being made salaried Governor of the Stanley Falls District. Then came the Emin Pacha relief expedition, where Tippoo's carriers mutinied and killed Major Barttelot.

TOBBACK, Comdt., late of the Carabineers, who succumbed to influenza early in 1905 at Brussels, commanded at Stanley Falls in succession to Capt. Bia in 1892, and took an active share in the Arab campaign. In fact, he narrowly escaped being one

of its first victims, as he left Riba Riba on May 9, 1892, a few hours before the assassination of Michiels and Noblesse, and but a few days before the massacre of Hodister and his companions.

The following year, after the capture of Riba Riba and the defeat of the Arabs of Kasuku by Chaltin, Comdt. Tobback was warned about the middle of May of an imminent attack on the Falls by Rachid, the nephew of Tippoo Tib, and immediately took such steps as were demanded by the critical position of the station. For some days he defended it, in spite of the crushing superiority in numbers of the assailants, with as much skill as courage, and was able to hold out until the arrival of reinforcements brought by Chaltin on May 18. The Arabs were completely defeated, and 1,500 of their number fell into the hands of Chaltin and Tobback. The campaign terminated at the end of August, 1893.

TRUMAN, Major-General William Robinson, who died on Nov. 6, 1905, joined the Army in 1862. During the war in South Africa he was head of the Remounts Department, and a serious scandal arising out of the excessive prices paid for horses obtained abroad and their inferior quality, resulted in the appointment in Feb., 1902, of a Court of Inquiry into the conduct of the Department. General Truman had a few days previously been asked to resign. This he consented to do provisionally, asking for a Court of Inquiry. The report of the Court was a practical exoneration of the General from serious blame. On July 17, 1903, Major-General Truman was placed on the retired list on account of age.

UDAL, Lieut. Evelyn Routh, of the Indian Army, serving with the 36th Sikhs at Peshawar, who died in 1905 of enteric fever, aged twenty four, joined the Welsh Regiment from the Embodied Militia in 1901; served all through the South African War, receiving the Queen's medal with one clasp and the King's with two; and was transferred to the Indian Army in 1903.

WAGSTAFFE, Fleet-Paymaster S. St. S., who died in 1905 in his seventy-ninth year, served in the *Penelope* on the West Coast of Africa at the capture of Lagos in 1851, and in the same vessel in the

Baltic during the Russian War in 1854-5. In 1859 he was wounded while secretary's clerk on the *Chesapeake* at the attack on the Peiho forts.

WATSON, William, late of Ladysmith, Natal, who died on April 28, 1906, was born at Headingley, near Leeds, Dec. 4, 1834, and was son of the late William T. Watson, of Leeds. Mr. Watson was the oldest inhabitant of Ladysmith, and was greatly esteemed throughout Natal.

WISSMANN, Major Herman von, late Governor of German East Africa, who died on July 15, 1905, was born in 1853, and joined the Army twenty years later. He made his first journey to Africa in 1880, subsequently making an exploration to the Congo for the Belgian Govt. He was spoken very highly of by the German Press, which described him as one of the most successful discoverers, path finders, and heroes connected with German Colonial development. Prince Bismarck's summary of Major Wissmann's character was that he had returned from the Darkest Continent with his waistcoat still white. He retired from his position as Governor of German East Africa in 1896, owing to illhealth.

Index

Surname in capitals (e.g. A'COURT, Lieut. Col. Charles) denotes a biography entry.

King Williamstown, 35, 93, 94, 182, 262, 288, 335, 338, 360, 363, 371, 381, 385, 434

KING, Godfrey James, 211

KING, Henry James, 211

KING, Thomas Burnham, 211

KING, William Joseph Harding, 211

King's African Rifles, 148, 196, 212, 355, 375, 376

KING-HARMAN, Sir Charles Anthony, 211

KIPLING, Rudyard, 212

KIRK, J. W. C., 212

KIRK, John, 212

KIRKMAN, Hon. Thomas, 212

Kitchener of Khartoum, General Viscount Horatio Herbert, 39, 83, 93, 133, 145, 148, 154, 186, 187, 189, 205, 213, 241, 259, 288, 314, 317, 342, 381, 384, 394, 433

KITCHENER, of Khartoum, General Viscount Horatio Herbert, 212

Kitchener's Fighting Scouts, 16, 45, 189, 391

KITCHIN, Joseph, 213

Kiva, 125

Klerksdorp, 45, 88, 90, 99, 105, 149, 273, 352, 356, 383

KLIMKE, Joseph, 213

KLINGENBERG, Dr. Georg Ernst, 214

Klip River, 17, 89, 159, 303

KNAPP, Major George Harvey, 215

KNIGHT, Edward Frederick, 215

KNIGHT, James Hartley, 215

KNOX, Charles Edmund, 216

KNOX, William George, 216

Knysna, 17, 188, 292, 332, 360

KOCK, Antonie Francois, 416

Koffyfontein, 308, 328, 339

KOHLER, Hon. Charles William Henry, 216

Kokstad Mounted Volunteers, 249

KOLBE, Rev, 216

Komatipoort, 296

KOOPMANS, Mrs. de Wet, 417

Kordofan, 110, 125, 175, 413

Kotze, John Gilbert, 155

KOTZE, John Gilbert, 216

KRAUSE, Dr., 217

KRIGE, Gideon Johannes, 217

KRIZINGER, Commandant, 217

Kroonstad, 33, 40, 49, 84, 285, 308, 350, 363

Kruger, Stephanus Johannes, 39, 71, 107, 109, 119, 121, 129, 130, 136, 153, 193, 217, 221, 226, 244, 246, 259, 269, 281, 291, 303, 309, 322, 325, 340, 342, 350, 355, 366, 397, 410, 415, 417, 419, 426, 427, 428

KRUGER, Stephanus Johannes, 417

KUHN, Peter Gysbert, 217

Kumasi, 8, 62, 143, 219, 223, 368, 396, 436, 437

Kuruman, 18, 50, 233, 263

LABISTOUR, Gustave Aristide de Roquefeuil, 217

LABUSCHAGNE, Casper Jeremiah, 217

Ladysmith, 6, 9, 29, 30, 33, 42, 44, 52, 60, 75, 85, 90, 91, 105, 141, 147, 148, 149, 152, 166, 167, 172, 176, 184, 186, 194, 216, 220, 234, 236, 237, 246, 247, 249, 252, 265, 270, 293, 296, 297, 307, 314, 315, 322, 327, 334, 339, 351, 357, 362, 366, 367, 370, 371, 375, 380, 381, 382, 400, 406, 412, 416, 417, 438

LAGDEN, Sir Godfrey Yeatman, 217

Lagos, 6, 11, 32, 100, 112, 158, 161, 166, 183, 228, 231, 233, 235, 237, 240, 263, 267, 273, 289, 295, 298, 302, 330, 334, 339, 343, 352, 362, 363, 425, 437

LAIDLEY, J. E., 219

LAING, J. M., 219

LAING, W. T., 219

LAIRD, Major Robert Montgomery, 219

Lake Chad, 110, 161, 223, 356

Lake Nairascha, 191

LAMBRECHTS, Alphonse, 219

LAMBTON, Charles, 220

LAMBTON, George Charles, 220

LAMBTON, Hedworth, 220

LAMBTON, William, 219

Lamu, 128

LANE, Capt. A. H., 220

Also available from Jeppestown Press

The Bulawayo Cookery Book and Household Guide
Mrs N. Chataway

First published in 1909, Zimbabwe's earliest cookery book will
entrance you with over 230 recipes for African delicacies:
aromatic green-fig preserve; spicy bobotie; zesty lemon pudding
and warm, comforting gingerbread. More than 50 contemporary
advertisements for companies like Puzey and Payne, Maskew
Miller and Haddon and Sly lend vintage Edwardian style to this
enchanting book.
ISBN: 0-9553936-2-0

www.ingramcontent.com/pod-product-compliance
Lightning Source LLC
Chambersburg PA
CBHW080409270326
41929CB00018B/2955